ISBN 0-7876-1911-6

90000

Twentieth-Century Literary Criticism

Guide to Gale Literary Criticism Series

When you need to review criticism of literary works, these are the Gale series to use:

If the author's death date is:	You should turn to:
After Dec. 31, 1959 (or author is still living)	**CONTEMPORARY LITERARY CRITICISM** for example: Jorge Luis Borges, Anthony Burgess, William Faulkner, Mary Gordon, Ernest Hemingway, Iris Murdoch
1900 through 1959	**TWENTIETH-CENTURY LITERARY CRITICISM** for example: Willa Cather, F. Scott Fitzgerald, Henry James, Mark Twain, Virginia Woolf
1800 through 1899	**NINETEENTH-CENTURY LITERATURE CRITICISM** for example: Fedor Dostoevski, Nathaniel Hawthorne, George Sand, William Wordsworth
1400 through 1799	**LITERATURE CRITICISM FROM 1400 TO 1800** *(excluding Shakespeare)* for example: Anne Bradstreet, Daniel Defoe, Alexander Pope, François Rabelais, Jonathan Swift, Phillis Wheatley
	SHAKESPEAREAN CRITICISM Shakespeare's plays and poetry
Antiquity through 1399	**CLASSICAL AND MEDIEVAL LITERATURE CRITICISM** for example: Dante, Homer, Plato, Sophocles, Vergil, the Beowulf Poet

---

Gale also publishes related criticism series:

CHILDREN'S LITERATURE REVIEW

This ongoing series covers authors of all eras. Presents criticism on authors and author/illustrators who write for the preschool through high school audience.

SHORT STORY CRITICISM

This series covers the major short fiction writers of all nationalities and periods of literary history.

ISSN 0276-8178

R

Volume 27

Twentieth-Century Literary Criticism

**Excerpts from Criticism of the
Works of Novelists, Poets, Playwrights,
Short Story Writers, and Other Creative Writers
Who Died between 1900 and 1960,
from the First Published Critical Appraisals
to Current Evaluations**

Dennis Poupard
Editor

Paula Kepos
Marie Lazzari
Thomas Ligotti
Associate Editors

 Gale Research Inc. • *DETROIT* • *LONDON*

STAFF

Dennis Poupard, *Editor*

Paula Kepos, Marie Lazzari, Thomas Ligotti, *Associate Editors*

Joann Prosyniuk, Keith E. Schooley, Laurie A. Sherman, *Senior Assistant Editors*

Faye Kuzma, Sandra Liddell, Timothy Veeser, *Assistant Editors*

Carolyn Bancroft, Denise Michlewicz Broderick, Melissa Reiff Hug,
Jay P. Pederson, Anne Sharp, Debra A. Wells, *Contributing Assistant Editors*

Sharon R. Gunton, *Contributing Editor*

Jeanne A. Gough, *Permissions & Production Manager*
Lizbeth A. Purdy, *Production Supervisor*
Kathleen M. Cook, *Assistant Production Coordinator*
Cathy Beranek, Suzanne Powers, Kristine E. Tipton, Lee Ann Welsh, *Editorial Assistants*
Linda M. Pugliese, *Manuscript Coordinator*
Donna Craft, *Assistant Manuscript Coordinator*
Jennifer E. Gale, Maureen A. Puhl, Rosetta Irene Simms, *Manuscript Assistants*

Victoria B. Cariappa, *Research Supervisor*
Maureen R. Richards, *Research Coordinator*
Mary D. Wise, *Senior Research Assistant*
Joyce E. Doyle, Kevin B. Hillstrom, Karen D. Kaus, Eric Priehs,
Filomena Sgambati, Laura B. Standley, *Research Assistants*

Janice M. Mach, *Text Permissions Supervisor*
Kathy Grell, *Text Permissions Coordinator*
Mabel E. Gurney, Josephine M. Keene, *Senior Permissions Assistants*
Eileen II. Bachr, H. Diane Cooper,
Anita L. Ransom, Kimberly F. Smilay, *Permissions Assistants*
Melissa A. Kamuyu, Martha A. Mulder, Lisa M. Wimmer, *Permissions Clerks*

Patricia A. Seefelt, *Picture Permissions Supervisor*
Margaret A. Chamberlain, *Permissions Coordinator, Pictures*
Pamela A. Hayes, Lillian Tyus, *Permissions Clerks*

Special thanks to Sharon K. Hall for her assistance with the Title Index.

Library of Congress Catalog Card Number 76-46132
ISBN 0-8103-2409-1
ISSN 0276-8178

Printed in the United States of America

Published simultaneously in the United Kingdom
by Gale Research International Limited
(An affiliated company of Gale Research Inc.)

Contents

Preface

It is impossible to overvalue the importance of literature in the intellectual, emotional, and spiritual evolution of humanity. Literature is that which both lifts us out of everyday life and helps us to better understand it. Through the fictive lives of such characters as Anna Karenina, Jay Gatsby, or Leopold Bloom, our perceptions of the human condition are enlarged, and we are enriched.

Literary criticism can also give us insight into the human condition, as well as into the specific moral and intellectual atmosphere of an era, for the criteria by which a work of art is judged reflect contemporary philosophical and social attitudes. Literary criticism takes many forms: the traditional essay, the book or play review, even the parodic poem. Criticism can also be of several types: normative, descriptive, interpretive, textual, appreciative, generic. Collectively, the range of critical response helps us to understand a work of art, an author, an era.

Scope of the Series

Twentieth-Century Literary Criticism (TCLC) is designed to serve as an introduction for the student of twentieth-century literature to the authors of the period 1900 to 1960 and to the most significant commentators on these authors. The great poets, novelists, short story writers, playwrights, and philosophers of this period are by far the most popular writers for study in high school and college literature courses. Since a vast amount of relevant critical material confronts the student, *TCLC* presents significant passages from the most important published criticism to aid students in the location and selection of commentaries on authors who died between 1900 and 1960.

The need for *TCLC* was suggested by the usefulness of the Gale series *Contemporary Literary Criticism (CLC)*, which excerpts criticism on current writing. Because of the difference in time span under consideration *(CLC* considers authors who were still living after 1959), there is no duplication of material between *CLC* and *TCLC*. For further information about *CLC* and Gale's other criticism series, users should consult the Guide to Gale Literary Criticism Series preceding the title page in this volume.

Each volume of *TCLC* is carefully compiled to include authors who represent a variety of genres and nationalities and who are currently regarded as the most important writers of this era. In addition to major authors, *TCLC* also presents criticism on lesser-known writers whose significant contributions to literary history are important to the study of twentieth-century literature.

Each author entry in *TCLC* is intended to provide an overview of major criticism on an author. Therefore, the editors include fifteen to twenty authors in each 600-page volume (compared with approximately forty authors in a *CLC* volume of similar size) so that more attention may be given to an author. Each author entry represents a historical survey of the critical response to that author's work: some early criticism is presented to indicate initial reactions, later criticism is selected to represent any rise or decline in the author's reputation, and current retrospective analyses provide students with a modern view. The length of an author entry is intended to reflect the amount of critical attention the author has received from critics writing in English, and from foreign criticism in translation. Critical articles and books that have not been translated into English are excluded. Every attempt has been made to identify and include excerpts from the seminal essays on each author's work.

An author may appear more than once in the series because of the great quantity of critical material available, or because of a resurgence of criticism generated by events such as an author's centennial or anniversary celebration, the republication or posthumous publication of an author's works, or the publication of a newly translated work. Generally, a few author entries in each volume of *TCLC* feature criticism on single works by major authors who have appeared previously in the series. Only those individual works that have been the subjects of vast amounts of criticism and are widely studied in literature classes are selected for this in-depth treatment. Eugene O'Neill's *Long Day's Journey into Night* and Edith Wharton's *Ethan Frome* are examples of such entries in *TCLC*, Volume 27.

Organization of the Book

An author entry consists of the following elements: author heading, biographical and critical introduction, list of principal works, excerpts of criticism (each preceded by explanatory notes and followed by a bibliographical citation), and an additional bibliography for further reading.

- The *author heading* consists of the author's full name, followed by birth and death dates. The unbracketed portion of the name denotes the form under which the author most commonly wrote. If an author wrote consistently under a pseudonym, the pseudonym will be listed in the author heading and the real name given in parentheses on the first line of the biographical and critical introduction. Also located at the beginning of the introduction to the author entry are any name variations under which an author wrote, including transliterated forms for authors whose languages use nonroman alphabets. Uncertainty as to a birth or death date is indicated by a question mark.

- The *biographical and critical introduction* contains background information designed to introduce the reader to an author and to the critical debate surrounding his or her work. Parenthetical material following many of the introductions provides references to biographical and critical reference series published by Gale, including *Children's Literature Review, Contemporary Authors, Dictionary of Literary Biography, Something about the Author,* and past volumes of *TCLC.*

- Most *TCLC* entries include *portraits* of the author. Many entries also contain illustrations of materials pertinent to an author's career, including manuscript pages, title pages, dust jackets, letters, or representations of important people, places, and events in an author's life.

- The *list of principal works* is chronological by date of first book publication and identifies the genre of each work. In the case of foreign authors where there are both foreign language publications and English translations, the title and date of the first English-language edition are given in brackets. Unless otherwise indicated, dramas are dated by first performance, not first publication.

- *Criticism* is arranged chronologically in each author entry to provide a perspective on changes in critical evaluation over the years. All titles by the author featured in the critical entry are printed in boldface type to enable the user to ascertain without difficulty the works being discussed. Also for purposes of easier identification, the critic's name and the publication date of the essay are given at the beginning of each piece of criticism. Unsigned criticism is preceded by the title of the journal in which it appeared. When an anonymous essay is later attributed to a critic, the critic's name appears in brackets at the beginning of the excerpt and in the bibliographical citation. Many critical entries in *TCLC* also contain translated material to aid users. Unless otherwise noted, translations within brackets are by the editors; translations within parentheses or continuous with the text are by the author of the excerpt. Publication information (such as publisher names and book prices) and parenthetical numerical references (such as footnotes or page and line references to specific editions of works) have been deleted at the editors' discretion to provide smoother reading of the text.

- Critical essays are prefaced by *explanatory notes* as an additional aid to students using *TCLC.* The explanatory notes provide several types of useful information, including the reputation of a critic, the importance of a work of criticism, the specific type of criticism (biographical, psychoanalytic, structuralist, etc.), a synopsis of the criticism, and the growth of critical controversy or changes in critical trends regarding an author's work. In some cases, these notes cross-reference the work of critics who agree or disagree with each other. Dates in parentheses within the explanatory notes refer to a book publication date when they follow a book title and to an essay date when they follow a critic's name.

- A complete *bibliographical citation* designed to facilitate location of the original essay or book by the interested reader follows each piece of criticism.

- The *additional bibliography* appearing at the end of each author entry suggests further reading on the author. In some cases it includes essays for which the editors could not obtain reprint rights.

An appendix lists the sources from which material in each volume has been reprinted. It does not, however, list every book or periodical consulted in the preparation of the volume.

Cumulative Indexes

Each volume of *TCLC* includes a cumulative index listing all the authors who have appeared in *Contemporary Literary Criticism, Twentieth-Century Literary Criticism, Nineteenth-Century Literature Criticism, Literature Criticism from 1400 to 1800, Classical and Medieval Literature Criticism,* and *Short Story Criticism,* along with cross-references to the Gale series *Children's Literature Review, Authors in the News, Contemporary Authors, Contemporary Authors Autobiography Series, Dictionary of Literary Biography, Concise Dictionary of American Literary Biography, Something about the Author, Something about the Author Autobiography Series,* and *Yesterday's Authors of Books for Children.* Readers will welcome this cumulated author index as a useful tool for locating an author within the various series. The index, which lists birth and death dates when available, will be particularly valuable for those authors who are identified with a certain period but whose death date causes them to be placed in another, or for those authors whose careers span two periods. For example, F. Scott Fitzgerald is found in *TCLC,* yet a writer often associated with him, Ernest Hemingway, is found in *CLC.*

Each volume of *TCLC* also includes a cumulative nationality index. Author names are arranged alphabetically under their respective nationalities and followed by the volume numbers in which they appear.

New Index

An important feature now appearing in *TCLC* is a cumulative index to titles, an alphabetical listing of the literary works discussed in the series since its inception. Each title listing includes the corresponding volume and page numbers where criticism may be located. Foreign language titles that have been translated are followed by the titles of the translations—for example, *Voina i mir (War and Peace)*. Page numbers following these translated titles refer to all pages on which any form of the titles, either foreign language or translated, appear. Titles of novels, dramas, nonfiction books, and poetry, short story, or essay collections are printed in italics, while all individual poems, short stories, and essays are printed in roman type within quotation marks. In cases where the same title is used by different authors, the author's surname is given in parentheses after the title, e.g., *Collected Poems* (Housman) and *Collected Poems* (Yeats).

Acknowledgments

No work of this scope can be accomplished without the cooperation of many people. The editors especially wish to thank the copyright holders of the excerpted criticism included in this volume, the permissions managers of many book and magazine publishing companies for assisting us in securing reprint rights, and Anthony Bogucki for assistance with copyright research. We are also grateful to the staffs of the Detroit Public Library, the Library of Congress, the University of Detroit Library, the University of Michigan Library, and the Wayne State University Library for making their resources available to us.

Suggestions Are Welcome

In response to various suggestions, several features have been added to *TCLC* since the series began, including explanatory notes to excerpted criticism that provide important information regarding critics and their work, a cumulative author index listing authors in all Gale literary criticism series, entries devoted to criticism on a single work by a major author, more extensive illustrations, and a title index listing all literary works discussed in the series since its inception.

Readers who wish to suggest authors to appear in future volumes, or who have other suggestions, are cordially invited to write the editors.

Authors to Be Featured in *TCLC*, Volumes 28 and 29

Mikhail Artsybashev (Russian novelist)—Artsybashev was notorious for works promoting the principles of anarchic individualism and unrestrained sensuality. His erotic novel *Sanin* produced an international sensation and inspired cults dedicated to the destruction of social convention.

Henri Bergson (French philosopher)—One of the most influential philosophers of the twentieth century, Bergson is renowned for his opposition to the dominant materialist thought of his time and for his creation of theories that emphasize the supremacy and independence of suprarational consciousness.

George Douglas Brown (Scottish novelist)—Brown is the author of *The House with the Green Shutters,* a chronicle of the tragic decline of a Scottish family and one of the first works to depict the baser aspects of life in rural Scotland.

Edgar Rice Burroughs (American novelist)—Burroughs was a science fiction writer who is best known as the creator of Tarzan. His *Tarzan of the Apes* and its numerous sequels have sold over thirty-five million copies in fifty-six languages, making Burroughs one of the most popular authors in the world.

Samuel Butler (English novelist and essayist)—Butler is best known for *The Way of All Flesh,* an autobiographical novel that is both a classic account of the conflict between father and son and an indictment of Victorian society.

Joyce Cary (Anglo-Irish novelist)—Regarded as an important contributor to the trilogy as a literary form, Cary wrote trilogies noted for their humor, vitality, sympathetic characterizations, and technical virtuosity.

Willa Cather (American novelist and short story writer) Cather combined knowledge of Nebraska with an artistic expertise reminiscent of the nineteenth-century literary masters to create one of the most distinguished achievements of twentieth-century American literature. She has been compared to Gustave Flaubert and Henry James for her sensibility, emphasis on technique, and high regard for the artist and European culture, and to the "lost generation" of Ernest Hemingway and F. Scott Fitzgerald for her alienation from modern American society.

Anton Chekhov (Russian dramatist and short story writer) Praised for his stylistic innovations in both fiction and drama as well as for his depth of insight into the human condition, Chekhov is the most significant Russian author of the generation to succeed Leo Tolstoy and Fedor Dostoevsky. *TCLC* will devote an entry to Chekhov's plays, focusing on his dramatic masterpieces *The Seagull, Uncle Vanya, Three Sisters,* and *The Cherry Orchard.*

Stephen Crane (American novelist and short story writer)—Crane was one of the foremost realistic writers in American literature. *TCLC* will devote an entry to his masterpiece, *The Red Badge of Courage,* in which he depicted the psychological complexities of fear and courage in battle.

Finley Peter Dunne (American journalist)—Dunne was the creator of Mr. Dooley, a popular character whose witty and insightful comments on social and political issues were a regular feature of American newspapers at the turn of the century. One of the best-known figures in America during the early decades of the century, Mr. Dooley inspired songs, plays, and musical comedies, as well as numerous imitators.

F. Scott Fitzgerald (American novelist)—Fitzgerald is considered the principal chronicler of the ideals and disillusionments of the Jazz Age, and his *Tender is the Night* is one of his most celebrated novels. In an entry devoted solely to this work, *TCLC* will present major critical essays examining its meaning and importance.

Edmund Gosse (English novelist and critic)—A prolific man of letters in late nineteenth-century England, Gosse is of primary importance for his autobiographical novel *Father and Son,* which is considered a seminal work for gaining insight into the major issues of the Victorian age, especially the conflict between science and religion inspired by Darwin's *The Origin of Species.* Gosse is also important for his introduction of Henrik Ibsen's "new drama" to English audiences and for his numerous critical studies of English and foreign authors.

Muhammad Iqbal (Indian poet and philosopher)—Considered one of the leading Muslim intellectual figures of the twentieth century, Iqbal was a political activist and the author of poetry calling for social and religious reform.

Franz Kafka (Austrian novelist and short story writer)—Kafka's novel *The Trial* is often considered the definitive expression of his alienated vision as well as one of the seminal works of modern literature. *TCLC* will devote an entire entry to critical discussion of this novel, which has been described by Alvin J. Seltzer as "one of the most unrelenting works of chaos created in the first half of this century."

Dmitri Merezhkovsky (Russian novelist, philosopher, poet, and critic)—Although his poetry and criticism are credited with initiating the Symbolist movement in Russian literature, Merezhkovsky is best known as a religious philosopher who sought in numerous essays and historical novels to reconcile the values of pagan religions with the teachings of Christ.

John Muir (American naturalist, essayist, and autobiographer)—In such works as *A Thousand Mile Walk to the Gulf* and *The Mountains of California,* Muir celebrated the North American wilderness. He was also a prominent conservationist who was instrumental in establishing the system of national parks in the United States.

George Orwell (English novelist and essayist)—Designated the "conscience of his generation" by V. S. Pritchett, Orwell is the author of influential novels and essays embodying his commitment to personal freedom and social justice. *TCLC* will devote an entry to Orwell's first major popular and critical success, *Animal Farm,* a satirical fable in which Orwell attacked the consequences of the Russian Revolution while suggesting reasons for the failure of most revolutionary ideals.

Luigi Pirandello (Italian dramatist)—Considered one of the most important innovators of twentieth-century drama, Pirandello developed experimental techniques including improvisation, the play-within-the-play, and the play-outside-the-play in order to explore such themes as the fluidity of reality, the relativity of truth, and the tenuous line between sanity and madness.

Marcel Proust (French novelist)—Proust's multivolume *À la recherche du temps perdu (Remembrance of Things Past)* is among literature's works of highest genius. Combining a social historian's chronicle of turn-of-the-century Paris society, a philosopher's reflections on the nature of time and consciousness, and a psychologist's insight into a tangled network of personalities, the novel is acclaimed for conveying a profound view of all human existence.

George Saintsbury (English critic)—Saintsbury has been called the most influential English literary historian and critic of the late-nineteenth and early-twentieth centuries.

Ernest Thompson Seton (American naturalist and author) Best known as the founder of the Boy Scouts of America, Seton was the author of twenty-five volumes of animal stories for children as well as books on woodcraft and natural history.

Gertrude Stein (American novelist and critic)—Stein is recognized as one of the principal figures of literary Modernism, both as a brilliant experimentalist in such works as *The Autobiography of Alice B. Toklas* and *Tender Buttons* and as an influence upon a generation of authors that included Ernest Hemingway and F. Scott Fitzgerald.

Italo Svevo (Italian novelist)—Svevo's ironic portrayals of the moral life of the bourgeoisie, which characteristically demonstrate the influence of the psychoanalytic theories of Sigmund Freud, earned him a reputation as the father of the modern Italian novel.

Leo Tolstoy (Russian novelist)—Along with *Anna Karenina, War and Peace* is considered Tolstoy's most important work and one of the greatest works in world literature. *TCLC* will devote an entire entry to the critical history of this epic novel.

Thorstein Veblen (American economist and social critic)— Veblen's seminal analyses of the nature, development, and consequences of business and industry—as well as his attack on bourgeois materialism in *The Theory of the Leisure Class*—distinguished him as one of the foremost American economists and social scientists of the twentieth century.

Thomas Wolfe (American novelist)—Wolfe is considered one of the foremost American novelists of the twentieth century. His most important works present intense and lyrical portraits of life in both rural and urban America while portraying the struggle of the lonely, sensitive, and artistic individual to find spiritual fulfillment.

Additional Authors to Appear in Future Volumes

Abbey, Henry 1842-1911
Abercrombie, Lascelles 1881-1938
Adamic, Louis 1898-1951
Ade, George 1866-1944
Agustini, Delmira 1886-1914
Akers, Elizabeth Chase 1832-1911
Akiko, Yosano 1878-1942
Alas, Leopoldo 1852-1901
Aldrich, Thomas Bailey 1836-1907
Aliyu, Dan Sidi 1902-1920
Allen, Hervey 1889-1949
Archer, William 1856-1924
Arlen, Michael 1895-1956
Arlt, Roberto 1900-1942
Austin, Alfred 1835-1913
Bahr, Hermann 1863-1934
Bailey, Philip James 1816-1902
Barbour, Ralph Henry 1870-1944
Benét, William Rose 1886-1950
Benjamin, Walter 1892-1940
Bennett, James Gordon, Jr. 1841-1918
Berdyaev, Nikolai Aleksandrovich 1874-1948
Beresford, J(ohn) D(avys) 1873-1947
Binyon, Laurence 1869-1943
Bishop, John Peale 1892-1944
Blake, Lillie Devereux 1835-1913
Blest Gana, Alberto 1830-1920
Blum, Léon 1872-1950
Bodenheim, Maxwell 1892-1954
Bowen, Marjorie 1886-1952
Byrne, Donn 1889-1928
Caine, Hall 1853-1931
Cannan, Gilbert 1884-1955
Carducci, Giosuè 1835-1907
Carswell, Catherine 1879-1946
Churchill, Winston 1871-1947
Corelli, Marie 1855-1924
Cotter, Joseph Seamon 1861-1949
Croce, Benedetto 1866-1952
Crofts, Freeman Wills 1879-1957
Cruze, James (Jens Cruz Bosen) 1884-1942
Curros, Enríquez Manuel 1851-1908
Dall, Caroline Wells (Healy) 1822-1912
Daudet, Léon 1867-1942
Delafield, E.M. (Edme Elizabeth Monica de la Pasture) 1890-1943
Deneson, Jacob 1836-1919
DeVoto, Bernard 1897-1955
Diego, José de 1866-1918
Douglas, (George) Norman 1868-1952
Douglas, Lloyd C(assel) 1877-1951
Dovzhenko, Alexander 1894-1956
Drinkwater, John 1882-1937
Durkheim, Émile 1858-1917

Duun, Olav 1876-1939
Eaton, Walter Prichard 1878-1957
Eggleston, Edward 1837-1902
Erskine, John 1879-1951
Fadeyev, Alexander 1901-1956
Ferland, Albert 1872-1943
Field, Rachel 1894-1924
Flecker, James Elroy 1884-1915
Fletcher, John Gould 1886-1950
Fogazzaro, Antonio 1842-1911
Francos, Karl Emil 1848-1904
Frank, Bruno 1886-1945
Frazer, (Sir) George 1854-1941
Freud, Sigmund 1853-1939
Fröding, Gustaf 1860-1911
Fuller, Henry Blake 1857-1929
Futabatei Shimei 1864-1909
Glaspell, Susan 1876-1948
Glyn, Elinor 1864-1943
Golding, Louis 1895-1958
Gould, Gerald 1885-1936
Guest, Edgar 1881-1959
Gumilyov, Nikolay 1886-1921
Gyulai, Pal 1826-1909
Hale, Edward Everett 1822-1909
Hansen, Martin 1909-1955
Hernández, Miguel 1910-1942
Hewlett, Maurice 1861-1923
Heyward, DuBose 1885-1940
Hope, Anthony 1863-1933
Hudson, W(illiam) H(enry) 1841-1922
Huidobro, Vincente 1893-1948
Ilyas, Abu Shabaka 1903-1947
Imbs, Bravig 1904-1946
Ivanov, Vyacheslav Ivanovich 1866-1949
James, Will 1892-1942
Jammes, Francis 1868-1938
Johnson, Fenton 1888-1958
Johnston, Mary 1870-1936
Jorgensen, Johannes 1866-1956
King, Grace 1851-1932
Kirby, William 1817-1906
Kline, Otis Albert 1891-1946
Kohut, Adolph 1848-1916
Kuzmin, Mikhail Alexseyevich 1875-1936
Lamm, Martin 1880-1950
Leipoldt, C. Louis 1880-1947
Lima, Jorge De 1895-1953
Locke, Alain 1886-1954
López Portillo y Rojas, José 1850-1903
Louys, Pierre 1870-1925
Lucas, E(dward) V(errall) 1868-1938
Lyall, Edna 1857-1903
Machar, Josef Svatopluk 1864-1945

Mander, Jane 1877-1949
Maragall, Joan 1860-1911
Marais, Eugene 1871-1936
Masaryk, Tomas 1850-1939
Mayor, Flora Macdonald 1872-1932
McClellan, George Marion 1860-1934
McCoy, Horace 1897-1955
Mirbeau, Octave 1850-1917
Mistral, Frédéric 1830-1914
Monro, Harold 1879-1932
Moore, Thomas Sturge 1870-1944
Móricz, Zsigmond 1879-1942
Morley, Christopher 1890-1957
Morley, S. Griswold 1883-1948
Murray, (George) Gilbert 1866-1957
Nansen, Peter 1861-1918
Nobre, Antonio 1867-1900
O'Dowd, Bernard 1866-1959
Ophuls, Max 1902-1957
Orczy, Baroness 1865-1947
Owen, Seaman 1861-1936
Page, Thomas Nelson 1853-1922
Palma, Ricardo 1833-1919
Papadiamantis, Alexandros 1851-1911
Parrington, Vernon L. 1871-1929
Peck, George W. 1840-1916
Phillips, Ulrich B. 1877-1934
Pinero, Arthur Wing 1855-1934
Pontoppidan, Henrik 1857-1943
Powys, T. F. 1875-1953
Prévost, Marcel 1862-1941
Quiller-Couch, Arthur 1863-1944
Radiguet, Raymond 1903-1923
Randall, James G. 1881-1953
Rappoport, Solomon 1863-1944
Read, Opie 1852-1939
Rebreanu, Liviu 1885-1944
Reisen (Reizen), Abraham 1875-1953
Remington, Frederic 1861-1909
Riley, James Whitcomb 1849-1916
Rinehart, Mary Roberts 1876-1958
Ring, Max 1817-1901
Rivera, José Eustasio 1889-1928
Rohmer, Sax 1883-1959
Rozanov, Vasily Vasilyevich 1856-1919
Saar, Ferdinand von 1833-1906
Sabatini, Rafael 1875-1950
Sakutaro, Hagiwara 1886-1942
Sanborn, Franklin Benjamin 1831-1917
Santayana, George 1863-1952
Sardou, Victorien 1831-1908
Schickele, René 1885-1940
Seabrook, William 1886-1945
Shestov, Lev 1866-1938
Shiels, George 1886-1949
Södergran, Edith Irene 1892-1923

Solovyov, Vladimir 1853-1900
Sorel, Georges 1847-1922
Spector, Mordechai 1859-1922
Squire, J(ohn) C(ollings) 1884-1958
Stavenhagen, Fritz 1876-1906
Stockton, Frank R. 1834-1902
Subrahmanya Bharati, C. 1882-1921
Sully-Prudhomme, René 1839-1907
Sylva, Carmen 1843-1916
Thoma, Ludwig 1867-1927
Tomlinson, Henry Major 1873-1958

Totovents, Vahan 1889-1937
Tuchmann, Jules 1830-1901
Turner, W(alter) J(ames) R(edfern) 1889-1946
Upward, Allen 1863-1926
Vachell, Horace Annesley 1861-1955
Van Dyke, Henry 1852-1933
Villaespesa, Francisco 1877-1936
Wallace, Edgar 1874-1932
Wallace, Lewis 1827-1905
Walsh, Ernest 1895-1926

Webster, Jean 1876-1916
Wen I-to 1899-1946
Whitlock, Brand 1869-1927
Wilson, Harry Leon 1867-1939
Wolf, Emma 1865-1932
Wood, Clement 1888-1950
Wren, P(ercival) C(hristopher) 1885-1941
Yonge, Charlotte Mary 1823-1901
Zecca, Ferdinand 1864-1947
Zeromski, Stefan 1864-1925

Readers are cordially invited to suggest additional authors to the editors.

E(dward) F(rederic) Benson

1867-1940

English novelist, short story writer, essayist, biographer, auto-biographer, and dramatist.

An enormously popular and prolific author, Benson is best remembered for his creation of the characters Dodo and Lucia, each of whom was featured in a series of novels that are considered classic works of Edwardian comedy. Charming, witty, and superficial, Benson's comic heroines were enthusiastically received by the reading public and continue to attract a devoted audience. Benson also wrote other types of popular fiction, including mysteries and horror stories, and achieved a modest reputation as a biographer and memoirist whose gossipy portraits of his era retain much of their interest today.

Benson was the fifth of six children born in Shropshire to Mary Sidgwick Benson and Edward White Benson, headmaster of Wellington College, later Bishop of Truro and then Archbishop of Canterbury. The household was devoted to learning and literary pursuits: the Bensons circulated their own sketches and stories among themselves, and three of them—Arthur Christopher, Robert Hugh, and Edward Frederic—became well-known authors who produced a prodigious number of volumes.

Benson studied classical languages and then archaeology at Marlborough College, where he also edited a student publication, the *Cambridge Fortnightly*. He continued his archaeological studies at King's College, Cambridge, and from 1892 through 1895 was associated with the British School of Archaeology, supervising several excavations in England. During these years he began his first novel, *Dodo,* which he conceived as the story "of some fascinating sort of modern girl, who tackled life with uncommon relish and success, and was adored by the world in general, and had all the embellishments that a human being can desire except a heart." When the novel was published it caused an immediate sensation due to its strikingly original heroine and the rumor that Dodo was modeled after a prominent figure in London society, as well as the fact that an Archbishop's son had written a smart (and slightly risqué) "society" novel from an insider's perspective. Benson went on to write nearly eighty novels and collections of short stories, a handful of plays, and several volumes each of biography, autobiography, sketches, and reminiscences. Toward the end of his life, his production of fiction slackened somewhat, although he continued to write until infirmity made it too difficult. From 1934 until 1937 he served as Mayor of Rye, a responsibility he met with great seriousness and which demanded much of his time. Benson died in 1940.

The popular success of *Dodo* and its sequels—*Dodo's Daughter, Dodo the Second,* and *Dodo Wonders*—is often attributed to Benson's manner of depicting Dodo and telling her story. As Benson explained: "It was no use just informing the reader that here was a marvellously fascinating personality . . . or that to see her was to worship her, or that after a due meed of worship she would reveal herself as no more than husk and coloring matter. Explanations and assurances of that sort were now altogether to be dispensed with." She "was to reveal herself by what she said, and thus, whatever she did, would need no comment." There is little plot and no character de-

velopment in a Dodo novel, merely the portrait of the central character and a host of minor figures coming into contact, and often conflict, with her. While many critics have described Dodo as "fascinating," "delightfully wicked," "brilliant and charming," others find her thoroughly unlikable. One reviewer called Benson's first novel a "successful picture of an attractive but soulless woman." In another series of novels Benson developed a second memorable character: Lucia, otherwise known as Emmeline Lucas, a relentless, middle-aged social climber. Lucia has much in common with her fictional predecessor Dodo: she is vain, shallow, pretentious, a snob—and to hosts of readers, irresistible. The novels featuring this character—*Queen Lucia, Miss Mapp, Lucia in London, Mapp and Lucia, Lucia's Progress,* and *Trouble for Lucia*—have been praised as minor comic masterpieces, and Lucia herself is considered one of the most memorable comic creations in English fiction.

Benson's other writings include works of short supernatural fiction that are noted for their often graphic scenes of horror. Several—in particular "The Room in the Tower," "Mrs. Amworth," "The Face," and "Caterpillars"—are considered classics of the genre. During the later years of his career, Benson turned increasingly to writing nonfiction, particularly biography, and he wrote several volumes of reminiscences that have been characterized as lively, entertaining, and slightly malicious in their unabashed tale-telling. Benson's autobiography, *Final Edition*, appeared posthumously to a uniformly positive reception. Commentators and friends used the opportunity to review the career of this prolific popular novelist who had captured archetypes of an era in his mocking but good-natured novels, and concluded that his works were valuable reflections of his age.

(See also *Contemporary Authors,* Vol. 114.)

PRINCIPAL WORKS

Dodo: A Detail of the Day. 2 vols. (novel) 1893
The Rubicon (novel) 1894
Limitations (novel) 1896
The Babe, B. A. (novel) 1897
The Princess Sophia (novel) 1900
The Luck of the Vails (novel) 1901
The Image in the Sand (novel) 1905
The Angel of Pain (novel) 1906
The Room in the Tower, and Other Stories (short stories) 1912
Dodo's Daughter (novel) 1913
Thorley Weir (novel) 1913
Arundel (novel) 1914
Dodo the Second (novel) 1914
The Oakleyites (novel) 1915
David Blaize (novel) 1916
The Freaks of Mayfair (sketches) 1916
David Blaize and the Blue Door (novel) 1918
Our Family Affairs 1867-1896 (sketches and reminiscences) 1920
Queen Lucia (novel) 1920
Dodo Wonders (novel) 1921
Miss Mapp (novel) 1922
Colin (novel) 1923
Visible and Invisible (short stories) 1923
Colin II (novel) 1925
Mother (biography) 1925
Lucia in London (novel) 1927
Sir Francis Drake (biography) 1927
The Life of Alcibiades (biography) 1928
Spook Stories (short stories) 1928
As We Were: A Victorian Peep-Show (sketches and reminiscences) 1930
Mapp and Lucia (novel) 1931
As We Are: A Modern Review (sketches and reminiscences) 1932
Charlotte Brontë (biography) 1932
King Edward VII (biography) 1933
More Spook Stories (short stories) 1934
Ravens' Brood (novel) 1934
Lucia's Progress (novel) 1935; also published as *The Worshipful Lucia,* 1935
Queen Victoria (biography) 1935
The Kaiser and English Relations (historiography) 1936
Daughters of Queen Victoria (biography) 1939
Trouble for Lucia (novel) 1939
Final Edition (autobiography) 1940

THE SPECTATOR   (essay date 1893)

[*In the following excerpt from a favorable review of* Dodo, *the critic particularly praises the characterization of Dodo.*]

Dodo is a delightfully witty sketch of the "smart" people of society as it is in the Row and the "house-party" of the day. We know no cleverer "impression" of the jumble of old and new habits of life as they are mixed in the froth of "all London." The writer is a showman with keen insight and sympathy, and he is a true artist in his presentation and selection of materials, which speak for themselves without labels. They are of the slightest, but so truthfully given that they suggest their world, and its movement and colour, without a word of padding or moralising. There is probably portraiture in some characteristics of his personages, particularly in the women of the story; but while the whole book is a telling "human document," he never dissects, even when he introduces us to souls or "apostles" who are nothing if not subtle and psychological as they faintly echo Ibsen and Bourget. Mr. Benson's men are more satisfactorily "barbarian" than his women, if not as novel. They have what may be called the healthy open-air virtues of English gentlemen, which some popular and pessimistic, and let us add ignorant, painters of society have for some time back left out of their representations. It is true that the portrait of the heroine, Dodo, which is the most elaborate study in the book, is as little like our grandmothers as possible. She is lifted to higher, and not lower, levels by the man who adores her, and this is a satisfactory new departure in fiction, which, even at its worst, perseveres in the old convention that women are, or ought to be, superior beings, which, as a matter of fact, they have not been since Eden or before.

Dodo incarnates in a brilliant and charming fashion a new type,—woman as she has become since she cast herself loose from the customs built up during so many centuries. Dodo has beauty and the genius of fragmentary wit, but how intolerable would be a wilderness of women aping her and suffering from the same enfranchisement! She is meantime quite different from the creations of French fiction, and though her nerves are as highly strung and her heart as small as those of any Parisian heroine, she is as English as any breezy young woman who gallops early in the Park. She marries the Marquis of Chesterford for money and position, while she likes his cousin, Jack Broxton, better. As for love, she feels it only for her brilliant self, and even her love for herself is a shallow passion. Bore is the protagonist of the book. Bore is the origin of all its evil. Her baby bores her, and within three weeks of its death she goes to a ball as her only relief. . . .

She is adored by her loyal and chivalrous husband, who believes in her according to old-fashioned faith in women as angels,—a faith for the first time shaken by her indifference to their child. In vain she really tries to act her part properly as an attentive and agreeable wife, for she has the energy and perseverance which are gained by long habit of society. Bore overcomes all her intentions of fine performance of her part as Lord Chesterford's wife, and she suddenly asks Jack Broxton to run away with her, having previously ordered her carriage to take them to the nearest station the same evening. He refuses, in a well-drawn scene, and she forgets all about the carriage, and is as cheery as ever hunting next morning with her husband. This is all very shocking, yet it is touched with so light a hand that we are no more shocked than Charles Lamb was by the dramatists of the Restoration. We are chiefly sorry for the forlorn female intellect unballasted by love, drifting hither and thither among the quicksands of circumstance, unstayed by any unseen power even of passion. She is very pitiful in her in-capacity for any emotions except those which her "play-act-ing" provides for her. She is an inimitable comrade, but she should not have let herself be caught in the meshes of man's honest and faithful love. When she meets it face to face,—"I don't know what to do," she exclaims, "it isn't my fault that I am made like this. I want to know what love is, and I can't. I can't!" With wit free as the song of birds and that has some-thing of genius in its spontaneity, Dodo is absolute queen of her set, and her set is "all London." To amuse and to be amused is her aim in life, as it is of many in "all London," and she allows no echoes of the Catechism or even of Mrs. Grundy's voice to interfere with her whims. She is egotism *in excelsis*, egotism triumphant, for men and women alike delight in her. If she wrecks the happiness of others she is sorry, and can sob and cry as a child might for a broken toy, yet even to us in the seat of judgment she is charming, and we wonder what fresh victim Dodo will discover, with a sense that the victim is enviable. The author draws the two Lords Chesterford with a fine conception of young English gentlemen, the very flower of European civilisation. Dodo's husband, by his truth and tender strength and courage, enhances all her follies, and yet shields them to the reader; both he and his cousin are governed by the fine honesty of honour. "Surely there is some-thing divine in these men we thought most human," says the painter of them, and we agree with him.

The women of the sketch are altogether on a lower level, and as yet unknown in the weary mass of daily fiction, that lives by outraging the old traditions or flattering them, and always with some turnover of the old properties in search of novelty. (p. 810)

The brilliant little picture is so essentially English that when its figures are transported to Zermatt, much of the verisimili-tude of the novel is lost. It has less of fresh-air charm, and becomes commonplace, as a French story might be. The noisy wit of Dodo has, for the first time, a hint of vulgar inappro-priateness in the shadow of the Matterhorn. She herself feels that Swiss scenery is not her right background, and at the same time she becomes aware of her final defeat at the hands of Adam. It requires a somewhat melodramatic Austrian Prince to restore the supremacy of man over this emancipated Eve. We leave the story for our readers to guess, or probably not to guess, and only say that the sudden and irretrievable collapse of Dodo is excellent art. We feel curiosity and even pity for her leap in the very dark company of an "unmitigated scoun-drel." . . .

Certainly, since Cleopatra there has been no woman of more "infinite variety" than Dodo. (p. 811)

A review of "Dodo," in The Spectator, Vol. 70, No. 3390, June 17, 1893, pp. 810-11.

WILLIAM MORTON PAYNE (essay date 1893)

[*The longtime literary editor for several Chicago publications, Payne reviewed books for twenty-three years at the* Dial, *one of America's most influential journals of literature and opinion in the early twentieth century. In the following excerpt, Payne pre-dicts transitory popularity for* Dodo.]

Mr. E. F. Benson's *Dodo* shows us that the son of an Arch-bishop of Canterbury may display a bent anything but eccle-siastical, or even ethical. It also shows us that the writer is a keen observer of things and men (including women), and that

he has no little sense of humor. Dodo is a delightfully wicked creation, although we cannot take her quite as seriously as the author would evidently have us do. She clearly belongs to the world of conventional art of which Lamb discoursed in his essay on the dramatists of the Restoration; a world that lies apart from the one in which we actually live, a world whose people may do and say what they please without the remotest danger of influencing the conduct of anybody in the real world. A large part of the book simply reports Dodo's conversation, of which the following is a good example:

> "Yes, I know, but you do me an injustice. I shall be very good to him. I can't pretend that I am what is known as being in love with him— in fact, I don't think I know what that means, except that people get in a very ridiculous state, and write sonnets to their mistress's front teeth, which reminds me that I am going to the dentist to-morrow. Come and hold my hand—yes, and keep withered flowers and that sort of thing. Ah, Jack, I wish that I really knew what it did mean. It can't be all nonsense, because Ches-terford's like that, and he is an honest man if you like. And I do respect and admire him very much, and I hope I shall make him happy, and I hear he's got a delightful new yacht; and, oh! do look at that Arbuthnot girl opposite with a magenta hat. It seems to me inconceivably stu-pid to have a magenta hat. Really, she's a fool. She wants to attract attention, but she attracts the wrong sort."

This sort of thing is almost preternaturally clever, and there is a great deal of it in the book; in fact, there is little else that arrests the attention. But it palls after a hundred pages or so, and most of the other characters are lay figures. *Dodo* has been, we understand, a great success in England, which is not sur-prising, but it will be equally surprising to find anybody reading it a few years hence. It has the meteoric quality of such books as *Mr. Isaacs* and *Helen's Babies*, and its brilliancy is but for the hour.

William Morton Payne, in a review of "Dodo: A Detail of the Day," in The Dial, Vol. XV, No. 179, December 1, 1893, p. 340.

WILLIAM MORTON PAYNE (essay date 1894)

[*In the following excerpt, Payne for the most part derides* The Rubicon.]

[The heroine] of **The Rubicon** is more seriously wicked than **Dodo**, and far less attractive in her wickedness. But she has at least the grace to put an end to her destructive career by suicide, and the action becomes her, however little the ethical finality attaching to it. The only merit of this novel is afforded by its occasional bits of bright observation and satirical comment; as a piece of construction, it is slovenly both as to style and to composition in the larger sense. What is meant for a tragic climax (the scene in the opera box) is ludicrous in its ineffec-tiveness and inadequacy. "You are a wicked woman," says Reggie, and turns on his heel. The remark is truthful enough, but the particular instance offers nothing to occasion it.

William Morton Payne, in a review of "The Rubi-con," in The Dial, Vol. XVI, No. 192, June 16, 1894, p. 364.

LITERARY DIGEST (essay date 1920)

[*In the following excerpt, the reviewer praises the first of the Lucia books,* Queen Lucia, *for its satire.*]

None of the recent English novelists seems to possess quite the light touch that is Mr. E. F. Benson's when he chooses. The author of *Dodo* is admirably qualified to shoot folly as it flies, and in *Queen Lucia* he has a merry time with some of the fads of a small but advanced community, and especially with Mrs. Lucas, the lady who bears aloft the torch of culture therein.

Riseholme is a small village whose fine old Elizabethan cottages had afforded Mrs. Lucas her opportunity when, her husband having amassed a comfortable fortune at the Bar, they were looking about for a country home. Three of these cottages had been bought, and, with the aid of a sympathetic architect, they had been made into a comfortable dwelling, the new owners "subsequently building onto them a new wing that ran at right angles at the back and which was, if anything, a shade more inexorably Elizabethan than the stem onto which it was grafted, for here was situated the famous smoking-parlor, with rushes on the floor, a dresser ranged with pewter tankards, and leaded lattice-windows of glass so antique that it was practically impossible to see out of them." In this charming abode dwell Mr. and Mrs. Lucas, perfect examples of the self-conscious, affected, shallow culture that is so characteristic of the first two decades of this century.

Mrs. Lucas's first name is Emmeline, but she is known to her friends and admirers as Lucia, pronounced in the Italian way— La Lucia, wife of Lucas. Her husband, tho a solid citizen, sufficiently practical to have made a comfortable fortune, is now devoting himself to literature, writing little prose poems, offering up incense to his wife, and reflecting complacently upon the pleasure he feels in leading the higher intellectual life. His wife keeps up her music, discourses upon the delights of Bach and Scarlatti, pities the poor Londoners for their feverish and unsatisfactory existences, and puts the finishing touch to the atmosphere of culture that pervades the domain by exchanging a few Italian sentences with her husband from time to time. They don't know much Italian, but they love to use the few phrases which they have acquired.

In such a village as Riseholme Mrs. Lucas is easily the queen. In all amusements she takes the lead, and especially is she the first to perceive and tread paths where the expansion of the mind and soul forms the goal. (pp. 101-02)

The book is lacking in what we are constantly told is necessary for a good novel. There is not much plot; there is no love interest; there is no climax—the book just stops (much to our regret) after chronicling one more Riseholme failure in the line of spirit manifestation. But it is long since one has seen such a masterly bit of satire, such a piece of character-study as Lucia. (p. 102)

"A Fearful Spectacle," *in* Literary Digest, *New York, Vol. LXVI, No. 12, September 18, 1920, pp. 101-02.*

ALICE SESSUMS LEOVY (essay date 1921)

[*In the following excerpt, Leovy favorably reviews the first three Dodo novels, noting that the characters and events of the books remain vivid and memorable.*]

Most people have read *Dodo*. If not, they seldom acknowledge the fact. They laugh or look wise and make vague, safe comments on Archbishop's sons or the great change in Mr. Benson's style, and let it go at that. For practically everyone knows enough about *Dodo* to hazard a few remarks. After thirty years some people can still speak of it with a certain scornful contempt. However, they read it—and, what is more, *they still remember it.* Not every Dodo of the minute can be Dodo for a generation. Novels of the day before yesterday are easily forgotten.

When Mr. Benson created Dodo—by the way, he did create her; the book was written, finished, before he had the pleasure of meeting Miss Margot Tennant for the first time—he did a very daring thing. For the book was an experiment, a new departure in style and treatment. And he was doubtful. But the ayes had it and *Dodo* became the rage. Whether one liked it or not, one read it. He established a precedent, and coined many quite inimitable phrases that have been duly appreciated by other writers. (Read *Dodo* again if you don't believe it.) He gave us a society novel—"a detail of the day"—in which the author stood back without comment and allowed his characters to speak for themselves. He did not egg them on, as it were, and interrupt them with sly observations and deductions of his own.

He let Dodo talk—incessantly—and when she paused to catch her breath, Edith talked. Delightful, ridiculous, lovable Edith! They are both alive, vivid, and so are most of the minor characters. But Chesterford is unconvincing at times; Jack is vague; and Prince Waldenech simply is not there at all.

Surely everyone remembers the opening scene—the announcement of Dodo's engagement and her conversation with Jack. Remembers how Dodo, fond of Jack, loving him as much as she can love anyone not herself, but greedy for position, marries his cousin. Lord Chesterford is a simple soul, dull and estimable. Dodo, of course, is neither. But she plays her part to perfection until things combine to force her hand. She finds Chesterford unutterably boring; and her baby, a comparative stranger; he is so young, dies at the height of the London season. During the three weeks of her seclusion—not her mourning—before her tempestuous reappearance in society, Jack is much in evidence. Then she has a foolish quarrel with her husband about Prince Waldenech. Finally she and Jack decide that it would be wiser to see less of one another in the future and Chesterford, a true gentleman, dies as the result of a hunting accident. But instead of marrying Jack she quarrels with him, at the last moment, about Prince Waldenech; and when he returns the next day "to make it up" he is told that— "Her Serene Highness left for Paris this morning." And that was the end of Dodo for many, many years.

Then, in the halcyon days of the Edwardian era she returned to England [in *Dodo's Daughter*]. She was accompanied by a grown daughter, but minus the Prince, whom she had divorced because he proved to be rather more than less of a beast. She is the same Dodo, unchanged in spite of her troubles. Clever, kind, deliciously amusing, and with about as much capacity for real emotion as a gold-fish. Light-heartedly and joyously, she prepares to reconquer England. She succeeds, of course. No one can resist her, not even Edith. And eventually she marries Jack, as she should have done years before, and becomes Marchioness of Chesterford for the second time. In spite of Waldenech, who follows her to England, there is a triumphant wedding, with royalty present, at which Edith's music is played.

Waldenech reminds one of the Countess of Cardigan's friend—whatever his morals were, his manners were perfect. Except, that is, for his one lapse; the moment when he so far forgot himself as to indulge in a little gunplay.

This is really the story of Nadine and her friends, but Nadine's mother dominates the scene instead of remaining decorously in the background. And who can imagine Dodo in the background? The people who missed *Dodo's Daughter* missed a rare treat. It is a collection of portrait studies; some charming, some refreshingly funny, all delightful, done by the hand of a real artist. Not that Mr. Benson is always an artist, but there are certain types that he can depict with even more skill than his imitators.

And now we meet Dodo again [in *Dodo Wonders*] in the spring of 1914. She is fifty-four, has tried to wear useless horn-rimmed spectacles and be frankly middle-aged, but it was a total failure. So she rattles merrily along, not by any means a "grizzly kitten," because for one thing, she has never annexed a boy. "And nothing makes a woman look so old as that." She has settled down, in matters of affection, to loving Jack and her young son, but she does and says as much as ever. And by the end of the war has actually discovered that the world is different—*that she is different*. In everything the war has "made the most immense difference. For instance—nowadays—we're all as poor as rats, though we trot along still. Nowadays . . . we all have parlor-maids. . . . Oh, that reminds me, Jack, I interviewed a butler this morning, who I think will do. He wants about a thousand a year. . . ."

Perhaps one is a snob, like Dodo, but it is nice to read about people who take the amenities of daily life for granted. Who have their meals in the dining-room as a matter of course, instead of in the kitchen. Who have long, clever conversations about nothing in particular over the tea table—and continue them while other people wash the tea things. It is restful. One realizes that it is all quite archaic, that Dodo and her friends are creatures of another age—but it is a very pleasant age.

One "gets nothing" from Dodo—except amusement—and it is not a book for those who take their fiction sadly. (pp. 281-82)

> *Alice Sessums Leovy, "The Dodo Saga," in The Double Dealer, Vol. II, No. 12, December, 1921, pp. 281-83.*

E. F. BENSON   (essay date 1921)

[*In the following excerpt from his first book of reminiscences, Our Family Affairs: 1867-1896, Benson outlines the beginnings of his literary career.*]

Young gentlemen with literary aspirations usually start a new University magazine, which for wit and pungency is designed to eclipse all such previous efforts, and I was no exception in the matter of this popular gambit. Another freshman lodging in the same house as myself was joint-editor, and so was Mr. Roger Fry, two or three years our senior, and some B.A. whose name I cannot recollect. Mr. Roger Fry certainly drew the illustration on the cover of the *Cambridge Fortnightly,* which represented a tremendous sun of culture rising behind King's College Chapel. O. B. contributed a poem to it, so also did my brother Arthur, and Mr. Barry Pain sent us one of the best parodies in the language, called "The Poets at Tea," in which Wordsworth, Tennyson, Christina Rossetti, Swinburne and others are ludicrously characteristic of themselves. He also tried to

galvanize the *Cambridge Fortnightly* into life by one or more admirable short stories, and Mr. G. Lowes Dickinson applied the battery with him. But the unfortunate infant was clearly stillborn, and considering the extreme feebleness of most of its organs, I do not wonder that it was, after the lapse of a term or so, quite despaired of. It had really never lived: it had merely appeared. My share in the funeral expenses was about five pounds, and I was already too busy writing *Sketches from Marlborough,* which was duly and magnificently published within a year, to regret the loss. Fearing to be told that I had better attend to my Greek and Latin, I did not inform my father of this literary adventure; then, when a local printer and publisher at Marlborough, to my great glee, undertook its production, I thought he would consider it very odd that I had not told him of it before and so I did not tell him at all. The book had a certain local notoriety, and naturally enough, the fact of it reached him, and he wrote me the most loving letter of remonstrance at my having kept it from him. There was no word of blame for this amateur expenditure of time and energies, but I divined and infinitely regretted that I had hurt him. And somehow I could not explain, for I still felt that if he had known I was working at it, he certainly would have suggested that I might have been better occupied. Already, though half-unconsciously, I knew to what entrancing occupation I had really determined to devote my life, and though I might have made a better choice, I could not, my choice being really made, have been better occupied than in practising for it. The book in itself, for the mere lightness which was all that it professed, was not really very bad: the ominous part about it (of which the omens have been amply fulfilled) being the extreme facility with which it was produced. (pp. 231-32)

My third year at Cambridge . . . I had resolved to devote to a strenuous course of the classical tongues, and the autumn of 1889 saw me provided with a shelf of interleaved Latin and Greek authors (in order to make quantities of profound notes on the opposite page); with a firm determination to remember every crabbed phrase in case of finding some approximate English equivalent in passages set for translation from English into Baboo Latin or Greek, and triumphantly dragging it in; with pots of red ink to underline them, and with an optimistic determination of getting a first in my Classical Tripos. (p. 243)

Having taken a first (such a first!) my father was more than pleased that, pending the choice of a profession, which I had already secretly registered, I should stop up another year and attempt to perform a similar feat in some other branch of knowledge (p. 245)

There were some weeks of long vacation . . . which I now know to have been loaded with fate so far as my own subsequent life was concerned, though at the time those scribblings I then indulged in seemed to be quite as void of significance as any particular number of the *Saturday Magazine* had been. For one morning, at Cambridge, where I had returned for a few weeks before we went out to Switzerland in August, I desisted from the perusal of Miss Harrison's *Mythology and Monuments of Ancient Athens,* and wrote on the top of a piece of blue foolscap a word that has stuck to me all my life. For a long time there had been wandering about in my head the idea of some fascinating sort of modern girl, who tackled life with uncommon relish and success, and was adored by the world in general, and had all the embellishments that a human being can desire except a heart. Years ago some adumbration of her had occurred in the story that Maggie [Benson's sister] and I wrote together; that I suppose was the yeast that was now beginning to stir and bubble in my head. She must ride, she must dance, she must have all the nameless attraction that attaches to those who are as prismatic and as hard as crystal, and above all she must talk. It was no use just informing the reader that here was a marvellously fascinating personality . . . , or that to see her was to worship her, or that after a due meed of worship she would reveal herself as no more than husk and colouring matter. Explanations and assurances of that sort were now altogether to be dispensed with. Scarcely even was the currrent of her thought, scarcely even were the main lines of her personality to be drawn: she was to reveal herself by what she said, and thus, whatever she did, would need no comment. There is the plain presentment of the idea that occupied my youthful mind when I wrote *Dodo* at the top of a piece of blue foolscap, and put the numeral ''one'' on the top right-hand corner; and where this crude story of mine still puts in a plea for originality, is in the region of its conscious plan. Bad or good (it was undoubtedly bad) it introduced a certain novelty into novel-writing which had ''quite a little vogue'' for a time. The main character, that is to say, was made, in her infinitesimal manner, to draw herself. In staged and acted drama even, that principle—bad or good—is never consistently mantained, because other people habitually discuss the hero and heroine, and the audience's conception of them is based on comment as well as on self-spoken revelation. Also in drama there is bound to be some sort of plot, in which action reveals the actor. But in this story which I scribbled at for a few weeks, there was no sort of plot: there was merely a clash of minor personalities breaking themselves to bits against the central gabbling figure. Hideously crude, blatantly inefficient as the execution was, there was just that one new and feasible idea in the manner of it. What I aimed at was a type that revealed itself in an individual by oceans of nonsensical speech.

I wrote with the breathless speed of creation (however minute such creation was), almost entirely, but not quite, for my own private amusement. It was not quite for that internal satisfaction alone, because as I scampered and scamped, I began to contemplate a book arising out of these scribblings, a marketable book, that is to say, between covers and for sale. Eventually, for the information of any who happen to remember the total result, I got as far as the lamentable death of Dodo's first husband, and that, as far as I knew then, was the end of the story. Dodo would be thus left a far from disconsolate widow dangling in the air like a blind-string in front of an open window. On the last page of the book, she would remain precisely as she had been on the first; she had not developed, she had not gone upwards or downwards in any moral course; she was a moment, a detail, a flashlight photograph flared on to a plate without the smallest presentment of anything, except what she happened to be at that moment. All this I did not then realize. . . . There it was anyhow, and having finished it, I bundled the whole affair into a drawer, and with that off my mind, concentrated again over the *Mythology and Monuments of Ancient Athens*. (pp. 247-49)

At Cambridge the study of archæology had forcibly taken possession of me by right of love, and at last I was working at that which it was my business to be occupied in, with devotion to my subject. (p. 255)

Once again I made a triumphant tripos in the matter of archæology, was given an open scholarship at King's, and immediately afterwards applied for one of those grants that seemed to hang like ripe plums on the delightful tree of knowledge. Hitherto those branches had waved high above my head,

but now they graciously swept downwards and I plucked at the first plum I saw, and applied for a small grant to excavate in the town-walls at Chester. . . . To my intense surprise some grant—from the Würtz Fund, I think—was given me, for the purpose of discovering, if possible, new facts about the distribution of Roman legions in Britain. (p. 263)

Six weeks' exploration was enough to exhaust my funds, and I carried my squeezes and my sketches back to Cambridge, there to put the results into shape. . . . And there I found, and re-read with a suddenly re-kindled interest those pages of blue foolscap on the first of which was the heading *Dodo*. I had written them chiefly for my own amusement, but now, rightly or wrongly, I had the conviction that they might amuse others as well. But I really had no idea, till I took them out again, what they were like; now it occurred to me that the people in them were something like real people, and that the whole in point of agitating fact was something like a real book, that might be printed and bound. . . . But I instantly wanted another and if possible a story-teller's opinion about it, and sent it off to my mother, asking her to read it first, and if it seemed to her to provide any species of entertainment, to think whether she could not manage to induce Mrs. Harrison (Lucas Malet) or Henry James, to cast a professional eye over it. She managed this with such success, that a few days afterwards she wrote to me to say that Henry James had consented to read it, and give his frank opinion. The packet she had already, on his consent, despatched to him.

Now this MSS. which thus had reached the kindest man in the world, was written in a furious hurry and covered with erasures, that exploded into illegible interpolations, and was indited in such a hand as we employ on a note that has to be dashed off when it is time already to go to the station. This was genially hinted at when late in November the recipient announced to me his judgment in the matter; for he prefaced his criticism with an apology for having kept it so long, and allowed that, in consenting to read and criticize, he had ''rather overestimated the attention I should be able to give to a production in manuscript of such substantial length. We live in such a world of type-copy to-day that I had taken for granted your story would come to me in that form.'' . . .

I should like to call the attention of Mr. Max Beerbohm, our national caricaturist and parodist, to this unique situation. Henry James at that time had lately evolved the style and the method which makes a deeper gulf between his earlier books and his later than exists between different periods of the work of any other artist. Nearest perhaps in this extent and depth of gulf comes the case of the painter Turner, but the most sober and quiet example of his early period is not so far sundered from the most riotous of Venetian sunrises, as is, let us say, ''Roderick Hudson'' from ''The Ivory Tower.'' Just about now Henry James had realized, as he told my mother, that all his previous work was ''subaqueous'': now, it seemed to him that he had got his head above water, whereas to those who adored his earlier work he appeared to have taken a header into some bottomless depth, where no plummet could penetrate. At this precise moment when he had vowed himself to psychological analysis so meticulous and intricate that such action as he henceforth permitted himself in his novels had to be sifted and searched for and inferred from the motives that prompted it, he found himself committed to read a long and crabbed MS., roughly and voluptuously squirted on to the paper. With what sense of outrage as he deciphered it sentence by sentence must he have found himself confronted by the high-spirited but harebrained harangues of my unfortunate heroine and her wordy friends! Page after page he must have turned, only to discover more elementary adventures, more nugatory and nonsensical dialogues. At the stage at which my story then was, I must tell the reader that the heroine was far more extravagant than she subsequently became: She was much pruned and tamed before she made her printed appearance. The greater part of her censored escapades have faded from my mind, but I still remember some occasion soon after her baby's death when she was discovered, I think by Jack, doing a step-dance with her footman. It must all have seemed to Henry James the very flower and felicity of hopeless, irredeemable fiction and still he persevered. . . . Or did he persevere? He wrote me anyhow the most careful and kindly of letters, following it by yet another, delicately and delightfully forbearing to quench the smoking flax.

"I am such a fanatic myself," he writes in the earlier of these, "on the subject of form, style, the evidence of intention and meditation, of chiselling and hammering out in literary things that I am afraid I am rather a cold-blooded judge, rather likely to be offensive to a young story-teller on the question of quality. I'm not sure that yours strikes me as quite so ferociously literary as my ideal. . . . Only remember that a story is, essentially a form, and that if it fails of that, it fails of its mission. . . . For the rest, make yourself a style. It is by style we are saved."

In case the reader has given a glance to *Dodo*, can he imagine a more wisely expressed opinion, that opinion, in fact, being no opinion at all? Never by any possibility could that MS. have seemed to him worth the paper it was written on, or two minutes of his own time. With what a sigh of relief he must have bundled it into its wrapper again!

I suppose I was incorrigible on this question of scribbling, for I was not in the least discouraged. But for the time the further adventures of the book were cut short by its author's Odysseys, for directly after Christmas my father and mother, Maggie, Lucy Tait and I started for Algiers, through which we were to journey together as far as Tunis. After that I was going on to Athens to spend the spring there studying at the British School of Archæology, and it was with a light heart that I clapped Dodo, after this austere outing, back into a drawer again to wait till I could attend to her. (pp. 272-75)

Dodo had been put back in her drawer, after her expedition to Henry James: now for the second time I took her out and tasted her, as if to see whether she seemed to have mellowed like a good wine, or become sour like an inferior one, in which case I would very gladly have poured her on the earth like water, and started again. But I could not, reading her once more, altogether cast her off: she had certain gleams of vitality about her, and with my mother's connivance and help again I submitted her to a professional verdict. This time it was my mother's friend, Mrs. Harrison, known to our admiring family as "Lucas Malet," author of the adorable *Colonel Enderby's Wife*, who was selected to pronounce on my story, and again, I am afraid, it was without the slightest realization of this highway robbery on the time of an author that I despatched the book. Anyhow those two assaults on Henry James and Lucas Malet have produced in me a fellow-feeling for criminals such as I was a quarter of a century ago, so that now, when, as occasionally happens, some light-hearted marauder announces that he or she (it is usually she) is sending me her manuscript, which she hopes I won't mind reading, and telling her as soon as possible exactly what I think of it, and to what publisher she had better send it (perhaps I would write him a line too)

and whether the heroine isn't a little overdone (but her mother thinks her excellent), and would I be careful to register it when I return it, and if before next Thursday to this address, and if after next Friday to another, etc. etc., I try to behave as Lucas Malet behaved in similar circumstances. I do not for a moment say that I succeed, but I can still remember how pleasant it should seem, from the point of view of the aspirant scribbler, that somebody should be permitted to read what has been written with such rapture and how important it all is. . . .

But I can never hope to emulate Lucas Malet's tact and wisdom in her genial, cordial, and honest reply (when she had had the privilege of wading through these sheets), for they still remain to me, who know her answer almost by heart, to be the first and the last word in the true theory of the writing of fiction. Her deft incisions dissected, from lungs and heart and outwards to the delicate fibre of the skin that protects and expresses the life within, the structure of stories, short or long, that are actually alive. First must come the "idea," the life that is to vitalize the complete animal, so that its very hair and nails are fed with blood. . . . And then, since I cannot possibly find words as apt and as sober as hers I will quote from the letters themselves.

> First the idea, then the grouping, which is equivalent to our drama—then a search for models from whom to draw. Most young English writers—the artistic sense being a matter of experience, not of instinct, with most of us—begin just the other way about. Begin with their characters . . . rummage about for a story in which to place them, and too often leave the idea out of the business altogether. . . . One evil consequence of this method—among many others—is that there is a distracting lack of completeness and *ensemble* in so much English work. The idea should be like the thread on which beads are strung. It shouldn't show, except at the two ends; but in point of fact it keeps the beads all together and in their proper relation.

Then, to one already hugely interested in this admirable creed of the art of fiction, Lucas Malet proceeded to a dissection, just and kind and ruthless, of the story as it stood. She hurt in order to heal, she cut in order that healthy tissue (if there was any) might have the chance to grow. She showed me by what process (if I applied it seriously and successfully) I might convert my Dodo-doll into something that did not only squeak when pressed in the stomach, and gave no other sign of vitality than closing its eyes when it was laid flat. In consequence, greatly exhilarated by this douche of cold water, I collected such fragments of an "idea" as existed, revised what I had written, and wrote (in pursuance of the "idea") the second volume, as it subsequently appeared, in those days when novels were originally issued in three or two volumes at the price of a guinea and a half or a guinea. I finished it that autumn, sent it to the publisher recommended by Lucas Malet, who instantly accepted it. It came out in the following spring, that of 1893. I was out in Greece . . . at the time, and though it was my first public appearance (since *Sketches from Marlborough* may be considered as a local phenomenon) I feel sure that from the time when, with trembling pride, I corrected the long inconvenient galley sheets that kept slipping on to the floor, I gave no further thought to it at all. Bad or good, I had done my best; what happened concerned me no more, for I was quite absorbed in the study of the precinct of Asclepios on the slopes of the Acropolis, in the life at Athens, and in a volume of short stories that I began to write with a pen still wet, so to speak, with the final corrections on the proof sheets of *Dodo*. She was done with, so far as I was concerned, and it was high time, now that I was twenty-five, to get on with something else, before the frosts of senility paralysed all further effort. (pp. 290-92)

I came home to find to my incredulous and incurious surprise, that in the interval I had become, just for the focus of a few months, famous or infamous. One of those rare phenomena, less calculable than the path of a comet, which periodically is to destroy the world, had occurred, and there was a "boom" in *Dodo,* and no one was more astonished than the author, when his mother met him arriving by the boat train at Victoria, and hinted at what was happening. All sorts of adventitious circumstances aided it: it was thought extremely piquant that a son of the Archbishop of Canterbury should have written a book so frankly unepiscopal, and quite a lot of ingenious little paragraphists invented stories of how I had read it aloud to my father and described his disconcertedness: the title-rôle and other characters were assigned to various persons who happened then to be figuring in the world, but apart from all these adventitious aids, this energetic and trivial experiment had—in those ancient days—a certain novelty of treatment. There were no explanations; whatever little life its characters were possessed of, they revealed by their own unstinted speech. That, as I have already explained, had been the plan of it in my mind, and the execution, whatever the merits of the plan might be, was in accordance with it. It went through edition after edition, in that two-volume form, price a guinea (against which shortly afterwards the libraries revolted) and all the raging and clamour, of course, only made it sell the more. It had received very scant notice in the Press itself; what (as always happens) made it flourish so furiously was that people talked about it.

But its success apart from the delightful comedy of such a first act to its author, led on to a truly violent situation when the curtain rose again, for the critics, justly enraged that this rare phenomenon called a "boom" should not have been detected and heralded by their auguries and by them damned or deified, laid aside a special pen for me, ready for the occasion when I should be so imprudent as to publish another novel; and they all procured a large bottle of that hot ink which Dante dipped for,

> When his left hand i' the hair of the wicked,
> Back he held the brow and pricked its stigma
> Bit unto the live man's flesh for parchment,
> Loosed him, laughed to see the writing rankle. . . .

If they had not noticed *Dodo,* they would at least notice her successor. Indeed the fairy godmother who presents a young author at his public christening with a boom, brings him a doubtful gift, for when next I challenged attention all these little Macaulays and Dantes uncorked their hot ink, and waited pen in hand till Mr. Methuen sent them their "advance copies." Then, saying "one, two, three—go," they all produced on the birth-morning of the unfortunate book columns and columns of the most blistering abuse that I remember ever beholding in God-fearing journals. This blasted infant was a small work called *The Rubicon*, now so completely forgotten that I must ask the reader to take my word for it that it was quite a poor book. It was not even very, very bad: it was just poor. Critics have hundreds of poor books submitted to their commiserated notice, and they are quite accustomed to that, and tell the public

in short paragraphs that the work in question is "decidedly powerful," or "intensely interesting" or "utterly futile," and there is an end of it as far as they are concerned. Had this blasted infant been a first book it would naturally have recieved no more than a few rude little notices, and perhaps a few polite little notices. But as it was the successor to the abhorred comet it was concertedly singled out for the wrath of the Olympians. The *candidatus exercitus* of the entire Press went forth with howitzers and Maxims (in both senses), with cannons of all calibres, with rifles and spears and arrows and sharp tongues to annihilate this poor little May-fly. (pp. 294-96)

No book, however bad, could possibly have called forth, in itself, so combined an onslaught: every gun in Grub Street was primed and ready and sighted not on *The Rubicon* at all, but on the author of *Dodo*. But herein is shown the inexpediency of using up all your ammunition at once, on so insignificant a target. It was clear that if the respectable journals of London made so vigorous an offensive, that offensive had to be final, and the war to be won. Still more clear was it that, if this was not a preconcerted, malicious and murderous campaign not on a particular book, but on an individual, the entire columns of the London Press must henceforth be completely devoted to crushing inferior novels. *The Rubicon* was but one of this innumerable company: if the Press had determined to crush inferior novels, it was clear that for a considerable time there would be no room in its columns for politics, or sport or foreign news or anything else whatever. Not even for advertisements, unless we regard such attacks as being unpaid advertisements. . . .

So there was no more firing for the present, and it was all rather reminiscent of the tale of how Oscar Wilde went out shooting, and fell down flat on the discharge of his own gun.

The Press, after that, had nothing more to shoot at me, for all their heaviest shells had been launched; so the blighted author walked off, as Mr. Mantalini said, as comfortable as demnition, and proceeded vigorously to write *The Babe, B. A.* and other tranquil works, just as if he had not been blown into a thousand fragments. (pp. 300-01)

> *E. F. Benson, in his* Our Family Affairs: 1867-1896,
> *George H. Doran Company, 1921, 336 p.*

THE NEW YORK TIMES BOOK REVIEW   (essay date 1924)

[*In the following excerpt, the critic reviews Benson's supernatural stories in* Visible and Invisible.]

A sound classification of modern "hair-raising" novelists would put Henry James at one extreme of the scale and, shall we say, Bram Stoker at the other. Mr. E. F. Benson's series, *Visible and Invisible* never reaches the depths of *Dracula,* but it is still further from the heights of *The Turn of the Screw*. For all their preoccupation with the occult the Benson brothers seem to lack the allusive faculty necessary to secure conviction when dealing with manifestations of the unseen world. There is a blunt objectivity in their treatment of psychic phenomena which passes the borders of contrast and leaves us in the domain of discrepancy. The psychic motive is a tenuous motive and overtones is its abiding peril. In the hands of a master of the genre a footfall heard on stairs or garden path, an accustomed and inexplicable sound caught in the stillness of night (who that has read it will forget James's "high, light cry"?) even an inpalpable presence needing no explantion beyond the tortured nerves of the watcher, will be quite sufficient to secure the desired effect. It is not in this suggestive spirit that Mr. Benson develops his themes. His vampires are robust creatures who tunnel their way up from unquiet graves to the surface, and who can only be allayed by apt incineration's artful aid. His ghostly gardeners "brush past" leaving a touch that is "that of ice." They stalk into quiet parlors where piquet is being played and exhibit a severed carotid that is full explanation for nocturnal "walkings."

Mr. Benson is too veteran a craftsman not to give us a book that is eminently readable. *Visible and Invisible* falls into the category of literature designated in advance for "fireside or hammock reading." In other words it is addressed to the uncritical spirit. There is the homely country side (Cornwall—that witch-land of England for choice) with its pleasant and well-ordered social life, golf, bridge, motoring—unsophisticated farm-folk or fisher-folk. Then, intruding their horrible and dubious Medusa heads, witch and were-wolf, family doom or half-forgotten local legend supply the thrill. Science is a useful and dependable ally. The impersonal, almost inhuman hermit of research, with his retorts and batteries, who can develop the image left upon glazing eyes, or release the cry choked back in the strangled throat, is a familiar, not to say domesticated, figure in the mystery story. Mr. Benson knows how to handle him to advantage.

The author of *Visible and Invisible* is most successful where he is content to be happily inconclusive. In **"Negotium Perambulans"** he does come near producing an authentic reaction of terror. The thing "like a gigantic slug" crudely and darkly painted upon the rood-screen of a remote Cornish church, which haunts the farmhouse built impiously out of the ruin of a more ancient fane, has its abiding place where all such things should have it, in the twilight of the half-perceived. In **"The Horror Horn,"** a theme which M. Edouard Esmé has developed into a long novel just published in American dress, is presented with a picturesqueness of detail that may be partly due to the accident of Mr. Benson, like his French brother in letters, M. Henry Bordeaux, being an enthusiastic Alpinist. On unclimbed peaks, in the region of eternal snow, there dwells, it seems, the last remnant of an extinct race, cave men and women of incredible strength, and incredible bestiality. In a raging snowstorm (wonderfully described) with the path to safety blotted out by whirling flakes, meet, with Mr. Benson, the Neanderthal woman.

> In one hand she held by the horns a chamois that kicked and struggled. A blow from its hind-leg caught her withered thigh, and with a grunt of anger she seized the leg in her other hand, and as a man may pull from its sheath a stem of meadow grass, she plucked it off the body, leaving the torn skin hanging round the gaping wound. Then, putting the red, bleeding member to her mouth she sucked at it as a child sucks a stick of sweetmeat. . . . She craned forward her neck, she dropped her prey and, half rising, began to move toward me. As she did this, she opened her mouth and gave forth a howl such as I had heard a moment before.

For fireside reading, you see, but, perhaps it would be as well to add, not alone and too late at night. (pp. 24-5)

"For Fireside Reading," in The New York Times Book Review, *May 11, 1924, pp. 24-5.*

GILBERT SELDES   (essay date 1936)

[Seldes was an American journalist, television scriptwriter, and critic. In the following excerpt from his introduction to an omnibus volume of the Lucia novels, he praises the vitality of the character of Lucia.]

The trouble about writing an introduction to the four masterpieces [*Queen Lucia, Miss Mapp, Lucia in London,* and *Mapp and Lucia*] . . . is that I can do one of two things, and either one is bound to be fatal to me. If I do not recount the great episodes and quote the wittiest lines, the comparison between the introduction and the text can do me nothing but harm. Whereas if I do recount and retell, it will be perfectly clear that all the good things are not mine, and I will only have spoiled the reader's pleasure. Everyone recalls, of course, what happened to Sir James Barrie when he wrote the introduction to *The Young Visiters;* he so obviously enjoyed writing down all the best bits of Daisy Ashford's book that, in the end, everyone believed that he himself was Daisy Ashford. As Mr. E. F. Benson is a famous writer, I do not run the risk of ever being flattered by the thought that I am Benson; and he is far too honest a writer for anyone to suspect that he chose another name to write this introduction himself.

The reason for having an introduction at all is that there ought to be a Lucia Society, just as there is a society which devotes itself to the most detailed research into the life and times of Sherlock Holmes—the principal object of which, if I am not mistaken, is to prove that Conan Doyle never existed, but was only a character created, between shots of dope, by Mr. Holmes. Where Holmes was educated, whether Watson was shot in the arm or the leg, how many housekeepers worked at their Baker Street lodgings, and who was Holmes's favorite composer, are subjects which these enthusiasts have discussed and answered. But the age of Lucia and her maiden name, the year in which Miss Mapp visited Riseholme, the exact constituents of the lobster recipe, and what became of Georgie's needlework when it was finished, are equally worthy of scholarship. And if there is a plaque on any house in Baker Street, there should be a statue, at least, in a certain English village in honor of the queen who left there and—as you may discover by reading [*Lucia's Progress*]—became the mayor of Tilling.

It is my opinion that these books about Lucia and Miss Mapp are the most enchantingly malicious works written by the hand of man. Few authors have been so unsparing of their own characters, and few have exposed them so gleefully to humiliation. The triumph of art over life is really remarkable, because, although I feel that I would do almost anything to avoid meeting either Lucia or Miss Mapp in person, I have in the past ten years gone to considerable pain to meet them again and again in the novels which Mr. Benson has written about them.

Mr. Benson's achievement will always be a trap to novelists who imagine that they can break the tradition of sequels. It is a formula of reviewing that sequels are never as good as the first work, but after writing *Queen Lucia* Mr. Benson wrote *Lucia in London,* and then, introducing Miss Mapp in a volume devoted entirely to herself, wrote a sequel in both series, and, as if that were not enough, published last season, fifteen years after the first of this series, *The Worshipful Lucia,* and they are all so magnificently done that it is hard to say, even with all the sentiment in the world in favor of a first appearance, that any one is better than any other. It is my own opinion that somewhere in the writing of *Lucia in London* the easy malice of the other works turned into actual unkindness. Lucia was out of place in London, and her author rather belabored her for going. But this is the only flaw in a perfect series.

I read *Queen Lucia* shortly after I read *Main Street,* and it was perfectly natural to compare the dictator of the arts and social graces in Riseholme with Carol Kennicott, who was doing much the same work in the Middle West. Sinclair Lewis, I felt, really thought his heroine admirable, but he was in a state of such violent fury about everything that he made her detestable. And Mr. Benson was so urbane about the absurd and magnificent woman he had created that she becomes completely fascinating. There is no doubt that she is a cheat and a liar and a snob and an appalling hypocrite. What is more—the reader will find out soon enough, and it might as well be faced—she breaks at moments into the most deplorable baby talk. She is so arty as to make you wish never to hear her "divine Beethoven" again. You want to gloat with profound satisfaction when she gets her come-uppance—and yet, a moment later, when on the rebound she soars higher than ever and dominates her court more ardently than before, you are as pleased as if one of your own sly social maneuvers had succeeded.

What this means is, of course, that Lucia has vitality. She is not only alive as a character is alive. She has energy, she is charged with powerful human impulses. Even when she is being a pretentious bore to her friends, she has a high magnetic power. She operates on a small scale, like a commander in the days before war was mechanized, but her marches and countermarches, and even her retreats, have the decision and brilliance of a master of strategy.

Her allies and her enemies are, with one conspicuous exception, almost as agreeably detestable as she is herself. That exception is Olga Bracely, the great soprano, who without even knowing it pulls the throne of Riseholme from under Queen Lucia, with never a thought of sitting on it herself. Because of her, Lucia wrests disaster from the very arms of defeat, and catastrophe from the arms of disaster, one magnificent climax of misfortune following on another—until peace (which by that time is virtually a victory) comes to her. It is rumored that Olga Bracely was drawn from life; from, in fact, an admirable American actress who many years ago settled in rural England. (There is a contrary rumor that the notable American actress was the original of Lucia herself, not of Lucia's conqueror—and this is one of the problems with which the Lucia Society may well busy itself.)

Among Lucia's allies, there is her husband, who binds his own poetry in limp leather tied with leather thongs. The reader will derive little satisfaction from the activities of Mr. Lucas. But in Mr. George Pillson he will, I am sure, take infinite pleasure, and I hope he will discern how cunningly Mr. Benson has kept this figure constantly on the edge of the absurd without making him completely into a figure of fun. These three allies are completely surrounded by enemies. In the case of Olga Bracely, the hostility comes entirely from Lucia herself, but Daisy Quantock, Godiva Plaistow, Mrs. Weston, and Elizabeth Mapp, whose face was "corrugated by chronic rage and curiosity," are not passive resisters to the tyranny of Queen Lucia. They are not as clever as she is, but they are endowed with the same almost super-human capacity for carrying on a social war.

The country which was afterwards to establish the British Empire once went to war because a sailor's ear had been cut off; in the Balkans there was a war once, for which the occasion, or the pretext, was pigs' bristles; so that Lucia's war over a

recipe for lobster or the rejection of a painting has ample precedent. I have a suspicion that, like Nietzsche, she reversed Franklin's dictum and believed that there never was a good peace or a bad war. Certainly in her moments of quiet she is most a fool. But when she is arrayed, as she usually is, like an army with banners, she is magnificent. (pp. ix-xiii)

Gilbert Seldes, in an introduction to All About Lucia: Four Novels *by E. F. Benson, Doubleday, Doran & Company, Inc., 1936, pp. ix-xiii.*

LEONARD WOOLF   (essay date 1936)

[*Woolf is best known as one of the leaders of the "Bloomsbury Group" of artists and thinkers, and as the husband of novelist Virginia Woolf, with whom he founded the Hogarth Press. A Fabian socialist during the World War I era, Woolf became a regular contributor to the socialist* New Statesman *and later served as literary editor of the* Nation *and the* Athenaeum, *in which much of his literary criticism is found. Throughout most of his life, Woolf also contributed essays on economics and politics to Britain's leading journals and acted as an advisor to the Labour Party. In the following excerpt, Woolf questions Benson's psychological interpretation of his subject in* The Kaiser and English Relations.]

It is so easy to write an interesting book about the Kaiser that the biographer is naturally tempted to take the line of least resistance and so to miss writing a really good book. Mr. Benson has not resisted the temptation. His book [*The Kaiser and English Relations*] has many admirable qualities in praise of which one might comfortably fill a column of this paper. . . . It is extremely interesting and eminently readable. It is written by a skilled writer—though it should be added that Mr. Benson is always liable to extraordinary linguistic or stylistic lapses, e.g., "the warmth of the Emperor's sentiments towards England and his uncle suffered a wintry refrigeration." Almost any reader will find some hours' entertainment in this lively portrait of the German Emperor and in the less detailed portraits of Queen Victoria, King Edward, the Tsar, and the lesser royal fry. The more sophisticated and more "serious" reader will also find the book interesting, even if there is little which is new in it. He may occasionally be rewarded by discovering some small historical facts hitherto unknown to him. For instance, Mr. Benson gives an account, based apparently upon private information, which I do not remember to have heard before, of how Bülow came to pass the Kaiser's appalling gaffe, the *Daily Telegraph* interview, and subsequently put the blame upon Freiherr von Müller. The point is of some historical importance. (p. 634)

There is ample evidence that, when they wanted to do so, Bülow and others prevented the Kaiser's imbecile gaffes, and in the crucial days of July, 1914, when they wanted to muzzle him, they completely muzzled him. When they wanted a gaffe for their own political purposes, the Kaiser was always given his head. (pp. 634, 636)

The Kaiser in his shining armour was far more the puppet of the "realists" who pulled the strings behind the puppet-show in the War Offices, the Admiralties, the Foreign Offices, the banks, and the purlieus where "heavy industry" is accustomed to pull its strings, than he realised or Mr. Benson realises. The shining armour was a cloak for less romantic things than mediaeval, monarchical nonsense. With those things Mr. Benson is, perhaps rightly, not concerned. He confines himself to the psychological rather than the political problem of the Kaiser. He finds the solution of that problem . . . in the withered arm and the inferiority complex, the discovery of which has done as much for biography and biographers as the internal combustion engine for locomotion. I have little doubt that this psychological interpretation is seventy-five per cent. correct, though I am not sure that the most interesting part of the Kaiser's character would not be found in the twenty-five per cent. which is missed or misinterpreted by Mr. Benson. This inferiority complex business is so terribly overworked these days that it must be almost as tired of itself as we are becoming of it. Nevertheless there are some extremely good things in Mr. Benson's portrait, particularly his convincing sketch of the Kaiser in retirement and the clever, sympathetic portrait of what he might have been, had he been born a country gentleman in tweeds instead of an emperor in shining armour.

As a serious historical biography, the book is of little importance. There is an extremely interesting and important book which might now be written, investigating the part which the Kaiser really played in determining German policy, but Mr. Benson has not written it. Where he approaches the kind of problem which would have to be discussed in such a work, he is, more often than not, I think, wrong in his judgments. For instance, he writes more than once as though there was one fixed point in the Kaisers' foreign policy, "his sincere desire to be allied with England." There is really no evidence of this. All the evidence goes to show that his mind was so unstable that it was perilously near insanity and that he was constitutionally incapable of any fixed policy or of any "sincere" desire which did not turn into its opposite every twenty-four hours. Of course, he did quite often have a "sincere" desire to be allied with England, but he also often had a desire to lead a European coalition which would destroy her. The relative sincerity of contradictory desires is not of much importance, and extremely difficult to determine; what was important about the Kaiser's contradictory desires was that they followed one another with bewildering rapidity and were expressed with almost imbecile violence. The whirling mind of a distracted weathercock is another thing which had to be concealed by the shining armour. (p. 636)

Leonard Woolf, "Shining Armour," in The New Statesman & Nation, n.s. Vol. XII, No. 296, October 24, 1936, pp. 634, 636.

ALBERT BRITT (essay date 1936)

[*In the following excerpt, Britt offers an extensive comparison of Benson's biography of Charlotte Brontë with that of Elizabeth Gaskell, judging Benson's to be more accurate and unbiased.*]

Biography and fiction are related but different arts.

The gap can be bridged and occasionally is. A case in point is . . . E. F. Benson's *Charlotte Brontë.* Its chief weakness lies in the fact, too obvious throughout, that Mr. Benson's chief reason for writing is to confound the first and great biographer of Miss Brontë, Mrs. Gaskell, another novelist. Mrs. Gaskell's *Life of Charlotte Brontë* has for the most part been accepted hitherto as an authentic, usually accurate, and entirely fair portrayal of the great woman novelist of the Victorian time. To be sure, by modern standards she was hardly qualified for such a task. She was a sympathetic, admiring friend, who wrote at close range of a kindred spirit perplexed in many ways by similar problems, doubts, and handicaps. It is only in our time that this state of affairs would be held to constitute a disability. In fact, in the time in which Charlotte lived and Mrs. Gaskell wrote of her, friendship, sympathy, contemporary experience

were all held to be superior qualifications for such authorship, if not, in fact, the only desirable and reliable qualifications.

It is to Mrs. Gaskell that we owe the picture of Miss Brontë as in part the victim of an unfeeling, erratic, and at times cruel father and at most times of a drunken brother. Mrs. Gaskell has shown us Charlotte with her sister, lonesome, unhappy, and unappreciated in the girls' school in Brussels, first as a pupil and then as a teacher. It is to Mrs. Gaskell's pen that we are indebted for the account of the hardships of the Brontë sisters in the school at Cowan Bridge and the long struggles through which they passed to such success as was theirs. Then appears Mr. Benson, having had access to the Brontë letters in the Clement Shorter collection, to offer direct contradiction of many of the statements which contribute to build the pathetic, frequently tragic, always moving story of the Brontës.

To begin with, there is the account of the father's aristocratic Irish pedigree. Mrs. Gaskell implies that the Brontës trace their line from an old Irish family antedating the Cromwellian occupation of Ireland but in Victorian times fallen upon evil days. Mr. Benson assembles evidence that the father's father was an Irish peasant farmer, Brunty by name, and implies that the later spelling was suggested by the accident of Nelson's being made Duke of Brontë in 1799. The discovery of an aristocratic pedigree is an amiable and almost universal weakness and it is probable that most such lines have a peasant origin nearer than most genealogists or ancestor worshipers would be willing to admit. The case against Mrs. Gaskell, however, is somewhat stronger in other and more specific respects.

The picture of Patrick Brontë, the father, as cruel, at times as insane, tyrannizing over his family, forcing them to live on potatoes for days on end, carrying a loaded pistol about the house, and otherwise behaving like a madman with a sadistic tendency, is frequently contradicted by the testimony of Brontë servants who were in the family for years. Mrs. Gaskell's material on this point seems to have been drawn largely from a discharged servant who had been a member of the household for a comparatively short time. There is abundant evidence that the father was of a hot temper, subject to moods of depression, tortured through many years by the fear of blindness, and broken in spirit by the early death of his wife. But that his attitude toward the family was in any material respect different from that of thousands of other parents afflicted with poverty and depressed by sorrow rests only on the evidence of Mrs. Gaskell.

The drunkenness of Bramwell, the brother, is another favorite theme of Mrs. Gaskell. As a matter of fact, Mr. Benson shows that a literal acceptance of the Gaskell record on this point makes Bramwell a confirmed drunkard at the age of fourteen. Drunkard he was at the end of his life, but before that tragedy came there were several years in which his association with his sisters appears to have been of the most agreeable sort, clouded only by his own thwarted ambition, his lack of agreeable companionship of his own age, and a vague and futile process of experiment in several fields of intellectual effort.

Mr. Benson pays his respects to Mrs. Gaskell's account of the writing of the sisters, particularly of Charlotte, and rather cruelly makes literal calculation from one of Mrs. Gaskell's statements. This process shows that according to Mrs. Gaskell, Charlotte's youthful unpublished writing over a period of fifteen months must have amounted to more than two and one-quarter million words, equaling in volume approximately twenty-two modern novels.

Mrs. Gaskell makes considerable use of the overshadowing influence of the school at Cowan Bridge, which all of the Brontë sisters attended as children. She pictures the school as swept by a typhus epidemic. According to Mr. Benson the records show that only one girl died as a result of the illness and that the cause was probably influenza.

But it is in the Brussels period that Mr. Benson is most destructive of the Gaskell structure. The facts of the Brussels experience, according to Mr. Benson, are that Charlotte Brontë fell deeply in love with Monsieur Heger, and that her apparently unwilling return to Brussels the second time, this time as a teacher, was due entirely to her feeling for the master of the school and her desire to be with him. Mr. Benson quotes from letters in the Shorter collection which can be read only as love letters and cites evidence to the effect that the recipient of these letters replied briefly and coldly and only through his wife as amanuensis. As a matter of fact, the Brontë letters which were preserved were saved by Madame Heger who rescued them from a wastebasket where Heger had thrown them. The most damaging aspect of this part of Mr. Benson's discussion is in the evidence that Mrs. Gaskell had access to some of these very letters in Brussels and quoted carefully selected passages in cases where a reproduction of the entire letter would have put an entirely different face on Charlotte's attitude toward the school and the headmaster.

The most complete proof of Mrs. Gaskell's overenthusiastic advocacy of Charlotte Brontë is in the fact that several of her statements, notably those about the father and about the school at Cowan Bridge, were eliminated or altered in a later edition of the *Life.* Unfortunately for Monsieur Heger there was no one to speak so firmly for him and the Brussels experience as portrayed by Mrs. Gaskell, and Charlotte herself in her novel, *Villette,* remains substantially as first presented.

In spite, however, of Mr. Benson's destructive criticism of Mrs. Gaskell, Charlotte Brontë emerges from his book rather more vivid, compelling, and unusual than from the pages of the too kindly friend. The friend's effort is apparently directed toward a justification where no justification was needed and toward an explanation which tended logically to reduce erratic genius to the dead level of ordinary talent. It is a fair assumption that the picture of Charlotte Brontë presented by Mrs. Gaskell as an abused, misunderstood, tortured spirit, beating her wings against the bars of poverty and cruelty, is largely one that the egoistic Charlotte herself presented.

Throughout her life she lived in two worlds, one the rather sordid, dull, empty world of the Haworth parsonage and the moors that surrounded the village; the other the highly colored, exciting, stimulating world of her imagination. The characters and to a considerable extent the events of her novels were drawn out of the everyday life in which she lived. But the plots, particularly the major episodes and relationships, were often those of the dream world. The result was frequently a powerful, realistic clothing draped on an absurd melodramatic frame, as in the case of *Jane Eyre.*

The amiable, unsophisticated, ambitious Jane about to be married to a man already handicapped with a mad wife is undoubtedly Charlotte herself as she liked to conceive herself. The basic incident of *Jane Eyre,* the finding of the unknown cousin living in the lone house on the moors to which she wanders in the typical stage storm of the Victorian novel, the fortune of which they tell her, the burning house in which the mad wife is consumed, the blind Rochester, the marriage and

Rochester's surprising and miraculous recovery of his eyesight, all these are the rankest melodrama and quite characteristic of the writing of such a suppressed, unsophisticated, imaginative character as Charlotte Brontë was.

To accept Mr. Benson's conclusions rather than those of Mrs. Gaskell is to conceive of Charlotte Brontë as something near a genius instead of a rather commonplace, mildly talented, hard working, misunderstood, mistreated mid-Victorian lady.

Parenthetically, the reader of *Jane Eyre* and *Villette* would probably be willing to agree that, if the spirit of Charlotte could be asked to select which of these two pictures most pleased her egotistic soul, it would be Benson's and not Mrs. Gaskell's that would receive the award. (pp. 119-27)

Albert Britt, "Scott and Brontë," in his The Great
Biographers, *Whittlesey House, 1936, pp. 116-27.*

MAX BEERBOHM   (essay date 1940)

[*Although he lived until 1956, Beerbohm is chiefly associated with the fin de siècle period in English literature, more specifically with its lighter phases of witty sophistication and mannered elegance. His temperament was urbane and satirical, and he excelled in both literary and artistic caricatures of his contemporaries. "Entertaining" in the most complimentary sense of the word, Beerbohm's criticism for the* Saturday Review—*where he was a longtime drama critic—everywhere indicates his scrupulously developed taste and unpretentious, fair-minded approach to literature. In the following excerpt, Beerbohm provides a memorial tribute to Benson.*]

The book [*Final Edition*] is one that makes me wish I had known the writer much better than I did. I knew him for many years, and we had many friends in common, but I think we were not personally much interested in each other's doings. I had read *Dodo,* of course, when it burst upon the world, and thought it very brilliant—as, indeed, in a rather garish way, it was. And *The Babe, B. A.,* was a very bright affair also. But nobody pressed me to read the rather more serious novels that followed, year after year, though they too were very popular. Two or three of them I did read. Very bright they seemed to me, but thin, not very real. And now I find that Benson himself, in later years, felt as I did about them. "They lacked," he says, "the red corpuscle. . . . I had often tried to conceal my own lack of emotion in situations that were intended to be moving, by daubing them over with sentimentality." He excepts three or four works from this candid indictment, "but," he says, "I had lost or was fast losing any claims to be called a serious novelist," and the spirit moved him to roam away into fresh fields of labour. He does not claim to have made in them any important discovery. Nevertheless he made one. He found himself.

He found also Charlotte Brontë. His book about her (the first of his biographical books) was an admirable study of character and circumstance. It was what we reviewers call "penetrating." It was tenderly acute and, with all due deference to the foregoing Mrs. Gaskell, inflexibly judicial. In fiction he had been hampered by lack of power to create significant men and women. But here, created already *for* him, was Charlotte, and here Emily and those others; and his keen intelligence could work freely, at case; and his innate gift for narrative shone as never before. He then strode, briskly, firmly, from Haworth Parsonage to Balmoral, where he abode with equally good results: his Victoria rivalled his Charlotte. And presently he gave us those two fascinating works, *As We Were* and *As We*

Are, the ripe fruits of social experience and observation—the wisdom of a man in love with things past, and in charitable touch with present things. There was plenty of autobiography mixed in with those musings. And now, in *Final Edition* (the best, I think, of all his books), there is no lack of pensive digressions in what is mainly the story of Benson's own life.

For autobiography there is a huge demand nowadays, and a not less huge supply. But many of the autobiographists are, alas, gravely handicapped. They have not had interesting lives, or haven't very good memories, or aren't in themselves obviously interesting or charming persons, or haven't a gift for writing. Some of them, indeed, have all these handicaps, and so their perseverance is all the more creditable to them. It is not for doggedness that Benson can be extolled. He had not had to wrestle with any of those awful drawbacks. He had lived in the centre of things, he had a keenly discriminating eye, he knew intimately many people well worth knowing, he had a very clear memory for anything that mattered, anything characteristic or illuminating or amusing; and he could write: he had become, in course of time, master of a lucid, concise, light, flexible prose that exactly fufilled his purposes; a prose abundant in natural felicities; a prose greatly superior to that of either of his brothers, who never were able to curb or chasten their immense facility. . . . As a matter of fact, of course, the three were very fond of one another, though none of them ever was able to admire the works of the other two. One of the most amusing scenes in *Final Edition* is that in which the three sit reading to their mother, one evening, at Tremans, caustic burlesques of one another's works. Each of the parodied was rather puzzled than pained, angrier than hurt. But "Oh, you clever people," said Mrs. Benson, "why don't you all for the future write each other's books instead of your own? You do it so much better."

But amidst all the fun that pervades this book, one is conscious of a serious, a gallant and even noble character. E. F. Benson, unlike his respectively academic and ecclesiastic brothers, had always been a man of the world, a lover of society, and of various sports, and of travel. Twenty years ago he began to have symptoms of arthritis. Gradually he was crippled, but in the fell process he never lost heart, and he writes of it with complete stoicism—and even with blithe wit. Only once does he repine—and then, I am bound to say, without good reason. "The presence of him who shuffles along on a stick, and who cannot pick it up if he drops it, does not promote gaiety. . . . He may feel, among many faces and the alert movements of acquaintances, that he is a tiny speck of tarnish on their silver hours, and will wonder if they are not suffering him rather than welcoming." The last time I met him was at a luncheon party given not long ago by an old friend of ours. Of course one couldn't help feeling sorry for him. But how could one not have delighted in his talk, of which the sparkle was as gay, and the point as keen, as ever?

Max Beerbohm, "Last and Best," in The Spectator, *Vol. 165, No. 5862, November 1, 1940, p. 446.*

ALEXIS LYKIARD   (essay date 1974)

[*Lykiard is a Greek-born English novelist, poet, and critic. The following excerpt is from Lykiard's introduction to a selection of Benson's best stories of supernatural horror.*]

The decade 1904-14 proved fertile imaginative soil for a last extraordinary flowering of fantastic or macabre minor classics. It was as if these hothouse blooms now so sought after by the contemporary connoisseur formed—with their entwined horrors and enchanted perversities, their tendrils of poetic dread—garlands for the Great Horror itself, the apocalyptic holocaust of War. Much of the best work of writers like Arthur Machen, Algernon Blackwood, M. P. Shiel, Bram Stoker, Rider Haggard, Richard Middleton, Oliver Onions, M. R. James, F. Marion Crawford, Violet Hunt, "Vernon Lee," "Baron Corvo" and William Hope Hodgson appeared during this period, and to their exotic ranks must be added Edward Frederic Benson, whose first ghost story collection, *The Room in the Tower,* was published in 1912. (p. 7)

[Apart] from the occasional story reprinted in an anthology, Benson's macabre writings have been virtually unobtainable—an injustice which this edition [*The Horror Horn and Other Stories: The Best Horror Stories of E. F. Benson*] culled from his four collections seeks to redress. The task of selecting the dozen or so "best" weird stories (less than a quarter of his total output) has been a difficult one.

The memorable vampire stories **"The Room in the Tower"** and **"Mrs. Amworth"** *must* be included. So of course, must **"Caterpillars,"** that spine-chilling fable of fear and disease. From there on, each to his own taste. H. P. Lovecraft in *Supernatural Horror in Literature* [see Additional Bibliography] praised Benson's versatility and singled out for special mention **"Negotium Perambulans"** "whose unfolding reveals an abnormal monster from an ancient ecclesiastical panel which performs an act of miraculous vengeance in a lonely village on the Cornish coast, and **'The Horror Horn,'** through which lopes a terrible half-human survival dwelling on unvisited Alpine peaks." Both these are included here, as is **"The Face,"** which Lovecraft considered "lethally potent, in its relentless aura of doom." Here too are other unforgettable creepy tales dealing with murders and mutants, obsession and repression, mediums and ghost-hunters, spectres, satanists and things that do far more than just go bump in the night.

Fantasy writers urge us to face hidden and irrational fears. Exaggerators, caricaturists, they work towards that deeper shock of recognition that comes *after* the initial shock, but as well as being entertainers they are moralists, who seek to extend mental frontiers and revise our views of life and death. Which probably accounts for their timeless popularity.

Confronting what Benson himself called "fear of what might be coming out of the huge darkness which lies on all sides of human experience," the choice of reaction (a laugh or a shudder) depends largely upon the reader's own temperament, but these stories carry conviction because E. F. Benson writes in a terse, no-nonsense style which tellingly contrasts with his wide-ranging and horrific subject-matter. Here he resembles his distinguished contemporary M. R. James: in the ever more sceptical twentieth century, understatement (Lovecraft's own luxuriant and archaic style excepted) is probably the most convincing narrative technique one can use when writing about the supernatural. Certainly Benson at his best causes the reader to suspend disbelief: these stories do linger in the mind and distil their unease with real art. (pp. 8-9)

Alexis Lykiard, in an introduction to The Horror Horn and Other Stories *by E. F. Benson, edited by Alexis Lykiard, Panther, 1974, pp. 7-9.*

NANCY MITFORD   (essay date 1977)

[*Mitford was an English novelist and critic. In the following excerpt, she notes the artful simplicity of the Lucia novels, which renders them enjoyable to modern readers.*]

Lucia (Mrs. Emmeline Lucas) is a forceful lady who lives in the South of England in two small country towns—that is, when we meet her first, in the late Twenties, she is the Queen of Riseholme, but half way through her story (which ends just before the war) she transfers, presumably so that her creator can pit her against the formidable Miss Mapp, to Tilling. Tilling, I believe, is Rye, where E. F. Benson himself lived in the house formerly occupied by Henry James; this is the very house which Lucia finally worms out of Miss Mapp.

Lucia's neighbours in both towns are almost all, like herself, middle-aged people of comfortable means. Their occupations are housekeeping, at which most of them are skilled (there is a good deal about food in the books, and lobster à la Riseholme plays an important part), gardening, golf, bridge and bickering. None of them could be described as estimable, and they are certainly not very interesting, yet they are fascinated by each other and we are fascinated by them.

All this fascination is generated by Lucia; it is what happens with regard to her that counts; she is the centre and the driving force of her little world. As she is a profoundly irritating person, bossy, horribly energetic and pushing, the others groan beneath her yoke and occasionally try to shake it off: but in their heart of hearts they know that it is she who keeps them going and that life without her would be drab indeed.

The art of these books lies in their simplicity. The jokes seem quite obvious and are often repeated: we can never have enough of them. In *Lucia in London,* Daisy gets a ouija board and makes mystical contact with an Egyptian called Abfou. Now Abfou hardly ever says anything but "Lucia is a Snob," yet we hang on his lips and are thrilled every time Georgie says, "I am going to Daisy's, to weedj." Georgie is the local bachelor who passes for Lucia's lover. Then there is the Italian with which Lucia and Georgie pepper their conversation: "Tacete un momento, Georgie. Le domestiche." It never, never palls. On at least two occasions an Italian turns up and then we learn that Lucia and Georgino mio don't really know the language at all; the second time is as funny as the first.

I must say I reopened these magic books after some thirty years with misgivings; I feared that they would have worn badly and seem dated. Not at all; they are as fresh as paint. The characters are real and therefore timeless; the surprising few differences between that pre-war world and its equivalent today only add to the interest. Money of course is one of them—the characters speak of £2,000 as we would of £20,000. At least two people have Rolls-Royces; everybody has *domestiche.* When listening-in begins, Lucia refuses to have a wireless until Olga, a prima donna whom she reveres, owns to having one and listens-in to Cortot on it. None of them ever thinks of going abroad. When Lucia and Georgie want to get away from Riseholme for a little change they take houses at Tilling for the summer; that is what leads to them settling there.

But the chief difference is that, in Lucia's words, "that horrid thing which Freud calls sex" is utterly ignored. No writer nowadays could allow Georgie to do his embroidery and dye his hair and wear his little cape and sit for hours chatting with Lucia or playing celestial Mozartino, without hinting at Boys in the background. Quaint Irene, in her fisherman's jersey and knickerbockers, would certainly share her house with another lesbian and this word would be used. There are no children in the books—"Children are so sticky," says Georgie, "specially after tea." After the death of Mr. Lucas both Georgie and Lucia are afraid that the other may wish for marriage; the idea

gives them both the creeps. However, the years go by and they realize that nothing is farther from the inclination of either than any form of dalliance. Marriage is obviously the thing; Georgie remembers that he is a man and proposes it.

I was a fellow guest, at Highcliffe, with Mr. E. F. Benson soon after Lucia had become Mayor of Tilling. We talked of her for hours and he said, "What must she do now?" Alas, he died in the first year of the war; can we doubt that if he had lived Lucia would have become a General? (pp. vii-viii)

Nancy Mitford, in an introduction to Make Way for Lucia *by E. F. Benson, Thomas Y. Crowell Company, 1977, pp. vii-viii.*

V. S. PRITCHETT (essay date 1980)

[*Pritchett is a highly esteemed English novelist, short story writer, and critic. Considered one of the modern masters of the short story, he is also one of the world's most respected and well-read literary critics. Pritchett writes in the conversational tone of the familiar essay, approaching literature from the viewpoint of a lettered but not overly scholarly reader. In his criticism, Pritchett stresses his own experience, judgment, and sense of literary art, rather than following a codified critical doctrine derived from a school of psychological or philosophical speculation. In the following excerpt, he characterizes the Lucia novels as "a comically insinuating diagnosis" of some Edwardian psychological aberrations.*]

One of the characteristics common to Edwardian comedy is that it is a fairy tale for adults—indeed in the double meaning of the word. Its characters are seen as sexless. We can put this down to convention rather than to Puritanism, but the artifice does not mean that the novelist does not know or cannot insinuate what is going on under the surface of manners. It may be the point in the *Lucia* comedies of E. F. Benson that his people are neutered and that they are exhilarated and liberated by taking part in a useful psychological fraud. His enormously popular *Lucia* novels, now published in one fat volume [*Make Way for Lucia*], may even be a comically insinuating diagnosis.

What does Lucia, his self-appointed Queen of Riseholme, want as she sits in her fake medieval house or her garden where only Shakespearean flowers are allowed to grow? Certainly not sex. Not even connubial sex; her ruling passions are for power and publicity; she wants the gossip columns to mention her. She wants to dish her rivals. What about her husband, Peppino, writing his privately printed and artily bound little poems? No sex there or, we can guess, elsewhere. The pair have sublimated in dozens of little affectations, their happy marriage consolidated by the lies of baby talk and in snobbish snatches of Italian they have picked up from waiters in Italy. When an Italian singer comes to stay they can't understand a word he says.

And what about Georgie, Lucia's devoted *cicisbeo,* always on the go socially when she commands, playing his bits of Mozart to her, listening to her playing the first movement of "dear Beethoven's" *Moonlight* Sonata—the second is too fast. Georgie keeps changing his clothes, sits in his doll's house, doing his embroidery, painting a little picture or two, and being "busy at home" one day a week when he is having his toupee fixed and his hair dyed. Homosexual probably, but no boys in sight; certainly a Narcissus. There is no need to tell us; he gives himself away in his frenzied cult of youth, his fuss about his bibelots, his malicious pleasure in seeing through "*cara*" Lucia's snobbery, her frauds, and her lies instantly, enjoying his horror of her as a sister figure he cannot do without. And then there are the various loud masculine ladies of the clique in Riseholme: hearty butches in combat with Lucia's bitcheries; even the surrounding overweight wives with their sulking or choleric husbands are without children and exist in stertorous comic relief. The servants are faithful. The monstrous Lady Ambermere calls hers ''my people,'' as if she were an empress. The obsequious tradesmen of the town seem to be the only people engaged—but oft the scene—in the vulgar task of begetting their kind.

Since it is not sex that makes this world go round, what does? Gossip above all, spying from windows, plotting about teas and dinner parties, a genteel greed for money and news, and above all matching wits against Lucia's ruthless gifts. Our culture hound, who poses at her window, swots up in the Encyclopedia before distinguished guests arrive, pretending to have read Nietzsche or Theophrastus, can't distinguish between Schumann and Schubert. She steals a guru from Daisy Quantock, hooks a medium—a fake Russian princess—and although these things lead to farcical disaster, she rises above it and is on to the next fad like a hawk. Her dishonesty is spectacular, her vitality endless; and if Riseholme tears her to pieces and is deeply hurt when she inherits a small fortune and takes a house in London to conquer Society there with the same assurance, they long for her to return and, when she does, welcome her with joy. After all, Lucia may have made herself ridiculous but she has come back: she is Life.

Lucia's bids for power in London lead to disasters far beyond the mishaps of Riseholme; but her resilience in intrigue grips us. At the centre of the novels is Georgie—''*Georgino mio*''— and their close relationship is based on fascination—she needs his spite, he needs her deceits. Each is the other's mirror. At one point a delightful opera singer almost snatches him because she can see Lucia as a joke; but this infidelity is nominal. When she shows signs of wanting to be cuddled in Le Touquet, he sheers off in terror and returns to Lucia, forgiven.

We see into the absurd shallows of Lucia's emotional life in two of the central novels in the series. In Riseholme Lucia's social battles are provincial, her artiness is distinctly non-metropolitan, where the medieval revival has become derisively passé and middle class: she had better try to ''keep up.'' If she is chasing titled notorieties and Prime Ministers she must drop the Daisy Quantocks who have only just got around to clock golf, and see what smart picture exhibitions, a top gossip writer, or a fashionable divorce case can teach her. The last is a revelation. We see the court scene through her silly mind:

> Certainly, Babs Shyton, the lady whose husband wanted to get rid of her, had written very odd letters to Woof-dog, otherwise known as Lord Middlesex, and he to her. . . . But as the trial went on, Lucia found herself growing warm with sympathy for Babs. . . . Both Babs and he [Middlesex], in the extracts from the remarkable correspondence between them which were read out in court, alluded to Colonel Shyton as the S.P., which Babs (amid loud laughter) frankly confessed meant Stinkpot; and Babs had certainly written to Woof-dog to say that she was in bed and very sleepy and cross, but wished that Woof-dog was thumping his tail on the hearthrug. . . . As for the row of crosses [at the end of her letter], she explained frankly that they indicated she was cross. . . . Babs had pro-

duced an excellent impression, in fact; she had looked so pretty and had answered so gaily. . . .

As for Woof-dog he was the strong silent Englishman, and when he was asked whether he had ever kissed Babs, replied:

> ''That's a lie'' in such a loud fierce voice that you felt that the jury had better believe him unless they all wanted to be knocked down.

Always a positive thinker, Lucia draws the correct moral: it is no good, it is abhorrent, to take a real lover. Even in marriage her bedroom door is locked and her husband is content. The important thing is to have the *reputation* of having a lover: it gives a woman cachet. In the ensuing folly we see her pursuing a gossip writer who, when he tumbles to her plot, is determined not to be made a fool of like *that*! Gossip writers don't like gossip about themselves; it kills their trade and in any case he is a neuter not unlike *''Georgino mio.''*

Like so many of her enterprises the London venture is a series of disasters from which she recovers fast. Her husband dies of general neglect and a rather despicable inability to keep up with her. She chucks Riseholme and moves to Tilling—which is in fact Henry James's Rye—to deal with a rival more formidable than Daisy Quantock and with lesbians tougher than the Riseholme set. The lady is Miss Mapp, a woman in her forties whose

> . . . face was of high vivid colour and corrugated by chronic rage and curiosity; but these vivifying emotions had preserved to her an astonishing activity of mind and body, which fully accounted for [her] comparative adolescence. . . . Anger and the gravest suspicions about everybody had kept her young and on the boil.

As a spy on what is going on she can read the significance in every woman's shopping basket, every window lit or unlit, every motor that passes, what everyone eats, drinks, and thinks, what every woman has got on, on top and underneath. Every English village has its Miss Mapp. She intends to be mayoress of Tilling: Lucia has more hypocrisy and subtlety and beats her to it. And if admittedly this petticoat war is long drawn out it does lead to one splendid drama. Tilling (Rye), as everyone knows, is close to the sea marshes; it is liable to tidal floods. Miss Mapp is caught trying to steal a recipe in Lucia's kitchen just as the sea wall carelessly breaks its bank and she and Lucia are carried into the Channel on an upturned kitchen table and vanish into the sea fog for several weeks. They are presumed drowned. There is even a memorial service. Georgie has erected a cenotaph and a plaque recording their deaths— Miss Mapp's name is carved in smaller letters than Lucia's! Of course the two rivals turn up looking very healthy: they have been rescued by fishermen and have been fed on disgusting cod. Each gives unflattering accounts of the other's behaviour on the raft and with the seamen, and gives rival public lectures on the subject. Bitching is the permanent incentive to Benson's invention and his feline mind.

At the death of Lucia's husband and despite Georgie's total mistrust of Lucia, he marries her after an enthusiastic agreement that they will never go to bed together. They have that horror in common. It is noticeable that their affection declines at once, but their need for each other is increased. Miss Mapp marries the usual Colonel who, as she knows, is grossly after her money. But one must not be deceived into thinking that

Benson hates the idiots he is writing about or suffers from *Schadenfreude*. Far from it, the sun of comedy shines on his pages; he adores his victims.

The period is surprisingly the post-1918 one, but that beastly war is not mentioned. Pockets of Edwardian manners survived long after that war, for inherited money is the great preserver of dead cultures. Many of his characters—notably minor ones like Lady Ambermere, a woman of slowly enunciated and grandiose rudeness—were in action fifty years ago. I can remember their accents and their syntax. And here lies part of Benson's absurd spell: his ear for the dialogue of cliques is quick and devastating, for he understands the baby talk of fairyland which, of course, sex and our four-letter words have destroyed. (Unless mass society's own nonstop chatter about "fucking," "screwing," and the boys "having it off" is itself a new fairy-tale jargon.) The minor catchphrases preserve their cracked notes. "How tarsome!" exclaims Georgie. "Au reservoir" spreads like measles in place of *"au revoir."* There is a key to Benson's wicked mind in the following passage between Lucia and *"Georgino mio"*:

> *"I domestichi* are making *salone* ready."
>
> *"Molto bene,"* she said.
>
> "Everybody's tummin'," said Georgie, varying the cipher.
>
> "Me so *nervosa!"* said Lucia. "Fancy me doing Brunnhilde before singing Brunnhilde. Me can't bear it."

The key word is "cipher." Benson knew the cipher of all his characters. His pleasure was in the idiotic gabble of life. Is he too tepid for export? Years ago Gilbert Seldes compared Benson with the Sinclair Lewis of *Main Street* but pointed out that Lewis spoiled his book by his violent fury [see excerpt dated 1936]. Benson was never furious when he killed an age. He believed that love lasts longest when it is unkind. (pp. 18-24)

> V. S. Pritchett, "E. F. Benson: Fairy Tales," in his
> The Tale Bearers: Literary Essays, *Random House,*
> *1980, pp. 18-24.*

MIKE ASHLEY   (essay date 1984)

[*Ashley is an English critic specializing in horror, fantasy, and science fiction. In the following excerpt from an essay on the horror fiction of Arthur Christopher, Robert Hugh, and E. F. Benson, Ashley discusses some of Benson's best horror stories.*]

E. F. Benson did not set out to establish any special place for himself in the horror genre. If anything he was an imitator . . . , but with sufficient imagination to lend his stories an individuality. He wrote ghost stories because he enjoyed that *frisson* of fear himself. He felt that "the narrator must succeed in frightening himself before he can hope to frighten his readers." Perhaps for that reason Benson composed many of his stories in the first person.

When he used an idea that he liked, it was not unusual to find him borrowing it again and again. As a result a steady diet of E. F. Benson, unless selected carefully, can pall. In some stories Fred let the bare boards show through, with too little attempt to make them convincingly real (try, for instance, **"And the Dead Spake—,"** an utterly absurd story in which a man likens the human brain to a gramophone record and tries to replay deep-seated memories). But these are minor infractions

which one must expect from an author as prolific as Benson. They are far outweighed by his more polished and inventive tales.

One fine example is **"The Room in the Tower,"** the title story of his first collection. It grows out of a recurrent dream which plagues the narrator's adolescence and early manhood, but which never reaches a conclusion. The narrator only knows that he enters a room in a tower and is confronted by something terrible. At length the events in the dream begin to enact themselves, and the narrator finds himself in the room. Awakened in the pitch darkness of night during a storm, he sees fleetingly in a flash of lightning "a figure that leaned over the end of the bed, watching me," wearing a "close-clinging white garment, spotted and staid with mould." In the stygian blackness and deathly stillness that follows, he hears "the rustle of movement coming nearer." (p. 69)

Dreams are used to good effect. . . . [Benson], in fact, used the device on many occasions. In **"The Face,"** the events are almost replayed scene for scene as a young girl's recurrent dreams lead inevitably to her doom. In fact, if any single theme pervades E. F. Benson's works, it is that of fate, of one's unswervable destiny, both in life and beyond it. It recurs most pointedly in **"The Outcast,"** which makes full use of the idea almost tossed away at the end of **"The Room in the Tower,"** that of a coffin which refuses to be buried. In **"The Outcast"** we follow the life and death of a Mrs. Acres, whose body houses a spirit cursed in a former life never to rest or find shelter. As a consequence all things reject Mrs. Acres, and even after her death on board ship, when she is buried in the English Channel, the sea will not allow her rest, and she is cast up on the shore. When laid to rest again in the local churchyard, even the earth rejects her.

Unlike some of Benson's contemporaries, who left much unsaid in their stories, Benson liked to dwell on the more grotesque and gruesome details, as in **"The Horror Horn."** . . . But Benson's greatest predilection was for things glutinous and slimy, especially worms and slugs. They appear as the manifestations of evil in several stories. **"Negotium Perambulans,"** which H. P. Lovecraft thought possessed "singular power" [see Additional Bibliography], is really a rather weak attempt at imitating M. R. James. It presents a remote Cornish village with a house cursed by an ancient evil in the form of a gigantic slug which sucks the body of all its blood. In **"And No Bird Sings"** we find a wood devoid of all animal and bird life due to the presence of an elemental. Two men set out to rid the wood of this unseen evil and find themselves assailed by something "cold and slimy and hairy," like a giant worm. The same sluglike elemental reappears in **"The Thing in the Hall,"** while the victim in **"The Sanctuary"** is afflicted by a grey worm. Psychologists may well interpret the constant reference to worms as a reflection of Benson's own suppressed sexuality, but nevertheless he found it a profound store for horror tales. The frequent reworking of the theme does tend to diminish any authentic terror, but there is one story in particular in which Fred employed the theme to stunning effect: **"Caterpillars,"** a tale many consider his masterpiece.

Set, for once, in an Italian villa, it tells of the terrifying dreams that the narrator suffers. First, entering an unoccupied bedroom, he sees that the four-poster bed is a mass of writhing greyish-yellow caterpillars, all a foot or more in length and with crablike pincers instead of suckers. The caterpillars become aware of his presence and turn their attention to him, pursuing him back to his own room. The next day just such a

Illustration by Stephen Lawrence for Benson's short story "Caterpillars." From Terror: A History of Horror Illustrations from the Pulp Magazines, *by Peter Haining. A & W Visual Library, 1976. Reproduced by permission of the author.*

caterpillar, though of normal size, is found by another of the guests, a painter called Inglis. The following night the narrator suffers another dream, and this time is forced to witness a relentless tide of caterpillars as they mount the stairs and force their way into the painter's bedroom. Later, the symbolic significance of "the crab" is brought home to the narrator when he learns that from that second evening on, Inglis has contracted cancer.

Being so prolific, E. F. Benson turned to most of the traditional horror themes for his stories. **"Mrs. Amworth,"** for instance, is a fairly typical vampire story. **"The Man Who Went Too Far"** employs the back-to-nature theme that was rather common in late Victorian fantasies, especially in the work of Algernon Blackwood and Arthur Machen . . . , and it was a theme he expanded in his novel *The Angel of Pain.* **"In the Tube"** and **"The Bed by the Window"** show that he shared with H. G. Wells and again with Algernon Blackwood a fascination for time and other dimensions. **"Gavon's Eve"** uses witchcraft as its central theme, while there are any number of stories involving séances and spiritualists. His novel *The Image in the Sand* concerns a vengeful Egyptian spirit; *Colin* and *Colin II*—actually one long novel split in two—tell of a man who sells his soul to the devil, while *The Inheritor* deals with a family curse in which alternate generations are born hairy and cloven-hoofed. Curiously, though his novels contain some of his best

writing, they are long out of print and are virtually forgotten. Only *Raven's Brood,* his last weird novel, has seen any recent revival, and even then it was misrepresented as a typical paperback gothic, complete with lighted turret window and backward-glancing fleeing maiden on the cover.

Benson was at his best when producing genuine ghost stories, for which he earned an enviable reputation in the 1920s, with magazines proudly declaring on their covers, "Another Spook Story by E. F. Benson." It was this blurb that inspired the titles of his last two collections, and indeed *Spook Stories* contains much of his best work. Apart from the already mentioned **"And No Bird Sings," "The Face,"** and the very excellent **"Naboth's Vineyard,"** there are tales of spectral retribution such as **"The Tale of an Empty House," "Expiation," "Home, Sweet Home"** with its chilling vision of a piano that starts to play silently by itself, **"The Corner House,"** and the oddly titled **"Spinach,"** which is set in and around his beloved Rye. (pp. 69-70)

Mike Ashley, "The Essential Writers: Blood Brothers," in Rod Serling's The Twilight Zone Magazine, *Vol. 4, No. 2, May-June, 1984, pp. 63-80.*

STEPHEN KNIGHT   (essay date 1986)

[*In the following essay, Knight characterizes* The Luck of the Vails *as an ironic social novel typical of Benson that is also a well-crafted thriller.*]

The nondescript name E. F. Benson hides a model literary gentleman. Son of an Archbishop of Canterbury, educated at Marlborough and Cambridge, resident at the British School in Athens, Benson seems to have glided through life writing books about sport and history as well as his social novels and "tales of the macabre." These last are neither exactly crime fictions nor yet Gothic novels; they consistently deal with sensational feeling and personal oppressions, often presented through a respectable and rather inexperienced young man.

Not all have admired them. Norman Donaldson commented rather acidly [see Additional Bibliography] . . . that "Benson's many tales of the macabre are too mild to set today's more sophisticated readers shuddering," and noted in an equally needling vein, "That Benson, a life-long bachelor, created as the central figure of many of these stories a large cheery woman with a secret depravity is not without interest."

However that may be, or not be, Bensons's long-unconsidered stories are being once more printed, read and even dramatised. His new favour seems to rest, for the most part, on the wry and dry flavour of his writing and his ironic negativism—suitable, perhaps, for our new *fin de siècle.* But several of Benson's books, without abandoning the characteristic tone, come close to being serious thrillers. Perhaps the best known is *The Blotting Book,* which even the pawky Donaldson admired (though he pilloried its punctuation, for reasons too punctilious to follow). An equal to that, both as a thriller and in its quirky Bensonian quality, is *The Luck of the Vails.*

It opens with a characteristic sequence of leisured description; the prose lounges up to the Vail country. This book is for those with time to read at length and no lust for the rapid fire of saturation plotting. Similarly, the hero is no dynamic, sure-footed detective like Sherlock Holmes, nor a mercurial citizen out of John Buchan. Harry, Lord Vail, is, when we meet him, stuck fast in immobilising gloom and he can hardly be said to quicken into much activity at any stage of the story.

Like the all-sensing prose style, Vail is a watcher and re-
sponder, someone to whom things happen. And they do indeed
happen; black events cross his path most forcibly. Genuine
accidents, planned misadventures, straightforward attempts at
murder, they all fall upon this decent, depressed and puzzled
man, almost the last of the Vails.

As it develops, the book is neither peaceful nor self-indulgent.
It starts in that mode to make more emphatic the various dis-
ruptions which occur in Harry Vail's life. As well as the accidents and quasi-accidents, he must confront human problems:
the almost frenetic cheerfulness of his uncle and notional heir;
the quizzical and sometimes disturbing presence of his only
friend Geoffrey; the onslaught of love for someone estranged
from his family; the acerbic and erratic force of Lady Oxted,
his beloved's duenna.

So much activity boring into Harry Vail's quiet centre would
make a diverting society novel, and Benson shows his art in
that amiable but often friendless form—extended conversation,
enigmatic gesture, mild humour, puzzling but unsensational
turns of plot, shifts of time and place to process changes in
tone and theme. But something graver than that lightweight
mode is embodied in this book and in Lord Vail's life. It centres
on the strange disturbance created by the Luck of the Vails
itself.

This remarkable object, a combination of the Holy Grail and
the Maltese Falcon, is rediscovered up in the attic. Brought in
to dinner, toasted as the visible presence of the line and its
fortune, it is at once heirloom, symbol of antique family and
cause of disruption in the present. The Luck brings luck of
two sorts, so Harry is told and comes to believe. He has so
much misfortune at first that he knows good must develop: it
is his true and happy love for "one of the greatest heiresses
in England." Luck indeed.

Yet the Luck-related accidents grow quite unaccidental. Its
reputation is a delusory snare to catch Harry's life. But the
Luck becomes more than a Gothick whimsy or a would-be
murderer's stalking horse. Its disruptive presence meshes with
other oddities in the story; together they trace a socially symbolic complex beneath the surface of the tale. The thriller mode
has made Benson himself thrill to his story's inner tension.

The striking thing about the world of Harry, Lord Vail, is that
he has so few people about him: one relative, one friend; one
girl-friend and one older woman; one house servant, one out-
servant—and the last is actually his double. About Vail there
is a world of minimal relations in which he is the only centre,
and the thriller plot gives him cause to suspect, in turn, every
single one-to-one relationship as being fraudulent, perhaps
aimed only at his disgrace and defeat.

This is far from the extensive socialisation of the aristocratic
past, a ghostly absence at the strange, lonely dinners where
the Luck presides. Equally, Harry's world is quite cut off from
modern formations, urban, capitalist and democratic alike: the
poor are only glimpsed as the train whisks past the backs of
mean houses. The social essence of the story, the ultimate base
of its tight spring of tension, is the world of individualism,
where everyone is inherently alone and in implicit competition
with all others.

Just as he is so thinly and nervously socialised, Harry is beset
by a horrible world. In embattled Vail, the place and the peer,
Benson has sketched and filled with dark and, for once, un-
satirised emotion the world, that Agatha Christie turned into

potent formulae, a world, that is, where every hand and object
may be turned against the isolated human intelligence, especially if it controls money and property; the world of compet-
itive individualism is re-formed into dynamic and compulsive
fiction.

Inscribed strongly throughout *The Luck of the Vails* is the painful paradox between the real comforts of bourgeois life and
the disconcerting acquisitive competition on which they are
based. That duality is realised in the novel's form: a spark is
struck by the friction between a leisured and luxurious prose
style and the enigmatic off-putting incidents that are consistently interjected. Such duality is, of course, the essence of
that strange symbol, the Luck itself.

What Harry Vail hopes for in the end, however, is not to
retrieve his family's lost glories nor yet recover its fortune—
he hopes to avoid the disturbing paradox of profit and conflict
by entering that other bourgeois formation, the dream of domestic peace. This mixture of social awareness and positive
ideals is not typical of Benson's work as a whole and may
surprise the reader. The self-exposing task of inventing a plot
and moulding characters usually sent Benson retreating into
all-round irony. But the set patterns of the thriller seem to have
relieved him of such embarrassment and so freed his imagination to plumb the nervous depths of this ambient world. Much
the same, with much steeper gradients, were the contours of
Conan Doyle's literary career; the most formulaic work can be
the most imaginatively vivid through the release it brings from
a censoring self-conscious.

The Luck of the Vails had another level of distance from the
author's persona: Benson notes that his brother provided the
idea for the story. But he gave it his own finely-judged variations of style, well-paced narrative, skilled management of a
mystery within a limited plot; above all, he revealed a perhaps
unsuspected power to craft a story that beneath a merely fluent
surface surges with deep imaginative vitality. Among the crime
fiction giants of the turn of the century a little room, at least,
should be made for E. F. Benson. (pp. iii-vi)

> *Stephen Knight, in an introduction to* The Luck of
> the Vails *by E. F. Benson, The Hogarth Press, 1986,
> pp. iii-vi.*

HUGH LAMB (essay date 1986)

[*Lamb, an English critic and editor, is best known for his numerous anthologies of supernatural stories. In the following excerpt, he discusses Benson's career as a supernatural writer and
mentions Arthur Christopher Benson's and Robert Hugh Benson's
contributions to this genre.*]

No other family has approached the Bensons for sheer volume
of printed words. Among them, the three Benson brothers
wrote over one hundred books.

Ghost stories formed the merest fraction of the Bensons' output, yet they produced some of the best in the literature of the
uncanny. (p. 28)

[Despite an early leaning toward archaeology, Edward (Fred)
Benson] became what can only be described as a social butterfly. The secret of Fred Benson was that he never really grew
up. Even in his last book, written just before he died, the same
youthful irreverence comes across as in his first. After a massive success with *Dodo,* he became a full-time writer and produced a string of novels for nearly fifty years. As the end of

his career approached, he tended more toward scholarship, but his heart was always in the social whirl—and this shows in his books, even in his ghost stories. (p. 29)

The current revival of interest in the Bensons was spearheaded by the reprinting of many of Fred's social novels and the publication of extracts from Arthur's diary (locked up for fifty years after his death, on his instructions, for fear of offending those discussed in it). For many years the Bensons were in literary obscurity, their name kept alive only by the reprinting of some of their ghost stories in various anthologies. Arthur's ghost stories remained undiscovered by anthologists until Hugh Lamb used them in the 1970s.

That they would all write ghost stories was almost certain. Arthur was a lifelong friend of M. R. James; Fred attended James's first reading in 1893; it was the fashion to write such things among many of their Eton and Cambridge set. The brother's individual aims in writing ghost stories, however, varied enormously. Fred wrote his for entertainment and money. Arthur wrote his in the main as allegorical tales for his pupils and kept his grimmer stuff well hidden (it only emerged after his death). Hugh wrote his as glorifications, often unctuous, of the Catholic faith. That all three managed to come across as masters of the craft and purveyors of good, scary material speaks worlds for their talents.

The Bensons' family and background provided them with much overt material. For instance, all three wrote of rooms in towers: Arthur in "The Closed Window" (from *The Hill of Trouble,* 1903), Fred in the title story of his 1912 collection [*The Room in the Tower*], and Hugh in "Father Maddox's Tale" (from a *A Mirror of Shalott,* 1907). The tower room was a feature of their home at Lis Escop, the bishop's residence in Truro when their father held that office.

Fred poured his longing for the past into his story "Pirates," in which the fictional setting Lescop *is* Lis Escop, down to the last tree and bush. Fred, in particular, showed in his stories where his life had led him. Almost all his narrators are single men with no roots, who find ghosts and monsters in their travels (a characteristic of M. R. James's stories noted by Jack Sullivan). When Fred's characters are married, the circumstances are not always happy—"Christopher Comes Back" is a nasty littly story of marital murder and ghostly revenge. Sex in Fred's stories either is unspoken or leads to trouble. (pp. 29-30)

[Of] the three brothers, Fred made the most lasting impression as a ghost story writer. His work, at its best, is among the finest in the literature, as excellent as James's at times.

Fred was not interested in moral lessons; he wrote his stories to frighten and said so in the introduction to his first collection, *The Room in the Tower.* By far the best of his four books of ghost stories, this contains seventeen tales, each almost too well rounded to fault. The title story is a genuinely chilling exercise in both prophecy and vampirism. In this book we find all the themes Fred would return to in ghost stories throughout his life: Egypt ("At Abdul Ali's Grave"), sluglike elementals ("The Thing in the Hall"), the psychic residues of murder ("The House with the Brick-Kiln") and suicide ("Gavon's Eve"), humor ("How Fear Departed from the Long Gallery"), and disease ("Caterpillars"). The impact of Fred's stories at the time must have been interesting. Familiar with his carefree material, like *Dodo,* Fred's readers must have sat up with a jerk when they encountered a story in which cancer stalks an Italian villa in the form of yellowish-gray caterpillars.

Fred kept up this standard through three other books: *Visible and Invisible, Spook Stories,* and *More Spook Stories.* He also contributed ghost stories to magazines; many stories remain uncollected. On occasion, he surpassed his previous efforts. "The Step" is quite bizarre, with its terrifying phantom whose face is a "slab of smooth yellowish flesh . . . empty as the oval of an egg without eyes or nose or mouth." "Mrs. Amworth" is one of the best vampire stories written, gaining in its effects from its homely village background. "Negotium Perambulans," featuring the author's favorite slug elemental, sees a blasphemer reduced to "no more than a rind of skin . . . over projecting bones."

The narrator of "A Tale of an Empty House" not only hears and sees the ghost of a murderer, but finds himself wrestling with it. And here we come to one of the keys to Fred's success in this field: his ghosts are *very* physical. Not for him the flashes and glimpses of James's thin ghosts; Fred's ghosts are more often than not mistaken for real people, or are known to the characters who see them. They sport cut throats, which they show the narrators, or they return to avenge a murder. Hardly ever are they like many of James's ghosts, the result of tampering with things best left alone.

Sardonic humor permeates much of Fred's work, and he was not averse to trying his hand at humorous ghost stories, generally mocking spiritualism, such as "The Psychical Mallards" or "Mrs. Andrews' Control." He also wrote a string of macabre novels, ranging from the light warning against spiritualism in *Across the Stream* to a lurid tale of rural witchcraft and thinly veiled sex in *Raven's Brood.*

Fred's stories have been well anthologized over the years and are thereby easily accessible; his brothers have suffered undue neglect. It is a shame, for among them they created a body of work in this genre that repays careful attention, has moments of genuine terror, and is never—even at its most tenuous— uninteresting. (pp. 30-1)

> *Hugh Lamb, "Robert Hugh Benson," in* The Penguin Encyclopedia of Horror and the Supernatural, *edited by Jack Sullivan, Viking, 1986, pp. 28-31.*

ADDITIONAL BIBLIOGRAPHY

Askwith, Betty. "The Bensons." In her *Two Victorian Families,* pp. 108-222. London: Chatto & Windus, 1973.
    Family history of Edward White Benson, Mary Sidgwick Benson, and their six children. The critic had access to unpublished family papers, including letters and diaries, in composing this work.

Review of *Dodo,* by E. F. Benson. *The Athenaeum,* No. 3430 (22 July 1893): 126.
    Proclaims Benson "a writer of quite exceptional ability" on the strength of his first novel, praising in particular the "pointed and natural" dialogue.

Donaldson, Norman. "E(dward) F(rederic) Benson." In *Twentieth-Century Crime and Mystery Writers,* edited by John M. Reilly, pp. 100-04. New York: St. Martin's Press, 1980.
    Lists biographical facts about Benson and provides an inclusive bibliography of his works. Donaldson briefly mentions *The Blotting Book* as Benson's one detective novel, and maintains that "Benson's many tales of the macabre are too mild to set today's more sophisticated readers shuddering."

Hamilton, Cosmo. "E. F. Benson: The Incredible Nineties." In his *People Worth Talking About*, pp. 197-204. 1933. Reprint. Freeport, N. Y.: Books for Libraries Press, 1970.

Outlines Benson's literary career and recounts anecdotes from his volume of memoirs *As We Were*.

Lacon. "Mr. Edward Frederic Benson." In his *Lectures to Living Authors*, pp. 209-16. London: Geoffrey Bles, 1925.

Essay in the form of an address to Benson, praising him as a workmanlike author of "very readable, well-written, well-constructed stories."

Lovecraft, H. P. "The Weird Tradition in the British Isles." In his *Supernatural Horror in Literature*, pp. 76-86. 1927. Reprint. New York: Ben Abramson, 1945.

Briefly lists and comments on some of Benson's best horror stories.

Maurois, André. "Life of a Peacemaker." *The Saturday Review of Literature* X, No. 10 (23 September 1933): 127.

Favorable review of Benson's biography *King Edward VII*.

"Real Children and a Family." *The New York Times Book Review* (20 March 1921): 2.

Reviews Benson's childhood memoir *Our Family Affairs*, maintaining that Benson is unequalled in recounting "screamingly funny" as well as touchingly true-to-life memories of youth.

Parrish, Anne. Foreword to *All About Lucia: Four Novels*, by E. F. Benson, pp. v-vi. Garden City, N. Y.: Doubleday, Doran & Co., 1936.

Discusses the pleasures of reading and rereading the Lucia Books.

Payne, William Morton. Review of *The Angel of Pain*, by E. F. Benson. *The Dial* XL, No. 476 (16 April 1906): 264.

Criticizes Benson's introduction of "an element of the most fantastic superstition" into an otherwise skillfully told story of English life, concluding that "if he does not pull himself together in time, he will come near to ruining his hitherto creditable reputation as a minor novelist."

Review of *Visible and Invisible*, by E. F. Benson. *The Times Literary Supplement*, No. 1139 (15 November 1923): 773.

Favorably reviews a volume of Benson's supernatural horror stories, noting that "Mr. Benson is very clever in scene-setting and conveying a subtle sense of the mysterious in the surroundings of his incidents, and of course he writes well."

Von Beselen, D. "The Kaiser and English Relations." *The Quarterly Review* 268, No. 531 (January 1937): 1-17.

Lengthy negative review of Benson's *The Kaiser and English Relations*.

Weathered, H. N. "Twentieth Century: Benson." In his *The Curious Art of Autobiography: From Benvenuto Cellini to Rudyard Kipling*, pp. 211-27. New York: Philosophical Library, 1956.

Finds that Benson's *As We Were* contains primarily lively information about interesting people other than himself.

Weygandt, Cornelius. "The Lesser Late Victorians." In his *A Century of the English Novel*, pp. 273-368. New York: Century Co., 1925.

Characterizes *Dodo* as the "one novel of any vitality" to issue from the prolific Benson brothers, a "book of the hour" that retains a limited interest, "if it interests at all, as a slice of life of its time."

Williams, David. *Genesis and Exodus: A Portrait of the Benson Family*. London: Hamish Hamilton, 1979, 236 p.

History of the Benson family focusing on Mary Sidgwick Benson.

R(ichard) D(oddridge) Blackmore

1825-1900

(Also wrote under pseudonym of Melanter) English novelist, short story writer, and poet.

Blackmore is the author of *Lorna Doone,* a classic novel of adventure that is widely admired for its evocative setting, memorable rustic characters, and richly descriptive prose style. Although these are characteristics of Blackmore's fiction generally, none of his other works approached the critical or popular success of *Lorna Doone.* Nevertheless, Blackmore's many novels earned him distinction as one of the most outstanding rural portraitists of his period, and his works are often compared with those of Sir Walter Scott and Thomas Hardy for their shared concerns with the importance of nature and the timeless traditions of rural England.

The son of an Anglican curate and his wife, Blackmore was born in the Berkshire village of Longworth. Following the death of his mother while Blackmore was still in infancy, he was placed in the care of an aunt. Several years later he returned to live with his father, who had by then remarried. While he was growing up, Blackmore visited often with relatives in the Berkshire region, which enabled him to learn much about his family and local history. During childhood visits with his grandfather and uncle, for example, he heard the legends that provided the basis for *Lorna Doone.*

Blackmore graduated from Exeter College in 1847 without the first-place honors that would have qualified him for a scholarly career. He studied law in London and was called to the bar in 1852. Because he suffered from epilepsy, he avoided the courtroom and began his legal profession earning a meager income writing deeds. The following year he married, and shortly thereafter published his first book, *Poems by Melanter.* This work, and two subsequent volumes of poetry, attracted little critical or popular attention. In 1855 Blackmore began teaching classics at a grammar school, continuing in this occupation for three years until an inheritance enabled him to purchase sixteen acres of land in Teddington, where he built a modest house and began growing and marketing fruit. Blackmore made little money from his produce and so turned to writing fiction to support himself and his farm. Although his first two novels sold poorly, the great success of his third, *Lorna Doone,* convinced Blackmore that fiction writing could provide him with an income, and for the rest of his life he worked jointly at farming and writing. He died in 1900.

Lorna Doone has attained such critical and popular success that despite his thirteen other novels Blackmore is generally regarded as a one-book author. The novel's initial surge of popularity—occuring nearly two years after its first publication—has been attributed to the rumor that it was based on the history of a noble family then much in the news because of intermarriage with England's royal family. However, its continued success has been ascribed to its intrinsic merits. *Lorna Doone* is a long, adventurous romance set in seventeenth-century Exmoor, a wild rural region of southwest England. Although the novel contains both historical background and meticulously drawn local color, Blackmore did not strictly adhere to historical fact, maintaining that he had romanticized the

factual bases of the work for the purpose of telling a story. The continuing appeal of the novel derives from the interest of the plot and the hero, John Ridd, who recounts his love for the orphan Lorna Doone, held captive by an outlaw band, and his rivalry with the villainous Carver Doone, whom he defeats in battle at the novel's dramatic climax. Ridd's many exemplary qualities make him, according to John Steuart, the embodiment of "perfect English manhood," and many critics have concurred. A notable flaw that commentators have found in the narrative is the imprecise characterization of the ostensible heroine, Lorna Doone. She is described in vague terms of female perfection due to the narrator's infatuation with her, and is therefore less interesting than the novel's many finely drawn and well individualized minor female characters.

Critics often commend the poetic quality of Blackmore's meticulously detailed descriptions of nature and of Exmoor locales in *Lorna Doone.* Thomas Hardy expressed his appreciation of Blackmore's "exquisite ways of describing things" in a letter to the novelist, adding that "little phases of nature which I thought nobody had noticed but myself were continually turning up in your book." Blackmore is also commended for his representation of rural dialects; Herbert Warren noted that "he came just in time to catch and fix much of the dialect of Somerset and Devonshire." George Saintsbury concluded that "the way in which he had turned a striking, but not extraordinary, and certainly not very extensive West Country glen into an *Arabian Nights* valley, with the figures and action of a mediaeval romance and the human interest of a modern novel, is really wonderful.''

With the exception of *Lorna Doone*, Blackmore's novels are virtually unknown to modern readers, for, according to critics, none compare in quality. Among the flaws that mar these novels, critics have cited awkward, at times absurd plots, an excessive reliance on coincidence as well as providence, and lengthy digressions from the main story. Nevertheless, critics have pointed out that Blackmore's novels possess a number of praiseworthy attributes, including keen observations of people and nature, lifelike depictions of the lives of rural villagers, and an ability to bring a scene vividly to life. Despite the artistic and structural deficiencies of his novels, however, critics agree that Blackmore's descriptions of the English countryside—from minute, easily overlooked details to vast landscapes—are outstanding. Furthermore, he created a host of memorable rustic characters and some lively, entertaining portrayals of rural community life. His works preserve some images of bygone England and attest to Blackmore's skill, described by Kenneth Budd, as an ''observer and listener in obscure corners of forgotten places.''

(See also *Contemporary Authors*, Vol. 120, and *Dictionary of Literary Biography*, Vol. 18: *Victorian Novelists after 1885*.)

PRINCIPAL WORKS

Poems by Melanter [as Melanter] (poetry) 1854
Epullia [as Melanter] (poetry) 1854
The Bugle of the Black Sea; or, The British in the East [as Melanter] (poetry) 1855
Clara Vaughan (novel) 1864
Cradock Nowell (novel) 1866; rev. ed. 1873
Lorna Doone (novel) 1869
The Maid of Sker (novel) 1872
Alice Lorraine (novel) 1875
Cripps, the Carrier (novel) 1876
Erema (novel) 1877
Mary Anerley (novel) 1880
Christowell (novel) 1881
The Remarkable History of Sir Thomas Upmore Bart MP, Formerly Known as ''Tommy Upmore'' (novel) 1884
Springhaven (novel) 1887
Kit and Kitty (novel) 1889
Perlycross (novel) 1894
Fringilla (poetry) 1895
Slain by the Doones (short stories) 1895; also published as *Tales from the Telling House*, 1896
Dariel (novel) 1897

THE SATURDAY REVIEW, LONDON (essay date 1864)

[*In the following excerpt, an early reviewer of* Clara Vaughan *maintains that ''not a few incidental touches and turns of phrase'' reveal an inexperienced female author.*]

[*Clara Vaughan*] is the product of a highly fertile imagination, revelling in the ease and wealth of its creations, without showing much trace of having been disciplined in the logic of probabilities, or of being over-scrupulous in the handling of ordi-

nary motives. There is great freshness and vivacity in the way in which the story is carried through, and, so far as simply keeping up the reader's attention is concerned, it may be pronounced as full of materials for amusement as almost any novel of the season. It does not aim at illustrating any deep or lofty theory of ethics, and on the whole its pervading moral tone is nothing higher than that of wild untutored impulse, blindly working out an end in itself righteous by the mere native straightforwardness of passionate instincts. The plot of the tale is the fierce, unswerving pursuit, by a feminine will, of a savage purpose. It is the *vendetta* of a *vendetta*—a Corsican revenge carried out with English sense and spirit. We have the detection and punishment of a mysterious criminal—the devotion of a daughter, with the keenness of a sleuth-hound and the self-sacrifice of a fanatic, to avenge her father's murder. (p. 539)

[*Clara Vaughan* is] not a work belonging to the highest order of intellect, or showing the results of even a disciplined and thoughtful cast of mind. It is, however, original in conception, besides being occasionally brilliant in flashes of fancy. The characters are drawn mainly by touches of outward description, not by means of mental analysis, or the delineation of subjective or internal motives. In works of the nature of autobiographies, written like that before us in the first person, this must needs be a serious drawback on the writer's part. For the hero or heroine to describe himself or herself thus is too much like drawing with a looking-glass always before the eyes, or retailing scraps of descriptive flattery casually overheard. Such qualities as beauty, cleverness, or wit—presupposed, as they must needs be, on the part of the leading personages of a tale like the present—cannot of course be the subject of direct description, though we are not long in finding out that the imaginary writer is as conscious of possessing them as any young lady similarly gifted in reality might be.... The hand of an inexperienced writer is easily detected.... Not a few incidental touches and turns of phrase will, moreover, be found ... to bear out a further inference, suggested by the general framework of the plot and by the entire cast of characters. The primary conception of the personages, the situations in which they are introduced, and the tone of speech and sentiment prevalent throughout, are unmistakably the creation of a female mind. The inconsecutive logic by which each stage of the discovery is connected with those going before, and the weak and wavering purposes, not only of the dark villains of the piece, but of the virtuous victims themselves and their feminine avenger, are scarcely less characteristic in this respect than the ''brooch-eyed'' look which wide-mouthed astonishment is capable of suggesting to the writer, or the ''maiden thoughts'' conjured up by the temporary blindness brought on by a bold experiment in the course of tracking the guilty party. Never more to know ''where her teacup stands,'' or when her hands are clean, ''except by smelling soap,'' how her dress becomes her, or when her hair ''is right,'' never to ''see her own sad face, in which she has been fool enough often to glory,'' never—''and this is worst of all—never catch another's smile''—in all this there seems to speak something more than a mere man's impersonation of the other sex. ''Here am I,'' is the complaint, ''a full grown girl, full of maiden's thoughts and wonderings, knowing well that I am shaped so but to be a link in life; must I never think of loving or of being loved, except with love like Isola's—sweet affection—very sweet, but white sugar only?''

Another decided feature by which our lady novelists are wont to betray the secret of their authorship is the characteristic mode in which they unconsciously make sport of the simplest principles of physics, and of the most elementary rules or usages of the law. No small portion of the plot of **Clara Vaughan** is absolutely made to turn upon the liberties which are coolly taken with what are generally regarded by men as fixities of nature and equity. Mere degrees of improbability are as nothing by the side of this contempt for technical truth. (pp. 539-40)

We are not called upon to spoil the story by initiating our readers into the development of a plot which begins with so many promises of sensation, or preparing them for the surprises which await them as the burden of crime is gradually shifted off the original shoulders. Neither can we pretend to adjust the measure of probability with which events are made to run on toward their ultimate goal, or to discount the blessings of fortune which, when the depths of suffering and patience are once sounded, begin to flow in upon the heroine with such profusion as well nigh to pall upon us. Recovered sight, love, wealth, the mystery unravelled, revenge sated, peace restored with the unjustly suspected uncle, charming cousins brought to light, a gifted and romantic husband among them—so many good things falling in, several of them in a day, almost overpower and melt even the obdurate, headstrong, and somewhat cynical Clara, as they certainly take away the breath of the more prosaic and commonplace reader. So rich is the tissue of surprises, so wonderful the way in which events fit into one another, that long before the close we are too *blasés* to admit the designed or expected sensation. In Thessaly, we are told, in the palmy days of incantation and magic, people had got so used to marvels every day that a head might go on talking as it rolled along the ground without anybody thinking it worth while to pay attention to it. The situations and conceptions which crowd upon each other in **Clara Vaughan,** clever and exuberant in fancy as they are, are strange if not magical enough in quality to weary us of so perpetual a strain upon our sense of what is within the bounds of reason. The writer, at all events, seems to have lived so long in a self-created atmosphere of romantic glamour as almost to have lost the power of distinguishing and enjoying things as they should be. A more stringent mental discipline, as well as a more chastened style, might yet lead, we cannot doubt, to productions of genuine and permanent value. (pp. 540-41)

A review of "Clara Vaughan," in The Saturday Review, *London, Vol. 17, No. 444, April 30, 1864, pp. 539-41.*

THE ATHENAEUM (essay date 1869)

[*In the following excerpt, the critic favorably appraises* Lorna Doone, *noting in particular the vivid, attractive descriptions of rustic life in seventeenth-century England.*]

Lorna Doone really deserves its title as a romance. The story is well told; and although some impatient readers may call the pace too leisurely, we think that even they, if they once fairly begin it, will read on to the end, and close the book with regret. There is a reality and truthfulness about the story which gain upon the reader as he proceeds. The period is laid in the time of James the Second, and we are completely transported out of the present day to the England that was when there were no roads at all across Exmoor; and for a man to travel safely from one town to another required not only a thorough knowledge of all the bogs, pit-holes, soft places and sloughs, but much wary walking and great good luck besides. Mr. Blackmore is quite at home in the local aspects of Somerset and Devonshire,

and he is thoroughly acquainted with the rustic life of England as it was in those days, when there was no communication between one town and another except by pack-horses for goods and stout nags for men, and when the people from another parish were foreigners instead of neighbours, when highwaymen flourished, and the gibbets which studded Exmoor told that some of them fell victims to their profession. The story takes us completely into a bygone world. The rustic life of England as it was led at Plover Barrow Farm is set forth in a way to make one wish we might have paid a visit to that worthy and stalwart yeoman, John Ridd, the owner of the place and the hero of the story. Plover Barrow Farm seems to have been a rustic Paradise: it is pervaded by a sense of honest labour and wholesome tranquillity, with such a wealth of plenty and comfort and warmth that the reader is made to feel as if he had been carried far away from London, and was breathing the pure air of Exmoor, and luxuriating in the good country fare so well and vividly described. (p. 534)

[The story] is narrated in a quiet and veracious style, with unconscious touches of character and the introduction of persons who are not only historical but life-like.

Some of the incidents are narrated with great power—such as the outrage by the Doones, which at last aroused the long-suffering country people to avenge themselves, and to destroy the whole race of Doones; and the final attack and destruction of their stronghold. The death wrestle between John Ridd and his enemy, Carver Doone, is terrible, and yet keeps clear of being melo-dramatic. (p. 535)

A review of "Lorna Doone: A Romance of Exmoor," in The Athenaeum, *No. 2164, April 17, 1869, pp. 534-35.*

THOMAS HARDY (letter date 1875)

[*Hardy is considered one of the greatest novelists in English literature. His work resembles that of earlier Victorian novelists in technique, while in subject matter it daringly violated literary traditions of the age. In contrast to the Victorian ideal of progress, Hardy depicted human existence as a tragedy determined by powers beyond the individual's command, in particular the external pressures of society and the internal compulsions of character. Hardy's desire to reveal the underlying forces directing the lives of his characters led him to realistically examine love and sexuality in his fiction, a practice that often offended the readers of his time and endangered his literary reputation. In the following excerpt from a letter to Blackmore, Hardy expresses enthusiasm for Blackmore's descriptions of nature in* Lorna Doone.]

I have just read your finest book (as I think)—*Lorna Doone,* & I cannot help writing just one line to tell you how astonished I was to find what it contained—exquisite ways of describing things which are more after my own heart than the "presentations" of any other writer that I am acquainted with. It seems almost absurd that I had never read it before, considering the kind of work I attempted in *Far from the Madding Crowd,* & it has been a continual regret to me—since I have found out what the book contains—that I had not read it before meeting you. Little phases of nature which I thought nobody had noticed but myself were continually turning up in your book—for instance, the marking of a heap of sand into little pits by the droppings from trees was a fact I should unhesitatingly have declared unknown to any other novelist till now. A kindred sentiment between us in so many things is, I suppose, partly because we both spring from the West of England.

I congratulate you on the reception of your new book. (pp. 37-8)

Thomas Hardy, in a letter to R. D. Blackmore on June 8, 1875, in his The Collected Letters of Thomas Hardy: 1840-1892, Vol. I, *edited by Richard Little Purdy and Michael Millgate, Oxford at the Clarendon Press, Oxford, 1978, pp. 37-8.*

GEORGE BARNETT SMITH   (essay date 1879)

[*Smith was an English journalist and nonfiction writer. In the following excerpt, he discusses some general characteristics of Blackmore's novels through* Erema.]

[It] is one of the highest effects of the novelist's art to secure the illusion of reality. The real man is the heroic man, wherever and under whatever circumstances he may be placed. Now that novelist who has the rare gift and power of grasping real humanity, and making it appear real to others, is undoubtedly the highest of his craft. (p. 406)

[How does Blackmore] meet this chief and most essential requirement of the novelist? The charge has been brought against him that though his men and women are fresh and vigorous, they are not very real; but it is impossible fairly to sustain such an objection. Can any one contemplate Mr. Blackmore's characters, and not perceive at a glance that they have been photographed, as it were, upon the retina of a plastic imagination? Is it possible for heroines to be more real than Lorna Doone, Amy Rosedew, or Erema Castlewood? or heroes to have more of the semblance of flesh and blood than John Ridd, Cradock Nowell, David Llewellyn, or even Cripps the Carrier? His objectors would seem to require town manners and peculiarities grafted upon local and provincial characters; but Mr. Blackmore has too clear a perception of his art to make his *dramatis personæ* other than what they are. Take, for example, John Rosedew, the clergyman, who bears all the weight of his Oxford learning lightly like a flower: there is none of the superciliousness of fastidiousness of the town about him; he is lovable, simple, unsophisticated,—better known and beloved by those who perceive only his humanity and know nothing of his learning than by those who frequent the best circles, or by those who are competent to argue with him some abstruse passage in Lucretius or the Greek poets. So, too, in John Ridd we see preserved strictly to the letter—even under the most trying circumstances in the metropolis—the honest, homely yeoman of the West of England. In Lorna Doone is to be witnessed a beautiful, natural refinement, which clings about her like the bloom upon the peach, and exhales from her like the odor of flowers. But any one can see that this refinement is natural; and we instinctively feel both with regard to this and other female creations of Mr. Blackmore, that any seeming idealization of character is really only the subtle grasping of the true identity.

It is easy to perceive, nevertheless, why Mr. Blackmore's characters are said to be somewhat unreal. It is because of the overwhelming presence of the personality of the author in the connecting matter of his narrative. Put this out of sight, and the naturalness and *vraisemblance* of his creations themselves are at once apparent. But many critics have failed to do this, and have consequently lost the perception of the real human character of his men and women. Mr. Blackmore is undoubtedly a mannerist: he cannot shut himself out of his romances. He is probably as easily to be recognized as is any other living author in his or her own special work. Deprived of his name

upon the title-page of most of his stories, it would yet be easy for us to supply the deficiency. We should do it intuitively, for no writer has more distinct moods of thought, or more pronounced forms of expression. Yet would not every sentence of what we have just written apply equally well to Thackeray or Dickens,—certainly to the latter? Dickens is the greatest of all mannerists in fiction,—a child might almost discover him in any disguise; yet who would say that he could not depict most truthfully the humorous or grotesque aspects of human nature? A Daniel Peggotty, a Mr. Dombey, a Captain Cuttle, a Mrs. Gamp, a hundred varying types of mankind are not only possible, but seem to every reader exact and startling realities. It may be said that Dickens's characters are caricatures; if it be so, it is only because the original characters from whom they are drawn are themselves, as it were, caricatures of humanity. They are true to nature,—such nature as it is; yet the books in which they appear are saturated with the personality of the author. So we must not push the complaint of Mr. Blackmore's mannerism so far as to deny his strong and obvious faculty of representing types of human character with accuracy and fidelity.

Mr. Blackmore's imagination is lucid and energetic. . . . Though we may frequently find a love of Nature without an active and vigorous imagination, yet wherever we discover the latter we never find it divorced from the former. The two equally developed go largely towards constituting the poet. So in our author there is clear evidence of the poetic faculty, not always restrained within the inharmonious elements of prose. Sometimes, indeed, as in all impassioned writers of prose,—writers like Burke, for example, who have the poetic cast of mind without poetic culture,—we find that Mr. Blackmore becomes as truly the poet in his descriptions as do any of our professed writers of verse. There is in his mind also a curious disorder in orderliness, which is the characteristic of many of our poets. No one will deny him the presence of imagination. His trees and flowers are English trees and flowers; his bucolic Devonshire and Somersetshire worthies would be impossible elsewhere; his transcripts from the scenery of the New Forest would do for no other forest; and it is impossible mentally to detach the actions and speeches of his characters from the characters themselves, or to imagine for a moment the transplanting of these characters to other scenes. The sense of local color is in this writer unusually strong and keen; and when we add to this his undoubted power of reproducing indigenous character, what is this but admitting that he is entitled to one of the highest distinctions of the novelist? (pp. 408-09)

[Blackmore] is destined to no mushroom popularity, for each of his novels is a distinct accession to literature. There is in all his works not only much poetic freshness, but a robust manliness which is sadly wanting in numbers of the vapid novels which teem from the press. He has a high conception of the value of his art, and consequently does not write for the mere sake of production,—the most dangerous and insidious custom which can creep over a popular writer, though one, unfortunately, too frequently witnessed. (p. 425)

There is a quaintness in our author which ever and anon reminds us of the writers of the Elizabethan era; but it is not unpleasant, and seems in harmony with the eccentric characters which Mr. Blackmore so frequently delights to draw. But what are the minor and occasional defects of incongruity, quaintness, and eccentricity in the presence of such sterling qualities of a much higher type, possessed by the author? His humor is true and genuine,—no other writer at all approaches its peculiar flavor.

He has the soul and eye of the poet; he reads a weighty lesson in every flower that blows, and converses with Nature as a child with its parent, gently drawing from her the secrets of her mighty heart. He has much of worldly wisdom, but more still of the wisdom of humanity, unsophisticated by the false-hoods and prevarications of society. If his genius has somewhat the appearance of a gnarled and knotted oak, it has the oak's massiveness and strength. He has written novels which will live because of their honesty and truthfulness of purpose, as well as for their imagination, their observation, and those num-berless touches of true genius which may be apprehended, but cannot be defined. All the world is to Mr. Blackmore a large garden filled with variegated flowers of divers hues and quality, but all yielding suggestions of the beautiful. And besides his active love of humanity,—without which no writer ever yet established a permanent claim upon the world's attention and regard,—he is not ashamed to own that with him the old-fashioned idea of faith in God, now so freely assailed by a weak and puny scepticism, has not yet grown obsolete. (pp. 425-26)

George Barnett Smith, "Mr Blackmore's Novels," in The International Review, Vol. VII, September, 1879, pp. 406-26.

JOHN A. STEUART (essay date 1890)

[*In the following excerpt, Steuart analyzes the charm of* Lorna Doone, *maintaining that the most outstanding element of this novel is Blackmore's characterization of John Ridd.*]

While the public are so tolerant and indulgent with a popular favourite as generally to read all his works, they have a singular predilection for judging him by one, for making a particular book the touchstone by which to try all his other writings. The book by which they have chosen to judge you is *Lorna Doone*. But, though that is by far your most popular book, I, for one, am not quite prepared to say it is your best. At any rate, it cannot make me forget that you are the author of *Springhaven* and *Christowell*. However, since it is the popular choice, I am quite willing to accept it as mine also, and to make it the ground on which briefly to examine the claim your admirers advance for you, of being the first of living English novelists. (p. 239)

What, one is often tempted to ask, is the singular charm that fascinates us in that Romance of Exmoor? Is it in the style, or in the characters, or in the scenery and action of the story? Doubtless it lies in all these, for it is subtle and manifold. But if one were forced to lay one's finger on a particular feature as the chief one, I think it would be concluded that that gentle and humane giant, John Ridd: gentle and humane, yet full of a volcanic fire and force, and capable on occasion of being stern enough to deal out terrific justice—I say there are obvious reasons why he should be considered the central attraction of the book. And, as a matter of fact, I believe he is. A friend of mine, and one of the most discriminating of your admirers, recently spoke of the book, as a whole, and John Ridd in particular, as follows, and in so doing voiced the popular ver-dict:

Lorna Doone is one of those books which are national in character. The atmosphere is the free air of our English moors. The situations are always interesting, such common occupations as sheep-shearing and working in the fields never being prosaic. The apotheosis of brute force is

natural, or it would be mean. It might still be mean if it were not allied with perfect courage and undeniable honesty and chastity. John Ridd is the type of our perfect English manhood; he has within him the element of all that is noble; nothing but manliness could dwell in his great heart. Martyrdom he would bear, but freedom he must have. He would fight like a fiend for freedom, but he would not be a libertine. It is of the John Ridds of the world that you cannot ask, "Is he a gentleman?" Such a character as Mr. Blackmore's hero stands above all ques-tions of the kind. He is a man. . . . Neither can criticism touch Lorna Doone herself. She is the proper partner of John, and when that is said you have given her her due.

It might be said that she is a very perfect heroine indeed whom criticism cannot touch—more perfect than even that sweetest and most perfect piece of fictitious womanhood, the master-piece of the master, the beautiful, the peerless, the almost faultless Imogen. However, let it be granted that Lorna Doone is the fit companion for the doughty yeoman of Devon. Though for myself, if I were disposed to be captious, it is on Lorna I should fasten. . . . It may be that I have failed to fully grasp your intentions, or fully comprehend some of the very peculiar circumstances of the story, some of the circumstances in which Lorna is particularly involved, but to me she is not the most satisfactory female character you have drawn. Nay, I hardly think her the most satisfactory female character in the book to which she gives her name. Though palpitating with life to the finger-tips (and that, of course, is the first essential) she is not in *all* respects so fine in my eyes as either Annie or Mrs. Ridd. There are times when I think even Ruth Huckaback better. Perhaps, indeed, no character so slightly sketched as Ruth was ever truer or more intensely alive. She has a woman's heart in that little body of hers, a heart that swells with big passions, and such aspirations as only a woman can have, and, little as we see of her, we know her thoroughly, and what is more, sympathise with her deeply.

Lorna Doone we also know thoroughly, and in most of her trying situations sympathise with. But she hardly commands complete and perfect sympathy and admiration. How is it that a creation, in most respects so charming, fails to make the reader, as it were, her own, through at least the first half of the book? Is it because, like Juliet, she is sometimes too much the untutored child of nature to suit the modern taste, or is it because the over-generous John, seeing her with the eyes of infatuation, makes her just a little too angelic, and thus some-times lifts her beyond the sphere of our sympathy? Perhaps the latter is the true explanation. It would be interesting to find that once in a while, however long the intervals might be, John was aware of some slight human imperfection in his adored inamorata. It is so human to be fallible, that when we encounter a creature of divine perfection, much as we admire her, we can hardly feel that bond of equality and kinship which alone makes one child of Adam interesting to another. Perhaps the fact that John Ridd is unable to discover, or at any rate declines to reveal any trifling defect in Lorna, is a strong argument against the autobiographical form of fiction. John is always ready enough to dwell, and dwell with emphasis, on his own imperfections, but it evidently is a sheer impossibility to see any fault, hardly so much as a foible in the goddess of the Doone Glen. . . . After all the objections that might justly be taken to what is styled the analytical school, a little more of its spirit would have saved the delineator of Lorna Doone from giving us an angel instead of a woman. But let it be frankly owned that, even with her fault of a too elaborate perfection, Lorna Doone is a splended creation, noble in all her instincts, and hardly suffering in a comparison with any heroine of any novelist living or dead, except, perhaps, some of the heroines of Goethe, and one or two of Mr. Howells's.

Concerning the hero, the titanic John, there can, I think, be but one opinion, the opinion given by the critic I have already quoted, namely, that he "is the type of our perfect English manhood." A grand, massive character he surely is, the embodiment of English strength, English solidity, English generosity, English fair-play—a right sound piece of stuff, true as the best-tempered steel, not to be shaken by adversity, nor spoiled by prosperity—a yeoman of whom one would be proud to say that his limbs were made in England. It is hard to speak of John Ridd without going into superlatives. He is so frank, so genial, of such vast dimensions in mind and body, so caressing in his gentleness, so terrific in his anger, so just, so honourable, so fierce in his hatred of all that is mean, so constant in his loyalty to all that is noble, so perfectly admirable in his strength and his weakness, that it is admiration first and criticism nowhere. Some of Scott's characters would, I dare say, equal him in strength and kindliness of nature. He somewhat resembles Dandie Dinmont. Not that there is the least trace of imitation in him, but that great natures are pretty much the same the wide world over, and that when they are faithfully drawn there must be points of similarity in the pictures. Others of Scott's characters, too, might match him in most of his best qualities—many of them are much more romantic,—but since the days of Scott I doubt if any novelist has given us a character fit to stand beside John Ridd, except it might be the creators of Christian Christianson and Daniel Mylrea.

For one of his physical proportions John Ridd is gentle almost beyond example. As the saying is, he would not hurt a fly if he could help it, and his behaviour towards Lorna and his mother and sisters is very beautiful. At the same time, though gentleness is admirable in a giant, I don't know that I like Ridd's softness best. Dr. Johnson professed to like a good hater, and I own that I am partial to a man who knows how to be angry on occasion. A man's mettle is shown by the manner in which he deals with an enemy; and perhaps no incident in Ridd's career is more impressive than that final meeting with Carver Doone, after the chivalrous outlaw had shot Lorna at the altar. It was a situation to try a man; but John rises magnificently to the occasion. Not long after the outlaw has taken his base revenge, John is able to announce that

> "the black bog had him by the feet, the sucking of the ground drew on him like the thirsty lips of death. In our fury we had heeded neither wet nor dry; nor thought of earth beneath us. I myself might scarcely leap with the last spring of o'erlaboured legs from the engulfing grave of slime. He fell back with his swarthy breast (from which my grip had rent all the clothing) like a hummock of bog oak, standing out of the quagmire; and then he tossed his arms to heaven, and they were black to the elbow. I could only gaze and pant, for my strength was no more than an infant's, from the fury and the horror. Scarcely could I turn away while joint by joint he sank from sight."

John Ridd can be gentle, but he knows how to avenge a wrong.

Nor with all his delicious self-depreciation, his apparent heaviness and ignorance of life and literature (except the Bible and Master William Shakespeare), is he wanting in what the Scotch call "wut." Like Falstaff, he hath a very pleasant humour. It rises spontaneously and unexpectedly, as the best humour always does and must, and ripples like sunshine over scenes which would otherwise be exceedingly grim indeed. His accounts of his own escapades, especially in the early portions of the book, are done with a delightful sense of the charm of lightenment. But this quality of humour is one which is ever present in all your works. You cannot even make a parson arrest a thief without indulging in a little jocoseness, just enough to give savour to the scene without destroying the excitement of it.

Besides the quality of humour, your characters are usually endowed with very considerable powers of observation and reflection. John Ridd, indeed, is a second Sancho Panza in the liberal fashion in which he lets pearls of wisdom drop by the way. (pp. 239-49)

One great charm, not only of **Lorna Doone,** but of all your works, lies in the warmth of tone that pervades them. Not only are your creations vital (in **Springhaven** they are fairly exuberant with life), but we seem to feel the pulse of Nature in your scenic pictures as well. At the start I asked whether the charm of **Lorna Doone** lay in the style. I think it might be answered that, if the chief pleasure in reading your writings is not derivable from style, at least your style gives no small pleasure to every reader with any appreciation of culture. It is a style that is peculiar and hard to analyse. Sometimes, in its expressiveness, it reminds one of the style of John Bunyan, at other times its circumstantial minuteness reminds one of Defoe's; but, as a whole, it is infinitely richer than Bunyan's, and infinitely more poetic than Defoe's. Perhaps its power is shown nowhere as well as in the descriptions of Nature which abound in all your writings. The following, I think, gives evidence of what is called the poetic sense:—

> The rising of the sun was noble in the cold and warmth of it; peeping down the spread of light, he raised his shoulder heavily over the edge of gray mountain and wavering length of upland. Beneath his gaze the dewfogs dipped, and crept to the hollow places, then stole away in line and column holding skirts, and clinging subtly at the sheltering corners where rock hung over grass-land, while the brave lines of the hills came forth, one beyond other gliding.
>
> Then the woods arose in folds, like drapery of awakened mountains, stately, with a depth of awe and memory of the tempests. Autumn's mellow hand was on them, as they owned already, touched with gold and red and olive; and their joy towards the sun was less to a bridegroom than a father.
>
> Yet before the floating impress of the woods could clear itself, suddenly the gladsome light leaped over hill and valley, casting amber, blue, and purple, and a tint of rich, red rose according to the scene they lit on, and the curtain flung around; yet all alike dispelling fear and the cloven hoof of darkness; all on the wings of hope advancing, and proclaiming, "God is here."

Somehow I imagine that your success as a portrait-painter hinders a due appreciation of your merits as a landscape artist. It is a pity to think that such a passage as the above should be skipped. (pp. 250-52)

John A. Steuart, "To Mr. R. D. Blackmore," in his Letters to Living Authors, *United States Book Co., 1890, pp. 236-52.*

GEORGE SAINTSBURY (essay date 1894)

[*Saintsbury has been called the most influential English literary historian and critic of the late nineteenth and early twentieth centuries. His studies of French literature, particularly* A History of the French Novel *(1917-1919), have established him as a leading authority on such writers as Guy de Maupassant and Honoré de Balzac. Saintsbury adhered to two distinct sets of critical standards: one for the novel and the other for poetry and drama. As a critic of novels, he maintained that "the novel has nothing to do with any beliefs, with any convictions, with any thoughts in the strict sense, except as mere garnishings. Its substance must always be life not thought, conduct not belief, the passions not the intellect, manners and morals not creeds and theories. . . . The novel is . . . mainly and firstly a criticism of life." René Wellek has praised Saintsbury's critical qualities: his "enormous reading, the almost universal scope of his subject matter, the zest and zeal of his exposition," and "the audacity with which he handles the most ambitious and unattempted arguments." In the following excerpt, Saintsbury offers a largely favorable review of* Perlycross.]

It is hardly possible to exaggerate the sense of "most exceeding peace" that comes upon the reviewer when he opens in these days a novel of Mr. Blackmore's. We know that not only will he be able to share the poet's boast—

> We asked no social questions, we pumped no hidden
> shame,
> We never talked obstetrics when the Little Stranger
> came;
> We left the Lord in Heaven, we left the fiends in
> Hell—

u.s.w., but that these immense negative merits will be accompanied by positive ones hardly less satisfactory. A style racy and quaint, without excessive affectation; a good old-fashioned scholarship; a perpetual fount of humour; a store of English patriotism, sense, and sanity—these are some of the good things which Mr. Blackmore always gives us, but which he seems (we do not know whether it is by contrast or not) to give us in *Perlycross* to an extent surpassing most of his later gifts. To the central incident—the disappearance of the coffin of Sir Thomas Waldron, and the consequent imputations of body-snatching or other foul play on the parish doctor, on Lady Waldron, and others—it might be possible, if it were worth while, to make some unimportant demurs. It may seem a little odd that such an intelligent as well as excellent person as Mr. Penniloe, the curate, bound by special ties to the Waldron family, and anxious for the doctor's well-being, should not have made stricter search to see whether the mortal remains of the good Sir Thomas had actually disappeared; but no one can say that his failure to do so is wholly improbable. A certain complication too, an in-and-outness of sub-plots and minor interests, which is not uncommon with Mr. Blackmore, may offend those who like either a very simple and straightforward story or else one the ravelments of which are unravelled in a strictly mathematical and orderly fashion. But these are mere technical objections; the merits of the book for reading are as

indisputable as ever—more so indeed, as we have hinted, than those of some of its immediate predecessors. The author's gift, not merely of creating a character or two, but of filling a whole village and almost a whole district with live people, has seldom been better shown. Sometimes his personages are oddities and almost "humours": but they are always live oddities, humours that move and breathe. And it is a proof of Mr. Blackmore's strength that one has some difficulty in deciding whether his most elaborate or his slightest sketches are the best. For instance, the Rev. Philip Penniloe, the resident curate of Perlycross (for 'tis sixty years since) is the central figure of most of the scenes in the book; and the Rev. John Chevithorne, his rector, non-resident, but by no means bloated or tyrannical, though a little unspiritual, appears at most in one or two. Yet it may be doubted whether the Rev. Philip or the Rev. John is the neater and completer presentation of an entire person. And this cardinal faculty of vivification—the chiefest and by far the rarest faculty of the novelist—is very nearly all-pervading. You may not be extraordinarily enamoured of any one. Christie Fox, the doctor's sister; Lady Waldron herself (whose Spanish-English is a real addition to the few and difficult successes in such a kind), and the "pupil" Pike are perhaps the most engaging; but they are all real people. And how many of our clever novelists nowadays can make real people at any time; how many can make them all the time? The story of *Perlycross* is too complicated and the characters too numerous for it to be possible to do anything like justice in such a notice as this. But what we have said of it is equivalent to saying that the intending reader need fear no mistake in it, seeing that he is in the hands of a master. (pp. 299-300)

George Saintsbury, in a review of "Perlycross," in The Academy, *Vol. XLVII, No. 1172, October 20, 1894, pp. 299-300.*

EDEN PHILLPOTTS (essay date 1901)

[*Phillpotts was an English novelist and poet whose series of Dartmoor novels have often been compared with Hardy's Wessex novels. An admirer of Blackmore, Phillpotts had in common with him a love of gardening as well as of nature. In the following excerpt, Phillpotts presents a favorable overview of Blackmore's works, praising in particular his representation of country life.*]

As summed in his books and reflected in his sequestered life, the message of Blackmore can be easily gleaned. He taught, as the artist must, without intention, and his lesson was how a man may be modest and self-reliant. Of late, no demand has existed for these virtues; and consequently during the last few years of his career Blackmore enjoyed a seclusion and peace that would render our successful modern story-tellers most uneasy. His inner life and his home were sacred in his opinion, and that antiquated idea he chose to maintain against all comers. So the unthinking supposed that he had retreated from the van of the fight; whereas, in reality, he stood there to the end, watching the progress of his beloved art with critical eyes—stood there beside the two remaining great novelists still left to us. In subtlety the others exceeded him; in the quality of a sea-deep, sane humor and tolerance of humanity, he stood far above either.

The old, spacious treatment of fiction—the long story that demands time for the telling, and winds like a noble, natural valley amid high hills and under various skies—will presently vanish. For those who are heard seldom paint upon big canvases to-day. But Blackmore belongs to the voluminous men in this respect, and, without pretending to any special admiration for bulk, yet in a generation of mediocrity, where the writers who count at all are so often engaged upon mosaic and miniature painting, one loves these spacious stories full of clean air, broad light and shade, and honest laughter from the lungs.

Blackmore was an artist first and last. Unconsciously—because conviction laid at the root of his philosophy and dominated him at his tree-pruning, trout-fishing, and story-telling—he taught faith, courage, honesty, and clean living. His heroes were men of no finical complexity; his heroines were women upon the noble, feminine, and gracious lines of Shakespeare's women. Clear-eyed, pure-spirited, and stately they move through their loves and sorrows. He set forth the beauty of healthy manhood and womanhood; and he was thankful that the canker he had seen fasten upon literature and art—that passing glorification of decay and disease—had already begun to dry up and heal before he died.

It is the fashion to speak of Blackmore as the writer of *Lorna Doone* rather than as an artist who produced a dozen great stories, and another dozen, amply sufficient for the passport of any novelist in the second rank. *Lorna Doone* indeed has the life-blood of the author, and John Ridd stands as near to him as ever a character stood to its creator; but his work abounds in men as great and single-hearted; while of humorous personages John Ridd is by no means first. Perhaps Davy Llewellyn in *The Maid of Sker* enjoys pride of place from that standpoint, for the old sailor is Shakespearian in his surprises, in his breadth, boldness of outline, and glorious humor.

Absolutely without fear, Blackmore answered to none but his own ideal, and no critic ever handled his work with such severity as he did himself. His humor kept him sound on all self-estimates; his modesty alone misled him to rate himself too low. His work will surely endure. *Lorna Doone, The Maid of Sker, Perlycross, Springhaven, Mary Anerley, Alice Lorraine, Christowell,* and other stories—because they give a true picture of our national life and character at various great periods in history—will take their proper rank with the enduring fiction of the nineteenth century; and it may well be that, weary of the "short long story," or the "long short story," or whatever the particular production in question is called, with its straining and its fever, its neurotics, its "problems," and its frantic pursuit of the phrase, that scanty party of the elect among novel-readers, which requires to be taken seriously in each generation, will turn again to Blackmore and find in his broad sweep, like the roll of an ocean wave, his manliness, his laughter, his detestation of what is mean, and small, and dirty, a sort of tonic they may come to cry for in years not far distant.

Full of the very sap and scent of country life are all his stories, and long before the advent of Richard Jefferies, you shall find Blackmore noting the details of rural scenery through the procession of the seasons and setting them forth, as only an artist can, in their due relation to the mass of mountains, to the volume of rivers, to the life of men and women. Indeed, while to appreciate the greatest in Blackmore one needs only to be a student of our common nature, there is another quality in which he stands absolutely alone; and for understanding his achievement in this sort, a man must know the country and know it well. The love and appreciation of green growing things is a fruitful secret of his inspiration. His harvests of the years are painted in such mellow colors as only autumn knows, and his fruit pieces have not been equalled in the language. The welfare of fruit was near his heart. . . . The cherry, the strawberry, the peach, and the vine flourish in his works as no artist shall ever make them upon canvas, for Blackmore paints with

dawns and twilights, the varying warmth of the sun and the diamond dews born of starry nights. For him the garden filled no small part of life, and, out of sheer love, he studied all natural things from the seed and egg to their full accomplishment. Such love all may indeed share, but his inner knowledge and understanding only a lifetime of frank service can win, and only genius yield again in adequate literary form. But we are prone to be sceptical concerning high qualities in a writer which we lack the catholicity or knowledge to appreciate, and these real triumphs are not understood by many urban critics who have discussed Blackmore. Mr. W. E. Henley, for example, does not know whether *Lorna Doone* is a great book. So Hazlitt, had he appreciated the difference between an oak and an ash, or ever picked a primrose, or trodden a west country lane, could not have written what he wrote about Robert Herrick. But the writers of the soil have all to endure the indifference of your brick-and-mortar men. The latter do not fully appreciate the significance of environment. (pp. 413-15)

[One] ventures to hope that an adequate memorial of Richard Doddridge Blackmore may shortly be undertaken. His memory meantime is safe enough, and his faith in goodness and manly optimism shall long hearten us upon the road of life. He was of the pith and marrow of his native land—a great artist, a great Englishman. (p. 415)

> *Eden Phillpotts, "Richard Doddridge Blackmore: A Note," in* The Critic, *New York, Vol. XXXVIII, No. 5, May, 1901, pp. 413-15.*

JAMES BAKER (essay date 1908)

[In the following excerpt from an essay by a friend of Blackmore, Baker reminisces about Blackmore and offers a favorable commentary on his novels.]

The varied experiences of [Blackmore's] life are utilized in all his books. The Church, from his home life—his father was a Devon clergyman—college life, from his Exeter College days. How he loved Oxford! I once spoke to him of a son of mine who was going in for a scholarship exam. "Send him to Oxford! send him to Oxford!" was his emphatic exclamation. Then came his schoolmaster trials, with all the capabilities of boys for worrying. Then the law, and, lastly, his great love, the Grower's occupation, fully described in that quaint novel *Kit and Kitty.* How minutely and intently he studied man and Nature! Some novelists who, either by their own efforts or their publishers' assiduity, have been paragraphed and puffed and birthday-booked, must strive in vain to produce from their work such a wealth of quaint, incisive phrases that in a line picture phases of life and thought. Take his description of England in *Alice Lorraine,* as "bounty from the lap of beauty, and that cultivated glory which no other land can show," or "the joy of all things dies in the enjoying" on the same page.

To the charm of quaintness he adds the charm of the unsuspected, and a depicting of the virtues and foibles of humanity in phrases that are ever fresh, yet fitting to the characters uttering them.

His wild bits of Nature he describes with a minute power that brings the scene and all the living things that people it vividly before one. What a charm there is in that marvellous description in the *Maid of Sker* of an October evening on Barnstaple River, off Braunton Burrows. Old Davy Llewellyn has been set by Parson Chowne to watch Sir Phillip Bampfylde from his schooner, as the Parson calls it. "Ketch, your reverence," interrupts Davy; "the difference is in the mizzen mast," proving Mr. Blackmore's care with local terms and titles. But in this task Davy has time to look about him, and the author has, therefore, time to make the reader feel the atmosphere of the scene of action; and in Chapter XXX. how those who know the district seem to breathe the very air of Taw and Torridge. In few words the waning day is pictured. "The full moon, lately risen, gazed directly down upon the river; but memory of daylight still was coming from the westward, feeble, and inclined to yield." One feels the gleam of orange light in the west, over stretch of sand and rivers, being overmastered by the silver gleams of the moon in the east. (pp. 32-3)

One interesting phase of Mr. Blackmore's work is his habit of interthought. An idea is caught, and in expressing it an interloping thought comes, modifying the idea. A habit this that in this snippet age, irritates the reader, whose brain is so weakened by the snippet dram that it can scarcely grasp one idea, and a secondary developing of that idea is wholly too much for it. A very simple example of this occurs in *Cradock Nowell*, where the very lovable John Rosedew, rector and tutor, is arguing a point with his practical sister, Aunt Eudoxia: "John always yielded at once whenever Eudoxia tried to argue, and the lady had the pleasure of feeling—until she began to think a little—how much she had the best of it." That interloping sentence makes the reader think also, and see a little deeper into the character of Miss Eudoxia. Or take the passage from *Dariel* upon the respect due from man to woman: "For drop as we may—and the ladies too often call upon us now to drop it—the sense that is inborn in us of a purer and higher birth in them." How the whole bent of modern woman life comes sweeping into the mind in this interjected sentence.

Sometimes Mr. Blackmore gives, like Balzac, just the minute touches that call up the whole picture of the scene, as that of a labourer's home in evening. He is describing in *Springhaven* Caryl Carne's hatred of the homely life of the little port; his waiting for the home-going labourers and "truant sweethearts who cannot have enough of one another," to get out of his way. "He let them get home, and pull their boots off, and set the frying-pan a-bubbling; for they ended the day with a bit of bacon whenever they could cash or credit it." One can see the good wife at the fire and the whole interior of the cottage by this touch, and how delightfully he depicts the scenes wherein his characters move and have their being. For these are not puppets; you do not see the author pulling the strings: we get to know them. The pretty, self-willed, vivacious Dolly in *Springhaven* is a very real character, as is the old Admiral Darling, with his discourses on himself and his unselfishness. Captain Stubbard and Dan Tugwell, the well-built and stalwart, are all as real as are the better-known Squire Faggus, and the gentle Lorna, or "girt" Jan Ridd the immortal; and whether he is describing the Hampshire heaths in *Cradock Nowell*, the Surrey gardens in *Kit and Kitty*, or even the wild Titanic ice-capped passes of the Caucasus, "the land of Prometheus," as in *Dariel*, one is enveloped in the scene. The curious fault in *Dariel* is that the atmosphere of the story is of bygone days, but certain incidents make it a story of to-day. If the history had been antedated by a century the book would have been more real, and yet one forgets this fault in the passion of it. The great charm of Mr. Blackmore's work is now in the story, now in the setting. The storm and passion of life is in all his work; aye, and the delicate love passages, and the gradual forging of the links that bind soul to soul, or body to body; but the artistic interest, the mind interest, lies in his rich de-

scriptive powers, his sense of condensation, and his quaint aphorisms and epigrammatic phrases. (pp. 34-6)

Springhaven is full of epigrammatic phrases. "Little cares, which are the ants that bring heavy grief." "All gentlemen hate to have a tree cut down, all blackguards delight in the process." "To achieve unmerited honour is the special gift of thousands, but to deserve and win befalls some few in every century."

What a capital description is that of James Cheseman, the successful grocer and butterman, who "was patted on both shoulders by the world whilst he patted his own butter"; and how the quiet humour ripples out in the self-denying Admiral, when there is a French alarm. "For my part, if I can only manage this plate of soup, and a slice of fish, and then one help of mutton, and just one apple fritter or some trifles of that sort, I shall be quite as lucky as I can hope to be. Eat your dinners, children, and don't think of mine."

There is a cutting sarcasm in the allusion to the suicidal growing dislike to work in the words "for the one" sacred principle of labour "is to play"; or, to go to one of his earlier works, there is much expressed in the words, "A thousand winks of childhood widen into one clear dream of age." Is not the domineering crabbedness, often begotten by the continuous teaching of troublesome boys, well expressed by, "Strange though it is, it is equally true that the duty and practice of teaching the young idea how to shoot, drive many good and benevolent people to long to shoot one another"? (p. 39)

Mr. Blackmore was a rare worker. The list of the literary work produced by him since the year 1864 would be considered ample work for most men—sixteen novels, several volumes of poems, occasional contributions to current publications, and the translation of the *Georgics*. And Mr. Blackmore's were no snippet novels written in a month, but well-developed works, full of incident that compels the reader to know his characters. In one of his letters in 1892 he writes of one of my own books: "I see that you give honest measure, which is more than most of us do now." But the "us," modestly inserted, did not include himself, for are not *Perlycross* and *Dariel*, written after this date, both honest measure and honest, delightful work, each double the length of a snippet novel?

Modesty, a positive disowning of any great qualities in his own work—in fact, a constant dissatisfaction with himself that he had not done better—was one of Mr. Blackmore's great characteristics. Repeatedly in his letters came this note of aiming at the best, yet non-contentment at the result.

But how full is his work of all that makes greatness! Intense dramatic force, tension of interest, and yet the power to snap that tension and still carry the reader on in some gentle bypath, by force of power of description or subtle humour. (pp. 44-5)

[Blackmore] loved the earth and its products, and to see Nature's development under his care. He had to send his products to Covent Garden, where, as I read in one of his letters, he was "fair game, and fair game never gets fair play." In *Alice Lorraine* is a capital chapter on Covent Garden in early morning in years gone by. "The market in those days was not flooded with poor foreign produce, fair to the eye, but a fraud on the belly, and full of most dangerous colic . . . a native would really buy from his neighbour as gladly as from his born enemy." He makes one feel the breath of the country coming into the sweltering city, following the lines of country produce, and lingering about "the Garden." Master John Thorne, on the top of his wagon, has sold out all his cherries, but still has "some bushels of peas and new potatoes, bunches of colewort and early carrots, besides five or six dozen of creamy cauliflowers, and several scores of fine-hearted lettuces."

Whether in market or in garden, by rush of Devon stream or on Glamorgan sands, or mid the frosty Caucasus as in *Dariel*, Mr. Blackmore lived amidst his scenes, and made his readers live there also. His close watching of Nature is exemplified by such passages as "The earth has a dew that foretells a bright day—whenever the dew is of the proper sort, for three kinds are established now." (pp. 50-1)

Mr. Blackmore's aim in life was always to get at the best, to do good work, to hate shams, and to revere honest purpose and aim, and he was so often dissatisfied with his own work because he ever strove to outdo himself. But let those who have read his work for the stories, re-read them for the philosophy of life, the rippling humour they so richly contain; and they will no longer say that Mr. Blackmore was a one-book author, although [*Lorna Doone*] is a mighty masterpiece in all the love and passion, tragedy and humour, and powerful description that build up a great novel. (p. 54)

James Baker, "R. D. Blackmore and His Work," in his Literary and Biographical Studies, *Chapman and Hall, Limited, 1908, pp. 24-54.*

WILLIAM LYON PHELPS (essay date 1910)

[*An American critic and educator, Phelps was for over forty years a lecturer on English literature at Yale. His early study* The Beginnings of the English Romantic Movement *(1893) is still considered an important work and his* Essays on Russian Novelists *(1911) was one of the first influential studies in English of the Russian realists. From 1922 until his death in 1943 he wrote a regular column for* Scribner's Magazine *and a nationally syndicated newspaper column. During this period, his criticism became less scholarly and more journalistic, and is notable for its generally enthusiastic tone. In the following excerpt, Phelps praises the narrative, plot, characters, and poetic descriptions of the country in* Lorna Doone *as elements of this novel that assure its continuing popularity.*]

[*Lorna Doone*] is not only one of the best-loved books in English fiction, and stands magnificently the severe test of re-reading, it is bound to have even more admirers in the future than it has ever yet enjoyed; it is visibly growing in reputation every year. It may be interesting to analyse some of its elements, in order to understand what has given it so assured a place. The main plot is simplicity itself. It is a history, however, that the world has always found entertaining, the history of the love of a strong man for a beautiful girl. They meet, he falls in love, he rescues her from peril, she goes up to London, becomes a great lady, returns, is dangerously wounded on her wedding-day, recovers, and they live happily for ever after—*voilà tout*. A very simple plot, yet the telling fills two stout volumes, with the reader's interest maintained from first to last.

It is told in the first person—the approved method of the historical romance. . . . Now, the great advantage of having John Ridd speak throughout is the gain in reality and vividness; it is as though we sat with him in the ingle, and obtained all our information at first hand. What is lost by narrowness of experience is made up in intensity; we follow him breathlessly, as Desdemona followed Othello, and he has every moment our burning sympathy. We participate more fully in his joys and

sorrows, in the agony of his suspense; we share his final triumph. He is talking directly to us, and John Ridd is a good talker. He is the kind of man who appeals to all classes of listeners. He has the gentleness and modesty that are so becoming to great physical strength; the love of children, animals, and all helpless creatures; reverence for God, purity of heart, and a noble slowness to wrath. Such a man is simply irresistible, and we are sorry when he finishes his tale. The defect in this method of narration, which Mr. Blackmore has employed with such success, is the inevitable defect in all stories written in this manner, as Professor Raleigh has observed: "It takes from the novelist the privilege of killing his hero." When John Ridd is securely bound, and the guns of hostile soldiers are levelled at his huge bulk, with their fingers actually on the triggers, we laugh at ourselves for our high-beating hearts; for of course he is unkillable, else how could he be talking at this very moment?

The plot of *Lorna Doone*, which, as we have observed, is very simple, is, nevertheless, skilfully complicated. It is not a surprise plot, like that of *A Pair of Blue Eyes;* we are not stunned by the last page. It is a suspense plot; we have a well-founded hope that all will come right in the end, and yet the author has introduced enough disturbing elements to put us occasionally in a maze. This artistic suspense is attained partly by the method of direct discourse; which, at the same time, develops the character of the hero. Big John repeats incidents, dwells lengthily on minute particulars, stops to enjoy the scenery, and makes mountains of stories out of molehills of fact. The second complication of the plot arises from the introduction of characters that apparently divert the course of the story without really doing so. There are nineteen important characters, all held well in hand; and a conspicuous example of a complicating personage is little Ruth Huckaback. She interferes in the main plot in an exceedingly clever way. The absorbing question in every reader's mind is, of course, Will John marry Lorna? Now Ruth's interviews with the hero are so skilfully managed, and with such intervals of time between, that on some pages she seems destined to be his bride. And, admirably drawn as her character is, when her artistic purpose in the plot is fully accomplished, she quietly fades out, with the significant tribute, "Ruth Huckaback is not married yet."

There is also a subsidiary plot, dovetailed neatly into the main building. This is the story of the attractive highwayman, Tom Faggus, and his love for John's sister, Annie. Many pages are taken up with the adventures of this gentleman, who enters the novel on horseback (what a horse!) at the moment when the old drake is fighting for his life. Besides our interest in Tom himself, in his wild adventures, and in his reformation, we are interested in the conflict of his two passions, one for the bottle, and one for Annie, and we wonder which will win. This subsidiary love story is still further complicated by the introduction of young De Whichehalse; and in the struggle between John Ridd and the Doones, both Tom Faggus and the De Whichehalse family play important parts. It is interesting, too, to observe how events that seem at the time to be of no particular importance, turn out later to be highly significant; when, at the very beginning of the long story, the little boy, on his way home from school, meets the lady's maid, and shortly after sees the child borne away on the robber's saddle, we imagine all this is put in to enliven the journey, that it is just "detail"; long afterwards we find the artistic motive. In fact, one of the most notable virtues of this admirable plot is the constant introduction of matters apparently irrelevant and due to mere garrulity, such as the uncanny sound, for example, which prove after all to be essential to the course of the narrative.

As for the characters, they impress us differently in different moods. For all John Ridd's prodigious strength, marvellous escapes, and astounding feats, his personality is so intensely human that he seems real. His *soul*, at any rate, is genuine, and wholly natural; his bodily activity—the extraction of Carver's biceps, the wrenching of the branch from the tree, the hurling of the cannon through the door—makes him a dim giant in a fairy story. When we think of the qualities of his mind and heart, he comes quite close; when we think of his physical prowess, he almost vanishes in the land of Fable. I remember the comment of an undergraduate—"John Ridd is as remote as Achilles; he is like a Greek myth."

The women are all well drawn and individualised—except the heroine. I venture to say that no one has ever seen Lorna in his mind's eye. She is like a plate that will not develop. A very pretty girl with an affectionate disposition,—what more can be said? But so long as a Queen has beauty and dignity, she does not need to be interesting; and Lorna is the queen of this romance. John's mother and his two sisters are as like and unlike as members of the same family ought to be; they are real women. Ruth Huckaback and Gwenny Carfax are great additions to our literary acquaintances; each would make an excellent heroine for a realistic novel. They have the indescribable puzzling characteristics that we call feminine; sudden caprices, flashes of unexpected jealousy, deep loyal tenderness, unlimited capacity for self-sacrifice, and in the last analysis, Mystery.

The humour of the story is spontaneous, and of great variety, running from broad mirth to whimsical subtlety. The first concerted attack on the Doones is comic opera burlesque; but the scenes of humour that delight us most are those describing friendly relations with beast and bird. The eye of the old drake, as he stared wildly from his precarious position, and the delight of the ducks as they welcomed his rescue; above all, Annie's care of the wild birds in the bitter cold. (pp. 235-41)

Whatever may be the merits of Mr. Blackmore's published verse, there is more poetry in *Lorna Doone* than in many volumes of formal rime. The wonderful descriptions of the country in shade and shine, in fog and drought, the pictures of the sunrise and the falling water, the "tumultuous privacy" of the snow-storms,—these are all descriptive poems. Every reader has noticed the peculiar rhythm of the style, and wondered if it were intentional. Hundreds of sentences here and there are perfect English hexameters; one can find them by opening the book at random, and reading aloud. But this peculiar element in the style goes much farther than isolated phrases. There are solid passages of steady rhythm, which might correctly be printed in verse form.

Mr. Blackmore's personal character was so modest, unassuming, and lovable, that it is not difficult to guess the source of the purity, sweetness, and sincerity of his great book. If he were somewhat surprised at the utter coldness of its first reception, he never got over his amazement at the size and extent of its ultimate triumph. . . . Mr. Blackmore lived long enough to see an entirely different kind of "local colour" become conventional, where many a novelist, portraying his native town or the community in which he dwelt, emphasised with what skill he could command all its poverty, squalor, and meanness; the disgusting vices and malignant selfishness of its inhabitants; and after he had thus fouled his nest by representing it as a mass of filth, degradation, and sin, he imagined he had created a work of art. The author of *Lorna Doone* had the satisfaction of knowing that he had inspired hundreds of thou-sands of readers with the love of his favourite west country, and with an intense desire to visit it. (pp. 241-43)

William Lyon Phelps, " 'Lorna Doone'," in his *Essays on Modern Novelists*, *The Macmillan Company, 1910*, pp. 229-43.

GEORGE SAINTSBURY (essay date 1913)

[*In the following excerpt, Saintsbury expresses admiration for Blackmore's novels, but questions their classification as masterpieces.*]

A very interesting subject for examination . . . is Mr. Blackmore. . . . Few of our modern novelists have combined so much scholarship with so much command of mother wit and racy English, so much close study of minor character and local speech with such wealth of romantic fancy; such a thorough observance of "good form" with so complete a freedom from priggishness and prudery. To this day there are lively controversies whether he worked up the Doone story from local tradition or made it "out of his own head." But whichever he did (and the present historian owns that he cares very little about the point) the way in which he has turned a striking, but not extraordinary, and certainly not very extensive West Country glen into an *Arabian Nights* valley, with the figures and action of a mediæval romance and the human interest of a modern novel, is really wonderful. And there is hardly a book of his last thirty years' production, from *Clara Vaughan* to *Perlycross,* which has not vigour, variety, character, "race" enough for half a dozen. In such books, for example, as *The Maid of Sker* and *Cripps the Carrier* the idiosyncrasy is extraordinary; the quaint and piquant oddity of phrase and apothegm as vivid as Dickens, rather more real, and tinged somehow with a flavour of literature, even of poetry, which was Dickens's constant lack.

And yet when one comes to consider the books critically, either one by one, or in pairs and batches, or as a whole, it is somehow or other difficult to pronounce any one exactly a masterpiece. There is a want of "inevitableness" which sometimes amounts to improbability, as in the case particularly of that most vivid and racy of books, *Cripps the Carrier,* where the central incident or situation, though by no means impossible, is almost insultingly unlikely, and forces its unlikeliness on one at almost every moment and turn. Never, perhaps, was there a better instance of that "possible-improbable" which contrasts so fatally with the "probable-impossible." In not a few cases, too, there is that reproduction of similar *dénouements* and crucial occurrences which is almost necessary in a time when men write many novels. In almost all there is a want of central interest in the characters that should be central; in some an exaggeration of dialect; or of quaint non-dialectic but also non-catholic locutions on the author's part. One rather hates oneself for finding such faults—no one of which is absolutely fatal—in a mass of work which has given, and continues to give, so much pleasure: but the facts remain. One would not have the books *not* written on any account; but one feels that they were written rather because the author chose to do so than because he could not help it. Now it is possible to exaggerate the necessity of "mission" and the like: but, after all, *Ich kann nicht anders* ["I can do nothing else"] must be to some extent the mood of mind of the man who is committing a masterpiece. (pp. 284-86)

George Saintsbury, "The Fiction of Yesterday—Conclusion," in his The English Novel, *J. M. Dent & Sons, Ltd., 1913, pp. 273-314.*

SIR HERBERT WARREN   (essay date 1914)

[*Warren was an English educator and writer. In the following excerpt, he compares Blackmore with several of his contemporaries, discusses the epic qualities of* Lorna Doone, *and notes Blackmore's affinity for classical writers as well as for ancient languages.*]

[*Lorna Doone*] has done for the limited but specially beautiful region of Exmoor, where Devon and Somerset meet, what Scott did for the Highlands, or in a sense for Scotland, what on a smaller scale Kingsley did for Devon, what Mr. Eden Phillpotts has done for Dartmoor, and Mr. Thomas Hardy for the so-called "Wessex," another part of the same ancient kingdom.

Of Watchet and Minehead, of Dunkery and Porlock, of Oare and Simonsbath and Dulverton, Blackmore is the *vates sacer*. Hotels, coaches, steamers, and that not in Somerset alone, bear the name of his heroine. (p. vii)

Blackmore wrote many other stories. Perhaps none was a failure and many proved decided successes. But it was by *Lorna Doone* that he became known, and it is by *Lorna Doone* that he lives. This alone of his works has any claim to be a classic. Is it a classic? Will it endure? It seems likely that it will. An historic or geographic story is weighted at the start with certain drawbacks. It does not make a simple and wide appeal to all men of its own time. But if it once succeeds, then its success is likely to be the more lasting, for its vogue does not depend on a passing fashion. It is a picture of an interesting time and place, interesting to all times that care for the past or for local legend and association. An admirable example of this is Thackeray's *Esmond*. Blackmore himself was aware of the difficulty.

In the preface already quoted he says, "In shaping this tale the writer neither dares, nor desires, to claim for it the dignity, or cumber it with the difficulty, of an historic novel."

He was well advised. Herein lies the secret of its success. He himself calls *Lorna Doone* a "romance." It is in reality a poem though in prose. Blackmore's first ambition was to be a poet. Somehow, though like Dickens at times he came very near realizing this ambition, he did not quite realize it. He failed as a poet in verse, but he succeeded as a poet in "that other harmony," as Dryden so happily calls it, "of prose."

Lorna Doone is an epic, a prose epic. It has the epic size. It is distinctly a long book. You can "cut at it and come again." It has the epic structure, large, loose, at times almost rambling and desultory, with all the licence, and the easy-going, prattling narrative of the old chronicler. It has its separate "stories within a story," the successive *aristeia*, as the Greeks called them, the "innings" of the different heroes, when now Jan Fry, now Tom Faggus, now Jeremy Stickles, now the Counsellor, now Carver, now Reuben Huckaback, successively has his "show." And each has his individual character, the dashing highwayman, the stout and loyal, if limited soldier, the villains of craft, the villain of brutal and cunning force.

And so it is with the women, from the mother still young and comely, her woman's amiability steeled by sorrow, to the domestic sweet-tempered Annie, the literary and critical Elizabeth, the prudent yet tender little Ruth.

The story again can afford to turn aside, to depict with a loving hand and lingering brush, the scenery, the hues of the region, the tradition of the great frost, or to introduce local legends, like that of the magician and the saint.

The author's turn for verse too, if it does not quite amount to poetry, enables him to interweave once and again effective ballads and refrains, like the Exmoor Harvest Song.

It can give us enough, but not too much of the history and colour of the time. London under Charles II and James II, the Battle of Sedgmoor as it appeared to the country folk, Judge Jeffreys in his court or on the Bloody Assize, Kirke with his "Lambs," and the Duke of Marlborough in his early days as "General Churchill." There is, too, a real and a fine plot. Through all, as in a great epic, runs the dominant thread knitting the narrative into an artistic whole, the passion, the true love, of Jan Ridd and Lorna.

Like the "wrath of Achilles" or the constancy of Ulysses, this is the motive and secret of the composition. And like the true hero of the epic, the central character, for all his foibles, towers not only physically but morally over all the other figures, while the fact that he tells his own story in his own way adds to the illusion and probability.

The style and language, too, have an epic character, poetic, rich in varied elements, picturesque. There is a considerable element of dialect which tinges the whole and yet is not overdone. Blackmore had a *flair* for unusual and effective words and phrases—his poetic gift gave him that—circumfere, flotage, mux me! yelloon, goyal, tallat, linhay, telling-house, dap, antre, mostacchio, eyesen, toesen, rhaine; "Cross the rhaine and coome within rache!" Some are words of dialect, some are old English, some Elizabethan. "The Bible and Master William Shakespeare," Jan Ridd tells us, are the sources of his diction. His idiom, too, has the value of a phonographic record. He came just in time to catch and fix much of the dialect of Somerset and Devon, the strength and force of which those who knew it in childhood fifty years ago will remember with regretful affection. (pp. viii-x)

> *Sir Herbert Warren, in an introduction to* Lorna Doone: A Romance of Exmoor *by R. D. Blackmore, Oxford University Press, London, 1914, pp. v-xviii.*

WALDO H. DUNN   (essay date 1926)

[*Dunn, an American educator and writer, was a good friend of Blackmore and later became his first biographer. In the following excerpt, Dunn discusses the appeal of* Lorna Doone, Perlycross, *and* Dariel, *and considers Blackmore's writing style as a reflection of the author's nature.*]

[For] most people, Blackmore's name will always suggest *Lorna Doone*. It is well for us to remember that *Lorna* did not spring into immediate popularity, and the reason is not far to seek. Its quality is too high. Moreover, it is a long romance; the narrative moves in most leisurely fashion, lingering with love over the most insignificant details, pressing all the sweetness out of the most trivial incidents of life. The book contains bits of description as gorgeously woven as rare tapestries. . . . [The] style of *Lorna Doone* is ornate, quaint, archaic. The author frequently "stays his haste" and "makes delays." One is inclined at times to say that the style has in it the very elements that militate against popularity—especially in an age like this. And yet the book grips the attention, and seems to attract to itself more and more readers. Again, the reason is not far to seek. The story has in it everything to appeal: bearded bandits and a beautiful kidnapped maiden, hairbreadth escapes, love-making in the face of heavy odds, dark caverns, treacherous bogs of quicksand; difficulties and dangers alternate with peaceful rural scenes; the movement of a mighty life is always felt beneath the deepest calm. If great literature be a means of escape from the humdrum of everyday duties, from the dust and heat of the present, *Lorna Doone* offers just that escape. It takes us away from the rush and whirl of the twentieth century, away from factories and airplanes, into a beautiful, leisurely, remote corner of England's out-of-doors; back to the glens and the valleys of Devon and Somerset, to the white, drifting clouds, the clear, sparkling streams, the singing birds. Men with great spurred boots and plumes on hats gallop by on horseback; creaking stage-coaches rumble along the highways. It is a world of throbbing human life against a background of unsubdued nature. Every valley holds its secret; every woodland corner may conceal an enemy. The book rests upon the bedrock of elemental human passions. It seems to me that it has in it almost everything that good narrative demands, and an added something that is the very essence of Blackmore's nature. (pp. 48-50)

Lorna easily surpasses every other novel that Blackmore has written, having in it "the little more" that means "what worlds away." In it Blackmore reached the very culmination of his narrative method and style. (pp. 50-1)

His pen never lost its cunning, even though he was not able again to attain to the magic that marks his masterpiece. In many ways I consider *Perlycross* . . . one of the best of his novels from the point of view of humour and skilful delineation of Devonshire and Cornwall rustics. He may very fairly divide honours in this respect with Thomas Hardy at Hardy's best. He writes from the most intimate first-hand knowledge. "Each place has its own style, and tone, vein of sentiment, and lines of attitude, deepened perhaps by the lore and store of many generations." In such wise he speaks of differences among the parishes in south-western England, and he never fails to mark these differences with the greatest delicacy and precision. Two brief passages will show that his peculiar turn of humour was undimmed by age. The first bit crops out in a descriptive passage:

> Southward stretched the rich Perle valley, green with meadows beloved by cows, who expressed their fine emotions in the noblest cream.

The other centres about an ultimatum delivered by Parson Penniloe to workers on the parish church:

> Silence was enjoined three times by ding-dong of bell and blare of trump, and thrice the fatal document was read with stern solemnity and mute acceptance of every creature except ducks, whom nothing short of death can silence, and scarcely even that when once their long valves quiver with the elegiac strain.

(p. 51)

[*Dariel* was] the work of Blackmore's old age; twenty-six months later he was dead. The uninitiated reader would never suspect, however, that it was the work of a man in his seventy-second year, unless, perchance, he should stop to consider that the deep wisdom of the story could emanate only from long and varied and rich experience. I am glad that the best of Blackmore persisted to the end. *Dariel* is the work of a man who is not yet disillusioned, a man whose spirit is still young; the beauty

and the magic of love continue to thrill him; the earth and the sky speak to him as of old; his faith is undimmed. "What is truly great," he asks, "unless it be concerned with love, or valour, freedom, piety, or self-denial, and desire to benefit the world at large?" I feel as I close *Dariel* that its author never betrays one of his readers; he always gives something upon which the soul may rest.

I have mentioned the narrative method and style of Blackmore. What is it in his writing that marks it as his own, that makes it possible for a reader at once to recognize it as Blackmore's? It would, perhaps, require too much space to enter upon a learned analysis of his writings—an analysis which would in the end, I fear, as most analyses do, leave the reader as much in the dark as before. But this much may be said: Blackmore's novels sprang out of the deep, rich soil of a rare and wholesome spirit, and the qualities of that spirit blossomed in what we call the characteristics of his style. To be more specific, we may say that Blackmore was sturdily English; he loved every highway and byway of his native land, and most of his stories grew out of the soil of rural England, and could have been written only by one who was thus English to the core. Then, too, he had the Englishman's intense love of the outdoors, and, like Wordsworth, "was rapt away into a region of immeasurable astonishment" by the beauty and the glory of the smallest manifestations of Nature. (pp. 53-4)

Strong love of country, unusual sensitiveness to beauty, native healthiness of spirit, deep reverence, overflowing good humour, clear insight into human nature, calm trust and confidence—these are the qualities of his soul that blossom in his style. In the midst of narrative he often pauses to reflect thus:

> The happiest of mankind is he whose stores of life are endless, whose pure delights can never cloy, who sees and feels in every birth, in every growth or motion, his own Almighty Father; and loving Him, is loved again, as a child who spreads his arms out.

In the closing paragraph of *Cradock Nowell* he writes:

> And in the spreading of that realm beyond the shores of time and space, when at last it is understood what the true aim of this life has been, not greatness, honour, wealth, or science, no, nor even wisdom—as we unwisely take it—but . . . a flowing tide whose fountain is our love of one another, then shall we truly learn by feeling (whereby alone we can learn) that all the cleaving of our sorrow, and cuts into the heart of us, were nothing worse than preparation for the grafts of God.

It is in such passages that we lovers of Blackmore recognize the essential man speaking. We feel the sincerity of the thought and the emotion behind the words. Such expression is not sermonizing; only the bursting into bud and bloom of an abiding faith.

And so we may say that Blackmore is wholesome. Ugly things and sad things appear in his books, sins and sorrows and disappointments confront us in his pages, we often glimpse the dark places of the human soul; but there is a faith in him that subdues all terrors. The light of his faith is like the light of the sun; darkness flees before it. The mantle of his faith is like the mantle of the ivy; it clothes a ruin with beauty. Blackmore calms and refreshes the restless human spirit. . . . I feel that his interpretation of life is more illuminating, more satisfying than that of many present-day novelists, because it is founded upon a more comprehensive view; I believe that Blackmore not only saw life steadily, but that to a remarkable degree he saw it whole, and saw it, too, under a light that is vouchsafed only to the romantics. (pp. 55-6)

Waldo H. Dunn, ''Richard Doddridge Blackmore,'' in The London Quarterly Review, *Vol. CXLV, January, 1926, pp. 44-57.*

QUINCY GUY BURRIS (essay date 1930)

[*In the following excerpt from his biographical and critical study of Blackmore, Burris compares Blackmore with Sir Walter Scott, Charles Kingsley, and George Eliot, then examines some merits and weaknesses of his novels.*]

Scott's particular field was history. Within this field he portrayed periods from that of the Crusades down to that immediately preceding his own; his world embraces at once the sphere of the cavalier and that of the lowly dweller in his own beloved heaths. His pages are rich with characters from all levels, but his emphasis is placed upon the class of the political great, except where he sought to portray his own countrymen of humble station. The truth is that, knowing all sorts and conditions of men, he drew them all with skill, though his best portraitures are those of lowly people. All his fiction was charged with the purpose of giving a picture of a people in a particular age, the spirit of that people in a crisis of its existence; and that other purpose, of painting men and their lives as they have been since civilization came to be.

Blackmore had this much in common with Scott: He took a small corner of England and painted it, with its peace, its people, and their eccentricities. Like Scott, he placed his humor in his peasant characters, whom he drew with great skill. (pp. 150-51)

Blackmore followed the program, laid down by Scott, of striking an intelligible mean between the language of a past age and that of the present, although there is nothing to indicate that he got the program from Scott. It is a parallel, innocent of derivative significance, and the similarity goes no further. Blackmore shunned the history of great society; he would have none of your strutting captains, none of the pomp and pageantry Scott loved so well. Neither did he write of any nation or people at a crisis in their affairs, religious or otherwise, except in *Springhaven,* where he drew upon the report that Napoleon contemplated an invasion of England from the south. He had no rigid pattern of historical interpretation; he neither affirmed nor denied the history of his story, except to declare that the incidents and characters alike were romantic.

He did not, as did Scott with Scotland, deliberately try to express the genius of a whole nation. Rather he drew the unpretentious life of the obscure yeoman who loved his land beyond all things else, and stayed quietly at home, out of the brawls and perils of a civil war, until the folly of his hotter brother-in-law forced him to go to his rescue. He drew a little corner of England, and somehow, it is true, he managed to infuse the whole of English spirit in the figures who appeared in it.

But the chief difference between Scott and Blackmore is yet undisclosed. The former was something timid about approaching a scene in which the tender passions were involved, because, some assert, he had himself been disappointed in love.

Be the reason what it may, his aversion to such scenes is well established. His heroes woo coldly, and are never so lyric and so lush with praises as John Ridd, when he dwells upon the perfections of Lorna. Blackmore was never timid about his love scenes.

As distinct from Kingsley, he wrote but little of the great folk of his age. And he sought, not so much to catch the spirit of the English nation in such an age as that of Elizabeth, as to catch the spirit of the yeoman landholder in all ages—the spirit of devotion to the farm, love of his flocks, and a passion for simple and unobtrusive life. The Spensers and the Raleighs of *Westward Ho!* find no parallels in Blackmore's novels. Amyas Leigh is, however, in some things akin to John Ridd, though not in many. He is huge, as John is; he is of a shrewd practical brain, as John is. But he is the son of a gentleman. He is moved as much by romance in new lands and upon the seas as he is by the love of woman; and he is more moved by these things than he is by any love of the land. John wants nothing of battles, or adventures. Each of these characters is the expression of a sturdy English spirit; the one, the lust of adventure; the other, the quiet contentment of staying at home, keeping peace in the county, and tilling broad fields.

It is significant that Kingsley, although he wrote feelingly of Devon scenery, did not approach the caressing delicacy, the almost passionate adoration of growing things characteristic of Blackmore's description. (pp. 151-52)

With the world of George Eliot [Blackmore] has more in common. The world of the simple farmer, the rustic life, the dairy and the kitchen scenes are Blackmore's own demesne. *Adam Bede* is more nearly like John Ridd than either Dandie Dinmont or Amyas Leigh. They are both shrewd and mighty yeomen, great of muscle, and quiet, though Adam is not a lover of the soil. He is rather of a religious turn, more sombre and more ardent than John; and he is subjected to a harrowing experience in the seduction of Hetty, his betrothed, beside which the life of John seems a blithe thing. In the main, however, the quiet scenes of the farm or the rustic mill are of a oneness with those of John's own farm. Yet there is a strong difference in their descriptions of natural scenes. It is this: As [descriptive passages in her work are] . . . burdened with details which speak the analytic mind of George Eliot, so the following quotation from Blackmore illustrates the unanalytical pleasure he took in similar descriptions:

> There was a little runnel going softly down beside me, falling from the upper rock by the means of moss and grass, as if it feared to make a noise, and had a mother sleeping. Now and then it seemed to stop, in fear of its own dropping, and waiting for some orders; and the blades of grass that straightened to it turned their points a little way, and offered their allegiance to wind instead of water. Yet before their carkled edges bent more than a driven saw, down the water came again with heavy drops and pats of running, and bright anger at neglect.
>
> This was very pleasant to me, now and then to gaze at, blinking as the water blinked, and falling back to sleep again.

But there is a difference more vast than any I have thus far discussed. In Blackmore there is no doctrine of the cumulative good or evil of a deed. There is no psychological analysis, no conviction that the human lot is hard. After the obstacle is hurdled, after the abducted heroine or child is restored, joy is the order of the day in his novels. The tragedy which is inevitable in George Eliot's novels is unthinkable in Blackmore's. There is no tragedy; that which has threatened is averted, the goodly are joined, and there is peace at the end of his stories. Love, not sacrifice, is his theme; romance, not analysis, his forte. The evil train of events which followed in the wake of Hetty's seduction has no place in his world. His novels, beside those of George Eliot, are light of texture; they have nothing of the somberness of her mind. They want her depth of insight, her philosophy. (pp. 153-54)

We have seen that Blackmore has many of the qualities we find in his contemporaries. He has the skill with the lowly that was Scott's; he has a hero in some things similar to Kingsley's Amyas Leigh; and he has the same world of unassuming people that George Eliot portrayed, with a hero not unlike Adam Bede. But the differences between his novels and those of the novelists just mentioned are so vast and of such a significance that the similarities we have discovered are pigmied.

What then, you may well ask, did Blackmore give the Victorian reader which pleased and satisfied him, and which he could not find elsewhere? The answer is this: Blackmore used many of the same materials, scenes, and characters as the other novelists. But he combined them in a different way. He fused these materials in such a fashion that where the emphasis before lay heavily upon history, or upon the problem of seizing the spirit of a people in a crisis, or upon psychological investigation of cause and effect; in his own it lay upon other things. He took the simple yeoman, loving his land; he set him down in his native element—the element above all else loved by Blackmore himself—the bosom of nature, the broad fields, the sheep huts, the skirling streams, the blossoming orchards, and the hearty harvesting. He pictured him in his love-time, in the adoration of a pure woman. In the story of this love among simple people is all the essence of Blackmore.

It is no great wonder, then, that the Victorian reader, wearying of the histories of great men, sated with realism, finding onerous the cry of reform, and irked by much heavy scientific thrusting and groping, turned gladly to the sheer romance, the idyllic peace, and the quiet loves of Blackmore's novels. (pp. 154-55)

Blackmore's view of the world embraced all things natural; and to him all things natural were good. He wrote to portray humanity as it has been in all ages and in all places. The evil in humanity he regarded as unnatural, and therefore frowned upon it; the good he thought the natural state of man, and gave it his approbation. More particularly, of course, he strove to limn the firm English character of a class of folk not high in social affairs, but themselves the salt of the earth. He identified himself with the locality in which they lived, with its scenes, its peculiarity of dialect, its very weather. He was himself all these things. Above all, he knew and loved the humanity upon which he wrought out characters who have the solid tangibility of timeless human attributes. His method in this was to show pure love, to him the most benign force in the world, beleaguered by the evil of the world, and in the end triumphant. Naturally, he placed this struggle in a world of diametrical hostilities, in a world sharply divided between good and bad. In this world love was good; lust, shallow desire, or cupidity were evil. It does not matter that the actual world is not wholly of that order; it does not matter that good and bad are commingled in it. For the purposes of romance, Blackmore must have such a world, and have it he did. This force of love he

made operative in simple people of the landed yeoman class; people lowly, faithful, honest, of clean lives, strong and sturdy masculinity, solidity of character, kindliness, and tolerance of human foibles so long as they were not base. These people, wrought upon by love, he set down in rustic places, beyond the artificiality of metropolitan life, in places of natural beauty such as he himself loved, and such as were fitted to reflect the glamour of their love-time and the storm of anguish to which they were sometimes subjected. He imbued these characters with quiet English solidity of person, and with a love of old England. Though they move in remote places, they have the human interests which are peculiar to folk everywhere, and which leave the impression not so much of English people as of humanity at large.

His faults flow out of the very essence of his merits. He had no mission, no conscious purpose beyond the presentation of life as he loved it. He was not caught up with any desire to present a people in a crisis of their history. History of that kind held no interest for him. (pp. 159-60)

His purpose, as I have indicated, was to portray humanity in England, and to show humanity in its love-time. And all this, he undertook to do with no higher aim than entertainment of his readers. (p. 160)

[Blackmore's] really significant aim is the presentation of human life in a romantic setting.

The only real fault into which this world led him was a certain sentimental lushness when writing of love. The early restraint upon this which he observed was removed in his old age, and sentimentality grows rampant in his late novels. This sentimentality manifests itself in an excessive gentleness, a profuseness of praise for women, and an absurd humility on the part of the heroes when in the presence of those they love. Kit Orchardson in *Kit and Kitty* is a sentimental ass over his sweetheart, and is infinitely more absurd than John Ridd in his wooing. He is thrilled to stand beneath a tree which once sheltered him and his love from the rain; and he values a coat inordinately because her dear head has lain upon it. This instance is an index to Blackmore's later manner, as a whole, although it is true that in all of his novels he is sentimental. John Ridd himself is lush over his Lorna, but he is not so extravagant as Kit.

The most important merit of Blackmore's character-building is that, having created a character, he is able to breathe life into it. He quickens it. Even such eccentrics as Rufus Hutton and John Rosedew are sufficiently human so that their eccentricities seem not the whole of their characters, but only a large part of them. These characters, moving about the remote demesne of Nowellhurst, add to their pedantry a fund of human kindness, such as was plain in John Rosedew's giving Cradock Nowell money in London. This capacity of Blackmore's for quickening his characters is most clearly evident in his portrayal of the men of the soil; the parsons; the women of slightly minor rôles, such as Annie Ridd and Julia Touchwood, the latter in *Christowell*; and the very minor figures of the servant class, who speak in dialect, and smack strongly of humble, soil-bound lives.

The method by which he manages to make his heroes live and breathe is frequently the use of the first person. He puts the tale in the mouth of John Ridd himself, who, despite a modesty that was Blackmore's own, manages to convey a very decent impression of his own character. This method, which he employs in about half of his novels, has the added advantage of allowing the narrator to suggest characteristics by denying or slighting them—a practice which increases the reader's opinion of his own astuteness in analysis of the character. The heroes who tell their own stories are the best characters in all of Blackmore's novels. The others are characterized by action and speech rather than by overt description, not clumsily, but with skill and dispatch. There are, to be sure, occasional passages of character description, but the verisimilitude of his characters is due not to such passages, but to their action and speech.

Indeed, Blackmore sired a very swarm of characters, big and little, major and minor. As Saintsbury points out [see excerpt dated 1894], it is difficult to determine whether Blackmore is more successful with characters fully drawn or with those drawn briefly, for he has the knack of giving the one touch needed for quickening slightly drawn characters. His ability to handle and enliven so many characters of small part is extraordinary and rare among novelists. These characters serve, by ordinary, a very subordinate end in the novel, for apparently it was Blackmore's skill to call up and round a character whenever any slight *impasse* in the continuity of the tale demanded a new character to lead it out into the main current again. These minor folk are all real, all with the touch of earthy reality about them, all simple, breathing, human. Even the hosts of the inns visited in *Lorna Doone* are genuine people, however casually introduced. It would be useless to enumerate the names of his minor characters, but from Pugsley in *Christowell* to Mrs. Huxtable in *Clara Vaughan,* they have the solidity of people we might have known in the flesh.

His faults are in some measure the results of certain of his merits. His heroines, though they share a little in the life of the other characters, are dim. They sweep mistily, and, Blackmore tells us, beauteously before us. They are not so vibrant, they do not live so fully as his other characters. Lorna and Kitty Fairthorne, though they pace graciously enough through their parts, do not light the pages with their passing. I believe that this is due to the fact that they are characterized solely by the praises of their lovers, who tell the tales. If John had not been so utterly in love with Lorna, we might have had a more convincing portrait of her. I say this because he does give excellent character to those with whom he was not in love. With Lorna, however, he is deaf to everything but superlatives.

That same skill which enabled Blackmore to endow the very slightest character with life proved a pitfall in his novels. He has too many minor characters, taken up, quickened, and abandoned when their efficacy in the story is spent. . . . This is true of such a character as the brother of Mary Anerley, who thought himself an inventor, but accomplished nothing. What this character actually did in the novel was to bring out the practical side of Stephen Anerley, and the maternal indulgence of Mrs. Anerley, though Mary herself evoked these traits quite as well. The character himself, however well drawn, has only his futile flair for invention to distinguish him, and he is soon dropped. That these characters should appear in the guise of consequence, and then be given such unceremoniously short shrift, is a genuine fault in the novels of Blackmore. (pp. 161-63)

Blackmore's villains are usually well enough motivated; but in certain instances their viciousness has too little explanation. Parson Chowne's innate evil is hardly sufficient to explain all his villainy, though a large part finds its explanation in the exigencies of the tale itself. Downy Bulwrag, in *Kit and Kitty,* is a most vicious young man, and the excess of his badness is hard to justify with the motivation at hand. As characters the villains are all of a piece, they are excellently drawn; but there is always that Iago-like want of purpose in viciousness to create doubt in the reader's mind.

Blackmore's plots are well-built, and well-joined. . . . The host of his characters, and the consequent multitudinous incidents which involve them, have already been pointed out as a fault. But the fashion in which these incidents and characters are built into the tale, and made to hinge securely on the main plot,— even made to sustain the main plot over a longer period than would otherwise be possible—this is unimpeachable. William Lyon Phelps points out the excellence of the architecture of *Lorna Doone,* in the fact that there are nineteen important characters, all well handled and made of some consequence in the main plot of the novel. He goes on to show how the affair of Ruth Huckaback and John Ridd is used to heighten the interest of the reader by making him believe that John may marry her [see excerpt dated 1910]. Now Ruth is distinctly a minor character, but she is none the less made to carry and prolong the main interest of the novel. . . . Wherever there is a question of joining and building, Blackmore wrought well in his novels, although he never quite escapes a touch of melodrama in his plots.

Concerning the use of the first person, there are different opinions. Mr. Phelps . . . says that the use of the first person limits the range of the novel and intensifies the dramatic interest of the plot. I believe that it does all this. . . . If we take such a novel as *The Maid of Sker* as an instance of the excellence of this usage, we cannot object to the method at all. Davy Llewellyn, who tells this tale, is essential to the story in a large way, but his social station, as compared with that of the principals of the love-story, would have made him a minor character in any other form of narrative. Wishing to give him conspicuity as an important and interesting character, Blackmore inverts the order of the characters, and puts the story into the mouth of this rascally old sailor. It is a master-stroke of skill, for it gives the reader a point of view, and the best point of view, in a story in which the real interest is Davy, although that interest would have been obscured if the story had been told either through the mouths of any other characters or in the third person.

The plots are simple and direct in the main, though occasionally cluttered with irrelevant matter. The major fault, in my opinion, is his repetition of motives and situations. Although his genius was rich enough in the invention of minor incidents, it was not rich in the invention of large situations for the novel. He depended almost wholly on three motives, three situations, and the attendant results. The first of these is abduction by means of forged letters or notes. In fully half of his novels this is the main situation. The plots, as I have said, are simple, and the whole suspense of the action centers in the rescue from abduction. The heroine, or perhaps it is a child, is beloved of certain people; certain other people find it desirable to do away with the heroine or the child, at least for a time, and they effect this removal by means of a forged note. The hero rescues the heroine or the child. The device itself is not objectionable, but Blackmore used it too often.

The second situation to which Blackmore is given is the problem of the disputed inheritance, which is at times coupled with the abduction *motif.* . . . This motive is present in one form or another in [*Craddock Nowell*], *Clara Vaughan, The Maid of Sker, Alice Lorraine, Cripps the Carrier, Christowell,* and *Mary Anerley.*

The third situation of Blackmore's novels is the use of a long and rather belated interlude which tells the story up to the time of the beginning of the novel, which, as the novels are constructed, must necessarily appear where it does. Aside from the fact that these interludes are sometimes too long, they are occasionally irrelevant, and are used much too frequently. The most conspicuous examples of excessive length are in *Clara Vaughan* and *Dariel,* and of irrelevance, in *Springhaven.*

Beyond these faults, the motivation of certain actions is sometimes too tenuous and feeble to seem probable. For instance, in *Kit and Kitty,* Kitty is led away from her husband to her father by a note from Downy Bulwrag, who desires her for himself. The note implies that Kit Orchardson is given to dangerous mental lapses, and is urgent. It is true that it removes her from Kit's house, but it does not secure her to Downy. If this is merely a piece of villainy, it wants purpose even for that.

Sometimes the process of abduction is absurdly simple; the bird falls too easily into the fowler's hands. Kitty walked too serenely into what was hardly an abduction, though there is a real one in the novel; but she walked into a situation which, so far as Kit was concerned, was equivalent to an abduction. (pp. 163-66)

The host of important characters which Blackmore managed with such skill gives rise to yet another fault. Emphasis is confused in some of the novels, among the subplots to which these characters give occasion. Sometimes figures which should be of a central interest are plundered of their right by the obtrusion of other figures. This is true in *Perlycross,* in a measure, where the main interest is that of clearing Dr. Jemmy Fox of the charge of grave-robbing, so that he may marry the daughter of Sir Thomas, whose body has disappeared from its burying-place. This is spun out and cluttered with a great deal of irrelevant matter and pleasantry, interesting enough in itself, but not to the purpose. Other love plots loom large in the reader's mind, too large for the reader to be very much absorbed in Dr. Jemmy. The situation is worse in *Mary Anerley,* where two stories are carried on side by side, with very little to join them, except here and there a feeble span. These two stories in turn are interrupted by subplots, fastened cleverly enough upon the main stories. But there is too great a confusion of emphasis. When the reader has finished, he is not sure to what part of the novel he should have given his best attention. The whole is confused in his mind.

Finally, the plots want *vraisemblance,* they want inevitability. That Lorna Doone should have recovered to grace John's old age after Carver's attack at the church is not too much for credulity. One can concede that much. I have already pointed out several instances which strain the reader's willingness to believe; but I must add the fact that the last link of the story usually seems flawed. Blackmore could never forego a completely poetic justice; he could never forego having a man's sins recoil upon himself. In *Christowell,* when George Gaston is killed in the village church by a terrific bolt of lightning, and the evil figure of the novel is thus hurried off the stage, we cannot help doubting its verisimilitude. The end of Gaston is too utterly and terribly just. The same thing is true of Downy Bulwrag's violent death, in *Kit and Kitty,* and of Caryl Carne in *Springhaven,* and Parson Chowne in *The Maid of Sker.* They die horribly and a little incredibly, Downy through the return of his leprous father, Carne in the explosion of his own castle, and Chowne of hydrophobia.

Beyond all this, the late novels of Blackmore were prolix and wordy and labored. He himself realized this fault in his novels,

and spent a great while culling pages from *Dariel* before it was published. The waste fertility and the amazing fund of characters and incidents with which his novels are filled are responsible for this imperfection. In most of his stories there is material enough for two respectable novels.

If diction were the whole stuff of style, I should have very little to cavil at in Blackmore, for in so far as the mere manipulation of words is concerned, he has few betters. But style is not so simple as that. What distinguishes style, even more than the ability to state a thing well, is the *esprit* behind the words, the spirit that informs them, and which they express in addition to the overt meaning they bear. For this I cannot always feel admiration, although in a great many instances I cannot withhold it.

These latter instances usually occur in his descriptions of natural scenes, for which, in *Lorna Doone* particularly, he is justly celebrated; and which do not, in his other novels, abate their excellence. So far as my own reading goes, Blackmore has no master in the wealth of feeling, keen observation, poignancy of effect, and minute accuracy of detail, all set down with skill, and delicate, nervous exactitude. . . . (pp. 167-69)

In the matter of dialect, Blackmore is excellent; and in reproducing the speech of former centuries he follows the dictums laid down by Scott in the preface to Ivanhoe that the novelist should use the language of past times only as it aids the illusion of reality, without forcing the necessity of a translation upon the reader.

Against these excellences of style and spirit, we must consider the much repeated charge that Blackmore's prose falls into metrical beats; it is even charged that he writes blank verse. True, one cannot escape the impression of measure in certain passages. (p. 170)

[The] following illustrates [Blackmore's rhythmic] manner of utterance:

> Then I swung me on high to the swing of the
> sledge, as a thresher bends back to the rise of
> the flail, and with all my power descending
> delivered the ponderous onset. Crashing and
> crushed the great stone fell over, and threads
> of sparkling gold appeared in the jagged sides
> of the breakage.

There is rhythm here, certainly. In [this] passage, the first two lines scan in anapaest, but the meter is not sustained further. It resumes the same meter at a later time, and then shifts to trochée. This is generally true of Blackmore's prose. Short and disturbing flashes of actual meter occur, but they are not sustained. Few of his sentences scan for more than half their length. The effect this creates, I think, is partly due to rhythmic lines, and partly to the presence of alliterative and onomatopoetic words. . . . In the following passage, these qualities are even more marked:

> Then the golden harvest came, waving on the
> broad hillside, and nestling in the quiet nooks
> scooped from out the fringe of wood. A wealth
> of harvest such as never gladdened all our coun-
> try-side since my father ceased to reap, and his
> sickle hung to rust.

(pp. 170-71)

One cannot scan [Blackmore's] passages by a single meter. There are several meters mingled, but the rhythm is not consistently the beat of any single design. The frequent brief flash of metrical words, combined with a skilful use of alliteration and tone-color, is responsible for the strong impression of rhythm in these lines. It is a maddening thing to analyze; it is there and not there. One finds it, and it has fled. It is too strong and obvious, I think, for real prose rhythm; and yet it is hardly consistent enough for verse. (p. 171)

[There] are times when Blackmore's emotions are too lush, too replete with superlatives, and without their proper effect. It is usually in praise of women that these passages occur. . . . (p. 172)

The sentimentality of Blackmore, which I mentioned earlier, is responsible for these weaknesses. There are some further marked absurdities of style, all in a sentimental vein. He calls a pig "a greedy quadruped;" he says "the little doggie wagged her tail."

But these are really trifles which I am half ashamed to mention. For the most part his style is excellent, clear, robust, and pregnant with feeling. On the whole, his merits outweigh his faults. Most of the things we have called faults are trifles; and most of the things we have called merits are considerations of some weight. It is hardly fair to range the one category against the other. But they stand so; and it is my belief that the weight of his merits is far greater than that of his faults. (pp. 172-73)

> *Quincy Guy Burris, in his* Richard Doddridge Blackmore: His Life and Novels, *1930. Reprint by Greenwood Press, 1973, 219 p.*

MALCOLM ELWIN (essay date 1934)

[*Elwin was an English author, critic, and editor who specialized in nineteenth-century literature. In the following excerpt, he discusses some characteristics of Blackmore's prose.*]

The blight afflicting Blackmore's reputation has gained no ground; it was firmly settled there during his lifetime, and *Lorna Doone,* the only blooming of his art then to escape its ravages, continues to hold up its head, ranking as a classic of prose fiction. Blackmore justly resented the disparity in popularity between this and his other books. He was not a "one-book" writer; he maintained a high standard of quality in his work, but the rest of his books were unfairly handicapped because he excelled himself in one. He was like a good horse, which, having won a big prize in company of the highest class, is subsequently handicapped out of any chance of winning another race.

Blackmore was a good horse. He was not in the Derby or St. Leger class—not a Thackeray, a Dickens, or a Walter Scott— but he belonged to the top class of handicappers, ranking below Charles Reade and rather above the Kingsleys, on the same mark as Anthony Trollope. With Trollope, he invites comparison on so many points of similarity that he seems, consciously or involuntarily, to have taken him as a model in some of his later books. While *Clara Vaughan* was frankly an essay in "sensation" fiction, *Cradock Nowell* an approximation to Henry Kingsley, and *Erema, Mary Anerley* and *Tommy Upmore* all differently reminiscent of Reade, such books as *Christowell* and *Perlycross* tend closely to Trollope's manner. Both take their titles from an imaginary village on the verge of Dartmoor, the original of each being Culmstock, where his father had held a curacy and where much of his boyhood was spent. Both have the tranquil, parochial atmosphere of Trollope's Barset books, dealing with the same types of provincial society, though

Blackmore characteristically introduces more plebeian and fewer patrician characters than Trollope. Rarely looking higher than a baronet, his landscape is narrower than Trollope's, whose hunting gentry of the "county" class had houses in town and worldly connections, which facilitated an occasional shift of scene to London. His ecclesiastics are vicars and curates, not canons and bishops, and domestic servants and rustic villagers, though incidental characters, are drawn with such particularity that they usually loom large in the story. *Christowell* and *Perlycross* are realistic pictures of village life, quiet, subdued, peaceful as a summer's day, when the hot sun blazes upon the dusty village street, glinting golden upon stray wisps of straw clinging to the hedgerows, and no sound breaks the pleasant stillness save the buzzing of the flies; they are not of Blackmore's best, but they offer congenial reading for the idle holiday-maker, and there is no reason why they should not sell for their local colour in South Devon, as *Lorna Doone* sells on the north coast of the county.

In an age of middle class snobbery, revelling in Ouida's counts and princes of fabulous magnificence, Blackmore's habit of writing about ordinary people of everyday life contributed to his unpopularity. The crowning evidence of the fact appears in *The Maid of Sker,* which failed to follow up the success of *Lorna Doone* merely because the autobiographical narrative was put into the unromantic mouth of an old fisherman. Blackmore's rustic types compare with any in the body of English literature. Picturesquely they wander against the background of all his books, like Pugsley, the village carrier in *Christowell,* who, when his horse stumbled into a hole, casting a wheel from his cart and tipping the load of garden-pots into the lane, sits comfortably down at the roadside to eat his breakfast, having thus reflected:

> All men is clay; and the Lord hath not intended us to putt His material into these here shapes, with a C.R. upon 'em, maning carrier's risk. Wull, a carn't brak' no more of 'un nor there be, now can 'e, Teddy? Smarl blame to thee, old chap. We'll both of us toorn to our brexass. This hosebird job hath coom, I rackon, 'long of doing of despite to the gifts of the Lord.

With such incidents and characters plentifully sprinkled throughout his books, Blackmore may be claimed to have brought to bear the same humorous observation upon rustic types as Dickens upon the cockney. Testimony to the living likeness of his characters was implied in the accusation charged against *Perlycross* that the author had deliberately caricatured real people, resident at Culmstock in his youth.

His principals are less convincing than his minor characters on account of their sameness. His heroes are almost always cast in the mould of Jan Ridd, "girt," honest, and chivalrous; his heroines, similarly, re-duplicate Lorna Doone in her demure and winsome innocence, beauty, and charm. His villains are almost equally stereotyped, bold, resolute, ruthless, usually as strong in intellectual as physical equipment.

> Though I am not a judge of men's faces, there was something in his which turned me cold, as though with a kind of horror. Not that it was an ugly face; nay rather it seemed a handsome one, so far as mere form and line might go, full of strength, and vigour, and will, and steadfast resolution. From the short black hair above the broad forehead, to the long black beard

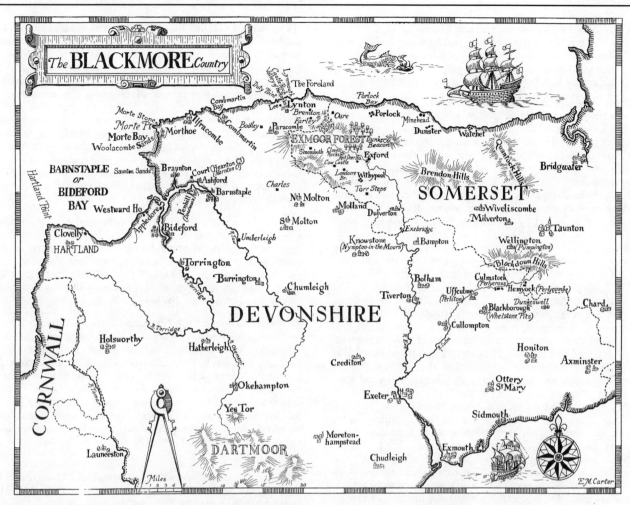

Map of the English countryside that figured in Blackmore's novels.

descending below the curt bold chin, there was not any curve or glimpse of weakness or of afterthought. Nothing playful, nothing pleasant, nothing with a track for smiles; nothing which a friend could like, and laugh at him for having. And yet he might have been a good man (for I have known very good men so fortified by their own strange ideas of God): I say that he might have seemed a good man, but for the cold and cruel hankering of his steel-blue eyes.

Such was Carver Doone, and George Gaston of *Christowell*, Downy Bulwrag of *Kit and Kitty*, Parson Chowne, and the dark, handsome, haughty and disdainful, almost heroic villain of *Springhaven*, Caryl Carne, are variations on the same theme. Parsons loomed large in Blackmore's life and family, and they inevitably appear in his novels, usually playing a prominent part, though with the exceptions of Chowne in *The Maid of Sker* and downright, sturdy little Tom Short, the true hero of *Christowell* ("no other preacher in the diocese could say so much in the time allowed, which was never more than five minutes; and no other congregation listened with attention so close, and yawns so few," though he himself declared that he always invited over a neighbouring clergyman, whose sermons lasted three quarters of an hour, "for collection Sundays," as "he draws half a crown where I draw a shilling. My farmers

say, 'short time makes short wages',") none take a central place in the plot. Usually, as in the cases of Twemlow in *Springhaven*, studious, absent-minded John Rosedew of *Cradock Nowell* (said to be a pen-portrait of Blackmore's uncle, the Rev. Hey Knight), the bluff and sporting Struan Hales of *Alice Lorraine*, and Philip Penniloe of *Perlycross*, they function as benevolent advisers and arrangers of affairs, fulfilling the traditional office which parsons habitually assumed in those spacious Victorian days, when a living was a living, and a squire's dinner-table was laden with good food and fine wine.

Finally, there are the men of the soil, whom Blackmore loved and inspired with much of his own personality—Farmer Lovejoy, the fruit-grower of *Alice Lorraine*, Captain Larks of *Christowell*, Kit Orchardson, the hero of *Kit and Kitty*, and his Uncle Corny, all loving and reverently revelling in the beauties of nature, living cleanly and honourably, and looking on life with tolerant humour, cheerful optimism, and solid good sense. Blackmore delighted in introducing details of his beloved gardening and fruit-growing, blissfully suspending the movement of his story to dilate on the glories of rose-growing or a fine auricula, as in the dialogues between Captain Larks and his daughter, who lectures Tom Short on the crime of nailing "the young wood of a wall-tree down the trunk," driving "the great nails into the poor thing's breast!" But his love of nature went beyond a pleasant crankiness; no writer in the language has left more eloquent and inspired descriptions of English scenery. . . . Not only Devon inspired him to conjure up . . . splendid landscapes before the readers' eyes; he wrote equally well of Oxfordshire in *Cripps the Carrier,* of Kent in *Alice Lorraine,* and Sussex in *Springhaven.* For such gems of descriptive beauty, even his fatally inevitable habit of digression may be forgiven.

For prolixity was Blackmore's besetting sin, apparent even in *Lorna Doone* and *The Maid of Sker,* and noticeably aggravated in his later novels. The digressive habit of old Dyo in *The Maid of Sker* is adopted less picturesquely and more perversely by many of his senior characters, who soliloquize and expound their views upon things in general, much as Blackmore himself may have done in the seclusion of his garden. In *Clara Vaughan, Alice Lorraine,* and *Dariel,* he follows the old eighteenth-century manner of introducing stories within stories, frequently utilized by Scott and by Dickens in *Pickwick,* but long since rejected in the vogue of the serial as an impediment to narrative. All who remember the shooting of Lorna Doone will readily recognize that he has an excellent sense of dramatic situation, but he is nevertheless capable of irritating loitering in his story, as in *Springhaven,* when the reader is agog to learn the *dénouement* of Carne's plot to initiate the French invasion of England, and the author tantalizingly wastes the better part of a chapter in relating the amusing device by which Erle Twemlow rid himself of the amorous attentions of an African negress. Such digressions could hardly be intended as tragic irony, like the knocking at the gate in *Macbeth* or the watchman in the *Agamemnon;* if so, they are clumsily prolonged beyond their function. It seems rather that, unlike Wilkie Collins and Trollope, who planned their entire books before writing the first chapter, Blackmore allowed his story to grow at will under his hand, thus courting the temptation to allow his fancy to run away with him. Consequently, there is a tendency to "skip" when reading his novels, though much of incidental interest may be missed in doing so. A just enjoyment of his work necessitates a leisurely mood—a long winter evening or a deckchair on a hot afternoon; the reader must not expect to race after the characters, as with Wilkie Collins or Ouida. (pp. 274-80)

> Malcolm Elwin, *"Wallflower the Eighth: 'Lorna Doone,' Blackmore,"* in his Victorian Wallflowers, Jonathan Cape, 1934, pp. 254-81.

KENNETH BUDD   (essay date 1960)

[*Budd was an English critic and religious writer. In the following excerpt, he surveys Blackmore's prose works with the exception of* Lorna Doone.]

[Blackmore's first novel], *Clara Vaughan,* set chiefly in Gloucestershire, but giving us glimpses of London and the North Devon area Blackmore was to make so much his own, is told in the first person singular by the determined and highly emotional young lady who gives her name to the book. The dominating passion of her life, stimulated by many a morbid reverie, is to discover the person who murdered her father in his bed shortly after the celebration of Clara's tenth birthday. By repeated visits to the scene of the crime Clara finds some clues which lead her into a number of sensational adventures, involving the disclosure of a Corsican vendetta, imprisonment in a vivisection chamber, and the sight of the violent end of the villain before wedding bells ring over her in the last chapter. The plot has no particular claim to originality, and there is a long story within the story which takes the reader off to Italy, and which for lushness and melodramatic sentimentality could

not have been excelled by any contemporary authoress. But if the book has no memorable characters, it has its memorable moments. There is a magnificent description of the Western countryside in the long drought of 1849, and there are sketches of an "old-fashioned" Christmas and a London fog which could have come straight out of Dickens. The account of a wrestling-match between the Northern Champion and John Huxtable of Devon is a fine piece of writing, reminding us of the exceptional ability always shown by Blackmore in communicating the excitement of physical combat and the poetry of motion, whether of animal or man. But perhaps the special interest of the book is in its presentation of a character whose appearance in these pages makes Blackmore in a particular respect one of the pioneers. (pp. 33-4)

Four years before Wilkie Collins published *The Moonstone* (1868) with Sergeant Cuff, based on Inspector Whicher of Scotland Yard, as the man who plays the decisive part in the solution of the mystery, Blackmore, in *Clara Vaughan,* had produced his Inspector Cutting. . . . Blackmore was one of the earliest English novelists to make use of the newly-created "Detective Force." . . . (p. 36)

The book has one other distinction and point of interest. Blackmore succeeded, in his creation of Clara Vaughan, in making a heroine who is more real and living to us than any other of the many heroines he produced from a single mould of celestial perfection. Many years later he told a friend that he "knew two people who prefer Clara to the more popular Lorna." Their reason must have been that Clara Vaughan, long since lost in the oblivion of minor Victorian literature, reveals at least one or two of the faults common to our imperfect human nature; whereas the immortal Lorna Doone apparently has none to show. (p. 38)

The plot of *Cradock Nowell* is unoriginal and clumsy, and in essence may be found in many other novels of the period. The story is hinged upon the fact that the twin sons of the owner of the great estate of Nowelhurst were confused by a nurse shortly after their birth. Cradock had expected to be the heir before the error was discovered, and when his brother Clayton is shot close to a place where Cradock is hunting, suspicion inevitably falls upon the latter. The problem of the disputed inheritance is one that Blackmore used in his plots several times, and the fact is not really surprising. There had been litigation in his own family, and he had had plenty of examples in his legal training to provide him with good material in this line. Judging from the extent to which lawyers and their disputing clients figure in the great mass of Victorian fiction, few citizens of that period had no experience of the courts and their preliminaries.

Blackmore had no initial success to follow up when he wrote *Cradock Nowell,* and his second effort made no better impression than his first. (pp. 42-3)

The long sentences, the many digressions, the scores of classical allusions and quotations, must render the book unreadable today by any except those who can endure such things for the sake of the occasional felicities of description of field and forest, in which Blackmore was so comfortably at home. He can never in *Cradock Nowell,* and but rarely in his other novels, speak simply of a simple person, but must expend to the full every image and every comparison in relation to that person which comes into his mind; he is so determined to make us picture the unearthly charm of his heroine or the manly power of his hero that he takes us and stuns us with such a force of adjectives and similes that we are left in no condition to perceive a creature of flesh and blood at all. (pp. 43-4)

Cradock Nowell has some magnificent passages, especially in the long description of a storm in the New Forest. Conrad never drew a storm at sea more vividly than Blackmore has painted this one in a series of pictures, beginning with the "blobs of cloud" which "threw feelers out, and strung themselves together, until a broad serried and serrate bar went boldly across the heavens." At the end the reader is left breathless from the fury of a storm that has smashed and wrecked and killed from Christchurch to the Goodwins. Blackmore was as apt at describing the violence of nature as the violence of man, and the digressions which ruin so many of his novels find no place when he has his eyes on bending trees or straining limbs.

In the Rev. John Rosedew, Rector of the little New Forest parish of Nowellhurst, Blackmore has created a country parson of the finest type. He is the servant of the simple, the bosom-friend of the Squire, the beloved friend and pastor of his small self-contained community, with a good taste in wines, an accomplished classic, a man who can swim and fish and row and (with some misgivings proceeding from his Christian charity) also shoot. . . . He is the figure in the rural scene whom Thomas Hardy has completely forgotten. There were too many parsons of another sort (and Blackmore had met them), but the John Rosedews have existed and their influence has been a large factor in shaping a way of life that had the roots our civilisation so tragically lacks. In *Cradock Nowell* Blackmore affirms the robust Christianity, the personal and enthusiastic conviction of an essential justice and purpose in the world, which Browning was proclaiming in his poetry. (pp. 47-8)

Unfortunately, however, for the nineteenth-century reader, and fatally for the reader of to-day, Parson Rosedew, "who always thought in Greek, except when Latin hindered him," is made the mouthpiece of Blackmore's own classical erudition. The Greek and Latin references and quotations run into scores, and Blackmore, until he had learned a little more about readers who had neither a University education nor a personal library, scorned to translate.

So *Cradock Nowell* made only a very slight ripple in the wide sea of Victorian fiction, and Blackmore went on with his pruning and his planting and his chess-playing. (p. 49)

It is difficult to understand why a number of critics, and indeed Blackmore himself, have held [*The Maid of Sker*] in such high esteem. The plot strains the reader's credulity, and relies on chances and coincidences even more strongly than *Cradock Nowell*. The striking descent from *Lorna Doone* in this respect is evident also in the character-drawing. The child Bardie is Blackmore's contribution to the gallery of frail and frilly children produced in the romantic period. (p. 66)

Bardie is the incarnation of holiness as Parson Chowne is the incarnation of evil, but the latter is too melodramatically over-drawn to terrify us, and it is certain that Bardie's "quaintness" will be judged by most modern readers to be tedious whimsy.

Sentiments and opinions are put into the mouth of old Davy which he could never have expressed as Blackmore, so obviously speaking in many instances through the sailor's lips, makes him express them. But it is interesting to have in this way further glimpses into Blackmore's mind, and into the spirit and outlook we call Victorianism. There is, for example, an attitude to war which the present generation, even allowing for what we have seen of the horrible reality of human conflict

since those days when it still had its conventions, would pronounce nonsense and blasphemy. (pp. 67-8)

Some pleasant descriptions of the region of Braunton Burrows brighten the early parts of the book, and there is undeniable vigour in the account of the naval engagements; but never are we convinced, as by *Lorna Doone,* that Blackmore had the time and the place and the loved one all together, and knew precisely how and what to tell us about them. (p. 69)

[Malcolm Elwin] has declared that *Alice Lorraine* "displays a remarkable poverty of incident, vitality, gusto, and dramatic motive." But Blackmore, always a stern critic of his own work, thought very highly of it, and Professor J. W. Mackail declared in 1925 that it was his best book after *Lorna Doone.* The novel's chief attractions are in two or three of its characters and in some descriptive passages which again reveal Blackmore's fine art and knowledge welded in an appraisal of the rural scene. The story itself, set partly in Kentish orchards and partly in the South Downs country near Steyning, with an interlude in Spain, moves slowly, and for a long way the reader must feel that the author ought to obey the injunction of his own reflections in Chapter 30, that "it is high time to work, to strengthen the threads of the wavering plan, to tighten the mesh of the woven web, to cast about here and there for completion."

There is a loving and lively picture of the Rev. Struan Hales, the sporting Rector of West Lorraine, and a convincing description of some of the trials and triumphs of the British troops in Spain after Salamanca. Hilary, the central character of the story, here becomes involved with two Spanish nurses, and all but marries the designing one. The letters from home, seeking to restrain him, are remarkable examples of the Victorian attitude towards "foreigners." Hilary's sister Alice seems destined by family pressure to marriage with a Captain Chapman whom she cordially dislikes, but is saved "from the saddest doom that can befall proud woman—wedlock with an object," by the discovery of an astrologer's ancient treasure. The best chapters in the book are the last dozen. They contain a magnificent description of the severe winter of 1813, "remarkable not only for perpetual frost, but for continual snowfall," as it affected the inhabitants of the little village beneath the Sussex Downs. Here one notes again Blackmore's power of observation, his skill in the description of the behaviour of natural phenomena so that the reader can enter fully into the experience. (pp. 75-6)

Although [his] next novel, *Cripps the Carrier,* had no particular success, it is a good example of the field in which Blackmore's best work was done—the small, self-contained community of the English village in the 18th or early 19th century, with a number of outstanding "characters," living their tranquil lives against the background of Nature lovely in herself and magnificent in her constant witness to God-given laws.

Sub-titled "A Woodland Tale," *Cripps the Carrier* is set in the village of Beckley, a few miles north-east of Oxford, and now within easy reach of the tentacles of Headington's "development." It was an area which Blackmore knew well and, with benefit to his tale, he does not move outside it. The plot, hinging upon the disappearance of the Squire's daughter, is thin enough, and there are fewer than usual of Blackmore's rhapsodies upon the seasons, but the book does something to disprove the general notion that he was "an artist of externals, not of psychological nuances." The character of Zacchary Cripps is finely observed, and the chief people in the little community, with their simple beliefs and sometimes exasperating superstitions, are drawn with a care for detail that gives the romance the stamp of verisimilitude. Glimpses of local events, such as the May Day singing of choristers from the tower of Magdalen College and a cricket match between Islip and Beckley, assist the impression of sunlight always too strong for the dark plans and deeds of men to be concealed. Destiny in this village, in strong contrast to what it is generally doing in Hardy's Wessex, is working always towards the triumph of a simple and persevering righteousness. (pp. 78-9)

The failure of *Erema* to please the reviewers or to attract readers was a bitter disappointment to its author, who called it his "most unlucky book." ... Blackmore's tales sometimes remind one of the joke about the publisher who declared that the many novels of a best-selling author on his list had one thing in common—the same plot. It is all here, in the prose counterpart of innumerable Victorian paintings—the father wrongfully accused of another's crime, the prolonged searching of legal documents, the "just retribution," the "faithful and soft-hearted nurse" of childhood, the revelation that little Erema is mistress of the great estates of Castlewood—the library subscribers knew the whole mixture and were becoming allergic to it. In many, distaste must have been intensified by the sympathies Blackmore expresses for the cause of "the noble South" in the American Civil War. It was typical of the spiritual myopia with which so many Victorians were afflicted in the sphere of the ethical implications of their religion, that Blackmore should declare, in a letter to Paul Hamilton Hayne, that "the outcry against 'Slavery' has always seemed to me a sample of ignorant clap-trap, such as makes hideous this British air." In another letter to the same correspondent, he is indignant because "the blessed Nigger ... seems to be a horrible pest among you, & destroys your tranquillity." ... [The] book as a whole leaves one wondering how it could have been written by the same hand that created *Lorna Doone*. (pp. 81-3)

Mary Anerley must rank high in the list of Blackmore's novels. It shows an unaccustomed discipline in its creator's unfolding of the plot, has many witty comments on human frailties, and minor characters who are credible and sometimes memorable.... Once more ..., it is in his description of the changing moods of earth and sky and sea, and the crispness of his observation of little, secret things (a crispness coming unexpectedly at times on the heels of a particularly involved passage) that Blackmore "finds" us. Examples in *Mary Anerley* are the beautifully etched picture of the vast and sudden activity in Hamborough when the mackerel arrive in the bay, and the vignette of a corner of the farm on a warm day in August. (pp. 85-6)

Christowell, set a little south of the Christow which gave Blackmore some features of the story, and while only "five leagues off from the dark square towers of Exeter Cathedral," yet "as remote from a day as the central sahara," is simply "A Dartmoor Tale." A mile from the village, under a jagged tor, stood a lonely cottage whose solitary occupant had helped the hand of nature to secure his quietude. This person, known to the village as "Captain Larks," is the most firmly-drawn and convincing character in the book, largely because while he was being drawn Blackmore was looking at himself in a mirror. The curiosity of the villagers in a little place "where everybody knows, twice a day, how everybody else's cough is; and scarcely can the most industrious woman find anything to say, that she has not said thrice," and the reserve of the "Captain," who had come out of another world and wanted only to be left alone to cultivate his fertile garden, gave Blackmore ample scope

for sly reflections on human peculiarities and for good advertisement of his accurate knowledge of the Devonshire dialect. There is some fine prose in *Christowell,* and nowhere is Blackmore's nature-realism seen to greater advantage than in his magnificent account of the storm which accounts for the villain and passes into a horrifying memory handed on from one generation to another. (p. 88)

Christowell has another claim on the modern reader's interest, in its glimpses of the happy simplicity of village life at the beginning of the reign of Queen Victoria. Blackmore was wrong in his criticism of certain aspects of the contemporary scene, but profoundly right in others. He knew something about the compensations offered in "the quiet runs of shadow, where poor people live and are content." He knew that shepherds and woodmen are "giant symbols of everlasting truth," and that the seasonal rejoicings, made from the intertwining of Christian and pagan beliefs, of these small communities, came spontaneously from man's poetic and truth-finding imagination. (p. 91)

Blackmore chose as the period of his [next novel, *Springhaven,*] the opening years of the nineteenth century, when Napoleon, in his scheme for reorganising Europe as a commonwealth under French hegemony, planned to begin it with the invasion and conquest of England.... [It] was upon a small community in Sussex, close to Hastings with its record of a successful invader who had landed there nearly eight hundred years earlier and changed our history, that Blackmore focused his interest in those tense and exciting days "when England trusted mainly to the vigour and valour of one man, against a world of enemies."

"Springhaven" is Newhaven, then a quiet little fishing village in a tranquil Sussex valley, and, according to Blackmore's Nelson, "the place of all places in England for the French to land." To Springhaven came one Caryl Carne, to store French arms in the vaults of his ancestors' disintegrating castle and to seek to dissuade local folk from their allegiance to their king. One of his special targets in this connection was Dolly Darling, daughter of Admiral Charles Darling and god-daughter of Lord Nelson, who was an old friend of the family. (pp. 97-8)

In Caryl Carne Blackmore has drawn a rather more credible character than most of his other villains, and the spell he casts over Dolly is one that is fully understandable in the light of the psychological make-up of the man and the girl; Blackmore took more pains with his creation of both of them than was usual with him. Strongly noticeable, too, in this book is his sense of *compassion* for all human creatures; he had something of that "vast universal charity" which is the greatness of Dickens and Dostoevsky and always the mark of the greatest writers. However contemptuous of his rogues and however strongly he underlined their sheer and abominable wickedness, one always detects in Blackmore's attitude to them this note of infinite pity; for the purpose in the heart of the Person who made the world is not the destruction of evil, but its redemption. (pp. 99-100)

Blackmore took care with his historical portraits, and particularly in the case of Nelson.... (p. 101)

[Blackmore portrays Nelson as] a man utterly confident and entirely convinced of his own brilliance as a naval tactician, and sometimes speaks in a way which would fill the average man, who likes some modesty in his heroes, with keen distaste. "If God Almighty prolongs my life—which is not very likely— it will be that I may meet that scoundrel, Napoleon Bonaparte, on dry land. I hear that he is eager to encounter me on the waves, himself commanding a line-of-battle ship. I should send him to the devil in a quarter of an hour. And ashore I could astonish him, I think, a little, if I had a good army to back me up. Remember what I did at Bastia, in the land that produced this monster, and where I was called the Brigadier; and again, upon the coast of Italy, I showed that I understood all their dry-ground business.''

Blackmore's skill as an observer and listener in obscure corners of forgotten places, by which as a writer he is specially distinguished, is often at work in this novel. (pp. 102-03)

[*Springhaven*] has merits of plot, character-drawing, humour and narrative power that no other writer dealing with that period of our history has equalled. (p. 104)

The motive for the writing of *Kit and Kitty* was undoubtedly Blackmore's desire to recapture some of the bliss of his early days with his "Kitty," [his wife Lucy, who died in 1888,] and to find some solace in the unfolding of a tale of love triumphant over adverse circumstance. (p. 106)

It would be pleasant indeed to be able to record that out of this sorrowful time came a work of note and importance. But *Kit and Kitty* merely tells with fair competence a tale that many would judge scarcely worth the telling. Set chiefly in Sunbury, but touching also the Thames-side regions of Shepperton, Hampton, and Hanworth, it has none of those memorable descriptions of the countryside which are found so often in most of Blackmore's other books. There is sometimes a bathos worse even than the sudden descents of Thomas Hardy, and there are passages of fantastic sentimentality which would be joyfully plucked by someone looking for examples of Victorian fiction at its worst, such as those describing the reunion of the lover and his beloved, after a number of quite incredible mistakes and misunderstandings:

> She was threatened with hysterics; but I soothed her gently, and she rested on my breast with her eyes half closed. As I looked at her, I felt that in this rapture I could die.
>
> "Darling, I can hardly believe it yet," she whispered, playing with my fingers to make sure; "see, this is my wedding-ring, I never took it off. What fine gold it is, not to tarnish with my tears. The drops that have fallen on it—oh, I wonder there is any blue left in my eyes at all! Do you think they are as blue, dear, as when you used to love them?"
>
> "They are bluer, heart of hearts. They are larger and deeper. The tears of true love have made them still more lovely."
>
> (pp. 106-07)

The chief interest of the book is in the portrait of the market-gardener, "Uncle Corny," for it is clearly in many respects a portrait of Blackmore himself. For this honest, rugged, and downright character, "few things vexed him much, except to find his things sold below their value; and that far less for the love of money than from the sense of justice." "If ever there was a man who gave good change for sixpence, ay, and took good care to get it, too, you will own it was my Uncle Corny." (p. 108)

Kit and Kitty will always have some special appeal to those who know well the region of the Thames Valley which is the scene of the story, and they will note with interest Blackmore's references to such long-vanished things as "the great wax-works at Teddington," and "Woking Road Station." But Blackmore nowhere communicates the beauty of the neighbourhood at blossom-time as vividly as George Meredith, nor the sombreness of the flat lands in autumn twilight as strikingly as Mrs. Riddell, who was writing about them in prolific fashion in this very year. . . . (pp. 108-09)

Looking back upon Culmstock [where his father had served as a curate-in-charge] across the span of nearly sixty years, Blackmore was inspired to write *Perlycross*, perhaps his finest work after *Lorna Doone*, and certainly one of the best pastoral novels in our language. Once again he teased the critics and the guide-book makers with a good measure of topographical liberty mixed with the drawing of characters based upon the remembrance of actual persons; "Perlycross" is Culmstock, and "Pumpington" is recognisably Wellington, but some fine estates are removed by Blackmore many miles from their real situation. The plot, hinging upon the disappearance of the body of Sir Thomas Waldron from a vault beneath the church and a false accusation of body-snatching against the local doctor, is no stronger than most of the slender, and sometimes thread-bare, plots in Blackmore's other novels. Remarkably enough, there is scarcely any love-interest worth mentioning, reflecting perhaps the decline of the heroine which had been taking place in the literary world over the past three decades.

But with all this, *Perlycross* is so clever and so observant a study of a little community that it reflects Blackmore at the height of his powers. In Sergeant Jakes (the village schoolmaster), old Clerk Channing, and Parson Penniloe (modelled on his own father), Blackmore has created characters perhaps more real than any others in his books; he was, in any case, always more successful in this way with his men than with his women. The character-drawing in *Perlycross* was praised by no less a critic than George Saintsbury [see excerpt dated 1894], and the whole vigorous gallery of persons in the novel not unexpectedly involved the author in many denials as to the originals confidently "discovered." With a good dénouement and a fair absence of those digressions which the reviewers had so often deplored in his earlier works, *Perlycross* succeeds in presenting us with a small world in which the adventures of simple people contribute to the general impression of peace, inward and outward, that reigned in this corner of the West country in the third decade of the nineteenth century. Local legends and customs are skilfully interwoven in the narrative. (pp. 110-12)

Blackmore's skill in describing the countryside is particularly noticeable in *Perlycross*. (p. 112)

Blackmore's description is as evocative as Thomas Hardy's of Egdon Heath in *The Return of the Native*. Comparison with Hardy is inevitable; for Blackmore has in *Perlycross* done for the Culm Valley what Hardy did for Stinsford in *Under the Greenwood Tree*. "How admirable are Blackmore and Hardy!" wrote Gerald Manley Hopkins in a letter to Robert Bridges (October 1886). "But these writers only rise to their great strokes; they do not write continuously well." This true judgment could be applied to every other major English novelist; but one must point to *Perlycross* as representing a peak, inferior only to *Lorna Doone*, in its author's range of achievement. (p. 113)

Tales from the Telling House, [published] in America as *Slain by the Doones,* consisted of four short stories and a Preface.

The first story alone gave Blackmore's readers the background and the characters they "had been clamouring for," and little enough of either. Here Blackmore made use of one of the reputed exploits of the Doones, when they were said to have attacked and murdered a Squire who lived in a lonely part of Exmoor Forest called "The Warren." (p. 117)

Lorna does not appear at all, and the brief showing of Carver Doone adds nothing to what we already know about his villainy and his "horrible visage." Blackmore, yielding to the pressure of his public and his publisher, probably wrote the story with a renewed feeling of annoyance that in general estimation he was bound hand-and-foot as a literary artist to his Romance of Exmoor. In truth, he gave his expectant admirers very little in the way of a second helping; and the title of the book could not have helped to stimulate sales. The ordinary public could scarcely be expected to know that the "Telling House" denoted the place in which lost sheep, when found and brought thither, were sorted out and attached to their rightful owners.

Some compensation, however, for the disappointing Doone episode should have been found by Blackmore's readers in the dramatic story of **"George Bowring."** Set in North Wales, it tells of a student friendship carried on in after years until brought to a tragic conclusion when the narrator's friend was murdered in a remote spot near Cader Idris. . . . The strange tale witnesses to Blackmore's strong sense of the numinous and his sympathetic understanding of those in whom, through ignorance, superstition has to serve for faith. In **"Crocker's Hole"** Blackmore makes use of a Culm legend, and reveals his intimate knowledge of angling, but the whole is little more than an incident retailed with a rather strained attempt at humour. **"Frida; or the Lover's Leap"** is based on a legend of the coast near Lynton. . . . (pp. 118-19)

[These] tales provide interest and good examples of Blackmore's craft for those who will be ready to find such pleasures outside the pages of *Lorna Doone.* In this volume the novelist could very fittingly have taken leave of his readers, and been gratefully remembered in this last excursion to fields he had made so much his own. The pity was that only a few months after the book had appeared he was struggling with the composition of his final novel, which by style and manner was doomed even before it had started on its fruitless rounds of the American magazines. (p. 120)

Dariel is sub-titled "A romance of Surrey," but the locality is not precisely indicated; the situation of Crogate Hall, the narrator's home, seems to have been somewhere in the neighbourhood of Leatherhead, perhaps not far from the old farm of Meredith's *Diana of the Crossways.* Occasionally in the descriptive writing where Surrey is concerned, there is a flash of the old skill, but the plot, making use of the vendetta motive which was prominent in *Clara Vaughan,* is tediously involved, and the characters bear little resemblance to human beings. The hand that moved the puppets in this last work was plainly one that was very tired. When, at the end of the story, the ample ghost of John Ridd turns up in the Caucasus to save the day and rout the loathsome ruffians, it is difficult to believe that it is the same pen which so graphically described the battles between virtue and lawlessness on Exmoor that is now trying vainly to give reality to a pasteboard contest in a sham moonlight. (p. 121)

[It] was always when dealing with a rural "corner" of England that Blackmore's best work was done. When he strayed abroad in his writings, handicapped as he was by his own complete lack of experience as a traveller and by the prevalent conception of "foreigners" as mostly dishonest and treacherous, he achieved little of value and was rarely able, in fact, to rise much above melodrama. In *Lorna Doone, Perlycross, Christowell,* and *Cripps the Carrier,* Blackmore mercifully made no expeditions overseas, but established a claim by these books to be, after Thomas Hardy, our finest exponent of the pastoral novel. It may be that as the time and manners they depict recede still further from us, and our unfulfilled longing for what was best in that far away simplicity increases as our rural regions are gradually engulfed, we shall rediscover some of these books and be grateful for them, as we are grateful for Hardy himself, and for Quiller-Couch and Walter Raymond and William Barnes. (pp. 121-22)

Kenneth Budd, in his The Last Victorian: R. D. Blackmore and His Novels, *Centaur Press, 1960, 125 p.*

MAX KEITH SUTTON (essay date 1979)

[*Sutton is an American educator and critic. In the following excerpt, he appraises Blackmore's achievement as a novelist.*]

[In 1894 Blackmore wrote], "Sometimes I am afraid of doing miserable work, & am reduced to the belief that I have done too much of that character already. . . ."

The novelist's fears of doing "miserable work" invite the question of how well those fears were founded. Certainly they reflect his difficulties in composition and his increasing sense in the 1890s that public taste was going against him. It was, and to try now to evaluate his fiction calls not only for a look at the bases of his self-doubt but also for an awareness of the critical assumptions that elevated realism over romance, and irony over sentiment and humor in the years after his death. . . . [As] the name of a genre with special conventions and functions, "romance" can be usefully descriptive in dealing with the question of Blackmore's artistry. It names the tradition in which he struggled with the essential elements of his craft: plot and character, setting and style.

In plotting a narrative, Blackmore often seems like something of a crude concoctor. His letters on this point anticipate the objections of his harshest critics. How to conclude a story was a continual problem for him, one which he seldom solved so well that a "sense of the ending" permeates the total work. How could it, when the author began writing with no clear sense of it himself, or changed his mind as he did in *Alice Lorraine*? His uncertainty of direction must have stretched the length of the novels, which in surviving cheap editions of over 400 or 500 close-set pages discourage casual reading. "My difficulty," he confessed, "always is to stop, & wisely shut up shop, when I get into full swing of business. My plan enlarges, & my lines fill out & a lot of little cross tracks lead me off, & I find it harder & harder to pull up." (He has trouble stopping even here.) With his penchant for digression, for stories within stories, and clauses within clauses (his "habit of interthought"), he resembles his garrulous Mrs. Snacks, whose "largeness" of mind embraced "a family of fifty narratives, during the production of a single one."

Any plot that emerges from such largeness of mind is apt to be oddly multilinear, ending arbitrarily without the "verisimilitude" and "inevitability" that realism demands. But these terms are more appropriate to naturalistic fiction than to romantic comedy. To make them a standard for judging his work is to risk condemning a whole genre along with the author. Knowing his difficulties in plotting, Blackmore relied upon the conventions of romance to give his fiction form, and he seldom tried anything unsanctioned by long use. The story within a story appears in ancient, Elizabethan, and nineteenth-century romances, while the tradition of last-minute rescues and elaborate discovery scenes left the writer free from the demand to plot out a realistic chain of cause-and-effect events. Trying to write romance during an age of realism, Blackmore had bravely said, "Improbabilities are nothing"; Hardy would say, more carefully, "It is not improbabilities of incident but improbabilities of character that matter. . . ." In positive terms, what counts in romance is the author's "rhetorical skill" in filling the space between beginning and end with appropriate characterization, lively incidents, and, for Blackmore, loving evocation of landscape, plant-life, animals, and weather.

His most famous book proves the wisdom of accepting romantic conventions in order to enjoy the humor, excitement, and quickened sense of life that floods John Ridd's narrative. But *Lorna Doone* is the most openly romantic of Blackmore's novels and one of the earliest. The rise of realism in the eras of Thackeray, George Eliot, and Henry James made any suspension of disbelief increasingly lowbrow, if not more difficult. Addressing readers with a "discriminating" rather than an "omnivorous taste in fiction," a hostile critic in 1887 could not forgive Blackmore's use of "matters only suited to a fairy tale." The crime would look especially glaring in books like *Springhaven* which are not obvious romances; in fact, Blackmore's characterization and his attention to local and historical detail sometimes suggest attempts at realism. The contrast between a realistic texture and an improbable romantic plot bewildered even a friendly reviewer of *Cripps, the Carrier*, leaving him caught between his delight in the book and his sense of its absurdity. To summarize a novel with an abduction in Oxfordshire, three rescues from imminent death, and an elaborate discovery scene would "turn the story . . . into ridicule." His resource was to separate the plot from the "charm" of characterization, dialogue, and description.

Such indulgence still is easy enough for an unpretentious book like *Cripps* but very difficult when the characters lack interest and the plot seems only a means of prolonging tedium. At his worst, Blackmore deserves the parody of *Kit and Kitty* in which the elderly orchardman says, "Bear up, Chris my boy. We're all right because we're in a novel." They have every reason to feel snug, for Blackmore's authorial providence is at least as predictably protective as Hardy's fate is destructive. But unless the book offers something more than the plot, the price of their security will be the reader's boredom, unrelieved by stilted pages of genteel conversation or the narrator's grouching about Free Trade.

In itself, the romantic plot of loss and recovery neither breaks nor makes Blackmore's fiction. He can handle it impressively in *Lorna Doone* and *Perlycross*, perfunctorily in *Alice Lorraine*, and comically in *Cripps*, but the success of his books depends upon more than this ancient pattern. Much depends upon his characters, and here he offends the canons of realism in a way that Hardy does not. The offense comes mainly with his heroes and heroines, who fall in love at first or second sight, seldom stray from their romantic goals, and behave with the decorum of courtly lovers. From the modern viewpoint, they are stereotypes, unbelievably simple when set beside the "real" characters of Henry James and George Eliot. With its tacit assumption that to be "real" is to be complex and probably confused, the modern view was attacked by late-Victorian defenders of romance, who complained that James's endlessly introspective women and "emasculated" men were only the "specimens of an overwrought age": they were not embodiments of essential humanity. The real man or woman was altogether different—simple, straightforward, even heroic; and "any seeming idealization of character," according to one admirer of Blackmore's heroines, was "only the subtle grasping of the true identity."

The realist's view triumphed in this controversy, and it still puts readers of Blackmore, Haggard, or Stevenson on the defensive. But the issue is not whether John Ridd is more or less real than some Prufrockian center of consciousness in Henry James. The basic questions in romance are whether and why the hero and heroine appeal to the reader. The answers will reflect individual tastes, obviously, but much depends on how well these characters are tested. Whether they are comic like Daphnis and Chloe or tragic like Romeo and Juliet, the hero and heroine must be tested in order to act out the experience of romantic love. Blackmore's mistake after *Lorna Doone* was to shield his well-behaved young ladies and gentlemen until they rarely seem vulnerable to the dangers or the silliness of the experience. The threats to their happiness seem manufactured for the occasion in *Christowell* and *Kit and Kitty*, while the return to perilous romance in *Dariel* partly fails because the lovers do not face dangers together in scenes like those in the Doone Valley. By playing an overprotective providence, Blackmore almost deprives the young couples of their essential role, for love without risk is hardly romantic. Certainly it makes an inadequate plot for a long novel.

But most of Blackmore's later fiction takes shape from a more public and less stylized action than a love story. The love between a young hero and heroine becomes only one thread in a design that represents the experience of a whole community. If *Christowell*, *Springhaven*, and *Perlycross* seem unusually digressive and baggy, that is because the community is the protagonist. A multitude of characters and incidents is essential to the story. To represent country life in a single, steadily focused plot, as Hardy does, calls for an immense effort of stylization, not only in paring away lesser characters and details but also in speeding up rural time to cover the career of one central figure. Since rural experience is marked by the movement from seedtime to seedtime, a story of the countryside naturally moves with the seasons, like *Under the Greenwood Tree*, the loosest-knit of Hardy's novels. Blackmore times his plots by the seasons, letting the movement from winter to summer support his stories of loss and renewal. Even then, the full-scale novels of community nearly break under the weight of accumulated characters. But at the very point of threatened artistic chaos lies the earthy treasure of his fiction—the farmers, fishermen, sailors, servants, landladies, shopkeepers, and schoolchildren who more than make up for the tedium in the squire's garden or the vicar's parlor. For every fainting heroine there is an unblushing Betty Muxworthy or a Mrs. Tugwell; for every modest hero there is a John Fry, a Clerk Channing, or a grumbling Uncle Cornelius. These little people, if not always the salt of the earth, are the needed seasoning for Blackmore's idealizing imagination.

Each of these characters brings to his fiction a personal landscape, a field of being, charged with particular human energies. Not only does the heroine have her springtime bower and the villain his waste moorland: the little people also fill spaces that both illuminate and reflect their presence. In *Perlycross* alone, the interplay between person, place, and season occurs at the rotting mill in December where Mrs. Tremlett is dying, and along the ditch of dead weeds haunted by the half-witted poacher; it can be felt on the morning of melting frost in the potato field where the blacksmith tells his scary story and on the May morning of the closing fishing scene. Being, for his characters, is the concrete act of filling a certain spot in time and space, weighting both with individual human presences. Finding "the very sap and scent of country life" in Blackmore's stories, Eden Phillpotts singled out his gift for "noting the details of rural scenery through the procession of the seasons, and setting them forth, as only an artist can, in their due relation to the mass of mountains, to the volume of rivers, to the life of men and women" [see excerpt dated 1901]. The last phrase points to the achievement that makes Blackmore a novelist, and not a describer only, of the countryside.

But the elaborate wordpainting which Hardy and Hopkins also admired can prove an obstacle to any reader who wants to get on with the story. Blackmore himself realized the danger and disciplined an early impulse to outdo Ruskin. Even so, his verbal landscapes sometimes sound showy and precious, like George Meredith's, and suggest a lack of Hardy's genius for keeping description subordinate to the narrative as a whole. Their contrast with Hardy's landscapes makes obvious an essential feature of Blackmore's vision. His is openly impressionistic, fluid, and responsive to change, while Hardy's is poetic in a quieter, more stable way and focused on longer-lasting marks of being. The famous description of Blackmore Vale in *Tess of the d'Urbervilles* (ch. 2) presents a landscape "like a map" before an unspecified traveler, outlines its enduring pattern, and treats its colors as if they would always stay the same. The pattern consists of a "network of dark green threads" formed by the hedgerows, with "a broad rich mass of grass and trees, mantling minor hills and dales within the major." The atmosphere is unchanging; the scene stays essentially static as it is laid out in a series of main clauses that assert being only. Things either are or seem; they do not appear in distinctive action.

A more impressionistic writer could never conclude, with Hardy's finality, that "such is the Vale of Blackmore." For any landscape, even this green Dorset one, changes with the light, the seasons, and the weather. Blackmore treats change as essential. To evoke the movement of things, his verbs are active and his long sentences eddy and flow with the large variety of the movement. Describing a huge view from east Dartmoor in *Christowell,* he puts a more specific traveler on the scene, gives him a good breakfast (since a person's mood colors what he sees), and lets him look outdoors by the "light of an average morning." At once, the scene begins to act. Beyond the stable landmarks of Exeter Cathedral, Powderham Castle, and the coastline, "the broad sweep of the English Channel glistens, or darkens, with the moods above it, from the Dorset headlands to the Start itself. Before he has time to make sure of all this, the grand view wavers, and the colours blend; some parts retire and some come nearer, and lights and shadows flow and flit, like the wave and dip of barley, feathering to a gentle July breeze." Then, just as Blackmore seems most emulous of Ruskin and Turner, he stops without even saying which colors are blending. He has evoked the movement of a landscape, not a static pattern.

Furthering the sense of movement is his rhythmic phrasing and echoing of like sounds. His cadences are far more emphatic than Hardy's, not only in the metrical passages of *Cradock*

Nowell and *Lorna Doone,* but here in "the flow and flit" of barley or the "sweep of upland" in *Perlycross,* "black in some places with bights of fired furze, but streaked with long alleys of green, where the flames had not fed, or the rains had wept them off." Hardy does not write with this springiness of rhythm; Meredith comes closer to it in his moments of ecstatic prose. But Blackmore achieved his distinctive lilt at the risk of sounding self-conscious, like Meredith, as in this passage from *Christowell,* when the eye moves down the slopes of Fingle Vale: "Deep in the wooded bottom quiver, like a clue of gossamer, sunny threads of the twisted river, wafted through the lifts of gloom." Rhyming at one point, the first three cadences keep the rhythm restless with their weak final syllables, until the eye returns from the swift water to the still "lifts of gloom."

The trouble with this bit of buried Tennyson is the way it calls attention to itself. Momentarily the style counts for more than either the setting or the story. Poetic description continues in the next paragraph until the narrator, as if embarrassed by his own eloquence, undercuts it all with humor. Scenic grandeur now contrasts with low-bred tourists' cries of "come here, Harry," and "oh larks, Maltilda" in the degenerate present—unlike the time of the story when "Our good British race had not yet been driven, to pant up hill, and perspire down dale, for the sake of saying that they had done it." Humor dissipates the poetry and eventually leads back to the characters, who are still miles from Fingle Vale. Rather than advancing the plot, as description generally does in Hardy, this little essay into and against the picturesque serves as a resting place between narrative and dialogue. But to stop and look round a landscape is a delight in Blackmore, who tries hard to make it worthwhile and more than matches his lapses into metrical pomposity with cadences elsewhere of strong poetic force. When John Ridd tells how the reapers swept the field "like half a wedge of wildfowl" or describes the great snowdrift "rolling and curling beneath the violent blast," the language moves with the energy of nature itself, and the effect seems worth the rhetorical effort. Hardy can also evoke this power, but not with Blackmore's springing rhythms and the lilt of a narrator's voice.

In depicting the intricate life of nature, Blackmore can stand comparison with any British novelist of his century. But only here, and perhaps in humor, does he surpass his master in historical fiction, Sir Walter Scott, with whom he was compared more often than with Hardy. Like Scott, he helped to clothe a land in its own history and legend. But he writes from a narrower perspective and covers far less time and space. Scott's vision is not only wider but more balanced. Scott does not grumble about contemporary politics like the omniscient narrator of *Springhaven*; he sounds far more Olympian, at once more detached from political issues and more understanding of them than Blackmore, and he speaks with far less eccentricity of rhythm, imagery, and syntax. His fame rests on many historical novels, while Blackmore won popular success with only one book. As an avowed "romance" and not "an historical novel," *Lorna Doone* stays closer to local legend than to the national events that would have concerned Scott. Though Judge Jeffreys and James II make brief appearances, Monmouth's Rebellion happens almost entirely offstage, becoming real only when a peace-loving young farmer strays among the dead and wounded after the Battle of Sedgemoor. The author of *Waverley* would have put him nearer to the intrigue and the fighting.

When Blackmore does invite comparison with Scott in *Springhaven,* his greatest achievement is not in portraying Nelson or

Napoleon but in making the village a microcosm of the nation. As a historical novelist, he is less concerned with grand events than with their repercussions among the little people in a particular neighborhood. Writing of fishermen on the Sussex or Yorkshire coast or of farmfolk on Exmoor, he brings to life the manners, customs, and speech of people whom the noted historians long ignored. Scott provided a model for extending the historical vision to include ordinary folk, and Blackmore learned the lesson so well that Victorian reviewers saw his books as a means of holding images of rural life against the time when all the villages in England should have died out or spread into towns. Although these pictures need to be balanced by less humorous and romantic ones, they form his most impressive approach to history. (pp. 123-30)

As a writer of less romantic narratives than *Lorna Doone,* Blackmore is more closely linked with the early George Eliot, whose *Adam Bede* (1859) helped to start the regional novel in England, and with Hardy, who entered the field with *Under the Greenwood Tree* in 1872, after Blackmore had already dealt with rural life in North Devon, Hampshire, and Somerset. Independently of each other, they started exploring the countryside of southern England. At the time each began admiring the other's work in 1875, the two men were not so far apart as they would seem by the 1890s, when they stopped writing novels. *Under the Greenwood Tree* could have been the model for *Cripps, the Carrier* and the dance in *Christowell*; Hardy found it "almost absurd" that he had not read *Lorna Doone* before writing *Far from the Madding Crowd* [see excerpt dated 1875], for both stories represent shepherding and farming, the festivity of harvest, and the subtler changes of plant-life and weather. Drawn to the past, to folklore and West Country speech, both writers were conscious rural historians, trying, in Hardy's words, "to preserve . . . a fairly true record of a vanishing life."

Both saw it vanishing, but where Hardy's vision turned bitter and tragic, Blackmore's remained comic, despite his anger at the fate of British agriculture once the nation began to rely upon imported food. Hardy went on to show the decline of the village culture; Blackmore almost never dealt with it directly and seldom set his novels later than 1840. Only the grumbling asides of his narrators suggest the contrast between present rural distress and the stability of an imagined past. In the grief, irritation, and lameness of old age, he kept celebrating an outdated vision of rural society along with the growth of things in fiction, while tending the apple and pear trees of his unprofitable orchard. Often disappointed, he never reached Hardy's conviction "that it was better not to have lived than face the ordeal of life as a conscious being." He did not blame suffering upon an Aeschylean "President of the Immortals" (Gladstone was a more likely scapegoat), or writes as coolly as Hardy about the coming of a new springtime: "Another year's instalment of flowers, leaves, nightingales, thrushes, finches, and such ephemeral creatures, took up their positions where only a year ago others had stood in their place when these were nothing more than germs and inorganic particles." To the last, he stayed true to his love for "green and growing things," the "secret of his inspiration." (pp. 131-32)

If time has erased or painted over the world that Blackmore remembered, the changes make his vision all the more worth preserving. The lost, cart-horse's pace of village life can still be felt in *Cripps, the Carrier* and *Perlycross,* though the wheel-ruts have long been paved and milk-lorries roar between the hedgerows. Where John Ridd turned to wade up Bagworthy

Water, touring coaches unload beside a gift shop; and in the gorge at Fingle Bridge a shop and inn provide shelter for any picnickers caught in rains like those that spoiled Julia Touchwood's "gipseying" in *Christowell.* Tourism long ago replaced fishing as the major industry at Flamborough Head, the Yorkshire setting of *Mary Anerley,* and the current heroes of the North Sea are more likely to be the men on the oil rigs than any dashing smugglers. But Blackmore's vision is not entirely of things past. The sea breaks against the cliffs, snow drifts on the moors, and men still fish. The green patchwork of the Devon hills still nourishes sheep and cows; where farmyards hum with milking-machines and high-banked lanes resound with tractors, the ancient pastoral work of man goes on, despite the Common Market imports of butter, lamb, and bacon which would have dismayed the Victorian enemy of Free Trade. Fewer now, the thatched houses still stand in sheltered combes and in the villages that are always said to be dying. The thatch sprouts television aerials as well as moss, and the calm BBC voice in the low-beamed sitting-rooms tells of more abductions and murders than the Doones ever inflicted upon Exmoor. While life goes on this way, with times of peace and of terror in the long "procession of the seasons," Blackmore has a part with greater artists, like Hardy and Wordsworth, who teach "our eyes to see." (p. 133)

> *Max Keith Sutton, in his* R. D. Blackmore, *Twayne Publishers, 1979, 156 p.*

ADDITIONAL BIBLIOGRAPHY

"Rhythmical Form in *Lorna Doone.*" *Atlantic Monthly* 65, No. 388 (February 1890): 284-85.
    Predicts "a secure, distinguished place in literature" for *Lorna Doone* in a review that especially notes the novel's rhythmical prose.

Barbour, Albert L. Introduction to *Lorna Doone: A Romance of Exmoor,* by Richard Doddridge Blackmore, pp. vii-xvi. New York: Macmillan Co., 1919.
    Discusses Blackmore's life and various occupations in law, literature, and horticulture. Barbour notes some reasons for the enduring appeal of *Lorna Doone.*

"The Novels of Mr. Blackmore." *Blackwood's Edinburgh Magazine* 160, No. 971 (September 1896): 409-22.
    Discusses the presence of Blackmore's social, political, and religious views in his novels, and examines the style, characterization, and descriptive qualities of these works.

Buckler, William E. "Blackmore's Novels Before *Lorna Doone.*" *Nineteenth-Century Fiction* 10, No. 3 (December 1955): 169-87.
    Traces the relationship of Blackmore with his first publisher, Macmillan and Company, focusing on the commercial failure of *Clara Vaughan* and *Cradock Nowell.* Buckler employs unpublished correspondence between Blackmore and Macmillan to demonstrate that Blackmore's concessions to his publisher's guidelines as well as his opposition to Victorian prudery resulted in tension and frustration.

Burton, S. H. *The Lorna Doone Trail.* Dulverton: Exmoor Press, 1975, 65 p.
    Provides illustrations and annotations for numerous excerpted passages from *Lorna Doone,* noting "how often the complexities of the plot and Blackmore's heightened treatment of scene and place baffle the explorer."

Dunn, Waldo Hilary. *R. D. Blackmore: The Author of "Lorna Doone."* New York: Longmans, Green and Co., 1956, 316 p.
    Noncritical biography by a friend of Blackmore.

Elliott-Cannon, A. *In Quest of the Doones*. Dulverton: Breakaway Books, 1981, 48 p.

Discusses the historical facts and oral traditions on which Blackmore probably based *Lorna Doone*.

Ellis, S. M. "R. D. Blackmore." In his *Wilkie Collins, Le Fanu, and Others*, pp. 117-39. 1931. Reprint. New York: Books for Libraries Press, 1968.

Biographical and critical study of Blackmore.

Garvin, J. L. "One Hundred Years of Lorna Doone." *The Living Age* 326, No. 4228 (18 July 1925): 142-46.

Discusses reasons for the continuing popularity of *Lorna Doone* and describes the region that figures in the novel. Garvin concludes that "like Wordsworth in the Lake District, [Blackmore] identified himself with a great landscape, where the shapes of his fancy mingle with every sight and sound, and common memory keeps his name alive."

Graham, Richard D. "Earlier Victorian Novelists." In his *The Masters of Victorian Literature: 1837-1897*. Edinburgh: James Thin, 1897, pp. 9-104.

Mentions Blackmore's most important works and briefly appraises *Lorna Doone*, stating, "Local character and dialect Mr. Blackmore is able to give with a much nearer approach to accuracy than even Mr. Hardy can lay claim to." Graham describes *Lorna Doone* as "a work which after Scott it would be hard to beat among the historical romances of English literature."

Harding, James. Introduction to *The Maid of Sker*, by R. D. Blackmore, pp. vii-xi. London: Anthony Blond, 1968.

Biographical discussion, focussing on Blackmore's classical education, his various occupations, and his love of nature. Harding considers *The Maid of Sker* a sprawling novel with awkward plotting that is enjoyable because of Blackmore's masterful descriptions.

Jones, Sally. "A 'Lost Leader': R. D. Blackmore and *The Maid of Sker*." *The Anglo-Welsh Review* 25, No. 55 (Autumn 1975): 32-45.

Discusses Blackmore's use of his Welsh family background in writing *The Maid of Sker*.

Reid, Stuart J. "Mr. Blackmore." *The Cornhill Magazine* VII (April 1900): 533-36.

Personal reminiscence of Blackmore by a man who knew him well during the last ten years of his life. Reid recalls Blackmore's love of solitude, his sense of humor, his kindness, and his attitude toward fame.

Rideing, William H. "In Country of Lorna Doone." *New England Magazine* X, No. 5 (July 1894): 610-19.

Description of the English countryside which inspired the setting of *Lorna Doone*. Rideing comments on some changes in the area since the time the novel was written and defends Blackmore's alteration of certain facts to fit his fictional purposes.

Ryan, Lawrence V. "The Classical Verse of R. D. Blackmore." *Victorian Poetry* 23, No. 3: 229-47.

Surveys the subjects, styles, and themes of Blackmore's poetry.

Snell, F. J. *The Blackmore Country*. London: Adam and Charles Black, 1911, 288 p.

Illustrated presentation of the geography, landmarks, history, and legends portrayed in Blackmore's novels.

Sutton, Max Keith. "Blackmore's Letters to Blackwood: The Record of a Novelist's Indecision." *English Literature in Transition, 1880-1929* 20, No. 2 (1977): 69-76.

Discusses the relationship of Blackmore with his publishers John and William Blackwood, quoting from Blackmore's correspondence to illustrate his frustration and indecision, as well as his artistic compromises, in the writing of *Alice Lorraine*.

————. "*The Prelude* and *Lorna Doone*." *The Wordsworth Circle* 13, No. 4 (Autumn 1982): 193-97.

Suggests that *Lorna Doone* was influenced by Wordsworth's *The Prelude*. Sutton compares and contrasts these works, noting similarities that include their "rural viewpoint," their "positive vision of the child in nature," their affirmation of the "'renovating virtue' of certain early memories," and "shared images."

Thornicroft, L. B. *The Story of the Doones in Fact, Fiction and Photo*. Tauton: Wessex Press, 1939, 90 p.

Examines the history and legends on which Blackmore based *Lorna Doone*, in an effort "to sift the fact from fiction." Thornicroft also provides a guide to the region and traces the history of Exmoor District from the tenth through the twentieth centuries.

Ward, H. Snowden. Introduction to *Lorna Doone: A Romance of Exmoor*, by R. D. Blackmore, pp. xiii-li. New York: Harper & Brothers, 1908.

Biographical and critical discussion of Blackmore and the novel, including examination of the local legendry from which Blackmore drew in writing *Lorna Doone*.

Charles (Montagu) Doughty

1843-1926

English travel writer, poet, and nonfiction writer.

Doughty is the author of *Travels in Arabia Deserta,* a classic work of travel literature that is distinguished by its idiosyncratic prose style. Considering nineteenth-century English the vitiated form of a once expressive language, Doughty attempted to reproduce in his work the English of the fourteenth and fifteenth centuries. Specifically, this linguistic practice was intended as a remedy for the overly abstract nature of the English language during the Victorian Era, a problem later addressed by such Modernist writers as T. S. Eliot and James Joyce. After completing *Travels in Arabia Deserta* Doughty wrote a number of epic poems, including *The Dawn in Britain* and *Adam Cast Forth.* Critical consensus holds that with the exception of *Adam Cast Forth,* Doughty's stylistic eccentricities and archaism mar his poetry, but that in *Travels in Arabia Deserta* he employed these devices to create a preeminent work of autobiography, exotica, and social commentary.

Doughty was born into an aristocratic family: his father was a minister and his mother a baron's granddaughter. Both of his parents died when Doughty was a child, and he was raised by his uncle. Following a tradition in his mother's family, Doughty was directed toward a career in the navy; however, he failed the navel medical test due to a slight speech impediment. From 1861 to 1865 Doughty studied geology at Cambridge, taking a year's leave to make a scientific examination of the glaciers in Norway, but found himself more interested in the poetry of Geoffrey Chaucer and Edmund Spenser and in English philology than in his natural science curriculum. By 1865 Doughty had determined to revive the language of Chaucer and Spenser, as well as the epic form in poetry, and began private study at Oxford. Five years later he left England to visit the countries that would later provide the setting for his literary work, as well as to study their various languages, an experience which gave him greater perspective on the form of English he wished to write. He traveled through Holland, Italy, Spain, and Greece, and arrived in Egypt in 1874. Doughty spent two years learning Arabic in order to transcribe and translate Arabic manuscripts previously inaccessible to English scholars. Joining the Haj, or pilgrim's caravan to Mecca, he became the first European to enter the interior of Arabia, beginning the two-year journey which he recorded in *Travels in Arabia Deserta.* Doughty wrote the expansive work over several years while living in the Middle East and later in Italy. He returned to England to publish *Travels in Arabia Deserta,* but encountered difficulties because of its archaic style. When Cambridge University Press suggested that the book be rewritten in contemporary English by another writer, Doughty stated that he considered his style more important than his matter. Cambridge University Press ultimately acceded, publishing *Travels in Arabia Deserta* as it was written. Doughty spent the remainder of his life in England, devoting himself to the composition of heroic poetry. He considered *Mansoul,* his last poem, to be his greatest achievement, and he continued to revise the poem until his death in 1926.

The most conspicuous feature of Doughty's works is their archaism of vocabulary and grammatical construction. Doughty believed that the English language had achieved its greatest

power of expression during the fourteenth and fifteenth centuries with the poetry of Chaucer and Spenser, and that nineteenth-century Victorian English represented a severe decline from this standard. While Doughty's literary style was most strongly influenced by Middle English, especially in its stress on individual words reflecting vital human experience, scholars also note the influence of Arabic, which is similarly vivid and concrete. Doughty preferred this use of language to that of modern English, which had become increasingly abstract, full of associations with literature rather than life, and which, instead of utilizing words as distinct units of meaning, emphasized their interrelationships and various shades of meaning. Doughty's detractors view his literary style as an affectation which had a debilitating effect on his work, while his supporters consider it an innovation, resolving the problem of worn-out Victorian English. Critics agree, however, that Doughty's literary style was most successful in his masterpiece, *Travels in Arabia Deserta.*

Composed over a ten year period, *Travels in Arabia Deserta* is an account of Doughty's sojourn in the Arabian Peninsula. In the course of this work, Doughty presents his experiences with the culture, customs, and geography of Arabia with a detail unprecedented in a work written for an English-speaking audience. Doughty's trip was initially undertaken as a brief excursion to study ancient Hebrew and Aramaic writing, as well as to retrace the origins of English culture and civilization, including the origins of Christianity, by observing the land in which the Bible originated. Doughty remained in Arabia for almost two years, however, and scholars disagree over his reasons for such an extended stay, as *Travels in Arabia Deserta* itself raises the question of Doughty's motivation in its first sentence and never adequately answers it. Inferring that Doughty was not fully aware of his own reasons, scholars have postulated several theories ranging from Doughty's apparent fascination with the primitivistic language, culture, and terrain of Arabia to an interpretation of the journey as an invitation to martyrdom, as reparation for having lost his early faith in Christianity. The latter idea purports to explain Doughty's insistence on proclaiming himself a "Nasrâny," the most offensive Arabic term for a Christian. While many other explorers to Arabia feigned Islamic belief, Doughty refused to do so, thereby risking his life on several occasions. Much of the narrative of *Travels in Arabia Deserta* centers on these threats to Doughty's life.

Although the conception of writing an epic poem based on early English history had taken shape in his mind when he was a young man, Doughty was in his sixties when *The Dawn in Britain* was published. In this work set in first century England, Rome, and Palestine, Doughty combined early English history and myth to relate the origins of Christianity in the British Isles. A difficult and extremely long poem, *The Dawn in Britain* is considered much less successful than the far shorter and less linguistically complex *Adam Cast Forth*. Considered Doughty's greatest poetic achievement, *Adam Cast Forth* takes for its subject an Arabic myth concerning the wanderings of Adam and Eve after they were expelled from the Garden of Eden. Encompassing subjects similar to those in John Milton's *Paradise Lost*, critics have found that *Adam Cast Forth* nevertheless attains a thematic and stylistic originality and is in many ways a comparable poetic achievement to Milton's work. Doughty's archaic style, however, proved less successful in poems that concerned modern topics. *The Cliffs* and *The Clouds*, while surprisingly prophetic in their depictions of modern warfare, are felt by many critics to be unnecessarily remote due to Doughty's archaism. Doughty's admirers also tend to disparage these works, though not for their archaic style, but rather because they feel that in them Doughty devoted himself to subjects unworthy of his talent. Doughty's last poem, *Mansoul*, relates a Dantesque journey into the underworld, in which the narrator tries to gain truth by questioning history's great philosophers and religious leaders. Though containing memorable passages, it is regarded as less successful than *Adam Cast Forth*, largely because Doughty's vague theistic beliefs are unable to answer the spiritual and philosophical questions posed by the poem, thus creating the appearance of confusion and purposelessness.

While Doughty's poetry remains controversial and little read, his *Travels in Arabia Deserta* has retained its interest and has gained high critical stature as a work of English prose. Doughty became a widely acknowledged influence on such later travelers to Arabia as T. E. Lawrence and Wilfrid Blunt, the latter of whom called *Travels in Arabia Deserta* "the best prose written in the last two centuries." Although Doughty is now known almost exclusively for this work, his prose and poetry alike are championed by a group of ardent devotees who claim that he has been wrongly neglected in modern criticism, and that all of his works will ultimately find a place among the greatest of nineteenth- and twentieth-century literature.

(See also *Contemporary Authors,* Vol. 115 and *Dictionary of Literary Biography,* Vol. 19: *British Poets, 1880-1914.*)

PRINCIPAL WORKS

On the Jöstedal-brae Glaciers in Norway   (nonfiction) 1866
Documents épigraphiques recueillis dans le nord de l'Arabie (nonfiction) 1884
Travels in Arabia Deserta. 2 vols.   (travel memoirs) 1888; also published as *Wanderings in Arabia* [abridged edition], 1908
Under Arms 1900   (poetry)   1900
The Dawn in Britain. 6 vols.   (poetry)   1906-07
Adam Cast Forth   (poetry)   1908
The Cliffs   (poetry)   1909
The Clouds   (poetry)   1912
The Titans   (poetry)   1916
Mansoul   (poetry)   1920; also published as *Mansoul* [revised edition], 1923

RICHARD F. BURTON   (essay date 1888)

[*An English traveler famed for his sojourns in India, the Middle East, Africa, and the Americas, Burton published over eighty books, including his* Personal Narrative of a Pilgrimage to Al Madinah and Mecca *(1855), in which he recounted his travels in Arabia and pilgrimage to Mecca disguised as a Moslem. Burton also translated the Portuguese epic* The Lusiads *of Vaz de Camões and produced the first unexpurgated translation of the* Arabian Nights. *In the following excerpt, Burton reviews* Travels in Arabia Deserta.]

[Despite] its affectations and eccentricities, its prejudices and misjudgments, [*Travels in Arabia Deserta*] is right well told. The characters stand out in high relief—*e.g.,* the hot-hearted ruffians of the Kal'ah (fort-tower of) Madáin Sálih, not to mention a host of others. The contradictory nature of the half-feminine Badawi—with his frantic loves and hates, his cowardice and his reckless courage, his griping greed and his lavish generosity and hospitality; his courtesy and churlishness, his nobility and vileness, his mild charity and his furious vindictiveness—is almost a puzzle to the European mind, but we all can vouch for its truth. The adventures are tedious because mostly unnecessary; but the scenery is sketched with a broad touch and a firm hand; and scattered about the two volumes are wise "dictes," fresh views appreciative of trite subjects, and many scraps of information, such as the northern limits of the rainy monsoon, which are novel as they are valuable. Whether Mr. Doughty is justified in adopting, for a prosaic *recit de voyage,* a style so archaic, so involved, and at times so enigmatical, however fitted it may be for works of fiction, and however pleasant for the reminiscences of days when English was not vulgarised and Americanised, the reader must judge for himself. (p. 47)

> Richard F. Burton, "Mr. Doughty's Travels in Arabia," in The Academy, *Vol. XXXIV, No. 847, July 28, 1888, pp. 47-8.*

THE SPECTATOR (essay date 1908)

[In the following excerpt, the critic reviews the abridged version of Travels in Arabia Deserta.*]*

Mr. Edward Garnett has done a public service in issuing an abridgment of what is one of the greatest travel-books in literature. The present writer once happened on Doughty's work in a country-house library, and has ever since ardently desired to possess a copy. No book of Arabian travel, not even those of Sir Richard Burton, Palgrave, and Lady Anne Blunt, is comparable to it in romantic interest. We would go further, and say that not since the Elizabethan voyagers has there been any parallel to it either in style or in Quixotic adventure. A man taking it up casually might imagine that he was reading one of Hakluyt's volumes. It is a great story told in the great manner, a masterpiece of style, and a record of heroic doings. We trust that in its new form it may find many readers, for no modern book is so worthy of the attention of Englishmen. We have one piece of advice to give these readers. Doughty was no wandering romancer, but a serious and scientific traveller. His work deserves to be read with care. . . . (p. 377)

To appreciate the full magnitude of Doughty's achievement one must remember that the period he chose for his travels was the worst conceivable, since Turkey was fighting Russia, and there was a violent feeling against the infidel; that most of the time he was sick and feeble; that he was almost without money; and that he persisted in calling himself a Christian and testifying everywhere for his faith. He even chose the most aggressive and contumelious name for his faith, Nasrâny, instead of the milder Messihi,—a fact of which he was perfectly conscious (Vol. I., p. 240). With the Bedawin he had little trouble. He read them like a book, and his simplicity wakened a responsive note in their natures. But in the towns, where every type of fanatic congregated, it is amazing that the poor and friendless stranger should have passed with his life. Not many were of the belief of Amm Mohammed, who said: "The Yahûdy [Jew] in his faith, the Nasrâny in his faith, and the Moslem in his faith; aye, and the Kafir may be a good faithful man in his belief." Perhaps his intransigence was his salvation. In a land of supple tongues veracity may command unwilling respect, and, as he says himself, "in such hazards there is nothing, I suppose, more prudent than a wise folly." (pp. 377-78)

The style of this great book is . . . Elizabethan of the Elizabethans. Old words and constructions are moulded into the stateliest prose of our generation. Another man would have been merely dull. But Doughty is so free from egotism, so sincere and earnest in his work, so inspired with the true spirit of romance, that before we have finished the book we cannot conceive such a tale told in any other manner. (p. 378)

"The Epic of the Desert," in The Spectator, *Vol. 100, No. 4158, March 7, 1908, pp. 377-78.*

EDWARD GARNETT (essay date 1908)

[Garnett was a prominent editor for several London publishing houses and discovered or greatly influenced the work of many important English writers, including Joseph Conrad, John Galsworthy, and D. H. Lawrence. He also published several volumes of criticism, all of which are characterized by thorough research and sound critical judgments. In the following excerpt from an essay first published in the Academy *in 1902 and revised in 1908 to form an introduction to* Wanderings in Arabia, *Garnett sum-*

marizes the action of Travels in Arabia Deserta *and approvingly comments on Doughty's literary style.]*

*[**Travels in Arabia Deserta** is]* a masterpiece second to none in our literature of travel. . . . And here the writer must confess that he knows no other book of travel which makes him so proud that the author is an Englishman. Gentleness, courage, humanity, endurance, and the insight of genius, these were the qualities that carried Doughty safely through his strange achievement of adventuring alone, a professed Christian, amid the fanatical Arabians. That he proclaimed his race and faith wherever he went is a supreme testimony to the firmness of his spirit and to the magnetism of a frank and mild nature that evoked so often in response the humanity underlying the Arabs' fanaticism. His narrative, indeed, testifies how much milk of human kindness the solitary stranger could count upon finding in the breast of all but the most fanatical Mohammedans. But it is surely less the author's valuable discoveries than the intense human interest of his book that will bring him enduring fame? What an unforgettable picture it is, that of this Englishman of an old-fashioned stamp adventuring alone for many long months in the deserts of Arabia, going each day not very sure of his life, yet obstinately proclaiming to all men, to sheykhs and shepherds, to fanatical tribesmen in every encampment, that he is a Nasrâny, a Christian! With a pistol hidden in his bosom, and a few gold pieces in his purse, with a sack of clothes and books and drugs thrown on the hired camel of his rafîks, or wandering guides, he goes onward, a quiet man of peace, a scholar of scholars, applying his stores of learning to interpret all the signs and tokens of the Bedouins' life, gaining thereby a draught of camel's milk in the sickness of exhaustion, and now drawing on himself an Emir's irony by his rough bluntness of speech. He goes, this good man, this Englishman, alone into the heart of hostile Arabia, insularly self-conscious yet lost in the sensation of his adventurings, keenly alive to every sight and sound, very shrewd in his calculations, often outwitted and sometimes despitefully treated, a great reader of men's characters, always trusting in God, yet keeping a keen watch on the Arabians' moods; and as he journeys on, this scholar, geologist, archaeologist, philologist, and anti-Mohammedan, we see Arabia as only a genius can reveal it to us; we see, hear, and touch its people as our most intimate friends. And all these Arabs' characters, daily cares, occupations, pleasures, worries, their inner and outer selves, are closer to us than are the English villagers living at our own doors. It is a great human picture Doughty has drawn for us in **Arabia Deserta,** and not the least testimony to the great art of the writer is that we see him in the Arabians' minds. But wherever the wandering Englishman goes he cannot stay long. He must move on. From town to village, from village out into the wilderness, from Nomad's tent to Nomad's tent he is carried, fetched, dropped, left by the wayside by his uneasy rafîks. The fingers of the most fanatical itch to cut the Nasrâny's throat, but with the chief sheykhs and the rich elders of the towns it is an instinct of living graciousness and humanity to shelter him, show him true hospitality, and drive away the mob of base-born fellows clamouring at the stranger's heels. So Doughty makes strong friends wherever he journeys, finds kindly shelter with liberal-hearted hosts who love to sit and question him about the wonders of the Western world, and hear him speak his learned mind on Eastern ways; until at last, a little tired of the Nasrâny's power of sitting still, tired of the constant clamour of the town, and of their own growing unpopularity because they shelter him, they open suddenly some postern gate, pack the Nasrâny and his saddle bags upon some worthless beast, and send him forth into the desert with some brutish

serving-man to act as faithless guide. So Doughty goes, protected by the stars, by his own shrewd weakness, by chance and by his sturdy obstinacy; he goes quite safe, yet ever in jeopardy, trusting in Arab human nature, and in his own command of Arab lore, yet humanly alarmed and ready to cry out when his fanatical companions eye his bulging saddlebags and feel the edges of their knives.

The style in which Doughty brings before us a mirage of the strange wilderness of the upland stony deserts of Arabia, a land of rocky lava drifts girt in by savage crater pits and interspersed here and there with green valley oases, where villages and walled towns have been built because there, only there is water,—the style by which Doughty communicates to us the strange feeling of his traveller's days and nights, his hourly speculations and agitations, his inner strength, his muttered doubts, his own craft and purpose, is the style of a consummate master of English. Many are the travellers and few are the styles. Palgrave's style is flat and colourless and tame beside Doughty's; Burton's style is ordinary, vigorous, commonplace. Doughty has surely succeeded better than any other English traveller in fashioning a style and forging and tempering it so as to bring the reader into intimate contact with the character of the land he describes, while contrasting with it artistically the traveller's racial spirit. Doughty forges and smelts words as only a learned man can; he goes back to the Old Testament for a plain, smiting simplicity of speech; he lifts straight from the Arabic the names of the creatures, the plants that Arabia has fashioned in her womb, the names for the weapons, the daily objects, the slang and the oaths that are in the mouth of the Arab. And into this rich medley of idioms he mixes the old English words, the Norse words he loves as only a cunning craftsman in language can. He is an artist therein, for the main vision his book leaves on the mind is that of a stubborn latter-day Norseman (mixed with the blood of an Old English cleric) adventuring forth amid the quick-witted, fierce, fanatical, kindly and fickle Arabians. Doughty's style is that of a man with a great instinct for the shades of language; his vocabulary is very rich and racy. If there be a spice or more of affectation in his speech, we welcome it as a characteristic ingredient in the idiomatic character of the whole. (pp. 107-11)

> *Edward Garnett, "Mr. C. M. Doughty: 'Arabia Deserta'," in his* Friday Nights: Literary Criticisms and Appreciations, *first series, Alfred A. Knopf, 1922, pp. 105-11.*

EDWARD GARNETT   (essay date 1908)

[*In the following excerpt from an essay written in 1908, Garnett champions the linguistic style and epic subject matter of Doughty's poetry.*]

A curious study might be made of the early efforts of men of genius whose inborn forces have long struggled with an environment of aesthetic fashions and traditions to which they are hostile. Luckily, genius is like a winged seed which floats, on favouring airs, past many obstacles till it finds a congenial soil to nurture it, and Mr. Doughty's was determined by his early wanderings in Arabia, and by his ambition, conceived in youth, to create for his own country a national epic, which, in style and texture of language, should derive from the ancient roots and stem of the English tongue, and not from those latter-day grafts, which to the critical taste of some, bear doubtful fruit. Of the language of *Travels in Arabia Deserta* a critic, Mr. Hogarth, has said, "It has the precision and inevitableness of

great style . . . it must be allowed that archaistic effort sustained by Doughty's genius through more than a thousand pages of his *Arabia Deserta,* is curiously in keeping . . . with the primeval society he set himself to describe" [see Additional Bibliography].

The implication here that our modern literary language cannot boast of a style of austere force is just. Modern English, which has long shed hundreds of simple idioms and a great part of the racy vocabulary that was in familiar use from Chaucer's to Shakespeare's time, exhales the uncertain atmosphere of a complicated civilization. It is, therefore, folly in the critic to complain that the linguistic horizon of Mr. Doughty's epic [*The Dawn in Britain*] is not bounded by the practice of our poets of today or of yesterday. The subject itself precludes it. The extraordinary feat of conjuring up before our eyes the struggle of the Celtic and Teutonic aristocracies of barbaric Europe against the Roman arms (B.C. 450—A.D. 50) is one that only a great genius, confident in its resources, could have planned and achieved. But it could not have been accomplished before our period. Though many generations of scholars and students have cultivated with assiduity the fields of archaeology, philology, and folklore, the right of the latter to rank as exact sciences is but recent. Mr. Doughty has surveyed this enormous field of research, and the fabric of his epic is built upon the knowledge of the life of our barbaric forbears, unearthed by the labours of a great band of scholars. As for the language in which the vision of *The Dawn in Britain* is embodied, it is obvious that there is no instrument in the whole armoury of our English poets ancient or modern, that could fittingly have moulded it. A new weapon had to be forged, and Mr. Doughty's blank verse, concentrated and weighty, great in its sweep and range, rich in internal rhythms, if sometimes labouring, and sometimes broken, is the product of his theme, a theme of heroic strife, vast and rugged as a mountain range, titanic in breadth and in savage depth of passion. As a critic, Mr. Edward Thomas says, "The test of a style is its expressiveness and its whole effect" and one might as well criticize what Mr. Doughty's style expresses as the style itself, *e. g.,* the face of the primeval landscape with its dense forests and boggy valleys, marshlands and fens, the tribal settlements in stockaded villages, raths and dunes, and rude walled towns, or the battles, sieges, tumults, famines, the shock of racial invasions, the dynastic customs and religious rites, the poetic myths and legends, the marriage feasts, and funeral ceremonies of this barbaric civilization in all its uncouth wildness and rude dignity. The heroic grandeur and strange wild beauty of this great pageant of life, resolving swiftly into new changing forms, are conveyed to us in a style that makes no concessions to the indolent reader.

One of his critics, Mr. R. C. Lehmann, has asked, "What reason was there, either in the nature of things, or in the purpose of the book, which could compel Mr. Doughty to this violent excess of archaism, to this spasmodic arrangement of truncated phrases with all their baldness of expression and strenuous inversion of order?" The answer to this is, simply, that you cannot make an omelette without breaking eggs, and that if the style can bring before us by direct poetic images the mysterious forces of elemental nature, the clash of nations in conflict, the physical character and spiritual breath of a thousand varied scenes, that style, with its "obscurities," "inversions," "baldness," "mannerisms," "truncated phrases" and what not, is a style of epic greatness. So unerring is the force of the author's imagination, so mysterious his creative insight that in the whole twenty-four books of his epic there is not a single event narrated that we do not accept and believe in as implicitly as though it had passed before our eyes. All has the inevitableness and actuality of nature. And we dare not question the artistic method, even in the broken waters of truncated phrases and obscurities, or in the prosaic stretches of the narrative, any more than we can hope to smooth away the lines from a man's face and yet retain its character.

Mr. Doughty's verse raises questions of vital interest today when so many modern poets by their predilection for the rarefied moods of cloistered emotions, by their retreat into aesthetic sanctuaries and inner shrines, shut out the common air and life, and abandon character and gesture in order to create cunningly carven images. Poetry, always a matter of high artifice, grows pale and languid as a plant which is sheltered indoors from the forces of wind and weather. Without the constant revolt of the great, free spirits who are the innovating forces in art, against the petrifying tendency of tradition, we know that the fairway of the main channel would gradually be silted up by time. Mediæval Irish poetry, for example, after its fresh and forceful youth, stagnated for centuries, sinking to the level of a mere game of skill in metrical technique. Mr. Doughty's verse shows life, movement and interplay of character and spontaneous force, in a measure that transcends the example of all but the great immortals. Its rugged, strange, uncouth beauty, repellent at first sight, bears with it an air of actuality that soon weakens a reader's taste for the smoother, more graceful styles of verse. The strangeness of the achievement is that the author has preserved the flow and stress of real life on the scale of epic grandeur. Even Cæsar Claudius, the unready epicurean, trembling at the din of battle, shows that mysterious vitality which the great artists always stamp upon their portraits. It is the spirit of a man, the genius of the people or place, the essence and atmosphere of things visible and invisible that Mr. Doughty paints with intensity and force, and with such breadth and freedom of handling as to impair, by comparison, creations of admirable artifice but of less character. Examine, for example, this speech of Cæsar Claudius at the banquet of Asiaticus, his host, and note how the genius of Roman civilization, its imperial outlook and the flavour of patrician luxury are all here together in twenty lines:

> Good is this loaf, of sheaf reaped by our soldiers!
> We also some will fraught in ship, to Rome.
> Which grind shall Briton captives, and thereof
> Be loaves set, on all tables, in Rome's streets;
> What day to Rome's citizens, we shall make,
> (As erewhile *divus* Julius), triumph-feast.
> Thy maidens, Friend, be like to marble nymphs,
> Of Praxiteles, fecht to Rome, those which
> Stand in *impluvium* of our golden house:
> Swift Cynthia's train, with silver bows; that seem,
> And rattling quivers, on their budded breasts,
> Leaping their high round flanks, on crystal feet,
> Follow, with loud holloa! the chase in heaven.
> This, which beside me, my Valerius, hath
> So bright long hair-locks like ringed wiry gold,
> And gracious breast, whereon sit wooing doves,
> Meseems that famous Cnidian Aphrodite,
> Great goddess mother of our Julian house;
> Whereby now Thermæ Agrippæ are adorned.
>
> What damsel! mix me cup of Lesbian wine;
> And give, with kiss of Venus' lips, of love.
> Ha, these, that skill not of our Latin tongue,
> Hold scorn of Caesar, Asiaticus!

(pp. 117-23)

[The] appeal of the style lies in the cumulative effect of the whole image; and what wealth there is in the strange spiritual depths of this human ocean! To take one Book only out of the twenty-four: Book XX. unfolds the shipwreck of Britain's fortunes, the agony of Caractacus, his night frenzy in the gravefields, his capture by the plotted treachery and subtle spells of Cartismandua, the harlot queen, the madness and punishment of her paramour, Prince Vellocatus, the transportation of Caractacus and his queen overseas, and their incarceration in the prison pit of Servius Tullius. Another perhaps more amazing feat of the poet's imagination is the wild passage in which Belisama, the British goddess, incites the warrior Camulus to save Caractacus. We know nothing in literature like this, in its astounding insight into the conceptions of a primitive society.

It is not by subject, not by his form merely, that we must rank a poet, but by the original creative force and beauty of his whole vision. In *The Cliffs,* a modern drama of the invasion of England by a fleet of Dreadnoughts, and aerial ships of a hostile European Power, Mr. Doughty shows as great imaginative insight in his treatment of an old shepherd, a Crimean veteran walking the shore by night, and of the strife of factitious politicians in Parliament, as in his picture of Caractacus in Rome. The sharp, homely pathos of the veteran's memories of the trenches, the biting satiric invective and fantastic mercilessness of the picture of the politicians, the aerial delicacy and poetic humour of the elves' marriage, all this is great poetry, poetry that seizes on the spiritual essences of human life and feeling and weaves them into an original tissue of rich imagery. We do not claim that *The Cliffs* is an achievement comparable with *The Dawn in Britain. The Cliffs* is a poem written with a patriotic purpose, and wherever the purpose becomes obtrusive, as in certain speeches of the invading foreigners on the Anglian cliff, and in the last sixty pages of the poem describing how news is brought of the repulse and retreat of the invading foe, winding up with the patriotic Te Deum of "Sancta Britannia" which is sung by the English villagers, the vicar and all good Englishmen, we drop abruptly from poetry to prose, and the effect is the more marked, since it is not the details that are unfit for poetic treatment, but the vision that has grown ordinary in spirit and imagery through over accentuation of the national, patriotic purpose. Extraordinary in its marred, imperfect achievement as is *The Cliffs,* one has only to place it beside *Adam Cast Forth* to see that the latter in imaginative intensity and creative loftiness is the crown of the poet's creations. In sublimity, in native austerity, in the qualities of elemental awe and pity the sacred drama of the earthly fate of Adam and Eve, after they have been cast forth from Eden, vies with the Miltonic drama. The Judæo-Arabian legend on which *Adam Cast Forth* is founded is, no doubt, a product of the same deserts from which the awful Monotheism of the Bible sprang. After the whirling fiery blast of Sarsar, the rushing tempest of God's wrath has reft Adam and Adama (Eve) apart, Adam is hurled over sharp rocks, and buffeted through thickets of thorns to desolate Harisuth, the sweltering land of fiery dust and burning stones, a sun-beat wilderness; where he lies, blackened and sightless, fed by ravens for a hundred years, bowed to the scorching earth, in agony of bruised flesh, piteous and groaning. The drama opens with the appearance of Ezriel, the Angel of the Lord's Face, who tells of the Lord's mercy. Now to the blinded man comes Adama, whom he recognizes by her voice, and entreats that she will bind their bodies together so that he may not lose her again. The originality and exquisite quality of the poem lie in the contrast between the naked sublimity of the awful landscape, this waterless, sun-blackened, high, waste wilderness over which broods the Wrath of God of the Hebraic conception, and the pitiable defencelessness of the "naked and simple fleshling Adam." We have said that *Adam Cast Forth* vies in sublimity with Milton's epic, and certainly not only is the picture of primeval Arabian landscape wrought with an austere force that no poet could command who had not himself known the horrors of its savage desolation, but the figure of Adam in elemental simplicity and force of outline, "mixt of the base ferment of beasts' flesh," and "the breath of the Highest," is both a grander and more humanly credible "world father" than the scholastic creation of Milton. In its dramatic development *Adam Cast Forth* shows the inevitability of great art. A Voice proclaims that the years of Adam's punishment are ended, and Adama guides her helpmate to a palmgrove, where, bathing in a spring, he recovers sight and strength. To prove their hearts, "Whether, indeed, ye will obey His Voice," Adam and Adama are bidden to leave the valley of the Lord's Rest and journey perilously through Harisuth, the Land of the Lord's Curse. The narrative of their tormenting march and augmented sufferings among the glowing crags of this vast waste of desolation is inspired by a deep tenderness and pity for human sorrow, born of an extreme sensitiveness united to a natural austerity of vision. What is to be remarked in the character of all our author's works is this dualism of mind which penetrates into the spirit of all harsh and terrible forces in nature, and on the other hand sheds mild, beneficent and healing rays of loving kindness. (pp. 126-30)

> Edward Garnett, "Mr. C. M. Doughty: Mr. Doughty's Poems," in his Friday Nights: Literary Criticisms and Appreciations, first series, *Alfred A. Knopf, 1922, pp. 117-31.*

T. E. LAWRENCE (essay date 1921)

[*Popularly known as Lawrence of Arabia, Lawrence was the author of* Seven Pillars of Wisdom *(1922), an account of his experiences as a military intelligence officer involved in the Arab Revolt against the Turkish Empire during World War I. Written in the tradition of Homeric epic,* Seven Pillars of Wisdom *betrays medieval and chivalric influences while retaining a modern perspective. Its various narrative modes allow* Seven Pillars of Wisdom *to be read as military history, poetic autobiography, self-created myth, spiritual confession, and journal of psychosexual pathology.* Seven Pillars of Wisdom *has been compared to the works of Marcel Proust, Franz Kafka, and James Joyce, and is recognized as a modern classic. Lawrence was an ardent admirer of Doughty, and* Seven Pillars of Wisdom *is highly indebted in its mannered prose and panoramic grandeur to* Travels in Arabia Deserta. *In the following excerpt from an introduction to the second edition of* Travels in Arabia Deserta, *Lawrence praises Doughty's portrayal of Middle Eastern people, customs, and environment.*]

It is not comfortable to have to write about *Arabia Deserta*. I have studied it for ten years, and have grown to consider it a book not like other books, but something particular, a bible of its kind. To turn round now and reckon its merits and demerits seems absurd. I do not think that any traveller in Arabia before or since Mr. Doughty has qualified himself to praise the book— much less to blame it. The more you learn of Arabia the more you find in *Arabia Deserta*. The more you travel there the greater your respect for the insight, judgment and artistry of the author. We call the book "Doughty" pure and simple, for it is a classic, and the personality of Mr. Doughty hardly comes into question. Indeed, it is rather shocking to learn that he is a real and living person. The book has no date and can never

grow old. It is the first and indispensable work upon the Arabs of the desert; and if it has not always been referred to, or enough read, that has been because it was excessively rare. Every student of Arabia wants a copy. (p. 17)

I have talked the book over with many travellers, and we are agreed that here you have all the desert, its hills and plains, the lava fields, the villages, the tents, the men and animals. They are told of to the life, with words and phrases fitted to them so perfectly that one cannot dissociate them in memory. It is the true Arabia, the land with its smells and dirt, as well as its nobility and freedom. There is no sentiment, nothing merely picturesque, that most common failing of oriental travel-books. Doughty's completeness is devastating. There is nothing we would take away, little we could add. He took all Arabia for his province, and has left to his successors only the poor part of specialists. We may write books on parts of the desert or some of the history of it; but there can never be another picture of the whole, in our time, because here it is all said, and by a great master.

There have been many well-endowed Englishmen travelling in Arabia, and most of them have written books. None have brought away a prize as rich as Doughty brought, and the merit of this is his own unaided merit. He had many things against him. Forty years ago the desert was less hospitable to strangers than it is to-day. Turkey was still strong there, and the Wahabi movement had kept fanaticism vivid in the tribes. Doughty was a pioneer, both as European and Christian, in nearly all the districts he entered. Also he was poor. He came down a lone man from Damascus with the pilgrim caravan, and was left behind at Medain Salih with scant recommendation. He struck out into the desert dressed like the very poor, travelling like the very poor, trying to maintain himself by the practice of rational medicine, in a society more willing to invest in charms.

Then he was a sick man. His health was weak when he started, and the climate of the plateau of Arabia is a trying one, with its extremes of heat and cold, and the poverty of its nourishment. He had been brought up in England, a fruitful country of rich and plentiful food. He came as a guest to the Arab tents, to share their lean hospitality, and to support himself on the little that sufficed them. They treated him to what they had themselves. Their skinny bodies subsisted well enough on a spring season of camel-milk, and rare meals of dates or meat for the barren months of the year, but such a diet was starvation for an Englishman. It would be short commons to a sedentary man; but Doughty was for ever wandering about, often riding from sunrise to sunset, if not for half the night, in forced marches across rocky and toilsome country, under a burning sun, or in keen exhausting winds. Travel in Arabia in the best circumstances, with a train of servants, good riding-beasts, tents and your own kitchen, is a trying experience. Doughty faced it native-fashion, in spite of his physical disadvantages, and brought home more booty than we all. The sheer endurance of his effort is wonderful. (pp. 17-18)

The realism of the book is complete. Doughty tries to tell the full and exact truth of all that he saw. If there is a bias it will be against the Arabs, for he liked them so much; he was so impressed by the strange attraction, isolation and independence of this people that he took pleasure in bringing out their virtues by a careful expression of their faults. "If one live any time with the Arab he will have all his life after a feeling of the desert." He had experienced it himself, the test of nomadism, that most deeply biting of all social disciplines, and for our sakes he strained all the more to paint it in its true colours, as a life too hard, too empty, too denying for all but the strongest and most determined men. Nothing is more powerful and real than this record of all his daily accidents and obstacles, and the feelings that came to him on the way. His picture of the Semites, sitting to the eyes in a cloaca, but with their brows touching Heaven, sums up in full measure their strength and weakness, and the strange contradictions of their thought which quicken our curiosity at our first meeting with them.

To try and solve their riddle many of us have gone far into their society, and seen the clear hardness of their belief, a limitation almost mathematical, which repels us by its unsympathetic form. Semites have no half-tones in their register of vision. They are a people of primary colours, especially of black and white, who see the world always in line. They are a certain people, despising doubt, our modern crown of thorns. They do not understand our metaphysical difficulties, our self-questionings. They know only truth and untruth, belief and unbelief, without our hesitating retinue of finer shades.

Semites are black and white not only in vision, but in their inner furnishing; black and white not merely in clarity, but in apposition. Their thoughts live easiest among extremes. They inhabit superlatives by choice. Sometimes the great inconsistents seem to possess them jointly. They exclude compromise, and pursue the logic of their ideas to its absurd ends, without seeing incongruity in their opposed conclusions. They oscillate with cool head and tranquil judgment from asymptote to asymptote, so imperturbably that they would seem hardly conscious of their giddy flight.

They are a limited narrow-minded people whose inert intellects lie incuriously fallow. Their imaginations are keen but not creative. There is so little Arab art to-day in Asia that they can nearly be said to have no art, though their rulers have been liberal patrons and have encouraged their neighbours' talents in architecture, ceramic and handicraft. They show no longing for great industry, no organisations of mind or body anywhere. They invent no systems of philosophy or mythologies. They are the least morbid of peoples, who take the gift of life unquestioning, as an axiom. To them it is a thing inevitable, entailed on man, a usufruct, beyond our control. Suicide is a thing nearly impossible and death no grief.

They are a people of spasms, of upheavals, of ideas, the race of the individual genius. Their movements are the more shocking by contrast with the quietude of every day, their great men greater by contrast with the humanity of their mass. Their convictions are by instinct, their activities intuitional. Their largest manufacture is of creeds. They are monopolists of revealed religions, finding always an antagonism of body and spirit, and laying their stress on the spirit. Their profound reaction against matter leads them to preach barrenness, renunciation, poverty: and this atmosphere stifles the minds of the desert pitilessly. They are always looking out towards those things in which mankind has had no lot or part.

The Beduin has beeen born and brought up in the desert, and has embraced this barrenness too harsh for volunteers with all his soul, for the reason, felt but inarticulate, that there he finds himself indubitably free. He loses all natural ties, all comforting superfluities or complications, to achieve that personal liberty which haunts starvation and death. He sees no virtue in poverty herself; he enjoys the little vices and luxuries—coffee, fresh water, women—which he can still afford. In his life he has air and winds, sun and light, open spaces and great emptiness. There is no human effort, no fecundity in Nature;

just heaven above and unspotted earth beneath; and the only refuge and rhythm of their being is in God. This single God is to the Arab not anthropomorphic, not tangible or moral or ethical, not concerned particularly with the world or with him. He alone is great, and yet there is a homeliness, an every-day-ness of this Arab God who rules their eating, their fighting and their lusting; and is their commonest thought, and companion, in a way impossible to those whose God is tediously veiled from them by the decorum of formal worship. They feel no incongruity in bringing God into their weaknesses and appetites. He is the commonest of their words.

This creed of the desert is an inheritance. The Arab does not value it extremely. He has never been either evangelist or proselyte. He arrives at this intense condensation of himself in God by shutting his eyes to the world, and to all the complex possibilities latent in him which only wealth and temptation could bring out. He attains a sure trust and a powerful trust, but of how narrow a field! His sterile experience perverts his human kindness to the image of the waste in which he hides. Accordingly he hurts himself, not merely to be free, but to please himself. There follows a self-delight in pain, a cruelty which is more to him than goods. The desert Arab finds no joy like the joy of voluntarily holding back. He finds luxury in abnegation, renunciation, self-restraint. He lives his own life in a hard selfishness. His desert is made a spiritual ice-house, in which is preserved intact but unimproved for all ages an idea of the unity of God.

Doughty went among these people dispassionately, looked at their life, and wrote it down word for word. By being always Arab in manner and European in mind he maintained a perfect judgment, while bearing towards them a full sympathy which persuaded them to show him their inmost ideas. When his trial of two years was over he carried away in his note-book (so far as the art of writing can express the art of living) the soul of the desert, the complete existence of a remarkable and self-contained community, shut away from the currents of the world in the unchanging desert, working out their days in an environment utterly foreign to us. The economic reason for their existence is the demand for camels, which can be best bred on the thorns and plants of these healthy uplands. The desert is incapable of other development, but admirably suited to this. Their camel-breeding makes the Beduins nomads. The camels live only on the pasture of the desert, and as it is scanty, a great herd will soon exhaust any one district. Then they with their masters must move to another, and so they circulate month by month in a course determined by the vegetation sprung up wherever the intermittent winter rains have this season fallen heaviest.

The social organisation of the desert is in tribes, partly because of original family-feeling, partly because the instinct of self-preservation compels large masses of men to hold together for mutual support. By belonging to a recognised tribe each man feels that he has a strong body of nominal kinsmen, to support him if he is injured; and equally to bear the burden and to discharge his wrong-doing, when he is the guilty party. This collective responsibility makes men careful not to offend; and makes punishment very easy. The offender is shut out from the system and becomes an exile till he has made his peace again with the public opinion of his tribesmen.

Each tribe has its district in the desert. The extent and nature of these tribal districts are determined by the economic laws of camel-breeding. Each holds a fair chance of pasture all the year round in every normal year, and each holds enough drinking-water to suffice all its households every year; but the poverty of the country forces an internal subdivision of itself upon the tribe. The water-sources are usually single wells (often very scanty wells), and the pasturages small scattered patches in sheltered valleys or oases among the rocks. They could not accommodate at one time or place all the tribe, which therefore breaks into clans, and lives always as clans, wandering each apart on its own cycle within the orbit of the tribal whole.

The society is illiterate, so each clan keeps small enough to enable all its adults to meet frequently, and discuss all common business verbally. Such general intercourse, and their open life beside one another in tents makes the desert a place altogether without privacy. Man lives candidly with man. It is a society in perpetual movement, an equality of voice and opportunity for every male. The daily hearth or sheikh's coffee-gathering is their education, a university for every man grown enough to walk and speak.

It is also their news-office, their tribunal, their political expression, and their government. They bring and expose there in public every day all their ideas, their experiences, their opinions, and they sharpen one another, so that the desert society is always alive, instructed to a high moral level, and tolerant of new ideas. Common rumour makes them as unchanging as the desert in which they live; but more often they show themselves singularly receptive, very open to useful innovations. Their few vested interests make it simple for them to change their ways; but even so it is astonishing to find how whole-heartedly they adopt an invention fitted to their life. Coffee, gunpowder, Manchester cotton are all new things, and yet appear so native that without them one can hardly imagine their desert life.

Consequently, one would expect a book such as *Arabia Deserta,* written forty years ago, to be inaccurate to-day in such little respects, and had Doughty's work been solely scientific, dependent on the expression rather than the spirit of things, its day might have passed. Happily the beauty of the telling, its truth to life, the rich gallery of characters and landscapes in it, will remain for all time, and will keep it peerless, as the indispensable foundation of all true understanding of the desert. (pp. 21-5)

I believe [*Arabia Deserta*] to be one of the great prose works of our literature. It is a book which begins powerfully, written in a style which has apparently neither father nor son, so closely wrought, so tense, so just in its words and phrases, that it demands a hard reader. It seems not to have been written easily; but in a few of its pages you learn more of the Arabs than in all that others have written, and the further you go the closer the style seems to cling to the subject, and the more natural it becomes to your taste.

The history of the march of the caravan down the pilgrim road, the picture of Zeyd's tent, the description of Ibn Rashid's court at Hail, the negroid village in Kheybar, the urbane life at Aneyza, the long march across the desert of Western Nejd to Mecca, each seems better than the one before till there comes the very climax of the book near Taif, and after this excitement a gentle closing chapter of the road down to Jidda to the hospitality of Mohammed Nasif's house, and the British Consulate.

To have accomplished such a journey would have been achievement enough for the ordinary man. Mr. Doughty was not content till he had made the book justify the journey as much as the journey justified the book, and in the double power, to go and to write, he will not soon find his rival. (pp. 27-8)

> *T. E. Lawrence, in an introduction to* Travels in Arabia Deserta *by Charles M. Doughty, 1921. Reprint by Random House Publishers, 1937, pp. 17-28.*

EDMUND GOSSE (essay date 1921)

[*Gosse's importance as a critic is due primarily to his introduction of Henrik Ibsen's "new drama" to an English audience. He was among the chief English translators and critics of Scandinavian literature and was decorated by the Norwegian, Swedish, and Danish governments for his efforts. Among his other works are studies of John Donne, Thomas Gray, Sir Thomas Browne, and important early articles on French authors of the late nineteenth century. Although Gosse's works are varied and voluminous, he was largely a popularizer, with the consequence that his commentary lacks depth and is not considered in the first rank of modern critical thought. However, his broad interests and knowledge of foreign literatures lend his works much more than a documentary value. In the following excerpt, Gosse examines positive and negative aspects of Doughty's poetry as exemplified by* Mansoul.]

On the principle, I suppose, that in these days you must make a very loud noise in order to be heard at all, . . . [*Mansoul*] has been ushered into the world with shawms and trumpets by the little clan of his enthusiastic admirers. The most exorbitant claims have been made for recognition of its merit, and its author has been named as an equal with Chaucer, Spenser, and Milton. At the same time, remarkably little explanation has been vouchsafed of the grounds on which this glorification is founded. We merely have had repeated such epithets as "sublime" and "magnificent," and such nouns as "genius," "splendour," and "beauty." We are told that Mr. Doughty's vision is "beyond the compass of ordinary seers," but not in what it consists. We are told that he rewards students of great poetry "as no one else living rewards" them, and we are haughtily informed that not every reader is worthy of approaching his "unparalleled mastery." To find defects in him is "not to be quite equal" to the privilege of making his acquaintance.

This browbeating of the cultivated public is insufferable, and it is foolish from its own point of view, since the reader who turns from the reviews to the text, and is bewildered by peculiarities which he has not been led to expect, will be very likely to throw the book aside in anger and dismay. I greatly admire the verse of Mr. Doughty, though I prefer the prose of his wonderful *Arabia Deserta,* but I admire the former with certain reserves. I think it essential to admit that his poetical system offers various difficulties and provokes objection from perfectly honest and highly cultivated readers.

Nothing about Mr. Doughty is commonplace. . . . [All of Doughty's poetic works] are remarkable for the broad and grandiose effects which they produce, for their archaic stateliness, and for their sumptuous colour; they stalk, like Collins's phantom kings, "in pageant robes and wreath'd with sheeny gold." They are remarkable, too, for their independence of all contemporary or even modern influence, and for a uniformity of execution which is impressive at first, and which grows a little importunate and fatiguing at last.

On the other hand, a course of initiation is required before the poetry of Mr. Doughty can be appreciated at all. In his reaction against inane and flatulent phraseology he hurls the speech of

England back six hundred years, and in doing so, and by juggling in the most extraordinary manner with syntax and punctuation, he introduces elements of strangeness and awkwardness which are undeniable. Poetry ought to give immediate pleasure to the ear and mind, and specimens of it which demand systematic defence are so far shown to be of doubtful success. Mr. Doughty is a revolutionary who affects to be a restorer of ancient manners; and who will be more kingly than the King himself. But it is not right that we should have to force ourselves to admire fine poetry. It is the drawback to a full appreciation of Mr. Doughty that he has attempted to create a new poetic language without sufficient consideration of the passage of time or the requirements of the age he lives in. He runs the danger of incurring the blame which Ben Jonson gave to a reforming poet of his own age—namely, that, in trying to improve our speech, he "writ no language at all."

Let us endeavour to do full justice to the object which Mr. Doughty has had in view in writing his new poem, and to the degree in which he attains it. *Mansoul* is an epic in six books and in blank verse. The poet speaks in his own person and describes a vision, in the mediæval manner made familiar to us by Chaucer and *Piers the Plowman*. He is seated one summer's day on the terrace of a house, when he falls into a trance, in the course of which he prays, being surrounded by the turmoil of opinion in the market-place of Mantown, for moral guidance. His prayer is immediately answered by the apparition of a virgin of divine stature, "with eyes of living light, as stars of God." The poet instantly recognises her as the Muse of Britain, who taught him his art long since when he was the disciple of Colin Clout—that is to say, of Spenser. She leads him through a brazen desolation, where Minimus is sleeping, with whom the Poet seems to be henceforth identified. He enters the Cave of Hertha, in whose garden he falls asleep, and enjoys a vision within a vision of the Sister Muses (I have dared to modernise the punctuation):—

> Whilst yet I in that Pleasaunce roamed and gazed,—
> Cool rumbling brook, sliding with liquid foot
> 'Twixt flowery banks, trembling like watery light,—
> I came to a fishpool, mirror of clear skies,
> Where wont the Sisters tire their jacinth locks
> And wind them in thick tress; where feed their hands
> A golden-scalèd voiceless finny drove.
> Then, angry at mine intruded stranger foot,
> Knee-deep in water-mists, loose-strife, flowering rush,
> A ruffling swan, proud warden of that plot,
> Plunged from his nest and vehement breasts outforth.

Conducted out of the garden, he finds the Muse of Britain again, now seated in an ivory stall outside a temple, and she consents to conduct him through the world, as Dante was accompanied by Virgil. They descend to the rusty doors of "Hell's Tremendous House," which fly open and clap to behind their backs. There is a very fine conception of the gate of Death, and of the abysmal gulf beyond Death, where the Poet (and indeed the reader also) is not a little startled to find the ex-Emperor Wilhelm, "werewolf" and "warmonger," bound to a stake of adamant, and gazing in a mirror at his own

> coxcomb visage and enormous deeds
> Till Time shall cease,

While an ever-accusing Voice

> Rings and reverberates in his being's ears.

The pilgrims pass on through the thoroughfare of the world's

Doughty in 1922. From The Life of Charles M. Doughty, *by D. G. Hogarth. Doubleday, Doran & Company, Inc., 1929. Courtesy of Doubleday & Company, Inc.*

dead, and meet Buddha, Socrates, the disciples of Plato, Confucius (introduced as "King"), and Zarathrusta. They are spectators of the majestic scene of the Crucifixion of "Jeshúa"; and see, but do not visit, Japan. The close of the poem deals principally with English poetry, with Cædmon, with Chaucer and Langland, and with Spenser. The poet wakes out of the underworld vision, and the poem ends with a solemn mystical celebration in the Cathedral of British Verse.

Such, very rudely and briefly told, seems to be the plot or subject-matter of *Mansoul*, which is built up with a sort of Cyclopean masonry of thought and expression which has no recent counterpart. Mr. Doughty's originality as a poet consists in his consistent employment of a lumbering and almost clumsily massive style, seldom lacking in a vague grandeur, and sometimes, as in the passage I first quoted, extremely rich, but always remote from our present habits of expression. This is embodied in a ponderous versification which shows no evidence of the author's having read anything later than the beginnings of blank verse at the close of the sixteenth century, as found in *The Misfortunes of Arthur* and in *Tamburlaine*, but here broken up with elisions and arbitrary innovations of accent. The verse moves like a heavy body leaping from slab to slab across a stream.

The general character of Mr. Doughty's style may be described as displaying an apparent simplicity which is really extremely sophisticated. The effect, it is impossible to deny, is excessively fatiguing to the attention, from the uniform artificiality of language, but the reader is rewarded and refreshed by frequent passages of unusual beauty, and by a certain general upliftedness which is the ambrosia in the hard and heavy cup of Mr. Doughty's uncompromising poetry.

One of the unflinching enthusiasts has said that Mr. Doughty carries on the great tradition of British verse. No compliment could be more unlucky, nor fit the recipient of it less conspicuously. With a rougher hand than any other poet of the last hundred years Mr. Doughty scornfully and haughtily breaks with the tradition of British verse. For him our poetry ceases with Spenser. The tradition comes down to us through Milton and Dryden, through Pope and Burns, through Wordsworth and Keats. These writers do not exist for Mr. Doughty, who admits and reveres the genius of Spenser, but descends no lower in the scale. What he seems, if I may conjecture, to wish to do is even to restore a much earlier condition of thought and language. His poetry is really more in keeping with the fourteenth century than with any later age, and he is careful to resemble no modern writer, except Blake in the Prophetic Books (and this may be an accident).

Mr. Doughty's actual coevals are the nameless bards who wrote unrhymed and alliterative romances, such as *William of Palerme* and *Cleanness,* although he likes to avoid the monotonous amble of the fourteenth century by breaking his verses with a very strong irregular pause.

Mr. Doughty has never read Wordsworth, and therefore does not remember that poetry should be "the language really used by men in a state of vivid sensation." The readers of *William of Palerme* (which is positively not more difficult than whole pages of **Mansoul**) actually spoke the language of the poet, but who now except Mr. Doughty says "see" for "seat," or "sue" for "follow"? What is the use of flooring the unhappy reader with words like "craigstewed" and "scruzed" and "derne"? Mr. Doughty is very fond of "derne"; his pilgrims are "all-suddenly dasht on a derne cliff." It sounds like a mild American expletive. We say "glowworms"; what is gained by writing "glade-worms"? Mr. Doughty is a writer of noble imagination and great force of temper, but he is also fantastic and preposterous. Let us admire in him what is admirable, but not allow ourselves to be bullied into subjection to his eccentricities. (pp. 267-72)

Edmund Gosse, "Mr. Doughty's 'Mansoul'," in his Books on the Table, *Charles Scribner's Sons, 1921, pp. 265-72.*

SAMUEL C. CHEW   (essay date 1925-26)

[*Chew is an American eductor and critic. In the following excerpt, he favorably discusses each of Doughty's epic poems.*]

Doughty's "incessant labor" during the decennium 1879-1888 was the composition of the **Travels in Arabia Deserta**. . . . It is not my present purpose to attempt any "appreciation" of that incomparable record. . . . More profitable, did space serve, would be some indication of the relation of the book to other narratives of travel—Burckhardt's *Travels in Arabia,* Burton's *Personal Narrative,* Palgrave's *Narrative,* Warburton's *The Crescent and the Cross,* Curzon's *Monasteries of the Levant,* and Kinglake's *Eothen.* Considered more broadly, Doughty's work might serve as the culmination of the entire history of the influence of the Levant upon English literature.

One pictures the poet-traveler, conscious of a vocation as yet unfulfilled and meditating the theme of a long poem as he lay

out upon the desert sands beneath the stars. His championship of Christianity among the Moslems may have suggested a Christian subject; association with the nomads directed his thoughts to life in primitive society; pride in England impelled him to choose an English theme. These three motives—Christianity; Primitivism; England—are intertwined in the story of the bringing of Christianity to Britain. Years passed while the travel-book was written. Then the idea of his epic poem took shape slowly in his mind. The assembling of materials was the work of several years, and the actual writing of the epic, Mr. Doughty has told me, occupied nearly a decade. In 1906 **The Dawn in Britain,** an epic poem in six volumes, was published.

The reception given this long, ambitious, and difficult work resembles that accorded to *The Dynasts;* but whereas Mr. Hardy's epic-drama has won its way to recognition as the greatest English poem of this age, **The Dawn in Britain** remains little read and seldom spoken of. There are serious stumbling-blocks in the reader's path, for Doughty makes no concessions to ignorance of semi-legendary British history. The involutions and contortions of the style, the archaistic vocabulary (for which he had the great precedent of Spenser), and the syntactical peculiarities, have alienated benevolent readers who are, moreover, irritated by the suppression of the apostrophe in the genitive case and by similar eccentricities. The abundant use of secondary ictus necessitates the employment of accents as guides to the proper scansion of the lines. An additional difficulty is the punctuation, which is not grammatical or syntactical but rhythmical and elocutionary, following a system not very logically worked out. (pp. 27-9)

The stately monotony of the blank verse, like the tread of unnumbered hosts, harmonizes with the remorseless and monotonous passing of the human generations who appear and vanish again during the vast epoch (from the taking of Rome by Brennus to the revolt of Bonduca) covered by the story. An effect is gained of vague grandeur, but there is confusion in the reader's mind as the narrative wanders on, as king gives way to king, as now Briton and now Roman triumphs, and as the new faith out of Syria wins converts from the ancient religion of the isle. An ill-defined allegory of the struggle of the forces of light, symbolized by the meek Syrian missionaries, with the forces of darkness, symbolized by the woad-stained devotees of Druidism, may be read into the poem; but in general it is singularly objective, without hidden meaning and with no purpose save the grand one to tell the tale of the dawn of civilization in the poet's well-loved land.

Defective in the larger matters of composition, the epic is rich in striking and beautiful episodes. The following is a characteristic example of Doughty's manner. At a time when mighty Julius had become "an handful of common cinders," in far-off Syria a new Light dawned upon the world:

> Pass other years: and seemeth that her first peace,
> Returned to earth; and truce in weary hearts!
> Then, in a night, which lightsome seems as day,
> Sounded in Mona's temple-cave, divine
> Voice, saying; Him worship, all ye Briton gods!
>   Dear Muse, which from this world's beginning, was
> Seated, above, in heavenly harmonies;
> Reveal that Radiance to mine hungry ears,
> Thine eyes behold; what sacred Light, far off,
> Like new wide Dawn (for which, men's eyes have
>   watched,
> From age to age) now kindled on the earth!
> Whiles Night lies, as a cloak, whelmed on our Britain;

Tell me of Land, under East bent of heaven;
Wherein, is born, the Everlasting Prince
Of Peace, Sun of night-darkness of our hearts!

I would gladly quote a score of passages from this poem; but
it must suffice to send my readers to such episodes as that of
the first meeting of Brennus and Fridia (Book ii); the descent
of Brennus's armies upon Italy (Book iii); the story of the
nymph Agygia (Book iii); the coming of the second Brennus
to Delphi (Book v); the voyage of Joseph in Mauson's ship
(Book vi). In book vii there is a tremendous vision of Hell
where fiends gather in council how to prevent the coming of
the saints to Britain. "Disdain, tiptoe-stalking demon," "blind
blasphemous Despair," "heart-nipping Envy" and other devils
gather with a rabblement of—

Skrats, woodwives, goblins, of earths forlorn night;
Punks, spectres, bugs; earth, well and mountain sprites,
In guise of werewolves, fitchews, and strange shapes.

In Britain battles innumerable are fought and "sounds of insult,
shame, and wrong" echo through the poem. The characterization of the Emperor Claudius (Book xiv), though not confirmed by modern research, is a remarkable revitalization of
tradition. The harangue of Caractacus to his "blue barbare
host" before the battle (Book xvi) is a fine example of Doughty's rugged eloquence; and the picture of the same chief, a
prisoner in Rome (Book xx), reflects the poet's own large-
hearted patriotism. In the end, there sounds again the motive
of the gentle human love which has been brought to war-worn
Britain by the Syrian saints—

Love is here lowest stair to the Infinite Good,
Love-labour easy is: is aught so hard,
But will attempt it love? with panting breast!
For love, love lightly would forsake the world!

There is much evidence in the *Arabia Deserta* of Doughty's
interest in folk-traditions, especially such as, possessed in common by various branches of the Semites, illuminate the Old
Testament narrative. One such legend, picked up from the
nomads, tells how Adam and Eve, "cast forth from the Paradise, fell down in several places of the Earth: whence they,
after age-long wandering, meet together again, upon a Mountain." This is the theme of *Adam Cast Forth,* a sacred drama
published in 1908. The simple story is told in rude and unadorned fashion, yet with much of primitive nobility. The rock-
strewn wilderness through which our first parents move and
the smiling oasis to which they come are alike suggestive of
Arabian landscape; and the unquestioning obedience to the will
of God is characteristic of "the tented Children-of-the-East."
But the drama is too remote from Occidental ways of thought
and life ever to be popular or widely read. And equally alien
to our lives is the narrative poem of *The Titans. . .,* the opening
lines of which are typical of Doughty's austere grandeur—

Neath Heavens high stars, whereof we some see cease,
To shed their light, whilst other some increase;
There nothing is at any stay. This House
Of Middle-Earth, which Time brought lately forth;
Our Inn, in bosom of Gods Universe;
Is full of variance, tiding ever forth.
Alone the everlasting Throne stands stedfast.

But this Dantesque sublimity of utterance is not sustained
throughout. The Titans, defeated in warfare with gods and men,
are cast into a pit. In after ages the "living corse" of one
"great Eothen-statue" is found by men who remove it to their
market-place, where buried loin-deep the Titan returns to life
and, as a yoked laborer, is subdued to the service of man.
There is an allegorical suggestion of man's gradual conquest
and utilization of the forces of nature; but it is not clearly
realized and the general impression is confused. Despite passages of power and beauty, *The Titans* is the least excellent
and most difficult of Doughty's poems.

Meanwhile Doughty's intense patriotism and love of England—her past, her traditions, her greatness, her countryside—were leading him to take anxious thought for her immediate future. In politics he had adopted an idealistic Toryism
which attributed to other Conservatives a high-mindedness and
disinterestedness equal to his own. Of mere blatant imperialism
there is no trace in his thought; but, for all his long dwelling
in the East, he does not see eye to eye with such opponents
of British policy as his fellow traveller in Arabia, Wilfrid
Scawen Blunt. Doughty viewed with increasing alarm the growth
of German power and accepted as sincere, and as bound before
long to be put into practice, the enunciations of German world
policy. He came to believe that his mission was to arouse
England to an awareness of her imminent danger and to utter
a call to national service. In 1909 he published the dramatic
poem *The Cliffs,* and in 1912 its sequel, *The Clouds.* The first
of these was written while the earliest German dirigibles were
circling above Lake Constance. Doughty voices a passionate
prophecy of war's imminence and of the terrible part to be
played in it by the new astounding inventions of science. Few
things are stranger in literary history than the fulfillment of
this vision; not merely in such details as the actualities of
submarine and aerial warfare but in the clairvoyant sense of
the spirit of a people threatened with immolation—the horrors
of invasion, the confusion of an undisciplined country, the
realization of the world-shaking ambitions of the foe, the kin-
dling consciousness of the necessity of self-sacrifice. The theme
is the secret landing of German spies upon the coast of Kent
on the eve of war; the drama ends with the warding off of the
danger from overseas. The poet seems to have felt that the
warning was not sufficiently drastic; and in *The Clouds* he
depicts "War, invading war! in England's midst." With scathing satire he attacks in both poems the bungling and selfish
politicians in charge of England's destiny. Intense moral indignation and austere patriotism are combined with a naïve
belief in the absolute justice of his country's cause and the
utter malignity of her enemies. In both poems are many passages of great eloquence, such as the magnificent soliloquy of
old John Hobbe with which *The Cliffs* opens (perhaps the finest
lines in all Doughty's poetry); or the chant of the Sacred Band
with which the same poem closes; or the vision of the Muses'
Garden in *The Clouds.* Both poems are lightened and varied
by quaint and charming interludes in which, during the night
while the human actors sleep, the gnomes and dapper elves
come from their hiding-places to disport themselves and to
play their part in the protection of England. A whimsical and
tricksy fancy which one might not have associated with Doughty
save for odd hints in the *Arabia Deserta* creates in the fantastic
play of these sprites the very atmosphere of *A Midsummer
Night's Dream* and of *Nymphidia.* The scene of the elfin wedding is as pretty a bit of fairy poetry as is to be found in our
literature.

It remains to say something of the latest and noblest of Doughty's poems—*Mansoul; or the Riddle of the World;* though the
less need be said since it has secured comparatively wide recognition. All Doughty's life has been a spiritual quest, a cease-
less groping for light through the murkiness of the world. At

home, as in Arabia, he has pursued (in Pater's words) ''a dimly discerned mental journey.'' The sense of this is one of the many impressions made by a perusal of the *Arabia Deserta,* for, as Dr. Hogarth well says, ''reading Doughty's personal adventures, one feels him to be less an individual than a type of all his kind undergoing a certain trial of spirit'' [see Additional Bibliography]. Joseph of Arimathea and his companions are upon such a journey in which the blindly groping, woad-stained Britons join them. Adam, cast forth from Paradise, pursues his quest, as do the Dawn-Men who wage war against the Titans. Through the centuries Britain, ever groping, has followed the same quest; and the two prophetic war poems are appeals to the younger generation to persevere upon the path. *Mansoul* is yet another and more definite allegory of the way of the soul. The poet, Minimus, traveling in the company of Mansoul, enters the world of the dead and confronts the old prophets, sages, and founders of religions with the persistent question: ''What were indeed right paths of a man's feet?'' Zarathustra, Buddha, Confucius, and Socrates give answers characteristic of their thought, but all the sages bow in ignorance before the final mystery of death; and the words with which the poem closes and which ''abide, a Perfume, in our hearts,'' are those of Jesus: ''Fear ye not, little flock; God is Love.''

Mansoul contains many other elements. There are grand passages of Syrian and Arabian landscape. The elves and gnomes reappear at their graceful sports. And there is a vision of Man's City, a City which hath foundations, towards which humanity is painfully making its way. . . . It was in his lovely Kentish garden that I last saw Mr. Doughty; and as I call to mind the old poet's kindly eyes, his gentle voice, and serene bearing, and majestic head, he assumes the dignity of a type or abstract of all humanity, a stranger and pilgrim upon the road. (pp. 29-37)

Samuel C. Chew, ''The Poetry of Charles Montagu Doughty,'' in American Criticism, 1926, *edited by William A. Drake, Harcourt, Brace, and Company, Inc., 1926, pp. 19-37.*

JOHN MIDDLETON MURRY   (essay date 1926)

[*Murry is recognized as one of the most significant English critics and editors of the twentieth century. Anticipating later scholarly opinion, he championed the writings of Marcel Proust, James Joyce, Paul Valéry, D. H. Lawrence, and the poetry of Thomas Hardy through his positions as the editor of the* Athenaeum *and as a longtime contributor to the* Times Literary Supplement *and other periodicals. As with his magazine essays, Murry's book-length critical works are noted for their unusually impassioned tone and startling discoveries; such biographically centered critical studies as* Keats and Shakespeare: A Study of Keats' Poetic Life from 1816-1820 *(1925) and* Son of Woman: The Story of D. H. Lawrence *(1931) contain esoteric, controversial conclusions that have angered scholars who favor more traditional approaches. Nevertheless, Murry is cited for his perspicuity, clarity, and supportive argumentation. His early exposition on literary appreciation,* The Problem of Style *(1922), is widely revered as an informed guidebook for both critics and readers to employ when considering not only the style of a literary work, but its theme and viewpoint as well. In it Murry espouses a theoretical premise which underlies all his criticism: that in order to fully evaluate a writer's achievement the critic must search for crucial passages which effectively ''crystallize'' the writer's innermost impressions and convictions regarding life. In the following excerpt, Murry compares the differing philosophies of life conveyed by Doughty's early and later works.*]

In a grave and dignified review of Mr. Hogarth's *Arabia,* written not many months before his death, Charles Montagu Doughty once more described the grim country whose secret he had sought with so great suffering, wherein like Adam cast forth, of his own poem, he had wandered over desolate basaltic wastes till ''the thick warm salt living blood brast forth his nostrils.''

> The bulk of that huge peninsula [he wrote] lies within the earth's rainless belt. Under a perpetual grey more than blue heaven the immense upland is seen everywhere as a parched and bald treeless landscape, which to unwonted eyes seems to be nearly without herbage. Rain rarely falls, and that is always partial. Her drought and barrenness nourished few wild creatures; on man's pate beats all day a blazing sun, and seldom is there the relief of any overshadowing cloud.

—sentences heavy with reminiscence for minds which have endured the terrible and intoxicating experience of wrestling day after day with the immortal narrative of *Arabia Deserta;* and, for those who know well all Doughty's work, thrilled also with subtler correspondences. Not only is that ''overshadowing cloud'' the self-same which I AM for moments of brief mercy stretched over the face of the else immitigable sun, when Adam and Adama strove to pass that grisly region.

> Which wing not overflies; nor foot of beast
> Doth tread; vast Wasteness burned of the LORD's
> WRATH . . .

but over the austere rhythm of the final sentence hovers the memory of more opulent sonorities:

> Grave is that giddy heat upon the crown of the
> head; the ears tingle with a flickering shrillness,
> a subtle crepitation it seems, in the glassiness
> of this sun-stricken nature: the hot sand-blink
> is in the eyes, and there is little refreshment to
> find in the tents' shelter; the worsted booths
> leak to this fiery rain of sunny light.

Nearly fifty years lay between those two memories. The Doughty who wrote *Arabia Deserta* was a young man—the book over which he laboured so many years was published before he was forty; the Doughty who returned to literature in 1906 with an epic poem was an old one.

But the difference between those two memories is not at all the difference between prime and decline: there is a change, but not towards decrepitude. The touch is firm, and the hand full of cunning in the later picture as in the earlier; what has intervened is a change, or a sublimation, of temper. The strange immediacy of sensation which makes *Arabia Deserta* so overpowering has given way to a spiritual remoteness. The same things are remembered, yet how differently! Between *Arabia Deserta* and Doughty's subsequent writing there is a division which is almost a gulf. Though there were twenty-five years between *Arabia Deserta* and *The Dawn in Britain,* it is not a temporal division; though *Arabia Deserta* is prose and the rest of Doughty's writing poetry, it is not a division of literary kinds; it is a spiritual metamorphosis. In fact it must have been gradual; but in the long silence of twenty-five years there is nothing to prepare us, nothing to mediate by gentle transitions the sudden shock of his uncouth epic.

And, when we have meditated upon it, we begin to see how fortunate was the accident which gave us *Arabia Deserta*. In the nomad life of the inhospitable desert Doughty had found, by a premonitory instinct, the only human society he could accept. When he went to the Arab peninsula he was driven, scarce consciously, by the impulse to struggle his way backward through time away from the works of modern man; and he all but died in the effort. Why, we ask ourselves again and again, as we read his story, does he stay? Why does not he escape? The inscriptions that were his nominal excuse meant little or nothing to him; there was no thought of profit, none even of "experience." He was there, he knew not why nor how; for the cause lay deeper than his consciousness. If he was to live active in the world of men, it was among such men that he must live, men who believed fiercely and loved and hated simply—men who were truly of one substance with the earth wherein they lived. He stayed among them to the moment when, if he stayed longer, he would have died, because it was a real world to him: in it he *lived*. In it were men and women he understood and who understood him, and his pictures of them have a direct Homeric truth. In the pages of *Arabia Deserta* the society of men among whom he could *live* lives again. When that book was finished Doughty's work was over: he had done perfectly what no other man could have done at all; he had carved an enduring image of a simple Semitic people whose hate was more real to him than a European's love.

After many years *The Dawn in Britain* appeared. It was an epic on the grand pattern in twenty-four books, telling of men and gods and godlike men. But Doughty had already written his epic. The Arab and Beduwy with whom he had lived were real men; he had had but to describe them as he had known them. Not so with his primitive Britons, who were the work of his imagination. His Arabs live, his Celts do not. *Arabia Deserta* has the actuality of Homer; *The Dawn in Britain* is, after all, wholly artificial. So, one might say, is the *Aeneid*. But, first, the world of Aeneas was by no means so remote from Virgil as that of Caractacus from Doughty; second, Virgil used his story as the means by which every tremor of a subtle consciousness might find expression; and, third, he was creating at once a new poetry and a new language. So Doughty himself in *Arabia Deserta* had struck new fires out of the English speech; he is fanatical, but not in his language. In *The Dawn in Britain* his fanaticism has invaded his art.

Whatever the language of *Arabia Deserta* may be, it is not primitive: it has the richness of a fine eclecticism and a sure sense of propriety. To secure his effects Doughty freely chose the finest tools. But by the time he had begun to write poetry he had become possessed by a theory of diction, derived not from any consideration of the language itself, but wholly from moral prepossessions. In Spenser, he held, English had reached its brief perfection, and in him already had begun to decline. Chaucer he could with an effort accept, but he could never mention him without heaving a sigh over the broadness of Geoffrey's humour. But with these two men the English language began and ended for Doughty the poet. Such a phrase as "a subtle crepitation" became impossible to him.

There may seem to have been a certain wisdom in his deliberate archaism. He had determined to write of early Britons: then why not use the English language when it is nearest to its simplicity, yet still an English language? Perhaps it was with some such argument that Doughty first persuaded himself; but it is an argument which forgot that when Spenser himself was writing he was using all the resources of language as freely as

Doughty himself had done in his prose. A poet cannot deny himself this freedom if his imaginations are to be made real. But, in Doughty, the distinction between asceticism of spirit and self-denial in the use of language seems to have been obliterated; moreover, he had come to regard himself as a man with a mission, to restore to a degenerate nation the virtues and the speech of olden time.

Doughty's poetry, in conception and in diction, is the poetry of a fanatic; the spirit, which had served him so well by steeling him to endure extreme hardship in the desert at nature's hands and men's, now hardened within him. In Arabia, and in writing of it, he had expanded; now he contracted. There is in all his poetry an intense patriotism, but it is a patriotism which loves an ideal England and abhors the actual; the bitterness in his denunciations of the democratic polity is vitriolic, and it has a defect graver than its mere excess; it is repellent even to those who might share his aversion because it shows clearly that, if Doughty could have had his way, he would have replaced democracy by something worse—a rigid and tyrannous theocracy. For in his imagination God and England were one, precisely as God and Israel were one to the Jews of old; and in *The Cliffs* . . . he pushes his idea relentlessly to the point of savagery. In that poem the image of "Sancta Britannia" is precisely as the idol of a savage tribe; with the decay of the warrior spirit it languishes, with the revival under stress of invasion of the berserk mood it regains power; but even at the last the image remains blindfold. The veil can be removed from its eyes only by the hands of the only child of a young widow, and the child must die the moment its fingers touch the veil. And the child is sacrificed accordingly, as Mesha, King of Moab, slew his eldest son. Doughty had come to be unconscious of the distinction between patriotism and Moloch worship; and, more strangely still, he makes the horrible imagination worse by putting forward a chorus of elves who promise to the mother, while she holds the murdered baby in her arms,

> She widow shall not want, whilst elves can work:
> We would we might, in honey of wild bees,
> Embalm her blossom babe; whose little mound
> Will elves each summer night bestrew with flowers . . .

The man who could make fairies condone that inhuman sacrifice had become estranged from the spirit of the country he loved: his zeal had eaten him up.

To the rigour and perversity of his mind inevitably corresponded a rigour and perversity in his use of language: he became not merely archaistic, but insensitive and tyrannous. With a kind of frenzied implacability he would torture English syntax and compel words to do his bidding. Scarcely can a page be found of his poetry without lines of this kind:

> No more I knew: under a flag of truce
> Gathered at day the fallen were; and when us
> The surgeons had inspected one by one;
> I on the dead-cart was 'mongst soldiers dead
> Laid; and that driven then to the grave-trench was.
> There on the brinks those, shrouded in their cloaks
> White with night-rime, were in long rows, outlaied.

It is no use mincing words: that is something worse than idiosyncrasy; and it is never far away in Doughty's poetry. Sometimes the effect, if we can regard it in complete detachment, is comic (. . . burst were the water and gas Mains): but for the most part the manner is too much of a piece with the matter to permit such facile relief. Doughty is terribly humourless—

it is never easy to laugh at a man whom one can never laugh with.

No criticism of his work would be adequate which did not insist that his poetry, in content and form alike, is of a lower order than *Arabia Deserta:* from beginning to end, save for one remarkable exception, it is warped. It is the poetry of a sectary, of a man of intense and narrow genius, who had once, and once for all, breathed a full breath among his semblables. The life that he had lived he rendered again: he lavished himself on the one human reality he had loved. The completeness of *Arabia Deserta* is narrow; but it is an absolute completeness; within those amazing pages is a universe, simple, primeval, but one where men are born and have their being and are gathered to their fathers. And Doughty's one great poem sprang directly from his experience of that eternal world. *Adam Cast Forth* is in essence a sublime simplification of all that he lived and learned in the Arabian desert. There he had become as the first man; under that implacable sun he had been as it were dissolved away into an elemental essence of mortality, he had become the I AM of man, the plaything yet the equal of his own ineffable but jealous God. If the pure sublime has ever been achieved in English poetry it is achieved in *Adam Cast Forth:* for in it man and God become almost indistinguishable in majesty, yet not, as in Milton, with a diminution of God. Man the creature is lifted up to his Creator. Again and again Doughty challenges Milton, and comes away, if not victorious, completely without scathe. Milton's glory of language is counterpoised by Doughty's intensity of realization. When Adam tells the story of the Fall, and says simply: "Then God was weary of us," the effect is overpowering: one feels that in those six words is somehow crammed a vision of the whole of human destiny. And Doughty can meet Milton at the very pinnacle of his own perfection: he dares to rewrite Eve's encounter with her own mirrored image. Here is the Milton:

> I thither went
> With unexperienced thought, and laid me down
> On the green bank, to look into the clear
> Smooth lake, that to me seemed another sky.
> As I bent down to look, just opposite
> A shape within the wat'ry gleam appeared,
> Bending to look upon me. I started back;
> It started back: but pleased I soon returned;
> Pleased it return'd as soon with answering looks
> Of sympathy and love; there had I fix'd
> Mine eyes till now, and pined with vain desire
> Had not a voice thus warned me. What thou seest,
> What there thou seest, fair Creature, is thyself.

All the resources of Milton's art are in motion there. What can Doughty do against it? This is what he does:

> Therein I saw then, like an heavenly vision,
> Some Being more even than art thou O Adamu fair!
> The appearance of an Angel, that I knew not:
> Which, whilst I looked, seemed woman. I outstretched
> Mine hand: she likewise hand put forth toward mine.
>   Down, at the water's brink, to view more near
> This thing, I kneeled: she kneeled! I gazed upon her
> I laughed, I spake: she laughed then, but not spake.
> And in her other hand were fruits as these,
> And flowers like to mine. Surprised mine heart,
>   I startling leapt; and plashed therein my foot.
>   Marred then the image was: she fled, alas!
>   I saw her not again; though I descended
>   To seek her, in the pool.

There is not in this the opulent, sensuous loveliness of the Milton; the rhythm, as ever in Doughty, is harsher and more abrupt: and yet Doughty exists, even beside Milton, sovereign in his own right. Doughty's Adama is not the equal of Milton's Eve, of course; but neither is Milton's Adam the equal of Doughty's Adamu.

Let us leave the swaying issue, remembering that *Adam Cast Forth* is not Doughty's epic poem. Would it had been! It is simply a poem of a little over a hundred pages, intense and sublime, written out of the knowledge of one who had been driven from oasis into desert and stumbled back to an earthly Eden again. Was it, we wonder, simply because Milton had preceded him, that Doughty sought his subject in ancient Britain? If it was, we have lost a masterpiece through a misconception; what Adamu might have been Milton did not know, and Doughty did. But he turned aside and plunged into the misty beginnings of these islands—a long, vague, intricate story which he, who had little or no architectonic gift, could not control. As we wander through its tortuous passages we have frequent glimpses of loveliness and grandeur: loveliness as in the tale of Crispin and Ogygia in Book I, or of Elsa and Cloten in Book III, or the fleeting pictures of England's graciousness which are given only to be snatched away, as this of the arrival of the Christians in England:

> Behold new birth of the long dying night,
> How day, with cheerful face, is springing wide!
> Sounds, of small fowl, the mingled sweet consent
> From river-brinks, of Britain's underwoods,
> Warbling God's love, among their leafy bowers.
> On trembling, lightsome, wings blithe lav'rock mounts.
> With *iss-iss!* shrill, sheen swallows flit aloft;
> And chants, from thicket-grove, lone nightingale.
> And golden bees borne-by, on dawn's sweet breath,
> To dewy hills. Hark cushots, sobbing soft.
> Like unto bride seems this fair land adorned.

Within the ruggedness of their surroundings such lines as these seem soft and gentle; but they also have in them an unrelenting rigour, a rhythmical austerity that reminds us that even the fairies of this poet's imagination smile upon blood-sacrifice. Yet Doughty was fond of fairies: they appear in both *The Cliffs* and *The Clouds;* but they are the fairies not of the delighted fancy, but of some queer theology, sisters to daemons, daughters of principalities and powers, unbending ministers of Doughty's grim tribal god. We are told they dance, we never feel they dance; we are told they sing, we never hear them singing. These are a new kind of fairies in whom one must believe on pain of excommunication, or worse, who would not pinch us black and blue, but torture us with red-hot pincers.

Doughty's real poetic splendours are not to be found in such passages as these, not even in a passage of loveliness so sustained as the Muses' garden with which *The Clouds* opens; they are grim and grey, and pass almost unperceived, yet they shine with a strange solemnity, like the dark glint on steel. Such is this description of the morning after a storm on the Christians' voyage to England:

> Though long be, till crude winter season change,
>   Dear to the saints, are their seafaring days;
> .Wherein new birth and childhood of their lives.
> Fair is that fleeting fullness of the seas,
>   In whose round molten bosom their keel rides.
> Falls now the storm, and sleep grey dapple waves:

Or these like fallows, and much furrowed field.
Whose springing blade is wallowed of the wind.
And aye sea's infinite bruit is in their ears,
Like to an everlasting voice of God. . . .

In still grimmer vein is this brief glimpse of the Pillars of Hercules:

They see, where their keel fleets, thick bedded ribs:
(Clothed with long tangle-locks, of wild sea-wrack,
And shells,) of many drowned and broken ships:
And under rumbling caves strewed the white sand,
With skulls and dreary bones of mariners;
That to and fro, washed in cold-sliding billows,
Do make their everlasting moan, to God.

Such sudden things as these, and they are many, are high poetry indeed. But Doughty, who could never have become a little poet, lacked two things necessary to the great one: comprehensiveness of mind and a receptive sensibility. We feel that, after his great book, he ceased to experience; he had taken one long gulp at the cup of life that was offered him in his youth and drained it to the lees. It was never refilled for him, or if it was he put it away from him like a desert anchorite. What he had known and suffered was life to him, and there was no other. The primeval struggle of man against the elements—this was real and true: the rest of life was an ugly and evil dream. He set his face and shut his heart against it. There is something magnificent in the indomitable spirit of this lonely hero who, like Ajax in the Underworld, stalks away and will not speak; and his unbending spirit is in the steely monotony of his verse. Doughty had received his revelation, once for all, in the Arabian desert: to it nothing might be added, from it nothing taken away. (pp. 104-14)

> John Middleton Murry, ''Charles Montagu Doughty,'' in his Countries of the Mind: Essays in Literary Criticism, first series, *revised edition, Books for Libraries Press, 1968; distributed by Arno Press, Inc., pp. 104-14.*

ANNE TRENEER (essay date 1935)

[*Treneer was an English poet, autobiographer, and critic. In the following excerpt, she discusses Doughty's prose and poetry, focusing on his ideas about the English language that led to his archaic style.*]

The fame of C. M. Doughty has been circumscribed by the very merits of his first book. *Travels in Arabia Deserta* is so completely achieved that it has a kind of anonymity, an independent life of its own as though it never had an author. Yet in another sense it has swallowed up its author's name, since *Arabia Deserta* and Doughty have become synonyms, and it is felt almost as an affront that he should have written anything else. Nothing else could be so good. There is a natural shrinking, a fear of an anticlimax in approaching other work by any author of a book peculiarly loved; and this fear is intensified in the case of Doughty, whose other work consists of poems, and long poems at that. The thought of long poems makes the heart sink.

But once the reluctance to begin is overcome, and the shortest of the poems, *Adam Cast Forth,* is read, fear is lost in the recognition that here again is something which has become itself, separate and complete, with an integral life of its own. One is encouraged to read the other poems, and then to explore what is known of Doughty's life and intention. Then it becomes clear that poetry was primarily his aim; that *Travels in Arabia Deserta,* not *The Dawn of Britain* was incidental to his plan. This does not mean that *The Dawn in Britain* is necessarily the better piece of writing; the demon that controls pens is unaccountable, and is often better provoked by accident than purpose. But it does mean that Doughty's work as a whole needs to be viewed in the perspective he himself intended; and it was on poetry he was bent, and the right use of words. (pp. 11-12)

His experiment with words is especially interesting in our own time when many are conscious of the exhaustion of common English, and seeking a remedy for it. Doughty is not so much their forerunner as an unregarded individualist who solved in his own way the problem they are attacking. Although he was born in 1843, only six years after Queen Victoria came to the throne, he hated what came to be known as Victorian English, and fought against it unremittingly from the time he left Cambridge in 1865 until he died in 1926. (p. 12)

[Doughty] cared for words. There are few experiences more conducive to humility and at the same time more exhilarating than to go over his manuscript notes—covering a time soon after he left Cambridge to the time of his death—and to feel the integrity of a workman in letters. He gave much of his life to the study of words. But he studied them in his own peculiar way, his idiosyncrasy is felt in his very method. Anything more unlike a professional philologist than Doughty can hardly be imagined; his aim was different. He sought words and studied their history not to formulate the laws of their relationship but to decide which were good sound words to use. Not that he shunned theories altogether. That a knowledge of philology is an aid to good writing is itself a theory, and in the eyes of many a pernicious one. Doughty's knowledge of words is an amateur's knowledge—''amateur'' being used in a good sense. He had an interest that penetrated into odd corners and his knowledge was come by in so individual a way as to form part of the colour of his character. He was a private scholar with the private scholar's pleasure in starting hares. Had he not, in addition to his theories about words, had a poet's sensibility to, and perception of, what he was to call ''the glory of the world''?—

. . . he saw, again, then
Glory of the world,

he was to write of a man dying reluctant—he might easily have become one of the many Englishmen of his kind who spend their lives coursing after some stubbornly held theory, and filling the library shelves with the results of their chase. Any catalogue of books yields some spoil of this sport—very curious, pleasant spoil in the eyes of some people—*The Effect of the Mis-use of Familiar Words on the Character of Men and the Fate of Nations,* by David Urquhart, for example.

As it is, there is a trace of the eccentric investigator in Doughty's work which has prejudiced some clear minds against him. Like David Urquhart, whose book was published in 1856, just at the time when Doughty was refused for the navy, he held that the English of his day, and the mode of thinking which the preponderant use of abstract terms implied, was thoroughly bad. Urquhart, who had been much in the East, praised the concrete qualities of Turkish, and contrasted with it unfavourably the generalities too current in English. He relates that he told an English politician how a man had befriended him in the East because of the bread and salt between them, and the politician said, ''Hospitality is the concomitant of barbarism.'' Doughty may or may not have read Urquhart; but it was language of this kind which helped him to decide that his work in life would be to help towards a better understanding and use of the mother tongue. He studied words no less as a moralist than as a poet, believing that the right use of vital language was essential to the health of individuals and nations. "Words are almost the elements of human thoughts," he wrote in his Notes; and on another page he jotted, "The old manly English, full of pith and stomach." One of the duties of a poet was to preserve the elements from decay, and keep the notation clear, warring against loose use of words as a thing perilous to thought and feeling, and as an insidious means to undermine the inegrity of individual persons and finally of whole peoples.

For a poet to fulfil his duty towards language in the nineteenth century he must, Doughty considered, study the language of the past. Accordingly, three years after leaving Cambridge, during which little is known of his movements, we find him working as a private scholar in the Bodleian library and concerned wholly with the study of English literature. A list of some of the books ordered by him in the Bodleian is printed in the Appendix at the close of Hogarth's *Life;* and in addition Doughty's extracts from his reading have been preserved. It is a strange experience to go through these extracts, written by an eager student in his youth, and to see underlined words and phrases which were to find new life in his own creative work; words, for example, like *smell-feast* from the sixteenth-century Latin-English dictionary of Sir Thomas Elyot. *Smell-feast* was a word with the right flavour to attach to the Beduin lad who looked in at the casement upon the "mighty trays of victual" provided for breakfast by the rich host at ed-Doeh. Doughty remembered it from Elyot, from a definition he had copied out together with many others in the days when he was a student in the Bodleian. He liked dictionaries. He knew the fascination of words as mere words; he studied their origin and relationships; but above all he studied their use in the English writers up to the beginning of the seventeenth century. He learnt old English by reading Latin-Saxon versions of the Psalms and Gospels. There are long extracts in his notes from the Anglo-Saxon *Chronicle,* and from Aelfric's *Glossaries;* and Doughty's own glossaries have been preserved. He read Middle English, especially Chaucer, the lyrics, *Piers Plowman* and Gavin Douglas, whose *Æneid* he admired; and he was widely read in early Tudor and Elizabethan literature, especially Skelton and Spenser. He studied particularly the drama and sermons, where the written word comes nearest to the spoken.

Through his close study of medieval and of sixteenth and seventeenth century writing he came, I think, to a clearer comprehension of the effect of the Renaissance on the vernacular languages and on thought than was common among the scholars of his time. Mr. Ezra Pound has well summed up the profit and loss of the Renaissance: "What the Renaissance gained in direct examination of natural phenomena, it in part lost in losing the feel of and desire for exact descriptive terms." In some ways Doughty was a very son of the Renaissance, particularly in his instinct for the direct examination of natural phenomena, in which he is rather the heir of Bacon than of the Middle Ages; he is at one with the great Renaissance scholars, too, in his enthusiasm for his country and his fervour. He had read Du Bellay's *La Défense et Illustration* and copied out the famous passage beginning "Qui veult voler par les mains et bouches des hommes." But with this passionate devoting of himself to the cause of writing his likeness to Du Bellay ends. In his ideas about language he is the opposite of the Renaissance poet. Whereas Du Bellay would extend vocabulary and swell the vulgar tongue with terms borrowed from the classics, steal-

ing from the ancients to enrich the present, Doughty would go back beyond this period of expansion, and contract the flow in order to regain definiteness and exactitude. His idea was to make a fresh channel for English direct from the upper reaches, from the vernacular as it was before the Renaissance, and so freshen and purify the corrupt main flood. Most of the words he tried to revive—especially the words he revived in prose—fell out of use between the time of Wyclif and Purvey's translation of the Bible and the Authorized Version. Not that the revival of obsolete words is of main importance in Doughty's experiment. Much more important is his scrutiny of known words, and his close fitting of word to sense. He did not fall into what Bacon calls the first disease of learning, that men hunt words rather than matter; but neither did he neglect the warning of his favourite Ascham, "Ye know not what hurt ye do to learning, that care not for words but for matter, and so make a divorce betwixt the tongue and the heart." (pp. 15-19)

Nowhere in [Doughty's] letters which relate to his own prose and verse does he express so clearly what it was he sought in words as in his chance remarks about the diction of Arabia. What he yearned to do himself may be divined from what he praises in others. He liked the "perspicuous propriety" of good Arabic, but it must be united with "quick significance." Words must get to the heart of the matter. He detested Abdullah of Kheybar, and with good reason; but he praised his stories. In him he said, "was that round kind of utterance of the Arabic coffee-drinkers, with election of words, and dropping with the sap of a human life." He praised, too, the young man of Shuggera, who told tales while he twisted bast and made strands. "He put life in his words, as a juggler can impress his will on some inert matter." He knew that their art was learnt not from books but from life; their tales were "of the marrow of human experience," the tales of men who were unlettered yet wise in speech and practised. The coffee-gatherings were as a school for them. There, apart from the women (with the hareem, says Doughty, they had no "reasonable fellowship"), they met and discoursed; and these gatherings were as a school of infinite observation where they learned to "speak to the heart of one another." The power to "speak to the heart of one another" was in common speech, and in the prose "taling" with which the Arabs whiled away the long hours. The Arabic rhyming poets were held by Doughty in less regard. The only remark he makes of them which had relation to his own poetic style is that they used a language quite apart from the popular speech. "There are," he said, "turns and terms of the herdsmen poets of the desert which are dark or unknown in any form to the townling Syrians." For the most part the endless spinning of the rhymers wearied him. [Doughty's] attitude towards verse and scholarship in Arabia is an amusing contrast to his attitude towards those same things in England. In Arabia he laughed at them; in England he praised them. In Arabia he was in the position of the man in the street. He was not bookish. He never wearied of praising the easy speech of the Beduw and placing it above the school-taught language. His whole reliance was on the current spoken word. He told the Italian scholar who had turned Moslem, and was making a pilgrimage to Mecca, that he could never find better than a headache in the farrago of the Koran. The more the Italian exalted the Scriptures and dispraised the easy babble-talk of the Arab the more Doughty supported the one and belittled the other. This is amusing as coming from a man who was to rely so much in his own prose on the language of the Bible and to praise unweariedly the 'antique tongue' of his own nation. Some criticism of his own diction in later days might be taken as a nemesis on him for his light-hearted dismissal of the Italian's school Arabic.

But it is easy to see that although there is a surface difference in this matter between Doughty in Arabia and Doughty in England, the two are fundamentally consistent. Current English and current Arabic were, he considered, at two different stages. The qualities to be found in the best Arabic speakers were to be sought not in current English, but in the English of Chaucer, a copy of whose *Canterbury Tales* he carried with him into Arabia. He buried some of his books when he found his baggage an intolerable burden, but he kept his Chaucer; and when he reached India after his long pilgrimage one of his first actions was to write to the Secretary of the Asiatic Society for the loan of the volumes of Chaucer other than the *Canterbury Tales*. He agreed that Chaucer sometimes spoke "full broad"—though the markings in his copy show that it was not the *Parson's Tale* he enjoyed most himself; but he reverenced in Chaucer "the justness and directness . . . which touches men's hearts," and the "diligent searching out and observation of natural human things." To Chaucer, he said, belonged the secrets of humanity, but to Spenser it was given to know the harmony of the spheres.

Doughty came home from Arabia with the theories about language, which he had cherished before he went out, grown only the stronger; and he was ready now to put them into practice. He was not yet prepared to write his long poem, but he had abundant other matter to express, and more than an inkling of the way in which he would express it. He returned to England in 1879, when he was thirty-six, after wandering for nine years. For the rest of his life he was a writer, spending the winters in Italy until 1898, after which he made his permanent home in England. He first wrote an account of his Arabian travels in prose which appeared in 1888. In letters he set out explicitly his aim. Writing to D. G. Hogarth in 1902 he said:

> In writing the volumes *Arabia Deserta* my main intention was not so much the setting forth of personal wanderings among a people of Biblical interest, as the ideal endeavour to continue the older tradition of Chaucer and Spenser, resisting to my power the decadence of the English language: so that whilst my work should be the mere verity for orientalists, it should also be my life's contribution so far to literature.

Again in 1913:

> The *Arabia Deserta* volumes had necessarily a personal tone. A principal cause of writing them was, besides the interest of the Semitic life in tents, my dislike of Victorian English; and I wished to show, and thought I might be able to show, that there was something else.
>
> (pp. 23-6)

With the exception of one or two short articles Doughty wrote no more prose after *Arabia Deserta*. He was free now to be a poet. He first made the poem which had been at the back of his mind since 1865; it was an epic dealing with the history of Britain during about 450 years, from the taking of ancient Rome by the Gauls to the destruction of Jerusalem by Titus; the language being, as nearly as he could make it, of the days of Spenser. The making of this poem took many years. It appeared in six volumes (twenty-four books), 1906-7, when Doughty was just over sixty. He published five more poems: *Adam Cast Forth*, 1908; *The Cliffs*, 1909; *The Clouds*, 1912; *The Titans*, 1916; and *Mansoul*, 1920. In 1923 he issued a revised edition of *Mansoul*, and was engaged on further re-

vision up to the time of his death in 1926. The diction of his poetry varies in different poems and in different parts of the same poem, but in all he followed the practice of the Arabic rhymers and of Spenser in using a language differing from the language of prose.

The poetry, in spite of the efforts of Mr. Edward Garnett, the first to delight in it, and of other staunch admirers, has made much less progress in public regard and affection than the prose. It is a pity; for whereas parts of *Arabia Deserta* can only be fully appreciated by experts like Hogarth, the poetry could be received into the hearts and minds of all people. It has a universal appeal, although a too prolonged reading of the successive volumes refreshes a taste for Byron. One yearns for something flippant, or something without too much sense in it; something dashed off happily, something to make us laugh out; careless, sudden, rushing along; something unstudied; a muse not on the lead. Doughty is consistent and moral, not governed by his moods, and sometimes we look for what is heady if not first rate. Then, the manner of his verse is always likely to revive an ancient controversy. There will always be some to maintain that Doughty, like Spenser, in copying the ancients, "writ no language"; recently we have been able to hear the voice of Gerard Manley Hopkins, who did not live to see Doughty's verse, and probably tasted the prose only in extracts, raised emphatically against the principle of archaism. While admitting that Victorian English is a bad business, he "cannot away with any form of archaism" or any diction "sicklied o'er" with Elizabethan English. "But come now," he writes to Bridges who had recommended *Arabia Deserta*, "is it not affectation to write obsolete English? You know it is." What Hopkins could not realize was that Doughty was engaged on a process for which the word "archaism" as applied, say, to the poetry of William Morris, is unsuitable. Yet it was a process possessing its own dangers of which Doughty himself was aware, since he wrote in his Notes, "All art is harmony"; and on the same slip he jotted, "handiwork"; "skill of instruments"; "of rare device"; "to fashion Adam"; "Ah art is a manner, an affectation; an eclectic.". . . But Doughty's manner cannot be considered apart from the matter which gave it birth, or apart from his generating imagination which could create, not merely furbish up a myth, and which also led him, in an age dominated by the short poem, to choose the grand form. The very largeness of his endeavour gives vigour and nobility and breadth to his achievement. He is something more than a private poet. From what at first glance seems an especially idiosyncratic style he is able to rise to an impersonal beauty, to poetry beside which the work of some of his contemporaries sounds provincial or improvised. He could get the authentic ring. (pp. 28-30)

Anne Treneer, "Introductory: Doughty's Attitude as a Writer," in her Charles M. Doughty: A Study of His Prose and Verse, *Jonathan Cape, 1935, pp. 11-30.*

BARKER FAIRLEY (essay date 1935)

[*Fairley was an English-born Canadian educator and critic. In the following excerpt, he contends that despite archaisms of diction and syntax, Doughty's use of language in his poetry was innovative and modern.*]

Doughty seems to have been quite unaware of his own modernity. Rejecting all Victorian standards of literature he went back into Elizabethan English, Pre-Elizabethan, Anglo-Saxon, even Dutch and Danish in his passion to find a world and a vocabulary that suited him. His whole life might be interpreted and has been interpreted as an escape into the dark backward, into the world of early man, into the world before man. At every turn he seems to look behind—further, more consistently, it may be, than anyone, but always behind. His ramifications, literary and historical, are astonishing.

Yet he ended by doing a new thing and becoming a "modern" in spite of himself. Those who have commented on him thus far have been struck more by his unlikeness to his avowed master, Spenser, than by his likeness, more by the novelty, the drastic novelty, of his style than by his conformity to any tradition; and all readers will find that when the first archaic impressions are dissipated and his verse becomes familiar the sense of what is radically new in it asserts itself with growing strength and shows him finally in a sharp contemporary light. (p. 128)

In Doughty, the spatial, visual, physical sense of metre—as opposed to the more exclusively musical—seems to be stronger than in any other English poet, making him care more than others for the opportunity that metre affords him of arranging significant words in significant positions—at beginnings and ends, closely joined or widely separated. Rhythm and music he has in plenty; he can write orthodox lines with the best, whether it be to describe a love-sick swain sprinkling flowers in a brook, all amorous and swooning.

> And, as they mingle, or those swimming blooms
> Be sunder drawn; so rise his hopes and wane,

or elephants pulling a plough, all massive and stubborn.

> Lo, garlanded Claudius' sacred plough, with flowers,
> Whose glittering share draw, yoked instead of beves,
> With slow foot forth, huge Afric elephants.

But this is not what we read Doughty for; behind the impulse that seems to dictate this sort of line is a stronger, deeper, more pervasive one which gives his poetry its unique character.... For illustration I would prefer to instance the six volumes of *The Dawn in Britain* in full, since it is only in this extended way that a new epic style can be acquired and appraised; but something of its underlying quality will appear in these lines describing the leading of Caradoc and other captives from their Roman dungeon to the place of execution.

> Behold then, on set day, those Royal Britons,
> Sad, squalid, chained, are lifted, bleak of hew,
> Up, from that dreadful lower prison-pit,
> Of Servius Tullius; (which, four-paces deep,
> Is ceiled with stone, beneath the Roman street;)
> Into sun's blissful ray, to march, from weight
> Of night, to death.

Here it is the positioning of the significant words rather than any metrical skill . . . that gives the lines their strength; the spacing-out of "Britons," "up," "into,'" the obstructing relative clause, then the proximity of "sun" and "death"; all of these are essentially effects of position. Rhythm and music, the management of feet and stresses, play their part, but it is a smaller part and it explains less. Metre is used here less to submerge words than to isolate them, less to speed them than to slow them down and it is when words are isolated and slowed-down in this way that the spatial sense asserts itself.

It is the same in these very simple lines describing Adam as first seen in *Adam Cast Forth*

>   I behold,
> (Out of the Tempest, is he fallen down,
> In mountain border of murk HARISUTH)
> Adam, blind, bowed together: blackened is
> His visage and his flesh.

Here is a deliberate parenthesis, separating verb and object and palpably setting Adam at a distance, followed by the huddling together of "blind, bowed together: blackened." Again the power of the lines can be better analysed physically than musically, though the music is not lacking; and, similarly, in this description of a woman-archer shooting it is the physical act that breaks the rhythm and, as it were, forces its way through the words.

> She, priestess, murmuring, vows the foes of Brennus,
> To gods of death: so swart-winged scudding shaft,
> To her bow-string fits; draws, and she it loost forth,

while for a more violent singling-out and juxtaposing and wrenching asunder of words there are these lines from Doughty's tale of the wars of gods and giants

> Reeled earth's wide mould, sunk, neath gods' mighty tread.
> They Titans smote: and had of them just gods,
> Full vengeance. Giants, gods, in the meres, thus made,
> To the everlasting ground-rocks, left then, chained.

It will be apparent from these instances that in spite of his having written almost exclusively in blank verse and in an archaic vocabulary the basic principle of his writing is radically new or at least radically modified and must be accepted as such, especially in dealing with his excesses of style. It is a principle which Hopkins, alone of Doughty's contemporaries, may give a hint of now and then, but there is no question of his adopting it. This was left for Doughty who with quite extraordinary courage and force of character used it consistently from first to last and left his poetry to stand or fall by it.

It is easy to see that the change of sensibility which we find in Doughty brings poetry nearer than before to the visual arts, to sculpture and to painting—though not in any easy pictorial sense. Not only is there an inviting comparison to be made between *Adam Cast Forth* with its elemental speech-accents and the primitive sculpture that the twentieth century has unearthed and imitated; a significant affinity has been suggested . . . between Doughty and Cézanne—an affinity which, if it can be upheld, serves the very welcome purpose of placing Doughty more firmly with contemporaries in the modern world, Cézanne being only four years his senior.

In one respect the comparison is convincing. Just as after a picture of the Cézanne school all other pictures seem to lie—two-dimensional—on the surface of their canvases and to have either no depth at all or else a spurious depth, so after a spell with Doughty all other poets seem to merge and dissolve their words and to destroy that solidness and separateness which is a vital part of their character. In Doughty the significant words seem to stand out in relief against their metrical bed; so that as we read we are startled again and again by the sight of simple things rather than by the sound of simple words. It may be "sea-waves" or "olive-beam" or "clay" or "grass" or "brink" or "bruised," the words come round and full with a force that no traditional prosody can explain. No other English poet has managed to use words in this way.

It is here rather than in any theory of poetry that the key to Doughty's way of writing must be sought; he has an extraordinary word-sense—a sense of words separate and self-contained, quite unlike the groups and fusions of words that we call Shakespearean, and he devotes his whole art to the exercise of this gift. It was not for arbitrary reasons that Doughty wrote so differently from his contemporaries; it was because he had a different, a more elemental word-sense and had no choice but to submit to it. His technique fits it exactly and is the outcome of it. Poetry, he reminds us, is made of words first and last—words which we may blend or separate, flood with rhythm or lift high and dry out of rhythm. Nothing matters for poetry, as distinct from prose of the utilitarian sort, save to release the virtue, the lost or unsuspected power, the rare, the added qualities that reside in words, in words joined or separated. To make words rhythmical is one way of poetry, to make them unrhythmical may be another; it all depends on the sensibility of the author and the virtue in words which he proposes to release. Poetry is not rhythm, it is "making words do things." Rhythm is one of the resources, a chief resource, a necessary resource, of poetry, but it is not the basis of it. Poetry is words, it is built with words.

No English poet reminds us of this with Doughty's force and in one respect it is a timely reminder and once more shows Doughty in a contemporary light. In his hands words, when he chooses, become primal and young again and affect us as if they were being used by him for the first time, even his most archaic words taking on this new and underivative character. It is not enough that Doughty should write of Adam without involving Milton, that he should write some of the things that Milton wrote—Eve's first sight of her reflection in the water or Adam's prophetic vision of war—as if there had never been a Milton; he writes without becoming so much as Biblical. He seems to come before the Authorized Version, not after it, and to reach back into an older mentality, as in that passage in which Eve or Adama, as he calls her, sees death for the first time and Adam comments on it

> I have seen death; birds fugitive and fleet beasts,
> By crooked lightnings, smitten to Earth's dust.
> Those fell and moved no more: but stink came up,
> As blackness, from their earth. Fly we from death.

Or in this brief statement of autumn in the early world

> Earth's fruit hangs ruddy on the weary bough;
> In all the fallow field, the bearded herb,
> Stands sere, and ripeneth seed: fall russet leaves
> Cumbering clear brooks, which bitter flow thereof.

Here signally it is the choice of the key-words for autumn that matters. There is no trick of rhythm, none of the ordinary dexterities. Yet such is Doughty's art that he almost persuades us that we have only to hit on the right word, the Sesame, for autumn, and autumn, the vision of autumn, will come; and both here and in Adam's words on death and prevailingly throughout the poem, whether in its bare humanities or in its pictures of desert and oasis, the words are stripped of literary allusiveness, of clustered reminiscence, of age and wornness and triteness—in short, of all the diseases that infest the vocabulary of the modern poet. In *The Dawn in Britain* the radiant words leap out of every page and in their larger context disturb us with their energy.

> Joyous, on her bright wings, that heavenly maid
> Leapt forth. She stooped, soon, from her aery voyage,
> Runs-on, like partridge, in earth's green hill-sides.

The strong words seem to come single and intact and to catch the reader's or the listener's mind before they have spent their force on one another, involving him strenuously in what they say and do, drawing him into their life and their creativeness, instead of teasing him intellectually with their ambiguities.

Apart from Doughty poetry is at the other extreme; its words are so rubbed with usage, so scored and dinted with the past, so full of associations and memories of one sort or another that poetry after thriving on this condition for generations has now been brought almost to a standstill by it. It is as if poetry itself were getting worn out. Mr. T. S. Eliot, it is clear, has only succeeded in wresting another vital poem from the language—*The Waste Land*—by frankly accepting this aged allusiveness in the words and phrases at his disposal and by carrying it to its limit. By making it excessive he makes it for the moment new and strange. At no other point in English poetry would it be possible to compose an original poem largely out of quotations from other poems, allusions to other poems, catchwords from the street, the publichouse, the music-hall. When asked for explanatory notes he furnishes chiefly a list of allusions, as if to say that these are the stuff of the poem. And this is what they are; there is no irony in the notes except in so far as the poem itself is ironical. The more one reads the poem, the more allusive, the more reminiscent it becomes, till one ends by believing that every line and every word is packed with the most sophisticated associations. When he writes

> But at my back from time to time I hear
> The sound of horns and motors, which shall bring
> Sweeney to Mrs. Porter in the spring.
> O the moon shone bright on Mrs. Porter

he is, as he reminds us himself, echoing Marvell, Day, and a popular song. The eight closing lines of the poem are compounded of quotations in five languages, English, Latin, French, Italian, Sanskrit.

It is a sort of inspired *reductio ad absurdum*. What makes it important is that Eliot has made a virtue of this necessity and has expressed through his technique of allusion a condition of the spirit intensely personal to himself and peculiarly representative of the decadent forces of the modern world in which, he seems to say, nothing stands between man and chaos except these fragments of a dying tradition, this "heap of broken images," which he shores against his ruins.

Poetry can go no farther in this direction. *The Waste Land* is an end, not a beginning; it brings the poetry of allusion to a conscious climax and thereby forces poetry to change its course. For once we see poetry homoeopathically cured of a long ailment; by dosing poetry with the associations that were sapping it Eliot has, so to speak, saved its life—for others, if not for himself. Poetry must now seek other ways and, since *The Waste Land* blocks the backward road, it must go forward.

Seen in this light Doughty post-dates Eliot, though he was nearly half a century older—a view which Hugh MacDiarmid seems to corroborate in his lines "On a raised beach" (*Stony Limits*), 1934. Here he explicitly draws away from Eliot and towards Doughty; first he dissociates himself in his geological mood from Eliot, saying "This is no heap of broken images" and later allies himself to Doughty's "seeing of a hungry man" (*Arabia Deserta*) and his "supreme serenity," for it will be clear from MacDiarmid's fine commemorative lines on Doughty in the title-poem of the same volume that the serenity he has in mind must be Doughty's serenity. Perhaps there is a further suggestiveness in the fact that it is Eliot who leads the way into the desert

> Here is no water but only rock
> Rock and no water and the sandy road.

And Doughty who leads the way out again

> See where a well-spring floweth in the white sand.

for granted that Eliot's desert is mainly symbolical, while Doughty's is a sublimation of Arabia, the two quotations—and the two poems from which they are taken, *The Waste Land* and *Adam Cast Forth*—exactly characterize their authors. Eliot, whether we enjoy him or not, leaves us with mouths parched or drives us elsewhere for refreshment; Doughty, if we yield to him at all, is a fountain to the spirit, being one who, in Edward Garnett's words, whilst penetrating into all the "harsh and terrible forces in nature" also "sheds mild, beneficent and healing rays of loving kindness." (pp. 132-36)

> Barker Fairley, "Charles Doughty and Modern Poetry," in The London Mercury, *Vol. XXXII, No. 188, June, 1935, pp. 128-37.*

F. R. LEAVIS (essay date 1935)

[*Leavis is an influential contemporary English critic. His critical methodology combines close textual criticism with predominantly moral and social concerns and emphasis on the development of "the individual sensibility." Leavis views the writer as that individual who represents "the most conscious point of the race" in his or her lifetime. More importantly, the writer is one who can effectively communicate this consciousness. Contrary to what these statements may suggest, Leavis is not specifically interested in the individual writer per se, but rather with the usefulness of his or her art in the scheme of civilization. The writer's role in this vision is to eliminate "ego-centered distortion and all impure motives" from his or her work and to promote what Leavis calls "sincerity"—or, the realization of the individual's proper place in human society. In the following excerpt, Leavis refutes the claims of Anne Treneer (see excerpt dated 1935) and Barker Fairley (see excerpt dated 1935 and Additional Bibliography) that Doughty was a precursor of Modernist poets and that his poetic style is comparable to that of Gerard Manley Hopkins.*]

To find Doughty in his dealings with the English language at all akin to Hopkins is to betray a complete inappreciation of Hopkins's poetry. It should not have been necessary to say this, but plainly it is. The word is being passed round that Doughty and Hopkins, Victorian rebels, will go bracketed (Blake-Burns, Dryden-Pope) down to posterity. They are both extravagantly and wilfully odd, uncouth, crabbed, and defiant of common English usage—that seems to be the argument. "One looks forward," says Miss Treneer, and she has the endorsement of eminent reviewers, "to the day when young poets and critics such as Mr. Cecil Day Lewis will number the author of *Adam Cast Forth* with Wilfred Owen, Gerard Manley Hopkins and T. S. Eliot among their immediate ancestors."

Now to appreciate Hopkins is to lose all sense of oddity; but Doughty, in the very nature of his achievement, remains insistently and essentially odd—that is why there is not the slightest danger of his having any influence at all, in verse or prose. He is a nobly massive eccentric, a great English Character. Hopkins is central and a great English poet. His apparent oddity disappears because he is working in the spirit of the living English language; all his efforts are to realize this spirit in all its vigour and at its highest intensity. He condemned archaism as manifesting a wrong attitude towards the language—the

language as spoken in the poet's time. It is significant that Bridges, who would have nothing to do with his friend's "oddity," should have gladly acclaimed Doughty's rebellion against "Victorian English": Doughty was merely odd and eccentric and of scholarly interest and not in the least disturbing (though he is a rich and an easy subject for academic treatises and lectures). At the best, with the aim he served, he could succeed merely in creating an impressively eccentric monument. To talk of his refreshing or renovating the language is absurd; there was not the slightest chance of his having any effect whatsoever upon it or upon subsequent literature (if there had been he would have needed denouncing as a pernicious influence).

Even to talk, with Miss Treneer, of his effecting "a scholar's enrichment of current language" is a radical misrepresentation. Doughty pursued his word-hoarding in a spirit of rejection of current language: that comes out forcibly in his constant, extreme and wanton defiance of English idiom and word-order. He collected his words (and both Miss Treneer and Mr. Barker Fairley insist that it was individual words he was interested in) because they were strange, odd, antique and not current. What advantage did he gain by putting "spirituous" for "spiritual," "charret" for "chariot," "drenched" for "drowned," "girdlestead" and "middle" for "waist," "contrast" for "resist," "maidenchild" for "girl," "rumour" for "noise," "carol" for "dance," or by writing: "The truant smiling Beduins have answered again that they could no tales"? His style, in prose and verse, carries to an extreme the spirit of Victorian romanticism—except that, as Miss Treneer says, "he did not spend his time sighing for heroic days, he tried to recreate them." And he does marvellously succeed in making Victorian romanticism look truly heroic. But the heroism that affects the English language, English poetry and us is Hopkins's. (pp. 316-17)

[It] is enough to say (while admitting that there are interesting passages) that Doughty's verse exhibits an utter—and not merely a Miltonic—rejection of English idiom.

As for *Travels in Arabia Deserta*, it will remain a respected but little-read minor classic. (p. 317)

> F. R. Leavis, "Doughty and Hopkins," in Scrutiny, *Vol. IV, No. 3, December, 1935, pp. 316-17.*

CORNELIUS WEYGANDT (essay date 1937)

[*A historian and critic, Weygandt was one of the first American scholars to examine contemporary Irish drama, introducing its major practitioners to American readers in his* Irish Plays and Playwrights *(1913). In the following excerpt, Weygandt discusses what he finds to be the failures of Doughty's poetry.*]

There is not nearly so much poetry in the verse of the epics and dramas of Charles M. Doughty . . . as there is in the prose of his *Arabia Deserta*. . . . The book of travel has the proportions and structure and unity of the epic. It is dominated by the long-suffering Nasrany, Khalil, as the Arabs called him, a figure as truly heroic as that of any famed warrior of *Iliad* or *Song of Roland* or *Volsunga Saga*. The journeyings of Doughty, his changing adventures day by day from the November of 1876 to the July of 1878, his patient determination, hold all the divergent elements of his material together, center all the interest in him, write him large against the background of wild life in high desert and teeming oasis. (p. 284)

Doughty regarded *Arabia Deserta* as only a by-product of his life, the real purpose of which was the restoration to England of a poetry based on that of Chaucer and Spenser. He ignored practically all poetry after Milton, and he owed almost nothing to him; or to Shakespeare, for that matter, unless it be in the handling of the elves and fairies he is so fond of introducing into his writing. Doughty lived so apart from the literary world of his own day that he had never heard of Hardy until he saw mention of *The Dynasts* in a review of his own epic, *The Dawn in Britain*. . . . (pp. 284-85)

The Dawn in Britain, the most ambitious of [Doughty's poems] is weakest of all, save *The Titans* . . . , in its plan and in the execution of its plan. It is longer than any other English poem known to me, save Bailey's *Festus* (1839), but it can be read, as *Festus* cannot be, at least by me. *The Dawn in Britain* cannot all be read with pleasure, however. The mere fact that I am discussing its length before any of its poetical qualities shows that its author has defeated his own ends by letting it wander on to such interminable extent.

I shall never forget my disappointment over the first two volumes. I had the books ordered by our University Library from advance notices, and I requested they be reserved for me as soon as they were catalogued. I could hardly wait for their arrival, and I badgered the Library staff to put them through quickly for me. I had read *Arabia Deserta* entranced, with more zest than I had read any book of comparable length, novel or what not. I looked through the first volume of *The Dawn* going out in the train. It didn't look succulent as I turned over the pages. I opened it further on at hazard, and came on unhelmeted warriors paying reverence to the dead. That was dull chronicle. I was afraid I was not going to have an evening lost in antiquity as I had anticipated. The volumes were worse than I had anticipated. I found only few passages of high poetry in either Volume I or Volume II. I hadn't the courage to tackle the remaining volumes when they came in, and ten years afterwards they were hard sledding for me, though I found more passages I liked than in the first two volumes. The basic trouble with it all is that the stories which compose it have not been made a part of himself by Doughty. They are a jumble of loosely related incidents, outside of him, unabsorbed, all more or less illustrating the long struggle between Rome and Britain. We meet Cæsar and Christ, Caractacus and Messalina, Joseph of Arimathea and Manannan, Son of Lir, but few familiar figures loom large in the story, and none of the invented figures have personality enough to fix themselves in memory. Nor has Doughty always been able to make his heroes grand. Too often they remain grandiose, more grandiose, even, than the heroes of Macpherson's *Ossian*. I should much like to know what those two poets Dr. Robert Bridges and Squire Wilfred Scawen Blunt, who wrote Doughty such appreciative letters about *Arabia Deserta*, thought of *The Dawn of Britain*. I know that Blunt liked the white cattle that swam with the wain after them from Belgic shores to Britain, as I liked them because they suggested the white oxen of the Campagna, and the Chillingham cattle, the survivors of the wild cattle of Britain. I suspect that he liked, too, if he read far enough to meet them, the ferocious sow, big as a bison, that Titus slew, and that talking raven that the witch-wife fed on rowan berries and the flesh of men. I wonder what Dr. Bridges found to like.

Adam Cast Forth . . . has its moments, moments that recall now the prophetic books of Blake and now certain of his illustrations. Other passages recall the declamation of some of the oratorios. Satan is Miltonic even if his conception owes

nothing to Milton, but he is, I have to say it again, grandiose rather than grand. The whole conception of the poem seems but a reimagining of Khalil's own wanderings in Arabia, but with himself blind for a time, and with a woman in tow. There are passages of tenderness and bits of description like crude friezes from primitive temples. These have little of the dignity and Greek grace of related friezes in Sturge Moore. There are few lyric passages, and the raptures are carefully restrained. It is only rarely that there is music. Indeed music is rare everywhere in the epics and dramas of Doughty. There are a few chants of pomp and circumstance, some lamentations unto the Lord, more brass than woodwind. There are pipes, however, now and then, once even in *Adam Cast Forth:*

> The beasts have shelter and the birds have nests.
> The Lord giveth us an hollow cliff, to house,
> Flits in the chiddering swallow, and white dove;
> And the sweet honey-flies, they lodge with us.

In these words of Adama, there is none of the cluttering-up of the verses with adjective on adjective, and less of inversion and the archaic use of words than is his wont. As is usual in long poems without largeness and solidity of design, the lyrical interbreathings are the best parts of Doughty's. Here is a characteristic one, a cross section of his *Mansoul*, which shows how like he was at his best in 1920 to what he had been in 1908:

> I slumbered till a turtles' gentle flock,
> That feared not yet Man's shape; folding from flight
> Their rattling wings; lighted on vermeil feet;
> Jetting, with mincing pace, their iris necks;
> With crooling throat-bole; voice of peace and rest;
> All round about me, at that drinking place.
>   Thence faring upward, toward that water's source;
> Which, full of sunbeams, gurgles from hid grot,
> In ivy-embowered mossy steep above:
> And sunk oft up, reneweth as oft her course;
> In channels clear; surging from gilded sand:
> I stayed, where pleasant grassy holms depart;
> Those streaming water brooks, bordered all along;
> With daphne and willow-herb, loose-strife, laughing robin;
> With woodbine garlanded and sweet eglantine,
> And azure-hued in creeky shallows still,
> Forget-me-nots lift our frail thoughts to heaven.
>   Broods o'er those thymy argots drowsy hum;
> Bourdon of glistering bees, in mails of gold.
> Labouring from sweet to sweet, in the long hours
> Of sunny heat; they sound their shrill small clarions.
> And hurl by booming dors, gross bee-fly kin;
> Broad-girdled diverse hued, in their long pelts:
> That solitary, while eve's light endureth,
> In Summer skies, each becking clover-tuft haunt.

(pp. 285-88)

There was never poetry higher in intention than this of Doughty. *The Dawn in Britain* and *Adam Cast Forth, The Cliffs* and *The Clouds, The Titans* and *Mansoul* are largely conceived, but they are indifferently planned in detail, and they are often poorly executed. The archaisms and the eccentricities are less irritating after you become used to them, and begin to read on without noticing them, but they have to be gotten over each time you return to the reading of Doughty after a lapse of years. There is lofty imagination in the man, if he cannot always get lofty imagination into his poems, and a sweep of vision over wide areas of the earth and of time. The poems stand out in memory, however, as new ruins rather than as old, and new ruins have, somehow, a rather artificial impressiveness. They are like low fortifications of Mid-Victorian years half blown to pieces by target practice, rather than like Stonehenge with rude shafts and trilithons lonely against the sky.

I find more in *The Cliffs* and *The Clouds* than in the earlier epic and the earlier drama. *The Cliffs,* save as prophecy, is not imposing on the whole, but it has parts that arrest and delight. The reviewers, as a rule, did not praise it, largely because of what they were pleased to call its jingoism. The pastoral at its outset is to me the most appealing poem in all Doughty, the pastoral of John Hobbe that ends with his killing by the German aëronauts who have descended on the headland on which he is herding sheep. *The Cliffs* is drama in form, but in structure it is a conglomeration of several sorts of poetry. Hobbe is, of course, Hodge the peasant we have known in one guise or other from Langland to Mary Webb. This particular peasant gives his life for England, as he has in the past given everything else he had to give, the best of his young years, what energy his wounds have left him, and the lives of two of his sons. Could his devotion and his sacrifices and his faithfulness have been summarized in a short poem with those simplicities and that music which catch the popular ear, Doughty might have succeeded in rousing England to the German menace in 1909. But as part of the formless mass of *The Cliffs* the symbolic pastoral of Hobbe passed almost unnoticed.

The Cliffs is thoroughly "up to date" with its airships and submarines. The man who had never heard of Hardy knew what the German war lords were planning. Those years on the Riviera, with their many meetings with foreigners of all sorts, gave Doughty a knowledge of doings on the Continent that stay-at-home Englishmen could not bring themselves to consider. There is not invasion in *The Cliffs,* only naval action off shore, and the threat of invasion. In *The Clouds,* however, England is invaded south and north by German armies, and London itself invested. Only the timely arrival of help from the Five Britains overseas saves the Motherland from catastrophe.

Doughty saw what was to happen in certain aspects of the fighting in the world war with startling accuracy of prevision. He foresaw how large a part submarines and airships were to play, he foresaw the purpose of the German North Sea fleet, and he foresaw the German frightfulness. He foresaw conscription, and he foresaw the welding of the discordant elements of class and faction in England into one whole to meet the threat of the war. The fact that his mother's people, the Hothams, were navy people, and that he was intended for the navy in his youth, no doubt supplemented those talks at Bordighera in making him aware of the intentions of Germany. (pp. 288-90)

Mansoul was the preoccupation of [Doughty's] old age. It was first published in 1920, and then worked over, despite ill health and the weakness of his years until 1923, when its final version came out. It is that I own, with Doughty's crabbed but legible signature in it. It is the most marked of my Doughtys, though I would not claim it, for that reason, the best of him. The subject of the epic is "The Riddle of the Universe," and it may be said at once he has no solution for the riddle. Yet a man of his experience in earlier years and of his long brooding in later years has much to say on the Whys and Wherefores and Whither of life. As Hogarth quotes him in a letter to Edward Garnett, "What of this very old solar Earth-planet . . .? How came it into being? What of man's later World therein; and what of aught beyond? has long been to me the Question of

questions.'' Mansoul goes all over the world, and under the world, with a Merlin's glass that enables him to see through solid earth. In the abodes of the dead he encounters and questions Zarathustra (Zoroaster), Buddha, Kung (Confucius), and Socrates. Socrates helps him as much as any one with his observations on the constitutions of things, but he does not help very much at that. Returning to himself from a trance, Socrates cries out:

> live in Faith of the Eternal Good.
> Who dares impeach His Justice! No man knoweth;
> To what intent Gods made and marred the World.
> Nor whether Gods made men, or Man made Gods.

On the whole, however, Doughty is no safer a guide in religion and philosophizing than he is as a critic of literature. It is for his power over words that conjure our emotions, and for his descriptions of the external beauty of the world, that those who love literature will go to him in the years to come. His prophecy of the World War will have a page in history, and certain passages of his will have place in the anthologies of those poems that catch and preserve the beauty of English countryside and the faithfulness of English men. (p. 292)

Cornelius Weygandt, "Charles M. Doughty, Sturge Moore and Gordon Bottomley," in his The Time of Yeats: English Poetry of To-day against an American Background, *D. Appleton-Century Company, Inc., 1937, pp. 284-305.*

WALT TAYLOR   (essay date 1939)

[In the following excerpt, Taylor provides a philological examination of Doughy's prose in Travels in Arabia Deserta.*]*

[Doughty] set out to write pure English. It seemed to him, as to many of his contemporaries, that the middle style of Victorian English was not good enough, not sufficiently expressive; that some other form of English must be substituted for it. "The Arabia Deserta volumes," he wrote, had necessarily a personal tone. A principal cause of writing them was besides the interest of the Semitic life in tents, my dislike of the Victorian English; and I wished to show, and thought I might be able to show, that there was something else." The pre-Raphaelites felt the same. Morris thought to improve English by a return to an Anglo-Saxon vocabulary, Meredith by setting aside some of the rules of the grammarians, Bridges by a careful choice of diction used according to accepted grammatical usage. Doughty created an idiom of his own which it is our purpose here to discuss.

Doughty's style was at once modern, Chaucerian, Elizabethan, and Arabic; its Chaucerian and Elizabethan quality is no mere pastiche; it is Arabic; it is "pure" English written by a modern writer of genius. Now "pure" English certainly is not Arabic. For a writer to write one language in the manner of another language would seem at first sight to be a strange and dangerous thing to do; but we must remember that throughout the history of English there have been many writers who have written English prose as though they were writing Latin prose, some who have deliberately thought in Latin and then translated their thought into English, many who have used Latin grammar and vocabulary and method of expression as a touchstone for the correct usage of English.

If it seems natural to us that Gibbon's *Decline and Fall of the Roman Empire* (partly because of its subject) should be written in a highly Latinized style, it should not be strange that Doughty's *Arabia Deserta* (if only because of its subject) is written in a highly Arabicized style: the strangeness will not be in the fact of the Arabicized style but in the effect of that style; for Gibbon is only one of many who have based their English style on Latin, whereas Doughty has been unique among English writers in basing his style on Arabic.

I do not suggest that Doughty wrote in an Arabicized style merely because he was writing about Arabs and Arabia. He was too great a master to play such a trick with the English language. His justification is much more important and much more subtle: it was precisely in Arabic that Doughty found his model for pure English. He was not a philologist; but he felt intuitively, what the philologists now confirm, that a primitive language is more concrete and emotional than a more civilized language; that a civilized language is addressed more to the reason, and is therefore more abstract. He had felt while he was still up at Cambridge (1861-6) that Victorian English was too abstract and lifeless, and that for his poetic purposes he must master a more primitive form of English. For this reason we find him reading Early English texts in the Bodleian from 1868 to 1870. "The next year out of reverence for the memory of Erasmus, Jos. Scaliger, &c., I passed in Holland learning Hollandish—which with Danish (I was nearly a year in Norway in '63-4) gave me a philological feeling in English."

Living abroad enables an Englishman to see English objectively, as he sees a foreign language; and living in the countries where Germanic languages are spoken will bring him into contact with elements from which modern English has developed. Doughty's mind was naturally antiquarian: at Cambridge he had read Geology in order to see the origins of the world; now, as a preparation for writing, he was deliberately studying the origins of English.

In Doughty's mind there was no clear distinction between literature and language. A philologist can succeed in removing his studies from the reading of literature; but this line of study never attracted Doughty. To him "English" was both the English language and its best use in literature, from Old English times to his own times. When he wrote "My work is not intended for the philologically uneducated, untuned Victorian and present common English sense" he did not imply that his work was addressed to formal philologists, but to those readers of English who have a philological (i.e. word-loving) sense of the right use of English. (pp. 1681-83)

When we think of the origin of English (using the word in this sense) we at once realize that English is not entirely Germanic. It contains other important elements—French, Italian, Spanish, Roman, Greek, Hebrew. And we see Doughty leaving Holland, wandering in France, Italy, Spain, Greece, and finally to the Bible Lands, making a literary and linguistic pilgrimage, tracing back his literary and linguistic heritage to its origins. And study of the origins of the religious heritage led him, as all Semitic studies must lead, into Arabia. He left England in 1870 to study the Low German sources of English. Five years later he was in Sinai seeing Arabia in little; and next year he entered the Desert itself.

In this wilderness he found his ideal language. Arabic seemed to him a language "rich in spirit," and "dropping with the sap of human life." Here was a nation of word-lovers, enunciating their language with great care, and speaking with "perspicuous propriety," emulating each other, as they talked round the coffee-hearth, in "election of words." Doughty himself joined in their philological discussions. "Having a vocabulary

in my hand, now and then I read out a page or two to the company. Certainly I could not err much in the utterance of many words that were before well known to me; but no small part of these town and bookish terms were quite unknown to all my nomad hearers! of some it seemed they had not the roots, of many they use other forms. They wondered themselves and as Arabs will (who have so much feeling in their language and leisure to be eloquent) considered word after word with a patient attention."

Arabic, to be spoken well, must be clearly enunciated. Generalizing from the "imperfect and unready speech" of Doughty, a certain Abu Rashid in Arabia said: "These Franks labour in the Arabic utterance, for they have not a supple tongue: the Arabs' tongue is running and returning like a wheel, and in the Arabs all parts alike of the mouth and gullet are organs of speech; but your words are born crippling and fall half dead out of your mouths." Miss Treneer suggests a psychological reason for Doughty's interest in the clearness of Arab speech: that his own hesitation in speech would heighten his admiration for, and sharpen his ear to, the sound of the Arabs' voices. But it is not necessary to have Doughty's consciousness of the poverty of one's Arabic, or Doughty's quick ear, to be struck by the clarity of Arab pronunciation. The first thing which any European learns about Arabic when he undertakes the study of that language is that he must articulate his consonants with much more vigour than in his own language; and not debase the quality of his vowels.

What attracted Doughty in the speech of the Beduins was not only its clear utterance but also the fact that each word was deliberately chosen. There is perhaps no language in which the individual word has so much power as it has in Arabic. There are words in Arabic which are regarded as good in themselves, so that a hearer may interrupt the thought of the speaker to say "Ah! Such, that is a good word,' or, "Such-and-such, those are good words." There are other words which go to the heart of the hearer: words of tremendous emotive power, such as only great orators can find in other languages. Arabic, like Hebrew, can do what no European language can do: it can without any great strain reach the sublime. (pp. 1683-84)

[The] "pure" Arabic which he heard daily in the Desert was an inspiration to Doughty. As already hinted, it took such hold on his imagination that he wanted to write "pure" English in the manner of "pure" Arabic. For this purpose he had to create an English language for himself in which the word should be the unit of speech and writing—the individual word, chosen for its aptness and its emotional force and for the historical tradition behind it. For this reason he made his own lists of words good to use . . . his private thesaurus of English words and phrases. He chose words old or new, preferably old, but if new, made from an old root, words which struck him as being poetic. "Is not ποιησις ["poiēsis"]," he asked, "an architecture of elect national words and eternal human thoughts; raised upon a well-devised foundation, and builded of none but diligently found, chosen, and wrought, goodly stones, all truly laid: built up into a temple which shall be in harmony with the human aspect of things, as is a tree, in the landscape?"

That there is a close connexion between the nature of a language and the nature of the literature produced in it has long been recognized. We may call French, for example, a logical language, meaning both that the grammatical structure of the language is logical and that it is an easy language in which to express oneself logically: indeed, a difficult language in which to be vague. From another point of view we may call French

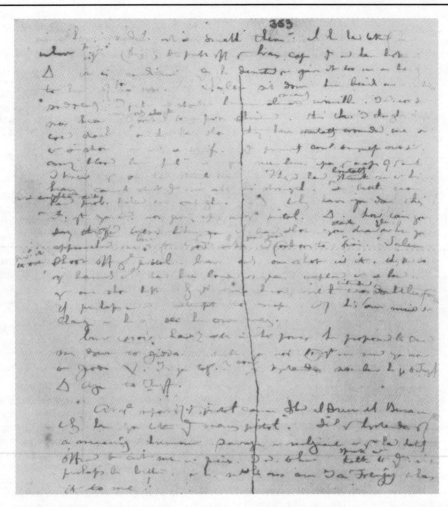

Facsimile of a page in Doughty's Arabian diary. From The Life of Charles M. Doughty, *by D. G. Hogarth. Doubleday, Doran & Company, Inc., 1929. Courtesy of Doubleday & Company, Inc.*

a sophisticated language, with reference both to its artificiality, its sense of knowing what it is about (controlled as it is by an Academy), and its excellence as a medium, for example, for witty speech. So we may call German heavy, meaning both that its phonetic and grammatical nature is heavy, and that its literature has a certain peculiar seriousness. Professor Jespersen in a similar manner has called English a masculine language, and its literature also masculine.

But when we ask what is the essential and peculiar nature of Arabic, we are at a loss for a word. If we can find one it will possibly help us to understand the nature of Doughty's English, for the peculiar nature of Doughty's English is its Arabic quality. By adding a semantic value to an already existing English word I think we might call Arabic an "elemental" language.

By "elemental" I do not mean only that the language is in its grammatical structure composed of certain knowable and comparatively few elements, through that is true in so far as it is a language of verbal roots and of few "parts of speech." I mean also that for literary purposes it is a language which naturally expresses fundamentals; that its vocabulary refers to *things* which exist, and to deep-seated emotions: not to abstractions, notions, or ideas. In a sense it is the most expressive language, because in Arabic it is easiest to express what I should like to call elemental things; the elements or funda-

mentals of Nature and of human nature. It has what Doughty calls a "quick significance," which enables the Arabs to "speak to the heart of one another." And that is precisely the ideal which Doughty aimed at in his use of English. He was using what we may call "elemental" English. He sought to create an English which would be as expressive as Arabic, and expressive of the same fundamentals.

The purely literary criticism of Doughty's work is outside our province in this place. But we can examine his attempt to write "elemental" English, at any rate from a philological point of view. I think we shall find that he preferred a word the sense of which could be referred to that of its root; that he preferred the Germanic to the Latin word and the looser Germanic syntax to the more formal Latin syntax of English; that he liked words which had gathered round them emotional associations. Above all, his English is elemental in that he exalted the power of the individual word. His thought was conceived and expressed not as the paragraph in prose and the stanza in verse, nor as the sentence which is a unit in itself, but as a sequence of carefully chosen and placed but separate words.

Doughty gave himself freedom to use any word which served his purpose, whether that word were current or obsolete, or a dialect word or a colloquialism; and where existing words failed he made new ones from English roots, or Latin, or French, or

Arabic; or he gave a new meaning, where that was convenient, to an existing English word.

The archaism in Doughty is merely incidental: he was not a seeker after archaisms such as Lamb was. He usually avoids, for example, the *-eth* ending of the third person of the present tense, and *be* for *are,* those easiest tricks of the writer of "quaint" English. He took words and grammatical constructions from Old and Middle English and from early Modern English writers; but his English might be called "futuristic" with as much justice as it could be called "archaic." His *Arabia Deserta* is a treasure-house of good old words but it is a treasure-house too of good new ones. What he aimed at was not a revival of earlier English but a renaissance of modern English. (pp. 1687-90)

> *Walt Taylor, "Doughty's English," in* S. P. E. Tracts: *LI-LXVI, Vol. IV,* Oxford University Press, n.d., *pp. 1679-1724.*

JOHN HOLLOWAY (essay date 1954)

[*An English poet, autobiographer, and critic, Holloway is best known for his poetry, which demonstrates a mastery of many traditional verse forms. In the following excerpt, he defends Doughty's use of archaic language.*]

"Come, is it not an affectation to write obsolete English? You know it is." This is how Gerard Manley Hopkins wrote of Doughty's prose book, the *Travels in Arabia Deserta,* when it came out in 1888 [see Additional Bibliography]; and the point he made is one that has led many readers to turn away from Doughty's prose, and turn away still more from the long poems that he wrote between 1888 and his death in 1926. At the present time, there is a principle which we almost take for granted: that the language of prose or of poetry must have its roots in the language of common speech. But Doughty's verse runs plain counter to this principle; and that fact, as Hopkins implied, seems enough by itself to discredit him.

It is, though, the very thing which makes his verse peculiarly interesting. This is because, by its extra-ordinary language, it brings out the fundamental reason why poetry is likely to be enriched by ordinary language. It enables one to get to the heart of a whole major critical problem. And furthermore, Doughty's verse is not instructive in this way, because it is a typical, a classic example of failure. It is instructive because, at least within a certain well-defined range, it has a definite but very peculiar kind of success, and it illuminates the general principle about ordinary language and successful poetry by being a remarkable exception to it.

The arguments for this principle are not often reviewed: it is too firmly accepted for them to seem to need it. But when one begins to review them, Doughty's peculiar situation shows at once. Hopkins himself, for example, objected to archaism as an affectation, and to affectation as something not *manly;* and he rejected inversions as well as archaisms in poetry, because they destroy the "in-earnestness of the utterance." But "not manly" and "not in earnest" are the last words one could use even of Doughty's worst failures—on the contrary, perhaps; and when Hopkins goes on to attack poets who affect a shallow and diluted *Shakespearean* diction, one sees clearly that his dislike of archaisms originated in poetry of quite another kind from Doughty's, and a kind moreover against which Doughty fulminated himself. Indeed, the relation between Hopkins's argument and Doughty's practice is more complicated still.

Doughty wrote in a language that drew heavily upon Chaucer and Spenser. But when he says "How can a newsboy's cry be a prosaic line?" or "perfection is simplicity," he gives the impression of having been over Hopkins's ground, of knowing the risk that archaism runs. And he goes further: he actually appropriates Hopkins's very word, giving it a good sense, and writing "art is a manner, an affectation"; which emphatically shows that he was not a thoughtless derivative writer, but a conscious literary artist who had considered the fundamentals of his task, knew its dangers and difficulties, and tried to meet them in his own distinctive way.

Doughty's theory of language deeply influenced his work. His main purpose in composing the *Travels* was not to write a scientist's or geographer's account of Arabia, but (as he puts it himself) "resisting . . . the decadence of the English language." The same attitude shows in his verse. . . . All of [Doughty's poetry was] written in the belief that English was at its best in Chaucer and Spenser, and had since then suffered a complete degeneration. To Doughty, writing prose was a preparation for writing poetry; it was the latter that he called "my true life's work." His travels were a preparation for poetry too; and he studied philology and languages because, in his view, "epic language in any tongue cannot possibly be the decadent speech of the streets." No paradox is created by his having been, in the earlier part of his life, the most travelled of English poets, and in the later part of it perhaps the most studious and sedentary.

It is important to recognize the central place that poetry had in Doughty's life, and not to put his interests in poetry and in philology the wrong way round. He did not write poems so as to coax picturesque verbal curiosities back to life, but he cared for philology as a poet's instrument. What he praised in Chaucer was his justness and directness; in Spencer, his "golden intimate tongue," not the quaintness that the eighteenth century so strangely found instead. He laboured incessantly in revising his work; he aspired to make *The Dawn in Britain* "perfected in form"; he saw a long poem as like music, with a complete harmony going right through it. In other words, he had crossed that frontier which exists between those who see that the literary art is *art,* and those who think of it as some other kind of thing. And this is surely why he eludes Hopkins's attack. For the core of the argument against archaisms, as Hopkins put it is "We do not speak that way; therefore if a man speaks that way he is not serious, he is at something else than the seeming matter in hand." About this argument, however, there are several things to be said. First, the usually astute Hopkins has fallen into more than one logical slip. He assumes that the normal speaker is the typically earnest speaker, which is in itself questionable enough; and (even allowing this) he assumes that there could not possibly be any way of speaking in earnest except the normal way. Perhaps another point, though, is even more important. What, after all, *is* the "matter in hand"? It is clearly not one and the same for the man living through an experience, and for the poet making a poem around a perhaps imaginary experience; and, perhaps because the poet's "matter in hand" is primarily to make a poem, everyone who advocates ordinary language for poetry sooner or later invents a formula which lets the poet deviate from it. Hopkins's formula was that the current language could be "to any degree heightened and unlike itself"; Wordsworth tried "a *selection* from the language really used by men"; Ezra Pound's formula is more telling—and also more obscure: "(Poetry's) language must be a fine language, departing in no way from speech save by a heightened intensity (i.e. simplicity)." In other words, deviation from common speech is allowed even by the keenest advocates of it. But what is it a deviation towards, and what purpose does it serve? These are the questions that Doughty's anomalous verse, with its anomalous successes, help to answer.

The language of speech is necessarily that in which what is new, striking, and vivid in experience is likely to get its initial record; and therefore the idiom of speech is constantly being vivified, its power to communicate a real impact is constantly being preserved or restored. A literary language, on the contrary, might be called a language of illustrious *cliché:* expressions earn a place in it when their meanings (in both the narrower and wider senses) are fixed and controlled by the literature of the past. Whatever advantages this may have been thought to bring, the realistic vividness of such a language must almost necessarily be slight. But if this is so, then Doughty is using neither ordinary nor literary language, but some third thing: for there is no doubt that his twisted, abrupt, extraordinarily condensed style has its own impact. It is infinitely removed from the *cliché:*

> What hour I fell down-forth, out of that blast,
> To the dim Earth, behold it empty was,
> A wailing-place of dragons. Cumber was
> Of burning stones there strewed, beneath my feet,
> Cast out from heaven, against those perverse spirits,
> Whereunder smitten, lay, like unto green trunks,
> Fell dragon brood. Still seeking thee, shut up
> Mine heart in anguish, I like worm, crept forth;
> Till lean my flesh and dry was, as a leaf.
>
> *(Adam Cast Forth . . .)*

Here, certainly, is a divergence from ordinary speech. But it is in a direction opposite to that of poetic diction in the usual sense; for, by comparison with it, ordinary speech is not more, but perhaps even less direct and blunt and emphatic.

Doughty's verse might still be worthless, if the reader had to persevere through its dense grain and occasional archaism for nothing but a triviality of substance. So far from this, by a detail, or an image, or simply by the organization of its language, *The Dawn in Britain* at least shows that fuller, keener, more deeply felt vision of his subject which is surely the creative writer's vital possession. Doughty does not merely rearrange the known poetical effects; he writes with his own genuine vision, and his poem speaks in its own direct voice. Examples of this are not hard to find; there are the lost souls that are not even worth punishing, and that hang neglected on the walls of Hell, *like drowsy moths;* the two human sacrifices who, at the very instant they fall dying on the altar-stone, seem half to turn to embrace each other; the Emperor Claudius, who one night, to escape a skirmish, climbs alone to the top of a siege-engine's tower, and then hears nothing at all except the night wind in the cords of the engines all round him. . . . Like all real poets, Doughty constantly adds the quickening, life-giving touch, constantly tells more about the subject than we know already, simply from what it is; whereas the trivial and derivative poet constantly tells less.

But this is only to make the preliminary point that Doughty has something to say of his own, that he is not rehashing clichés from books already written. It might still be true that his strange and difficult style only impeded his real gift. On the contrary, it is not in spite of, it is through the eccentricities of his style that he creates the originality of what he has to say. He makes inversion, for example, control the order of his ideas, and it is this order which creates the whole that they make up together.

Here is a fragment where he is briefly handling a conventional epic device, and it is what makes the style eccentric that creates the speed and animation, that through its order makes the scene vivid, and that at last fixes upon the tiny vital point:

> Tumbles aloft, as tosst of windy gusts,
> The arrow. It, snatcht the feathered fiend, in flight,
> And guides the bitter forkhead . . .
>
> *(The Dawn in Britain . . .)*

And in these lines about Roman ships crossing the Channel, it is Doughty's syntax, rhyme or half-rhyme, and repetition, which create the movement, the stop-and-go-on, of the verse, and this which creates the monotony and expectancy and strangeness of the scene:

> All rowing, they the wind-bound Briton hoys,
> At length outgo; and, sithen, lose from view.
> Till night, when covered are the stars, they row.
> Then weary they lie to; not daring show
> Light, in their lanterns. Mariners shout, from ship
> To ship, all night; and clarions softly blow.
>
> *(The Dawn in Britain . . .)*
> (pp. 58-63)

[Poetry] needs ordinary language not because this has some talismanic quality all of its own, but because it is the normal and the readiest vehicle for what is really grasped and lived by the writer. Doughty had that grasp, and at its best his verse gives it real expression. At its best, it eludes the ordinary objections to a special language for poetry, because in its own strange way its achieves what ordinary language is relied on to achieve. It crystallizes what has been sharply realized and seen afresh by the writer, and indeed, further than this, it is not simply a ready-made counter for that realization, but by its immediacy and subtlety is what actually constitutes it. Doughty's anomalous success shows the real nature of the normal success, when the poet avoids a "literary" vapidity by relying on ordinary language; and if this is what the normal success essentially is, then it follows that at the point where ordinary language ceases to speak with this directness and reality (or some other language begins to do that better), it ceases to be what poetry demands. This explains why the advocates of ordinary language have usually found reasons for leaving it behind when doing so suited their purpose. In fact, the principle that poetry should use the language of common speech, often treated as if it were fundamental, is quite derivative, and merely applies the really important principle, which is that literature is not parthenogenetic. (pp. 69-70)

John Holloway, "Poetry and Plain Language: The Verse of C. M. Doughty," in Essays in Criticism, *Vol. IV, No. 1, January, 1954, pp. 58-70.*

JONATHAN BISHOP   (essay date 1960)

[*In the following excerpt, Bishop discusses a series of incidents in* Travels in Arabia Deserta *in which Doughty refuses to defend himself even when his life is threatened, thereby displaying Christian virtues of self-abnegation and rejecting traditional heroic attributes such as self-assertion and self-determination.*]

Anne Treneer's book on Charles Doughty [see excerpt dated 1935] . . . is more than twenty years old. One cannot, of course, vouch for the impression later readers of the *Arabia Deserta* may have had, but it is perhaps permissible to speculate. Would a responsible reader nowadays end on this note?

A peculiar feeling of exultation results from the reading of *Arabia Deserta* as an adventure story. The hero—with whom unconsciously we identify ourselves—is undefeated. The vulnerable body of the man is not finally crushed by inimical, elemental powers, nor are his individual mind and will subdued by the common mind and will of a hostile people. He wandered in an alien society, in a part of the world where the natural forces seemed arrayed against man— a lonely spirit in a frail body against a spiritually and physically hostile world. And he came through.

This passage defines the protagonist of the *Arabia Deserta* as the traditional hero of adventure in foreign parts, a Victorian who triumphed. But is this the only definition of heroism there is? And in any case, does Doughty fit it?

At one point in her study, Miss Treneer does indeed seem to qualify her position: "It is because in *Arabia Deserta* the sense of man's power in weakness disengages itself—disengages itself from the story, not from some adjoined statement about it—that the book has its peculiar place in our own time." The phrase "power in weakness" disengages itself from Miss Treneer's remarks, but the context seems to suggest that she does not put much weight on the preposition, and means only, "power to survive in spite of weakness." Miss Treneer's insight, taken in a more strictly paradoxical sense, gives us a juster view of the style of heroism presented to us in Doughty's book than her considered judgment.

The first place to look to substantiate this view, it seems to me, is the story itself. This may appear a perverse method of attack on a book in which the surface of the language, with its stylistic peculiarities and chaos of detail, attracts so much of every reader's attention. Yet beneath this surface there is a story, a sequence of meaningful actions, and an examination of these, besides giving us a firmer grasp of the structure of the book, may serve indirectly to explain some part of the role linguistic oddity plays in its economy.

Doughty, it will be recalled, joins the Moslem pilgrimage caravan at Damascus with the view of traveling down into Arabia as far as Medáin Sâlih. There he hopes to investigate rumors of inscriptions on old tombs. The venture is initially successful, and he finds himself living in a *kella*, or water-fort, while he records the inscriptions he finds in the vicinity. At this point a curious incident occurs, the first in which Doughty, hitherto so retiring, plays an active part:

> Upon the morrow I asked of Mohammad Aly to further me in all that he might; the time was short to accomplish the enterprise of Medáin. Sâlih. I did not stick to speak frankly; but I thought he made me cats'-eyes. "You cannot have forgotten that you made me certain promises!"—"I will give you the gun again." This was in my chamber; he stood up and his fury rising, much to my astonishment, he went to his own, came again with the carbine, turned the back and left me. I set the gun again, with a friendly word, in the door of his chamber,— "Out!" cried the savage wretch, in that leaping up and laying hold upon my mantle: then as we were on the gallery the Moorish villain suddenly struck me with the flat hand and all his

> mad force in the face, there wanted little of my falling to the yard below.

The quarrel arises because Mohammed Aly has promised to take Doughty on an expedition in return for a carbine. He does not (for reasons that are left obscure) wish to keep his promise. Doughty reminds him, first by word, then by gesture. This precipitates a mad reaction. Now Doughty here seems to have all the advantages of the man who is keeping his word, in contradistinction to the other, who is breaking it. He is testing to see if another man will behave honorably. Yet the insistence, and perhaps the passivity, with which he does this have the effect of making Mohammed Aly lose his temper. To be sure, we have learned that Mohammed Aly is always on the verge of an outbreak, which he excuses by alleging the hot temper of all Moors. He is susceptible to slights, and Doughty's reminder is a criticism of his good faith. His paroxysm of rage seems due to guilt combined with anger at Doughty's own mildness, the frustration of a man who would rather be cuffed than be accused so gently. We can, I think, comprehend Mohammed Aly's feelings and see Doughty's very passiveness as a kind of aggression. To Doughty himself, however, the slap comes as a complete surprise; he is not sensitive to the meaning of Mohammed's wish to return the gun. Yet he does not respond in the way we might expect:

> He shouted also with savage voice, "Dost thou not know me yet?" He went forward to the kahwa, and I followed him, seeing some Beduins were sitting there;—the nomads, who observe the religion of the desert, abhor the homely outrage. I said to them, "*Ya rubbâ*, O fellowship, ye are witnesses of this man's misdoing."

He does not burst out in abuse or strike Mohammed in return. Indeed, two sentences intervene between the act and his response. And when this comes, it takes the form of an appeal to the bystanders to be witnesses, to recognize that a wrong has been done by their own code. His first act is, as it were, to put in his moral claim, to establish his moral position in their eyes. The response of the Bedouins to this request, as well as the reaction of Mohammed to being reminded of his promise, demonstrates the moral climate of the world in which Doughty is traveling. It is the other party that acts—Doughty retires from action, placing himself in the role, first of a man to whom promises have been made, then of a man who has been wronged.

> The nomads looked coldly on aghast; it is damnable among them, a man to do his guest violence, who is a guest of Ullah. Mohammed Aly, trembling and frantic, leaping up then in his place, struck me again in the doorway, with all his tiger's force; as he heaped blows I seized his two wrists and held them fast. "Now, I said, have done, or else I am a strong man."

"Carry this too far and I shall behave normally." But the "or else" is ironic, for his strength is not in his hands, and if he were to use them, he would lose the paradoxical authority his willingness to suffer humiliation gives him. Mohammed Aly stops, and the bystanders do not engage themselves. The tide of Doughty's meditations turns to a pistol he carries on a thong around his neck, but he knows that if he did kill, and had to wander out alone into the desert, he would be lost. It is this consideration, he says, which leads him to bear with "dastardly" insults of this kind.

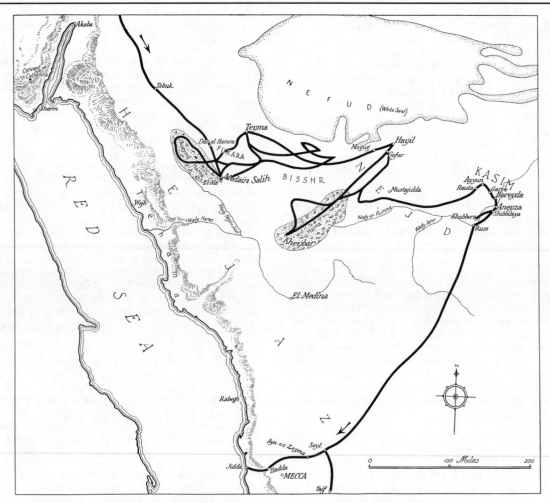

Map of Doughty's travels in Arabia. From The Life of Charles M. Doughty, *by D. G. Hogarth. Doubleday, Doran & Company, Inc., 1929. Courtesy of Doubleday & Company, Inc.*

We may suspect here that the announced motive does not suffice to explain the behavior with which he links it. His unwillingness to hit Mohammad Aly back gives him an ambiguous power; he saves himself from death, but at the expense of provoking fresh humiliations, for it is always a temptation, when a man professes humility, to indulge his virtue by enjoying the complementary vice and stepping on him. If Doughty had hit back, he might, to be sure, have roused the religious passions of the bystanders against him and lost his life; but he might alternatively have cowed them. Straightforward power is at least comprehensible: the power effective as weakness is maddening to men like Mohammed Aly and potentially, at least, destructive to the protagonist. Doughty is courting martyrdom. We feel that behind the affectation of surprise he expects the blow he has provoked.

The excess of humiliation is obliteration. There is an interesting passage toward the end of the first volume which we may read as a commentary on the incident at Medáin Sâlih. An Arab has committed suicide, a rare act among Mohammedans. Doughty interjects:

> In the ferment of our civil societies, from which the guardian angels seem to depart, we see many every moment sliding at the brink. What anguishes are rankling in the lees of the soul, the

heart-nipping unkindness of a man's friends, his defeated endeavours! betwixt the birth and death of the mind, what swallowing seas, and storms of mortal miseries! And when the wildfire is in the heart and he is made mad, the incontinent hands would wreak the harm upon his own head, to blot out the abhorred illusion of the world and the desolate remembrance of himself.

The violence of the language, the exclamation points, and the mixed metaphors suggest clearly enough an interest going beyond the immediate occasion, and we have no trouble reading this as a call for sympathy directly from Doughty to us. Suicide is here a temptation, the result of wrong feelings bursting out in action against the self. In Medáin Sâlih this violence is, as it were, distanced from the actor; Mohammed is Doughty's surrogate, and acts for him, expressing all the violence he himself might feel; he can retire, passive, and await the blow, conscious that the guilt which he would otherwise suffer has been transferred to another. Besides, death has dwindled to a slap. It remains in Doughty's consciousness only as a practical danger he must be sure to avoid.

Doughty hopes to escape the ambiguous strains implicit in such adventures by withdrawing into the desert with the Bedouin, away from the treachery of the Turkish kella-keepers. At first he finds a freer life and a more unqualified hospitality. But as the months pass and his traveling plans go awry and his money and health diminish, he begins to find himself in a more dangerous situation than any he escaped at Medáin Sâlih. He is relatively safe as long as he is able to keep moving from town to town and from tribe to tribe, being passed on from one half-friendly sheik to another; when, however, he is forced to return upon his tracks, he finds suspicion redoubled. Made to leave the town of Kheybar by the hostile townspeople, he returns to Hâyil. But the deputy of the Emir refuses to accept him again. Despairing, he turns once more toward Kheybar, guided by men who have good reason to think no one now cares what they do with their Christian employer. They force him to travel barefoot while they ride the camels he has paid for; he has to drive himself to keep up with their mounted pace, for fear that if they once get out of sight, the last tenuous string of obligation would break, and he would be left to die alone in the desert.

> So it drew to the burning midst of the afternoon, when, what for the throes in my chest, I thought that the heart would burst. The hot blood at length spouted from my nostrils: I called to the rafiks who went riding together before me to halt, that I might lie down awhile, but they would not hear. Then I took up stones, to receive the dropping gore, lest I should come with a bloody shirt to the next Aarab: besides it might work some alteration in my rafiks' envenomed spirits!—in this haste there fell blood on my hands. When I overtook them, they seeing my bloody hands drew bridle in astonishment!

Their astonishment changes to disgust; "Now is this not a kafir!" which Doughty endeavors to turn into pity and shame: "Are ye not more than kafirs, that abandon the rafik in the way?" They justify themselves with the observation that there is no need to keep faith between Moslem and Christian. They slow their pace, and halt; one kindles the cord of his matchlock and prepares to prime. When Doughty questions this action, he is told it is to kill a hare, but seeing them confused, he speaks out: "by the life of Him who created us" he will kill them both the instant a gun is turned against him. They fall silent and ride on, obviously puzzled, for they do not know he is armed. Do they suppose he has magical powers he can use against them? He himself reviews again the desperate character of his predicament: if he kills them, he must flee alone through the desert, a solitary man suffering from ophthalmia, on a weak camel, not knowing the way to the remote safety of Syria, apt to die at the hands of anyone he meets. Besides, as he wonders the next day when the uneasy situation recurs, would it be just to kill them? "—in this faintness of body and spirit I could not tell; I thought that a man should forsake life rather than justice, and pollute his soul with outrage."

The components that strike us as significant here are the same as those we read in the incident at Medáin Sâlih, with this difference, that the feelings of the actors never quite rise to the threatened climax, but subside only to recur over and over through agonizing days, with the same medley of impotence, shame, violence, and humility. Here, as before, there is a promise which the Arabs have broken or are about to break; here, too, Doughty's ambiguous authority, increased by his very helplessness; here, too, the calm acceptance of humiliation, not merely in the eyes of the Arabs, but perhaps also in the eyes of the reader. At the edge of the experience is death;

Doughty's, or the death enclosed in the pistol, the power that is never quite used. And our consciousness of the presence of death reinforces our acceptance of the role he adopts, supporting our respect for his humility and our willingness to allow him his enormous moral claim: to be, in effect, a saint, a man who willingly subjects himself to higher laws than he expects those with whom he deals to obey. He practices ideal justice, even as a victim; they who prosecute him will not even keep ordinary good faith. We feel this is fair, because, as we are reminded again and again, hospitality is the prime Arab virtue, and good faith with one's fellow man their chief moral boast; if, we think, a stranger should go among them, and find them deficient in just those virtues in which the world was willing to allow them preëminence, then, indeed, they are judged, and judged fairly. There is, in fact, no equality between Moslem and Christian, though not in the sense the Moslems suppose. In their eyes Doughty is beneath them; in ours, they are beneath him. We believe the second statement true in morals, because we see the first true in fact.

His next adventure of this kind is in Boreyda, Doughty's farthest penetration into the interior of the peninsula. Arriving alone and at night, he is stripped and beaten, and his papers and baggage are ransacked by fanatics who demand he make the Moslem confession. He cries out for help; at the last moment an officer rescues him. Again the feelings of the townspeople make it impossible for the better class to protect him indefinitely from the mob, and he is put out of Boreyda to travel on to Aneyza. His guides abandon him there with only eight reals left. He finds a liberal friend in Aneyza who for a while makes life easier, but the inevitable tension builds up and he must leave. Called out of the house in which he is staying in the middle of the night, he pleads sickness, lack of money, debts in the town for medicine which he has not collected; to all this the sheik who leads the hostile party answers with violent and scornful orders to leave.

> "Ha-ha! what is that to us, I say come off": as I regarded him fixedly, the villain struck me with his fist in the face.—If the angry instinct betray me, the rest (I thought) would fall with their weapons upon the Nasrâny:—Aly had pulled his sword from the sheath to the half. "This, I said to him, you may put up again; what need of violence?"

As the pattern of events recurs again and again, the pace quickens. Within three pages of his exit from Aneyza he faces another crisis with a mutinous guide. Half by accident Doughty's pistol is exposed to view; the sight is enough to terrify the guide into momentary compliance. It is the first serious use he has made of the long-threatened pistol. Very soon comes the familiar dialogue, with accusation and rebuttal, provoking the inevitable blow on the face, this time followed by threats of a stoning. A young man, once a patient of Doughty's, comes up "by chance" and stems the tide for a while.

By this time the adventure of traveling in Arabia is over. Doughty is now anxious only to escape from the country by the nearest possible route, before his illnesses and poverty combine with Arab hostility to destroy him. He has pursued as direct a journey as he can toward the seaport of Jidda, but now that he has a definite goal and compelling reasons to reach it, he finds himself almost entirely without control of his actions. Besides, his route necessarily takes him close to Mecca, and the dangers he has been running are understandably most acute when he finds himself on the outskirts of the sacred city confronting a madman with a knife:

> When he came thus with his knife, and saw me stand still, with a hand in my bosom [gripping the pistol], he stayed with wonder and discouragement. Commonly among three Arabians is one mediator; their spirits are soon spent, and indifferent bystanders incline to lenity and good counsel: I waited therefore that some would open his mouth on my behalf!—but there was no man. I looked in the scelerat's eyes; and totter-headed, as are so many poor nomads, he might not abide it; but, heaving up his khánjar, he fetched a great breath (he was infirm, as are not few in that barren life, at the middle age) and made feints with the weapon at my chest; so with a sigh he brought down his arm and drew it to him again.

The fanatic raises his knife again, and again the arguments of prudence and anger pass through Doughty's mind, and again someone interrupts. The new element here simply confirms the impressions we have derived before. We see how thoroughly Doughty's mere passiveness has paralyzed the fanatic's arm, a passivity reflected in the language of the passage describing the incident, with its parenthetical generalizations on the health of middle-aged Arabs. The rabbit has charmed the snake.

Soon after this, though, he catches his tunic on an acacia bush and exposes his pistol. "Show me!" cry his companions, and in spite of expostulations he is forced to draw it and point it toward them. One of the ringleaders of the fanatic party closes in on him, and

> I gave back pace for pace: he opened his arms to embrace me!—there was but a moment, I must slay him, or render the weapon, my only defence; and my life would be at the discretion of these wretches.—I bade him come forward boldly. There was not time to shake out the shot, the pistol was yet suspended from my neck, by a strong lace: I offered the butt to his hands.

We could scarcely expect any other denouement. It is consistent with the character and progress of his adventures that he should, if challenged, yield his only remaining weapon, after health, money, and respect have failed. The suspense induced by the repetition of so elementary, yet so ambiguous, a pattern of action has not been of any practical use to us as readers; we have had nothing to look forward to but more humiliation, since we know that Doughty survived to write the tale we are reading. The protracted agony does, however, convince us of the importance of this mode of confrontation and makes us willing to see it as the typical action of the book, the essential adventure of the self Doughty records, the metaphor in which his meaning finds embodiment. Despairing repetition, inhibited will, helpless appeal: what are we to make of these?

It ought by now to be plain how very unlike the commonplace Victorian hero Doughty is. Ordinary adventures move from a clear start to a clear goal. The intervening incidents are helps toward this goal. Sufferings are bearable because they are provisional. The protagonist is superior to his surroundings. Crises occur when he proves this superiority. Morally the adventurer conducts an experiment in which the values of his home culture are tested against a neutral background. Finally, the story is told in plain prose to a wide audience. Doughty has reversed every one of these defining characteristics. He has criticized the ideal by turning it upside down. (pp. 59-65)

The journey down into Arabia is a pilgrimage for Doughty as well as for the Moslems he accompanies in the early part of his journey, and we are never unaware that he is a solitary Christian in a land of infidels. With the same determined perversity that characterizes so much of his behavior in Arabia, Doughty called himself "Nasrâny," apparently the most provocative of the available names for a Christian. His private belief amounts to a reserved and tolerant agnosticism: publicly, he puts himself in a position to incur the full weight of religious fanaticism. The Arabs thought him a contemptible Nasrâny; very well, a Nasrâny he would be, to the death if necessary. It is plainly one of the signs of the ethical insufficiency of Islam that it should permit concealment of faith to those whose faith is so bigoted. A higher standard of belief requires a stricter integrity in Doughty, whose personal religion is so much weaker than that of the most skeptical Moslem. Such an irony turns against the self which enjoys it. The imitation of Christ, stripped of its sacramental character by unbelief, is slow suicide.

The moral residuum of this process is a judgment, not of Doughty, but of his world. We have observed that the ordinary hero conducts an experiment in which the home values are tested in his own person. Here it is Arabia that is being tested. Doughty is himself the blank background which throws into sad relief the moral inadequacy of Islam. The hero has proved, not that he is heroic, but that his environment is inhuman. By simply wandering about, Doughty has given a world its chance, and perhaps, by extension, all worlds their chance. To reach this point of moral leverage, Doughty must throw away every normal advantage. The more extreme his humiliation the more successful his redefinition of the heroic ideal. Upon this paradox Doughty has staked his claims for his strange book. (pp. 67-8)

Jonathan Bishop, "The Heroic Ideal in Doughty's 'Arabia Deserta'," in Modern Language Quarterly, *Vol. XXI, No. 1, March, 1960, pp. 59-68.*

RICHARD BEVIS   (essay date 1972)

[*In the following excerpt, Bevis speculates on possible reasons for Doughty's journeys through the Arabian peninsula, proposing that Doughty was attracted to the religious, cultural, linguistic, and geological primitivism that he discovered there.*]

Critical speculations and inferences about Doughty's motives [for his Arabian journey] have been plentiful, and most of them can be supported in some degree from the text [of *Travels in Arabia Deserta*]. No one has entirely overlooked, and none can afford to ignore, the religious dimension of Doughty's Arabian venture. In his prefaces he declares his interest "in all that pertains to Biblical research," and tells us that he felt himself "carried back to the days of the nomad Hebrew patriarchs" when among the Arabian bedouin. Throughout the text he never tires of citing Old Testament parallels or attacking the religion of the Prophet Mohammed. Most impressive of all, he continually flaunts the name of Christian in the faces of his Muslim hosts, despite the vexation and danger involved, when outward renunciation would have been easy and convenient.

But to argue that Doughty moved through Arabia chiefly as a Christian—that his Christianity kept him going, as it were—involves serious difficulties, unless we take the extreme position that he was a saint seeking martyrdom. For it is precisely his profession of Christianity which causes Khalil (as Doughty called himself in Arabia) most of his grief, predictably enough; one can hardly imagine a less propitious place and time to practice Christianity than the Arabian peninsula in the 1870's. Doughty keeps going *despite* his religion, not *because* of it. Furthermore, the exact content and nature of Doughty's Christianity remain shadowy. His biographer, Hogarth, described him (on the basis of personal acquaintance) as "an agnostic Humanitarian of heart-felt piety and deep reverence for any *credo* based on Reason"—a remark whose implications have been surprisingly neglected by writers on Doughty. Indeed, what is striking about Doughty's Christianity in Arabia is the extent to which it is formal and intellectual only; his real emotions seem to lie elsewhere. Reverence and spirituality abound in his narrative, but whether they are *Christian* is highly problematical, and Professor Assad's choice of "Nasrâny" as a label for Doughty is balanced by John Middleton Murry's vision of Doughty as "veritably an Ishmael, who would find a home for his soul in the desert, or nowhere at all."

Faced with these difficulties, other writers have sought secular motives for his soujourn in Arabia. David Hogarth insists that "throughout the Arabian enterprise and in all the labours of relating it, Doughty was inspired primarily by a scientific purpose . . . ," while Barker Fairley would shift the emphasis towards race history, and Sir Ronald Storrs says flatly that for Doughty, as for T. E. Lawrence, the "spell of Arabia" was "the past." All of these theories strike me as being somewhat circumscribed, a bit too cold and (except for Storrs) superficial, to explain satisfactorily the peculiar power of the book, or Doughty's self-description as "*Saiêhh,* 'a walker about the world,' 'God's wanderer, who, not looking back to his worldly interest, betakes himself to the contemplative life's pilgrimage.'" This statement seems to turn us back towards Christian piety, tempered by a certain philosophic and humanitarian breadth.

At this apparent impasse, surely the safest course is to seek a way out through Doughty's own text. In his "Preface to the Second Edition" of *Arabia Deserta* he describes the inception of his nomadic interval thus:

> The pilgrims come again [up from Mecca to Mada'in Salih], I did not return with them to Syria; but rode with a friendly *sheykh* of the district Beduins, to live with them awhile in the high desert. I might thus, I hoped, visit the next Arabian uplands and view those vast waterless marches of the nomad Arabia; tent-dwellers, inhabiting, from the beginning, as it were beyond the World.

Laconic enough, yet not lacking in significant clues which are echoed elsewhere in the book. A land and a people "beyond the World" and before time: are they what held and fascinated Doughty? These tribesfolk, he goes on, "continue to observe a Great Semitic Law, unwritten; namely the ancient Faith of their illimitable empty wastes." This law he shares with them, despite their menaces and revilings of the Nasrâny, and his equally narrow and fanatical detestation of Wahhabi Islam. Moreover, Doughty and the bedouin share a broader cameraderie transcending religion, since all participate in what he calls "the great antique humanity of the Semitic desert," a brotherhood of men in extremis:

> The traveller must be himself, in men's eyes,
> a man worthy to live under the bent of God's

heaven, and were it without a religion: he is such who has a clean human heart and long-suffering under his bare shirt; it is enough, and though the way be full of harms, he may travel to the ends of the world.

Forty years later Doughty gratefully recalled many good moments of "human fellowship" in Arabia; it is perhaps the chief weakness of Edward Garnett's fine abridgment of *Arabia Deserta* that it somewhat magnifies the proportion of distress in the full narrative, journalistically sacrificing the dull and normal to the spectacular.

And yet, it would be fully as difficult to make out a case for human associations as Doughty's "moving cause" in Arabia as it would be for Christianity: both made him suffer at length. It was not only a question of religion; Doughty was radically ambivalent about the race itself. "The Semites are like to a man sitting in a cloaca to the eyes, and whose brows touch heaven," runs his famous epigram. Such moments of balance, or the more positive statements quoted above, are deeply compromised by a multitude of ill-tempered assaults on Arabian minds and manners scattered throughout the narrative. The self-proclaimed student of the past is soon disillusioned with the "tent-dwellers" . . . beyond the World."

But the "vast waterless marches" do not disappoint him; the land itself impresses him profoundly, awakening the poet and the religious philosopher in him. Doughty himself draws our attention to this aspect of his book:

> Of surpassing interest to those many minds, which seek after philosophic knowledge and instruction, is the Story of the Earth. Her manifold living creatures, the human generations and Her ancient rocks.

Note the "divine capitals," and his characteristic way of setting all life firmly within its geological context. Elsewhere "Faith" and "humanity are both said to be "of" the desert wastes, and the Banu Sakhr tribe are "children of sandstone." Even among Arabian travellers, a very land-conscious group, Doughty's responsiveness to topography is exceptional. Many writers on the desert have, for example, compared it in passing to the ocean, but in *Arabia Deserta* the analogy is elaborated and extended into a pervasive metaphor. Mountains become "coasts," the oasis village of Khaybar is "an island," and (in the Mudawwarra plain between Ma'an and Aqaba) "sometimes the soil is a flaggy pavement of sandstones, rippled in the strand of those old planetary seas." Deep in Arabia Doughty catches sight of the summit of Jabal Anaz, "riding as it were upon the rocky tempest . . . I despaired of coming thither, over so many vulcanic deeps and reefs of lavas. . . ." One major function of Doughty's unorthodox style is the impressionistic conveyance, not only of images of the landscape, but of the emotions which that landscape evokes in the wanderer. Arabia, "that vast mountainous labyrinthine solitude of rainless valleys," assumes the proportions of a first cause, towering above, before and beyond man:

> We look out from every height, upon the Harra, over an iron desolation; what uncouth blackness and lifeless cumber of vulcanic matter!—an hardset face of nature without a smile for ever, a wilderness of burning and rusty horror of unformed matter. What lonely life would not feel constraint of heart to trespass here! the barren heaven! the nightmare soil! where should he

> look for comfort?—There is a startled conscience within a man of his *mesquîn* begin, and profane, in presence of the divine stature of the elemental world!—this lion-like sleep of cosmogonic forces, in which is swallowed up the gnat of the soul within him,—that short motion and parasitical usurpation which is the weak accident of life in matter.

This passage is additional testimony to Doughty's unusual preoccupation with topography, of course, but it has other aspects as well, whose common denominator is elusiveness. Each time we sense it approaching some familiar mode of thought our expectations are violated. Clearly this was a moment of deep religious (or quasi-religious) feeling for Doughty, a kind of epiphany, but was it a Christian perception? Hardly: "heaven" is "barren," life only a "weak accident" in matter, and there is no answer to "where should he look for comfort?" According to Genesis God gave man dominion over the earth, while here is a suffocating tyranny of the material world.

Is it deism then, that frequent resort of Romantic poets and nature-writers, the process by which the "book of nature" leads us inevitably to nature's God? At first glance it may appear so, but we must be wary. For the deist, nature is generally transcendental: a means to an end (whether religious or spiritual), an optical aid to view a higher truth. Wordsworth among the daffodils or atop Mount Snowdon, Coleridge in the Vale of Chamonix, Shelley in his bleak Caucasian ravine or Keats before a flower, take off from nature as from a springboard, and end up somewhere else. But in the ***Arabia Deserta*** passage, if there is anywhere else to go, any divinity beyond nature, we must infer its existence for ourselves; Doughty himself does not even suggest it. In fact, he seems deliberately to locate the deity within this "hard-set face of nature": man finds himself "in presence of the divine stature of the elemental world," though he himself is "profane."

Doughty in Arabian attire.

Another possible classification might be Darwinism, for there are notable affinities between Doughty's vision of man dwarfed and threatened by hostile nature, and Darwin's picture of an unending struggle for survival. But the dissimilarities are equally striking: Darwin's "nature red in tooth and claw" is mainly a struggle between competing organisms, whereas in ***Arabia Deserta*** the emphasis falls rather on inanimate nature. Doughty is known to have studied and maintained an interest in the natural science of his day. It was not the "new biology" which claimed his attention, however; it was the "new geology," which burst upon Europe a generation before Darwin, with Sir Charles Lyell as its chief apostle. "I was as much Geologist as Nasrâny," Doughty wrote to Hogarth in 1904. It is this early and lifelong devotion to geology—and the attitudes connected with it—which I propose as the starting point for understanding Doughty, his travels and his book. Though this facet of Doughty's thought has not been entirely overlooked by writers on his work, it has not been sufficiently emphasized either, nor its ramifications adequately explored. In the end the "Story of the Earth"—*geo-logos*—is the story of ***Arabia Deserta***—but *finis origine pendet*. (pp. 164-68)

The great confrontation of religion and science in the nineteenth century did not begin with Darwin; the strife between theologians and biologists after 1859 was preceded by a less well-known but equally virulent controversy between theologians and geologists which formed a prologue to the drama of Darwinism. Tennyson's "In Memoriam," often invoked as a convenient literary manifestation of the Victorians' agonizing reassessment of faith in the light of empirical reason, was published nine years before *The Origin of Species,* and it is more concerned with terrestrial science than with anthropology:

> There rolls the deep where grew the tree.
> O earth, what changes hast thou seen
> There where the long street roars, hath been
> The stillness of the central sea.
>
> The hills are shadows, and they flow
> From form to form, and nothing stands;
> They melt like mist, the solid lands,
> Like clouds they shape themselves and go.
>
> (CXXIII).

The trouble (already more than half a century old) was over the increasingly successful efforts of some geologists to impugn the so-called "Mosaic geology"—the creation and flood narratives in Genesis—and to substitute for it a naturalistic earth history based on observed data. In 1788, when James Hutton, a brilliant Scottish lawyer, farmer and natural historian, published his *Theory of the Earth,* fossils were still supposed to have been deposited by Noah's Flood. Hutton, however, insisted that the geological past and present could be explained wholly in terms of forces still at work and observable by anyone who would "go and see," thus earning for himself the title of "the father of modern geology." He estimated that the earth was vastly older than Biblical geology made it out to be, and argued strongly for the importance of earthquakes and volcan-

oes in effecting changes on the earth's crust throughout its existence.

Hutton's views were of course fiercely attacked by those whom Lyell would later call "physico-theologians," but, supported by other geologists, made gradual headway: a Geological Society was formed in London in 1807, and a topographical map of Great Britain, made in 1815. Yet in 1820 a young geology student named Charles Lyell was still being taught by "catastrophists" and "diluvialists" that the earth was formed by a series of great floods and upheavals unlike anything now known, and as late as 1826 he seems to have believed them. But his reading and field work of the next few years changed his mind completely; he swung over to "the adequacy of present causes," and with the publication of *The Principles of Geology* in 1830 emerged as the leading spokesman for "uniformitarianism," the view that geological forces are now what they were in the past—in other words, roughly Hutton's theory, more fully exposited and documented. Lyell's position, though rather a synthesis of other men's ideas than a new departure, proved a convenient focus for the controversy, his insistence on taking nature, not Scripture, as his authority being furiously assaulted. But his references to Scripture were so circumspect, his field evidence in successive editions so overwhelming, and his non-geological utterances on religion so conservative, that his opponents were disarmed and forced to retreat from point to point. In 1835, when Lyell was elected President of the Geological Society, his party gained the field, and British science was relatively peaceful until organic evolution became an issue in the mid-1840's.

Today we can read *The Principles* without a quickening of the pulse, and uniformitarian geology seems mere induction. Lyell (like Darwin) emerges from his writings as a cautious scientist given to understatement, not as a revolutionary; he did not even accept biological evolution until he read *The Origin of Species*. And despite all the efforts to divorce religion and science they remained intertwined (as they are in Doughty); Lyell was among those who agreed that the laws of nature, while immutable and in no need of miraculous intervention, are of divine origin. Thus in some respects uniformitarianism suggests another avatar of Deism, which had been around for a century and a half and should have bothered no one.

But the impact of Lyell's argument at the time on Doughty and other Victorian scientists was powerful, and understandably so, for the implications were enormous. Deism had simply argued that the book of nature as well as the book of God (the Bible) could lead man to God's truth; it had assumed there was only one truth and that the two books were therefore in harmony. But here in the new geology was a reading of the book of nature which contradicted the book of God and seemed to point towards a different truth, and its advocates, instead of shying away from this clash, seemed determined to press the new truth to its conclusion, whatever that might be. Fully grasped and accepted, the uniformitarian position "logically required the rejection of the whole framework of conventional natural theology," and the deep concern shown by many sincere lay Christians is no more surprising than the hysteria of Lyell's "theological sophists." In this atmosphere of challenge and crisis the young Doughty sought to work out his own convictions and establish harmony between his religious piety and his passion for natural science.

In *Arabia Deserta* we have evidence of the nature of that reconciliation, while, reversing the token, the symbiosis of science and religion helps explain the book's unique qualities. The explanation lies in Doughty's particular response to the implications of uniformitarianism. For the average nineteenth-century Christian, Lyell's geology undermined the accounts of nature and history in the Book of God; therefore, it somehow threatened God Himself—or at least removed Him from human knowledge, like the deities of Lucretius, aloof in interstellar space. But there was another way out, virtually the polar opposite in that it did not distance God but brought Him closer, locating Him in nature and even identifying Him with it. This was not a difficult leap for faith to make. Among the manifestations of the Christian God, His role as the Creator, or the creating force, is paramount; to the Deist, this is perhaps His only knowable manifestation. But Lyell and the uniformitarians claimed that they had discovered the shaping and creating forces of the planet, not in the dim inconceivable past, not in some revelation accessible to faith alone, but all around us new, still at work, observable by anyone who would "go and see," and, best of all, open and convincing to the empirical intelligence. The Deists of the European Enlightenment, elaborating Descartes, liked to say that God had wound up the watch of the universe and had then withdrawn somewhere to let it run by itself, but they were now seen to be wrong: He was still present and active, as volcano, earthquake and glacier, as wind and water action, only Christians had not recognized Him previously in this guise. The creation was yet proceeding in many areas, and even where it was quiescent one could see evidence of similar creations in the relatively recent past (such as folding and faulting and overthrusting in mountain ranges) which elucidated the continuing processes and were the hand, as well as the handiwork, of the Creator. It was unorthodox, it might even be heretical—certainly some attributes of God and terms in the divine equation were being changed—but it was here and it was dynamic. No wonder that, under the influence of this perception, a sensitive youth such as Doughty responded by attaching to nature the kind of emotional reverence we normally expect to encounter in a religious context.

Much about Doughty's life now falls into place. Why did he spend nearly a decade of his young manhood in "studious travel"? Partly, of course, to steep himself in the cultural past of Europe and the Mediterranean and thus prepare for his projected epic on the history of Britain. But, also, Lyell had written:

> If it be true that delivery be the first, second and third requisite in a popular orator, it is no less certain that to travel is of first, second and third importance to those who desire to originate just and comprehensive views concerning the structure of our globe.

And both the Christian and the natural scientist in Doughty would want to do just this. Why the special attachment to Arabian topography, when other areas held more historic and archeological interest? Here other travellers to Arabia are helpful, for many of them have remarked on a striking feature of the geological structure of the Peninsula: that it seems to be the "bare bones" of the planet. Richard Burton, like Doughty, noticed this, and also the spirituality associated with it:

> This day's march was peculiarly Arabia. It was a desert peopled only with echoes,—a place of death for what little there is to die in it,—a wilderness where, to use my companion's phrase, there is nothing but He. Nature scalped, flayed, discovered all her skeleton to the gazer's eye.

And this is to take only one example of dozens, the basic idea always being that in Arabia—and the Middle East generally— one could inspect the skeleton or structural foundations of the earth, the fundamental building materials, whereas in Europe this architectural or anatomical lesson was usually buried beneath a layer of terrestrial skin and flesh. Thus in Arabia one was closer to, because more aware of, the Creator. (This idea was supported by a touch of the Rousseavian misanthropy about civilized, progressive, overcrowded Europe which one encounters in many nineteenth-century desert travellers, and perhaps by a general fascination with the Near East as the cradle of early civilization, though one finds little of the latter in Doughty's pages.) "Why," asked Hogarth, "did such as these hazard themselves in a land so naked . . .?" The answer, which was before him, should now be clear to us: that nakedness was precisely its attraction.

Lyell's view of nature also seems to have influenced Doughty's view of man. We should expect to find Doughty's anthropology colored by *The Origin of Species,* and indeed phrases like "natural selection" and "survival of the fittest" do seem to describe an important aspect of human existence in the book. But, as I suggested earlier in discussing Doughty's description of the Harra, on close examination his outlook proves not to be that of Darwin; it is merely "darwinesque." The adversary of man in his struggle for survival is not man, or any other species, but *inanimate* nature, which is savagely "red in tooth and claw," but at the same time spiritualized, granted the attributes of God the Creator and thereby imbued with holiness. Man is seen as locked in a fierce struggle with God-as-Nature, a personal confrontation which nevertheless results in blood brotherhood between them, as in the Semitic myth of Jacob, who wrestled with the angel and was named Israel, "he who strives with God."

Nature in Doughty's Arabia, then, could be said to play the role of a Scourge of God. It turns on man a face of awful and seldom-relenting hostility, but from this clash is born a rapport with the divine, so that the encounter is religious and ultimately beneficial for man. Doughty notes that physical suffering on the Muslim *haj* is not an unwanted by-product but an integral part of the process of purification, and thus "meritorious"; "there are many whom their old pain so enamours of the sacred way, that they will fare anew and cannot forsake it." Having heaven smite one's brows is, evidently, one way of having one's brows touch heaven. Finally, just as in Darwin the grimmest struggle selects the finest survivors, so in Doughty the more bitter the opposition of man and nature, and the hotter the purging crucible, the stronger will be the links with the divine thus forged. Hence, for Doughty, "Arabia Felix" becomes "Arabia Phoenix": a trial by fire leading to spiritual rebirth. The entire cycle of cosmic animus, followed by peace, renewed life and renewed trial, is visible in his set piece on a summer day in the Nafūd waste:

> The summer's night at end, the sun stands up as a crown of hostile flames from that huge covert of inhospitable sandstone bergs; the desert day dawns not little and little, but it is noontide in an hour. The sun, entering as a tyrant upon the waste landscape, darts upon us a torment of fiery beams, not to be remitted till the far-off evening.—No matins here of birds; not a rock partridge-cock, calling with blithesome chuckle over the extreme waterless desolation. Grave is that giddy heat upon the crown of the

head; the ears tingle with a flickering shrillness, a subtle crepitation it seems, in the glassiness of this sun-stricken nature: the hot sand-blink is in the eyes, and there is little refreshment to find in the tent's shelter; the worsted booths leak to this fiery rain of sunny light. Mountains looming like dry bones through the thin air, stand far around about us: the savage flank of Ybba Moghrair, the high spire and ruinous stacks of el-Jebal, Chebad, the coast of Helwan! Herds of the weak nomad camels waver dispersedly, seeking pasture in the midst of this hollow fainting country, where but lately the swarming locusts have fretted every green thing. This silent air burning about us, we endure breathless till the assr: when the dazing Arabs in the tents revive after their heavy hours. The lingering day draws down to the sun-setting; the herdsmen, weary of the sun, come again with the cattle, to taste in their menzils the first sweetness of mirth and repose.—The day is done, and there rises the nightly freshness of this purest mountain air: and then to the cheerful song and cup at the common fire. The moon rises ruddy from that solemn obscurity of jebel like a mighty beacon:—and the morrow will be as this day, days deadly drowned in the sun of the summer wilderness.

Here the blend of Lyell with Darwin is evident, but to see clearly the spirit of religious philosophy in Doughty aroused by this environment we must complete the cycle and hear his nocturne:

> The summer night's delightful freshness in the mountain is our daily repast; and lying to rest amidst wild basalt-stones under the clear stars, in a land of enemies, I have found more refreshment than upon beds and pillows in our close chambers.—Hither lies no way from the city of the world, a thousand years pass as one daylight; we are in the world and not in the world, where Nature brought forth man, an enigma to himself, and an evil spirit sowed in him the seeds of dissolution. And, looking then upon that infinite spectacle, this life of the wasted flesh seemed to me ebbing, and the spirit to waver her eyas wings unto that divine obscurity.

If this seems to have more of St. Augustine ("the city of the world") and Christian *contemptus mundi,* with less geology than I have been premising, note that "Nature brought forth man" and that nature, not revelation, gives rise to these reflections. "Our daily repast" is given by Nature, while stars and stones refresh him in the valley of the shadow of death. Taken together, the two passages exhibit the mixture of natural science with spirituality which is characteristic of *Arabia Deserta.*

But reverence for the land is not quite the bedrock of Doughty's thought. His religion of nature is only one important manifestation of a deeper impulse which informed all of his work, and to recognize this impulse is to perceive the unity of all he did from about age twenty onwards. This ultimate substratum is "primitivism," the drive to get back to simplest beginnings, and it underlies every aspect of his prose, his poetry and life.

The passage quoted above from *Arabia Deserta* may well call to mind, among other things, the early Christian desert hermits, and the next paragraph confirms this inference:

> . . . I mused in these nights and days of the old hermits of Christian faith that were in the upper desert countries—and there will rise up some of the primitive temper in every age to renew and judge the earth; how there fled many willfully from the troublesome waves of the world, devising in themselves to retrieve the first Adam in their own souls, and coveting a sinless habitation with the elements, whither, saving themselves out of the common calamities, they might accomplish the time remaining of their patience, and depart to better life. A natural philosophy meditates the goodly rule and cure; religious asceticism is sharp surgery to cut away the very substance of man's faulty affections. . . .

Though Doughty is ostensibly speaking of ancient hermits here, there is an obvious self-portrait as well: the man of "primitive temper" come to "renew" the earth; yet also the man who flees the world to seek a prelapsarian sinlessness, like "the first Adam," the common denominator of both being "religious asceticism." T. E. Lawrence observed that Doughty was "keen" only "on life and death," while he himself cared for "psychology and politics" (but we find the same "sharp surgery" of asceticism, the yearning to reduce life to its bare essentials, in Lawrence and other desert travellers as well).

This primitivist outlook is apparent everywhere in Doughty's career: in his piety, in his nationalism, in his approach to literature and science. As a Christian, first, he was interested in his religious origins; this was one of the attractions for him of the Near East. For the "back to the Bible" fundamentalism of the Methodists could not satisfy his intellect, though he shared the evangelists' preference for the Old Testament. No bookish devotion was enough: he must visit the lands where Christianity originated. But here again, the venerable pilgrimage to Egypt and Palestine would not suffice; he must go beyond, to the desert, to see the patriarchal ways surviving among the bedouin. Nominally an Anglican, Doughty was a Puritan in the extremes to which he would press a point. (A fine irony of the book is that his troublesome opponents in Arabia were the Puritans of Islam, the zealous Wahhabis.) Sinai and Syria and Arabia Petraea still did not content him, though he saw nomads there: he pressed on into the interior, anxious to reach the oasis of Khaybar, chiefly because of the reputed antiquity of its Jewish settlement. Though other motives also played a part, the logic of this sequence is that of religious primitivism, and Doughty is outspoken in his narrative and prefaces about his desire to know at first hand the life of the Pentateuch. (pp. 170-77)

The primitive . . . is the unifying idea of Doughty's thought and labours, linking his interest in science, his religion, his patriotism and his writings. Doughty found a congenial home for that idea in the land of the Arabs, and its various manifestations are fused in the prose-poem named for that land. The archaic diction is suited to filial piety for Mother England and Mother Nature; the "Story of the Earth" is the final "rearwall," the backdrop to man and the origin of his religion, and the more bare and skeletal the landscape becomes the more deeply the spiritual geologist is moved. The patriot, the Judaeo-Christian, and the natural scientist are satisfied that they have found their sources, and call upon the artist to embody their perception in suitable language. At that point *Arabia Deserta* begins:

> A new voice hailed me of an old friend when, first returned from the Peninsula, I paced again in that long street of Damascus which is called Straight, and suddenly taking me wondering by the hand "Tell me (said he), since thou art here again in the peace and assurance of Ullah, and whilst we walk, as in the former years, toward the new blossoming orchards, full of the sweet spring as the garden of God, what moved thee, or how couldst thou take such journeys into the fanatic Arabia?"

This question encircles the journey: though asked afterwards, it occurs at the start of the book and seeks the prior motive. It is the question that began my essay, and one that both Doughty and I, in our own ways, try to answer. (pp. 180-81)

> *Richard Bevis, "Spiritual Geology: C. M. Doughty and the Land of the Arabs," in* Victorian Studies, *Vol. XVI, No. 2, December, 1972, pp. 163-81.*

STEPHEN ELY TABACHNICK (essay date 1981)

[*Tabachnick is an Israeli educator and critic specializing in the literature of the British empire. In the following excerpt, he analyzes the narrative complexities of* Travels in Arabia Deserta.]

At first glance, the narration of the autobiographical *Arabia Deserta* would seem to present no problems. As narrator of the book Doughty always refers to himself as "I" and the Arabs call him "Khalil," exactly as they did in Arabia. What could be more straightforward? But all observers have noticed a certain difference, or distance, between the narrative voice that tells the story and Khalil, the protagonist who acts in it. Barker Fairley explains this felt difference in the following way: "It goes without saying that when Doughty looked back at those extraordinary days, they seemed unbelievably strange to him and that he was unable to work with a complete sense of identity between himself who was writing and the man whose astonishing story he was telling." The distance between the narrator and Khalil the protagonist can be seen in three areas of the text itself. First, "Khalil" is not just any name, a mere phonetic equivalent of "Charles," but a highly symbolic name, meaning "Friend," and referring to Islam's "Friend of God," Abraham. By continually calling him this, the Arab characters in *Arabia Deserta* transform the protagonist into a kind of allegorical Everyman, thus giving him a quality not found in the narrator's descriptions of him. And, in fact, Khalil as we see him in *Arabia Deserta* is an idealized artistic construct who represents the best in Doughty's personality. Further, we find that Khalil—as in his conversations with Abdullah El Kenneyny in Aneyza—comes out with declarations of universal love and religious tolerance in addition to more prejudiced remarks, while the more bitter and ironic retrospective narrator, who is never of course under social pressure since he is only a voice, never admits Islam to the inner circle of civilized religions and only very rarely or never shows the tolerance that we see in some of Khalil's conversations. Finally, the narrator occasionally offers forward-looking information—as for instance when he mentions the Bombay Jews whom Doughty was to meet only after leaving Arabia—which the Khalil who is limited to knowledge of the present cannot know about. Thus, whether or not he precisely intended this separation between narrative voice and protagonist, Doughty the artist created it, and the reader feels it more and more as the book progresses.

As the use of the term "Doughty the artist" indicates, we find yet another distinction operating in the narrative texture of *Arabia Deserta*: that between the narrative voice, which describes and comments on the characters and action, including Khalil's thoughts, and reports the dialogue, and Doughty the artist, who almost like a novelist controls both Khalil and the narrative voice. It is Doughty the artist who creates the dialogue of the characters, decides which characters will be included in the book, which incidents concerning Khalil and other characters the narrator will report, which words the narrator will use, which qualities of the characters the narrator will stress, when things will happen, where the chapter divisions, illustrations, appendixes, index, and map will be, and speaks directly to us in the prefaces.

D. H. Lawrence noticed the difference between artist and narrator when he commented about Melville that "the artist was so much greater than the man." By this, he meant that Ishmael, Melville's mouthpiece-narrator in *Moby Dick,* is frequently preachy and tiresome and that the book is much more complicated than Ishmael is. . . . It is Doughty the artist, with his conscious and subconscious integrity and desire to respect the "truth" and deep human empathy, who has made this shift of sympathy possible, because he is much "greater" than either the narrator or Khalil. He has put powerful words in the mouths of the Arab characters, and has made the narrator (who strikes us in his dogmatism and moralizing as very much a limited Victorian) include incidents and statements which do not always support his case, even when he thinks they do. In other words, as conscious teller of his tale, Doughty reveals his own Victorian narrowness and limitations; but as deep artist, he has shown much more sympathy and understanding than he consciously knows, and this appears in many ways.

For example, Sirur, Abdullah's lieutenant at Kheybar, is depicted as a stupid and brutal bully in the narrator's report of his actions, the narrator's assessment of those actions, and in Khalil's dialogues with him. But in at least one incident the modern reader will side with Sirur rather than with the narrator and Khalil. Khalil tries to determine the ethnic origins of the people of Kheybar, using his crude, pseudo-scientific nineteenth-century physical anthropology:

> Seeing these more Arab-looking, and even copper-coloured village faces, and that some young men here wore their negro locks braided as the Nomads, I enquired, had they no tradition of their ancestry. They answered me: "We are Jeheyna;—but is there nothing of Kheybar written in your books?"—"Are not the Kheyâbara from the Sudàn?—or from whence have they these lips and noses?"

Sirur responds to Khalil's comment about "lips and noses" as follows: "*Sirûr* (with his ribald malice), 'Come up, each of ye people of Umm Kida! and let this wise stranger feel each of your noses (khusshm), and declare to you what ancestry ye be of, and where is every man's natural béled'." Despite the narrator's obvious intention of denigrating Sirur ("with ribald malice" indicates the narrator's view of Sirur's intentions), the modern reader, knowing the dangers of Khalil's badly based "racial" anthropology, will find Sirur's comments more wise than malicious, or properly malicious. The narrator wants us

to take sides against Sirur, but the artist in Doughty has made it possible for us to do the opposite. In Sirur's remarks we feel his justified resentment against the white man's "scientific" racism and perhaps against Khalil's superior tone when uttering "'these lips and noses,'" all of which Doughty the artist has captured perfectly and preserved for the alert reader. Somewhat more obvious examples of the same phenomenon of artist outflanking narrator and Khalil are the well-stated defense of polygamy by the Beduin and Mohammed Ibn Rashid's intelligent suspicion of colonialism, both of which views the characters state powerfully while the narrator and Khalil fail to agree with them.

We can sum up the narrative forces operating in *Arabia Deserta* in the following convenient manner: (1) *Khalil:* The protagonist who acts and speaks and is addressed by other characters in the present, and whose thoughts, actions, and dialogue are reported and described by the narrator. An idealized Everyman version of Doughty's personality. (2) *The narrator:* The highly intelligent but moralistic and prejudiced voice which describes and comments on the characters (including Khalil and his thoughts), and on the action, sometimes looking ahead of it or to a period before it occurred. He also reports and comments on the dialogue. Doughty as conscious Victorian. (3) *Doughty the artist:* The force which created and controls all the elements in the work, of which Khalil and the narrator are only two. He decides on the narrator's tone and thought and the style of the whole work, and precisely what Khalil or another character will say and do, and when they will say or do it. Because of the power he gives them in dialogue, the Arab characters frequently appear in a more favorable light than Khalil and the narrator (who reports the dialogue) think they do. Doughty as conscious and subconscious artist.

Because Doughty the artist is far greater than Doughty the man of his times (whom we see in the narrator's voice), his book becomes capable of continual self-renewal in all circumstances and periods, like any masterpiece. We perceive clearly the narrator's and Khalil's prejudices but can read through these to a greater sympathy with the Arabs and a more complex enjoyment of the book that Doughty the artist has made possible.

While we praise Doughty the artist of *Arabia Deserta* for his human sympathy, we must note that Doughty reveals a very different side of his artistic personality in the poetry, with the possible exception of *Adam Cast Forth*. In *Arabia Deserta*, Doughty had real people to work on, and by portraying them in all their complex detail as they appeared to him he surpassed his own narrow preconceptions of how they should be. The deep artist predominates over the Victorian narrator, as we have seen. Furthermore, Khalil becomes a saint—despite his faults—owing to his sufferings. If we wish to translate Doughty's artistic personality in *Arabia Deserta* somewhat simplistically, we can say that the book on the whole reveals his "masochistic" side, and that it is by far his best side. Desert sufferings seem to have liberated in him unknown artistic depths of sympathy not just for Khalil, but for the Arabs as well.

In the poetry, on the other hand, we find an overt sadism and almost fanatic chauvinism which can never sympathize with the perceived enemies of England, and which results in too many very bloody battle scenes in *Dawn in Britain* and the extremity of child sacrifice for Britain's sake in *The Cliffs*. It is as if only the moralizing and prejudiced narrator of *Arabia Deserta,* pushed to an extreme, exists in the characters, action, and speaker's voice of the poetry, without the qualifying greatness of the artist of *Arabia Deserta.* Only in *Adam Cast Forth,* where Doughty recapitulates his desert sufferings, do we feel a truly human note. In the rest of the poetry, where he creates his own fictional or semihistorical beings without deep auto-biographical connections, the result is either black and white stereotyping and wooden characters, or vapid abstractions. In short, in *Arabia Deserta,* Doughty reaches subconscious artistic depths of his personality, while in the poetry he remains the conscious, boring, and simpleminded Victorian patriot who addresses us directly through speaker's voice and characters as well. The distinction between the three narrative elements of *Arabia Deserta* and the difference between *Arabia Deserta* and the poetry noted here are worth keeping in mind. . . . However, these are only literary distinctions used to facilitate precise discussion of the works, and we should always remember that they represent only different aspects of the man Charles Montagu Doughty, himself. (pp. 48-52)

Stephen Ely Tabachnick, in his Charles Doughty, *Twayne Publishers, 1981, 183 p.*

ADDITIONAL BIBLIOGRAPHY

Assad, Thomas J. "Charles Montagu Doughty—Nasrâny." In his *Three Victorian Travellers: Burton, Blunt, Doughty,* pp. 95-132. London: Routledge & Kegan Paul, 1964.
    Contrasts Doughty's objective description of Arabian life with his subjective reaction to it.

Blunt, Wilfrid Scawen. "Siwah." In his *My Diaries: Being a Personal Narrative of Events 1888-1914,* pp. 242-76. New York: Alfred A. Knopf, 1921.
    Contains an entry dated 5 March 1897 calling *Travels in Arabia Deserta* "certainly the best prose written in the last two centuries."

"A Sacred Drama." *The Bookman* 34, No. 201 (June 1908): 113-14.
    Early review praising *Adam Cast Forth.*

Brittain, Mary Z. "Doughty's Mirror of Arabia." *The Moslem World* XXXVII, No. 1 (January 1947): 42-8.
    Discusses the wealth of information about Arabia contained in *Travels in Arabia Deserta.*

Brown, Alec. "C. M. Doughty, Poète Malgré Lui." *The Calendar* IV (April-July 1927): 111-25.
    Finds Doughty a brilliant lyric poet whose work was marred by his insistence on epic subjects for his poetry.

Colum, Padraic. "Epic of the Sea and Epic of the Desert." In his *A Half Day's Ride; or, Estates in Corsica,* pp. 175-84. New York: Macmillan Co., 1932.
    Compares Herman Melville's *Moby Dick* and *Travels in Arabia Deserta* as prose epics, emphasizing the heroic nature of Doughty's characterization and language.

Cournos, John. "Charles M. Doughty—The Supreme Traveler." In his *A Modern Plutarch; Being an Account of Some Great Lives in the Nineteenth Century, Together with Some Comparisons between the Latin and the Anglo-Saxon Genius,* pp. 119-26. Indianapolis: Bobbs-Merrill Co., 1928.
    Biographical discussion of Doughty calling *Travels in Arabia Deserta* "the greatest work of prose written in English during the nineteenth century."

Douglas, Norman. "*Arabia Deserta.*" In his *Experiments,* pp. 1-22. New York: Robert M. McBride & Co., 1925.
    Discusses the strong emotional content of *Travels in Arabia Deserta.*

Fairchild, Hoxie Neale. "More Mavericks." In his *Religious Trends in English Poetry: 1880-1929, Gods of a Changing Poetry,* Vol. V, pp. 296-346. New York and London: Columbia University Press, 1962.
    Contains a discussion of *The Dawn in Britain* and *Mansoul,* emphasizing the "modernism" of Doughty's archaic language and theistic beliefs.

Fairley, Barker. *Charles M. Doughty: A Critical Study.* London: Jonathan Cape, 1927, 256 p.
    Influential examination of *Travels in Arabia Deserta* and Doughty's poetry. Fairley relates Doughty's stylistic eccentricities to the subject matter of his work and notes the concrete, specific nature of Doughty's writing in contrast to the allusive, suggestive nature of much post-Shakespearian literature.

———. "Charles Doughty (1843-1926)." *University of Toronto Quarterly* XIII, No. 1 (October 1943): 14-24.
    General examination of Doughty's works written for the centennial of his birth.

———. "*The Dawn in Britain* after Fifty Years." *University of Toronto Quarterly* XXVI, No. 2 (January 1957): 149-64.
    Summarizes *The Dawn in Britain,* speculates on its date of origin, and examines its critical reputation.

Freeman, John. "Charles Montagu Doughty." *The London Mercury* XIV, No. 82 (August 1926): 368-82.
    Memorial tribute to Doughty with a general discussion of his work.

Heath-Stubbs, John. "Beyond Aestheticism." In his *The Darkling Plain: A Study of the Later Fortunes of Romanticism in English Poetry from George Darley to W. B. Yeats,* pp. 179-214. London: Eyre & Spottiswoode, 1950.
    Includes a discussion of *The Dawn in Britain,* considering it a great modern epic and Doughty's most important work.

Hogarth, D. G. *The Life of Charles M. Doughty.* Garden City, N.Y.: Doubleday, Doran & Co., 1929, 216 p.
    Biography written by a longtime correspondent of Doughty.

Hopkins, Gerard Manley. "CLXIII" and "CLXV." In *The Letters of Gerard Manley Hopkins to Robert Bridges,* pp. 282-84, 289-90. London and New York: Oxford University Press, 1935.
    Objects to Doughty's archaism. Hopkins maintains, "He writes in it, I understand, because it is manly. At any rate affectation is not manly, and to write in an obsolete style is affectation."

Jackson, Laura (Riding). "On C. M. Doughty." *PN Review* 10, No. 4 (1983): 34-8.
    General essay introducing readers to Doughty's work.

Lehmann, R. C. "An Amazing Epic." *The Bookman* 30, No. 177 (June 1906): 107-08.
    Early review of *The Dawn in Britain* acknowledging Doughty's talent while lamenting his archaism.

MacDiarmid, Hugh. "Charles Doughty and the Need for Heroic Poetry." In his *Selected Essays of Hugh MacDiarmid,* pp. 75-85. Berkeley and Los Angeles: University of California Press, 1970.
    A Marxist perspective on Doughty's poetry.

McCormick, Annette M. "Hebrew Parallelism in Doughty's *Travels in Arabia Deserta.*" In *Studies in Comparative Literature,* edited by Waldo F. McNeir, pp. 29-46. Baton Rouge: Louisiana State University Press, 1962.
    Compares the prose style of *Travels in Arabia Deserta* with that of Old Testament literature.

———. "An Elizabethan-Victorian Travel Book: Doughty's *Travels in Arabia Deserta.*" In *Essays in Honor of Esmond Linworth Marilla,* edited by Thomas Austin Kirby and William John Olive, pp. 230-42. Baton Rouge: Louisiana State University Press, 1970.
    Discusses the influence of sixteenth-century travel books on the composition of *Travels in Arabia Deserta.*

"Dead Doughty." *New Verse* 17 (October-November 1935): 21-2.

Denigrates Doughty's work and attacks favorable comparisons between Doughty and Gerard Manley Hopkins offered by Anne Treneer and Barker Fairley.

Pritchett, V. S. "'Arabia Deserta'." *The New Statesman and Nation* LII, No. 1330 (September 8, 1956): 285-86.
    Discusses Doughty's attempt to factually portray Arabia.

Thomas, Edward. Review of *The Dawn in Britain. The Bookman* 30, No. 180 (September 1906): 222-23.
    Laudatory early review.

Tidrick, Kathryn. "Charles M. Doughty (1843-1926)." In her *Heart-beguiling Araby,* pp. 136-56. Cambridge, England: Cambridge University Press, 1981.
    Interprets Doughty's insistent proclamation of Christianity during his travels in Arabia as an invitation to martyrdom due to his guilt over having lost his faith.

Van Doren, Mark. "*Arabia Deserta.*" In his *The Private Reader: Selected Articles and Reviews,* pp. 119-27. Henry Holt and Co., 1942.
    Examines the poetic quality of *Travels in Arabia Deserta,* applauding its rich language and completeness of detail.

Weygandt, Cornelius. "The Birds of *Arabia Deserta.*" In his *Tuesdays at Ten: A Garnering from the Talks of Thirty Years on Poets, Dramatists, and Essayists,* pp. 108-17. Philadelphia: University of Pennsylvania Press, 1928.
    Discusses Doughty's descriptions of birds and his onomatopoeic representations of their calls.

Zwemer, Samuel M. "Islam in *Arabia Deserta.*" *The Moslem World* XXXIII, No. 3 (July 1943): 157-64.
    Discusses Doughty's treatment of Islamic culture, quoting extensively from *Travels in Arabia Deserta.*

Fyodor (Vasilyevich) Gladkov

1883-1958

Russian novelist, short story writer, essayist, and dramatist.

Gladkov is best known for his proletarian novel *Tsement (Cement),* in which he documented the changes that occurred in Russia following the revolution of 1917. As a member of the Communist party, Gladkov strongly supported the postrevolutionary regime, and in *Cement* he enthusiastically endorsed governmental plans for reorganizing Russian society. However, despite the generally affirmative tone of the novel, Gladkov did not refrain from exposing what Gleb Struve has called ''the seamy side of this new life.''

Gladkov was born in the village of Chernavka to a peasant family only one generation removed from serfdom. Although his parents were too poor to send him to school, a family friend taught him to read and write; soon after, he began reading the classics of Russian literature, including the works of Leo Tolstoy, Fyodor Dostoevski, and Mikhail Lermontov. At the age of seventeen, Gladkov began to write for local newspapers and to work as a tutor, earning enough money to attend the Normal School in Tiflis, where he quickly became involved in the burgeoning revolutionary movement. Gladkov's subsequent activities during the abortive revolution of 1905 resulted in his exile to Siberia.

Returning to Russia after three years in exile, Gladkov settled in the Black Sea port of Novorossiysk, and it was there that he wrote his first novel, *Izgoi.* Upon completion of the manuscript, he sent it to Vladimir Korolenko, who was then editor of the liberal journal *Russkoe Bogatstvo.* Korolenko rejected the manuscript but encouraged Gladkov to submit the work to the smaller journal *Zavety,* where it was published in 1912. Gladkov continued to write and teach until the outbreak of the revolution in 1917, whereupon he abandoned both to resume his revolutionary activities.

After participating in the revolution and the ensuing civil war, Gladkov devoted himself exclusively to literature, hoping to aid in the creation of a new national literature for his newly transformed country. However, *Ognennyi kon',* his first postwar novel, fell far short of his expectations, and it was only with the publication of *Cement* in 1925 that he succeeded in producing a novel that celebrated the life of the proletariat in a manner favored by the government. The book was immediately popular with readers and critics, while its pro-communist sentiments earned the approval of the government and thus allowed him freedom to continue writing and publishing in the Soviet Union. Gladkov subsequently produced a number of other works, but he was never able to duplicate the success of *Cement,* and at his death in 1958 he was still known primarily as the author of that novel.

In *Cement,* Gladkov sought to describe in a realistic and inspiring manner the emergence of a new socialist society from the turmoil of war and revolution, focusing in particular on the collectivization of Russian industry and the transformation of traditional values. Although he was thoroughly optimistic about the eventual success of the former, he foresaw major difficulties in altering centuries-old Russian social institutions. These attitudes are reflected in *Cement,* where the characters' efforts

to rebuild and restart a cement factory as a collective endeavor are significantly more successful than their efforts to collectivize their interpersonal relationships. Nevertheless, the primary message of the novel remains, as Marc Slonim has described it, ''the victory of confidence over skepticism, of effort over indolence, of labor over inactivity.''

Observers note that the major reason for the initial popularity of *Cement* in Russia was the relevance of the plot; Russian citizens, struggling to rebuild their own cities and factories, were indeed inspired by the triumph of Gladkov's workers. Critics, however, were divided on the question of its merits, and continue to be so. Many of Gladkov's socialist contemporaries found his prose style no different from that of nineteenth-century romantic fiction, while non-socialists found his overt didacticism unpalatable. The majority of critics today find Gladkov's characters unconvincing and his prose style stilted, but they concede that the work as a whole is powerful in its effect and acknowledge its influence on the development of Soviet socialist literature.

PRINCIPAL WORKS

Izgoi (novel) 1912
Ognennyi kon' (novel) 1923

Tsement (novel) 1925
  [*Cement,* 1929]
Staraya sekretnaya (novel) 1927
Novaya zemlya (novel) 1931
Energiya (novel) 1932-38
Tragediya Lyubashi (novel) 1935
Malen'kaya trilogiya (short stories) 1936
Opalyonnaya dusha (short stories) 1943
Klyatva (short stories) 1944
Povest' o detstve (novel) 1949
Vol'nitsa (novel) 1950
Likhaya godina (novel) 1954
Myatezhnaya yunost' (unfinished novel) 1958
  [*Restless Youth,* 1959]
Sobranie sochineniya. 8 vols. (novels, short stories,
    dramas, and essays) 1958-59

V. SACKVILLE-WEST (essay date 1929)

[*Sackville-West was an English poet, novelist, and biographer associated with the Bloomsbury group, a circle of English writers, artists, and intellectuals who held informal artistic and philosophical discussions in the Bloomsbury district of London, from around 1907 to the early 1930s. The Bloomsbury group adhered to no uniform aesthetic or philosophic beliefs, but did commonly express an aversion to moral prudery, a desire for greater social tolerance, and an aesthetic appreciation of beauty. In the following excerpt, Sackville-West discusses* Cement, *focusing on Gladkov's characterizations.*]

[*Cement*] is a confused, violent, and occasionally horrifying book, written by a man who—judging by the brief autobiographical preface—has seen war, revolution, and the harsher sides of life, and to whom probably many of the scenes and events described were familiar. Among the numerous characters, the mechanic Gleb Chumalov and his wife Sasha are the most prominent, and in the end it is into Sasha's mouth that the author puts these words, a summing-up of the stormy chapters that have gone before:—

> It's not our fault, Gleb. The old life has finished
> and will not return. We must build up a new
> life. The time will come when we shall build
> ourselves new homes. Love will always be love,
> Gleb, but it requires a new form. Everything
> will come through and attain new forms, and
> then we shall know how to forge new links.

The words apply not only to their personal relationships as man and woman, but to the social and political strife which they have witnessed and in which they have taken their part. It is obvious that Gladkov intends to draw the picture of his country in a state of painful transition, and the interest of the book lies perhaps in this aspect of it, rather than in its merits purely as literature. Its fault, considered as literature, is that the characters are presented more as a mass than as individuals; not one of them detaches himself at all clearly from his fellows— a very common and almost inevitable failing in novels of this type, where the author perhaps loses sight of human nature in his ardent desire to express his convictions.

> *V. Sackville-West, in a review of ''Cement,'' in* The Nation and the Athenaeum, *Vol. XLIV, No. 18, February 2, 1929, pp. 620, 622.*

JOSHUA KUNITZ (essay date 1929)

[*A Polish-born critic, Kunitz was the author of several respected works on Russian literature and history. He also served as literary editor of* New Masses, *one of America's leading socialist journals, between 1926 and 1948. In the following excerpt, Kunitz discusses the merits and shortcomings of* Cement.]

Cement, though an important novel, is not by any means a great novel. The author is woefully addicted to pathos and ornamentation; and not infrequently his pathos degenerates into bathos, and his ornamentation into a heap of obstructing details. His characterizations, too, are not always felicitous: not one of the main heroes is clearly delineated. Many situations are absurdly treated (the Party cleansing is a good example). The two lines along which the story unfolds—the factory and the home—are never welded into an artistically convincing whole.

The historic moment presented in the story is the spring and summer of 1921, the days of the first faltering attempts at economic rehabilitation after the civil war. Poverty, hunger, disease, lack of faith among many of the workers, sabotaging tactics on the part of the few remaining ''bourgeois'' specialists, bureaucracy in the most responsible offices of the Communist Party—these are some of the main obstacles which Gleb Chumalov, the central character of the novel, encounters in his mighty efforts to rebuild the cement factory. Needless to say, Gleb finally emerges victorious. After three hundred closely printed pages we finally come to the scene of his great triumph— the celebration of the reopening of the factory.

Parallel to his victorious struggle on the economic front, the hero of the story wages a much more cruel, perplexing, and desperate battle on the marital front. A disciplined Communist, a civil-war hero belonging to the Order of the Red Flag, Gleb, in his connubial relations, is conservative, traditional. He still feels a proprietary right to his wife's undivided affections. He still wants his Dasha to be the old-fashioned female—wife, mother, cook. But Dasha has changed. Three years of activity in the revolutionary party have made a new woman of her. She is free and independent and places her social and Communist duties above those of wife and mother. ''I love you, Gleb,'' she says, ''but perhaps sometimes I love others, too . . .'' Gleb is overwhelmed, while Dasha continues: ''I don't know, Gleb; everything is broken and smashed and become confused. Somehow love will have to be arranged differently . . .'' How simple political and economic revolutions are when compared with the ruthless civil wars and revolutions people have to fight out in their own souls!

Gleb's victory on the economic front is somewhat spoiled by his partial defeat on the ''domestic front.'' He reestablishes the old factory; he fails to reestablish the old family. With the death of their only child, his wife leaves him in order that she may function unhampered as a free woman and a consecrated Communist. Yet even here Gleb is only partly beaten, for he finally succeeds in transcending the atavistic emotion of jealousy. In the exultation at the restarting of the works, he forgets his bitter hatred for the man who had once possessed Dasha. The moment is glorious—enmities are hushed, jealousies waved aside, doubts resolved in a splendid outburst of comradely enthusiasm. The two erstwhile antagonists shake hands. The personal is merged in the general, the individual in the social. (pp. 695-96)

> *Joshua Kunitz, ''Russian Romance,'' in* The Nation, *New York, Vol. CXXIX, No. 3361, December 4, 1929, pp. 695-96.*

GLEB STRUVE (essay date 1935)

[*A Russian-born educator and critic, Struve is internationally known for his studies of Slavic literature. In the following excerpt, he discusses Gladkov's place in Soviet literature and the literary and sociological value of* Cement.]

[Gladkov's] literary career began before the Revolution, but his pre-revolutionary works attracted no attention: they did not rise above the average and rather low level of the Populist magazine fiction.

One of his earliest post-revolutionary works, the novel *The Fiery Steed,* was a mixture of revolutionary ideology with a cheap imitation of Dostoevsky in the presentation of morbid amorous psychology. Even in his later works Gladkov could not quite rid himself of this latter tendency. His literary reputation was made in 1924 when his *Cement* was published. This was an outstanding event in the history of proletarian literature. On the general plane of development it was a fact parallel and similar to the novels of Leonov and Fedin, it signified a transition from purely descriptive works to a work of grand style, of great psychological and social significance. So it was meant to be at least. Soviet critics have praised Gladkov's novel beyond all measure; it was translated into several foreign languages and had a great success outside Russia, its sales reaching an unheard-of figure of 500,000 copies. On its title-page one could see the inscription reminding of the good old times when certain books used to be approved by the Ministry of Education or some other competent authority and recommended for inclusion in school libraries. On Gladkov's *Cement* we read: "Recommended by the Head Department of Political Education for mass public libraries. Admitted by the State Learned Council into school libraries."

It is certainly an interesting novel. Its subject is the transition of Communism from the Civil War, which had disorganized and disintegrated the life of the country, to the period of peaceful but unromantic reconstruction, and more particularly the resumption of work on a big cement factory (it is easy enough to recognize that the action of the novel takes place in Novorossiysk with its well-known cement works). Parallel with this we are shown the disintegration of the old framework of life, the dissolution of family relations, the birth of a new morality and new ways of life. The novel is full of enthusiasm for revolutionary construction, but one cannot reproach Gladkov for looking at the things through rosy spectacles. He does not shirk from branding that which he dislikes or disapproves in the conditions which prevailed at the time, even though he does so within the reasonable limits of so-called "self-criticism," so popular once among the Communists.

The principal characters of the novel are the workman Gleb Chumalov and his wife Dasha. Chumalov has spent nearly the whole of the Civil War at the front and has been decorated with the Order of the Red Banner; he now plays the main part in restarting the cement factory. A good Communist, he has not yet succeeded in overcoming in himself some of the old moral instincts and "prejudices." This conflict between his political and his moral nature is one of the psychological pivots of the novel. His wife Dasha, on the other hand, personifies a new "ideal" emancipated woman with whom political convictions and moral views go hand in glove. But as is often the case with "ideal" characters, she is the least convincing, the least plausible, the most wooden in the whole novel, and some of the incidents in her career touch on melodrama. There are in the novel many well-drawn secondary characters, simple unsophisticated workmen, disillusioned Communists from the intelligentsia who after the ascetic period of War Communism believe that the country is going to the dogs because of the iniquities of the newly introduced NEP. But in the depiction of the two principal characters, especially in the dialogues, there are many notes that sound false and unnatural. The novel is certainly too long-drawn, especially as there is no real plot and the author does not succeed in making the story of the resumption of work at the cement factory sufficiently exciting. Yet as a document, as a picture of conditions of life and of moods prevailing in the Communist Party at a certain period in its history, it is valuable. Its weakest point as a work of art is its style, an irritating mixture of old-fashioned Realism with ill-digested modernist devices. Gladkov, who came originally from the school of Gorky and the Populists, has been influenced by the technical methods of the modern Russian prose. But he has not assimilated them properly, he seems to parade, to flaunt them, and most of his descriptions and dialogues make an irritating reading—they are affected, unnatural. This defect is not so noticeable in translations which probably accounts for the success of Gladkov's novel outside Russia, but in the original it spoils the effect of the whole. As a literary work Gladkov's *Cement* is no doubt greatly inferior to the novels of Fedin, Leonov and Kaverin. The colossal figure of its sales need not deceive us, if we remember the official recommendation; its enormous success was certainly to a great extent artificial; on the other hand, it was due to the fact that here was the first modern proletarian novel written on a grand scale, going beyond pure description, attempting psychological analysis and yet quite orthodox from the political, ideological point of view. It came as an answer to the demands of the *On Guard* group, and they used it as a proof of the existence of proletarian literature. (pp. 88-91)

*Gleb Struve, "The Proletarian Writers: Gladkov,"
in his* Soviet Russian Literature, *Routledge & Kegan
Paul Ltd., 1935, pp. 88-91.*

VYACHESLAV ZAVALISHIN (essay date 1958)

[*In the following excerpt, Zavalishin presents a survey of Gladkov's works.*]

Gladkov's novel *Cement* was serialized in the review *Krasnaya nov'* (*Red Virgin Soil*) in 1925. Soon afterwards it was published in book form. By mid-1927 it had already gone through ten editions. Bolshevik publicists were making the most of the novel as evidence that a genuine proletarian literature was at last arising to outweigh the efforts of the fellow travelers.

The critic Lebedev-Polyanski hailed *Cement* as a true reflection of reality, "a living refutation" of allegations that proletarian literature was tendentious, focusing only on the facts which justified Soviet policy and rejecting those which contradicted its preconceived ideas.

P. S. Kogan maintained that after the revolution the literature of emotional experience was being replaced by the literature of practical action. The "new man" had not yet come into being, but new relations between men were being established where labor was concerned. This labor wholly absorbed man's spiritual life; since in life emotional experience was being replaced by action, literature could not but follow suit. To Kogan the significance of *Cement* was that Gladkov had presented in it a romantic view of the social necessity for practical action.

Each opinion contains a grain of truth. Gladkov did indeed reject the principle of passing over certain facts for the sake of propaganda—he even brought into his novel Party members who are vicious men—and in this respect he compares favorably with Libedinski and Serafimovich. Gladkov's treatment of the Cheka agent Chibis, a ferocious sadist, also bears out Kogan's interpretation. Chibis' fanatic devotion to the Communist idea is portrayed so that his personal character seems to be unimportant or, in any case, excusable. It seems of no significance whether a man was noble or vicious by nature— the system obliterated his individuality. By aggrandizing the system, which conquers man's personality, Gladkov was able to forego the usual idealization of individual Bolsheviks and still produce ideologically acceptable fiction.

Cement is an account of the reconstruction of a partially wrecked industrial plant in the period following the Civil War. Gladkov devoted far more attention to Party meetings and planning than to actual scenes of labor and industrial processes. The Proletcult objected to his method, and on this count compared *Cement* unfavorably with Lyashko's *Blast Furnace*.

Gleb Chumalov, protagonist of *Cement* and rebuilder of the plant, is the hero of *Toilers of the Sea* (that working bible of the Proletcult school) turned Russian Communist. He is filled with romantic enthusiasm, and he comes to life. Gladkov is in general unsurpassed among postrevolutionary writers in portraying workers.

Chumalov's activity as organizer and Party member is in dramatic contrast to his private life. As an organizer he profits greatly by the revolution, but as a man he is even more unhappy than under the tsarist regime, which he fought to overthrow. The contradiction between public and private life which Gladkov saw besetting the makers of the revolution in general exemplifies the philosophy censured by Soviet critics as "an unnatural blend of Marxism and Freudianism."

It is true that Gladkov was perhaps more deeply influenced by Freud than by Marx. Gladkov saw the unbridled sexual instinct asserting itself in an endeavor to offset the effects of the revolution. The lust of the flesh translated man's attempt to make the loss of his ego, swallowed up in the storm, relatively painless, to rob it of its sting by indulging in a feast of the senses. The reverse side of the medal was the elimination of spiritual love, and the resultant suffering on the part of women. But sensual passion might also be transmuted into dynamic energy and thus lead to creative activity. Such a transmutation facilitated the process of dissolution of the personality and permitted the individual to become a small but integral part of the storm which raged about him. It is on this basis that the characters Dasha Chumalova, Gleb's wife, and Bad'in in *Cement* were evolved.

Gladkov was haunted by the image of the same woman. Marina in *Steed of Flame,* Nastya in the play *The Gang* and Dasha in *Cement* are all variations of that image. This woman is a slave to household drudgery who tries to fight her way to freedom and becomes the captive of a man's sensual passion, caught in a vicious circle.

Bad'in, the chairman of the executive committee, is a proletarian Sanin, who makes his prototype look like a callow youth, a sniveling intellectual. After seducing the teacher, Sanin at least makes some attempt to set her mind at peace. Bad'in rapes Polya Mekhova, but when she is expelled from the Party he will not raise a finger to help her. Gleb Chumalov, a Communist of moral decency, turns on Bad'in in disgust. At the same time Bad'in is an energetic and able executive and does a good job for the Party. In recompense, Gladkov granted him

a remission of all his sins and whitewashed him precisely as he did Chibis.

In the character of Sergei Ivagin, blood brother to Yuri Svarozhich in Artsybashev's *Sanin*, Gladkov criticized the intelligentsia and portrayed it as merely pathetic and downtrodden.

From the point of view of style and its system of imagery *Cement* is a mediocre imitation of Andrei Belyi's *St. Petersburg*. What Belyi turns into a symbol, Gladkov tried to interpret in a materialistic and realistic way. Stylistically *Cement* suffers from the author's attempts to achieve epic scope. The value of the novel lies not in Gladkov's craftsmanship but in his powers of observation and in the story he tells.

Gladkov is not a very important writer, but he has brought home with force—if only by virtue of dogged repetition—the important theme in postrevolutionary Russian letters of the dissolution of the individual personality in the storm of the revolution and the subsequent attempt of those carried to power— the organizers who had retained the storm's dynamic energy— to impose their will, to suppress and obliterate the individuality of the executors, who had lost their energy and strength of will.

Gladkov, born of peasant parents, is a typical self-made intellectual. As a boy, he worked for a pharmacist; later he became a typesetter and then a teacher. He had been a provincial newspaperman for a long time before the revolution. Soon afterwards he joined the Communist Party and was an active member of the Smithy.

An early story **"The Fallen"** (**"Izgov"**), written in 1912 but not published until after the revolution, described the life of political exiles in Siberia and introduced one of the themes to which Gladkov was to return again and again. He contrasted doubting and vacillating intellectuals with the proletarian Ivanyuk, who is able to suppress his own doubts and to devote himself wholly to revolutionary work. *Old Secret (Staraya sekretnaya)*, a short novel written in the mid-1920's, repeated the same theme, greatly elaborated, apparently for the purpose of tracing the current outbreak of doubts and vacillations—rightist and leftist deviations—to roots in the past and of showing it as an organic outgrowth of prerevolutionary contradictions.

Gladkov's prominence came with the novel *Steed of Flame (Ognennyi kon')*, 1923, a story of the Civil War in the Kuban'. The Cossack Andrei Guzi vacillates between the Reds and the Whites and finally sides with the latter. His death is a foregone conclusion. His friend, Gmyrya, another Cossack, is torn between hatred and pity for Andrei and tortured by passion for the Cossack girl Marina, who welcomes the revolution as liberation from domestic slavery and fights against Gmyrya's passion for fear of falling into another captivity, but in the end unwillingly succumbs. The Bolshevik Globa deludes his own reason with talk about the "Scythian element" in the revolution; but his disquisitions are merely a way of quieting the unease he feels over the incipient shipwreck of the human ego.

Gladkov's strong point is revealed in this novel—his acute sensitivity to, and dramatic presentation of, the new forms of life after the revolution. Stylistically, however, he lacks originality. He has always imitated other writers. In *Steed of Flame* the influences are those of Andreyev and Artsybashev.

Gladkov's intellectuals have decency and integrity, but an inner emptiness and an acute awareness of their own maladjustment and impotence. They have lost contact with the soil and lack the strength which comes from it. Already half dead, the intelligentsia as a class faces inevitable extinction in the new world.

Gladkov's play *Uprooted by the Storm,* 1921, dealing with the inadequacies of the Russian intelligentsia, even those who laid the groundwork for the revolution, is reminiscent of Artsybashev's play *Jealousy,* particularly in the characterization of the hero. Ugryumov, a former Party member and political exile, now a teacher, can find no safe place for himself under the new order. "The intelligentsia," says another character, is nothing but "the remains of outdated formations, and its whole life is spent in continuously looking for a safe harbor."

All Gladkov's negative qualities are concentrated in his plays, which are very poor theater. They suffer from an amorphous and overburdened composition, a confusion between the personal and the social planes, and a crude naturalism of speech. *The Gang (Vataga),* 1923, is the most chaotic of his plays, so confused that it is not always comprehensible. Several conflicts are presented, but none of them is fully thought out and developed. In the character of Shatalov, Gladkov intended to portray a transcendental peasant rebel, a modern Sten'ka Razin, but Shatalov remains no more than a red flag waving over a drab fisherman's village.

Pride, 1935, is an unsuccessful dramatization of his novel *Power.*

Gladkov intended *Power,* 1932-1938, to be a sequel to *Cement* and reintroduced the character Gleb Chumalov, but there is little connection between the two books.

Power is an archipelago of scenes of industrial life vaguely and unconvincingly related. The scene is the construction site of the hydroelectric power plant Dneprostroi.

Osip Brik once said about *Cement* that Gladkov was a slave to "the heroic cliché." The defect is far more obvious in *Power* than in the earlier novel. *Power* is, generally speaking, Gladkov's greatest failure. The defects are more conspicuous in later editions than in the original version, for the author was compelled to revise several times to meet new censorship requirements. A comparison of the original form of *Power,* as serialized in *Novyi Mir* (New World) in 1932 and 1937-1938, with the edition of 1939 shows that the book suffered considerably from the changes. The 1939 version omits Chumalov's conversation with the German workers' delegation—the anti-Fascist attitude expressed in the incident had already become embarrassing. Further, the author excised a chapter entitled "The Tournament" ("Turnir"), in which the engineer Khabi was unmasked prematurely and too crudely. In this excision—dictated by the fall of Yezhov and the rise of Lavrenti Beriya, who eliminated some of the excesses of his predecessor—Gladkov was toeing the Party line and abandoning any claim to truthful representation.

There are a great many characters in *Power,* but few living people. The brains of the organizers act as so many dynamos, producing the energy and will power needed to set into motion thousands of robots. The character of Kostya Gromov, a gypsy, a free son of the steppes, natural and spontaneous, stands out in contrast to his mechanized environment: "I've traveled all over the whole country. Everyone working, fuss and bother everywhere. Not like before. And I don't like it—it's shameful."

Gladkov is an unusually prolific writer, but only a few of his remaining works deserve attention—the stories *Drunken Sun* and *Lyubasha's Tragedy,* the sketch "Heart's Blood," and the two satiric tales "The Cephalopod" and "Inspired Goose," from *A Little Trilogy.*

In *Drunken Sun,* 1927, Gladkov managed to shake off Artsybashev's influence and indeed to argue and joust with his former mentor. At first glance Akatuyev, the protagonist of *Drunken Sun,* a high Party official, has a good deal in common with Bad'in in *Cement,* but the resemblance is merely external. Akatuyev is ashamed of the beast in himself, and, repressing his lust, transforms it into energy, action and leadership.

The setting is a rest sanatorium surrounded by people who hate the guests—a symptom of the growing antagonism between the common man and the privileged class. It is the NEP period, and the country is going through a crisis. The executors are weary unto death, not merely in body. They have lost faith in the cause and interest in their work, and seek oblivion in drunkenness and license.

Among the young people at the sanatorium not all are depraved. Marusya, the heroine, and Yasha are repelled by the heartlessness of the new order. Marusya, a new feminine type for Gladkov—the woman who forces men to accept her not as a female but as a human being—is another Isanka, not so highly educated but with the same instinctive protest against the crudely materialistic attitude and with an inclination toward a naive and touching pantheism:

> From the unreachably far horizon, where the sea merged with the sky and was as ethereal as the sky, came an endless series of small and rhythmical ripples and a distant sound of deep and pietous sighing. It was a siren-buoy out in the harbor, and Marusya liked to think that it was the depths of the sea moaning, tired from doing some mysterious important work somewhere far out in the blue inhuman distance. . . . When she was alone, she felt sad and a little frightened, and was obsessed by vague thoughts about the unknown distances that she would never attain.

Lyubasha, the heroine of *Lyubasha's Tragedy,* 1935, one of Gladkov's best pieces, represents a further development of Marusya and yet is a type known in Russia since time immemorial, the peasant-woman whom Nekrasov called "the regal Slav" and of whom he said that, although she walked in the selfsame road as all, the dirt of the shabby surroundings did not stick to her.

After the devastation of the village such peasant women went off to work in factories. But whereever they went, nothing could break their pride and independence. *Lyubasha's Tragedy* is a tale of the inevitable conflict of one of these Russian women with the Soviet regime.

Lyubasha is a weaver, a Communist. She wins respect not through making speeches at meetings or currying favor with her superiors, but through stubborn and inspired hard work. The habit of working and of doing everything well is in her blood, a heritage from her ancestors. Suddenly Lyubasha begins to turn out poor-quality textiles. The department in which she works is being supplied with poor yarn. To explain away defective output—the deterioration of flax, cotton and silk as a result of the collectivization of agriculture is of course not to be hinted—scapegoats must be found. Lyubasha is one of the victims. The foreman says to her:

> "You are not here as a decoration, this is no glasshouse. Turn your soul inside out, if you

have to, but turn out stuff that does the heart good.''

"Do you expect me to feed myself into the machine?''

"If that's good for production, go right ahead!''

"A human being is nothing to you—you judge him by the quality of the cloth.''

Indignant at the callous treatment of human beings, Lyubasha comes into conflict with the Party and her fellow workers. A secret agent in the factory resorts to forgery to deliver her over to the OGPU on charges of "plunder of socialist property.'' She is alone in her trouble. Even her husband fails to understand what she is going through—to him she is merely a source of sensual pleasure.

Like Marusya, Lyubasha unconsciously turns from Marxism as a religion to pantheism:

> She listened to her heart, to the blood singing in her ears, and it seemed to her that her heart was everywhere in this far blue sweep of space.... The sparkling lake, the wood and the sky were filled with the ringing of distant bells.

The long-drawn out happy ending is altogether unconvincing. As often, Gladkov set his sights on a bold idea but suddenly lowered his rifle, afraid to press the trigger. His work in general is crippled by fear of the censor.

Lyubasha's Tragedy is refreshingly free of the deliberate crudities and clumsy language with which Gladkov's style is frequently pock-marked. The "cosmic" imagery of his earlier work—Gladkov had frequently done in prose what Kirillov and Gerasimov did in poetry—has also become less stilted in this story. When the weavers' looms remind him of "harps clad in grey work-clothes," the second half of the simile suitably tones down the first.

One piece of Gladkov's written during the NEP period is remarkable for its blunt speaking. Gladkov chose to call his **"Heart's Blood"** a short story, but it is a piece of literary criticism nonetheless. At the end of a literary soirée given by a workers' club for a popular writer, the writer is taken to the club's library to have some tea and to indulge in a friendly discussion. One of the workers listens unobtrusively to the discussion for a long time. Finally the librarian introduces him to the writer with the remark that Comrade Chizhov is a typesetter and the library's most faithful reader.

"How strongly are you aware of the responsibility your fame carries with it?" Chizhov asks the writer without preliminaries.

The writer is a connoisseur of men. He understands instantly that Chizhov is one of those rare readers who open a book not for a pleasant pastime but in order to find an answer in its pages to the question of what is worth working and living for.

The writer admits to himself that he does not deserve such a reader, that he is weak in spirit, a coward, like other Soviet writers given over to hypocrisy and self-delusion. Chizhov realizes that his question has seriously disturbed the writer, who is already torn by doubts and vacillations, and seizes the opportunity to pour out the grievance he has on his mind. The greater part of **"Heart's Blood"** consists of a monologue in which Chizhov berates Soviet literature, accusing current writ-

ers of failing as prophets and teachers, of being cringing little men:

> "You are too poor and mediocre to make us follow you....
>
> "Where is the inextinguishable fire that people used to have? ... The classics stirred in people a spirit of indignation, protest and rebellion. What did you learn to understand from them? Nothing. You are ignoramuses and pitiful imitators....
>
> "Are we to believe that the wooden images you describe ... were the makers of ... the revolution? Are we to think that this dreary and obscure existence which you praise to the skies is indeed the nucleus and foundation of the human society of the future? ...
>
> "And you, you bureaucratic scribblers, you kill the living spirit of protest in man. You waste paper by covering it with patent lies: We are so wonderful! We live in a paradise! We are unique ... in the universe! ... You get drunk on self-praise to the point of not noticing how blind and nauseating you are....
>
> "You try to make even art live in a barracks.... You oversimplify until you reach the level of primitives, of illiterates. You forget that the creative act is a glance into the future; its whole point is in depicting not what is, but what must be....
>
> "You forget that the path we have traveled is strewn with the corpses of the fallen, with the dirt and abomination of our struggle."

The writer has nothing to say in refutation.

During the NEP period there were still among the highly skilled workers self-educated men who thought for themselves and were not afraid to offer harsh criticism of the new regime. Gladkov's **"Heart's Blood"** might now be fittingly retitled "In Memoriam."

A Little Trilogy, published in the thirties but containing three stories written earlier, can hardly be called true satire. Gladkov imitates Shchedrin, but the Shchedrin of *The Golovlyovs (Gospoda Golovlyovy),* which is also not a satirical work.

The hero of the first story in *A Little Trilogy,* **"The Cephalopod,"** is a wire-pulling careerist capable of any immoral action, of any crime, if it will win him a promotion.

Comrade Budash, hero of **"The Inspired Goose,"** is a type which fills the ranks of Soviet editors, agitators and propagandists—men without principles or original ideas but with a "practiced agility of mind." Through the efforts of men like Budash, "the Press ... has a wonderful way of transforming a mediocrity into a hero ... you may kill a talent that the Republic could well use—but no matter!"

The remaining story of *A Little Trilogy,* **"The Immaculate Devil,"** relates the adventures of a fool obsessed with sex. The whole thing sounds like a dirty story and lends a tinge of vulgarity to the entire book.

After *Lyubasha's Tragedy* Gladkov's powers began to decline. During the war, he published a series of patriotic stories, all inferior to his earlier work.

Gladkov's postwar books *Story of My Childhood,* 1949, and *Free Men,* 1951, each of which was awarded a Stalin Prize, are novelized reminiscences, in which the reader senses the suffering of a spiritually depleted man. Gladkov's philosophy, his peculiar combination of Marxism and Freudianism, is still shallow and incoherent.

Nevertheless, to pay Gladkov his due, he was a keen observer and in his accurate recording of characteristic national types after the revolution he has few rivals. (pp. 288-98)

Vyacheslav Zavalishin, "The New Realists," in his Early Soviet Writers, *Frederick A. Praeger Publishers, 1958, pp. 269-98.*

EDWARD J. BROWN (essay date 1969)

[*Brown is an American educator and critic who has written extensively on post-Revolution Soviet literature. Notable among his studies is* Russian Literature since the Revolution *(1963), which some critics consider the standard work on the period. In the following excerpt from that study, Brown compares passages from the original and revised versions of* Cement *to illustrate the compromises Gladkov made with changing political regimes in the Soviet Union.*]

Cement lacks both verbal artistry and psychological power, yet it had an emotional impact on the Soviet reader, and it became the model and prototype for the vast novels of industrial construction written during the thirties. It was a favorite of Stalin, and as such was circulated in millions of copies. It contained an explicit statement of Marxist philosophy, and in successive editions it quite unsubtly reflected changes in Party policy. Gladkov's fundamental indifference to his novel as a literary product is shown by the ease with which he altered both content and style as times and fashions changed. One example of these alterations is amusing evidence not only of the Soviet reader's changing taste in the matter of naturalistic detail, but of the Party's changing doctrine on the relative position of the sexes. The parallel passages are from the 1925 edition and the 1950 edition, and the later version reflects in a brutal image the return to a more conventional relationship, in contrast to the woman's struggle for emancipation in the early days:

1925 Edition

From the other side of the narrow street muffled drunken voices could be heard coming from the open window of a building. It was the heavy voice of the cooper Savchuk and his hysterical wife Motia, who was cackling like a hen. Gleb left his kit near the fence and crossed over to Savchuk's place. The walls of the room were filthy with soot. Overturned chairs lay helter-skelter on the floor, and clothing was strewn about . . . Because of the sun in his eyes Gleb could not immediately distinguish any person. Then he made out two dirty, convulsed bodies rolling and fighting on the floor. Taking a closer look he saw that it was the Savchuks, man and wife. The man's shirt was torn to bits, his back was bent and his ribs stuck out like barrel hoops . . . The woman's full breast heaved violently as they struggled together.

1950 Edition

On the other side of the street the drunken cooper, Savchuk, was making a row. His wife Motia was screaming hysterically. Gleb listened to it a moment then sprang into action. He got up and went over to Savchuk's quarters. There was dirt and stench in the room. Stools and clothing were strewn about on the floor. A tin tea kettle lay on its side. Flour was scattered all over everything. Motia was lying on a potato sack and hugging it to her bosom, and Savchuk, in a torn and ragged shirt and bellowing like a bull, was punching Motia with his fists and kicking her with his bare feet. Gleb grabbed him from behind under the armpits and dragged him away from her.

A second example of political editing was applauded by a Soviet critic, and it illustrates Gladkov's responsiveness to the demand for intelligible and didactic prose even in the remarks of a character under emotional stress. A sudden sharp attack of White "bandits" has just been repulsed. Several workmen have been killed in the action, and Gleb, choked and panting, addresses the proletarian crowd:

1925 Edition

Again Gleb raised his arms on high.

"Comrades, listen! A sacrifice to labor . . . With our united strength . . . No tears or crying! The victory of our hands . . . the factory. We have won . . . We shall make ourselves heard with fire and machines. The great labor of constructing the Workers' Republic . . . Ourselves, with our brains and hands. . . . The blood and suffering of the battle—these are our weapons for winning the whole world."

1950 Edition

Gleb shouted through his palms as through a megaphone: "Comrades! This has been a sacrifice in labor and struggle. No tears and sobs, but the joy of real victory . . . Soon the factory will begin to roar with its furnaces and machines. You and I are beginning the mighty construction of socialism. Yes, blood has been spilled, and there has been much suffering. There have been many trials on our path and there will be many more. But this path of struggle leads to happiness, to the final victory over the world of violence. We are building our own world with our own hands. With the name of Lenin on our lips, with faith in unlimited happiness let us double and treble our efforts for the conquest of the future."

The earlier variants provide evidence that Gladkov's style possessed originally a kind of rude emotional power. In an article entitled **"My Work on the Novel** *Cement"* Gladkov describes the systematic "normalization" of that style undertaken so that the book's message might be intelligible and acceptable to as many Russians as possible. In successive operations on the text of the novel, Gladkov excised substandard vocabulary, vulgar language, and almost all traces of class or local dialect. (pp. 131-33)

Gladkov's novels, chiefly his proletarian "classic" *Cement,* are read in many parts of the world by the recently literate masses to whom the strictures of cultivated critics or the amused contempt of a Formalist writer such as Osip Brik are understandable, probably, only as evidence of their malice. (p. 134)

Edward J. Brown, "The Proletarians, II," in his Russian Literature since the Revolution, *revised edition, 1969. Reprint by Cambridge, Mass.: Harvard University Press, 1982, pp. 126-52.*

MARC SLONIM   (essay date 1977)

[Slonim was a Russian-born American critic who wrote extensively on Russian literature. In the following excerpt, he examines the reasons for the popularity of Cement *in the Soviet Union.]*

The defects of *Cement* are quite obvious. Its impressionism is cheap and incongruous; there are scenes of torture and various episodes of violence and death that remind one of Andreyev—or, even worse, of Artzybashev; Gleb and Dasha, the pivotal characters, are stilted and two-dimensional, and the secondary ones, such as Ivolghin the intellectual, are weak and stereotyped. Nevertheless, all those literary shortcomings did not prevent *Cement* from scoring a tremendous success in Russia as well as abroad. Translated in all the languages of the Soviet Union, it had sold 2 million copies by 1937 and still continues to be widely read.

There are several reasons for its popularity. This truly "proletarian" novel emphasizes the main theme of Communist literature—the victory of confidence over skepticism, of effort over indolence, of labor over inactivity. And it established a pattern that had nothing to do with literary perfection: the most important thing for fiction of Communist persuasion was to express faith and to show the triumph of hope. Moreover Gladkov pointed at constructive work as a vehicle for the resumption of normal life, and this was on everybody's mind in the 1920's. The fellow-travelers talked too much about the holocaust of the Revolution and civil war: and here was a novel about material reconstruction and new ethics. Gladkov also attempted to introduce a new hero—his greatly romanticized Gleb begins a long series of strong-willed, purposeful Communists—and a new heroine, the woman who rejects the old code of morality and does not want to be "just a housekeeper and a wife." *Cement* dealt with all these themes in a rather primitive way—a way that proved to be accessible to the masses, who were interested in direct representation.

The mechanics of making a best-seller in Russia are much the same as in capitalist countries, the difference being that social content and an affirmation of incorruptible conviction, rather than an adventurous or salacious story, form the basis of mass appeal. In the U.S. (and in the West, in general) large sections of the public seek in books primarily entertainment, excitement, or escape, but the Russians have been so conditioned by tradition and by the Revolution as to expect in their reading an echo of their own thoughts and an answer to their perplexities and anxieties—or at least an indication of what is good or evil. New audiences in the Soviet Union, less sophisticated than those of the pre-revolutionary epoch, yet much more numerous, demand moral and social inspiration from works of fiction—hence the fact, that while second- or third-rate Western literature offers simple trash, poor Soviet literature produces tendentious and didactic trash. (pp. 176-77)

Marc Slonim, "Literature of Communist Persuasion: From Furmanov to Ostrovsky," in his Soviet Russian Literature: Writers and Problems 1917-1977, *second revised edition, Oxford University Press, 1977, pp. 169-87.*

HALINA STEPHAN   (essay date 1979)

[In the following excerpt, Stephan examines popular and critical reaction to Cement.]

Despite numerous translations and large foreign editions of *Cement,* the novel has had limited impact abroad. Admittedly, the colorless character of the later versions gave little reason for an abstract esthetic appreciation. The lack of an alternate perspective, however, arose from an absence of information on the trend-setting position of the novel in the early debates on the direction of Soviet literature. As a result, a foreign reader saw *Cement*'s revolutionary romanticism as an attempt to gloss over the real problems of the post-revolutionary period. The glorification of industrial labor, a part of the esthetic program of both the proletarian writers and their opponents from the avant-garde, was received as Communist propaganda, and the cult of the machine which Gladkov brought from his association with the "Smithies" evoked a baffled response. Quite frequently, *Cement* was regarded as a compilation of socialist realist clichés despite the fact that the novel was written almost ten years before the introduction of socialist realism.

Meanwhile, in the Soviet Union, the success of *Cement* only increased with time. When the first version appeared in 1925, *Cement* was acclaimed as one of the most significant, although still debatable, creations of young Soviet literature. Those who objected to the novel expressed formal reservations, criticizing it as a stylistic "cookbook," a combination of ingredients borrowed from various literary schools. Thematically, however, the book was without blame; Stalin himself was among the many who praised it. The popularity of the novel was such that by 1930 *Cement* was already translated into eight European languages, and into Chinese and Japanese. In Russian, the novel has been regularly republished in very large editions which, however, considerably differ from the original version. (p. 86)

The main reason for the impact of *Cement* in the 1920s was the relevance of the plot. The story deals with the crucial moment of the economic, social, and psychological transition from the revolutionary romanticism of War Communism to the implementation of socialism. In 1925-26, when the book appeared, this topic occupied critics and readers. Historically, its emphasis on the construction of the new society coincided with Stalin's efforts to consolidate political power. In the literary life, the success of Gladkov, a proletarian writer, came at the time when the All Russian Association of Proletarian Writers (VAPP) championed the cause of proletarian hegemony with increasing determination.

Because of its timeliness, *Cement* was welcomed by those like Lunacharskii and Gor'kii who were influential in cultural politics. Lunarcharskii, the Commissar of Education, greeted it as one of the fundamental manifestations of the new Soviet literature. Gor'kii applauded the novel because he found a reflection of his own romanticism in the positive attitude of an author who dared "to see the reality as a raw material and from the bad which prevails [created, HS] the good which is wished for."

Beyond the historical significance of the plot and its political optimism, Gladkov's monumental projection of the industrial theme represented a pioneering effort at the creation of new literature. Gladkov had already proposed the epic approach to the Soviet themes in 1924, in an essay **"The Picture of Lenin,"** where he advocated "artistic synthesis" as an alternative to the fragmented, analytic art of the immediate post-revolutionary period. In his opinion, the new times needed "monumental generalizations" and powerful abstract types fit for "the revolutionary avant-garde of world literature." The schematism of characters and conflicts evident in *Cement* was then a result of the search for the typical rather than the individual manifestations of the transition period. The exaggerated emotional intensity of the protagonists reflected Gladkov's intention to give his story a larger-than-life dimension in order to create an epos of the new era.

The new objectives lacked, however, a corresponding artistic solution. Gladkov presented the new theme in the tradition of ornamentalism popular in the immediate pre- and post-revolutionary period. The language of *Cement* was rich in poetic figures which were not integrated in the narrative. The story was set against a "lyrical landscape borrowed from Bunin, Gor'kii, Vsevolod Ivanov, and the Smithy poets." Machinery was personified in the mode of the *Proletkult* writers which neither ideologically nor stylistically answered the tone of the middle 1920s. The dialogues showed the characters as torn by powerful emotions which failed to translate into psychological depth. As Robert Maguire somewhat harshly pointed out [see Additional Bibliography], the novel indeed relies on literary stereotypes: "*Cement* pretends to be a novel, but is really a romance. Everything passes immediately into action. The love theme comes out of pulp fiction; the reconstruction theme merely renames the clichés of military fiction; the shock troops of industry storm objectives defended by wily enemies. There are no hidden thoughts, no ambiguities. Although the characters take on a semblance of complexity by moving from situation to situation, in themselves they lack depth and consistency."

The combination of *Cement*'s popularity with the obviousness of its shortcomings invited critical responses as soon as the novel appeared. Gladkov, as a proletarian writer, found his novel interpreted as a proletarian alternative to developing socialist art. Literary groups and organizations which had earlier abstractly discussed the question of the form and function of art in the new state were eager to respond to a concrete model. The proletarian critics and the "fellow travellers," who essentially adhered to the realistic notion of literature, welcomed Gladkov's new interpretation of realism, his epic glorification of work. In *Novyj mir,* D. Gorbov called the novel the most outstanding literary event of 1925 and praised *Cement* because it reflected "the melody of the epoch." He credited Gladkov as the first to present the motif of the factory in an epic narrative instead of in the traditional lyric-romantic approach typical of the earliest Soviet period.

Some objections, however, were expressed about the psychological aspects of the novel, its excessive ornamentalism, and a few political nuances. A. Lezhnev, writing in *Pechat' i revoliuciia,* valued the monumental design of *Cement,* but could not reconcile it with the lack of psychological depth. The conflicts, in his opinion, were too schematic and the characters functioned as personifications of ideas rather than as individuals. Another critic, A. Gorbachev, while generally praising the novel, astutely saw that its schematism was not an innovation, but derived from Gladkov's earlier admiration for the Symbolists and for Andreev's Expressionism. Such an influence, in Gorbachev's opinion, created in *Cement* a blend of "revolutionary thematics and ideology" with "psychopath-

ology in the Dostoevskian vein and the metaphysics of the Symbolists."

Other supporters of realism were hesitant with their objections in the face of the increasing drive for the development of proletarian literature. One of those was the editor of *Krasnaia nov',* Aleksandr Voronskii, who played an influential role in early Soviet cultural politics. Although the first version of *Cement* appeared in his journal, Voronskii allegedly considered the text "devoid of literary merit," but accepted it for its topic. In publishing it, Voronskii toned down an aspect of Gladkov's ideological message. In his role as a semi-official supporter of the non-communist "fellow-travellers," he deleted a chapter of the novel which might have antagonized his ex-bourgeois contributors. The section, "Meeting of the Repentent," described the return of the contrite, disoriented White officers who, together with their Cossack soldiers, sought forgiveness from the Reds and permission to stay in Russia. Gladkov had personally observed this scene while he was a commissar of education in the Black Sea region, and in his novel he stylized it into a monumental tableau in the vein of folk ballads. Although Voronskii probably appreciated the folkloristic dimension, his "fellow-traveller" readers could have been offended by the scenes such as "from Golgotha to Canossa" [sic] and "Toothless Wolves" which depicted the crushed onetime opponents of the system prostrating themselves in front of the Communist victors. The deletion of this chapter was a political compromise meant to offset the concession to the proletarian literature made by *Krasnaia nov',* which was dominated by the "fellow travellers."

Despite the objections to *Cement*'s excessive ornamentalism and some questionable political accents, the general direction of the novel found almost uniform approval. Among the critics, only the group known as the Left Front of the Arts ("Lef") rejected the novel entirely. Formed by the avant-garde writers and critics, "Lef" fought realism as a direction for the new Soviet literature. The "Lef" members—former Futurists and Futurist sympathizers—tried to infuse the emerging Soviet culture with the anti-traditionalism, anti-psychologism, and anti-estheticism which originated with Futurism. Instead of realism, they propagated "operative art," which had a modern, fragmented form designed to stimulate the analytic capacities of the audience. Through an appeal to the intellect of the audience, such a form could ideally help to transfer the artistic message into the realm of social action. Obviously, from the avant-garde perspective, an epic novel could not contribute to the conscious reorganization of life demanded of the new times. For this reason, Gladkov's *Cement* conflicted with the "Lef" vision of Soviet art: its revolutionary subject matter lacked an appropriate modern form. Yet, in 1925, the success of Gladkov's novel was an indication that the "Lef" notion of "operative art" was losing ground against the growing tendency toward an epic narrative.

Osip Brik, next to Vladimir Maiakovskii, the leading member of "Lef," explained the avant-garde attitude toward Gladkov's novel in an astute, polemical essay, "Why was *Cement* liked?" Since the entire direction of Gladkov's writing was unacceptable for the avant-garde, Brik intended to discredit both Gladkov's artistic synthesis and his monumentalism. He did so by attacking the narrative structure of *Cement* and the portrayal of the characters in the novel. The plot, in his opinion, lacked unity. It contained two parallel themes: that of Gleb building the factory and that of Dasha building the new life. Neither plot line affected the other; the existence of two plots was not motivated by any logical ties. To make matters worse, the two themes were supplemented by a variety of episodes which did not belong to either one. In Brik's opinion, the synthesis which Gladkov originally promised was completely illusory. The romance of Gleb and Dasha was not integrated with the rebuilding of the factory, and the chain of disconnected episodes failed to create a panorama.

Brik also criticizes the portrayal of the construction of the factory, because he believes that Gladkov's synthesis glosses over the real difficulties of the post-revolutionary years. In the novel, Gleb, a heroic leader, overcomes problems with a fairy tale ease. Brik ironically compares his trials to a hurdle chase in which Gleb as a pure-blooded proletarian race-horse, effortlessly takes hurdle after hurdle. From the ideological point of view, Brik insists that Gleb's central position in the novel represents an individualistic heroism instead of the modern heroism of the collective. To Brik, such treatment is unsuitable for Soviet literature: "Heroics is a literary device with the help of which the sum of accomplishments of a number of people is ascribed to an individual hero. This device is very old and its social roots have been revealed with sufficient clarity by Marxist criticism."

Gleb's heroic role in the construction of national economy was paralleled by Dasha's role as the proletarian heroine working for the emergence of a new daily life, of the new byt. In Brik's view, their roles develop with matching simplicity. Dasha decides to free herself from the dominance of men in order to live freely for the benefit of the collective. In her position as a free woman, she accepts neither jealousy nor love. Sex for her is purely physical, incidental, and implies no commitment. The straightforwardness of her attitude in the novel, according to Brik, has no relation to the inevitably complex consequences of such a position in real life.

In addition to the synthetic problems and simplistic solutions presented through the protagonists, Brik found a similar illusory synthesis in Gladkov's concept of literary form. According to Brik, in Cement Gladkov tried to fulfill opposing demands made of Soviet literature. He attempted to present both "heroism and daily life," both "proclamation and protocol." Yet, instead of synthesizing these elements, he simply put the heroic, the proclamatory element, into the presentation of Gleb and Dasha and devoted the remaining parts of the novel to the depiction of a seemingly real life. In order to present the heroic, to give his protagonists a monumental dimension, Gladkov turned to literary stereotypes, to "a Greco-Soviet stylization." In Brik's words, Gleb was stylized into "Gleb-Achilles, Gleb-Roland, Gleb-Il'ia Muromets," and Dasha into "Joanne d'Arc." The real Gleb Chumalov and Dasha Chumalova fail to materialize in the novel. From Brik's point of view, any attempt to find a heroic, monumental form for the theme of the reconstruction obscures the features unique to the revolutionary subject matter.

As an alternative to Gladkov's semi-mythological approach, to his illusory realism, the "Lef" group propagated the modern genre of "biography of a thing." In his essay "Biography of a Thing," Sergei Tret'iakov, a major theoretician of "Lef" and writer of literatura fakta, attacked the traditional narrative and contrasted it with "Lef's" proposals for the new prose. Tret'iakov believed that a novel, like Gladkov's Cement, which viewed the world through the prism of psychology, traditionally presented socio-political conflicts as sins against ethics, and depicted protagonists as suffering "neuropathological" qualms of conscience. In a modernized Soviet version, such literature

uses an individual protagonist to illustrate the totality of change and so inevitably distorts the patterns of the revolutionary turnover. Instead of showing the contradictions and new directions visible in the society, it presents emotional turmoils experienced by individual characters who show "fully irrational features."

Tret'iakov himself refused to grant the primacy of emotions and fictional situations over man's intellect, man's knowledge and his technical-organizational ability. A "biography of a thing" was, in his opinion, better fit for the new scientific-technological age than was the traditional psychological novel. In a "biography of a thing," a production process occupies the central place in the narrative, and the story expands to the group of people and the incidents connected with production. Tret'iakov compared this genre to a conveyer belt transporting a raw element which changed into a useful product through collective human efforts. Through such an encompassing focus, the author could give a picture of social and economic interactions without the distortion which occurs when an individual is put in the centre of the narration and made to stand for the masses. Cement not withstanding, Tret'iakov maintained that real "biographies of things" such as "Wood," "Grain," "Coal," still needed to be written.

And so, in the late 1920s between the adherents of realism and the supporters of the avant-garde, Gladkov's Cement was viewed through two conflicting standards. One side wanted art to be a reflection of reality, with the accompanying psychological insight into the characters and a belief in the role of art as an affirmative example for the social change. The other side stood for art as a construct, an analyzable model, with a corresponding experimental form functioning as an incitement toward open analysis of the societal processes.

The further fate of Gladkov's novel and of the proposals made by his critics was determined by the introduction of socialist realism in 1932. Cement survived the next decades in numerous, but thoroughly revised, editions. In these revisions, the mystique of the machine reminiscent of the Smithies and the romanticism of War Communism were rejected as typical mistakes of the initial revolutionary enthusiasm. The ornamental style was smoothed out; passages dealing with sexual freedom were deleted; the importance of the family was re-established; and a socialist realist positive perspective supplemented the plot.

While the revised Cement gained a new prominence as a classic of Soviet literature, the criticism of the novel by the proponents of the avant-garde had no immediate impact. "Lef" theories of operative art came to an end with the suicide of Maiakovskii in 1930 and the imprisonment of Tret'iakov a few years later. (pp. 88-93)

> Halina Stephan, " 'Cement': From Gladkov's Monumental Epos to Müller's Avant-Garde Drama," in Germano-Slavica, No. 2, Fall, 1979, pp. 85-103.

BERTA BRAININA   (essay date 1981)

[In the following excerpt from her introduction to a 1981 English-language translation of Cement published in the Soviet Union, Brainina praises the artistic and ideological achievements of Gladkov's novel.]

Cement is already well over 50 years old. Essentially it is a novel about people at work—working from inner motivation—which makes it both a social and historical document and a significant literary breakthrough. This theme touched Gladkov more deeply than any other: as he himself put it, *Cement* tells more about his life than do his autobiographical tales.

In his article **"The Genesis of *Cement*,"** Gladkov wrote that he had intended to produce "something on the lines of an epic" from the very first. And 23 years later he told the Second Soviet Writers' Congress that his novel was indeed an epic, a work which bore the "fiery imprint" of his youth.

Youth—yes, but not only youth. *Cement* is a repository of all that was dearest to Gladkov's heart from the beginning of his conscious life until the day he died. "*Cement* was my first love—and my last," he once said to me.

He worked on the novel throughout his life, making improvements in composition and style but retaining the original pattern of images and the ideological and stylistic kernel of the work.

The verve and immediacy of *Cement* escaped none of its contemporaries. To Alexander Serafimovich *Cement* was "the first sweeping portrayal of a revolutionary country in the making. The first fictionalised overview of a new way of life, born of revolution. And the picture is not angled, not fragmentary, but broad, bold and sure."

Cement took the Soviet reading public by storm. Gladkov once showed me a letter he had received from Alexei Zakharyev, a young worker. They later became friends and kept in constant contact until the Second World War, when Zakharyev perished in a burning tank. "You've hit it just right . . ." the young man wrote. "I did my apprenticeship under your Gleb Chumalov—though his name was Pyotr Tikhonov. And we had a Chibis and a Zhuk, a Zhidky and even a Badin, only they all had different names. So much joy and sorrow, tears and laughter! And all of us, except Badin (Toropov) were so happy and so inspired that we felt we could move mountains. . . ."

The letter was dated 1926; it was yellow with age. Gladkov had kept it safe for over 30 years. . . .

In an autobiographical note written in the early thirties, Gladkov gave his own explanation of the immediate and remarkable popularity of his novel:

"The working class and the Red Army simply rearmed, and, rifles in hand, went off to do battle on the economic front. Tempered in the fires of war, in their bloody and heroic clashes with the class enemy, they carried the same heroism and enthusiasm into the struggle to restore all sectors of the ravaged economy and to construct a new, Soviet economic system.

"New people were born, new forms of existence, of social relations, arose. The struggle was life and breath to me, a rank-and-file Party member and working man. And in that struggle, for the first time, a new pattern of images blossomed within me; I was completely wrapped up in my epic, *Cement*. I wrote it in a state of extreme tension, of utter involvement. A new theme, new characters, new problems—all without precedent in Soviet fiction and all hot off the anvil of the Civil War—assured *Cement* its immediate and 'remarkable popularity'."

Not surprisingly, *Cement* made a deep impression on Maxim Gorky too. On 23 August 1925 he wrote to Gladkov: "I would like, if I may, to say a few words about *Cement*. I believe that it is a highly important, very good book. For the first time since the Revolution we are offered a firm grasp on and a clearsighted view of the most significant theme of the present day—the theme of work. None of your predecessors has tackled this theme with such vigour. Or so cleverly."

A few months later Gorky returned to *Cement*, writing to Gladkov: "I'm pleased that *Cement* is a success. I'm quite convinced that it will have a great social and practical import. I wrote once before, I think, to congratulate you on being the first to take the theme of work and invest it with emotion. That is to your credit."

Gladkov's novel is not only a milestone of Soviet literature. It has stood the test of time, and lives on. And faces the future undismayed.

We are immediately thrust into a unique, a legendary time—the years immediately following the October Revolution of 1917. Gleb Chumalov, a fitter, returns from the front and visits the plant he left three years before. Walking along a "wildly overgrown path," he sees in the distance the desolate, hungry sea, the cheerless wharves, sees the exhausted faces of the workers and hears that many of them have become peddlers and are keeping chickens, pigs and goats near the plant and on the plant premises. But Gleb, in his forage cap with its crimson star, the Order of the Red Banner on his chest, does not break his disciplined, undeviating, confident stride. . . .

Gladkov's description of the scene, besides fixing the action in time and space, reveals his hero's fundamental qualities. A courageous, noble man, who has defended the Revolution, his native land and his own home tooth and nail, comes back to his little nest—and finds only chaos and ruin. Yet Gleb is not one of those adamantine heroes that were so common in the literature of those days, but an uncomplicated, human figure; who is not immune to loneliness and depression. Suddenly worn out, full of bitter thoughts, he sits motionless outside his house. And this inner conflict, this pain, this lack of confidence in his own strength continue to dog his steps. We read later a deeply moving monologue, an unspoken conversation with his scrupulous, ever-alert conscience.

"Did he really have the strength to push for an organised labour front when everything around, from the machines down to the last nail, had gone to rack and ruin, been stolen or left to rust, when there was no fuel, no bread, no transport, when the wagons stood still as death on the railway tracks and no ships would come steaming to the jetties for so very long? . . . A Johnny-come-lately. A botcher. A hamfisted fool. People still could not keep a grip on the tiniest little thing; the very existence of the workers' state was still under threat. So how could anyone possibly plan to revive the plant? Surely it was absurd to even think of it at a time when the workers were on drastically reduced rations, so far gone that a full working day was well beyond their strength? What point was there in producing anything when the economic life of the Republic was in a state of chronic paralysis and the country was dying of starvation?"

But Gleb, a soldier and a Communist, who even under fire had dreamed of the plant, of working there when the fighting was done, cannot simply give in and let himself go. Gladkov is well aware that a true revolutionary is not one who never experiences weariness and doubt, but one who knows how to overcome them.

One of the most valuable qualities of the working man who devotes himself to the Revolution is strength of spirit. The confrontations Gleb engages in and the obstacles he surmounts are fundamental to his growth as a militant creator of a new world.

The novel's internal tension is deepened by a subtle orchestration of action-packed scenes, leading up to the natural and inevitable climax—the reopening of the plant.

Cement has been constructed as a co-ordinated whole. The fight to save the plant, to have it producing within the shortest possible time is the touchstone of our understanding of Gleb and all the other major characters.

Crowd scenes are usually pivotal. While presenting Gleb as a courageous revolutionary, a noble figure, Gladkov never sets his hero against the people: Gleb the Communist directs the people and yet feels total unity with them.

At the outset the workers, though apparently glad to see Gleb, keep their distance from him. But his first serious talk with them breaks the ice. Though he really gives them a piece of his mind, they can see his point and understand that he is motivated by a genuine concern for their future and the future of the Revolution.

Gleb gets through to them because not only with his mind but with the very depths of his being he grasps that the most vital, the most noble quality of the working man—the absence of which brings degradation and moral and physical death—is his capacity for work. Work is the linchpin of human life, as vital to a man as air itself.

"You see," Gladkov told me, "I know from personal experience that the very idea of inactivity paralyses the lungs. There's nothing to breathe—so you just lie down and die ... 'Unemployment' is a fearful word—a catastrophe, a tragedy, an abyss opening up beneath your feet. . . ."

Psychological realism is without doubt one of the novel's finest features.

"In *Cement* I wanted to bring out, above all, my characters' 'spiritual dialectic'." Gladkov wrote on 15 May 1954. "Psychology is an essential part of man, and hence of art. And in this my prime example was, and always has been, Lev Tolstoy."

That seems rather questionable at first glance. *Cement* defies the precepts of classical proportion, of classical reticence. The novel is split into 17 separate novellas, which only habit prompts us to call chapters. The novellas are divided into subsections; the story line often makes sharp turns between one subsection and the next. The novel abounds with dialect expressions, hyperbolic epithets and the other violations of the classical norms that were the heritage of the "stylistic revolution" and reflected the contradictory influences of the time, the upheavals in the literary world—what Konstantin Fedin called "the literary measles."

But the core of *Cement*—its flesh and blood—is psychological analysis, the tracing of psychological developments. Commenting on Gladkov's ability to get inside his characters and show their thoughts and emotions in action, Gorky wrote: "All your characters sparkle with life."

Various artistic devices contribute to this depth of psychological insight: use of the omniscient narrator, internal monologue, impersonal direct speech, and, most important of all, dialogue. Gladkov's dialogues are always psychological duels, lively exchanges in which new character traits are revealed.

The novel's mainstay is the principle of militant humanism; Gleb Chumalov, champion of all the author holds most dear, remains true to that principle throughout.

In his fight for the plant, Gleb, now secretary of the plant Party group, comes up against Zhidky, secretary of the district committee. Zhidky, a man whose mental horizons are limited in the extreme, advises Gleb to drop his plans for the plant and concentrate for the time being on what he sees as the priority issue—fuel.

The conflict between them reveals two things: Gleb's unerring political sense and his ability to view things nationwide; and the personality traits of the blinkard Zhidky type, those people who were forced by life itself to abandon their hair-splitting ways, to take a new perspective on life. Gradually Zhidky develops a liking for Gleb, comes to share his viewpoint that the plant must come first—then there will be fuel, and food, and everything that the Revolution needs.

"I assure you," Gladkov told me, "that the Revolution literally remade the Zhidkys. It stirred them up, and they grew before my very eyes. And it stirs them still—unless, of course, their consciences are fast asleep."

But while it is relatively easy for Gleb to overcome Zhidky's limitations—since the man is actually capable of self-criticism and genuinely wants to live and work as part of a collective—Badin, the chairman of the executive committee, is a different proposition altogether. Badin is ambitious, one hundred per cent dedicated to himself, to his strength and his power over others. A former revolutionary, he is intelligent, dynamic and even honourable in his own way, since he honestly believes that he is serving the cause of the Revolution. In actual fact he betrays the Revolution with his degenerate lifestyle, his inability to grasp the needs and future perspectives of the time and the deliberate and uncouth way in which he distances himself from the people.

Gleb was Soviet literature's prototype worker-Communist, committed to the creation of a new, socialist society. Yet Badin, a predominantly negative figure, was no less powerfully conceived. In bringing Gleb face to face with a dangerous and clever opponent, Gladkov not only underlines his hero's political sensitivity but also intensifies the drama of the situation and depicts yet another complex source of friction which faced Gleb and all other revolutionaries in their struggle for Soviet power and revolutionary justice. Gleb's clearsightedness, the depth of his militant love of mankind are revealed in his interaction with various types of people.

The problems to be faced were tremendous—but strong and devoted Communists like Gleb tackled them, and in so doing helped others overcome the same obstacles. They had a profound faith in their fellow-men, a faith which persisted throughout the life-and-death struggles of those days. It was a marvellous faith. And its leitmotif was the magical, inimitable "music of the revolution."

That faith meant a great deal to Lenin. As the ultimate truth of the Revolution, Lenin is an invisible presence in the book, just as he was constantly present in Gladkov's consciousness.

"I never met Lenin," Gladkov said to me once, "but he's alive in my mind's eye and I ask his advice when things get tough. . . ." (pp. 7-16)

Sergei Ivagin, the Communist, his father, Ivan Arsenich, a member of the pre-Revolutionary intelligentsia, and Kleist, the engineer, illustrate the problems of the intelligentsia face-to-face with the Revolution. This supercharged issue is a facet of the broad theme of humanism in the new world, the novel's ideological and artistic kernel.

During the confiscation of the local bourgeoisie's belongings, Gleb comes to Ivan Arsenich's house, where two workers, Loshak and Gromada, are carrying out their duties, and listens as the old man holds forth on the need to renounce worldly goods, on man's powerlessness in the eye of fate—a morbid, abstract monologue which rouses only confusion and pity. Loshak treats Ivan Arsenich with patronising bonhomie, while Gromada mutters: "Comrade Chumalov, you could go daft listening to all that clever stuff."

Gleb's pity is rather more effective. He leaves the old man's things alone, calms him down, shakes his hand and leaves.

While Ivan Arsenich is pitiful, his son, Sergei, is an entirely different prospect—dedicated heart and mind to the Revolution, in defiance of his upbringing and his milieu. The son has left his father far behind.

Sergei knows that man is capable of refashioning society. He himself and his comrades in the Bolshevik Party are doing precisely that. Yet, when Gleb shakes his hand for the first time, the fingers he touches are soft and timid as a young girl's. That inborn softness and timidity also reflect Sergei's fear of the demands of the day, of the headlong sweep of the Revolution. Sergei's feverish activity has more than a touch of hysteria about it, as though he is driving himself on, submitting to his hard and glorious duty, doing all that he must—and yet is haunted by the suspicion that he lacks the force to reach his goal.

His obedience, proof of his utter dedication to the Revolution, is at the same time symptomatic of this fear and lack of faith in himself. It is as if he is continually wondering if he has strength enough, time enough. . . .

Sergei needs to keep on the move in order to assuage the constant pain within, the pity for all those (including himself) who, in his view, must turn against their own selves or be swept to their death by the Revolutionary whirlwind.

For all this, though, the story of Sergei Ivagin might well have had a happier ending had he not fallen foul of the "walking skeleton," the chairman of the Party purge commission.

Here Gladkov's satire is given full rein. The "skeleton" is a heartless creature who should never have attained a position of such responsibility in the Party. Gladkov wastes no good words on him.

The approach to Kleist, the bourgeois engineer, is completely different. Here Gladkov lifts Gleb to the heights of Communist consciousness, to the stage at which social ideals take precedence over individual feelings and subjective reactions to others. Gleb, realising that Kleist is vital to the plant's future, concentrates heavily upon him—a man he dislikes and with whom he shares no common ground at the outset—to the detriment of Sergei Ivagin and Polya Mekhova—his own people, his dear friends. He is simply too busy, too preoccupied to give them their due attention.

Gladkov liked to tell the story of an engineer, "a talented and educated person who did not want to emigrate because he could not imagine life outside his homeland. He told me that life without a homeland was as unthinkable as life without oxygen. Now, this engineer—we'll call him Ivan Pavlovich—was opposed to the Revolution at the beginning, but he did not leave his plant, which had suffered terribly during the Civil War. Later he became a highly valued specialist and was decorated for his services to the state. He's an old man now, we're still

friends . . . Now, that engineer was one of my models for Kleist. I say 'one,' because I'm sure there's no such thing as a pure, unadulterated model. At least, not in my work."

When Gleb catches sight of Kleist, the man who had once betrayed him to the White Guards, his first instinct is to rush out of the room full of workers, to confront the engineer face to face, and enjoy watching him squirm with terror: "There was the man he would gladly have strangled at any moment, and that moment would have been a highlight of his life."

But can Gleb, a Communist, give way to hatred and a thirst for revenge? His soul becomes a battleground, until the wisdom of the Party, the militant humanism of a true revolutionary, take the upper hand: far from taking revenge on Kleist, Gleb actually ensures that this gifted engineer will go on living and working.

Kleist is to a large extent the victim of class prejudices: he sees the Socialist Revolution as a tragedy, a harbinger of chaos and death; he goes into "secret emigration," hiding from people and from life itself in his office, behind dusty windows that are firmly and, he thinks, eternally shut.

Gladkov's sure touch reveals itself in the psychological resonance of his images: nothing in the novel offends against life or art, and the reader therefore questions no change, no volte-face, however unexpected.

Kleist, when confronted by Gleb, does indeed squirm:

"'You . . . you . . . Chumalov, for pity's sake do what you have to do quickly, but please, you . . . please don't torture me . . .'."

'Gleb went up to Kleist and laughed.

"'Comrade engineer, what are you talking about? You can forget all that rubbish right now . . . You're no good to me dead!'"

Gleb immediately gives Kleist certain specific tasks: to get the cable-road working, put the power-house in order and repair the buildings. And Kleist recognises the hand of friendship, sees new horizons opening, understands that life goes on.

Kleist is reborn: "In this last gruelling struggle for life, Kleist realised that those fearful hands, those death-dealing hands, had nailed him, forcibly and firmly, to life. . . ."

Later, during a weekend of voluntary work on the cable-road, Kleist is shown wholly committed to the new life. Gladkov uses his considerable talent for psychological analysis to show what Kleist and Gleb have in common—that is, a burning desire to create and a love of work. Once again Gleb, with his militant humanism and inherent ability to organise others, stands tall before us, at one with the working people.

"'Well now, Herman Hermanovich—remember you said that this lot would take at least a month to finish? Just look what people can do with a bit of enthusiasm. They've only been at it three days and they've nearly done.'

"Kleist smiled, and, sedate as ever, said drily: 'Oh yes indeed. Going at it like this you can work wonders. But it's such a waste of energy—no planning, no organised division of labour. Enthusiasm's like a thunderstorm—shortlived and harmful.'

"'When things are in this state we have to start this way. Once we've laid a firm foundation and got it all sorted out, then we can start planning our industrial processes. Besides, enthusiasm isn't a thunderstorm. It's a fire, a fire in the soul, and our fire'll never go out'."

Let me digress for a moment.

From 1918 to 1921 Gladkov was in Novorossiisk, where the novel is set: until March 1920 he helped direct the Civil War partisan movement from the underground. After Soviet power had been declared in the area, all efforts were concentrated on restoring the economy. Enthusiasm—Gleb's "fire in the soul"—was vitally, sometimes even decisively, important at that time. Lenin called it "heroic initiative."

Initiative and creativity, new ways of working, those famous days of voluntary labour . . . When Gladkov spoke about such things he was transformed, the years dropped away from him, his back straightened and he actually became taller. For he too had spent his free time working on the cement plant in Novorossiisk, he too had wielded picks, crowbars and shovels in a bitter north-easterly that literally swept people off their feet.

Gladkov showed me a local newspaper dated 9 October 1921: "On Sunday, 2 October, the cementworkers, along with the entire proletariat of Novorossiisk, were able to congratulate themselves on a magnificent victory on the industrial front: the cable-road went into operation . . . Glowing faces all around . . . They looked at the road with affection and proprietorial pride, repeated, time and again: 'Beat it, then, didn't we? There'll be fuel for the winter. We've won'."

Gleb Chumalov is one of those ordinary working men, one of those pioneers who took matters into their own restless hands, who created a new life—thus, all unawares, became heroes, legendary figures, called upon by history to perform miracles.

A hero of the twenties, a champion of Soviet power, a motive force of the economy, he walks straight out of the pages into our lives.

But Gleb does not belong only to the twenties: an image of such breadth and depth must necessarily retain its vigour far outside its immediate context. *Cement* has been translated into all the languages of the Soviet Union and almost every world language. And new translations keep on appearing.

The novel's impact on Soviet literature had been immense: every fictionalised treatment of the working class which takes a serious and speculative view of reality shows the influence of *Cement*.

And through this industrial epic, a whole slice of history, a whole complex of attitudes and emotions, comes to life. We learn about the New Economic Policy, the Party purges, the defeat of petty-bourgeois anarchy, the destruction of the old and creation of the new, the recruitment of bourgeois specialists, the assimilation of advanced technical expertise, and the battle with the external enemy, the last remnants of the White Guards.

The title of the novel itself reflects the essence of the age. Cement symbolises the unbending will of the Party—cementing, strengthening, directing the people to victory.

The life of *Cement* is hard, full of conflict, intensely dramatic and, as Gladkov put it, "simply staggering." It demands preternatural yet co-ordinated intellectual and physical effort; in it the most menial labour becomes an intellectually satisfying pursuit, brings an almost aesthetic pleasure.

Here Gladkov—novelist, citizen, revolutionary—clearly sees himself answerable not only to his own age but also to the future, to history.

I have already noted that the characters of *Cement* were living people, Gladkov's contemporaries, past and present. And they live for us all, because *Cement* is a paean to the creative intellectual energy of the working class—a theme which reverberates through the world to this very day. (pp. 17-24)

> *Berta Brainina, in a foreword to* Cement: A Novel *by Feodor Gladkov, translated by Liv Tadge, 1981. Reprint by Raduga Publishers, 1985, pp. 7-24.*

MARGOT K. FRANK   (essay date 1983)

[*In the following excerpt, Frank compares the original and revised versions of* Cement.]

Gladkov's account of post-revolutionary change [*Cement*] continues to be popular. It has even been cast into dramatic form and was recently staged in West Germany. As originally written in 1925, Gladkov's outspoken criticism of party, government, and certain approaches contrasts pleasantly with the dull tone usually reserved for topics dealing with working class consciousness. The vitality and immediacy with which the author chronicles the confusion of social upheaval, using a boldly experimental style, have made the novel into a Socialist Realism classic. Only part of Gladkov's verve comes across in [the] new Soviet translation, which is based on a 1958 revised version. During the Stalin decades, the author himself undertook a number of major and minor reworkings, each time eliminating or softening references critical of the regime and its policies. The first edition has not been released by Soviet publishing for reprinting. Fortunately, the novel still makes its point, even in truncated form. Gladkov disapproves, not through overt theorizing or explicit description, but by skillful manipulation of the text. He introduces a number of topical issues, traces their implementation, and has the characters sing their praises. A look at the subtext, however, reveals that these policies are unworkable, bring unhappiness to the participants, and cause unnecessary deaths. They are ethically unwholesome in that they tear natural relationships apart, and force people into artificial unions. In addition, the policies are carried out by corrupt party leaders. Among the items questioned or rejected by Gladkov are: the emancipation of women and the dissolution of the family; the early purges; the treatment of former middle class intellectuals; the idolization of technical specialists; the dispossessing of the bourgeoisie; the emerging weight of the bureaucracy; the avarice and immorality of regional Soviet leaders.

Of special interest is the author's critical stance in regard to female emancipation, which is depicted as leading straight to family disintegration. The metamorphosis of a formerly docile housewife into an independent, social activist is portrayed in harsh terms, focusing on the heartlessness with which the erstwhile loving mother abandons her child to die in an incompetent children's home so that she can advance her career without obstacles. The rewritten version, reflecting later pro-family policies, attempts to modify the devastating effect of the heroine's communization on family life. In her foreword to the English-speaking audience, Gladkov specialist Berta Brainina does not even mention the family issue, the liberated wife, or any of the female topics so prominently foregrounded in the novel [see excerpt dated 1981]. Readers would do well to compare the original version, available in English in an Ungar edition, with the current book for an excellent demonstration of how literature, written in the censorially benign 1920s, had to be altered to suit changing policies and ever more severe restrictions on artistic expression. (pp. 303-04)

Margot K. Frank, in a review of "Cement," in The Modern Language Journal, Vol. LXVII, No. 3, Autumn, 1983, pp. 303-04.

ADDITIONAL BIBLIOGRAPHY

Brewster, Dorothy. "Engines as Gods." *New York Herald Tribune Books* (14 July 1929): 2.
    Descriptive review of *Cement.* Brewster comments that "the book is written in a vigorous dramatic style, with a rapid tempo."

Friedberg, Maurice. "New Editions of Soviet Belles-Lettres: A Study in Politics and Palimpsests." *American Slavic and East European Review* XIII (1954): 72-88.
    Examines textual emendations in the various Soviet editions of *Cement* in a discussion of how such alterations in a number of works reflect the changing attitudes and restrictions of the Soviet government.

Maguire, Robert A. *Red Virgin Soil: Soviet Literature in the 1920s,* pp. 126ff. Princeton: Princeton University Press, 1968.
    Study of *Red Virgin Soil,* a major Russian literary journal of the 1920s. Includes mention of Gladkov as a peripheral member of the group surrounding the journal and a brief discussion of *Cement* as an unsuccessful novel.

"Fiction Notes." *New Republic* LVIII, No. 754 (15 May 1929): 367-68.
    Positive review of *Cement,* which the critic finds "clear-cut and lucid." The critic further states that "if the Soviet Republic can inspire such literary work as is revealed in this book, then under Communism, Russian letters will not suffer."

"Shorter Notices." *New Statesman* XXXII, No. 824 (9 February 1929): 576-78.
    Negative review of *Cement.* The critic complains that Gladkov "sees Russia in terms of sweat and filth."

Struve, Gleb. "Proletarian Novelists." In his *Russian Literature under Lenin and Stalin,* pp. 130-40. Norman: University of Oklahoma Press, 1971.
    Briefly discusses Gladkov's literary career, focusing primarily on *Cement.*

Hayashi Fumiko

1904-1951

Japanese novelist, short story writer, journalist, essayist, and poet.

At the peak of her career Hayashi was the most popular female writer in Japan. In her works she depicted the lives of the poor and dispossessed—the social class from which Hayashi herself came. Her post-World War II fiction is especially praised for its vivid evocation of the plight of the poor during that time and is distinguished by Hayashi's skillful creation of female characters who are economically dependent upon improvident and unreliable men.

Hayashi's mother and stepfather were itinerant peddlers. Although their livelihood depended upon almost constant travel, the family maintained a home in Onomichi for seven years, and Hayashi was able to attend a girls' school there for four years. In her teens, Hayashi supported herself while pursuing a secondary education. In 1922, at eighteen, she moved to Tokyo to live with a university student who had promised to marry her but ultimately abandoned her; Hayashi subsequently engaged in many affairs and several marriages with similarly unhappy outcomes. She continued to support herself, and often a lover or husband as well, through domestic or factory work and an occasional return to the hard and uncertain life of the homeless peddler. A diary she kept during her first years in Tokyo provided much of the material for her first novel, *Hōrōki (Journal of a Vagabond)*. The success of the book enabled Hayashi to live abroad for six months, but not lavishly: she suffered from malnutrition and had to borrow money for her return fare.

Returning to Japan in 1932, she found that her first novel was still extremely popular. Publishers solicited further works from her, and she eventually produced more than two hundred books and numerous short stories, essays, articles, and poems. At the outbreak of the second Sino-Japanese war in 1937, Hayashi became a war correspondent for the magazine *Mainichi* and later served as a member of the Japanese press corps during World War II. She remained deeply committed to her writing career, rarely refusing a request for a literary contribution—possibly driven, some commentators speculate, by memories of early poverty and uncertainty about the future. She was supplying serials to three magazines when she died of a heart attack in 1951.

Hayashi has received little critical attention from commentators writing in English. Chiefly noted are her first novel, *Journal of a Vagabond,* and two postwar works: the short story "Bangiku" ("Late Chrysanthemum") and the novel *Ukigumo (Floating Cloud)*. The largely autobiographical *Journal* tells the story of a poor young woman who is undaunted by her precarious existence as a street peddler and optimistic despite her often disastrous encounters with men. "Late Chrysanthemum" established Hayashi's reputation as a postwar writer. This story of an aging geisha and her disagreeable reunion with a former lover is praised for its evocation of the depressing mood of Japan in the years following World War II, as well as for Hayashi's depiction of the lovers' emotions as they meet

again and realize that nothing remains of the attraction that they once felt for each other. The novel *Floating Cloud* similarly presents a powerful vision of Japan after World War II. In this work, Hayashi portrays two lovers who are unable to find fulfillment in their relationship or in any other aspect of their bleak lives. *Floating Cloud* is generally considered Hayashi's finest work. The lovers' resignation to their unsatisfying lives is considered symbolic of a general mood of hopelessness that pervaded postwar Japan.

Critics generally find Hayashi's avoidance of sentimentality to be the outstanding characteristic of her fiction. She never descended to the maudlin or the bathetic in her treatment of potentially sentimental subjects, themes, and plots: "No romantic banality" is found in Hayashi, wrote Armando Martins Janeira, "even when risking a difficult subject." Ivan Morris has commented that "Given its dominant subject and approach, it is inevitable that Hayashi Fumiko's writing should frequently verge on the sentimental; yet there is a simple, poetic quality about her language and a directness about her telling method that save her work from ever becoming maudlin." Although Hayashi's works are no longer as widely read or critically esteemed as they were during her lifetime, her portraits of postwar Japanese life still retain interest for contemporary readers.

PRINCIPAL WORKS

Hōrōki (novel) 1930
  [*Journal of a Vagabond,* 1951]
''Bangiku'' (short story) 1948
  [''Late Chrysanthemum'' published in *Japan Quarterly,*
  1956]
''Shitamachi'' (short story) 1949
  [''Tokyo'' (partial translation) published in *Modern
  Japanese Literature,* 1956; also published as
  ''Downtown'' (partial translation) in *Modern Japanese
  Stories,* 1962]
Ukigumo (novel) 1951
  [*Floating Cloud,* 1957; also published as *The Floating
  Clouds,* 1965]
Hayashi Fumiko zenshū. 23 vols. (novels, short stories,
  and poetry) 1951-52

YOSHIKAZU KATAOKA (essay date 1939)

[*In the following excerpt, the critic discusses the structure and
prevailing mood of Hayashi's novel* Hōrōki.]

[*Hōrōki*] is a kind of novel made up of twenty-nine chapters . . . , including an introduction, ''Hōrōki Izen'' (Prelude),
and an epilogue, ''Hōrōki Igo no Ninshiki'' (After-Percep-
tions). Primarily an account of the wanderings of the author
herself, it is a collection of fragmentary notes which she jotted
down between hurried moments at different times and at different places, and is not, therefore, a work that has been developed fully in accordance with the scheme and composition
of the novel form. Aside from the introduction and the epilogue, the twenty-seven chapters which constitute the narrative
itself are all written in the form of a diary. They are all, of
course, given a certain measure of coherence, yet there are
numerous instances in which both unity and continuity are
lacking, either in the matter of content or of time, in bringing
the various chapters into a close relationship. So that those
cases, for example, in which an incident which breaks out in
one chapter is directly taken up in the following chapter, occur
rather less frequently than those in which it is not. At the same
time, though each of the short chapters may be said to have
been given a fairly coherent treatment, yet only a few of them
are so arranged as to conform to the standard short-story form.
In short, the work may be a diary that savours of fiction, but
a good deal of the contents is such that it cannot be called a
story in the form of a diary. Therefore, it would perhaps be
better, after all, to characterize it as ''a novel formed by an
accumulation of prose-poem diary entries.'' (p. 192)

In this work is described the manner of living of a woman who
exists in a society, not perhaps of the lowest, but at any rate
of a very low station, and the varied occupations to which she
can cling for her subsistence. It is, in a word, a world of
degeneration, of humiliation, of instability. Here are occupations that have been debased through the intricacy and corruption of a highly developed capitalist system. Liberalism faces
a crisis, threatened with an early, forcible extinction. Above
all, men tyrannize over women, whom they regard as semi-
subordinate creatures, and the women are apathetic. Helpless
women are surrounded by temptations, by violence, by filthy
favours. Unable in view of her desire to live in peace in such
a world, the heroine of this work leads a wandering life, but

the more she roams about the greater is her disillusionment
and disappointment, no matter where she goes. Indeed, it is
the kind of gloomy world in which egoism and individual
freedom and all such considerations are doomed to a crushing
extinction. The heroine herself is prone to be hysterical, mut-
tering that ''man is such a brute that I cannot believe in him;''
bewailing, ''how can I make plans for the future with any
pretensions to seriousness?'' and screaming, ''I wish the earth
would crack in two with a bang!''

Yet, in spite of this, a faintly genial mood and a spirit of
optimism run through the work. This is due to the fact that,
though the heroine roams about and leads a gloomy life, she
nevertheless brings it under control with the desire to rise in
the world and the fierce will to survive. And because, also,
she seeks to reorient her relations with human beings and her
modes of living through self-perfection. The tenacity of this
will-power reminds one of a sort of sheer imperviousness.
Many a time it contemplates death and once it even goes so
far as actually to attempt self-destruction. Yet, in the end, it
vigorously pushes the thought away. Such being the case, the
heroine herself, for all that she exists in the midst of corruption
and humiliation, is always in a healthy state. It would seem
only natural, therefore, that a genial mood and a bright optimism should permeate the work. Nevertheless, this volition,
instead of being linked with a thoroughgoing critique of human
life based upon intelligence and hence with the orientation that
should logically result from it, is confined to the limits of a
much simpler will-to-live which borders on instinct, or sensibility—an uncritical, purblind will that merely reflects and
repels outward influences. So that in seeking to orient itself,
it frequently falls into aberrations, and the effect of placing the
girl's wanderings in an even more chaotic state is considerably
in evidence. When she becomes indignant over human life
which reeks with corruption, she returns to the ''native place
of her travels,'' but soon leaves the place and goes on a distinctly aimless pilgrimage of life. If she is disillusioned by a
man she runs to another, and if she is betrayed by the latter
she returns to the affections of the former. If the life of womankind as she observes it seems all too wretched, she forthwith
seeks the protection of men whom she had up to then treated
contemptuously. While strongly feeling the cheerfulness and
friendship of a world sunk to the very bottom of the social
scale and sympathizing with a strike in progress, she yet exclaims that ''no matter what sort of revolution occurs which
is inconsistent with my own idea, and though a million men
point their arrows at me, I will still live in accordance with
my mother's ideas.'' All these aberrations bear witness to the
chaotic state of her world which it is impossible to set aright.

And this, in short, accounts for the fact that in the present
work there is frankly projected a realm which, while sentimentally holding freedom and individual character in high regard and trying to realize this principle with the innate and
primitive will-to-live, is nevertheless destitute of profound reflections, of speculative thoughts, of a unified view of human
life. The confusion of that realm naturally borders on nihilism
and anarchism, and the heroine herself is frequently given to
making nihilistic and anarchistic utterances. Yet it is not compounded of a systematized ideology, but merely of explosive
expressions of moods of self-abandonment and of ironies and
resentment directed at others, which are ejaculated at different
moments. Accordingly, it also tends, on the contrary, to stimulate the inverse development of an egotism which springs from
individual character and stubbornness of will.

While this work contains delineations of all sorts and conditions of living, and of a great variety of human beings, they are all confined to the circumstances of the heroine's own life, and one fails to discover any scheme calculated to observe society on a wide scale, or an incisive and thoroughgoing exposé of society derived from such a scheme. Instead of these things, the whole range of interest that, in the final analysis, can be savoured from this work is the mental agitation of one exhausted in the struggle between the purblind will-to-live amid the kind of life that has been crushed and warped on the one hand, and the varied bits of reality that obstruct it on the other— of becoming nihilistic, of trying to shut oneself up in the narrow, empty realm of egotism, of pining for the embrace of travel, of native soil, of mother, of father—together with the lyrical exclamations uttered against the chaos compounded of these elements. (pp. 197-99)

[All] this indicates an aspect of life which results from something that originates in self-love. . . . [As] is characteristic of the author, instead of trying to consider her subject as a problem to be resolved, she indulges in exclamations of sentimental poetic feelings which savour of a reckless sense of self-abandonment. (p. 199)

> *Yoshikazu Kataoka, "'Hōrōki' (A Roving Record): 1922-1927, by Fumiko Hayashi," in* Introduction to Contemporary Japanese Literature: 1902-1935, *edited by the Kokusai Bunka Shinkokai, Kokusai Bunka Shinkokai, 1939, pp. 192-200.*

IVAN MORRIS   (essay date 1961)

[*Morris was an English educator and critic noted for his studies of Japanese history, politics, and culture. In the following excerpt, he characterizes Hayashi's fiction as realistic and compassionate, finding that she avoids sentimentality through her use of simple language and direct narrative.*]

In her stories and novels Hayashi Fumiko portrays with realism and compassion the hardships of the Tokyo lower classes, with which she was so intimately acquainted from her own youth. She shows us a world of degeneration, humiliation, and instability in which men tyrannize over women and women themselves are, all too often, merely apathetic. Yet, tough as this world is, Miss Hayashi suggests that there is a surprising degree of cheerfulness and hope in the lives of the members of the lower stratum that she describes. Her principal women characters are of the humble, yet undaunted, type. . . . [Their] impulses of despair are almost always balanced by a strong will to live and a faith in the future. Given its dominant subject and approach, it is inevitable that Hayashi Fumiko's writing should frequently verge on the sentimental; yet there is a simple, poetic quality about her language and a directness about her telling method that save her work from ever becoming maudlin. (pp. 349-50)

> *Ivan Morris, in an introduction to "Downtown" by Hayashi Fumiko, translated by Ivan Morris, in* Modern Japanese Stories: An Anthology, *edited by Ivan Morris, Charles E. Tuttle Company, 1961, pp. 349-50.*

ARMANDO MARTINS JANEIRA   (essay date 1970)

[*In the following excerpt, the critic notes Hayashi's skillful characterization and plotting.*]

Floating Cloud is the story of a young secretary, chased by lustful and selfish men, who, like her, suffer from living lonely lives without friends, money, work, and source of support. Yukiko's lover looks for her but then leaves her, not even knowing if he loves her. He hurts his wife with his infidelity. Attached to his home and at the same time unsatisfied with his sad, insipid married life, he is himself uncertain and lost:

> Warmed by the body of Tomioka, Yukiko remained fretful, seeking something more violent, more vigorous, out of the whole of the man. It was the same thing with Tomioka. Hugging the girl with all his strength, he still felt lonely. He could not be at ease. He too wanted something, something stronger, more solid, more tangible, and holding out one hand, he repeatedly drank cups of sake, while with the other hand, he held the body of Yukiko. She picked up sushi from time to time, and munching, was attacked by a cutting sense of emptiness. Indeed there were abundant memories of the past that they alone could cherish and enjoy. They both fought to call them back and fill the cavity that lay between their feelings. But it was altogether a difficult task, and the night, long autumn night, had just begun.

The atmosphere of poverty, sadness, and human abandonment prevails in this story, showing the author's great capacity for kindness as well as her unusual skill to describe the feelings of a feminine heart most subtly. There is an echo of the deep humanity of some characters of Gorki. Hayashi's destitute heroes can attain a rare feeling of happiness through mutual devotion and selflessness.

In her short story **"Tokyo,"** a tea pedlar called Ryo is portrayed with truth and tenderness in her poverty. Hayashi herself had made her living as a streetstall pedlar at one time. The woman in the novel has not heard from her husband, a prisoner in Siberia, for six years and she is caring for her six-year-old son. She possesses nothing, not even a room to sleep in, and still she can generously give love without asking for love in return. Of the same human generosity is the worker with whom she falls in love; he is unexpectedly killed in a lorry accident. He fought in war, survived the hardships of a prisoner camp in Siberia to die in an accident when coming back from work. Ryo accepts the loss without despair or romanticism. She continues to sell her tea. Then one day a woman asks her "'How much does it cost?'" Seeing the pedlar's rucksack she adds, "'Come in and rest a while, if you like. I'll see how much money we've got left. We may have enough for tea.' Ryo went in and put down her rucksack. In the small room four serving-women were sitting on the floor around an oil stove, working on a heap of shirts and socks. They were women like herself, thought Ryo, as she watched their busy needles moving in and out of the material. A feeling of warmth came over her."

It is this human warmth that gives the stories of this writer such a deep human quality. She has an extraordinary gift for developing a tight plot and creating a living atmosphere.

There is no romantic banality, even when risking a difficult subject, as in **"Hone"** (**"Bones"**). In it a young war widow, Michiko, has her first experience as a prostitute. She had to get money to feed the selfish family consisting of her senile father and young brother dying of tuberculosis:

She could not help feeling terribly guilty. Staring blankly at the frosted glass which had brightened to blue-green, she felt like asking some god if this was human fate.

It is curious to note that this short story opens with a quotation from the Bible and ends with Michiko and her daughter carrying the casket with the ashes and bones of the young brother, while the child sings "Jesus Loves Me." At that moment Michiko only wonders when her father will die. What is most admirable about Hayashi is that unlike most proletarian writers, she wrote not with ideological tirades or theories, but with understanding for real people. (pp. 173-74)

> Armando Martins Janeira, "Western Influence on Contemporary Japanese Writers," in his Japanese and Western Literature: A Comparative Study, *Charles E. Tuttle Company, 1970, pp. 142-83.*

DONALD KEENE (essay date 1984)

[*Keene is one of the foremost American translators and critics of Japanese literature. In the following excerpt, he presents a discussion of Hayashi's principal works of fiction available in English, together with comment on some of her best-known untranslated works.*]

[Many] details of Hayashi's life are presented in her first book, *Hōrōki (Journal of a Vagabond),* published in 1930. She wrote that she had been inspired to write this book after reading Knut Hamsun's *Hunger;* but apart from the poverty she describes there is little similarity between the two books. *Journal of a Vagabond,* though it might be called an "I novel" because of the many details drawn directly from the author's personal experiences, was written in an idiom quite unlike that of the usual "I novel." Sometimes it recalls the New Sensationalists in the jumps and seeming non sequiturs; but it is noteworthy especially for its lively narration. Almost any episode would do equally well to illustrate this point: the following passage, which occurs early in the book, is typical:

> People were still noisily coming in or going out even after it got late.
>
> "Excuse me," said a woman with her hair done up in the gingko-leaf style. She clattered open the shōji and unceremoniously pushed herself inside my thin bedding. The next minute I heard a loud sound of footsteps, and a greasy-looking man, who wasn't even wearing a hat, opened the shōji a crack. He called, "Hey, you! Get up!"
>
> The woman, muttering something under her breath, got up and went out into the hall. I could hear the sound of somebody being slapped in the face, over and over. Then it became quiet outside, an eerie, cloudy silence, like dirty water. The atmosphere in my room, which the woman had disturbed, still had not reverted to normal.
>
> "What've you been doing up to now? Address? Destination? Age? Parents? . . ."
>
> The greasy-looking man came into my room again and stood by my pillow, licking his pencil.
>
> "Do you know that woman?"

> "No, she burst in without a word of explanation."

> I'm sure not even Knut Hamsun ever got into such a predicament. After the detective left, I stretched out my arms and legs. I tried touching the wallet stuck inside the pillow. My remaining money: one yen, sixty-five sen. The moon looked as if it were being blown around by the wind, and I could see through the crooked window high up on the wall a rainbow, in all colors of light.

The woman who without warning crawls into the narrator's bed, the sinister man, the strange image of silence like dirty water, and the unexplained reference to Knut Hamsun all suggest the influence of Modernism, but the success of the book with the general public was due not to Hayashi's use of new literary techniques but to the absolute frankness with which she described her relations with men and her struggles to earn money. She wrote of herself, "The only ideal I ever had was to get rich quick." Her detached, rather humorous way of looking at herself is the most attractive feature of *Journal of a Vagabond.* She conveyed to her readers the love of life that had enabled her to triumph over the misery that seemed to be her destiny.

The writing in *Journal of a Vagabond* is lively, at times even brilliant, and full of variety. Most of the book is in the form of a diary, no doubt because the materials were derived from the extensive diary that Hayashi had kept since 1922, the year of her arrival in Tokyo. But although the months of the entries are given, the years and days are not, and the effect is kaleidoscopic. Sections are in poetry, both Hayashi's own and other people's, but whatever the style or content, the whole is unified by the immense verve of her personality. (pp. 1139-41)

Virtually all of her early works were directly based on personal experiences; she had enough to provide materials for many, many books. By the time of her death in 1951 at the early age of forty-eight she had published over 270 books, most of them autobiographical. But Hayashi was resolved to prove that she could create stories even without specific models. In 1934 she published the novel *Nakimushi Kozō (Cry Baby),* the account of a boy who is unwanted by his widowed mother and shunted from one relative to another while the mother amuses herself with a lover. No doubt Hayashi's experiences as a child were projected onto her portrayal of the boy, but the story is not autobiographical in any other sense. A somewhat later work, *Kaki (The Oyster),* was not only free of autobiographical elements but remarkably successful as the depiction of an inarticulate, retarded man who is driven into a shell of madness that seals him off from the world. Hayashi was so pleased with the reception accorded to *The Oyster* that she gave an elaborate party to celebrate the publication. She had arrived as an author; no longer would her works be read mainly for what they told about a woman who had fought with tooth and nail and her whole body to gain a foothold in a world dominated by men. She was now a full-fledged author, and although she continued to publish a prodigious outpouring of articles, essays, stories, poems, anything she was asked to write, she was capable of producing works that startled the literary world into remembering her ability.

In 1937, with the outbreak of the China Incident, Hayashi threw herself into the war effort. She traveled to China in December as a correspondent for the *Mainichi Shimbun,* and was proud to be the first Japanese woman inside Nanking after its fall that month. In the following year she again visited the front, but under different auspices: she was so irritated that the Mainichi had chosen her rival, Yoshiya Nobuko, to cover the fall of Hankow that she leaped aboard the first *Asahi Shimbun* truck she saw in the fighting zone, and thus had the added distinction of being the first Japanese woman to set foot inside *that* city after its fall.

During the Pacific War Hayashi was sent to Southeast Asia as a member of an information unit whose objective was to raise morale at home by writing stirring accounts of Japanese victories. She observed the fighting in French Indo-China, Java, and Borneo, always making a point of living with local civilians in order to gain an understanding of what their lives were really like. Her stay in Dalat, a highland city in what later became known as Vietnam, was particularly important because it provided materials for her most impressive novel, *Ukigumo (Floating Cloud)*. (pp. 1142-43)

Some of her novels, notably *Journal of a Vagabond*, had been banned during the war by the authorities because the content did not accord with the selfless consecration that was expected of wartime Japanese. . . . But she was far from being forgotten. A story appeared in the inaugural issue of the magazine *Ningen* (*Humanity*) in January 1946, and this was followed by many others. In 1947 she began serializing the novel *Uzushio (Swirling Currents)* in the *Mainichi Shimbun*, the first such serial published in the press after the war. This novel, though not one of Hayashi's best, is of interest because it treats the problem of war widows, some of whom were hardly married before their husbands were sent overseas and killed in the fighting. The novel is in this sense antiwar, but Hayashi tended to see the tragedy of war in terms of the particular, rather than (in the manner of Miyamoto Yuriko) in terms of the evil inherent in war.

Hayashi's most accomplished writing was done after the war. The stories **"Bangiku"** (**"Late Chrysanthemum"**), and **"Dauntaun"** (**"Downtown"**), and the novel *Floating Cloud* demonstrated her firmness of artistic purpose even when she seemed to be squandering her talents most heedlessly. (She published nine full-length novels and innumerable shorter works between 1949 and 1951.)

"Late Chrysanthemum" was acclaimed as soon as it was published, and established Hayashi's credentials as a specifically post-war writer. The story opens as Kin, a geisha who is remarkably well preserved for a woman in her late fifties, has a telephone call from Tabe, a man with whom she had a passionate affair four or five years earlier, before he was sent to Burma as a young officer. Kin, nostalgically recalling his charm and youthful body, carefully prepares herself to look as attractive and young as possible. But when Tabe appears she sees that he has lost all his charm. He asks her to lend him some desperately needed money, but she fends off the request with a transparent lie that she is penniless. Her love turns to contempt: a man without money is no man at all. Tabe, for his part, feels no lingering attachment for Kin and, as he gradually becomes drunk on the whiskey he has brought as a present, he feels tempted to kill her for her money. She shows him a photograph of himself in bygone days. The contrast is all too painful; when he goes to the toilet she burns the picture. Tabe is too drunk to leave, so Kin has bedding laid out for him in the guest room. She will make sure that he leaves the next day.

Of the innumerable stories about geishas, written by both women and men, none rings truer than **"Late Chrysanthemum."** The details of Kin's life, of her constant concern for her beauty and her skill at handling men, and each thought that flashes through her mind as she converses with Tabe have incontrovertible authority. The relationship between Kin and her former love is beautifully communicated in such a passage as:

> Exposure to the years had engraved a complex and different pattern of emotions on both their hearts. They had gradually grown older, he in his way, she in hers, and the old fondness was gone beyond recall. Plunged in a sense of disillusion, they took silent stock of each other as they were now. They were weary with a host of different emotions. Nothing could be less like the storybook meeting with its charming fictions than this reality. It would all, without doubt, have been made much prettier in a novel— the truth about life was too subtle. To reject each other—this had been the only purpose of their coming together today.

"Late Chrysanthemum" alone, even if Hayashi had written nothing else, would have earned her a reputation. **"Downtown"** makes a greater appeal to the reader's sympathy and is specifically linked to the landscapes of postwar Tokyo, but it lacks the psychological insights that make **"Late Chrysanthemum"** so memorable.

Floating Cloud is usually treated as Hayashi's finest work. It is not so finely wrought as **"Late Chrysanthemum,"** but the brilliance of a short story naturally could not be sustained through a full-length novel. This is the story of lovers who are drawn together at first by physical passion but at the end by a kind of resignation. The book opens as Yukiko returns to Japan from French Indo-China after the war, where she has worked as a typist for a Japanese forestry survey. She meets Tomioka in the hill station of Dalat, and they fall in love, she more strongly than he; Tomioka not only has a wife in Japan but a Vietnamese mistress with whom he has had a child. Tomioka is repatriated to Japan before Yukiko, but to her great disappointment he does not answer her telegram announcing her arrival. It is a bad omen for their future. When eventually she visits his house, she sees how sadly he has changed: the assured and urbane man she knew in Dalat now looks haggard. He is desperately trying to earn enough money in wintry Japan to support his parents and wife. They meet occasionally and resume their physical relations, but nothing is the same. Memories of Dalat, where it was warm and they enjoyed the amenities of colonial masters, contrast with the gloom of defeated Japan and keep them apart. Tomioka's business fails, his wife dies, and at a loss where to turn, he decides to take Yukiko with him to a hot spring where he will kill her and then himself. But he does not go through with the plan because he finds another woman who arouses his passion, the young wife of a local barkeeper. His happiness with the woman does not last long: she is killed by her enraged husband.

Tomioka finally takes a position with the forestry service on Yaku Island, at the time the southernmost point administered by the Japanese government. Yukiko insists on going with him, though she is still recovering from an abortion. It rains almost uninterruptedly on Yaku, and as Yukiko lies on her sickbed, listening to the rain, her thoughts wander to Dalat and even to the American soldier with whom she sometimes slept in her little apartment. She dies and Tomioka feels a surge of affection for her, which is mingled with relief that he no longer has to bear a heavy burden. He is free, but there is nowhere to go. He will live like a drifting cloud, the traditional metaphor for an aimless life.

Floating Cloud is not only an effective novel but a moving evocation of postwar Japan. Tomioka is drawn particularly well. In a sense he is another Tabe, but the greater amplitude of the novel permitted Hayashi to develop his character more compellingly. Hirabayashi Taiko, who knew Hayashi . . . , wrote of *Floating Cloud*, "The novel deserves its reputation as a novel of the defeat in which it is attempted to find some refuge for the collapsed morale of a vanquished Japan. To write this novel alone was sufficient reason for Hayashi to have been born."

Hayashi died while still writing her most ambitious novel, *Meshi (Food)*. At the time she was simultaneously publishing one newspaper and three monthly magazine serials, as well as many articles for popular consumption. She had driven herself mercilessly, in her last years no less than in the days of her vagabondage. (pp. 1143-46)

> *Donald Keene, "The Revival of Writing by Women,"*
> *in his* Dawn to the West: Japanese Literature of the
> Modern Era, Fiction, Vol. 1, *Holt, Rinehart and Winston, 1984, pp. 1113-66.*

ADDITIONAL BIBLIOGRAPHY

"About the Authoress." In *Floating Cloud (Ukigumo)*, by Fumiko Hayashi, translated by Sho Tanaka, p. v. Tokyo: Information Publishing, 1957.
  Brief biographical essay.

Johnson, Eric W. "Modern Japanese Women Writers." *Literature East and West* XVIII, No. 1 (March 1974): 90-102.
  Biographical and critical sketch. Johnson characterizes Hayashi's fiction as possessing "a kind of passionate despair and hopelessness that is often touching, bordering on sentimentality but avoiding it."

"Hayashi Fumiko." In *Modern Japanese Literature in Translation: A Bibliography*, pp. 61-2. Tokyo: Kodansha International, 1979.
  Contains complete bibliographic information for translations of Hayashi's fiction and poetry.

Vincas Krėvė (Mickevicius)

1882-1954

(Also wrote under pseudonym of Vincas Baltausis) Lithuanian short story writer, novelist, dramatist, poet, and critic.

Krėvė is considered Lithuania's greatest modern writer. Portraying heroic figures from medieval legends as well as the common people of his own day, Krėvė dedicated his fiction to expressing the independent spirit of the Lithuanian people. During the late nineteenth and early twentieth centuries, Lithuanian literature was devoted to creating a revival of national consciousness in order to counteract the long-standing cultural influence of Poland and political domination by Russia. When a forty-year ban on all publications in the Lithuanian language was repealed by the Russians in 1904, the desire to establish a national culture motivated Lithuanian writers to focus on the past greatness of their country. Influenced by authors who celebrated the development of Lithuania as a powerful European empire during the Middle Ages, Krėvė based his earliest works on heroic legends, medieval history, and folklore, while his subsequent works included depictions of Lithuanian peasant life and the political plight of modern Lithuanians.

Born in the village of Subartonys, Krėvė grew up hearing the folksongs and folktales of southeastern Lithuania. His early education was conducted at a seminary in Vilinius, and at the age of twenty-two he entered the University of Kiev to study philology. He went on to graduate work in the same field at the University of Lvov in the Soviet Ukraine. Concerning his experiences as a student, Krėvė later wrote: "When, while studying at the university, I had occasion to meet students of a different national background who boasted about their glorious past history, I was seized by a desire to show the others that our history is greater than theirs." After his graduation in 1908, Krėvė taught Russian language and literature at secondary schools in the Ukraine. He also began writing adaptations of folktales which he included in his first collection of stories, *Dainavos šalies senų žmonių padavimai*. On returning to Lithuania in 1920, Krėvė became professor of Slavic literatures at the University of Kaunas. Over the next two decades, he played a major role in the cultural affairs of his country by founding and editing several journals. In 1940, when Soviet control was reinstated after twenty years of Lithuanian autonomy, Krėvė entered Lithuanian political life by becoming Prime Minister of Lithuania's foreign affairs. In the satirical novel *Pagunda* (*The Temptation*), he related in fictional form some of his frustrating experiences in dealing with the totalitarian Soviet regime. Regarding this work, Charles Angoff has written: "It is surely one of the best portraits of what it means to be a Communist functionary and a Communist intellectual that has yet appeared in print." In 1944, Krėvė resigned from his office and left Lithuania. He spent the next three years living in exile in Austria before ultimately emigrating to the United States, where he accepted a professorship at the University of Pennsylvania. From 1947 until his death in 1954, Krėvė devoted himself to teaching and writing.

Throughout his career Krėvė utilized Lithuanian legend and folklore in developing his central subject: the independent spirit of the Lithuanian people. In his earliest works, Krėvė depicted figures from Lithuanian legends, such as medieval princes and

knights, in order "to re-create that Lithuania of old which with one hand fought off the onslaught of Western Europe while with the other it conquered the large part of that country which is now Russia." Krėvė described the heroic figures in his work as "giants" who represented the "spirit and soul of old Lithuania." One of Krėvė's most successful illustrations of this spirit is the drama *Šarūnas, Dainavos kunigaikštis*, in which the legendary prince Šarūnas leads his country into battle in an attempt to unite the tribes of Lithuania. Although he is defeated, the struggle to consolidate Lithuania's tribes is continued after his death. In another dramatic work, *Skirgaila*, Krėvė again delineated the struggle for independence and political unity in Lithuania, a struggle now carried on by the wrathful prince Skirgaila, who led Lithuania into battle against invading Teutons. Critics have seen in Krėvė's emphasis on the turmoil medieval Lithuania experienced in the struggle for political unification and independence an analogy to the situation of modern Lithuania.

The spirit of the Lithuanian people is further defined in Krėvė's stories of peasant life. These works focus primarily on the peasants living in Krėvė's native region of Dzūkija at the turn of the century, emphasizing their essential goodness and primitive faith in the life-giving powers of nature. Together with his renditions of Lithuanian legends, Krėvė's peasant stories made him one of his country's most representative and beloved authors. Praising Krėvė's part in the renewal of a Lithuanian national consciousness, Alfred Senn wrote in 1956: "Krėvė has indeed created a new spiritual world for the Lithuanians. He has given Lithuanian culture a new physiognomy. No other Lithuanian in the entire course of Lithuanian history can boast a similiar success."

PRINCIPAL WORKS

Šarūnas, Dainavos kunigaikštis (drama) 1911
Dainavos šalies senų žmonių padavimai (short stories) 1912
Sūtemose (short stories) 1921
Žentas (drama) [first publication] 1921
Vinco Krėvės raštai. 10 vols. (short stories and dramas) 1921-30
Šiaudinėj pastogėj (short stories) 1922
Likimo keliais. 2 vols. (drama) [first publication] 1926-29
Rytų pasakos (short stories) 1930
Mindaugo mirtis (drama) [first publication] 1935
*Skirgaila (drama) [first publication] 1935
Raganius (novel) 1938
Miglose (short stories) 1944
Dangaus ir žemės sūnūs (drama) [first publication] 1949
Pagunda [as Vincas Baltaūsis] (novel) 1950; published in journal *Naujienos*
   [*The Temptation,* 1950]
The Herdsman and the Linden Tree (short stories) 1964

*This work was originally composed in Russia and published in 1918.

VINCAS MACIŪNAS (essay date 1952)

[*In the following excerpt, Maciūnas explains the cultural background to the development of Lithuanian literature and provides a survey of Krėvė's fiction, giving particular attention to Krėvė's storytelling methods in characterizing heroic figures from Lithuanian legends and folklore epics.*]

The small nations have produced creative talents no less important than those of the acknowledged leaders in the field of writing, but the lack of good translations has formed the barrier which prevents these writers from becoming internationally known figures of world literature. Their work usually can be appreciated and understood only by their own compatriots. That's the fate of Vincas Krėvė, one of Lithuania's greatest writers.

In order to understand better his position in Lithuanian literature, let us turn back and survey its development. The historical conditions which helped to create ancient Lithuania as a great political power in Eastern Europe, were not favorable for the development of Lithuanian art and literature. After the majority of the Lithuanian aristocrats were Polonized, Lithuanian literature was represented for a very long time only by religious pamphlets and booklets for the peasants. In the 19th Century Lithuania was shaken by that wave of nationalistic revival which was sweeping the whole of Europe. It appeared in Lithuania and elsewhere as a natural revival of old historical traditions, of the native language, national culture and literature.

After the unsuccessful uprising in 1863, severe reprisals were taken by the Russians. Not only were many Lithuanian hanged and deported to Siberia, but the Russians sought to destroy Lithuanian culture as well. One of the most depressing means for Russification of the Lithuanian nation was that famous decree which prohibited the printing of Lithuanian books and newspapers in the usual Latin characters. The Russians believed that by getting accustomed to the Russian alphabet the Lithuanians would gradually become Russians. This oppression lasted 40 years. However, resistance to Russification spread the nationalistic revival, increased the will for freedom and filled Lithuanian literature with deep patriotism. But those conditions, under which even the simplest Lithuanian prayer book or language primer had to be printed abroad and smuggled into the country where their distribution was prohibited, could not be very favorable to the development of Lithuanian literature, although even these darkest hours produced some well-known authors, among them the most popular poet of the national renaissance-Maironis.

Finally the Lithuanians won the fight for their own press. The decree was withdrawn by the Russians in the year 1904 when they became convinced of its failure. The revolution of 1905 shook the regime of the absolute monarchy. Representatives from the whole of Lithuania met in a convention in Vilnius in the same year and asked for a full autonomy for their country. That was probably the strongest sign of the nationalistic revival in the country. The intelligentsia was already numerous and strong and, of course, did not hesitate to further the growth of the national culture, in order to fill in the gaps caused by such a long oppression. The results were very promising in the different sections of the cultural life. It was at this time that the Lithuanian painter, M. K. Čiurlionis, rose to international fame.

These efforts to reach the cultural level of other nations naturally were noticeable in the growth of the Lithuanian literature. And here came Vincas Krėvė, the greatest of that generation, fulfilling the hopes for literary works of a high level. He became known and beloved in the entire country and his writings became classical works in Lithuanian literature. They were read and discussed in schools, printed and reprinted many times.

Many artists of that time turned more and more to folk art, regarding it as original and specifically Lithuanian, and by using it as a source for their own creation hoped to add something new to the art treasures of the world. M. K. Čiurlionis wrote on the occasion of a Lithuanian art exhibition: "The folk art must be the fundamental of our individual art. The specific Lithuanian style is bound to originate from this folk art which we must be proud of because the beauty expressed in folk art is pure and exceptionally Lithuanian."

Authors also often used folk poetry as their inspiration. Lithuanian songs were always famous for their poetical gentleness. Already Lessing and Herder admired them and Goethe used a Lithuanian folksong in his "Die Fischerin." In the 19th Century many foreign linguists who were interested in the Lithuanian language because of its scientific importance also collected and published Lithuanian folksongs. Although enthusiastic appreciations of the beauty of Lithuanian songs were quite numerous, still the interest was chiefly of philological and folkloristic nature. However, at the beginning of the 20th Century literary critics expressed the belief that folk poetry should not only be collected, published and appreciated, but it also should be used in creating new literary works. Soon the folklore motives could be found in much new poetry, but Vincas Krėvė, in using folk art motives for his works, achieved the greatest literary results in his *Dainavos šalies senų žmonių padavimai* (*Old Folk Legends of Dainava*), which is considered one of the most truly Lithuanian literary creations.

The Lithuanian folksongs are purely lyrical. Lithuanians do not have any such heroic epics as the *Nibelungenlied* or anything like the Russian byliny. However, historical sources prove that there were songs describing the heroic deeds of the warriors. At the time of Romanticism there were those (e.g. the Czech, V. Hanka) who tried to forge such heroic epics, not finding them in their national literature.

Using the old legends preserved among the people of villages and rural areas, lending stylistic forms from Lithuanian folksongs, and, always keeping the characteristics of the epic fundamentals, Krėvė tried thus to recreate the old Lithuanian, already vanished epodes. These legends are written in a poetical prose.

Thus the poetical world of legends arises in Krėvė's work: The girl crying for her dead beloved becomes a stone at the side of the highway and her tears appear as a salty well; a beautiful castle is swallowed up by a suddenly-appearing lake because its owner had committed a crime in his youth, and he appears in the moonlight with his beloved wife diving and playing in the shimmering, secretive waters of the bewitched lake; in a bewitched mountain are heard the heart-breaking wails of a duke; the old castle ruins tell the stories of ancestoral battles against the iron-clad Teutonic knights for the freedom of their native land. We hear the author saying through the lips of an old folksong singer, "Oh ye, dear young ones, ye gray falcons, be still for a moment. Be still, and listen to me. Listen to my sad, sad story, to my wailing words. I, the old one, will sing to ye. . . ."

The heroic epic elevates its people and their actions out of everyday levels into a festive world. The life in the legends of Dainava seems to be like eternal festivity: noisy hunting parties, large banquets, severe battles, and the people, heroic fighters who inspire admiration. They have only a few fundamental emotions, mostly love, revenge and the passionate pursuit of happiness and honor. But these are immensely towering passions worthy of real giants: ". . . giant men who never knew, never understood what is human fear, low, unhappy slavery; their hands were more powerful than their desires, and their actions and deeds were faster than their thoughts: the thoughts were not yet thought, already their hands had fulfilled them."

The portrayal of such heroic life can be fully expressed only in noble language. And thus is the language of the legends of Dainava very poetical and rich. As is the case in folklore, the language is rich in permanent epithets and comparisons, many beautiful parallelisms, mild diminutives, colorful metaphors, impressive antitheses and repetitions, and many hyperbolic figures of speech so beloved in the heroic epics. The use of so many poetical figures broadens the style. But the author of epical poems loves such richness in his style. He is not anxious to tell the events in the quickest way. On the contrary, he wants to enjoy the story-telling itself. It is like a wide river which flows quietly and steadily. This ever-flowing stream is never stopped by the most painful worries or the joy of endless happiness. The sentences are carefully arranged and often varied by long and musical-sounding periods, thus giving the impression of a pleasant, rhythmic fluctuation. Not until the appear-

ance of the legends of Dainava had the Lithuanian literature such a beautiful musical prose.

The dramatic work *Šarūnas, Dainavos kunigaikštis* (*Šarūnas, the Prince of Dainava*) seems to be an expanding of one of the legends. Šarūnas is a legendary, not an historical prince. He is depicted here by Krėvė in a romantic spirit: Šarūnas is an individual who shapes the history of the whole country. His mission is to unite Lithuanians into one powerful state. This idea is not at first clear even to Šarūnas himself. He feels punished by nature: he is an ugly hunchback. Everyone laughs at him and he does not find happiness in love and joy in his own family, but he is very proud. As if in revenge, his heart is inflamed by a passion for great deeds and endless honor: "I would gladly give away the blood and tears and life not only of the entire world, but also my own for just that one moment of such honor which has never been bestowed upon any human being since this world of ours came into existence."

In those heroic days such an honor could be found only on the battlefield. And thus Šarūnas throws the whole Dainava country into a turmoil by his wars, battles, and by the blood which is being spilled on the battlefield. He wants to "fly in the world as only the eagle does." By and by, under the influence of the Bard Rainys, Šarūnas forms for himself the final aim for his restless struggles. "There is only one sun in the sky, there is going to be only one ruler in Dainava, or the soil will not keep me alive." The older people cannot understand his plans. They curse him because of the sufferings of the constant wars. Only the younger generation, attracted by the coveted honor of the battles, lines up with him. His aim becomes clear to everyone only when he has fallen in the final battle in which he crushes the Teutonic knights which appear for the first time on Lithuanian soil. Šarūnas falls but his idea remains alive. All understand now that only political unity can save them from that new and powerful enemy.

The most important thing in this drama is not the political problem of establishing a united state, but the character of Šarūnas. He is not a simple, one-sided hero of a heroic epic, but rather a complicated and deeply tragic figure. He not only battles his enemies, he struggles against the inner conflicts of his own contradictory wishes and emotions. He is wavering and, therefore, suffering. He is a fighter for power and honor; he is a man filled with a mad desire for revenge, but he also is one who longs for quiet happiness and silent joy. Alas, he never achieves that and his heart is filled with more hatred.

Akin to Šarūnas is Skirgaila in Krėvė's drama *Skirgaila*. He is known to us from history, a brother of Jogaila and his regent in Lithuania. In Krėvė's drama he is, like Šarūnas, a prince of wrathful character: "There is no other will around here as soon as I express mine." But Skirgaila is not so impulsive as Šarūnas. He suppresses his passionate nature by his willpower. His greatest wish is a powerful and great Lithuania, but he sees that the old pagan Lithuania, surrounded by powerful and numerous Christian enemies, will never be able to withstand pressure from without. He understands that the old gods cannot defend Lithuania. Here is the essence of the tragedy of Skirgaila: ". . . I am a scoundrel because openly I am forced to honor and respect the unjust god of that hated and foreign nation. He flooded Lithuania with blood; he forced us to bow under the sword and fire." Since Skirgaila no longer respects himself, he despises others, especially when the false news reaches him that an old and sturdy pagan priest, Stardas, became a Christian just before he died. At the same time, deeply in his heart he starts to doubt the gods. Skirgaila, who respects only power and might, who can even enjoy the success of a courageous enemy, cannot respect gods after they have lost their power to revenge and punish those who have betrayed them.

Skirgaila's tragedy is increased by troubles in his own family. In order to keep Lithuania united, he forcibly marries the princess of Lyda—Ona Duonutė. He knows that she does not love him and at the same time he longs for a few moments of idyllic peace in his own family to offset the worries and troubles of the helm of state. But force bears no love, only hatred. Ona Duonutė is about to flee, helped by Keller, a Teutonic knight. When he discovers this, Skirgaila is enraged. For revenge, he orders—to the horror of a few who know the story—that the heroic knight sacrifice himself for his beloved woman and be buried alive. "I carry out every deed to the end, and so with revenge," Skirgaila says grimly. With regard to its dramatic suspense, *Skirgaila* can rightfully take its place among the best known tragedies.

In his drama *Mindaugo mirtis* (*The Death of Mindaugas*) Krėvė depicts another powerful personality from Lithuanian history. The whole history of the nation finds its symbolical expression in Krėvė's mystical drama *Likimo keliais* (*On the Path of Destiny*).

Šarūnas and Skirgaila appear in Krėvė's works as giants out of the past enshrouded by historical mists. But not only great historical personalities attracted Krėvė's attention. A simple peasant also is close to Krėvė's heart. Born and raised in a South Lithuanian village, Krėvė not only grew up with the beautiful folksongs and enchanted legends about secret lakes and castlehills, he also became well acquainted with the simple village life and its people with their joys and troubles, with their thoughts and emotions.

In a collection of short stories *Šiaudinėj pastogėj* (*Under the Thatched Roof*) Krėvė shows not only his deep psychological insight into the soul of simple people, but at the same time his deep love for the people he describes. This love allows him to discover and portray the unsophisticated beauty of soul which lies unsuspected in simple, uneducated village people. As an example we can mention "**Bobulės vargai**" ("**The Worries of Grandma**"). In it we see maternal love, goodwill and forgiveness shining through the everyday troubles and worries of this old woman, and giving moral warmth to the story.

A constant pursuit of good purpose, a natural feeling for truth shines subconsciously in the depths of the people in these stories. Take for instance a small, naughty shepherd boy who, in anger, kills a pig with a stone and then hides himself from the angry farmer. Finally, surprised by the farmer, he not only does not try to run away, but he starts to cry because he is sorry to have done such an awful thing.

Another farmer, Dvainis, is tortured by all kinds of bad luck, but the hard life does not hurt him so much as the fact that his belief in truth is shaken when he sees that bad people get along fine in the world, while he, who tries to be truthful in every matter, is punished by God! And here appears in his heart the flame of Šarūnas' revolting spirit: "Well, dear Lord," says Dvainis, "if thou treatest me like that, I'll repay thee in the same way. Thou givest nothing to me for my prayers so I'll not pray unto Thee any more, but, behold, I will do this. There the priest sings mass and I will fell the tree. That's it!" But he was not able to carry out his threat. A bird, which was sitting in the tree which he started to fell, suddenly flew away uttering strange cries and the superstitious farmer ran away

badly frightened. He remembered so many stories about the miraculous and horrible happenings in the woods.

Dvainis and others in Krėvė's stories see nature as an alive being, full of spirits. It is the same animistic belief in nature which so frequently occurs in Lithuanian folklore. Thus nature in these stories is not only beautiful landscape, it is active and plays a decisive role in the lives of the people. It is actually nature that prevents Dvainis from fulfilling his revenge. It is nature which keeps the farmer, Kalpokas, from spanking the small boy who had killed his pig. He is impressed by that gray, rainy, autumn day in the forest. He not only does not spank the boy, he tries to sooth his weeping. It is nature itself which gives "atheist" Vainoras such a surprising peace of mind and tranquillity that he appears to us like a sage who has discovered the secret of life.

The head shepherd, Lapinas, is almost completely united with nature. He identifies his long life with an old and mighty linden tree. He believes he will live so long as that tree stands. He is very old, but unusually energetic and full of natural youthful vitality. Although his hair is white as an apple tree in bloom, he does not feel the burden of his years. Nor does he long for the peaceful and quiet life of old age. Just the contrary is true: he loves noise, children's fights, the quarreling of grown-ups. Wherever he goes, noise and turmoil follow. However, Lapinas is old-fashioned in his philosophy of life. He is not touched by modern culture. He appears as a survivor of the time of half-paganism. Children tease him that he does not know the catechism. He even does not know how many gods there are.

And suddenly farmer Grainis fells his linden tree. Lapinas dies soon after that. We could, of course, explain his death as occurring through natural causes: he gets drunk, falls asleep in an orchard, catches a severe cold and does not recover. But that is, so to say, only the superficial cause of his death. The primary cause is that the felling of his tree brings to an end his desire to live. "Eh, if these people can fell such a tree as this linden tree, if they do not pity such a tree, they won't pity anything. It is better to die than live among such people!" He suddenly realizes that he has outlived his age, that he does not fit into these new times. This short story ends with a note of melancholy: everyone is saddened because the shadow of death fell across his path. Not only did Lapinas die, the "old times" died.

Old Lapinas, just as Šarūnas, became one of the most popular characters in Lithuanian literature. He also was dear to the author himself who later described him in a longer story *Raganius* (*The Sorcerer*).

Lithuanian history, Lithuanian folklore and life in a Lithuanian village are the main motives in Krėvė's works. But that is not all. He studies diligently Oriental thought and Oriental poetry. To him we owe the most beautiful examples of the Oriental style in Lithuanian literature: the charming Indian legend "**Pratjekabuddha, šventųjų Gango vilnių pasaka**" ("**Pratjekabuddha, the Story of the Holy Waves of the Ganges River**") and a beautiful Oriental parable "**Indas, kuriame karalius laiko savo geriausią vyną**" ("**The Dish in Which the King Keeps His Best Wine**") and other writings. Out of these stories the collection *Rytų pasakos* (*Tales From the Orient*) was published. The most important work of this series is "**Dangaus ir žemės sūnūs**" ("**The Sons of Heaven and Earth**") wherein, in partly Biblical style, Kreve portrays the life of the Jews in Christ's time. Until now only the first part has been published—from Christ's birth till the death of Herod.

The setting of the prologue of this work is in Heaven. Here, as in Goethe's *Faust,* the author tries to find the explanation of human existence in the form of a legend. Goethe wanted to show the moral principle which lies deeply in man's soul: ''A good man, through obscurest aspiration has still an instinct of the one true way.'' The most important human trait to Krėvė is the human undecisiveness between good and evil. His men are those revolting angels of the Old Testament. They are banished to their exile which is our earth: ''Therefore you shall go down to the earth. You shall cover yourselves with bodies and you shall go and go until you shall stop hesitating which way you will choose—the one which leads to me or that which leads to him who is my enemy.'' The people in this work do hesitate which way to choose. Some of them are modest and shy, others are proud revolutionists. Some of them are truthful beings, others are horrible hypocrites. Some are full of love, others think only of revenge. A few do not ask for any luxury on this earth, others are slaves of their own passions. All of them are real ''sons of heaven and earth.''

The prologue naturally has only symbolic meaning as a beautiful legend because the work itself is carried out in a realistic manner. The author is primarily concerned with giving a full and broad picture of the Jewish life of that time when the Jews felt the Roman oppression more and more and the longing for the promised Messiah-Redeemer was growing stronger and stronger. Christ is not shown much in this first part of the work. But the people of all the segments of Jewish life are pictured with all their passions, feelings, wishes, with all their worries and troubles—the peaceful shepherds of Bethlehem and the fishermen on the lake of Gennesaret, the laborers toiling at the huge buildings of Herod, the fanatical fighters rallying around the pseudo-Messiah, the peaceful Essenes, the quarreling Sadducees and Pharisees in the Sanhedrin, the cosmopolitan people at Herod's court: Herod's Greek advisors, the deceitful head of his spies, the hardened chieftain of the hired military guards of Herod and many others.

Herod towers above all these people. He is a passionate and strong character, and many writers have tried out their talent depicting him. There are more than 40 dramas written about him and his wife, Marianne. Krėvė touches only upon the last years of Herod's life. His Herod is a strong-willed and emotional man, a severe and despotic ruler, at the same time, though, a very unhappy man. Not only does a horrible and incurable disease eat his body and soul; not only does he have to suffer under the memory of his beloved wife whom he, himself, has doomed, but he is most unhappy because he was misunderstood by the people he ruled and whom he wished to elevate to great honor. He is passionately hated by the Jews and he repays them with a matching hatred. He tries to console himself by speaking to one of his Greek advisors ''Oh, Hellene, Hellene, thou canst not understand how difficult it is to rule upon a nation which one hates.'' After he loses his moral balance he pathologically enjoys revenging himself in the most horrible fashion. His tragedy lies in the fact that he had to live at the crossroads of two completely different worlds: that of the enlightened and tolerant Greeks and that of the fanatically isolationist and self-conscious Jews. His Greek courtier talks about him: ''Here is his unhappiness; in his soul he is a Hellene, in his feelings he is a Jew and he hates the Jews.''

Krėvė started to write *The Sons of Heaven and Earth* before the First World War, but the first part did not appear in print until 1949. It is really surprising that this work—written in the difficult surroundings of a Displaced Persons camp in Austria

after the Second World War, and especially since the author was no longer young and had lost all his manuscripts—should be so full of youthful fire. That encourages still higher hopes for the last two parts of the work which are now being written. (pp. 11-21)

Vincas Maciūnas, ''Vincas Krėvė's Place in Lithuanian Literature,'' in Studi Baltici, n.s. Vol. 1, 1952, pp. 11-23.

ALFRED SENN (essay date 1956)

[*Senn is an American historian, educator, and critic whose works include several studies of modern Slavic history. In the following excerpt, he focuses on the distinction in Krėvė's work between stories based on heroic legends and folklore and those that are realistic depictions of Lithuanian peasants.*]

Ever since the end of World War I, Lithuanian literature has been dominated by the towering figure of Vincent Krėvė. I call him a towering figure in spite of the fact that physically he is no giant at all, actually less than five feet in height. I consider Krėvė the greatest Lithuanian poet and writer of all times. His rivals for first place are Donalitius and Maironis, but there is no question in my mind about the outcome of this rivalry. Donalitius must be eliminated because of his lack of originality. His hexameters were made in imitation of a literary fad prevailing at that time in western Europe. One might say that Donalitius wrote German poetry in Lithuanian words but added his own realism for which there was no German model at the time. Donalitius was a great poet, but Krėvė is greater. Even Maironis must come out second best in a comparison with Krėvė although Maironis is undoubtedly original in the content, though not the form, of his poems. However, Maironis succeeded only in one genre, namely, the lyric poem but failed in the epic and the drama in which he tried his skill also. Krėvė, on the other hand, succeeded at least in two genres, namely, the short story and the drama. (pp. 175-76)

In his writings Krėvė displays a dual personality, depending on the subject matter or topic. He is now an exuberant romanticist, now an observant and even critical realist. He is a realist with deep psychological insight when in his short stories he describes Lithuanian peasants or peasant children of the twentieth century and their everyday chores and worries. There is nothing heroic about the personages of these short stories. These personages impress the reader because they are real, they are true human beings with hopes and frustrations, with virtues and weaknesses. On the other hand, Krėvė is a romanticist in his tales placed into pagan antiquity which are based on Lithuanian folklore material, such as semihistorical legends and fairy tale motifs. He uses even different styles for the two types of short stories. While the realistic short story dealing with modern Lithuanian life is written in a pure and noble everyday prose, all his legends or ethnical tales appear in a melodious rhythmic prose, an imitation and refinement of the style of folklore literature.

The same dual personality as in the short stories can also be found in the plays. Definitely realistic, even with a tendency to point out existing evils, is the play *Son-in-Law* which deals with a young wastrel, the son of a well-to-do farmer. Against the better judgment and advice of his elders, the young man runs away to America where he apparently expects the gold to grow on trees. His experiences in the coal mines of Pennsylvania bring him to his senses and he returns home to his duties and obligations as a reformed character and a sensible man. If

Krėvė had written nothing but this realistic play and the realistic short stories, I would consider him worthy of highest praise and recognition, even the Nobel Prize. However, to his own people, the Lithuanians, Krėvė has endeared himself much more by his romantic writings than these realistic portrayals.

In Krėvė's life the romantic period came first. He first wrote poems in the style of the Lithuanian folk song. Then he turned to prose, cultivating both the short story and the drama. The realistic phase of Krėvė's literary work comes later in his life and shows a more mature stage of development.

Krėvė's romanticism is expressed most strongly in two early works, the drama *Sharunas, Prince of Dainava: The Tale of a Life According to the Ancient Poets* and the collection of tales or legendary short stories first published in 1912 under the title *Stories Told by Old People of the Dainava Country*. (pp. 177-78)

Sharunas is a drama merely by its external form, being written in dialogue. It could just as well be called a lyric novel. Its main purpose is to exhibit the wealth of Lithuanian folklore material which the author had collected and which is used as background for an action that is projected into pagan antiquity. This is done on the assumption that almost any detail of modern Lithuanian folklore dates back into the most ancient times, an absolutely faulty assumption if judged by standards of historical truth. However, disregard of historical facts is quite natural to the romanticists. For a description of the plot of the *Sharunas* drama I am going to quote from [an] article of Maciunas [see excerpt dated 1952].

> Sharunas is a legendary, not an historical prince. He is depicted here by Krėvė in a romantic spirit: Sharunas is an individual who shapes the history of the whole country. His mission is to unite the Lithuanians into one powerful state. . . . Sharunas feels punished by nature: he is an ugly hunchback. Everyone laughs at him, nor does he find happiness in love and joy in his own family; but he is very proud. As if in revenge, his heart is inflamed by a passion for great deeds and honor. . . . In those heroic days such honor could be found only on the battlefield. And thus Sharunas throws the whole Dainava country into a turmoil by his wars, battles, and by the blood which is being spilled on the battlefield. He wants to "fly in the world as only the eagle does." By and by, under the influence of the Bard Rainys, Sharunas forms for himself the final aim for his restless struggles. "There is only one sun in the sky, there is going to be only one ruler in Dainava, or the soil will not keep me alive." The older people cannot understand his plans and curse him because of the sufferings brought about by constant wars. Only the younger generation, attracted by the coveted honor of the battles, lines up with him. It is only after his death that his aim becomes clear to everyone. He falls in a battle in which he crushes the Teutonic Knights who appear for the first time on Lithuanian soil. Sharunas dies but his idea remains alive. All understand now that only political unity can save them from that new and powerful enemy.

It is interesting to note that today the whole of central and western Europe is in a similar situation as the Lithuanians were in the times of Sharunas, except that today the danger threatens from the East. As was stated above, Sharunas is not a historical person. The *Sharunas* story is absolute fiction. No trace of this personage is found in Lithuanian literature or historical sources prior to the first appearance of Krėvė's *Sharunas*. Since then, however, Prince Sharunas has become the Lithuanian national hero, a real person for most Lithuanians, similar to the role Wilhelm Tell plays in the hearts and minds of the Swiss. There is a difference, however, between these two national heroes: Wilhelm Tell is the defender of human rights, but Sharunas is the protagonist of nationalism.

Even more romantic than *Sharunas* are Krėvė's *Dainava Stories* which are written in the style of fairy tales and in rhythmic prose throughout. In the introduction we find the author's assertion that he is only relating what he has been told by old people living in that region. This assertion is similar to the statement included in the full title of *Sharunas* where we are assured that the truth of the *Tale of Sharunas* is vouched for by ancient poets. All the tales are definitely connected with actual localities in the Dainava Country that is an area extending to the south of Alytus, in the southernmost part of Lithuania. (pp. 178-80)

The theme treated first in *Sharunas* is resumed in the drama *Skirgaila*. . . . Unlike *Sharunas*, *Skirgaila* is absolutely perfect from the point of view of dramaturgy. The plot is more condensed and better organized. Actually, I cannot see how it could be criticized from the point of view of dramaturgic technique. It is the best historical play ever produced for the Lithuanian stage. This success is to a large extent due to the almost complete absence of the romantic tinsel prevailing in the earlier works. (p. 182)

From the standpoint of dramatic structure, I consider the *Son-in-Law* and *Skirgaila* as Krėvė's best plays. They show Krėvė's greatness as a playwright. They are not the only real and great plays written by our poet. There are for instance *On the Path of Destiny* in two volumes and *The Death of Mindaugas*. Both these plays deal with Lithuanian problems.

Other works of Krėvė deal with Oriental motifs. Actually, Krėvė has been a diligent student of Oriental thought and poetry all his life. The latest attempt in this field is the biblical drama, *The Sons of Heaven and Earth*. Since our presentation is limited to works which bear specifically on Lithuanian history and folklore, we have to forego a discussion of the other aspects of Krėvė's creative activity.

On the occasion of the celebration of his seventieth birthday anniversary on October 19, 1952, Vincent Krėvė made the following statement to the assembled admirers and well-wishers:

> When, while studying at the university, I had occasion to meet students of different national background who boasted about their glorious past history, I was seized by a desire to show the others that our history is greater than theirs. I was then impelled to re-create that Lithuania of old which with one hand fought off the onslaught of western Europe while with the other it conquered the larger part of that country which is now Russia. I wanted to show that through those battles Lithuania became the largest and most powerful state of that period. It seemed to me that, if those people could achieve such deeds, they must have been giants in spirit. And

I made up my mind to portray the spirit and the soul of those giants, that is the spirit and soul of Old Lithuania. I did it, not in order to become famous myself, but in order that the Lithuanians, especially the young people, might obtain some self-respect and the conviction that we are not inferior, but rather superior to many nations which at present consider themselves great. . . . We are a heroic nation and powerful in spirit. This was all I had in mind when I created the *Dainava Stories, Sharunas, Skirgaila,* etc. This was my one and only idea. . . . And I am very happy today to see that I was understood the way I wanted to be understood.

It is an unusual thing to hear such words from a creative writer, "I am very happy to see that I was understood the way I wanted to be understood." These are words from the mouth of a man who has changed a whole world and has lived to see the dreams of his youth realized. Krėvė has indeed created a new spiritual world for the Lithuanians. He has given Lithuanian culture a new physiognomy. No other Lithuanian in the entire course of Lithuanian history can boast of similar success. (pp. 183-84)

> *Alfred Senn, "Vincent Krėvė, Lithuania's Creator of Heroes," in* World Literatures *by Joseph Remenyi and others, University of Pittsburgh Press, 1956, pp. 170-84.*

KOSTAS OSTRAUSKAS (essay date 1964)

[*In the following excerpt, Ostrauskas finds Krėvė's fiction predominantly romantic with only touches of realism.*]

Vincas Krėvė appeared on the literary scene at the time when Lithuanian literature, after a period of playing a subordinate role to the cause of national revival, was about to become a creative endeavor for its own intrinsic values. Krėvė realized the new vistas opened by this transformation and, at the dawn of the twentieth century, became one of the pathfinders of modern Lithuanian literature. As its foremost representative, at the peak of his creative life, he had attained the stature of a classic. Already in 1926, on the occasion of twenty years of Krėvė's literary work, Vincas Mykolaitis-Putinas—himself an outstanding poet, novelist, dramatist, and critic—observed that, "Among all our [Lithuanian] contemporary writers Vincas Krėvė in his works has embraced, undoubtedly, the widest variety of themes and genres, and has expressed the most diverse scale of moods."

Basically a late romanticist with touches of realism, Vincas Krėvė first drew inspiration and material for his works from the treasures of Lithuanian folklore and from the distant past of Lithuania. This was evident already in most of his earliest writings (collected and published later under the title *Sutemos* [**Dusk**]) which otherwise were rather fragmentary and still immature. These sources found their best expression in *Dainavos šalies senu žmoniu padavimai (The Old Folk Tales of Dainava)* and two plays, *Šarūnas* and *Skirgaila.* With *Dainavos padavimai* Krėvė created in a folk ballad style the legends of the ages long gone by, while the two plays revived in heroic manner both the legendary and historic past. Significantly, the dramatic works are not based just on mere skirmishes of bygone times. Although drawn on a wide canvas, they are not historical "spectaculars," either. Krėvė chooses some of the most crucial and problematic periods of Lithuanian history and evolves his own creative interpretation. Moreover, these momentous periods of history are not introduced just for their own sake. They serve more as background and influencing factors on the leading characters who are not the puppets governed helplessly by the forces of history, but the conscious architects of the present and future. Men of flesh and blood, of manifold and complicated egos, with their deep-rooted personal problems, they are tragic figures struggling valiantly with their own times. Thus the legendary prince Šarūnas is caught in throes of the birth of the medieval state of Lithuania, while the historic Skirgaila is torn by the dichotomy and struggle between the pagan and the Christian worlds. The raging Šarūnas has already become a byword, while *Skirgaila,* a tragedy of masterfully knit composition and Shakesperean overtones, remains an unsurpassed masterpiece of that genre in Lithuanian literature. The cycle of Krėvė's historical plays is completed with *Mindaugo mirtis (The Death of Mindaugas)* and *Likimo keliai (On the Path of Destiny),* the latter being a lengthy, ambitious mystical drama which interprets symbolically, in rather involved and sometimes obscured images, the entire history of the nation.

Concurrently, not to bypass his own time and reality, Vincas Krėvė has explored with a keen eye and deep psychological insight the rustic life of Lithuania, especially of his own region of Dzūkija, as it existed at the turn of the century. To this category, somewhat less romantic in approach and treatment of the subject, belong the collection of short stories, *Šiaudinėj pastogėj (Under the Thatched Roof),* its sequel, *Raganius (The Sorcerer),* and the play, *Zentas (The Son-in-Law).* The first one contains some of the best examples of the Lithuanian short story. Their characters, in contrast to the heroic figures of Šarūnas and Skirgaila, are simple country folk almost untouched by modern civilization and its inhibitions, though with their own peculiar beliefs and philosophies. We encounter in these stories the unorthodox, self-interpreted morality of the farm maid Marcelė ("Silkės"—"The Herrings"), the complete affinity with nature of the animistic, half-pagan old shepherd Lapinas ("Skerdžius"—"The Shepherd"), the pantheism of the country philosopher Vainoras ("Bedievis"—"The Atheist"), etc. The village life between the two World Wars was further explored in *Miglose (In the Fog),* though less successfully than in the previous volumes.

All these works have taken roots in Lithuanian soil. However, this is not the entire range of Krėvė's writings; indeed, it extends far beyond his native material and milieu. A man of diverse interests and wide erudition, Krėvė was particularly well acquainted with Oriental thought and literature, as well as with the history of Christianity, especially with its origins and initial rise. As the creative outgrowth of these interests, two works were born; namely, the collection *Rytu pasakos (Tales of the Orient)* which introduced the Oriental style to Lithuanian literature, and *Dangaus ir žemės sūnūs (The Sons of Heaven and Earth),* a Biblical epic of major proportions. Krėvė has been working on this epic on and off throughout the entire course of his literary life: the earliest chapters date back to 1907, while the last ones are, in fact, the last fragments ever to come from his pen. However, of the projected three volumes only the first two were completed (vol. I was published in 1949, vol. II, posthumously in 1963). In this work (its introduction is somewhat akin to the prologue of Goethe's *Faust*), employing partly Biblical style, Krėvė paints a wide and vivid panorama of the world of Jews in Christ's time and gives a rather unorthodox interpretation of the wellsprings of Christianity. Of particular interest is the tragedy of Herod woven into the epic in dramatic form, so that it comprises a complete drama by itself. As conceived by Krėvė, Herod's tragedy, in the final analysis, lies in the collision of the two widely different worlds—the Jewish and the Greek—within himself and his milieu. This interpretation of Herod's doom adds a new dimension and contributes substantially to the treatment of the Herod theme in literature. (pp. 265-67)

> *Kostas Ostrauskas, "Vincas Kreve: A Lithuanian Classic," in* Books Abroad, *Vol. 38, No. 3, Summer, 1964, pp. 265-67.*

CHARLES ANGOFF (essay date 1965)

[*A naturalized American citizen born in Russia, Angoff was a prolific writer who is most famous for his series of novels describing the Jewish experience in American life. Also a prominent journalist, he was associated with many American newspapers and magazines, serving as editor of the* American Mercury *and the* Literary Review, *among others. In the following excerpt, Angoff discusses* The Temptation *as a fictional autobiography.*]

Logic and *Realpolitik* have often been the worst enemies of decency and progress. It's possible to give reasons for almost any evil purpose, as the kept philosophers of the Hitler regime proved. And it's possible to whitewash, at least temporarily, almost any cruelty on the ground of *Realpolitik*. This is exactly what Lenin did and what Stalin did and what Khrushchev did—and what every tyrant, proletarian or otherwise, has done throughout the ages. Add diplomatic finesse to *Realpolitik,* and you have the whole history of the Bolshevik slave state from the beginning to the present.

Mr. Krévé knew this very well. In some mysterious way he tried to "come to terms" with Moscow, when the Communists tried to "liberate" his beloved Lithuania. But on his very first trip, as Lithuanian Foreign Minister, to Moscow in 1940 he saw at once that it is impossible to come to terms with an adversary who submits to no code of honorable conduct in international affairs. His bitter disillusionment eventually sent him into exile, where he devoted himself to teaching and writing till his death in 1954, at the age of seventy-two. Happily he wrote a great deal, and one of his compositions is *The Temptation*. . . . (p. 3)

The Temptation is a novel solidly based on fact. Indeed, it is thinly fictionized slice of autobiography. Yet it is not reporting, however factual it may be. Genuine fiction writer that he was—and one of the finest of our time—Mr. Krévé used his own life as a framework for his story, and from that framework he drew, so to speak, the essence of his body of insight into the totalitarian mentality. The result is a brief work of huge dimensions. It is surely one of the best portraits of what it means to be a Communist functionary and a Communist intellectual that has yet appeared in print.

Mr. Krévé's actual tale is simplicity itself. Victor Lemain, of Russian-French origin, but born in St. Petersburg, is deeply in love with his native land. The aftermath of World War I saw the Bolsheviks come to power, and he yearned to participate

in the "noble experiment." His efforts were interrupted by the anti-intellectual wave that swept Russia, and he escaped to his second mother-land, France. There he became a journalist—and here Mr. Krévé gives us a horrifying peep into the ethics of a good deal of French journalism. World War II revives Victor's love to Russia, and soon he is an honored member of a French delegation to Russia. By this time he had learned to hate America, "a nation that not only has no culture of its own, but has not the slightest understanding of what we Europeans mean by culture."

It wasn't long before Victor began to learn what Russian culture was. The functionaries tried to imbue him with the nobility of the Communist ways, which included, though of course they did not say so, opening his suitcases in his hotel room, during his absence, and hunting for "dangerous" documents and weapons. All the while Victor kept a note-book which he filled with his candid observations on people and places, and he saw at once that preserving this note-book would present great difficulties. What presented even greater difficulties was fighting off the Communist attempts to turn him into a virtual spy for Russia and a journalistic prostitute for the Soviet totalitarian leaders. The Communists promise him fabulous fees and "status," and then, in effect, threaten him with death if he dares publish any of his "lies" about Russia in France or elsewhere. They give him instances of others who had been unwise in this respect; they all died mysteriously.

Victor's verbal duels with his tormentors is little short of a masterpiece of psychological probing. So vivid is this whole section that it probably reflects an actual series of incidents in Mr. Krévé's personal life.

But there are other excellences in the book, which, I believe, will be read both as a work of literary art and as a document of our times long after scores of other books on the same subject are forgotten. *The Temptation* is truly an important book. (pp. 3-5)

> *Charles Angoff, in an introduction to* The Temptation *by Vincas Krévé, translated by Raphael Sealey, Manyland Books, Inc., 1965, pp. 3-5.*

ADDITIONAL BIBLIOGRAPHY

Angoff, Charles. Introduction to *The Herdsman and the Linden Tree,* by Vincas Krėvė, translated by Albinas Baranauskas, Pranas Pranckus, and Raphael Sealey, pp. 9-12. New York: Manyland Books, 1964.
  Discusses the five stories in this collection, concluding that the title story alone "places Vincas Krėvė in the front rank of modern fiction writers."

Senn, Alfred. "On the Sources of a Lithuanian Tale." In *Corona: Studies in Celebration of the Eightieth Birthday of Samuel Singer,* edited by Arno Schirokauer and Wolfgang Paulsen, pp. 8-22. Durham, N.C.: Duke University Press, 1941.
  Traces folklore sources and motifs in Krėvė's short story "Gilše."

Henry (Archibald Hertzberg) Lawson

1867-1922

(Also wrote under pseudonym of John Lawrence) Australian short story writer, poet, and autobiographer.

Lawson is highly regarded for his pithy, realistic short stories about the Australian "bush," or inland wilderness. Although he was best known during his lifetime as a poet, modern critics contend that his poetry is conventional and unextraordinary, while his fiction prefigures the work of many mid-twentieth-century writers in its unadorned style and vivid realism. A common theme in Lawson's work is that of "mateship," a lofty Australian conception of loyalty in friendship which Lawson championed. Although Lawson produced only two important short story collections, he nonetheless exerted a profound influence on later writers and is considered a landmark figure in Australian literature.

Lawson was born near Grenfell in New South Wales, where his father, a Norwegian sailor, was prospecting for gold. Lawson's father was a heavy drinker and willing prey for get-rich-quick schemes, while his mother was a radical activist who fluctuated from feminist and socialist concerns to religious devotion and asceticism. Dissension within the family, as well as the onset of deafness during his early teens, contributed to Lawson's tendency toward isolation and such solitary activities as writing. He left school at fourteen to work with his father as a painter and builder, and when his parents separated in 1883 he moved with his mother to Sydney, where she became involved in radical politics, bought the *Republican,* a socialist propaganda sheet, and founded the feminist periodical *Dawn.* Lawson published his first poem in 1887, and his first short story the following year, in the national literary magazine the *Bulletin.* While his early work was primarily social and political in content, Lawson's artistic focus changed permanently as the result of a trip to the frontier town of Bourke in 1892, where he encountered the "outback" wilderness for the first time. Lawson was struck by the barren landscape and harsh life of the bush, which contrasted sharply with the lush and romantic depiction of the outback in Australian literary tradition. Most of Lawson's subsequent writing was devoted to correcting the false portrayal of outback life that he found in Australian fiction.

Lawson published his first book, *Short Stories in Prose and Verse,* in 1894. A slim volume of poetry and short fiction privately printed on his mother's press, it attracted little critical attention, although it contained stories which would be recognized as among Lawson's best when reprinted two years later in *While the Billy Boils,* a collection that made him nationally famous. Earlier that year Lawson had married, and in 1897 the couple moved to New Zealand for a year, where Lawson was temporarily able to overcome incipient alcoholism and concentrate on writing. He continued to publish both fiction and poetry, and became most renowned in Australia for his nationalistic and politically radical poetry, although his short stories were the vehicle by which his reputation grew beyond the boundaries of his own country. In 1900 Lawson traveled to England, seeking a wider audience and fresh stimulation from new surroundings. There he published his most successful short story collection, *Joe Wilson and His Mates.* Lawson

returned to Australia in 1902, alienated from his wife due to his progressing alcoholism, to find that a young woman with whom he had fallen in love before leaving Australia had died. This misfortune, coupled with the separation demanded by his wife a few months later, caused Lawson to increase his drinking as a refuge from despondency. The fiction and poetry that he wrote for the next twenty years shows a marked decline from his early work. Lawson was found dead at his home in Sydney in 1922.

Although best known during his life as "the poet Lawson," most critics dismiss Lawson's poetry as conventional balladeering, although some contend that Lawson freed Australian verse from the formal language, archaisms, and elevated topics common to poetry at the turn of the century. Critics agree, however, that Lawson's best work is contained in the short story volumes *While the Billy Boils* and *Joe Wilson and His Mates.* The best stories of *While the Billy Boils,* including "The Drover's Wife," "The Bush Undertaker," and "The Union Buries Its Dead," are early works written while the inspiration of Lawson's trip to the outback was still fresh in his mind. Concerned with the hardships of living in the bush, several of these early stories describe the inherent obstacles to human habitation of the region and portray the roughness and cruelty which people living in such difficult conditions exhibit. Lawson's harsh, realistic descriptions countered a tradition in Australian literature that romanticized the outback and idealized its inhabitants. In many of the stories, however, Lawson also depicted kindness in his characters and celebrated the idealistic concept of "mateship." Mateship involves a strong bond of loyalty and trust which makes desertion in adversity, selfishness, or failure to defend a "mate" unthinkable, yet in practice carries few of the trappings of the chivalry it implies and, in its attention to form, can be as cruel as the outback itself. Lawson successfully depicted the harsh reality of bush life and the unromantic code of mateship in his early fiction. For example, in "The Union Buries Its Dead," a group of men loyally attend the funeral of a fellow union member whom they do not know simply because he has no family or friends in the area, but nevertheless callously allow a farce to be made of the ceremony and do not even recall the man's name after they learn it. Lawson's early stories contain the best examples of his distinctive writing style. During his lifetime it was considered an artless, journalistic style encouraged by the editorial policies of the *Bulletin*, but modern critics believe that Lawson made a conscious attempt to rid his prose of Victorian accoutrements, and that this attempt foreshadowed modern developments in the short story.

The stories of *Joe Wilson and His Mates*, begun in New Zealand and finished in England, are generally considered Lawson's finest. While lacking some of the energy and vivacity of his early work, they probe more deeply into complex human emotions and relationships. The central stories—"Joe Wilson's Courtship," "Brighten's Sister-in-Law," " 'Water Them Geraniums'," and "A Double Buggy at Lahey's Creek"—plot the course of courtship, marriage, hardship, the loss of affection, and tentative reconciliation. Many critics consider Joe Wilson a persona of Lawson, and the story cycle an autobiographical portrayal of the breakdown of Lawson's marriage, completed by a later Joe Wilson story, "Drifting Apart." Joe Wilson's function as narrator of the stories also creates interest in his perception and interpretation of events. In *Joe Wilson and His Mates*, critics saw Lawson on the edge of an artistic breakthrough that never occurred. In Lawson's remaining years his work became increasingly mawkish, predicated on the glorification of mateship and lacking the keen-edged realism which mitigated the sentimentality of his earlier stories. While many critics attribute this decline solely to personal causes, some believe that these weaknessess exist throughout his career, although they were more carefully suppressed in the early stories. Others believe that the increasing distance from his source of inspiration in the outback was the primary factor in Lawson's decreasing artistic power.

Lawson's achievements in *While the Billy Boils* and *Joe Wilson and His Mates* are highly regarded in Australia. In seeking to overturn false and romantic conceptions of Australian life, he came to write realistic stories which led to his acceptance as a spokesman for the Australian people. His deceptively simple writing style foreshadowed that of many later writers and his vivid realism and exploration of the concept of mateship influenced an entire generation of Australian writers.

PRINCIPAL WORKS

Short Stories in Prose and Verse (short stories and poetry) 1894
In the Days When the World Was Wide, and Other Verses (poetry) 1896
While the Billy Boils (short stories) 1896

On the Track (short stories) 1900
Over the Sliprails (short stories) 1900
*On the Track, and Over the Sliprails (short stories) 1900
Verses Popular and Humorous (poetry) 1900
The Country I Come From (short stories) 1901
Joe Wilson and His Mates (short stories) 1901
Children of the Bush (short stories and poetry) 1902
[Also published in two volumes as *Send Around the Hat* (1907) and *The Romance of the Swag* (1907)]
When I Was King, and Other Verses (poetry) 1905
The Rising of the Court (short stories and poetry) 1910
The Skyline Riders (poetry) 1910
A Coronation Ode and Retrospect (poetry) 1911
For Australia, and Other Poems (poetry) 1913
Triangles of Life, and Other Stories (short stories) 1913
My Army! O, My Army! and Other Songs (poetry) 1915
[Also published in a different order as *Song of the Dardanelles*, 1916]
Poetical Works of Henry Lawson. 3 vols. (poetry) 1925
The Prose Works of Henry Lawson (short stories) 1937
The Stories of Henry Lawson. 3 vols. (short stories) 1964
Collected Verse. 3 vols. (poetry) 1967-69
Henry Lawson: Letters 1890-1922 (letters) 1970
Henry Lawson: Autobiographical and Other Writings (autobiography and nonfiction) 1972
Henry Lawson: Short Stories and Sketches (short stories and sketches) 1972

*This work is a compilation of *On the Track* and *Over the Sliprails*.

[JOHN LE GAY BRERETON] (essay date 1894)

[*In the following excerpt, Brereton pronounces Lawson a great Australian poet.*]

If you mention Australian poetry to the average man who has not been tainted by looking at Sladen's anthologies, two names occur to his mind, and probably only two. He is right. Even the length of *Convict Once* will not save Brunton Stephens from oblivion, and yet Stephens has a fine humour. Unhappily, humour and an easy-flowing pen are not all that is required. Kendall and Gordon deserve to be remembered for one or two things they have written—"Araluen," for example, and "The Rhyme of Joyous Garde"—but even they, our first authentic poets, are, in a sense, failures. Their lack of success is, in both cases, to be traced to the egotism, the eternal self-reference of the men. . . .

Both these men have entered the dark arch of death. Who is there to take their places? Is there anyone who, with ability equal to or greater than theirs, is guided by a brighter star, inspired by nobler aspirations? There is. We have the man among us, and his name is Henry Lawson. Here at last is one who has within him the elements of greatness. He may not have the galloping rush that marks the most spirited of Gordon's verses, nor the calm aesthetic meditation of Kendall's melancholy songs, but he has what they had not—an intense power of sympathy that forces him to realise the struggling efforts of human nature upwards, the various hopes and fears of his fellow men. From the ranks of the workers his voice rises up, full of comfort and of hope. He knows what the poorer classes of our country have to fight with, for he too has had no thornless path of life to travel. The workers should hail him as their God-sent prophet, for he has worked with them, hoped with them, suffered with them. He has seen them at their best and at their worst, and in spite of their too frequent displays of bigotry, narrowness and coarseness, he is willing to celebrate their nobler qualities in living song, and to figure their just claims in letters of fire upon the heavens. Let them beware that they do not drive him from their camp. Let them take care lest they prove unworthy of their champion. There are signs in his work of a strong revulsion of feeling, a bitter awakening to sordid reality. Nothing can quench the love that inspires him, but the tendency of his poetry is changing. Let us turn to the verse of his earlier phase, and what do we find? Here is an ardent boy, full of enthusiasm and fire. He is inexperienced, and his views of life are illogical and fiercely revolutionary. He worships an abstraction which he knows by the name of THE PEOPLE. The sight of misery fills him with savage indignation. Poverty is a visible evil. Men starve, and look in vain for work. Yet there are some who enjoy riches and luxury. The impulsive spirit of the youth sees the main facts and leaps at once to what he regards as the immediate and obvious solution. Bloody Revolution will clear the stagnant air. Madness? Then youth is always mad. At least he is terribly in earnest:

> Once I cried: ''O God Almighty! if thy might doth still
>   endure,
>   Now show me in a vision, for the wrongs of Earth, a
>   cure.''
> And lo! with shops all shuttered, I beheld a city's
>   street,
> And in the waning distance heard the tramp of many
>   feet,
>   Coming near, coming near,
>   To a drum's dull distant beat,
> And soon I saw the army that was marching down
>   the street.''. . .

He does not publish such powerful, ringing verses now, because his mind is in a state of transition. He used to shout loud announcements of the distant but approaching tramp of ''red revolution's feet,'' and longed to carry a scarlet rag on a pole and lead an army of THE PEOPLE against the hirelings of tyranny. Probably deeper experience has taught him that THE PEOPLE were only ''such stuff as dreams are made of.'' His ideal has been shattered, and he hardly knows what to believe in, or where to place his trust. But there are signs that he is beginning to see that his mistake lay in his exclusiveness. He is beginning to take a more concrete view of things. He seems at length to realize the fact of universal brotherhood, and looks forward to the time that must come at last,

> When the people work together, and there ain't no fore-
> 'n'-aft.

Let him cling to his faith. Let him steadily seek for good, not ignoring the evil in men, but recognising it as dirt which may be washed off. Let him view all things with the eyes of love. He is at the parting of the ways, and if he is true to himself success is certain. But he must remember that his soul is not his own. We, too, have our share in it, and we shall, when the time of reckoning comes, demand a strict account. Genius is neither a plaything nor a minting machine. But I know that the soul of the man is essentially unselfish, and with confidence I hail him as one whose name will wake feelings of love and reverence in thousands of hearts. And so for a moment I take leave of Henry Lawson. (pp. 1-3)

[John Le Gay Brereton], ''Poetry in Australia,'' in Henry Lawson Criticism: 1894-1971, *edited by Colin Roderick, Angus and Robertson, 1972, pp. 1-3.*

A. G. STEPHENS   (essay date 1896)

[In the following excerpt Stephens criticizes the arrangement and fragmentation of the collection While the Billy Boils, *while acknowledging the talent evident in Lawson's best work.]*

Many of Lawson's sketches are written in series: there is a ''Mitchell'' sequence, a ''Steelman'' sequence, a bush sequence, a city sequence, and so on. The obvious way of dealing with these was the best way. They should have been classified and put in sections, so that continuity might be unbroken and the characters might gain force and distinctness from the massing of impressions. Exactly the opposite course has been followed. The book [*While the Billy Boils*] is like a bad cook's ragoût. You get here a mouthful of salt, there one of pepper, the next is meat uncondimented. Not only is power lost, but the haphazard mixture jolts the mind like an unexpected bottom step.

The pity of it is greater because with the best arrangement the matter would seem scrappy and disconnected. Written for occasional publication, these detached sketches have no unity of idea or treatment. Their appeal was bound to be diffused and vague: the least that could be done was to concentrate the interest as far as the slight skeins of similarity permitted, and instead of half-a-hundred taps to strike half-a-dozen *blows*. It was not done.

Lawson might conceivably have written many of his fragmentary impressions into a single plotted, climaxed story which would make a permanent mark. Or if even he had contrived a set of characters to pass from chapter to chapter, as Mark Twain manages, and hung his matter on their pegs, his result would have been stronger. As it is, the reader is perpetually getting up steam for a five-minutes' journey which brings him back to starting-point. And only half-a-dozen of these sketches—as printed—are something like literature. The rest are frequently good journal-work, good material for literature—nothing more.

Yet the standard for criticism of Lawson is rising as he rises. We ask from him better things than we asked a year ago. Hitherto he has only had to make a reputation—with his endowments an easy task: now—O labor of giants!—he has to maintain it.

And Lawson's public reception has been quite equal to his deserts. . . . [His] volume of poems has been noticed by a hundred critics anxious to forget blemishes, keen to discover beauties; the rolling snowball of his fame has been kicked onward by a thousand eager feet. Thanks in part to this zealous ardor, there is not a corner of Australia where his name is unknown; not a town in which he will not find some strange hand stretched to grip his, some honest face shining with pleasure to greet the poet of the bush. (pp. 51-2)

But reputation, like rank, has its responsibilities. If Lawson's is not to wane, he must wax continually.

The charm of Lawson's prose is essentially that of his poetry. Art he has none; his artifices are of the feeblest. For the most part he might say with Antony:

> I only speak right on;
> I tell you that which you yourselves do know.

But what others merely know, Lawson feels. He is indeed abnormally sensitive: the trifles which make evanescent impression on ordinary minds draw blood (and ink) from his. Then ordinary minds with pleasure recognise his own impressions. "Why, these are *our* thoughts; these people are *our* people; these scenes and places are the scenes and places we have known for all our lives."

Precisely; yet until Lawson pictured, revealed, and vitalised them, those thoughts, those people, those ordinary places and scenes never really existed for ordinary minds. Which is, of course, but a variation on the well-worn apothegms that beauty is in the eye of the gazer, that we get out of everything exactly what we put into it, that one man's meat is another man's poison, and the rest. The ordinary mind lives all a life behind horn windows: genius has invented glass. Its senses are acute to the point of ecstasy; it sees the rays of the human spectrum to grosser eyes invisible; like the beautiful Norse god Baldur, it can hear the grass growing. And Lawson, as before enunciated, has a touch of genius.

His instincts of assimilation and selection are matched in his later work by his instinct of expression. His quaint simple style suits his themes and modes of thought. And his manner is strengthening. The happy word and phrase come to him easily: the incidents fall without effort into place: his picture is made before he knows. Lawson is beginning to find himself.

Yet his impressionable mind often reflects the color of the medium through which it has been flowing last. There are hints of Bret Harte and Dickens in his earlier work; of Mark Twain and *Bulletin* humorists in his later. And the work is none the better for them. Regard for Lawson's reputation would, indeed, have excised a good half of the book—especially stories in which the pathos is deliberately manufactured, like **"Arvie Aspinall's Alarm Clock"**; and valueless sketches like **"Bogg of Geebung"**, with similar imaginative effects; and undistinguished journalism like **"For Auld Lang Syne."** The remainder, in their class, would be very good indeed: as it is, the level of the volume is a long way below its best pages.

Not the best, but the most promising are those which tell **"An Unfinished Love Story."** Here, for the first time, Lawson ceases to describe characteristics and starts to create characters. (pp. 52-3)

> A. G. Stephens, "Lawson's Prose," in Henry Lawson Criticism: 1894-1971, *edited by Colin Roderick, Angus and Robertson, 1972, pp. 51-3.*

THE SPECTATOR   (essay date 1897)

[*In the following essay the critic commends Lawson for powerful, energetic writing and candid realism in* While the Billy Boils.]

In these days when short dramatic stories are eagerly looked for, it is strange that one whom we would venture to call the greatest Australian writer should be practically unknown in England. Short stories are his—none shorter—scrap-sketches indeed, but biting into the very heart of the bushman's life, ruthless in truth, extraordinarily dramatic, and pathetically uneven. That they should not be read on this side of the world seems to point either to a contemptuous indifference to European opinion or to an unusual ignorance on the part of their writer as to his own merit. He is apparently content to let what he has to say drift through the sheets of Australian and New Zealand newspapers, and be gathered into a volume by a Sydney publisher, under the name of *While the Billy Boils*. We

may remember that Mr. Rudyard Kipling began his literary career in the same track, and perhaps it has its advantages. At any rate, both men have somehow gained that power of concentration which by a few strong strokes can set place and people before you with amazing force. Mr. Lawson is a less experienced writer than Mr. Kipling, and more unequal, but there are two or three sketches in this volume which for vigour and truth can hold their own with even so great a rival. The men and their mates pass before you, violent, brutal, with that horrible familiarity with profane oaths which is a curse of the land; yet with "grit" in them, enduring, loyal to their companions,—hiding, in fact, a little gold in a good deal of wash dirt. Macquarie, the drunken shearer, staggered ten miles to the hospital, with three fractured ribs and a cracked skull, and would have staggered away again in his agony if they had refused to set his dog's leg, smashed in the same row. **"Macquarie's Mate,"** broken-down sot as he was, leapt to passionate life again in defence of the chum he thought dead. Other sharply drawn sketches are **"Rats"** and **"Brummy Usen,"** while for dreary description of a dreary country take the railway journey in **"In a Wet Season,"** where, as night drew on, the bush grew darker, and the plains more like ghastly oceans, and here and there the "dominant note of Australian scenery" was acccentuated, as it were, by "naked, white, ring-barked trees standing in the water, and haunting the ghostly surroundings." Here you get Australia, actual Australia, seen and put down as it is, and not as it is imagined. Most incisive, most impressive of all is **"The Bush Undertaker,"** a gruesome story of an old shepherd (and his dog, "Five Bob") whose idea of a holiday was grubbing among blackfellows' graves. So doing, he comes across the dried-up mummy of a former chum, and takes it back to his hut to bury as decently as he could. After several ghastly incidents:—

> "It's time yer turned in, Brum," he said, lifting the body down. He carried it to the grave and dropped it into one corner like a post. He arranged the bark so as to cover the face, and by means of a piece of clothes line, lowered the body to a horizontal position. Then he threw in an armful of gum leaves, and then, very reluctantly, took the shovel and dropped in a few shovelfuls of earth.—"An' this is the last of Brummy," he said, leaning on his spade and looking away over the tops of the ragged gums on the distant range. This reflection seemed to engender a flood of memories, in which the old man became absorbed. He leaned heavily upon his spade and thought.—"Arter all," he murmured sadly; "arter all—it were Brummy."— "Brummy," he said at last, "it's all over now; nothin' matters now—nothin' didn't ever matter, nor—nor don't. You uster say as how it 'ud be all right termorrer" (pause); "termorrer's come, Brummy—come fur you—it ain't come fur me yet, but—it's a comin'." He threw in some more earth.—"Yer don't remember, Brummy, an' mebbe yer don't want to remember—*I* don't want to remember—but—well, but yer see that's where yer got the pull on me." He shovelled in some more earth and paused again. The dog rose with ears erect, and looked anxiously first at his master and then into the grave. "Theer ought to be somethin' sed," muttered the old man; "'tain't right to put 'im under like a dog. There oughter be some sort

o' sarmin.'' He sighed heavily in the listening silence that followed this remark, and proceeded with his work. He filled the grave to the brim this time, and fashioned the mound carefully with his spade. Once or twice he muttered the words, ''I am the rassaraction.'' He was evidently trying to remember, as he laid the tools quietly aside, and stood at the head of the grave, the something that ought to be said. He removed his hat, placed it carefully on the grass, held his hands out from his sides and a little to the front, drew a long, deep breath, and said with a solemnity that greatly disturbed Five Bob, ''Hashes ter hashes, dus' ter dus', Brummy—an'—an' in hopes of a great and gerlorious rassaraction!'' He sat down on a log near by, rested his elbows on his knees, and passed his hand wearily over his forehead,—but only as one who was tired and felt the heat; and presently he rose, took up the tools and walked back to the hut. And the sun sank again on the grand Australian bush,—the nurse and tutor of eccentric minds, the home of the weird, and of much that is different from things in other lands.

This is strong writing, the best, perhaps, in the book. But there is in other of the papers enough rough pathos, fire, and tragic realism to draw the eyes of literary men upon the author. (pp. 665-66)

''An Australian Story-Teller,'' in The Spectator, *Vol. 78, No. 3593, May 8, 1897, pp. 665-66.*

EDWARD GARNETT   (essay date 1902)

[*Garnett was a prominent editor for several London publishing houses, and discovered or greatly influenced the work of many important English writers, including Joseph Conrad, John Galsworthy, and D. H. Lawrence. He also published several volumes of criticism, all of which are characterized by thorough research and sound critical judgments. In the following essay Garnett discusses Lawson as an accurate interpreter of Australian life.*]

What Henry Lawson's talent is it would be impossible to discover from his poetry. His verse, to put it bluntly, is the verse of a thousand-and-one vigorous versifiers of today, writing humorously or picturesquely it may be, but producing work thereby which shows the stamp of the literary artisan rather than that of the artist. To consider Lawson's verse is, however, interesting, because through its medium his characteristic humour, sentiment and outlook on life struggle vainly to express anything that others have not put as well. Lawson's verse is that of a third-rate writer; his prose is that of a writer who represents a continent. Like a voice speaking to you through a bad telephone, the poems convey the speaker's meaning, but all the shades of original tone are muffled, lost or hidden. There is plenty of evidence of rattling humour and sentimentalism in the poems, and these indeed show the skeleton of his talent, but all its delicate nerves and tissues and the ligaments that make the writer truly original, one must look for in his prose.

I have said that Henry Lawson's sketches bring before us the life of a continent, and if my readers like to qualify this high praise by putting it thus: ''In the absence of great writers he is the writer who best represents the Australia of today,'' I shall not object. No writer, of course, stands for the whole of his nation, but only for a part; and if Australia had now a flowering time of national genius, with a representative group of creative talents appearing, Lawson, undeniably, might find his place marked *proxime accessit*. A writer's place in the national life cannot, however, be assessed by any official handicap, or by including him in an Olympian contest of merit between the modern writers of all nations. Lawson's special value to us is that he stands as the representative writer of a definite environment, as the portrayer of life on the Australian soil, and that he brings before our eyes more fully and vividly than any other man the way the Australian settlers' life has been going, its characteristic spirit, code and outlook, the living thought and sensation of these tens and hundreds and thousands and millions of people who make up the Australian democracy. And here, to place Lawson rightly, I must make a distinction between ''representative'' writers. Thousands of modern writers are typical of their surroundings, and are, indeed, products of the environments they envisage for us. There are, perhaps, over a hundred clever French writers today who consciously and acutely analyse the spirit of their generation; but a writer must not only reflect life, he must *focus* and typify, and the more he can focus of life the more significant he becomes. Thus, there are many clever novelists, but only one Anatole France. Lawson, as an artist, is often crude and disappointing, often sketchy and rough, but many of his slightest sketches show he has the faculty of bringing life to a focus, of making it typical. Further, the point is, What is the artist's commentary on the life he represents worth? What depth of human nature does his insight touch? To answer these elementary questions is to explain why we place to such representative writers as Balzac and Eugene Sue, the one fairly high in the scale, the other decidedly low, and why we place Fielding higher than Smollett. And to answer it is also to explain why Australia can really show us a national writer in Henry Lawson, while Canada is sending us an ingenious, theatrical story-teller in Mr. Gilbert Parker. Lawson's journalistic sketches establish fresh creative values of life, but the merely ingenious story-tellers only re-affirm stale valuations. It is in the sense, then, of being a national writer that Henry Lawson's work deserves careful attention from the English people. We hear a great deal today of ''The Empire,'' and of ''Hands Across the Sea,'' but in truth English people seem to care much more about expressing fraternal emotions than in ascertaining what is in their kinsmen's heads.

To turn to Lawson's art. If we are to measure his tales chiefly by their sketchiness, by their inequalities, by their casual air of being an ingenious reporting of entertaining incidents, if we are to lay stress on the caricaturist and the sentimental writer in him, we must in that case join hands with the academic critics who may affirm that Lawson's work really falls within the province of those ephemeral story-tellers who serve only to amuse their generation. The answering argument is that Lawson through these journalistic tales *interprets* the life of the Australian people, typifies the average life for us, and takes us beneath the surface. His tales are not merely all foreground. His pictures of life convey to us a great sense of the background of the whole people's life; their struggles and cares, their humour and outlook, live in his pages. Nothing is more difficult to find in this generation than an English writer who identifies himself successfully with the life of the working democracy, a writer who does not stand aloof from and patronize the bulk of the people who labour with their hands. This no doubt is because nearly all our writers have a middle-class bias and training, and so either write down to or write up to their subject when it leads them outside their own class, and accordingly their valuations thereof are in general falsified. Mrs. Humphrey Ward describes her own class admirably, for example, but her working people are ludicrous. Gissing's lower-middle-class people are generally good, but his working men are feebly drawn. Even Hardy's West-country rustics are idealized at times to suit the middle-class taste. We have no English writer so true as Miss Wilkins is to the life of "the people," and she does not profess to write as one of them. Lawson, however, has the great strength of the writer writing simply as one of the democracy, and of the man who does not have to climb down from a class fence in order to understand the human nature of the majority of his fellow men. I have never read anything in modern Englegh literature that is so absolutely democratic in tone, so much the real thing, as **"Joe Wilson's Courtship."** And so with all Lawson's tales and sketches. Not even Maupassant himself has taken us so absolutely inside people's lives as do the tales **"Joe Wilson's Courtship"** and **"A Double Buggy at Lahey's Creek."** And it is this rare, convincing tone of this Australian writer that gives him a great value now, when forty-nine out of fifty Anglo-Saxon writers are insisting on *not* describing the class they were born in, but straining their necks and their outlooks in order to describe the life of the class which God has placed beyond them. Hence the comparative decay and neglect of true realism, the realism of *Tom Jones,* and of *Emma,* of *Barchester Towers,* and of *Middlemarch.* Our commercialized public, intent on "rising," instinctively prefers to nourish itself on Mr. Anthony Hope rather than on Mrs. Mary E. Mann. It is therefore an immense relief to the unsophisticated critic, after looking East and West and North and South for writers untainted by the ambition to be mentally genteel, to come across the small group of able democratic writers on the *Sydney Bulletin,* of whom Mr. Lawson is the chief. In *The Country I Come From,* in *While the Billy Boils,* in *Joe Wilson and His Mates,* in *On the Track, Over the Slip Rails,* we have the real Australia, the real bushman, "selector," "squatter," "roustabout," "shearer," drover, shepherd, "spieler," shanty-keeper and publican, the real Australian woman, mother, wife and girl, the real "larrykin," the real boy, the real "Boss," and the real "mate." Read **"The Union Buries Its Dead,"** in *The Country I Come From,* if you care to see how the most casual, "newspapery" and apparently artless art of this Australian writer carries with it a truer, finer, more delicate commentary on life than do the idealistic works in any of our genteel school of writers. It isn't great art, but it is near to great art; and, moreover, great art is not to be found every "publishing season." Read **"An Oversight of Steelman's,"** if you want humour, the real thing, and read **"No Place for a Woman"** if you want pathos, also the real thing. If you want a working philosophy of life, read **"How Steelman Told His Story,"** and if you want to see how admirably a man can sum up his own country in ten careless pages, read **"His Country After All,"** and **"The Little World Left Behind."** There is a little sketch in *While the Billy Boils* called **"The Drover's Wife,"** a sketch of a woman in the bush, left for months alone with her four children while her husband is up-country droving. If this artless sketch be taken as the summary of a woman's life, giving its significance in ten short pages, even Tolstoy has never done better. Lawson has re-treated this subject at length in the more detailed picture in **"'Water Them Geraniums'";** I leave it to mothers of all ranks and stations in life to say how it affects them, and whether it has not universal application to the life of working women wherever the sun goes down. Art stands for much, but sincerity also stands for much in art, and the sincerity of Lawson's tales

nearly always drives them home. There is another little sketch called **"They Wait on the Wharf in Black,"** which artists may call sentimental. Well, it is sentimental; it is on a sentimental subject, and I have never found anywhere a tale that so well describes the meeting of a father with his children: it is all there in the last two pages, the family meeting, and the family feeling, and I invite the sceptical reader to turn to it. I leave it to more competent critics to say how far mere sketches of human nature, such as **"The Shanty-Keeper's Wife,"** can vie with the art of literary pictures carefully arranged in studio lights, with real models posed "from the life," *à la* Mr. Marion Crawford. I have not laid much stress on Mr. Lawson's humour, as the public is likely to lay such stress on it as to fail to see that his vision of life cannot be summed up by the term "humourist." But, undoubtedly, Mr. Lawson is pre-eminent among modern humourists. Humourists, so luckily common in life, are uncommonly scarce in literature—the reason being that the intonation and the gesture of the living man can only be reproduced by writers who have a racy language of their own. Lawson has this racy language and an extremely delicate observation of those tiny details which reveal situation and character. His minute appreciation of individual peculiarities is as well shown in the sketch **"Mr. Smellingscheck"** as is his power of idiomatic language in the "Stiffner" stories. His weakness as an artist lies chiefly in his temptation to introduce sentimental touches that mar his realism—see, for example, in his admirable **"Two Larrykins"** and the last page of **"Telling Mrs. Baker."** To come back to my main point—that Lawson is a national writer, of whom the Australians may be proud—I should be inclined to pair him with Miss Wilkins, who is also a national writer, if I did not find that his canvas, his range, his experience of life are richer and wider than the American authoress's. The difference between the two writers is largely the difference of masculine and feminine. Miss Wilkins—none better—can describe the indoor life of women, and Lawson—none better—the democratic life of the road, the bush, the track, the shearer, the "selector," the "pub," the wharf, the river, and the street.

If Lawson's tales fail to live in another fifty years—and where will be much of Kipling's, Stevenson's, Hardy's, and Henry James's fiction then?—it will be because they have too little beauty of form and there is too much crudity and roughness in their literary substance. Henry Lawson's matter is more interesting than his form and matter in general only survives through its form. This admitted, it may be claimed for Lawson that he of the Australian writers best pictures for us and interprets democratic Australia today, and that he is one of the very few genuinely democratic writers that the literature of "Greater Britain" can show. (pp. 177-86)

Edward Garnett, "Henry Lawson and the Democracy," in his Friday Nights: Literary Criticisms and Appreciations, first series, *Alfred A. Knopf, 1922, pp. 177-86.*

ARCHIE JAMES COOMBES   (essay date 1938)

[In the following excerpt Coombes favorably assesses Lawson's poetry, especially praising the philosophy of "mateship" expressed in it and its portrayal of bleak elements of Australian life at the turn of the century.]

Up to 1880, nothing in the nature of a school of poetry had emerged in Australia. The generative force necessary for such a development did not exist in the community. Politically, the six States were more or less antagonistic to one another, and thought, where not merely parish-wide, was seldom, if ever, more than State-wide. But the last twenty years of the century witnessed a gradual breaking down of provincial prejudices, and the growth of something approaching a national spirit manifested itself, and finally found expression in the political unity of the Commonwealth.

Within the same period also, a vigorous influence was at work, which succeeded to a considerable degree in organizing, and to some extent in unifying, the poetic energy of Australia. That influence was provided by the *Bulletin,* a weekly journal established in Sydney in 1880, which for many years, wherein it saw the hey-day of its formative impulse, was conducted by J. F. Archibald. Added value was also imparted to the journal as a literary medium by A. G. Stevens's long association with it.

The *Bulletin* gave something of a status to the poet's profession. It demanded good work and paid a price. It waged a merciless warfare upon sham and humbug. Its literary criticisms were corrosive of trash, but stimulating and constructive for meritorious verse. It was aggressively Australian in sentiment, and insisted on first-hand Australian thought and experience in its poets. In short, it educated a race of poets to a forceful, honest, and interesting treatment of subjects likely to appeal to the progressive and virile elements of the Australian community. Moreover, it educated a body of readers to a level which ensured the appreciation of its pages, so that when the best of its poets came to issue their collected verses in volume form, the demand for the work was extraordinary in comparison with the apathy that had previously blighted poets' hopes.

Though the *Bulletin* prescribed no single standard of style and set no specific limit upon subject, except that it should be Australian, yet a certain convention both of style and of subject speedily developed. The "bush" became a kind of poets' El Dorado. Like an alluvial goldfield it was fossicked from end to end for pay-dirt, and literature was enriched by as much as a vigorous native balladry has in it, perhaps, to bestow. (pp. 59-60)

Foremost of the versifiers of the *Bulletin* school, Henry Archibald Lawson is also the most forceful personality in the whole course of Australian literature. In range, variety, and volume, his literary product exceeds that of every other Australian writer, and his singular fidelity in presenting various aspects of Australianism, entitles him to rank nearest to national among our literary men. (p. 61)

To be a patriot in the eighties, one had also, by the dictates of ordinary intelligence, to be something of a rebel too, for public opinion, in its most prevalent mode of expression, both then and later, was so heavily overlaid with mid-Victorian conventionalism, and so hypnotized by the spell of the Empire's greatness, that to assert the claims of preference to Australian interests was in general to invite contempt and ridicule, if not to precipitate the penalties of treason. Could any sane man fail to be convinced otherwise than that all was well with Australia, since Australia was a unit in the grandest Empire the sun had ever shone upon? Smug self-complacency could grow nobly sentimentalized on such a thought, but that did not solve the problem as to whether all was right with Australia. Passionate in his conviction to the contrary Henry Lawson took a genuinely Australian stand in countering hypocrisy, sham, and fatuous humbug with some of the most ruthless presentations of the reality of things that ever flowed from an Australian pen. He

began his poetic career as a rebel-patriot, voicing the anguish, the indignation, the resentment, and the impassioned will of the masses submerged and stifled by adverse economic conditions. Two poems among many will serve to illustrate him in this role, namely **"The Army of the Rear,"** and **"Faces in the Street,"** both of which were originally published in the *Bulletin* in 1888. With those poems also should be read **"My Army, O, My Army!"** written after an interval of over a quarter of a century.

In verses of this class Lawson shows a mingled power, sincerity, and passion unique in Australian literature. His aim is to carry conviction of the truth of things alive into the hearts of his readers; and even though the truth be harsh, or unpleasant, or fouled to ugliness by oppression, he nerves his utterance so fervidly with moral purpose as to establish that very ugliness in its right to be seen and heard among men. In the life he depicts, beauty has no place, for the emotional conditions within which alone beauty can exist are too jangled by distress and too harrowed by injustice to function. His poetic impulse therefore finds its goal in revolution as the only means of restoring suffering humanity to its natural right to emotional content. His ideal has in it the realization of beauty in life; and for that reason he lays bare the failure of his age in its human duty. He shows his love of his fellow-men by showing his hatred of their oppression.

There is a fine intellectual courage, a type of heroism, in this work of Lawson's. He speaks with authority and in a tone and manner, not parish-wide, but Australia-wide in its appeal. He stands above class, and ranks as a national figure in his advocacy of what are essentially national principles. The extent of his influence in shaping and informing public opinion can never be calculated. It is more likely to be under-estimated than over-estimated. Persistent, sincere, and urgent, his voice, heard over a series of years throughout the length and breadth of the land, has done no mean national service in steeling and tempering the rectitude inherent in normal men, and in converting apathy into active will for social sympathy.

However, it would be idle to assert that every sordid scene presented by Lawson is nobly motived. The white heat of his early zeal ultimately cooled; and whereas in the first place he loved humanity and hated to see it sunk in squalor, and looked through that squalor for the cause or the remedy, yet he came in time to exploit squalor as an end in itself. It provided good "copy." Hence, there is in a proportion of his work a lack of elevation and an element of the cant of hard luck as a profession.

Lawson possessed a happy genius as a story-teller. His *Bulletin* training had exercised him in the necessity for relevance, significance, and reasonable brevity, and he found his finest literary vehicle in the Short Story. But many elements of his art in prose are employed with success in his verse. His dramatic sense vitalizes his narrations. He draws his inspiration direct from experience; and character, motive, action, and setting are as a rule presented with life-like reality in moments and conditions unmistakably Australian in themselves, and more deeply, perhaps more subtly, Australianized by the author's personality, whether by its humour, or sentiment, or sympathy, or regret, or other mood. One feels on having read a Lawson scene that dramatic values have been justly gauged both in the design and presentation of the subject. It therefore imparts the freshness, variety, and impact of life as it is lived.

That life, however, though being a dramatic moment, is very far from being representative of the heart and core of Australianism from which have developed the fine prosperity and the bouyant and healthy spirit of the community of to-day. Swagmen and rouseabouts, poverty-stricken selections, and wayside shanties have been essentially a feature of Australian out-back life, but the Australian race had not won its right to nationhood on what they have added to its well-being. As driftwood or wreckage on the shore they provided Lawson with a source of picturesque speculation in which the flow of the vital stream is unrecorded or unobserved. His heart abounded with sympathy, but it was a sympathy lacking in universality. It gave him a rare insight into forms of failure, but it left him blind to the soul of success.

Australian life in its hardships, its cruelties, its disappointments, its droughts, starvations, and despairs has never been more truly or more feelingly depicted than by him. He has recorded faithfully what he has seen. In that fact lies his triumph and his failure; for in what he has not seen, the deeper significances of life in Australia reside.

Lawson's philosophy of life was beaten out of his experience; and as that experience was endured, especially in his fluid and formative years, under the shadow of economic need, so his philosophy prescribes as its highest good an ideal that will fortify the spirit in adversity and gild the gloom in distress—the simple creed of "mateship." His conception of the perfect man is the true and tried and unwavering mate. Mateship with him is a form of applied Christianity. The Good Samaritan is a brother of the craft. "Bear ye one another's burdens" is the essence of many an illustration he furnishes of his creed in action. As a solvent for selfishness and an insurance against morbidity and despair the doctrine is indispensable to the man "on the track." Given a mate, though all the world should fall in ruin round him, life still may sustain him to beauty of conduct and nobility of act. Bereft of a mate, he is face to face with that land of lost souls, the land of "the hatter," the world of the "Jimmy Woodser."

Lawson was tireless in the exposition of his creed, and as he applied it, it is pregnant with moments of fine morality. Nevertheless, its limitations as a philosophy of life are obvious, even as its values are.

In its normal environment mateship was an implicit contract between two parties, embodying a mutual suspension of disbelief in one another, coupled with mutual service "for better or for worse, for richer or poorer, in sickness and in health" till circumstances did them part, and, like the holy bond of matrimony, it admitted no intrusion of a third party. And as "Me and my mate, and the rest go hang," to parody a Lawson line, its possibilities for Christian sublimity he dressed to such advantage as to render almost impertinent any suggestion of its non-Christian exclusiveness.

Lawson, too, was in his way an exponent of a philosophy of clothes. The world of his philosophy was principally the world of the unskilled labourer, and, as a rule, the world of the unskilled labourer in his non-labouring periods. And, granted that it would not be wholly just to argue that admission to his fold was pre-conditioned by dirty linen and a grouch, yet in the main the skilled worker happy in his work remained above his line of vision, even as the harmless virtue that finds expression in a clean collar was beyond his will for recognition.

The zeal and honesty of soul that drove him to attack oppression and hypocrisy and sycophancy in life as he saw it was too full of onset to leave unbeaten any bush that might shelter a sham. Hence in the polish of manners he sees moral verity supplanted

by standards of elegance; in cuffs and collars he reads the fatuous superciliousness that sneers at honest toil; in literary taste he finds the purblind pedant, or "culchaw," that poor hollow ass; and in forms and ceremonies of every kind he discloses the lurking of the snob and the rogue and the fool. Therefore, finding in appearances nothing but food for contempt and ridicule, he figuratively strips humanity of its sartorial sheathing, and finds reality only in the hearts of men face to face with the stark experience of failing to make a living.

A career such as Lawson's would have been impossible to a man without a sense of humour. It is his humour, perhaps, more than any other of his literary qualities, that endears him to the majority of Australian readers, for the Australian temperament finds its true reflection, not in the alien glooms and griefs and leaden-eyed despairs that poets have libellously thrust upon it, but in the joyous intelligence of the laughing heart that is resilient to adversity, and too generously motived to seek its expression in old men's fears. And Lawson's humour flows from the intelligence of a laughing heart.

Moreover, Lawson is an artist in humour. He moulds it with the justest sense of dramatic values. It is invariably the humour of character in action, and thereby possesses a richer significance than mere humour of incident. And that significance he colours and deepens with an imparted atmosphere that breathes with colloquial ease through the spirit of his scenes. Character, incident, setting, and the atmosphere of the laughing heart behind them, all belong as naturally to the order of things Australian as the cheerful incense of woodland campfires or the profuse gold of tufted wattle.

The fact that Lawson was generously endowed with a sense of humour proved a happy circumstance for Australian literature in another direction. It guaranteed him to sanity and saved him from excess in dealing with sentiment. To the literary policy of the *Bulletin* and to the natural endowments of its school of writers are due the thanks of those lovers of Australian verse who hate the cant of pity-mongers and despise the vulgarity of private woe exhibited as a public spectacle. Morbid egoism and the abasement of tear-worship as being doubly false, for they were false to art as well as to life, disappeared under the corrective influences of the eighties and nineties, and sentiment grew robust as the miasma of sentimentalism vanished.

Sentiment plays a prominent part in Lawson's verse. He senses the truth of feeling accurately. He gauges its force and its moment of impact justly, but does not elaborate its subtleties. He is neither sensitive nor sensuous, but characteristically sensible in his emotional contacts, and there is a healthy pleasure in the glow imparted, even when the theme is a sad one. His tender and yet robust fancy is at its best in these bush surroundings that he both knew and loved. It lingers with happy affection in his reminiscence of the romance of the past, of the colour and movement and ever-impending incidence of good-fortune of the Roaring Days. With equal affection too it lingers upon individual types, such as Harry Dale, and Andy, and the bush-girl of **"The Sliprails and the Spur"**; and in those and similar instances, he dramatizes situation, character, and sentiment so effectively as to attach and intensify sympathy and esteem through the individual to the manhood and womanhood of the bush in general.

Along with its warmth, the sincerity of Lawson's feeling is always a natural counterpart of the reality of the subject matter he is dealing with. Everywhere in his verse he is in direct contact with nature and with life as he knew them; and the emotional accompaniment is as much the truth of experience as the recorded impression is the truth of fact.

Consistent with his philosophy of clothes, Lawson's chief concern in his verse was with the significance of his subject matter, with its inner content rather than with its outward form; and therefore he provided it with no shining raiment, but from a kind of democratic preference dressed it serviceably for workaday wear in the sober tones selected for strength and not for delicacy. Hence one finds in his verse none of the subtleties of metrical effect, either in movement or in music, such as exhilarate the sense of beauty in the work of artists more graciously endowed. While his personal choice in music was given to the brass band, his preference in movement seems to have been for the march; and in the mechanics of his verse these two predilections prevail. He can never be said to "foot it featly here and there." In his metrical gait he never departs from democratic decorum so far as to "Trip it . . . on the light fantastic toe." In fact, although he did not stress the point, beauty, in many of its forms, appears to have languished as a suspect under his surveillance. As a potential begetter of aesthetic priggery it carried its condemnation in its face, within the world of his wayfaring. One does not, therefore, read Lawson for beauty of rhythm or melody. His metres are robust and vigorous and carry in them the ring of sincerity. They are suited to their themes, and are the honest echo of the soul of the man. One would not wish to have them other than they are, for to do so would be to desire that Lawson should be un-Lawsonian. They are not detachable elements but are integral with his personality, as the form in which it naturally flows when rendered fluid by contact with experience.

Lawson's work is the most vital and significant reflection of one aspect of Australian life that our literature possesses. As an exponent of the truth of fact he ranks as the greatest of our realists. That entitles him to pre-eminence as an Australian among poets; though not necessarily to pre-eminence as a poet among Australians. In the more purely poetic necessities he is surpassed by Kendall and Daley and others, but in spite of that, what Lawson has left us is all so admirably characterized that it will survive as the most graphic record of an interesting period of our development. (pp. 68-76)

Archie James Coombes, "Henry Lawson," in his Some Australian Poets, 1938. Reprint by Books for Libraries Press, 1970; distributed by Arno Press, Inc., pp. 59-76.

ARTHUR A. PHILLIPS (essay date 1948)

[*Phillips is an Australian literary critic and educator. In the following excerpt he demonstrates that Lawson's short stories display a purposeful, controlled style.*]

The work of Lawson, Furphy and their contemporaries—the first generation of the Australian born—is a land-mark in the history of Anglo-Saxon culture. Almost for the first time, fiction in our language has abandoned a middle-class attitude. Dickens, Hardy and Bret Harte had, it is true, already written sympathetically and knowledgeably of the unpossessing; but they had written from middle-class minds. It is significant that Oliver Twist was a gentleman by birth and ultimate destiny, that Jude's tragedy was his unescapeable obscurity. Such writers were essentially observers of a life strange and interesting to their middle-class readers, to whom they were reporting it—

often with a passionate sympathy. But to Lawson and Furphy the middle-class were foreigners—and they the often jingoistic nationalists of the poor. They wrote of the people, from the people, and even—by grace of the *Bulletin*—for the people. In that task almost their only precursor in Anglo-Saxon fiction, later than Bunyan, was Mark Twain; and he lacked the consistent courage of his perceptions.

This revolution in attitude and in audience was a natural enough expression of Australian society in the nineties. It needed no conscious renunciation for Lawson and his Australian contemporaries to write of the working-man, as it does for the modern "proletarian" writer whose subject-matter is determined by his political theory. But it did require a new technique. Middle-class fiction had largely relied on the sophistication and articulateness of its characters for its interest; and it had naturally developed a sophisticated and self-conscious method of presentation. If the Australian proletarian writer was to achieve an artistic correspondence between matter and method, he had to find simpler patterns of form to suit his home-spun material.

Furphy shirked that task—and only his intense vitality saves him from consequent disaster. The sense of restlessness, the over-ornate shape of his work, springs partly, one may guess, from a half-recognised contradiction. He accepted the contemporary assumption that fiction should be overtly intellectual— to a writer of the nineties the alternative would have seemed to be a relapse into the merely narrative aim of Scott and the early story-tellers; but his chosen material was not intellectual—or even articulate. So he tries to establish the height of his brow by the devices of digressive commentary, an allusive style, and the involutions of his plot. His misconceived methods were inspired, not by conceit, but by what probably seemed to him the necessity for intellectualism if he was to reach an intelligent audience—which did not, to his mind, imply a middle-class audience.

Lawson, less tempted because he was less a reader, found the necessary unity of matter and method. The completeness of that achievement is shown by the persistence with which his critics have ignored it. The conventional view of Lawson assumes that he triumphs by virtue of his warmth of heart and perceptiveness of eye, and in spite of his technical deficiencies. He is regarded, with affectionate patronage, as a grand backyard cricketer who sees the ball so well that he does not need a straight bat. The truth, I believe, is precisely the opposite; his style looks easy (non-existent to David McKee Wright [poetry editor for the Sydney *Bulletin* in 1917]), because it has the confident unobtrusiveness of a developed technique. We should not need the evidence of Bertha Lawson that he took great pains in the shaping of his work; to anyone with a feeling for craftsmanship it should be obvious—unless the conventionality of much of his verse leads us to ignore the originality of most of his prose.

For Lawson's prose form at its best is not only admirably conceived—it is his own invention. To a superficial view Lawson seems simply to have adopted the media which lay nearest at hand. If he was to reach his intended audience, the *Bulletin* was his only practicable vehicle. That fact edged Lawson towards the use of the bush-ballad and the short story. The former was ill-adapted to his finer powers. Lawson is fundamentally an observer, even when he is writing of himself; his specific talents are for precision, economy, the restraint which reveals emotion rather than the declamation which asserts it—and these are the talents of the prose-writer. Moreover the bush-ballad had developed too rigid a form to be easily adapted to new

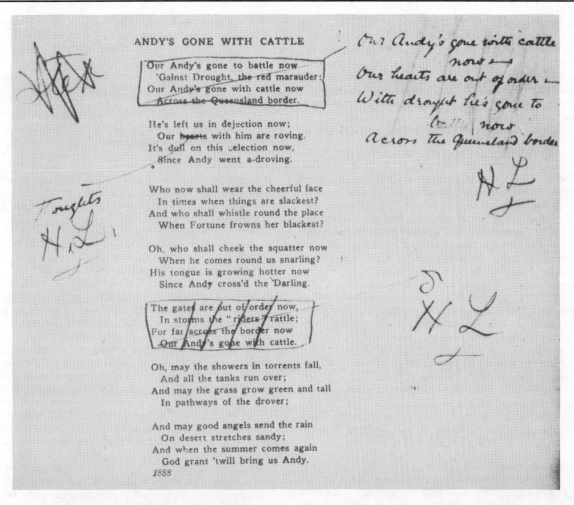

Lawson typescript with alterations imposed by his editor. From The Real Henry Lawson, *by Colin Roderick. Rigby Publishers, 1982.*

purposes. The conventional ruts of its rhythm had been worn deep, compelling the same trundling pace on all users. Lawson's verse is often interesting and effective, occasionally masterly; but its successes are the triumphs of his prose qualities over an ill-suited form. **"The Sliprails and the Spur"** is a superbly compressed short-story, aided, it is true, by some evocative use of rhythm. **"The Star Of Australasia"** lives rather by the clarity of its human pictures than by the prophetic chant which half a dozen of Lawson's contemporaries could have contrived as effectively.

In the short story Lawson is at home; but only because he has re-built it to suit himself. It is easy for us to underestimate his architectural achievements, because his designs have been adopted by later builders. In Lawson's time, the short story had not escaped from an essentially narrative purpose—as the novel had, thirty years earlier. That purpose did not suit Lawson who wanted, not to tell stories for their own sake, but to reveal the Australian way of living and the ethic informing it. Too heavy plotting would have distracted attention from the real matter he was expounding, would have dissipated the simplicity and naturalism which belonged to the way of life he was revealing. He had to learn how to be successfully 'slight,' to find just how little plot he could afford to use without risking the collapse of the structure. The bones of episode and development are always there in his more careful work—Lawson

does not serve up his slice of life filleted, in the flabby modern manner—but they are used only for their right anatomical purpose. It is a delicate problem of craftsmanship which Lawson had set himself—to find the minimum weight of frame-work which will hold the story erect—but he solves it at his best with a sure tact.

In **"That There Dog o' Mine,"** for example, the purpose of the story is to delineate the relationship between dog and man, as it reveals the spirit of the bushman. Its essential material is Macquarie's monologue; but the monologue, baldly presented, would lack shape. So Lawson contrives a fairly strong, but economically presented episode as his opening, further stiffening the frame-work by the not too obtrusive element of conflict over the dog's right to hospitality. He has now a firm enough structure to carry the monologue without over-shadowing it. The monologue having made its impact, the symmetry of the shape is completed by a resolution of the conflict. If it was sheer intuition which evolved that confident adequacy of the structure to the story's purpose—then heaven help the writer who hopes to succeed by conscious thought.

This is a typical sample of Lawson's general method, although he varies its application from story to story. The solidity of plot is increased in the comedies of incident, daringly diminished in such stories as **"Going Blind"** and **"Drifted Back,"** occasionally misjudged in a too slight sketch; but, save in the pieces of reportage and the obvious pot-boilers, there is usually a delicate balance between the danger of distraction of interest from the real content on the one hand and of collapse into shapelessness on the other. To his contemporaries, of course, accustomed to the narrative-centred story, Lawson's lightness of build seemed evidence of his technical imcompetence; a later generation, well aware of Chekov's similar method of solving the same problem, should show more discernment.

Further evidence of the deliberateness of Lawson's methods may be found in their growth and change. Certain stories in *On the Track, and Over the Sliprails* are at first puzzling. Such tales as **"The Hero of Redclay"** are longer and far more heavily plotted than the earlier sketches. It seems as if Lawson had lost his delicacy of touch. But when we read *Joe Wilson*, we realise what has been happening. Lawson has been searching for a more sustained form—every writer at times feels the need for a larger canvas; his fumblings have been the attempts to find a structural method for the roomier story. In *Joe Wilson* he has learnt how to adapt the old principle to the new scale. Plot is still kept slight enough to be undistracting—in **"The Hero of Redclay"** it had hopelessly obscured the purpose—but the episodes are stronger, more dramatically presented, to prevent a sagging of the more extended material. Observe, for instance, in **"Joe Wilson's Courtship"** how the incident of the fight is used to tighten the interest at the precise point where further easy reminiscent trivialities might become tiresome; or how the reflective philosophising of **"Brighten's Sister-in-Law"** is stiffened by drama at the corresponding stage. Yet Lawson's usual tact prevents us from reading with a concentration on the drama instead of on the evocation of the quality of married living which is the real purpose of the stories.

In using the first person in these stories, Lawson has set himself a particularly difficult problem—for his selector hero is not the sort of person who can be permitted to "talk like a book." How many later proletarian writers have been wrecked on this reef? Trying to set down the thoughts of their uneducated characters in an "unliterary" way, they have achieved only an irritating syntax and a brittle staccato. Lawson, with no model to help him, strikes the note accurately. The meditations are completely natural, never seeming too articulate for the character, and yet entirely revealing, and charged with emotional weight:

> You never saw a child in convulsions? Well, you don't want to. It must be only a matter of seconds, but it seems long minutes; and half an hour afterwards the child might be laughing and playing with you, or stretched out dead. It shook me up a lot. I was always pretty high-strung and sensitive. After Jim took the first fit, every time he cried, or turned over, or stretched out in the night, I'd jump: I was always feeling his forehead in the dark to see if he was feverish, or feeling his limbs to see if he was "limp" yet. Mary and I often laughed about it—afterwards. I tried sleeping in another room, but for nights after Jim's first attack I'd just be dozing off into a sound sleep when I'd hear him scream, as plain as could be, and I'd hear Mary cry, "Joe!—Joe!"—short, sharp, and terrible—and I'd be up and into their room like a shot, only to find them sleeping peacefully. Then I'd feel Jim's head and his breathing

> for signs of convulsions, see to the fire and water, and go back to bed and try to sleep. For the first few nights I was like that all night, and I'd feel relieved when daylight came. I'd be in first thing to see if they were all right; then I'd sleep till dinner-time if it was Sunday or I had no work. But then I was run down about that time: I was worried about some money for a wool-shed I put up and never got paid for; and besides, I'd been pretty wild before I met Mary.

If that is an achievement of "natural" writing, how comes it that, when he is speaking through the mouth of Joe Wilson, Lawson's style has a different pace and texture from his direct narratives?

At this point, when Lawson's power seemed to be reaching maturity, his development ceased. His touch henceforth became less sure, his vitality faded. It is difficult to estimate the influences which led to his early decline. Possibly he had exhausted his material—he was never an inventive writer and seems to have needed a pretty strong hint from fact before he could develop a story or a character. Perhaps beer and personal shipwreck weakened his confidence and his power to concentrate—and forced him to a proselytism which overcame his artistic perception. His own desperate need called him to preach his ethical faith, instead of letting it reveal itself as the spirit of the life he was presenting. To these probable influences, one other should be added which may have aided their disintegrating effect—the imperceptiveness of his academic critics. They hopelessly underestimated the conscientiousness and skill of his craftsmanship, either patronising what they took for an inspired naiveté or nagging him to adopt conventional methods. They did not convince him; but they may have shaken his faith in his own methods, and hardened in him a belief that methods do not matter so long as the spirit is humane and true. Writing would be an easier and less exciting craft if that were true.

It was natural enough for his contemporaries to underestimate Lawson's deliberated skill as a craftsman; his methods were too original to be quickly appreciated. The modern student, as he examines Lawson's writing, grows progressively more confident that he knew pretty accurately what he was doing—though it remains impossible to judge how explicitly he defined his methods to himself. His practice was too consistent, too closely allied to his artistic purpose, to be the product of happy accident or unguided intuition. A controlled intention is as clear in his handling of detail as in his general design.

Test him at the crucial points—the beginnings and endings of his stories. In finding how to open a story, Lawson once again had to abandon the established conventions of his time, which leaned towards a formal and self-conscious beginning—the studied elegance of the elocutionist's bow before he gets to his deadly work. Such a start would have jarred with the simplicity which was essential to Lawson's aim. Set him beside his contemporaries and the originality of his conception and the smoothness of its execution become almost startlingly apparent. Here is an F.A.Q. example of the openings used by Lawson's contemporaries:

> I never pass through Chalk Newton without turning to regard the neighbouring upland, at a point where a lane crosses the long straight highway dividing this from the next parish; a

sight which does not fail to recall the events which once happened there. . . .

Once upon a time, very far from England, there lived three men who loved each other so greatly that neither man nor woman could come between them. They were in no sense refined, nor to be admitted to the outdoor mats of decent folk, because they happened to be private soldiers in Her Majesty's Army; and private soldiers of our service have small time for self-culture.

Supper was over, and there had fallen upon the camp the silence that accompanies the rolling of cornhusk cigarettes. The water-hole shone from the dank earth like a patch of fallen sky.

Of all the problems which had been submitted to my friend, Mr. Sherlock Holmes, for solution during the years of our intimacy, there were only two which I was the means of introducing to his notice.

And here are the openings of the first three stories in *While the Billy Boils:*—

You remember when we hurried home from the old bush school how we were sometimes startled by a bearded apparition, who smiled quietly down on us, and whom our mothers introduced, as we raked off our hats, as "An old mate of your father's on the diggings, Johnny," And he would pat our heads and say we were fine boys or girls—as the case may have been—and that we had our father's nose but our mother's eyes or the other way about.

The Western train had just arrived at Redfern railway station with a lot of ordinary passengers and one swagman.

He was short, and stout, and bow-legged, and freckled and sandy. . . .

We were tramping down in Canterbury, Maoriland, at the time, swagging it—me and Bill—looking for work on the new railway line. Well, one afternoon, after a long, hot tramp, we came to Stiffner's Hotel—between Christ-church and the other place—I forget the name of it—with throats on us like sunstruck bones, and not the price of a stick of tobacco.

That easy natural slide into the story is, to modern ears at least, a great improvement on the stiff gesturing of Lawson's contemporaries. It may be supposed that it is simply the triumph of the naive writer over the self-conscious. Such a view shows little appreciation of the difficulties of simplicity. Again it is with the closely deliberated method of Chekov that Lawson shows the closest correspondence, as a random selection of the Russian writer's openings may suggest:

Ivan Alexeyitch Ognev remembers how on that August evening he opened the glass door with a rattle and went out on to the verandah. He was wearing. . . .

One day when she was younger and better-looking and when her voice was stronger, Ni-

kolay Petrovitch Kolpakov, her adorer, was sitting in the outer room in her summer villa.

The Superintendent said to me, "I only keep you out of regard for your worthy father; but for that you would have been sent flying long ago." I replied to him: "You flatter me too much your Excellency, in assuming that I am capable of flying."

The coincidence is certainly remarkable if we are to regard Lawson as "artless," as having merely fluked the method of his technically accomplished contemporary.

In his handling of the ending, there can be even less doubt of Lawson's purposeful craftsmanship. Again his aim raised for him difficult problems. The elegantly rounded off close would not have suited his simplicity of atmosphere. On the other hand, the snap finish, the last triumphant clap of the hammer on the nail driven home, would not do either. Lawson's aim, I have said, was not to tell a story but to evoke the quality of Australian living; and the evocative tale must end, not with a bang but an echo. The stone having plunged in the pool, the ripples must widen quietly out to vanish in mystery.

Lawson is a master of this final reverberation. His stories seldom end at the point which the merely narrative interest suggests. Thus **"Joe Wilson's Courtship"** has its obvious—and neat enough—winding-up.

"Why won't you kiss me Mary? Don't you love me?"

"Because," she said, "because—because—I—I don't—I don't think it's right for a girl—to kiss a man unless she's going to be his wife."

Then it dawned on me! I'd forgot all about proposing.

"Mary," I said, "would you marry a chap like me?"

And that was all right.

But Lawson does not end there; he goes on to the little dialogue with Black (Black, it will be remembered, was the squatter—Mary's guardian—who had "married an Englishwoman after the hardships were over, and she'd never got any Australian notions.")

Next morning Mary cleared out my room and sorted out my things, and didn't take the slightest notice of the other girls' astonishment.

But she made me promise to speak to old Black, and I did the same evening. I found him sitting on the log by the fence, having a yarn on the quiet with an old bushman; and when the old bushman got up and went away, I sat down.

"Well Joe," said Black, "I see somebody's been spoiling your face for the dance." And after a bit he said, "Well, Joe, what is it? Do you want another job? If you do, you'll have to ask Mrs. Black or Bob" (Bob was his eldest son); "they're managing the station for me now you know." He could be bitter sometimes in his quiet way.

"No," I said, "it's not that, boss."

''Well, what is it, Joe?''

''I—well, the fact is, I want little Mary.''

He puffed at his pipe for a long time, then I thought he spoke.

''What did you say, boss?'' I said.

''Nothing, Joe,'' he said. ''I was going to say a lot, but it wouldn't be any use. My father used to say a lot to me before I was married.''

I waited a good while for him to speak.

''Well, boss,'' I said, ''what about Mary?''

''Oh, I suppose that's all right, Joe,'' he said. ''I—I beg your pardon. I got thinking of the days when I was courting Mrs. Black.''

The tail-piece not merely avoids an over-abrupt and too conventional finish; it gives added depth to the whole story, suggesting the universality of the experience and the precariousness of human happiness.

Lawson uses this method often and with a loving care, too often and too carefully for it to be accident or intuition. Any student of the art of fiction could learn much of craftsmanship by looking for the point where he would have been tempted to end a Lawson story—and observing how, with a further touch, Lawson prolongs the over-tones. Let him beware of imitation, though; for unless the echo contains the inimitable touch of humane wisdom, the mechanical device will not become the mode of an artist.

Often Lawson's final echo is ironic in tone; and in his use of irony he shows again a delicate sense of design. His work was openly and unashamedly sentimental. Without its sentiment, indeed, it could have expressed neither his own sense of values nor the quality of bush life. But Lawson is determined that he shall not degenerate into sentimentality—which would have suited neither the manliness of his tone nor the honesty of his art. At least until the period of his decline begins, he walks this tight-rope with a confident balance—what other sentimental writer of the nineteenth century escapes mawkishness so consistently as he?

That is mainly due to the steadiness of his vision; but it is aided by two consciously used devices—effective understatement, and the ironic twist at the danger-points. The first adds weight to the feeling, as well as a saving moderation. To have said, for instance, that the bushmen ''kept the memory of Doc. Wilde evergreen in their hearts'' would have been weak as well as cloying. To say ''They buried him with bush honours and chiseled his name on a slab of blue-gum—a wood that lasts'' suggests the strong tug of under-currents. The ability to use understatement effectively, be it noted, is seldom the possession of the naive. (pp. 80-7)

Finally, let me pose to the exponents of the ''artless'' assumption, one question of—I hope—a devastating simplicity. Here is the last sentence of **The Drover's Wife**:

And she hugs him to her worn-out breast and kisses him, and they sit thus together while the sickly daylight breaks over the bush.

Was there ever a naive writer who could have resisted the temptation to put an epithet before that last word—at least in Australia, where flux of adjectives has been an endemic literary disease?

I have not completed the tally of Lawson's technical equipment—that has not been my aim. On the evidence presented, the defence can, I believe, confidently rest. It remains only to wonder whether the case was worth stating. To stretch Lawson's stories on the dissecting-table of analytic criticism is a gruesome process. Perhaps he was more fittingly praised by those critics who, loving him, denied his mere skill. The painter may be satisfied with the cunning of his brush-work when the beholder sees only the picture, and forgets the paint.

And yet perhaps the false estimate needs to be denied, lest it be used to deduce a fallacy—the sentimental fallacy that in art, ardour is everything and arduousness beside the point. What Lawson said, thousands of his contemporaries knew and felt to be the truth. His mates had as intimate a knowledge of the country and the people, they shared his humane warmth, his recognition—half angry, half proud—of the harsh environment, his sense of the importance of the individual, his feeling for the mystery of life. Lawson's highest value is that he could set down fairly what every bushman back o'Bourke knew to be the truth. He is distinguished from them by two qualities only—the artist's sharper sensitiveness, and the power to write. That power is only in part a magic gift for the right word, the right shaping to hold the fluid thought; it is also the inspired determination not to rest until the word, the shaping, have been achieved. (pp. 89-90)

*Arthur A. Phillips, ''Henry Lawson as Craftsman,''
in* Meanjin, *Vol. 7, No. 2, Winter, 1948, pp. 80-90.*

T. INGLIS MOORE   (essay date 1957)

[*Moore is an Australian poet, novelist, dramatist, and critic. In the following excerpt he examines the achievement of Lawson's early work and the decline of his later fiction.*]

An English friend of mine used to classify people as belonging to one of four abbreviated categories. People, he said, were either TS, NQQ, AGC, or SAS. There were the exceptional few who were TS—Top Shelf. Then a larger number who were good also, but Not Quite Quite. The great mass of persons could be characterized simply as AGC—Also God's Creatures. Lastly, there was the small band of objectionables of whom one could only say SAS—Shoot at Sight!

These broad categories define Henry Lawson's short stories with remarkable aptness. A few—say a baker's dozen—of the stories are undoubtedly TS, standing firmly on the Top Shelf. These would include, to name a few examples, such stories as **The Drover's Wife,'' ''The Union Buries Its Dead,'' ''Joe Wilson's Courtship,'' ''The Loaded Dog,'' ''Brighten's Sister-in-law,''** and **A Double Buggy at Lahey's Creek.''**

Then come a considerable number of NQQs, stories that are good but just miss the first grade because of a slight defect or two, such as **Settling on the Land,'' ''A Geological Spieler,''** and **Mitchell on Matrimony.''** A good example of this Not Quite Quite story is **Telling Mrs. Baker,''** a small gem of combined irony and pathos spoilt only by a false sentimental touch near the end. There are, of course, many stories of simple average quality, and then an unfortunate collection of tales which are repetitious, obvious, thin, artificial, sentimental, and even maudlin. A few of the inferior stories occur early in Lawson's career, but most of them come after the period of his maturity in 1901. Examining the stories as a whole, we find different stages of Lawson's development as an artist, and a clear rise and fall in his artistry in this field. I wish to trace briefly the stages of this development and decline, and indicate at the same time the special qualities—good and bad—which characterize each stage. (p. 365)

I should say that the line rises sharply in the very first tentative volume, the *Short Stories In Prose and Verse* of 1894, since, despite many weaknesses, it contains some of Lawson's best stories. The line rises again in average quality to the large collection of *While the Billy Boils,* 1896, which has a very good general standard, together with a wide variety of theme and mood and type of story. There the line falls to the two inferior collections of *On the Track, and Over the Sliprails* of 1900, which contain only one outstanding sketch—**"They Wait on the Wharf in Black."** Then in 1901 comes the volume showing Lawson at his maturity, *Joe Wilson and His Mates,* and the line rises to its peak. If not as varied as *While the Billy Boils,* this book has a higher standard throughout. Then comes the fall, beginning with *Children of the Bush,* 1902, a serious decline that continues sharply with the two later volumes, *The Rising of the Court,* 1910, and *Triangles of Life,* 1913, except that the last book shows a slight rise from its predecessor. Lawson's fruitful period as a short story writer, then was mainly limited to about a decade, from 1891 to 1901. It is represented best by two volumes, *While the Billy Boils* and *Joe Wilson and His Mates.*

Let us look more closely now at the evolution of Lawson in handling the short story. In his earlier tales there are, I think, three influences at work which helped to shape the mood and treatment of his themes. These were Dickens, Bret Harte, and the *Bulletin.* All encouraged him to exploit sentiment, especially pathos. But I suspect that Lawson may also have picked up from Harte the effective device of staving off sentimentality by an adroit touch of saving humour. Lawson developed this device later till it became characteristic and in his maturity he used it with a delicate subtlety far beyond the power of Bret Harte. That is one reason why the American writer now seems dated and sentimental, and Lawson emerges as the superiior artist. It was probably from Bret Harte, moreover, that he learned to substitute for the orotund, rather elaborate ending then customary in the literary short story a sharp dramatic finish, often with a dash of dialogue and a final terse sentence. Take, for instance, the ending of Bret Harte's tale "A Monte Flat Pastoral" where the old man, who for years had talked of going hime to his family, when confronted at last with his wife and daughter brought to him by the miners of Monte Flat, angrily protested: "Let me go: d'ye hear? Keep them women off me! Let me go! I'm going—I'm going home!"

> His hands were thrown up convulsively in the air, and, half turning round, he fell sideways on the porch, and so to the ground. They picked him up hurriedly; but too late. He had gone home.

Now turn to the ending of **"His Father's Mate,"** Lawson's first story published in the *Bulletin* in 1888. After the death of the child Isley, Bob Sawkins brought to the hut of Mason the father, a stranger, his other long-lost son.

> For a moment the stranger paused irresolute, and then stepping up to the table he laid his hand on Mason's arm, and said gently: "Father! Do you want another mate?"

> But the sleeper did not—at least, not in this world.

Lawson's story **"When the Sun Went Down"** ends with the same type of terse sentence as "A Monte Flat Pastoral," with its "He had gone home" paralleled by Lawson's "And the sun went down." So, too, the ending of Harte's story "Miggles" sounds almost pure Lawson. There is strong internal evidence that Lawson learned this part of his technique from Harte, although later, of course, he developed it from one of dramatic but rather obvious effect to a subtler one of suggestive evocation.

Another early influence on Lawson, the *Bulletin,* then the most important local market for short stories, laid down special demands for its stories—and its contributors had to meet them. Its first demand was brevity. It told one contributor in its columns, "Be terse. Boil it down," and another, "The *Bulletin* is only a little paper and not one to maunder in. We wouldn't allow three and a half columns to William Shakespeare." This demand was good for Lawson in that it encouraged him to develop a fine economy in his style. It was thanks to Archibald that Lawson learned to pack a lot in a little space. The demand for brevity, however, had also a narrowing influence, since it gave little room for any development of depth in character or significance. It tended to produce sketches and fragments rather than well constructed stories. Thus Lawson later rebelled at its limitations when he originated the longer, more leisurely, and richer stories of the Joe Wilson cycle. He could to this because *Blackwood's Magazine,* in which he published some of them, gave him room to elaborate his tales—room denied him by the *Bulletin.*

The *Bulletin,* again, demanded other qualities which are well described by A. G. Stephens when he wrote of the stories in the *Bulletin Story-Book* of 1901 in his Introduction: "Usually they are objective, episodic, detached—branches torn from the Tree of Life . . . many are absolute transcripts of the Fact, copied as faithfully as the resources of language will permit." From following this genre Lawson gained objectivity, the truth of realism, and an honest fidelity to fact. But this genre also encouraged the *Bulletin* writers to be content with reportage, to be episodic, slight, and scrappy. These weaknesses remained with Lawson in many of his stories.

But his original talent rose in the best stories, even in his very first volume, above the *Bulletin* limitations, so that he stands far above the other short story writers of his period. Of these only three writers—and two of them stood outside the *Bulletin*—have real distinction: Barbara Baynton (who comes next to him in power), Dowell O'Reilly, and Ted Dyson. Lawson transcended the *Bulletin* form because he brought to his reportage other elements. The realism was illuminated with imagination, the objectivity was combined with depth of sympathy, the sentiment was salted with humour, and the casual episode or sketch was given a wider significance. Above all, he displayed the gift of focussing a scene or character so that it became universal. He went beyond the bushmen or bush women to humanity. As the French critic Professor Emile Saillens put it well: "there is in his work abundant evidence of the spirit that makes the classics, a genuine comprehension of what is deeply and eternally human." And we find all these original elements in Lawson given richly in such outstanding stories in his very first volume as **"The Drover's Wife"** and **"The Union Buries Its Dead."** The pictures given here are unforgettable. The same creative force, if of less intensity, is felt in his two vivid representations of the strength of mateship in **"The Bush Undertaker"** and **"Macquarie's Mate."**

In *While the Billy Boils* Lawson gives us a rich plentitude. Apart from the stories reprinted from *Short Stories in Prose and Verse,* he ranges from the genuine pathos of "A Visit of Condolence" and "Jones's Alley" to the harsh irony of "Settling on the Land" and the humour of the Mitchell and Steelman tales. Here are character sketches, descriptive vignettes, contructed tales of sentiment or farce, and dramatic stories of emotion. The comments of that bush philosopher, Mitchell, are superb in their kind.

There are weaknesses in this collection. A number of the stories are too slight and fragmentary; others fall into sentimentality. On the whole, however, the collection is notable for its good level of quality and the way in which Lawson obtains a wealth of feeling and characterization from a narrow field of subject matter.

One of the best examples of Lawson's uncompromising, incisive realism, for example, is the bush sketch "The Union Buries Its Dead," which contains the ironic, hardy wryness of the men on the land who had reached a fatalistic indifference after they had battled for years against drought and flood, rabbits and pests and bushfires. Its spirit reminds me of a passage in D. H. Lawrence's *Kangaroo* where Lawrence uses Somers to express his own idea of Australia and Australians:

> . . . this speechless, aimless solitariness was in the air. It was natural to the country. The People left you alone, They didn't follow you with their curiosity and their inquisitiveness and their human fellowship. You passed, and they forgot you. You came again, and they hardly saw you. You spoke, and they were friendly. But they never asked any questions, and they never encroached. They didn't care. The profound Australian indifference, which still is not really apathy . . . the basic indifference under everything.

It is this particular aspect of the Australian character described by Lawrence that seems to me the essence of the sketch, whilst the concept of Union loyalty also expressed is only secondary. It is, for instance, weaker than a bush thirst:

> The departed was a "Roman," and the majority of the town were otherwise—but Unionism is stronger than creed. Liquor, however, is stronger than Unionism; and when the hearse presently arrived, more than two-thirds of the funeral were unable to follow.

The "basic indifference" of Lawson is cynical in his picture of the funeral:

> The procession numbered fifteen, fourteen souls following the broken shell of a soul. Perhaps not one of the fourteen possessed a soul any more than the corpse did—but that doesn't matter.

> Four or five of the funeral, who were boarders at the pub, borrowed a trap which the landlord used to carry passengers to and from the railway station. They were strangers to us who were on foot, and we to them. We were all strangers to the corpse.

Later, it turns out that the name on the coffin plate wasn't the real name of the dead man—only "the name he went by." So Lawson concludes:

> We did hear later on, what his real name was; but if we ever chance to read it in the "Missing Friends column," we shall not be able to give any information to heart-broken mother or sister or wife, nor to anyone who could let him hear something to his advantage—for we have already forgotten the name.

As Lawrence put it, "You passed, and they forgot you." Elsewhere in *Kangaroo* Lawrence spoke not only of the Australians' indifference but also of their "sardonic tolerance." "The Union Buries Its Dead" might also be termed a pungent essay in "sardonic tolerance."

In contrast, showing the rich variety of Lawson's writing in the *While the Billy Boils* series, "The Drover's Wife" has a deep sympathy behind the simple, direct picture of the courage shown by a woman of the bush in facing loneliness, hardships, and danger. Lawson brings out the pathos of the drover's wife dressing herself up to go for a walk with the children in the bush on Sunday afternoon, and he stresses the bush's monotony. But this is not allowed to give the story the unrelenting harshness we get in Barbara Baynton's "Scrammy 'And" and "Squeaker's Mate," since he also gives two touches of humour, one cynical and one tender, in the story of the blackfellow who built the woodheap hollow and the drover's wife putting her thumb and finger through the holes of her handkerchief. These touches provide chiaroscuro for the general picture. Thus Lawson's delicately balanced combination of sympathy and humour makes "The Drover's Wife" a moving, memorable, and authentic sketch.

It is significant of the breadth of his range that it is followed in *While the Billy Boils* by a very different story with a different type of humour in "Steelman's Pupil." Here we have the humour of the clever trickster, a type common to frontier literatures. It is frequent in Mark Twain, for instance, in his American frontier tales, and O. Henry used it neatly with his stories of Jeff Peters, bagman and spieler. In our own literature the two best exponents of the trickster humour are Paterson, who depended largely on it in his comic ballads, and Lawson in his Steelman stories. Like O. Henry, Lawson is particularly effective because he does not depend on the force of the trick alone but gives it an extension of richness through characterization. Steelman, like Jeff Peters, is a character developed in the round, who has various aspects to his personality beside the adroitness with which he lives by his wits. Here Lawson's "How Steelman Told His Story" is paralleled by O. Henry's story "Cupid à la Carte." Steelman's partner Smith is another individual, although less developed. In the story "Steelman's Pupil," however, he turns the tables on his master. Here it is the trickster who is tricked in the end. The same thing happens in the best of the Steelman stories, "The Geological Spieler," and in another excellent humourous story "The Man Who Forgot." (pp. 366-70)

While the Billy Boils is a wide-ranging collection in which Lawson, as Edward Garnett put it, "represents a continent" [see excerpt dated 1902]. It also represents the kaleidoscope of Lawson's art as a short story writer.

Lawson's high level falls perceptibly, however, in the next two collections of stories which were combined in one volume, *On the Track, and Over the Sliprails.* this seems a scraped-up collection, an impression deepened by the inclusion of early stories from the 1894 book which Lawson evidently did not consider worth reprinting in *While the Billy Boils,* such as the inferior

"Bush Cats" and "The Mystery of Dave Regan." There are only a bare half dozen stories or sketches of distinction, like "They Wait on the Wharf in Black," "Middleton's Peter," "Mitchell on Matrimony"—an excellent ironic sketch—and the effective tale of "A Gentleman Sharper and Steelman Sharper." There are few bad stories, but too many are undistinguished.

This volume is a transitional one, a breathing space between *While the Billy Boils* and *Joe Wilson and His Mates*. It is also a tentative groping towards the latter, since in "The Hero of Redclay," "The Selector's Daughter," and the Oracle stories Lawson is obviously experimenting with a longer, more firmly articulated story with a developed plot. This point has been well seized upon by Mr. A. A. Phillips in his article "Henry Lawson as Craftsman" [see excerpt dated 1948], the best critical analysis of Lawson as a short story writer. Unfortunately, Lawson's tales in this new form are unsuccessful apprentice efforts, giving the impression of artificial contrivance rather than genuine construction. Indeed, it is remarkable at this stage how Lawson's fumbling for the longer, more leisurely, and more strongly articulated story was followed immediately by his success in the mature first-class tales of *Joe Wilson and His Mates*. These, it is true, have not the freshness, incisiveness, and sharp, vivid impact of the outstanding stories in *While the Billy Boils*, but they are richer in texture and firmer in construction. They strike deeper. "Joe Wilson's Courtship" is a deeply satisfying story in which characters, setting, action, and emotion are beautifully blended. Lawson is particularly skilful here—as throughout the four long stories of the Joe Wilson cycle—in rendering sentiment naturally, with a universal connotation, whilst escaping sentimentality. Take, for instance, the exquisite ending to "A Double Buggy at Lahey's Creek," a moving story that all married couples should appreciate, perhaps the finest story in this collection. Here Joe Wilson, the selector, has finally bought the double buggy for Mary, his wife, which would free her from the loneliness of the isolated selection. He tells of its reception.

> When we were alone Mary climbed into the buggy to try the seat, and made me get up alongside her. We hadn't had such a comfortable seat for years; but we soon got down, in case anyone came by, for we began to feel like a pair of fools up there.

> Then we sat, side by side, on the edge of the veranda and talked more than we'd done for years—and there was a good deal of "Do you remember?" in it—and I think we got to understand each other better that night.

> And at last Mary said, "Do you know, Joe, why, I feel tonight just—just like I did the day we were married?"

> And somehow I had that strange, shy sort of feeling too.

When Lawson feels that there is a danger of too much sentiment he throws in a touch of humour. At his best he walks the tightrope of sentiment with masterly ease, using humour as his balancing rod.

In the story "Telling Mrs. Baker" the irony is maintained skilfully throughout as Andy and Jack, the two drovers who had seen their boss Bob Baker die of the D.Ts., lie manfully to Mrs. Baker in order to save her feelings and protect the

name of a dead mate. The contrast between the truth we know and the lies spun by Andy and Jack is developed adroitly in point after point as the two drovers stare for relief at Mrs. Baker's picture of Wellington meeting Blucher on the field at Waterloo. Then in "The Loaded Dog" we have an uproarious masterpiece in pure farce.

It is the depth of feeling and understanding, however, the simple warm humanity, of Lawson's stories here that makes them so memorable. In these particular qualities Lawson is superior, for example, to Maupassant, who, except for a few stories like "Boule de Suif" and "La Maison Tellier," has a hard, objective brilliance rarely touched by pity or tenderness. On the other hand, we feel a natural affinity between Lawson and the Russian storytellers—Chekhov, Turgenev, and most of all, Gorki. With Lawson as with them the short story is used, not for the narrative itself, but as a means of presenting life. The London *Academy* discerned this aim of Lawson's when it compared him with Bret Harte:

> Both are concerned with rough and ready pioneers and struggle-for-lifers; but the Californian writer thinks of the story before everything else, the Australian, of the human document.

Lawson, indeed, had his own original aim of rendering "the human document," and to carry out his aim he developed an original form of treatment and an original style—a style which seems deceptively simple and natural, casual, and even artless, but which has been deliberately shaped by an artist as the best medium for treating his particular themes for his own special purpose. It is a flexible instrument that succeeds in achieving its effect without the reader becoming conscious of the technical artistry. Its surface simplicity masks the complexity that can compass sympathy or sentiment, delicate tenderness or harsh cynicism, farce or dry irony. Above all, its economy and understatement can be richly evocative. Its leanness is imaginative, charged with undertones and suggestiveness. It can sum up a character in one laconic sentence, as when Andy the drover is described: "Andy was a chap who could keep his word—and nothing else."

The style's evocation is of emotion, however, rather than of the stirrings of the spirit. It is perhaps a national as well as a personal characteristic that it realizes humanity, but not infinity. It has not the sense of spiritual issues and the concept of cosmic space as background that we find in Gorki. In the last resort, therefore, Lawson never quite achieves the greatness of the Russian masters. His vision is luminous, but limited. Perhaps the creed of mateship, however sincerely felt and convincingly expressed, was no adequate substitute for a full metaphysics or religion. Perhaps the realism is too earthy, too matter-of-fact. (pp. 371-73)

Turning from the best of Lawson in *Joe Wilson and His Mates* to the later collections, we find a lamentable fall in his art. *Children of the Bush*, later reprinted in two volumes as *Send Around the Hat* and *The Romance of the Swag*, contains, I feel, only one story of real quality, "Send Around the Hat." This leans to the sentimental but has the excellent character sketch of "The Giraffe," that lovable long-legged shearer and incorrigible samaritan. Lawson balances sentiment here with his characteristic dry humour. Unhappily this does not occur often enough in the *Children of the Bush* stories. Most of them suffer from sentimentality, Lawson's main weakness in his period of decline. When he attempts to construct a story of plot as in "Buckolt's Gate" the result is weak and unconvincing. The tales of Peter McLaughlan, the bush missionary, are good up to a point, but they lack the surety of the earlier Mitchell sketches. More and more Lawson falls back on a rather crude exploitation of pathos and turns lachrymose. The fondness for boozers and derelicts and failures grows maudlin. The booze, in fact, seems to have dragged Henry down in art as in life. (p. 374)

The Rising of the Court, a handsel of only eight stories, continues the decline. There is some vigour but too much sentimentalism in "**Roll Up at Talbragar**" and "**Wanted by the Police.**" The humour has grown painfully thin in "**The Hypnotised Township,**" as a comparison with such excellent stories of humour as "**The Loaded Dog**" and "**The Geological Spieler**" soon shows. The essay on "**Mateship in Shakespeare's Rome**" presents a fresh and original argument, but it shows the didactic weakness again. As an expression of mateship, for instance, compare the sermonizing of this essay and the one on "**Mateship,**" published later in *Triangles of Life,* with the earlier dramatic narratives such as "**The Bush Undertaker,**" "**Macquarie's Mate**" and "**That There Dog of Mine**" which appeared in *While the Billy Boils.* Where the later stories preach, the earlier ones show mateship in action—a much more artistic form of expression.

The last published collection, *Triangles of Life,* is a poor one redeemed by flashes of the true Lawson. "**A Child in the Dark, and a Foreign Father**" is a moving sketch in which the writer goes back to his own childhood days for his theme. It is significant, however, that this is an early story published in the *Bulletin* in 1902. "**Drifting Apart**" and "**James and Maggie,**" two stories which continue the Joe Wilson saga, show flickers of the old artistry. These were probably written in an earlier period. Other tales are sketchy. The story "**Triangles of Life**" is another attempt at the long constructed story of plot, with the setting partly in England, partly in Australia. It is readable but little else, since it lacks force and intimacy. It remains superficial, like the "**Letters to John Cornstalk,**" which hardly rise above average journalism. Lawson's hand has lost its old skill. (p. 375)

[Lawson's] decline was due, it seems, to two main factors: the kind of life Lawson led after his return from the disastrous visit to London; and the fact that he had used up his stock of material. On his return to Sydney he succumbed to the drink habit, separated from his wife, and drifted aimlessly without regular employment or purpose except for the brief interlude at Leeton. It is worth noting that, in comparison, his best work, *Joe Wilson and His Mates,* was written when he lived in New Zealand, near Kaikoura in 1897 and 1898. Here he enjoyed peace and quiet, away from the pubs and his boon companions, with leisure to concentrate on his stories, since his wife carried out most of the work in the Maori school to which he had been appointed teacher.

Again, Lawson drew the material for his best work from his memories of his boyhood in the bush, supplemented by the trip, provided by Archibald, which he made in 1892 out to Bourke and from there to Hungerford. By about 1901 he had largely exhausted this material. The gold had been worked out, and in later years he depended on mere "tailings." His Sydney experiences were severely limited by his mode of living, and he never found in themes of the city the inspiration which he had discovered in the bush. Unfortunately he never sought new material by going to the bush again, when he might possibly have recovered the freshness and intimacy of his early work.

He became as rootless in his writing as in his living. It is no wonder that his art deteriorated in the way it did.

Although Lawson was extremely unequal in his stories, it is the best of a writer that counts, after all, and at his best he was an artist of both power and subtlety, a master of his medium. A. G. Stephens writing of the short story once said: "Every story of a man or woman should be a microcosm of humanity; every vision of nature should hold an imagination of the Universe." Henry Lawson did not attain to "an imagination of the Universe," but he had the rare vision that made his stories of the men and women of the bush a true "microcosm of humanity." (p. 376)

T. Inglis Moore, "The Rise and Fall of Henry Lawson," in Meanjin, *Vol. XVI, No. 4, December, 1957, pp. 365-76.*

H. M. GREEN (essay date 1961)

[*In the following excerpt from an essay originally published in his* A History of Australian Literature: Pure and Applied, 1789-1923, *Green discusses Lawson as a poet, assessing his verse as inferior to his fiction and evaluating Lawson as essentially a talented lyricist who occasionally rose to the level of a true poet.*]

Lawson was preacher and prophet as well as balladist, and it is this that was responsible for the idea, once held very widely, that he was a poet, even the national poet of Australia; it was rationalized by his old friend Professor Brereton. After admitting what as a cultivated writer himself and a Professor of English Literature he would have been the last person to deny, the superiority of Lawson's prose to his verse, Brereton went on:

> Other Australian authors have more often and more completely succeeded in capturing the essentials of poetry than he. But the instinct of the people is not at fault . . . at the present stage in our history "the poet Lawson" may well stand alone as the typical figure of Australian literature. . . . By him are made articulate not so much the thoughts of Australia as her feelings . . . here and now he is for us the national poet.

It is easy to understand how those for whom Lawson was preacher and prophet, particularly if poetry was not much in their line, might confuse a sympathetic with an aesthetic appeal; and it is easy to understand how his old friend Brereton might sympathize with them emotionally though not intellectually, and make the most of their case; but representative capacity, even where it is combined with deep and sincere emotion and a talent for simple and ringing verse, are not enough to make a poet. Fundamentally, Lawson lacked as a writer of verse imaginative penetration which is capable of bringing life to the glowing focus that is poetry: there is a glow in "**In the Days When the World Was Wide,**" but it is a diffused and windy glow; and in pieces like "**Faces in the Street**" the excitement that is aroused in the sympathetic reader is not primarily a poetic excitement. In a few odd verses, as for example in a fine image from "**Scots of the Riverina,**"

The old man ploughed at daybreak and the old man ploughed till the mirk—
There were furrows of pain in the orchard while his household went to the kirk;

perhaps in part of **"The Roaring Days,"** by reason of its breadth and clarity of view rather than of its tinkling music, and certainly in the image with which the poem ends,

> The mighty Bush with iron rails
> Is tethered to the world:

in these and in a few other instances Lawson has written poetry, but it is absurd to speak of him as "the poet Lawson." There was in him a primary impulse towards story-telling that made him in verse essentially a balladist, though he was also sometimes a little more than that; it is significant that the title of his first book was *Short Stories in Prose and Verse*. He turned readily, at first anyhow, to either form, and, as will be seen later, he sometimes used the same theme in both; but the full expression of his talent far overflowed the capacity of verse, at least of the quality that he could command. Yet prose by itself would not have been enough either: Lawson's intense indignation at human wrongs and hardships and his intense ideal enthusiasm found their most natural expression in rhetoric of a kind that called inevitably for verse. With the reservation that the feeling, the atmosphere, the movement of the ballad animate almost all his verses, so that in a sense they may all be called ballads, they fall roughly into two main groups: ballads and ballad-like poems, and poems of revolt. It was the second group that brought Lawson his most enthusiastic followers; they include all those verses in which he expresses a merely weary or an active and sometimes explosive indignation of man's inhumanity to man; in them it is the humanitarian who is uppermost, the ultra-democrat, the reformer, the revolutionary, the Lawson who suffered as Arvie Aspinall in Grinder Brothers' factory, who sympathized and worked with Lane of Paraguay, and went almost mad when he was told that troops might be used against the strikers. Overworked and bullied, a lonely country boy in Sydney, leaning out of the window of his room after the day's work was done, he watched the monotonous drift of the **"Faces in the Street"**; he heard the monotonous tramp of **"The Army of the Rear"**; his own sensitiveness and the melancholy streak in him deepened the colours of what he had himself seen and experienced, so that they blended with what he had read in Dickens of life in the London slums a couple of generations earlier. He wrote, too, in revulsion against such foolish "patriotic" assertions as that

> . . . want is here a stranger, and that misery's unknown,

and if in his generous indignation he exaggerated the Australian facts, he became the more widely representative; but his ultra-democratic attitude was more emotional than intellectual and could not be confined within the limits of any political creed. In the most characteristic of the poems of revolt he looks with regret to the great days of the past or with prophetic fire to some imagined future, discovering in each a freer, brighter, more heroic world. But he pays far less attention to the

> . . . dull, brown days of a shilling-an-hour

than to the glorious age when

> . . . the North was hale in the march of Time, and the
> South and West were new,

turning almost at once to what he regards as the age of honour and faith and courage, to the great explorers by sea and land, to

> The good ship bound for the Southern seas when the
> beacon was Ballarat,
> Wtih a "Ship ahoy" on the freshening breeze, "Where
> bound?" and "What ship's that?"—
> The emigrant train to New Mexico—the rush to the
> Lachlan side—

to Westward Ho and the Eureka Stockade; and he ends with a call like a trumpet, though the trumpet is of brass, not gold:

> The march of Freedom is North by the Dawn! Follow,
> whate'er betide!
> Sons of the Exiles, march! March on! March till the
> world grows wide!

With this rousing appeal to all who hope for the future may be grouped **"The Star of Australasia"** and the other fragments in which Lawson looked forward to the brightening and unifying effect of a great defensive war fought for a high ideal, as in the early days of the first World War that was to come, before the appearance of the doubt and disillusionment that emerged later. In such poems as **"Faces in the Street"** on the other hand, and **"My Army, O, My Army"** the primary motive is indignation at the wrongs of the poor; it is these that occupy the greater part of the poem, and only at the end that revolution brings redress. Sometimes the revolt is against not social ills but individual misfortunes, even though, as in **"When Your Pants Begin to Go,"** the misfortunes may be connected with the structure of society; and there are such up-country parallels as **"Out Back,"** with its ringing refrain:

> For time means tucker, and tramp you must, where the
> scrubs and plains are wide
> With seldom a track that a man can trust, or a mountain
> peak to guide;
> All day long in the dust and heat—when summer is on
> the track—
> With stinted stomachs and blistered feet, they carry
> their swags Out Back.

Still, the last two of these are primarily ballads, because after all they are stories, occupied mainly with action. This is true also of **"Peter Anderson and Co."** and **"The Cambaroora Star,"** in spite of their atmosphere of revolt. But about Lawson's verse in general there is an air if not of revolt at least of dissatisfaction with life, so that the two groups merge without sharp margins; in this matter the contrast between the tone of Lawson's and of Paterson's ballads is most marked. Where Paterson accepts and ignores, Lawson accentuates and regrets; where Paterson gives the effect of a life that is bright and bubbling over, with Lawson as a maker of verse it is a life that is either tragic or at least clouded and repressed by pain. As a maker of verse, though not as a story-writer, it may be said that when Lawson looked at life itself it saddened him; it was only in rhapsodizing about some golden past or future that he was able to break free into a bright enthusiasm. His ballads reflect the countryside as strongly as Paterson's, but it is a different countryside: instead of the horseman racing down a mountainside or jogging after cattle over the western plains, there is the heavy swag and the dusty bush track, the bush shanty, the rougher side of droving, the poor selection and the lonely shearer's wife. To Paterson life was a game, played mainly on horseback, though he did not ignore its falls and hard knocks; to Lawson life was a battle: his concern was with those who fought on foot, and the echoes of that battle ring throughout his verse. Yet in Lawson's ballads, and indeed in all his verses "the energy of the rhythm defies the gloom that it describes": his verses are as vigorous as Paterson's, though the motive that inspires them is quite different: with Lawson that motive is human sympathy; with Paterson it is love of the land and of those who live by and upon it, types that represent it and that it has helped to produce. And whereas Paterson, as befits the balladist pure and simple, concerns himself mainly with action, Lawson, even in his ballads, devotes a good deal of his energy to moralization, which is often rhetorical; their gloomy note, though dominant, is relieved however by glimpses of sardonic humour and by a wide sympathy and fine enthusiasm. Lawson's range is wider than Paterson's, and he can handle a tragic theme as Paterson cannot, though he runs sometimes into sentimentality and melodrama. He took verse-making as he took everything else, more seriously than Paterson, and is never so clumsy as Paterson at his worst, though some of his verses are crude enough and they are full of journalistic clichés; the occasional touches of rhythmic and pictorial magic with which Paterson opens small windows on the Australian countryside are far rarer with Lawson, but he has a deeper insight into human motive and a deeper sympathy with human misfortune. And Lawson's literary antecedents were only less different from Paterson's than his experience of life. He too, of course, owed something to the stimulus of the modern ballad revival, and he may have read something of the old folk-ballads; but the Old Bush Songs had little if any influence upon him: as a boy he had heard many of them sung, along with other old songs, but they do not seem to have stood out in his mind. There is no reflection of Kipling in any of his verses, except perhaps in the rhetorical swing of some of his poems of revolt. There are occasional traces of Bret Harte, who did not influence Paterson at all; and Gordon might never have existed for Lawson, in spite of his own streak of temperamental melancholy. The influence of Dickens, of which also there is no trace in Paterson, is as strongly marked in Lawson's verse as in his prose. The best of Lawson's ballads are full of swift action and spirited enough: **"Jack Dunn of Nevertire"** for instance, and **"Talbragar,"** with its rousing refrain, though both, like almost all the best of Lawson's ballads, end in tragedy. And once in a way there is the devil-may-care spirit that is characteristic of Australian ballads in general and in particular of those of Paterson and Morant: the best example of this is **"Taking His Chance,"** which begins,

> They stood by the door of the Inn on the Rise;
> May Carney looked up in the bushranger's eyes:
> "Oh! why did you come?—it was mad of you, Jack;
> You know that the troopers are out on your track."
> A laugh and a shake of his obstinate head—
> "I wanted a dance, and I'll chance it," he said.

"The Sliprails and the Spur" is filled with the tragedy of character, in which

> . . . he rides hard to dull the pain
>   Who rides from one that loves him best . . .
> And he rides slowly back again,
>   Whose restless heart must rove for rest.

Only a couple of Lawson's best ballads, **"Andy's Return"** and **"The Lights of Cobb and Co."** are light-hearted throughout:

> Fire lighted; on the table a meal for sleepy men;
> A lantern in the stable; a jingle now and then;
> The mail-coach looming darkly by light of moon and
>   star;
> The growl of sleepy voices; a candle in the bar;

> .   .   .   .   .

> Past haunted half-way houses—where convicts made the
>   bricks—
> Scrub-yards and new bark shanties, we dash with five
>   and six;
> By clear, ridge-country rivers, and gaps where tracks
>   run high,

> Where waits the lonely horseman, cut clear against the
>   sky;
> Through stringy-bark and blue-gum, and box and pine
>   we go—
> New camps are stretching 'cross the plains the routes of
>   Cobb and Co!

None of Lawson's character-sketches in verse is comparable with his corresponding work in prose. The best of them are of old people, and in particular there is the affectionate reminiscence of **"Black Bonnet,"** the old lady who was his mother's mother; there are also the poor old ladies in **"Past Carin'"** and **"When the Children Come Home"**; and there are **"The Old Jimmy Woodser"** and the old bush publican in **"Where the Army Prays for Watty."** Lawson's love poems, except the one that has been quoted, are not among his best, and the only other kind of verses that need be mentioned here is that in which the subject is for once not man but nature. Among the best of these, setting aside the ballads in which nature-description is more or less incidental, is **"The Song of the Darling River,"** with its striking opening:

> The skies are brass and the plains are bare,
> Death and ruin are everywhere.

A couple of pieces that deal with the Blue Mountains are faintly reminiscent of Kendall, and in one, **"The Water-Lily,"** which possesses a curious, most uncharacteristic and rather fascinating refrain, there is a suggestion of a poet of whom Lawson had probably never heard: Rossetti. (pp. 350-56)

> *H. M. Green, "Lawson as Poet and Short Story Writer," in* Henry Lawson Criticism: 1894-1971, *edited by Colin Roderick, Angus and Robertson, 1972, pp. 350-70.*

STEPHEN MURRAY-SMITH   (essay date 1962)

[*Murray-Smith is an Australian educator and critic. In the following excerpt he acknowledges Lawson's deficiencies as a poet while defending Lawson from critics who dismiss his poetry entirely.*]

The critics of today who regard Lawson's verse as beneath contempt betray an aloof particularity that chills the blood. This verse cannot be considered *per se*, neglecting the circumstances of its writing and reception and its effect on the Australia of the day. For instance, the derogatory critic of today, perhaps a poet who likes to think of himself as unwedded to convention and as a genuinely creative force in his own country, owes much of the favourable ground on which he stands to Lawson and Lawson's contemporaries. Today, perhaps, we often feel the need to revolt against what many have come to feel is the dead hand of the nineties holding us back from uninhibited cultural expression; and it is true, as I have said, that the success of Lawson has encouraged to this day a host of worthless imitators. Yet in their time, we must remember, Lawson and his friends were bold and daring innovators; it was *they* who prepared and brilliantly carried through the most profound and searching revolution in literature that our country has seen.

Take Kendall, Gordon and J. B. Stephens, three poets who would have been acclaimed in 1885 as among the typical poets of their day. A random opening of their books reveals poems on Autumn, on Sunlight on the Sea, on Mountain Moss, The Story of a Soul. And it is not only the subject matter, for Stephens and Kendall in particular often wrote on Australian subject matter, and in Kendall's case often quite well. But their phrasing is mannered, derivative, distant and redolent of the accepted poetic etiquette of the time: "For, ere the early settlers came and stocked / These wilds with sheep and kine . . . ," or "Upon the utmost orient of the land, / Enfranchised of the world, alone, and free. . . ." Often, if the phrasing is not at fault, we find the sentiments cloy, trite and sticky in the worst Victorian tradition.

Too much can be made of a "clean break" with the earlier tradition, and certainly it is time that literary fashion swung round so that we can have another and more unbiassed look at such poets as these. Yet the fact remains that within ten years the poems that people who opened books of verse were likely to light on dealt with Store Cattle from Nelanjie, Kylie's Run or The Glass on the Bar! The rhythms of the verse were new—a faster moving ballad metre owing something to the anonymous bush ballad of earlier years—the vocabulary was racily contemporary and the phrasings and ideas unorthodox and relaxed. In fact an epochal event had occurred—an event which at that time had perhaps not occurred in any other land, and from the implications of which we are still retreating in fright—poetry had been given to the people. A *prima facie* case had been made out for a "majority culture."

Lawson's first published poems, like **"The Army of the Rear,"** while in no way greatly superior to much radical sloganising of the period, contained some lines that rang in the ears ("I hate the wrongs I read about, I hate the wrongs I see"), they fitted the mood of the day and they meant that the young man received literary encouragement at a critical time. When such poems as **"The Faces in the Street"** appeared (a poem which Lawson later came to hate because of its success) it was clear that the *Bulletin* had played its hunches correctly: here was a young writer with furious fancies and a burning spear. He was also a trailblazer: it comes as something of a shock to realize that, despite the fact that Paterson was two years older than Lawson, "Clancy of the Overflow" did not appear in the *Bulletin* until 1889, two years after Lawson's first poem.

As Lawson received praise running the gamut from the warm to the adulatory for his poems as they appeared in the *Bulletin* in the five years or so from 1888, it must have appeared to him that any verse that flowed from his pen had poetic merit of its own right. He possessed, too, the conviction that he was writing in the people's cause: the strongest draught ever lifted to a poet's lips and one of the most dangerous. Democracy being so manifestly the logic of nature, did a writer have to do more than open the gates and let nature in?

Thus Lawson's verse as a whole, as well as many of the individual poems, is marred by a lack of selectivity that we do not find in his prose. This fault—an insensitivity where one would least expect it—is expressed in a demeaning naturalism and a range of emotion and expression so uncontrolled that it can switch from profound and moving insight to banal sentimentality within a few lines, or even words.

"Black Bonnet," for instance, is as good an example as any. The idea of sketching in verse an old pioneer woman, and of catching in words that indefinable sweetness and wisdom of many old people, was a good one. But to any sensitive reader the poem presents so many conflicting and alternating impressions that one is finally stricken with a kind of literary mal-de-mer. The scene is set in the first four lines:

> A day of seeming innocence,
>   A glorious sun and sky,
> And, just above my picket fence,
>   Black Bonnet passing by.

The lines immediately present a vivid picture of an old woman in a black bonnet walking along past the fence, but the total effect is spoiled by the first line. Why "seeming" innocence? Is there something sinister in the scene after all? (The reader's eye wanders ahead to forestall shock.) It soon becomes clear that the completely inappropriate phrase is placed there because it was docketed in Lawson's mind as "poetic" and intangible.

Even if a case can be made out for this word, a few lines down we have the inelegancy of "Her hair is richly white, like milk, / That long ago was fair—," and within another six lines the harsh jangling of "to-day," "days gone by" and "old days" within three lines. ("The martyred rules of prosody can only shriek desperately in his determined clutch," A. G. Stephens unkindly said [in the January 12, 1901 Sydney *Bulletin* in Roderick, Colin, ed., *Henry Lawson Criticism: 1891-1974* (see Additional Bibliography)]).

The story proceeds, liberally sprinkled with capital letters, through most of the romantic cliches of the day: "the dangers of the Track," the "little home Out Back," and the "barren creeks the Bushman loves" (why?). In the true tradition of Victorian sentiment we are told that "God gave her beauty back again / The more her hair grew white." Two resounding pairs of words are now flung in—they must have been hackneyed long before Lawson's day—immediately to be offset by two lines of real observation and simple, attractive expression:

> By verdant swath and ivied wall
>   The congregation's seen—
> White nothings where the shadows fall,
>   Black blots against the green . . .

Following this Lawson cleverly brings in two little girls and uses them to "set" a natural conclusion for the poem:

> To them her mind is clear and bright,
>   Her old ideas are new;
> They know her "real talk" is right,
>   Her "fairy talk" is true.
> And they converse as grown-ups may,
>   When all the news is told;
> The one so wisely young today,
>   The two so wisely old.

Despite the defects here (the weak sixth line, for instance, and the undesirable repetition of "wisely") this stanza is not a bad climax for the poem. But Lawson, in distinction to the instinctive grasp he has of the short story ending, now adds two strained and bathetic verses which detract from the impact of the whole poem, ending with:

> There's scarce a sound of dish on dish
>   Or cup slipped into cup,
> When, left alone, as is her wish,
>   Black Bonnet "washes up"!

So much for the sins of editors who pay for poetry on a lineage basis.

As we have just seen, it is easy to denigrate Lawson's verse. However well Lawson may have been served by the *Bulletin*'s editors, he was badly served by those who prepared his *Selected Verse* for publication. In the form in which it is available today Lawson's poetry is printed with no indication of the (often revealing) chronological order in which it was written; it has been extensively edited (not always to bad effect, of course); and, above all, it includes a great deal of material which should never have been lifted from the pages of the periodical press in which it first appeared. "Casual newspaper verses, so many jaundiced reflections of bitter hours," A. G. Stephens calls them.

It is only fair, however, to consider the case for Lawson's verse at its best. We have already said that Lawson was an important poetic innovator. He was also a poet of Democracy, at a time when that word was more likely to be spelt with a capital initial than it is now; and, as a poet of Democracy, he struck an immediate chord and response in the hearts of thousands of his countrymen:

> Once I showed it to a critic, and he said 'twas very
>   fine,
> Though he wasn't long in finding glaring faults in every
>   line;
> But the poem sang of Freedom—all the clever critic
>   said
> Couldn't stop that song from ringing, ringing, ringing
>   in my head.

Lawson's more directly political calls to action not only gave form to bitter resentments but carried with them that apocalyptic breath that long nourished Australia Militant and its utopian hopes, frustrated in a society in the hands of the bankers, wool-kings and overseas capitalists, where little else than revolutionary change seemed conceiveable:

> And, lo, with shops all shuttered I beheld a city's
>   street,
> And in the warning distance heard the tramp of many
>   feet,
>   Coming near, coming near,
>   To a drum's dull distant beat—
> 'Twas Despair's conscripted army that was marching
>   down the street!

Indeed it has been persuasively argued that at no time before or since has Australian society been in such a "revolutionary situation" as it was in the nineties.

In poems such as **"The Faces in the Street," "The Army of the Rear"** and **"The Men Who Made Australia"** Lawson, at the height of his radical passion and indignation, is capable of maintaining a sustained level of poetic writing—especially if we refrain from judging the poems as if they had been written in 1960 and try to relate them to the time, and the literary and social possibilities of the time. There have been few more moving, dignified and poetically effective lines in our literature than:

> In the shearer's hut the slush-lamp shows a haggard,
>   stern-faced man
> Preaching war against the Wool-King to his mates:
> And wherever go the billy, water-bag and frying-pan,
> They are drafting future histories of States.

But even more important to Lawson's democratic audience than these were the poems in which he brought into the light of day, and in some alchemical way typified, the homely and human emotions of *people*. Daley, Brady, Paterson and others were better poets—in a purely literary sense—than Lawson, but they never managed to do this. Such emotions are often sentimental, for sentiment is vicarious longing, and Lawson's people had much to long for; they are sometimes banal—but banality is recognized as a vice only by the sophisticated; sometimes they seem excessively simple—but the apparent simpleness may in fact be simplicity, as with:

> And I thought—there are times when our memory
>   trends
>   Through the future, as 'twere, on its own—
> That I, out-of-date ere my pilgrimage ends,
> In a new-fashioned bar to dead loves and dead friends
>   Might drink, like the old man, alone.

There is an underlying poignancy here which is not too simple.

Nor is Lawson being simple or obvious when he writes:

> 'Tis a class of men belonging to those soul-forsaken
>   years;
> Third-rate canvassers, collectors, journalists and
>   auctioneers.
> They are never very shabby, they are never very
>   spruce—
> Going cheerfully and carelessly and smoothly to the
>   deuce.
> Some are wanderers by profession, turning up and gone
>   as soon,
> Travelling second-class, or steerage (when it's cheap
>   they go saloon);
> Free from all the "ists" and "isms," undisturbed by
>   faith or doubt—
> Lazy, purposeless, and useless—knocking round and
>   hanging out.

Lawson demonstrates here his ability to depict with nerveless accuracy a type, a category of the human condition familiar enough—unhappily—to him, and familiar enough to the rest of us too. While it is true that—as A. G. Stephens several times remarked—Lawson's engagement covered only a small arc of the Australian horizon, within that arc he demonstrated time and time again his deep and pervasive understanding and insight into people. (pp. 32-6)

> *Stephen Murray-Smith, in his* Henry Lawson, *Lansdowne Press, 1962, 48 p.*

COLIN RODERICK   (essay date 1966)

[*Roderick is an Australian educator and critic who has written extensively on Lawson and edited volumes of his poetry and fiction. In the following excerpt Roderick defends Lawson as a poet.*]

When Henry Lawson's book of verse, **In the Days When the World Was Wide,** appeared in February 1896, critics throughout Australia hailed him as a poet. A. G. Stephens, who had already spoken kindly of a little book of Lawson's verse and short stories brought out by his mother in 1894, wrote of him in the Sydney *Bulletin*: "His capacity for emotion is his best gift: it is because he feels so deeply that he writes so strongly." In Lawson and Paterson, Stephens held, "we see something like the beginnings of a national school of poetry." John Farrell said in the *Daily Telegraph:* "There is not the grace and richness of artisanship in his verse which characterized that of Kendall; but it has not been equalled in its class." To Victor Daley he was "the tribal poet of the down-and-out." He was compared with Burns as "a minstrel of native fire." (p. 11)

These observations were made when Lawson was at his best as an interpreter of man in society. After 1896 his flashes of poetic insight were less frequent; but Australians of his generation never ceased to think of him as "the poet Lawson."

This was still true fifty years ago, when he had lost the power of bringing consistent artistic discipline to his verse. By the

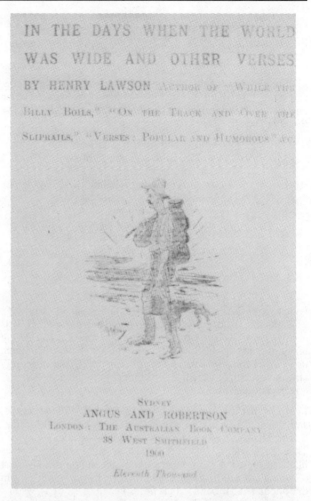

The Tent and the Tree

"I had a dreamy recollection of the place as a hut; some of my people said it was a tent, on a good frame — for Father was a carpenter, but Mother tells me that he built a little bark room in front, lined with scrim, papered with newspapers, with a white-washed floor with mats; a fire place in front, by the side of the door, and a glass door! — relic of the rush, I suppose. The tent was the same that I was born in on the Grenfel goldfield, some three years before, and had been brought back to Pipeclay. Then

Manuscript page of Lawson's autobiography. From The Real Henry Lawson, *by Colin Roderick. Rigby Publishers, 1982.*

Title page of In the Days When the World Was Wide.

time of his death in 1922 a new generation of critics had arisen; but they still thought of him primarily as a poet. (p. 12)

Nowadays most of our critics think otherwise. They say today that as a poet Lawson is hardly worth reading. A great gulf, they say, yawns between his verse and his prose; and his verse is represented as being little better than inspired doggerel.

H. M. Green wrote in 1961: "It is absurd to speak of him as 'the poet Lawson'" [see excerpt dated 1961]. (p. 13)

Mr A. A. Phillips, in the *Australian Tradition*, 1958, completely disregarded Lawson as a poet. . . . Mr Phillips had an article entitled "Henry Lawson Revisited." This article explains a great deal. Mr Phillips begins by asking himself: "What constitutes the significant part of Lawson's work?" He goes on to answer his own question. "First," he writes, "I have ignored his verse. That is only partly because it is not consistently good enough to be patiently readable in quantity. Mainly I have set it aside because I am uncertain how truly it contains the mind of its writer. Too often, one feels, the ballads are not by Henry Lawson. They are the work of a persona, bearing his name and cashing his cheques, who assumed the rôle of the Australian folk-voice."

What are we to believe in the face of all that?

"The ballads are not by Henry Lawson but by a persona bearing his name." "It is absurd to speak of him as 'the poet Lawson'." "Lawson's poetry hardly merits critical attention."

Truly these are damning dicta, so confidently affirmed that they have led to the common belief that as poet Lawson has fallen from a state of grace. With one or two exceptions, notably Mr Vincent Buckley of Melbourne, teachers of literature have accepted this condemnation. Mr Buckley thinks of Lawson as a poet, but a poet "simple, crude, and narrow"; and in support of his opinion he selects these two stanzas from **"The Roaring Days":**

Ah, then their hearts were bolder,
    And if Dame Fortune frowned,
Their swags they'd lightly shoulder
    And tramp to other ground.
Oh, they were lion-hearted
    Who gave our country birth!
Stout sons, of stoutest fathers born,
    From all the lands on earth!

Those golden days are vanished,
    And altered is the scene;
The diggings are deserted,
    The camping-grounds are green;

The flaunting flag of progress
    Is in the West unfurled;
The mighty Bush with iron rails
    Is tethered to the world.

Mr Buckley says of this that despite its being "simple, crude, narrow," "it is hard to resist the temporary excitement when one reads it." Well then, let us take another stanza from **"The Roaring Days"**:

Oh, who would paint a goldfield
    And paint the picture right—
As we have often seen it
    In early morning's light:
The yellow mounds of mullock
    With spots of red and white,
The scattered quartz that glistened
    Like diamonds in light;
The azure line of ridges,
    The bush of darkest green,
The little homes of calico
    That dotted all the scene.

Is that *simple?* Yes, as simple as the simplest of Wordsworth's little poems. Is it *crude?* I think not. Is it *narrow?* If it is narrow, so is Robert Bridges's "London Snow"; and so are many of the songs of Robert Burns. Nowadays, when so much that passes for poetry is *un*-natural, contorted, and obscurely allusive, we might welcome something of this alleged "simple, crude, and narrow."

I suspect that Lawson is too often considered "simple, crude, and narrow" because he is classified nowadays as a bush balladist. That he wrote ballads is quite true; so did Tennyson. That the narratives of these ballads were set in the bush is likewise true; but these bush ballads, the simplest and truest of which are still distinguishable by their literary quality from the popular bush ballad, bulk little in the mass of Lawson's verse. He wrote ballads of the city, too, as well as ballads of the sea and of war—true ballads as distinct from minor descriptive or lyrical verse.

If Lawson were in fact confined to the bush ballad, there might be some justice in describing him as "simple, crude, and narrow." The truth, it seems to me, is elsewhere.

Lawson was an unlettered poet: he attended no university; he probably never knew the meaning of the word "metaphysical." His latter-day critics, while admitting his genius in the short story, found his verse lacking in the rhythms and allusions of the later English tradition, and therefore rude and unpolished.

When I hear Lawson's verse described as rude, I think of John Skelton, *poeta laureatus* of Oxford in the fifteenth century. Much the same thing was said of him by some of his critics, both during his lifetime and soon afterwards; and you will remember his comment in *Colyn Cloute:*

Though my rhyme be ragged,
Tattered and jagged,
Rudely rain-beaten,
Rusty and moth-eaten,
If you take well therewith,
It hath in it some pith.

Which would not be a bad retort for Lawson, who hath in him some pith, the pith of social criticism, the pith of humanity, and who, despite his ignorance of courts, cloisters, and cathedrals, resembled Skelton in the satirical cast of his mind. Nei-

ther was Lawson silent before pedantry. You will recall the savage lines to his cultured critic, John Le Gay Brereton:

You were quick to pick on a faulty line
    That I strove to put my soul in:
Your eyes were keen for a dash of mine
    In the place of a semi-colon—
And blind to the rest.

It was because David McKee Wright, editor of the Red Page of the Sydney *Bulletin* in 1917, thought Lawson "simple, crude, and narrow," because he, too, was "blind to the rest," that he altered and "improved" the poet's lines: the result often was crudity. Some of Lawson's best poems were omitted from Wright's collected edition of his verse: the result of this was a suggestion of narrowness. The analytical simplicity of his best work was too often obscured or converted into doggerel. Far from being undeserving of critical scrutiny, as Todd wrote, the restoration of Lawson's text requires keen critical application. Todd was deceived by the spurious versions of Lawson that we read today: his strictures are apt, for example, if we apply ourselves to the poem that passes muster as **"Andy's Gone with Cattle."** In the version now available the opening stanza reads:

Our Andy's gone with cattle now—
    Our hearts are out of order—
With drought he's gone to battle now
    Across the Queensland border.

That is not merely simple; it is simple doggerel, well deserving of the epithet "crude." *But it is not what Lawson wrote.* It is true that Lawson wrote all the words that are in it, but he did not write either the words or the lines in that order. Look at it again:

Our Andy's gone with cattle now—
    Our hearts are out of order—
With drought he's gone to battle now
    Across the Queensland border.

Now let us see what Lawson did write:

Our Andy's gone to battle now
    With Drought, the red marauder:
Our Andy's gone with cattle now
    Across the Queensland border.

How did the line

    Our hearts are out of order—

get in?

It was manufactured by David McKee Wright in 1917. He took the words "Our hearts" from Lawson's original second stanza—from the lines which previously ran:

He's left us in dejection now:
    Our hearts with him are roving.

"'Our hearts'," Wright said, "must become 'our thoughts' because 'hearts' was used in the previous alteration." He overlooked the natural poetic antithesis implied in the two lines; he forgot that the heart is figurative of the emotions: we are in dejection because our feelings, our sympathies, not our intellectual diversions, are roving with Andy.

What now of the rest of the line—the words "are out of order"? These come from one of Lawson's original stanzas, which Wright omitted entirely from the poem, very likely because he didn't known what Lawson was talking about.

The stanza omitted reads:

> The gates are out of order now,
>   In storms the "riders" rattle;
> For far across the border now
>   Our Andy's gone with cattle.

So you see, all that you have to do to ruin a poem is to substitute the condition of the farm gates for the condition of the farmer's emotions, look on the poem as a meccano toy, take the toy apart, then put it together to suit your own fancy. In this case the result was hardly what Coleridge would have thought "the best words in their best order." Coleridge, I imagine, would have left the poem alone.

As for the mutilated opening stanza, critical barbarism could scarcely have defaced it more efficiently. David McKee Wright subscribed to the archaic rule of rhyme then current that "marauder," which had no "r" before the "d," could not be allowed as a rhyme with "border." (Perhaps he rolled his "r's.") Nowadays, with phonetics to back us up, we may rhyme "Harry Lauder" with "rank disorder" and never raise an eyebrow.

Is Lawson's stanza poetry?

> Our Andy's gone to battle now
>   With Drought, the red marauder;
> Our Andy's gone with cattle now
>   Across the Queensland border.

I suggest that the little attention we have been able to give it in these few minutes has enabled us to discover that what he writes here is poetry. Simple? Yes, with the strong simplicity of Hebrew poetry, and reminiscent of the parallelism that marked much of that poetry:

> He clave the rocks in the wilderness and gave
> them drink as out of the great depths: he brought
> streams out of the rock and caused waters to
> run down like rivers.

Crude? Narrow? I leave it to you to decide; to my mind it is pregnant with suggestion.

So much for the suggestiveness of Lawson's expression. What now of the cast of his mind?

It was his refusal to take an idealized view of life that first exposed him to a charge of gloomy narrowness, a charge that has stuck. He never was as popular a poet as the breezy Paterson. The well-known debate on the merits of the city and the bush that occupied these two in 1892 gave rise to Lawson's reputation as a narrow poet of gloom. But again, the truth has been obscured. This debate was, in fact, hatched up by them to create public interest in their *Bulletin* poems.

"We ought to do pretty well out of it," Lawson told Paterson. "We ought to be able to get in three or four sets of verses each before they stop us."

"This suited me all right," Paterson recollected, "for we were working on space, and the pay was very small, so we slam-banged away at each other for weeks and weeks."

Although the debate began in friendly vein, both poets reacted more and more acidly to each other's barbs as the debate went on, and Paterson ended up by saying:

No doubt, the bush *is* wretched if you judge it by the groan
Of the sad and soulful poet with a graveyard of his own.

Lawson has never quite shaken off this description of him. Yet it is only part of the truth, and a small part at that.

There is nothing "soulful"—or doleful—about such pieces as **"For'ard,"** or **"The Boss's Boots,"** or **"The Boss over the Board,"** **"The God-forgotten Election,"** **"The Greenhand Rouseabout,"** **"The Jolly Dead March,"** or **"Robbie's Statue."**

The greater part of the truth is that Lawson saw deeper into the nature of things than Paterson ever could. Where Paterson saw what was on the surface, Lawson penetrated beneath. He was analytical where Paterson was merely responsive. He interpreted where Paterson described. He heard what Wordsworth called "the still sad music of humanity." He saw man acquainted with grief, often self-created, as in **"Dan the Wreck"**; but he saw through the shabbiness to the good in man, and he brought it to the surface:

> We may be—so goes the rumour—
>   Bad as Dan;
> But we may not have the humour
>   Of the man;
> Nor the sight—well, deem it blindness
>   As the general public do—
> And the love of human kindness
>   Or the *grit* to see it throught.

It is when Lawson is at his simplest that he is at his best. In the declamatory mood he is windy: it is then that his verse is suspect as poetry, however valuable it is as the expression of a social attitude. (pp. 13-21)

[When] Lawson falls into the heroic strain, you are entitled to distrust the result as poetry and to look elsewhere for Lawson the poet. When he says, in **"The Writer's Dream"**—

> I was born to write of the things that are! and the
>   strength was given to me;
> I was born to strike at the things that mar the world as
>   the world should be—

you may be sure that he is assuming a posture, the posture of a latter-day Hamlet, cursed to put the world to rights.

When he says in **"The Uncultured Rhymer to His Cultured Critic"**—

> I come with strength of the living day, and with half
>   the world behind me—

he is speaking not as a poet but as an advocate, the social advocate of that half; and like any other advocate, he is only half right. (pp. 24-5)

We might go on, finding line after line, piece after piece, that come from Lawson the self-appointed prophet, Lawson the rhetorician, Lawson the Member for Utopia; they are not from Lawson the poet. But when we come to lines like these—

> And the sunlight streamed in, and a light like a star
> Seemed to glow in the depth of the glass on the bar—

we commune with a poet, we look with his eyes past the object and the circumstance to the essential poetry that he discerns in them.

Here are a few more lines by which we may recognize the poetry that was in him. This line, from **"Knocked Up"**:

I'm lyin' on the barren ground that's baked and cracked
    with drought;

or this, from **"Marshall's Mate"**:

You almost *heard* the surface bake, and *saw*
    the gum-leaves burn.

You hear the note of genuine poetry in the whole of **"Reedy River"**:

Ten miles down Reedy River
    A pool of water lies,
And all the year it mirrors
    The changes in the skies;

or again, in idyllic vein, in the later poem, **"Do They Think That I Do Not Know?"**:

When the love-burst came, like an English spring,
    In the days when our hair was brown,
And the hem of her skirt was a sacred thing
    And her hair was an angel's crown;

or in the grim prison lines:

The great round church with its volume of sound, where
    we dare not turn our eyes—
They take us there from our separate hells to sing of
    Paradise;
The High Church service swells and swells where the
    tinted Christs look down—
It is easy to see who is weary and faint and who wears
    the thorny crown.

The range of experience exposed in what I take to be the poetry of Lawson is far from narrow. His heart goes out to the haggard woman of **"Past Carin',"** who symbolizes long-suffering humanity:

My eyes are dry, I cannot cry,
    I've got no heart for breakin',
But where it was in days gone by,
    A dull and empty achin'.
My last boy ran away from me,
    I know my temper's wearin',
But now I only wish to be
    Beyond all signs of carin'.
        Past wearyin' or carin',
        Past feelin' and despairin';
    And now I only wish to be
    Beyond all signs of carin'.

At the other end of the scale, in **"Hannah Thomburn,"** he catches the poetry in the face of a beautiful woman:

Her eyes were the warm grey venetian
    That comes with the dawn of the day;

and, in **"The Lily of St. Leonards,"** the poetry of a pure heart and mind:

As fair as lily whitness,
    As pure as lily gold,
And bright with childlike brightness
    And wise as worlds of old.

Her heart for all was beating
    And all hearts were her own—
Like sunshine through the Lily
    Her purity was shown.

                                        (pp. 26-8)

Lawson's verse is many things: it is the direct speech not only of Lawson the poet, but also of Lawson the social reformer, Lawson the politician, Lawson the seer identifying himself with Australia, Lawson the apologist for himself.

It is not easy to sift the poetry in his verse from the rhetoric and the propaganda, mainly because the rhetoric and the propaganda are in terms that closely resemble his poetic expression. What shall we say of such a piece as **"The Great Grey Plain,"** written in 1893? It begins with rhetoric:

Out West, where the stars are brightest,
    Where the scorching north wind blows,
And the bones of the dead gleam whitest,
    And the sun on a desert glows.

It ends with propaganda:

'Tis a desert not more barren
    Than the Great Grey Plain of years,
Where a fierce fire burns the hearts of men,
    Dries up the fount of tears:
Where the victims of a greed insane
    Are crushed in a hell-born strife—
Where the souls of a race are murdered
    On the Great Grey Plain of Life!

The true poetic equivalent of **"The Great Grey Plain"** is a line in a letter Lawson wrote to his aunt, Emma Brookes, from Hungerford in January 1893 describing the horrors of life in the drought-stricken west: "Men tramp and beg and live like dogs." Lawson's vision of that bitter life is expressed poetically in **"Out Back."** I would today prefer **"Out Back,"** as poetry, to **"The Great Grey Plain."**

One's own estimate of Lawson as poet inevitably changes as one learns more about the inner life of the man and as one studies his original manuscripts.

Twenty years ago it seemed to me that Lawson could be adequately represented as a poet by seven poems. Today I am not so sure. . . . I would certainly add at least ten more, but in the text Lawson wrote, not that of David McKee Wright.

What are these poems?

The five that I would retain are **"Past Carin',"** **"The Teams,"** **"The Water-Lily,"** **"The Sliprails and the Spur,"** and **"After All."** The one I would discard is **"In the Days When the World Was Wide,"** which today I consider valuable as a social document, but not poetry.

Remembering that the personality we seek is that of Lawson the poet, what other poems ought we to admit as his best? From what I have said so far, you will know my reasons for including such poems as these—I name half-a-dozen in the order of composition—**"Andy's Gone with Cattle,"** **"Faces in the Street,"** **"Taking His Chance,"** **"Knocked Up,"** **"Since Then,"** **"Dan the Wreck,"** **"One Hundred and Three."** They are not all, of course; but what I have said so far will suggest others in the same vein, for example, **"Middleton's Rouseabout."** (pp. 31-3)

Colin Roderick, in his Henry Lawson: Poet and Short Story Writer, *Angus and Robertson, 1966, 70 p.*

LIVIO DOBREZ   (essay date 1976)

[*In the following excerpt Dobrez analyzes two of Lawson's short stories, "The Drover's Wife" and "The Bush Undertaker," as representative examples of what is best in Lawson's work.*]

Lawson is in some respects a very simple artist and very much a man of his time—and place—with all the limitations that implies; indeed his is a flawed talent. But before concentrating on his failures one has to account for the immense dramatic force of many of the stories and for their depth of human feeling. (p. 375)

[**"The Drover's Wife,"** a] portrait of a woman who is both stubbornly and movingly individual and a type of Outback endurance, is one of the finest in Lawson and, understandably, it takes all our attention as we read. At the same time it is evident that its success depends very much on its dramatic context. Obviously there is the setting as well, or rather the partial identification of the woman and her environment, the tension of belonging and not belonging to the harsh landscape, handled so gently and yet powerfully by Lawson: on the one hand the woman's assertion of difference, that is, of human-ity—wonderfully expressed in the pathos of the formal Sunday walk in the midst of desolation—on the other, her stoic ac-ceptance of those experiences of pain which root her to the environment and make her indistinguishable from it. Every-thing is contained in the image of the primitive house and its surroundings which opens the story and, in an unexpectedly poetic way, in the surely not fortuitous reference to she-oaks which follows: Nothing to relieve the eye save the darker green of a few she-oaks which are sighing above the narrow, almost waterless creek. But in terms of dramatic technique the most important thing is the utterly simple means used to initiate the exploration of the woman's mind. The snake, that is to say, the action of the story, is simply an excuse, and a very suc-cessful one, for the protagonist's vigil which in turn gives Lawson the opportunity to concentrate on his real subject. Again and again he introduces the sense of passing time: "It is near sunset . . ."; "Near midnight"; "It must be near one or two o'clock"; "It must be near morning now"; "It must be near daylight." In other words, the acute awareness of time, justified as it is by the continuing menace of the snake, creates the kind of dramatic tension which is necessary to give the silent meditation its astonishing immediacy and reality. After-wards, action resolves this tension, at least in part, and, at a symbolic or emotive level, the larger tensions in the woman's life, so that it is possible to end in a passive mood of relief as we watch the snake quietly burn. In one sense the entire story depicts a symbolic act, of course. Likewise the snake, however real, gathers symbolic overtones as the story proceeds. In the end, it sums up in its presence nothing less than the enduring reality of danger and suffering in the woman's life. It is, in other words, an embodiment of pain and of the bush, signif-icantly *invading* the area of the human—the small house set in the wilderness. We may even say it is a diabolic presence because the possibility that a reference to the myth of *Genesis* is at the back of the author's mind is shown in the description of the dog's killing the snake: "He shakes the snake as though he felt the original curse in common with mankind."

A woman and a snake—only the man is missing. And indeed the absent husband is there, at the centre of the story. In her reverie the woman is aware of him, anxiously so, since she has had no word from him in six months. On the face of it she feels no resentment: "he is careless, but a good enough husband," willing to give her all he has but equally able to

"forget sometimes that he is married." Whereas as a young wife she suffered from the solitude of the bush, she is now hardened by an acceptance that has no need to distinguish between pain and joy: "She is glad when her husband returns, but she does not gush or make a fuss about it. She gets him something good to eat, and tidies up the children." What weight of unacknowledged bitterness lies behind this stoic mask? Nat-urally we cannot discuss the drover's wife as if she were a reality outside the bounds of Lawson's story. But, in spite of a seeming refusal on the author's part to assign any guilt to the absent drover, there are elements in the tale itself suggestive of at least an ambivalence in this regard. One of these is the extraordinary outburst of the woman's son, significantly placed at the very end. The snake is dead, the woman weeps, the boy is awake: "Presently he looks up at her, sees the tears in her eyes, and, throwing his arms round her neck, exclaims: 'Mother, I won't never go drovin'; blast me if I do!'" Granted the dramatic justification for such a response, why a reference to *droving,* why a consciousness—and a damning one at that—of the *father* at this particular point? One might expect an expression of love or of relief. Yet the whole emotional weight of the experience of fear and horror shapes itself into something else, for which we have not evidently been prepared: a judge-ment, brutal with all the simplicity of a child's view, upon the absent drover. Without taking the point too far I would suggest that **"The Drover's Wife"** is more concerned perhaps than the author realizes with the protagonist's relation to her husband, in fact that it is in part a study of (unsatisfactory) human relations in the context of marriage and the Australian bush. From this angle we may be forgiven the surmise that Lawson's snake, that personification of menace and the bush, is also closely, if obscurely, linked in the author's mind with the careless but good enough husband. Is the conclusion so sur-prising in a writer we *expect* to be greatly concerned with the relationship of male and female? **"The Drover's Wife"** reflects Lawson's constant internal debate; its moral is complex but on the whole the antithesis of that put forward in **"A Child in the Dark, and a Foreign Father,"** where sympathy is directed towards the male victim of female dominance. It may be ob-jected that Lawson's approach to life and literature does not allow for symbols—but this is simply not true. Like much good writing in the realist tradition, Lawson's suggests undercurrents of emotion not by crude or mechanical appeal to symbol but by symbolic resonances, by a synthesis of objective and sub-jective truth such that external action takes on a wider and more allusive significance. Lawson's best known story is not only a small masterpiece of sympathetic humour and grim psycho-logical realism: it is subtly and carefully constructed as a dra-matic piece and, to its credit, its life in a real sense escapes the artist's control.

And yet, having said this, one has to admit the partial failure. As usual, Lawson walks the tightrope of Victorian sentiment, liable at any point to turn the story into a sentimental melo-drama. The ending betrays him; after the gesture of the child's outburst, there is the sensationalism of: "And she hugs him to her worn-out breast and kisses him; and they sit thus together while the sickly daylight breaks over the bush." But this is not the main problem, which is Lawson's failure to pursue and to face squarely some of the issues implicit in his own treatment of his material. The boy's final cry is as unexpected to the writer as it is to us, as if Lawson were unaware of the emotional undercurrents of his story, or only dimly aware of them, willing to allow the tale its obscure direction but unable to contemplate it directly. So we have the curious mixture of subtlety and crudeness, of insight and fumbling confusion which is characteristic of all Lawson's work.

The touch is more sure in **"The Bush Undertaker,"** where Lawson's emotional range is narrower but his evocative power equally evident. This story dispenses even with the minimal action of **"The Drover's Wife."** Again the setting is important: a primitive hut and its surroundings, a dry creek, brown hills. And in this solitude, an old shepherd and his dog. The old man leaves the house to dig up an Aboriginal grave. After collecting the remains of bones he comes upon the corpse of a white man, his friend Brummy—killed by hard drinking presumably and accompanied by a bottle of rum—whom he takes back to the hut and buries nearby. There is one other macabre detail: the shepherd sees a number of mysterious black goannas on his way; during the night he is frightened by sounds around the hut; he fires and to his surprise brings down a goanna, realizing at last that it is the one goanna he has been seeing all day and, rather horribly, that the creature has followed Brummy's body because it has been feeding on it. The simple tale is deliberately anti-climactic: when the entire episode is buried with Brummy's corpse, the old man passes "his hand wearily over his forehead," but not with overt signs of emotion—"only as one who was tired and felt the heat." Lawson spoils the effect a little by an unnecessary last sentence which suggests that the story is merely eccentric, like its protagonist—it is nothing of the sort. **"The Bush Undertaker"** is a casually superb study of life and death, or rather of the easy relationship that exists between the two in the bush—and anywhere else, for that matter. It has a broad religious dimension. For example, we are told it is Christmas Day. On this day of birth the protagonist encounters first the remains of an Aboriginal, then of his friend. Now Brummy's body is preserved (by the dry heat—and the rum); it is twice casually referred to as a mummy—and indeed its name suggests a combination of the two words, rum and mummy. Moreover the story is full of comic and grotesque indications of *life* in the corpse. To begin with the shepherd talks to is as if it *were* alive, but more than that it is remarkably lively in its own right: it frightens him with its piercing gaze when he first discovers it; it strikes him from behind when he props it up incorrectly against the hut; it gives him another shock with another horrifying look when the bark covering its face suddenly slips. And there is a further oblique variation on the theme of life-in-death in the form of the ghostly night visitor, the goanna. By the time we reach the end these recurrent half humorous, half grim hints on the preservation of life after death give a remarkable depth to the simple burial, itself described with warm, sympathetic irony combined with reverence and a perfect sense of dramatic timing and pace:

> "It's time yer turned in, Brum," he said, lifting the body down.
>
> He carried it to the grave and dropped it into one corner like a post. He arranged the bark so as to cover the face, and, by means of a peice of clothes-line, lowered the body to a horizontal position. Then he threw in an armful of gum leaves, and then, very reluctantly, took the shovel and dropped in a few shovelfuls of earth.
>
> "An' this is the last of Brummy," he said, leaning on his spade and looking away over the tops of the ragged gums on the distant range.
>
> This reflection seemed to engender a flood of memories, in which the old man became ab-

sorbed. He leaned heavily upon his spade and thought.

> "Arter all," he murmured sadly, "arter all—it were Brummy."
>
> "Brummy," he said at last, "it's all over now; nothin' matters now—nothin' didn't ever matter, nor—nor don't. You uster say as how it 'ud be all right termorrer" (pause); "termorrer's come, Brummy—come fur you—it ain't come fur me yet, but—it's a-comin'."
>
> He threw in some more earth.
>
> "Yer don't remember, Brummy, an' mebbe yer don't want to remember—*I* don't want to remember—but—well, but, yer see, that's where yer got the pull on me."
>
> He shovelled in some more earth and paused again.
>
> The dog rose, with ears erect, and looked anxiously first at his master, and then into the grave.
>
> "Theer ougther be somethin' sed," muttered the old man; "'tain't right to put 'im under like a dog. There ougther be some sort o' sarmin." He sighed heavily in the listening silence that followed this remark, and proceeded with his work. He filled the grave to the brim this time, and fashioned the mound carefully with his spade. Once or twice he muttered the words, "I am the rassaraction." As he laid the tools quietly aside, and stood at the head of the grave, he was evidently trying to remember the something that ought to be said. He removed his hat, placed it carefully on the grass, held his hands out from his sides and a little to the front, drew a long deep breath, and said with a solemnity that greatly disturbed Five Bob, "Hashes ter hashes, dus ter dus, Brummy—an'—an' in hopes of a great an' gerlorious rassaraction!"

Everything is summed up in the ridiculous and yet deeply serious "I am the rassaraction." **"The Bush Undertaker"** is a grotesque and touching picture of man's decay and of his hopes for life beyond the grave, above all of the homely familiarity of death to a man like the old shepherd. More than that it suggests the naturalness of death as a part of life, the fact that all human beings must live with the reality of death. So closely are the two poles of human existence, birth and death, related in the cycle of nature that they become one and the same: thus, in a grotesque metamorphosis and a parody of resurrection and new life, Brummy becomes the goanna's "Christmas dinner," dies as Brummy to live in the life of the goanna. Not that we are to interpret this as bitter scepticism about the Christmas hope of rebirth. The tone of Lawson's story is gently satirical only, acknowledging equally the immanent power of nature in its cycles of generation and decay and the desperate longing for transcendence and freedom within the human being. In this framework of natural and human forces interacting and opposing, the goanna is of crucial significance. It functions in a semi-symbolic way much as does the snake in **"The Drover's Wife,"** evoking a sense of horror and at the same time ironic humour. In short, it comes to represent the land itself with all its heartless indifference to human aspirations and so in a more general sense nature, the forces of life and death, a nagging presence at the edges of consciousness: the true undertaker of the bush. These chill connotations are unmistakable every time it makes an appearance, first as a "great greasy black" creature standing guard on the blackened corpse, then as a scurrying, ubiquitous spy, puzzling and disquieting to the old man. The dog will not touch it: it is stuffed with rotting human flesh, indeed it seems to be *composed* of decay. In the end its presence is exorcised—but not altogether. It remains in the image of the grave which swallows Brummy and, after all, like the snake in **"The Drover's Wife,"** continues its existence in its true habitat as an elusive fear within the mind. Not surprisingly, the protagonist faces it, as any man must, in utter solitude. But the mood is not despairing. In the face of the Bush Undertaker Lawson's shepherd asserts with tragicomic vigour those pathetically frail and yet not easily dismissed human qualities of endurance and hope. Even more important he asserts, ludicrously and movingly, the reality of consciousness in an alien environment—the bush, or finally, nature in general—consciousness incessantly, absurdly *active*, bursting with warmth of human feeling and optimism, endlessly offering itself in communication to another of its kind. This aspect of the story is never sentimental, although full of sentiment; it is deeply ironic without cynicism and handled so lightly and unobtrusively we scarcely notice Lawson's art: the dramatic device of the soliloquy. The old shepherd never stops the flow of talk which is nothing more than an extension of his thinking—but it is no more than a soliloquy. He talks, with endearing complexity of tone and mood, from beginning to end, to—a *dog*, a *corpse* and to *himself*. So vital and convincing is his communication that we are hardly aware of the discrepancy. Brummy comes to life in the stream of words, the dog becomes a human being, a solitary consciousness discovers otherness within itself and shapes the wilderness in its own image. As a result the alien reality of the goanna is kept at a distance and human values are reaffirmed in what from one point of view might have seemed an impossible context. Incredibly, as in Beckett's *Happy Days,* we are satisfied that the protagonist is actually enjoying his lot. It is an exciting, encouraging Christmas, to discover a body ("Me luck's in for the day and no mistake!"), a bottle of rum ("me luck's in this Christmas, an' no mistake") and to lug a friend home for burial ("I ain't a-spendin' sech a dull Christmas arter all").

After this admirable handshake with the void, however, we do not expect a faltering apology. This is the last sentence of **"The Bush Undertaker"**: "And the sun sank again on the grand Australian bush—the nurse and tutor of eccentric minds, the home of the weird, and of much that is different from things in other lands." Lawson's lapse is as inexplicable as it is banal. There is no need for the sun to sink, certainly not on the grand Australian bush—and what purpose other than confusion and debasement of his theme is served by the author's use of inappropriate terms like "eccentric" and (worse) "weird"? The sentence reads like an excuse for what has gone before. As in **"The Drover's Wife"** Lawson is clearly out of step with his own considerable imaginative powers. It is as if the truths *implicit* in his story eluded him with the same tantalising regularity with which the goanna avoids the protagonist of **"The Bush Undertaker."** (pp. 375-81)

Livio Dobrez, "The Craftsmanship of Lawson Revisited," in Australian Literary Studies, *Vol. 7, No. 4, October, 1976, pp. 375-88.*

JOHN MADDOCKS (essay date 1977)

[*In the following essay Maddocks discusses the narrative and interpretive functions of the character Joe Wilson, as exemplified in "Brighten's Sister-in-Law" and "Water Them Geraniums."*]

While the Joe Wilson stories are generally considered to represent Henry Lawson's prose style at its best, little attention has been paid to the narrative technique on which that style depends.

Joe, as narrator, attains the successful balance of objectivity and imaginative evocation sought in Lawson's previous stories. The older Joe Wilson maintains an almost objective detachment in the narration of his own earlier life. This tone of detachment is struck in the generalizing reflections of the opening of **"Joe Wilson's Courtship"**: "There are many times in this world when a healthy boy is happy." The balance between this objective tone and that of personal reminiscence is soon introduced: "I wasn't a healthy-minded, average boy." . . . The balance created by the narrative voice allows for shifts in perspective throughout the story. Whenever there is a danger that the self-revelatory aspect of the narration may approach indulgence, as when Joe tells us that

> I reckon I was born for a poet by mistake, and
> grew up to be a Bushman, and didn't know
> what was the matter with me—or the world—
> but that's got nothing to do with it.

there is a shift to a detached generalization like "There are times when a man is happy." . . . The obvious depth of the revelation about not being average, and being born for a poet, has, of course, everything "to do with it," and the attempt to gloss over this aspect of personality in fact creates a strong impression about Joe's nature. We are drawn away from the impression for the moment by a return to the objective "There are times."

What may appear to be a discursive introduction is actually a skilful evocation of the tone and content of the story, and an establishing of the quality of Joe's narrative voice.

Joe Wilson is a man of considerable experience, an older, but not necessarily wiser, married man. Joe attempts to express his experience and the depth of his personal feelings in a detached manner, and to cover his more emotional reflections with generalizations. Having claimed that

> the happiest time in a man's life is when he's
> courting a girl and finds out for sure that she
> loves him and hasn't a thought for anyone else

—having exposed a gentleness—he turns to a tone of almost patronizing distance: "Make the most of your courting days, you young chaps." . . . The effect of this alternation of tone is to create an impression of Joe as a sensitive man who has been hurt by experience. But those who miss the purpose of this technique, and who mistake the instruction to "young chaps" for moralizing from the point of view of the cheap advantage of age will not be able to explain the equanimity of "In short he is—well, a married man. And when he knows all this, how much better or happier is he for it?"

This discontinuous and apparently rambling narrative has in fact effectively and economically introduced the theme of the major Joe Wilson stories—an attempt to portray uncompromisingly the range of Joe's personal experiences within marriage, to speak of the woe, and the happiness. In the space of a few paragraphs we have been given an impression of Joe as father and husband, have glimpsed his youth, and been given hints of his possible adultery and marriage failure. All these aspects of Joe's experience are portrayed in the ensuing stories. And, most importantly, the balance of the narrative voice is established, a balance by which Joe, a sensitive and reticent character, is able gradually to reveal his deepest personal emotions.

One of the finest achievements of the Joe Wilson stories is the full realization of a personality and his experiences by means of an impressionist technique. This impressionism is created by the position of memory in the narrative, a memory which selects in its reflective processes the primary material to be included in the story. The narrator, as vehicle for memory, also interprets and includes glimpses of the present in relation to the past, which results in not merely a flashback effect, but a shifting perspective closer to superimposition in film. In describing the "first glimpse I got of Mary," Joe uses such a superimposition:

> There was a wide, old-fashioned, brick-floored verandah in front, with an open end; there was ivy climbing up the verandah post on one side and a baby-rose on the other, and a grape-vine near the chimney. We rode up to the end of the verandah, and Jack called to see if there was anyone at home, and Mary came trotting out; so it was in the frame of vines that I first saw her.

> More than once since then I've had a fancy to wonder whether the rose-bush killed the grape-vine or the ivy smothered 'em both in the end. I used to have a vague idea of riding that way some day to see. You do get strange fancies at odd times.

There is in this passage the initial framing of Mary in the vines, the recall of a first impression, followed immediately by the movement to a later time, with its impression of decay and death in "whether the rose-bush killed the grape-vine." The purpose of the later impression is, of course, to contrast some of the bitterness and harshness of the love relationship with its first glowing freshness. And the contrast is masterfully achieved. The superimposition of the later impression on the earlier, which appears to be merely the inclusion of a rather casual reflection, creates a depth of insight for the reader which would be difficult to achieve any other way. The technique allows us a passing, but penetrating, glimpse of Joe's strange fancies, and of the course of the relationship of Joe and Mary that produces their presence in Joe's mind.

Joe Wilson as narrator is an essentially psychological construct. The narrative is centred in the processes of Joe's consciousness, in his reactions to people and events recorded internally. This is demonstrated by the way that external events are described succinctly whilst passing on to the central concern—Joe's recalled impression: "Jack asked her if the boss was in. He did all the talking." These preliminary facts being dispensed with, we move to the recollection of Mary:

> I saw a little girl rather plump, with a complexion like a New England or Blue Mountain girl. . . . She had the biggest and brightest eyes I'd seen round there, dark, hazel eyes, as I found out afterwards, and bright as a 'possum's. No wonder they called her 'Possum.

This highly selective description gives the reader a mere impression of Mary; of the aspects of her which Joe notices. That is, we see only, and consciously, Joe's Mary—a record available only through the process of his visual perception, and not a literal accumulation of detail. The external world in these stories is presented only by the impressions arising from Joe's response to it, refined through the processes of memory. Joe himself is included in the picture of past events by means of such recalled responses: "I felt a sort of comfortable satisfaction in the fact that I was on horseback: most Bushmen look better on horseback." The effect of this remembered feeling is to create an image of the younger Joe as a Bushman, as a type. But the image itself is a product of the function of memory.

Although the story appears to unfold sequentially—with a linear progression from Joe's introduction to Mary to his proposal—there are constant changes in the time perspective which qualify and overlay the sequential narrative. The opening of the story, with its mature reflections on marriage, tends to contain (but not reduce) the impact of the emotions of the younger man. Joe's impetuosity, his romanticism, his bashfulness are fully presented, but are continually placed in a balanced perspective by the discontinuous interpretative entries of the older Joe. An example is the reflective comment on the fight with Romany:

> Looking back, I think there was a bit of romance about it: Mary singing under the vines to amuse a jackaroo dude, and a coward going down to the river in the moonlight to fight for her.

The effect of the shifting perspective is to ensure that any romance is eclipsed, and to create a tone of world weariness, of the dissolution of youthful hopes. This effect is most successfully achieved in the ending of **"Joe Wilson's Courtship."** The romantic climax of the clumsy proposal with its innocence and naïvety is completely placed by the final scene depicting Joe's approach to Old Black for Mary's hand. Black's bitterness towards his wife is made evident, and the story ends with a masterfully evoked sense of impermanence, of the inevitable dissolution of romantic aspiration. We are left with the final image of an old man conveying that feeling of inevitability to a younger man. And it is conveyed by impression only, by hint, and with unusual power:

> "What did you say, Boss?" I said.

> "Nothing Joe," he said. "I was going to say a lot, but it wouldn't be any use. My father used to say a lot to me before I was married."

The failure of Black's marriage, and more than mere failure, a sense of disillusion for which no one can be prepared or forewarned, is carried by these sentences. And that important Lawsonian device, the reflective pause, is used to convey the unspeakable:

> I waited a good while for him to speak.

> "Well, Boss," I said, "What about Mary?"

> "Oh! I suppose that's all right Joe," he said. "I—I beg your pardon. I got thinking of the days when I was courting Mrs Black."

The nostalgia of Black for his courting days has, of course, already been undercut by his present position and bitterness towards his wife. This ends the story neatly on the theme of the transitory joy of courtship. But there is a further significance in Black's "that's all right, Joe." It is an echo of the statement that would have been the climax of the story had it been merely romantic: "'Mary,' I said, 'would you marry a chap like me?' And that was all right." The very different tone of "all right" in Black's later statement gives the phrase a strongly ironic quality.

It is clear from a close reading of **"Joe Wilson's Courtship"** that Lawson was trying to achieve an intensification of experience of a different nature from that of the full dramatic presentation of a novel. His use of discontinuous narrative enables him to escape the confines of a strictly sequential time scheme and plot development, and to include only those events and characters important to his impressionistic style.

In the Joe Wilson sequence of **"Joe Wilson's Courtship,"** **"Brighten's Sister-in-Law,"** **"'Water Them Geraniums',"** **"A Double Buggy at Lahey's Creek"** and **"Drifting Apart,"** intensification of experience is centred upon an event or character, and is depicted in terms of Joe's responses. The fight with Romany, little Jim's convulsions, the strangeness of Mrs. Spicer, stimulate Joe's gaining of insight into existence. These incidents and characters also force Joe to reflect on his own psychological processes. On his way to fight Romany, for example, Joe, in hastily deciding that this incident is to be the turning point of his life, reflects that "A man can think a lot in a flash sometimes." A major aspect of the story becomes a study of Joe's psychological reactions to the stress of the fight. We gain impression after impression of these reactions, which take precedence in Joe's memory:

> I was thinking fast, and learning more in three seconds than Jack's sparring could have taught me in three weeks. I fancy that a fighting man, if he isn't altogether an animal, suffers more mentally than he does physically. . . . I thought hard into the future, even as I fought the fight only seemed something that was passing.

In **"Brighten's Sister-in-Law"** we again find this type of "flash" insight of Joe's, which occurs while little Jim is being attended to by the nurse: "I thought of Mary and the funeral—and wished that that was past. All this in a flash, as it were." Joe's recorded psychological reactions are not merely mundane or conventional, but have a revelatory, confessional tone:

> I felt that it would be a great relief, and only wished the funeral was months past. I felt— well, altogether selfish. I only thought for myself.

Joe is aware that this is not the way he is supposed to be thinking, and that a more normal feeling would be to be thinking only of his sick child. But this is not merely an attempt to be confessionally honest or coldly realistic. It is a continuation of a theme of these stories concerning unusual or extreme states of mind emanating from intense experiences. In **"Brighten's Sister-in-Law,"** the aspect of strangeness is accentuated from the beginning. Jim is described as being an "old-fashioned child," and Joe implies some connection between this aspect of personality and Jim's convulsions. Jim's disjointed conversation and behaviour become a progression of signs of impending illness:

> When I went to lift him in he was lying back, looking up at the stars in a half-dreamy, half-fascinated way that I didn't like. Whenever Jim

was extra old-fashioned, or affectionate, there was a danger.

Joe, alone in the Bush at night with a sick child, has become involved, as in his fight with Romany, in a decisive struggle which will severely test his mind and emotions. The internal narrative allows the reader to experience this struggle in terms of responses and feelings:

> I was mad with anxiety and fright; I remember I kept saying, "I'll be kinder to Mary after this! I'll take more notice of Jim."

The sense of strangeness and tension would probably become melodramatic if it was not for the narrative viewpoint. The inclusion of the apparition pointing to Brighten's farm would be almost ridiculous if not for Joe's consciousness being the vehicle for its interpretation:

> —Now, it might have been that I was all un-strung, or it might have been a patch of sky outlined in the gently moving branches, or the blue smoke rising up. But I saw the figure of a woman, all white, come down, down, nearly to the limbs of the trees, point on up the main road and then float up and up and vanish, still pointing. I thought Mary was dead! Then it flashed on me—

What would otherwise be a rather clumsy piece of plot machinery, or too strenuous a concession to the supernatural and strange elements of the story, becomes a means of possible psychological insight because of Joe's own account of his state of mind immediately before the hallucination:

> Then I lost nerve and started blundering back-ward and forward between the waggon and the fire, and repeating what I'd heard Mary say the last time we fought for Jim: "God! don't take my child! God! don't take my boy!"

In this context the hallucination becomes the manifestation of a severely distracted state of mind. It is as if Joe's memory, which already holds the information about Brighten's Sister-in-Law, fails to operate rationally under stress, and his mind instead throws out an image revealing the information.

The success of **"Brighten's Sister-in-Law"** is dependent on the fidelity of the narrator in recording his responses and impressions. Joe is regarding his consciousness with detachment, as if its functions are not really under control, but merely *happen:*

> I felt cold all over then and sick in the stom-ach—but *clear-headed* in a way: strange, wasn't it? I don't know why I didn't get down and rush into the kitchen to get a bath ready.

This confessional honesty, only possible in an internal narra-tive, is undoubtedly a great achievement of the Joe Wilson stories. It is a very convincing form of psychological realism.

It is, then, the consciousness of Joe Wilson, as presented in his narrative, that is the subject of these stories. Neither Bright-en's Sister-in-Law, or even Mrs. Spicer, are the true subjects of the stories in which they feature so prominently. These characters become ultimately important because of what they represent for Joe at the time of their appearance, and for the significance of the impressions of them created in Joe's con-sciousness.

Mrs. Spicer is undoubtedly important as a representative type: the downtrodden Bushwoman. But if she is representative, like, say, the Drover's Wife, she is not representative in the same way. Mrs. Spicer is most important as representing something for Joe. She is a symbol of the wretchedness awaiting him, and particularly, awaiting Mary. The full sketch of Mrs. Spicer in Part Two of "**'Water Them Geraniums'**" would be of greatly reduced significance, and in no real way different from, say, the portrait of the Bush Undertaker (another mad or "ratty" inhabitant of Lawson's Bush) if we did not have the preceding knowledge of Joe's depressed state in Part One before she makes her real appearance.

Mrs. Spicer is introduced after Joe and Mary have their first argument at Lahey's Creek. The argument is chiefly interesting because of the insight we gain into Joe's character and personality, an insight gained by the technique of allowing the reader to experience the gap between what Joe is saying to Mary and what he is thinking in response to her words:

> "And what sort of a place was Gulgong, Joe?" asked Mary quietly. (I thought even then in a flash what sort of place Gulgong was. A wretched remnant of a town on an old abandoned gold-field. . . .)

The distance between Joe's words in argument with Mary, and his actual recognition of his own weaknesses and wrong views, creates an impression of discontent which far exceeds the particular subject of the argument. The sense of discontent is heightened dramatically by the intervention of the older Joe with a bitter reflection:

> But the time came, and not many years after, when I stood by the bed where Mary lay, white and still, and, amongst other things, I kept saying, "I'll give in, Mary—I'll give in," and then I'd laugh. They thought that I was raving mad, and took me from the room.

This dismal image of the end of Joe and Mary's relationship, a vision of Joe's ultimate discontent, failure, and even madness, sets the tone of the narrative for the introduction of Mrs. Spicer as a symbol of desperation, the introduction of the bushwoman who precedes Mary to the state of being "past carin'."

Joe's feeling of marital failure is matched by his recognition of the personal weaknesses which he feels underlie his general failure: "I was not fit to 'go on the land' . . . I had only drifted here through carelessness, brooding, and discontent." And into the midst of these reflections on failure, this mental landscape of desolation, is introduced the figure of Mrs. Spicer, the "gaunt haggard Bushwoman."

Mrs. Spicer represents even more than "what Mary would come to if I left her here." She is the embodiment of the madness of the Bush, the representation of a mind driven beyond "carin'," beyond normal feelings and responses. And rather than being a merely individual study of this condition, she is presented as being an extension of a state of mind common to all who spend a long time alone in the Bush:

> I think that most men who have been alone in the Bush for any length of time—and married couples too—are more or less mad.

The commonness of madness in the Bush makes Mrs. Spicer less an eccentric to be identified as outside normal experience, and more a natural development of the conditions common to all Bush inhabitants. It is significant that Joe himself has had some experience of Bush madness, and can thus act as a credible interpreter of Mrs. Spicer's condition. Mary, however, is outside this experience, and this intensifies the relationship of shared understanding between Joe and Mrs. Spicer: "Mary thought her a little mad at times. But I seemed to understand." Joe's understanding of Mrs. Spicer is crucial to the creation of her as a character of stature.

Mrs. Spicer, as reflected in and presented by Joe's narrative consciousness, represents not so much a fully drawn character as a state of being. She is the true objective correlative of the desolation of the Bush, and of Joe's discontent with Bush life. Her disjointed conversations, with their bitter reflections on a harsh existence, and their anecdotes of men hanging themselves in despair, create the impression of a personality that has lost its full range of normal response, that has gradually narrowed in the face of a limited and harsh environment. Mrs. Spicer is in the state of being (progressively) "past carin'." But this state does not have any equanimity or philosophical resignation of a positive kind. It is rather an almost total disintegration of human sensibility. For example, when Mary asks Mrs. Spicer about her loneliness during the long absences of her husband, she replies "'I don't mind—I somehow seem to have got past carin'." Mrs. Spicer's self-awareness has been reduced to the knowledge that she is "past carin'," and "ratty," or mad.

Mrs. Spicer represents, then, the disintegration of civilized habits in the harsh Bush environment. That Mrs. Spicer had once had such habits is indicated when Mary notices that she "had been used to table napkins at one time in her life." This observation both places Mary at a considerable distance from the experience of Mrs. Spicer's present condition, adding to the former's aura of innocence, and skilfully creates an impression of the early Mrs. Spicer and the extent of her downfall. And it is Joe who possesses and conveys the full knowledge of what Mrs. Spicer's state of being really is. Mary is largely outside this knowledge, gaining only a partial insight into its full significance, and this increases her potential as a victim of the Bush.

Mrs. Spicer herself indicates to Joe both her awareness of his recognition of the cause of her state of mind, and their complicity in the implications that the recognition may have for Mary:

> She said nothing for a long time, and seemed to be thinking in a puzzled way. Then she said suddenly:
>
> "What-did-you-bring-her-here-for? She's only a girl."
>
> "I beg pardon, Mrs. Spicer?"

Joe's politely evasive "I beg pardon" attempts to conceal what is in fact a feeling shared by both Joe and Mrs. Spicer. For the reader already has the record of Joe's reaction on first encountering Mrs. Spicer:

> I felt—and the thought came like a whip-stroke on my heart—that this was what Mary would come to if I left her here.

It is this relationship of Joe, as narrator, with Mrs. Spicer and their shared knowledge of the possible effect of the Bush on human sensibility, which makes "**'Water Them Geraniums'**" the finest story of the Joe Wilson series. Lawson has achieved a narrative balance which allows a powerful creation of impression with a minimum of conventional plot. **"Joe Wilson's Courtship"** and **"Brighten's Sister-in-Law"** have a far greater element of plot development than **"'Water Them Geraniums'."** The creation of Mrs. Spicer does not rely on the pretext of an event like courtship or the sickness of a child, or on any sequential development of such events. **"'Water Them Geraniums'"** records the interaction of characters in a shared experience—living in the Bush. And in this interaction we see most clearly the personality and consciousness of the narrator. Unlike, say, the fight with Romany, or the midnight dash to Brighten's house, the events of **"'Water Them Geraniums'"** are comparatively unexceptional.

What is conveyed most strongly by the story is a sense of depression, of a type of grinding anguish. And Lawson, in so doing, has created his "strange dream" of the Bush:

> It is when the sun goes down on the dark bed of the lonely Bush, and the sunset flashes like a sea of fire and then fades, and then glows out again, like a bank of coals, and then burns away to ashes—it is then that old things come home to one. And strange, new-old things too, that haunt and depress you terribly, and that you can't understand.

Joe and Mrs. Spicer share this mystical knowledge of the Bush, a knowledge which may lead to anguish and madness, and which is incomprehensible to the uninitiated. It is the exploration of this anguish through the narrative consciousness of Joe, located most powerfully in his reaction to and relationship with Mrs. Spicer, that gives the story such a depth of insight into human nature. Lawson has here most successfully presented his preoccupation with the intricacies and manifestations of the deep suffering of existence, and the attempts of the human spirit to come to terms with that suffering. The quality of narrative in the Joe Wilson sequence is undoubtedly the high point of Lawson's literary production. (pp. 97-107)

John Maddocks, "Narrative Technique in Lawson's Joe Wilson Stories," in Southerly, *Vol. 37, No. 1, March, 1977, pp. 97-107.*

KEN STEWART (essay date 1983)

[*In the following excerpt Stewart examines two chief characteristics of Lawson's fiction, "human gregariousness" and "the hardness of things."*]

Lawson's emphasis on gregariousness is obvious and elusive: obvious, because we attest to it in every story about loneliness, isolation, mateship, neighbourliness, and masculine bush ethos, love, husband and wife, madness, the bush itself as humans experience it; potentially elusive, because we may so easily fail to perceive that he alone among authors of recognised stature writes of little else: this instinct and need within the human species, its potential and limitations, the forms it may take and the effects of its repression, are virtually his exclusive subject, determining action and plot, or passivity and plotlessness, and the complexity of his narrative tone, as well as defining the area in which his insight into human behaviour and human nature operates. It is possible for characters to live by themselves in Furphy's fiction, for example, without becoming mad, or eccentric, or intolerably deprived; and if, like Tom Collins, the loner may be judged as rather fussy, pedantic and self-deluding—then, such is life. Such *isn't* life for Lawson: the gregarious impulse, in his view of the nature of things,

is dominant and paramount; the loner is to be perceived as a curious individual, like Mr Smellingscheck, whose mystique and mystery derive from the fact that he is *not* gregarious. The isolate in Lawson is eccentric; or mad; or sulky, sullen and selfish; or intolerably deprived. The salvation of the Bush Undertaker, and of the swagman "Rats," is that they create their own gregarious reality from illusion. The Drover's Wife is an archetypal image of maternal isolation and loneliness—intolerably deprived. The urgency and extensiveness of Lawson's preoccupation with the gregarious impulse is artistically valid (his art validates it) but it is almost exclusive: nobody climbs Mount Everest, or experiences an epiphany or invents the wheel, or is "justified" through romantic love or religious experience, or occupies himself in any way satisfactorily, unless it be gregariously; and the author's values and priorities adjust themselves to this perspective on human lives.

Lawson's subject, then, is the instinct of human beings for human company and contact: to huddle, to be, and to interact, preferably warmly, with others of the species. His first person narrators are "insiders." They write critically, ambivalently and loyally from inside the group, accommodating themselves to the bullies and big kids, like Barcoo Rot and One Eyed Bogan; the innocuously stupid, like Tom Hall; and the hard cases, like Mitchell. The relationship of the narrator to the group establishes the paradox of conformity as a theme or problematic element within many of the stories, (for example, **"Lord Douglas," "The Union Buries Its Dead,"** and **"Telling Mrs. Baker"**), but gregarious solidarity must win, or at least continue. In **"The Union Buries Its Dead"** it is not the loner's death that is disturbing; it is Lawson's evocation of the fear that a man, or all men, could be cut off from the human race, unredeemed by the gregarious impulse, locked without recognition within the individual self. His Union is a huddle of schoolboys; the verandah of the Bourke Imperial is like the quadrangle of a segregated boys' secondary school. Although the characters in these settings are not "types," they are realised psychologically only to the extent that social rituals and the breaking of them permit and define. They are real people whom the reader gets to know socially, but not intimately; and their mores and routines, the unwritten rules for gregarious behaviour, are, as Hal Porter would write, "equally of air and of iron." From time to time a fight breaks out in the quadrangle; and occasionally, as in **"That Pretty Girl in the Army,"** a strange foreign creature called a girl wanders into alien precincts, and you have to patronise her delicately and watch your language. (pp. 152-53)

Lawson's second pervasive assumption is "the hardness of things." The most universal practice amongst sane people in his fiction is overt worry, in the manner of Joe Wilson, or the suppression of outward concern, as with Mitchell. His celebrated "realism" is flecked with constant emotional regret: external reality is not his subject—the narrator's emotional response, his voice, is the subject. The difference between Lawson's "Ah, well" and Furphy's "Such is Life," or rather his many "Such is Life"'s, is that Lawson's expresses a direct emotional avowal, whereas Furphy's characters offer a more cerebral diversity of clinching observations in the face of the variety and enigma of life itself. "Ah, well" expresses *felt* resignation: it is a kind of sad moan. The contrast with "Such is Life" is illustrated inadvertently by Manning Clark in Volume IV of *A History of Australia:*

> Ned Kelly walked to his death in the Old Melbourne Gaol in the morning of 11 November

1880. His mother had urged him to die like a Kelly. Some said he looked frightened and morose and only managed to utter a lame "Ah well, I suppose it has come to this." Others said he summed it up in that sardonic Australian remark "Such is Life."

Lawson's positives, then, charity, neighbourliness, even madness, toughness and shrewdness, are really the valued arms of struggle against the hardness of things. Lawson never states despair: he intones something grim. Even "It didn't matter much—nothing does" is a fluctuation of the voice, rather than a considered conclusion; and it is a voice which is not so much meditating, as actually expressing the moment's reaction to a continuing burden. There is an undefined or lost ideal behind Lawson's writing: it is life *without* the hardness of things; it is the relief of that pressure which creates his narrator's burdened tone.

That Lawson, unlike Furphy and Baynton, implicitly uses such an ideal as a gauge of the quality of reality is illustrated by his attacks on the romanticism and optimism of other Australian writers. These attacks in fact indicate his self-delusion, because they illustrate *his* romantic longing:

> They put in shining rivers and grassy plains, and western hills, and dawn and morn, and forest boles of gigantic size—everything, in fact, which is not and never was in bush scenery or language; and the more the drought bakes them the more inspired they become. Perhaps they unconsciously see the bush as it should be, and their literature is the result of craving for the ideal.

The angry bitterness is revealing. It is as though Lawson would really like to "put in shining rivers and grassy plains" but the truth prevents him, and makes him angry with those who do. In the phrase "they unconsciously see the bush as it should be," he gives himself away, by implying that the bush "should be" an Arcadian dream world. Clearly, and ironically, Lawson's literature is equally "the result of a craving for the ideal" of the optimists he attacks, albeit in conjunction with his constant emotional rediscovery that the world is not ideal. (p. 154)

Lawson's fascination with ideal and real, and with illusion and reality, triggers the creative impulse behind several of his best known stories. It leads him to examine perspectives on a seeming innocence or state of grace, a condition in which the Hardness of Things dissolves or loses its oppressiveness, and in which altruism and generosity are unsullied by hard experience, and may work as an agent of good. These stories, however, work to conclude that the Hardness of Things itself explains or modifies any initial, magical *appearance* of innocence or grace, and reduces it to the status of very unmagical experience. "That's the way of it," comments Donald McDonald at the end of **"That Pretty Girl in the Army,"** "with a woman it's love or religion; with a man it's love or the devil." That Pretty Girl, whose initial mystique is of altruism, beauty and spiritual quality, so far from transcending the Hardness of Things through some unusual bestowed grace or inherent innocence or goodness, is eventually to be perceived as simply the product and the victim of this ordinary hardness in life: apparent innocence becomes an explicable delusion. Mrs. Baker, too, must remain deluded: the hardness of things is *too* hard for her to be told. The Giraffe, to whom we have begun to respond for his innocence and natural generosity, is as close as Lawson gets to

sainthood. But in Lawson's world, where therre are many martyrs and no saints, the Giraffe has to start saving his money, and is despatched on the train to marriage, which in Lawson is virtually a synonym for Paradise Lost. "I wish I could immortalize him!" writes the narrator, longing for the ideal, but thereby confirming that he cannot. The Giraffe has never really changed hardbitten humanity; it has changed him. (p. 155)

Ken Stewart, "'The Loaded Dog': A Celebration," in Australian Literary Studies, *Vol. 11, No. 2, October, 1983, pp. 152-61.*

BRIAN MATTHEWS (essay date 1983)

[*In the following excerpt Matthews discusses Lawson's depiction of women.*]

In his harsh review of **While the Billy Boils** [see excerpt dated 1896] A. G. Stephens makes so many damaging criticisms that it is easy to overlook one of the strangest and most quixotic of them, especially as it occurs in the last two sentences and is more or less a "throw-away." "Not the best," he suggests, "but the most promising [stories] are those which tell 'An Unfinished Love Story'." "Here, for the first time, Lawson ceases to describe characteristics and starts to create characters." This is a rather gnomic pronouncement in several ways. What are the other stories which, it is implied, also tell an unfinished love story? Even interpreted as literally as possible, the remark could only refer to a very few stories: **"He'd Come Back"** perhaps; **"Bogg of Geebung," "The Drover's Wife," "Drifted Back," "Some Day"** . . .? These would at least be candidates but they are not at all obvious or even satisfactory choices. Outside of them, it's difficult to see what else might qualify. Moreover, even when Stephens's implied definition is stretched to breaking point, only two of these could remotely be regarded as creating characters rather than describing characteristics. The other three, **"He'd Come Back," "Drifted Back"** and **"Bogg of Geebung"** are, on the face of it, some of the slightest pieces in the whole collection. They are precisely the sort of thing to which Stephens takes energetic exception elsewhere in the same review: ". . . here a mouthful of salt, there one of pepper," "scrappy and disconnected," "detached sketches," "slight skeins," "half-a-hundred taps to strike half-a-dozen blows," etc.

What did Stephens see in **"An Unfinished Love Story"?** Probably not much. It is the last point he makes in his review and it has all the hallmarks of reviewer's twitch—that surrender to home-grown aphorism, slick generalization, neat phrase-turning or cavalier throwaway which casts little or no light on the work but makes the reviewer look rather good so long as no one reads too closely. Stephens's special trick here is to adapt the story's title neatly to his own apparent purpose, but in doing so he commits himself to a generalization about **While the Billy Boils** which will not stand a moment's scrutiny. And yet . . . *Something* caught Stephens's attention even if almost subliminally, and it was something more intriguing, more substantial than can be conveyed by the glib distinction between describing characteristics and creating characters. If Lawson is creating characters in **"An Unfinished Love Story,"** Brook is not one of them. He is a thoroughly recognizable figure—the world-hardened city man returning with only contempt or at best weary curiosity to his bush origins, who takes advantage (just exactly what advantage is not clear) of an inexperienced farm girl. There is something desolating and deathly about Brook. In a collection where names and characters recur constantly, Brook, whose "father was dead [and whose] other relations had moved away" is never heard of or mentioned in any other story. His return to the city where, "'after hours,' he staggered in through a side entrance to the lighted parlour of a private bar" is like a grateful descent into a subworld. But Lizzie is much more interesting and perhaps it is only the relative mediocrity of the story, *pace* Stephens, that makes it seem extravagant to see her not as a new departure in Lawsonian characterization (which, as far as I can see, she is not) but as an example of a pattern the recognition of which is crucial to our understanding of Lawson's portrayal of women.

There is a certain passiveness about Lizzie, but it is more like what *The Dawn* referred to as feminine "passive force" than anything describable as submissiveness. Lizzie's demeanour is constantly characterized as "grave," "solemn," "reflective," "thoughtful," "pondering"; she deliberates and her essential innocence is communicated by this deliberation which is always suggesting that she has no ready-made reactions drawn from pleasant or bitter experience in life or love. Her answers are carefully and reasonably thought out; they are not recollections or interpretations of experience. Lawson skilfully enhances this impression of an innocent, unspoiled mind addressing complex and personal matters with untutored genuineness, by reporting much of what she decides and replies in short, scrupulously unambiguous sentences. This method has the added effect of making her appear silent, withdrawing, but also self-contained. We don't often, as it were, hear her voice:

> She thought a while, and then she asked him if he was glad to go.
>
> She thought a good long while, and then she said she was.
>
> She reflected so as to be sure; then she said she hadn't.
>
> She pondered over this for some minutes as a result of which she said she thought that she did.

Lizzie accepts Brook's attentions "with the greatest of gravity." After the first kiss, during which her lack of emotion gives way to "agitation," she "obeys" Brook's further urgings "just as a frightened child might." Her breathless confusion, her sudden torrent of words ("We must go now" / "We really must go now" / "I don't know—I can't promise" / "I don't like to promise" etc.) stand in pointed contrast to her earlier reticence and deliberation. Yet with all this, and despite her acceptance of Brook's urgent authority and ready rationalizations, Lizzie's "passive force" seems always more impressive, more substantial than Brook's persuasions: it is not that she won't be hurt by him but that she remains—no matter what the outcome of their insignificant encounter—on another plane from him, *profoundly* different. As for the outcome, it is always obvious Brook will abandon her: every move he has made has been both calculated and shallow and in response to her sense of "wonder" he feels only curiosity. When the truth can no longer be avoided, she shows "some emotion for the first time, or perhaps the second—maybe the third time—in that week of her life." "They say Lizzie broke her heart that year," the story concludes, "but, then, the world does not believe in such things nowadays."

It seems, though, that Lawson does. If anything distinguishes the story it is the kind of love which it is within Lizzie's power to bestow: "the wonder in her expression—as if something

had come into her life which she could not realize" has a transforming effect upon her presence in the story. Her innocence, which Lawson has been at pains to establish and which is not simple sexual inexperience or ignorance but a kind of pristineness (she has never loved anyone but she knows what love is), is enhanced by this incipient transformation. There is something utopian in this view of woman and the sense of utopianism disappointed informs the saddened conclusion as well as the ruthless realism of the portrait of Brook and his motives. Brook—and the disbelieving "world"—are Experience to her Innocence. Lawson seems to have a personal investment in the idealism of his portrait of Lizzie while, at the same time, sadly admitting and demonstrating that this is not the kind of world in which such idealism can long live untainted. He returns to the point in the sequel story, **"Thin Lips and False Teeth,"** in which Brook dreams of Lizzie during a feverish, hung-over sleep:

> He begin to dream pretty coherently. He thought he was back on the old selection where he had spent a holiday some two or three years previously. He was sitting, in the twilight, on a log among some saplings, with the selector's niece—a country girl of nineteen—by his side . . . Next he was on his knees in the dirt before the log, with his arms folded on top of it, and his forehead resting on his wrists. He seemed crushed down by some horrible load of trouble. A light girlish hand was laid gently on his bowed head . . . She understood, then! She understood! The simple, innocent bush girl! Oh God!

It is Lizzie's brand of innocence here which makes her the healer of his ills. She has nothing of his experience of the world, she is a "country girl," only "nineteen," "girlish," "simple," "innocent," a "bush girl"—one could scarcely miss the emphasis—but she "understands." From some resource that is not reason, experience, the lessons of the years, she derives her healing knowledge. The source seems to be what Lawson sees as a uniquely feminine innocence.

Awake, Brook resolves to seek out this "something pure," the "rest and peace" represented by the vision of Lizzie; he will "breathe awhile in an atmosphere of innocence." But it is too late. Lizzie has already been tainted by the world—by his previous rejection—has already written him a pathetic, pleading and vulnerable letter, has already—as a result of having given in vain "the first love of her life"—married the oafish James Bullock. "How cruelly dull and dreary her life must be in such a place," Brook reflects, before retreating once more to the city.

Lizzie's story adds, in retrospect, further substance and some explanation to **"The Drover's Wife."** The two stories are placed almost together in the second half of *While the Billy Boils*, separated—perhaps as a kind of momentary relief—only by **"Steelman's Pupil";** so if the book is read in sequence it is almost inevitable that some connections between them will become evident. The drover's wife is well advanced along a road on which Lizzie has taken only the first fatal steps. She is long past bestowing her life's first love. "As a girl she built the usual castles in the air; but all her girlish hopes and aspirations have long been dead." She has known great hardship and "has few pleasures to think of"; she has learned so well to endure the loneliness she once hated that she would now "feel strange away from it." Her husband, who may "forget sometimes that he is married'' is ''careless, but a good enough husband.'' ''She is glad when (he) returns, but she does not gush or make a fuss about it . . . She seems contented with her lot.'' Nevertheless, her plight is truly desperate and her tears at the end of the story are silent recognition of the knowledge that she is doomed forever to this life of successive crises, of loneliness, of gradual decline as her strength and her will to endure are eroded. Tommy's assurance that he ''won't never go drovin'' only twists the knife. She knows, as does the reader, that he will go his own way, inevitably. ''How cruelly dull and dreary her life [is] in such a place.''

There are some important similarities between these two portrayals. While the nature of the bush and bush life is a powerful force in the imminent disintegration of both women, so also is the nature of man. Both are in one way or another abandoned by a man (the drover's wife has been alone for six months at the time the incident takes place); both have a husband who is at best ''good enough''; both have suffered the destruction of innocent visions—the drover's wife's ''girlish hopes and aspirations'' are dead; Lizzie's sense of ''wonder . . . as if something had come into her life which she could not realize'' has been brutally dissipated leaving her broken-hearted. Explicitly in **''An Unfinished Love Story''** and less obviously in **''The Drover's Wife,''** there is a suggestion that a crucial factor in the actual or imminent decline of the woman has been her involvement with an unworthy man. Even in **''The Drover's Wife''** such an inference is available and receives more than bare emphasis when Tommy makes his vow: the actual emptiness of his impulsive assurance, the certainty that he *will* go away, seems to point to something in the nature of things between men and women. Tommy's outburst is implicitly a criticism of his father as a man unworthy of the wife who endures so much because of his absence. But Tommy will do the same thing. In **''An Unfinished Love Story,''** of course, the unworthiness of Brook is unmistakable.

There aren't many other women in *While the Billy Boils* but Lizzie's small tragedy does seem to have a brief prefigurement in **''Some Day.''** Here, the redoubtable Mitchell tells of the ''one little girl'' he ''was properly stuck on'':

> I think she was the best little girl that ever lived, and about the prettiest. She was just eighteen, and didn't come up to my shoulder; the biggest blue eyes you ever saw, and she had hair that reached down to her knees, and so thick you couldn't span it with two hands—brown and glossy—and her skin was like lilies and roses. Of course, I never thought she'd look at a rough, ugly, ignorant brute like me, and I used to keep out of her way and act a little stiff towards her; . . . I thought . . . she pitied me because I was such a rough, awkward chap. I was gone on that girl and no joking; and I felt quite proud to think she was a countrywoman of mine.

The pattern is the same: the man either is or, as in this case, fancies he is unworthy of the woman. She for her part is perfection. Lizzie was not physically striking but had an innocence, a pristine quality as I have called it, which Brook—belatedly—recognized as setting her absolutely apart. Edie Brown is physically beautiful with ideal attributes: lustrous hair, blue eyes, perfect skin fit for comparison with the lilies and roses of tradition; and so on. Her innocence, her unspoilt quality, is suggested by the twice-used term ''*little* girl.'' The real or imagined unworthiness of the man in both **''An Unfinished**

Love Story'' and **''Some Day''** destroys the possibilities which the woman's transcendent qualities put within his reach. In each case, the woman is forced to make a declaration which is painful to her pride and natural modesty: she abandons momentarily and with difficulty what Lawson portrays as a natural demureness that comes not from subservience but from self-awareness, in an attempt to begin the process of realizing the potential she feels rightly or wrongly exists in the relationship. In each case the man rejects this plea and leaves her. Lizzie's life is ruined by it; we don't hear about Edie though the experience will clearly do her no good judging from the intensity of her reactions. And in each case it is, in the final judgment, ''the world''—the nature of things between men and women—that is the problem: ''the world does not believe in such things nowadays''; ''Damn the world, say I,'' concludes Mitchell.

On the evidence of these three stories, together with the fleeting glimpses one gets in sketches and vignettes like **''Drifted Back,''** **''Bogg of Geebung''** and others, it begins to look as if, in Lawson's eyes, men are simply not worthy of women. He tends to place women on a pedestal or alternatively, portray them as if they have been treated shamefully if not so placed. Thus idealised, they are basically beyond the reach of men, either because the men are frankly no good or because in the presence of ideal womanhood, they think they are no good. When women leave their pedestals to enter the world of men, it is like leaving Eden: their innocence becomes permanently scarred by rejection or other kinds of ill-treatment; the vision of love either disintegrates completely or degenerates to mere propinquity; loving sacrifice collapses into a dogged endurance that might well appear more and more meaningless as time passes. There is, it seems, rarely a middle way. That, at any rate, is how it looks in *While the Billy Boils,* a work which, considering its deservedly classic status, has remarkably little to say about the relationships between men and women, or, more particularly, about women. Nevertheless, what it does say tends to linger in the mind: **''Some Day''** is the bitterest of the earliest group of Mitchell sketches; **''The Drover's Wife''** is a fascinating, endlessly challenging portrait; and as for Lizzie, it is not surprising she caught A. G. Stephens's jaundiced eye even if he didn't pause to work out what it was he had glimpsed. In these three pieces, and very tenuously elsewhere, Lawson begins to worry around the edges of a conflict—that between woman as ideal (because that is the way he inclines to see her) and a world, a reality, in which, as he clearly realizes, that ideal cannot continue to exist without some concessions, some deterioration from its pristine original. Men inhabit the evil world. Women—the women he values—are beyond it and are tarnished almost invariably by entering it. In *While the Billy Boils* this conflict is barely sketched; if he'd said no more on the matter it would have been impossible to proceed even this far. But in fact, he has a great deal more to say: in later books it becomes a major preoccupation and the pattern arguably visible in *While the Billy Boils* becomes familiar and entrenched.

On the Track, and Over the Sliprails have much to say about women and the woman problem (or ''the sex problem'') mostly through the medium of Mitchell. There are discussions on the matter (**''Mitchell on Matrimony,''** or **''Mitchell on the 'Sex' and Other 'Problems'''**—the very titles have a didactic ring) and cases and examples are canvassed (**''The Story of the Oracle,''** **''A Case for the Oracle''**). There are more ambitious, plotted stories (**''The Selector's Daughter''** and **''The Hero of Redclay''**) but these owe a great deal to standard melodramatic plots and much less to Lawson's own inspiration which, for

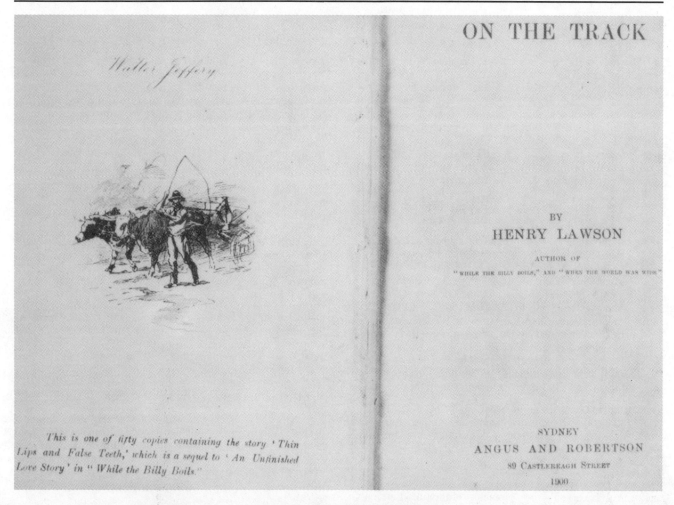

ON THE TRACK

BY
HENRY LAWSON

AUTHOR OF
"WHILE THE BILLY BOILS," AND "WHEN THE WORLD WAS WIDE"

This is one of fifty copies containing the story 'Thin Lips and False Teeth,' which is a sequel to 'An Unfinished Love Story' in "While the Billy Boils."

SYDNEY
ANGUS AND ROBERTSON
89 CASTLEREAGH STREET
1900

Frontispiece and title page of On the Track.

various reasons, is faltering in both these books. (Even so, Ruth Wilson in **"The Hero of Redclay"** is "pretty, and ladylike, and [keeps] to herself" and "most of the single men . . . and some of the married ones . . . were gone on her" but could not bring themselves to approach her; she gives herself to Jack Drew who is unworthy of her but whom she hopes will reform and who finally leaves her rather than have her name besmirched. She never recovers from the shock and dies of brain fever: a familiar pattern grafted onto a borrowed situation.)

In the Mitchell sketches—which incidentally lose much of their punch and profundity as they become more diffuse and didactic—Mitchell grapples with the problem of understanding women and makes a poor fist of it. In **"Mitchell on Matrimony"** he decides that trying to understand women "would be only wasted brain power that might just as well be spent on the blackfellow's lingo; because by the time you've learnt it they'll be extinct, and woman'll be extinct before you've learnt her." The rest of his reflection, fragmented and even a little muddled, consists of musings on how a woman's inevitably domestic career might be made more comfortable by a thoughtful husband! In having Mitchell put these views, no matter how sympathetically, Lawson was at odds even then with much feminine (and not only feminist) opinion and entirely in conflict with his mother who, only a year before the composition date of this sketch, had thundered in *The Dawn* editorial:

A woman's life should not be bounded by domesticity, not as a means of showing her dislike for that sphere, but for the highest good of those within it. The true mother gathers the riches of intellect, education, and ethics that she may administer them to those at home.

But it is evident that Lawson could not have accommodated such views even had he been ideologically inclined to because he was haunted by the sense that once the woman became part of the man's world the result was a Fall. His vision of her was such that no man was worthy of her. Mitchell's meanderings in **"Mitchell on Matrimony"** are shot through with this assumption: "I don't think we ever understood women properly . . . I don't think we ever will"; ". . . a man changes after he's married . . . it comes like a cold shock to her and all her air-castles vanish"; ". . . a woman's love is her whole existence, while a man's love is only part of his." Equally, his listener, Joe, who is heading home to his wife, can tell a story only of subtle decline: "I might have made a better husband than I did" he admits "seriously and rather bitterly"; "I might have made her a good deal more happy and contented without hurting myself much." His stern avowal that he is "going to try and make up for it" when he gets back "this time" makes little headway against this prevailing impression of decay, an impression intensified by the final revelation that Mitchell, for all his apparent awareness of women's needs, lost his wife to "another kind of fellow."

In **"Mitchell on the 'Sex' and Other 'Problems'"** the muddle is much greater. This is partly because the "sex problem" is confusedly mixed up with several other unrelated matters, but also because, it seems, Mitchell is frustrated by the imponderability of the whole thing: ". . . the rotten 'sex-problem' sort of thing is the cause of it all," he says vaguely, attributing to the "sex problem" most of the world's political and social ills. Once again, there are strong indications of a "Fall" mentality, a strengthening conviction that when unworthy man does more than worship a good woman from afar, only decline and destructive complexities can result. Polygamy, monogamy, promiscuity—none has really provided an answer to the corrosion that eats into relationships between men and women:

> In the Bible times they had half a dozen wives each, but we don't know for certain how *they* got on. The Mormons tried it again, and seemed to get on all right till we interfered. We don't seem to be able to get on with one wife now . . . The "sex problem" troubled the Turks so much that they tried three. Lots of us try to settle it by knocking round promiscuously, and that leads to actions for maintenance and breach of promise cases and all sorts of trouble. Our blacks settle the "sex problem" with a club, and so far I haven't heard any complaints from them.

The last alternative is, both in its extremity and its underlying desire to have the whole problem somehow go away, as good an indication as any of a strain of desperation never far from the surface of this diatribe.

The lack of control in this sketch, its muddle and indecisiveness, may be attributed, of course, to a number of causes, but one of them is certainly the "problem" of the title. Lawson's own frustrations and confusions are evident: they are caused by his inability or, at best, profound reluctance to see any middle ground between Ideal Woman and the inevitably fallen and deteriorating state which follows upon that woman entering the world of reality, the evil world, the world of men. This is why the conclusion of the sketch, which might conceivably have been mildly humorous, is so significant: it makes explicit at last the anguished desire for simplicity, for a utopia of the sexes, which was recognizable to varying degrees in **"The Drover's Wife," "An Unfinished Love Story," "Some Day"** and **"Mitchell on Matrimony"**:

> Trying to find out things is the cause of all the work and trouble in this world. It was Eve's fault in the first place—or Adam's rather, because it might be argued that he should have been master. Some men are too lazy to be masters in their own homes, and run the show properly; some are too careless, and some too drunk most of their time, and some too weak. If Adam and Eve hadn't tried to find out things there'd have been no toil and trouble in the world today; there'd have been no bloated capitalists, and no horny-handed working men, and no politics, no free trade and protection—and no clothes. We'd have all been running round in a big Garden of Eden with nothing on, and nothing to do except loaf, and make love, and lark, and laugh, and play practical jokes on each other . . .

> That would have been glorious. Wouldn't it, Joe? There'd have been no "sex problem" then.

Here is simplicity—don't try to find out things—and utopia—"nothing to do except loaf and make love . . ."—and no sex problem at all. The fact that it is men's ills that are catalogued now comes as no surprise. The blame for the loss of Eden, traditionally seen as beginning with Eve, is transferred to Adam with a deliberation which draws to it maximum attention. It is man who is unworthy, it is man's transgressions and omissions from which evils flow. The fallen world is characteristically man's world. Eve has been exonerated.

In other stories of **On the Track, and Over the Sliprails** a similar tendency is discernible though there are variations on the basic pattern. In **"No Place For a Woman"** the entry of the woman into the man's world is an actual, physical event: Mary, "a jolly girl when [he] married her," insists on joining Howlett in the remote bush. He, in common with so many of Lawson's men, resists her descent into his world—it's "no place for a woman." But she does come and decline and disaster follow. (pp. 37-46)

Of course, much else can be said about these stories. The bush, the *place* hastens and exacerbates the rifts between men and women as Lawson sees it. It might not be so bad elsewhere, away from loneliness, hardship, uncertainty. It is, literally, no place for a woman. But it is obviously not *only* that which works the evil: the fault is in the nature of the universe and, above all, in the nature of man; not woman.

Lawson's finest work, **Joe Wilson,** is among other things a detailed working out of this pattern which comes to dominate his fiction wherever it deals seriously with love between man and woman. This quartet of stories begins with a clear statement of the "fall" theme: love begins to decline almost as soon as it is born:

> I think the happiest time in a man's life is when he's courting a girl and finds out for sure that she loves him and hasn't a thought for anyone else. Make the most of your courting days, you young chaps, and keep them clean, for they're about the only days when there's a chance of poetry and beauty coming into this life. Make the best of them and you'll never regret it the longest day you live. They're the days that the wife will look back to, anyway, in the brightest of times as well as in the blackest, and there shouldn't be anything in those days that might hurt her when she looks back. Make the most of your courting days, you young chaps, for they will never come again.

Innocence is replaced by Experience: "A married man knows all about it . . . if he's inclined that way, (he) has three times the chance with a woman than a single man has . . . he knows just how far he can go . . . he takes (women) and things for granted . . . And, when he knows all this, how much better or happier is he for it?" **"Joe Wilson's Courtship,"** edenic as it is at one level—with "the Possum's" beauty and innocence and Joe's stumbling transformation as he falls in love—is shot through with sombre reminders of inevitable decay, of "fall." The older Joe, who is narrating the story, pauses often to lament the failures and regrets that have burdened their lives since those days of courtship; and old Black, whose permission Joe must ask in order to marry Mary, sadly prefigures the decline that will inevitably be the lot of Joe and Mary, for all their present commitment to each other.

> "Well, what is it, Joe?"
>
> "I—well, the fact is, I want little Mary."
>
> He puffed at his pipe for a long time, then I thought he spoke.
>
> "What did you say, Boss?" I said.
>
> "Nothing, Joe," he said. "I was going to say a lot, but it wouldn't be any use. My father used to say a lot to me before I was married."
>
> I waited a good while for him to speak.
>
> "Well, Boss," I said, "What about Mary?"
>
> "Oh! I suppose that's all right, Joe,"he said. "I—I beg your pardon. I got thinking of the days when I was courting Mrs Black."

Like other Lawson women before they descend into the world of men, there is something (and it does not have to be obvious physical beauty) which distinguishes Mary from all around her, which makes her seem unspoilt:

> I saw a *little girl,* rather plump, with a complexion like a New England or Blue Mountain girl, or a girl from Tasmania or from Gippsland in Victoria. Red and white girls were very scarce in the Solong district. She had the biggest and brightest eyes I'd seen round there, dark hazel eyes, as I found out afterwards, and bright as a "'possum's". No wonder they called her Possum. I forgot at once that Mrs Jack Barnes was the prettiest girl in the district (my emphasis).

Like other Lawson men at this point of decision, Joe feels unworthy and therefore reluctant:

> . . . somehow, whenever a girl took any notice of me I took it for granted that she was only playing with me, and felt nasty about it.
>
> "My wife knows little 'Possum'," said Jack. "I'll get her to ask her out to our place and let you know."
>
> I reckoned that he wouldn't get me there then, and made a note to be on the watch for tricks.
>
> "What did you tell her?"
>
> "Oh, nothing in particular. She'd heard all about you before."
>
> "She hadn't heard much good, I suppose," I said.
>
> "Well, that's true as far as I could make out."
>
> . . . I reckoned that I was a fool for thinking for a moment that she might give me a second thought, except by way of kindness.

But unlike so many of his predecessors in Lawson's fiction, Joe does win Mary. The stories that follow the courtship anatomize their life together and represent certainly Lawson's most extended attempt—but in some ways his *only* real attempt—to portray in detail and to understand the middle way that lies between, on the one hand, an ideal of woman, woman "on a pedestal," for whom no man is worthy and, on the

other, the inevitably disastrous result of that woman's descending into a world of unworthy men. It is not only a near-novel; it aspires to be, at last, a finished love story. Joe and Mary function in "the world"—that world that Mitchell damns and that doesn't believe in such things as heart-broken women. But the pattern of their relationship, though much elaborated in comparison with earlier stories and sketches, remains quite recognizable. Their marriage, despite moments of tenderness and intimacy, is a process of decay and decline. This is partly and powerfully due to the nature of the bush in which they live which implacably wears away at their resilience, their mutual tolerance and love and their sense of meaning; but it is also the fault of that larger "world" in which men, including Joe, are simply unworthy of and unable properly to love and cherish women like Mary. His weakness for drink, his indecision, his stubborn pride, his spurning of Mary's "passive force," his rejection of that strange "understanding" which Brook, in his dream, saw in Lizzie—all these are contributors to their failure. (It is significant that, when "not many years after" he stands "by the bed where Mary lay, white and still," he repeats over and over to her, "I'll give in, Mary—I'll give in.") Their moments of closest understanding and their important reconciliations are not so much the results of a process of relationship in which bonds strengthen and can withstand pressures, as ecstatic but necessarily momentary returns to their own Eden—that time of courtship when life was uncomplicated and there was a chance for poetry and beauty:

> . . . I think we got to understand each other better that night. And at last Mary said, "Do you know, Joe, why, I feel tonight just—just like I did the day we were married."
>
> And somehow I had that strange, shy sort of feeling too.
>
> . . . when the train swung round the horn of the crescent of hills in which Haviland lay there wasn't any need for acting. There was the old homestead, little changed, and as fair as it seemed in those faraway days . . . when that lanky scamp, Joe Wilson, came hanging round after "Little Possum," who was far too good for the likes of him . . .
>
> There was no need for humbugging now. The trouble was to swallow the lumps in my throat. Mary . . . was staring out with wide-opened eyes, and there were tears in them . . . Then suddenly she turned from the window and looked at me, her eyes wide and brimming . . .
>
> I jumped up and sat down by her side, and put my arm around her; she put her arms around my neck and her head down on my chest, and cried . . .

It seems to me true to say of Lawson's fictional women that they "become not so much a complementary sex as a separate species" and if, as I think is also true, "Lawson's treatment of women lacks sexual intensity" (in comparison, say, with Barbara Baynton who is superior to Lawson in this respect alone) this may well be importantly due to the fact that his particular presentation of them rarely allows of their being for long, or even at all, in clearly sexual contexts. They are either idealized—creatures in comparison with whom men feel, fancy themselves to be or indeed are, unworthy—or they enter into the world of men, the real and un-ideal world, only at the price of decay and decline precisely because they have thrown in their lot with the unworthy.

Why Lawson should have developed this view of women in his fiction is a question which can no doubt be answered in a number of ways. It does, however, seem to me consistent with his weakness for the romantic and the melodramatic. The impulse to put women on a pedestal is both romantic—because it seeks to turn the flesh and blood human being into some sort of vision—and melodramatic—because it removes her from the real and complicated world into the realm of starkly opposed good and bad. Such idealization is above all a simplifying move: if woman will only stay on her pedestal she can be properly adored without the necessity of coping with the complexities of relationships, the difficulties of understanding her, and oneself in relation to her. "Trying to find out things is the cause of all the work and trouble." . . . Lawson was constantly wanting woman on a pedestal while just as constantly conceding that she could not and would not stay there, reality dictated this. Thus, so many of his women are portrayed initially in idealized terms and yet come to grief and decay and loss and rejection subsequently. He sees that they must "enter" the real world but that entry, as far as he is concerned, can lead only to their being tainted. (pp. 46-50)

Expecting impossibilities of women, Lawson was doomed to disappointment. Descending into the world of men his women, even the best and most admirable of them, become like men. It is a hallmark of Lawson's enduring, slowly disintegrating women that they lose their femininity, they become rather masculine. The drover's wife wears her husband's trousers to fight the fire and is attacked, in mistake, by the dog; her "surroundings are not favourable to the development of the 'womanly' or sentimental side of nature." Mrs. Spicer wears "an old coat of her husband's" and is "gaunt and flat-chested . . . her face . . . 'burnt to a brick'." It is not the bush alone that causes these ravages: Mrs Aspinall who lives in Jones's Alley, is

> a haggard woman. Her second husband was supposed to be dead, and she lived in dread of his daily resurrection. Her eldest son was at large, but, not being yet sufficiently hardened in misery, she dreaded his getting into trouble. . . . She could buy off the son for a shilling or two and a clean shirt and collar, but she couldn't purchase the absence of the father at any price—*he* claimed what he called his "conzugal rights" as well as his board, lodging, washing and beer. She slaved for her children and nag-nag-nagged them everlastingly. . . . She had the spirit of a bullock. Her whole nature was soured.

It is not only the bush, not only the remorseless city and slums that produce these effects. It is, just as importantly, life with men. Even the frankly "bad" women in Lawson's fictional world are, most often, originally the victims of men: the Giraffe's comment on the prostitutes in Bourke is typical: "I s'pose they're bad, but I don't s'pose they're worse than men has made them."

Henry Lawson's love stories are almost always unfinished: communication between man and woman always breaks down, or often enough, scarcely begins. The Giraffe may *possibly* be heading for marital bliss; *perhaps* Jack Moonlight will have a successful reunion with Hannah. But the picture overall is grim:

men and women stand little chance of successful, sustained loving communion because Lawson seems unable to shake himself free of the conviction that such involvement represents for the woman a descent, an entry into a kind of world which can only undermine and possibly destroy her. No continuity, no "finish" is possible in his depictions of women encountering men, because the inevitable "fall" that is the fate of women entering the world of men breaks off relationship, sours and destroys it. (pp. 51-2)

> The wife is well. She's a gem. Matrimony is good and right, but . . . Oh, Jack! "it plays hell with your notions of duty"—to your chums.
>
> And what were our notions of duty, in the abstract? Never mind, Jack. I think the creed of the Chaps, Coves, and Fellows is the grandest of all.

So wrote Lawson to [John Le Gay] Brereton from New Zealand (April 1897). The letter was probably dashed off (it was certainly overdue) and shouldn't be burdened with a second glance. Yet, like A. G. Stephens's throw-away aside with which this essay opened, this concluding paragraph of the letter is curiously revealing, irresistably arresting. All Lawson's women are gems. And the creed of the chaps, coves and fellows is so earth-bound, so shot through with failures, regrets, shames and self-blame, that aspiration towards the pure world of gems is scarcely possible, and if persisted with, results only in the dulling of the gem. (p. 54)

> *Brian Matthews, "Eve Exonerated: Henry Lawson's Unfinished Love Stories," in* Who is She? *edited by Shirley Walker, St. Martin's Press, 1983, pp. 37-55.*

ADDITIONAL BIBLIOGRAPHY

Adcock, A. St. John. "Henry Lawson." *The Bookman,* London LVI, No. 336 (September 1919): 195-97.
> Review of Lawson's *Selected Poems,* calling Lawson the most typical and representative Australian poet of his time.

Barnes, John. "Lawson and the Short Story in Australia." *Westerly,* No. 2 (July 1968): 83-7.
> Discusses the influence of Lawson on the short story in Australia.

———. "'What Has He Done for Our National Spirit'—A Note on Lawson Criticism." *Australian Literary Studies* 8, No. 4 (October 1978): 485-91.
> Discusses criticism on Lawson by Frank Dalby Davison and Vance Palmer, two writers who were influenced by Lawson, concerning Lawson's effect on Australian self-perception.

———. "Henry Lawson in England." *Quadrant* XXVII, No. 8 (August 1983): 60-9.
> Biographical and critical examination of Lawson's literary decline during and after his trip to England in 1900.

Clark, Manning. *In Search of Henry Lawson.* South Melbourne: Macmillan Co. of Australia, 1978, 143 p.
> Romanticized biography of Lawson.

Heseltine, H. P. "Between Living and Dying." *Overland* 88 (July 1982): 19-26.
> Discusses Lawson's cultural significance as a representative Australian writer.

Kiernan, Brian, ed. Introduction to *Henry Lawson,* pp. ix-xxiii. St. Lucia: University of Queensland Press, 1976, 393 p.

Examines autobiographical themes and the realistic representation of Australian life in Lawson's short fiction.

Matthews, Brian. *The Receding Wave: Henry Lawson's Prose*. Melbourne: Melbourne University Press, 1972, 196 p.
A close examination of Lawson's major work, and an explanation of his decline. Matthews demonstrates that the sentimental excesses that mar Lawson's later work, present throughout his writing, are carefully suppressed in his best stories.

Pearson, W. H. *Henry Lawson among Maoris*. Canberra: Australian National University Press, 1968, 224 p.
Examines racism in Lawson's story "A Daughter of Maoriland," and discusses the limitations of Lawson's creed of "mateship."

Phillips, A. A. *Henry Lawson*. New York: Twayne, 1970, 159 p.
Biographical and critical study.

Roderick, Colin, ed. *Henry Lawson Criticism: 1894-1971*. Sydney: Angus and Robertson, 1972, 514 p.

Thorough compilation of criticism on Lawson, with a lengthy and informative biographical and critical introduction. This is an excellent source for many early critics, particularly A. G. Stephens. Several essays from this source are excerpted in the entry above.

———. *The Real Henry Lawson*. Adelaide, Australia: Rigby, 1982, 208 p.
Critical biography of Lawson.

Turner, Graeme. "Mateship, Individualism and the Production of Character in Australian Fiction." *Australian Literary Studies* 11, No. 4 (October 1984): 447-57.
Examines the type of "flat," nonindividuated character often created by Lawson and Joseph Furphy in presenting their conception of mateship.

Wilkes, G. A. "Henry Lawson Reconsidered." *Southerly* 25, No. 4 (1965): 264-75.
Discusses Lawson's work as representative of distinctly Australian literature.

Eugene (Gladstone) O'Neill

1888-1953

American dramatist, poet, and short story writer.

The following entry presents criticism of O'Neill's drama *Long Day's Journey into Night,* written in the early 1940s and first performed in 1956. For a discussion of O'Neill's complete career, see *TCLC*, Volumes 1 and 6.

Long Day's Journey into Night is regarded as O'Neill's masterpiece, and many critics consider it the greatest dramatic work written by an American. For more than a quarter century, O'Neill's career was marked by bold experimentation with dramatic form and content, including the use of masks, lengthy asides reflecting his characters' thoughts, choral exposition, and innovative sound and lighting effects. With *Long Day's Journey* he resorted to the simplest of staging effects, using a single set and minimal props and relying on dialogue to convey the meaning and emotion of his autobiographically inspired play. According to Frederic I. Carpenter, "the tremendous acclaim that greeted this play was both immediate and international in scope" and inspired a resurgence of interest in O'Neill.

The son of a professional actor, O'Neill was brought up on the road and acquired a precocious knowledge of the theater. His early years were profoundly affected by the pressures of his mother's recurring mental illness and drug addiction and by his tempestuous relationship with his father, a discordant family situation that he later drew upon when writing *Long Day's Journey into Night.* Although he was a voracious reader, O'Neill was a poor student, preferring to spend his adolescence in barrooms with his profligate older brother James. After expulsion from Princeton University and a brief, unsuccessful marriage, O'Neill embarked on a life at sea. For two years he lived alternately as a seaman and as a panhandling drifter in several South American ports, experiences that provided material for many of his early plays. During this period he unsuccessfully attempted suicide by taking an overdose of barbiturates. A turning point in his life came in 1912, when he suffered a mild attack of tuberculosis. While convalescing in a sanatorium he resolved to become a dramatist, and spent the next several years assiduously studying his craft.

O'Neill's career can be divided into five somewhat distinct periods that include, after a term of dramatic apprenticeship, a second period during which he wrote primarily one-act plays about the sea. According to some critics, O'Neill's first performed play, *Bound East for Cardiff,* marks the initial departure in America from nineteenth-century melodrama and the beginning of serious American theater. During a third phase of his career, which lasted from 1920 through 1924, O'Neill began writing longer plays. Foremost among these is *Desire under the Elms,* one of his few conventional tragedies and one of his most critically acclaimed dramas. Throughout this period O'Neill utilized many experimental theatrical techniques. *The Emperor Jones,* for example, is considered one of the principal dramatic works of the time executed in a symbolistic style, and *The Hairy Ape* is regarded as a prominent example of Expressionism in the American theater. O'Neill's fourth, sometimes called his "cosmic," period extends from 1924 to 1935.

The plays of this period are often much longer than traditional productions, and demonstrate O'Neill's continuing experimentation with theatrical technique. The most important among these plays, the trilogy *Mourning Becomes Electra,* retells the Oedipus and Electra myths with Freudian psychosexual drives replacing fate as the motivating factor in the characters' lives. Despite his award of the Nobel Prize in literature in 1936, O'Neill's reputation declined steadily after 1935. It was not until after his death that the plays of his last period gained critical and popular recognition of a high order. These plays— *The Iceman Cometh, Long Day's Journey, A Moon for the Misbegotten, A Touch of the Poet,* and *Hughie*—employ most directly the realistic dramatic styles of Henrik Ibsen and August Strindberg, whom O'Neill had always cited as primary influences. These last plays received little attention until after the initial performance of *Long Day's Journey* in 1956, but once "rediscovered," they led many critics to call for a reevaluation of O'Neill's entire career.

O'Neill's third wife and literary executor, Carlotta Monterey, to whom *Long Day's Journey into Night* is dedicated, recounted that O'Neill's oldest son asked his father that the play not be published or performed because of the negative light it cast on his father's family. O'Neill acquiesced, depositing the play with his publishers with the injunction that it not appear until twenty-five years after his own death. However, according to

Monterey, O'Neill believed his son's suicide removed this constraint. After O'Neill's death, she authorized the play's production in 1956 in Sweden—a country O'Neill had always felt was particularly receptive to his drama—and it debuted in the United States later that year.

Many commentators agree with O'Neill critic and biographer Normand Berlin that *Long Day's Journey into Night* was "the play that he *had* to write . . . it was psychologically necessary for him to confront his family by way of art." It is unquestionably the most directly autobiographical of his plays, although commentators have discerned autobiographical elements in nearly all of his works. The early one-act plays, for example, draw from his years as a seaman, and a waterfront bar that was central to his early bohemian life in New York appears in *Anna Christie* and *The Iceman Cometh*. The plot of *Long Day's Journey* and the facts of O'Neill's life to 1912 correspond fairly closely. Like the Tyrone family of the play, the O'Neills summered together in New England when O'Neill's father was not touring with his theatrical company. They continued to do so after the elder O'Neill retired, as do the Tyrones, and this is the situation upon which the play opens. The drama encompasses about eighteen hours of a summer day in 1912. James Tyrone, Sr., like James O'Neill, Sr., has retired from acting; Mary Tyrone, like O'Neill's mother, Ella, is succumbing once again to drug addiction; James Tyrone, Jr., called Jamie, is a directionless wastrel, as was James O'Neill, Jr.; and Edmund Tyrone, who wants to be a writer—but a poet, not a playwright—has discovered that he has tuberculosis, as did O'Neill himself during that summer. Central to the play's progression are growing indications that Mary has resumed her drug use, with the consequent reactions of the three Tyrone men, who alternately blame themselves and one another for her lapse. Most critics agree that O'Neill's life gave him the outline but not all of the details of his drama, and that the autobiographical details of the play are important only insofar as O'Neill utilized them artistically. According to Grant H. Redford, to regard *Long Day's Journey* "as an autobiographical record rather than as a work of dramatic art . . . does serious disservice to O'Neill's intention and accomplishment." A strictly autobiographical interpretation, according to Henry I. Schvey, "overlooks the importance of the creative impulse in shaping and selecting the raw material of life and moulding it into art." Leonard Chabrowe notes that although O'Neill "wrote under a directly autobiographical compulsion," he was, despite the intensely personal nature of his material, able to select, alter, and fit autobiographical facts into his aesthetic scheme.

The enormous stage success of *Long Day's Journey into Night* is often considered inexplicable. The play has very little plot and virtually no action—usual theatrical requisites. The scene remains the same throughout: the living room of the Tyrone's summer house. The four Tyrones engage in a series of discussions, arguments, and disputes that display a pattern of constantly shifting alliances between family members. For example, Edmund and Jamie teasingly support Mary's attack on Tyrone's snoring; when he reacts with anger, Mary becomes defensive, Edmund annoyed, and Jamie impatient. As the play's four acts unfold, the disputes become more and more heated and more serious and the family members more emphatic in their desire to assign blame for their various shortcomings to one another. Throughout the first three acts the audience is able to assess each character only in terms of how he or she is viewed by the others: Mary beloved but weak-willed, Tyrone an insensitive miser, Jamie a directionless drunkard, and Edmund an ineffectual dreamer. In the fourth act, however, the characters have the opportunity to explain their reasons for their self-destructive behavior, and they conclude, appropriately, that Mary's drug addiction may have been the result of her husband's penuriousness and the reason for her sons' failures.

Critics generally agree that as the play develops, loss of faith emerges as a central theme. Tyrone criticizes his sons for abandoning the church for the writings of Friedrich Nietzsche and the nihilistic, hedonistic philosophy of the saloon and streetcorner; however, Tyrone himself no longer attends church or lives by the precepts of his faith. The theme of lost faith—central to much of O'Neill's work—is most explicitly embodied in Mary, who intended to become a nun but left the convent to marry James Tyrone. Their union began the cycle of unhappiness and recrimination that is relentlessly examined in the play. According to Chabrowe: "What occurs is the final disintegration of the family and, in varying degrees, its individual members" as the other characters are defeated by Mary's final breakdown and return to drug addiction. Many critics contend that this family tragedy reflects a national crisis of disintegrated lives lacking the comforts of faith—what Harold Clurman termed the twentieth-century American tragedy of lost faith, stemming from the failure of traditional faith and the lack of any new articles of faith in modern society. This wider significance, in the opinion of many commentators, makes *Long Day's Journey* one of a very few modern American dramas that is also a tragedy in the classical sense. It has been observed that when O'Neill set out to update a classical tragedy in *Mourning Becomes Electra,* he largely failed, producing an oversized and generally unperformable white elephant of a drama; however, in composing the work which seemed an attempt to exorcize his personal demons, he produced a truly great tragic play that has been called the highest achievement of American realistic theater.

(See also *Contemporary Authors,* Volume 110; *Dictionary of Literary Biography,* Volume 7: *Twentieth-Century American Dramatists;* and *Authors in the News,* Volume 1.)

GEORGE WILLIAMSON (essay date 1956)

[*In the following excerpt from a review of the world premier of* Long Day's Journey into Night, *Williamson concludes that the play's compassion lifts it from a purely autobiographical work to a universal tragedy.*]

The world premiere of Eugene O'Neill's *Long Day's Journey Into Night* here on Feb. 10 is still resounding in the Swedish press.

Local critics, who are usually hard to please, have unanimously acclaimed the play. They call O'Neill the world's last dramatist of the stature of Aeschylus and Shakespeare.

The fact that some critics intimated that O'Neill ranks somewhere above Ibsen and Strindberg evoked sharp-edged editorial comment in a major Stockholm daily. The editorial recalled O'Neill's admitted debt to Strindberg.

Because of the autobiographical nature of the play the critics say it will give literary historians new insight into O'Neill's previous works. The characters closely parallel the family of James O'Neill, the playwright's father.

The four-and-a-half hour tragedy is a conflict between human disintegration and the cohesive effect of family love. It is a play of sympathy and forgiveness despite all the petty shortcomings and pathetic decay of the four main characters. There is no protagonist.

The action through four acts takes place in a single room on the day in 1912 that Eugene O'Neill, in this case Edmund Tyrone, discovered he had tuberculosis and was committed to a sanatorium.

There is no plot, but the dialogue reveals characters through a series of accusations, self-blame and self-justification. In the end no one is to blame.

The mother is a morphine addict who blames her condition on the birth of her younger son, Edmund. The parsimonious, drunkard father is blamed for having forced his older son into the theatre, where he failed. The older son is accused of leading the younger astray. The last hope of the sick soul-searching Edmund, the love and comradeship of his older brother, is crushed in the last act by the revelation of the elder's hate and jealousy. All hopes of the three men seem crushed by the mother's final flight into a morphine dream.

It is the human compassion of the drama that raises it from something autobiographical into something universal. It raises it from the ingrown pessimism of much contemporary drama into an unfolding of love and understanding. The final scene of stark, almost unbearable hopelessness dissolves all conflicting emotions of hate in a catharsis of compassion.

George Williamson, "Plaudits for O'Neill," in The New York Times, *February 19, 1956, pp. 1, 3.*

JOSEPH WOOD KRUTCH   (essay date 1956)

[*Krutch is widely regarded as one of America's most respected literary and drama critics. Noteworthy among his works are* The American Drama since 1918 *(1939), in which he analyzed the most important dramas of the 1920s and 1930s, and "Modernism" in* Modern Drama *(1953), in which he stressed the need for twentieth-century playwrights to infuse their works with traditional humanistic values. A conservative and idealistic thinker, he was a consistent proponent of human dignity and the preeminence of literary art. His literary criticism is characterized by such concerns: in* The Modern Temper *(1929) he argued that because scientific thought has denied human worth, tragedy has become obsolete, and in* The Measure of Man *(1954) he attacked modern culture for depriving humanity of the sense of individual responsibility necessary for making important decisions in an increasingly complex age. In the following excerpt, Krutch stresses the importance of* Long Day's Journey into Night *as autobiography.*]

[Eugene O'Neill's] *Long Day's Journey into Night* is intensely personal and directly autobiographical. Written in an agonized attempt to understand himself, and no doubt primarily for his own sake, it is terribly frank not only about himself but about his father and his mother as well. Because O'Neill was so essentially a dramatist, self-examination and the attempt to lighten the burden of the past inevitably took the form of a drama, but another man might have written what he has written here in the form of a statement for the eyes of some psychiatrist to whom he had gone for help.

As it stands, the play is a determined attempt to face those external circumstances which made him the desperate man (and perhaps helped make him the arresting playwright) he was. (p. 25)

Even if it were nothing more, *Long Day's Journey* obviously would be the most important document we have for any biographical approach to the interpretation of O'Neill as a writer. Actually it is a great deal more. Though both in method and style it is in some respects different from any of his other major plays, it will certainly assume a place among them on its merits. And because of the differences, that position will be almost unique.

With one exception, all of his other well-remembered plays have in one way or another transcended realism—sometimes through the use of various "expressionistic" techniques, sometimes merely by virtue of the fact that the themes and sentiments lifted them out of the realm of familiar reality. Their light is never merely the light of common day, and the scene, no matter what the stage directions may say, always moves sooner or later to Lear's blasted heath where man, stripped down to the poor forked radish, is naked before the wrath of heaven. Only once before did he ever attempt in any major play to stay within the framework of everyday happenings and merely rational thoughts. That was, of course, in *Ah, Wilderness!* which, as he once remarked to me, was written to purge some persistent memories which refused to allow him to get on with what he regarded as the more important work at hand. But *Ah, Wilderness!* is wryly comic, relatively slight and at moments playfully fanciful, rather than strictly realistic. At times it deliberately wraps events in a nostalgic haze, and at at least one moment (in the saloon scene) it just restrains a tendency to fly off to the blasted heath. It is also both a relatively slight play and one which seems to have grown out of a remembered incident relatively slight in itself and relatively easily purged from O'Neill's subconsciousness.

Long Day's Journey, on the other hand, digs deeper into far more painful events. Its subject is not the puppy love of a man who could not take puppy love lightly, but the agony of a sensitive man faced with the prospect of early death at the same time that he must face the truth of his relationship with parents whom he loves but cannot respect; also hates but cannot wholly blame for what he believes to be their share in the responsibility for reducing him to physical and spiritual desperation. Yet because of what must have been a carefully formed resolution, the treatment of this situation is never for a moment permitted any of the antirealistic devices to which O'Neill so habitually turned. Despite its deeper probing, *Long Day's Journey* is more consistently and unequivocally realistic in method than *Ah, Wilderness!,* and in fact one might be tempted simply to call it without qualification "a domestic drama."

The time covered is from morning to midnight of the same day in August of 1912, and the six scenes of the four acts are all set in the living room of the Tyrones' summer home. Outwardly this is a fundamentally united family, and despite dangerous tensions it is not obvious that these are not ultimately resolvable. The father is a popular Irish actor who has sacrificed his professed ambition, to be a great Shakespearean, to success in sensational plays, and he would be rich if it were not for a mania for improbable speculations in real estate. The mother is a once-beautiful Irish woman who is sensitive and loving but never quite reconciled to the bohemian ways of her husband. Of the two sons, both are, in similar but not identical ways, problems. The elder, called James, is something of a ne'er-do-well—like his father in his love for barroom companions but cynical rather than sentimental. Edmund, the younger son, is a third variation on the theme. Like his brother and like his father, he has the streak of recklessness which has its most obvious expression in that fondness for drink and for dubious companions, and which is a flight from reality; and in this his brother has encouraged him. But he is intellectual rather than cynical, though it is a disputed question between the two whether the philosophy he has learned from Baudelaire, Nietzsche and other moderns is essentially different from what James has learned from whores and drunkards. Edmund also has been suffering from a persistent "cold" upon which the doctor has promised that day to pronounce definitely.

The first act in which all this is set forth is rather quiet in tone. It is the essential unity of the family and the love which holds it together that one feels most strongly. Resentments are present but they are muted. Only an occasional flash of bitter frankness suggests the explosive potentialities. This, it seems, is a situation never to be resolved but possibly to be lived with in the future as it has been lived with in the past.

Then suddenly, with the beginning of Act II, the tension rises. Essentially it is Edmund's illness, which all are merely pretending to have any doubts about, that becomes the catalyst. This is a catastrophe which cannot be brushed aside or temporized with. It faces them all with their sense of guilt and the need for exculpation by the blaming of others. Each now gives free rein to his resentments and his bitterness. What previously was hinted or passed off as banter is now stated with fierce accusation. Things previously never acknowledged at all are now brutally admitted—notably the fact that the mother is slyly dosing herself with a narcotic too freely prescribed, to dull the pain of her arthritic hands. There is still some love mixed with the resentment, some pity and resignation with the anger and blame. But they no longer are effective; they are now merely further acerbities. The house of Tyrone is doomed. Nothing can ever make it a functioning unity again. It is destroying itself, and if one member of that household will flee from it into another life, he never will escape wholly from the memory of its horrors.

Who is to blame? Surely, so they all feel, someone not one's self must be. The mother blames the father (and the doctors) for both her own plight and for that of her son. James is "not to blame" for being a wastrel. "If he had been brought up in a real home, I'm sure he would have been different." She is not to blame for her addiction because doctors "will do anything to keep you coming to them." "They'll sell their souls! What's worse, they'll sell yours, and you never know it until one day you find yourself in hell." Perhaps, so she thinks, it all began when she consented to leave a home for the bohemian wanderings of a husband who understood hotel rooms and bars but never a home. Certainly family life was made intolerable by the streak of stinginess which has sent her and Edmund to cheap doctors while money was squandered in "conviviality." The head of the house must be to blame when the house falls. (pp. 25, 89-90)

But in reality, is the blame equally shared because all members of the family have, each in his own way, a tendency to run away from what is unpleasant? (p. 90)

Out of all this recrimination (which is also self-accusation), and which destroys the whole family as a family, one positive result arises. Shamed, the father consents to send Edmund to a better sanitarium than the state hospital to which he was resolved to consign him. Perhaps because of that fact we readers know that Edmund will survive. But we never can know whether or not the pain of that long day and the not-to-be

exorcised memories of it were what made him a playwright to be reckoned with.

So much, then, for *Long Day's Journey into Night* as a domestic play which is also an important contribution to the spiritual biography of O'Neill. What else, if anything, is it? To what extent is it also a tragedy? And if it is a tragedy, then what is its theme?

One answer might be that it is a tragedy whose theme is the one often said to be the dominant theme of our generation, namely, the theme of alienation; the sense, said to be more pervasive in our time than in any other, of *not belonging*. Edmund himself states that theme explicitly. "It was a great mistake, my being born a man, I would have been much more successful as a sea gull or a fish. As it is, I will always be a stranger who never feels at home, who does not really want and is not really wanted, who can never belong, who must always be a little in love with death!" . . .

Or perhaps the tragic theme, as distinguished from the autobiographic substance, is something even more fundamental and more ancient, something which is at the heart of every great tragedy: namely, the theme of freedom versus necessity, of guilt and guiltlessness, of man the victim versus man the maker of his own destiny. The Greeks talked of Fate; moderns talk of Heredity, of Social Determinants, of Psychological Traumas. All these concepts attempt to explain why the figures in tragedy could not help being what they were. Yet tragedy itself could not be written if this thesis were accepted as completely satisfactory.

The Greeks felt compelled to ask, "But is Fate really character, and is character to some extent self-determined?" Shakespeare never could answer once and for all the question whether our fate is in our stars, or whether it is in ourselves that we are thus and so. Moderns can write tragedy only in so far as they also cannot accept their own explanations without some question. Like Oedipus, all the Tyrones were looking for someone to blame. It is never certain that if their quest had been successful, they would not have discovered what Oedipus himself did. (p. 91)

> *Joseph Wood Krutch, "O'Neill's Last Play: Domestic Drama with Some Difference," in* Theatre Arts, *Vol. XL, No. 4, April, 1956, pp. 25, 89-91.*

KENNETH TYNAN   (essay date 1958)

[*Tynan was an English theater critic. In the following excerpt, he maintains that the power and impact of* Long Day's Journey into Night *stems from its autobiographical basis.*]

Many charges, during his lifetime, were levelled at O'Neill. . . . That he could not think; that he was no poet; that his attempts at comedy were even more pathetic than his aspirations to tragedy. The odd thing is that all of these charges are entirely true. The defence admits them: it does not wish even to cross-examine the witnesses. Their testimony, which would be enough to annihilate most other playwrights, is in O'Neill's case irrelevant. His strength lies elsewhere. It has nothing to do with intellect, verbal beauty, or the accepted definitions of tragedy and comedy. It exists independently of them: indeed, they might even have cramped and depleted it.

What is this strength, this durable virtue? I got the clue to it from the American critic Stark Young, into whose reviews I have lately been dipping. Mr. Young is sometimes a windy writer, but the wind is usually blowing in the right direction. As early as 1926 he saw that O'Neill's theatrical power did not arise from any "strong dramatic expertness," but that "what moved us was *the cost to the dramatist of what he handled.*" (My italics.) Two years later, reviewing *Dynamo,* he developed this idea. He found in the play an "individual poignancy" to which he responded no matter how tritely or unevenly it was expressed. From this it was a short step to the truth. "Even when we are not at all touched by the feeling itself or the idea presented," he wrote, "we are stabbed to our depths by the importance of this feeling to him, and we are all his, not because of what he says but because saying it meant so much to him."

Thirty years later we are stabbed in the same way, and for the same reason. The writing of *Long Day's Journey* must have cost O'Neill more than Mr. Young could ever have conceived, for its subject is that rarest and most painful of all *dramatis personae,* the dramatist himself. No more honest or unsparing autobiographical play exists in dramatic literature. Yet what grips us about it is not the craft of a playwright. It is the need, the vital, driving plaint, of a human being. (pp. 223-24)

Kenneth Tynan, "The British Theatre: 'Long Day's Journey into Night'," in his Curtains: Selections from the Drama Criticism and Related Writings, Atheneum, 1961, pp. 223-25.

ALAN S. DOWNER (essay date 1961)

[*In the following excerpt, Downer views* Long Day's Journey into Night *as the culmination of O'Neill's ambitions as a playwright.*]

[Eugene O'Neill's] heroes have been men of humble status, either members of, or in quest of, a family, a living room.

The quest in an O'Neill play is in fact a double one: O'Neill's own quest as a writer for a high and universal subject, and his character's quest for place, for home, for selfhood and identity. This double quest is announced in his earliest plays, like *The Long Voyage Home,* and it ends, not coincidentally, in his last work, *Long Day's Journey into Night.* To put it in most general terms, his constant theme is the journey of the common man to a kind of protean mirage. This is not the Augustinian journey to the City of God, or Pilgrim's Bunyan-heavy Progress; it is not until the very end that the character, or the author, knows what the goal is to be.

Whatever the specific plot or situations, there are many other constants in O'Neill's plays. Again and again we meet the contrasted young men, brothers or friends, the poet and the materialist. Over and over we meet the illusions, induced by dreams, madness, alcohol, the illusions which alone make living a tolerable experience. Again and again we meet the harsh father, miserly, remote from his children, driven by some Puritanical conviction of self-rightness. Again and again we meet the mother, idealized, romantically beautiful, mystically associated with the symbolic forces of nature, yet also curiously remote, unsympathetic with her sons. Other women may be vicious, perverted, Strindbergian, but not the mother.

Out of such materials came O'Neill's mystery play, *The Great God Brown,* that endless puzzle to students, and producers, and, I suspect, to O'Neill himself: an allegory of modern life enacted by Billy Brown, the commonplace success, Dion Anthony, the saintly ascetic frustrated into a kind of Mephistophelian Pan, the father, unheeding Jehovah, and the mother—idealized, romanticized, victimized, yet curiously cold and un-

sympathetic despite O'Neill's earnest intention that she be somehow the warm and sympathetic womb.

O'Neill's preoccupation with these reiterated elements grew greater after *The Great God Brown.* In rewriting the *Oresteia* into *Mourning Becomes Electra,* he translated it from an ethical-moral conflict between man and man, man and the gods, and god and god, into a conflict wholly among the individuals of a single, particular family. Ostensibly he was bringing the eternal values of Greek myth home to the modern audience by substituting Freud for fate. *Strange Interlude* is almost completely an examination of the ambiguous mother-figure. But after nine acts, the ambiguity is not removed; and if the audience accepted mysticism as a satisfactory conclusion, it is more to be credited to the author's theatrical power than to an American audience's willingness ever to accept the mystic as an answer. And at the center of the wild amalgam of *The Iceman Cometh* is the mysterious mother, the frustrated son, and alcohol-induced illusion.

In 1940, O'Neill finally reached the end of his own long voyage when he shut himself into his study and wrote *Long Day's Journey into Night.* His wife tells us that he would emerge from a day's writing with his face wracked by pain and tears in his eyes. In this play he drove himself to look upon the family that had always been masked in his earlier characters and situations, the O'Neill family, and to see clearly and hence to tear away the mystic mask from the mysterious mother. Mrs. Tyrone escapes from her younger son by becoming a narcotic addict. Only in his last play does O'Neill permit himself to employ narcotics as a dramatic device; the hypodermic needle administers a truth serum which put an end to his twenty-five year quest.

Although it is a very long play, it is written with an economy of means and an absence of gimmickery which gives it a kind of surface simplicity: a single setting, twelve hours of elapsed time, five characters. Four of these characters are the members of a family who must in this day face the facts, which all have evaded, that the mother is an incurable drug addict and the younger son tubercular. The setting is a living room dominated by a large circular table and the action around this table exemplifies one of the play's themes, the nature of familyness, *odi et amo.* The father is a great actor who cannot forget the poverty of his past as an Irish peasant; loving his family, he still begrudges every penny they cost him. The mother, loving her husband and her children, is still haunted by the unfulfilled dreams of her youth, to be a dedicated nun or an accomplished pianist. The older son, a failure in following his father's footsteps in the theater, sensitive to poetry and art, covers his failure in debauchery and cynicism. The younger son, idealist and artist, has known peace only in moments of mystic communion with nature while sailing or swimming in the ocean.

Thrown together in the living room around the family table they tear at each other's souls and give solace to each other's hearts as the morning sun dissolves in fog and the fog dissolves in night. And with the night comes the revelation that all have fought to avoid; while the men drink, the mother enters without awareness of their presence. She carries her wedding gown, which her husband takes from her as she advances to the front of the stage and relates her dissatisfaction with the Mother Superior who advised her against becoming a nun. Then, with a queer leap through the years, she seems to be looking back on her life: "That was in the winter of senior year. Then in the spring something happened to me. Yes, I remember. I fell in love with James Tyrone and was so happy for a time."

After some five hours, the curtain finally puts an end to revelation. But the audience does not leave the theater like a lot of exhausted peeping Toms. Although *Long Day's Journey into Night* is a perfect and complete explication of all the unanswered questions raised by O'Neill's earlier work, the audience's reaction is the reaction to tragedy not autobiography. You do not care, do not find the satisfaction of a curiosity seeker, in learning that the great romantic actor, James O'Neill, was in real life a penny-pinching peasant; you do not care that Mrs. James O'Neill took drugs. Curiosity about specific common men and women simply cannot be sustained with unbroken theatrical tension for all those hours.

I suspect the power of this play to hold and to move the contemporary audience lies in the fact that O'Neill, having finally forced himself to look upon his own family without masks, has discovered the quintessential family of which we are all members. Look at them again, briefly. James Tyrone, who has made his way in the world, was born to dig and delve in field and farm; but, success though he be, he is conscious of insecurity in this new world, this outside world to which he was not born. He is driven by a force that he cannot identify to a goal which he cannot see. On the other hand, his wife remembers only the past, the security, peace, of the world she had known before she joined her fortunes to the actor's and moved out into the greater world, a world which introduced her to birth and death and pain and unhappiness. The older son, cynical, barren of ideals, a failure, a doubter, is driven, unwillingly but unavoidably, to the destruction of his younger, still idealistic brother. O'Neill nowhere reveals that he is thinking of Adam and Eve and Cain and Abel and there is no suggestion of allegory or myth in the developing action. But in finding a mythical referent for his particular family, he found once again the voice and the vision of the tragedian.

Long Day's Journey into Night demonstrates convincingly the possibilities for the equivalent of tragic experience in the drama of the living room. Both words in that phrase are of equal importance: the room which limits and defines the action, and the living, which is the action. For nobody dies. This is the tragedy of survival; it is the tragedy that involves not so much acting (which can lead to murder, suicide, general violence), but sustaining. The forces that confront the characters are definable ones. They do not speak through sibyls and oracles, but with the domestic voice. They dwell not on Olympus but in Connecticut. We know them, we understand them, they are so—familiar. Science has liberated us from the Fates; we can no longer blame the gods for human failure. The Constitution and the Declaration of Independence have established our human rights, our individual importance; we can no longer blame a hierarchical code for human insecurity. But having eliminated the gods, the Fates, the Furies, and the political tyrant, we are still left with a greater enemy, one more mysterious than that confronting the Greeks, greater because he is partly under our control. We can split the atom, and wash the brain, and reconstitute the personality, and hence the mystery that lies beyond atom and mind becomes deeper and darker. We have not so much dethroned Fate as to make it, in part, our own instrument. In a sense the possibilities for tragic vision in our situation have increased as our power and knowledge have grown.

Long Day's Journey into Night is a tragedy, not because it obediently follows the precepts of Aristotle, but because it considers the possibilities for failure in the pursuit of happiness, a way of life of which Aristotle never dreamed. We must not

conclude, because Aristotle never spoke of it, that the pursuit of happiness is trivial hedonism, escapism. The failure to achieve happiness, the fullest realization of individual potentiality, can be for the contemporary audience of as great significance as the failure of King Oedipus to adjust to the way of life expected of him. This failure to achieve the happiness which it is the right of every man to seek, this failure can properly be the equivalent of tragedy as a dramatic experience for the contemporary audience-complex. (pp. 118-21)

Alan S. Downer, "Tragedy and 'The Pursuit of Happiness': 'Long Day's Journey into Night'," in Jahrbuch Für Amerikastudien, Vol. 6, 1961, pp. 115-21.

RICHARD E. LANGFORD   (essay date 1963)

[*In the following excerpt, Langford maintains that O'Neill has been consistently misunderstood as pessimistic and examines* Long Day's Journey into Night *and its sequel,* A Moon for the Misbegotten, *as affirmations of O'Neill's belief that people can overcome adversity.*]

Though generally recognized as the most important American dramatist of the twentieth century, Eugene O'Neill is misunderstood consistently by his critics. His plays are not the morose, pessimistic view of life that both his admirers and detractors say they are. (p. 65)

To accuse O'Neill of being a total pessimist—a prophet of doom—is to read him superficially. Usually the gloomy tone in O'Neill is but his way of expressing the tragic consequences that await those who are content with illusions; the gloom is not intended to be understood as an end in itself.

For O'Neill, the tragedy of man lies in the search for spiritual peace among the false gods of ambition, pride, security, physical love, etc. All of these human goals are unreal to O'Neill; they are the illusions that men live by, to avoid the difficulties of reality. His dramas are primarily attempts to depict man in the struggle to distinguish illusion from reality—attempts to restore man's perspective and offer him a solution to his predicament. (pp. 65-6)

[What] seems to be bitterness on the part of O'Neill is usually anger directed at those who will not even try to understand his thesis: that man must discard the comforting crutch of illusion if he expects to know any peace of mind in this world.

If the world were two-valued—all good or all evil—then it might make sense to place O'Neill in the pessimistic camp. Despite the fact that the world is likely to be merely a tenuous, on-going process, most people do orient themselves in a two-valued manner, if only for the sake of convenience—and the convenience becomes a snare. As a result of the pressure to label a man in one way or another, O'Neill is made headmaster of the "doom and gloom" school. Thus, many critics who are generally sensitive and percipient find nothing but pessimism in him.

But O'Neill reserves the traditional right of genius to be an innovator—to see the world in a unique way. (pp. 66-7)

The responsible artist is not blindly optimistic, nor is he futilely pessimistic; he must seek a form of expression which recognizes reality (what man is), and concurrently offers man some conception of the ideal (what man can become). From the need for such a form comes O'Neill's expressionism.

O'Neill tries to lift the audience above its ordinary thought patterns so that he may reveal a truth, while the mind of the audience is clear and perceptive. He tries to cut away symbolically what he called ''the banality of surfaces,'' deliberately destroying dramatic conventions, if necessary, to surprise his audience into seeing reality.

Men often mistake a label for an object—a name for a thing which the name only represents. Dramatic expressionism becomes O'Neill's way to suspend the operation of what man calls reality (illusion) so that man may be shown the truth that lies just beneath the surface. Often O'Neill shows the onlooker only the essence of what he usually thinks of as reality, then points out that the ''reality'' is only an illusion—a label—and is not real at all. (p. 67)

In his major dramas O'Neill is concerned pointedly with this conflict between illusion and reality. The key is found in the one major character, in almost every play, who sheds his illusions. One character gains insight, and at least begins to live with things as they are. (p. 68)

Two O'Neill dramas that are very often misinterpreted are *A Moon for the Misbegotten* and *Long Day's Journey Into Night*. The former is actually a sequel to the latter, though the sequel was published first. Both plays are largely autobiographical. Though each will stand alone artistically, they are best considered with their relationship in mind.

James Tyrone, Jr., in *Moon*, represents O'Neill's older brother. The play tells of the alcoholic degeneration of Tyrone, and of the compassion and understanding of Josie, who lives with her father, Hogan, in a tenant farmhouse on Tyrone's estate. Josie, in love with Tyrone, schemes with Hogan to trap Tyrone into marrying her. (pp. 69-70)

Josie's immoral scheme collapses; she fails deliberately to take advantage of Tyrone when the opportunity arises. Tyrone's faith in Josie—and in life—is sustained, and both Josie and Hogan see clearly that life is not to blame for their unhappiness. (p. 70)

When *Moon* is understood, it is not the gloomy play that many critics think it is. All three of the main characters face truth and realize the foolishness of measuring happiness against conventional standards only. Each decides to live as an individual, assuming the obligation to be patient with life and to try to comprehend and cope with the special predicament each of their lives presents.

As for *Long Day's Journey Into Night,* many think it leaves absolutely no hope for man. However, if one considers the play as a complete work of art, instead of as a series of distressing emotional episodes, one finds it to be a hopeful affirmation of O'Neill's belief that man can find a way out of the dilemma in which he exists.

Based on the dramatist's early life, *Journey* describes the emotioinal difficulties of the author (Edmund), his brother (James Tyrone, Jr.), his mother (Mary), and his father (Tyrone, Sr.). The audience sees these four people caught in a web of frustration and misery which is as much their own weaving as it is fate's.

Edmund, not entirely captured by illusion, is sick; the play ends as he is sent to a TB hospital. James is an alcoholic, almost hopelessly caught in despair, but still trying to find his own purpose in life and to extricate himself from him predicament by placing his faith in his mother's ability to cure herself

of dope addiction. He thinks that if his mother can win her battle with dope, then perhaps there is a chance for him to win his with alcohol. The older man, Tyrone, Sr., is a retired actor who lives a life of self-justification. His wealth is known to all of them, but he continues the pretense of poverty almost to the point of causing Edmund's death.

The four confront bitterly what appears to be a hopeless existence. Mary, excusing her weakness, says:

> None of us can help the things life has done to us. They're done before you realize it, and once they're done they make you do other things until at last everything comes between you and what you'd like to be and you've lost your true self forever.

Overhearing an argument between Edmund and Tyrone, Jr., she admonishes Edmund: ''It's wrong to blame your brother. He can't help being what the past has made him. Any more than your father can. Or you. Or I.'' (pp. 71-2)

Arguing with his father, Edmund tells him: ''Yes, facts don't mean a thing, do they? What you want to believe, that's the only truth!'' Edmund tells his father of the understanding of life which he has acquired slowly, in his travels around the world. In a lengthy and important soliloquy, he explains his search for and finding of reality:

> I was set free! I belonged, without past or future, within peace and unity and a wild joy, within something greater than my own life, or the life of Man, to Life itself!

Edmund sheds illusions—the mask behind which men hide their true natures—and sees things as they are: ''Like the veil of things as they seem drawn back by an unseen hand. For a second you see—and seeing the secret, are the secret. For a second there is meaning!''

Old Tyrone is moved by his son's sincere, emotionally charged words and says, confessing his own guilt: ''I've never admitted this to anyone before, lad, but tonight I'm so heartsick I feel at the end of everything, and what's the use of false pride and pretense.'' He explains that he could have been a great actor, but he gave up and accepted a highly remunerative, stereotyped role; he realizes that his life has been nothing more than a long series of rationalizations. Finally, he asks Edmund: ''What the hell was it I wanted to buy, I wonder, that was worth—well, no matter.'' Worth his soul? The old actor had sold his soul for a handful of illusions.

Letting go his rationalizations, seeing things clearly, James Tyrone, Sr., can say now: ''There's nothing wrong with life. It's we who . . .'' Old Hogan has said almost the same thing, in *Moon*. O'Neill is reiterating his basic theme: the man who mistakes form for substance, cheats himself.

All four characters gather for the final scene. Even James, Jr., confesses his guilt: he is jealous of Edmund and tells his younger brother how he has tried to corrupt him. Only Mary, the mother, is left alone in her drugged illusions. She enters, looking desperately around the room for something she says she has lost:

> Something I need terribly. I remember when I had it I was never lonely nor afraid. I can't have lost it forever, I would die if I thought that. Because then there would be no hope.

Mary has lost her faith and searches for it among memories of her youth:

> . . . so I went to the shrine and prayed to the Blessed Virgin and found peace again because I know she heard my prayer and would always love me and see no harm ever came to me so long as I never lost faith in her. That was in the winter of senior year. Then in the spring something happened to me. Yes, I remember. I fell in love with James Tyrone and was so happy for a time.

Mary has spoken the closing lines of *Journey.* O'Neill concludes this powerful play with the central idea implanted firmly in the mind of his audience: Mary has exchanged her spiritual faith for human love—a love that is a temporal illusion. When she married James Tyrone, she saw things as she wanted them to be, not as they were.

The rest of the family can no longer place faith in Mary. Each of them must face the truth; each must seek moral strength for himself. All hope for Mary's recovery is gone, and the play appears to end sadly.

But hope stems from the other characters, from their expressions of guilt and their decisions to accept responsibility for their actions. There is hope in the fact that three men face each other and speak the truth. And there is hope in the fact that James, Jr., will continue to try to "beat the game," as he transfers that desire from a dependence on Mary to an emotionally more acceptable relationship with Josie, in *Moon.*

The sadness and frustrations that envelop the characters in *Long Day's Journey Into Night* are to be considered as stepping stones to reality, not as indications of man's certain doom. O'Neill expresses in the play his understanding of man's position in relation to his creator: he portrays characters who face defeating human problems, but who become aware that human problems—and human joys—will end. Three characters in *Journey* face their dilemma and determine to go on trying to understand themselves and their world. It isn't that all men are doomed, says O'Neill—but some are: those who do not wish to see the truth, and will not try. For these, there is only the false, immoral comfort of dreams. (pp. 72-4)

Often torn between a desire to make God into a man and a desire to touch a spiritual something beyond man, O'Neill suffered the emotional anguish of all who search for a valid ultimate meaning for man's existence. Some of his searching is scarred by cynicism, as many critics have noted, but most of it is marked with genuine love—not of what man is—but of what man can become. His dramas are positive, noble expressions of one man's understanding of the human dilemma. With a genius for comprehending man's nature, and with compassion for man's failures, Eugene O'Neill affirms man's hope for meaning and beauty in life. (pp. 74-5)

> *Richard E. Langford, "Eugene O'Neill: The Mask of Illusion," in* Essays in Modern American Literature, *edited by Richard E. Langford, Stetson University Press, 1963, pp. 65-75.*

GRANT H. REDFORD (essay date 1964)

[*In the following excerpt, Redford maintains that O'Neill employed autobiographical elements in* Long Day's Journey into Night *solely as a means of expressing his themes, and that the play should therefore be appraised on the basis of its value as drama, not autobiography.*]

The recent film version of Eugene O'Neill's *Long Day's Journey Into Night* focuses attention on a problem which has surrounded this play ever since it was first known to have been written. That problem is the general tendency to regard the play as an autobiographical record rather than a work of dramatic art. This tendency does serious disservice to O'Neill's intention and accomplishment. (p. 527)

That he drew on personal experience is true, but it is not that the value of any of the plays depends on how closely they parallel that experience. The value as art of Leonardo da Vinci's painting, "The Last Supper" has nothing to do with whether the figures resemble those who lived several hundred years before the artist created the painting. And so with O'Neill's plays, or anyone's plays. *Long Day's Journey* should be judged as art. It would be better to regard the materials as irrelevant than to judge the play in terms of how closely the materials conform to historical fact. Not the source of the materials but their use should be the criterion. . . .

O'Neill and his wife Carlotta are somewhat responsible for the common tendency to approach *LDJ* as a record of personal experience. In his dedication of the play to her he says that her love had enabled him "to face my dead at last and write this play—write it with deep pity and understanding and forgiveness for all the four haunted Tyrones." (p. 528)

Other statements made by O'Neill have a bearing on his use of autobiographical material. But they reveal also—as an analysis of *LDJ* will show—that the material was only subject matter to be fashioned into dramas which would reveal his involvement in American life, his conviction that the United States was beset by escapism, pipe dreams, loss of old gods and the failure of science and materialism to supply satisfying new ones, and the struggle to "belong," to find the thread which would bind one to the fabric of life and make it meaningful.

Variations of these themes run through all his plays. O'Neill's struggle as an artist was to give dramatic formulation to these themes. An examination of *LDJ* shows this to be so, shows it to be a work of meticulous design and power embodying all the themes which have been given partial expression in each of his plays.

The clear and unified concentration of all his themes in one work is itself a notable artistic achievement but to have done so within the strict confines of the "faithful realism" he assigned himself makes his accomplishment even more impressive.

And yet observe how at least one critic has misjudged the work, attributing to the form the qualities of the subject matter. Croswell Bowen writes in *The Curse of the Misbegotten:*

> The play is essentially plotless. It is not so much a story as an experience. It is autobiographical, yet O'Neill has imaginatively heightened his material and rendered a genuine artistic experience. *Long Day's Journey* is undoubtedly too long—one long scene seems almost irrelevant; there is too much quoting of classic poetry; and the deliberate formlessness of it all is enervating. Still, it is a dramatic achievement of the finest order, a play that will survive, a play that

may well be O'Neill's greatest single work [see Bowen entry in Additional Bibliography].

In Mr. Bowen's defense it must be noted that he does not pretend to be writing a book of criticism. He deals with the plays primarily as particular ingredients in a much larger structure concerning the life of Eugene O'Neill and his children. But that he should have indulged in such double-talk about what he himself says "may well be O'Neill's greatest single work," seems irresponsible. If this is O'Neill's greatest single accomplishment and it is essentially plotless, not much of a story, too long and so deliberately formless that it is enervating, then all the rest of his work must be second rate indeed.

But Mr. Bowen doesn't think this nor is it a question here. The error he makes of confusing biographical materials with artistic achievement is one made by many. It is hoped that the following analysis will help correct that error and allow for a reading or a seeing of *LDJ* as a triumph of artistic form over the comparative formlessness of personal history.

Control and emphasis of themes—the heart of artistic form—accounts for the four-act structure, the changes in each of the four characters and the symbolic use of setting and time. The four acts provide the equivalent of an act for each member of the family during which the changes in the characters are symbolized by changes in both time and weather: first act, sunny New England morning; second act, slightly foggy noon; third act, foggy night; fourth act, fog-blinded midnight. The sus-

Typescript page from the manuscript of Long Day's Journey Into Night. *Collection of American Literature, Beinecke Rare Book and Manuscript Library, Yale University.*

tained use of fog to objectify the progress of escapism in the characters—fog is involved symbolically at least fifteen times—is one example of O'Neill's control of setting to intensify major themes.

Hamilton Basso has said that the major theme in the work of O'Neill's mature years is that greed, the devotion to materialism, corrupts all who succumb to it. O'Neill once quoted from the New Testament to express this view—he was speaking specifically of the United States—"For what shall it profit a man, if he shall gain the whole world and lose his own soul."

In *LDJ* this theme, that devotion to material things corrupts, is embodied in the father, James Tyrone. The theme is introduced on the second page of the play by Tyrone himself. He speaks of getting his cigars dead cheap. "It was McGuire put me on to them." His wife, Mary, questions his real estate transactions with McGuire and he replies, "But land is land, and it's safer than the stocks and bonds of Wall Street swindlers."

His obsession with material things is emphasized at seventeen other strategic points in the play. This emphasis reveals that his obsession is the force which has corrupted not only his life but through him the other members of the family. For example: his unwillingness to pay for a first-rate doctor is felt by the others to be the direct cause of Mary's drug addiction and of the progress of Edmund's illness. When Mary hears that Edmund is again to be sent to the local doctor, Tyrone's choice, she says:

> Oh, we all realize why you like him, James! Because he's cheap! . . . He understands nothing! And yet it was exactly the same type of cheap quack who first gave you the medicine—and you never knew what it was until too late!

Sixty-five pages later, Edmund, after having returned from seeing his father's doctor, repeats the same accusation. . . . (pp. 528-29)

If obsession with material wealth may have been the cause for the corruption of others in the home, it is that which has destroyed Tyrone himself. He confesses this to Edmund in their long scene together in the last act. But O'Neill's artistic use of Tyrone's confession of how love of money has destroyed him is best understood when it is seen in conjunction with another of O'Neill's themes: salvation through understanding and forgiveness, a theme of such importance to him that he wrote it into the play's dedication, as already noted. This theme, too, culminates in the last act. . . . (p. 530)

[It] is useful to recall another of his themes. This is one already mentioned which he formulated in 1928 at a time when the United States was in the grip of great financial prosperity and speculation. The passionate pursuit of wealth was a sickness, he said. One of his earliest plays, *Ile*, uses this theme. However, this sickness, he writes in his preface to *Dynamo*, was related to another of even greater importance: the death of the god whose existence had given meaning to life and comfort for the dying, and the failure of materialism and science to provide a satisfactory substitute. It is this latter theme which provides some of the most moving moments in *LDJ*, particularly where it is combined with that other concern of his: that pipe dreams, escape from reality, are all that is left to make life bearable after the death of the god.

These themes are embodied in the mother, Mary. Her tragedy results from loss of faith and her attempt to substitute an escape through lies, drugs, and pipe dreams. During the night before the play opens she has given herself "another shot in the arm" as Jamie describes it. As the play opens she begins to weave a fabric of lies to hide herself from having done so. The fabric of drugs, lies, and dreams is being created to hide herself from the fact of her youngest son's illness, tuberculosis, which had killed her father and which she now calls a "summer cold."

Drugs are, of course, her more violent methods of escaping, of producing the pipe dreams. They remove her, at least temporarily, not only from Edmund's illness but from a marriage and sons and an environment which provide her no sense of home, no security. Edmund says she does it "to get beyond our reach, to be rid of us, to forget we're alive!"

O'Neill selected a point of special structural importance at the center of the play—end of Act Two—to present a climax of this aspect of the escape theme. Here her habit of lying is joined to her drug addiction and climaxed by being combined with her loss of faith. The climax is created when Mary tries to tell Edmund that she isn't using his illness as an excuse for further indulgence in drugs, and he says what else can he believe. She answers:

> I don't blame you. How could you believe me— when I don't believe myself? I've become such a liar. I never lied about anything once upon a time. Now I have to lie, especially to myself. But how can you understand, when I don't myself. I've never understood anything about it, except that one day long ago I found I could no longer call my soul my own.

A page and half later, in the final lines of the fact when she is alone after Edmund has gone, she says,

> It's so lonely here. (Then her face hardens into bitter self-contempt.) You're lying to yourself again. You wanted to get rid of them. Their contempt and disgust aren't pleasant company. You're glad they're gone. (Then just as the curtain closes she cries,) Then Mother of God, why do I feel so lonely?

Cut off from those she needs to love, she needs to understand and to have love and understand her, she turns for comfort to a religious faith, to the Mother of God. But there is no comfort here because she has lost that faith and has no substitute but her drug-induced dreams, her lonely isolation.

Having ended Act Two with this theme of loss and loneliness, O'Neill devotes almost the entire third act to it and then uses it again to climax the unforgettable last scene of the play.

The third act begins about five hours after the second, near six-thirty in a fog-enveloping evening. During the afternoon, Mary has taken the maid with her for a drive to purchase more drugs. As the act opens, Mary is bribing the maid with whiskey so she'll stay and keep her company. Mary talks about the past "when she was happy." Her withdrawal into the past continues from this point until in the last act she has literally become a young girl again.

But this withdrawal is not made without suffering. At one point after the maid leaves and the fear of the news not-yet-received about Edmund's illness is able to assault her, she cries out: "If I could only find the faith I lost, so I could pray again." She tries to pray, but finds no comfort. She sneers at herself: "You expect the Blessed Virgin to be fooled by a lying dope fiend reciting words!" Finding only emptiness here she springs to her feet. "I must go upstairs. I haven't taken enough." Cut off from love, understanding, and faith in God, she clutches almost violently at the comfort of more drugs and more complete withdrawal into the past.

But all this is only O'Neill's preparation for the final scene of the play. Here he uses all his theatrical skill to emphasize and unify all these themes. The final scene takes place about six hours later, i.e., around midnight, and how many doses of drugs later we do not know. Mary has been upstairs alone all that time. Tyrone has devoted his day and the night to drinking and some soul-searching of his own in a long scene with Edmund; at the moment he has dozed off into alcoholic comfort; so has Jamie after his sad confession; only Edmund is awake and tensely aware.

This fog-bound, midnight quiet is now shattered by that hair-raising piano playing by Mary. This is followed by the appearance of Mary herself, a childlike woman in her night dress carrying her thirty-six-year-old wedding gown.

But just in case we've missed the implication of all this, missed how the play's themes of lost faith, loss of happiness and understanding, escape into pipe dreams, are embodied in these final moments of the play, O'Neill has Mary say, "What is it I'm looking for? I know it's something I lost. . . . Something I need terribly. I remember when I had it I was never lonely nor afraid." A few lines later and almost the last words of the play, she remembers the days of her happy girlhood when she was not lonely nor afraid. She had gone to the shrine to pray to the Blessed Virgin about whether she should become a nun and stay in the convent. "I knew she heard my prayer and would always love me and see no harm ever came to me so long as I never lost my faith in her." Having lost that faith, she now has lost that for which she gave up her faith. The last three sentences of the play follow almost immediately: "Then in the spring something happened to me. Yes, I remember. I fell in love with James Tyrone and was so happy for a time."

The play is a record of what happened to that happiness—that of the family and symbolically that of the whole country, of Western industrial society. This careful tying-up of an author's major themes into the visual, auditory, and verbal emphasis of the last scene is an impressive artistic accomplishment.

But in order to understand more about this artistic control one needs to recall that O'Neill was operating within a self-imposed attempt to achieve "faithful realism." Realism is not, as some people seem to think, merely the rendering of the morbid and unpleasant. It is an attempt to see and render what is real, the totality of an event. The event of the play's long journey into the night of loss and escape is balanced by O'Neill so that the journey into night becomes also a journey into light, into the healing light of understanding. Or maybe it is more accurate to say that to the degree that there is a journey into understanding by the characters there is a journey into light.

This thematic development is embodied most significantly in Edmund whose efforts to face-up to the circumstances of his life lead the audience to believe that he will survive where others have succumbed. Again and again Edmund is shown attempting to face life, to understand it. In Act One he and his mother are watching out the window as Jamie hides behind the hedge so passersby will not see him clipping the hedge. The mother sympathizes with Jamie but Edmund says he is a fool not to stand up and face them. In Act Two Jamie says of the mother. "The truth is there is no cure and we've been saps to hope—They never come back!'' Edmund denies it by scornfully parodying his brother's cynicism and concluding ''*(Disdainfully)* Christ, if I felt the way you do—!''

At least twice during Act One he and his mother make an effort toward understanding. Edmund tells his mother that he heard her up in the night and he says miserably, ''God, Mama, you know how I hate to remind you. I'm doing it because it's been so wonderful having you home the way you've been, and it would be terrible—'' She answers ''strickenly,'' ''Please, dear. I know you mean it for the best, but—'' This effort fails because she escapes into a lie.

A few pages later he tries to quiet her fears about his illness by attempting to deny it, and then by trying to help her face the situation.

''You know it's only bad cold,'' he says. And she replies, ''Yes, of course, I know that! . . .'' The scene continues:

> EDMUND. Listen, Mama. I want you to promise me that even if it should turn out to be something worse . . .
>
> MARY. *(Frightenedly)* I won't listen when you're so silly! . . . Of course, I promise you. I give you my sacred word of honor! (Then with sad bitterness.) But I suppose you're remembering I've promised before on my word of honor.
>
> EDMUND. No!
>
> MARY. I'm not blaming you, dear . . .

This effort toward understanding, their partial facing up to their past, present, and possible future, gives them a moment of closeness.

A scene in the third act between Mary and Edmund after he returns from seeing the doctor almost breaks through to understanding. He tells her that he must go away to the sanitarium and she says:

> No, I won't have it! How dare Doctor Hardy advise such a thing . . .
>
> EDMUND. Why are you so against my going away now? I've been away a lot, and I've never noticed it broke your heart!
>
> MARY. I'm afraid you're not very sensitive, after all. You might have guessed, dear, that after I knew you knew—about me—I had to be glad whenever you were where you couldn't see me.
>
> EDMUND. *(Brokenly)* Mama! Don't. *(He reaches out blindly and takes her hand.)*

But it is in Act Four where greater degrees of understanding are achieved. This results because, in the face of Edmund's illness and possible death, they all four make greater effort. This searching, these attempts to understand and absolve each other, account for the necessary length of this act, an act often described as too long by people failing to understand its realistic necessity.

Act Four begins, the very first lines of it, with two themes which are embodied in Tyrone, i.e., his subjection to materialism which has tended to destroy all he loves, and his resultant loneliness. These themes are used as subdued counterpoint to the theme of understanding. Tyrone has been sitting alone for hours, drinking and playing solitaire. He hears Edmund returning from seeing the doctor and calls to him out in the hall:

> Turn that light out before you come in. I'm glad you've come, lad. I've been damned lonely.
>
> [An angry exchange develops regarding the turning out of the light and the expense involved and Tyrone threatens to thrash Edmund. But he stops himself, remembering the illness.]
>
> TYRONE. Forgive me, lad. I forgot—You shouldn't goad me into losing my temper.
>
> EDMUND. Forget it, Papa. I apologize, too. I had no right to being nasty about nothing. I am a bit soused, I guess. I'll put out the damned light.
>
> TYRONE. *(Sadly)* I've never admitted this to anyone before, lad, but tonight I'm so heartsick I feel at the end of everything, and what's the use of fake pride and pretense. That God-damned play I bought for a song . . . it ruined me with a promise of an easy fortune. I didn't want to do anything else, and by the time I woke up to the fact I'd become a slave to the damned thing and did try other plays, it was too late.

(It is revealing of O'Neill's intentions and method to recall that these are almost the exact words Mary uses about her enslavement by drugs.)

This confession makes a great impression on Edmund. The stage direction says that he is moved and that ''he stares at his father with understanding [then answers] slowly: 'I'm glad you've told me this, Papa. I know you a lot better now.'''

But though this achievement of understanding is the climax of the act, two more confessional scenes follow, the last one between Edmund and Jamie. Jamie comes in after hours of escapist drinking in a whore house and says to Edmund:

> Listen, Kid, you'll be going away. May not get another chance to talk. Or might not be drunk enough to tell you the truth. So got to tell you now. . . . I've been rotten influence. And worst of it is, I did it on purpose. . . . Never wanted you succeed and make me look even worse by comparison. Wanted you to fail. . . . Feel better now. Gone to confession. Know you absolve me, don't you kid? You understand. . . . God bless you, K.O.

As one watches these people struggle to find meaning and direction in their lives, one is reminded of the cry of Oedipus 2500 years previously, '''Twas Apollo, friends, willed the evil . . . and yet the hand that struck was mine, mine only wretched. Why should I see, whose eyes had no more any good to look upon?'' And they, like Oedipus, find little good to look upon. Whatever life has given them, it is they, themselves, who've blinded themselves with drink and drugs and materialistic pipe dreams, and their lament fills the play. The father cries, ''I'd be willing to have no home but the poorhouse in my old age if I could look back now on having been the fine artist I might have been.''

Only Edmund does not lament. He looks back and tells his father of those moments when poetry or the sea had awakened him to life, and when he had been drunk with life. Even now, faced with an uncertain future in the tuberculosis sanitarium— and in 1912 tuberculosis was almost certain death—he contemplates the future; sees himself, and his father comes to see him too, as a poet who will stammer out his faithful realism, the native eloquence of fog people. His journey into light gives the audience confidence that his will-to-live will pull him through his illness.

The situation and the characters chosen for *LDJ* contain the themes which had shaped the work of O'Neill's mature years. That the material used is more intimately autobiographical than that used in other of his plays should not confuse the difference between biographical materials and the artistic use made of them. O'Neill assigned himself the responsibility of writing dramatic art. Biography attempts to discover and record the details of the years. Dramatic art chooses details of the moment, to illustrate, to emphasize, themes. Biography, or autobiography, is the truth of history—to use Aristotle's terms—while dramatic art is the truth of poetry. O'Neill wanted to tell the truth as he saw it about forces which waste life, destroy dignity, corrupt love; he was not concerned with drawing portraits of his family except as he was able to adapt those portraits, *distort* them, to illustrate the themes of his drama. Dramatic art involves the creation of valid characters. No important drama exists without them. But valid characters are not the objective of drama any more than photography is the objective of painting. Characters are a function of theme not portraits for the sake of portraiture. O'Neill turned personal history into the truth of poetry.

It is as poetry, as dramatic art, and not as autobiography that *Long Day's Journey Into Night* should be judged. Many people including myself consider it to be the best play written within the realistic convention in the United States. (pp. 530-35)

> Grant H. Redford, "Dramatic Art vs. Autobiography: A Look at 'Long Day's Journey Into Night,'" in College English, Vol. 25, No. 7, April, 1964, pp. 527-35.

JOHN HENRY RALEIGH (essay date 1965)

[*Raleigh is an American educator and critic whose writings on O'Neill's life and works have been highly praised. In the following excerpt from his study* The Plays of Eugene O'Neill, *he discusses the autobiographical aspects of* Long Day's Journey into Night.]

It sometimes takes generations of scholarship to prove it, but it usually turns out that most of the major characters in works such as [*Remembrance of Things Past, War and Peace, Middlemarch, and David Copperfield*] are based either directly on the author himself, as Pierre and Andrew in *War and Peace* represent two sides of Tolstoi, or as Dorothea Brooke and Mary Garth in *Middlemarch* represent two sides of George Eliot; or on someone the author knew well. . . . With Samuel Butler's *The Way of All Flesh* (1901) the novel became explicitly a way of settling accounts with one's self and one's family. In the twentieth century, with such directly autobiographical works as *Portrait of the Artist as a Young Man, Sons and Lovers, In Our Time,* Thomas Wolfe's entire production, and at least the first work of almost every modern writer, fiction and autobiography have become inextricably welded. But the difference between these admitted "confessions" and the mode of James or Dickens or Eliot or Tolstoi is one of degree, not of kind. Still it should be noted that seldom, even in the avowed confessions, are the autobiographical revelations so direct and literal as they are in *Long Day's Journey Into Night*.

O'Neill, then, was not an initiator of this tradition but a culminator of it. The hoots of derision that greeted Wordsworth's thousands of lines about himself were directed at what was to become a new and major mode of literary expression in the next two centuries of Western literature. [Nicola] Chiarmonte cites Maurice Blanchot on Rousseau (the French counterpart of Wordsworth, or vice versa), to the effect that Rousseau is the seminal figure for modern literature since he, rebelling against artifice, invented "sincerity" under which dispensation all art becomes "confession" [see Additional Bibliography]. The significant difference, according to Chiarmonte, between these two great, sad, mad writers, Rousseau and O'Neill, resides in the fact that O'Neill could never believe, as could Rousseau, that it was all—the whole, dark plight—"*the fault of others.*" Honesty, then, is at the root of O'Neill's power, but it must be added that only the naturalistic-realistic drama, the fourth wall removed, real people saying real things, could provide this ultimate illusion of reality and validity.

But having said this, we immediately encounter an ambiguity which necessitates a qualification, namely, that autobiographical art is not literal autobiography. In the first place—although this has nothing to do with *Long Day's Journey Into Night* as a play per se—life itself considerably mitigated the implications of that tragic fourth act of *Long Day's Journey:* it was almost as if Dickens had taken over to write an Epilogue [to *David Copperfield*]. Edmund-Eugene was only slightly ravaged by consumption, which was soon arrested, and he became eventually, after many other vicissitudes, a great playwright. Mrs. O'Neill did overcome her dope addiction ("Tiny Tim did get well"), and with the help of nuns at that, for her cure was effected by a stay at a nunnery, not a sanitarium. After James O'Neill's death, his eldest son stopped drinking and remained abstemious for two years. (Although when his mother became mortally ill he began drinking once more, and continued to, until his early death.) Moreover, at the time of the production of *Beyond the Horizon,* the family, especially Eugene, James, and Ella—Jamie at this time was still unregenerate—came together in a harmonious unit, and the father had the pleasure of seeing one son a very great success and, like himself, in connection with the theater. (pp. 86-8)

These details are irrelevant to *Long Day's Journey Into Night* considered as a dramatic document although they cast back some ironic light upon it as an autobiography. (p. 88)

[As] most serious art of the past two centuries is in great part autobiography, whether announced as such or not, explicitly autobiographical art, such as *Long Day's Journey Into Night,* is hardly ever, strictly speaking, "true," for the literary characters and events hardly ever correspond exactly and precisely with the actual characters and events. Here again *The Way of All Flesh* is the classic instance of the genre. When Butler's novel was first published, and for generations after, the book was taken, at least by the general reader, as a literal and accurate picture of the Butler family. Two recent collections of Butler letters, however, show quite clearly that neither his father, nor his sisters and brother, nor himself were, in the life, identical to the characters in *The Way of All Flesh,* nor was the general situation identical.

And there is always the further complexity and irony that complicated characters, such as the O'Neills, would not lend themselves to any kind of clear photography. Nor, finally, does it all matter: the O'Neills have all gone to their graves; while the play remains. The interesting aspect with *Long Day's Journey* is that seldom in literature, if ever, have we have a conjunction of such a nakedly autobiographical work juxtaposed with such an abundance of detailed knowledge about the people upon whom the play is based; and no doubt in the future there will be still more factual knowledge.

Besides the discrepancy between the rather shabby summer home of the imaginations of Mary, Jamie, and Edmund Tyrone in the play and the rather solid one of reality, there are various other, and curious, discrepancies between the play and reality: Edmund-Eugene's marriage and son are never mentioned, nor is his rather serious involvement with a "nice" girl, such as Mary Tyrone laments in the play her sons will have nothing to do with, nor they with her sons. (pp. 90-1)

The O'Neills themselves are, like all human beings worthy of the designation, impossible to type or categorize, although there are degrees in this matter, as in all other things. The least gap between the reality and the dramatization seems to be in the picture of Jamie, who appears to have been in life just about what he is in the play: cynical, libidinous, alcoholic, rebellious, passionately attached to all the other members of the family but especially to his mother; a monumental failure of considerable charm; simultaneously devoted to and jealous of his talented younger brother—and yet withal, and under all the bravado and verbal fireworks, a lost soul with some last traces of boyish sweetness, headed only, and as surely as Hickey of **The Iceman Cometh,** to extinction. Perhaps only his mother and his brother knew of the "soul" still there, which was why O'Neill could not let his portrait in *A Long Day's Journey Into Night* stand as definitive but had to go on to the portrait in *A Moon for the Misbegotten,* which by Acts III and IV he becomes, in effect, a little boy crying in the dark.

With Edmund (himself), O'Neill effected some suppressions both of fact and of character traits. The suppression of the marriage and the fact of his current romance have already been mentioned. In addition, like Joyce with his self-portrait in Stephen Dedalus, O'Neill emphasized his own somber, brooding and poetic side, to the exclusion of his extroverted, bawdy, outgoing side, for the existence of which, as with Joyce once more, there is plenty of evidence. It perhaps could be argued that this side would not show itself on such a day as the one described in *Long Day's Journey,* just as Stephen Dedalus can do nothing but brood over his sins against his dead mother on June 16, 1904 (the day of *Ulysses*). Nevertheless, there was a certain ruthlessness about O'Neill, as his conduct in his first marriage would indicate, that is absent from the character of Edmund Tyrone, the young poet perhaps facing extinction and therefore a figure of more pathos than the real Eugene O'Neill seems to have been. Likewise, at least so it seems to me, he is the one character in the play who is more sinned against than sinning, betrayed alike by his father, who will skimp on his medical care, his brother, who will try to make him fail, and his mother, who will reshatter the image of motherly purity by taking dope. His own aggression against them are, more or less, minimized although he does once mention the "rotten" things he has done to his father; he does not, however, get specific about these matters.

The most problematical characterizations are those of the father and mother. Almost everybody who knew James O'Neill, who was legendary for his good-looks, charm and generosity, was outraged by the portrait of him in *Long Day's Journey Into Night.* Yet it is a fact of life, as Samuel Butler's father (who was held in great esteem by his fellow citizens) attests, that a man may present one face to the world and another face to his family. It is also quite possible for a man, especially a self-

made man, to be an inexplicable combination of generosity and penuriousness, to squander thousands in real estate and always stand drinks for the house, as James O'Neill used to do, and pinch pennies in other areas, in the home, for example. Still it would seem that as O'Neill gave himself the better of the deal, morally speaking, he gave his father the worse, for the fact would seem to be that the father was not the almost total skinflint that he is made out to be in *Long Day's Journey Into Night.* O'Neill would not allow his father to be a "good Catholic" either. In the play it is said that he never attends church but, in fact, he was a regular Mass-goer. . . . (pp. 92-3)

But, it should be said, the play itself finally does full justice to James O'Neill, and I think his defenders often overlook or minimize this. In the great fourth act certainly his essential decency, and his charm, are convincingly dramatized, as is the very real motivation for any penuriousness that he may have had. If Eugene O'Neill had done in his early years some "rotten" things to his father, as he had, he more than made up for it in writing this play. And in *A Moon for the Misbegotten* he has Josie Hogan, whose words we may take for true metal, give a brief, but splendid, encomium to the character of James O'Neill.

The most shadowy figure in the play and the most shadowy figure in the family was the mother, Mary Tyrone-Ella O'Neill. There seems to have been some basis for this elusiveness in reality; . . . nobody did seem to know her. Her Irish relatives tended to think of her as "stuck-up." She also evidently remained aloof from the world of actors and actresses that her husband introduced her to. She was automatically shut out from the world of the wealthy New Londoners. Her morphine addiction would tend, of course, to make her even more of a pariah. That, isolated as she was, she tended to dwell upon the past would seem to be indubitable. Cancer and the removal of a breast at the age of twenty-nine could hardly have encouraged her to be optimistic and forward-looking. She was pretty and loved beautiful things. She was deeply loved and cherished by her "three men." For two of them, James and Jamie, she was enough for a lifetime. For her turbulent sons and her earthy husband she represented something indefinably feminine and delicate, if desecrated when taking "the poison." James O'Neill put her on a pedestal, from the day they were married, and she seems to have remained there. Again that fourth act, with the three men downstairs, drinking, wrangling, reminiscing, and the ghostlike mother rumaging around, set off and alone, on the second floor, must have some wide-ranging significance for the whole relationship. She had, when she wanted to, a good deal of charm, like the rest of the family. This quality is shown briefly as Act I of the play, and it was attested to by people who had met her. . . . She was somewhat of a Mona Lisa in life, and she is certainly the Mona Lisa of the play, aloof, apart, lost in a glorified and sentimentalized past. As Jamie is as gross and clear as earth, she is somnambulistic, wraithlike, disembodied.

As far as one can tell at this point, then, O'Neill in writing this play telescoped events, suppressed some facts, distorted others, invented some more, and transferred some others. . . . He seemed to have both simplified and heightened characters, Jamie perhaps excepted. He presented Jamie as is, or was, selected one side of himself and one side of his father and presented them in a rather exaggerated fashion; he made his mother shadowy and insubstantial, as was only fitting for someone existing in the twilight zone of a morphine stupor. He cut the O'Neill family off from the social connections they did have. He picked the year, 1912, when his father's career ended and his own began, or was at least determined on. Finally, he did not "blame" anybody, neither God, nor History, nor Man; and thus the play is, in a good sense, morally relativistic. Each of the characters is on some kind of treadmill that they did not create but which they certainly freely stepped on to. If I may be allowed to quote myself, from a previous essay on *Long Day's Journey,* "Nothing is to blame except everybody" [see Additional Bibliography]. (pp. 94-5)

> John Henry Raleigh, in his The Plays of Eugene
> O'Neill, *Southern Illinois University Press, 1965,*
> *304 p.*

JACKSON R. BRYER   (essay date 1970)

[*Bryer is an American educator and critic. In the following excerpt, he pronounces* Long Day's Journey into Night *one of the very few tragedies in modern American theater. Bryer prefaced his essay with the following epigram from Jean Anouilh's drama* Antigone: *"In a tragedy, nothing is in doubt and everyone's destiny is known. That makes for tranquility. There is a sort of fellow-feeling among characters in a tragedy: he who kills is as innocent as he who gets killed: it's all a matter of what part you are playing. Tragedy is restful; and the reason is that hope, that foul, deceitful thing, has no part in it. There isn't any hope. You're trapped. The whole sky has fallen on you, and all you can do about it is to shout."*]

One of the many ironies in the career of Eugene O'Neill is that, in 1931, when he deliberately tried to write a modern play which would approximate the Greek ideal of tragic drama, he produced *Mourning Becomes Electra.* This thirteen-act monstrosity is one of the great white elephants of our theater history. Not only does it lack the great dialogue of tragedy but it also fails because of its over-simplified view of characters entirely motivated by Freudian complexes which O'Neill substituted for the Greek idea of Fate. A decade later, however, when he simply sat down and wrote out the story which had been torturing him for years—that of his own family—O'Neill produced, in *Long Day's Journey Into Night,* one of the very few modern plays which we can see as tragic.

To talk about any modern play as a tragedy is immediately to enter what are at best muddy waters. For decades critics have quarreled over what constitutes a "modern" tragedy. A few distinctions are clear, however. One is that the strictures which Aristotle supplied in classical times no longer apply. The assumption of the Greeks that theirs was a universe controlled by the gods has never been less warranted than today, when the very existence of any deity is questioned. And there is little or no agreement as to the nature and omnipotence of a God even when His existence is acknowledged. But to remove Fate as the major cause in tragedy is not to suggest that, in the modern theater, we have been unwilling to substitute other forces for this Greek idea. Not surprisingly, we seem to have supplied causes which result from universally held notions of our day, as the idea of Fate deriving from the gods was held by the Greeks. Because we live in a highly scientific age—and because the beginnings of modern drama parallel the dawn of that age—our causes, principally heredity and environment, are major determinants in the lives of individuals and, hence, we accept them as irreversible and uncontrollable forces in the lives of dramatic characters. Thus, Ibsen in *Ghosts* and Chekhov in *The Cherry Orchard* represent the two germinal strands

of the modern theater, each writing plays of tragic proportions based primarily on heredity and environment, respectively.

But I would carry this one step further and suggest that for a modern play to be truly tragic we must have more than these uncontrollable forces operating on an individual. His demise must also be partially his own fault before a true ambivalence can exist. Again, the reason can be found in the assumptions of our society as opposed to the Greeks. We live in an essentially humanistic age. Because of this, while we accept the influence of heredity and environment, we do not see them as totally determining our lives. The Greeks, on the other hand, did see the gods in this way. We have a more sophisticated and complicated view of the causes for our actions and for the directions our lives take. To be convincingly tragic a modern play must reflect this more complex perspective. There are relatively few examples of American drama that meet this challenge; but where it is met we can see the attributes noted above. In Tennessee Williams' two great classics, *The Glass Menagerie* and *A Streetcar Named Desire,* and in Arthur Miller's *Death of a Salesman* and *The Crucible,* we see characters who are victims both of their backgrounds and environments and of characteristics within themselves.

Finally, it is possible to make some further observations about the nature of these characteristics which are partially responsible for the figurative or literal downfall of the tragic protagonist. In many cases, the character's flaw—to borrow from Aristotle—is often the quality which in another sense makes him exceptional. Laura's flaw in *The Glass Menagerie* is, at least to some extent, that she cannot exist in the real world (this is, in fact, the flaw of all three Wingfields); but is it not also her strength, the basis of her uniqueness? Similarly, in *The Crucible,* it is John Proctor's integrity and honesty which set him apart; but it is these very qualities which make him choose death instead of a false confession. Even in *Oedipus Rex,* if we discount for a moment the overall causative factor of Fate, Oedipus' outstanding quality is his inquiring mind which has enabled him to solve the riddle of the Sphinx; but it is the same spirit of inquiry which makes him continue to question Tiresias and thus bring about his tragedy. This, then, seems to be one of the paradoxes inherent in tragedy—that a man's weakness is also his strength and that this very quality which sets him apart from other men may cause his destruction—or at least be responsible for his unhappiness.

Long Day's Journey Into Night exhibits most of these characteristics of modern tragedy; and it goes beyond other plays of the modern American theater in two major respects: first, it involves four tragic characters whose lives are inextricably bound but who are nonetheless decided individuals, complexly and completely depicted and explored; and second, rather than offering only heredity and environment as the partial—and uncontrollable—elements in the destinies of these figures, O'Neill offers a far more profound and abstract additional factor—love. Love binds together the four Tyrones; but love is also at the basis of their tragedy. Were there not love between the members of the family, Jamie and Edmund could leave, James could detach himself from his wife's illness and his sons' problems, and Mary could, in a sense, return to the safety of her girlhood. But, as in Sartre's *No Exit,* hell for the Tyrones is other people, each other.

All of them in the course of the play express, either explicitly or implicitly or both, a yearning for an isolated existence. The most overt examples of this are Edmund's speeches at the beginning of Act IV in which he admits that all he wants is "to be alone with myself in another world where truth is untrue and life can hide from itself." For him, the sea is the epitome of this condition and in his long reminiscence about his experiences at sea he expresses total satisfaction with an existence in which he was alone with nature, with "none of the crew in sight," a time when he belonged "to a fulfillment beyond men's lousy, pitiful, greedy fears and hopes and dreams."

Jamie's continual state of drunkenness is an expression of *his* longing for isolation; just as Mary's drug addiction implies the same sort of desire to escape the real world and envelop herself in a protective fog. James' escapes are more subtle. In one respect, his refuge is *The Count of Monte Cristo,* the "big money-maker" on which he has squandered his talents. It has enabled him to stop living creatively. His pose as a patrician land-owner also provides him with an escape from his true heritage as a shanty Irishman and makes it possible for him often to dissociate himself from his contemporaries.

But at the same time that the Tyrones seek escape, they see that it is impossible; they realize that they are hopelessly tied to one another for life. This realization, combined with the desire to escape, produces what is perhaps the major tension in the play, a tension which is expressed primarily in a continual series of expressions of love and hatred on the part of each character. Throughout the play, each Tyrone says and does many things deliberately to hurt another. They strike out at each other like the caged animals that they are; but, in virtually the next breath, they profess deep and genuine affection. This ambivalence provides **Long Day's Journey** with one of its most complex elements.

In Act IV, Jamie drunkenly admits to Edmund that he deliberately introduced him to the dissolute existence that he, Jamie, relishes because he "never wanted you to succeed and look even worse by comparison." He then blames Edmund's birth for Mary's dope addiction and, while he admits that it is not Edmund's fault, he declares, "God damn you, I can't help hating your guts—!" But, almost immediately, he adds, "But don't get the wrong idea, Kid. I love you more than I hate you." Similarly, in Act I, when all three Tyrones are concerned about the possible return of Mary's habit, it is Jamie, whose love for his mother is the cause of his hatred of Edmund, who deliberately lets slip the fact that Edmund's illness is more than a cold, a disclosure which he knows is likely to help drive her back to morphine. Later in the same act, Edmund, who is even closer to Mary than Jamie is, unnecessarily tells her that he heard her go into the spare room the night before, a sure indication that she is back on the drug.

Mary and James accuse one another continually, Mary blaming her husband for not providing a home for his family and for being a miser, James bitterly blaming her for ruining their happiness. Yet, at the end of their most heated exchange, early in Act II, Scene 2, Mary exclaims, "James! We've loved each other! We always will!" And, in Act II, Mary reminds Jamie that he should have more respect for his father: "You ought to be proud you're his son!" Both Mary and James also reminisce often about how happy they were with one another once; and they do so in terms that make it very clear that they still love each other a great deal.

Both sons lash out at their father throughout the play. Mary even at one point tells Edmund, "I never knew what rheumatism was before you were born!" Yet, despite all this rancor, there is abundant evidence of abiding affection. This is ironically and appropriately symbolized at the very end of the play when Mary, completely under the influence of morphine, drifts in dragging her wedding gown and wanders about the room reminiscing about her girlhood. The reverie concludes with her memory of senior year when she decided to be a nun; but then, she recalls, "in the spring something happened to me. . . . I fell in love with James Tyrone and was so happy for a time." This brief passage sums up all of one aspect of the tragedy. Mary's love for James, and all the Tyrones' love for each other, is both their great strength and the cause of their torture. If they did not love each other so much, they could not strike out so cruelly, they could not hate. Edmund's remark about Mary—"It's as if, in spite of loving us, she hated us!"—might well be changed to read because she loves us, she hates us, and then applied equally to all the relationships in this family. And, finally, each character's desire to escape the others, to find an isolation away from the complications of other people, is really no more nor less than a wish to evade one of the major responsibilities of the human condition, contact with other human beings and all the conflicting emotions and attitudes that these contacts produce. As Edmund says in Act IV—and as many an O'Neill protagonist could and does echo—"It was a great mistake, my being born a man. I would have been much more successful as a sea gull or a fish."

But there are other tragic aspects to **Long Day's Journey.** An important one is suggested by my earlier remarks about the forces operating on an individual in modern tragic drama. In O'Neill's play, each of the Tyrones is both responsible and not responsible for the part he is playing. The best example of this is James. The three members of his family accuse him of being miserly and there is ample confirmation of this charge, most especially in his efforts to send Edmund to an inexpensive sanitorium. But, in Act IV, James admits to Edmund that perhaps he is a "stinking old miser" and goes on to explain this trait by describing his childhood when he "learned the value of a dollar" working twelve hours a day in a machine shop, a "dirty barn of a place where rain dripped through the roof," for fifty cents a week. With this disclosure it becomes clear that James is not entirely to blame for his penurious ways. It is not his fault that he was brought up in a penniless and fatherless family. This background understandably has made him overly sensitive to the evils of the poorhouse. And yet we cannot totally excuse this quality in James because we feel that, once he became financially successful, he should have developed more generous instincts in accordance with normal familial devotion. Clearly, however, the responsibility for James' weakness is divided between forces in his background over which he had no control and present factors which he should be able to alter.

The same sort of divided responsibility can be seen in the three other characters. Jamie's drunken and dissolute ways are certainly his own fault to an extent, but they can also be traced to the family situation. His father introduced him to drink and brought him up in an atmosphere where he could meet the cheap tarts and low types with whom he now associates. Jamie's failures in life can also be linked partially to his father's refusal to allow him to be a success. This is perhaps because James realizes that he has sold his own talents for a sure financial return and he must therefore keep his son from being any more successful than he is. Jamie's problems are also further compounded by his relationships with his mother and his brother. He feels, with considerable justification, that Mary dotes on Edmund and ignores him. He also is, as he admits to Edmund in Act IV, extremely jealous of his brother and of the possibility that he will succeed and make him look worse by comparison.

Mary also is both victim and causative factor. She is guilty of forcing her family into an almost death-like inaction by her drug addiction; but when we look at her background and the cause of her illness, we find ample extenuating circumstances. She is, in many ways, still the shy convent girl who, as O'Neill stresses in his long stage direction introducing her, "has never lost" her "innate unworldly innocence." Because of this she is totally unable to cope with the cruel realities of the world around her. In this she shares more than a literal kinship with Edmund, who also cannot face the world because of a sensitive poetic nature. Both Mary and Edmund feel a tremendous lack of belonging, a loneliness. It is difficult to decide whether Mary's addiction, like Laura's limp in *The Glass Menagerie*, causes her isolation or whether the addiction is merely an overt manifestation of the isolation which is already there. Mary has not been at peace since she left her father's house to marry James. While it is true that James has never given her the house she so desperately wants, she would undoubtedly have been unable to cope with one had she been asked to do so. Mary's retreat into the past through drugs is her way of going back to what was for her an ideal world, an escape from a real world which she cannot handle. Her addiction is probably no more than a means towards an end which she would have reached— or tried to reach—through another method had morphine not been available. Thus, we cannot totally blame her problems on James and the "cheap quack doctor" who attended her at Edmund's birth. Nor can we blame Edmund's present illness for her reversion to dope. Mary's difficulties are far more deep-seated than this. Her protected childhood has made her constitutionally and emotionally unable to deal with life. On the other hand, Mary *is* guilty of refusing to face her problem. Unlike James, she will not admit either to herself or to her family that she cannot exist in the real world and hence she is torturing her husband and her sons. James can look objectively at his background and see it as a major influence upon his present personality; but Mary, while she can realize that the "past is the present" and "the future too," cannot act on that understanding.

As I've already said, Edmund is much like his mother—and this probably accounts for the fact that he understands her more fully than anyone else. He is the typical O'Neill protagonist who, he himself realizes, "never feels at home, who does not really want and is not really wanted, who can never belong, who must always be a little in love with death." Unlike his mother and like his father, Edmund does try to face up to his inadequacies and attempts to understand why he does not belong. Mary totally rejects life because she cannot understand it and does not want to try; Edmund accepts life, understanding that he can never really be a part of it. In his long soliloquy midway through Act IV, after he describes the ecstasy of life at sea, he tells how, after that moment, "the hand lets the veil fall and you are alone, lost in the fog again, and you stumble on toward nowhere, for no good reason." But Edmund too is both the victim and the originator of his troubles. His sensitive nature makes him unable to deal with most of the world around him, just as so many O'Neill characters from the Mayo brothers in *Beyond the Horizon* and Yank in *The Hairy Ape* down to the denizens of Harry Hope's bar in *The Iceman Cometh* cannot belong in the real world with which they are faced. But he is also a victim of that world which is so insensitive to him and to his special needs. He is a poet in a world which rejects its poets. And his understanding of this fact is revealed in Act

IV, just as Jamie's and James' awareness are disclosed during this final explosive section of the play.

In fact, this last act serves to complicate our responses to these characters enormously in that their capacity to understand and articulate their own weaknesses makes them fit objects of our respect as well as our pity. Up to this point, we are quite ready to accept James as a miser who has repressed his family disastrously, Jamie as a wastrel who has been the major disappointment of his father's life, and Edmund as a foolish dreamer; for these are the pictures we get of them from the three other characters. But when, in Act IV, we hear their side of the story, we can no longer be content simply to dismiss them this easily. What we end up with is the sense of divided responsibility which I defined at the beginning of this essay. It is expressed overtly in *Long Day's Journey* through two brief passages. The first, appropriately enough spoken by Mary, expresses the forces over which she and her family have no control: "None of us can help the things life has done to us. They're done before you realize it, and once they're done they make you do other things until at last everything comes between you and what you'd like to be, and you've lost your true self forever." The second occurs when Edmund remarks to his father that life is "so damned crazy" and James corrects him: "There's nothing wrong with life. It's we who—*He quotes*. 'The fault, dear Brutus, is not in our stars, but in ourselves that we are underlings.'"

The consequence of this divided responsibility is that, as in any tragic play of the modern era, it is impossible to assign blame. Both controllable and uncontrollable forces operate on the lives of the Tyrones, with the added complication that the very family situation they live in is both a contributor to and a result of the tragic situation. Not only could each of these characters by himself be the subject of a tragic drama—as he could—but also a major share of the tragic element is attributable to their interrelationships. Unlike the Greeks who tended to center their tragedies on one flawed protagonist, O'Neill in *Long Day's Journey* (and, to a certain extent, other modern playwrights like Chekhov, Ibsen, and Williams), seem to see groups of individuals—most often families—caught in webs partially of their own devising but woven by outside forces as well.

The degree of struggle possible within these webs varies from play to play. In *Long Day's Journey* there seems to be very little. In the terms of the passage from *Antigone* quoted as the epigram to this essay, there is definitely a "tranquility" here, a "fellow-feeling" among the four Tyrones, who are, in numerous ways, on character. They are certainly all subject to many of the same tensions and ambivalences. There is, as I've stressed, no easily assigned guilt or innocence; we certainly can find no villain or hero in this play. While there may be some hope for Edmund, it is primarily medically-based or founded quite irrelevantly on the assumption that he is Eugene O'Neill who, after all, did become a successful playwright. Far more germane is the obvious fact that Edmund will never "belong" in the real world any more than his mother will; he will always be "the stranger" that he realizes he is now. Without hope, as Anouilh notes, a tragic play like *Long Day's Journey* is "restful." The characters are "trapped," as the single set for the play and the fog continually rolling in explicitly indicate. There is a good deal of shouting in the play, but most of it is the ultimately ineffectual beating at the bars

James O'Neill as the Count of Monte Cristo.

of four caged animals who have no other means of voicing their frustrations.

Just as in a later American play with which it shares many common elements, *Who's Afraid of Virginia Woolf?*, nothing really happens in *Long Day's Journey*. There is very little action, in the conventional dramatic sense of the term; and none of the characters change at all. The reason for this is simple: nothing can happen to four figures in this situation. All we can do is contemplate them in their web and endeavor to understand them with the assistance of the skill of the playwright who unfolds their lives to us. Because no American playwright has depicted more complex and complete characters with more compassion and sheer dramatic power than Eugene O'Neill in *Long Day's Journey*, it deserves a place among the great plays written in any age in any language. It is a further measure of its magnitude that it is also one of the few American plays which meet most of the measures of modern tragedy. That is does so within the framework of a generally conventional realistic four-character domestic drama, rather than through a consciously super-imposed classical mold, merely makes O'Neill's achievement that much more remarkable. (pp. 261-70)

Jackson R. Bryer, "'Hell Is Other People': 'Long Day's Journey into Night'," in The Fifties: Fiction, Poetry, Drama, *edited by Warren French, Everett/ Edwards, Inc., 1970, pp. 261-70.*

HAROLD CLURMAN   (essay date 1971)

[*Highly regarded as a director, author, and longtime drama critic (1953-80) for the* Nation, *Clurman was an important contributor to the development of the modern American theater. In 1931, with Lee Strasberg and Cheryl Crawford, he founded the innovative Group Theatre, which served as an arena for the works of budding playwrights, including Clifford Odets, William Saroyan, and Elia Kazan, and as an experimental workshop for actors. Together with Strasberg, Clurman also introduced the Stanislavsky method of acting—most commonly referred to as the "Method"—to the American stage. Based on the dramatic principles of Russian actor and director Konstantin Stanislavsky, the Method seeks truthful characterization through the conveyance of the actor's personal emotional experiences in similar situations. Clurman describes the Method as "a way of doing something with the actor . . . to enable him to use himself more consciously as an instrument for the attainment of truth on the stage." In addition, he wrote several works on the theater, including his acclaimed autobiography* All People Are Famous *(1974). In the following excerpt, Clurman pronounces* Long Day's Journey into Night *a masterpiece of "solidly constructed realistic drama" in which O'Neill expressed the national tragedy of loss of faith in terms of his personal experiences.*]

In the last act father-and-son scene of O'Neill's *Long Day's Journey into Night* James Tyrone says, "The praise Edwin Booth gave my Othello! I made the manager put down his exact words in writing. I kept it in my wallet for years. . . . Where is it now, I wonder? Somewhere in this house. I remember I put it away carefully—." To which his son Edmund replies, "It might be in the old trunk, along with Mama's wedding dress."

In the play's final moments the mother, benumbed by morphine, enters dragging a wedding gown on the floor. She doesn't recognize it as hers. James, her husband, takes it from her, pointing out that she might get it dirty, and she murmurs, "I remember now. I found it in the attic hidden in a trunk. But I don't know what I wanted it for. I'm going to be a nun— that is, if I can only find . . ." She breaks off and then resumes, "What is it I'm looking for? I know it's something I lost."

The four Tyrones are bedeviled by a terrible unnamed loss. The loss inspires guilt in them; they thrash about in a vain effort to identify it, though they hardly realize the nature of their quest. They blame one another for the absence of what is essential to them, and immediately thereafter apologize, knowing that the accusations are misdirected. Each is isolated in his or her sorrowful guilt. Only one of them, Edmund, may emerge from the morass—as Eugene O'Neill did later, through his plays.

The long day's journey is a bitter self-examination into the darkness of the self. The journey for the dramatist constituted a process of self-discovey. But the play's characters, bound together by their dilemma, which makes for a kind of tortured love, are rarely able to touch one another. Each suspects the others of being the cause of his sufferings. An audience sufficiently attentive, and aided by a wholly sound production, should comprehend the source of the Tyrones' tragedy.

They have lost their faith. Loss of faith is the main theme almost throughout O'Neill's work. For him it was more than a personal tragedy, it was *the* American tragedy. As individuals and as a nation, we have lost that spiritual coherence which makes men and societies whole. O'Neill declared that his *magnum opus*—the nine plays, of which he completed only *A Touch of the Poet*—was the dramatization of the question, "What shall it profit a man if he gain the whole world and lose his own soul?''

What innocent and trusting Mary Tyrone has lost is her religious faith, a faith in God which sustained her in the genteel home and the convent in which she was raised. She fell in love with James Tyrone, a star actor of romantically heroic roles, ''and was so happy for a time.'' But the actor in the crude theatre of that day (middle and late nineteenth century), with its long national tours in generally shoddy shows, stopping in every sort of hotel in numerous one-night stands, led a life that offered no haven for so delicate a being as Mary Tyrone. Her husband believed in the theatre, especially in Shakespeare; ''I studied Shakespeare,'' he says, ''as you'd study the Bible.'' Shakespeare was central to his religion, on whose account he rid himself of the brogue of his Irish birth.

But then he found a play which had an enormous success. His many years of immigrant struggle against poverty had made him acutely aware of ''the value of a dollar.'' This turned him to a miserliness to which his sons ascribe all the family's misfortunes. His anxiety to avoid the specter of the poorhouse caused him to abandon his deepest desire to be a great Shakespearean actor and give himself to the exploitation of the box-office hit which he played for more than twenty years to the exclusion of everything else. He betrayed his religion. ''What the hell was it I wanted to buy that was worth—'' He falters as he asks the question.

The vagrant life of the road led to Mary's intense loneliness (James's boon companions, his fellow actors, were no fit company for such as she) and so unwittingly she became addicted to drugs. On this account, her older son, James, Jr., lost faith in his mother, becoming a cynical drunk and patron of brothels, a blasphemer against his mother's religion and his father's profession, always a little jealous of his younger brother whom he also loves. Edmund is a seeker after truth. He declares himself not so much a poet as a faithful realist. Still, he feels that he will forever be less than whole if he is unable to recapture that sense of belonging to something ''greater than my own life, or the life of Man . . . to God, if you want to put it that way. . . .'' He experienced such a state at moments in his year at sea. It is this ecstatic relation to existence which Edmund says he lost—''and you are alone, lost in a fog again, and stumble on toward nowhere. . . .''

If the desolateness of this condition in the Tyrone household and the agonized quest for a light beyond the dark are not present in the production, it becomes only the chronicle of an unhappy family—though, even as such, very moving. The triumph is that here a solidly constructed realistic drama is rendered integral with social meaning as well as the soulful poetry of despair and forgiveness. That is what makes *Long Day's Journey into Night* O'Neill's masterpiece. (pp. 283-84)

Harold Clurman, in a review of '' 'Long Day's Journey into Night','' in his The Divine Pastime: Theatre Essays, *Macmillan Publishing Co., Inc., 1974, pp. 282-85.*

TRAVIS BOGARD (essay date 1972)

[Bogard is an American educator and critic. In the following excerpt from his study Contour in Time: The Plays of Eugene O'Neill, *he discusses both theatrical and autobiographical elements of* Long Day's Journey into Night.]

O'Neill used the stage as his mirror, and the sum of his work comprises an autobiography. In many of his plays, with a bold directness of approach, he drew a figure whose face resembled his own, and whose exterior life barely concealed a passionate, questing inner existence. Around this figure, he grouped other characters who served as thin masks for members of his close family and for his friends and significant acquaintances. On the stage, their grouping forms a structure of relationships through which O'Neill moved to discover what in his life gave him identity.

As elements of works of art, the characters live for the most part independent of their creator; they stand in the round at an appropriate aesthetic distance. Yet the shape of the drama is formed by private matters. O'Neill's experiments with masks, asides, soliloquies and long monologues evolve from his necessity to make his personal quest a theatrical reality. The intense subjectivity of the plays, conflicting at times with the need theatre has for relatively objective delineations, accounts in part for the lyricism that emerges unexpectedly in many of his earlier works and toward the end of his life comes to dominate his stage. In such late plays as *Hughie, Long Day's Journey into Night* and *A Moon for the Misbegotten,* the dialogue repeatedly assumes a lyric, rather than a dramatic mode; narrative is suspended, and voices borne out of silence and darkness speak a threnody of pain and loss. The lyricism is a token of the fact that no other dramatist in the world's history, not even excepting Strindberg with whom O'Neill felt particularly allied, continually turned the theatre to such personal purposes.

The result forms a partial paradox. Using the stage with such intimate intention, O'Neill yet managed to produce the greatest plays of American dramatic literature, and, in the world theatre of the first half of the twentieth century, can be compared only to Chekhov, Shaw, Pirandello, and Brecht, all of whom wrote with more intricacy, wit and style than O'Neill, but never with more deep-rooted involvement. (pp. xii-xiii)

[*Long Day's Journey into Night*] was begun shortly after the completion of *The Iceman Cometh* and, together with *Hughie,* was O'Neill's major creative effort of 1940. It was completed in September. Then, after a period of illness, he turned to its sequel, *A Moon for the Misbegotten.* He had written half of the first draft of that play when the Japanese bombed Pearl Harbor. O'Neill wrote to Dudley Nichols on December 16, 1941, that he had managed to finish the draft, but that the heart had gone out of its writing. Although he worked on it sporadically through 1943 and during the same period made revisions of *A Touch of the Poet* and developed the scenario of *The Last Conquest,* O'Neill's career as a playwright ended as the United States entered the war. By 1943, the tremor in his hand made sustained work impossible.

His illness and the war were real reasons for silence, but equally important was an underlying cause: having written the two plays about his family, O'Neill had no further place to go. *Long Day's Journey into Night* was the play he had been trying to write from the outset of his career; its achievement was his raison d'être as an artist. *A Moon for the Misbegotten* was an essential coda, an act of love, of charity and of contrition. Mrs. O'Neill recorded movingly what happened to O'Neill as he wrote. His work day was a long one, five hours in the morning and additional hours in the afternoon. As she described him, he was a man ''being tortured every day by his own writing. He would come out of his study at the end of a day gaunt and sometimes weeping. His eyes would be all red and he looked ten years older than when he went in in the morning.'' O'Neill said not without irony that he was writing plays he knew he could finish, but the Tyrone plays were more than substitutes for the cycle. A lifetime's psychological and physical pressures had cornered him at last. It was a moment for truth and he told it.

When it was said, he was not entirely certain that it had emerged as truth. Edmund Tyrone, having told his father of all that has meaning for him, concludes his account of his quest by saying, "I couldn't touch what I tried to tell you just now. I just stammered. That's the best I'll ever do. . . . Well it will be faithful realism, at least. Stammering is the native eloquence of us fog-people." He was wrong. *Long Day's Journey into Night* is not the work of a stammerer, but of a man who had become a master of his art, and whose native speech—not the words only, but the full acted drama—had the eloquence of a poet. The technical experimentation of the 1920's often caused him to beat frenetically against the limits of the stage. In the last four plays, the stage did all he asked of it without strain. The result is the highest achievement of the American realistic theatre.

What he asks is deceptively simple. Ironically, O'Neill's ultimate "experiment" was a return to four boards and a passion—to in other words, a confident reliance on his actors. He, who had gone to such elaborate lengths to ensure that his actors would fulfill his purposes, loading them with masks, asides, choral support and an infinity of pauses, now removed all exterior pressures. He was still generous with stage directions suggesting intonation and attitude, but he no longer tried to enforce a performance with the impediment of the Art Theatre. Everything, now, is in the role. An actor in these plays cannot hide behind personal mannerisms, clever business or habitual stage trickery. O'Neill has stripped all but the most minimal requirements from the stage, leaving the actors naked. They must play or perish.

Essentially, what is needed as setting for the four last plays are table surfaces and chairs. Properties are few, mostly bottles and glasses. Costume requirements are negligible. The most elaborate of the plays is *The Iceman Cometh,* which requires the bar structure and the essentials of the birthday feast, but even these are minimal in view of the play's length and the size of its cast: What O'Neill makes from his simple materials is extraordinary. In the printed texts, he describes in elaborate detail each of the settings, listing titles of books on the shelves, giving the history of Hope's saloon and the hotel where Erie lives. It is information that he provides but does not insist on. An actor should know it, but an audience will perceive such details only through the filter of performance. It is said of Shakespeare that when he wishes the details of his setting to be specific, he makes it possible for the actor to show them. The same, despite the very different theatrical conventions, can be said of O'Neill in the last plays.

What an audience learns is surprisingly detailed, considering the limited means. The house of the Tyrones, its environment and the historical period are confidently set forth. Although the setting is bare, the audience knows that the house has four bedrooms and an attic and a cellar, that there is a big lawn ending in a hedge by the street, that the sea is near and that the town is a long streetcar ride away. The importance of the house to the action is evident, but it is through the action that the setting is fully evoked. So for the period. In creating the historical time for the two Tyrone plays, 1912 and 1923, O'Neill has relied on few specific historical details. The sinking of the *Titanic* or the arrival of Scott at the South Pole in 1912 might

well have provided imagery for the desperately isolated Tyrones. The point, however, is that they *are* isolated, and no superficial references to period are needed to testify to the fact that they live in a society that is not very complex, in which they can find such privacy. (pp. 422-24)

Like the details of setting and the historical period the time-scheme of *Long Day's Journey into Night* is simple and placed in the grain of the action without specific technical elaboration. In many earlier plays, O'Neill pretended that the carefully designed, detailed planning of the progress of time had meaning. Occasionally, as with the sunset-to-dawn pattern of *Lazarus Laughed,* a somewhat gratuitous symbolism was achieved, but more often, the time structure was arbitrary and vague in its significance.

The arrangement of time in the autobiographical plays, however, is anything but arbitrary or extraneous. Around the time plan, O'Neill marshals such "effects" as he uses. Both plays begin in the full light of day to the sound of laughter. In *Long Day's Journey into Night,* as the Tyrones enter from the dining room, laughter sounds gently. Sun pours through the windows, the fog and the sound of the foghorn that has kept the family awake through the night have gone. The moment is poised and normal, but almost at once O'Neill denies its normalcy and starts the progression that had been a hallmark of his style from the first work he did for the theatre. The light dwindles, the fog returns, the foghorn sounds again. Gradually, the space diminishes to the area defined by a single light bulb over the central table in the room. The Tyrones' world is seen in its barest essentials. The proposition is clear, both to the actors and their characters: if life is to be created it must be evolved from the simple elements in this limited space. There are no extraneous symbols—isolating actors in follow-spots, diminishing the room by pulling in the walls of the set. Everything is in the action as the fog becomes the physical evidence of the isolation of the Tyrones.

The view of human nature set forth in the plays is of divided beings—the conception that earlier occasioned O'Neill's use of masks and other devices to suggest outer and inner lives. The Tyrones, however, need no masks. In their nearly mortal extremity, they have nothing to hide. Their pain fills their being so completely that their essential natures lie close to the surface. Thus Tyrone's charm, his friendliness and grace have worn thin under the erosion of despair. His actor's carriage and voice are ingrained in his demeanor, but as the night wears on and as the whiskey sickens him without making him drunk, the hidden man comes clearly into view. Jamie's cynical mask is dropped as the whiskey begins to talk, permitting the defenseless child in him to be seen. In the same way, as Mary descends farther into the doped state, the young girl alive within the pain-wracked woman comes forth to haunt them all. Whiskey and morphine effectively remove all disguise.

The words that come when the masks are off are in the form of soliloquies and monologues such as were from the first a characteristic of O'Neill's playwriting. Now, however, there is no breaking of the play's realistic limits. When, for example, Mary is left alone at the end of the scene with Cathleen in Act II, she speaks of her past in a long monologue that arises naturally from her addiction. As the morphine takes effect it causes her to babble, but she is still sufficiently aware not to be entirely dulled to her condition. Her words rise involuntarily out of her loneliness and guilt and speak of her longing for the life of the girl she was. It is as if she speaks to the girl in the past so as to assuage the loneliness of the present. Similarly, the long monologues of Edmund and his father in Act IV evoke the past as the only surcease from the doped present. Over their words there hangs no hint of Art Theatre Show Shop. O'Neill has enabled his actors to motivate the monologues and make them convincingly natural, psychologically real.

The two Tyrone plays hold firmly to the best realistic theatre practice. Yet for all their "faithful realism," it should be remarked that the dramas more readily than many earlier works approach the abstraction and symbolism so characteristic of the expressionist mode. The quality and force of that abstraction is difficult to define. O'Neill does not try to convince his audiences that the world of the Tyrones is a microcosm, as he suggested with the typified chorus of *The Iceman Cometh*. The Tyrones and the Hogans are particular people, moving in a specific time, facing highly individual problems. Like many other works of the realistic American theatre—*Come Back, Little Sheba* or *A Hatful of Rain,* for example—the plays are contained and domestic, well-told case histories. Yet to call *Long Day's Journey into Night* a "domestic tragedy" is to underestimate seriously its emotional effect. It is enlarged, not in the sense of Aristotelian "heightening," but more by its unremitting movement "behind life," in the phrase O'Neill once used to describe Strindberg's expressionist dramas. For a play to move "behind life" means that it expands inward, through the surfaces, and toward the core of life itself. The inner enlargement of the Tyrone plays not only scrutinize the motives that produce the painful events, but somehow, also, they enlarge an audience's knowledge of the suffering these events produce. No drama of modern times contains more of pain's substance than *Long Day's Journey into Night,* but in the final analysis, it is not the events, shocking though they are, that grip the audience. The Tyrones suffer and the spectators are convinced that when suffering is the only reality, life is truly as it is depicted in the play.

Verisimilitude does not necessarily lead to a universal statement. However, when *Long Day's Journey into Night* is played, another dimension opens. In the theatre, the suffering of the playwright is more real, if that is possible, than that of his characters. The audience shares them both, and moves as in a dream that is both real and more than real along the course of this "Wander Play." Pain exists in a double layer, one that can seem a fiction, one that must be a truth as the truth of suffering has seldom been stated. An emotion appropriate to an aesthetic experience and an emotion evoked by reality join to create in the spectators a capacity for pity that extends well beyond the boundaries of the theatre and rises to an acknowledgment of exceptional purity: that the universality of pain makes pity and understanding and forgiveness the greatest of human needs.

At their climactic moments, both the Tyrone plays convey the qualities of a dream. The fog or moonlight, the whiskey or dope causes the characters to drift in slow emotional movements. Activity ceases, and each play becomes "a play for voices" that permits the lyrics of lamentation and loss to be heard clearly. Physical objects are only the source of reverie. Edmund and his father play cards. A bottle and glasses are on the table and above it an electric chandelier. Only these have substance in the room. The two men sit in near darkness and silence. A card is played or a drink is poured or a light bulb is turned on. Something in the outer world is touched, but it is a meaningless gesture. Then, as the object is touched, the mind recoils, moving away from that physical contact with the present into the past, wandering in a reverie that is as formless and far-reaching as the night outside. The reverie ended, the ballooning thought returns to the space where life is. Something else is touched; reverie begins again, in a movement that is like a man's swimming, sinking and touching bottom in order to rise up again into the currents of the water. In such scenes, time as an adjunct of reality has stopped; forward motion has ended. The slow turning of memory is the play's only action. Life becomes a dream of pain.

What the morphine brings to the surface in Mary Tyrone is awareness of the isolation that is both her need and her terror. As she appears in the first scene of the play, although small hints of what is to follow quickly become apparent, she seems a woman to whom her home and family are all. . . . The dependence of the men on her is marked, and not only in their concern for her health. She emerges in the few moments of normalcy as the source of life for them, the quiet hub around which they move, happy in her presence. The summer house seems to be truly a home, and the comforts it offers, though modest, are sufficient to their well-being. The illusion of the home is an essential image to establish at the outset, for it, of course, is not what it seems. The room is shabby, poorly furnished, a temporary residence at best. It is like the cheap hotels of Tyrone's road tours, where Mary has waited alone, unable to associate with theatre people, spending nights in idleness until her husband comes or is brought home from the theatre. Mary's life has taught her loneliness and provided her with the definition of a home as a place where "one is never lonely." She remembers having had in her girlhood a "real" home, yet the memory is illusory. Idealizing her father, she has obliterated whatever faults existed in him. Tyrone tells Edmund her home was an ordinary one and her father a steady drinker. His implied question is whether Mary's girlhood was indeed the happy time she remembers it to have been. O'Neill makes clear that her desire, even as a girl, was to escape into a lonely world—into the convent where she could be sustained by a vision and live a simple, virginal existence. That Mary loves her husband admits no question, yet in a larger sense, love has disturbed her spirit and violated her desire to retain her encapsuled purity. Love has led her into a world for which she was not and never could be ready. She needs to be alone in a protected silence. She blames her failure vaguely on life, and she is right to do so. She says,

> None of us can help the things life has done to us. They're done before you realize it, and once they're done they make you do other things until at last everything comes between you and what you'd like to be, and you've lost your true self forever.

In seeking her "true self," Mary is looking for a self that does not exist. Repeatedly she remarks that she cannot find her glasses and therefore cannot see to fix her hair. In other words, she cannot see what she is. She associates her Catholicism loosely with her need for morphine. Morphine is medicine to still the pain in her arthritic hands; the hands once played the piano; she studied music in the convent. "I had two dreams. To be a nun, that was the more beautiful one. To become a concert pianist, that was the other." But the dreams of lost faith and spent talent are dreams of escape which affect her as the morphine does by pulling her from the present, from the house, from the irony of Tyrone's buying property without providing a home, and from her indifference that is like hatred of her family.

In the course of the play, Mary shifts repeatedly from a young girl to a cynical embittered, self-contemptuous creature. Her guilt at failing to take care of her dead child, Eugene, is translated into insane hatred of her husband: "I know why he wants to send you to a sanatorium," she tells Edmund. "To take you away from me! He's always tried to do that. He's been jealous of every one of my babies! He kept finding ways to make me leave them. That's what caused Eugene's death. He's been jealous of you most of all. He knew I loved you best because—." Frantically babying Edmund does not prevent her from blaming him for being born and starting her on the dope habit. Edmund is her scourge and should never have been born. Her hatred of Jamie is less ambiguous. Jamie's need for her is by no means reciprocated. She hates his cynicism, turns from him in fear that he will discover her need of the dope and silently accuses him of murdering the dead child. When the morphine talks in her, she treats her husband with a mixture of love and contempt, dwelling on his failures and yet maintaining the truth of her love for him. . . . Mary needs to turn from them all, to find a path that will take her deep into the fog, hating the loneliness, yet wanting to be rid of the obligations the men's love place upon her. Edmund describes the blank wall she builds around herself:

> It's . . . like a bank of fog in which she hides
> and loses herself. Deliberately, that's the hell
> of it! You know something in her does it de-
> liberately—to get beyond our reach, to be rid
> of us, to forget we're alive! It's as if, in spite
> of loving us, she hated us!

Mary's refusal of all her responsibilities has bred in her a guilt she is incapable of bearing. The morphine must be used to wipe out "the pain—*all* the pain—I mean in my hands." In the morphine trance, she moves gently back in time, seeking to re-create the illusions of a happier world, before there was a past to make her what she has become. Her wedding dress . . . is a symbol of something that never was a substantial reality. Her quest is for a hope lost, a goalless search for salvation never to be attained.

The men around Mary are condemned as she is to hopeless questing. Her husband . . . is both poet and peasant. Under the graceful bearing of the aging actor, trained to eradicate the brogue, to gesture and speak with authority, there lies the fear of the poverty-striken past. O'Neill has falsified to a degree the penny-pinching qualities in his father in drawing Tyrone, yet the fear his father felt was undoubtedly a real one, as was the sense he expressed of having failed his potential as an actor. Like Mary, Tyrone is doomed to an endless life of regret for something lost in the past, holding to a hope that has no reality. "What the hell was it I wanted to buy?" he asks, and there is no answer unless it is protection and the quieting of irrational fears. His failure as an artist and as a husband had made him guilty beyond pardon. Like a lugged bear he stands as the target for all his family's recriminations. Yet, perhaps more than any of the others, he shoulders the responsibilities of their lives. He has kindness in him, and a devotion to his wife that overrides all her animosity. For Edmund he demonstrates little close feeling. A generalized, somewhat distant affection is the most he reveals for his younger son. For Jamie, however, he has a strong feeling that is so positive it can turn easily into hostility. The two months during which Mary has returned to normal he describes to Jamie as "heaven," and he adds, "This home has been a home again. But I needn't tell you, Jamie." O'Neill amplifies the sense of understanding with a stage direction:

His son looks at him, for the first time with an understanding sympathy. It is as if suddenly a deep bound of common feeling existed between them in which their antagonisms could be forgotten.

It is Jamie's sobbing in the final moments of the play that breaks Tyrone, and Jamie who evokes in him his only shows of violence and perhaps also his most bitter expression of sorrow. As his son lies drunk and unconscious he says with sadness,

> A sweet spectacle for me! My first-born, who
> I hoped would bear my name in honor and
> dignity, who showed such brilliant promise!

Tyrone, more than any other member of the family, honors the bonds of the home. He is capable of love but is often driven toward hatred. Even so, he never truly hates, but lives isolated within the frame of the bond, attempting to love in spite of everything. He turns from the pain of his life, to the local barroom; he buys bad real estate to purchase security he cannot find; he drinks to dope his mind to the point of forgetfulness. But he does not betray. He remains a simple man, free of cynicism, incapable of hatred. O'Neill's view of his father contains full charity.

O'Neill's picture of his younger self and of his brother Jamie is on the surface clear enough. Jamie, like his brother and father, is lost, embittered and cynical, wanting his mother whose rejection of him perhaps reaches farther back than the time when morphine forced her into drugged isolation. To compensate for her loss, he has sought to destroy himself with the profligate life of the Broadway rounder, and he has attempted to corrupt his brother, in the pretense of "putting him wise" to women and liquor. In Jamie, pain can have no anodyne. Liquor, far from dulling his loss, makes it unbearable, and, while Edmund is fussed over, even babied, no one tries to help Jamie. Nor is escape possible. Edmund can move into the fog—as he does in the third act—and find a kind of peace. The peace of belonging to a secret at the source of life, "the vision of beatitude" which he attempts to describe to his father, offers him a way out, just as Mary's dream of finding her girlhood faith and Tyrone's memory of Booth's praise have power to assuage the present. There is no vision of beatitude for Jamie in *Long Day's Journey into Night*. His need is always beside him, in Mary, but he cannot reach her. Like Tantalus, he has no refuge from desire. His is the howl of a soul lost in hell.

Edmund, as O'Neill presents him, is clearly drawn, and, as a dramatic character, offers adequate material to an actor, but there is perhaps less truth in his portrait than in the others. He is a strangely neutral figure, except in the scene with his father in Act IV. Even there he speaks out of a solitude that is unlike the isolation of the others. Although O'Neill has been at pains to show what the past has made his parents and brother, it is unclear what the past has made Edmund. . . . He mentions that Edmund has been to sea, and almost perfunctorily adds that he has lived in the sewers of New York and Buenos Aires and has attempted suicide. None of these events, except insofar as his having been to sea conditions his vision of belonging, bear heavily on what he is. He seems to be the victim of the family, unwanted, betrayed, led astray by his brother and, now, with tuberculosis, suffering under his father's penuriousness. It is easy—perhaps too easy—to sympathize with Edmund. He is no more than an embittered adolescent, certainly a pale copy of what Eugene O'Neill was at that time.

How deliberate the suppression of personal qualities was is difficult to estimate. In *A Moon for the Misbegotten,* Jamie's brother is mentioned, but many descriptions of his reactions to Jamie's behavior were deleted in final revision. For example a speech of Jamie's in Act III, reads in the printed text, "Don't want to touch me now, eh? (*He shrugs his shoulders mechanically*) Sorry. I'm a damned fool. I shouldn't have told you." In the typescript the speech contains a canceled reference to Jamie's brother:

> Don't want to touch me now? Well, I don't blame you. Except you promised. No, forget that. But you didn't know what you were letting yourself in for. My fault. I shouldn't have told you. Too rotten and horrible. Never told anyone except my brother. He said "You dirty bastard"—then tried to excuse me because we'd always been such close pals—blamed it all on booze. He knows the booze game from his own experience—the mad things you do. All the same he couldn't forget. He loved her, too. He's never felt the same about me since. Tries to. He's a pal. But can't. Makes excuses to himself to keep away from me. For another reason, too. Can't keep me from seeing that he knows what I'm up against, and that there's only one answer. He knows it's hopeless. He can't help wishing I were dead, too—for my sake. (*Rousing himself, with a shrug of his shoulders—self-contemptuously*) Nuts! Why do I tell you about him. Nothing to do with you. (*Sneering*) A little more sob stuff. . . .

The responses of Jamie's brother in the second play are justifiably deleted. Whatever reticence O'Neill may have felt in describing his reactions to his brother's behavior, his views are irrelevant to the moment in the play. However, the elimination of detail about his own character in *Long Day's Journey into Night* is of another order. Edmund's somewhat poetic inclinations to lose himself in the fog and his desire to enter into a state of Dionysian ecstasy are recognizable characteristics of the young playwright as his early plays showed him to be. Such melancholy, mingled with narcissim, is little more than a normal stage of the developing adolescent ego. (pp. 424-33)

Long Day's Journey into Night is a mirror, the last into which O'Neill looked, and it is of concern to explore what he found there when, for once, he committed himself to see himself unmasked and clear.

The characters most unambiguously drawn as self-portraits are the Poet in *Fog*, John Brown in *Bread and Butter*, Robert Mayo in *Beyond the Horizon*, Stephen Murray in *The Straw*, Michael Cape in *Welded*, Dion Anthony in *The Great God Brown*, Richard Miller in *Ah, Wilderness!* John in *Days Without End*, Simon Harford in *More Stately Mansions* and Edmund Tyrone in *Long Day's Journey into Night*. The physical portrait of each is that of a sensitive man, with big, wide-set dark eyes, a high forehead, dark hair brushed straight back, a dark, often sunburnt complexion, a narrow face with high checkbones, a straight, thin nose and a full-lipped, sensitive mouth, suggesting weakness. His physique is tall, slender and wiry, and his demeanour is shy, restless, rebellious and a little delicate. All the details are not mentioned for all of the characters, and there are some variations in the color of eyes and hair. Yet in general, the image conforms—with the interesting exception of the frequently mentioned weak, sensual mouth—to photographs of O'Neill taken throughout his lifetime.

The reflection he saw in the stage mirror was a strangely softened portrait of the saturnine, hard, disciplined man he became in his maturity. The theatrical face reveals consistently a softer man, a somewhat sentimentalized dreamer. With the exception of Michael Cape and John Loving, the character is young, in his late adolescence or early twenties. He is artistic, a writer, painter or poet, and he holds himself apart from a world that he views as his enemy. He loathes its materialism and seeks to escape it by "belonging" to something beyond life. In this, he reveals a pervasive deathwish suggesting that he will try to avoid undergoing the process of struggle and maturation. Certain of the characters develop positively. John Loving, for instance, finds his faith, but by and large, the course the character charts through his life is a downward one, leading to the destruction of the bright, adolescent dreams.

Setting Simon Harford momentarily aside, no one of the characters finds a significant sexual fulfillment. Indeed, each one of them turns away from sexual experience. As Dion Anthony makes love to Margaret, he denies life, and he seeks out Cybel for reasons other than her sexuality. Michael Cape hopes for something beyond sexual love, that will prove "a faith in which to relax," and he too refuses a sexual encounter with the prostitute. Richard Miller, who like Cape and Anthony turns away from the whore, is transfixed in innocence in a moment of presexual puppy-love. Stephen Murray refuses Eileen Carmody's love so long as it offers sexual possibility. John Loving's casual adultery produces a convulsion of spirit that rocks his faith. John Brown and Robert Mayo emerge from their minimal sexual encounters filled with hostility toward the women who have caused them to betray their dreams. The self-portrait is oddly antiseptic. None of the characters O'Neill cast in his own image, Dion excepted, reveals his tendency toward dissipation, nor displays his knowledge of life in the lower depths.

Reasons for his imaging of himself as an innocent might be attributed to personal reticence, or to fastidiousness that rejected public confession. It is also true that each of the characters *is* an image, formed for a specific theatrical occasion, but like any reflection existing without past or future and empty of physical and psychological depth. With this possibility there can be no quarrel. Self-portraits or not, they are creatures of the imagination, and O'Neill cannot be denied the editorial rights and privileges of any author.

With the creation of Edmund Tyrone, however, the conditions change. Edmund is more than an imaginary figure. He is a figure from history and one upon whose truth-to-life an audience has a right to insist. Yet he is cut in the same pattern as the earlier self-portraits and emerges as a curiously two-dimensional reflection, whose past has been bowdlerized and whose negative characteristics are only lightly touched. It cannot be. If Mary and Tyrone and Jamie are "true," then Edmund should be equally so. If the characters in the play are "what the past has made them," then Edmund's past is of grave concern, as are the ambitions and desires that will move him on in the future. The past, however, is not there as it is with the others. The future is never suggested. He remains a participating observer, a little apart, an eavesdropping creature of the imagination. The truth, whatever it was, is at least distorted.

To seek for a reason why O'Neill drew such a suppressed self-portrait is to move toward areas of psychoanalysis that are not relevant here. Whatever the reason, it was not only simple reticence at public self-exposure or a lack of frankness in dealing with some aspects of his own nature in other guises. To counter charges of mere shyness, there is the figure of Simon Harford, whose face is very like that of Edmund Tyrone. Moreover, there are three others, very different characters from the dreaming poet, in whose general aspect something of the essence of O'Neill's theatrical image may be noted: Eben Cabot, Reuben Light and Orin Mannon. (pp. 433-36)

The lives of the four are similar, their desires astonishingly special. Each is oedipally in love with his mother. Each is embittered by her loss and feels either that she has betrayed him, or that by seeking to possess her, he has betrayed her. Yet without her he is lost and must in compensation seek a surrogate. Eben, Reuben and Orin, each in revulsion from the attempt to find the mother in another woman, call the surrogate a whore. (p. 436)

The search for the surrogate mother turns each man toward a condition that is child-like. Reuben, Orin and Simon seek to become children again and to rejoin their mothers in death or in mad dreams. Eben, who in possessing Abbie has felt that he has also possessed his mother, moves toward a final position that is more resolute than the others. Yet midway in the play, the gratification of the child comes to him as well. (p. 437)

The dissimilarity between these four characters and the other portraits of the poetic dreamer of which Edmund Tyrone is a culmination is vast. Importantly, the difference is not one of increased revelation, of plunging deeper into the dreamer to reveal more of the man. The difference is really in kind, and it evolves from a difference in subject. Although they wear a face that resembles that of Edmund Tyrone, they are in fact another character, one who conforms closely to the characterization O'Neill drew of his brother in both the Tyrone plays.

In *Long Day's Journey into Night,* Jamie's need for his mother is the central explanation for his despair. His revulsion against her and himself is extreme. It is he who calls Mary a "Hophead" and who marks her final entrance with the "self-defensively sardonic" cry: "The Mad Scene. Enter Ophelia!" He confesses to hating Edmund because "it was your being born that started Mama on dope," and he dates his own dereliction from the day he first "got wise"when he saw her injecting herself with morphine. "Christ," he says, "I'd never dreamed before that any women but whores took dope." What he feels to be his mother's whore-like behavior has left him with no belief. That Mary had appeared to be beating the habit "meant so much," he says. "I'd begun to hope, if she'd beaten the game, I could too." When he realizes that she has defeated his hope, he heads for the local brothel and goes upstairs with the least attractive, and, it is to be assumed, the most maternal of the whores, Fat Violet, who drinks so much and is so overweight that the madam has determined to get rid of her. . . . The maternal whore and the mother whose addiction is a whore's addiction merge in Jamie's befuddled consciousness as the source of his self-digust and his need.

The Fat Violet episode served in all probability as the basis for a romantic fantasy surrounding that need in *A Moon for the Misbegotten.* Jamie's account of his actions with the whore on the train while he was bringing his mother's body home suggests the same pattern of loss, the same despairing self-destruction as the earlier play did. Not having the mother, he must expend his spirit on the most repulsive facsimile he can find in an orgy of self-defilement. Later, he finds peace with

Josie Hogan, the giant woman, who pretends to be a whore, but who is really a virgin, and who in the course of hearing Jamie's confession, holds him pièta-fashion through the long, calm night, as if she were a "virgin who bears a dead child in the night, and the dawn finds her still a virgin." In his drunkeness, Jamie sometimes confuses Josie with the "blonde pig" on the train, but at other times she becomes much more than a substitute for his lost mother: she becomes a mother in truth. As she kisses him, *"There is passion in her kiss but it is a tender, protective maternal passion, which he responds to with an instant grateful yielding."* Josie, finally, in her double role of mother and whore, can bring to Jamie his mother's forgiveness and blessing. As he sobs himself to sleep on her breasts she tells him she forgives him as his mother forgives and loves and understands them both. In his last play, it was fitting that O'Neill should create the woman who could be in reality for his brother what other of his characters—Eben, Reuben, Orin and Simon—had sought with such frenzy.

These four men, although they appear to have Eugene's face, are more nearly to be recognized as portraits of Jamie as the Tyrone plays depicted him. If this is, three explanations for the transference may be considered. The first is that the oedipal tendencies were in truth Eugene's and that in presenting them on stage, he could not be sufficiently honest to expose himself, and, for this reason, when the character became expressly autobiographical in the Tyrone plays, disguised his need as Jamie's. Against this stands the biographical evidence, especially the story of Jamie's behavior after his mother's death as it is accurately recounted in *A Moon for the Misbegotten.* Clearly Jamie was possessed of an overt oedipal drive, and the portrait in the Tyrone plays rings true.

A second possibility is that both brothers reacted to the situation in identical ways. (pp. 437-39)

A third alternative may be suggested: that what O'Neill saw and explored at first in self-portrait—through the figures of Eben, Reuben, Orin and Simon—and later, in the Tyrone plays, through Jamie, was both himself *and* Jamie. Or, more specifically, he inspected that part of himself that was in effect Jamie's creation, that to which Jamie referred when he told Edmund, "Hell, you're more than my brother. I made you! You're my Frankenstein!"

The implication of the Frankenstein image is that Jamie was both the creator and destroyer of his brother. Jamie reminds Edmund that it was he who first interested him in reading poetry and he who, because he wanted to write, gave his brother the idea of becoming a writer. By moulding Edmund's tastes and encouraging his talent, Jamie gave himself a kind of creative life. The negative aspect, however, appears as well, as Jamie brags how he introduced his brother to alcohol and to the whores with whom he found release. In the play, speaking in vino veritas, Jamie claims that he dragged Edmund down "to make a bum" of him, and that he did it in full consciousness:

> . . . Or part of me did. A big part. That part
> that's been dead so long. That hates life. My
> putting you wise so you'd learn from my mis-
> takes. Believed that myself at times, but it's a
> fake. Made my mistakes look good. Made get-
> ting drunk romantic. Made whores fascinating
> vampires instead of poor, stupid, diseased slobs
> they really are. Made fun of work as sucker's
> game. Never wanted you succeed and make me
> look even worse by comparison. Wanted you

to fail. Always jealous of you. Mama's baby,
Papa's pet!

Loving and hating his brother, Jamie has tried to create Edmund
in his own image, possessing him in an almost demonic way.
In the play, Edmund refuses to pay attention to Jamie's confession, but the Frankenstein image is nowhere denied.

The imagery implies that Jamie was responsible both for Edmund's positive qualities and also for their opposite, the neg-
atives that led him to follow a course of self-destruction. To
some extent these polarities exist in all of O'Neill self-portraits,
starting with a simple opposition of a poetic man with a crassly
materialistic society. Quickly, however, as O'Neill became
capable of more complex conceptions of human nature, the
creative and self-destructive forces were centered within the
hero, as in Stephen Murray and Michael Cape. As yet, however, there was no radical division of personality, but this was
to come and it was to be expressed in strange intermingling of
personalities. (pp. 440-41)

The image shifts, dazzles, puzzles, but the provocative possibility is that O'Neill believed that his brother had done as he
claimed, and that part of him *was* Jamie, and, therefore, that
Jamie was more than his brother, was somehow an image of
himself, an image that was a hostile double, bent on his destruction, a form of *doppelgänger*. (pp. 441-42)

The image of the poet destroyed by the materialist has multiple
recurrences, and characters return: the mother who is a betrayer
of her children and who resents being the object of their need;
brothers bound in opposition; wives who persecute their husbands; fathers and children fixed in a pattern of love and hate;
the maternal whore to whom men turn for surcease; men and
women who feed on dreams. The list is long, but it evolves
from a single, central source, the action of *Long Day's Journey
into Night,* in which O'Neill's whole creative life centered. He
had to write the play; literally, he lived to write it.

In the play's dedication, O'Neill thanks his wife for giving
him "the faith in love that enabled me to face my dead at last
and write this play—write it with deep pity and understanding
and forgiveness for *all* the four haunted Tyrones." Pity, understanding and forgiveness surely are there for three of them,
but for Edmund the understanding, the pity and perhaps the
forgiveness is less pervasive. Edmund is only a slightly more
mature version of the sentimental rebel O'Neill created in Richard Miller. Except in such episodes as his reaction to his father's
attempt to put him into a cheap sanatorium, his responses to
his family are not specifically defined. He repeatedly avoids
conflict, refuses to face issues, remains neutral and a little
passive. Partly the blandness may be because Jamie is now on
stage in his own person, and much that O'Neill had previously
explored of Jamie in himself is now, as it were, returned to
its source. About Jamie, as about his mother and father, O'Neill,
the playwright, is totally perceptive. Their relationships to one
another as well as to Edmund are strongly and clearly defined.
His to them are not. Perhaps, if *Long Day's Journey into Night*
may be called a "dream play," an explanation might lie in the
fact that Edmund is the dreamer's dream of himself. He moves
like a dream's protagonist in wonder and dread, but is uncommitted to the dream's occurrences. Commitment, finally, belongs to the dreamer and not the dream. The play is O'Neill's
last mirror, the last time he would look to see if he was "there."
In itself, the image of the young, gentle, unhappy man he saw
proved nothing, but having gone through the door in the mind
to the fogbound room in the past, he perhaps understood him-

self as his figure was illuminated by the pain and concern of
those about him. In the agony of the others, it is possible, the
playwright's identity was at last to be found.

Long Day's Journey into Night ended his search for identity.
Yet he remained concerned for the man who was so strangely
a part of his being—for Jamie, who was condemned to live
without love, and without any possibility of a sustaining vision
of beatitude. *A Moon for the Misbegotten* is an act of love,
supplying through its romantic fiction a blessing for a damned
soul.

The play is set in September, 1923. At that time, Jamie O'Neill
was in a sanatorium, where he had been carried in a strait
jacket the previous May. After his mother's death the year
before, Jamie had quite literally drunk himself to death. His
hair had turned white, he had all but lost his eyesight, and
when he died in the sanatorium on November 8, he achieved
perhaps the only beatitude he ever knew. In the play, Jamie
is a dying man, but about his presence there is no suggestion
of the physical horror that came to him in the end. O'Neill,
while he did not mitigate the agonizing psychological causes
of Jamie's behavior after his mother died, gave him in Josie
Hogan a gentler fate. (pp. 444-46)

In Jamie Tyrone, in Hickey and in Erie whose lives parallel
Jamie's in many particulars, and in Con Melody at the end of
A Touch of the Poet, O'Neill had shown that there was a depth
lower than that the misbegotten inhabited—a world where man
was entirely without the possibility of any sustaining illusion,
where he must live in isolation, unable to reach and touch
another human being, alone with his pain. However it is to be
described, in O'Neill imagery or otherwise, it was in fact the
depth in which his brother lived, and it was from this that
O'Neill attempted to redeem him.

A Moon for the Misbegotten is suffused with an elegiac tone,
and like an elegy, the play attempts to mitigate the fact of
death, both to assuage the sorrows of the living and to bless
him who has died. Beyond that, as is proper with an elegy,
the drama attests the value of the life that has been lived. Jamie
had lived beyond the possibility of blessing and his life, in any
absolute terms, considered as a perpetual source of pain for
others as well as himself, could not be said to have had value.
Certainly he was incapable of vision or gratifying memory.
What remedy, then was possible, except to create the vision
in the present? Or rather, to allow it to be created by his fictional
brother and Josie Hogan, who is symbolic of all the women
his brother slept with and also of the one woman he loved.
(p. 449)

[Josie] speaks the play's curtain line. In it can be read O'Neill's
wish for all the Tyrones:

> May you have your wish and die in your sleep
> soon, Jim, darling. May you rest forever in
> forgiveness and peace.

These are the last words O'Neill was to write for the stage and
they express what came in the end to be the consummation of
his tragedy. (p. 452)

Long Day's Journey into Night and *A Moon for the Misbegotten*
are companion pieces in more than subject matter. The second
Tyrone play, a romantic fiction which provides an act of grace
toward Jamie, is a necessary rounding off of the lives of all
the Tyrones. Not that *Long Day's Journey into Night* is brutal.
Its ending, as Mary Tyrone steps softly through the dark room
among the men frozen with pain, is gentle, erratic, rocking as

a feather falling. It is distillation of sorrow, pure, beyond tears, but it is also agony. The play has cried loudly and convincingly that God is dead. In tragedy, God cannot be dead. Men must reach their fates for reasons that are comprehensible and, in the long contour of time, just. But not here. In no other play has God been so needed. His absence is so palpable that tragedy is created, but in such a way that pity itself becomes like terror. *Long Day's Journey into Night* needs the resolution *A Moon for the Misbegotten* brings as it offers, finally, a pervading relief in the knowledge that death is good, and that in welcoming it, man can find respite from terror, and in love, transcend pity.

It may be, too, that in writing finally only of Jamie, O'Neill in his last play found something of himself. Josie Hogan, like Nora Melody, in her simplicity of love testifies to the presence of a value in life that O'Neill earlier had ignored as he wrote of the distorted, suffering world of the misbegotten. Jamie's sacrificial confession is a commitment beyond suffering, and one which O'Neill through his fiction may have been making for himself as well as for his fictional brother. The consciousness of the playwright broods over both plays in much the same way as the awareness of Strindberg moves behind *A Dream Play.* Nathan, years before, had spoken of O'Neill's ''presence'' as being one of the most exciting qualities in his dramas. O'Neill, before the mirroring stage, was always his own audience. Perhaps in this lies the reason he shunned performances of his plays before the public, fearing an invasion of the privacy he as spectator required. Who can know? Who can know why he came to loathe *A Moon for the Misbegotten?* At first, it was an essential work. To speak of Jamie with charity and to invent the giant woman to comfort him was initially an act of pity and of love. It may have come to more than this. Bringing peace to Jamie meant by extension bringing peace to all the haunted Tyrones. The doubles were separated, his own image was suppressed but, even so, O'Neill, knowing that Jamie's agony was his own, found that Jamie's peace was also his. It was a necessary consummation. (pp. 452-53)

> *Travis Bogard, in his* Contour in Time: The Plays of Eugene O'Neill, *Oxford University Press, 1972, 491 p.*

LEONARD CHABROWE (essay date 1976)

[*In the following excerpt from his study* Ritual and Pathos: The Theater of O'Neill, *Chabrowe finds* Long Day's Journey into Night *a modern work comparable to classical Greek tragedy.*]

Long Day's Journey Into Night was written immediately after *The Iceman Cometh* and is characterized by very much the same mood and thought. Life is understood to be ultimately unlivable, bringing man sooner or later to a choice between psychological and physical death. As in *The Iceman,* however, O'Neill's main concern was aesthetic rather than philosophic. And just as he had been able by ritual means to celebrate life even while despairing of it, he was able to make it tragic. At the same time he wrote under a directly autobiographical compulsion, which, like his despair, tended not to be tragic. But by treating the autobiographical facts freely—eliminating, condensing and changing different ones—he was able to fit them into his aesthetic scheme. (p. 169)

As with *The Iceman,* O'Neill constructed the play according to the three old unities of time, place and action. Everything occurs from 8:30 in the morning to about midnight on a day in August 1912 in the living room of the Tyrone family's New

London summer home. What occurs is the final disintegration of the family and, in varying degrees, of its individual members. The house is situated quite close to the harbor, allowing for a symbolism of the sea, the fog and the foghorn. This is the same symbolism first used many years before in *Bound East for Cardiff.* But where in the early play the meaning was intuitive and vague, here it is fairly well defined. (p. 170)

[The] sea generally signifies life itself. Yet the fog, which had once simply suggested mystery, now specifically signifies the psychological death of illusion. And the foghorn, instead of being just a reminder of inevitable defeat, now represents the unbearable pain of reality. This precise meaning isn't wholly manifest until the last act. It becomes increasingly obvious, however, along with the family disintegration. When the disintegration is revealed in all its finality, life itself is revealed in its psychologically fated aspect at the same time.

The primary figure in the revelation of both the family disintegration and the fate of psychological death is Mary, the mother. The rest of the family is dependent on her, disintegrating as a result of her breakdown and seeing their own defeat in the life struggle in hers. It is Edmund rather than Mary who finally makes the symbolism entirely clear. But what he sees in the abstract, Mary embodies in the flesh, and through her his revelations have significance for the whole family. There is an especially close bond between Mary and Edmund, and she is dependent in turn on him. Jamie is described as looking more like his father with Edmund looking more like his mother. As in *Mourning Becomes Electra,* these resemblances are psychic as well as physical.

Actually, Mary's state of mind is dependent to a large extent on Jamie and Tyrone also. She tells Edmund in the first act, ''It makes it so much harder, living in this atmosphere of constant suspicion, knowing everyone is spying on me, and none of you believe in me, or trust me.'' Yet allowing for this interdependency of Mary and the rest of the family, she is still the one on whom the family as a whole depends. When she relapses into her morphine addiction, Jamie, Tyrone and Edmund all suffer in their individual lives as a result. In the last act Jamie returns home drunk from the whorehouse uptown, and shortly afterwards he provokes Edmund into hitting him by referring to Mary as a hophead. Edmund apologizes for the blow, but Jamie admits he deserved it.

> JAMIE. *(huskily)* . . . My dirty tongue. Like to cut it out. *(He hides his face in his hands—dully)* I suppose it's because I feel so damned sunk. Because this time Mama had me fooled. I really believed she had it licked. She thinks I always believe the worst, but this time I believed the best. *(His voice flutters)* I suppose I can't forgive her yet. It meant so much. I'd begun to hope, if she'd beaten the game, I could, too. *(He begins to sob, and the horrible part of his weeping is that it appears sober, not the maudlin tears of drunkenness).*

Mary's failure to overcome her sickness has meant the loss of his hope that he would find the strength to struggle against his sickness of alcholism. The disintegrating effect of her failure on Tyrone is no less profound, though it isn't the basis of his own failure in life. When the still hearty Tyrone realizes Mary has gone back to taking morphine, he immediately gives way to a sad and bitter weariness. From that point on his mood varies between dull anger, grief-stricken pleading and hopeless

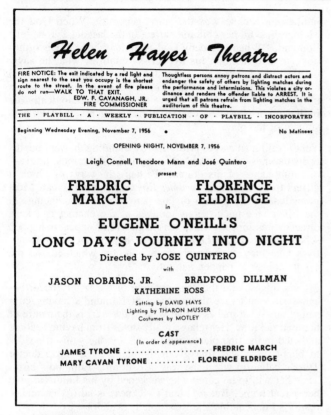

Playbill from the American premier of Long Day's Journey Into Night. *Playbill® is a registered trademark of Playbill Incorporated, N.Y.C. Used by permission.*

resignation. And by the end of the day it is apparent that the pain of Mary's failure is paralyzing. Her final defeat is his. As for Edmund, the disintegrating effect of Mary's defeat comes out in his bitter hurt and despair. It isn't altogether paralyzing, but at the very least he is left psychologically crippled by it.

So in a general way Mary's fate is the whole family's. She suffers a psychological death by finally withdrawing from the painful reality of life, and this withdrawal is symbolized by the fog. Her relapse begins the night prior to the disintegration when she takes some morphine because her anxiety over Edmund keeps her awake. As there is fog in the harbor, she is also kept awake by the foghorn. Then in the morning she tells Tyrone and Jamie she knows the fog will be coming back. And she explains self-consciously, "Or I should say, the rheumatism in my hands knows. . . . Ugh! How ugly they are! Who'd ever believe they were once beautiful?" To her the ugliness of her hands is the ugliness of what she has become over the last twenty-five years, which is why she uses the pain of the rheumatism in them as her reason for the morphine. When she takes morphine, she withdraws from the outer world of reality into the inner world of illusion, from the sight of her hands and the sound of the foghorn into the dense and muffling fog. In the third act she tells Cathleen, "It kills the pain. You go back until at last you are beyond its reach. Only the past when you were happy is real." More than a symbol of illusion in general, the fog is a symbol of the illusion of the past. The past is what displaces in her mind the reality of the present.

For Edmund the fog is even more of a retreat than for Mary. Around midnight he returns from a long walk he has taken to the beach and finds his father alone and half drunk. Tyrone

begins to chasten him about not having more sense than to risk making his consumption worse, but he interrupts.

> EDMUND. To hell with sense! We're all crazy. What do we want with sense! . . . *(Staring before him)* The fog was where I wanted to be. Halfway down the path you can't see this house. You'd never know it was here. Or any of the other places down the avenue. I couldn't see but a few feet ahead. I didn't meet a soul. Everything looked and sounded unreal. Nothing was what it is. That's what I wanted—to be alone with myself in another world where truth is untrue and life can hide from itself. Out beyond the harbor, where the road runs along the beach, I even lost the feeling of being on land. The fog and the sea seemed part of each other. It was like walking on the bottom of the sea. As if I had drowned long ago. As if I was a ghost belonging to the fog, and the fog was the ghost of the sea. It felt damned peaceful to be nothing more than a ghost within a ghost. *(He sees his father staring at him with mingled worry and irritated disapproval. He grins mockingly)* Don't look at me as if I'd gone nutty. I'm talking sense. Who wants to see life as it is, if they can help it? It's the three Gorgons in one. You look in their faces and turn to stone. Or it's Pan. You see him and you die—that is, inside you—and you have to go on living as a ghost.

The reality of life is unbearable. And existence is possible only in a state of psychological death or illusion where the fog is indistinguishable from the sea, the illusion of life indistinguishable from life itself. The illusion of life is composed of the past. But while Mary's illusion is of the conscious past, Edmund's is of the unconscious past. He says that the fog made him feel as if he were walking on the bottom of the sea. For the sea is the maternal sea, and the bottom of the maternal sea is the source of life, the libidinal depths. He says that he felt as if he had drowned long ago, suggesting the very waters of the womb out of which he first came forth and to which in the fog he returns. Being psychically like his mother, he loves the fog and finds peace only by withdrawing from reality into it. The irony is that the pain of reality is unbearable to him primarily because of her withdrawal. After Tyrone is led by an argument over his miserliness to tell Edmund about some of the things in his past, Edmund responds in a like way. He describes the experiences of mystical union he has had, and the play's vision of life is made complete.

> EDMUND. . . . Then the moment of ecstatic freedom came. The peace, the end of the quest, the last harbor, the joy of belonging to a fulfillment beyond men's lousy, pitiful, greedy fears and hopes and dreams! And several other times in my life, when I was swimming far out, or lying alone on a beach, I have had the same experience. Became the sun, the hot sand, green seaweed anchored to a rock, swaying in the tide. Like a saint's vision of beatitude. Like the veil of things as they seem drawn back by an unseen hand. For a second you see—and seeing the secret, are the secret. For a second there is meaning! Then the hand lets the veil

fall and you are alone, lost in the fog again, and you stumble on toward nowhere, for no good reason! *(He grins wryly)* It was a great mistake, my being born a man, I would have been much more successful as a sea gull or a fish. As it is, I will always be a stranger who never feels at home, who does not really want and is not really wanted, who can never belong, who must always be a little in love with death!

The veil of things drawn back is the individual appearance of things concealing the oneness of all life, the oneness of Nature. It is the same veil of Mâyâ which O'Neill first read of in Schopenhauer or in *The Birth of Tragedy.* The secret is of that oneness, or of what Nietzsche called "the mysterious Primordial Unity," here symbolized by the universal womb of the sea. But almost immediately the veil falls, and he who has seen the oneness is lost in confusion again, caught between his endless desires and frustrations, longing vainly to return where he was whole. Edmund says he would have been much more successful as a sea gull or a fish, by which he means if he had never come out of the womb of the maternal sea at all.

This despairing vision of life in *Long Day's Journey* is parallel to the hopeless outlook in *The Iceman.* Moreover, the parallel extends beneath the surface. The sickness of modern life underlying the sickness of the individual characters is the same in each play. It is the sickness caused by the death of the old God and the failure of the new. At one point Tyrone tells his two sons that their denial of Catholicism, the faith they were born and raised in, has brought them nothing but self-destruction. They retort that, for all his pretending, he is no better a Catholic than either of them, and Edmund asks him sarcastically if he has prayed for Mary. After replying that he has always prayed for her Tyrone says, "If your mother had prayed, too—She hasn't denied her faith, but she's forgotten it, until now there's no strength of the spirit left in her to fight against her curse." In part the family sickness Mary embodies is the loss of spiritual strength that comes from not having anything to believe in. At the end of the second act she is alone with Edmund and breaks down under his suspicion of her relapse.

MARY. . . . I've become such a liar. I never lied about anything once upon a time. Now I have to lie, especially to myself. But how can you understand, when I don't myself. I've never understood anything about it, except that one day long ago I found I could no longer call my soul my own. *(She pauses—then lowering her voice to a strange tone of whispered confidence)* But some day, dear, I will find it again—some day when you're all well, and I see you healthy and happy and successful, and I don't have to feel guilty any more—some day when the Blessed Virgin Mary forgives me and gives me back the faith in Her love and pity I used to have in my convent days, and I can pray to Her again—when She sees no one in the world can believe in me, and with Her help it will be so easy. I will hear myself scream with agony, and at the same time I will laugh because I will be so sure of myself.

Mary's loss of will, or loss of faith in herself, is really due to her loss of faith in the Blessed Virgin Mary. Her withdrawal into the past even takes the form of a search for her lost faith. And this relationship between her withdrawal and lost faith

implies the sickness of the spirit generally. When God the Mother dies, all her children suffer. In the last act Tyrone tells Edmund, "When you deny God, you deny hope." His orthodoxy, not to mention his hypocrisy, qualifies what he says, but the remark emphasizes the underlying dilemma. As life in a godless world without faith or hope is unlivable, man is ultimately led to the point where he must psychologically die in illusion or physically destroy himself. Such is the total pessimism of the play.

Yet O'Neill manages to justify life by sounding the very depths of its darkness. *Long Day's Journey* is even the most tragic—or triumphant—of his dramas. Perhaps the ways in which it differs from *Mourning Becomes Electra* make this clear. Most immediately, the pattern of fate here is more convincing. In the trilogy the unconscious motives of the characters take a direct expression, for which reason the events appear to happen schematically. But in *Long Day's Journey* the unconscious motives take only an indirect expression, for which reason the events appear to happen naturally.

Mary's relapse and the disintegration of the family occur because she can't face the prospect of Edmund's having consumption. What makes her so weak, however, is the nature of her own sickness. Her relapse really stems from having become addicted in the first place, and for this Tyrone's miserliness is to blame. She was first given morphine by a cheap doctor Tyrone called in when she was in pain after Edmund's birth. Then her will to be cured was weakened by his failure to give her a real home. But Edmund's sickness is still what makes reality so unbearable she must totally withdraw from it. And the dependence of her state of mind on Edmund's well-being is tied up in a strange way with her past dependence on her father. Tyrone remarks early to Jamie, "What makes it worse is her father died of consumption. She worshipped him and she's never forgotten." When she is completely back in the past at the end, she says she loves Mother Elizabeth in her convent school better than her own mother. Taken together with her adoration of her father, this means a much closer attachment to him than to her mother. By inference the tie between her attachments to her father and Edmund is Oedipal.

This Oedipal element in *Long Day's Journey* is different in degree, if not in kind, from the Oedipal element in *Mourning Becomes Electra.* In the earlier work the attachments making up the fate pattern are pathologically Oedipal. They are all-motivating; there is nothing else. In the later work the pattern has other elements, and the Oedipal attachments are only what may be called normal or latent. For example, Mary says to Edmund, "All you need is your mother to nurse you. Big as you are, you're still the baby of the family to me, you know." And the lasting nature of her attachment to her father is suggested by the simple fact that Tyrone was friendly with him and was introduced to her by him. At one point Mary tells Tyrone that, while she couldn't help loving him, she would never have married him had she known he drank so much. This is curious in view of what Tyrone subsequently tells Edmund, although he speaks somewhat resentfully.

TYRONE. . . . you must take her memories with a grain of salt. Her wonderful home was ordinary enough. Her father wasn't the great, generous, noble Irish gentleman she makes out. He was a nice enough man, good company and a good talker. I liked him and he liked me. He was prosperous enough, too, in his wholesale grocery business, an able man. But he had his weakness. She condemns my drinking but she forgets his. It's true he never touched a drop till he was forty, but after that he made up for lost time. He became a steady champagne drinker, the worst kind. That was his grand pose, to drink only champagne. Well, it finished him quick—that and the consumption—*(He stops with a guilty glance at his son).*

The intimation is that he and her father had more in common than Mary admits, which, along with her naiveté and romantic imagination, must have been a factor in her falling in love with him. The Oedipal nature of Mary's attachments as daughter to father and as mother to son is only implied, but the implication is both forceful and essential. For it characterizes the loss of her father by consumption as a traumatic shock from which she has never fully recovered. And it makes the threatened loss of her son by the same disease understandable as something too painful for her to face, combining as it does with the pain of her father's loss in the past. When Edmund tries to tell her he is seriously ill and likens himself to her father, she responds angrily, "Why do you mention him? There's no comparison at all with you. He had consumption. . . . I forbid you to remind me of my father's death, do you hear me?"

So the cause-and-effect pattern comes down to why Edmund has consumption, which is also explained in part by Oedipal forces. The basic reason, according to Mary, is that he was born with a nervous constitution which made him susceptible to physical breakdown. And the reason for this is the state of mind she was in when she was carrying him. She was afraid of what his not having a real home would do to him, afraid something terrible would happen as had happened three years before when her second baby, Eugene, died. She still felt guilty over the second baby's death and was fearful over having another one to take its place.

The death of Eugene, then, indirectly caused Edmund to be born nervous and overly sensitive. Further, it made the birth itself difficult enough for Mary to be in pain afterwards. In this way it was an originating factor in both Edmund's consumption and Mary's addiction. Eugene had died from measles contracted while Mary was on the road with Tyrone, who had written her to join him because he missed her and was lonely. But the real cause of Eugene's death was Oedipal jealousy on the part of Jamie, and to a lesser extent on the part of Tyrone. Jamie had gone into the baby's room when he had been sick with measles himself, which is how the baby had caught them. Mary says he did it on purpose, explaining, "He was jealous of the baby. He hated him. . . . Oh, I know Jamie was only seven, but he was never stupid. He'd been warned it might kill the baby. He knew. I've never been able to forgive him for that." Then when Edmund tells her he must go to a sanatorium, she accuses Tyrone of wanting to take him away from her out of a similar jealousy.

> MARY. *(Dazedly, as if this was something that had never occurred to her)* Go away? *(Violently)* No! I won't have it! How dare Doctor Hardy advise such a thing without consulting me! How dare your father allow him! What right has he? You are my baby! Let him attend to Jamie! *(More and more excited and bitter)* I know why he wants you sent to a sanatorium. To take you from me! He's always tried to do that. He's been jealous of every one of my babies! He kept finding ways to make me leave

them. That's what caused Eugene's death. He's been jealous of you most of all. He knew I loved you most because—

The other reason for Edmund's breakdown is that, on top of his susceptibility to it, he has led an unstable life. The main influence acting on him in this has been Jamie's. In the first act Jamie accuses his father of picking Doctor Hardy for Edmund only because Hardy is the cheapest doctor around, and Tyrone tries to defend himself by bringing up the ill effects of Jamie's influence. Jamie denies them, but before the argument is over his jealousy of Edmund comes out. And later, while drunk, he admits his jealousy to Edmund along with always having been aware of it deep down.

The question naturally arises why Jamie is the way he is. The reason for his failure to overcome his alcoholism lies with his dependency on his mother and her failure to overcome her addiction. But the reason he became an alcoholic rather than something less destructive lies with Tyrone. Mary recalls how Jamie always saw his father drinking, how there was always a bottle of whiskey around, how Tyrone's remedy for whenever Jamie had a nightmare or stomach ache was to give him a teaspoonful of whiskey to quiet him. Still she tells Edmund that his father didn't know any better since the Tyrones were such a poverty-stricken and ignorant family.

Actually, Jamie began to drink seriously when he found out about his mother's addiction. Yet his inclination to drink was developed in childhood by his father, who in the same unwitting way also encouraged Edmund to drink. Edmund's consumption has been brought about by a whole complex of things, including his own self-willed adventures as a beachcomer in Buenos Aires and a down-and-outer in a New York waterfront dive. But by one route or another they all lead back to Tyrone, to his jealousy, his ignorance and especially his miserliness. At the same time Tyrone is no less a victim of his own family past. He is a victim both in his personal life and in his career as a serious actor, which he sacrificed to a compulsive need for security. Consequently, in the last analysis it is impossible to know where the cause-and-effect pattern began or for that matter will end.

Like the Mannons [in *Mourning Becomes Electra*], the Tyrones are defeated by a determining force beyond their control. But as the force is more complex and subtle here than in *Mourning Becomes Electra,* their defeat has a greater reality and evokes a deeper emotional response. Moreover, *Long Day's Journey* is set off from the trilogy by its compassion. Where the Mannon Puritanism was condemned, Tyrone's miserliness is forgiven. Edmund forgives him when, moved by his father's memories, he says with understanding, "I'm glad you've told me this, Papa. I know you a lot better now." Mary expresses her forgiveness several times, as when she says to Cathleen, "I've loved him dearly for thirty-six years. That proves I know he's lovable at heart and can't help being what he is, doesn't it?" Jamie fails to understand, but that is because he is so much the victim of his Oedipal feelings, being wholly dependent on his mother and hostile to his father. In addition, he is helplessly embittered by the failure of his own life. But though he can't redeem himself by forgiving, he is at least absolved by being forgiven. At one point Mary upbraids Edmund for turning on Jamie, telling him in her detached tone, "It's wrong to blame your brother. He can't help being what the past has made him. Any more than your father can. Or you. Or I." The past alone is unforgivable, there is no one to blame. The Tyrones, who are fuller characters than the Mannons, still hold to one another in their despair. The current of emotion in the play runs in all directions and on all levels.

In fact, what mainly separates *Long Day's Journey* from *Mourning Becomes Electra* is its pathos, which derives from its music acting on its pessimism. By the time O'Neill started writing the later play his darkened outlook had done away with every possibility of a triumph over defeat, whether personal on the part of the characters or symbolic on the part of audience. Along with the Nietzschean process of Eternal Recurrence, the Jungian process of psychological rebirth had become just one more formula or pipe dream. To be sure, the figure of the Blessed Virgin in *Long Day's Journey* is another manifestation of God the Mother. Yet the loss of faith in the old God has destroyed her life-giving power, and Mary's return to her is a psychological withdrawal or death. The maternal sea is a manifestation of the old life-giving Mother, a manifestation of life itself. Yet life itself is now understood to be unlivable for the individual, notwithstanding its cycle of birth, death and rebirth for the race. And Edmund's ecstatic sensations of union with it have no value beyond what he experiences while they last—they are too fleeting and fragile to redeem his own life in any significant way. So there is no personal triumph over defeat by means of a transforming inner conquest. Nor is there a symbolic triumph by means of the very size or grandeur of the defeat. The tragic effect of *Long Day's Journey* comes rather from another aspect of the defeat, the aesthetic quality as against the quantity of it.

Despite the final disintegration of the family the Tyrones love one another as before. Edmund even has a greater understanding of his family and love for them than previously. The hostility between Jamie and his father is perhaps more rancorous, but underlying the rancor is the frustration of their love for Mary. This is emphasized at the climax by the appeal each one makes to her to come back to them, though they all know it is hopeless. Similarly, Mary is a victim of the frustration of her love for them. More than anything else it is the pain of being unable to prevent herself from hurting them, especially Edmund whom she loves most, which makes her withdraw from them entirely. The sum of this unrequited love on all sides is suffering. And suffering generates pathos, the aesthetic equivalent that O'Neill had long been striving for but always missing to an extent. In *The Birth of Tragedy* Nietzsche had stated the following.

> The effect of tragedy never depended on epic suspense, on a fascinating uncertainty as to what is to happen now and afterwards: but rather on the great rhetorical-lyric scenes in which the passion and dialectic of the chief hero swelled to a broad and mighty stream. Everything was directed toward pathos, not action; and whatever was not directed toward pathos was considered objectionable.

O'Neill didn't pretend to any great rhetorical-lyric scenes, at least not in his later plays. But considering its naturalistic idiom, the last act of *Long Day's Journey* comes closer to being one than anything else he ever wrote. This is because of the poetry that Edmund and Jamie quote. O'Neill used the poetry to achieve a lyrical effect such as he himself as a writer of prose, or for that matter the modern prose theater, was incapable of. The poetry was a ritual device designed to get "more composition (in musical sense) into inner structure," as he had noted his intention somewhat vainly for *Mourning Becomes Electra*. Many of the poems are lamentations for a lost love,

corresponding in their elegiac mood to the emotions of the characters in the dramatic situation. And the lyrical intensity of the poems serves the purpose of gradually swelling these feelings to the point where the audience is submerged in a pathos that is general.

The lyrical climax coincides with the dramatic climax. It is achieved by Jamie's bitter quoting from Swinburne's "A Leave-taking," following Mary's dreaded entrance when completely lost in the fog of the past. Jamie recites three verses, the first after Tyrone's desperate appeal to her to come back to them, the second after his own, and the third after Edmund's. The Swinburne poem is made to express the unrequited love of the whole family. The tragic image is of all four Tyrones, and a pathos of tragic proportions is released at the very moment the final disintegration of the family is revealed. The disintegration isn't overcome by the feeling of unrequited love on stage, but it is by the audience's experience of the pathos called up by that feeling.

As in *The Iceman,* both the Apollonian and Dionysian artistic principles are embodied in the play. The dramatic image is Apollonian, a conscious view of individual experience, but the aesthetic effect is Dionysian, an emotional upsurge which is communal. And this Dionysian aesthetic effect is achieved by means of ritual intensifying the action from within. The ritual used in *The Iceman* consists of singing and dancing, the ritual in *Long Day's Journey* of singing only. The singing in the latter, however, is present in more than just the lyricism of the quoted poetry. It is embedded in what amounts to an operalike structure of the whole drama. Throughout the first three acts there is only a suggestion of this, though it becomes stronger as the action deepens. In the first act there are no really long speeches, but in the succeeding ones Mary's become longer and longer as she recedes more and more into the past. They become like arias, as it were, set off by interludes of recitative. Then in the last act, in which there are longer speeches by Edmund, Tyrone and Jamie as well, the operatic structure becomes manifest.

The beginning of the last act is much like a long duet between Edmund and his father. The middle part is like a duet between Edmund and Jamie, this second duet giving way to a trio on Tyrone's return. The two duets and the trio all contain outbursts of poetry. Edmund and Jamie recite Dowson, Baudelaire, Wilde, Rosetti and even Kipling. Tyrone quotes Shakespeare, as does Jamie a couple of times rather mockingly. As for the probability of the poetry, it is always in character. Tyrone's being an actor allows for his quotes, and the reading Edmund and Jamie have done allows for theirs. The setting helps in this regard with two bookcases containing among other works those quoted. In addition, the conversation either prepares for the poetry in advance or justifies it as it comes. Shortly before quoting from "A Leave-taking" Jamie says to Edmund, "And who steered you on to reading poetry first? Swinburne, for example? I did!" The last part of the act begins with Mary's entrance. The pathos is heightened just before she comes in by her awkward playing of a Chopin waltz that she remembers from her convent days. She enters immediately after, and in the ensuing quartet, the tragic ensemble of all four Tyrones, the pathos reaches its climax.

So just as the utter despair of life in *The Iceman* is celebrated aesthetically, the inevitability of defeat in *Long Days's Journey* is made tragic aesthetically. How can the ugly and the unharmonious, the substance of tragic myth, excite aesthetic pleasure?" Nietzsche asked. If the ugly and unharmonious are taken in this case for hopelessness and pain, the answer of Nietzsche's quoted by O'Neill in the program to *The Great God Brown* again applies:

> Here it becomes necessary to raise ourselves with one daring bound into a metaphysics of Art. Therefore I repeat my former proposition that only as an aesthetic phenomenon may existence and the world appear justified: and in this sense it is precisely the function of tragic myth to convince us that even the ugly and unharmonious is an artistic game which the will plays with itself in the eternal fullness of its joy.

With *Long Day's Journey* O'Neill finally succeeded in creating a modern tragedy equivalent to the ancient Greek. The Freudian and Jungian experiment had led him to the abstract perfection of *Mourning Becomes Electra* and then to a drama of psychological inevitability on the individual level. And through the inspiration he had first found in Nietzsche—together with the impetus given this inspiration by his pessimism—everything was finally directed toward pathos, not action. His concept of fate becomes moving to the point of exultation as well as intellectually acceptable. Like *The Iceman,* the play brought both emphases of his idea of the theater together. In its naturalistic form the ritual of *The Iceman* was a celebration of the individual life struggle, and in its musical composition the life struggle of *Long Day's Journey* was a ritual of celebration. (pp. 170-87)

> Leonard Chabrowe, in his Ritual and Pathos—the Theater of O'Neill, *Bucknell University Press, 1976, 226 p.*

JEAN CHOTHIA   (essay date 1979)

[*In the following excerpt, Chothia demonstrates that O'Neill's use of language in* Long Day's Journey into Night *is an essential element of the play.*]

Many commentators, attributing the roundedness of the characters of *Long Day's Journey Into Night* to the autobiographical origins of the play, have been concerned to describe O'Neill's private relationships in the period in which the play is set. But this is to slide away from the crucial questions about how the play works, since autobiographical writing is not, *per se,* binding on its audience. Although the personal nature of the material may well quicken the writer's imagination, it can only speak to the audience when it has been shaped by that imagination into an artistic form with its own unity, apart from the life.

If the play is an emotionally harrowing experience, it is so because of the stage characters and the stage action. However lifelike they seem, characters have their existence only in relation to the stage action, and exist in their particular form because of the way the writer has selected and organized words and gestures. The dramatist writes dialogue, not speech, and presents not the O'Neills, who are people, but the Tyrones, who are characters. (pp. 144-45)

[O'Neill] develops an idiosyncratic language pattern for each character, thus differentiating them and giving each an identity. He then proceeds to vary and occasionally break these patterns so that each speaks with several different and even conflicting voices. Each appears many-faceted, an unpredictable amalgam and yet, at any given moment, still himself, distinct from any other figure on the stage.

James Tyrone's speech mode in *Long Day's Journey Into Night* varies according to his emotional state and, at times, both sons echo his manner. Mary Tyrone's . . . speech changes under the influence of the drug she takes and is actually different from act to act. Changes in her speech serve to mark the passage of time . . . , from present to remembered past. Jamie uses two distinct and conflicting registers, one of which is usually consciously adopted but sometimes seems to take demonic possession, whilst Edmund, still a young man with several paths open to him, has a range of voices some directly imitative of Jamie or of the writers he admires, but none so distinct as those of the other members of the family. (p. 146)

When he creates a stage presence for his characters, O'Neill is conscious of the effect of their speech and of their physical being. In the stage directions, he notes not only costume and appearance, but bearing and quality of voice. Tyrone

> is sixty-five but looks ten years younger . . . his bearing . . . has a soldierly quality of head up, chest out, stomach in, shoulders squared . . . a big, finely shaped head . . . His voice is remarkably fine, resonant and flexible . . . There is a lot of solid earthy peasant in him.

and the description is complemented by a speech mode that is equally robust and straightforward.

The majority of Tyrone's sentences fall into the subject—verb—complement pattern of the normal English sentence. The subject is usually a personal pronoun and only rarely a nominal phrase or clause. The sentences are usually simple or co-ordinating and there are few adjuncts. When O'Neill wants to intensify Tyrone's speech he does so by adding one or two new elements or by concentrating the habitual syntax and making it strikingly regular. In act IV, for example, when Tyrone in one of the crucial speeches of the play confesses to Edmund that he has betrayed his dreams for financial security, his self-searching is conveyed by just such grammatical intensification:

> I've never admitted this to anyone before . . .
> *That God-damned play* I bought for a song and made such a great success in—a great money success—*it* ruined me with its promise of an easy fortune. I didn't want to do anything else, and by the time I woke up to the fact I'd become a slave to the damned thing and did try other plays it was too late. They had identified me with that one part, and didn't want me in anything else. They were right, too. I'd lost the great talent I once had through years of easy repetition, never learning a new part, never really working hard. Thirty-five to forty thousand dollars net profit a season like snapping your fingers! It was too great a temptation. Yet before I bought the damned thing I was considered one of the three or four young actors with the greatest artistic promise in America. I'd worked like hell. I'd left a good job as a machinist to take supers' parts because I loved the theatre. I was wild with ambition. I read all the plays ever written. I studied Shakespeare as you'd study the Bible. I educated myself. I got rid of an Irish Brogue you could cut with a knife. I loved Shakespeare. I would have acted in any of his plays for nothing, for the joy of being alive in his great poetry. And I acted well in

him. I felt inspired by him. I could have been
a great Shakespearian actor if I'd kept on. I
know that!

The confession begins with a more complicated construction
than is usual in Tyrone's speech. The subject is not a simple
noun ("The play") but is a nominal group ("That God-damned
play . . .") which contains besides adjectives and nouns, two
post modifying clauses ("[which] I bought . . ." and "[which
I] made such a. . . ." It is disjoined from its verb and placed
in apposition to the pronoun, "it." [In his *The English Language and Images of Matter*] Randolph Quirk has noted that
this type of construction is common in spoken English where
it is used for emphasis and clarity and, certainly, the unusually
complicated syntax here, does suggest Tyrone's anxiety to
communicate a difficult insight into himself as accurately as
possible. The impression is reinforced by Tyrone's use of parenthetical intensifiers, "They were right, too"; "I know that,"
and, later in the speech, "And it was true"; "Ask her what I
was like in those days." Tyrone's speech seems to become
more animated when he recalls the crucial period in his past.
His normally preferred construction becomes completely dominant, "I read . . . I studied . . . I educated . . . I got rid of . . .
I loved . . . ," and the succession of short parallel sentences
makes the distant experience seem close, until the simple past
tense gives way to the hypothetical past tense in two conditional
clauses, "I *would* have acted . . . for nothing . . . I *could* have
been . . . a great Shakespearean actor," reminding us that all
the effort and devotion was forfeit and pushing the events back
into the distant past.

Syntax is similarly important in structuring our response to the
words of the other characters. O'Neill seems to take us into
Jamie's mind in the course of his confession in act IV. After
a sequence of boisterous camaraderie, Jamie introduces a more
serious note into the conversation:

> Nix, Kid! You listen! Did it on purpose to make
> a bum of you. Or part of me did. A big part.
> That part that's been dead so long. That hates
> life. My putting you wise so you'd learn from
> my mistakes. Believed that myself at times,
> but it's a fake. *Made* my mistakes look good.
> *Made* getting drunk romantic. *Made* whores
> fascinating vampires instead of poor, stupid,
> diseased slobs they really are. *Made* fun of
> work as a sucker's game. Never wanted you
> succeed and make me look even worse by com-
> parison. Wanted you to fail. Always jealous of
> you. Mama's baby, Papa's pet! (*He stares at
> Edmund with increasing enmity.*) And it was
> your being born that started Mama on dope. I
> know that's not your fault, but all the same,
> God damn you, I can't help hating your guts—!
>   (. . . my italics)

The parataxis at the beginning has much the same function as
the complicated syntax at the opening of Tyrone's speech.
Jamie is reaching around for his meaning. Then, in a succession
of parallel sentences beginning "Made . . . ," we are presented
with a catalogue of Jamie's self-blame until, at the end of the
passage, the self-blame is suddenly replaced by accusation.
The shift in thought is marked by the significantly childish
insult, "Mama's baby, Papa's pet!," after which we have the
impression of a deeper, darker impulse overcoming the original
goodwill of the confession. A syntactical shift underlines the
change, signalling that we have moved to a different level of

Jamie's consciousness. He himself says later that he had not
meant to tell "that last stuff," adding "Don't know what made
me." Obviously, we do not respond to the grammar at a conscious level noting, "Ah, parataxis! Ah, a syntactical shift!,"
but we can see how instrumental the syntactical shift is if we
try to rewrite the passage substituting a continuation of the
elliptical pattern of the earlier part of the speech for the complete sentences with which the passage concludes in O'Neill's
text. If we read, for example, "Wanted you to fail. Always
jealous of you. Resented your being born. Said started Mama
on dope. Know not your fault, but can't help hating you," we
find that the change from self-blame to self-justification is lost
and, with it, the impression the last part of the passage gives
of suppressed thoughts spilling over into speech. In both
confessions, O'Neill communicates the secret emotion of his
characters through his structuring of their speech. The audience
is made to feel something about the characters without being
conscious of the machinery that shapes their feeling.

Tyrone is given an alternative register of speech, which is used
when he is hurt, embarrassed or angry, and acts as a kind of
subliminal preparation for his confession. Although he is given
particularly resonant quotations from Shakespeare to roll around
the theatre with his fine and flexible voice, his alternative
register is not the prose of Shakespearean drama but that of
the melodramatic stage. In this mode, colourful nominal phrases
replace the pronouns—Shaughnessey, for example, is "that
blackguard"—and a string of synonymous verbs or a succession of imperatives replace his normal verb pattern. In act II,
for example, Tyrone berates Jamie:

> You ought to be kicked out in the gutter! But
> if I did it, you know damn well who'd weep
> and plead for you, and excuse you and complain
> till I let you come back.

On such occasions, he adopts not only the speech structure but
the attitudes of melodrama. The register is made to appear
more flamboyant because it is used most frequently in argument
with Jamie, whose speech on such occasions is terse.

O'Neill uses the histrionic side of Tyrone to bring vigour and
variety to the play's surface. We enjoy Tyrone's delight in
recitation and fine words and relish his flourishing gestures
when we see them or hear them described, as for instance by
Mary who describes the stage bow she sees him direct towards
haughty neighbours passing in their smart car. In act IV, O'Neill
produces a brilliant *coup de théâtre*. A squabble between Tyrone and Edmund, developed from a petty clash of wills over
whether the lights should be turned off or not, becomes bitter
when Edmund taunts his father with his meanness and bigotry.
The angry tirade with which Tyrone replies is stilled on his
recollecting his son's illness and, in one of those moments of
sudden quiet which O'Neill creates from time to time between
the members of this family, Edmund, ashamed, gets up to turn
out the lights. He is forestalled by his father whose anger is
replaced by an equally overstated self-pity, accompanied by a
magnificent gesture:

> Let it burn! (*He stands up abruptly—and a bit
> drunkenly—and begins turning on the three bulbs
> in the chandelier, with a childish, bitterly dra-
> matic self-pity.*) We'll have them all on! Let
> them burn! To hell with them! The poorhouse
> is the end of the road, and it might as well be
> sooner as later! (*He finishes turning on the
> lights.*)

The whole quarrel has collapsed into broad comedy.

But O'Neill does not create such a dramatic moment without integrating it into the structure of the play. Drinking and brooding over Mary, occasionally returning to their card game, the two men again become hostile when Edmund accuses his father of planning to send him to a cheap sanatorium in order not to waste money on attempting to cure a fatal disease. The vicious aspect of Tyrone's meanness is felt more sharply because the audience has enjoyed its comic aspect. This cruel exchange exposes a rawer level of emotion and, in order to make the return from this extreme position, O'Neill must present us with something as intense in a positive instead of a negative way. It is here that he introduces Tyrone's confession. When Tyrone concludes with the wry inquiry, "What the hell was it I wanted to buy, I wonder?", his claim on our sympathy has been re-established. But, suddenly, the initial obstinacy and the splendid gesture are recalled and the audience are shifted back to the humour of the beginning of the sequence, when Tyrone says:

> The glare from those extra lights hurts my eyes. You don't mind if I turn them out do you? We don't need them, and there's no use making the Electric Company rich.

The conflict between our recognition of Tyrone's uncertainty and broken dream and our sense of the ridiculous ensures that our response to James Tyrone will remain ambivalent. If we recall the melodramatic stage clichés which swamped O'Neill's writing at the beginning of his career when he attempted to convey strong emotion . . . and compare the strategic use to which they are put here, we have some measure of the kind of control O'Neill is exerting.

O'Neill uses contrast between the melodramatic and the plain-speaking register, to create an impression of heartfelt sincerity in Tyrone in sentences which, out of context, would seem neutral enough. He sometimes does this by a direct juxtaposition as in this utterance, for example, when the register of Tyrone's attempt to comfort Edmund in the first part contrasts with that in his apostrophizing of Jamie in the second part:

> don't take it too much to heart, lad. He loves to exaggerate the worst of himself when he's drunk. He's devoted to you. It's the one good thing left in him. (*He looks down on Jamie with a bitter sadness.*) A sweet spectacle for me! My first born, who I hoped would bear my name in honour and dignity, who showed such brilliant promise!

At other times, our recognition of what Mary's surrender to the drug means to the family is sharpened because words fail the usually fluent Tyrone. In act II i, when it is apparent that Mary has yielded to the drug, Tyrone remains slumped and silent. One of the most moving moments of the play comes later when Tyrone simply cries out his wife's name, and then adds a brief appeal, "For the love of God, for my sake and the boys' sake and your own, won't you stop now?" The actor in the theatre uttering the cry, can hardly fail to make use of the long gliding dipthong in the final word, drawing on the very sound of the word to express the pain. (pp. 147-51)

At the beginning of the play, O'Neill emphasizes how normal the manner and matter of Mary Tyrone's speech is. She has the preoccupations and the slang of polite middle class America. . . .

She is self-possessed, rarely speaking except to pacify. In the first draft of the play, O'Neill made Mary's speech tense and erratic at the outset, but he later cut the explicit signals of her anxiety so that now the implication that she is not as calm as she might appear filters in only slowly and does so primarily through gesture—a hand patting hair, fingers drumming on the table top, and through two quickly curtailed outbursts. A hardly stated impression of resentment is conveyed through a series of comments which, individually, would appear as light teasing of Tyrone but, taken together, form a complaint. The audience are alerted to her unease by the conversation between Jamie and Tyrone during Mary's first absence and, from this point onwards, have a new sensitivity to the implications of her utterance. At her return, Mary replies to Jamie's comment that Hardy is not a good doctor:

> Oh. No, I wouldn't say he was either. (*Changing the subject—forcing a smile.*) That Bridget! I thought I'd never get away. She told me all about her second cousin on the police force in St Louis. (*Then with nervous irritation.*) Well, if you're going to work on the hedge why don't you go? (*Hastily.*) I mean, take advantage of the sunshine before the fog comes back. (*Strangely, as if talking aloud to herself.*) Because I know it will. (*Suddenly she is self-consciously aware that they are both staring fixedly at her—flurriedly, raising her hands.*) Or I should say, the rheumatism in my hands knows. It's a better weather prophet than you

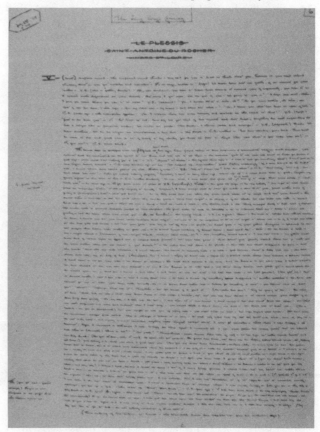

Page from O'Neill's scenario for Long Day's Journey Into Night. *Collection of American Literature, Beinecke Rare Book and Manuscript Library, Yale University.*

are, James. (*She stares at her hands with fascinated repulsion.*) Ugh! How ugly they are! Who'd ever believe they were once beautiful.

In such a speech, O'Neill rewards the expectations he has created and stimulates further concentration. We miss Mary's earlier coherence. The individual sentences are neutral enough, what makes them striking is their erratic combination. She seems to respond to some private significance in her seemingly commonplace remarks which she hastens to qualify. Each sentence begins with a conjunction or a parenthetical phrase, as though she were beginning mid-sentence. The distracted movement of her speech is ominous, following the men's discussion, and so is the harshness with which she rebuffs Jamie's attempt to reassure her at the end of the scene.

Towards the end of the first act, therefore, Mary's probable return to the drug is signalled by the shape of her speech. In the subsequent acts, the fragmentation of her personality under the drug is also imaged in the structure of her speech. In acts II and III, O'Neill presents us with an extraordinary study of the human mind under the influence of morphine. Freed from the normal restraints of intercourse, Mary speaks her fears and harboured resentments, her impulsive warmth and her perceptions about the personality of others. She moves in panic between the present and the past in search of the explanation of her suffering until, in act IV, she comes to rest, cut off from reality, at a point of security in the distant past.

Four main patterns alternate in Mary's speech in acts II and III, and one slowly comes to dominate. One pattern recurs when Mary is obliged to deal with present anxieties. Her speech then becomes frenetic, a combination of excited protests and nagging questions, with which she torments both herself and the men:

Why is that glass there? Did you take a drink? Oh, how can you be such a fool? Don't you know it's the worst thing? You're to blame, James. How could you let him? . . .

I won't have it! Do you hear, Edmund? Such morbid nonsense! . . . Your father shouldn't allow you . . .

I won't have it! How dare . . . ! How dare . . . ! What right . . . ?

The busy persistence of such speeches and the uniformity of their tone make them hard to listen to and present a distressing contrast with the peacemaking Mary of act I. O'Neill establishes a guilty allegiance between the audience and the listening characters by following such outbursts with an abrupt and unsympathetic demand for peace from one of the men: "Mama, stop talking!"; "Stop talking crazy," and, more harshly, in protection of a third person, 'Mary! Hold your tongue." When Mary finally arrives at her resting place, isolated from the present, the audience's response is qualified by a feeling of relief at being able to listen easily to her words.

There is also a vein of quiet sharpness in Mary's speech. She utters words lightly which are not light for the character who hears them. Nothing is explicitly stated—the onus of making the connection between the two figures present before them on the stage being put on to the audience, who thus becomes acutely conscious of the emotion of the silent listener. This is not a new device for O'Neill, although it is used more consistently here than elsewhere. . . . Mary's words can seem . . . cutting, as they do, for example, in the sequence which comes

after Mary has recalled her first meeting with Tyrone. He replies to her query, "Do you remember?":

TYRONE. (*Deeply moved—his voice husky*) Can you think I'd ever forget, Mary?

(*Edmund looks away from them sad and embarrassed.*)

MARY. (*Tenderly*) No. I know you still love me, James, in spite of everything.

TYRONE. (*His face works and he blinks back tears—with quiet intensity.*) Yes! As God is my judge! Always and forever, Mary!

MARY. And I love you, dear, in spite of everything.

(*There is a pause in which Edmund moves embarrassedly. The strange detachment comes over her manner again as if she were speaking impersonally of people seen from a distance.*)

But I must confess, James, although I couldn't help loving you, I would never have married you if I'd known you drank so much.

The calmness of the repudiation after the moment of intimacy makes it seem particularly cruel. Later in the same act, O'Neill uses the device over an extended sequence of the action, rousing and then undercutting the audience's feelings of hostility to Mary. Edmund exposes his misery to his mother in a desperate attempt to draw sympathy from her. She rebuffs him with a light denial:

You're so like your father, dear. You love to make a scene out of nothing so you can be dramatic and tragic. If I gave you the slightest encouragement you'd tell me next you were going to die—

and then, when her son has left in despair, replies with shocking indifference to Tyrone's query about him, "Perhaps he's going uptown again to find Jamie. He still had some money left, I suppose." The constrast between this and her sudden bare cry, "Oh, James, I'm so frightened. I know he's going to die," which is accompanied by her reaching out for physical contact and then sobbing, is distressing, and confuses our certainty of who is strong and who weak, who caring and who cruel. The emotional force of the device depends on the audience's consciousness of the listener and, therefore, belongs peculiarly to the drama where we can watch one character whilst listening to the other. (pp. 151-54)

Sometimes O'Neill shows us a Mary who veers within a single speech from one line of thought to another, from one emotion to another, contradicting in one sentence the idea of the previous one. This third pattern in her speech gives us the impression of her incoherence without ever being allowed to become itself incoherent because O'Neill limits its use to few strategic points in the action. It occurs in the utterance which tells Tyrone she has returned to the drug; again, immediately after the three men have left; immediately before they re-enter; at the end of her long recollection of the past, when her excursion to buy the drug is discussed; and, finally, when she briefly faces the truth about Edmund's illness. These are all occasions on which the present intrudes on her reverie about the past or she is forced to acknowledge her close ties with one of the three men.

My example is the monologue spoken before the men's entrance in act III:

> You're a sentimental fool. What is so wonderful about that first meeting between a silly romantic schoolgirl and a matinee idol? You were much happier before you knew he existed, in the Convent when you used to pray to the Blessed Virgin. (*Longingly.*) If I could only find the faith I lost, so I could pray again! (*She pauses—then begins to recite the Hail Mary in a flat, empty tone.*) "Hail, Mary, full of grace! the Lord is with Thee; blessed art Thou among women." (*Sneeringly.*) You expect the Blessed Virgin to be fooled by a lying dope fiend reciting words! You can't hide from Her! (*She springs to her feet. Her hands fly up to pat her hair distractedly.*) I must go upstairs. I haven't taken enough. When you start again you never know exactly how much you need. (*She goes toward the front parlour—then stops in the doorway as she hears the sound of voices from the front path. She starts guiltily.*) That must be them—(*She hurries back to sit down. Her face sets in stubborn defensiveness—resentfully.*) Why are they coming back? They don't want to. And I'd much rather be alone. (*Suddenly her whole manner changes. She becomes pathetically relieved and eager.*) Oh, I'm so glad they've come! I've been so horribly lonely!

Clearly, the interpretation and voice control of the actress are extremely important in creating the effect of such speeches but the dramatist guides her with his structuring of the passage as well as with his stage directions about tone and bearing. Mary uses the second person pronoun to address herself in her expressions of self-contempt at the opening of her speech. This somewhat impersonal form gives way to the first person pronoun when she speaks longingly and the thrusting questions and accusations are replaced by the conditional form of the verb. The epithets she applies to herself, "sentimental fool," "silly romantic schoolgirl," are bitter enough when contrasted with the joyfulness we heard in her account of that meeting a few speeches earlier but they are, nevertheless, the same kind of language. When, soon afterwards, she calls herself a "lying dope fiend" we have the impression that there has been a real mental shift, because Mary is now using a different and cruder kind of slang. In the last section of the monologue, her contradictory response to the men's return is expressed by the juxtaposition of a snatch of Mary's nagging, questioning, with a snatch of the register which we have heard frequently in the central acts and which will dominate her speech at the end of the play.

We are prepared for the state of withdrawal which Mary will have achieved at the end of the play by her own testimony and by that of the men. "She'll listen but she won't listen. She'll be here but she won't be here," says Jamie, and Tyrone endorses this, "Yes . . . there'll be the same drifting away from us until by the end of each night—." . . . As we listen to the various passages of reverie, we realize that it is not one particular event Mary is trying to retrieve, but a state of mind: of faith, perhaps, but faith in herself as well as in the Deity, and faith that there is meaning and purpose in existence. She searches back into her past until she finds a time when life was forward looking, and there were still choices to be made.

O'Neill underlines this by using as the language of reverie, the eager, effusive elements of girlish speech. "Lovely," "beautiful," "dreadful" are recurrent adjectives. The same word is repeated with a different function or meaning within a brief section of her utterance: "All" is used like this in act III, "I forgot *all* about . . . *All* I wanted was . . . And in *all* those thirty-six years . . . ," and "sure" in the final speech of the play, "how *sure* . . . to make me *sure* . . . as *surely* as . . . I must be more *sure* . . . If I was so *sure* . . . If I felt *sure*. . . ." The impression of trusting naïveté, so moving when heard from the mouth of the white-haired woman, cruelly worn by her experience of the world, is conveyed by the use of "and" to pile up adjectives in descriptions of people and events: of Tyrone, for instance, who was "simple, and kind, and unassuming, not a bit stuck up or vain." . . . We begin to see here how effectively O'Neill uses the seemingly insignificant words in presenting a verbal image of personality. Indeed, the use of the intensifier "so" recurs at crucial moments of the play and becomes remarkably expressive as a result. "I worked *so* hard," "I was *so* bashful," "I was *so* excited and happy:" such remarks occur frequently in the reverie and show us Mary at her most girlish, untouched by disappointment. To express Mary's present desolation, O'Neill uses the same construction, but combines "so" with "alone," "lonesome," or "lonely," . . . The echoing cry "so lonely" is fixed more securely in the auditor's mind because not only are these the last words Mary speaks before the men enter in act III, but they have also been uttered as the final words of act II, scene ii, the mid-point of the play, and the most probable place for the interval in a stage production. That this effect was consciously produced by O'Neill is evident from alterations he made to the first draft of the play, in which he cut away the original ending until these words were prominent. The parallelism of the phrases "so happy" / "so lonely" means that each calls the other to mind. It is no mistake that the final line of the play should be, "I fell in love with James Tyrone and was so happy for a time."

Mary's affliction, which makes a ghost or a fog person out of a flesh and blood human being, is the result of chance and circumstance and, as such, is a peculiarly powerful image through which O'Neill can project the tension between received ideas of order and experience of disorder, between faith and unwilled scepticism. On paper, Jamie Tyrone would seem to be one of the weaker elements of the play, his condition a paler version of his mother's, since alcohol is less strange to us then morphine, its effect less immediately drastic and its influence less clearly the result of accident or of a single blow of Fate. The characterization is more vulnerable to distortion in the event of any looseness on the part of the author because the audience are likely to have preconceptions about alcoholism which may sway them towards sympathy, sentimentality or hostility, making this figure seem less real than the other three. The characterization is similarly threatened by the traditional stage stereotypes of the charming wastrel and of the drunken buffoon. In the event, O'Neill demonstrates how complex Jamie is in contrast to the stage stereotypes and so draws the character as to leave no room for any private gloss by the audience. Jamie is as credible and as mysterious as the other three characters, and his presence is as essential in creating the fine balance which exists between them.

Jamie is presented as living a death-in-life but the "dead part" of him is responsible for his sharp tongue, from which much of the humour and vigour of the play derives. The audience, therefore, responding to his recitation, his jokes, his startling but frequently apt remarks about the other characters, finds itself drawn into partial collusion with him. Moreover, since a large part of the information about Jamie derives from the testimony of other characters which must be modified subsequently in the light of actual words and deeds, we are continually forced to recognize that he is more complex than the testimony allows. We are constantly confronted with the positive elements of a largely negative figure.

In the opening scene of the play, Jamie compliments his mother, laughs at his brother's joke, shrugs off his father's attacks, but actually says very little. What he does say is commonplace enough. The audience is thus alerted to the disparity between what they observe and the hyper-sensitivity of the other characters towards Jamie. Edmund is quick to notice and parry attacks on him; Mary becomes defensive when she catches him looking at her, Tyrone attacks him without noticeable provocation. Prompted by the testimony, we are led to see that Jamie's neutrality is a deliberate withdrawal from any demanding situation: "Let's forget it," "Oh, all right, I'm a fool to argue." "All right, Papa, I'm a bum. Anything you like so long as it stops the argument." If this seems to support Tyrone's opinion of his son's shiftlessness, the few times when Jamie does initiate the conversation present a different picture. In the atmosphere of mystification, we find that his impulse is towards the truth: "The Kid's damned sick"; "I think it's the wrong idea to let Mama go on kidding herself"; "He thinks it's consumption, doesn't he, Papa?"; "God, this ought to be the one thing we can talk over frankly without a battle." When the promised sneers do come, therefore, late in act I, the audience is prepared to find accuracy as well as malice in them. Their vigour is probably more surprising.

O'Neill couches Jamie's sneers in New York City slang drawing particularly on its habit of hyperbole and extravagant abuse: "If Edmund was a lousy acre of land you wanted, the sky would be the limit." . . . His words are, therefore, projected forcefully, drawing our attention to the accuracy beneath the sneer. We begin to recognize that the other characters fear the sneers themselves less than the possibility that they represent the truth, and suspicion and appreciation conflict in our response to him. It is Rocky's rather than Harry Hope's kind of slang [in *The Iceman Cometh*] that Jamie usually speaks. We are conscious of the note of abuse even when no deliberate insult is intended. A man is "a louse," "a sap," "a boob," "a sucker," "a dumbell," living in a world of "hick burgs," "hooker shops," "cheap dumps" and talking "the bunk" or "drunken bull." . . . At its lightest, the humour is uncomplimentary, achieving its effects through bathos, "I was half-way up the walk when Cathleen burst into song. Our wild Irish lark! She ought to be a train announcer," or derisive incongruity, "I shall attain the pinnacle of success! I'll be the lover of the fat woman in Barnum and Bailey's circus." But the slang usage is developed differently here from in the earlier play. (pp. 155-59)

Jamie's slang indicates his alienation from his own home where no-one shares his language. His "foul tongue," his "rotten Broadway loafer's lingo" is specifically rejected by the other characters and the gulf is the wider because of the half-echo we find in Edmund's speech. The younger man occasionally adopts the lexis but never the spirit of the slang and it is from him that the sharpest repudiation of it comes in his scornful parody:

> They never come back! Everything is in the
> bag! It's all a frame-up! We're all fall guys and

> suckers and we can't beat the game! . . . Christ,
> if I felt the way you do—!

The other difference is that Jamie is not limited to a single variety of English. In the first act, slang words and attitudes are loosely interspersed with Standard and do not become persistent until after Mary's return to the drug. It is only rarely used with full force. . . . The shock of his sudden brutal coarseness ("Another shot in the arm!" "Where's the hop-head?") is reinforced by the response of the stage listeners, by Tyrone's anger and by Edmund's swift physical reflex action, as well as by Jamie's own subsequent collapse into silent sobs. When O'Neill wishes Jamie's words to carry conviction he uses no slang. To Tyrone's accusation that his son sneers at everyone except himself, Jamie replies, "You can't hear me talking to myself, that's all" and, in explanation of his bitterness towards his mother, "She thinks I always believe the worst, but this time I believed the best. I suppose I can't forgive her—yet. It meant so much." The simplicity of the language here gives the actor the cue to the tone in which they must be spoken. As so often in this play, it is the contrast with what occurs elsewhere which makes the particular words moving.

Jamie's absence during act III has a realistic explanation, but it is also strategic. He is removed at the point in time when his tongue, were he to remain on stage, must become most callous. His harshness is communicated by means of reported rather than direct speech and so is tempered. The references to Jamie are frequent but usually brief, "You say such mean bitter things when you've drunk too much. You're as bad as Jamie or Edmund;" "That loafer! I hope to God he misses the last car and has to stay up-town." Two are rather more extended: Mary in her reverie projects a picture of Jamie's childhood. There is no didacticism here because the information about Jamie is given almost by the way—our recognition of his early emotional deprivation is gleaned between the lines of Mary's telling of her own tragic experience of life. Edmund's discussion of Jamie in act IV is more direct. He presents a hypothetical image of Jamie's actions off-stage at the moment of speaking. The presentation is ambivalent because Jamie's thought is satirized through the quotation of two poems with whose writers Edmund, only a short time before, has identified himself. Edmund's own position is again in question, as it was when he parodied Jamie's "lingo." We gather that the relationship between the brothers is less straightforward than either claims, and that the intimacy between the two can be betrayed by the younger as well as by the older. When Jamie enters, the reality of his action is superimposed on the image. Since image and reality almost coincide, our attention is fixed on the few differences. Jamie has indeed been reciting poetry to a fat whore in a brothel but his wry recognition of the humour in the situation shows us a self-knowledge greater than had been allowed. Where Edmund's account was narrated and generalized, Jamie's is particularized and delivered as a series of performances: Mamie beefing, Fat Vi giving a "grand bawling out," Jamie crying and sentimentalizing whilst conscious of the reactions of the onlooker. We find a vitality in the speech of the man, who is able to produce nothing, that is lacking in the words of the incipient writer. (pp. 159-61)

If we are repeatedly made to feel that there is more to Jamie than meets the eye, we find that his younger brother continually eludes our grasp. Edmund's identity seems to be unformed rather than shifting like those of the other members of the family. He is ten years younger than Jamie, but seems a lifetime away from brother and parents because he is the only one for whom possibilities remain. He is the one link the Tyrones have with the future. He stands at that point in time to which Tyrone and Mary both look back and which Jamie can never experience. O'Neill casts a particularly dark shadow on this seemingly doomed family by making him the character whom tuberculosis will possibly kill.

O'Neill achieves this effect of Edmund's being not quite formed, not yet an adult, by emphasizing his clumsiness and enthusiasm. His eagerness to reassure Mary, at the end of act I, is for her the signal of mistrust which finally pushes her back to the drug, whilst his inexperience and optimism make him slow to realize that she has returned to it, in act II, scene i. He is stoutly optimistic, but when he attempts to act on his hope, we see at once that there is no substance to it. He cannot begin to talk on equal ground with his mother. She manipulates him verbally in act I, and avoids his appeal in act III. The awkwardness of his revolt against his father invites comparison with Jamie's verbal dexterity. In reply to Tyrone's quotation of Prospero, for example, Edmund rephrases Shakespeare's words:

> Fine! That's beautiful. But I wasn't trying to
> say that. We are such stuff as manure is made
> on, so let's drink up and forget it. That's more
> my idea. . . .

Edmund's inexperience is revealed, too, when his sensitivity to the response to the outside world breaks through incongruously at moments when private grief would be expected to be uppermost. It is the character who in the bright morning had declared in support of Tyrone's independent attitude ("He's right not to give a damn what anyone thinks. Jamie's a fool to care about the Chatfields . . . whoever heard about them outside this hick burg?") who later cries to his mother, "For God's sake, Mama! You can't trust her! Do you want everyone on earth to know?" and says to his father:

> to think when it's a question of your son having
> consumption, you can show yourself up before
> the whole town as such a stinking old tightwad!
> Don't you know Hardy will talk and the whole
> damned town will know?

When he is not talking a great deal, as in his narration of the joke in act I or during the vigil he shares with Tyrone in act IV, he talks noticeably little. Indeed, of his eighty-five separate utterances in acts II and III, sixty-three consist of only one or two terse sentences or half sentences, and only nine of five or more sentences. Since it is in these acts that the family afflictions become apparent, this brevity helps to indicate the difficulty he finds in coping with the situation. Many of his utterances are appeals to the others for silence. . . . "Cut it out, Papa"; "Don't, mother"; "Stop talking, Mama." And, of all the characters, it is he who resorts most often to gesture because words have failed him. He twice attacks Jamie physically and once recollects having done so and in his misery at the end of act III, he runs out to hide himself in the fog.

We catch echoes of all the other characters in Edmund's speech: of Jamie's slang, Mary's vocabulary, Tyrone's delight in the sound of words. He adopts Jamie's slang, for instance, particularly in conversation with or about his brother, but his usage is woolly. Expressions like, "Nix on the loud noise"; "Don't look at me as though I'd gone nutty," lack the callousness but also the pungency of Jamie's idiom. They are sufficient to indicate both the influence of brother on brother and the limits of that influence.

The characterization is not as negative as my discussion so far suggests. What at one moment we call "unformed," at the next we might describe as "not fixed." His retreat from the word might equally be seen as self-assertion through physical action. His sensitivity to the situation implies a degree of feeling not hardened by habit. Although the other characters fear Jamie's tongue, the most cutting comments on the situation come from the lips of the naïve son. His mockery of Jamie's melancholy self-analysis stops his brother short; his appeal at the end of the play, almost impinges on Mary and it is he who shows Tyrone that his symbol of the past is to be equated with Mary's when, in what is in its implications one of the cruellest lines of the play, he suggests that Booth's praise for Tyrone's Othello "might be in an old trunk in the attic, along with Mama's wedding dress." (pp. 161-63)

One of the more firmly fixed dramatic conventions is that there should be a hero, a central figure. Much of the emotional intensity of this play derives from O'Neill's deliberate breaking of the convention. The audience's impulse to identify with one character is continually satisfied and then frustrated. At any given moment, one of the four dominates the action revealing his thought in such a way that our sympathy is engaged but, immediately, his words and gestures alienate that sympathy and his place is taken by another. The resulting tension binds the audience to the action by insisting that they hold the claims of all four characters in mind and delay judgement on what they see. Even as one figure expresses his spiritual isolation, we find ourselves relating his words to each of the other three and, by extension, to all human experience. The relationship between the four characters, from which none can wholly separate himself, is as much O'Neill's subject as is the quest of each for individual meaning. As the play proceeds, we recognize that each character is both supported and crippled by the relationship and that these elements are tightly enmeshed. O'Neill uses particular linguistic devices to create what might be called a "family rhythm." These are responsible for much of the surface variety of the play and also for its underlying coherence, since they permeate the action, seeming to root the characters together in their shared past.

Most obviously, but nevertheless importantly for the tone of the play, the characters address each other familiarly. They tease each other about little personal matters, snoring, reducing, digesting. . . . Quarrels : . . . flair out of nothing and are quickly deflated, allegiances shift and each character puts in his word in a manner possible only amongst people with a history of such interactions. O'Neill is confronting the audience with the pattern of its own familiar conversations and asking them to leap its grasp and understand its shared assumptions. Something of this can be seen in a fairly lighthearted exchange early in act I: Edmund breaks into a conversation about other matters with a reference back to Mary's earlier complaint about Tyrone's snoring:

> EDMUND. I'll back you up about Papa's snoring. Gosh, what a racket!
>
> JAMIE. I heard him, too. (*He quotes, putting on a ham actor manner.*) "The Moor, I know his trumpet."
>
> (*His mother and brother laugh.*)
>
> TYRONE (*Scathingly*). If it takes my snoring to make you remember Shakespeare instead of the dope sheet on the ponies, I hope I'll keep on with it.

MARY. Now, James! You mustn't be so touchy.

(Jamie shrugs his shoulders and sits down in the chair on her right.)

EDMUND. *(Irritably).* Yes, for Pete's sake, Papa! First thing after breakfast! Give it a rest, can't you?

(He slumps down in the chair at left of table next to his brother. His father ignores him.)

MARY. *(Reprovingly)* Your father wasn't finding fault with you. You don't have to always take Jamie's part. You'd think you were the one ten years older.

Jamie caps Edmund's words, Edmund Mary's and the dialogue flows quickly from statement to reaction, the alternation of second and first person pronouns helping the movement of the sequence. Each utterance endorses, contradicts or extends the preceeding one. The startling personal attack by father on son and the speed with which the other two characters intervene, suggest that there is knowledge involved which predates the play and alert us to meanings beyond the common core of the words spoken. Using the predisposition of the audience to seek out significance, O'Neill embeds his exposition of situation and character into the flow of the dialogue. There is no narration in this play of the kind spoken by Larry to Parritt at the opening of *The Iceman Cometh*. There are only fragments which the audience must piece together. The use, here, of the continuous form of the verb, and of adverbs of time, such as Mary's "always," suggest that we are witnessing a habitual response, and this impression will be reinforced when these two features recur, as they frequently do, in expression of irritation between the characters.... We gather specific information, too, about Jamie's wastrel life, the relative ages of the two brothers, Tyrone's respect for Shakespeare, and we can deduce that both brothers must have been awake during the night although the significance of this will only become apparent with the accumulation of several such hints. Similarly, we hear a comic distortion of a quotation and an irritable response to it—the first piece of a pattern which will be elaborated during the play.

The open method of exposition is particularly appropriate to this play. What the audience learns about the past might be detailed, but it can never be fixed because it is refracted through the consciousness of one or other of the characters and, far from endorsing any one account, O'Neill lets each contradict the others. Whilst some details are allowed to seem fairly stable, other topics—homes, doctors, the electric light, the fog, alcohol—are raised, dropped and taken up again by each character, each new reference modifying the audience's viewpoint until, by the end of the play, each topic is fraught with suggestion. (pp. 168-70)

We catch echoes of one character's speech in that of another. The speech of both Tyrone and Mary has an Irish shape ... which appears most noticeably when they tease each other affectionately or dream of the past. This helps to suggest the warmth of their feeling at such moments and also marks the experiential gap between parent and child.... Elsewhere, shared language can mark the deep, unacknowledged bond between parent and child. (pp. 170-71)

Denials and barriers of silence occur frequently. They are as telling as the shared language in revealing what the characters have in common and, as they accumulate, we become aware of their thematic significance. Certain truths are avoided by the Tyrones as firmly as others were in Hope's bar. Things are implied but not stated, a topic is suddenly changed, a speaker falls silent in mid-sentence and the listener forbears to comment. During the first act, for example, we observe the men's concern for Mary, we hear her demands that they trust her and their eager reassurances and we also piece together a grimly comic picture of all three men simulating sleep on the night before the action of the play whilst listening intently to Mary's restless moving about. When any of the men attempts to discuss this the others deny having been conscious of anything extraordinary. The audience's curiosity is aroused. In the second act, the anxiety and shirked confidences of the men are recalled, just before Mary's entrance, in the pause which occurs during this brief exchange:

EDMUND. She didn't get much sleep last night.

JAMIE. I know she didn't.

(A pause. The brothers avoid looking at each other.)

EDMUND. That damned foghorn kept me awake, too.

The admissions which flood into such silences are more marked because they are spoken only in the minds of the audience. They are ominous because they draw attention to but do not solve the mystery already sensed. Euphemisms are used in the play, with similar effect. Tyrone refers to the drug as "the poison," "her curse," and the other characters avoid naming it. All use the euphemism "summer cold" to disguise their fear of Edmund's illness from themselves and each other. If, in his anxiety, one character forgets the tacit agreement, the others quickly remind him and the pattern of reticence and uneasy collusion is reinforced. For example:

MARY. You mustn't mind Edmund, James. Remember he isn't well.

(Edmund can be heard coughing as he goes upstairs.)

(She adds nervously.) A *summer cold* makes anyone *irritable.*

JAMIE. *(Genuinely concerned)* It's not just a cold he's got. The Kid is damned sick.

(His father gives him a sharp warning look but he doesn't see it.)

MARY. *(Turns on him resentfully).* Why do you say that? It is *just a cold!* Anyone can tell that! You always imagine things!

TYRONE. *(With another warning glance at Jamie—easily)* All Jamie meant was Edmund might have *a touch of something else,* too, which makes his cold worse.

JAMIE. Sure, Mama, *that's all* I meant.

TYRONE. Doctor Hardy thinks it might be *a bit of* malarial fever he caught when he was in the tropics. If it is, quinine will soon cure it.

Such passages help to show the guilt and panic underlying the relationship. The soothing words, which infiltrate the speech of all the characters, as my italicizing in the extract demonstrates, represent a shrinking from the deeper reassurances and admissions for which all long. The euphemisms make us sen-

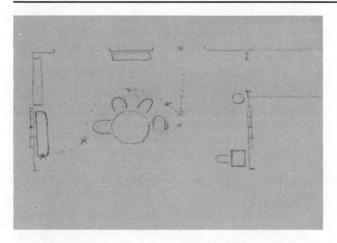

O'Neill's sketch plotting the characters' stage movements for the last scene of Long Day's Journey Into Night. *Collection of American Literature, Beinecke Rare Book and Manuscript Library, Yale University.*

sitive to the family's private taboos, and it is the effect of a taboo being broken as much as the sudden coarse slang which makes Jamie's bitter attacks on Mary so shocking, or Edmund's cry, "Mama, it isn't a summer cold! I've got consumption," so piercing and Mary's refusal to respond so final.

Throughout the play such denials occur, shifting attention from facts and events to their emotional effect, and infiltrating our consciousness with the looming despair of the Tyrones. We are made painfully aware that the time will never be ripe, that opportunities will always be missed, because O'Neill juxtaposes some of the cruellest denials with moments of brief sympathy, frustrating the expectations of change which are beginning to be shaped. So, in act I, Jamie and Tyrone break apart with mutual recriminations after their brief understanding. And, when one character tries to break through to another by crying out an appeal, the other retreats in confusion or resentment, as Tyrone does from Mary in act II and she from him in the following act. Such withdrawal, as we have seen, becomes a dominant pattern in Mary's speech.

A similar pattern of accretion underlies our impression that the relationship also has its positive aspect. This is most immediately apparent in the confessions of act IV, in which, one after another, each character reveals his trust by attempting to expose his deepest thought. (pp. 171-73)

Our sense of the necessity of the family unit to each member, despite all the horrors it holds for them, is established in part by the image we are given of the Tyrones keeping face before the outside world and revealing their fragmented, uncertain selves only to each other. When Tyrone, in act III, quiets Mary with the words, "Hush now! Here comes Cathleen. You don't want her to see you crying," he bears witness to the existence of an intimacy which does allow her to cry before him. (p. 174)

The unfolding action of **Long Day's Journey Into Night** has a greater coherence and the dialogue is more absorbingly complex than that of [**Mourning Becomes Electra**]. The ending, when it comes, comes as the culmination of the meanings, the undertones and overtones we have absorbed during the play, and it is couched in words and images made potent by their use within the play. (p. 181)

O'Neill altered act IV in its second draft to keep Mary offstage until the last few minutes of the play. In doing so, he increased the suspense of the act and the subsequent impact of Mary's appearance. Throughout the act her entrance is anticipated, by the listening attitude of the men, by their comments on her restless pacing above them and by their very presence on the stage, since we recognize that their vigil must continue until she has become still.... The underlying pattern of the action demands Mary's presence for its completion. Edmund and Tyrone have moved three times from hostility to understanding, reaching a deeper level of mutual confidence at each stage. Then, the relationship between the two brothers has been presented with comparable intensification as Jamie has moved from bonhomie to threat, to self-revelation. Each of the three men having in turn exposed his secret thought to one of the others, there is a hiatus. Exhausted, they drowse. The balance in which the characters have been held until now makes Mary's entrance inevitable. But it is also startling because of the way in which it takes place. There is a moment of silence and then Edmund jerks up, listening intently. A burst of light at the back of the stage, when all five bulbs of the chandelier flash on, is followed by a burst of sound, when a Chopin waltz is played on the piano. When Mary appears in the doorway, her hair is long and braided girlishly, she wears a sky blue night gown, and carries a wedding dress. O'Neill succeeds in creating a poetry of theatre here ... because each visual and aural impression arouses in the audience some memory of the dialogue. Things which through repeated naming have become emblems of the private mythology of the family are suddenly present before us in solid form. Jamie's words, which break the silence, have the force of words which should not have been spoken but, having been, cannot be expunged from the mind and Mary's failure to react to them signifies how dissociated from the present she has become. (pp. 181-82)

Here, as throughout the play, the verbal and visual level are integrated with each other, so that when words leave off the stage image speaks. Once we have absorbed the impact of Mary's final entrance, the stage picture has significance not because, like that, it is startling or spectacular, but because of the way it complements the dialogue. Watching the final moments of the play, we are scarcely aware of how carefully movement and gesture have been organized and how much they contribute to the feeling of the scene. As can be seen from O'Neill's sketch of this sequence ..., the men remain still so that our eyes follow Mary as she crosses from the door to the front of the stage. Mary's seemingly aimless movement, in fact takes her past each of the men in turn, taking our attention with her from one to the other of them. In the single other movement, shortly after Mary's entrance, Tyrone approaches Mary who carries her wedding dress that has lain in the old trunk in the attic and that, described with delight by Mary earlier in the play, had become an emblem of her lost girlhood and her reproach to Tyrone. Because we have experienced this, Tyrone's simple gesture of taking the dress from her and holding it protectively is remarkably moving. When Mary comes to rest it is, as the sketch shows, at the front left corner of the stage which leaves the silent characters at the focal point in the centre. This divides the audience's attention during Mary's final speech and so acts as preparation for the last line of the play. (pp. 182-83)

Mary has given herself over to the past, obliterating her menfolk with her colloquialisms, her girlish intensifiers.... Her naïve and trusting words, "I knew She heard my prayer and would always love me and see no harm ever came to me as long as I never lost my faith in her," are almost unbearable for the stage listeners, and for the audience observing the stage listeners and knowing that their perspective is from a different point in time from hers.

The overwhelming effect of the last four lines of the play comes, I think, because, just when it appears that the play has drawn to its conclusion and has reached some kind of resting place, however dismal, the sentence, *"That was in the winter of senior year,"* pushes the interview back into the distant past and returns Mary to the present and the family, from which there can be, after all, no escape for any of the four Tyrones. The quiet ending of the play is not a conclusion but another relentless beginning:

> That was in the winter of senior year. Then in the spring something happened to me. Yes, I remember, I fell in love with James Tyrone and was so happy for a time.

> (pp. 183-84)

> *Jean Chothia, in her* Forging a Language: A Study of the Plays of Eugene O'Neill, *Cambridge University Press, 1979, 243 p.*

ADDITIONAL BIBLIOGRAPHY

Barlow, Judith E. "*Long Day's Journey into Night:* From Early Notes to Finished Play." *Modern Drama* XXII, No. 1 (March 1979): 19-28.
    Compares and contrasts the final text of *Long Day's Journey into Night* with early drafts of the play.

————. *Final Acts: The Creation of Three Late O'Neill Plays.* Athens: The University of Georgia Press, 1985, 215 p.
    Traces the composition of *The Iceman Cometh, Long Day's Journey into Night,* and *A Moon for the Misbegotten* from random notes, early drafts, and holograph manuscripts to published texts, noting the kinds of changes O'Neill made during the composition of this play.

Berlin, Normand. *Eugene O'Neill.* New York: Grove Press, 1982, 178 p.
    Biographical and critical study, with a chapter devoted to *Long Day's Journey into Night.*

Bowen, Croswell. *The Curse of the Misbegotten: A Tale of the House of O'Neill.* N.Y.: McGraw-Hill, 1959, 384 p.
    Extensive biography written with the assistance of O'Neill's son Shane.

Carpenter, Frederic I. *Eugene O'Neill.* Boston: Twayne, 1979, 192 p.
    Biographical and critical study with a selective bibliography of O'Neill criticism.

Chiaromonte, Nicola. "Eugene O'Neill (1958)." *The Sewannee Review* 68 (1960): 494-501.
    Defines O'Neill's chief characteristic as "an honesty, sincerity and integrity which can only be defined as 'romantic'," and contends that this sincerity makes the "monotonous and obstinate round of suffering" portrayed in *Long Day's Journey into Night* bearable.

Clurman, Harold. Review of *Long Day's Journey into Night. The Nation* 183, No. 21 (24 November 1956): 466.
    Views *Long Day's Journey into Night* as painfully honest autobiography.

D'Andrea, Paul. "'Thou Starre of Poets': Shakespeare as DNA." In *Shakespeare: Aspects of Influence,* edited by G. B. Evans, pp. 163-91. Cambridge: Harvard University Press, 1976.
    Discusses "Shakespeare's significance as an icon" quoted and referred to by the characters in *Long Day's Journey into Night.*

Eldridge, Florence. "Reflections on *Long Day's Journey into Night:* First Curtain Call for Mary Tyrone." In *Eugene O'Neill: A World View,* edited by Virginia Floyd, pp. 286-87. New York: Frederick Ungar, 1979.
    Brief reminiscence by the American actress who first enacted the role of Mary Tyrone in the United States.

Fitzgerald, Geraldine. "Another Neurotic Electra: A New Look at Mary Tyrone." In *Eugene O'Neill: A World View,* edited by Virginia Floyd, pp. 290-92. New York: Frederick Ungar, 1979.
    Explanation of the actress's interpretation of the role of Mary Tyrone, based on her research into morphine addiction and its effect upon personality.

Floyd, Virginia. "*Long Day's Journey into Night.*" In her *The Plays of Eugene O'Neill,* pp. 532-54. New York: Frederick Ungar, 1985.
    Pronounces *Long Day's Journey into Night* "the supreme achievement of both O'Neill and the American theater" in a discussion focusing on the play's autobiographical aspects.

Gelb, Arthur, and Gelb, Barbara. *O'Neill.* New York: Harper & Brothers, 1960, 970 p.
    Thorough biography quoting from the reminiscences of many friends, acquaintances, and contemporaries of O'Neill.

Frenz, Horst, and Tuck, Susan, eds. *Eugene O'Neill's Critics: Voices from Abroad.* Carbondale: Southern Illinois University Press, 1984, 225 p.
    Collection of European, Asian, and South American critical essays about O'Neill. Discussion of *Long Day's Journey into Night* appears in essays by B. Nagy László of Hungary and Oscar Fritz Schuh of Germany.

Kern, Walter. Review of *Long Day's Journey into Night. New York Herald Tribune* (8 November 1956): 20.
    Autobiographical interpretation of an early United States performance of *Long Day's Journey into Night,* praising the performances of Frederic March, Jason Robards, Florence Eldridge, and Bradford Dillman.

McDonnell, Thomas P. "O'Neill's Drama of the Psyche." *The Catholic World* 197, No. 1178 (May 1963): 120-25.
    Calls *Long Day's Journey into Night* "clearly an autobiographical drama—and the greatest one we have," seeing it as the fitting culmination of a long career in which O'Neill repeatedly explored his personal tragedies in powerful dramas; McDonnell concludes that it is "the greatest play written by an American."

Miller, Jordan Y. *Eugene O'Neill and the American Critic.* Rev. ed. Hamden, CT.: Archon Books, 1973, 553 p.
    Most complete annotated bibliography of American criticism on O'Neill.

Nethercot, Arthur H. "The Psychoanalyzing of Eugene O'Neill." *Modern Drama* 3, Nos. 3 and 4 (December 1960 and February 1961): 357-72.
    Examination of O'Neill's use of psychological themes in his dramas.

————. "The Psychoanalyzing of Eugene O'Neill: Postscript." *Modern Drama* VIII, No. 2 (September 1965): 150-55.
    Study of what was revealed about O'Neill's personal conversance with psychological theory in the Arthur and Barbara Gelb biography *O'Neill* (see Additional Bibliography item above).

————. "The Psychoanalyzing of Eugene O'Neill: P. P. S." *Modern Drama* XVI, No. 1 (June 1973): 35-48.
    Further examination of O'Neill's knowledge of psychoanalysis and the extent of its influence on him and his plays.

Raleigh, John Henry. "O'Neill's *Long Day's Journey into Night* and New England Irish-Catholicism." *Partisan Review* XXVI, No. 4 (Fall 1959): 573-92.
    Considers the importance of O'Neill's Irish-Catholic background to the composition of *Long Day's Journey into Night.*

Ranald, Margaret Loftus. *The Eugene O'Neill Companion.* Westport, CT: Greenwood Press, 1984, 827 p.

Valuable study guide, listing all of O'Neill's plays and characters with plot summaries and descriptive commentary. Three appendices offer a chronology of plays, a listing of adaptions of O'Neill's works in other genres, and an essay discussing his theory and practice of the theater.

Scheibler, Rolf. "*Long Day's Journey into Night.*" In his *The Late Plays of Eugene O'Neill,* pp. 102-41. Bern: Francke, 1970.
Provides a close examination of the structure, action, and characterization of *Long Day's Journey into Night,* focusing on the characters' relationships with one another and to the major symbols of the play.

Schvey, Henry I. " 'The Past is the Present, Isn't It?': Eugene O'Neill's *Long Day's Journey into Night.*" *Dutch Quarterly Review of Anglo-American Letters* 10, No. 2 (1980): 84-99.
Discusses the ways in which the past is responsible for the present and, presumably, future unhappiness of the Tyrones in *Long Day's Journey into Night.*

Sewall, Richard B. "*Long Day's Journey into Night.*" In his *The Vision of Tragedy,* pp. 161-74. New Haven: Yale University Press, 1980.
Interpretation of *Long Day's Journey into Night* as an expression of O'Neill's personal quest for meaning in his life, extraordinary in particular because of its effectiveness in balancing four main characters of equal importance.

Sheaffer, Louis. *O'Neill: Son and Playwright.* Boston: Little, Brown, 1968, 543 p.
Major biography. This first of two volumes covers O'Neill's life to 1920.

————. *O'Neill: Son and Artist.* Boston: Little, Brown, 1973, 750 p.
The second volume of Sheaffer's biography, covering O'Neill's life from 1920 until his death.

Sinha, C. P. *Eugene O'Neill's Tragic Vision.* New Delhi: New Statesman Publishing Co., 1981, 176 p.

Examines O'Neill's early "sea plays" and his autobiographically inspired final plays as "the end product" of the playwright's own "private agonies" and "the prevailing futilitarianism of the time."

Stamm, Rudolf. " 'Faithful Realism': Eugene O'Neill and the Problem of Style." *English Studies* 40, Nos. 1-6 (1959): 242-50.
Contends that O'Neill's thematically linked posthumous plays *The Iceman Cometh, Long Day's Journey into Night, A Moon for the Misbegotten,* and *A Touch of the Poet,* necessitate a favorable reevaluation of his contribution as a dramatist.

Weissman, Philip. "Conscious and Unconscious Autobiographical Dramas of Eugene O'Neill." *Journal of the American Psychoanalytic Association* V, No. 3 (July 1957): 432-60.
Freudian psychoanalytic discussion of *Long Day's Journey into Night* as revelatory autobiography.

Whicher, Stephen. "O'Neill's Long Journey." *The Commonweal* LXIII, No. 24 (16 March 1956): 614-15.
Review of an early performance in the United States of *Long Day's Journey into Night,* suggesting that the play's greatest strength lies in its character portrayals.

Winther, Sophus Keith. "O'Neill's Tragic Themes: *Long Day's Journey into Night.*" *The Arizona Quarterly* 13, No. 4 (Winter 1957): 295-307.
Discounts the importance of the autobiographical element of *Long Day's Journey into Night,* maintaining that the drama's greatest significance lies in its development of four themes: the father, the mother, the home, and the poet-philosopher's world view.

————. *Eugene O'Neill: A Critical Study.* Rev. ed. New York: Russell & Russell, 1961, 319 p.
Early full-length study of O'Neill, originally published in 1934. Winther examines O'Neill as a social critic and as a tragedian who portrays his characters' "heroic will to live." The 1961 edition includes a chapter on O'Neill's later tragedies, including *Long Day's Journey into Night.*

Wilfred (Edward Salter) Owen

1893-1918

English poet.

One of the leading English poets of the First World War, Owen is primarily remembered for realistic protest poems inspired by his experiences at the Western Front in 1916 and 1917. Regarding the true subject of his poems as "the pity of war," he sought to present the grim realities of warfare and its effects on the human spirit. His unique voice—he is considered less idealistically patriotic than Rupert Brooke though more compassionate than Siegfried Sassoon—is complemented by his unusual and experimental technical style. He is recognized as the first English poet to fully utilize para-rhyme, that is, rhyme achieved by matching the initial and final consonants of words while altering the vowel sounds. This distinctive technique and the prominent note of social protest in his works influenced the poets of the 1920s and 1930s, most notably W. H. Auden, C. Day Lewis, and Stephen Spender.

Owen was born in Oswestry, Shropshire, the eldest son of a minor railroad official. Described by his brother as a "grave, healthy little boy," Owen was a serious student, profoundly influenced by his Calvinist mother. A thoughtful, imaginative youth, he developed an interest in poets and poetry, especially in John Keats, whose influence can be seen in many of Owen's poems. After attending schools in Birkenhead and Shrewsbury, Owen hoped to enter a university in 1911; however, he failed to win a scholarship and instead became a lay assistant to the Vicar of Dunsden in Oxfordshire. He tried unsuccessfully for a scholarship again in 1913 and subsequently accepted a position teaching English at the Berlitz School in Bordeaux. In France he was befriended by the Symbolist poet and pacifist Laurent Tailhade, whose encouragement affirmed Owen's dedication to poetry. Leaving the language school to tutor privately, Owen remained in France until September 1915, more than a year after the First World War began. Shortly after his return to England, he enlisted in the Artist's Rifles and, while training in London, frequently visited Harold Monro's Poetry Bookshop, becoming acquainted with Monro and regularly attending public poetry readings. At the end of his training, he was commissioned as a lieutenant in the Manchester Regiment; in late 1916 he was posted to the Western Front where he participated in the Battle of the Somme.

Suffering shell-shock after several months of service at the front, Owen was declared "unfit to command troops." He was invalided out of action in May 1917 and in June he was admitted to Craiglockhart War Hospital in Edinburgh. One of the most important events of his poetic career was his meeting there in August with fellow-patient Siegfried Sassoon, an outspoken critic of the war who encouraged him to use his battle experiences as subjects for poetry. The poets quickly became friends and spent many evenings together discussing their latest works. Critics often emphasize that the realistic presentation of war and the use of colloquial phrasing in Sassoon's poems greatly influenced Owen's works at the time, and Sassoon's respect and encouragement confirmed for Owen his ability as a poet. He wrote most of his critically acclaimed poems after this meeting in the fifteen months prior to his death. After being discharged from the hospital, Owen rejoined his regiment in

From Wilfred Owen, by Jon Stallworthy. Oxford University Press and Chatto and Windus, 1974. Reproduced by permission of Oxford University Press.

Scarborough. He returned to the front in early September 1918 and shortly afterwards was awarded the Military Cross for gallantry. He was killed in action at the Sambre Canal in northeast France on November 4, 1918—one week before the Armistice. He is buried at Ors, France.

At the time of his death only a handful of Owen's poems had been published, and his early works are generally considered derivative and undistinguished, though they do indicate his developing interest in various rhyme techniques. Even his first war verses are regarded as conventional, patriotic songs of valor. Critics generally date Owen's mature period from his encounter with Sassoon at Craiglockhart Hospital, for under Sassoon's guidance Owen first adapted his poetic techniques to non-traditional war subjects. He added compassion to the pronounced anger of Sassoon's satiric verses, and, according to Jon Silkin, Owen's more complex emotional response "permitted a more flexible understanding of war." He based new works solely on his personal experiences, making the expression of the truth of war the aim of his poetry. Shortly before his death Owen began preparing a collection of his works for publication, and the preface he drafted is considered the chief statement of his aesthetic principles. In the preface Owen wrote "This book is not about heroes. My subject is War, and the pity of war. I am not concerned with Poetry. The Poetry is in the Pity. Yet these elegies are to this generation in no sense consolatory. They may be to the next. All a poet can do today is to warn.''

Critics view that statement as a key to understanding the motive behind Owen's poetry. He viewed his literary role as the voice of infantrymen who were unable to effectively articulate their own experiences and emotions. Many of Owen's poems assail those in England who continued to write conventional verses espousing the traditional values of wartime heroism and the appropriateness of dying in battle on behalf of one's country.

Among his best known poems are ''*Dulce et Decorum Est*,'' ''Anthem for Doomed Youth,'' and ''Strange Meeting,'' an uncompleted poem which is considered by many critics to be the finest of the First World War. An elegy, ''Strange Meeting'' presents Owen's historical, humanistic, and mystical themes, while considering the conflict between ego and conscience in war. In a dreamlike vision the narrator of the poem encounters a soldier whom he has killed, and the ensuing dialogue renders Owen's protests of the futility of war. By not identifying the nationalities of the two soldiers in the poem, Owen achieved an ambiguity that allows the verses to be viewed as commentary on World War I or on the universal nature of war and suggests analogies between the soldier and Christ and between the enemy and oneself. In this and other poems, the Christian ethical principle of ''greater love,'' based on the New Testament teaching ''Greater love hath no man than this, that a man lay down his life for his friends'' (John 15:13), is considered highly significant. Many critics have noted that while Owen rebelled against the strict institutional religion of his mother, he retained a deep love of Christ, with whom he often identified the young men sacrificed on the battlefields.

Owen's reputation as a poet was firmly established in the years immediately after the war by the publication in 1920 of a volume of his poems edited by Sassoon, and he subsequently gained a wide audience through collections edited by Edmund Blunden and C. Day Lewis as well as the inclusion of his poems in numerous anthologies. However, for several decades after his death, Owen scholars were limited in their analyses by a lack of biographical information, and the tentative research that followed resulted in confusion and invalid claims over the dates of the various poems and the progress of Owen's development as a poet. With the publication of several biographical studies, including Harold Owen's three-volume memoir of his family, more definitive critical studies have been made possible.

Generally critics have agreed that Owen's verses represent a unique, emotional response to war and a masterful technical achievement. This consensus was challenged by W. B. Yeats, who omitted Owen's poetry from his anthology *The Oxford Book of Modern Verse* (1937), commenting that ''passive suffering is not a theme for poetry.'' However, the exclusion of Owen's verses was challenged by numerous commentators, who questioned Yeats's selection criteria. Perhaps the greatest indicator of Owen's importance lies in the influence he had on poets of the next generation; W. H. Auden has named Owen, along with Gerard Manley Hopkins and T. S. Eliot, as one of the poets who most affected him and his fellow-writers of the 1930s—Day Lewis, Christopher Isherwood, Louis MacNeice, and Stephen Spender. The younger poets were especially impressed by Owen's versatile rhyme techniques and compassionate protests against suffering and war. According to John H. Johnston: ''[Owen's] youth, his small but eloquent body of verse, his intense dedication to the truth, his untimely and

unnecessary death—all of these factors combined to make him an irresistible figure to the succeeding generation, whose 'stable background' of traditional forms and values had, like Owen's been destroyed by the war.'' Modern scholars tend to judge Owen's work as the limited but nonetheless real achievement of a poet who made rapid progress over the course of his brief and unsettled career. In the words of Richard Hoffpauir: ''Rather than bemoan what might have been, we should perhaps marvel that the few successful but minor poems (those of vivid description and honest feeling) were written at all at such a disruptive time. But we should also not overvalue the achievement . . . for then we do a disservice to all poetry and especially to those few poems that do meet the poetic demand of the difficult and extraordinary conditions of war.''

(See also *TCLC*, Vol. 5; *Contemporary Authors*, Vol. 104; and *Dictionary of Literary Biography: British Poets, 1914-1945*, Vol. 20.)

PRINCIPAL WORKS

Poems (poetry) 1920
The Poems of Wilfred Owen (poetry) 1931
Thirteen Poems (poetry) 1956
The Collected Poems of Wilfred Owen (poetry) 1963
Collected Letters (letters) 1967
Wilfred Owen: War Poems and Others (poetry) 1973
The Complete Poems and Fragments (poetry) 1983

THE TIMES LITERARY SUPPLEMENT (essay date 1921)

[*In the following excerpt, the critic favorably reviews the first collection of Owen's poetry.*]

The main drift of Wilfred Owen's verse is the shattering of the illusion of the glory of war, and its mood is not free from a scathing bitterness for the men who nurture this illusion. We ask ourselves in vain where among English readers these men are to be found. The suggestion is that a nation is divided into two parts, one of which talks of war and ordains it, while the other acts and suffers. We can understand how such a thought might arise, but not how it can persist and find sustenance. And does the illusion of glory still hold any one? The only glory imperishably associated with war is that of the supreme sacrifice which it entails; the trumpets and the banners are poor humanity's imperfect tribute to that sublime implication. So far as the details of military action are concerned, the horror of them has descended upon the whole world like a nightmare; and if any man is not now pacifist it is not because he relishes the thought of battle, but only because of a paralysing apprehension that war is inexorably necessary. Above all, the idea that lack of experience explains militarism is baseless. The nation that has been most proved by the war and has most intimately felt its devastations and agonies is the nation that has the greatest difficulty in throwing off the obsession. And what shall we say finally of the strange intimation that the old men sacrifice the young? As if any father would not face death sooner than send his boy to face it for him. . . .

Wilfred Owen's poetical gesture springs in part from an error of judgment, and we cannot appreciate his poems as they deserve without calling attention to that error. He might have been less a poet if he had not made it, for no doubt it was his sensitiveness that played him false. It was made, and it enters into and colours his whole poetical expression. His moral revolt is largely misplaced; certain wider horizons, seen for example by Whitman as a poet of war, are not revealed to him. There is one direction, however, in which he opens up and exposes to us a great range of realities, realities which, because of the horror and anguish associated with them, men do conspire to glose over and hush up. War, in a word, involves savagery; it demands of men such cruel outrage against their human instincts that as a moral experience it is essentially unbearable. There is, consequently, a permanent division between those who have and those who have not passed through the furnace; and it has been a part of Wilfred Owen's aim to bridge the chasm and represent to the mind of peace the inconceivable, arid atrocity of the mind of war, with the suffering and death-in-life which it entails. One might have supposed that this was an impossible task for poetry; yet he has passages in which he achieves it, showing us together, by a wonderful mastery of the associations of words, both the wilderness and wreckage and the tender, trustful loveliness they have displaced:—

Red lips are not so red
  As the stained stones kissed by the English dead.
Kindness of wooed and wooer
Seems shame to their love pure.
O Love, your eyes lose lure
  When I behold eyes blinded in my stead! . . .

In so far then as Wilfred Owen passes a moral judgment upon imaginary non-combatants, he is beside the issue; in so far as he endeavours to evoke and perpetuate the memory of "that execrable, wild, callous abomination called fighting" (whose accompanying virtues he also deeply understands), so as to strengthen our determination to redeem the world from it, all the strength of Truth is with him. For war is brought about not by the last decisions and the dispatch of the ultimatum, but by those innumerable, imperceptible strivings for private advantage which, taken in their bulk, place rival nations at last in positions which they find mutually intolerable; and for the prevention of catastrophe, what we need most is some motive strong enough to act through all those intervening periods of seeming calm, when the course of events is deciding whether the crisis is to come or not. If we could possess ourselves permanently of the vision of that crime in which we are tempted to connive, our egotism might be checked and our more generous motives fortified. Owen offers us such a vision, for a warning at once terrible and salutary; but he is too true a poet not to have recognized that peace is something other than the avoidance of war, and that detestation of war is not enough to assure us of it. He gives hints and indications of a constructive message in a poem only partially worked out, but characterized by an ardour and compactness of expression which suggest the tone of veritable "prophecy":—

Let us forgo men's minds that are brute's natures,
Let us not sup the blood which some say nurtures. . . .
Let us lie out and hold the open truth.
Then when their blood hath clogged the chariot wheels
We will go up and wash them from deep wells.
What though we sink from men as pitchers falling,
Many shall raise us up to be their filling,
Even from wells we sunk too deep for war
And filled by brows that bled where no wounds were.

Moreover, a sustaining impulse of his poetry—here, again, is a positive feature of unimpeachable worth—is sympathy and pity. He is pitiless with his readers, but for the sake of utter

truth and faithfulness where pity belongs. And the tenderness behind his relentlessness gives the hard brutal words a strange, improbable beauty; they live, they breathe out a redemptive virtue, searing us with an anguish, which, nevertheless, they transcend:

Happy are those who lose imagination:
They have enough to carry with ammunition.
Their spirit drags no pack.
Their old wounds save with cold can not more ache. . . .
Their senses in some scorching cautery of battle
Now long since ironed,
Can laugh among the dying, unconcerned. . . .

Wilfred Owen's technique has one specially remarkable feature, which readers will have already noticed in our quotations. He invents a peculiar type of rhyme to aid him in the expression of that prevailing emotion of disgust, of weariness of illusion, of insistence on the bleak realities which he is determined to drive home. To put it briefly, he substitutes for vowel identity, with its pleasing music, a consonantal identity which neither pleases nor is intended to please, except with that remote pleasure we derive from a recognition of a true adaptation of means to ends. The intention is to chastise our sensibility, as it were, to shake and wake us, as has been done not infrequently through certain alliterative devices, regularly, indeed, in the old Saxon metres. But our ear being now tuned to vowel-rhyme, the poet avails himself of our disappointment to increase the biting severity of his strokes; and so, profiting not only by what he gives but also by what he withholds, he gets an effect of total desolation, as in this soliloquy of a wounded soldier:—

My arms have mutinied against me—brutes!
My fingers fidget like ten idle brats,
My back's been stiff for hours, damned hours.
Death never gives his squad a Stand-at-ease.
I can't read. There; it's no use. Take your book.
A short life and a merry one, my buck!
We said we'd hate to grow dead old. But now,
Not to live old seems awful: not to renew
My boyhood with my boys, and teach 'em hitting,
Shooting and hunting,—all the arts of hurting!

The question may possibly be canvassed whether these are rhymes at all. Should controversy arise it would be endless: for the question at issue would be one either of terminology or of taste. We have here a novel device used for a purpose which it fulfils. We may wish the purpose had been different or hesitate to decide what name to give to this feature in its embodiment. But we see quite clearly what was intended and what has been accomplished; and that is all that matters. Let us add that the device is applied systematically and has a cumulative effect. Naturally, it is not every pair of lines that assault us as does the first of those we have just quoted; but as the poem proceeds and vowel assonance is persistently refused, the sense of mournful barrenness grows heavier and heavier, and we more and more feel what an immeasurable distance divides this mud, this monotony, this slow torture from the stuff of conventional verse, how far the "troops who fade" are from those flowers which are "for poets' tearful fooling."

"Wilfred Owen's Poems," in The Times Literary Supplement, No. 990, January 6, 1921, p. 6.

SIR HENRY NEWBOLT (letter date 1924)

[*Newbolt, one of the most popular English poets of the early twentieth century, is best known for his poems on naval and patriotic subjects. In the following excerpt from a letter to an unidentified correspondent dated 2 August 1924, Newbolt disagrees with the underlying sentiment of Owen's verses.]*

This week-end, ten years ago—nothing in all my life seems further away, but I can still recall the feeling of it—the splendid epic calm and tingle of every act and word. Much as I hate the idea of war and waste, and clearly as I see the obvious crash, still I imagine we are we, and if next time came we should just shoulder it again.

That's really what Sassoon said to me on Tuesday—*he* would go again, and if he then everybody. He has sent me Wilfred Owen's *Poems*, with an Introduction by himself. The best of them I knew already—they are terribly good, but of course limited, almost all on one note. I like better Sassoon's two-sided collection—there are more than two sides to this business of war, and a man is hardly normal any longer if he comes down to one. S. S. says that Owen pitied others but never himself: I'm afraid that isn't quite true—or at any rate not quite fair. To be a man one must be willing that others as well as yourself should bear the burden that must be borne. . . . Owen and the rest of the broken men rail at the Old Men who sent the young to die: they have suffered cruelly, but in the nerves and not the heart—they haven't the experience or the imagination to know the extreme human agony—''Who giveth me to die for thee, Absalom my son, my son.'' Paternity apart, what Englishman of fifty wouldn't far rather stop the shot himself than see the boys do it for him? I don't think these shell-shocked war poems will move our grandchildren greatly—there's nothing fundamental or final about them—at least they only put one figure into a very big equation, and that's not one of the unknown but one of the best known quantities. (pp. 314-15)

> *Sir Henry Newbolt, in a letter to A. H. on August 2, 1924, in his* The Later Life and Letters of Sir Henry Newbolt, *edited by Margaret Newbolt, Faber & Faber Limited, 1942, pp. 314-15.*

SIEGFRIED SASSOON   (lecture date 1948)

[Sassoon was an important war poet, chiefly remembered for his satirical protest poems of 1917 and 1918 which realistically reflected the sufferings of soldiers on the Western Front. The verse he wrote expressing the horror of war strongly influenced the direction of Owen's poetry. Following their meeting in August 1917, Sassoon served as Owen's literary mentor until Owen's death in November 1918. He later collected, edited, and published the first volume of Owen's poetry. In the following excerpt, Sassoon recalls his association with Owen at Craiglockhart War Hospital and outlines Owen's subsequent poetic development.]

One sunny morning in the first week of August, 1917, I was sitting by a bedroom window in a War Hospital near Edinburgh, sand-papering my clubs. For, although the War Office had diagnosed my anti-war protest as due to shell-shock, I was spending most of my days in sampling the local golf courses. Anyway, there I was, meditating on an encouraging letter I had just received from H. G. Wells, and quite unconscious of the significance of the ''Come in'' with which I now responded to a gentle knock on the door. The young officer who entered was wearing the badges of the Manchester Regiment. (p. 34)

For him, as he afterwards wrote to his mother, the occasion was a momentous one. For me, though I took an instinctive liking to him during the half-hour he was with me that morning, he was, so far, merely a nice mannered young man with a pleasantly modulated voice and a charming honest smile, who had confessed that he wrote poetry, none of which had yet appeared in print. . . . It was indeed an extraordinary bit of luck that we should have got to know one another, with several million chances against it ever happening. But life is an affair of fortuities; and so it came about that we two, whose names are now inseparably associated, were together in that hospital until the beginning of November, when he rejoined a Reserve Battalion of his regiment.

Our companionship very soon became an ideal one. Our temperaments were harmonious; and it was a confederacy of two writers intent on the same purpose, to reveal the front-line realities of the war. I cannot remember that we ever discussed or compared our active-service experiences; but we were, both of us, working steadily, and at intervals submitted the results to each other—Owen doing so with a modesty which now seems more remarkable than it did to me at the time—For instance, he has recorded in a letter that, on September 7th, I condemned some of his poems, amended others, and rejoiced over a few. He added that he was not worthy to light my pipe—an observation which posterity will firmly repudiate. I must mention, however, that some of the poems he showed me were survivors from his juvenilia which he contemplated destroying. I censured the over-luscious writing of these immature pieces, though his skill in rich and melodious combinations of words was already apparent in them.

It may have been on that evening—I can remember going through the manuscripts with him as we sat in a corner of the cavernous hall of the requisitioned Hydro which we inhabited—that I first became aware of the masterly quality of his verse. He had handed me a newly-written sonnet called **"Anthem for Doomed Youth."** There was enough in it to indicate the power and originality of what he afterwards produced, and I rejoiced in my discovery of an authentic poet. (pp. 34-5)

I could see that this was the sort of poetry I liked. But at that time my critical perceptions were undeveloped, and I was slow in realising that his imagination worked on a larger scale than mine, and that in technical accomplishment and intellectual approach he was on a higher plane. My trench-sketches were like rockets, sent up to illuminate the darkness. They were the first thing of their kind, and could claim to be opportune. It was Owen who revealed how, out of realistic horror and scorn, poetry might be made. My judgment was to some extent affected by his attitude of devoted discipleship. I knew that I could write epigrammatic satires better than he could, and he was attempting, in a few of his pieces, to imitate them. This has sometimes caused my influence on him to be exaggerated. The truth of the matter was that I arrived just when he needed my stimulation and advice. It was my privilege to be in close contact with him while he was attaining a clear view of what he wanted to say and deploying his technical resources to a matured utterance. I was, he assured me, the one man he had longed to know. And I count it among my most satisfactory performances that I was able to be of service to his genius. Nearly six months before we met, he had written the first draft of **"Exposure,"** one of his most dynamically descriptive war poems. This—after his usual process of drastic revision—he had now perfected. Here, for the first time, he used with fullest effect, those para-rhymes or alliterative assonance endings through which he brought a new element to verse technique. (p. 36)

He wrote [**"Exposure"**] while away from the front-line for a few weeks, after enduring the arctic weather of January, 1917.

The experience is described in one of his letters. His platoon was occupying an advanced post in a heavily shelled sector. There were no dug-outs, and one of his party froze to death. In March he fell into a deep cavity in a devastated area. A month later he was blown up by a shell during a particularly harassing twelve days in the Line. At the beginning of June, he was sent to England, suffering from nervous breakdown and the effects of concussion. By the time I met him he appeared to have completely recovered. He could now record what he had seen and suffered in an objective fragment comparable to one of Hardy's scenic introductions in *The Dynasts*.

"THE SHOW"

We have fallen in the dreams the ever-living
Breathe on the tarnished mirror of the world.
And then smooth out with ivory hands and sigh.
                                    W. B. YEATS

My soul looked down from a vague height with Death.
As unremembering how I rose or why,
And saw a sad land, weak with sweats or dearth,
Gray, cratered like the moon with hollow woe,
And pitted with great pocks and scabs of plagues.

Across its beard, that horror of harsh wire,
There moved thin caterpillars, slowly uncoiled.
It seemed they pushed themselves to be as plugs
Of ditches, where they writhed and shrivelled, killed.

By them had slimy paths been trailed and scraped
Round myriad warts that might be little hills.

From gloom's last dregs these long-strung creatures
        crept,
And vanished out of dawn down hidden holes.
(And smell came up from those foul openings
As out of mouths, or deep wounds deepening.)

On dithering feet upgathered, more and more,
Brown strings, towards strings of gray, with bristling
        spines,
All migrants from green fields, intent on mire.

Those that were gray, of more abundant spawns,
Ramped on the rest and ate them and were eaten.

I saw their bitten backs curve, loop, and straighten,
I watched those agonies curl, lift, and flatten.

Whereat, in terror what that sight might mean,
I reeled and shivered earthward like a feather.

And Death fell with me, like a deepening moan.
And He, picking a manner of worm, which half had hid
Its bruises in the earth, but crawled no further,
Showed me its feet, the feet of many men,
And the fresh-severed head of it, my head.

Let it be remembered that, when this was written, all truthful reportings of experience were regarded as unpatriotic and subversive to War Effort. Officialdom suppressed, and the great majority of non-combatants shunned and resented, such revelations. Sensitive people couldn't bear to be told the facts. This was understandable—though not always comprehensible to the young. What Owen and I found intolerable was the selfishness and humbug apparent among many types of civilians. We could not agree with the old men that it was sweet and decorous to die for one's country. Inevitable, no doubt, but not edifying. Several of his poems were deliberately written to shock complacency, and were part of his plan for the volume

Owen's mentor, Siegfried Sassoon, 1915. BBC Hulton/The Bettmann Archive.

which his death in action prevented him from completing. In these he dramatized the disabled soldier of all ranks and the dumbly enduring conscript, optimistically assured by politicians that he was engaged on a war to end war. Among his papers we found a few notes for the Preface to this volume. "This book is not about heroes," he wrote, "My subject is War, and the pity of War. I am not concerned with Poetry. The Poetry is in the Pity. Yet these elegies are to this generation in no sense consolatory. They may be to the next. All a poet can do today is to warn." His warnings were, mostly, impersonally rendered. For himself, he testified to the spiritual compensations which he had experienced through the comradeship of active service. (pp. 37-8)

Siegfried Sassoon, "Wilfred Owen—A Personal Appreciation," in *A Tribute to Wilfred Owen*, *edited by T. J. Walsh, n.p., n.d., pp. 34-41.*

EDMUND BLUNDEN   (essay date 1958)

[*Blunden was associated with the Georgians, an early twentieth-century group of English poets who reacted against the prevalent contemporary mood of disillusionment and the rise of artistic modernism by seeking to return to the pastoral, nineteenth-century poetic traditions associated with William Wordsworth. In this regard, much of Blunden's poetry reflects his love of the sights, sounds, and ways of rural England. Blunden is also considered one of his generation's leading war poets—he was gassed while serving in World War I and the horror of war is a major theme in his work. As a literary critic and essayist, he often wrote of the lesser-known figures of the Romantic era as well as the pleasures of English country life. In the following excerpt, he characterizes Owen's poetry as richly imaginative and distinguished by a "spiritual and mental dignity."*]

The poems of Owen on war express many aspects . . . but perhaps pity is the one he felt most. (p. 32)

[Preparing a preface for his first volume of poetry], Owen insisted, "Above all, this is not concerned with Poetry. The subject of it is War, and the pity of War. The Poetry is in the pity." Be it noted that Owen had no tolerance for amateurish elegies such as the time teemed with—calling them "poets' tearful fooling." Finally a true word on Owen's quality of pity is found in [Siegfried Sassoon's] introduction to the selection of poems published in 1920. "He never wrote his poems (as so many war poets did) to make the effect of a personal gesture. He pitied others; he did not pity himself." (p. 33)

In 1914, when he was aged only twenty-one, his immature verse at any rate spoke for his breadth of vision and his ability to sum things up. After 1914 when as poet he had shed a certain weak luxuriousness through his ordeal by battle, with intervals for reflection and analysis, his intellectual advance was swift. In many respects Owen was what is called a typical young officer, well in control of his duties, meeting emergencies with good sense, at the same time ready with the usual dry comments on the daily round and idle authority. But very few young officers had also his profound interest in the great subjects of the world's destiny. We meet with a spiritual and mental dignity, with a solitariness of imaginative purpose, in many of his poems; by that quality, it may be, his individual genius is most clearly distinguished.

"The Show" is one of the poems referred to, with its opening line "My soul looked down from a vague height with Death" and its unveiling of a stupendous, automatic, painful scene of modern war—almost the hieroglyph of the end or the denial of our civilization. This is of the order of those panoramas in Thomas Hardy's *Dynasts*, or of the Vision of Dante. The poet's high imagination is voiced with a clear certainty. Such compositions might justify wonder even in a critic when it is remembered what the author's situation was, either involved in the mud-pits and barrages he describes or about to be among them. Imagination triumphs.

But it is not only in such allegorical pieces that Owen the poet is seen above the battle in which as a soldier he was desperately engaged. A number of original and understanding essays or odes on human nature—for instance, **"Insensibility," "Greater Love"** or the more pictorial **"Spring Offensive"**—were written with singular devotion. Wisdom and art in them were united while the poet as his first editor remarks quite forgot his own case. This richness of thought and word reminds us always that Keats was his idol, and if Keats could know that he had a worshipper so congenial and so equally capable of taking his themes far beyond his own actual afflictions he would be happy. In Keats's lines on negative capability in "Hyperion" something very like the selfless power of Owen's war poems is defined:

> to bear all naked truths,
> And to envisage circumstance, all calm,
> That is the top of sovereignty.

It is true, of course, that some of the poems are not calm, but imprecatory and scalding; it could not have been otherwise,

the urgency being that of a cry from the depths, as one devastating day or night seized the humble heroes or conscripts.

Nothing has yet been said here of the radiant art of poetry which Owen practised, and which was progressive. It is not out of place to glance at it, for deeply considered technique itself was part of the offering that this soldier-poet made to eventual peace and mercy. He was what Wordsworth called Coleridge, "an epicure in sound," he gathered a copious and various vocabulary partly because of the musical values of words. With Keats he delights in slow movements, full tides of stresses. He plays with alliteration finely, and with internal rhyme. Owen's assonances in place of rhymes have made him a name among later poets and prosodists. Verlaine, whose poems like many others by French writers were part of his inner life, may have helped him to think over this novelty of assonances, which in **"Strange Meeting"** especially is so integral. The bitterness of his heart required some discord in the utterance. Lastly, what an excellent writer of sonnets he became! To concentrate meaning and metaphor within that enduring form was no doubt a pleasure to him, a trial of art, even if the topic was pain and grief. (pp. 33-5)

Edmund Blunden, "Mainly Wilfred Owen," in his War Poets: 1914-1918, *1958. Reprint by The British Council, 1969, pp. 29-36.*

JOHN H. JOHNSTON (essay date 1964)

[*An American educator and critic, Johnston is the author of* English Poetry of the First World War. *In the following excerpt from that work, he surveys Owen's later war poetry and discusses Owen's concept of "greater love."*]

Most World War I poets dealt only with material that was subjectively or experientially important, since their purposes ranged from that of simple self-dramatization to that of shocking the British public out of its ignorance and apathy. Owen, however, seemed to realize the limitations of a narrowly subjective or experiential approach; the numerous revisions in the British Museum manuscripts, according to D. S. R. Welland, reveal a "progressive movement toward impersonality in the gradual elimination of pronouns in the first and second person in favor of less personal constructions." By controlling the subjective element in his verse, Owen sought a greater freedom in exploring the larger moral and spiritual aspects of the conflict. His rapid poetic growth during the Scarborough period [a period of light duty at a military hotel in Scarborough where he was stationed from November 1917 to Spring 1918] is also visible in his gradual mastery of an individualized lyric technique that embodied the discords of modern warfare and in his rejection of the rather narrow experiential bias implicit in **"Apologia pro Poemate Meo."** Instead of insisting upon the exclusive nature of the soldier's experience, Owen was henceforth to dwell upon its universality.

Although Owen's **"Greater Love"** is undated, its relationship to other poems indicates that it was composed in the spring or summer of 1918. The theme of pity touched upon in **"Apologia pro Poemate Meo"** (November 1917) and fully developed in **"Miners"** (January 1918) is here combined with Owen's most eloquent statement of the "greater love" ideal. In **"Miners"** the poet associates himself with the pathos of a sacrifice forgotten by future generations; the centuries "will not dream of us poor lads / Lost in the ground." In **"Greater Love,"** however, he has abandoned his earlier self-concern and assumed the responsibility of "pleader" for those too dedicated or too inarticulate to plead for themselves. At first an observer, Owen becomes a deeply involved participant, then advances to the more demanding and more disciplined role of intermediary. Thus the emotional force of an experienced truth submits to the control of a maturely conceived poetic purpose in **"Greater Love."**

The structure of the poem involves a point-by-point contrast between sensuous love and the "greater love"; the poet evokes the familiar imagery of the one in order to bring fresh meaning to the other. The contrast, therefore, is more than a revelation of pathetic discrepancies; it is the re-definition of a spiritual concept in terms of its lesser physical counterpart. Sensuous love is aroused by the beauty of lips, eyes, and limbs, and it is expressed through the voice, the heart (the emotions), and the hands. Owen uses each of these images to draw out the contrasting implications of sacrificial love. . . . The consuming intensity of the "greater love" is described in terms of an explicit sexual analogy. Just as the sexual act represents the fruition of sensuous love, so the agonies of the dying represent the fulfillment of the "greater love." The analogy, of course, evokes a whole range of opposed associations that are too profound for irony:

> Your slender attitude
>   Trembles not exquisite like limbs knife-skewed,
> Rolling and rolling there
> Where God seems not to care;
> Till the fierce Love they bear
> Cramps them in death's extreme decrepitude.

The fourth line touches another, less obvious contrast that embodies the spiritual doubts which had troubled Owen since his first exposure to the sufferings of war. Since God—in whom man finds the perfection of love—is apparently indifferent to the fate of the dying, man himself becomes the real exemplar of the "greater love." Thus the deeper levels of the poem reveal an irony that turns upon man's capacity for a love greater than sensuous love and greater, apparently, than the love that God bears for man. (pp. 191-93)

Life, of course, is the corollary of sensuous love; death is the corollary of the "greater love," the purity and intensity of which shame the ordinary expressions of love between man and woman. If, as the poet believes, "God seems not to care," Christ himself—the original exemplar of the "greater love"—voiced the same sense of dereliction that is implicit in Owen's attitude: "My God, my God, why hast thou forsaken me?" Thus the poem advances on two closely related levels of meaning. The first level involves a complex pattern of contrasts between sensuous and spiritual love; the second level suggests an analogy between two manifestations of the "greater love": Christ and the modern infantryman. Owen's basic purpose, of course, is definition. Only when we comprehend the nature of the "greater love" can we begin to understand the terrible demands that are made upon those whom that love destroys.

"Greater Love" is a key utterance because it marks a stage in the development of Owen's ability to give his inner conflicts an explicit and compelling poetic form. Another key utterance is **"Strange Meeting."** . . . Here the major concept is not the "greater love" but the truth upon which the "true Poets" must base their appeal to posterity. In the absence or inadequacy of other standards, the "greater love" may be the only positive guide for man in modern warfare; the self-sacrifice implicit in the "greater love" may never be necessary, however, if future generations heed the warnings of the "true Poets."

Although it takes the form of a possibly unfinished colloquy, **"Strange Meeting"** opens with a dramatic incident which was almost certainly inspired by Sassoon's "The Rear-Guard." Sassoon's brief narrative, it may be recalled, deals with the experience of a solitary soldier lost in the darkness of a tunnel below the Hindenburg Line; when he attempts to arouse a recumbent figure, he is confronted with the agonized face of a dead German soldier. . . . Sassoon emphasizes only the physical and psychological shock of his experience in the Hindenburg tunnel; he retreats with the "sweat of horror in his hair," "unloading hell behind him step by step." Owen, however, goes far beyond the experiential effects developed by Sassoon; he remains in hell and confronts the truth behind the horror. In **"Mental Cases"** (written in May 1918), Owen had employed Dante's rhetorical and dramatic technique. In **"Strange Meeting"** he utilizes Sassoon's experience as a background for a colloquy that is again appropriately Dantesque in method and effect. In the profound silence of the tunnel ("no guns thumped, or down the flues made moan") he isolates himself from the tumult and distractions of battle ("no blood reached there from the upper ground") in order to assess the personal, artistic, and historical implications of the conflict. (pp. 194-96)

[In **"Strange Meeting"**] Owen forecasts the social and economic crises of the postwar years as well as the rise of the totalitarian state. More remarkable than the prophecy, however, is his conception of the role of the poet amid the evils of chaos and regimentation. Had he lived, the apparition would have had the insight and the skill to voice his protest, to tell the "truth untold" about war, to assert his faith in the values that men relinquish for the "vain citadels" of political absolutism and militarism. It is in this re-definition of the poet's role that **"Strange Meeting"** reveals a dramatic transition between the general attitudes of nineteenth-century poetry and those of the poetry written in the twenties and thirties. When men "boil bloody," the poet may no longer hunt "the wildest beauty in the world"; his function is broadly social rather than personal or aesthetic. . . . When "none will break ranks" from the march that leads inevitably to war, the poet emerges as seer and spokesman; he has access to a truth that immunizes him against the passions of nationalism. Thus he may no longer endorse imperialism, as did Kipling; it is not his duty to fight as a soldier or, as a poet, to deal with the external phenomena of war. This completely independent attitude is a measure of the poet's sensitivity rather than of his objectivity: "Foreheads of men have bled where no wounds were." Yet it is only through the exercise of his objectifying power (his courage and wisdom) that the poet has been able to renounce traditional claims upon his art as well as the more recent claims advanced by the stunning physical realities of modern warfare. Those physical realities must be "distilled" rather than crudely transmitted as experiential effects; the metaphor carries over to the "sweet wells" of truth, which represent a distillation of the poetic experience.

"Strange Meeting" concludes with a poignant revelation that makes pity and the "greater love" a part of the "truth untold" which must perish with the poet:

> I am the enemy you killed, my friend.
> I knew you in this dark; for so you frowned
> Yesterday through me as you jabbed and killed.
> I parried; but my hands were loath and cold.
> Let us sleep now. . . .

Although we assume that the two soldiers are British and German, they are not identified as such; it is the bond of humanity that must now be stressed and not the opposition of rival nationalities. Sorley described the tragic blindness of such an opposition in his 1914 sonnet "To Germany"; that blindness is now lifted, ironically, in the darkness of the "profound dull tunnel" where the truth of war lies buried with those who yearn to tell it. The lack of national identification also permits an alternative or additional interpretation of the poem; the "enemy" is the poet himself, seen as the slayer and the slain and sharing the guilt of murder as well as the innocence of the "greater love." . . . This interpretation, however, alters neither the basic meaning of the poem nor its external literary significance. With **"Strange Meeting"** Owen joins the small company of English poets who have been privileged to speak for their art in a time of crisis and change. He was the only war poet who seemed to be conscious of the implications of "war poetry" for poetry in general. The change in his own conceptions anticipates a radically altered conception of poetic purpose and method, itself a product of inadequacies which the war— and the poetry of the war—clearly revealed. The summary of nineteenth-century traditions which the Georgians represented could not cope with the moral and physical complexities of the twentieth century; poetry, if it would live, must change. Owen had time only to mark the transition, to lament the "undone years," to prophesy—as did Matthew Arnold in "Dover Beach"—the effects of absolutism and anarchy. (pp. 197-99)

Owen's arrival in France in September 1918 coincided with preparations for the last great offensive of the war, the effort that was to result in the breaking of the Hindenburg Line. Just prior to or during his participation in the September attacks, the poet produced **"Spring Offensive," "The Sentry,"** [and **"Smile, Smile, Smile"**]. . . . (pp. 199-200)

"Smile, Smile, Smile" records, after the colloquial manner of Sassoon, the secret derision of the wounded as they read distorted newspaper accounts of the war, which is still being managed as if a "victory" were possible. Sassoon's *Counter-Attack* had appeared only two months before this poem was completed, so possibly Owen felt justified in renewing his own "counter-attack" on the misconceptions encouraged by the daily press. In **"Spring Offensive"** and **"The Sentry,"** however, Owen seems to be experimenting with the possibilities of the brief narrative form. **"The Sentry"** is related in the first person by a participating observer; the fluent colloquial style is Sassoon's, as well as the range of blunt physical notation. . . . (p. 200)

In **"Spring Offensive,"** on the other hand, the story is told in the third person with the poet as an omniscient but remote narrator. The style is formal, elevated, and controlled. Apparently Owen had some misgivings about the contrasting effects of **"The Sentry"** and **"Spring Offensive,"** for he feared that the latter poem, because of its deliberately "poetic" technique, would evoke a *"No Compris!"* from the ordinary soldier. (p. 201)

In **"Spring Offensive"** Owen attempts to encompass the objective as well as the subjective reality of war. In so doing he seems to have been developing a technique that would represent the significant aspects of both external and internal realities. "I do not doubt that, had he lived longer," writes Sassoon, "he would have produced poems of sustained grandeur and ample design." Certainly the narrative technique employed in **"Spring Offensive"** would have been equal to the conceptions involved in any such poems.

Both **"At a Calvary near the Ancre"** and **"Le Christianisme"** are explicit in their indictments of formal Christianity. In poems

such as **"Anthem for Doomed Youth"** and **"Greater Love,"** Owen had explored the implications of his disillusionment with Christianity as an external symbol, but in these two late lyrics he writes with the casual bitterness of a man whose doubts have settled into convictions. (pp. 202-03)

"The End" may also be read as a rejection of orthodox Christianity. . . . The mood of **"The End"** is clearly pessimistic, but its personifications and rhetorical tenor represent an abstract treatment of the subject rather than a spontaneous confession of disbelief:

> After the blast of lightning from the East,
> The flourish of loud clouds, the Chariot Throne;
> After the drums of Time have rolled and ceased,
> And by the bronze west long retreat is blown,
>
> Shall life renew these bodies? Of a truth
> All death will He annul, all tears assuage?—
> Fill the void veins of Life again with youth,
> And wash, with an immortal water, Age?
>
> When I do ask white Age he saith not so:
> "My head hangs weighed with snow."
> And when I hearken to the Earth, she saith:
> "My fiery heart shrinks, aching. It is death.
> Mine ancient scars shall not be glorified,
> Nor my titanic tears, the sea, be dried."

Aside from its formal excellence as a sonnet, **"The End"** is interesting because the poet's mother chose lines 5-6 for his tombstone at Ors. In the epitaph, however, the second question mark is omitted, thus reversing the pessimism of the sestet:

> Shall life renew these bodies? Of a truth
> All death will He annul, all tears assuage.

Thus a final ambiguity rounds off what has proved to be (aside from textual problems) the most perplexing aspect of Owen's poetry. Disputes about his orthodoxy are likely to continue until a full biography and an edition of his letters are available. It is obvious, however, that his finest work was inspired not by cynicism or despair but by a doctrine close to the heart of Christianity. This fact itself is responsible for the complexities and ambiguities that trouble so many of his readers. Owen's grasp of the implications of "pure Christianity" inevitably led to his rejection of an "impure" Christianity buried under "its rubbish and its rubble"; he held to the concept of the "greater love" as the only spiritual and poetic truth which could illuminate and possibly redeem the sufferings of the modern soldier. We may sometimes feel, however, that in doing this Owen has drawn the virtue of the "greater love" so far out of its Christian context of faith and hope that it stands in his poetry only as a source of ironic reproach or anguished appeal.

Despite Owen's extraordinary sensitivity and his efforts to reconcile that sensitivity to the demands of formal poetic art, his achievement does not measure up to the vast tragic potentialities of his material. His sense of personal involvement in the war resembled Rupert Brooke's in that it was a motive for as well as a source of poetry. Although he moves far beyond the Georgian attitude with his vision of pity, that vision was not enough. His compassion and his concept of the "greater love" grew out of his perhaps too exclusive concern with the aspects of suffering and sacrifice; these aspects do not assume their place or proportion in the total reality. Unlike Blunden, whose poetic interests range less intensely but more widely over the field of war, Owen cannot shift his eyes from particulars that represent merely a part of an enormous complex of opposed human energies comprehensible only on the historic or tragic scale. Although he attempts to give these particulars a universal significance, his vision of pity frequently obscures rather than illuminates the whole; we are likely to lose sight of the historical reality as well as the underlying tragic values that inspire the pity. In Owen's case the pity produces the poetry; only in a partial and sporadic fashion does the poetry produce pity as an effect of tragic events. Furthermore, if it is true that an enlightened compassion was apparently the only poetically fruitful point of view permitted by the nature of modern warfare, is it not also true, as Stephen Spender suggests in his essay on Owen [see excerpt dated 1935 in *TCLC*-5], that "poetry inspired by pity is dependent on that repeated stimulus for its inspiration"? The best of Owen's lyrics are necessarily developed in terms of a single emotion—an emotion that cannot be maintained or repeated without psychological strain or aesthetic loss. How many successful poems can be written in the tenor of **"Disabled"**? The very intensity of the author's compassion tends to exhaust both the emotion and the force of its stimulus. Unless pity is generated and objectified within a large tragic context, it cannot of itself support a tragic vision; as a motive for lyric poetry, it tends to become sentimental or obsessive regardless of the eloquence with which it is developed. When the compassionate attitude is apparently the only attitude with which war can be truthfully described, the possibilities of poetry are severely restricted: only passive suffering and death can provide its materials.

William Butler Yeats excluded Owen's poetry from his *Oxford Book of Modern Verse* on the basis of his judgment that "passive suffering is not a theme for poetry." A "pleader" for the sufferings of others necessarily makes those sufferings his own; "withdrawn into the quicksilver at the back of the mirror," he loses his objectivity and his sense of proportion: "no great event becomes luminous in his mind." The function of the epic narrative, of course, was to communicate that luminous effect; the epic poet, dealing with and illuminating great events, interpreted his tale in the light of heroic values. These values affected the form as well as the materials of the narrative; the epic vision determined the attitude and technique of the poet as well as the motivations and actions of his characters. In Owen's poetry we have the physical background of war, the sense of hazard and duress, the pathos of suffering, and even a perception of tragic extremity. But these, at best, are but fragmentary aspects of the whole. They appear not as products of a unified and comprehensive poetic vision but as effects of a lyric sensibility vainly attempting to find order and significance on a level of experience where these values could not exist—where, in fact, they had been destroyed. Owen and his contemporaries inherited a sensibility deprived of vision and value; their experiences—so alien to anything dealt with by the romantic tradition—required an intellectual and imaginative discipline far beyond that provided by the vision of pity, which was itself a product of tortured sensibility. Unlike Sassoon, Owen recovered from an early experiential bias; this bias, he discovered, was as poetically unproductive as the Georgian "retrenchment" from which it was an abrupt and sensational reaction. His ironic use of romantic terms and concepts indicates the conflict between a sensibility long devoted to "Poetry" and experiences that demanded the truth. Lacking a positive and comprehensive lyric vision, Owen drew his poetry from this inner conflict while attempting to find his bearings in a period of rapid historical and artistic transition. **"Strange Meeting"** is his final word on the social responsibilities of the "true Poet"; but even in this statement, where the "truth untold" is seen as the pity—"the pity war distilled," Owen

can present no further justification of the poet's new role than his sensitivity to suffering. (pp. 204-07)

Owen's influence on the postwar poets has been summarized by C. Day Lewis [in *A Hope for Poetry* (1934)], who nominates Hopkins, Owen, and Eliot as the "immediate ancestors" of the Auden group. Owen's contribution, however, was less technical than inspirational. Auden, Day Lewis, and Louis MacNeice employed Owen's most notable innovation—half-rhyme—for a variety of effects, but with the exception of Day Lewis they did not seriously explore the musical possibilities of this device, which does not lend itself to every poetic purpose. It is rather as a prophet that Owen earns Day Lewis' designation as "a true revolutionary poet." Owen's protest against the evils of war has been rather unwarrantably extended to the social and economic evils of modern life; he "commends himself to postwar poets largely because they feel themselves to be in the same predicament; they feel the same lack of a stable background against which the dance of words may stand out plainly, the same distrust and horror of the unnatural forms into which life for the majority of people is being forced." Owen is actually a symbol rather than a prophet; his youth, his small but eloquent body of verse, his intense dedication to the truth, his untimely and unnecessary death—all of these factors combined to make him an irresistible figure to the succeeding generation, whose "stable background" of traditional forms and values had, like Owen's, been destroyed by the war. He is a "revolutionary poet" not in the sense that he deliberately undertook any radical reformation of his art but in the sense that his work embodies, more dramatically than that of any other poet, the changing values of the time. (pp. 208-09)

John H. Johnston, "Poetry and Pity: Wilfred Owen,"
in his English Poetry of the First World War: A Study

Owen at age nineteen.

in the Evolution of Lyric and Narrative Form, *Princeton University Press, 1964, pp. 155-209.*

JOSEPH COHEN (essay date 1966)

[*Cohen is an American educator, journalist, and critic whose works reflect his interests in Jewish studies and the literature of the First World War. In the following excerpt from an essay that originally appeared in* English Literature in Transition, *December 1965, he argues that a form of homosexuality dominated Owen's sexual nature and that it provides the key to understanding his poetry.*]

A decade of research has suggested to me that our wide lack of information concerning Owen's military life and its relationship to his poetry is not accidental. There seems almost to have been a conspiracy of silence punctuated over the years by the occasional release of carefully chosen materials designed to create an image not of a human being but of a self-sacrificing soldier-hero who in a brilliant and poignant protest bequeathed his eloquent wisdom to posterity. No one denies the eloquence, but the guarded and controlled dissemination of information has prevented our viewing the poet in all his human dimensions. (pp. 3-4)

Prior to 1960 I had established contact with Harold Owen, and in a long series of letters between 1954 and 1960 he iterated over and over the view that any information obtained outside of the poet's immediate family about their private lives was suspect and almost certain to be incredibly misleading. The truth, he argued, would have to be set forth by a member of the family. Until that time came, the world had no alternative but to wait and indulge in fruitless speculation over the autobiographical content of the poems. (p. 4)

The results of this over-zealous protection have unquestionably impeded the natural development of Owen's reputation. Correct critical assessment has been difficult; and a number of commentators, myself included, have advanced interpretations which need adjustment. I must now, for example, repudiate the view I published in 1956 that the key to understanding Owen was to be found in "his conscientious retreat into the 'pure Christianity' of his youth" [this view is advanced in Cohen's "Wilfred Owen's Greater Love," *Tulane Studies in English*, VI, 1956]. The religious element, it is clear to all, is certainly significant, but the key to Owen, I am now convinced, lies elsewhere.

Another result of the protection accorded Owen's private life is that one begins to suspect that there may be a skeleton rattling in the closet. I have long believed there is one in Owen's locker, that it needs airing, and that while some of its aspects may appear to be sinister, it is insufficiently spectral to justify being guarded. The primary purpose of this paper is not to lay this particular ghost but to use it in attaining deeper insight into Wilfred Owen. (p. 5)

I believe that . . . it can be demonstrated that a form of homosexuality dominated [Owen's] sexual nature and that its presence can be confirmed. I submit that it is the final key to understanding Owen's achievement, and that the position he took toward the war was almost entirely motivated by homosexual elements.

If this motivation can be demonstrated, we will be able to view Owen in a new, more complex dimension than any that have been advanced in the past. Moreover, the dimension itself is one that demands our attention. It has only become apparent

in recent years that one of the dominant motifs, perhaps *the* dominant motif, to evolve in war literature after the Battle of the Somme is an erotic one. The imagery of war turned from figures of heroic sacrifice, of valor, honor, might and patriotism to images of sexual fulfillment. When war became an overwhelming and crushing totality, the trench poet and later the war novelist found they could combat the sense of genocidal menace only by opposing to it the terms of procreation. The phallic symbolism of weaponry, the symbolic return to the womb in the trenches of Mother Earth, the descriptions of infantry units from induction through training to baptism under fire and death in terms of virginity and consummation rites, and the bridal paeans to the infantryman's truest companion, his rifle, are all more commonplace images than we have realized. Since Owen is regarded as the most important of the war poets writing in English, it is all the more necessary to investigate the nature of his sexuality and its influence on his poetry.

Homosexuality is usually initiated through a family pattern wherein a close and very strong tie is developed and continued between mother and son from early childhood. The son identifies with the mother to such an extent that the masculine role of the father is negated and his authority is questioned and subsequently limited. As the son becomes estranged from the father he fails to develop his own masculine identity and in time adopts the familiarly comforting and reassuring feminism of the dominant, adoring mother. Consequently, the identification becomes complete and the son turns to the same love objects natural to the mother, i.e., other boys, concentrating his attention upon them. This begins with himself in narcissism and develops into homosexuality. The son continues to reject the father, but if the father and son are under the same roof continually competing for the mother the rejection produces guilt in the son, which generally is assuaged through suffering the pain and punishment invited by an aggressive hostility toward paternal authority. A pattern is established whereby the guilt must continually be assuaged through the absorption of invited pain; hence, the description of homosexuals as injustice-collectors. At the same time, another rejection also takes place. Adoring the mother and identifying with her completely, the son cannot love another female without being unfaithful not only to his mother but to himself as well, having adopted the mother's role. The rejection of women permits the transference of affection to boys or men of equivalent age.

If one asks how much of this can be applied to Owen, the answer is that all of it applies. The documentation is in the first and second volumes of Harold Owen's *Memoirs* and in Owen's published excerpts from his letters and his poetry. Keeping in mind that religious and literary restraints existed to prevent Owen's becoming a practicing homosexual, we may confirm his inverted development by identifying and documenting the following elements in turn: overattachment to the mother accompanied by estrangement from the father; narcissism; injustice-collecting; rejection of women; and transference of affection to male equivalents. (pp. 7-9)

Though Harold Owen insists that Wilfred and his father reached . . . [an] amicable understanding during the war, there can be little question but that they were sufficiently estranged during the formative years of the poet's life to affect seriously his total outlook. His war poems are filled with patriarchal distrust and disdain.

The most obvious example of Owen's anti-paternalism is, of course, **"The Parable of the Old Man and the Young."** In retelling the Old Testament story of Abraham's near-sacrifice of Isaac, Owen transforms this civilizing legend in the abandonment of human sacrifice into ritual murder. The father is cold, heartless, misdirected, bloodthirsty, and bent on destruction; the son accepts his fate passively. There is no escape. He allows himself to be tied to the altar and slain. Through this ritual murder, Owen would have us believe that the only gift fathers have to pass on to their sons is blood-lust. In **"A Terre"** he was to make this assumption more specific. His multiple amputee thinks of the child he will never sire and says:

> I suppose
> Little I'd ever teach a son, but hitting,
> Shooting, war, hunting, all the arts of hurting.
> Well, that's what I learnt,—that, and making money.

Nowhere in Owen's poetry are there references to gentle, humane, adoring fathers. The images are all hostile. In **"S.I.W."** (Self Inflicted Wound) the soldier son is sent to war with the admonition to "show the Hun a brave man's face"; "Father [Owen says] would sooner [see] him dead than in disgrace"; and it is this particular soldier son who after unrelieved months in the trenches commits suicide by shooting himself in the mouth:

> With him they buried the muzzle his teeth had kissed,
> And truthfully, wrote the Mother, "Tim died smiling."

In **"Smile, Smile, Smile,"** fathers hypocritically prolong the war to satisfy their own blood-lust at the fatal expense of their boys. "Peace," Owen has them argue, "would do wrong to our undying dead,— / The sons we offered might regret they died / If we got nothing lasting in their stead. / We must be solidly indemnified." Even father-surrogates at the Front are depicted by Owen as being heartless. In **"The Dead-Beat,"** the doctor, a conventional father-image in modern war literature, celebrates casually the death of a soldier whose courage had broken and who had been taken to the field hospital: "Next day I heard the Doc's well-whiskied laugh: / 'That scum you sent last night soon died. Hooray'."

Owen associated patriarchal blood-lust not only with prolongation of the war in France, but with war-profiteering and the general superciliousness of the Home Front. Critics have largely missed Owen's motivation in making the extension. One father, a poet of the older generation himself when the Great War began, did recognize essentially Owen's central position. In a letter written in 1924 on the tenth anniversary of the outbreak of war but not published until 1942, Sir Henry Newbolt said:

> [Sassoon] has sent me Wilfred Owen's *Poems,* with an Introduction by himself. The best of them I knew already—they are terribly good, but of course limited, almost all on one note. I like better Sassoon's two-sided collection— there are more than two sides to this business of war, and a man is hardly normal any longer if he comes down to one. S.S. says that Owen pitied others but never himself: I'm afraid that isn't quite true—or at any rate not quite fair. To be a man one must be willing that others as well as yourself should bear the burden that must be borne . . . Owen and the rest of the broken men rail at the Old Men who sent the young to die: they have suffered cruelly, but in the nerves and not the heart—they haven't the experience or the imagination to know the extreme human agony—"who giveth me to die

for thee, Absalom, my son, my son." Paternity apart, what Englishman of fifty wouldn't far rather stop the shot himself than see the boys do it for him? [See excerpt dated 1924.]

Owen's extension of patriarchal blood-lust did not end, however, with the Home Front. There is a special antipathy in his poetry reserved for God, the ultimate Father-figure, as opposed to Owen's thoroughgoing love of Jesus. Allusions, direct and indirect, to God occur in numerous poems. Some are ambiguous while others are openly hostile. In the **"Parable"** God offers Abraham the opportunity of exorcising the Ram of Pride but when Abraham ignores the offer God does not interfere further to save Isaac. This is a basic, negative theme in Owen's poetry: God, if He is not openly antagonistic to the young, is indifferent to their destruction, which is just as bad. **"Greater Love"** cites this indifference: the limbs of young men are being "knifeskewed" where "God seems not to care"; while **"Exposure"** develops the theme pointedly:

To-night, His frost will fasten on this mud and us,
Shrivelling many hands, puckering foreheads crisp.
The burying-party, picks and shovels in their shaking grasp,
Pause over half-known faces. All their eyes are ice,
    But nothing happens.

At other times, Owen leaves the interpretation to the reader. In **"Arms and the Boy"** he tells us God will grow neither talons nor antlers for young soldiers to use in fighting but they have instead the bayonet "keen with hunger of blood" and "blunt bullet-leads / Which long to nuzzle in the hearts of lads," implements remarkable, incidentally, in their phallicism. In **"Asleep"** and **"Apologia pro Poemate Meo"** and **"Spring Offensive"** other contradictory juxtapositions of God's attitude are found: **"Asleep"** describes a dead soldier whose body is shaded by "Calm pillows of God's making" yet under these clouds are "sleets of lead" and "the winds' scimitars"; **"Apologia"** begins with the line, "I, too, saw God through mud," which hints at His glory but emphasizes the hell in which it must be perceived; while **"Spring Offensive"** describes God's having caught soldiers during an attack "even before they fell," posing the question whether the gesture is one of tender recovery or of compelling blood-lust.

If these interpretations are open both to positive and negative assumptions, allusions to God in the poems **"Inspection"** and **"Soldier's Dream"** are not. Dennis Welland's commentary on the first of these poems is particularly illuminating: he calls it another **"Parable of the Old Man and the Young."** This time, however, "the inspecting Deity [Welland notes] wants the sacrifice" not openly demanded in the **"Parable."** Owen's soldier victim in this poem has been "confined to camp" for being "dirty on parade," the dirt being dried blood:

> "Blood's dirt," he laughed, looking away
> Far off to where his wound had bled
> And almost merged for ever into clay.
> "The world is washing out its stains," he said.
> "It doesn't like our cheeks so red:
> Young blood's its great objection.
> But when we're duly white-washed, being dead,
> The race will bear Field-Marshal God's inspection."

"Soldier's Dream" is even more explicit. This poem, unpublished until 1963, gives us an unusual example of Owen's compulsion in indicting God, the Father, attributing to Him the continuation of the carnage. In an early version . . . it is curious to note that Owen's first choice of a villain who prolongs the war is political; he is the militant "pro patria" father figure who has fresh blood to spill: "a man from U.S.A. / Stopped us, and said: 'You go right back this minute' [into the trenches]." In the later revised version the poem shifts the blame, as follows:

> I dreamed kind Jesus fouled the big-gun gears;
> And caused a permanent stoppage in all bolts;
> And buckled with a smile Mausers and Colts;
> And rusted every bayonet with His tears.
> And there were no more bombs, of ours or Theirs,
> Not even an old flint-lock, nor even a pikel.
> But God was vexed, and gave all power to Michael;
> And when I woke he'd seen to our repairs.

Owen's animosity is so strong he can serve it only by creating a powerful clash of interest between Jesus and God, a clash that is hardly supported by Christian theology. It is understandable only in the light of Owen's attitude toward his own father and his transference of affection to Jesus, i.e., one who is young and suffering and passively subjected, as Owen felt he was, to an overwhelming authority.

We have always regarded Owen as a poet filled with compassion. Yet he had none for fathers or their images. Nor did he spare parents in general except mothers recalled in the memories of their doomed sons. A particularly relevant example occurs in the opening lines to **"Happiness."** The ultimate bliss the son has known in the mother's bond is confirmed in a question Owen poses: "Ever again to breathe pure happiness, / The happiness our mother gave us, boys?" The attachment to the mother is perfect in the memory but the bond itself is no longer present. "The former happiness," Owen says in the same poem, "is unreturning." Coupled to the loss of this happiness or innocence is the assumption of experience revealed by the awareness and threat of guilt: "Have we not wrought too sick and sorrowful wrongs / For her hands' pardoning?" The guilt loosens the bond leaving only the memory of its pure pleasure overshadowed by the omnipresent estrangement from the father.

Having idealized one parent years before and rejected the other, Owen's psychosexual arrest was inevitable. Its first pronounced manifestation was in narcissism, the self-love that grew out of his adoption of the maternal role. The self-love, the self-concern that Sir Henry Newbolt detected, remained a part of the poet all his life. It explains the extreme lushness of his juvenilia and his gross inability to deal anywhere in his verse affirmatively and maturely with the theme of heterosexual love. Of love he has plenty to say, but it is the love plaint of the adolescent, the sensitive, introspective lad in love with love, in search of Eros, with shaft unhurled:

> But when I heard his singing wings expand
>   My face fell deeply in his shoulder.
> Sweet moons we flew thus, yet I waned not older
> But in his exquisiteness I flagged, unmanned
> Till, when his wings were drooping to an end,
> Feeling my empty hand fulfilled with His,
> I knew Love gave himself my passion-friend.
>   (**"To the Bitter Sweet-Heart: A Dream"**)

Harold Owen goes to great lengths in the *Memoirs* to assure us that Wilfred was not an adolescent prig. His protests, understandable as they are, give credibility to this aspect of the poet's personality. The self-love was there, and it was accompanied by a healthy contempt for others: the Philistines Owen had to contend with, and later, the callous Home Front. In fairness, however, it must be remembered that apart from his mother's staunch but narrowly-visioned support the young poet carried alone the burden of preparing himself for his future achievement against the crushing vicissitudes of his limited existence. He was victimized by poverty, by discouragement, by harassment, and by the severity of the English winters. It is no wonder that he secured himself partly through priggishness or that he became morose, sullen, and subject to sieges of depression. The worst effects of his adolescent situation and the narcissism it engendered moved him rapidly toward injustice-collecting.

The injustice-collector is said to find satisfaction in defeat, humiliation, privation, and depression. Self-pity is fundamental. In his youth, Owen propelled himself toward situations filled with despair. (pp. 11-16)

The slings and arrows of peacetime, partly self-inflicted by Owen, nurtured his sensitivity toward suffering and injustice. When he entered the war it was only natural that he would respond to the horrors of the Western Front, almost in a sense of negative fulfillment. Practically all of his best known trench poems can be legitimately read as studies in injustice-collecting.

Since Owen's poems first appeared, critics have applauded his restraint and his ability to turn his anger into art. He was a quiet, gentle person not given to indecorous postures, windy propagandizing, or heated verbal outbursts. His anger ran deep. In rising to the surface, it was cooled and controlled by long experience in privation and exploitation. Owen knew the world in its harshness, apathy, and cruelty, and he knew that it would be useless to lash out aimlessly at its evil. He realized poetry was his only weapon and he agonized endlessly over his efforts to fashion a vehicle powerful enough to contain his anger and use its force to carry his message across the generations. His struggle to achieve mastery of expression is well known, but what is most impressive in the struggle is the degree to which he cloaked in irony his anger and bitterness toward patriarchal bloodlust, war-profiteering, women, a conception of a merciless Old Testament God, and the madness of war.

Accompanying Owen's anger is his pity. These are the two basic elements in his poetry. Self-concerned as he was, his ability to cloak in compassion his view of himself as victim may be even more remarkable than his channeling anger through irony. Sassoon says Owen was not concerned about himself. The poems, as Sir Henry Newbolt intimated, suggest otherwise. Had Owen not been convinced that the world would crucify him before he had accomplished his mission—he knew all too well the life expectancy of an infantry officer on the Western Front—he would not have attacked so passionately the supreme apathy of the Home Front, or complained so bitterly over the patriarchal blood-lust he attributed to God.

In the despair of combat, in the humiliation of living in mud and vermin amid unburied bodies, in the generally putrifying primitiveness of that first modern theatre of the absurd, the Western Front, Owen would have been less than human if he hadn't felt sorry for himself as well as for his suffering fellows. It is a wonder he didn't develop fully into a psychic masochist, exposed and vulnerable, being hurt, and hurting others in turn. His carrying photographs in his shirt pocket of mutilated soldiers to shock the complacent citizenry at home is evidence enough that he approached this brink though he never fell from its edge.

Since there can now be little doubt that Owen was an injustice-collector, and since there are in many reviews and articles ample commentaries on his protests, we need catalogue only a few of the more outstanding instances of injustice-collecting that appear in the poems. The **"Parable"** and **"Inspection"** have already been cited. **"Strange Meeting"** laments the unjust deprivation of future fulfillment. **"Insensibility"** rails against those "dullards whom no cannon stuns" and who "By choice . . . made themselves immune / To pity and whatever mourns in man." **"Apologia pro Poemate Meo"** exalts combatants at the expense of non-combatants whose humanity Owen denies: "These men are worth / Your tears. You are not worth their merriment." **"Anthem for Doomed Youth"** records the injustice of battle-zone burial in which dead soldiers are denied even conventional religious rites, false, Owen says, though they may be: "No mockeries now for them; no prayers nor bells." **"Exposure"** details the pain and suffering inflicted by the natural elements: icy winds, soaking rains, stormy clouds, blackened snow. **"The Show"** expounds victimization on several levels in its depiction of the battle-front as a dead male body—no identification with Mother Earth here—being devoured by strings of brown and gray worms, the opposing armies, of whom one, whose head is "fresh-severed," is the poet's own. **"Mental Cases"** in its anger, compassion and self-pity, for Owen was a "mental case" for a time himself, bitterly expresses the absorbed horror of war-ravaged minds and nervous systems. Finally, **"Dulce et Decorum Est,"** the least restrained of Owen's poems, denounces the injustice of gas attacks and even worse, the injustice of those who ignore them and continue to prate about war as a patriotic and necessary adventure. . . . (pp. 17-18)

Homosexuals, whether inverts or perverts, it should be observed, have no monopoly on injustice-collecting. Heterosexual injustice-collectors are found throughout all levels of society. Injustice-collecting is, nonetheless, one aspect of the homosexual's makeup. If this were the only evidence of homosexuality in Owen it would be ridiculous to pursue the point. Other elements, however, have already been documented, and still others remain: the rejection of women, and the transference of affection to male equivalents. (p. 19)

Owen clearly revealed his hostility and distaste for women in several important poems. In **"Strange Meeting"** he rejects the traditionally romantic peacetime quest for an idyllically successful love relationship by emphasizing that "the wildest beauty in the world" for which both soldiers before their deaths "went hunting wild" was not to be found "calm in eyes, or braided hair." In **"Apologia pro Poemate Meo"** he rejects the love that consists of "the binding [by Joy] of fair lips / With the soft silk of eyes" in favor of the love that grows out of soldiers suffering together. In **"The Sendoff"** he asks if the troops at the Front "mock what women meant / Who gave them flowers," as they marched away, again rejecting the value inherent in the women's symbolic gesture. The bitterness of **"Dulce et Decorum Est"** arises partly from its being a reply "To a Certain Poetess" (Jessie Pope) who was publishing stirring but superficial jingles of the war. **"Disabled"** dwells on the infidelity and ingratitude of women who, though attractive with their "slim . . . waists" and "warm . . . subtle hands," now touch the multiple amputee as though he had "some queer disease." Earlier, the amputee had volunteered, partly "to please his Meg; / Aye, that was it, to please the giddy jilts," and now that he has returned, their eyes pass "from him to the strong men that were whole." **"The Dead Beat"** describes a soldier who just gives up and dies and Owen explains again that the cause is likely to be this same infidelity and ingratitude:

> A low voice said,
> "It's Blighty, p'raps, he sees; his pluck's all gone,
> Dreaming of all the valiant, that aren't dead:
> Bold uncles, smiling ministerially;
> Maybe his brave young wife, getting her fun
> In some new home, improved materially.
> It's not these stiffs have crazed him; nor the Hun."

Owen's major pronouncement on the value of women is found in **"Greater Love,"** a work that has come to be increasingly recognized as pivotal in Owen's trench poems and one that should equal **"Strange Meeting"** in interest. A number of commentators, myself included, have described the several levels on which the poem operates through its juxtaposition of sexual love against the conditions of the Western Front. In the poem the speaker contrasts his beloved's erotic charms: lips, eyes, limbs, voice, heart, and hands, with his own spiritual reflections produced by his experience in combat. Through apostrophe the poet seems thoroughly to be establishing a love relationship with the woman of the poem as real as the greater love he feels for his comrades in the trenches. Several critics have allowed themselves to be swayed by the suggested realism of the poem, assuming that because Owen creates a heterosexual love relationship it actually existed externally. (pp. 19-21)

It can be argued, of course, that Owen establishes the lady's existence by directly addressing her and that he embodies her presence with the terms "your eyes," "your slender attitude," and "your voice." Yet the embodiment remains within the poetic context. It is simply not true historically, in view of the fact that two of the surviving manuscripts of **"Greater Love"** contain cancelled subtitles to "any" attractive woman. Obviously, the beautiful woman never existed. She is the abstract foil to the poet's greater regard for his army comrades. In my view, the success Owen achieved in **"Greater Love"** can be explained only by his absolute lack of experience with women. If he had known heterosexual fulfillment, **"Greater Love"** would have lost its fine edge, if indeed, it had been written at all. Without realizing it, Owen obtained a sense of sterility and barrenness by rejecting sexual love, a sterility which easily coalesced with the sense of destruction at the Front, giving a heightened value to his transference of love to his fellow men.

Owen's narcissism throughout adolescence kept him from those normal day-to-day activities which would have brought him closely into contact with other boys. It was not, then, until he entered the Army that he developed a capacity for sustained friendship with his fellows and a concern for them. Such affection as he possessed before this time was lavished not on his father or brothers but on the figure of his suffering, often-denied, God-hero, Jesus. It was to a living concept of Jesus that he turned for friendship, and in the concept he found strength and understanding (to say nothing of a restraining moral force that would have negated any possibility of his inversion being extended to perversion). Moreover, he found in this concept a union of friendship and compassion. Together they confirmed the necessity of sacrifice, a basic theme of the war poems. (pp. 21-2)

If there is a plausible answer to Owen's willing return [to the Front in the summer of 1918], it must lie in his attraction to injustice-collecting, and his compulsive affection for the troops. That affection permeates **"Greater Love,"** where we have observed, sexual love is rendered valueless next to Owen's regard for the comradeship of men. Moreover, the implication is that sexual love is sordid and degrading: "Kindness of wooed and wooer / Seems shame to their love pure," Owen says in contrasting the two disparate groups of lovers, reminding the beautiful girl at the close of the poem that the second group, the soldiers, are beyond her tainted reach: "Weep, you may weep, for you may touch them not." At the same time he is demolishing the validity of the heterosexual relationship, he invests the love of men, as he cherishes it, with Christian resignation: "And though your hand be pale, / Paler are all which trail / Your cross through flame and hail." By identifying this male companionship with Jesus, it was sanctified in purity.

"Apologia pro Poemate Meo" and **"Strange Meeting"** are further testimonials to Owen's transferred affection. In **"Apologia"** he confirms again the view that the ultimate relationship is between men in arms; and in **"Strange Meeting"** he extends that comradeship to the enemy, again in Christian resignation. This spirituality makes it difficult to think of Owen in homosexual terms, yet it will be remembered that he carried in his shirt pocket his famous pictures of mutilated men just as other soldiers carried pictures of their girl friends, and he grieved over those men in poem after poem.

Any final assessment of Owen's achievement must now take into account the strong evidence that he was [according to Robert Graves in *Goodbye to All That* (1957)] "an idealistic homosexual with a religious background." His homosexual proclivities play a major role in the expression of anger and pity and love in the poetry, and their presence cannot be denied. His war poems have their own individual stamp. His work is vastly different from Isaac Rosenberg's, who came closest to him in promise if not in achievement; and for all they had in common, the fundamental difference between them is in their use of sexual imagery. Rosenberg, who is known to have been heterosexually experienced, everywhere pays his respects to the White Goddess, and it would have been inconceivable for him to describe the terrain of France in masculine terms as did Owen in **"The Show."** Neither could he have created the image as Owen did in **"Spring Offensive"** of soldiers going into battle taking a last look at the sun "like a friend with whom their love is done." To Owen's **"Greater Love"** Rosenberg would have opposed his "Daughters of War" and his play "The Unicorn," in which the power and fury of the war is dramatized in terms of female sexuality. In this same respect Owen's work is significantly different from Herbert Read's "End of a War," which uses the rape of a French girl by a German soldier as one of the chief symbolic nightmares of the Western Front. Owen stands apart also from David Jones, whose *In Parenthesis* relies heavily on feminine imagery in revealing the conflict.... Owen brought to the war a separate genius marked by those proclivities which have been the subject of this inquiry. Their presence is in no way condemnatory. Owen's contribution to English literature is obviously safe. Indeed, we may appreciate that contribution more by identifying it with a human being psychosexually arrested whose struggle and whose agonies are known to us rather than with the windy and empty legend of a self-sacrificing, dominantly masculine hero who never existed. (pp. 23-4)

> *Joseph Cohen, in his* Owen Agonistes, *revised edition, n.p., 1966, 24 p.*

TIMOTHY O'KEEFFE (essay date 1972)

[*In the following excerpt, O'Keeffe discusses ironic allusions to literature and the Bible in Owen's poetry.*]

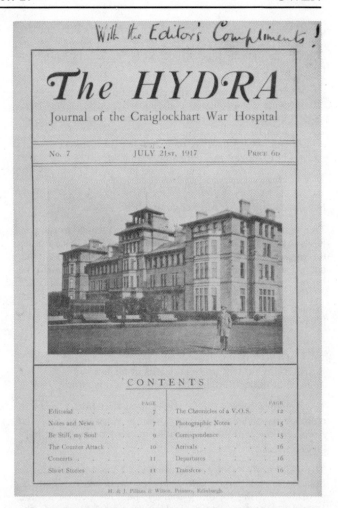

An inscribed issue of "The Hydra," which Owen edited while a patient at Craiglockhart. From Wilfred Owen, *by Jon Stallworthy. Oxford University Press and Chatto and Windus, 1974. Reproduced by permission of Oxford University Press.*

Faced with the incredible horror of warfare in the trenches, Wilfred Owen sought to find some yardstick with which to measure its carnage. He had been nurtured on the aestheticism of the Georgians, of Tennyson, and particularly of Keats, but the irrelevance of poetry of excessive self-pity and beauty to Owen's life on the Western Front became distressingly clear. (p. 72)

Although Owen often echoes the poets he had read in a straightforward manner, many of his more effective poems depend upon ironic allusions not only to past British poets but also to at least two Roman authors and to the Bible. The irony of these allusions consists in the enormous distance between the sense of values of the writers of the past and their naive conception of war and Owen's immediate knowledge of its mindless obscenity. Byron, among the English poets of the past century, had anticipated Owen with his description of the siege of Ismail in *Don Juan*.

Owen also criticizes the religious establishment through references to the Bible which project the disparity between the gentle teachings and example of Christ and the English Church's support of the war. The irony is telling because of the unquestionable authority of the soldier-poet in speaking of life and death on the battlefield. In a letter from a hospital on the Somme, he indicated the distinction he made between Christianity and Christ:

> And am I not myself a conscientious objector with a very seared conscience?... Christ is literally in "no man's land." There men often hear His voice: Greater Love hath no man than this, that a man lay down his life for a friend. Is it spoken in English only and French? I do not believe so. Thus you see how pure Christianity will not fit in with pure patriotism.

For Owen the past could not comprehend the present.

Two patriotic poems of Classical literature provide ironic parallels to poems by Owen. **"Arms and the Boy"** clearly parodies the opening of the *Aeneid*, Virgil's claim, "Arma virumque cano," and his flattery of Augustus's apparent descent from a line of gallant Trojan warriors. In Owen's poem the innocence of the boy is caustically contrasted with the Classical allusions to harpies and (possibly) to Actaeon, who had violated with his eyes the chastity of Diana:

> For his teeth seem for laughing round an apple.
> There lurk no claws behind his fingers supple;
> And God will grow no talons at his heels,
> Nor antlers through the thickness of his curls.

The young soldier's innocence is despoiled by his need to embrace bayonets and bullets. Owen is as aware as Shaw in *Arms and the Man* of the specious glow surrounding military glory.

The well known **"Dulce et Decorum Est"** was written to Jessie Pope, a contemporary British poetess who had extolled the pleasure of dying for one's country, but Owen chose a more formidable poet to oppose in Horace, who had written the prototypical poem on the subject. Owen's tactic is simple: to portray the death of a soldier from chlorine gas in the most graphic terms and then bitterly end the poem with the admonition that if anyone had seen the sight of this horrible death,

> My friend, you would not tell with such high zest
> To children ardent for some desperate glory,
> The old Lie: Dulce et decorum est
> Pro patria mori.

At this early stage of Owen's career, he allows the ironic contrast to remain relatively undeveloped, or at least to develop only one side of the parallel. In later poems he juxtaposes correspondences in scrupulous detail.

Most of Owen's ironic references to the poetry of the past are to the works of the Romantics, who had influenced him deeply, particularly Keats. These allusions indicate the poet's disillusionment with the ideals of the Romantics, which sounded rapturous and inspiring in peacetime but which, to Owen, echoed hollow and fatuous in war. Just as Owen's preface emphasized the distinction between the literature of beauty and of war, an earlier poem, **"On My Songs,"** although written in sonnet form, manifests the poet's growing disenchantment with the poetry of his predecessors:

> Yet are there days when all these hoards of thought
> Hold nothing for me. Not one verse that throbs
> Throbs with my head, or as my brain is fraught.

This effort was composed long before Owen had been involved in the stark realities of war.

Several war poems exhibit an ironic incongruity of allusion to poems of the past. The eerie **"Strange Meeting"** describes the man the narrator has killed (just as Hardy had done in "The Man He Killed") as the slain soldier speaks in the role of a *Doppelgänger,* reminding the narrator of all the profitable things left undone because of his death:

> Then, when much blood had clogged their chariot-wheels,
> I would go up and wash them from sweet wells,
> Even with truths that lie too deep for taint.

The last line here parodies the last line in Wordsworth's "Intimations Ode," "Thoughts that do often lie too deep for tears," in that the speaker in Wordsworth's poem depicts the therapy that nature offers to the soul that has lost some of its original grandeur. In **"Strange Meeting,"** on the other hand, the speaker would attempt a cleansing therapy in the world above which would make it see the futility of war, but death has incapacitated him, preventing him from remedying the conditions which caused both his death and the deaths of others to follow.

"Apologia pro Poemate Meo" defines beauty in a context far different from that of Keats's Odes which appear as an ironic background to Owen's portrayal of the ugliness which achieves a strange beauty in war because of human courage. Truth may be beauty, according to Owen, but not because the subject in the poem is aesthetically attractive like an urn, but because a beauty is born to the human spirit amidst the ugliness of war. The poem pictures

> ... Joy, whose ribbon slips—
> But wound with war's hard wire whose stakes are strong;
> Bound with the bandage of the arm that drips;
> Knit in the webbing of the rifle-thong.

The echo here of **"Ode on Melancholy"** is most apropos in a grimly ironic sense; Keats's "And Joy, whose hand is ever at his lips" even contains the same rhyme (*lips—drips*) as Owen's portrait of Joy. Keats is saddened by the vanishing of pleasure in its act of consummation, but Owen sees a sturdier beauty in undesired human suffering.

"A Terre" and its sub-title, ("Being the Philosophy of Many Soldiers"), laconically provide a grimly witty joke at the expense of Shelley, who continually desired some kind of annihilation because life was too arduous. Owen had little patience with such self-pity and explains how the British soldier under bombardment agreed with Shelley's desire for union with the earth:

> "I shall be one with nature, herb, and stone,"
> Shelley would tell me. Shelley would be stunned:
> The dullest Tommy hugs that fancy now.
> "Pushing up daisies" is their creed, you know.
> To grain, then, go my fat, to buds my sap,
> For all the usefulness there is in soap.

In trench warfare it was difficult to distinguish who was alive, who dead, who above, and who below the earth. D.S.R. Welland remarked about this poem that

> obliged to live in close proximity to them. Many who were buried suffered an untimely and grisly resurrection through a bursting shell, a land subsistence or a digging party, and many became visibly assimilated into the squelching

mud. There was no escaping the sight or smell of this putrescence.

"Inspection" recalls Lady Macbeth's pathological need to remove the spot of blood on her hands, which was symbolic of her guilt. In Owen's poem the spot is also symbolic of the guilt of those who send soldiers to be killed. The dramatic irony in the poem depends upon the obtuseness of the sergeant-speaker, concerned only with the ritual of cleanliness and not with the meaning of the bloodstains he finds on the soldier's uniform during an inspection. He relates his own insensitivity without comprehending its myopia:

> Some days "confined to camp" he got,
> For being "dirty on parade."
> He told me, afterwards, the damnéd spot
> Was blood, his own. "Well, blood is dirt," I said.
>
> [Note how the acute mark in *damnéd* emphasizes the allusion.]

Like Pilate, who insisted upon immaculate hands, the sergeant is interested in cleanliness because it is a proper virtue. The meaningless theatricality of army inspections is exposed here, but more subtly the poem suggests the metamorphosis of blood into clay, an image without irony since the trenches were continually stained with blood.

An allusion more difficult to ascertain appears in **"Soldier's Dream,"** in which a soldier dreams that all the weapons of war have become fouled or jammed and the war can no longer continue. Owen may have had Book Six of *Paradise Lost* in mind when at the end of the poem God sees to it that the war can continue:

> But God was vexed, and gave all power to Michael;
> And when I woke he'd seen to our repairs.   ·

The pun on "our repairs" indicates that the soldiers will be fixed as well, so that they can no longer function as whole human beings. It is significant that Michael becomes the symbol of divine military power and not Christ, for in *Paradise Lost* Christ is the supreme military conqueror in Heaven. Either Owen was not thinking of Milton at all but instead working from tradition, or else he had the epic specifically in mind and wanted to reserve Christ for a gentler symbolic role as the sacrificial soldier, to be discussed under the category of Biblical allusions.

The final literary reference with ironic overtones is to Gray's *Elegy:* "The paths of glory lead but to the grave." The line was commonplace enough, and in Owen's **"Fragment: Not One Corner . . ."** the allusion, although agreeing in spirit and concept with Gray's elegy (The title of the fragment was to be "An Imperial Elegy" or "Libretto for Marche Funèbre"), ironically contrasts the concept of a glorious path with a vision of Europe as a vast soldier's cemetery:

> I looked and saw.
> An appearance of a titan's grave,
> At the length thereof a thousand miles.
> It crossed all Europe like a mystic road,
> Or as the Spirits' Pathway lieth on the night.
> And I heard a voice crying,
> This is the Path of Glory.

Humphrey Cobb's novel, *Paths of Glory,* also exploited the irony of Gray's phrase, but it is also possible that Owen is ridiculing the traditional *Via Mystica* in the phrase, "mystic road," since the Christian mystics attempted to reach God

through this process while the soldier reaches God with the speed of a bullet or shrapnel fragment. The soldier, however, dies not a mystical but a literal death.

Owen grew more and more to reject traditional, or perhaps the better word nowadays is "establishment," Christianity because it was enthusiastically supporting the war, at least in its early stages, as a Crusade. Eventually he distinguished Christ from Christianity and identified Christ with the soldiers in the trenches through their shared suffering. In a letter written on 4 July 1918, he recounts his training the troops:

> For 14 hours yesterday I was at work—teaching Christ to lift his cross by numbers, and how to adjust his crown; and not to imagine his thirst till after the last halt. I attended his Supper to see that there were not complaints; and inspected his feet that they should be worthy of the nails. I see to it that he is dumb, and stands at attention before his accusers. With a piece of silver I buy him every day, and with maps I make him familiar with the topography of Golgotha.

D. S. R. Welland points out [in his *Wilfred Owen*] how in **"Strange Meeting"** the soldier bleeds without a wound:

> I would have poured my spirit without stint
> But not through wounds; not on the cess of war.
> Foreheads of men have bled where no wounds were

Welland explains, "The implied reference to Christ's 'agony and bloody sweat' is inescapable, illuminating, and wholly successful." The common experience of Christ and the soldier is sacrifice (as Owen's letter quoted above, indicated), not the militancy of "Onward Christian Soldiers." (pp. 72-8)

["At a Calvary near the Ancre"] clearly exploits the Gospel accounts of the Crucifixion as a foil to the horrors of war. The first stanza depicts the ironic situation of the image of Christ "wounded in action":

> One ever hangs where shelled roads part.
>   In this war He too lost a limb,
> But His disciples hide apart;
>   And now the Soldiers bear with Him.

The civilian Christians are nowhere to be seen, just as many, including Peter, denied Christ when danger was imminent, and even more ironically, the modern soldiers bear a load just as Christ bore his cross. In the second stanza the priests who have been seduced by the sins of pride and of the flesh are "flesh-marked by the Beast," the Anti-Christ, who opposes the suffering Saviour. In the final stanza the poem expands to condemn the noisy war propagandists in contradistinction to the quiet soldiers who offer their lives in love, like Christ:

> The scribes on all the people shove,
>   And brawl allegiance to the state,
> But they who love the greater love
>   Lay down their life; they do not hate.

The scribes and pharisees correspond perfectly to the war propagandists because both groups protest too much about their fervor.

The last poem illustrating ironic allusion to the Bible, **"The Parable of the Old Man and the Young"** (in some MSS "Old Men"), has been too often superficially examined because of the obviousness of the reference to the twenty-second chapter of Genesis, the story of Abraham and Isaac. Just as in other poems suggesting the sacrifice of Christ, **"The Parable"** utilizes the intended sacrifice of Abraham. The irony of this allegory, however, emanates from the contrast between the relieved humanity of Abraham and the wilful homicide of the leaders of Europe. The contrast is sharpened by a rather close ironic correspondence between the Biblical text and the poem; that is, the subtle differences between the two indicate that Owen probably had the text of Genesis close by when he wrote the poem and that he intensified the irony scrupulously. Thus, in Genesis Isaac remarks on the preparations of "fire and wood," but in the poem he observes the "fire and iron" of the battlefield; in Genesis Abraham simply "bound Isaac" but in the poem:

> Then Abram bound the youth with belts and straps,
> And builded parapets and trenches there.

Further, in the original Abraham sees the ram caught in a thicket as a possible sacrifice, but in the poem Abram is too blind to see, and an angel, representing a good spiritual impulse, tells Abram to "Offer the Ram of Pride instead of him." The ending of the poem then offers an obvious contrast in the slaying of "half the seed of Europe, one by one" with Abraham's saving of his son. Genesis xii. 17 deepens the irony in the blessing given by God to Abraham's seed as opposed to the sterility and destruction effected by the old man of Europe: "That in blessing I will bless thee, and in multiplying I will multiply thy seed as the stars of the heaven, and as the sand which is upon the sea shore; and thy seed shall possess the gate of his enemies." Clearly the opposite, Owen prophesies, will be the result of the sacrifice in **"The Parable."**

Owen also took advantage of what is now called folk culture, as in his picture of the maimed and wounded reading the optimistic propaganda from home in **"Smile, Smile, Smile."** Every soldier knew the lines from the marching song,

> Pack up your troubles in your old kit bag
> And smile, smile, smile.
>   .   .   .   .   .   .
> Smile, boys, that's the style.

But the smile of the casualties in the face of the glorious programmes for the youth of England depends upon the realization that the future of England was really in France:

> That England one by one had fled to France,
> Not many elsewhere now, save under France.

For the poet this was the true "Lost Generation."

Wilfred Owen in his poetry found ironic allusions to literature and the Bible effective in driving home to his readers the horror of war and the inability of the values and morality of Western Christian civilization to comprehend the nature of World War I. Originally seeking the traditions of his past and its literature to support his poetry and writing an often too derivative verse, the poet discovered that the traditional support he was seeking simply wasn't extant, and so he paradoxically found sustenance in those traditions by displaying their impotence in explaining the cataclysm of modern warfare. (pp. 79-81)

> Timothy O'Keeffe, "Ironic Allusion in the Poetry of Wilfred Owen," in Ariel, (The University of Calgary), Vol. 3, No. 4, October, 1972, pp. 72-81.

JON SILKIN   (essay date 1972)

[*Silkin, an English poet and critic, edits the poetry review* Stand, *which he founded in the 1950s. In the following excerpt from his* Out of Battle, *a study of the English poets of the First World War, he discusses the group of poems that represents Owen's poetic responses to nature and those poems that use anger and satire to treat warfare.*]

Owen's crucial poems—those concerned with war, and two or three others—can be grouped under three headings, without violating their complexity. Firstly, poems in which nature, if one excludes war, is the principal element: **"Exposure"** (February 1917), **"Anthem for Doomed Youth"** (September 1917), **"Miners"** (January 1918), **"Asleep"** (November 1917), **"The Show"** (November 1917), **"Hospital Barge at Cérisy"** (December 1917), **"Futility"** (June 1918), **"Spring Offensive"** (September 1918). Also, I would add **"The Last Laugh"** (February 1918) for its last two lines which are, in this context, important. Secondly, come the Sassoon-like poems protesting against the war, in which anger, satire, or irony is especially directed against its continuation: and thus, directed also at the civilian who seems to have little understanding of war's horrors. Also included here are the poems which recreate such horror: **"Le Christianisme"** (April 1917), **"The Dead-Beat"** (August 1917), **"Dulce et Decorum Est"** (October 1917), **"Soldier's Dream"** (October 1917), **"Wild with All Regrets"** (December 1917), **"The Last Laugh"** (February 1918), **"A Terre"** (April 1918), **"Mental Cases"** (May 1918), **"Arms and the Boy"** (May 1918), **"The Sentry"** (September 1918), **"Spring Offensive"** (September 1918), **"Smile, Smile, Smile"** (September 1918). The following poems are also grouped here, but apart from the above because their dating is problematic: **"The Letter," "Conscious"** (January-March 1918), **"Disabled"** (?October 1917), **"The Chances," "S.I.W.," "Inspection," "The Parable of the Old Man and the Young," "At a Calvary near the Ancre," "On Seeing a Piece of Our Artillery Brought into Action," "The Next War."** Thirdly, poems whose originating impulse is compassion or pity: **"Anthem for Doomed Youth"** (September 1917), **"Miners"** (January 1918), **"Asleep"** (November 1917), **"The Calls"** (May 1918). And also here, poems whose dating is problematic: **"The Send-Off," "Greater Love," "Strange Meeting."** A fourth category contains poems which do not fit any of the others: **"Apologia pro Poemate Meo"** (November 1917), **"Insensibility"** (March 1918), **"Futility"** (May 1918). Needless to say, these headings are to be taken as no more than ways in which the poems may be helpfully explored. D. S. R. Welland has observed that "Owen's poetry may come to be of increasing value as a bridge between the poetry of the nineteenth century and that of the twentieth." Certainly his use of nature is a pertinent instance of such a bridge. On the other hand, the Sassoon-like mode of anger and satire is very unlike anything in nineteenth-century poetry, apart from Byron. (pp. 206-07)

[What his association with Siegfried Sassoon did for Owen] perhaps was to give him the confidence to draw into his work a greater realism, a more stringent anger and satire, which in their turn may have helped him more fully to realize his compassion. The colloquial element present in Sassoon's work would also have constituted a learning point for Owen, as much as *Le Feu,* "which set him alight as no other war book had done." Yet what is interesting, if the classifications I have attempted are at least temporarily granted, is that the largest number of poems comes under the second heading of anger and satire. This would seem to refute the commonplace assertion that Owen was overwhelmingly the poet of compassion.

I am not suggesting, of course, that he was not, but I am indicating a large body of work that gets ignored, or is at least not accommodated in the popular image of him, an image which in its turn forces upon the poems a reading that emphasizes the very weaknesses that Owen I think was partly aware of. That is, anger and compassion are complementary elements in his work, and exclusion of the former throws the latter into radical weakness of quite the wrong kind. The weakness itself amounts to a certain "haloesque" quality, which can obscure the horror of war that Owen in other poems was committed to recounting, but which pity is always I believe held in right concord and activity by the simultaneous presence (when it occurs) of anger.

The poems subsumed under the heading of compassion can be considered as being in some senses versions of Owen's responses to nature. They are composed partly of what he inherited, from Keats, Shelley, and Tennyson, for instance, and from the versions of pastoral current through Arnold and the whole of the nineteenth century. The pacific and the pastoral are closely interrelated syndromes, but what is interesting about Owen's use of the pastoral as a pacific attribute is that with a poet's proper intensity he proceeds to make literal a conversion which lesser, more immediately sophisticated writers would have seen as metaphor. He is deeply and directly in touch with a fundamental constituent or reflecting image in nature, and which is basically important to human concerns. Wrath of course has its ample counterpart in nature and he clearly incorporated this aspect in such poems as **"Exposure"** and **"Spring Offensive."** But to repeat what might risk becoming a formula, to be angry at destruction is to put a value on what is destroyed; thus, the richest response of compassion is one that also contains anger. It is an anger that includes those who have been corrupted by war, the anger directed not at these but at those in society who are in a position so to expose human beings to such corruption:

> some for love of slaughter, in imagination,
> learning later . . .
> some in fear, learning love of slaughter. . . .

That Owen attributed responsibility to the civilians more than to the soldiers (of either side) is confirmed not only by his earlier version of "I am the enemy you killed, my friend," which read "I was a German conscript, and your friend," but also by a letter written in August 1918 from Scarborough:

> this morning at 8.20 we heard a boat torpedoed
> in the bay about a mile out, they say who saw
> it. I think only 10 lives were saved. I wish the
> Bosche would have the pluck to come right in
> & make a clean sweep of the Pleasure Boats,
> and the promenaders on the Spa, and all the
> stinking Leeds & Bradford War-profiteers now
> reading *John Bull* on Scarborough Sands.

This passage has a political perceptiveness, which Welland is inclined to deny Owen, who admittedly lacked Sassoon's ability to translate it into action. In this respect, one might compare Sassoon and Owen with Byron and Wordsworth. Byron criticized Wordsworth for writing but not joining action to it. Wordsworth's intelligence and imagination, however, were richer on the whole than Byron's, as Owen's were richer than Sassoon's. To Sassoon's anger, Owen added compassion, and advances a further term into the perspective on war. In so doing, he also qualified his version of pastoral, as Wordsworth had done before him, "fostered alike by beauty and by fear."

Nevertheless, Owen often kept his compassion and anger in separate poems, and to my mind this is his principal weakness. Nevertheless, his complex consciousness was an advance on Sassoon's and permitted a more flexible understanding of war. (pp. 208-09)

[In the poems of the first group] Owen sees nature in one of two ways: either as a benign sustaining entity (which may or may not be the handiwork of God—as it *was* for the Deists), or as a force hostile to man for as long as he makes war. Unlike Blunden, he does not make nature in war a principal sufferer; for him, man is war's central victim. And in this scheme of man and nature, man is responsible for his own suffering, and nature merely endorses his error with her own retribution. That at least is principally his scheme, and rarely is nature permitted to take matters into her own hands. If she does, the whole scheme alters in emphasis. Then hostile nature is one more punitive act by God for violating His moral laws, but with the sense of God directly intervening in man's affairs. Once that happens, man's direct control over his fate suffers reciprocal diminution as God's direct intervention increases. It takes from man not only a sense of his own actions being his own, but of their consequences being a direct result. If you introduce into man's actions an alien and for ever incalculable factor that is outside man's capacity to effect, you diminish his sense of his own ability to act effectively. And with this diminution you absolve him of responsibility for his actions and their consequences and make of him a child. This would not do for Owen who came I think, whatever his religious upbringing, to believe that man's actions were what affected man. Thus, nature's variousness or duality *may* be a reflection of God's attitude, but it is also an image of man's actions and his own judging of them. The point at which nature is seen to be most at variance with her usual benignity is the point at which man's self-destructiveness is most intense.

If rage is a primary response to the inflictions of war, then Owen's poems of anger are more truly "war poems" than any others he wrote. Perhaps this is the meaning of Blunden's remark that Owen "was, apart from Mr. Sassoon, the greatest of the English war poets. But the term 'war poets' is rather convenient than accurate. Wilfred Owen was a poet without classifications of war and peace." One might add that, even in his poems of anger, Owen is often more complex than Sassoon. Interestingly, with regard to Sassoon's influence on Owen, one of the first of the poems in this category . . . [**"Dulce et Decorum Est"**] is amongst his harshest and most didactic; one, that is to say, most akin to Sassoon's war poetry. (pp. 219-20)

Perhaps, as one of his earliest poems of anger, it represents the tapping of a fresh source of energy (fresh in the sense of a previously unworked area) with confidence for the undertaking newly acquired through his *contact* with Sassoon. The language, although not yet colloquial, is, as it is in some of Sassoon's poems, nearer to speech than the language of **"Exposure,"** for example. Perhaps this change underscores Owen's recognition in himself of a tendency, especially in his poems of sacred pity, to use a poeticized, over-aureate language and tone that has recognizable affinities with the language of sanctification and euphemism. There is nothing of this in **"Dulce et Decorum Est."** The title itself points to one of the poem's targets: the sacredness of the sacrifice, and the glamorized decency of the danger ("adventure") one's own side undergoes. By contrast, the poem opens rawly:

Bent double, like old beggars under sacks,
Knock-kneed, coughing like hags, we cursed through
    sludge,
Till on the haunting flares we turned our backs
And towards our distant rest began to trudge.
Men marched asleep. Many had lost their boots
But limped on, blood-shod.

This has the dignity of honestly reported fact and implicitly acts as a corrective to the reporting of most journalists, whom both Sassoon and Owen loathed. Then comes the gas attack and Owen heightens our sense of terror by using, and thus making complex, a word that has associations contrary to the context in which it is used: "Gas! Gas! Quick, boys!—An ecstasy of fumbling." Ecstasy can produce fumbling, but this is not the ecstasy that accompanies the knowledge of the possibility of escape, but the fevered sense of the terrified fumbling itself, which *appears* akin to that of joy, but is in fact so opposite to it. Owen uses this bifurcated yoking together in other poems, but this is a comparatively early instance of it. One soldier fails to fit on his gas-mask in time. His agony haunts the narrator, as it horrifies the reader in front of whom it passes as though it were the experience itself. The intensity of it is such that, with the narrator, we have a sense not merely of being there but of identity with the gassed man. The scene shifts finally to where it is evident that the experience itself has melted into a narration of it and a ruminating on it (as well as into the narrating of the false subsequent narrative), and this shift, from experience to recall, contains the didactic element:

If you could hear, at every jolt, the blood
Come gargling from the froth-corrupted lungs,
Obscene as cancer, bitter as the cud
Of vile, incurable sores on innocent tongues,—
My friend, you would not tell with such high zest
To children ardent for some desperate glory,
The old Lie. . . .

The recall is folded into rebuke. And as the experience cancers the innocent flesh of its victims, so the thoughtless retelling of the story to children, and to adults, corrupts their imagination; and this, quite apart from the distortion of the suffering. Had the chauvinist been a participant, it is implied, he would not be perpetuating the old Lie that it is sweet and fitting to die for one's country, whatever the death.

"The Dead-Beat" reports the fate of a man whose body has apparently collapsed under the strain of war, although the medical officer chooses to believe he is malingering. In fact, the collapse is even more pervasive, although the mind in its desperation retains some convictions so strongly—that the ruling powers on both sides are callously responsible for the war's continuation—that it is able to voice its aggression.

—Didn't appear to know a war was on,
Or see the blasted trench at which he stared.
"I'll do 'em in," he whined. "If this hand's spared,
I'll murder them, I will."
                    A low voice said,
"It's Blighty, p'raps, he sees; his pluck's all
    gone. . . ."

In the *Collected Poems*, C. Day Lewis provides both an earlier draft of the poem and a note. The latter reads: "In a letter to LG [Leslie Gunston, the poet's cousin] dated 22 August 1917, enclosing this draft, Owen said, *after leaving him, I wrote*

something in Sassoon's style." his is the second stanza of the earlier draft:

He didn't seem to know a war was on,
    Or see or smell the bloody trench at all . . .
Perhaps he saw the crowd at Caxton Hall,
And that is why the fellow's pluck's all gone—

Owen's comment—"in Sassoon's style"—is shrewd self-criticism, and certainly the final version, paragraphed narrative, in comparison with the earlier draft in stanzas, shows a move away from Sassoon. Yet, interesting though the changes are, the matter perhaps owes something to Sassoon's concerns. Especially interesting is the reference to Caxton Hall, where some pacifist meetings were held. The point here is that, although the pacifists are blamed for causing the man's pluck to vanish, and are even, it is implied, in themselves lacking courage, the hint from the poet that comes through is that perhaps the soldier only too well recognizes and understands both what the pacifists have to say and the contingent political implications. Needless to say, the imputations put on the pacifists were not shared by Owen, if his own pacifist declarations provide any guide. (pp. 220-22)

"Soldier's Dream" . . . works by opposing the "kind Jesus" with an efficient vindictive God who has something of the character of Blake's "Selfish Father of Men!" ("Earth's Answer"). Kind Jesus "fouled the big-gun gears," but God empowers Michael to repair them, which he does. In . . . [an] earlier version, the prototype of an efficient God had been an authoritative "man from U.S.A." In a sense the poem remains on the level of fantasy, since no one in a battle would want the guns to be in disrepair unless the enemy's were also. As with **"The Dead-Beat"** and **"Strange Meeting,"** the significant alterations are away from particularity and towards universalizing statements. With the first poem especially, one regrets, for both the matter and expression, some of the inevitable loss of particularity. Yet in this poem, the shift is at least towards its proper subject and towards real considerations. The poem is concerned not with man's ploys with respect to a passive ludditism, but with attitudes. Of these, one symbolizes the kind, merciful, pacific; the other an impersonal, efficient bureaucracy.

"Wild with All Regrets" and its later version, **"A Terre,"** together with **"Disabled,"** **"Mental Cases,"** and in a certain sense **"The Chances,"** expose and examine the effects of war on survivors, wounded, maimed, and often doomed to early death or the asylum. Sassoon had written what are in some ways similar poems, such as "Does it Matter?" and "Repression of War Experience"; and Owen, consciously I think, acknowledges his debt in his reference to the "buffers." In **"A Terre"** Owen's "I'd willingly be puffy, bald, / And patriotic" recalls Sassoon's scarlet majors in "Base Details," who are "fierce and bald," have "puffy petulant" faces, and are of course patriotic. Owen's officer in **"A Terre,"** however, has little of the staff officer's illusions, pretensions, or even patriotism, but merely a tragic disablement. (p. 223)

"Disabled" . . . remembers, like Sassoon's "Does it Matter?," the former civilian health of those who are now maimed. Comparison is made between the pre-war heroics of the football field and those of the battlefield, the telling discrepancy between the two achieved in "blood-smear":

One time he liked a blood-smear down his leg,
After the matches, carried shoulder-high.
It was after football, when he'd drunk a peg,
He thought he'd better join.—He wonders why.

This last line echoes the close of Sassoon's poem "In the Pink," "And still the war goes on—*he* don't know why." Characteristically, Owen makes more attempt to enlarge the man's motive—pride that imagines it will do as well on the one field as the other; pride, excited by drink, and the presence of his woman.

> Someone had said he'd look a god in kilts,
> That's why; and may be, too, to please his Meg. . . .

His disabling wounds expose the reality of male vanity:

> To-night he noticed how the women's eyes
> Passed from him to the strong men that were whole.

If the subsequent judgements on his motives for enlisting are harsh, the feeling for the man himself in his disillusioned and disabled condition is compassionate. This sets Owen apart from Sassoon who will only imply compassion in his anger. The implied sexual incapacity, which the women sense, is the test of how little they really comprehended the sacrifice the men made in enlisting, and that which they have since made. It was not the sacrifice but the glamour of heroism which kindled them. They want their heroes, but they want them whole. Their attitude is not the same as that found in Newbolt's *"Vitai Lampada,"* but it stems from a similar lack of insight. For Newbolt the necessary heroisms of the two fields were identical, but Owen's remorseless contrast is followed through to the poem's end:

> Some cheered him home, but not as crowds cheer Goal.
> Only a solemn man who brought him fruits
> *Thanked* him; and then inquired about his soul.

Owen seems to imply that the pious visitor is as much—if not more—concerned with his own do-gooding as with the patient's spiritual welfare. The passive suffering, which Yeats rejected as a theme for poetry, is emphasized by the rhyme "Goal" (something actively achieved) and "soul" (whose condition is drastically qualified by the bodily one). The tactless inquiry as to the soldier's spiritual condition, when it is his physical one that is so overwhelmingly evident, indicates the real neglect that he suffers.

The same "blood-smear" appears in **"Mental Cases,"** another poem about disability. Physical mutilations and distortions are seen as the outward and visible evidence of inward dereliction:

> Drooping tongues from jaws that slob their relish,
> Baring teeth that leer like skulls' teeth wicked?
> Stroke on stroke of pain,—but what slow panic,
> Gouged these chasms round their fretted sockets?

As in **"The Chances,"**

> —These are men whose minds the Dead have ravished.
> Memory fingers in their hair of murders,
> Multitudinous murders they once witnessed.

We get some sense of their madness functioning as an index of their guilt or even, perhaps, as retribution for their murderous acts; but this compassionately gives way to a sense of their madness resulting from what they have witnessed and endured. In such a double situation of murderer and sufferer the soldiers' duality is never glossed over by Owen, but compassion is never finally withheld. As conscripts, they are essentially victims.

"Smile, Smile, Smile," probably Owen's last poem, makes a fairly detailed analysis of the clichés current in the justifications for continuing the war. A press that aimed at promoting its circulation and civilian morale habitually made the casualties seem less grievous by insisting on the gain in captured machinery (only of use in winning the war):

> Head to limp head, the sunk-eyed wounded scanned
> Yesterday's *Mail;* the casualties (typed small)
> And (large) Vast Booty from our Latest Haul.

The promise of "Cheap Homes" for the deserving soldiers after the war—and therefore "not yet planned"—gives way to a consideration of their present requirements. If they are to win the war, they will . . . need to be better and better equipped:

> Meanwhile their foremost need is aerodromes,
> It being certain war has but begun.
> Peace would do wrong to our undying dead. . . .

More men must be sacrificed to obtain that victory for which the dead have died. The official voice speaks carefully of the "undying," lest the sacrifice of millions seem a disproportionate price for victory. The euphemism "undying," which means "immortal through noble actions," also attempts to diminish the sense of loss which death brings the relatives. Thus, "undying" has it both ways; the dead continue to fight for us (some literally believed this) while we continue to fight and die for them so that their deaths (why then "undying"?) shall be vindicated. The contemptible manipulations of these illogicalities are familiar enough, but it is worth following the twist which Owen gives to them:

> The sons we offered might regret they died
> If we got nothing lasting in their stead.

"Lasting" is a loaded word, since it brings mortality to mind, but how can the dead be compensated for their "unlastingness"? They die, and we are given material compensation. "Lasting" also associates with the cliché, "lasting peace," which I believe Owen thought society was unlikely to obtain. It should also be noted that the quasi-religious terminology, used self-justifyingly by the modern state, underlines the active dissociation from Christianity as Owen understood it. (pp. 226-29)

[The] theme of war's corrupting influence—found also in Herbert Read's "The Happy Warrior," for instance—is present in both **"At a Calvary near the Ancre"** and **"Le Christianisme."** Both poems, in their different ways, are attacks upon the Church which, Owen felt, had become erastian. Blunden must surely have felt something similar when he prefaced his *Undertones of War* with the Article of the Church of England (No. xxxvii), 1553: "It is lawful for Christian men, at the commandment of the Magistrate, to wear weapons, and serve in the wars." Placed in this context, the Article draws to the Church some of the dubious morality of the State.

Owen wrote of the role of the Church:

> Already I have comprehended a light which will never filter into the dogma of any *national* church [my italics]: namely that one of Christ's essential commands was: Passivity at any price! Suffer dishonour and disgrace; but never resort to arms. Be bullied, be outraged, be killed; but do not kill. It may be a chimerical and an ignominious principle, but there it is. It can only be ignored: and I think pulpit professionals are ignoring it very skilfully and successfully indeed. . . . And am I not myself a conscientious objector with a very seared conscience?

The "pulpit professionals" ignored the question because, he implies, the Church as a body had become erastian and found it expedient to be so. Certainly, in **"At a Calvary,"** the contrast is between the "gentle" Christ and the priests who "were fleshmarked by the Beast." It is the soldiers (by paradox but not only by paradox) who are now Christ's suffering disciples:

> But His disciples hide apart;
> And now the Soldiers bear with Him.

The third verse makes all these ideas explicit:

> The scribes on all the people shove
> And brawl allegiance to the state,
> But they who love the greater love
> Lay down their life; they do not hate.

The last two lines, however, might seem to agree with the proposition that the "greater love" and patriotism are synonyms, but in the letter quoted above Owen wrote also: "Greater love hath no man than this, that a man lay down his life for a friend." In the poem, the phrase "Lay down their life" is admittedly ambiguous, in that it might mean by extension "for their country," but it seems highly unlikely that the poet intended this.

"Le Christianisme" also rebukes the Church; but here, for its failure to extend its powers of sympathy and beneficent perception to those enduring the war:

> So the church Christ was hit and buried
> Under its rubbish and its rubble.
> In cellars, packed-up saints lie serried,
> Well out of hearing of our trouble.

The implication is that the Church, with "its rubbish and its rubble" and its inanimate statues, is oblivious to human need and that, by its present nature perhaps, it cannot be otherwise. The Church has retained its "immaculate" spirituality and unworldliness, but at the price of inhumanity.

Owen's difficulties are partly located in his perplexed self-questioning, "And am I not myself a conscientious objector with a very seared conscience?" If he indicts the Church for its failure to accommodate this "light," he also accuses himself. A combatant conscientious objector shares in the suffering but also in the killing. Owen did not and could not resolve the "Victor-victim" paradox, but he tried. By fusing anger with compassion, he indicated that the only solution lay in people so rethinking their attitude to war that they would never wage it again. The sense of physical horror, anger, and pity must co-exist as mutually qualifying and interacting constituents. The presence of the anger and the physical horror prevents the sacred pity, which seems to be Owen's especial contribution, from neutralizing or shrouding war's enormities. But where the pity tends either to exclude the horror, or to operate in isolation, Owen risks our sense of the horror being dissolved in euphoria or religiosity, through his own incapacity (as I see it) or through others' (sometimes deliberate) misreading. By indulging the "haloesque," readers are released from the horror and the guilt, or, at the least, their awareness of what has been done, and are thus enabled to accept fresh wars whenever it is expedient for their governments to start them.

It seems possible that Owen coped with the dual role of pacifist-killer partly by encompassing the miseries of the German, French, and English soldiers in a universal pity. The Allies' victims are given pity, which in some sense acts as a neutralizer to the excruciating pain he must have felt as their slayer. This

antimony, this situation where the killing seems unavoidable and the pity necessary, perhaps accounts for the tendency of the poems of pity, and those of horror, to exclude each other's constituents. Pity, however, needs anger and physical horror; they are its material source. Conversely, if the anger is not to become a fiery hatred reducing the person to an entirely destructive particle, pity, if for the sacrificed alone, needs to be present. It too, in a qualified and active way, can order and direct the intelligence, and re-direct it towards the victims themselves. (pp. 232-34)

> *Jon Silkin, "Wilfred Owen," in his* Out of Battle: The Poetry of the Great War, *1972. Reprint by Routledge & Kegan Paul, 1987, pp. 197-248.*

PAUL FUSSELL   (essay date 1975)

[*An American educator, historian, and critic, Fussell is most often recognized for his* The Great War and Modern Memory, *a historical work in which he examines "the British experience of the Western Front from 1914 to 1918 and some of the literary means by which it has been remembered." In the following excerpt from that work, Fussell considers the "homoerotic sensuousness" of Owen's poetry, comparing his works to those of Gerard Manley Hopkins and A. E. Housman.*]

It is most conspicuously in the poetry of Wilfred Owen that [the] . . . impulses of Victorian and early-twentieth-century homoeroticism converge, and it is there that they are transfigured and sublimated with little diminution of their emotional warmth. If the boys of Owen's early imagination begin as interesting "lads," ripe for kissing, they end as his "men" in France, types not just of St. Sebastian but of the perpetually sacrificed Christ. The route Owen negotiates leads him from a world something like Baron Corvo's to one resembling that of Hopkins. The tradition of Victorian homoeroticism teaches him how to notice boys; the war, his talent, and his instinct of honor teach him what to make of them. (pp. 286-87)

[Owen's] pre-war psychological state can be estimated from his poem **"Maundy Thursday,"** which registers the tension he is beginning to feel between Establishment theology and homoerotic humanism. The kissing which is the leitmotif of the poem became one of Owen's favorite images:

> Between the brown hands of a server-lad
> The silver cross was offered to be kissed.
> The men came up, lugubrious, but not sad,
> And knelt reluctantly, half-prejudiced.
> (And kissing, kissed the emblem of a creed.)
> The mourning women knelt; meek mouths they had,
> (And kissed the Body of the Christ indeed.)
> Young children came, with eager lips and glad.
> (These kissed a silver doll, immensely bright.)
> Then I, too, knelt before that acolyte.
> Above the crucifix I bent my head:
> The Christ was thin, and cold, and very dead:
> And yet I bowed, yea, kissed—my lips did cling.
> (I kissed the warm live hand that held the thing.)

It would be hard indeed to ignore the ways in which that poem allies itself with the tradition of Symonds, Wilde, Rolfe, Charles Edward Sayle, John Francis Bloxam, and other writers of warm religio-erotic celebrations of boy-saints, choirboys, acolytes, and "server-lads." Hopkins's "The Handsome Heart: At a Gracious Answer" is in the tradition. As early as January, 1916, it was available in Bridges's anthology *The Spirit of*

Man. That Owen knew some of Hopkins seems likely from certain moments in his diction and meter. For example,

> But all limped on, blood-shod. All went lame; all blind
> ("**Dulce et Decorum Est**")

and, from "**Spells and Incantation,**"

>   . . . wrathful rubies
> You rolled. I watched their hot hearts fling
> Flames. . . .

Hopkins's affectionate physical notice of the boy who has helped him in the sacristy is like that at which Owen will become adept:

>   . . . more than handsome face—
> Beauty's bearing or muse of mounting vein,
> All, in this case, bathed in high hallowing grace. . . .

But Owen did not have to wait until 1916. Before he had seen any of the war he had already made his own the sentimental homoerotic theme which his greatest poems of the war would proceed to glorify. (pp. 287-88)

[Owen] had been a strikingly optimistic, cheerful young man, skilled in looking on the bright side and clever at rationalizing minor setbacks. But with his first experience of the trenches in the middle of January, 1917, everything changed. What he encountered at the front was worse than even a poet's imagination could have conceived. From then on, in the less than two years left to him, the emotions that dominated were horror, outrage, and pity: horror at what he saw at the front; outrage at the inability of the civilian world—especially the church—to understand what was going on; pity for the poor, dumb, helpless, good-looking boys victimized by it all. He was in and out of the line half a dozen times during the first four months of 1917, but what finally broke him was an action in late April, when he had to remain in a badly shelled forward position for days looking at the scattered pieces of a fellow officer's body. No one knows exactly how he reacted or what he did, but he was evacuated and his condition was diagnosed as neurasthenia. (p. 289)

Owen's poetic response to the war is unique. Unlike Sassoon, Blunden, and Graves, with their "university" bent toward structured general ideas, Owen, as Bergonzi has noted, "rarely attempts a contrast, nostalgic or ironic, between the trenches and remembered English scenes." Rather, he harnesses his innate fondness for dwelling on the visible sensuous particulars of boys in order to promote an intimate identification with them. His method is largely a de-sexed extension of his kissing "the warm live hand" of the "server-lad." With a most tender intimacy he contemplates—"adores" would perhaps not be too strong a word—physical details like eyes, hair, hands, limbs, sides, brows, faces, teeth, heads, smiles, breasts, fingers, backs, tongues. Loving these things, he arrives by disciplined sublimation at a state of profound pity for those who for such a brief moment possess them. He seems skilled in the deployment of the sympathetic imagination as defined by Keats. He is practiced in the art of throwing himself into another thing. The physical attributes of others, if sufficiently handsome, become like his own.

Whether he acts to identify himself with a homogeneous group of men ("**Insensibility,**" "**Apologia pro Poemate Meo,**" "**Greater Love,**" "**Anthem for Doomed Youth,**" "**The Send Off,**" "**The Last Laugh,**" "**Mental Cases**") or more warmly with one single unfortunate young male ("**Arms and the Boy,**"

"**Dulce et Decorum Est,**" "**Asleep,**" "**Futility,**" "**The Sentry,**" "**Conscious,**" "**A Terre,**" "**Disabled,**" "**The Dead-Beat,**" "**S.I.W.,**" "**Inspection**"), it is the features of the palpable body that set him off. This is noticeable even in so "ideal" a poem as "**Anthem for Doomed Youth,**" where the generalized accessories of funeral services (anthems, prayers, bells, "choirs," candles, and palls) are made to seem supremely irrelevant next to "the hands of boys" and—most tellingly—"their eyes."

Owen's favorite sensuous device is the formula "his——," with the blank usually filled with a part of the body. Thus "**Disabled,**" with its numerous echoes of "To an Athlete Dying Young," a poem in which Housman also has made certain that we see and admire the boy's eyes, ears, foot, head, and curls. Owen's former athlete, both legs and one arm gone, sits in his wheelchair in a hospital convalescent park listening to the shouts of "boys" playing at sunset. He can't help recalling the excitements of former early evenings in town before the war, back then "before he threw away his knees." His attributes, now all changed, move into focus:

> There was an artist silly for his face,
> For it was younger than his youth, last year.
> Now, he is old; his back will never brace;
> He's lost his color very far from here,
> Poured it down shell-holes till the veins ran dry,
> And half his lifetime lapsed in the hot race,
> And leap of purple spurted from his thigh.

(In one draft these lines were preceded by the following, which may remind us of Hopkins's Harry Ploughman. Their autoerotic tendency would seem to assure us that the artist who was silly for this boy's face is not being imagined as female:

> Ah! he was handsome when he used to stand
> Each evening on the curb or by the quays.
> His old soft cap slung half-way down his ear;
> Proud of his neck, scarfed with a sunburn band,
> And of his curl, and all his reckless gear,
> Down to the gloves of sun-brown on his hand.)

As the final draft resumes, it resumes Housman:

> One time he liked a blood-smear down his leg,
> After the matches, carried shoulder-high.

Why, in the midst of such triumphs, did he enlist? Physical vanity:

> Someone had said he'd look a god in kilts,
> That's why; and may be, too, to please his Meg;
> Aye, that was it, to please the giddy jilts
> He asked to join. He didn't have to beg;
> Smiling they wrote his lie; aged nineteen years.

But after his disaster, his return home was not as triumphal as the traditional athlete's. When Housman's athlete returned to his town,

>   Man and boy stood cheering by,

but when Owen's came back,

> Some cheered him home, but not as crowds cheer Goal.

Indeed his main welcomer was one curious not about his face, his youth, his back, or his color, but about a sexless attribute not at all visible:

> Only a solemn man who brought him fruits
> *Thanked* him; and then inquired about his soul.

After quoting C. Day Lewis as saying, "Owen had no pity to spare for the suffering of bereaved women," Bergonzi quite correctly notes, "Male fellowship and self-sacrifice is an absolute value, and Owen celebrates it in a manner that fuses the paternal with the erotic . . . : Owen's attitude to the 'boys' or 'lads' destined for sacrifice has some affinities with Housman's" [see excerpt dated 1965, *TCLC*-5]. And as the verbal echoes of Housman in **"Disabled"** suggest, he derives from Housman more than an attitude. In fact, Owen's early poem on the noble sacrifice of soldiers, **"Ballad of Purchase Moneys,"** suggests that he learned to write by imitating Housman as well as Keats. Here is the last of the ballad's three stanzas:

> Fair days are yet left for the old,
> And children's cheeks are ruddy,
> Because the good lads' limbs lie cold
> And their brave cheeks are bloody.

If the eighth line of **"Anthem for Doomed Youth"** were a foot shorter (by, say, the omission of *for them*), it could be Housman's:

> And bugles calling for them from sad shires;

and the *sad shires* might seem a not entirely unconscious inversion of Housman's joyous *colored counties* in "Bredon Hill." Whatever his verbal borrowings, Owen could have derived from *A Shropshire Lad* a whole set of tender emotions about young soldiers, their braveries, their deaths, their agonies, and even their self-inflicted wounds. (pp. 291-93)

Owen's other poems about individual victims ground themselves likewise in physical attributes. In **"Arms and the Boy"** the final stanza, which explains the outrageous instructions of the first two, does so by making us intimates of *his teeth, his fingers, his heels,* and *his curls.* In **"Dulce et Decorum Est"** it is *his face.* Indeed, until a late stage of revision, the lines,

> If you could hear, at every jolt, the blood
> Come gargling from the froth-corrupted lungs,
> Obscene as cancer, bitter as the cud
> Of vile, incurable sores on innocent tongues,

presented a considerably more attractive picture:

> If you could hear, at every jolt, the blood
> Come gargling from the froth-corrupted lungs,
> And think how, once, his head was like a bud,
> Fresh as a country rose, and keen, and young.

Again, as in **"Disabled,"** the effect of the revision is to efface indications of the poem's original Uranian leanings, to replace the pretty of 1913 with the nasty of 1917. In **"Asleep,"** we are offered his *brow, chest, arms, head,* and *his hair.* In **"Futility,"** his *limbs* and *sides.* In **"Conscious,"** *his fingers, his eyes,* and *his head.* In **"A Terre,"** *hands, fingers, eyes, back, legs,* and *arms' tan.* In **"The Dead-Beat,"** *his feet* and *hand.* The final two lines of **"S.I.W."** tell us how the victim of the self-inflicted wound was buried and how his mother was informed, but not without a lingering on attributes and on kissing:

> With him they buried the muzzle his teeth had kissed,
> And truthfully wrote the Mother, "Tim died smiling."

Another young male smile at the moment of death—this time more painful-ecstatic and hence Swinburnean—is that which concludes **"Has Your Soul Sipped"?** Eight stanzas develop a sequence of lush comparatives of "sweetness" (what could be imagined sweeter than the nightingale's song? the smell of leaves? the martyr's smile?) in order to arrive at an answer. Sweeter than them all, says Owen,

> was that smile,
> Faint as a wan, worn myth,
> Faint and exceeding small
> On a boy's murdered mouth.
> Though from his throat
> The life-tide leaps
> There was no threat
> On his lips.
>
> But with the bitter blood
> And the death-smell
> All his life's sweetness bled
> Into a smile.

And in **"Inspection"** the "dirt" on a man's tunic which the officer-speaker unimaginatively reprehends proves to be *blood, his own.* The *his* naturally becomes *their* in the poems depicting groups of the pitiable. Thus the opening of **"Insensibility"**:

> Happy are men who yet before they are killed
> Can let their veins run cold.
> Whom no compassion fleers
> Or makes their feet
> Sore on the alleys cobbled with their brothers.

(Is *their brothers* an intimate attribute? Owen would insist that it be seen as such—that is his whole point.)

Owen's extraordinary talent for imagined sensuous immediacy can be measured by contrasting the abstractions offered by Herbert Read when, in "Ode Written During the Battle of Dunkirk, May, 1940," he recalls the rhetorical structure ("Happy . . . happy . . . but") of Owen's **"Insensibility"** and ventures to bring it up to date:

> Happy are those who can relieve
> suffering with prayer
> Happy those who can rely on God
> to see them through.
>
> They can wait patiently for the end.
>
> But we who have put our faith
> in the goodness of man
> and now see man's image debas'd
> lower than the wolf or the hog—
>
> Where can we turn for consolation?

Owen's mind goes in the opposite direction, feeling always towards male particulars. To speak of "sufferings" is not enough; one must see and feel the bloody head cradled dead on one's own shoulder. In early October, 1918, he writes his mother to explain why he has had to come to France again: "I came out in order to help these boys—directly by leading them as well as an officer can; indirectly, by watching their sufferings that I may speak of them as well as a pleader can." And then, sensing that "their sufferings" is too abstract to do the job, he indicates what he's really talking about: "Of whose blood lies yet crimson on my shoulder where his head was—and where so lately yours was—I must not now write." But he does write about it to a less shockable audience, Sassoon: "The boy by my side, shot through the head, lay on top of me, soaking my shoulder, for half an hour." *His head. My shoulder.* An improvement over *watching their sufferings.* (pp. 294-96)

Paul Fussell, ''Soldier Boys,'' in his The Great War and Modern Memory, *Oxford University Press, 1975, pp. 270-309.*

DESMOND GRAHAM   (essay date 1984)

[*Graham is an English educator and critic whose works examine the place of war in twentieth-century poetry. In the following excerpt from his study* The Truth of War: Owen, Blunden, Rosenberg, *Graham discusses the experiential nature of Owen's poetry.*]

The context of war, perhaps more extensively and drastically than any other context, transforms language; not only through its own immense array of technical terms, coinages and jargon. It shifts the meaning of the simplest and commonest words, awakens to new and generally vicious life, dead metaphors and clichés and has the ability to disturb and redefine the whole relationship between what is metaphorical and what literal. How far the poet invokes this context is his decision within each poem he writes. Invoking it in every poem he wrote after experience of the trenches, Owen's understanding of its transformation of language is the centre of his art, the reason for its force, its directness of impact and its depth.

Owen's work does not offer the kind of obscurity which requires the intervention of professional explicators. What it does possess is the kind of complexity which we can comprehend emotionally, in a single reading; the kind of subtlety through which our feelings are accustomed to move. (p. 24)

How thoroughly the context of war transforms language, and how thoroughly Owen understood this fact, is revealed by what happens to some lines from Yeats's play *The King's Threshold* when Owen uses them as epigraph to a poem of war. Following the title, **''S.I.W.,''** an official military abbreviation for a ''self-inflicted wound,'' the lines from Yeats carry an obvious connection with the subject of wounding or killing oneself, but we can make little of their tone or point as we first read them:

> I will to the King,
> And offer him consolation in his trouble,
> For that man there has set his teeth to die,
> And being one that hates obedience,
> Discipline, and orderliness of life,
> I cannot mourn him.

We depend upon the ensuing poem for elucidation.

Owen's opening is immediately discordant beside the Yeats; we seem to have descended a long way, towards the commonplace and the casually colloquial:

> Patting goodbye, doubtless they told the lad
> He'd always show the Hun a brave man's face;
> Father would sooner him dead than in disgrace,—
> Was proud to see him going, aye, and glad. . . .

Outside the context of Owen's own work, the lines bring a response which is dependent upon the politics of the reader. The quick, simple rhythms, the clichés of expression and attitude, we could read as an encouragement to register and endorse familiar militaristic myths: only the slowing down and the emphasis brought by the last three words disturbs the harmony, and even these could be accommodated by the most resolutely militaristic. Read from any other ideological position, however, the first line's ''doubtless'' hints at irony, the clichés of the next two lines seem ironically exposed and the final three words reveal the viciousness truly behind the father's

attitude. What Owen's poem will do, in the twenty-four lines which comprise its ''Prologue,'' is ensure that we comprehend the ironic reading, by bringing us evidence of the real world in which militarism's clichés are lived through:

> . . . once an hour a bullet missed its aim.
> And misses teased the hunger of his brain.
> His eyes grew old with wincing, and his hand
> Reckless with ague. Courage leaked, as sand
> From the best sandbags after years of rain.
> But never leave, wound, fever, trench-foot, shock,
> Untrapped the wretch. And death seemed still withheld.

The evidence is extensive, bringing us not only the one man's experience but a wider view of trench life. The metaphor of courage leaking as sand from sandbags ''after years of rain'' directs us, if we are capable of taking the lead, to the larger time-scale of the war; and the varieties of suffering in the trenches, all presented as positives to be welcomed for the release they bring, are made clear: lack of leave, ''wound, fever, trench-foot, shock.''

From what we can now see as the satirical portrait of the poem's opening lines, through to the evidence of the lines just quoted, Owen's tone has been increasingly tinged with anger but it has remained impersonal. It remains so in the second section of the poem, ''The Action,'' though now his voice has become that of the active participant:

> One dawn, our wire patrol
> Carried him. This time, Death had not missed.
> We could do nothing but wipe his bleeding cough.
> Could it be accident?—Rifles go off . . .
> Not sniped? No. (Later they found the English ball.)

Even the personification ''Death'' is not out of place in this soldier's story: it takes up a cliché which had been quoted in a previous line: ''Death sooner than dishonour, that's the style!' / So Father said.''

At this point Owen introduces his third section with the surprising heading, ''The Poem.'' His heading, and there is evidence that he did not choose it casually, encourages us to look closely at the lines which follow, as they may help us towards an understanding of what he thinks of as a poem:

> It was the reasoned crisis of his soul
> Against more days of inescapable thrall,
> Against infrangibly wired and blind trench wall
> Curtained with fire, roofed in with creeping fire,
> Slow grazing fire, that would not burn him whole
> But kept him for death's promises and scoff,
> And life's half-promising, and both their riling.

The whole texture of his verse has changed: insistent aural and rhythmical patterns are developed, metaphor is extended and repetitions of syntax and phrase make rhetorical figures. His object is no longer to satirize or to report, but to dramatize for us the man's feelings so that we can imaginatively understand what he underwent. We could remain detached and observant in the first two sections, accumulating evidence and registering its points to understand as we understand a case. Here we must understand through our aroused feelings.

Yet at this very point where Owen has heightened his style, he has done so through language which is uniquely connected with the trench world. He deploys his pattern of repeated syntax and the pattern of rhyme, to draw us from the archaic word ''thrall,'' to the literal and technical term, ''blind trench wall'' (a *blind trench*: one with no outlet). The following metaphor grows from a pun on the military term *fire,* and is built upon two more technical terms: "Curtained with fire": a *curtain of fire* was a bombardment put down to cover troop movements or an attack; "roofed in with creeping fire": a *creeping barrage* was a barrage which advanced a specific distance at a specific time. We must enter the terms with which the trench soldier lived, in order to understand his experience.

Because of the military context the third part of the extending metaphor, "slow grazing fire," becomes a pun: its meaning first literal, the fire only *grazes* the skin, then metaphorical, bringing an exact description of the fire which neared and receded, stayed in the area at its own purpose and with its own undecipherable course, "grazed" there. To understand this metaphor we leave behind, either through suppression or through a momentary awareness and rejection, the pastoral source, the kind of grazing, on which it is based. So Owen has led us to give priority to literal meanings and to be aware of how thoroughly pacific associations are out of place. To end his "Poem," Owen leads us, our minds now alerted to punning, through a whole play upon the word "promise" which defines how its meaning is reduced and parodied in the world of war. All its potential affirmation lost, the word "promise" is left to express the doom of the man's situation and its torment as death teases him by postponing its desired arrival and life mocks him with its equivocation.

Two lines comprising "The Epilogue" conclude the poem. Schooled to see through cliché, to respond to the pun and to see literal meanings within metaphor, we have been brought by the language of the poem to comprehend immediately the multiple ironies of these concluding lines. "With him they buried the muzzle his teeth had kissed, / And truthfully wrote the Mother, 'Tim died smiling'."

To return to the epigraph from this, is to find Yeats's lines transformed by the context of war within which Owen has placed them:

> I will to the King,
> And offer him consolation in his trouble,
> For that man there has set his teeth to die,
> And being one that hates obedience,
> Discipline, and orderliness of life,
> I cannot mourn him.

The tough stance of the metaphor, "set his teeth to die" is confronted with grotesque, literal fact. The definition of why the man cannot be mourned comes to us as inhuman self-regard, a dedication to the authoritative voice of principle which shuts out sensitivity and enjoys the callous conviction of a moral posture. The abstract principles themselves, obedience, discipline, orderliness, are mocked and redefined as we hear within them the contrasting views of actual military authority and actual soldiers. The misdirection of pity towards the ruler is absurdly dutiful; the directive, "that man there," coldly, perhaps brutally impersonal.

Within this overall shift of emphasis and response, each detail of language is transformed by war's context. First, the war invites a specific historical context—I will to the King (George V) to console him (for this soldier's death)! Second, it creates a new, relative gauge for suffering: how trivial is the king's "trouble," whatever it may be, beside the soldier's experience. Third, it makes the directive, "that man there," an insensitive *officerly* command. Fourth, it transforms the abstract values, obedience, discipline, orderliness, into items within an au-

thoritarian and specifically military code. In thus transforming language, the context of war has exposed a new politics and a new morality, each set against what is abstract, official and authoritarian, each derived from the evidence of how the individual actually lives through what authority assumes and creates. This is the politics of Owen's work.

The purpose of my discussion of Yeats's lines was not, of course, to criticize Yeats—Owen took the lines out of context and I did so, too; it was to show the extent to which awareness of the war's context changes language, and to show the extent to which Owen understood this. There *is* a literary critique potentially within his transformation of Yeats's words, as there is one directly in the assertion in one of his letters from the Front, that but for the experience of the trenches at Beaumont Hamel he, like Tennyson in the poem "Crossing the Bar," would have been a great child; and it is a critique enforced through his later comment in another letter: "every word, every figure of speech must be a matter of experience"—the full associations and physical weight of the experience behind the words should be known and understood. But Owen's own creative understanding was too naturally in touch with the literary tradition he inherited, to see a simple repudiation of it as possible or worthwhile.

Owen's relationship with literary tradition—reworking and mixing styles, facing the grand aspirations and abstractions and harmonizing cadences of romantic language with other, more down-to-earth voices—is vividly presented within the monologue of the officer of his poem **"A Terre."** This man, blind, both his legs amputated, and near to dying, heightens his speech for the benefit of his audience—a poet, visiting him in hospital. The occupation of his visitor encourages him towards grandiloquence, philosophizing and arresting speech, both because the company of a poet brings this out, and because, with the skill of the truly desperate, he sustains the kind of talk which will keep his visitor at his bedside. I quote only the middle of the monologue, an extraordinary amalgam of pretention, crass self-pity, despair and truth:

> O Life, Life, let me breathe,—a dug-out rat!
> Not worse than ours the lives rats lead—
> Nosing along at night down some safe rut,
> They find a shell-proof home before they rot.
> Dead men may envy living mites in cheese,
> Or good germs even. Microbes have their joys,
> And subdivide, and never come to death.
> Certainly flowers have the easiest time on earth.
> "I shall be one with nature, herb, and stone,"
> Shelley would tell me. Shelley would be stunned:
> The dullest Tommy hugs that fancy now.
> "Pushing up daisies" is their creed, you know.

The speaker at times latches on to vivid expression (the rats, "Nosing along at night down some safe rut"). He makes truly provocative thought out of a reductive cliché of expression ("Certainly flowers have the easiest time on earth"). His opening words ("O Life, Life") take a romantic apostrophe and make it the half self-parodying cry of a man literally calling for life as he is near death, whose desire for breath ("let me breathe") is a desire for freedom, a cry against the claustrophobic tension of fear, and the literal demand for breath, of a man who has only one lung. His use of the word "stunned" has some strange and terrible ironic force, playing the colloquial, slang expression (Shelley would be shocked) against the impact of war on the imagination (stunned into silence) and the dark humour which alludes to the physically stunning impact of a bombardment. It is a kind of black joke against Shelley's innocence, a joke which is then enforced through the transformation of Shelley's high aspirations into trench soldier's slang, "pushing up daisies."

The terrible and down-to-earth knowledge of the soldier is a running commentary on the kinds of language which could previously be acceptable or harmless, and this certainly extends to the resonance and cadence of romantic poetry. But in his reference to Shelley here, Owen is quite literally "not concerned with poetry." What matters is the expression of this man's state and the knowledge of war he has to give us, what the subtitle of this poem refers to as "the philosophy of many soldiers." The style's exchange between contrasting ways of thinking and talking brings us the process of mind to which a man has been driven in the desperate attempt to keep from himself the knowledge that he is dying.

For Owen as poet, however, the absolute conflict in expression between the line quoted from Shelley's "Adonais" and the slang euphemism created by the trench soldiers, is pressingly relevant. The one was part of the language he had inherited from his reading, where he found expressed and endorsed the sensibility which turned him to poetry; the other was part of what he had heard around him at the Front, and expressed the knowledge of the men whose experience he had shared, and now wished to communicate in his poetry. It was a bold and essential ambition he voiced when, in a letter written after most of his war poems, he affirmed: "I don't want to write anything to which a soldier would say *No Compris!*": but given the place of poetry within the experience of most of the soldiers, and granted what he himself had to say as poet, this desire lived more as a passionate corrective than as a guiding principle. The force of his own experience, the particular kinds of articulacy which his reading and background had brought him, the extent and nature of his insights, led him to employ means of expression encompassing far more than reductive slang. In any case, his audience, the readers of poetry, not having experienced the trenches, could not possibly know what the soldier actually meant by such expressions as "pushing up daisies": a fact Owen directly brings home in the poem he drew from another cliché of the war, **"Smile, Smile, Smile."** (pp. 25-31)

[Poetry], as it was popularly understood and applauded at that time, was steeped in the political cant and illusions which helped to make and sustain war. This was not only a matter of the directly patriotic or military poetry in vogue before and during the war. The slackness and falsity of language which drove Ezra Pound to demand the purification of the language of the tribe, was regarded by most readers as an essential of what they considered to be poetry. It was not difficult for Owen to extend his poem **"Dulce et Decorum Est,"** originally written as an address "To a Certain Poetess," into an attack on the whole lie of heroic cant. The reassuring or uplifting rhythms, the manly violence or prejudice, the complacent pastoral dreams and resonant commonplaces, the whole sense that poetry was both nobler than real life and less real than life; were all expressions of political ideology. To work in a medium where readers sought and presumed they would find these, was to work at a source closely in touch with the sustaining mythologies of a society which brought about war.

Owen's essential effort in this, was to bring abstraction and metaphor back into contact with their sources in men's sensations and feelings, to use them in a way which was responsible to the world in which people live and act. Similarly, he strove to restore rhythms and forms to being functional and expressive, training them away from their tendency to affirm harmony and to suggest resolution. This narrowing of the gap between art and life depended for its honesty and its value upon a recognition that such a gap remained; a gap which Owen took pains to make clear and often made explicit in his poems. When he observed to Sassoon that his collection of poems, *Counter-Attack,* "frightened me much more than the real one," his contrast between the impact of the poetry and that of the actual battle was not a marvelling at the power of art, but a measuring, with residual dismay, of the depth of insensitivity to which taking part in battle had brought him.

The awareness of lies to answer, misunderstandings to correct, ignorance to supply with knowledge, gave fuel to Owen's creative energies. In support of his activities he had one further and inestimable encouragement: the conviction that what he wrote about was not the invention of his own imagination but communal and verifiable experience. To convey exactly one response of terror or confusion or betrayal would not be to convey an imaginative vision of his own making, but truths he knew to be shared truths. In the trenches, what he wrote about was common knowledge: at home, it was ignored or unreachable. From this, the extraordinary, confident, public directness of his work arose; from his knowledge that he could assume nothing in his audience except, at best, goodwill, he was driven to make an art which could so self-containedly speak for itself that it is able to speak across historical distance to us, with equal directness.

But it is an art which grows out of a specific manifestation of man's violence, the Great War, and is directed by awareness of a particular audience. For this reason care is needed to receive the precise terms of the messages he gives within his immediately accessible directness. One of those messages, and one which is both generally overlooked and essential to our understanding, concerns the darker side of the soldiers' knowledge that only those who were there, could understand.

Why the soldier believed no one outside could understand what he experienced at the Front was simple. When he first arrived at the Front, despite the hints or suggestions given to him through others who had been there, the soldier found misery and suffering more extensive and more extreme than he could possibly have imagined: the horror of what he saw there was simply inconceivable to him. The lies he read in the papers and heard in speeches, the misunderstanding, complacency, wilful lies or innocence he encountered if he was fortunate enough to have leave, gave him something on which he could focus his anger and bewilderment and bitterness; but it was the gap between what, with the best intentions and most sympathetic imagination, could be conceived from outside and the facts of what he saw, that convinced the soldier no one could understand. He himself would not have understood, if he had not seen for himself. Owen turned the despair of this realization into the active effort of trying to carry outside the trench-world as much of its knowledge as he could. Those who would read his work, however, must not be led into believing that they were facing the full truth of the experience or into resting on the belief that they understood. The poetry, however close it may bring them, through imaginative understanding, must also communicate the fact that such understanding was incomplete.

Twice Owen directly presents this realization in his poems, making explicit what elsewhere is implicit. On each occasion, his awareness of the impossibility of communication emerges from an attempt to hold within the poem some positive found on the battlefield. **"Greater Love"** partly expressing the grotesque and brutal form in which soldiers undergo the greater love of dying for others, also draws from Owen's mind a desire to hold true to the real comradely love he had seen and felt at the Front. Caught between these opposed and equally genuine impulses—to find a true expression for the new love and to expose, beyond redemption, the lie of patriotic cant—Owen turns to their one sure, common ground: the reader's inability to understand either. His tone takes on the assurance of exclusion, his point finally focusing the total physical and emotional distance in a pun on the word "touch": "Weep, you may weep, for you may touch them not."

In the second of the poems, **"Apologia pro Poemate Meo,"** he writes with a far stronger protection of irony, but again his awareness of positives which could never be truly understood leads him to rejection of the audience. This time by a direct insult. For seven stanzas he has tried to define the values which are found on the battlefield (exultation, beauty, merriment, fellowship, glory, joy and relief) trying to show how they are at once parodies of those forms as known outside the battlefield, and yet not totally perverse. Despite his ironies and the often brutal evidence he gives for the forms these values take, his awareness of how each of the terms could be absorbed back into cant and his awareness of the impossibility of anyone outside understanding the preciousness of such extraordinary survivals of humanity in a world which is totally inhumane, finally break out:

> Nevertheless, except you share
>   With them in hell the sorrowful dark of hell,
>   Whose world is but the trembling of a flare
>   And heaven but as the highway for a shell,
>
> You shall not hear their mirth. . .

The one criterion is a sharing of the soldier's experience. But with these lines alone, the reader could resist the implied exclusion by hopefully taking Owen to mean, not a literal sharing but an imaginative one. So that no mistake can be made, in his final lines, Owen seals the soldiers' experience back into its privacy by insulting his audience: "You shall not come to think them well content/By any jest of mine. These men are worth/Your tears. You are not worth their merriment." . . . The understanding of war which Owen employs his art to bring us, must be earned as we read, and as we read we are led towards its limits. These limits we must face in the unresolved ambiguities, the unanswered questions, the gestures and the facial expressions which Owen will not interpret for us. His most direct expression of the gap between the soldier's experience and the reader's understanding comes when he desires to affirm. But it is a gap to which he directs us no less explicitly when his desire is to record the darkest side of the soldier's knowledge, his guilt. We will find it in the survivors of **"Spring Offensive,"** and in those of **"Smile, Smile, Smile,"** who read of war in the *Daily Mail*: "The half-limbed readers did not chafe / But smiled at one another curiously/Like secret men who know their secret safe." (pp. 32-6)

Owen uses the language of war, not as a single area to be enforced, but as a shifting gauge, measuring the force of metaphor, the truth of cliché and idiom, testing the power of the poem to take form and pattern and enter the pleasing sphere of art. In his language it is the interplay between the different levels which he exploits, a layering and mixing of styles which brings about a directing of the reader's responses. What matters most in his art is the relationship between the artefact he makes and its source experience—direct experience of the Front. (p. 40)

Owen's exact measurement of the distance between the particular poem and the battlefield itself defines the nature of the experience he wishes the poem to convey to us about war. This experience may demand vivid immediacy of portrayal, sustained allusion to the literal facts, or a designed remoteness. Generally it will move between these things to bring us as readers towards something which we, as outsiders, cannot fully understand. **"Strange Meeting,"** so often discussed, and a cause of worry to many admirers of Owen, reveals most dramatically this shifting of distances. In the context of our discussion, the poem can be seen, not so much as a consistent ode, as a poem in parts, like **"S.I.W.,"** setting different spheres of experience in a single context to test their validity and significance by exposing them to each other.

From the first line, Owen portrays a removal from the battlefield, offering a prologue which finely fuses the worlds of dream landscape and Western Front, until the narrator, bewildered, realizes he is at a *safe* distance, and with the wisdom of the Front as shown in **"Asleep,"** finds no cause to mourn at being dead: death is an escape from torment. After this, the prologue, we have an answer to that reductive philosophy, as his envying of the peace of death is faced with the losses death has caused. For twenty-five lines this gives us "the poem": an elaborate account of ambition, largely "poetic" ambition, strengthened by its equation with the quest of the poet of war. Yet in these twenty-five lines we encounter a style not found anywhere else in Owen's war poetry. First the romantic terms which had been savagely transposed by Owen in **"Greater Love,"** are endorsed without ambivalence of attitude: "I went hunting wild/After the wildest beauty in the world,/Which lies not calm in eyes, or braided hair. . .". Then warfare is his subject: but it is mythological, literary warfare, calculatedly distanced from salients, barrages, entanglements and guns.

> Now men will go content with what we spoiled,
> Or, discontent, boil bloody, and be spilled.
> They will be swift with swiftness of the tigress.
> None will break ranks, though nations trek from progress.
> Courage was mine, and I had mystery,
> Wisdom was mine, and I had mastery:
> To miss the march of this retreating world
> Into vain citadels that are not walled.
> Then, when much blood had clogged their chariot-wheels,
> I would go up and wash them from sweet wells,
> Even with truths that lie too deep for taint.

Within the prophecy, there is reference to the way blood pours from the dying ("boil bloody, and be spilled"), numerous contemporary military terms are used—"break ranks," "the march," "retreating"—and a second reference is made to blood: but each of these elements is absorbed into a remote, literary context. The immediate knowledge of war is left far back, and no reader, certainly not the experienced soldier from the Front, would take up from such terms as they are used here, a comparison with the battlefields or the military life of the trenches.

In three lines Owen makes a transition at this point, turning the metaphor of pouring out one's spirit on to the literal fact of bleeding, through the use of the word "wounds." "I would have poured my spirit without stint/But not through wounds; not on the cess of war./ Foreheads of men have bled where no wounds were." The whole contemporary mythology of the soldier's sacrificial regeneration of his country by bleeding for it is invoked and dismissed: but we are led, through the repugnance which will not have anything to do with "the cess of war," to the image of Christ and a mental agony. That these lines have been a transition is only clear from what follows them. Despite their heightening of the previous emotions towards a physical disgust, and despite their reference to wounds, they retain the formal, literary indirect style of the meditation.

Without introduction, the whole tenor of the address changes. In what follows, "the epilogue," the immediate and the colloquial have taken over, and introduce the actuality of war more directly than anywhere else in Owen's work. The oxymoron of the first sentence ("enemy . . . friend") gives the moral point of a fact. The biblical overtone and echoing of *King Lear* in "I knew you in this dark" contribute their resonances within a literal recognition, defined through seeing again a facial expression.

> "I am the enemy you killed, my friend.
> I knew you in this dark: for so you frowned
> Yesterday through me as you jabbed and killed.
> I parried; but my hands were loath and cold.
> Let us sleep now. . . ."

The whole elaborate artifice of the meditation about ambition is severely and irreconcilably placed, its lost hopes and endeavours left far behind, remote echoes of some other world. What it has told us of youthful hopes and ambitions, however, focuses upon the word "enemy." "I," a man much like yourself, am the one you killed as "the enemy." The long monologue has therefore been turned into evidence against the central concept of militarism, that of the enemy. From that point, it is the depiction of killing which holds us. Much has rightly been made of the ambiguities of the last line, but none of its meanings offers consolation beside what Owen has shown us. Whether it is the dream-tossed sleep of the damned, the annihilation of the laid ghost, or a plea to be left in peace, what resonates through the phrase is not its ambiguity but its generous and hopeless conclusion to the exposure of what the poet, as fighting soldier, has done. It is the frown, the frankness of "jabbed," the half-hearted parry and the explanation, "my hands were loath and cold," which stay with us.

For us to call this the pity of war is to put the truth at hazard by couching it in a term which is easily sentimentalized. This is the pity of war, as could be conveyed in the expression "the pity of it," but the immediacy and vividness of Owen's final lines bring us to feel appalled rather than pitying. All the distance from which we heard the first person narrative of thwarted ambition has closed, as we are being made to understand. Humane reserve at murder has been reduced to a frown of anxiety as one kills: it leads, in the trap within which these men have been placed by their society, to being killed because one's hands are loath to strike. Yet the power of war's environment is even greater than this: it saps vitality to the point where not even survival matters—the hands were too cold to move swiftly; it demands a committed involvement so that the soldier frowns with concentration as he kills. (pp. 42-5)

Using all the force of his art to intervene between the experience of the soldiers and our ignorance, Owen's concentration is upon the soldier's feelings, and his persuasiveness comes in our imaginative understanding that we comprehend the difference between what the soldier undergoes in his world, and feelings with which we, as civilians out of war, are familiar. Weariness, pain, desolation, fear and horror, for example, all of us can

potentially understand, building from what is generally a limited acquaintance with such things a recognition of their more extreme and intense forms at the Front. There is the danger, however, that we will diminish the scale of those feelings by reducing them to proportions which we can comprehend from our first-hand knowledge; and there is the danger that finding such feelings brought to us through poetry, we will soften them into too easy and self-contained a sympathy.

Working on and through our feelings, Owen takes pains to school them, leading them, as at the end of **"Exposure"** and **"Strange Meeting,"** away from quiescent pity; or leading them, as in **"À Terre"** and **"S.I.W.,"** away from a sympathy which would like to find something attractive in those who are victims. The ruthlessness of the art to which this understanding leads Owen is nowhere more apparent than in **"The Last Laugh"**—a poem which, perhaps for that very ruthlessness, has aroused little comment from Owen's numerous interpreters.

The poem starts, as each of its stanzas will start, with the direct quotation of soldiers' words; in each case, their dying words. Beside this authentic evidence Owen uses the two devices he normally employed to help us towards the feelings of those in the trenches—personification and pathetic fallacy—to make a wholly artificial and consciously wrought poetry, brilliantly impressive in its transformation of the battlefield into art, and giving our emotions nothing. Owen helps us enter his poem by making his first quoted expression one of amazed horror: this we can reach, though it is at once reduced by the frankest banality. The second and third examples of dying words expose a nakedness of feeling which is so distressingly authentic and crass that it is almost impossible to find a voice for the words, when read aloud. All authority of speech has been taken from man, and transferred to the objects of war.

> "O! Jesus Christ! I'm hit," he said; and died.
> Whether he vainly cursed or prayed indeed,
>   The Bullets chirped—In vain! vain! vain!
>   Machine-guns chuckled—Tut-tut! Tut-tut!
>   And the Big Gun guffawed.
>
> Another sighed—"O Mother,—Mother,—Dad!"
> Then smiled at nothing, childlike, being dead.
>   And the lofty Shrapnel-cloud
>   Leisurely gestured,—Fool!
>   And the splinters spat, and tittered.
>
> "My Love!" one moaned. Love-languid seemed his mood,
> Till slowly lowered, his whole face kissed the mud.
>   And the Bayonets' long teeth grinned;
>   Rabbles of Shells hooted and groaned;
>   And the Gas hissed.
>
>   **"The Last Laugh"**

The audience of bullets, guns, splinters, bayonets and gas is blessed with the superior confidence of derision and a capacity for expressiveness which the poet's own art enforces. The sureness with which Owen evokes the sounds and sights of the battlefield, his hold on physical perceptions, enforces a mockery of all feelings. Here is the pity of war. A world in which emotion is ridiculed and made small; to which even our most deep-felt sensibilities cannot reach. It is the gap between our tender compassion and the reality of war which reveals the nature of its assault upon humanity. (pp. 65-7)

[Owen] brings us no single truth of war but the complex truths of our sensations and emotions. He brings us the physical facts of death, mutilation and pain, the effects on the mind which extend from madness through to protective insensibility. Through these he explores the meaning of the experience, and in them he finds that meaning. The cant, the myths and lies, the military and economic reckoning, the exploitation of religion and of all assumptions of value or honour are tested by the men's experience. In the end their experience remains secret: a secret even our compassion cannot claim fully to enter. A secret from which we must be excluded, not by silence or unwillingness to communicate; the whole effort of Owen's poems actively works against such despair: but by reminding us that we do not understand, because if we believe that we do, then any chance of understanding will be lost. (p. 77)

> Desmond Graham, in his The Truth of War: Owen, Blunden, Rosenberg, *Carcanet Press, 1984, 168 p.*

RICHARD HOFFPAUIR (essay date 1985)

[*In the following excerpt, Hoffpauir offers a negative assessment of Owen's poetry, finding "the diadactic demands of his poetic situations are rarely met by his poems."*]

It is difficult if not foolish to treat a poem as an isolated aesthetic object; this is even more intensely true of poems of and about war. While narrative, dramatic, and sometimes lyric structures may be foremost, war poetry by its very nature cannot, and most often cares not to, avoid being finally and essentially didactic. Realistic exposure and emotional intensity by themselves cannot satisfy the immense seriousness of a war poet's subject; sincerity can only be authorized by judicious commitment. Wilfred Owen, still considered by most critics the best of the English poets of the Great War (despite the recently growing reputation of Isaac Rosenberg), was acutely aware of his responsibilities: "All a poet can do to-day is warn." But if a poet expects his warnings to be heeded he must put his necessary verbal mastery to the service of the widest, sharpest, and most rational moral perspective possible. This is what Owen was for the most part unable to do: the didactic demands of his poetic situations are rarely met by his poems. . . . I refuse (I hope not too cold-heartedly) to be influenced by the fact of his premature death, by speculation over what might have been, by biographical considerations other than the conclusive one of the almost inevitable immaturity of his verse.

We should begin with two contextual reminders: Owen was a soldier-poet in the post-Somme phase of the war and he was closely associated with and influenced by Siegfried Sassoon. Like the other overtly protesting poets, and unlike for instance Rupert Brooke and Julian Grenfell, Owen and Sassoon lived through the disillusionments of 1916 and into the consequences of what became obviously by 1917 a war of attrition. But while we can understand why the broad, usually personal, Romantic glorifications of battle should give way to narrow, more impersonal, realistic exposures of the horrors of war, and why the mood should more often be anger than enthusiasm and the mode more often pathos than celebration, we can still require adequate moral perspectives. As frustration, weariness, and desperation increased, however, the poets usually sought blunt rhetorical weapons that finally kept their poetry from reaching a didactic plane higher than an immediately satisfying and emotional propaganda. What must be remembered is that despite much realistic description in his verse, Owen, like Sassoon, was not himself a realist, but rather a disheartened idealist. . . . Since Sassoon's avowed purpose as a war poet was not just to convey the suffering of soldiers but also to shame those at home, to attack the apathy and complacency that to some extent allowed the war to continue, his weapons were direct and sometimes brutal description, irony, and satire. Although Sassoon was an older and more experienced poet than Owen, whom he met in August 1917, and although Owen was for a while almost Sassoon's disciple, Owen's most accomplished verse is slightly broader and more complete in its moral treatment of the war, but only slightly. But if the emotional response is less strident, it is also more aesthetically indulged. Even though there is more to the emotion, as Owen tempered his anger with compassion, it is still as unrefined as Sassoon's. And there is little advance in intellectual complexity.

There is no doubting Sassoon's influence: there is the same colloquial directness, caustic irony, and easy indignation directed at insensitive and complacent staff officers and civilians (**"Inspection"** and **"Smile, Smile, Smile"**). **"The Dead-Beat,"** written consciously in Sassoon's style and very like Sassoon's " 'They,' " instances a similar debasing of moral language, but in a context that does not fully enough realize the poet's own reaction to the debasement. All we get is a final line that is embarrassingly crude and awkward. A soldier has a mental breakdown during a strafe:

>   A low voice said,
> "It's Blighty, p'raps, he sees; his pluck's all gone,
> Dreaming of all the valiant, that *aren't* dead:
> Bold uncles, smiling ministerially;
> Maybe his brave young wife, getting her fun
> In some new home, improved materially.
> It's not these stiffs have crazed him; nor the Hun."

He is sent to the field hospital, unwounded, and suspected of malingering. The poem closes with "Next day I heard the Doc's well-whiskied laugh:/'That scum you sent last night soon died. Hooray!'" What C. H. Sisson says of this poem [in *English Poetry 1900-1950: An Assessment* (1971)] applies to many of Owen's (as well as Sassoon's) explicit protest poems: "It is the voice of protest, but protesting against an attitude no adequate mind would defend."

On at least two memorable occasions Owen is able to broaden a Sassoon-like protest with the addition of a quiet poignancy. In **"The Send-Off"** the statement is obvious, but expressed with delicacy, due partly to the somewhat halting rhythm of alternating pentameter and dimeter lines and to a seamless structural movement from a detached description of soldiers boarding a train on their way to France to concerned speculation about the future of those soldiers. The third and fourth stanzas (curiously) prepare for the transition to a more personal voice by retreating momentarily through the view of the porters and a tramp to the animated but completely unemotional signals and lamp: "Dull porters watched them, and a casual tramp/ Stood staring hard,/ Sorry to miss them from the upland camp./ Then, unmoved, signals nodded, and a lamp/ Winked to the guard." So when comment comes in the next line it is tentative and cautious, moving to an assured, but subtle, and effective close, so unlike Sassoon:

> So secretly, like wrongs hushed-up, they went.
> They were not ours:
> We never heard to which front these were sent.
>
> Nor there if they yet mock what women meant
> Who gave them flowers.
>
> Shall they return to beatings of great bells
> In wild train-loads?
> A few, a few, too few for drums and yells,

May creep back, silent, to village wells
Up half-known roads.

The thought of the second stanza here is perhaps too easy (see Sassoon's "Glory of Women"), but this is a minor blemish on a finely poised poem. In **"S.I.W."** the situation is slightly more complex, and the expression more intense and (perhaps therefore) more uneven. An early reference to "disgrace" is undeveloped by a stereotyped context:

Patting good-bye, doubtless they told the lad
He'd always show the Hun a brave man's face;
Father would sooner him dead than in disgrace,—
Was proud to see him going, aye, and glad.
Perhaps his mother whimpered; how she'd fret
Until he got a nice safe wound to nurse.

The narrative of the poem does, however, finally deal ironically but still not adequately with the reference: the boy would rather commit suicide than give himself "a blighty one": "He'd seen men shoot their hands, on night patrol. / Their people never knew. Yet they were vile. / 'Death sooner than dishonour, that's the style!' / So Father said." That last line is a fine qualification, but isn't enough to prevent the poem from dismissing the idea of the previous line rather than the misapplication of it. And Owen can't resist a Sassoon-like close: "With him they buried the muzzle his teeth had kissed, / And truthfully wrote the Mother, 'Tim died smiling.'" But at least Owen in that section somewhat pretentiously called "The Poem" investigates the motive for the suicide (as Sassoon in "Suicide in the Trenches" does not). The blame is not grandly and sweepingly left at "this world's Powers who'd run amok"; there was in addition and more immediately "the reasoned crisis of his soul / Against more days of inescapable thrall," and against the "slow grazing fire, that would not burn him whole / But kept him for death's promises and scoff."

In those poems that distinguish Owen from Sassoon, there is, of course, the famous pity, which D. S. R. Welland attributes to an emotional, Romantic vision of "the tragic beauty of human suffering," and Paul Fussell to a "de-sexed extension" of his earlier homoerotic tendencies, and which led Jon Silkin to claim [in his Introduction to *The Penguin Book of First World War Poetry* (1979)] that "Owen must appear as one of the most authentic voices of compassion in English poetry." But, as these characterizations indicate, the pity is too often an end in itself, isolated from larger, less personal, social commitments. That is, there is a tendency rarely absent in even Owen's later poetry to concentrate too exclusively on the emotion. The tendency is evident, for instance, in the very early pre-war poem **"To Eros,"** and persists even into one of his most admired war poems, **"Greater Love,"** cited by Welland as a clear indication of his rapid maturation at the Front. **"To Eros"** is a protest against idealized love, and while one thinks immediately of the tradition of anti-Petrarchanism in the later Elizabethan period, Owen's sonnet has more to do with the disillusionment of a Byron than with the moral strictness of a Fulke Greville. The octave describes the intensity of his past dedication to the idea of love ("I sacrificed/ All of most worth") and includes an amusing and perhaps ironic simile: "Fair fame I cast away as bridegrooms do/ Their wedding garments in their haste of joy." The joy of a bridegroom may, of course, yield progeny, not the least important of the memorials one can hope to have. We get in the sestet the expected correction but unsubstantiated by an alternative: a laughing Eros pushes away the worshipping poet and retreats; without hope, the poet "starkly" returns "To stare upon the ash of all I burned."

The poem rests on the rejection, on the emotion of disillusionment. The self-pitying is perhaps kept in abeyance by the slight note of modest humor, but the judiciousness is still incomplete.

"Greater Love" also alludes to literary love conventions, but there is a more defined alternative. In a letter of May 1917, Owen writes, "Christ is literally in no man's land. There men often hear his voice: Greater love hath no man than this, that a man lay down his life—for a friend." Owen's poem specifies the compassion: the love of conventional love poetry is measured against the love of soldiers for each other. The poem is a simple list: red lips are not so red as "the stained stones kissed by the English dead," the kindness of heterosexual lovers "seems shame" next to the "pure" love of fellow soldiers, and so on. The list, however, is arbitrary (lips, kindness, eyes, attitude, voice, heart, and hand) and the statement tautological. Owen wants to shock his reader by contrasting the artificial and sentimental with the real and horrific. And that limited intention forces awkwardnesses, such as the crude self-conscious rhyming of the second stanza:

Your slender attitude
Trembles not exquisite like limbs knife-skewed,
Rolling and rolling there
Where God seems not to care;
Till the fierce Love they bear
Cramps them in death's extreme decrepitude.

(The fourth line of this stanza, incidentally, is gratuitous.) The theme of love has, indeed, widened to include pity, but the poet is still concentrating with rather forced intensity on the emotional response.

Just how limited this advance is can be realized if we compare **"Greater Love"** with a much less known poem by the much less famous Ivor Gurney. Here is the first and last stanza of "To His Love":

He's gone, and all our plans
Are useless indeed.
We'll walk no more on Cotswold
Where the sheep feed
Quietly and take no heed.

Cover him, cover him soon!
And with thick-set
Masses of memoried flowers—
Hide that red wet
Thing I must somehow forget.

While Gurney's lines are metrically less accomplished than Owen's, his less emphatic and obtrusive rhymes . . . combine with the numerous trochaic openings to keep the tone reserved *and* forceful. This more elegiac tone is appropriate to the wider consideration of the topic of death and sacrifice in war. Gurney is perhaps more securely universal by referring more concretely to a representative single "he" than is Owen, who is content with a generalized "they." Owen sets real horrors against artificial conventions; Gurney sets war's consequences in a context of past plans and future adjustments. (pp. 41-6)

The central problem for most of the later, protesting war poets was how to give significance to the experiential details they knew they had to present as vividly as possible, how to do more than what responsible war correspondents and journalists (had there been any free of censorship) would have done. Owen, like the rest, was consciously and avidly a propagandist. But as I have said, effective warnings must be more than emotionally charged details. Owen could distance himself from the recorded experiences and even from the initial outrage and loathing, but not from emotion itself. So when he structures a poem as a rational argument, when he tries to be less personal and more political, as in **"Dulce et Decorum Est,"** he falters. Silkin says, contrasting Owen with Sassoon, that "Owen doesn't allow his censoriousness or didactic impulse to dominate his sensuous life." In this instance he perhaps should have. There is no denying the skill with which Owen describes the man dying of gas poisoning in the first sixteen lines of the poem. But while the details continue in the last section of the poem (lines 17-28), the section offers itself as a rational statement of the effect of the scene on the sensitive reader. *If* you too could see and hear what I have seen and heard, *then* "My friend, you would not tell in such high zest / To children ardent for some desperate glory, / The old Lie: Dulce et decorum est / Pro patria mori." The poem tries to score didactic points too easily. It simply does not follow that because death in war can be horrible one should not die for one's country. Would he argue conversely that it is right to die for one's country as long as the death is clean and swift? The physical manner of death does not itself prove Horace's sentence a lie. But an unjust war with illegitimate and dishonorable aims led by incompetent or corrupt officers and politicians would prove it a lie, or more accurately prove it inapplicable in such a case. But Owen says nothing of this. [In his *Wilfred Owen: A Critical Study* (1978)] Welland generalizes that "the only call to which Owen answers is not that of the church but of human suffering. It is human suffering rather than abstract morality that determines his ethical position." That is, I think, too simple. Owen himself seemed to realize that the simple recording of suffering was not enough. But as this poem indicates, when he tried to place the descriptions within signifying moral contexts, his own intellectual limitations were exposed. . . . Morality is not itself the recognition of human suffering, though that may be where and how it begins; it is the set of defensible principles guiding our active (not just emotional) response to that suffering.

In **"Futility,"** however, he is able to add sound organizing thought to the graphic details and subjective responses:

> Move him into the sun—
> Gently its touch awoke him once,
> At home, whispering of fields unsown.
> Always it woke him, even in France,
> Until this morning and this snow.
> If anything might rouse him now
> The kind old sun will know.
>
> Think how it wakes the seeds,—
> Woke, once, the clays of a cold star.
> Are limbs, so dear-achieved, are sides,
> Full-nerved,—still warm,—too hard to stir?
> Was it for this the clay grew tall?
> —O what made fatuous sunbeams toil
> To break earth's sleep at all?

The poem is not much more than a complex mixture of tones, but it is unusual in Owen's work for being personal without being too subjective and for keeping the descriptive details plain and relatively bare. The organizing thought while simple is precise and important; it is similar to Wordsworth's "A Slumber Did My Spirit Seal," one of his finest lyrics for the same reasons Owen's little poem is noteworthy. Just as Wordsworth's poem moves from a past delusion about Lucy's immortality to a present realization of her mortality after her death, Owen's moves from an uneasy hope fed by past recur-

rences to a controlled bitterness, with frustration growing as his thought moves through the temporal divisions of the first stanza (from the distant past, to the near and then very near past, to a future prospect), and then in the second stanza through a series of more and more rhetorical questions. We are given the motive and the appropriate and complex emotional response; and while large philosophical questions are asked, they are not pretentious (as "fatuous" brilliantly indicates). They are asked within the confines of carefully and intricately formed stanzas to define the emotion, not to present the poet as a professional thinker. That is, while the context is broader, the poem is successful because Owen does not try for more than he is capable of, unlike the narrower **"Dulce et Decorum Est,"** which pretends to do more than it can.

But, as with most poets, it is the most aesthetically ambitious and least plain poems that attract the most critical attention and praise. With a young poet like Owen, however, we are sent to his weakest poems: the thought is still immature, so the literary devices are all the more obvious: the visionary melodrama of **"The Show,"** the ponderous symbolism of **"Hospital Barge at Cerisy,"** the vatic inflation of **"Six O'Clock in Princes Street,"** the earnest and repetitive ironies of **"Anthem for Doomed Youth,"** and the stiff archaisms of **"The Parable of the Old Man and the Young."**

The three most praised poems by Owen [**"Exposure," "Insensibility,"** and **"Strange Meeting"**] cannot so easily be set aside. None is free from the intellectual and emotional limitations we have been tracing, but they are richer and more interesting than most of his other poems. (pp. 46-8)

"Exposure" is predominantly a descriptive poem; Dominic Hibberd judges the first six stanzas "perhaps Owen's finest piece of descriptive writing." But the description is directed by a thematic opposition (nature and war), and in one non-descriptive stanza (the seventh) that opposition is briefly (too briefly) expanded into an abstract defense of the necessity for a Christ-like sacrifice. It is one of the few times when Owen seems to defend his involvement in the war. The main problem is one of proportion: too much space is devoted to description which is allowed to become too sensuous, and not enough to the defense, which remains ambiguous and unclear.

The poem is in a sense a commentary on the opening line: "Our brains ache, in the merciless iced east winds that knive us. . . ." For the first five stanzas the commentary reservedly goes no further than the Hardyesque suggestion that nature in its indifference to man's plight can on occasion aggravate that plight: "Watching, we hear the mad gusts tugging on the wire, / Like twitching agonies of men among its brambles." This metaphor introduces the idea by comparing the wire's barbs to a country hedge's brambles. In his figurative eagerness, Owen perhaps animates nature too much, for he begins to hint at an active malevolence in addition to the indifference: "Dawn massing in the east her melancholy army / Attacks once more in ranks on shivering ranks of gray." A mention of the snow flakes' "wandering" and the wind's "nonchalance" is followed two lines later by "Pale flakes with fingering stealth come feeling for our faces." One may defend the confusion by pointing to Owen's attempt to capture a collective sense of confusion and anxiety among the soldiers (there is no "I" in the poem, only "we"), but one thereby simply points to an inherent weakness in the dramatic mode; it explains the confusion, but does not justify it. Further minor confusions are caused by Owen's carelessness with possessives (is "the poignant misery of dawn" in line 11 the misery delivered by the dawn or the misery felt by the dawn?) and with punctuation (the period after ''silence'' in line 16 suggests that ''we,'' rather than the more obvious ''flights of bullets,'' are ''less deathly than the air''). The most serious problem with the descriptive stanzas is the tendency to aestheticize the scene of suffering soldiers with too insistent alliteration. (pp. 48-9)

In the sixth stanza the commentary comes forward and leaves momentarily the descriptive language behind. The soldiers, in that very fine phrase, ''back on forgotten dreams,'' their ''ghosts'' (an unfortunate word) ''drag home,'' where they imagine cozy fires, jingling crickets, and a late night house taken over for a few hours by innocent rejoicing mice. This movement to an imagined scene of nature and man in temporary harmony, a harmony denied the warring men on the front, ends in obvious symbolism: ''on us the doors are closed,— / We turn back to our dying.''

The seventh stanza then offers what seems syntactically a rational sequence, but . . . , because of careless expression, and, I suspect, incomplete thinking, it is far from being rationally clear:

> Since we believe not otherwise can kind fires burn;
> Nor ever suns smile true on child, or field, or fruit,
> For God's invincible spring our love is made afraid;
> Therefore, not loath, we lie out here; therefore were born,
> For love of God seems dying. . . .

Despite the eccentric punctuation, I believe the ''Since'' clause of the first line modifies the last line of the previous stanza, rather than the fourth line of this stanza: the first two lines here then give the reason why they turn back to the realities of the war instead of dreaming on about home fires, for the war must be fought to preserve the values symbolized (rather sentimentally perhaps) by those fires. Silkin suggests that the first line can be read as an independent clause by pausing after ''believe,'' with an implied ''in God.'' I find this a little forced even if it makes sense of Owen's punctuation. The poem has not prepared us for such a sudden declaration of religious faith, but it has for a tentative psychological and patriotic justification—we expect such a contemplative poem to answer the earlier question, ''What are we doing here?'' (pp. 49-50)

''**Insensibility**'' is a clearer statement about a more complex issue: wartime stoicism. The poet moves from sympathy with the forced insensitivity of front-line soldiers to criticism of the self-imposed stoicism of civilians. The first four sections comprise a catalogue of various kinds and causes of insensibility in soldiers (a lack of compassion for others, a cessation of feeling for themselves, unimaginativeness, inexperience). The fifth section is a somewhat indeterminate (and unironic) acknowledgment of the advantages of these deficiencies, and in its last two lines (''He cannot tell/ Old men's placidity from his'') acts as a transition to the sixth section, which declares such ''happy'' insensibility to be a curse if not forced on one, as it is not on noncombatants:

> But cursed are dullards whom no cannon stuns,
> That they should be as stones.
> Wretched are they, and mean
> With paucity that never was simplicity.
> By choice they made themselves immune
> To pity and whatever moans in man
> Before the last sea and the hapless stars;

> Whatever mourns when many leave these shores;
> Whatever shares
> The eternal reciprocity of tears.

The inadequacy here is not confusion but more obviously a limitation of the thought; this treatment of civilian insensitivity is too easy, a mere indignant gesture. With his disordered list, his loose, expansive, and undefining emotional rhythm of syntactical repetitions (''Happy are . . .'' throughout the first four sections, and in addition ''Their . . .'' throughout the third section), and his piecemeal sensuosity, he finally only laments a loss of emotional responsiveness, of an emotional sense of tragedy (''the eternal reciprocity of tears''), which reminds one of the melodramatic generalization in ''Ode to a Nightingale'' by the equally young Keats: ''Here, where men sit and hear each other groan.'' Owen regrets only the inability to respond sympathetically to the moaning; a more mature poet would also regret the loss of that which allows one to deal with the suffering and perhaps, limited as such actions are, do something about it. (pp. 51-2)

Most critics consider ''**Strange Meeting**'' Owen's greatest poem, but they also grudgingly admit that it obviously remains unfinished. The praise is based on that post-Romantic emphasis in this century on visionary intensity (even in the absence of finished thought) as the essence of poetic achievement. ''**Strange Meeting**'' is one of a small group of poems including the almost surreal ''**The Show**'' and the two fanciful sonnets, ''**The Next War**'' and ''**The End.**'' Owen was more successful when he found intensity in accurate pictures of the real war and its consequences (such as ''**Mental Cases**,'' ''**Disabled**,'' ''**Spring Offensive**,'' ''**The Chances**,'' ''**A Terre**,'' and ''**Miners**''), poems that may not rise above responsible journalism, but for the most part avoid pretentious prophecy. Young men should never try to be prophets. It was not a mode Owen was comfortable with, and while ''**Strange Meeting**'' is the best of the small group, the discomfort shows, however potentially powerful the imaginative situation is. Compassion for the common German soldier is not original with Owen, of course; one remembers Hardy's ''Often When Warring'' and Graves's ''Dead Boche.'' But what distinguishes Owen's poem and unfortunately also restricts its moral significance is that the poet is not sorry he has killed another human being, but only sorry he has killed a fellow Romantic poet.

The poem has two parts; lines 1-13 narrate a visionary descent into hell, which is effectively described as a permanent version of a World War I tunnel (''long since scooped/ Through granites which titanic wars had groined''). The only problem is the concept of hell, which is unconventional without reason: why are the dead smiling in hell (lines 9-10), and why would the visiting poet who knows this is hell think there is no cause for mourning (line 14)? Is not hell perpetual mourning for the loss of heavenly bliss? The poet seems to be confusing the state of being dead with the more specific state of being forever damned. The second part of the poem (lines 14-44) is a dialogue, or perhaps a monologue since the poet only speaks one line while the rest is the dead man's reply. The German soldier mourns the loss of hope, both his own and what his poetry, had he lived to write it, would have given others—not a hope for moral understanding or social stability or fullness of being, but for aesthetic extremes:

> Whatever hope is yours
> Was my life also; I went hunting wild
> After the wildest beauty in the world,

Which lies not calm in eyes, or braided hair,
But mocks the steady running of the hour,
And if it grieves, grieves richlier than here.

Welland has established Shelley's *The Revolt of Islam* as a
source of the poem, and Hibberd has suggested Keats's *En-
dymion,* Dante's *Inferno,* Sassoon's "Rear-Guard," and even
one line by Oscar Wilde. These particular lines, however, most
suggest Shelley's "Alastor," that long record of a pathetic
search by a poet for an unobtainable vision of fiery beauty.
The fourth line of the passage even recalls the Shelleyan poet's
rejection of the calm and sacrificing Arab maid. The next line,
of course, echoes Marvell's promise to his coy mistress of
sexual fireworks and the next the glutted sorrow of Keats's
"Ode on Melancholy." In the lines that follow, Owen quickly
and inexplicitly equates beauty with truth and truth with pity,
and thereby outdoes Keats. Meanwhile the speaker strongly
suggests that if poets had not been killed in the war the nations
would not, as he prophesizes they will, "trek from progress."
One therefore wonders about the nature of the "wisdom" he
claims for himself, and what "mystery" means in this context:

> Courage was mine, and I had mystery,
> Wisdom was mine, and I had mastery:
> To miss the march of this retreating world
> Into vain citadels that are not walled.

He seems to be saying, contrary to what he said earlier about
preventing the retreat, that as a poet he will be uncontaminated
by the inevitable decline of civilization, and only later ("Then,
when much blood had clogged their chariot wheels") would
he "go up and wash them from sweet wells,/ Even with truths
that lie too deep for taint./ I would have poured. . . ." The
sudden shift of tense (from "I would go" to "I would have")
also makes the passage very difficult to follow. The poem ends
with the dramatic revelation that this fellow poet is the enemy
killed by the narrator. The only thing that justifies "my friend"
is their shared view of the poet's function. The pathos is not
as sharp as it should be because it comes after such immature
and inflated claims. If we are at least to respect Owen's capacity
for pity and compassion and therefore his limited advance over
Sassoon's anger, we had best not invoke **"Strange Meeting"**
as representative of his best efforts.

Those best efforts amount, however, to a limited achievement.
Youthful poetry is usually and quite understandably morally
unfinished and stylistically uncertain, blunt, or pretentious. The
poetry of the soldier-poets of World War I is no exception.
Rather than bemoan what might have been, we should perhaps
marvel that the few successful but minor poems (those of vivid
description and honest feeling) were written at all at such a
disruptive time. But we should also not overvalue the achievement (as for instance does Welland in referring to Owen's
"mature, tragic vision of the disintegrative forces at work in
the modern world," for then we do a disservice to all poetry
and especially to those few poems that do meet the poetic
demand of the difficult and extraordinary conditions of war.
(pp. 52-4)

*Richard Hoffpauir, "An Assessment of Wilfred
Owen," in* English Literature in Transition: 1880-
1920, *Vol. 28, No. 1, 1985, pp. 41-55.*

R. P. DRAPER   (essay date 1985)

*[Draper is an English educator, scholar, and editor specializing
in British fiction from the sixteenth century to the present. In the*
*following excerpt, he discusses the reconciliation of objectivity
and subjectivity in Owen's verses.]*

["The Rear-Guard" by Siegfried Sassoon, "Dead Man's Dump"
by Isaac Rosenberg, and **"Dulce et Decorum Est"** by Wilfred
Owen] are realistic records of the most disgusting side of war,
which were meant to be, and even today still succeed in being,
deeply disturbing to the reader. They are also, of course, one-
sided, but one-sided as, for example, Swift's satire is, in that
they present a limited facet of war in intensive close-up, with
the purpose of shocking the reader out of any possible complacency of mind with regard to what death means in the conditions of modern warfare. Their justification lies in the sincerity of the moral indignation which is their driving force;
and in the fact that experiences of this order (their more recent
equivalents would perhaps be atrocities committed by the Na-
zis against the Jews, or the appalling effects of the atom bomb)
temporarily obliterate all other kinds of awareness, making the
criticism that they are one-sided seem, at least for a while,
irrelevant.

Owen seems to have taken this view himself, for in the intended
Preface to his poems he declares:

> Above all I am not concerned with Poetry.
> My subject is War, and the pity of War.
> The Poetry is in the pity.
> Yet these elegies are to this generation in no
> sense consolatory. They may be to the next.
> All a poet can do today is warn. That is why
> the true Poets must be truthful.

The urgency of the subject is placed before the means by which
it is expressed, as if there could be a simple division between
style and matter—a view which might be dismissed as critically
naive. But there are some fruitful contradictions in what Owen
says. He declares that he is "not concerned with Poetry,"
though he chooses to write in verse, and use many of the
traditional devices of poetry, as well as some interestingly
original ones such as half-rhyme and pararhyme. He then asserts that "The Poetry is in the pity." Poetry is thus reinstated,
but as a means to arousing a certain kind of emotional response,
not as an end in itself. This may be no more than a way of
recognising a greater seriousness and maturity in his own later
poetry as compared with the earlier; but it also suggests that,
like the Keats of the revised *Hyperion,* Owen has found a
deeper imaginative compulsion in themes which arouse feelings
of compassion, and which stimulate him to move compassion
in others. If so, this is close to recognising that his own bent
is towards lyric tragedy, and leads, understandably, in the next
line to the description of his poems as "these elegies." Owen
shifts again, however; for, having selected "elegies," he immediately seeks to cancel out the traditional association of elegy
with consolation, at least "to this generation." As far as his
contemporaries are concerned, his role will be to break through
poeticism, and shock them into realisation of the horror and
suffering which they unthinkingly condone; this is what, for
the time being, it means to be "truthful." Yet there is also
the concession that his "elegies" might be "consolatory" to
the next generation—a further recognition perhaps that they
do, after all, contain elements which properly arouse feelings
of grief and lament, and satisfy a permanent human need, rather
than merely serve to "warn."

Dominic Hibberd notes the use of the word "elegies" in Ow-
en's Preface, and relates it to what he sees as a development
away from Sassoon-like shock tactics to a more resonant lan-

guage of grief: "Satire aims to stimulate social action, elegy to arouse memory and grief. It did not take Owen long to perceive that his talent was more elegiac than satirical." And he adds that in December 1917 Owen read a translation of Bion and Moschus, and in 1918 "considered entitling a volume of his poems *With Lightning and with Music,* a phrase from Shelley's great elegy, or *English Elegies.*" This lends further support to the hint which the Preface itself contains that Owen was conscious of his place in the elegiac tradition, but wished to adapt it to the truth about modern war which he also felt a compulsion to express. It suggests that his aim was a kind of poetry which would be both immediate—a tract for the times—and in touch with the permanent realities of tragedy. If this is so, however, it does not mean that all his poems were meant to serve both these purposes—much less that they all succeed in doing so. There is considerable variety in his work, and much variation in individual poems, ranging over indignation, satire, horrific realism, visionary imagination, pathos, and at times sentimentality; but the distinguishing quality of his work at its best is just this combination of immediacy and distance. He is most himself when, without blurring or generalising vagueness, he is compassionately involved with his subject, but also sufficiently detached to reach the Vergilian "lacrimae rerum"—the permanent substratum of grief that is tapped by tragedy. It is the denial of this level of human awareness that he most severely condemns in the stay-at-home civilians whom he attacks in the last stanza of **"Insensibility"**:

> But cursed are dullards whom no cannon stuns,
> That they should be as stones.
> Wretched are they, and mean
> With paucity that never was simplicity.
> By choice they made themselves immune
> To pity and whatever mourns in man
> Before the last sea and the hapless stars;
> Whatever mourns when many leave these shores;
> Whatever shares
> The eternal reciprocity of tears.

In the foregoing stanzas of this poem the blunted state of feeling of the troops is seen as a blessing for them; their "insensibility" is necessary self-protection—though in the process of explaining why Owen also exemplifies the poetry of "pity" and "truth," and makes them real as "troops who fade, not flowers, / For poets' tearful fooling." But the civilians who wilfully insulate themselves from this truth not only fail in their duty to their contemporaries, but wither their own humanity. Recognising the one is an essential condition of the other.

Some of Owen's poems are directly about front-line experience; others focus on soldiers crippled and wasted by war, and have their setting behind the lines, or in hospital; still others are set at home, and deal with the civilians' response to the soldiers. It would be much too drastic a simplification to say that the further Owen retreats from the actual front line, the more he achieves tragic distancing of his material; but the conditions for that achievement do often seem to be more readily available when he is not directly evoking the horrors of battle. This is not a question of where Owen himself was at the time of writing any particular poem, but of the quality of his imaginative involvement. **"Dulce et Decorum Est,"** for example, was written when he was a shellshock patient at Craiglockhart hospital, near Edinburgh . . . , and its dramatic involvement may well have been the consequence of what Jon Stallworthy calls "nightmare memories." D. S. R. Welland, on the other hand, attributes it [in his biography of Owen] to "the white-hot in-

dignation to which [Owen] had been brought (as one manuscript reveals) by the patriotic lines of Miss Jessie Pope." It is highly successful in its purpose of jolting the complacent out of their complacency; and it is especially vivid and precise in its rendering of the sudden change from weary marching to the soldiers' frantic reaction to the gas attack. But its most remarkable lines are those which describe the struggles of the man who fails to get his mask on in time:

> But someone still was yelling out and stumbling,
> And flound'ring like a man in fire or lime. . . .
> Dim, through the misty panes and thick green light,
> As under a green sea, I saw him drowning.

The man and the first-person narrator are both vividly before us, but the suffering of the one, seen by the other through the clouded eyepiece of his own mask, which he has managed to put on, is transformed by perspective. Without it needing to be said, this points the isolation of the "drowning" man. Momentarily, he becomes a tragic Philoctetes, abandoned, though in this case unwillingly, by his comrades. By comparison the body flung in the wagon is not so much a tragic figure as an emotionally loaded image directed, as its syntactic containment within the double "If" clause indicates, at the ironic "friend" who deludes children with his ignorant glorification of war, summed up in the words of a dead poet, in a dead language, which Owen presents as culpably remote from the "truth" exemplified in the poem.

The colloquial satires which Owen wrote under Sassoon's influence—poems like **"The Dead-Beat," "The Letter," "The Chances," "S.I.W."** and **"The Inspection"**—are sardonic rather than tragic. The dialogue is realistic (though still an edited version of the language actually used by soldiers) and perhaps too deliberately prosaic, but, as intended, it is an effective antidote to romantic "Poetry" of the kind Owen declares himself not to be concerned with; and the abrupt endings, especially of **"The Dead-Beat"** and **"The Chances,"** leave a decidedly caustic impression:

> 'E's wounded, killed, and pris'ner, all the lot,
> The bloody lot all rolled in one. Jim's mad.

In some respects these are the poems most obviously in accord with the Preface's denial of elegiac consolation; in them the poetry has to be in the pity because anything more evidently "poetic" has been cut out. Nevertheless, this anti-poetic style plays an important part in achieving a certain kind of poetic effect; and in the more ambitious of these poems structures are employed which, despite the verbal astringency, add resonance and depth. Thus, **"S.I.W."** has an opening epigraph from Yeats, referring to the superficially similar death of one who "has set his teeth to die" and cannot therefore be mourned, only to intensify the real cause for mourning exemplified in this poem; and its division into sections, each with its own title (I. THE PROLOGUE; II. THE ACTION; III. THE POEM; IV. THE EPILOGUE), turns it into a kind of tragic drama. And in **"The Inspection"** (strictly speaking, not a front-line poem, but set in the rear) the smear of blood for which the soldier has to be rebuked prompts a gibe at the washing out of stains which deepens into a protest against militarism as such, which sacrifices the blood of youth on the altar of its own deified system.

In poems like **"Disabled," "Conscious," "Mental Cases"** and **"Smile, Smile, Smile,"** which are more removed from the immediacy of battle, pity takes on a tenderer form, though still stiffened with the sardonic quality of the front line pieces. Newspapers argue disingenuously for vast war indemnities on behalf of the national integrity which the dead and wounded are said to have preserved; but sufficient comment is made through the understated lines:

> Nation?—The half-limbed readers did not chafe
> But smiled at one another curiously
> Like secret men who know their secret safe.
>   (**"Smile, Smile, Smile"**)

A cripple sits in his wheelchair "waiting for dark," and, as the poem slides between his present and his past, and the "few sick years" which are now his future, it creates a context of both irony and pathos for the inappropriately heroic diction of

> He's lost his colour very far from here,
> Poured it down shell-holes till the veins ran dry,
> And half his lifetime lapsed in the hot race
> And leap of purple spurted from his thigh.
>   (**"Disabled"**)

The hectic language of **"Dulce et Decorum Est"** is echoed:

> Batter of guns and shatter of flying muscles,
> Carnage incomparable
>   (**"Mental Cases"**)

but this is the nightmare world inhabited by the "purgatorial shadows" of the insane, whose condition is made imaginatively compelling, not merely to horrify, but to arouse a sense of guilt in us who are responsible for it:

> Snatching after us who smote them, brother,
> Pawing us who dealt them war and madness.
>   (**"Mental Cases"**)

Further still from the front—at home, in fact—**"The Send-Off"** also has our guilt as its theme. Here the sardonic note of **"The Inspection"** is present in a muted form. A kind of ironic "Poetry" is suggested by the flowers given to the departing troops, whose "breasts were stuck all white with wreath and spray." Though perhaps meant as tributes to their courage, these flowers seem more like anticipatory funeral offerings for their predestined corpses—as the short, flat succeeding line, "As men's are, dead," implies. Their send-off is already a thing of the past: their present entraining is watched only by "Dull porters" and "a casual tramp" whose sorrow probably has more to do with the scraps he cadged from them at "the upland camp" than with compassion. The absence of feeling makes itself felt in a complex way in the lines:

> Then, unmoved, signals nodded, and a lamp
> Winked to the guard.

Life is ironically attributed to the signals and lamp, but in a form that suggests they are in complicity with the guard; and "unmoved" gives them a weird mechanical independence, but also suggests total lack of feeling. All this is an indirect comment on the indifference of society; and yet there is also a sense that society is guiltily uneasy. The giving of flowers becomes almost a propitiation of those who are being treated as scapegoats; the men are banished like secret crimes which "we" prefer to disown and forget:

> So secretly, like wrongs hushed-up, they went.
> They were not ours:
> We never heard to which front these were sent.
>
> Nor there if they yet mock what women meant
> Who gave them flowers.

Accordingly, the few who may return will "creep back," not to the accompaniment of "beatings of great bells," but furtively, "to still village wells / Up half-known roads." As Gertrude White remarks [in her *Wilfred Owen*], "we are left to wonder whether their village roads are only half-remembered by them because of the length of their absence or the intensity and terror of the events in which they have taken part." The unmentioned, and unmentionable, nature of their deaths is even more distanced than the crippling of the soldier in **"Disabled,"** and yet supplied with a context of before and after which endows it with the biting pathos of tragic irony.

Both battle front and home front come together in **"Anthem for Doomed Youth."** Its form is that of the Shakespearean sonnet, but modified in the third quatrain to rhyme EFFE instead of EFEF, and divided in the Petrarchan fashion between octave and sestet. The octave deals with the weapons of modern warfare, and the sestet with grief at home for the dead; but an elegiac tone is spread over the whole sonnet, unifying its two halves, and the religious mourning at home infiltrates the octave in a series of ironic substitutions of battlefield noises for such things as passing-bells, prayers and choirs. Instead of satire, however, this produces a mingled Shakespearean and Keatsian music of mourning (there are specific reminiscences of "the surly sullen bell" and the "Bare ruin'd choirs" of Sonnets 71 and 73 and the "wailful choir" of "To Autumn"), which aptly justifies the word "Anthem" in the title. A sense of indignation and outrage still makes itself felt, but it is blended into the double metaphor that creates "passing-bells" for the slain ("who die as cattle") out of guns which express "monstrous anger," and turns the onomatopoeic "stuttering rifles' rapid rattle" into the padre's hastily mumbled prayers for the dead. In the second quatrain this voice of protest is more muted still as "mockeries" soften into "mourning"—high-pitched in "The shrill, demented choirs of wailing shells," but receding funereally in the dying fall of "bugles calling for them from sad shires."

In the sestet the religious theme continues with a farewell ritual which, as Hibberd points out [in his *Wilfred Owen: War Poems and Others* (1973)], refers to the custom of "a household in mourning"; but warfare is left behind. The result, it must be admitted, is a little disappointing. An imaginative tension goes out of the verse, and the elegiac music comes perilously near to sentimentality as the ironic substitutions of the octave are replaced by alternatives to conventional grief which are themselves almost as conventional. Even the serious wit of "The pallor of girls' brows shall be their pall" cannot disguise the rather trite nature of the image; and the last couplet, though a beautifully sounding verbal coda to the "anthem," does no more than suggest a sadness which might be appropriate to any bereavement. It has lost touch with the youth doomed by modern war.

"Anthem for Doomed Youth" is thus a very fine experiment in combining the realities of war with more traditional elegiac mourning, but it is difficult to accept Gertrude White's judgement that it is a "wholly successful poem" and "perhaps the best that Owen wrote." It does much to satisfy the requirements of melancholy eloquence that Hume discusses in his essay on tragedy, and it has clearly learnt from Keats in this respect; but it is defective, at least in the sestet, in the Keatsian requirement of a "wakeful anguish" that sharpens and deepens melancholy into tragedy.

It is in another sonnet, **"Futility,"** that one can see a better and more consistent balance between distance and immediacy.

There is no direct mention, it is true, of the horrors of war, and even the fact that it is about a soldier who has just died is not made absolutely explicit. But the reference to France is sufficiently evocative; and the presence of a young war casualty paralysed in a wheel-chair, or hospital bed, and now beyond recovery, is strongly enough felt for him to be realised in the reader's imagination as both a particular and a general, representative case of tragic waste. Moreover, that it is a sonnet is not immediately apparent. It uses six-syllabled and eight- (or sometimes nine-) syllabled lines instead of the usual ten, and it breaks the fourteen lines into two seven-lined stanzas, each of which has a strangely haunting pattern of rhyme: ABAB (in half-rhyme or pararhyme); C(C)C (full rhyme, with pararhyme between). The result is a muted music rising to a broken climax which, even with its final full rhyme, interrupted as it is by the pararhyme in the penultimate line, never quite fulfils its promise.

This sense of unfulfilled promise is also the theme of the poem, worked out in the contrast between the two stanzaic halves which replace the usual division between octave and sestet. The first half presents the sun as a gently reviving power, "whispering of fields unsown"—"unsown," but none the less suggesting the sowing of seed, as "awoke" and "woke" (in "Gently its touch awoke him once" and "Always it woke him," lines 2 and 4) suggest its life-giving and restorative agency. The soldier, moreover, is felt to have always enjoyed a particularly strong relationship with the sun, both "At home" and "even in France"—with all that "France" summons up in the way of destructive antipathy to life. However, "Until this morning and this snow" hints that something especially ominous has happened to that relationship, introducing a coldness discordant with the warmth, tenderness and fertility which have so far been the keynote of the poem. The completion of the first half with

> If anything might rouse him now
> The kind old sun will know

counteracts that impression with a suggestion of continuing intimacy between soldier and sun that can still be relied on; yet the rhyming of "know" with "snow," the more hesitant "If anything might" and the slightly more desperate quality of "rouse," compared with "woke," and the patronising element in "The kind old sun," all point to a faltering confidence.

The second half seems to regain the lost, or fading, impetus with the urgent

> Think how it wakes the seeds,—
> Woke, once, the clays of a cold star.

The use of "wakes" and "Woke" more than echo their use in previous lines; they evoke the sun as a universal mover of what seems impossible, a bringer of life out of lifeless sterility. . . . It should have little difficulty, therefore, in reviving a human body with all the complexity of achievement it represents, and "still warm," not only with the heat of physical life, but with the conscious love it arouses. But the last five lines are question, not statement. The earlier, incipient doubt is now much more evident; and it reaches out not only to the sun's power to revive the soldier, but also to the purpose of human life, linked to the long, but now seemingly futile, evolutionary process via the echo in "Was it for this the clay grew tall?" of its beginning with "the clays of a cold star." And the final despairing question:

> —O what made fatuous sunbeams toil
> To break earth's sleep at all?

tinged, as it so often is in Hardy, with a sense of fundamental absurdity, completes the distancing of individual suffering to a universal tragic vision, while still leaving the pain of the particular situation uppermost.

"**Futility**" is as near as Owen came to achieving the right balance between distance and immediacy. It is all the answer that is needed to Yeats' notorious misjudgement in excluding him from the 1936 *Oxford Book of English Verse* on the excuse that "passive suffering is not a proper subject for poetry." There are, however, three front-line poems—"**Exposure**," "**Spring Offensive**" and "**Strange Meeting**"—which demand modification of the argument that he gains more tragic effect as he deals with subjects which are at more of a distance from actual conflict. The first of these, "**Exposure**," is descriptive verse, brilliantly onomatopoeic and almost luscious in its assonance and alliteration—surprising it would seem, only in that it applies this style to such distinctly untraditional poetic material as barbed wire, artillery and machine guns. But its recourse to a traditional style is by no means reassuring. It is modified by Owen's own use of pararhyme, with its sinister disappointment of expected rhyme; and its more usual association with the lavish and benevolent Nature of Romantic poetry serves as an ironic contrast in this Winter context, where natural forces are as inimical to the men in the trenches as the weapons of destruction used against them. Exposure to the elements becomes an extension of the suffering they endure in modern war, as Owen suggests by fusing the rigours of a cold, wet dawn with the grey military uniforms worn by the German soldiers:

> The poignant misery of dawn begins to grow. . . .
> We only know war lasts, rain soaks, and clouds sag stormy.
> Dawn massing in the east her melancholy army
> Attacks once more in ranks on shivering ranks of gray,
> > But nothing happens.

The perversion of Nature becomes something like a perversion of natural feeling. For example, in the description of the snow, "Pale flakes with fingering stealth come feeling for our faces," the language suggests that what is normally soft and caressing has taken on the groping menace of an assassin. Instinctively the men try to escape by retreating mentally "back on forgotten dreams" of a kindlier and more "Poetic" natural world:

> So we drowse, sun-dozed,
> Littered with blossoms trickling where the blackbird
> fusses

and to homes where "crickets jingle" and "the innocent mice rejoice"; but this is a sentimental illusion from which they are cut off by the unchanging reality of war. They believe, or have been persuaded to believe . . . , that the restoration of this illusion depends on the misery they endure—that somehow their perverted nature will bring the old idea of Nature back: "For God's invincible spring our love is made afraid." But the stanza ends with the suggestion that "love of God seems dying"; and the next, and final, stanza returns to the soldiers' immediate misery, which—depending on whether one reads "this frost" or "His frost"—may even be envisaged as the direct infliction of a God of Nature who is anything but benevolent. Their suffering is precisely rendered—the frost "Shrivelling many hands, puckering foreheads crisp"; but, as in "**Futility**," the individual's condition represents a tragic human condition: the wasteful reduction of life and energy to frozen immobility, symbolised in the corpses only half-recognised by the burying-party (''All their eyes are ice'') and the repeated refrain which forms the last words of the poem: ''But nothing happens.''

"Spring Offensive" and **"Strange Meeting"** are both unfinished, or at least not finally revised, and to that extent comment on them can only be provisional. But they seem to be front line poems which have deeply absorbed the tragically distancing process. It is perhaps significant that **"Spring Offensive,"** though written in September 1918, refers back to Owen's experience at Fayet in the offensive of 1917; and that **"Strange Meeting,"** written apparently a month earlier than **"Spring Offensive,"** is in the form of a semi-mythical encounter with an enemy-friend in an underworld which is both the world of the trenches and something like Dante's Inferno.

Like **"Exposure,"** **"Spring Offensive"** is rich in natural description, and as Keatsian as **"Anthem for Doomed Youth";** and with both it also shares elements of religious language. The attack becomes a leap into hell; and, though less obviously, there are hints of the Mass in ''the buttercup / Had blessed with gold their slow boots coming up'' and ''earth set sudden cups / In thousands for their blood.'' As Hibberd notes: ''Having refused the offered blessing of communion with the natural order, the men have become victims sacrificed to an outraged Nature.'' This use of religious language is continued in **"Strange Meeting,"** where the ''sullen hall'' in which the narrator finds himself is ''Hell,'' and the enemy-friend, ''Lifting distressful hands, as if to bless,'' and with his face marked with ''a thousand pains,'' is clearly a Christ-like figure, willing to give his blood in a purifying protest against the merely destructive bloodshed of war:

> Then, when much blood had clogged their chariot-wheels,
> I would go up and wash them from sweet wells,
> Even with truths that lie too deep for taint.
> I would have poured my spirit without stint
> But not through wounds; not on the cess of war.
> Foreheads of men have bled where no wounds were.

The biblical diction here, and the echo of Wordsworth's ''Thoughts that do often lie too deep for tears'' (''Immortality Ode,'' 204), like some of the phrasing in **"Spring Offensive,"** suggest a still imperfectly controlled desire to write ''Poetry,'' but the mythical and religious distancing do not produce a romanticised view of war. The consolation of courage in the face of death and the comfort of Christian redemption are hinted at only to be rejected. In **"Spring Offensive"** when the word of attack is given it is received with ''No alarms / Of bugles, no high flags, no clamorous haste''; and it is with an almost sardonic detachment that Owen reports the religious view that those who die in a just war are instantly redeemed:

> Of them who running on that last high place
> Leapt to swift unseen bullets. . . .
> Some say God caught them even before they fell.

The survivors themselves react very differently. Having been immersed in the extremely ambiguous heroism of fiendish battle, with its ''superhuman inhumanities'' and ''immemorial shames,'' they only crawl ''slowly back'' and by degrees regain ''cool peaceful air in wonder''; and it is left to the reader to answer the question, ''Why speak not they of comrades that went under?'' And even the aspirations of the new idealist who, in **"Strange Meeting,"** seems to have been reborn out of the horrors of war to preach the gospel, not of death, but of ''The pity of war, the pity of war distilled,'' are abandoned at the end, in lines which are the more quietly moving for

coming after the morally exalted (but also obscure) ecstasies which precede them:

> I am the enemy you killed, my friend.
> I knew you in this dark: for so you frowned
> Yesterday through me as you jabbed and killed.
> I parried; but my hands were loath and cold.
> Let us sleep now. . . .

The unemphatic quality of these closing lines is something different from what is to be found in either the elegiac music of **"Anthem for Doomed Youth,"** or the anguished final question of **"Futility."** Its nearest equivalent is the muted conclusion of **"The Send-Off":**

> A few, a few, too few for drums and yells,
>
> May creep back, silent, to still village wells
> Up half-known roads.

But **"The Send-Off"** does not have its own ecstasies as a contrast to the quietness of these lines; and it cannot, therefore, give the same impression of withdrawal even from the strenuous business of preaching a new moral heroism free from the taint of aggressive militarism. The broken last line, ''Let us sleep now,'' may, of course, be simply the result of the unfinished condition of the poem; but, if so, it seems peculiarly appropriate to what is being said, and the mood that is being evoked. By means of it the poem seems to turn its back on its own visionary prospects; and, like the prosaic, but deeply moving, lines spoken by Edgar at the end of *King Lear,* it gives the sense of obeying the weight of a sad time, and speaking what is felt, not what ought to be said. But there is also the particular sense in **"Strange Meeting"** of a quiet revulsion which is ambiguously at once the result of weariness with continuing bloodshed; the expression of a common humanity now recognised as beyond and above the temporary condition of hostility generated by war; and a turning from life to the inevitability of death. The old aggressiveness is there in association with the narrator of the poem, the first ''I,'' who ''jabbed and killed'' the second speaker, who is the ''I'' of the rest of the poem, from line 15 to the end. But these two ''I's'' are, essentially, both aspects of the poet himself—a self and anti-self suggestive of the two selves in [Edward] Thomas' ''The Other,'' but reconciled and brought to an understanding of each other. ''Yesterday'' they met and fought on the field of battle, where the second ''I,'' already reluctant, only ''parried.'' Here the first ''I'' addresses his alter ego as ''Strange friend,'' and the second declares his paradoxical identity as ''the enemy you killed, my friend,'' and adds his recognition: ''I knew you in this dark''—echoing the earlier lines in which he had sprung to meet his opposite ''With piteous recognition in fixed eyes.'' The two are finally joined together in the last words of the poem, where ''us'' is used for the first time; but what joins them is ''sleep,'' which in this context is death.

It is difficult to say whether **"Strange Meeting"** is tragic or not. As the two selves speak, both possibilities are suggested:

> ''Strange friend,'' I said, ''Here is no cause to mourn.''
> ''None,'' said that other, ''save the undone years,
> The hopelessness.''

It is tragic in its realisation of the waste and futility of war, and yet it seems to transcend tragedy in its acceptance of death as the ultimate remover of false barriers. In the long speech of the enemy-friend it becomes prophetic rather than tragic, but the impression given by the speaker's final words, of a disillusioned weariness with man's innate aggressiveness, is once more tragic. One must conclude that there is something unresolved in the poem's underlying purpose—that its mixture of earnest moral vision and resignation, like its uncertainty of tone and style, is a sign of its imperfectly finished state. But it remains in some respects uniquely moving. Less finely achieved than **"The Send-Off"** or **"Futility,"** it nevertheless seems Owen's most deeply introspective poem—the poem in which Owen is most profoundly engaged in the creative struggle to understand his own attitude to war and its tragic significance. It is his most ambitious attempt to reconcile distance and immediacy. (pp. 163-77)

> *R. P. Draper, "Wilfred Owen: Distance and Immediacy," in his* Lyric Tragedy, *The Macmillan Press Ltd., 1985, pp. 162-77.*

ADRIAN CAESAR (essay date 1987)

[*In the following excerpt, Caesar offers a modern reassessment of Owen's response to war.*]

Writing a review of Jon Stallworthy's biography of Wilfred Owen in 1975, Philip Larkin concluded that somewhere behind Owen's poetry "was a human problem that even after fifty years we are a long way from understanding" [see Additional Bibliography]. In the last ten years I do not think we have moved far forward. Owen's poetry is widely read and is taught on many High School courses throughout the English speaking world. His work is celebrated for what Larkin identifies as the "unique element of visionary compassion" which it is said to embody. Critics have thus far emphasised this, finding in Owen's work a humanist response to the horror of modern warfare, and a debunking of Imperialist notions of honour, glory and patriotism, which is much to their (and our) political taste. Owen's manner of writing is often described as "realistic." Bernard Bergonzi says of Owen that "his absorption in the concrete realities of the front is complete" [see excerpt dated 1965, *TCLC*-5]. Jon Silkin remarks that meeting Sassoon gave Owen "the confidence to draw into his work a greater realism." And one critic goes so far as to speak of the "straightforward reporting of experience" and the "starkly realistic" description to be found in Owen's poetry. This is all in despite of the obvious literariness of Owen's language and poetic form which both militate against any representationalist realism.

Nevertheless that Owen expresses attitudes of compassion and political rectitude through realism is in a fair way to becoming a critical commonplace which ignores the human problem that his work undoubtedly represents. It is to this latter conundrum that I wish to re-direct attention. By re-assessing Owen's complex reactions to the First World War I wish to challenge the nature and role of "pity" in his work; to re-evaluate his political stance and, where appropriate, demonstrate the absence of anything approaching realism in his work.

Owen's initial indifference to the outbreak of war has been well chronicled. He was, at the time, working as a private tutor in France and enjoying the sense of liberation which this exposure to a foreign culture afforded. He had neither written anything for a considerable period nor was he reading a great deal. But still his overriding ambition was to be a poet and it is this projected "career" which serves him as an argument for his staying free of the war. In two letters to his mother dated August and December 1914 respectively, he speaks of his life being worth more than his death to England. In these and other letters he speaks with an utterly unfeeling nonchalance of the Englishmen dying in France. "The guns," he

suggests to his mother, will "effect a little useful weeding"; the soldiers are referred to as "ten thousand lusty louts playing football." In a similarly unabashed manner he remarks: "I regret the mortality of the English regulars less than that of the French, Belgian, or even Russian or German armies: because the former are all Tommy Atkins, poor fellows, while the continental armies are inclusive of the finest brains and temperaments of the land." The lack of compassion here hardly requires comment and it is statements such as these that give the lie to those who seek to represent Owen as a politically aware spokesman for the left or for the oppressed.

As the war continued however, Owen felt some prickings of conscience, but these were allayed, not now by references to his value to England as a potential poet, but with reference to his past. His "conscience," he says, "is easily cleared by the recollection of certain happenings" in his past. And again two months later he writes: "I could not bear to draw comparisons with the life of the trenches and mine; unless I felt in a manner to have suffered my share of life. And I feel I have." It is impossible of course to either know or judge what recollections and sufferings Owen is referring to in these letters. His biography tells us of a nervous collapse which culminated in pneumonia at the end of 1913. This is the only instance of real suffering that has been recorded and clearly it bears little comparison with the slaughter and sufferings of trench warfare.

It can and has been argued that Owen at this stage was as blissfully ignorant of the realities of war as were the majority of non-combatant English people. But this is not the case. In a letter pre-dating the last two quoted he describes to his brother in elaborate detail embellished with pencil drawings the horrific wounds he has witnessed on a visit to the local hospital in Bordeaux with "the Doctor Sauvaitre." There is an odd sense of relish in this communication of Owen's as he dwells on the "crushed shinbone" which, "the doctor had to twist . . . and push . . . like a piston to get out the pus." Further details include a knee with a hole through it and "a head into which a ball had entered and come out again." The pencil drawings are large and graphic, complete with diagrammatic arrows and in one case, a label pointing to a foot "covered in dirt and blood." Following all this Owen says to his brother (who was then serving in the Merchant Navy under the threat of submarine attack), "I deliberately tell you all this to educate you to the actualities of the war." And, most curiously concludes that "I was not much upset by the morning at the hospital; and this is a striking proof of my health."

Apart from demonstrating that Owen had at least some inkling as to the "actualities" of war some twelve months before he enlisted, this letter I think, is also very illuminating with respect to Owen's rather morbid psychology and its attendant emotional confusions. There is clearly a pressure to communicate what he has seen yet an almost boastful expression of how little moved he has been by his encounter. And the ostensible motivation to educate his brother strikes one as a rationalisation rather than as a convincing imperative directing the discourse. There is an element of voyeurism here; of looking at horror through parted fingers and, most noticeably, a complete absence of anything approaching compassion.

What I wish to suggest is that Owen had an ambivalent interest in suffering (his own and others') which was not entirely conscious to him, which informs his writing both before and during his participation in the war and which was at least in part responsible for that participation. After all it was Christianity and Romantic poetry which (apart from his attachment to his mother) dominated Owen's intellectual and emotional development and both, in their different ways, tend to glorify suffering. By 1915 Owen had been through the crisis whereby he renounced institutionalised Christianity; a renunciation which significantly enough led him to a suffering in which, as we have already seen, he seems to have taken some pride. But his image of the "poet" was still very definitely the "Romantic Image" chronicled by Frank Kermode, wherein suffering is seen as a necessary condition of poetic creation. And although Owen's motivations for enlisting are mixed and to some extent obscure there is evidence to suggest that his poetic ambitions played a part.

It was in June 1915 that Owen began seriously to consider volunteering to fight. (pp. 67-9)

Despite some little vacillation Owen's enthusiasm to participate in the war rapidly developed. In . . . [a] letter of June 1915 he speaks of wanting "intensely to fight" and in July we find him again conceiving of war in connection with literature. He speaks of visiting the "battlefield of Castillon where, in 1453 Talbot Earl of Shrewsbury suffered the defeat which lost Guienne and Bordeaux to the English forever." Owen continues: "I can't understand it, but this battlefield will interest me as much as the field of the Marne;—and I am reading a tale of the Punic wars with more interest than the Communiques. There is only one cure for me! I am already quaking at the idea of Parade; and yawning with the boredom of it. *Now if I could make it a real, live adventure, a real old adventure, by flinging myself into Italy . . . ? [sic]."*

The thought of fighting had clearly captured Owen's imagination and the unstated conclusion of the conditional phrase here is surely to do with his poetry. If he can make it a "real" adventure yet an "old" adventure, (the paradox is telling) he may be able to create his own literature from the experience. From his role as a poet initially keeping him from the war, it has now become I think, a major reason for his going.

Owen enlisted on 21 October 1915 and there followed a period of training lasting a year before he was posted to the Second Manchester Regiment. By 1 January 1917 he was in France again; this time in uniform. Owen spent four months on active service until the beginning of May when, having been observed to be "acting strangely" by his commanding officer, he was sent back from the line suffering from "neurasthenia." Both the letters and the poems written during this four months are crucial in charting the ambivalence of Owen's response to his experience. In discussing these and Owen's subsequent writings it must be said that I am in no way attempting to deny or minimise the very real suffering that Owen and his many (too many) fellow soldiers underwent during the war. What I am anxious to demonstrate is the complexity of Owen's response to the fighting and suffering consequent upon it.

Before Owen's first experience of the front line his mood despite the physical discomforts of his position was ebullient. In his first letter from France to his mother he writes:

> This morning I was hit! We were bombing and a fragment from somewhere hit my thumb knuckle. I coaxed out 1 drop of blood. Alas! no more!!

> There is a fine heroic feeling about being in France, and I am in perfect spirits. A tinge of excitement is always necessary to my happiness.

However flippant this may be, the will to suffer together with a sense of heroism and excitement is clearly expressed. Ten days later Owen is describing a tour of the line which his regiment was soon to occupy. He speaks of his party being shelled and goes on: "I tell you *these* [sic] things because *afterwards* [sic] they will sound less exciting. If I leave all my exploits for recitation after the war without mentioning them now, they will be appearing bomb-shell-bastic." The same letter concludes: "Have no anxiety. I cannot do a better thing or be in a righter place. Yet I am not sainted therefore, and so I beg you to annoy . . . , [sic] for my wicked pleasure." Owen is not only thrilled with his proximity to danger but also expresses a sense of self-righteousness about his position. Although the tone of the closing sentence quoted above is again playful the choice of the word "sainted" is telling. The figure of the martyr lurks behind the prose and it is one that Owen is both attracted to and gratified by.

Owen's initial enthusiasm in France, like his remarks about the war in 1914-15, may be taken as the "innocence" of the as yet unblooded soldier. But his reaction to his first spell of action does not bear this out. Although he is horrified by his experience of battle, there is also an intensification of the excitement and the self-satisfaction of having suffered that we have noticed thus far. His next letter home was written after five days at the front. Owen "can see no reason for deceiving" his mother and therefore goes on to tell in detail of his and his comrades' sufferings. Neither pity nor self-pity direct the utterance; rather there is simply a need to tell, to share the emotional burden of what has been undergone. The letter ends with the following instructions:

> In conclusion I must say that if there is any power whom the Soldiery execrate more than another it is that of our distinguished countryman.

> You may pass it on Via Owen Owen.

> Don't pass round these sheets but have portions typed for Leslie etc.

Here is the first note of Owen's much-famed "protest" and an exceedingly self-conscious sound it makes. There is, as we shall see, an increasing division between Owen's private experience and the reactions he wishes to make public about that experience. In this letter we have the pertinent fact that he sees "no excuse" for deceiving his mother yet does not wish the letter to be read publicly. What may be made public is the soldiers cursing of David Lloyd George (then Minister for War). In referring to himself as "Owen Owen," our author is identifying himself with Owen Glendower, thereby both giving himself the elevated status of a national hero who can authoritatively challenge Lloyd George and, at the same time depersonalising his experience. The detail of his battle experience is too raw in this letter for Owen to want it disseminated.

Evidence for this last point may be gleaned from his next letter written three days later. Here he returns to a description of No Man's Land and the trenches, but now his response is much less immediate. His prose is drenched in the metaphor of high artifice. No Man's Land is "the eternal place of gnashing of teeth," it is worse than the "Slough of Despond" and the "fires of Sodom and Gamoorah." It is "pock-marked like a body of foulest disease and its odour is the breath of cancer." The letter concludes:

> Now I have let myself tell you more facts than I should in the exuberance of having already done "a Bit."

> The people of England needn't hope. They must agitate. But they are not yet agitated even. Let them imagine 50 men trembling as with ague for 50 hours!

Many of the unresolved dilemmas, the emotional complexities of Owen's war-poems are prefigured here as are the corresponding difficulties for the reader. Owen himself betrays uncertainty as to what should or should not be said and why. The reason for his highly metaphoric, notably non-realistic descriptions, is given as "exuberance." But then we have an expression of the need for protest rendered with an oddly bathetic image of fifty men trembling with illness. The point that Owen evades throughout the letter is that thousands of men were slaughtering each other. Nevertheless the horrors of the war as described earlier in the letter implicitly aggrandise and authenticate Owen's position and provide a basis for "protest." The paradox of course is that protest against the war depends upon participation in it.

Following his first spell of action Owen spent two months out of the line. . . . In April he was again involved in action which precipitated his neurasthenic attack and led to his evacuation via various field hospitals to Craiglockhart War Hospital in Scotland. It was from the 13th Casualty Clearing Hospital, after his neurasthenic attack, that Owen wrote one of his most famous letters. Thus far critics have declined to notice the irreconcilable contradiction at the heart of Owen's prose:

> Already I have comprehended a light which will never filter into the dogma of any national church; namely that one of Christ's essential commands was: Passivity at any price! Suffer dishonour and disgrace; but never resort to arms. Be bullied, be outraged, be killed; but do not kill. It may be a chimerical and an ignominious principle, but there it is. It can only be ignored: and I think pulpit professionals are ignoring it very successfully indeed . . . And am I not a conscientious objector with a very seared conscience . . . Christ is literally in No Man's Land. There men often hear his voice: Greater Love hath no man than this, that a man lay down his life—for a friend.

Not only the "pulpit professionals" were ignoring "Christ's essential commands"; so too was Owen. And though, given the historical context, we may sympathise with Owen's situation, we cannot condone it. His assertion that the claims of pacifism "can only be ignored" is simply not true. It is quite clear that Owen wanted to fight and came close to despising those who did not. Later he was to write, "I hate washy pacifists as temperamentally as I hate whiskied Prussianists." Owen's implicit justification for being a "conscientious objector with a very seared conscience" may be located in the value he placed upon suffering. Suffering is the agency of the "Greater Love." And where in human experience is suffering more widespread and self-evident than in wartime? The contradiction lies not only with Owen but also within Christianity. Both preach passivity but elevate suffering and sacrifice even as it is embodied in war, as a saving "spiritual" principle. And Owen's belief in the value of suffering was, I think, strength-

ened by his Romantic view of the artist as one who must suffer in order to create.

Owen's poems written during his first spell of action in France express this willingness to glorify suffering. **"Greater Love"** contrasts the "love" of the sacrificed soldier with that of heterosexual erotic love. Although the "greater love" of the dying soldiers is described as "pure" and above erotic passion, the language in which their dying is described is nothing if not sensual:

> Red lips are not so red
>   As the stained stones kissed by the English dead.
> Kindness of wooed and wooer
> Seems shame to their love pure.
> O Love, your eyes lose lure
>   When I behold eyes blinded in my stead!

> Your slender attitude
>   Trembles not exquisite like limbs knife-skewed,
> Rolling and rolling there
> Where God seems not to care;
> Till the fierce Love they bear
>   Cramps them in death's extreme decrepitude.

The pronoun here is directed against women as the last stanza of the poem makes clear:

> Heart, you were never hot,
>   Nor large, nor full like hearts made great with shot;

> And though your hand be pale,
> Paler are all which trail
> Your cross through flame and hail:
>   Weep, you may weep, for you may touch them not.

Paul Fussell has aptly noticed the "homoerotic sensuousness" in Wilfred Owen's poetry and its relationship to the late nineteenth-century tradition of "warm religio-erotic celebration" [see excerpt dated 1975]. All this is evident in the stanzas I have quoted. But in making a case for "homoerotic humanism" in Owen's work, Fussell fails to notice the misogyny implicit here, as well as the equation of sexuality with suffering; the "exquisite trembling" of "knife-skewed" limbs. (pp. 69-73)

"Happiness," another of Owen's poems written in early 1917, is unusual in so far as it has no religious allusions to lend it "spiritual" overtones. The poem is about innocence and experience. The "pure happiness / The happiness our mothers gave us, boys" is juxtaposed with the less equable emotional heights and depths of "youth":

> Have we not laughed too often since with joys?
> Have we not wrought too sick and sorrowful wrongs
> for her hands' pardoning? . . .

Here "joys" seem to be contrasted with "sick and sorrowful wrongs," but in the sestet it is implicit that the relationship between "joys" and "wrongs" is one of interdependence rather than contrast:

> But the old Happiness is unreturning.
> Boy's griefs are not so grievous as youth's yearning,
> Boys have no sadness sadder than our hope.
> We who have seen the gods' kaleidoscope,
> And played with human passions for our toys,
> We know men suffer chiefly by their joys.

"Human passions" clearly include "the sick and sorrowful wrongs" of the octet. By equating suffering with joy Owen is very close in this poem to an explicit expression of sado-masochistic tendencies.

Both **"Greater Love"** and **"Happiness"** are private poems in so far as they express personal beliefs and feelings rather than the more impersonal didacticism of his public utterances. **"Le Christianisme"** and **"At a Calvary near the Ancre"** move towards the public mode Owen experimented with after his meeting with Sassoon at Craiglockhart hospital. Nevertheless in **"Le Christianisme,"** an ironic attack upon the established Church, Owen concludes with an image of misogynistic violence; his private feelings intrude and disrupt the public point:

> One Virgin still immaculate
>   Smiles on for war to flatter her.
> She's halo'd with an old tin hat,
>   But a piece of hell will batter her.

"At a Calvary near the Ancre" takes up the theme of **"Greater Love"** with the soldiers taking the role of Christ whilst priests and politicians play the parts of the Biblical scribes and pharisees:

> The scribes on all the people shove
>   And brawl allegiance to the state,
> But they who love the greater love
>   Lay down their life; they do not hate.

In this stanza Owen castigates the reasons for fighting, but not the fighting itself. He locates value in the latter but not in the former. Fighting is the means to a glorious suffering, to the "greater love" of martyrdom and to homoerotic solidarity. Owen's political perceptions are completely at odds with his private feelings. If fighting is the means to an exalted spiritual suffering it hardly matters why one is fighting. Owen's public poems of pity and protest seek implicitly to justify this ethically compromised position whilst attempting to mask his private predilection for suffering.

Owen's poems written at Craiglockhart, Scarborough and Ripon, before he returned to France again bear witness to this. Sassoon's satiric poems with their blatant ironies and obvious didacticism seem to have influenced Owen for a time. Poems like **"The Dead-Beat,"** **"The Letter,"** **"The Chances"** and of course, **"Dulce et Decorum Est,"** though written with more verve than Sassoon could muster and showing Owen to be bravely exercising the vernacular in poetry, nevertheless are structured upon very unsubtle irony. This in itself does not constitute a valid criticism, but the neat construction of situational irony, rendered in rhyming couplets or in the ABAB/CDCD rhyme scheme of **"Dulce et Decorum Est,"** tends towards the glib and certainly militates against any arguments for the poems' realism. Owen also (and this is particularly true of **"The Letter"** and **"The Chances"**), though attempting to write in the language of the private soldiers is never terribly comfortable with the demotic, forcing it into poetic form and thereby sacrificing authenticity for didactic punch. This gives the poems an unremitting air of artificiality, the apotheosis of which may be discerned in the closing lines of the octet in **"The Chances,"** where "cushy" is made to rhyme embarrassingly with the word "mushy."

But more crucial to my argument is the response these poems are asking for. Owen is ostensibly detailing suffering in order to provoke a reaction of pity and indignation. The victims of war he portrays are implicitly innocent. We see men dying, we do not see the same men killing. Owen divests the soldiers of individual responsibility, his target being the politicians and the people at home who do not "understand." In other words the guilt of the audience is taken for granted, the guilt of the soldiers excised. This naivety with respect to ethics severely vitiates the public point of the poems.

"Dulce et Decorum Est" is justly regarded as one of Owen's finest didactic poems and, with less perspicacity, celebrated for its "realism." Not only its poetic form but also the use of metaphor and simile and the introduction of dreams force the poem away from realism. The gassed soldier's eyes "writhe" in his "hanging face" like a "devil's sick of sin." "Devils" clearly have no place in the arena of the reality principle. But for a moment Owen hints at the guilt of the victim. As the poem continues, however, the focus, and with it implicitly the blame, is shifted as Owen directs his utterance outwards to make his point. If we, the audience, had seen such terrible suffering we

> . . . would not tell with such high zest
> To children ardent for some desperate glory,
> The old Lie: Dulce et Decorum est
> Pro patria mori.

This needed to be said in 1917 in a way it does not need to be said now. The poem is undoubtedly powerful and to deflate the rhetoric of Imperialism was clearly salutary. But now, if we are not to react with complacent self-satisfaction, safe in the knowledge that we do not tell our children "old lies" we are, I think, obliged to recognise the tendency in a poem like this to substitute a different kind of glorification for the one which is being satirised. The poem seeks pity for its victim, but also tacitly asks for our admiration of the sufferings endured. The "greater love," which absolves the soldiers from all responsibility whilst elevating their experience in proportion to the sufferings sustained, needs to be called into question.

That Owen on the one hand celebrates suffering but on the other hand wishes to blame others for causing it, is a paradox which affects the role of "pity" in his poetry. In some poems he seems to demand a reaction of "pity" from his audience but in others he specifically denies or questions the adequacy of "pity" as a response to martyrdom.

We have already observed how the poem **"Greater Love"** concludes with the line "Weep, you may weep, for you may touch them not," at once describing the redundancy of tears and the exclusive nature of the male experience of war. Another central poem which elaborates this position is **"Apologia pro Poemate Meo."** Stallworthy suggests that this was written in response to a plea by Robert Graves that Owen should try to be more cheerful in his poems. Although they can hardly be described as "cheerful" the first seven stanzas of the poem do record Owen's positive experiences of warfare:

> I, too, saw God through mud,—
>   The mud that cracked on cheeks when wretches smiled.
> War brought more glory to their eyes than blood,
> And gave their laughs more glee than shakes a child.

> Merry it was to laugh there—
> Where death becomes absurd and life absurder.
> For power was on us as we slashed bones bare
> Not to feel sickness or remorse of murder.

The poem goes on to record the poet's having "dropped off fear," having "witnessed exultation," having "made fellowships— / Untold of happy lovers in old songs" and finally, before drawing his conclusion, the poet speaks of his aesthetic appreciation of war:

> I have perceived much beauty
>   In the hoarse oaths that kept our courage straight;
>   Heard music in the silentness of duty;
>   Found peace where shell-storms spouted reddest spate.
>
> Nevertheless, except you share
>   With them in hell the sorrowful dark of hell,
>   Whose world is but the trembling of a flare
>   And heaven but as the highway for a shell,
>
> You shall not hear their mirth:
>   You shall not come to think them well content
>   By any jest of mind. These men are worth
>   Your tears. You are not worth their merriment.

This "apology" is very telling. Having passionately expressed the glory, power, exultation, love and beauty of warfare Owen then attempts to subvert his own utterance with respect to his audience. The poem shifts from the private to the public. The audience are not "allowed" to hear the soldiers' mirth (despite Owen's vivid description of it), because we have not experienced "the sorrowful dark of hell" upon which the soldiers' "merriment" is predicated. To shed tears is our only proper role; we have to suffer like the troops in order to be "worthy." It has been said that Owen was "trying to convey the horror and pity of war to homefront readers." And this is, I think, how he saw his public role. But there is an unresolved tension between suing for peace and privately enjoying, even glorifying the fighting. How are we as an audience to feel pity when we are implicitly despised for being non-combatant. Owen wants peace but "hates" pacifists, he requires pity but implies that his audience is unfit to give it.

"Disabled," which seems to me one of Owen's finest poems in so far as it treats of the motivations of many young men for volunteering and, through carefully modulated sensuality uncovers the tragic irony of its now impotent victim, nevertheless places its audience in an untenable position:

> Some cheered him home, but not as crowds cheer Goal.
> Only a solemn man who brought him fruits
> *Thanked* him; and then inquired about his soul.
>
>   .   .   .   .   .   .
>
> Now, he will spend a few sick years in institutes,
> And do what things the rules consider wise,
> And take whatever pity they may dole.
> To-night he noticed how the women's eyes
> Passed from him to the strong men that were whole.

Irony is directed to expose the response of those at home as entirely inadequate to the soldier's tragedy; whatever "pity" is "doled" will be no good. Now this may be the case but it leaves the reader in an uncomfortable limbo because "pity" by implication seems to be the preserve of the fighters, if not of Owen himself. Behind the utterance lies the assumption that to be a real pacifist or feel real pity one has to go out and experience the fighting. Nowhere is this paradox given clearer expression than in another of Owen's poems of "protest," **"Insensibility."**

This is a poem which explicitly seeks ironically to contrast the fortunate and justifiable "insensibility" of some of the troops, with the unjustifiable "insensibility" of the "home front." But this is not all the poem articulates. Between the insensi-

bility of both soldiers and civilians is the sensibility of "Owen Owen"; fighter and poet:

> Happy are men who yet before they are killed
> Can let their veins run cold.
> Whom no compassion fleers
> Or makes their feet
> Sore on the alleys cobbled with their brothers.
> The front line withers.
> But they are troops who fade, not flowers,
> For poets' tearful fooling:
> Men, gaps for filling:
> Losses, who might have fought
> Longer; but no one bothers.

Despite his rhetorical gesture about "poets' tearful fooling," Owen projects himself here as the hero of his own poem; he is both "bothered" and has "compassion." The poem continues through sections II, III, and IV, to elaborate upon the "fortunate" soldiers who have "ceased feeling," "lost imagination," whose minds were "never trained"; they are not susceptible to the horrors that Owen "has" to endure. The poet argues that the "sensible" (or "sensitive") have to view their "task" in the same way as those who have lost their sensibility:

> We wise, who with a thought besmirch
> Blood over all our soul,
> How should we see our task,
> But through his blunt and lashless eyes?
> Alive, he is not vital overmuch;
> Dying, not mortal overmuch;
> Nor sad, nor proud,
> Nor curious at all.
> He cannot tell
> Old men's placidity from his.

This is supremely condescending towards the private soldiers as the poet's self-pity turns to self-congratulation. Although he has already demonstrated his sensibility, Owen argues that the "wise" (like him) are entirely justified in aspiring to insensibility under the circumstances. What cannot be justified, we find in the final stanza, is the position of those at home:

> But cursed are dullards whom no cannon stuns,
> That they should be as stones.
> Wretched are they, and mean
> With paucity that never was simplicity.
> By choice they made themselves immune
> To pity and whatever mourns in man
> Before the last sea and the hapless stars;
> Whatever mourns when many leave these shores;
> Whatever shares
> The eternal reciprocity of tears.

The effect of these grandiloquent gestures is to elevate the soldiers' experience (and particularly Owen's) indiscriminately at the expense of all non-combatants at home. The crux of this final stanza is in the line which begins "By choice," which neatly sidesteps the issue that he, and many of his fellow soldiers, volunteered. According to Owen fighting gives the soldiers the right to be insensible and also gives them (particularly those who remain "sensible" like Owen) the prerogative of "pity," "mourning" and the "eternal reciprocity of tears." The poem assumes an enormous moral rectitude which it cannot sustain. The ethics of the situation are far more complex than Owen's black and white "binary vision" allows.

During his time at Craiglockhart, Scarborough and Ripon, Owen gained recognition as a poet. He also became increasingly convinced that he "had" to return to France. Writing to his mother on New Year's Eve 1917 Owen wrote:

> I go out of this year a Poet, my dear Mother, as which I did not enter it. I am held peer by the Georgians; I am a poet's poet.
>
> I am started. The tugs have left me; I feel the great swelling of the open sea taking my galleon.

This is heady stuff and quite plainly Owen has lost none of the Romantic image of himself as a poet with a capital P. . . . Like his earlier decision to volunteer, Owen's motivations for wishing to return to France are clearly involved with his role as a poet. Fêted as he was by some of the leading literary figures in London, he could not but be aware that his experience of war had given rise to his finest poetry. To go out again and, as he later put it, "help these boys . . . indirectly by watching their sufferings that I may speak of them as well as a pleader can," was clearly what he wished to do. Owen wrote in another letter: "I am much gladder to be going out again than afraid. I shall be better able to cry my outcry, playing my part."

To "plead," to "cry his outcry," is the moral justification for his return to the war. But it is a highly irrational, personal justification. Apart from anything else it presumes that writing poetry was an effective means of "pleading" or crying one's outcry. In the immediate political situation of 1917-18 this was clearly untrue. Not only were very few of Owen's poems published during the war, but also Sassoon's public protest in the form of a letter caused more political impact than any poem did or could do. (pp. 73-80)

Returning to France made Owen content; it fulfilled his need to suffer and to write. What he did not wish to make public was this contentment. His private reaction to the war became ever more divorced from his public reaction to it. The following extracts from several letters, written during his second time on active service in France, make this abundantly clear:

> Serenity Shelley never dreamt of crowns me.
>
> Tell them [Harold and Colin Owen] and them only how peculiarly unreluctant I am to be back here.
>
> Do not inform friends and relations that I pass my hours reading, sleeping, conversing, and gathering roses from bewildered gardens. But so it is.
>
> . . . and may your peace be as divine as mine is tonight.
>
> Do not (as I afore-mentioned) undeceive the world which thinks I'm having a bad time.
>
> It past the limits of my abhorrence. I lost all my earthly faculties and fought like an angel . . . I only shot one man with my revolver (at about thirty yards); the rest I took with a smile.
>
> I live between the extremes of gross materialism—feeding savagely and sleeping doggishly—and of high spirituality suffering and sacrificing.

It should be noted that the last two letters quoted above are addressed to Owen's mother and marked "Strictly Private" and "Not for circulation as a whole," respectively.

I have said that I do not think that Owen was fully aware of his ambivalent attitude to suffering, and implied that his public poems mask their origins and motivations. But interestingly in two late and more private poems, **"Strange Meeting"** and **"Spring Offensive,"** there is evidence to suggest that Owen was beginning to battle with his own inward war. **"Strange Meeting"** has hitherto puzzled and fascinated critics. It is a difficult poem because it expresses deeply contradictory positions which are never reconciled. The poem portrays a vision of hell wherein two of the shades converse; they are dead soldiers. One suggests that "here is no cause to mourn," and the reply to this contention constitutes the rest of the poem:

> "None" said that other, "save the undone years
> The hopelessness. Whatever hope is yours,
> Was my life also; I went hunting wild
> After the wildest beauty in the world,
> Which lies not calm in eyes, or braided hair,
> But mocks the steady running of the hour
> And if it grieves, grieves richlier than here.
> And by my glee might many men have laughed
> And of my weeping something had been left
> Which must die now. I mean the truth untold,
> The pity of war, the pity war distilled.
> Now men will go content with what we spoiled. . . ."

The "wildest beauty in the world" surely pertains to art. The dead soldier-poet laments that his grief and joy have not been transmuted into what Yeats called "the artifice of eternity." The "truth" about the war is located in the "pity" that it "distilled." But this will now be left unspoken since the poet has been killed.

All this is coherent as far as it goes. But as the poem proceeds, the persona articulates a different position asserting that when alive he "had" the "courage" and "wisdom" to miss "the march of this retreating world" and "would" have played a different role:

> Then, when much blood had clogged their chariot-wheels
> I would go up and wash them from sweet wells,
> Even with truths that lie too deep for taint.
> I would have poured my spirit without stint
> But not through wounds; not on the cess of war.
> Foreheads of men have bled where no wounds were.

Since the poem makes clear that the persona had been killed in action the assertion of "courage" and "mastery" and all that follows has something of a hollow ring to it. It is never made clear to whom the pronoun in the first line quoted above refers. What is manifest is that the persona places himself above "them" and articulates a pacifist position implying that if he had his time again he would not fight. But this surely contradicts the persona's earlier lament. For there it is implied that the poet's art has a direct relationship to the "truth untold," the "pity" of war. The persona, like Owen, is caught between wishing he had been a pacifist and yet perceiving in warfare the materials of "truthful" poetry. It is also entirely significant that even whilst articulating the pacifist position, the persona implies that he still would have adopted the role of the Christ-like martyr in order to "pour his spirit," in order to write.

"Spring Offensive," like **"Strange Meeting"** is, I think, testimony to the fact that Owen could not resolve the opposing tensions which constituted his reaction to warfare. **"Spring Offensive"** describes an attack. We see the soldiers before, during and after the action. All three stages are deeply Romanticised. When the "little word" for the attack is spoken there are "No alarms / of bugles, no high flags, no clamorous haste,— / Only a lift and flare of eyes that faced / the sun." The "lift and flare of eyes" is surely as much an image of Romantic heroism as the "alarms," "bugles" and "flags." The subsequent slaughter is described thus:

> . . . And instantly the whole sky burned
> With fury against them; earth set sudden cups
> In thousands for their blood; and the green slope
> Chasmed and steepened sheer to infinite space.

It hardly needs to be remarked how "unrealistic" this is. Again Owen avoids the crucial fact that men were killing men; the earth and sky clearly had nothing to do with it! The crux of the poem however lies in the final stanza where a rhetoric of exaggeration echoes the extremity of the experience it describes and leads to a final unanswered rhetorical question:

> But what say such as from existence' brink
> Ventured but drave too swift to sink,
> The few who rushed in the body to enter hell
> And there out-fiending all its friends and flames
> With superhuman inhumanities,
> Long-famous glories, immemorial shames—
> And crawling slowly back, have by degrees
> Regained cool peaceful air in wonder—
> Why speak not they of comrades that went under?

There is a sense of the soldiers' volition here as they "rush" to their death. But the lines are fraught with paradox. It is the inability to resolve the tensions between "superhuman inhumanities," "glory" and "shame," which implicitly answers the final rhetorical question. The survivors are filled with wonder and with guilt; feelings impossible of synthesis or resolution. Therefore they are silent about their dead comrades. But beyond this is the further irony that Owen *does* speak of those who have "gone under" and the appropriate question is, to what purpose? On the one hand the poem seeks to express the emotional conflicts engendered by warfare, but on the other, the language of the poem tends to rescue human nature from indictment. Men are no longer men, they are "friends"; "inhumanities" become "superhuman." Although the poem goes further than much of his earlier work in directly giving voice to the ambivalent "glory" and "shame" Owen perceived in warfare, it still implicitly resists a bald recognition of the violence man is capable of, and tends to elevate this onto another plane of experience. Owen wishes to retrieve or preserve a notion of "humanity" which excludes the human potential for brutality.

Quoting Tagore, Owen said more than once, "What I have seen is unsurpassable." There is in this remark a sense of celebration which I think is crucial in attempting to understand the significance of Owen's work. For he not only criticised warfare, he also celebrated, even glorified it. Rupert Brooke's famous sonnet "Peace" has been castigated for seeing in war an answer to all the "little emptiness of love"; for perceiving the soldiers' venture in terms of a "swimmer into cleanness leaping." But there is something of this in Owen's attitude to the war as well. Although he saw the mud, blood and suffering, he found enormous value in it all. Critics have wished to make Owen into a humanist, a courageous political spokesman and above all a poet of pity and compassion. I have sought to show

that his "political" objection to the war was completely at odds with his private feelings on the subject. And that the "pity" in his work is severely compromised by his ambivalent attitude to suffering.

If we are to appreciate Owen's work, it should I think, be for the right reasons. I do not think his poetry is the vehicle of moral, political or spiritual rectitude. Rather the value of his best work resides in its undoubted and much remarked technical achievement and precisely in the complex of ambivalent feelings it expresses. For if we are to understand wars, not only do we have to study the politic-economic ideologies for which they are fought, we also need to understand ourselves and recognise that in the mind of humankind there is a potential for violence and a potential to glorify violence which needs to be part of our self-consciousness not our sub-consciousness. I have deliberately refrained from amateur psychoanalytic interpretation. What I have tried to suggest is that the "human problem" of Owen's work lies in those depths of the mind, not yet fully understood where, as Freud put it, the battle of "Eros" and "Thanatos," the creative and destructive principles is constantly waged. However much a part of the human condition pain and suffering are, to celebrate or enjoy one's own or other people's suffering belongs to the realm of the destructive element. We should not, I think, teach our children otherwise. (pp. 80-3)

> *Adrian Caesar, "The 'Human Problem' in Wilfred Owen's Poetry," in* Critical Quarterly, *Vol. 29, No. 2, Summer, 1987, pp. 67-84.*

ADDITIONAL BIBLIOGRAPHY

Bäckman, Sven. *Tradition Transformed: Studies in the Poetry of Wilfred Owen.* Lund, Sweden: C. W. K. Gleerup, 1979, 204 p.
    Examines Owen's relationship to poetic tradition and assesses his technical innovations.

Banerjee, A. "Wilfred Owen: A Reassessment." *The Literary Half-Yearly* XVIII, No. 2 (July 1977): 85-100.
    Supports William Butler Yeats's controversial negative view of Owen's poetry.

Bateson, F. W. "The Analysis of Poetic Texts: Owen's 'Futility' and Davie's 'The Garden Party'." *Essays in Criticism* XXIX, No. 2 (April 1979): 156-64.
    Considers "Futility" overrated and morally objectionable. According to Bateson: "If the proper reaction to trench warfare is to write elegantly about it then trench warfare becomes aesthetically desirable like a sunset, a primrose by the river's brim, or a model in the nude. *Quod est absurdum*. And worse than absurd—wicked."

Blunden, Edmund. "The Real War." *Athenaeum,* No. 4728 (10 December 1920): 807.
    Appreciative review of *Poems*. Blunden maintains that "in Owen we lost a poet of rare force. . . . The very make of his verse is hard and remorseless or strange and sombre as he wills."

Cohen, Joseph. "Wilfred Owen in America." *Prairie Schooner* XXXI, No. 4 (Winter 1957): 339-45.
    Discusses Owen's critical reputation in the United States. According to Cohen: "What reputation Owen currently possesses in America has arisen out of our poets' and critics' realization that his verses captured and expressed the essence of twentieth-century war, i.e., its totality, with more clarity, forcefulness, compassion and accomplishment than did the verse of his contemporaries."

————. "Owen's 'The Show'." *The Explicator* XVI, No. 2 (November 1957): No. 8.
Concludes that like "Strange Meeting," "'The Show' is identified geographically and chronologically with the Western Front, it is placed in a dream context, it develops the double image of the slain and the slayer in the same figure, it stresses dramatically the tragedy of armed conflict in both its personal and its cosmic manifestations, and it places precisely and emphatically the responsibility for war upon all mankind."

————. "In Memory of W. B. Yeats—and Wilfred Owen." *Journal of English and Germanic Philology* LVIII, No. 4 (October 1959): 637-49.
Examines the controversy surrounding Yeats's omission of Owen from his *Oxford Book of Modern Verse* (1936) and discusses Yeats's negative comments on Owen's poetry. According to Cohen: "Yeats clearly recognized if not Owen's own permanence, then the permanence of what he symbolized. Hence, we may conclude that Yeats's fight was never an entirely personal offense mounted directly against Owen, but a defense of a long cherished poetic principle no longer popular."

Das, Sasi Bhusan. *Wilfred Owen's Influence on Three Generations of Poets*. Calcutta: Roy & Roy, 1982, 282 p.
Examines Owen's influence on war poets of World Wars I and II and on major English-language poets of the 1930s.

Enright, D. J. "The Literature of the First World War." In *The Pelican Guide to English Literature, Vol. 7: The Modern Age*, edited by Boris Ford, pp. 154-69. Harmondsworth, Middlesex: Penguin Books, 1961.
General discussion of the work of Owen and his contemporaries.

————. "The Truth Told." *New Statesman* LXVI, No. 1698 (27 September 1963): 408, 410.
Discusses textual revisions in *The Collected Poems of Wilfred Owen*, edited by C. Day Lewis, and favorably assesses the first volume of Harold Owen's biography of his brother, *Journey from Obscurity*.

Fairchild, Hoxie Neale. "Toward Hysteria." In his *Religious Trends in English Poetry, Vol. 5: 1880-1920—Gods of a Changing Poetry*, pp. 578-627. New York: Columbia University Press, 1962.
Compares the war poetry of Siegfried Sassoon, Osbert Sitwell, Herbert Read, Isaac Rosenberg, and Owen. According to Fairchild: "Owen, by far the best poet of the group, is also essentially the most traditional. . . . He can be as savagely satirical as . . . Sassoon, but he uses his poetry not for the direct relief of a hysterical state of mind but as a means of controlling and sublimating his distress."

Fraser, G. S. "Two War Poets." *The New York Review of Books* II, No. 3 (19 March 1964): 6-7.
Reviews C. Day Lewis's collection of Owen's poems and a collected edition of poetry by Keith Douglas, an English poet who was killed in World War II.

Gregory, Horace. "A Dead Poetic Movement." *The Nation* CXXXIII, No. 3464 (25 November 1931): 577-78.
Adversely characterizes Georgian poetry in general and unfavorably reviews *The Poems of Wilfred Owen*, edited by Edmund Blunden. According to Gregory: "Owen's work was and still remains incomplete, poetry written by a man who died too soon and whose failure was characteristic of an entire movement in English poetry."

Griffith, George V. "Owen's 'Dulce et Decorum Est'." *The Explicator* 41, No. 3 (Spring 1983): 37-9.
Griffith maintains that "Owen's powerful indictment of Horace . . . is too neat, too simple. He uses poetry to exhort us not to believe poetry. If we accept that Horace is a lie, how are we to know that Owen is the truth?"

Grigson, Geoffrey. "Edited." *Saturday Review* 152, No. 3951 (18 July 1931): 95.
Condemns *The Poems of Wilfred Owen*, the volume of poems and memoirs edited by Edmund Blunden. According to Grigson: "If published at all" the verses in *The Poems of Wilfred Owen* "should have been decently bottled in an appendix and not allowed to water down the few vintage pints of lovely and matured poetry which Owen has left behind him."

Grubb, Frederick. "The Embattled Truth: Wilfred Owen and Isaac Rosenberg." In his *A Vision of Reality: A Study of Liberalism in Twentieth-Century Verse*, pp. 73-96. New York: Barnes & Noble, 1965.
Analyzes Owen's treatment of war as a subject, noting his apparent anti-war stance and his emphasis on the dehumanizing nature of war for those involved in battle.

Hepburn, James. "Wilfred Owen's Poetic Development." In his *Critic into Anti-Critic*, pp. 167-78. Columbia, S.C.: Camden House, 1984.
Studies Owen's technical and stylistic development, especially noting his experiments in off-rhyme. According to Hepburn: "Under the impact of horrifying experience he transformed himself from a priggish young Keatsian into a greatly original poet."

Hibberd, Dominic, ed. *Wilfred Owen: War Poems and Others*. London: Chatto and Windus, 1973, 158 p.
Includes an introductory biographical and critical sketch, notes on Owen's poems, Owen's own Preface to his poetry, a bibliography, and an index of first lines and titles.

————. "Wilfred Owen and the Georgians." *Review of English Studies* XXX, No. 17 (February 1979): 28-40.
Emphasizes the influence of Georgian poets Harold Monro, Siegfried Sassoon, and Robert Graves on the development of Owen's poetic style. In Hibberd's opinion: "All three attempted to curb his weakness for 'over-luscious' writing; they were fortunately only partly successful, and Owen is a transitional figure between Victorian and modern poetry."

Review of *The Poems of Wilfred Owen*. *Hound and Horn* 5, No. 4 (July-September 1932): 679-81.
Finds Owen's poetry flawed and incomplete, yet powerful. According to the critic, Owen's poems "have a toughness, a casual but not calculated violence."

Kaltembach, Michele. "Wilfred Owen's Personality as Revealed by His Letters." *Caliban* X (1973): 43-54.
Finds that Owen's letters demonstrate "how early in life Owen felt he had to fulfil a certain duty, how he prepared for it and how he came to realize precisely what his vocation consisted of."

Lane, Arthur E. *An Adequate Response: The War Poetry of Wilfred Owen & Siegfried Sassoon*. Detroit: Wayne State University Press, 1972, 190 p.
Examines the artistic milieu in which Owen and Sassoon were working, their poetic responses to the experience of war, and their relationship to poets Rupert Brooke, Charles Hamilton Sorley, and others who produced more traditionally patriotic verses.

Larkin, Philip. "The Real Wilfred: Owen's Life and Legends." *Encounter* XLIV, No. 3 (March 1975): 73-81.
Chiefly biographical commentary in a review of Jon Stallworthy's *Wilfred Owen*.

Lomas, Herbert. "The Critic as Anti-Hero: War Poetry." *The Hudson Review* XXXVIII, No. 3 (Autumn 1985): 376-89.
Finds that although Owen produced only "a handful of major poems" he "could hardly have gone farther at his age, in his time, under his pressures, though he might have turned into a worse fuddy-duddy than Sassoon surprisingly did."

Review of *Poems* by Wilfred Owen. *London Mercury* III, No. 15 (January 1921): 334-36.
Praises Owen's treatment of war as a subject. According to the reviewer: "His prime object was . . . the propagation of the truth about war, not in order that posterity might admire his powers of exact statement or his sensibility, but solely in order that they might quail from repeating such horrors."

MacNeice, Louis. "Out of Ugliness." *New Statesman* LX, No. 1545 (20 October 1960): 623-24.

Review of D. S. R. Welland's biography of Owen in which MacNeice comments on Owen's life and literary career, concluding that Yeats was incorrect in his unfavorable assessment of Owen's poetry.

McIlroy, James F. *Wilfred Owen's Poetry: A Study Guide*. London: Heinemann Educational Books, 1974, 124 p.
Handbook containing an introductory sketch, analyses, survey of critical opinion, and bibliography.

Muir, Edwin. "Poetry." In his *The Present Age from 1914*, pp. 43-128. London: Cresset Press, 1939.
Offers commentary on Owen's works and places him among early-twentieth-century English literary figures as a "poet of some influence, particularly on the newer generation." According to Muir: "The astonishing thing . . . is that Owen could suffer and reflect so deeply while he was suffering; that he could see what was unendurable, and yet stop and weigh it."

"English Poets of Today." *New York Times Book Review* (15 May 1921): 13, 27.
Includes an appreciative review of *Poems*, praising Owen's technical experiments and his objective treatment of war as a subject.

Norgate, Paul. "Shell-Shock and Poetry: Wilfred Owen at Craiglockhart Hospital." *English* XXXVI, No. 154 (Spring 1987): 1-35.
Chronicles the war experiences which led to Owen's neurasthenia, his meetings at Craiglockhart with Sassoon and Robert Graves, and his poetic development during his recovery at the hospital from June to October 1917.

Orrmont, Arthur. *Requiem for War: The Life of Wilfred Owen*. New York: Four Winds Press, 1972, 192 p.
An appreciative noncritical biography.

Pinto, Vivian de Sola. "Trench Poets." In her *Crisis in English Poetry: 1880-1940*, pp. 137-57. London: Hutchinson's University Library, 1951.
Introductory sketch placing Owen among his contemporaries. According to Pinto: "The greatness of Owen's poetry lies in its moral power. It is based on a morality that is the result of a profound exploration of the inner life, which strangely enough, in the misery of trench warfare has here found for an instant a more complete synthesis with outward experience than in any English poet since Hopkins."

Savage, D. S. "Two Prophetic Poems." *Western Review* 13, No. 2 (Winter 1949): 67-78.
Compares "The Second Coming" by W. B. Yeats with "Strange Meeting" by Owen. Savage concludes that "each of these poets, in his own way, penetrated to the heart of the human, historical situation, and defined in himself, with admirable devotion and clarity, one of the only two thoroughly consistent and coherent attitudes towards that course. Yeats wrote in affirmation of the Beast, of blood and of war. Owen . . . positively renounced brutalization and 'the blood which some (e.g. Yeats) say nurtures'."

Silkin, Jon, ed. Introduction to *The Penguin Book of First World War Poetry*, pp. 11-73. London: Allen Lane, 1978.
Discussion of various approaches to the theme of war in the poetry of Owen, Sassoon, Rupert Brooke, Isaac Rosenberg, and others.

Sinfield, Mark. "Wilfred Owen's 'Mental Cases': Source and Structure." *Notes and Queries* 29, No. 4 (August 1982): 339-41.
Determines that the soldier-patients in the poem represent paradoxically "both the saved and the damned." According to Sinfield: "[They] have to live with the guilt and horror of the 'mur-

ders' they have 'witnessed' . . . : we are not allowed simply to elevate them into saints and so pay them off with their acquired glory, but must recognize that we have required them to violate their humanity."

Sisson, C. H. "Edward Thomas; Wilfred Owen; Isaac Rosenberg; Harold Monro." In his *English Poetry, 1900-1950: An Assessment*, pp. 71-95. New York: St. Martin's Press, 1971.
Considers Owen's Preface to his collected poetry "an embarrassing statement" and pronounces Owen "a very limited poetic talent."

Stallworthy, Jon. "W. B. Yeats and Wilfred Owen." *Critical Quarterly* 11, No. 3 (Autumn 1969): 199-214.
Examines Yeats's influence on and disapproval of Owen's poetry.

———. *Wilfred Owen*. London: Oxford University Press and Chatto and Windus, 1974, 333 p.
An appreciative biography intended as a complementary volume to existing biographical sources including Harold Owen's *Journey from Obscurity* and the *Collected Letters*.

Thwaite, Anthony. "Wilfred Owen, Edward Thomas and D. H. Lawrence." In his *Contemporary English Poetry: An Introduction*, pp. 42-53. London: Heinemann, 1964.
Concludes that "Owen's poetry remains as both an important fragment of historical importance—an atmospheric picture of a particularly unpleasant and futile war—and as a body of work satisfying in itself."

Walsh, T. J., ed. *A Tribute to Wilfred Owen*. Liverpool: Birkenhead Institute, 1964, 62 p.
Includes biographical sketches and critical essays, as well as tributes by Sassoon, Benjamin Britten, Edmund Blunden, Herbert Read, Stephen Spender, C. Day Lewis, and T. S. Eliot, who called "Strange Meeting" a poem which "will never be forgotten, and which is not only one of the most moving pieces of verse inspired by the war of 1914-1918, but also a technical achievement of great originality."

Welland, D. S. R. "Half-Rhyme in Wilfred Owen: Its Derivation and Use." *Review of English Studies* 1, n.s., No. 3 (July 1950): 226-41.
Suggests antecedent literary and folk poets who may have inspired the use of half-rhyme by Owen and comments on the use of half-rhyme by poets who succeeded Owen, including C. Day Lewis and Louis MacNeice.

White, Gertrude M. "Critic's Key: Poem or Personality?" *English Literature in Transition, 1880-1920* II, No. 3 (1968): 174-79.
Attacks the thesis presented by Joseph Cohen in "Owen Agonistes" [see excerpt dated 1965] that the key to interpretation of Owen's verses lies in the poet's latent homosexuality.

White, William. *Wilfred Owen: A Bibliography*. Kent, Ohio: The Kent State University Press, 1967, 41 p.
Bibliography of and about Owen and his works.

Yeats, W. B., ed. Introduction to *The Oxford Book of Modern Verse: 1892-1935*, pp. v-xlii. New York: Oxford University Press, 1937.
Includes Yeats's derogatory comments on war poetry: "I have a distaste for certain poems written in the midst of the great war. . . . [The writers of war poetry] felt bound, in the words of the best known, to plead the suffering of their men. In poems that had for a time considerable fame, written in the first person, they made that suffering their own. I have rejected these poems for the same reason that made Arnold withdraw his *Empedocles on Etna* from circulation; passive suffering is not a theme for poetry."

Benito Pérez Galdós

1843-1920

Spanish novelist, dramatist, essayist, and journalist.

Galdós is considered the most important Spanish novelist since Cervantes and is one of the few Spanish writers to have achieved international recognition. Applying the techniques of the European schools of Realism and Naturalism, he created a portrait of Spanish society that critics find both accurate and comprehensive. A prolific writer, Galdós composed over seventy novels, the majority of which are divided into two groupings, the *Episodios nacionales* (*National Episodes*) and the *Novelas españolas contemporáneas* (*Contemporary Spanish Novels*); the latter are considered his best works and form the basis of his critical reputation.

Born in Las Palmas, in the Canary Islands, Galdós was the youngest of the ten children of a retired military officer and his wife. Galdós's mother hoped that her youngest son would emulate her favorite brother, a respected and wealthy attorney in Cuba, and when it was time for the young man to begin his secondary education it was she who decided he would study law at the University of Madrid. Galdós, however, had already decided to make writing his career and had in fact been publishing articles in Las Palmas journals for some time. Galdós enrolled at the university but seldom attended classes; instead, he spent his time discussing politics in student cafés, familiarizing himself with the street life of the city, and writing essays for leftist journals. Within three years he had abandoned the facade of university studies altogether and was making a nominal living as a journalist.

Galdós completed his first novel, *La sombra* (*The Shadow*), early in 1867, but he was so dissatisfied with the work that he did not attempt to have it published. Later that year, however, inspired by Honoré de Balzac's novel *Eugénie Grandet*, he wrote two historical novels, *La fontana de oro* and *El audaz*, and conceived the plan for the historical series *National Episodes*. Galdós worked at a feverish pace throughout the next decade, producing a total of twenty *National Episodes*. He also continued his journalistic activities during this period, and his acerbic attacks on the Bourbon monarchy and the Spanish Catholic church earned him the respect of the republicans, who responded by electing him to the Spanish congress in 1880.

While the *National Episodes* were a huge popular success and made Galdós a national celebrity, they failed to satisfy the author's artistic ambitions. As a result, in 1879 he announced his intention to abandon the series in order to concentrate on the creation of "contemporary types" in his fiction. One year later, he began writing his *Contemporary Spanish Novels;* working steadily and rapidly, he completed twenty of the twenty-four *Contemporary Novels* within a nine-year period. Although this series is today acknowledged as Galdós's crowning achievement, it was not well received during his lifetime, and he was forced by economic necessity to return to the production of *National Episodes*. Nevertheless, despite such concessions to financial exigencies, Galdós remained insolvent throughout the rest of his life.

Galdós continued to work on the *National Episodes* even after he became partially disabled by a stroke in 1905, and his writing

career ended only with the onset of total blindness in 1912. That same year, several of Galdós's colleagues attempted to gain the Nobel prize for him, but their efforts were blocked by civil and academic authorities who had been offended by his republican sympathies. Galdós remained active in politics throughout his final years; although he was unable to continue his journalistic activities, he frequently appeared at rallies for various liberal causes, where his presence often inspired a strong show of support. He died in 1920.

Critics find in Galdós's fiction the direct reflection of his liberal political ideology. In the *National Episodes,* which recount the events of Spain's turbulent history from 1805 through 1880, he attempted to show that the monarchy had proven itself unfit to rule the Spanish people, thus implying the inherent rectitude of the republican cause. Similarly, he revealed what he considered the moral bankruptcy of the Spanish Catholic church in the hope that such a revelation would help to decrease the enormous influence of the church in Spanish society. The narrative plan of the *National Episodes,* however, was necessarily shaped by the constraints of historical accuracy, and it was in the *Contemporary Novels* that Galdós was able to fully realize his didactic aims.

In creating the *National Episodes*, Galdós had been influenced chiefly by Balzac's *Comédie humaine,* attempting to vivify historical periods through the use of accurate detail. Before beginning work on the *Contemporary Novels,* though, Galdós read Emile Zola's "Rougon-Macquart" series and was deeply impressed by the French author's Naturalist theories. Like Zola, Galdós believed that fiction should frankly portray all aspects of human existence, whether pleasant or distasteful, noble or ignominious. Galdós further believed that honest depictions of social ills could serve as the first step toward their emendation. In Galdós's *Contemporary Novels,* the primary objects of social criticism are the pretensions of the Spanish middle class. In *Miau,* for example, Galdós exposes the greed and corruption of minor bureaucrats, while *La desheredada (The Disinherited Lady)* satirizes the aristocratic prejudices of an orphaned girl. Critics note, however, that the primary achievement of the *Contemporary Novels* is not their accurate identification of social evils, but their perceptive portrayals of the subtleties of human psychology and social interaction. Most notable in this respect is the novel *Fortunata y Jacinta (Fortunata and Jacinta),* in which Galdós explores the fierce rivalry of two women from drastically different social backgrounds who share the same man, one of them as his wife, the other as his mistress and the mother of his son. Critics agree that while *Fortunata and Jacinta* provides a comprehensive and realistic portrait of the manners and customs of nineteenth-century Madrid, the primary interest of the novel is in the characterization of the two women, and this work is universally acknowledged as Galdós's finest.

Although Galdós's contemporary Marcelino Mendenez y Pelayo called the *National Episodes* "one of the most fortunate and timely creations in Spanish literature," most critics today find them prolix and lacking in narrative coherence. Galdós's current reputation rests primarily on the *Contemporary Novels,* with critics citing *The Disinherited Lady, El amigo Manso, Tormento (Torment), La de Bringas (The Spendthrifts), Miau, Fortunata and Jacinta,* and *Angel Guerra* as the best of the twenty-four. Considered a major artistic and intellectual achievement, the *Contemporary Novels* are internationally esteemed by readers and critics, while their author is recognized as the most accomplished Spanish novelist of the nineteenth century.

PRINCIPAL WORKS

La fontana de oro (novel) 1870
La sombra (novel) 1870
  [*The Shadow,* 1980]
El audaz (novel) 1871
Bailén (novel) 1873
La corte de Carlos IV (novel) 1873
  [*The Court of Charles IV,* 1888]
El 19 de marzo y el 2 de mayo (novel) 1873
Trafalgar (novel) 1873
  [*Trafalgar,* 1884]
Cádiz (novel) 1874
Gerona (novel) 1874
Juan Martín el Empecinado (novel) 1874
Napoleón en Chamartín (novel) 1874
Zaragoza (novel) 1874
  [*Saragossa,* 1899]
La batalla de los Arapiles (novel) 1875
  [*The Battle of Salamanca,* 1895]
El equipaje del Rey José (novel) 1875
Memorias de un cortesano (novel) 1875
Doña Perfecta (novel) 1876
  [*Doña Perfecta,* 1895]

El Grande Oriente (novel) 1876
La segunda casaca (novel) 1876
El 7 de julio (novel) 1876
Los cien mil hijos de San Luis (novel) 1877
Gloria. 2 vols. (novel) 1877
  [*Gloria,* 1882]
El terror de 1824 (novel) 1877
La familia de León Roch. 3 vols. (novel) 1878-79
  [*Leon Roch: A Romance,* 1888]
Marianela (novel) 1878
  [*Marianela,* 1883]
Un voluntario realista (novel) 1878
Los apostólicos (novel) 1879
Un faccioso más y algunos frailes menos (novel) 1879
**La desheredada* (novel) 1881
  [*The Disinherited Lady,* 1957]
**El amigo Manso* (novel) 1882
  [*Our Friend Manso,* 1987]
**El doctor Centeno.* 2 vols. (novel) 1883
**La de Bringas* (novel) 1884
  [*The Spendthrifts,* 1952]
**Lo prohibido.* 2 vols. (novel) 1884-85
**Tormento* (novel) 1884
  [*Torment,* 1952]
**Fortunata y Jacinta.* 4 vols. (novel) 1886-87
  [*Fortunata and Jacinta,* 1973]
**Miau* (novel) 1888
  [*Miau,* 1963]
**La incógnita* (novel) 1889
**Torquemada en la hoguera* (novel) 1889
**Realidad* (novel) 1890
**Angel Guerra.* 3 vols. (novel) 1891
**La loca de la casa* (novel) 1892
**Tristana* (novel) 1892
  [*Tristana,* 1961]
**Torquemada en la Cruz* (novel) 1893
La de San Quintín (drama) 1894
  [*The Duchess of San Quentin* published in *Masterpieces of Spanish Drama,* 1917]
**Torquemada en el purgatorio* (novel) 1894
**Halma* (novel) 1895
**Nazarín* (novel) 1895
**Torquemada y San Pedro* (novel) 1895
La fiera (drama) 1896
**El abuelo* (novel) 1897
**Misericordia* (novel) 1897
  [*Compassion,* 1962]
De Oñate a la Granja (novel) 1898
Mendizábal (novel) 1898
Zumalacárregui (novel) 1898
La campaña del Maestrazgo (novel) 1899
La estafeta romántica (novel) 1899
Luchana (novel) 1899
Vergara (novel) 1899
Los ayacuchos (novel) 1900
Bodas reales (novel) 1900
Montes de Oca (novel) 1900
Electra (drama) 1901
  [*Electra,* 1902]
Narváez (novel) 1902
Las tormentas del 48 (novel) 1902
Los duendes de la camarilla (novel) 1903
El abuelo (drama) 1904
  [*The Grandfather,* 1910]
O'Donnell (novel) 1904

La revolución de julio   (novel)   1904
Aita Tettauen   (novel)   1905
Bárbara   (drama)   1905
Carlos VI en la Rápita   (novel)   1905
**Casandra*   (novel)   1905
Prim   (novel)   1906
La vuelta al mundo en la Numancia   (novel)   1906
La de los tristes destinos   (novel)   1907
España sin rey   (novel)   1908
***El caballero encantado*   (novel)   1909
España trágica   (novel)   1909
Amadeo I   (novel)   1910
De Cartago a Sagunto   (novel)   1911
La primera república   (novel)   1911
Cánovas   (novel)   1912
***La razón de la sinrazón*   (novel)   1915
El tacaño Salomón   (drama)   1916
Obras completas. 6 vols.   (novels, dramas, and essays)
    1941-42

*These novels comprise the historical series *Episodios nacionales*.

**These volumes comprise the series *Novelas españolas contemporáneas*.

W. D. HOWELLS   (essay date 1895)

[*Howells was the chief progenitor of American realism and the most influential American literary critic during the late nineteenth century. He was the author of nearly three dozen novels that, though neglected for decades, are today the subject of growing interest. He is recognized as one of the major literary figures of the nineteenth century: he successfully weaned American literature away from the sentimental romanticism of its infancy, earning the popular sobriquet "the Dean of American Letters." Through realism, a theory central to his fiction and criticism, Howells sought to disperse "the conventional acceptations by which men live on easy terms with themselves" that they might "examine the grounds of their social and moral opinions." To accomplish this, according to Howells, the writer must strive to record detailed impressions of everyday life, endowing characters with true-to-life motives and avoiding authorial comment in the narrative. Criticism and Fiction (1891), a patchwork of essays from* Harper's *Magazine, is often considered Howells's manifesto of realism, although, as René Wellek has noted, the book is actually "only a skirmish in a long campaign for his doctrines." In addition to his perceptive criticism of the works of his friends Henry James and Mark Twain, Howells reviewed three generations of international literature, urging Americans to read the works of Emile Zola, Bernard Shaw, Henrik Ibsen, Emily Dickinson, and other important authors. In the following excerpt, originally published in* Harper's *in November 1895, Howells assesses Galdós's achievement as a novelist, focusing on* Doña Perfecta.]

The very acute and lively Spanish critic who signs himself Clarín, and is known personally as Don Leopoldo Alas, says the present Spanish novel has no yesterday, but only a day-before-yesterday. It does not derive from the romantic novel which immediately preceded it, but it derives from the realistic novel which preceded that: the novel, large or little, as it was with Cervantes, Hurtado de Mendoza, Quevedo, and the masters of picaresque fiction.

Clarín dates its renascence from the political revolution of 1868, which gave Spanish literature the freedom necessary to the fiction that studies to reflect modern life, actual ideas, and current aspirations; and though its authors were few at first, "they have never been adventurous spirits, friends of Utopia, revolutionists, or impatient progressists and reformers." He thinks that the most daring, the most advanced, of the new Spanish novelists, and the best by far, is Don Pérez Galdós.

I should myself have made my little exception in favor of Don Armando Palacio Valdés, but Clarín speaks with infinitely more authority, and I am certainly ready to submit when he goes on to say that Galdós is not a social or literary insurgent; that he has no political or religious prejudices; that he shuns extremes, and is charmed with prudence; that his novels do not attack the Catholic dogmas—though they deal so severely with Catholic bigotry—but the customs and ideas cherished by secular fanaticism to the injury of the Church. Because this is so evident, our critic holds, his novels are "found in the bosom of families in every corner of Spain." Their popularity among all classes in Catholic and prejudiced Spain, and not among free-thinking students merely, bears testimony to the fact that his aim and motive are understood and appreciated, although his stories are apparently so often anti-Catholic.

Doña Perfecta is, first of all, a story, and a great story, but it is certainly also a story that must appear at times potently, and even bitterly, anti-Catholic. Yet it would be a pity and an error to read it with the preoccupation that it was an anti-Catholic tract, for really it is not that. If the persons were changed in name and place, and modified in passion to fit a cooler air, it might equally seem an anti-Presbyterian or anti-Baptist tract; for what it shows in the light of their own hatefulness and cruelty are the perversions of any religion, any creed. It is not, however, a tract at all; it deals in artistic largeness with the passion of bigotry, as it deals with the passion of love, the passion of ambition, the passion of revenge. But Galdós is Spanish and Catholic, and for him bigotry wears a Spanish and Catholic face. That is all.

Up to a certain time, I believe, Galdós wrote romantic or idealistic novels, and one of these I have read, and it tired me very much. It was called *Marianela,* and it surprised me the more because I was already acquainted with his later work, which is all realistic. But one does not turn realist in a single night, and although the change in Galdós was rapid, it was not quite a lightning change; perhaps because it was not merely an outward change, but artistically a change of heart. His acceptance in his quality of realist was much more instant than his conversion, and vastly wider; for we are told by the critic whom I have been quoting that Galdós's earlier efforts, which he called *Episodios nacionales,* never had the vogue which his realistic novels have enjoyed.

These were, indeed, tendencious, if I may anglicize a very necessary word from the Spanish *tendencioso.* That is, they dealt with very obvious problems, and had very distinct and poignant significations, at least in the case of *Doña Perfecta, Leon Roch,* and *Gloria.* In still later novels, Emilia Pardo-Bazán thinks, he has comprehended that "the novel of to-day must take note of the ambient truth, and realize the beautiful with freedom and independence." This valiant lady, in the campaign for realism which she made under the title of La Cuestión Palpitante—one of the best and strongest books on the subject—counts him first among Spanish realists as Clarín counts him first among Spanish novelists. "With a certain fundamental humanity," she says,

> a certain magisterial simplicity in his creations, with the natural tendency of his clear intelli-

gence toward the truth, and with the frankness of his observation, the great novelist was always disposed to pass over to realism with arms and munitions; but his aesthetic inclinations were idealistic, and only in his latest works has he adopted the method of the modern novel, fathomed more and more the human heart, and broken once for all with the picturesque and with the typical personages, to embrace the earth we tread.

For her, as I confess for me, *Doña Perfecta* is not realistic enough—realistic as it is; for realism at its best is not tendencious. It does not seek to grapple with human problems, but is richly content with portraying human experiences; and I think Señora Pardo-Bazán is right in regarding *Doña Perfecta* as transitional, and of a period when the author had not yet assimilated in its fullest meaning the faith he had imbibed.

Yet it is a great novel . . . ; and perhaps because it is transitional it will please the greater number who never really arrive anywhere, and who like to find themselves in good company *en route*. It is so far like life that it is full of significations which pass beyond the persons and actions involved, and envelop the reader, as if he too were a character of the book, or rather as if its persons were men and women of this thinking, feeling, and breathing world, and he must recognize their experiences as veritable facts. From the first moment to the last it is like some passage of actual events in which you cannot withhold your compassion, your abhorrence, your admiration, any more than if they took place within your personal knowledge. Where they transcend all facts of your personal knowledge, you do not accuse them of improbability, for you feel them potentially in yourself, and easily account for them in the alien circumstance. I am not saying that the story has no faults; it has several. There are tags of romanticism fluttering about it here and there; and at times the author permits himself certain old-fashioned literary airs and poses and artifices, which you simply wonder at. It is in spite of these, and with all these defects, that it is so great and beautiful a book.

What seems to be so very admirable in the management of the story is the author's success in keeping his own counsel. This may seem a very easy thing; but, if the reader will think over the novelists of his acquaintance, he will find that it is at least very uncommon. They mostly give themselves away almost from the beginning, either by their anxiety to hide what is coming, or their vanity in hinting what great things they have in store for the reader. Galdós does neither the one nor the other. He makes it his business to tell the story as it grows; to let the characters unfold themselves in speech and action; to permit the events to happen unheralded. He does not prophesy their course; he does not forecast the weather even for twenty-four hours; the atmosphere becomes slowly, slowly, but with occasional lifts and reliefs, of such a brooding breathlessness, of such a deepening intensity, that you feel the wild passion-storm nearer and nearer at hand, till it bursts at last; and then you are astonished that you had not foreseen it yourself from the first moment.

Next to this excellent method which I count the supreme characteristic of the book merely because it represents the whole, and the other facts are in the nature of parts, is the masterly conception of the characters. They are each typical of a certain side of human nature, as most of our personal friends and enemies are; but not exclusively of this side or that. They are each of mixed motives, mixed qualities; none of them is quite

a monster; though those who are badly mixed do such monstrous things.

Pepe Rey, who is such a good fellow—so kind, and brave, and upright, and generous, so fine a mind, and so high a soul—is tactless and imprudent; he even condescends to the thought of intrigue; and though he rejects his plots at last, his nature has once harbored deceit. Don Inocencio, the priest, whose control of Doña Perfecta's conscience has vitiated the very springs of goodness in her, is by no means bad, aside from his purposes. He loves his sister and her son tenderly, and wishes to provide for them by the marriage which Pepe's presence threatens to prevent. The nephew, though selfish and little, has moments of almost being a good fellow; the sister, though she is really such a lamb of meekness, becomes a cat, and scratches Don Inocencio dreadfully when he weakens in his design against Pepe.

Rosario, one of the sweetest and purest images of girlhood that I know in fiction, abandons herself with equal passion to the love she feels for her cousin Pepe, and to the love she feels for her mother, Doña Perfecta. She is ready to fly with him, and yet she betrays him to her mother's pitiless hate.

But it is Doña Perfecta herself who is the transcendent figure, the most powerful creation of the book. In her, bigotry and its fellow-vice, hypocrisy, have done their perfect work, until she comes near to being a devil and really does a devil's deeds. Yet even she is not without some extenuating traits. Her bigotry springs from her conscience, and she is truly devoted to her daughter's eternal welfare; she is of such a native frankness that at a certain point she tears aside her mask of dissimulation and lets Pepe see all the ugliness of her perverted soul. She is wonderfully managed. At what moment does she begin to hate him, and to wish to undo her own work in making a match between him and her daughter? I could defy any one to say. All one knows is that at one moment she adores her brother's son, and at another she abhors him, and has already subtly entered upon her efforts to thwart the affection she has invited in him for her daughter.

Caballuco, what shall I say of Caballuco? He seems altogether bad, but the author lets one imagine that this cruel, this ruthless brute must have somewhere about him traits of lovableness, of leniency, though he never lets one see them. His gratitude to Doña Perfecta, even his murderous devotion, is not altogether bad; and he is certainly worse than nature made him, when wrought upon by her fury and the suggestion of Don Inocencio. The scene where they work him up to rebellion and assassination is a compendium of the history of intolerance; as the mean little conceited city of Orbajosa is the microcosm of bigoted and reactionary Spain.

I have called, or half-called, this book tendencious; but in a certain larger view it is not so. It is the eternal interest of passion working upon passion, not the temporary interest of condition antagonizing condition, which renders *Doña Perfecta* so poignantly interesting, and which makes its tragedy immense. But there is hope as well as despair in such a tragedy. There is the strange support of a bereavement in it, the consolation of feeling that for those who have suffered unto death, nothing can harm them more; that even for those who have inflicted their suffering this peace will soon come.

"Is Pérez Galdós a pessimist?" asks the critic Clarín. "No, certainly; but if he is not, why does he paint us sorrows that seem inconsolable? Is it from love of paradox? Is it to show that his genius, which can do so much, can paint the shadow lovelier than the light? Nothing of this. Nothing that is not serious, honest, and noble is to be found in this novelist. Are they pessimistic, those ballads of the North, that always end with vague resonances of woe? Are they pessimists, those singers of our own land, who surprise us with tears in the midst of laughter? Is Nature pessimistic, who is so sad at nightfall that it seems as if day were dying forever? The sadness of art, like that of nature, is a form of hope. Why is Christianity so artistic? Because it is the religion of sadness.'' (pp. 133-38)

> W. D. Howells, " 'Doña Perfecta,' A Great Novel ,"
> in Criticism and Fiction and Other Essays, *edited by*
> *Clara Marburg Kirk and Rudolf Kirk, New York Uni-*
> *versity Press, 1959, pp. 133-38.*

J. D. M. FORD   (lecture date 1918)

[*Ford was an American critic who specialized in the study of*
Romance languages. In the following excerpt from a speech de-
livered in 1918, he laments Galdós's vehement anticlericalism,
finding that it mars his otherwise outstanding work.]

[Benito Pérez Galdós's] chief interests have lain within the domain of the psychological study of phases of Spanish life, rather than the simple recording of local manners, and within the field of the historical novel. As an historical novelist he has proved the truth of the dictum of Fernán Caballero that the historical attitude befits the Spanish story-teller. Taking his guidance from the scheme utilized by the Frenchmen Erckmann and Chatrian in their romances dealing with events of the Revolution and of the First Empire, Galdós has developed the successive stories of his *Episodios nacionales,* which, divided into decades, embrace many signal facts of the history of Spain from the reign of Carlos IV down through a large part of the 19th century. The volumes taken together form a sort of epopee, in which he has striven to show fidelity to the historic fact, and yet give the necessary air of romance to each book by interweaving with the fact love stories and other elements of his own invention. Not all the individual volumes strike the fancy; but the total effect is impressive.

Both at home and abroad Galdós has attracted less attention by his historical novels than by his many works of psychological fiction, typified by the *Doña Perfecta,* the *Gloria,* the *Familia de León Roch,* the *Fortunata y Jacinta,* etc. In these, unmistakable attributes of the author are his genius for observation, his skill in construction evinced in absolute unity of plot combined with diversity and fitness of incident, his inventiveness and large degree of plausibility in the creation of character, and his courage in urging his antipathies. And this last attribute is the more important in that his antipathies are directed against sore spots in the religious and social system of Spain, things that need medication for they demand a cure; but his courage is not one worthy of unqualified praise, for it is on occasion dangerously like the courage of the fanatic. He assails fanaticism in the religious constitution of his fellow Spaniards, and he exposes himself to the charge that he is himself a fanatic in his methods of doing so.

The *Doña Perfecta,* which out of all his novels has made most noise abroad, illustrates what happens when his antipathies take one of their most determined forms, anticlericalism, a corollary of which is for him that the faithful practitioner of Catholicism is always under the priestly thumb and is always a blind bigot. This corollary is apparently the thesis of the *Doña Perfecta,* and the author seeks to make it certain by creating a monster of a mother—who is plausibly possible—and by making her

ruthlessly sacrifice her own daughter and even countenance murder rather than depart one jot from her stiff-necked attitude of true believer and rigid practitioner. To put the issue plumply: bad faith appears to actuate Galdós, for in this book he gives but a perverted idea of religion, of Catholicism as practised in Spain. No one can prove a rule of life by basing his arguments upon the abnormal, the monstrous, the exceptional in human nature; and again the intrinsic goodness of a religious system is not vitiated by the excesses of a few fanatic and unintelligent believers. There are religious fanatics in Spain as out of Spain, and they ought to be attacked wherever they are, but not by unfair methods. It is unfortunate that the *Doña Perfecta* should enjoy such fame abroad; it gives too distorted an idea of a phase of Spanish life and that idea is one that the honest Spaniard should seek to destroy rather than confirm. Analysis of the *Gloria*—a Spanish *Daniel Deronda*—and of the *Familia de León Roch* would show Galdós again resorting to unfair methods under the spell of his anticlerical prepossessions and extending his attack so as to make his pictures of the Spanish-Christian wife and the Spanish-Christian family gross libels of actuality. All this is a great pity; Galdós is one of the most powerful novelists of the modern world, but he has let the spirit of propaganda betray him into injustice and unrighteousness. (pp. 238-41)

> J. D. M. Ford, "The Novel," in his Main Currents
> of Spanish Literature, *Henry Holt and Company, 1919,*
> *pp. 208-41.*

HAYWARD KENISTON   (essay date 1920)

[*In the following excerpt, Keniston discusses the personal qualities*
which allowed Galdós to create his characters with realism and
compassion.]

Galdós, like Cervantes, knew life by living it. For half a century he mingled with men of all classes, traveling into every corner of Spain—always in a third-class compartment—stopping at modest inns, penetrating the simple, daily life of people, and beyond the limits of his own land, visiting the other countries of Europe. Gifted with an uncommon power of observation and a memory which served him when the light had fled from his eyes, he brought to his task a wealth of detail, of the physical aspect of persons and things, of the speech of different types and classes of men, of the elemental psychology of his fellows, which few writers have possessed.

The mere power to observe the exterior manifestations of life is not sufficient to make a great artist. This is after all but an instrument. The great artist must also interpret the spirit of life. And here lies the greatest glory of Galdós.

What are the qualities which equip a writer to interpret this spirit? There are two which seem to me preëminent: the first is sympathy with man, the second is faith in man.

By sympathy I plainly do not mean only the ability to look at life without prejudice, coldly and dispassionately, but rather that instinct to see the other man's point of view, to find his acts and opinions reasonable and natural, even inevitable, or to use a phrase of Ramón Pérez de Ayala's, "to feel that you would have done the same thing, if you were in his place." And is not this in the end the spirit of democracy? It is often said the Spanish are the most democratic of all people. And that is undoubtedly true, if we mean by democracy that sympathetic regard for one's fellows which is the basis of all social equality. Among all of his nation, Galdós has justly deserved the title "The Great Democrat."

Perhaps I should make clearer too what I mean by faith in man, although since I am speaking of the spirit of life, there can be little room for doubt. Obviously I am not thinking of his material welfare, or his animal evolution, but a faith in man's spiritual development, in the ultimate triumph of the imponderable aspects of life, of the eternal ideals.

These, then, are the qualities which Galdós brought to his task. How are they evident in his work? The age which he set himself the task of interpreting was the nineteenth century, retrospectively in the *Episodios,* objectively in the *Novelas contemporáneas,* prophetically in the later semi-mystic novels and the drama. It is an age of pettiness, selfseeking and futility, in Spain as in the rest of Europe. Judged by its achievements, Spain of the nineteenth century is destined to stand in history as a record of unfulfilled aspirations. But as you read its story in the work of Galdós, you will nevertheless find in it at every point evidences of latent strength which point the way to a new future.

This anomaly, this gap between the vision and the realization, deep-rooted in Spanish life, emerges from every page of his work. In the *Episodios,*—that great national epic of the first half of the past century, none the less epic because its hero is the whole Spanish people rather than a single champion,—it is the contrast between the mighty impulse of a nation for political freedom and the betrayal of that impulse by personal and political selfishness. The cause fails, the high purpose is frustrated. But who can read this mighty poem without being kindled with a new faith in the cause itself, a new confidence in its ultimate triumph?

In the novels of contemporary life, Galdós turned his attention to another phase of modern life, its social problems. And here again, he finds the same anomaly. The world which he paints with such penetrating exactness is a banal one, the great middle class, emerging from the insignificance of the past, evolving into the democracy of the future. Judged by its acts this society is hopelessly decayed; conventionality, bigotry, materialism are dominant. Pepe Rey is the victim of reaction; Fortunata dies an outcast. The Madrid of Torquemada is a cess-pool of vulgarity and selfishness. This, and this only, is the image of modern society which you find in other novelists of the time, such as Leopoldo Alas or Padre Coloma. But it is precisely here that Galdós reveals his greatness. He has seen beneath the surface; there he has found a justification of his faith.

By temperament Galdós belongs to those who conceive life in terms of the emotions. And in his search for these fundamental emotional truths, he turned instinctively to the humble and the obscure, to those who, in the eyes of society, are outcasts, to the dreamers, to little children. There he found still vigorous the qualities which had disappeared from the conventional world. And so his work teems with these finely pathetic figures, like Marianela and Sor Simona, whose chief beauty lies in their primitive simplicity.

It is the contrast between these naïve types and the conventionally respectable folk, which forms one of the chief charms of his work, witness Casandra or "Pepet." Occasionally his propagandist zeal led him to present his sophisticated characters in an unfavorably exaggerated light, but in the greater part of his work there is a broad tolerance and sympathy even for those whose ideas were the antithesis of his own. At his best, as in *Fortunata y Jacinta, Angel Guerra,* or *La loca de la casa,* his

vision of life possesses that amplitude and serenity which marks the spirit of the Greek tragedy or of Shakespeare.

Galdós was never one who looked upon his art as a light or frivolous pastime. He felt called to be a teacher. The society which it fell to him to interpret was in many respects degenerate, decadent. But from that society he drew a lesson, for which we—and I mean all those who seek to solve the riddle of life—owe him a debt of eternal gratitude.

That lesson is a simple one, but it is as profound as time; it is the lesson that prophets and seers of all ages have taught. It is this: Despite oppression and tyranny, despite ignorance and idleness, despite selfishness and greed, there are certain eternal verities which are the abiding aspiration of men; the belief in these truths lies latent in the heart of the great mass of the community, aroused into action only in moments of stress; and in this latent consciousness lies the hope of the society of tomorrow.

Freedom, justice, love,—these are his themes. And the greatest of these is love. Again and again in his noblest works he tells the story of this triumphant love, a love that is greater than self, greater than honor, greater than death, the love of which Casandra says: "It is the only divine thing which I feel within me; divine, because it is imperishable, because I cannot conceive that it should cease to be what it is or have an end." (pp. 203-06)

A caricature of Galdós.

Hayward Keniston, "Galdós, Interpreter of Life,"
in Hispania, *Vol. III, No. 4, October, 1920, pp. 203-06.*

CLYDE CHEW GLASCOCK   (essay date 1923)

[*In the following excerpt, Glascock provides an overview of Galdós's novels.*]

Before the meteoric blaze of Blasco Ibáñez across the literary horizon it was generally thought that Pérez Galdós was the foremost modern Spanish novelist. Taking him for all in all, in view of the fertility and versatility of his production, the verdict seemed just, and it may still be so. There were those who preferred the brilliant, artistic, and idealistic realism of Valera the Andalusian, or the vigorous and profound realism of the painter of northern Cantabrian customs and characters, de Pereda, both of them his contemporaries; but the worldwide popularity of Blasco Ibáñez has for the moment eclipsed them all. In keeping to superlatives one might say that Valera is the most brilliant and charming, Pereda the most profound, Pérez Galdós the most versatile and fertile, Blasco Ibáñez the most popular and melodramatic.

Pérez Galdós was among the first to restore the Spanish novel to its pristine glory, though he was younger than his illustrious collaborators (Valera, Pereda, Alarcon). He was the most fecund, the one endowed with the richest invention, with the most virile creative power, he was the creator of the greatest number of life-like characters (running far over a thousand); he was sometimes styled the greatest of contemporary Spanish novelists, the Dickens or Balzac of Spain. (p. 158)

With unflagging energy he calmly and unostentatiously devoted himself to literary work, and as a result his productivity was enormous, like that of a few other Spanish writers; seventy-eight novels and a score of plays are enumerated in his output. For half a century he issued every year at least one volume, sometimes several.

Superior to all others in Spain in writing historical novels, in characterizing contemporary Spaniards of the middle class, in fertility of invention and in versatility of production, his fame appears secure, not merely for our day, but as well for time to come.

More than half of Pérez Galdós' novels, forty-six of them, belong to the province of the historical novel, in which we find a review of the history of Spain in the first three quarters of the nineteenth century. The tragedies and comedies of Spanish history in this period are faithfully related without invalidating facts by actors who took a prominent part in them. The author of these novels furnished them with the general title of *National Episodes* (*Episodios nacionales*).

These works have been thought to show similarity in part to French novels by Erckmann-Chatrian; but, Pérez Galdós displayed more energy and imagination, and by reason of increase in ability revealed in his second and third series, because of the intense life that animates them, the well studied portraits of historical personages, the picturesque details and the creation of a vast number of representative types, a comparison with Balzac (*Les Chouans, La Comédie humaine*) has been suggested by some. One may also catch unmistakably the spirit of Walter Scott in *Trafalgar,* and in *La corte de Carlos IV,* among the writer's early efforts. Scott's novels, however, reflect legendary history, whereas Pérez Galdós bases his novels on real history; the historical episodes and personalities are

kept true to facts so far as the author was able to ascertain them. Fictitious elements to enliven the interest are harmoniously interwoven.

These *National Episodes,* or historical novels, enjoyed great popularity with the Spanish people and they came when they were needed, for there was little reading in Spain at the time, and they taught many Spaniards all that they knew of the history of their own country. In these stories historical personages live again whose names were indistinctly engraven on the memory of Spaniards. He gave them precision and personality, a body and a soul. These books are indeed a faithful reproduction of the national incidents and characters of the epoch, of the inner and outer life of Spaniards during the nineteenth century.

Still greater fame and popularity were won by Pérez Galdós with a series of thirty-two novels on contemporary life in Spain, his *Contemporary Spanish Novels* (*Novelas españolas contemporáneas*), particularly with those of the second epoch or series, beginning with *The Untrained Women* (*La desheredada*) and concluding with *The Grandfather* (*El abuelo*). In this genre that depicts realistically the customs and people of the middle class in Spain, Pérez Galdós reigned as a master supreme.

Whereas other Spanish writers reproduced with more fullness and completeness customs and peculiarities of some definite region or locality in Spain, or were desirous of acquainting us with the flavor of this or that wild and isolated district Pérez Galdós made his permanent residence in Madrid, in the heart of the nation, to which all its lifeblood flowed, where there was much joy and much sorrow, where large numbers of Spaniards passing and repassing ceaselessly presented themselves for study to his observant gaze. He was not a believer in the leveling effect of life in a large city. He knew that one could find an infinite variety of temperaments and characters in the huge aggregations of the larger cities. He took pleasure in entering into the complex, in selecting people of humble station who by reason of their mediocrity and insignificance seemed doomed to be forgotten: modest middle class employees, humble people of every sort, even beggars and prostitutes. The plainness of bourgeois life in a fixed circle attracted rather than repelled him; in the monotony of daily fatigue and distractions he was able to discover passions as strong, virtues as sublime, vices as precise and intense as in any social sphere, and one may even say that the contrasts in these figures, the individualities that he was able to create and bring out on a seemingly indecisive background appear to have in reality extraordinary relief. In some of the novels of this series Pérez Galdós has gone for his material still deeper and lower in the life of Spaniards, reaching down into a world infernal of misery and of vice,—a feature of the naturalistic school.

Full of commiseration for victims of wretched Spanish institutions, for those who have been overborne in the cruel struggle for existence, for the weak, for the infirm, for outcasts, he caused flowers of delicious fragrance to flourish and blossom, often in a vitiated atmosphere, out of a soil of stench and putrefaction, such characters as Benina in *Misericordia,* and the adorable figure of the boy Luisito in *Miau,* or the exquisite and Christlike nazarín, "the most intense and Tolstoyan of creations by Pérez Galdós."

Though exclusively Spanish, so far as the description of customs is concerned, and although his characters are of the middle class and of the city, and though a full torrent of humanity flows around them, he interests and moves us more than some of his compatriots, the local color of whose writings, whose rustic customs and unusualness of thought and language alienate or confuse even Spaniards themselves.

But this author has other qualities that are admirable: his language, his style, is easy, natural and simple, especially adapted to his subjects that he treats; a style not altogether artless, however unadorned it may appear. He was usually inclined to reproduce reality, to say only what was necessary to set in relief a person, to present him to us as such and as we ought to see him, keeping at a distance from the usual style in books, which in Spain more than in most countries has been crystallized in moulds of former times and of other days. Some people of delicate taste may prefer a highly polished, literary style that is more curious and careful, or else "perfumed with the aroma of the mountains and of the sea, as that of Pereda," but we are told that the majority in Spain prefer Pérez Galdós, whose realism of a good and moderate sort captivates one with its frankness and absence of artificiality and affectation.

Another characteristic increases one's esteem for the man as well as for the writer. His work is usually sound and healthy. He was opposed moreover to affiliating himself with any political or religious party or faction; and he was usually opposed to an author's preaching under the mask of personages whose character and attitudes do not follow normal development, but are converted into champions of some cause—a thing which constantly happens to Fernán Caballero, and at times to Pereda—yet this vigorous and sincere painter of contemporaneous Spanish society, Pérez Galdós, possessed the highest ideals tending to morality, to the suppression of petty tyranny, bossism, and a thousand evils of a bad system of government and education. In religion he advocated sanity and the diffusion of true Christian charity without hostility to any form of established cult. He lacked moreover absolute confidence in any particular form of worship. He had no inclination to reticence nor to infantile prejudices, nor to affected discretion when it was a question of presenting vice and ugliness; but as a compensation, no parade or exhibition of obscenity; and everywhere, even in the most somber windings through this vale of tears, he gave us light, much light and joy; and his humor too, like a little star, shines above poor, grieving humanity, guiding and comforting it, snatching it often from suffering and woe, as the reader may see in *Misericordia,* one of the most sympathetic of his sympathetic books. This depicts the life of the servant woman Benina, who spends most of her existence begging and suffering in the streets of Madrid to save a lady, her proud and selfish mistress, from humiliation and privation, to the end, until she is even cast into the street by the indignant mistress, who thinks that her servant is negligent and indolent because of her long periods of absence, and that she is responsible for her former suffering and desperate poverty. Depressing though conditions revealed in this book may be, yet humor is ever there to relieve the darkening gloom with its radiant flashes. We are assured that the author was fundamentally religious and optimistic. The reader does not have to turn away in hopelessness and despair. (pp. 158-63)

Ultimately five series of [*National Episodes*] were completed, forty-six in all, presenting historical events of dramatic interest during the nineteenth century in Spain, running on down from the battle of Trafalgar (1805), which furnished the subject for his first masterpiece (*Trafalgar*) to the year 1880.

The ten novels of the first series are told in the first person by the leading character, Gabriel, who appears in *Trafalgar* as a poor boy; in the last work of the series, *La batalla de los Arapiles,* he has become a major. Feeling the limitations of

story-telling in the first person Pérez Galdós thereafter followed generally the fashion of narrating in the third person. The favorable reception accorded the second novel, *The Court of Charles IV* (*La corte de Carlos IV*), served as an inspiration, and suggested, together with the complete development of the *Episodios nacionales,* the interconnection of the ten works, reappearance of familiar characters, related subject matter, and the distribution of the subjects in such a way as to gain unity in variety. This linking together of the characters and events recalls a feature in *La Comédie humaine* by Balzac and in the *Rougon-Macquart* novels by Zola.

Though these historical novels, as a whole, are beyond comparison with any achievement of like kind in Spanish literature and may take their place among the best of the sort in any land, yet they are surpassed from the standpoint of literary art by his *Contemporary Spanish Novels* (*Novelas españolas contemporáneas*) dealing with contemporary Spanish life in the realm of pure fiction. These are the works that brought him greatest fame outside of Spain as well; in particular *Doña Perfecta, Gloria* in two volumes, *Marianela,* and *La familia de León Roch.* Although they are not quite equal to some of his later works, (e.g., *Fortunata y Jacinta, Angel Guerra*), yet they caused a tremendous stir in Spain by attacking fanaticism and clericalism, and by advocating enlightenment at a time when all Spain was agitated by an anticlerical struggle and by the progress of modern scientific ideas. These inner mental and moral struggles are no less intense than the external strife depicted in the *National Episodes,* nor are they peculiar to Spain. For the backwardness of country people in conforming to new conditions produced by the advance of education is found in every land. Likewise conservatism in religious matters everywhere when carried to excess results in bigotry. In *Doña Perfecta* this kind of narrow-mindedness, bigotry, and fanaticism are held up to scorn. The ill-feeling aroused in a little Spanish town because of difference in religious opinion due to differences of education and rearing might have been intense in almost any place if brought about by similar circumstances. And for this reason *Doña Perfecta* excited universal interest. Bigotry and fanaticism so monstrous however as that of Doña Perfecta, who permits her nephew, a free-thinker, to be murdered rather than have her daughter marry him, a tragedy that ends in her daughter's insanity, is beyond understanding today, but perhaps there was more need of drastic lessons like this when the book was published in Spain nearly fifty years ago. It then aroused a furious storm of controversy.

The fundamental thought in *La Familia de León Roch* (*The Family of Leon Roch*) is much the same as that in *Doña Perfecta,* the conflict between the old type of Spanish orthodoxy and modern scientific thought. María, who marries León, the scientist, is the counterpart of Doña Perfecta and like her is controlled by her confessor. . . . *Gloria* is built also on the problem of religious intolerance. The author has made a cultured English Jew the hero, as is the case in George Eliot's *Daniel Deronda.* The heroine, Gloria, a young Spanish girl, clings tenaciously to her traditional belief. The description of religious intolerance and feeling in a small Spanish town vies in vividness and interest with its parallel in the town of Orbajosa in *Doña Perfecta. Gloria* was considered the novel of his novels by many; but these critics were probably anticlerical partisans. Nevertheless *Doña Perfecta* and *Gloria* are, aside from the one fundamental fault of excessive anticlericalism, splendid artistic achievements. These novels have a clear purpose; they savagely arraign bigotry and fanaticism, and were interpreted by many as anti-Roman Catholic. They are certainly anticlerical, and their style, like most of the author's work, is realistic.

Marianela is more idealistic. It shows greater depth and tenderness of feeling, it is more pathetic and poetic than its predecessors. The value of sentiment as an essential factor is stressed in the emotions of Pablo and Marianela.

Pablo is a blind youth who recovers his sight after an operation and discovers the insuperable homeliness of Marianela, the girl whom he loves; he transfers his devotion to his beautiful cousin and Marianela succumbs to her despair. Toward the close of the story Marianela experiences the force of disillusion which she had always instinctively felt, and which Pablo could not conceive until he recovered his sight. Each is supremely happy while illusion lasts. The story is not only interesting from a psychological standpoint, but shows other characteristics of the author, especially his fondness for discussing problems of the day. In a mining town filled with poor toilers, earning their bread by the sweat of the brow, among whom there are only a few well-to-do people, the social problems concerning ignorance and education, poverty and wealth, selfishness and duty towards society, occur to the author's mind. These questions are treated with lucidity and vigor and reveal the writer's sympathy with progressive modern ideas.

After passing through a didactic, anticlerical stage Pérez Galdós began a series of more realistic novels in which he aimed to present truth as he saw it and let the reader draw conclusions. The purpose does not obtrude, or is supposed not to do so, and interfere with art. Yet the attitude of the author is clear even though he may no longer seem to be writing with a purpose, and the effect is decidedly ethical.

The Poorly Equipped Woman (*La desheredada*) portrays the evils that arise from defective education and training in characters who are unfit for performing anything successfully. We see how an attractive but inadequately equipped young girl, beginning her career in a comfortable, respectable station in Madrid on being left to her own devices may gradually sink to the bottom, to the dregs of society, to a life of nameless shame. *Tormento, Lo prohibido* (*Forbidden Fruit*), *Fortunata y Jacinta* his greatest novel, a wonderful picture of manners and customs among the middle and lower classes in Madrid, and *Tristana* follow a somewhat similar trend; in them illicit love and vice are extensively exploited. In these works the influence of French naturalism is visible, e.g. in details that are ugly, inartistic, repellent to the old-fashioned critic, who cares little for the life of the underworld in Madrid or any other city, and prefers to have pornography ignored. But at least we may say that Pérez Galdós deals sternly with vice in whatever guise it is concealed. His purpose is a good one. Social prestige, ever a fruitful field, is used to advantage morally and artistically in *El amigo Manso* (*Friend Manso*), *La de Bringas* (*The Wife of Bringas*), and in *Miau. La de Bringas* continues the story of a family of office-holders told in *Tormento,* and together with *Miau* deals with life among poorly paid government officials. These unfortunate people, in the vain and silly effort to maintain appearances, experience extreme distress. "It is not so much to the misery and woe involved in these situations that Pérez Galdós is desirous of calling attention, as to the folly or lack of intelligence which makes possible and perpetuates this state of things."

In *Angel Guerra,* one of his masterpieces, and in *Nazarín* exalted spiritualism and mysticism are studied. The priest in *Nazarín* is a quixotic, Christlike figure who ignores the dictates of practical common sense by protecting and sheltering an abandoned woman and he suffers disgrace in consequence. *Halma* is a sequel of *Nazarín*; the leading figure is now a nobly spiritualistic woman. Torquemada in four books presents the varying fortunes of the avaricious and successful usurer, Torquemada, who first appeared on the scene in *Fortunata y Jacinta. Misericordia* takes us among the beggars of Madrid. Pérez Galdós desired to arouse sympathy for deplorable social conditions, and so he portrayed their repellent features, believing as Zola professed to do, that some remedy would be found if they were sufficiently exposed. Blasco Ibáñez has adopted this principle in many of his novels. *El abuelo* in dramatic form embodies a study of heredity, and the disappointment that may ensue on adherence to popular notions of its processes. Foreign influence has been observed in *El abuelo* (of *King Lear*) *Nazarín* (of Tolstoy), *Realidad* (of Ibsen *and* Sudermann), but Pérez Galdós disclaimed that he was conscious of it. At any rate the characters in his books, the episodes, and the workmanship, are genuinely Spanish and often times recall the picaresque novel. (pp. 164-68)

In the light of recent naturalistic literature in Europe, and in particular since the appearance of Blasco Ibáñez' works that assail so savagely the government and church in Spain, the writings of Pérez Galdós seem by comparison mild and restrained enough; they would hardly cause a ripple on the surface of the waters now-a-days, but at the time of their appearance some of his novels were regarded by many as too advanced, as frankly revolutionary and hostile to the church, as deplorable and scandalous in spirit, demonstrating the weaknesses of a great faith by the fanaticism and wrong doing of individual adherents, proving a rule merely with exceptional and exaggerated cases.

In succeeding works a trace of naturalism was scented with its nervous pathology and vice, with its corrupt and immoral society of human beasts, with its "lethal and pornographic sensualism." Objection was also raised to his microscopic examination of life's pettiness, to his delving into abnormal psychology, to the absence of idealistic light and beauty, and to the lack of elevation and grandeur in his conceptions. Moreover, wearisome loquacity, the introduction of seemingly unimpressive and extraneous details, barrenness so far as beauty of description is concerned,—these defects are alleged as making the perusal of his novels laborious at times (Blanco García).

I cannot deny that some of the historical novels are tedious to a foreigner, and the contemporary novels are dull in places; the plot and the story of the lives of the leading personages occasionally move too slowly. The loquaciousness of his characters, however skilfully presented, is trying to an impatient reader. His prolixity is often marked. In addition, we of the present day are no longer profoundly stirred by efforts made in a comparatively moderate tone to bring about reforms in church and state; in fact the Roman Catholic Church and the governments of our day are no longer shaken by mild satire and criticism; nothing but viciously severe antagonism to church and state can arouse a storm. And so, in the light of recent history and of Bolshevism, much of Pérez Galdós' agitation for gradual reform seems a bit old-fashioned and by no means dangerously subversive. Opinion will differ of course as to the amount of vice that may be depicted in a novel. From the usual European point of view Pérez Galdós has not gone to extremes. In Spain, too, particularly in Madrid, there was great need of exposing vicious and putrefying influences in society. (pp. 172-73)

It is difficult to give in so short space any adequate idea of the varied and changing content and style of seventy-six novels, not to mention twenty-one plays by this author. The contemporary novels began in realistic style with religious problems as central themes, in particular with the conflicts engendered by bigotry and fanaticism, combative novels of frankly anti-fanatical tendency, didactic novels with a clear and somewhat revolutionary tendency that aroused heated controversy. Subsequently the author, veering toward naturalism, drew material from many social problems in all the walks of the middle class people: e.g., the struggling, poorly paid government official receives liberal attention, as in the works of so many Spanish writers; for like the beggar, and the monk and the nun, he has been long in evidence in Spain. Then, following the trend of naturalism in France, Pérez Galdós turned his attention to vice, with its stench, its filth, its pathology. His masterpiece perhaps, "one of the best novels of the century," *Fortunata y Jacinta,* falls in part within this realm, a wonderfully beautiful and pathetic book, but the story one of flagrant adultery, of forbidden love in which the weak man, Juanito, vacillates between his wife Jacinta and Fortunata, a woman of the semi-under-world. Exquisitely beautiful though this work undoubtedly is, yet it has been criticized on the ground of sensualism and for its pornographic elements. Notwithstanding this, *Fortunata y Jacinta* "is one of the grand efforts of the Spanish genius in our day, rivaled only by *Angel Guerra.*" "It is a book that gives the illusion of life. Its moral observation is at times so deep, its psychology so ingenious and pleasing, the principal action so interesting in the midst of its simplicity, the details so curious and picturesque, so ample the scene. In this book Pérez Galdós surprises the inmost feelings and interprets the hidden relation of things, raising them to a region more poetic and luminous. There is something epic in the whole thing."

Pérez Galdós was a very objective writer. He did not obtrude his own feelings, and one not versed in his art may think that there is a lack of grandly inspiring ideals in his work; but the author's purpose was to paint the average man of the middle class whose course does not appear to be guided always by grandly inspiring thought; his life is full of monotonous details that do not always lend to inspiring description. Nevertheless, profoundly beautiful comments may be suggested by the common things of life, as is so splendidly illustrated in the works of Gottfried Keller of Zürich, one of the world's greatest masters of the short story, one of the strongest writers of fiction in German after Goethe.

Pérez Galdós studied rather in living books than in libraries. He may have been "educated in part under the anatomical and physiological influence of Balzac, and in part in the study of English novelists, especially Dickens." English readers will at once notice a greater similarity to Dickens than to any other English or American novelist. In what is seen and in what is dreamed, details looked at through a microscope as it were, the attention given to what is humble and small, the poetry of children, the art of making them feel and speak, the portraiture of exceptional souls, mystics, fanatics of every sort, etc., not to mention the consummate art of reproducing ordinary conversation and loquacity, and in the whole style of the two men. But Charles Dickens made a more conscious effort to satisfy our longing for ideal moral beauty in man and for physical beauty in nature; he was more liberal in the use of comic and tragic effects, often blended; he makes us laugh or weep more frequently, he is not so strictly objective and impassive.

Granting the defects ascribed to Pérez Galdós, for almost every writer has his faults, yet his position as one of the foremost Spanish novelists is secure for all time.

He is "worthy of comparison with Balzac in France and with Dickens in England as well for the creative force with which he lends movement, life, and character to his personages, as for the faithful observation and the exactitude with which he paints the life of the middle class." (pp. 174-76)

Summing up we may conclude: No other modern Spanish writer has drawn more life-like portraits of men and women of his day, or excelled him in the delineation of character, no one has equalled him in depicting his contemporaries of the middle class, no other Spaniard and few foreigners have done so well in the field of the historical novel. No other Spanish novelist and very few foreigners are comparable in fertility of production. Fame enough for almost any man of literary aspirations, one would say. (p. 177)

> *Clyde Chew Glascock, "Spanish Novelists: Benito Pérez Galdós," in* The Texas Review, *Vol. VIII, No. 2, January, 1923, pp. 158-77.*

SALVADOR DE MADARIAGA   (essay date 1923)

[*Madariaga is widely considered Spain's outstanding intellectual figure of the twentieth century and was a prominent diplomat in pre-Revolutionary Spain, holding several government posts, including ambassador to the United States. Trilingual, he wrote criticism and political treatises, as well as novels, poetry, and plays in Spanish, French, and English, all of which have been praised for their clarity and elegance of style. Because of their liberal and humanistic stance, Madariaga's writings have consistently aroused discussion and controversy, particularly in his native Spain; his biography of Simón Bolívar has been called the "literary bombshell that caused Spain and Latin America to go to war again, with plenty of ink spilled on both sides." One of his best-known works,* Englishmen, Frenchmen, Spaniards *(1928), is a study of the obstacles national psychologies present to international relations. In the following excerpt, Madariaga examines the subject matter, artistic style, and philosophic vision of Galdós's fiction.*]

The novel may be defined as the æsthetic expression of life, and this definition naturally leads to a division of the study of a novelist into three heads, namely, the scope of his work, the quality of his æsthetic attitude, and his style; or, in other words, the subject, the artist, and the medium. It is hardly necessary to add that such a division cannot be understood nor even imagined literally. Matter, manner, and attitude in the work of an artist are as inseparable as body, soul, and environment in the life of a man. But it is the law of our intellect that, in order to analyse it must unfold in succession things that strike the mind at one and the same time, and so, at the risk of repetition, I shall deal in turn with each of these three aspects of Galdós's artistic personality.

The subject of Galdós's work could be defined thus; human nature as seen by an unprejudiced observer of nineteenth-century Spain.

Galdós's knowledge of Spain is complete and all-embracing. From this point of view—as from many others—he is the only truly national writer of the nineteenth century. Pereda belongs to a region, the Montaña; Valera belongs to a class, the refined aristocracy; Blasco Ibáñez is in manner and mind a cosmopolitan, if not a French, novelist. Galdós is Spanish, and he covers the whole of Spain, every province of its territory, every layer of its population, every shadow of its thought, and we may add, every year of its nineteenth century.

Curiously enough, this literary knight-errant of Spain was born in a land which only by a constitutional fiction can be considered as a part of the Peninsula. He saw the light in the Canary Islands, in 1845. But birth is an accident. From the age of twenty Galdós belongs to Madrid, and it is Madrid which he describes most willingly, and with a love which years of intimate knowledge did not abate. From his first work, *La fontana de oro* we begin to see under our eyes the unwieldy irregular town, full of an excitable and good-humoured population; its vast aristocratic mansions, low masses of granite and brick; its blocks of flats in which every *patio* is like a small village, bubbling with gossip and quarrels; its irregular, ill-paved streets which, like rivers dying in sands, radiate towards the desert over which, as our author says, "the heavens rise as spiritual life over the aridity of asceticism." But, though prominent in his books, Madrid takes no more important a place in them than it does in the life of the nation, and Galdós has succeeded in rendering with equal vividness and felicity the atmosphere of other Spanish towns, whether he conceals their features under an assumed name, as with his "Ficóbriga" in *Gloria* or his "Orbajosa" in *Doña Perfecta,* or reveals their whole identity down to the most vivid details of everyday life, as in his admirable rendering of Toledo in *Angel Guerra.* His knowledge of town and country is precise and detailed. Thus, he compares "the sudden harsh, strident outbursts of laughter" of one of his characters in *Lo prohibido* to "the tearing of cloth which one hears when passing along the Calle de Postas in shopping hours," a line which makes one pause and dream of his tall, gaunt figure, stealing along the streets of Madrid, a smile on his thin lips, his eyes lost in that waking dream of born observers, in which the mind is at rest but the instinct is alert and watching.

As he watched the life of the town and heard the tearing of cloth in the Calle de Postas, so he seems to have witnessed the life of the whole country during that nineteenth century which will perhaps some day be considered as the true Renaissance of Spain. Spain, like England, placed in the suburbs of Europe, has had a life of her own, subject to a historical rhythm quite different from that of the rest of the continent. Thus though the pioneer of municipal and parliamentary institutions in Europe, Spain arrives at the gates of the nineteenth century in a belated phase of development. Now the nineteenth century is in the history of Spain the constitutional century, not merely in the political, but in the national and cultural sense of the word. It is in the nineteenth century, through a calvary of civil wars, that Spain attains at last a full consciousness of her being. During the nineteenth century, Spain had to assimilate not only the French Revolution, but the Renaissance, and such elements of the Reformation as were not repugnant to her genius. It is a chaotic period of wars, which devastated the body no doubt but certainly stimulated the spirit of the nation. Galdós began to write almost exactly when the Bourbon Restoration initiated a period of relative stability, in reality the last phase of the struggle. He could look back on a vast field of romantic material which only awaited a great artist to be fashioned into immortal works. He saw his opportunity and proved himself worthy of it.

His *Episodios nacionales* are indeed an imposing work. All this romantic material of the nineteenth century is turned to account, from Trafalgar (the title of the first episode) to the beginnings of the present reign. In these forty-six volumes, many of which are admirable, and none of which can be passed over, Galdós gave us the history of Spain as seen from the drawing-room of contemporaries, not from the study of the historian. It is a living history, not the historical novel in the somewhat grandfatherly manner of Erckmann-Chatrian, nor again in the romantic and even romanesque manner of Walter Scott, but a vivid and dramatic interpretation of the life of the people through the events of the century, their hopes, feelings, thoughts, and disappointments.

Apart from their literary merit, the *Episodios nacionales* have been one of the most important elements in the formation of a Spanish national consciousness. Galdós was and is the most widely read of Spanish writers. His influence as an educator of the Spanish mind is incalculable.

A similar value must be attached to his nonhistorical novels, a series of thirty works the subject of which is the life of the Spanish people during the last quarter of the nineteenth century.

But though his immediate and concrete subject is the Spaniard of his age, his essential object is man. His outlook is human. If his characters are Spanish it is because creation is concrete and the Spanish genius never creates *ex nihilo* but from nature. His Spaniards, however, are as universal as those of Cervantes, for their life is woven with the eternal threads of love, destiny, and death.

If the novel is an aesthetic interpretation of life, it follows that novels may fail as works of art if conceived under ethical or intellectual preconceptions. Cervantes, it is generally admitted, set to work with an express ethical purpose when he wrote his *Don Quixote.* Fortunately, however, his creative instinct burst through his ethical intentions, and, as he proceeded, his end—the satire on chivalry books—soon became the means, while the means, the type of *Don Quixote,* became the real subject of the book and made it immortal.

Intellectual preconceptions were not yet strong in Cervantes' age. They had to wait till the nineteenth century, when Emile Zola tried to transform the novel into a branch of Natural History, closely connected with a veterinary science.

Galdós is almost a pure novelist, that is, he is almost free from both ethical and intellectual preconceptions. Yet, not quite. There is in him a strong political passion which now and then breaks out and upsets his artistic impartiality. His famous anticlerical series—*Doña Perfecta, Gloria, La familia de León Roch*—though admirable novels, are undoubtedly written in a spirit of passion and partisanship. This spirit was strong in him, since it inspired his famous play *Electra* in 1901, twenty-three years after the publication of *León Roch.* Yet the evolution from *Doña Perfecta* to *León Roch* shows a gradual refinement of his ethical preconception and an effort to raise the conflict of religious prejudices to the level of tragedy.

As for intellectual preconceptions, Galdós victoriously resisted the influence of his great French contemporary and never tried to turn his art into a science, probably because, fortunately, the notion that such a transformation could be an improvement of art could not enter his Spanish head. The pathetic belief in science which for several decades shed a melancholy light over the age, left however its mark on Galdós's work. We can see it in the choice of his heroes, who often, particularly in his first manner, belong to the noble scientist type—his José Rey, his León Roch, both mathematicians, astronomers, geologists. But Galdós is always greater than his creations, and it would be a mistake to imagine that his outlook was limited to that of his scientific characters, however noble and open-minded he portrayed them. He was saved from the religion of science by his sense of humour.

At bottom, and when he is writing free from the direct influence of public events, his work is purely aesthetic. Many of his friends have reproached him for his artistic impartiality, which they call impassivity. He knew best. He was true to his vocation, and true to the literary tradition of Spain, which from its earliest epics to its picaresque novel and to *Don Quixote,* has contemplated life with an artistic serenity rivalled only by the calm attitude of Shakespeare, the pole-star and model of all true artists. It is because he was able to look upon life with eyes clean from prejudice and kindled with love that his creations are so true. He has that universal sympathy of poetic souls—souls, that is, which carry within them the whole world.

A writer possessing that virtue can impart a permanent and universal value to any subject upon which he may chance to touch. Glimpses of Galdós's inner poetical vision shine here and there in his style, shedding a ray of light on the humblest, apparently most unimportant, facts; little touches which do not in the least disturb the quiet pace of the narrative, yet give it nobility and deepen and widen the interest of the plot, in which, we feel, God and nature and destiny are present and co-operate.

From such depth of intuition his characters are created. We must not go to him for that skilful analysis, that chemistry of the human soul, into which the modern novel seems to degenerate under the influence of intellectual culture and progress. Galdós's characters are not dissected, but alive, and they give us their actions, not their motives.

It follows that his art is mainly dramatic. Galdós has given Spain and the world a splendid galaxy of characters, creatures of flesh and blood who are known to us body and soul and quickly become familiar figures in our national life. In the skill and vigour of his dramatic developments he can stand comparison with any novelist old or new. He excels in the knitting of events into crises of admirable emotional strength, by means which are within the bounds of good taste and never fall into melodrama. Let us mention for instance the murder of Ángel Guerra, a *dénouement* as inevitable, and yet as skilfully brought to its close almost by surprise as the death of Othello. Galdós's dramatic ability, though not without a certain astuteness, is, however, essentially different from that almost mechanical ingeniousness with which Calderón contrived his plays. A novel of Galdós is to a play of Calderón what an organism is to a mechanism. In Galdós the crisis is brought about by the interplay of external circumstances and character. This non-interference before events leads him sometimes to awkward, almost childish inability of exposition, which is particularly observable in his plays.

Galdós's characters are not static. They grow, evolve, and develop as the work proceeds. And this tendency towards emphasizing growth probably explains why, though born above all a dramatist, he should have devoted most of his time to novel-writing. He undoubtedly found the modern stage—as Shakespeare himself would have done—too narrow for the delineation of character along the line of time. Our theatre has gradually contracted along the dimension of time. The last phase of this evolution is the Cinema, in spirit, no less than in matter, a mere film. The characters in Galdós are not cinematographic. They live and develop, and in this he is superior to all Spanish classics except Cervantes.

It goes without saying that since Galdós can make his characters develop, he knows them from within, and penetrates into the depths of their instinct and impulses. He puts in the mouth of one of his most admirable types, Ángel Guerra, a significant

word of his own coining: *impulsología.* No better name could be given to the branch of psychology that he knew best. There is little of the human underworld which he did not fathom and express with Wordsworthian penetration and felicity, and, in a sense, the whole of his work may be interpreted as the drama of impulse lurking under the comedy of action.

This central idea explains several of the most prominent features of his art, and particularly his frequent recourse to dreams and apparitions. With Galdós, dreams are not mere tricks for melodramatic effect. They are intimately linked up with the psychology of the character who dreams them, and act as small explosions from the subconscious, which throw up to the surface of consciousness shapeless fragments of the material below. In this, of course, Galdós anticipates the modern views of psycho-analysis. His treatment of dreams must be related to that of forebodings, or, as the Spanish language admirably says, *corazonadas.* The most famous instance of this is perhaps the secret expectancy with which Gloria, in the novel of this name, feels the arrival of Daniel, the unknown chosen of her heart who, without her knowing it, is being saved from the tempest by the priest of the parish while she is at prayer in the church. Another aspect of Galdós's "impulsological" manner is his tendency to picture those revulsions of character which take place when a natural group of tendencies has been repressed by education, environment, or self-deception and is suddenly released by a shock of fact giving back in one second all the energy locked up for years in the under-soul. Such dramatic reversions to type occur in practically every book of Galdós. In his very first novel, written when he was twenty-five, there is an admirable instance in Doña Paulita, the mystical bigot who has wasted her youth in what she thought to be divine love only to find her bigotry suddenly burnt away in the fire of her worldly love for Lázaro. The case of Ángel Guerra is similar in its essentials though treated with more subtlety. Ángel Guerra begins with worldly love, deviates towards mysticism under the fascination of his platonic mistress, the beautiful nun Leré, then, on his death-bed, murdered while in the exercise of a beautiful act of charity, he confesses that he has been the victim of self-delusion and that, all through, he loved Leré with earthly love. In the same novel, most skilfully arranged in parallel pattern with the case of Ángel Guerra, will be found the case of Don Tomé, the innocent, almost uncorporeal saint, who dies, also assisted by Leré, also in love with her, confessing his pure unearthly love to Ángel Guerra in terms of singular warmth expressive of ardent desire.

It is this wealth of impulse which gives his world its wonderful vigour. With him, weakness itself seems overflowing with vitality. In one of his best novels, ***Fortunata y Jacinta,*** Galdós has left us a type of a neurotic assistant chemist, of delicate body, average mind, and but little will, a type which it would seem almost impossible to endow with interest. Yet, he has made it live and move so admirably, with such abundance of motive and impulse, such variety of shades of feeling and passion, that Maxi is one of the great creations of the nineteenth century.

This creative miracle is due to the magic power of love. Galdós loved his characters, and that is why he saw into them. The people, quick to seize spiritual facts, had nicknamed him "El Abuelo" (the Grandfather). It was a true instinct which gave him that name. In the eyes of the Spanish people, Galdós stands surrounded by a crowd of living progeny—saints, adventurers, sweet maids, intriguers, passionate mothers, wives, and mistresses, criminals, and the motley variety of less definite types, all creatures whom he loved as the children of his heart, and in whom he will live as long as the Spanish language is spoken.

Galdós would not be a Spanish creative genius if he had taken the trouble to write well. No great Spaniard ever did. The style of great Spanish works reflects the influence of two conflicting tendencies: that of the creative instinct of the race and that of the literary preconceptions of the age. The first, a natural tendency, leads the writer to disregard mere form and to concentrate on the living substance. The second, an acquired tendency, checks the free flow of expression, and in extreme cases, as in the later development of Góngora or Calderón, overburdens the style with ornament.

There are now and then in Galdós traces of this unfortunate influence of literary preconceptions over style. At times, he seems to be trying to imitate Cervantes, as for instance in the opening chapters of *Doña Perfecta*. Later he passed through a fever of inversions. But, despite these witnesses to a national failing which could not be wholly absent from a writer so typically Spanish, Galdós's style flows clear like a river from a spring of creative inspiration. He is too great to treat style as more than a mere medium of expression. The cultivation of diction for the sake of diction is a sign of decadence, that is, of impotence; and we know that Galdós was anything but impotent. His prose is like a sail, more or less full according to the strength of the wind of inspiration. When he is moved, no one writes better; when he is dealing with unimportant facts or fulfilling those menial tasks which are necessary in dramatic and narrative literature, he lets expression fall to the simple level of the occasion. He is above all sincere and true.

With him, expression is subordinate to impression; words are tools. This is why we must not go to him for landscapes. His interest is in man, and to nature he gives exactly the same place which the painters of the Spanish school gave it, namely, the background. Not that his feeling for nature is poor or defective. Few writers speak of natural life with more sympathy and penetration than Galdós. But, being an eminently dramatic genius, he could not suspend the development of his action in order to indulge in a kind of pictorial *intermezzo*. He has left few but splendid descriptions of natural events, tempests, shipwrecks, sunsets. . . . But in these cases nature finds a place in the action as one of the characters thereof, and her intervention is admirably timed to the enhancement of dramatic interest. Moreover, the Galdosian bend towards picturing concrete persons leads him to attribute to trees, plains, rivers, and even buildings, human motives and attitudes. An excellent example of all these features of Galdós's treatment of nature will be found in the description of the tempest in *Gloria*. Nine-tenths of his style is the style of his characters, and in this, as in his interpretation of impulse, our great novelist shows how Protean his nature was. Just as he describes his characters by their own actions, so he expresses them by their own words. Often indeed, even in his early novels, the narrative form is dropped altogether and the characters are left to speak in dialogue, the author putting in a rare occasional indication as to gesture, voice, or attitude, mere stage directions. There are novels—*El abuelo* is a typical example—which are written in this form from beginning to end, a kind of writing which has no less a precedent than *La celestina*. At other times Galdós develops part or the whole of the novel (*La estafeta romántica*, for instance) in the form of letters purported to be written by the persons in the story, another direct, dramatic way of letting the characters speak for themselves. And it is not only what his characters say, but the manner and form of their speech,

which is theirs and living. He has worked so deep in this respect that, though he delighted in the presentation of urban types, whose tendency to slang is strong in all nations, his books have lost nothing of their power and freshness with years. For Galdós knew how to penetrate below the surface in language no less than in action, and, without losing in liveliness, to reach a level of expression which, being true, is in the real sense of the word classic. Now and then, and for purposes of illustration, he turns to account those little oddities of speech with which it is easy to give a type a certain external consistence, or a silhouette, such as the verbal infelicities of Mrs. Malaprop. But, in general, he seeks adequacy in language by the direct expression of character. As his own style flows from inspiration, his characters speak from the outpourings of their heart. Hence his simplicity and strength. Hence, also, his variety. His style is like a clear river which flows always even and the same, yet reflects whatever skies there are overhead in the author's mind.

In its dramatic quality, in its carelessness, in its swiftness, and in its humble subordination to the substance of action, Galdós's style is therefore classically Spanish. There is another Spanish quality which can be found in it to an eminent degree, namely, the power of forcible and condensed expression. A passage in *Doña Perfecta* may be given as an example. It is the last scene of the book. Midnight. While Rosario, Doña Perfecta's daughter, the victim of her mother's bigotry, is revealing to her in a moment of weakness that she has arranged to run away that night with José Rey, Remedios, the priest's sister, who wants Rosario to marry her son and feels a strong hatred against Rosario's lover, arrives at the house eager to impart to Doña Perfecta that José is in the garden, hidden, waiting for Rosario. She knocks at the front door. This is the way Galdós puts it:

> Rosario was on her knees. At that moment,
> they heard three knocks, three explosions. It
> was the heart of Remedios knocking at the door.

An admirable synthesis of the state of mind of Remedios, the action of her hand and the beating of her passionate heart in her breast. Such examples abound in Galdós's novels and dramas. They contribute to give his work its classical flavour.

In Spanish literature Galdós ranks as the greatest novelist since Cervantes. He has not created a type as universal as Don Quixote, but then Don Quixote is unique. He has, on the other hand, over Cervantes the advantage of three centuries of European life, so that he moves with greater philosophic and literary liberty; and, in these three centuries, perhaps the greatest event in literature—Shakespeare.

In European literature Galdós undoubtedly deserves to rank with the great novelists of the century, in line with Dickens, Balzac, and Dostoievsky.

A comparison between Galdós and Dickens has become quite customary in Spanish criticism. The two names are naturally related in the mind of the Spanish reader because Galdós is rich in humour, and Dickens owes perhaps most of his foreign popularity to his humorous vein. But, if I may venture a personal opinion which may not find ready acceptance, the comparison between Dickens and Galdós is not so much an honour to Galdós as an honour to Dickens. Galdós is superior to Dickens because his humour arises out of human, universal conditions, while Dickens's humour arises out of a social or conventional setting. Dickens deliberately mixes the comic element in the composition of his fables. In Galdós, humorous situations naturally result from the interplay of circumstance and character. Moreover, Galdós easily reaches that high pinnacle of dramatic art which Shakespeare and Cervantes alone were great enough to attain before him, namely, the interweaving of comic and tragic in one and the same scene and even in one and the same person. Many of his characters in fact live in a zone of changing lights, comic and tragic, and move to tears and laughter at the same time—thus, Maxi in *Fortunata y Jacinta,* Don Pio in *El abuelo,* and Pepet in *La loca de la casa.* It is doubtful whether Dickens ever rose to such heights of dramatic conception. Rather than tragic, his outlook might not unfairly be described as melodramatic.

With Balzac, the comparison suggests itself because Galdós wrote a real *Comédie Humaine* in a Spanish setting. His inferiority to the French master lies perhaps in that his works are more easy-going, and have in them less of that intensity, that appetite for life which is the secret of Balzac's creative power. Balzac is the more vigorous of the two, Galdós perhaps the better artist and certainly the more lovable mind.

Galdós resembles Dostoievsky in his preference for that zone of human nature where subliminal forces work obscurely in the shaping of action and character. As with Dostoievsky, his characters are often highly strung and at times unhinged. Maxi, Nazarin, are true Dostoievskian types. Both the Spaniard and the Russian seem to have a foible for depicting mystics and madmen. There is a Spanish saying that "children and madmen tell the truth." It is in search of truth that Dostoievsky and Galdós go to their abnormal types of humanity, hoping thus to evade the strict censorship of reason. Their main interest is in destiny. They are not so much concerned with man in his relation to society as with man in his relation to Eternity, and they instinctively feel that it is in exploring the subconscious depths that glimmers of truth may be seen shining here and there in moments of crisis. Hence there common preoccupation with religion. The three anti-clerical novels of Galdós are little more than a preliminary phase of his religious obsession, during which he, as it were, clears the ground of all political prepossessions before starting on his really religious work. He seems to have a marked preference for the mystical-practical type which St. Teresa immortalized and of which he gave such a lovable rendering in his Sor Lorenza or Leré in *Angel Guerra.* But he has studied almost every possible variety of the type with his usual penetration and impartiality.

Galdós does not reach the poignancy of Dostoievsky's tortured questionings. There is nothing in his work to compare with the tragedy of Ivan Karamazov. But he is calmer and more serene. This is due first to his Spanish common sense. In the Spaniard there is always a Sancho along with a Don Quixote, as Santa Teresa herself brilliantly proved by her own life. Then, the Spanish genius shuns that almost morbid tendency towards analysis which made Dostoievsky unhappy and his novels bibles of desperation. What in Dostoievsky is a problem, ever present to the intellect, never transcends in Galdós the aesthetic plane, and remains a tacit sense of tragedy contemplated in silence like the black heavens in a moonless night. Dostoievsky, moreover, never found an answer to his questionings, and to the end remained haunted by his unsolved problem of destiny. Galdós found in his nature a living answer which satisfied him. Galdós is the novelist of love.

The whole of his work is an illustration of the forms that love may take in the world, its triumphs, failures, disguises and transformations, its wanton playfulness and deep but fleeting joys. He is far from giving a rose-coloured version of love and life. Many of his novels—perhaps most of them—end in utter disappointment, despair, death. As if he wanted to prove how far he is convinced that love is a wanton, senseless passion, he shows in *Fortunata y Jacinta* a triangle of unrequited love: on each side, a man in love with a woman and these two women both in love with a third man, while this third man, the apex on which all these lines of love converge, is a perfectly inane creature who seems incapable of loving anybody. Yet the book is not cynical, not pitiless, not pessimistic, nor tragic. It is full of human sympathy and so overflowing with vitality that one shuts it after the death of Jacinta and the locking up of Maxi in a lunatic asylum with the sense that life is worth living when people can die and go mad in such a way.

Galdós, however, has no theory about love and does not claim to hold the secret of any panacea. With him love is not an idea but a living feeling which pervades all his work. He brings to Spanish literature a quality which is not very abundant in it, a delicate tenderness, wholly free from sentimentality, particularly noticeable when he speaks of children. No other writer ever treats children with so delightful a touch, light, tender, a little humorous. He speaks in *Gloria* of the sexton's little boy with "his dirty little fingers like rose leaves fallen in mud." In *León Roch,* when relating the infancy of María Egipciaca and her brother, he describes how, in imitation of St. Teresa, they decided to run away in order to perish as martyrs at the hands of the Infidels, and adds: "they fell asleep under the protection of a rock, and there, the Maker of all things, God

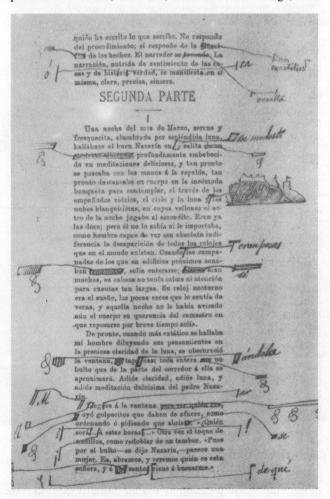

A galley page from Nazarín *with corrections by Galdós.*

Omnipotent, gave them a kiss and delivered them into the hands of the constabulary.''

He knew, therefore, what he was saying when in the mouths of so many of his characters he put words which expressed his faith in love as the one positive force of the world, the one force which made life worth living and unhappiness itself desirable. He looked on all forms of love with mystic eyes, and saw them as forms of the eternal love of God. ''The love of God''—he says in *León Roch*—''is nothing but the sublimation of the love of his creatures.'' Angel Guerra, on his death-bed, sums up this philosophy in words of admirable simplicity: ''The only thing one gets out of this life is the pleasure and the joy of loving.'' And Pepa Fúcar, in *León Roch*, when asked to renounce her happiness for conscience' sake, has force enough while bowing to destiny to utter this eloquent protest: ''My conscience is to love.'' An adaptation of this phrase might do for a brief description of Galdós's work: his art was love. (pp. 47-63)

Salvador de Madariaga, ''Benito Pérez Galdós,'' in his The Genius of Spain and Other Essays on Spanish Contemporary Literature, *Oxford at the Clarendon Press, Oxford, 1923, pp. 46-63.*

AUBREY F. G. BELL   (essay date 1925)

[*Bell was an English critic of Spanish and Portuguese literature. In the following excerpt, he notes the strengths and weaknesses of Galdós's fiction.*]

[Benito Pérez Galdós] faithfully caught the spirit of the times, and shortly after his arrival at Madrid in 1864 he had the inspiration to see that the historical novel might be renewed, not archæologically *à la* Walter Scott, but in the description of contemporary events and customs, as the *novela de costumbres* [''the novel of manners''].

His first novel, *La fontana de oro,* although not published until 1870, was written (1867-68), except the last few pages, before the Revolution of 1868. It deals with Madrid in 1821 and already shows the tendency to wrap the characters closely in contemporary history, as does the next novel, *El audaz,* the action of which lies in Madrid and Toledo at the beginning of the Nineteenth Century. The youth of twenty-five shows himself in this novel not insensible to the farce that may be enacted in the name of Liberty or to the iniquities of revolutions. In 1873 appeared the first *Episodio nacional, Trafalgar,* and the next five years were a period of amazing activity, for they included the best, the first twenty *National Episodes* and some of the most celebrated of the ''contemporary novels'': *Doña Perfecta, Gloria, Marianela* and *La familia de León Roch.* That was a prodigious effort, but his vein of invention was of marvellous fertility (in this respect he ranks with the greatest Spanish writers of all ages), and for the next twenty years contemporary novels flowed unfailingly from his pen, while in 1898 he took up the *National Episodes,* interrupted in 1879, and before his death in 1920 had added another twenty-six volumes to the twenty of the first two series.

It was impossible that all should be pure gold in so ample an output, yet there is gold to be found in every one of his books, although few of them are finished into so satisfying a completeness as *Doña Perfecta,* and, on a larger scale, *Fortunata y Jacinta* and *Angel Guerra.* It is usual to class Galdós among the realists, although a good deal of his writing is not strictly based on reality. In his first period the influence of the Nat-

uralistic school led him into an excessive or one-sided display of details (the description, for instance, of the night watchman of Orbajosa in *Doña Perfecta* shows a determination to look upon one side only: ''The Ave María Purísima of the drunken Sereno sounded like a wailing cry in the sleeping town.'' Later a cloudy symbolism and allegory manifested themselves, and a certain narrowness of outlook is evident throughout, without, however, the defect of insincerity or coldness.

Some critics have supposed Galdós to have been not only influenced by English novelists (chiefly Dickens) but possessed of an English temperament, that of the traditional type of cold and impassive Englishman. Such critics can scarcely have read very deeply in Galdós' voluminous works. We have only to consider the scene of the child's illness in *La familia de León Roch,* which is one of his great novels, since it is not merely a mordant attack on Madrid society, it is a moving story, human and intense; or his love of children generally, as shown so unmistakably and with delightful delicacy in many novels; Juan Jacobo in *Los apostólicos,* the most living portrait of Empecinadillo in *Juan Martín el Empecinado,* or the children, like flowers in a hailstorm, who play a prominent part, with such pathos and gaiety, in *Gerona.* We remember, too, the poignant story of Marianela, wild flower of a mining district of Cantabria, and the pathos of *El abuelo,* or the figure of Sola (akin to Señor Matheu's Eugenia) in *Los apostólicos:* she is presented with a naturalness and charm which he more often reserves for his child characters. His affectionate chivalry is shown also in humble but loyal figures, such as that of Casiana (thrown on the Madrid streets by her mother at an early age) in *Cánovas,* which abound in his pages; few writers have so successfully lit up with an inner significance such apparently dull or dingy lives.

Galdós is pre-eminently the novelist of Madrid, where he can find ''pictures worthy of the Potro of Córdoba and the Albaicín of Granada,'' and he had by heart all the changes and development of the life of the capital and court in the Nineteenth Century. If he laid bare some of the foibles of modern Spanish life, the love of talk, unbridled individualism, a positive dislike of reputations (the reputations of others), the ignorance of the women, of those sensible and energetic women whose ascendency he describes; the illiteracy of the orators, the inclination of even the most honest citizens to defraud the impersonal State, the contempt for manual labour, the regard for things foreign, the frivolous gaiety of the capital, the mingling of penury and ostentation; if he described Spain as lying beatifically asleep, he also paid constant tribute to the exceptional and splendid qualities of the race beneath those superficial defects, and no writer was more fervently patriotic or more national. His books are a treasury of Spanish prose, a perfect mine of familiar phrases. Style was never the principal consideration with him, but on great occasions it never failed him, and his prose is indigenous, completely free from gallicisms. (pp. 52-5)

Equipped with sound general knowledge, especially in medicine and astronomy, this industrious Spanish Balzac travelled over Spain observing keenly and filling in his notes with his acute reading of history. The dramatic events of the War of Independence and of the Carlist Wars lose nothing in the telling in the pages of the *Episodios nacionales,* which carry the history of Spain from the death of Churruca at Trafalgar to the Restoration. With the entry of Alfonso XII into Madrid at the beginning of *Cánovas,* he virtually brings this history of three-quarters of a century to an end, although he carries it on a few years further. Forerunners of the *Episodios nacionales* may be seen in the Erckmann-Chatrian novels and in those of Camillo Castello Branco; but the excellence of such a series of works produced almost mechanically, with unflinching persistence, has no precedent. The superiority of the early, the first twenty *Episodes* over the later twenty-six has often been noticed. Indeed, perhaps the merit of the later books is in danger of being ignored. The private story in these later *Episodes* is often of slighter interest, but the historical interest remains. Nevertheless, the old power of concentration, characterization and insistence on concrete detail, in a word, the creative vigour, had evidently diminished. The atmosphere becomes vaguer and dimmer, while the characters, so well brought out in the early works, fade into the background, and the story wanders on a little indefinitely, like a tale told by Padre Aleli.

The action of Galdós is impersonal and dramatic, the author keeps himself carefully behind the scene, unless we may see him in the dreams and hallucinations, ravings and disquisitions of his otherwise deliberately commonplace characters. These interludes were perhaps a half-unconscious refuge from the commonplace, devised by this homely, domestic novelist (is not one of his novels entitled *Miau*?) who devoted himself so relentlessly to potrayal of reality, when reality threatened to rise up in its drabness and materially smother him in bales of cotton and rolls of cloth and yards of lace. Then he would transplant the familiar figures, which charm us as presented in their ordinary life, into a nightmare of difficulties and adventures; Solita, for instance, searching for Monsalud in the Madrid streets during a night of insurrection (*7 de julio*). (pp. 55-7)

Other devices are adopted in order to present the characters as in a dream, ordinary persons in abnormal circumstances: magic, mystery, persecution, doubt, dreams, fever, famine, physical agony, blindness, allegorical figures, strange apparitions. In a passage of *Bailén* it is the moonlight, "disfiguring the things of Earth"; elsewhere the refuge from reality takes the form of asceticism: "There were moments in which he considered himself fortunate to be so unhappy" (*Montes de Oca*). In *Fortunata y Jacinta* he speaks of "certain devices absolutely necessary in order that the commonplace character of life should be converted into material for art." The introduction of the marvellous, which had already appeared in *Angel Guerra* and some of the earlier works, in the later novels is used as a deliberate mechanism to move the characters opportunely but with much needless magic to the vital historical points; but we feel in his work the truth of his earlier remark (in *El Grande Oriente*) that "it sometimes happens that the commonplace things are those most worth relating."

Some of the lucubrations, especially in the later works, are apt to be wearisome: not always can wisdom, as with Don Quixote, flow from the lips of the distraught. But more usually his characters are lifelike, natural and individual (the beggars and street urchins as individual as the rest) and are marked with a Dickensian emphasis, although ordinarily without caricature. Especially when the scene is Madrid, the city in which his observation was chiefly exercised, nearly every character is presented with some little trick or habit or physical peculiarity. How deftly these are underlined may be seen, for instance, in *Lo prohibido*, an account of the relations between a rich bachelor and three sisters (his first cousins) and their husbands. Few indeed are the novelists who have left so wonderful and abundantly stocked a gallery of portraits; in the true Castilian tradition, scenery and description are the mere background for the human figures. The new feature in Galdós is the multitude of these portraits. Instead of a few spinners or topers or Court buffoons, as with Velazquez, in the pages of Galdós a whole people invades literature and art: tramps, peasants, ploughmen, beggars, street *gamins,* shepherds of the uplands of Castile, priests and chaplains, monks and nuns, soldiers and volunteers, the prosperous bureaucrat or woebegone *cesante.* (pp. 57-8)

These are but a few of the hundreds, nay thousands of characters (the *Episodios nacionales* are said to contain a thousand characters and they swarm equally in the *Contemporary Novels*) which live, really live memorably in his pages and will keep them alive long after the more or less artificial religious or philosophical problems presented in *Gloria* (that "work written in a fortnight's enthusiasm," as its author described it) and *La familia de León Roch* and *Doña Perfecta*, or the socialism of *Angel Guerra* and *Halma* have lost their interest. (p. 59)

If we add the living, human, dramatic interest, the historic interest of Episodes such as those of the War of Independence, of which Southey prophesied truly in November 1808 that it would renew "such scenes as have never been witnessed in Europe since the destruction of Saguntum and Numantia''; the keen pathos and humour, the knack of unconventional but satisfactory endings, we may realize the hold maintained on countless readers and many younger writers by the greatest Spanish novelist of the Nineteenth Century after Pereda (whose friend he was and to whose "marvellous art" he paid a tribute in *Gloria*). It was indeed fortunate that he could round off a novel with some concession to the reader's interest in the characters, for in his faithful presentation of life he was inclined to publish his novels in lengths cut off almost at random, one might say, so that one must read his works entire for a full understanding. . . . Rationalism is an inartistic, analytical, dissolvent creed, and many of Galdós' novels are rather bundles of charming shreds and delicious patches than individual works of art. From time to time, however, the wizard could raise and concentrate a whole picture on a large canvas into a living masterpiece, as in *Angel Guerra,* the novel of Toledo (c. 1885), or *Fortunata y Jacinta,* the novel of Madrid (in the last third of the Nineteenth Century). (pp. 60-1)

Aubrey F. G. Bell, "The Novel: The National Novel, Pérez Galdós," in his Contemporary Spanish Literature, *Alfred A. Knopf, 1925, pp. 52-61.*

L. B. WALTON (essay date 1927)

[*In the following excerpt, Walton assesses Galdós's importance in Spanish literature.*]

[It] was Galdós who first seriously embarked upon the task of redeeming Spanish fiction from the deplorable state into which it had fallen since the great age of Cervantes and the "gusto picaresco" ["picaresque taste"]. It is true that Alarcón, Valera and Pereda were not unknown as writers prior to the appearance of *La fontana de oro*; but none of them had yet turned their attention to the novel proper. When Galdós entered the arena, he was faced with the task of creating the modern Spanish novel—and he met with such notable success in the performance of it that he has come to be regarded by many of those who are most competent to judge of such matters as the greatest Spanish novelist since Cervantes. In all the types of fiction which had been crudely essayed by his predecessors—the historical novel, the novel of customs and the *roman à thèse*—he attained signal distinction. To these he added the novel in dialogue and that curious species of imaginative literature to which Menéndez y Pelayo has given the name of "novela simbólica'' [''symbolic novel'']—both of which forms are, in spite of their many inconsistencies and absurdities, of considerable interest and importance.

The early cultivators of the historical novel lacked . . . both the psychological insight and the sound basis of erudition which this genre demands. In the majority of cases, they were content to reproduce, either in direct translation or in adaptation, the masterpieces of Scott and Dumas: and even those works for which originality is claimed bear obvious signs of foreign origin. The best of them are but pale reflections of a greater genius, and the worst of them are quite unreadable. These early novels of the Scott tradition are, however, with all their faults, preferable to the extravagant romances of chivalry seasoned to the taste of the modern palate which succeeded them; for the latter make no attempt to follow the dictates of common-sense. In the words of Menéndez y Pelayo: ''If the works in the first manner were usually conducive to slumber, although well written, those of the second period, in addition to being clumsy and awkward in their diction, were monstrous in their construction and even crazy in their plot.''

The *Episodios nacionales* of Galdós came, then, as a revelation to Spanish readers wearied of literary monstrosities; and they possessed, in addition to a firm basis of historical knowledge, a profound human appeal. So far as Spanish fiction was concerned, they were something entirely new—and they were hailed with intense enthusiasm by a public which has never been remarkable for intellectual curiosity. To his Spanish predecessors in the historical genre Galdós owes little or nothing; but the general scheme of the *Episodios* was almost certainly suggested to him by his reading of the brothers Erckmann-Chatrian. The novels of the latter were popular in Spain when Galdós conceived his project; and between the two series there is a clear external similarity. The French writers have a distinct advantage so far as background is concerned, for the French Revolution and the Napoleonic campaigns are events of transcendental significance in European history, while those of which Galdós treats in the *Episodios* are, with one or two exceptions, purely local in their appeal. He makes, however, the best possible use of his material; and out of many unpromising situations he succeeds in extracting the maximum of human interest. The *Episodios* are not . . . historical romances, in the orthodox sense of the term; but, inasmuch as they are an endeavour to interpret history in terms of the human spirit, they belong to the historical genre—of which, in modern Spanish literature, Galdós is, indisputably, the creator.

His position with regard to the novel of customs is not so clear. So far as the regional novel is concerned, the premier place must be awarded to Pereda; and the work of the early ''costumbristas,'' especially that of ''El Solitario,'' Mesonero, and Larra, is by no means negligible. If, however, we interpret the term ''novel of customs'' in its broadest sense, then, surely, to Galdós belongs the honour of having created it. In the words of Salvador de Madariaga; ''Pereda belongs to a region—the mountain; Valera, to a class—the aristocracy; Blasco Ibáñez is a cosmopolitan writer, if not a French one. Galdós is Spanish, and embraces the whole of Spain, all the colours and shades of her thought, and all the years of her nineteenth century'' [see excerpt dated 1923]. Galdós, then, takes the whole of Spain for his province, and for him ''the people'' does not signify, as it did, usually, for Calderón and Mesonero, the ''plebs'' merely, but the whole people—especially the middle classes, which in Spain, as he points out, are a synthesis of all classes. Although he has shown in many of his works that

he is as much at home in the country as in the capital, he concentrates especially upon Madrid—where all types meet. What sketch of local customs can compare in brilliance and human interest with the ''Visita al Cuarto Estado'' in *Fortunata y Jacinta*? Where is the atmosphere of an ancient Spanish city more realistically evoked than in the picture of Toledo in *Angel Guerra*? Where can we find more entertaining sketches of life in a small provincial town than those in *Doña Perfecta* and *Gloria*? It is true that Galdós has given us no ''regional'' novel in the conventional sense of the term; but he has infused into the ''género de costumbres'' [''genre of manners''] a human interest which transcends the merely local appeal of the earlier sketches. One has only to contrast *Doña Perfecta* with *La Gaviota* to appreciate the extent of the advance which had been made. How jejune and stilted Fernán Caballero's masterpiece appears beside that of Galdós! With all its undeniable merits, the former dates. The latter stands outside time.

Sr. Salvador de Madariaga has defined the subject-matter of Galdós' work as ''Human nature seen by an unprejudiced observer of nineteenth-century Spain.'' It can hardly be maintained, however, that Galdós approached the national problems of his day without any preconceived notions as to the cause of his country's ills and the best remedy for them. According to his own admission, he regarded the novel as a means of propaganda; and all his novels are, in a sense, thesis novels. There is, however, a great difference between the ''thesis novel'' as it was cultivated by la Avellaneda and the ''novel with a purpose'' as it was conceived by Galdós. We have seen how he humanised the ''género de costumbres''; and the didactic novel undergoes a similar process at his hands. The problem is not allowed, save in certain exceptional cases, to swamp the human interest of the work. In *Sab*, *Guatimozín* and *Espatolino* the ''thesis is the thing''; while in *Fortunata y Jacinta,* for example, one feels that the story gives rise to the problem, not the problem to the story. It is, of course, true that *Fortunata y Jacinta* is one of the least blatantly controversial of Galdós' works, but even where the ''thesis'' is emphatically apparent, as in *Doña Perfecta, Gloria* and *La familia de León Roch,* the author is interested in his characters as individuals. As we have seen, he falls at times into the error of using them as mouthpieces for his own opinions: but when he does so it is a lapse and nothing more. It is no exaggeration to state that Galdós is the greatest master of the novel of tendency in Spain. He purged it of its most objectionable characteristics and incorporated it into the novel of manners—which, in his view, must always have a ''purpose.'' What, in Galdós' case, was that purpose?

It was, in the first instance, we venture to suggest, the diagnosing of the spiritual malady from which he conceived Spain to be suffering. It is, in our view, a mistake to regard even the earlier novels as nothing more than clever pieces of anti-clerical propaganda. Clericalism is attacked merely because, in the opinion of Galdós, it fosters a certain attitude of mind, and it is that attitude of mind against which his shafts of irony are really directed. Bigotry and prejudice are the outcome of a spiritual provincialism which, in its turn, arises from mental laziness, a deep-rooted disinclination to think for oneself if someone else will do the work for one. The parochial spirit and the spirit of intolerance are, as we all know, very closely allied. The latter, indeed, arises out of the former. The Orbajosans of this world accept their immediate surroundings as beyond criticism very largely because they are too lazy to criticise, too indolent even to take stock of the platitudes which constitute their mental equipment. New ideas involve thinking—they may possibly involve an expenditure of physical energy. That, say the Orbajosns, would be a bore—so let us go on in the old way as our fathers did before us. What was good enough for them is good enough for us, and so on. It was this irrational, unthinking conservatism which Galdós lashed with relentless irony and not, as some might suppose, the conservatism which is born of mature reflection.

The malady of Spain, like the "mal du siècle" as it shows itself in the individual, is, Galdós seems to indicate, the result either of sheer laziness, or of lack of will ("abulia") or of the misdirection of energy. One form of such misdirection is to be found in a certain type of mysticism which alienates those who indulge in it (for Galdós, like certain modern psychologists, regards it as a form of sensuous indulgence) from the practical affairs of life. With this, as we can divine from so many of his books, he has no manner of patience. Whether it takes the form of orthodox piety, as in the case of María Sudre or Victoria, or of vague philosophising, as in the case of Maxí, it is equally to be condemned; for it is invariably a means of self-deception. The key to individual, as to national, health is—action. This must not, however, take the form of a vague physical unrest, a mere pointless "hustle." Even when disguised as philanthropy, this is pernicious. Energy is a valuable commodity, and it must not be expended without circumspection. Do good works by all means—but first of all make certain that your "good" actions will not defeat their own ends. The time for showy heroics is now past. How, then, can the individual and the nation best utilise their energies? The answer which Galdós offers to this question can, we think, easily be divined from his works. He has, however, left it on record in his Introduction to Salaverría's *Vieja España* where, after suggesting an epitaph for the Cid, he remarks: "The Spanish people retains the pattern of those virtues which gave it predominance in the age of heroic and glorious deeds. But the heroic ages are gone and we have come to live a peaceful and industrious life, without swords and all the rest of the flummery of Mars; *fighting human ills with the weapons of the arts and sciences.*" Since these words were written by Galdós events have given the lie to certain of his affirmations; but the ideal held forth is, possibly, one which the modern world has a right to claim as especially its own.

Galdós may justly be regarded as the founder of the new school of writers, which grew to maturity after the disaster of 1898. There is, indeed, little in Angel Ganivet's *Idearium Español* which we cannot find expressed either implicitly or explicitly in the *Novelas contemporáneas*; and Ganivet's work was the Bible of the spiritual renascence which followed the disaster. In it he uses the term "abulia" to designate the spiritual malady from which his country is suffering, and he seeks a remedy for the disease in the right use of the native energy of Spain. Like Galdós, he has no sympathy with a cosmopolitanism which pours scorn upon "las cosas de España." It is within, he affirms, that Spain must look for salvation. The *Novelas contemporáneas* also anticipate many of the views expressed by Ricardo Macías Picavea in his gloomy work, *El Problema Nacional*. Picavea attributes the national malady to two innate defects of character—the predominance of passion over will (cf. Ganivet's *Idearium*) and the lack of any sense of abstract justice. The first is responsible for the alleged Spanish tendency to live in the present without making adequate provision for the future; the second for the administrative corruption which disgraces the public life of Spain. Friendliness and family affection are admirable qualities—but they should not provide a motive for the filling of a public appointment! This prevalence of nepotism in public affairs was, as we have seen, admirably satirised by Galdós in his portrayal of Manuel José Ramón del Paz, "indefatigable apostle of that venerable routine upon which rests the noble edifice of our glorious national apathy," and his innumerable relations. Picavea suggests no remedy, for he conceives the malady to be incurable. A less pessimistic view was, however, taken by other members of the "generation of the disaster." (pp. 216-26)

The diagnosis of Spain's malady was further developed by Martínez Ruiz ("Azorín"), in his novel *La Voluntad,* and by his friend Pío Baroja in a number of works, especially *Vidas Sombrías* and *Camino de Perfección.* These two writers continue the work, initiated by Galdós in the *Episodios* and *Novelas contemporáneas,* of revealing Spain to Spaniards, and of making Spaniards intelligible to themselves. Both "Azorín" and Baroja agree with Galdós in tracing to "abulía" the source of their country's ills. Inspired, possibly, by the *Episodios* of Galdós, Baroja wrote his *Memorias de un hombre de Acción,* a series in which he studies the origins of contemporary Spain. The hero, Don Eugenio de Aviraneta, an historical figure, is essentially a man of action; a great promotor of sedition and revolt—the type of audacious adventurer which Baroja especially admires. Action is, indeed, the keynote of Baroja's work, but—and this is where he differs greatly from Galdós—the activity which Baroja extols is not necessarily either constructive or purposeful. He loves action for its own sake and demands from life, at any cost, "something dynamic." His is a vagabond spirit, and his love of wandering is reflected in nearly all his books—especially in *Zalacain, el Aventurero* and *Las Inquietudes de Shanti-Andía.* He also differs from Galdós in his attitude towards the poor and unfortunate. In *La Busca* and *Mala Hierba* he gives us a masterly picture of low-life in Madrid—but that life is studied with a detachment and a lack of sympathy which is almost inhuman. Galdós was, as we have seen, essentially Christian in his attitude towards the problem of poverty. Baroja is pagan, Nietzschean; but, again unlike Galdós, he never indulges in deliberate propaganda. He shares Flaubert's horror of didactic art; and it is this dislike of moralising which distinguishes his work from that of Korolenko, with whom he has been compared. Baroja is Galdós de-Christianised and purged of tendencious proclivities. Just as Galdós startled his countrymen of the post-revolution epoch by his attacks upon clericalism and conventional moral standards, so Baroja appears after the disaster of '98 with a more fundamental, if less resounding, challenge. While deploring the misinterpretation which he believes it to have suffered, Galdós holds fast to the Christian code of ethics. He does not doubt for one moment that life is worth while, nor does he question the general desirability of the existing social order. Baroja has a profound contempt for modern civilisation and for the moral teachings of Jesus Christ. He is the Spanish apostle of force, and the "relentless logic of facts." To the strong alone should come the "glittering prizes," and a society which exalts a Laodicean virtue as the ideal code of morality is both corrupt and foolish. "We must live the natural life, the savage, primitive life—we must bring up our children in the school of force. Let us despise empty ease. Life has no charm when we are not tormented by the spur of grief or wounded by the caress of love." Thus does González-Blanco sum up the philosophy which Baroja substitutes for the humanitarian positivism of Galdós. Although the two creeds are diametrically opposed, Baroja would have been impossible, or at least unlikely, without Galdós, who, by his revolt against what was evil in the existing order, prepared the way for an attack upon that order itself. He cannot be relieved of a certain responsibility for much that was thought, said and written by the "generation of '98," and almost all the great figures in contemporary Spanish fiction must look to him as their master. He is, indeed, a unique figure in the history of the modern Spanish novel.

His position in the history of modern European literature is more difficult to determine. To Spaniards, and to students in the Spanish field, he must always appear as a giant, if only by comparison with the pigmies whom he immediately succeeded. Is he, however, entitled to rank as a European novelist of the first order?

Some would deny him greatness of any description; while others, as we have seen, unite in according him the highest praise. Let us deal in the first place with the vexed question of originality. Galdós has been compared with Balzac, with Dickens and with Dostoievsky. What, if anything, does he owe to these writers? If he has borrowed, how far has he succeeded in employing the alien material to create something new, something indisputably Spanish?

No writer, however individual, can altogether fail to be influenced by the literary atmosphere of his age; and it is scarcely surprising that Galdós should have fallen under the spell of the great novelists of France, England and Russia. He has himself admitted that his reading of Balzac impelled him to write the *Novelas contemporáneas*—a Spanish "Comédie Humaine"—and with Balzac he has, naturally, frequently been compared. From Balzac he undoubtedly borrowed the general scheme for a series of inter-related novels; and in productivity he almost rivals the great French realist. Like those of Balzac, his plots develop innumerable ramifications, and he revels in genealogical trees! His observation is as minute and exhaustive as that of Balzac. No detail escapes his eye, and all is faithfully recorded. Like Balzac, he is especially interested in the bourgeoisie, and in money-making. The majority of his characters move, as do those of Balzac, in circles where financial soundness is one of the cardinal virtues and poverty one of the deadly sins. Hence the countless subterfuges and petty domestic meannesses to which many of his creations are obliged to resort for the sake of "keeping up appearances." And hovering in the background there is always a Gobseck or a Torquemada!

There are other general resemblances between the two "human comedies"; but it would not, in our opinion, be justifiable to conclude from such similarities that Galdós is to be dismissed as a mere imitator. The social conditions which he was describing were in many respects similar to those treated by Balzac, and a likeness between the works of the two is, consequently, only to be expected. While, however, he is no slavish imitator, Galdós lacks the creative force of Balzac, the intensity of genius which characterises the supreme artist. Acute psychologist as he was, Galdós could never have given us a Eugénie Grandet or a Père Goriot. He rarely becomes one, as it were, with his characters; rarely exhibits to a high degree a passionate sympathy with his creations. There is nothing of the poet in Galdós; and talent is only too frequently obliged to do the work of inspiration. He is also, as we have observed, too fond of the rostrum. It would, perhaps, be unkind rather than inapt to describe Galdós as Balzac turned schoolmaster.

The comparison with Dickens has, as Sr. de Madariaga remarks [see excerpt dated 1923], become a commonplace of Spanish criticism. It suggests itself naturally—for Galdós' affection for things English, and, especially, the novels of Dickens, is well known. There is a rich vein of humour in the work of Galdós which, in view of the fact that he admired that writer, has been dubbed somewhat too hastily, we think, "Dickensian." It is

difficult on closer examination to discover any relationship between the sly irony of Galdós and the hearty jollity of Dickens. The latter, as is well known, was prone to a certain exaggeration, almost amounting to caricature, in his delineation of humorous types. He is quite deliberately funny. With Galdós the humour is more subdued, and his comical situations seem to arise more naturally out of the incidents of the story. He does on occasions, as we have seen, deliberately imitate the mock heroics of the English writer; but there is, we venture to assert, no temperamental affinity between the two novelists. Dickens was the greater genius and Galdós, in many respects, the better artist. The characters of Dickens are on the move the whole time. They do not as a rule stop to analyse or be analysed; for their creator has no use for psychology which clogs the action. He does not trouble, as does Galdós, to unravel mixed motives. There are, however, certain similarities of method between the two writers. Dickens, like Galdós, frequently introduces his characters by giving us their "dossier." Like Galdós, also, he attaches great importance to details of dress; and, like Galdós, he is interested in abnormal psychology. He was himself subject to bad dreams, and was, he tells us, for long haunted by the face of a corpse he saw at a morgue. Abnormal states of consciousness play a large part in his work; and, as Sr. de Madariaga remarks, one of his best known heroes, Barnaby Rudge, is a half-wit. Dickens, however, unlike Galdós, is not concerned with these matters as a psychologist. He is attracted by abnormality because it is uncanny and supplies an atmosphere of dread. His "abnormals" are indeed, in the tradition of the "novel of terror," which enjoyed a great vogue at the time when he began to write and by which he was to some extent influenced. To these similarities of detail we must add the general resemblance which arises from the fact that both writers used the novel as a means of propaganda. In all essentials, however, they are utterly different. Dickens is a great lyrist. In his work emotion and sentiment predominate, while Galdós, as we have remarked, is rational, analytic—very rarely spontaneous in emotion.

Although his mildly benevolent and slightly academic muse fades into insignificance beside the sombre, terrible genius of Dostoievsky, Galdós is perhaps scarcely inferior to the Russian in his power of unravelling subconscious motives. Like those of Dostoievsky, his characters are usually neurotic or in some way mentally unstable. Like Dostoievsky, he is especially attracted by mystics and madmen, whom he regards as more closely in touch with the unseen world than are normal human beings. He did not, however, as did Dostoievsky in his cataleptic states, experience personally the curious ecstasies of the deranged. There is a detachment about his attitude which suggests at times the psychological laboratory; he is interested in his abnormals as "cases" rather than as human beings. His outlook on life is essentially sane and healthy-minded: free from morbidity himself, he cannot enter imaginatively into the psycho-pathological state which is unconscious of its own abnormality. Dostoievsky, like Spinoza, was a "God-tormented" man. Life to him was an insoluble problem, a problem which kept him continuously upon the rack of feverish introspection. He did not seek merely to portray human existence, but to justify that existence, which he found inexplicable. Galdós accepts life unquestioningly; and to all its problems he finds an answer in the exercise of charity. Charity, to him, is the central fact of human existence. He does not theorise about it or endeavour to explain its *raison d'être*. It is there: and that for him is enough.

In conclusion, it would, perhaps, be extravagant to claim for Galdós a place beside Balzac, Dickens, Tolstoy or Dostoievsky in the hierarchy of European letters. That he does, however, deserve an honoured place therein, and that he is, in the most significant sense of the word, the creator of the modern novel in Spain, we have here endeavoured to show. (pp. 227-34)

> L. B. Walton, in his Pérez Galdós and the Spanish Novel of the Nineteenth Century, *J. M. Dent & Sons Ltd., 1927, 250 p.*

GERALD BRENAN (essay date 1953)

[*In the following excerpt, Brenan discusses what he considers the best of Galdós's* Contemporary Novels, *beginning with* La desheredada.]

[*La desheredada*] owes its theme to a meditation on *Don Quixote*. It depicts the conflict, so deeply rooted in the Spanish character, between imagination and reality. Isidora Rufete is a girl of the lower middle classes who has been brought up by her uncle—a fantastic person who very appropriately lives at el Toboso, the village of Dulcinea—to believe that she is the daughter of a marquesa. She has what she supposes to be documentary proof of this and the novel takes her from her arrival in Madrid, to press her claim, through a long series of events that end in the failure of her lawsuit and in her sinking to the level of a prostitute. Isidora is a girl who, if she had not been brought up under false expectations, would have had a better fate. She has beauty: she is decent and honest and in many ways a likeable person, but she has one great vice that springs from her mistaken view of her origin—an unshakable conviction of her own transcendant value. *"Eso merezco yo,"* she says when she sees an expensive dress in a shop window, "I deserve to have that." Or, of a not sufficiently presentable suitor, *"Yo valgo infinitamente más que él,"* "I am worth infinitely more than him." This conviction gives her a loathing for everything that is vulgar, cheap and commonplace and makes her feel with every cell of her body that she was born for a life of ease and elegance. Thus, in spite of the efforts of her friends and relatives to help her, she passes on from lover to lover and, when at last she loses faith in her claim, finds it impossible to adjust herself to the narrow but respectable position that is offered her. She is a Manon Lescaut who is ruined by pride even more than by love of luxury.

La desheredada is the freshest, the most lyrical of Galdós' novels. The early chapters offer a picture, not usual in this author, of young life beginning, of adventures unrolling, of unshaped opportunities and possibilities. This is partly due to the presence of Augusto Miquís, a young doctor who is one of the few really witty characters in fiction. His flirtation with Isidora, their walk round Madrid together, their visit to the Zoo have a spring-like charm and gaiety. Then we are given a view of lower middle-class and working-class life. The girl's aunt keeps a shop in a very poor quarter, and her brother is a hooligan. These descents into squalor, where the atmosphere grows thick and dense as in a Dickens novel, and is shot by oblique lights, occur in most of Galdós' works. But meanwhile Isidora's character is developing. We see her unable to resist the temptations of the shop windows, unable to refuse the pleasures of new clothes and hot baths, unable to say no to any form of ostentation or luxury. With every fresh extravagance or folly her difficulties increase and she takes another step down. Galdós draws the struggle that goes on in her mind with wonderful tact and sensitivity. We are never allowed to forget her pride and egoism, her false refinement with its morbid dread of vulgarity or his essential hardness: they are not

pleasant characteristics, but they are redeemed for us by her sense of her destiny that drives her forward and by her reckless generosity. She pays in full the price of her faults and does it without remorse or self-pity. Ordinary though Isidora is, her story has all the cleanness and inevitability of classic tragedy.

Galdós' next book is *El amigo Manso*. It is a novel of a more conventional sort and lacks any dominating theme. The story is made by the rivalry of various men of the upper classes for a girl who, because she has no private means, becomes a governess. Young women in dependent positions often play the part of heroine in Galdós' novels, as they do in English ones, the chief difference being that in Spain they ran a great risk of being seduced and ruined. In this case the merit of the novel consists less in the story, which ends happily, than in the amusing scenes and characters that are thrown up by the way. There is, for example, the wealthy Indiano, Don José Maria Manso, with his Cuban family, who, in order to cut a figure in society, decides to use his money to found a new political party; the eminent nobodies who collect round him, their conversations and programmes and social functions, provide a rich comedy. Best of all is that mosquito-like horror, Doña Candida, a once wealthy widow who has squandered all her money and now supports herself by ingenious forms of pestering her old friends. With her lies and her snobbishness and her chatter, and her crude, virulent egoism, she is one of the high watermarks of Galdosian comedy.

El doctor Centeno, an interesting but uneven book, followed, and then, in 1884, two short novels that should be read in conjunction—*Tormento* and *La de Bringas. Tormento* is another novel on the subject of the impoverished young lady. Amparo Sánchez Emperador, who is also known as Tormento, is a poor relation who sews and does the shopping for a family of eminently respectable civil servants, the Bringas. A cousin of the Bringas', a millionaire who has made his money in the wilds of Mexico, falls in love with her and wishes to marry her. But Amparo has a secret past: as a young orphan in dire poverty, she had let herself be seduced by a dissolute priest. If she had confessed this to her fiancé, he would have forgiven her, but she cannot quite bring herself to do so. She is one of those humble, self-effacing, warm-hearted women who seem to owe their good qualities to the fact that they have no character and no moral courage. So the slow torture of the book begins. First the priest, who is still madly in love with her, blackmails her: then his sister, a sinister mahogany-faced *beata*, who spends her life in churches, throws out hints. But still she cannot confess. At last it comes out: the match is broken off and it is only on the final page that a bearable ending is provided by her fiancé carrying her off to Bordeaux as his mistress. Once again we get a picture of a young woman struggling with her character—this time, her weakness of will—and suffering cruelly over it. And in the background there is the magnificent comic spectacle of the Bringas family—Don Francisco, the perfect man of order and method, and Doña Rosalía with her envious, *agridulce* temperament.

La de Bringas, the novel that follows and continues *Tormento,* is Galdós' comic masterpiece. The centre of the picture is taken up by the Bringas couple and their young children. They are now living in the Royal Palace, a vast building which houses a heterogeneous population of court employees, ranging from ladies of the bedchamber and royal pensioners to charwomen. They have apartments there because Rosalía is an attendant of some unspecified sort on the queen, while her husband works in the Royal Commissariat for Holy Places. The book opens deliciously with a description of a fantastic work of art which Bringas has undertaken in his evenings—a picture of a classic mausoleum with angels, weeping willows, urns and garlands disposed around it, all made of human hair. It is to be a present to the wife of a high official, Don Manuel Pez, as a memorial of her dead son. It is a work requiring immense patience and a watchmaker's skill, but Bringas is an adept at every sort of domestic handicraft, from mending furniture to carving toys and polishing silver, so that making a picture of four different colours of hair, all taken from the heads of various members of the Pez family, is just the sort of task he likes. But while he works at his picture, his partner Rosalía enters on a new course of life. Hitherto she has always been a model wife and mother, prudent, economical and submissive to her husband and to his meticulous routine. But the presents given her (in *Tormento*) by her millionaire cousin and the envy aroused by Amparo's engagement to him have turned her head. She now longs to shine, to make the most of what is left of her youth and beauty, to dress well, and her spendthrift friend, the Marquesa de Tellería, urges her on. She is soon in debt and turning feverishly from one recourse to another.

The plot of the book consists in an alternation between her orgies of extravagant spending on clothes and a search for the means of preventing the debts thus incurred from becoming known to her husband. Never, I think, has a novelist introduced us so deeply or minutely to the secret of this feminine passion as Galdós here does. Rosalía cannot resist the lure of clothes, and the tale of her desperate borrowings and of those of her even more extravagant and bankrupt friend takes us from one crisis to another. As in *La desheredada* and *Tormento*, the main part of the novel consists of a description of the *passio* or suffering of the heroine, which she brings on herself by her inability to resist her leading vice. The alternations of hope and despair are skilfully arranged. For example, just as the whole thing seems about to come out, Bringas' eyesight, strained by the labours of his hair picture, gives way and he goes blind. Rosalía seizes on this to pawn the silver candlesticks and to abstract part of his private hoard, but, when his sight returns suddenly, there is a further crisis. The highest comic moment in the book occurs when, in spite of her strict principles, she decides to give herself to Don Manuel Pez in return for a "loan," which will allow her to replace what she has taken from the family savings. The Pez family—the word means "Fish"—are the type of the higher bureaucrats who appear in a number of Galdós' books. Don Manuel, elegant, poised, superior, is of a rank only just below that of minister. He has been courting her in a discreet way for some time and she has been flattered by his attentions. Oh that she had for a husband a really distinguished man such as he, who could afford to dress her as she deserves to be dressed! So she gives herself to him—clumsily choosing the wrong moment—but, when she asks for a loan, Pez has to confess that he is as much in debt as everyone else and at the moment cannot afford a penny. In the end Rosalía saves herself in the most humiliating way by borrowing from the sister of the despised Amparo, who is a dress-maker turned courtesan.

The story has taken place during the sweltering summer of 1868. Looking out from the windows of the Palace, the country lies white and inert in the heat. Now in September the curtain falls. The army, the navy, the middle classes and the workmen rise with one accord, and Queen Isabella takes the train to France. Rosalía and her husband lose their jobs and vacate their rooms in the Palace. And so this phantasmagoric society, so brilliant when seen from outside but built on poverty and debt

and emptiness, melts and disappears. The cold breath of reality puts an end to the brittle dream. We may say that *La de Bringas* is the application to Spanish society of the leading idea of *Don Quixote* and *La Vida es Sueño*.

In 1886-7 appeared Galdós' greatest novel, *Fortunata y Jacinta*. This enormously long book can be called the epic of Madrid: as we read its seventeen hundred or more dense pages, we become so caught up in the life of this self-absorbed city that we forget that there is anything outside it. Yet *Fortunata y Jacinta* is, like *War and Peace,* a universal book, giving, in Menéndez Pelayo's words, "the illusion of life itself, so completely have the characters and ambience been worked out." Unlike most of Galdós' previous novels, it has no simple or definite theme. Such guiding ideas as it can show are quite vague—a contrast between two women, the upper-class wife and the mistress who comes from the people, and behind these perhaps between civilized society and Nature. The plot, which in its main outline is simple, is complicated by an immense ramification of subsidiary events and characters.

Let us look at this main subject or plot. A young man, Juanito Santa Cruz, who belongs to a wealthy middle-class family, marries a girl called Jacinta from the same class as himself and has also a working-class girl called Fortunata for his mistress. The principal part of the novel consists of the description of his varying relations with both of them and in the feelings that the two women who are both in love with Juanito, have for one another. But not more than half the book is taken up in this way. Behind these three persons are grouped their numerous friends and relatives—rich on the one side and poor on the other—as well as the family of Fortunata's husband Maxi, who belongs to the respectable lower middle class; and the history and adventures of all these people are worked into the general picture.

Let us consider the three major characters first. Jacinta is sweet, refined, warm-hearted, generous girl—"an angel," as her friends put it—who has been brought up by adoring parents to a sheltered life. Fortunata, on the other hand, is a typical woman of the people—a term that means so much more in Spanish than it does in English. Although she is generous and warm-hearted too, she is much more full-blooded than Jacinta: her passions are stronger and she thinks and feels from instinct. Thus she believes that she is more truly married to Juanito than Jacinta is, because she has had a son by him, whereas Jacinta's great tragedy is that she is childless. This sterility of the wife—let us say in passing—has a symbolic value. Galdós had always castigated the frivolity of the upper classes, and here—with many reservations, no doubt—he is putting forward an idea that was widely held in Spain at the time—that the vital force of the country lay in "the people" and that the upper classes were feeble and decadent. As Cánovas, the restorer of the monarchy, expressed it, "the surface of our country constantly decays, but never the depths."

But if Galdós ever really held this rather simple view, he does not allow it to influence his sympathies as a novelist. His two women—Jacinta especially—are drawn with marvellous skill and delicacy. No writer, except perhaps Tolstoy, has shown such a deep and intimate understanding of women's characters and feelings. As we read, we forget the printed page and feel the living presence of this wife and mistress, and the tremors of love, jealousy, doubt and reassurance that pass through them. Juanito, on the other hand, is a poor creature. Handsome, agreeable, selfish, not exactly unkind but always putting his own pleasure first, the spoiled child of rich parents who takes the love of his wife and mistress for granted, he sums up for Galdós the whole class of *jeunesse dorée* ["gilded youth"].

One of the most delightful chapters in the novel is that which gives an account of the young couple's honeymoon. First Jacinta's feelings as she sits in the cab beside her new husband are described with a delicacy of intuition that Henry James would have envied. Then, a little later, we see her tantalized by the suspicion that she has not been the first woman in her husband's life and, half jealous and half merely curious, setting herself to wheedle out of him the story of his encounter a short time before with Fortunata. Serenely happy though these weeks are, all the seeds of the young couple's future discords come out and show themselves. And, as we read, we cannot help being amazed by the knowledge which this confirmed bachelor had of the intimate life of married people. Their conversations when undressing, their baby language, their half-affectionate discords and jealousies and reconciliations are revealed by him with the most complete naturalness. These are matters which other novelists, dazed perhaps by their own marriages, have rarely been able to present in their proper focus. He is fond too of showing us children. Most of his novels contain some, and these children have their own thoughts and characters and take their place in family life just like anyone else. Altogether I would say that there is no writer who gives us such vivid and detailed pictures—sometimes comic but in this novel straightforward—of the interior of middle class ménages. He is a master of the ordinary, the average, the commonplace, of life as it is lived by the majority of people, but—this is the peculiar triumph—under his touch it ceases to be commonplace and becomes alive and tremulous with human feelings and desires. To Galdós no human being, no moment of existence is unimportant.

However, the world contains exceptional people too, and Galdós, sometimes successfully, at other times less so, sets out to give them to us. *Fortunata y Jacinta* contains one character, Doña Guillermina Pacheco, who is very unusual indeed. She is a saint—a woman of the upper classes who devotes her life to works of charity. Galdós drew her from an actual person, well known in Madrid at the time, a sort of Catholic Florence Nightingale, and the portrait he gives of her, which has a superficial resemblance to Santa Teresa, is alive and convincing. I must single out too among the many vivid characters in this book that brilliant comic figure, Doña Lupe, *"la de los pavos."* She is Maxi's aunt, with whom he boards, and into her buxom, determined, matronly person are packed all the humours of Spanish lower middle-class women.

But there was something in Galdós that drew him away from the sphere that he knew best towards extreme types and situations. Already in *La desheredada* he had begun to show the fascination that slum life had for him. This melodramatic craving for scenes of poverty and degradation, inspired no doubt by Dickens, began to increase from now onwards till, at the end of his career of contemporary novelist, under the further impulse of a growing social conscience, he was to devote whole books to it.

At the same time he began to show a great interest in abnormal psychic states and in madness. The young heroine in *Doña Perfecta* was a hysteric: the father of Isidora in *La desheredada* was mad and its first chapter opens in a lunatic asylum: she herself had abnormal symptoms and her brother became an idiot. Many of the characters in his later novels are neurotics and we are often told their dreams. Dreams, indeed, occupy a large part in the technique of Galdós' character drawing.

Now, in *Fortunata y Jacinta,* we get a full-length history of a schizophrenic. Maxi Rubén is a man who, under a crushing sense of his own insignificance, has shut himself off from the world and taken refuge in day-dreams. He falls idealistically in love with Fortunata and persuades her to enter a convent for the redemption of Magdalenes. To get out of it she marries him. But marriage meant nothing to her and when Maxi realizes this he shuts himself up in his room to concentrate on the interior life. Here—he is to all intents and purposes mad—he invents a religious philosophy in which death is proclaimed as the only liberty and suicide the only duty. A new Messiah will come to announce this. But—here we have a remarkable anticipation of Freud—as soon as he realizes that this philosophy and the hallucinations that have accompanied it are due simply to his subconscious jealousy of his wife's lover—"jealousy fermented and putrefying," as he puts it—he becomes well again. Other border-line cases in the same book are José Ido, who has appeared in previous novels, and that strange Dostoevskian being, Mauricia la Dura. (pp. 392-400)

Miau, which came out in 1888, is on the classic subject of the *cesante. Cesantes* are Government officials who have lost their jobs because a new party has come into office. Owing to the clan-like way in which social and political life in Spain is organized, every change of Government is followed by a sort of musical chairs among the personnel of the bureaucracy. *Miau* is consequently a story of middle-class distress and ruin, brought about by no fault of the persons concerned. In this way it marks a change in the theme of Galdós' novels from the personal fault or vice to the social one. As a novel, it is one of the most condensed and painful that he wrote. From the way in which everything seems to combine to crush the unfortunate man who has lost his job, it reminds one of Balzac's *Le Cousin Pons*. The characters are all well drawn, one of the more original being an epileptic child who in his fits sees and talks with God. These conversations, reported in Galdós' dry manner, are extremely amusing, for the God whom Luisito talks with is the God of a small boy's imagination, something between a schoolmaster and a grandfather, and they are also interesting because they take us into the boy's mind and reveal to us what later physchologists have termed the super-ego. Where can Galdós have obtained his amazing knowledge of the workings of the abnormal mentality? We are also given a very entertaining picture of the interior of a Spanish Government office (compare it with the descriptions of the Royal Palace in *La de Bringas*) and of the system of nepotism by which promotions and jobs were obtained. But the book is a little too long. Galdós, like his contemporary Dostoevsky, could not always control his characters' loquacity.

La incógnita and its continuation, *Realidad,* are psychological explorations into a crime story. They reflect Galdós' interest in a sensational murder case that had just taken place, and their theme is that the psychological motives in crimes are always different from what they appear to be. Their chief defect lies in their form; the first is told in letters and the second in dialogue. Galdós' increasing interest in the drama was leading him to write novels in dialogue form, which he regarded as "purer" than narrative. But it did not suit him.

Angel Guerra, the second longest of Galdós' works, came out in 1890-1. It is a book on the theme of religious conversion, treated from a psychological angle and with sympathy. The plot is briefly as follows. Angel Guerra is a rich young widower who quarrels with his mother, plunges into a life of dissipation and takes part in a Republican rising. On the death of his mother he falls violently in love with Leré, who is governess to his child, and asks her to marry him. But Leré refuses, because she wishes to give herself to religion. She enters a convent at Toledo and Angel follows her there. The scene now shifts from Madrid to the religious capital of Spain. As a result of his constant conversations with Leré, Angel is converted from the agnostic philosophy he had previously professed to Catholicism. With the same impetuosity and whole-heartedness with which he had previously taken to revolutionary activities, he throws himself into his new faith and decides to devote his entire wealth to founding a Brotherhood of Mercy, of which Leré shall be the head of the female branch and he of the men's. But before this plan can be put into effect he is murdered by relatives of his former mistress.

As an account of a religious conversion this book is admirable. The gradual sublimation of Angel's love for Leré and the sudden, violent plunge into the new faith are convincingly drawn. Galdós would have nothing to learn from William James's *Varieties of Religious Experience,* which came out ten years later. Angel's abnormal character is presented in great detail and we are given not only his dreams, but also certain vivid experiences of his youth which had made a deep impression on him. Leré too, another pathological case, is excellent: she was not beautiful and her eyes were affected by a continual oscillation "which gave her the look of one of those mechanical dolls whose eyes move from right to left on a swivel"; yet we believe in her fascination. But the book, powerful and arresting though it is, fails, I think, to please. Unlike most of Galdós' novels, it contains little irony or humour. And among the subsidiary characters there are far too many criminal and neurotic types, some of them very repulsive. The physiognomies of these abnormals are presented to us with a sharpness and detail that is almost clinical. How different from the manner of Dostoevsky, who, though he fills his books with border-line cases, uses them to real imaginative effect. The neurotic storms that whirl and tear through his pages raise the action to a higher level of significance. Galdós, on the other hand, is confined to the limits of the realistic novel, and the comparison that occurs to our mind on reading *Angel Guerra* is rather to some of the veristic painting and wood sculpture done by Spanish artists in the seventeenth century. We feel a stress laid on morbid states of mind and on suffering that, artistically speaking, defeats its own purpose because it fails to liberate us. (pp. 400-02)

If the reader who does not know Spanish wishes to get a rough idea of what a novel by Galdós is like, let him take one of the better works of Balzac, add the warmth and colour and melodramatic sense of Dickens and the grave ironic tone of Cervantes, and he will have something that approximates to the picture. Galdós had in fact been deeply influenced by these three writers. Further, as I think I have already made clear, he is one of the great psychological novelists, endlessly curious about the varieties of human conduct and character. He keeps, however, within the range of what his very objective eye had seen: most of his characters are mediocrities, some are almost pitiful in their lack of personality and none are above life-size. We look in vain in his portrait gallery for outstanding figures, such as Prince Myshkin or Pierre Bezukhov or M. de Charlus. One reason for this is that he never treats his characters in isolation, but always as members of a class or group or family. He is a social historian who aimed at giving the pattern of a society (and what is more, of a society which he regarded as corrupt and frivolous) rather than an individualist seeking to

show to what magnificence of branch and leaf and root the human tree could grow.

He is especially good in his pictures of family circles. More than any other writer, he succeeds in conveying that peculiar, dense atmosphere that middle-class families, each in their own way, give off. He is able to do this because of his extraordinary eye for the significant detail of everyday life. In reading his books we are never far away from the sewing, the ironing, the children, the housekeeping and general economy of the ménage, and it is through these things that the feelings and idiosyncrasies of the various characters are made known to us. Then every member of one of his family groups is shown in relation to the other members; they are all the time acting on one another and being acted upon. No one is isolated. And since we have also had time to take a good look at the furniture of the house and to cast our eye over the dossiers of the relatives and friends, we end by having a sense of the corporate existence of the family such as no other novelist gives us. (p. 404)

Gerald Brenan, "Nineteenth-Century Prose," in his The Literature of the Spanish People from Roman Times to the Present Day, *second edition, 1953. Reprint by Cambridge University Press, 1976, pp. 377-416.*

SHERMAN EOFF   (essay date 1954)

[*In the following excerpt, Eoff traces the development of Galdós's narrative technique. Eoff later modified his theories concerning the primary characteristics of Galdós's fiction (see excerpt dated 1966).*]

Galdós in middle age. From Pérez Galdós: Spanish Liberal Crusader, *by H. Chonon Berkowitz. The University of Wisconsin Press, 1948. Courtesy of the publisher.*

Galdós showed considerable indecisiveness with regard to questions of form during his apprenticeship in the novel, embracing the years 1867 to 1873. . . . Briefly stated, the development begins with a decision to exploit the possibilities of a psychological study of character in relation to its social background, crystallizes momentarily in a plot of dramatic situation, changes to chronological narration of a protagonist's experiences, and then resumes partially an earlier practice by way of a mixture of the dramatic and the chronological plans. Although there are shifts of emphasis in the course of the developing method, at no time is character portrayal relegated to a secondary position with respect to happenings. For this reason, it is necessary to keep in mind the psychological nature of the novels. . . . (p. 5)

When Galdós began to write novels, he was preoccupied with the question of choosing between a historical and a social objective. *La fontana de oro* is essentially a historical novel, and the characters, largely surface delineations, are on somewhat the same level as local landmarks which fit into the picture of a given political epoch. The one exception is doña Paulitas. Her portrayal is limited to one brief moment of her life but includes basic causes of her behavior and a close view of her emotional and physical manifestations when she experiences a tense conflict between love for Lázaro, the protagonist, and the necessity of living up to the nunlike reputation which she has acquired in a sanctified atmosphere of seclusion. Doña Paulitas is merely incidental in *La fontana de oro*, but she is representative of what comes to be the major pattern of Galdós' characterization: the recording of a person's psychological reactions in close relation to the social background in which the person's behavior has been conditioned.

With *El audaz*, Galdós makes a definite advance toward utilizing social-psychological material for the basis of his narratives. Although he is obviously groping in this novel as he tries to combine historical and social objectives, the psychology of both the central characters presents complicating elements for the plot. The characterization of the young revolutionist Muriel is overshadowed by heavy attention to political background, in which personal motivations are insufficiently integrated with the sequence of events. But it is clear that the author wanted to show how youthful hardships and injustice to Muriel's father produced in the son an inflexibility which, directed toward personal ascendancy and social vengeance, leads to his downfall. The personality of Susana, daughter of an aristocrat and in love with the plebeian Muriel, is much more thoroughly portrayed. Though bearing the imprint of class prejudice, Susana's arrogance is tempered by a spirit of rebellion against convention, which causes her to disregard many of the traditional rules of conduct. The author carefully follows in his heroine the conflict between ideas imposed by a rigid social order and those based upon an independent sense of dignity and worth. Susana's portrayal receives relatively little space, especially in the latter part of the novel, but it is consistently traced, even to the catastrophic night of Muriel's failure and madness, when the heroine succumbs under the weight of conventional law and chooses suicide in preference to facing her family and her social group after having deserted them to follow her lover.

El audaz would have been Galdós' first psychological novel had its narrative been concentrated upon the love story of the main characters. As it is, it reveals a divided purpose and a resultant structural weakness. After the novelist decides to pursue the historical and social objectives separately, however, his contemporary novels gain artistically, becoming, primarily, studies in personality, in which the plot itself is an unfolding closely related to the characters' psychology.

It is easy to trace the course which Galdós followed in developing the narrative method most suited to his novelistic aims. There is a kind of plot that places a person in a situation which of itself demands decisive action and forces him to reveal his personality as he tries to extricate himself from a set of circumstances chosen by the author. In such a case the importance of the characterization, if it is psychological portrayal, will lie in the protagonist's reactions to the one immediate and dominating problem with which he is faced. This narrative form is essentially a plot of dramatic situation. It lends itself especially to the portrayal of character as seen in one climactic stage of its formation. Or again, a person may be visualized as moving along, perhaps casually most of the time, in an ordinary course of events in which arise the sundry situations that are probable in an extensive view of an individual's life. In this case the individual is led on by the necessity of living up to various circumstances of the moment, which nevertheless grow cumulatively in force and organization and assume a pattern of successive climactic episodes. This form, which may appropriately be called a biographical plot, is best suited to the portrayal of developing personality over a long period of time. The two kinds of plot here described typify, separately or in combination, all of Galdós' social novels. The first is adopted decisively in *Doña Perfecta*, and the second comes gradually to be the novelist's favorite method.

Of all of Galdós' novels, *Doña Perfecta* is structurally the most compact. It is an intense drama held within narrow limits of time, place, and personal motivations. The dramatic problem, which centers upon a mother's opposition to her daughter's marriage to a man of religious beliefs incompatible with her own, emerges quickly and develops rapidly as the battle of will against will leads to hatred and culminates in murder. With a prior conditioning of ecclesiastic rigidity and provincial narrow-mindedness, doña Perfecta immediately finds an opponent in her nephew Pepe, a freethinker with a marked tendency to brutal frankness. Rosario, the daughter in love with Pepe, enforces the latter's will to fight, even though she is completely dominated by her mother; while the priest don Inocencio, in a parallel though more important role, hovers in the background, inciting doña Perfecta to determined action and infuriating Pepe with calculated sarcasm.

The author's technique is one of progressive dramatic preparation along a single line of action. Caballuco's hostility to Pepe at the outset, don Inocencio's presence beside Rosario as Pepe arrives at his aunt's home, mention early in the story of the lawsuits with reference to Pepe's land, all point to impending trouble. As the intensification toward climax and catastrophe grows, all is excluded that does not bear on the central axis of the plot. Even the descriptive material pertaining to the countryside, the minor character types, and incidental scenes contribute to the background theme of provincial obscurantism, and harmonize with the intellectual inflexibility of doña Perfecta.

Though merged with the plot, the novel's ideological purpose accounts for its artistic weakness. Because of his own hostility to what doña Perfecta stands for, the author abruptly and persistently brings about unprovoked attacks upon Pepe from the moment that the latter sets foot in his aunt's house; and he deliberately, almost mechanically, accentuates his hero's difficulties, partly by overemphasis on his liberalism and partly by manipulation of events. The lawsuits, for example, are obviously invented for the sole purpose of instigating trouble for Pepe. If Galdós had allowed the conflict to develop gradually out of a slowly emerging incompatibility, his handling of plot and character would have seemed more natural. As it is, the novel reveals—to its detriment—the author's ideological passion in both its technique and its style.

The characterization of doña Perfecta, nevertheless, more than counterbalances the novel's technical flaws. The portrait of her personality overshadows all else in the story and bears strong testimony to the assertion that Galdós' fundamental strength as a novelist is psychological. The emotional disturbance begins in the protagonist as conflict between two desirable but mutually exclusive goals: one, a peaceful family relationship in which her established reputation for piety will remain undisturbed; and the other, the endorsement of and submission to her worship of ecclesiastic formulas, the indispensable basis of her integrity. The psychological picture is that of a struggle for emotional security on the part of one whose values force her into a violent defensive behavior, which passes through a state of ferment and frustration, and ends in a firm co-ordination of auxiliary motives toward the enforcement of her will. The plot follows the course of a developing passion of hate in an individual who personalizes a small segment of human nature trimmed down to one dominant compulsion. With justification the novel is said to have the classical stamp upon it.

Galdós never again in his novels achieved the compactness and tenseness of *Doña Perfecta*. His new orientation was in an important sense a turn to the realistic method, which at first, however, bore definite marks of romanticism. The transition begins with *Gloria*.

In Part I of *Gloria* a few events are chosen to provide a dramatic conflict between love and religious training. A young man (Daniel) is shipwrecked and brought to the home of a young woman (Gloria). The two fall in love but decide to part because of a difference in religious beliefs. At the time, the young man does not reveal what his religion is. Later he returns for the purpose of aiding a friend in trouble, finds an opportunity to urge his love upon the young woman, spends the night with her, and then discloses that he is a Jew, thus posing a problem of potentially tragic consequences. Depending heavily upon coincidence, especially in connection with the flood that washes away a bridge and keeps Gloria's father away from home, the author manipulates his plot so as to insure drama by making his heroine the victim of accidental happenings. Even so, he does not neglect characterization. Gloria is placed in a sufficiently large and varied number of circumstances to make her appear to be representative of a broad segment of human nature. Still more important, her portrayal has within itself the rudiments of a story, in that it shows how indoctrination with dogmatic religious beliefs emerges in moments of stress to distort natural inclinations.

Part II, written several months after the completion of Part I, is essentially an account of the correction of a mistake, and stresses more the effect of circumstances upon character than it does the drama of a given situation. The only events of real dramatic possibility are the sudden and ruthless intervention of Daniel's mother when her son is on the verge of carrying out his pretense of espousing Catholicism, and the final scene, in which Gloria pays one last visit to her child and dies in the presence of her lover.

Daniel, who at first was scarcely more than the symbol of a forbidden religious faith and an occasion for the conflict in Gloria between love and environment, comes to life in Part II, revealing in some detail his own conflict between love and moral responsibility on the one hand, and racial fervor on the other. Gloria, who was very alert in Part I, becomes meanwhile rather listless, but she remains the central personage in the plot. Galdós has merely altered his method, for the story is now an account of emotional and physical adjustment to the immovable weight of family and religious tradition. Weakened physically and dulled mentally, Gloria becomes more and more passive, while gradually absorbing her aunt's doctrine of martyrdom. The transition, from a spirited demeanor to a kind of stupefied resignation mixed with fanatical mystic zeal, is a psychological story in itself, which takes precedence over the sequence of events. Events serve primarily to bring latent developments to the surface or to effect a change of direction in personality growth. This is the method which Galdós follows in most of his novels subsequent to *Gloria,* though for a few more years he is rather reluctant to part with the dramatic plot which is inherent in a potentially explosive situation. (pp. 5-10)

The decisive orientation to a slow, sometimes tedious, but thorough approach appears in *La desheredada.* In a strict sense, this is Galdós' first realistic novel. Briefly, the narrative of *La desheredada* records events in the life of a woman (Isidora Rufete) who tries in vain to establish her claims to nobility, clinging meanwhile to her illusion of noble birth as her major standard of personal worth, living first with a man of aristocratic name and then with one who is financially able to satisfy her thirst for luxury, and eventually descending to the life of a prostitute when her illusion is irreparably shattered. The novel is plainly didactic in purpose, and it would be little more than a mediocre moralistic tale were it not also the psychological account of a degeneration in character. The descriptive, background material and the picture of social relationships are no substitute for narrative interest in a story that clearly is focused on one person. Nor are the events in this person's life so arranged as to produce dramatic interest in themselves. Only two episodes (Isidora's visit to the Marquesa, whose kinship she claimed, and her eventual imprisonment for a supposed falsification in connection with her claims on the Marquesa's family) are climactically presented. Considered as surface events, they appear in the whole as two widely separated and loosely connected occurrences. The full effect of continuity and progression is experienced only by recognizing the psychological movement, which shows how Isidora subordinates her wholesome inclinations of friendliness, sympathy, and honesty as she tries to prove her nobility; how she is increasingly tyrannized by the love of wealth and luxury; and how her integrity dissolves completely after the final disillusionment following her imprisonment. With the exception of the two decisive episodes mentioned above, the external happenings are scarcely more than occasions for revealing internal development; and even these two episodes are utilized to explain the change in character which follows them.

In one respect *La desheredada* is still a transitional novel. Just as the portrayal of doña Perfecta was an elaboration of one outstanding motive, so the portrayal of Isidora is concentrated on a single motivating force (the worship of a false value). For this reason, the novel has about it that abstractness which is characteristic of stories designed to prove theses. It thus retains some of the argumentative quality so noticeable in the narratives of 1876-1878. *El amigo Manso* may also be regarded as transitional, both in its thematic abstractness and its combination of dramatic situation and biography.

The chief modification in narrative method to be noted in the novels which follow *El amigo Manso* is the result of a relaxation in thematic demonstration. Social-moral themes are always present in Galdós, but with one or two exceptions, they "go underground" for the next fifteen years. The characters, meanwhile, become more representative of a non-specialized view of human nature, in that their portrayal exhibits not so much the development of a dominant compulsion or a given psychological state as multiple reactions to a variety of circumstances. It may be said, simply, that they are individual Spaniards portrayed with "sympathetic objectivity," and not symbols of Spanish social traits which, in the author's view, are undesirable. Moreover, Galdós broadens the framework of his plots by giving secondary characters important roles of their own. As a result, his novels sometimes appear to emphasize the depiction of society in its collective aspects. With all this broadening and, in some cases, loosening of structure, however, Galdós' major interest continues to be the study of individual personality.

In so far as method is concerned, *El doctor Centeno* is perhaps the most "plotless" of Galdós' stories; and yet it is fairly typical of the novelist's most fruitful period. The plot is a simple chronology of events in the life of a boy (Felipe Centeno) who sets out to make his way in the world. The main narrative steps are: Felipe's arrival in Madrid with high ambitions for a medical career; his first misfortunes, including service with the priest don Pedro Polo; his service and friendship with the visionary and poverty-stricken Alejandro Miquis, a relationship that constitutes the heart of the novel; termination of this association at the death of Miquis. There are many graphic scenes, numerous well-defined incidental characters, and certain dramatic episodes in the life of the unhappy Miquis. The story bears definite marks of kinship with *Lazarillo de Tormes* and *Don Quijote,* with an echo here and there from some of the tales of Charles Dickens. It thus has a certain charm apart from any thought of a centralized psychological study. To appreciate its meaning fully, however, it is necessary to realize that the author is actually depicting a maturing development in an individual who seeks to realize his own worth. With an initial drive for accomplishment and a pronounced need to belong in a satisfactory social relationship, Felipe consolidates for himself the values of work, perseverance, honesty, and loyalty. His sensible adjustment to a level of accomplishment befitting his own talents, as contrasted with the dream-world phantasy of Miquis, is a salient feature of the story. Even more important is the presentation of the friendship between the two persons, through which Felipe strengthens his sense of responsibility and, above all, experiences the edifying effects of sympathy and respect. Were it not for this underlying character development, *El doctor Centeno* might be regarded simply as another picaresque novel, recording as it does a series of adventures and misfortunes in the service of masters. Actually, the picaresque resemblance is purely superficial; for Felipe's rise above the average level of his environment is a development altogether contrary to the *pícaro's* facile adaptation to social evils. What takes place within the individual is the most important part of the story.

The structural pattern of *El doctor Centeno* is essentially the same as that of Galdós' maturest and most substantial works, including *Fortunata y Jacinta,* the Torquemada series, *Angel Guerra,* and *Misericordia.* The novelist broadens his range of vision and multiplies his secondary characters so as to embrace a large segment of urban life. In varying degree he supplies dramatic episodes having to do with frictional personal relationships; but his interest continues to be focused on the progress of one or two central characters whose "problems" arise from the cumulative vicissitudes of their day-by-day living.

When, out of deference to public taste, Galdós shortened his narratives and turned to the *novela dialogada,* he modified his method in two respects. He sharply curtailed the massive background material relating to setting and incidental characters, and he returned, partly, to the plot of dramatic situation. His intention was to combine the novel and drama in a more intensive psychological portrayal than was possible with the casual movement of his previous method. The result was a hybrid form that lacked the precision and tenseness of drama and added nothing to—if it did not actually dilute—the psychological study. The artistic weakness of these novels is explained primarily by the author's resumption of thematic abstractness. It can also be attributed to his inability to make full use of the slow biographical tempo on which he had depended so heavily in his characterizations. As he turns—reluctantly—away from his former practice, he now tends to follow his main characters separately, trying to visualize each of their personalities as a whole instead of exploiting the potential drama of the situation in which they are involved.

The indeterminateness of the hybrid form, which, incidentally, characterizes a number of Galdós' plays as well as his novels, can be seen in *Realidad,* the first of his *novelas dialogadas.* *Realidad* is above all a philosophical novel, whose meaning . . . is couched in the psychology of personal relationships. Its structure is of interest in the present connection because it shows Galdós' preoccupation with individual personality, to the disregard of what would usually be considered plot interest. The opportunity for dramatic action lies in the love triangle involving husband (Orozco), wife (Augusta), and wife's lover (Viera), who is also a friend of the husband. The author, instead of interesting himself in the solution of the dramatic problem, uses the love affair as a means of studying the characters individually in the light of their conceptions of truth and morality. Orozco, though participating in the activity befitting his social position, lives intellectually in a world apart from society, engrossed in the contemplation of ultimate reality and bent upon elevating his wife to his own level of spirituality, even after he discovers her infidelity.

Augusta, who respects but does not love Orozco, adheres to a philosophy by which she justifies her earthy, sensuous enjoyment of life, unable to sympathize with the cold otherworldliness of her husband. Viera, who lives an anchorless existence, torn between his pride in an aristocratic name, his Bohemian habits, and the guilt deriving from his betrayal of a friend, eventually terminates his conflict by committing suicide. The chief motivating force in Augusta's life is at first her rebellious independence of conventional standards, which nevertheless gives way to the common adjustment of preserving appearances after the tragic outcome of her illicit love affair. In her relation to her husband, she represents the triumph of earthiness over the supra-earthly attitude of one who personifies abstract metaphysics. Conversely, Orozco illustrates the failure of a self-appointed metaphysician in his efforts to put his theory into practice. Viera's story is primarily one of social maladjustment. Orozco's discovery of the love affair between his wife and Viera is a climactic episode that comes late in the story and brings to a conclusion three interdependent but essentially separate personality plots, in each of which the discovery of the love affair is a final test. The narrative movement in the novel thus follows the private interests of the several personages and converges upon but does not grow out of the conflict inherent in the situation. This structure, of course, is in keeping with the author's primary aim, which is to study questions of reality and morality from a variety of standpoints.

The structure of *La loca de la casa,* Galdós' second *novela dialogada,* is simpler and more clearly defined than that of *Realidad.* The narrative is a slow chronological development growing out of a domestic situation in which a daughter comes to the rescue of her aristocratic and bankrupt father, marries a rich but crude plebeian, and discovers the morally beneficial results of what promised to be an unbearable relationship. The few dramatic scenes are but steps in the developing psychology of the two main characters. In so far as method is concerned, *La loca de la casa* is plainly the incorporation of a situational problem in a biographical plot, of which adjustment to environment is an important component. Much the same can be said for *El abuelo,* except that its narrative is more compactly centered around a single emotional conflict. The last three of Galdós' contemporary novels (*Casandra; El caballero encantado; La razón de la sinrazón*), all of them in dialogue, are abstract and loosely constructed hybrids, which show definite marks of a decline in creative energy. But they, too, reveal a continued interest in individual psychology. Continuing his early aversion to the "novel of action," Galdós followed throughout his career a method in which the study of personality takes precedence over events. (pp. 12-16)

> Sherman Eoff, in his The Novels of Pérez Galdós: The Concept of Life as Dynamic Process, *Washington University Studies, 1954, 178 p.*

SHERMAN EOFF   (essay date 1966)

[*In the following excerpt, Eoff offers some qualifications to the view of Galdós's narrative development presented in his study* The Novels of Pérez Galdós: The Concept of Life as Dynamic Process, *noting that his initial interpretation failed to adequately acknowledge the social and historical emphasis in Galdós's novels. For Eoff's original comments, see the excerpt dated 1954.*]

The heading of the present essay might have carried as subtitle: "Thoughts on a socio-psychological approach to Galdós, eleven years afterwards." For the discussion to follow arises from the writer's questioning himself about the validity and possible significance of what he said in *The Novels of Pérez Galdós* published in 1954. In that book a demonstration was given of a specific method of analysis that visualizes the Galdosian social novel as being essentially the story of an individual character deeply planted in his social environment. It was a concentrated endeavor held within a single perspective and had perhaps the natural weakness of the usual thematic study in that it subjected each novel to a preconceived plan of appraisal. Needless to say, not all of Galdós' social novels follow the same narrative plan or exhibit precisely the same kind of techniques in character portrayal. Consequently, one may justifiably hold that a kind of analysis that adheres to a single avenue of approach can at best provide only a restricted view of any given novel.

A further understandable criticism could arise from the emphasis on personality change as having primary interpretive importance. In a good number of cases the author insisted that the change in a protagonist's personality constituted the essence of the "story"; a defensible viewpoint, it seems to me, with respect to some of the most important novels, though possibly to be regarded more as an aspect than as an indispensable

characteristic of the works as a whole. The psychological content of the novels, nevertheless, must surely be regarded always as paramount in Galdosian criticism; and it is equally plain that the kind of character portrayal confronting the critic is not typically an intensive analytical dissection of complex psychological activity. It is more often the rather casual recording of human experience that is based on the observation of an individual's normal interests and preoccupations.

The advantages of concentrating on this so-called socio-psychological approach probably are not to be found in the psychological analysis itself, which, after all, was a fairly simple application of common information; and certainly there was no intention of harnessing literary interpretation in scientific trappings. The important point is that the pursuit of a special kind of objective provided a useful vantage ground for viewing the novelist in a comprehensive way. It formed in effect a base on which a pyramid was constructed that reached into various strata of social, moral, and philosophical thought. One of the interesting results—for the author at least—was the great significance of Galdós' nineteenth-century background as a factor in the criticism of his works. This was largely a realization that grew out of the study and increased as it progressed. From the outset, however, the writer was thinking primarily of the intrinsic nature of the Galdosian novel as seen from within. Some note was taken, it is true, of various threads of thought that may have influenced Galdós. The insistence on developing character or personality change, for example, was partly out of deference to the heavy presence of evolutionism in the nineteenth century and the general emphasis on the concepts of adaptation, change, and growth. Yet no special effort was made to interpret the novelist in terms of his historical epoch.

Now, in retrospect, I am inclined to recommend what in a sense is a reversal of the former method, that is, the choice of nineteenth-century thought as a broad base on which to observe the intrinsic nature of a Galdosian novel. We like to think that a work of art in its own integrity commands our respect without reference to its particular location in time. At the same time we have to admit that an author's bonds of unity with his historical epoch may hold the qualities that make his art independent of history; and it is thus important to observe in Galdós that which is explained by his historical circumstances and is nevertheless free of them. His conception of human personality, for example, which is essentially socio-psychological and as such harmonizes with the trend in the social sciences during the last quarter of the nineteenth century, is also rich in the kind of moral and metaphysical thought that sees personality liberated from the very social ground in which it is nourished. The metaphysical aspects of the character portrayal, of course, are themselves colored by the philosophical ideas of the age. In short, we are forced to recognize that it is impossible to separate an author from his epoch. Probably we are inclined too often to take this fact for granted without exploiting its full significance.

In Galdós' case, especially, the author's identity with his age has a primary significance. The extension of thought involved reaches out in all directions to include physiology, psychology, sociology, the physical sciences, technology, the consequences of the Industrial Revolution, the prominence of the bourgeoisie, the rise of the proletariat; and over all this a philosophical consciousness attuned to a historical (evolutionary) conception of the universe. The student of Galdós is obliged to become a student of the nineteenth century.

A thorough investigation of this large area would undoubtedly reveal many specific aspects that are of interest in themselves. But the point I wish to emphasize is the desirability of holding the particular within a perspective of the general. A full appreciation of Galdós requires that we regard him in a comprehensive way, and the great amount of information uncovered by scholars must be centralized around certain major poles of orientation. For only by concentration on major ideas can an artist's deepest significance be understood. To look upon Galdós as being a product of the nineteenth century is one of the most profitable comprehensive ways of grasping his importance. In an effort to bring the subject into focus, let us consider for a moment two or three broad perspectives in which Galdós normally is observed.

Probably the most common tendency among those who study and discuss the novelist has been to identify him with Spain and things Spanish. Spanish writers of the twentieth century, especially, because of their intense preoccupation with their country's problems, have weighed their works heavily with national color; and Spanish critics themselves have found it difficult to appraise one of their own save in terms exclusively Spanish. Viewers from the outside, in their desire to understand, have necessarily been drawn into this vortex of self-examination. So it is that they have observed Galdós against the background of his personal circumstances and the locally controversial ideas of his own day; they have witnessed the general indifference to the novelist on the part of the generation of 1898; and since the civil war they have seen his name brought to the front once more, not with wide acclaim but at least with the recognition by some that he possesses a fundamental quality that could serve as basis for the restoration of national morale. In all this range of observation, the spectator from the outside is impressed above all with the picture of one Spaniard talking to another, sometimes apparently with little thought of a world beyond the national borders.

It is undeniably important to think of Galdós as a Spaniard located in a Spanish setting. He has left an unforgettable record of Spanish society and has in effect succeeded in creating a collective national character. He has demonstrated, sometimes overtly, sometimes subtly, ways of modernizing the thinking habits of his countrymen; and he has made us feel the presence, amidst numerous unfavorable features, of a strong national moral fibre. It is therefore necessary that scholars and critics examine this broad aspect of Galdós' novels. Such investigation is a natural continuation of attention to the novel of ideas, which, along with the subject of realism, occupied in large part the interest of critics among Galdós' contemporaries of the 1870's and 1880's.

As time removes us farther and farther from Galdós' epoch, questioning naturally increases concerning his place in literary history; and in recent years more and more thought seems to have been given to subject matter that tends to place the novelist in the relatively neutral perspective of "universality." What there is of wide and lasting value in an author's works, of course, is not as easy to define as his purely local features, but it is a question that is constantly with us. The subject no doubt can best be approached indirectly by choosing a concrete basis of judgment, such as an examination of the novelist's role as artist. Scholarship has in fact contributed in this way by investigating artistic and technical aspects of the Galdosian novel, having to do with methods, devices, style, narrative structure, character portrayal, and the like, all of which throw light on the breadth and texture of Galdós understanding of human nature. Through concentration on the novelist's art, visualized as art, insight is gained into the qualities that have universal appeal.

There is another way to find a solid footing on which to stand while appraising Galdós' place in history. As we shift our attention from its focus on a national writer toward emphasis on an artist of universal appeal, we can bring it to bear on a kind of middle ground that may properly be called European—of nineteenth-century Europe—, which not only is important to an understanding of Galdós the Spaniard but also helps to explain much of his lasting worth in the world of art at large. That he was very much a citizen of Europe as well as of Spain no one will deny. Bibliographical and biographical research continues to give evidence of his breadth of outlook. His affinity with certain European writers is known, and comparisons have been made, but this general nineteenth-century-European area remains perhaps the field of study that holds the greatest promise of results. Specifically, we may ask, is there not value in thinking still further of Galdós in comparison with Balzac in their roles of social historians; in placing him alongside Zola, with attention to the conception of literature as a social instrument, in addition to the question of naturalism; or in thinking of Tolstoy and his preoccupation with the common man, to say nothing of his interpretation of Christianity? In studies of this kind, let us insist, it is necessary to keep in mind that we are dealing with large areas, in which common bonds of interest lead different writers to express in their own way some of the ideals of an age. When we place Galdós against a common background with other great writers of his day, we can see clearly that his literary personality—perhaps at its best—bears the heavy mark of his century, that in fact it proclaims a substantial part of "the nineteenth-century message." In any case, concentration on the novelist in this single broad perspective can only deepen our understanding and appreciation of him.

I do not propose to draw the outline of a full picture, but I wish to suggest some of the advantages of thinking about generalities that may be too casually taken for granted. In the first place, the professional attitude with which Galdós regarded his mission as novelist was apparently a feeling of dedication to the new and what has proved to be—momentous literary movement known as realism. The youthful enthusiasm with which he embraced the general principles of realism may have decreased in his later years, but not the seriousness of purpose which led him through various phases of preparation and composition and which now seem to have entailed much more deliberateness than was once supposed. Research is constantly revealing evidence of the persistence with which Galdós worked, and one can be sure that he was a most serious and dedicated professional.

Now, it may be that some of the marks of professional thoroughness having to do with methods and techniques appear to a twentieth-century audience to be rather simple or at least unnecessarily obvious. But there is a great deal of subtlety in Galdós, and we can understand why scholars like to investigate multiple aspects of a novelistic production that continuously rewards them with new discoveries. The reward is greatest when we look for subtle connections in the realm of ideas. For the desire to keep up with modern thought, which the youthful Galdós showed, stayed with him through the most fruitful part of his career, and the roots of the ideational content of his novels reach deep into his intellectual environment. To what extent the novelist consciously incorporated contemporary ideas in his writing it may be difficult to say. But there can be little doubt that bonds of relationship and influence exist, and probably in every major ramification of nineteenth-century thought.

Perhaps the most fundamental way of approaching the study of Galdós in relation to nineteenth-century thought is through an examination of his reaction to the scientific rationalism of his age. We should keep in mind that the position which he maintained between a healthy respect for the physical and the social sciences and a loyalty to the human values that are independent of the sciences, was not a compromise between two contrary viewpoints but an effort to coordinate two possibly compatible ideals. The unifying, philosophical force in this seemingly dualistic world was the general idea of evolution. The novelist's own interpretation of various aspects of evolutionary theories unquestionably underlies not only his advocacy of material and social progress but becomes a potent influence in his study of human character and his vision of human destiny. Within this evolutionary perspective, for example, the novelist's liking for paradox can advantageously be regarded from the viewpoint of Hegelian theory. Without affirming that Galdós actually studied the big names of European philosophical thought in his day, we can be fairly certain that he was conscious of them and in some way absorbed their ideas. So it is that Kant, Hegel, and even Schopenhauer become important points of reference. It is easy, it seems to me, to think of Galdós as being an inveterate optimist, but there are moments in his career, possibly at the time of *Fortunata y Jacinta,* when a Schopenhauerian influence seems to be exerting its hypnotic spell. In the same novel, which is an exceptionally rich storehouse of possibilities for interpretation, one might even be inclined to look to Kierkegaard; an unusual intellectual companion for Galdós it would seem, but the more one studies this novelist the less one is surprised by the multiplicity and variety of his intellectual aspects.

As we think of the desirability of bringing Galdós into a sharper nineteenth-century focus than we have yet achieved, let us not forget that the advantages of comparative studies hold true with respect to writers of different centuries. Of special interest is a comparative view that places Galdós in perspective with decidedly twentieth-century writers like Baroja and Unamuno. For one thing, such a comparison makes us sharply aware of the importance, for interpretive purposes, of the question of meaning: the belief in the first place that the world has meaning, and in the second place, that the novel is an instrument with which to demonstrate meaning.

Emphasis on the fact that Galdós was the champion of a literature of meaning can hardly be overstated. Not content with merely depicting contemporary life and customs, he felt impelled to incorporate in his narratives a variety of social, moral, and religious themes, and these appear to have been always in accord with a controlling philosophical principle. It was not necessary for him to have a clear understanding of what the meaning of life is. It was sufficient only for him to believe that there is a meaning. Seeking after it thus became a challenge and a strong motivating force that is evident not only in the form of ideational themes, but in his novelistic methodology as well. His characters, for example, are generally driving ahead vigorously, sometimes futilely, but definitely, toward a goal. His narrative method, too, is characterized by purposiveness, virtually every chapter serving as a meaningful step toward a conclusion. At its worst, literature of strictly controlled meaning can be mere sermonizing, but it can also be subtle, with an appearance of perfect naturalness while being guided by a firm orientation that gives solidity and substance to the composition as a whole. In this connection, the contrast in methodology between Galdós and Baroja is strking. Although the latter seems always to be searching for meaning, he writes as though he considered the search hopeless. His protagonists, generally without firm orientation, appear to be going nowhere in particular, simply because there is no place to go. This by no means indicates that Baroja is less an artist than Galdós or less interesting to read. It may even help to explain why a reader can enjoy page after page of Baroja's fictional episodes without caring particularly whether he is headed in any definite direction. (The same can be said of Cela.) Writing is, in its effort to capture the present moment, its own excuse for being. With Galdós, on the other hand, seldom is a descriptive or narrative scene independent of the objective at which the author is aiming; and since the reader is conscious of this narrative purposiveness, he may sometimes become impatient with any appearance of unnecessary delay in arriving at the narrative goal that is known to await him.

This contrast in novelistic method is also a contrast between a philosophical outlook that sees the world as a purposeful process, and one that reflects above all the depressiveness of a lack of purpose. Even Unamuno, who is obsessed with a sense of responsibility to establish meaning, goes about his task with the emotional uneasiness of one who seeks by the brute force of his own personal will to wrest meaning from a so-called purposeful order in which he only halfway believes. The philosophical and emotional plague of the twentieth century, the dark shadow of unmeaning, of course, has its roots in the nineteenth-century, which was never able to shake off the heavy mesmerism of the natural sciences and ended with a marked spiritual tiredness. Galdós, however, from the beginning of his career, maintained a determined course of positive action, though losing in his later years his vigorous creative energy. He did not fall victim to scientific rationalism, and he consequently does not evince the anguish of such writers as Flaubert, Dostoevsky, and Tolstoy. A non-conformist within the area of his personal and purely Spanish environment, he was a most exemplary, and healthy, conformist within the broad perspective of modern scientific thought and hence made a remarkable adjustment to his century by cooperating with it.

Now, if Galdós has lasting appeal, it is most likely to be found definitely colored by certain aspects of his peculiarly nineteenth-century quality. Without doubt, his personal brand of realism, in so far as its outward form is concerned, has diminished in popularity, just as much of the nineteenth-century manner of writing novels has gone out of style. But even the casual reader must feel the strength of his character portraits, and the wholesomeness of his ideas about individual personality even though he may find nothing spectacular in the portraits themselves. The fact is that Galdós succeeded in elevating the humblest, most unspectacular kind of human being to a place of high honor in the human family and he did so simply and unpretentiously. He was able to create heroics out of the unheroics of life, and in this accomplishment he demonstrated the very essence of nineteenth-century realism.

Can we not say, further, that Galdós' philosophical posture lays claim to posterity's admiration, even though it may be temporarily out of style? Kierkegaard and Dostoevsky were precursors, it is said. They were precursors of the twentieth-century soul-searching anxiety, an unhappy confrontation with the human predicament. But did not Galdós see this same agitation as a mere step, a necessary and inevitably social step, in a larger view of existence? The cosmic vision which he held is vertical and dynamic; that is, it is essentially an evolutionary view of gradual development along a line from lower to higher states of being. The predominantly characteristic view of the twentieth century is horizontal, as of a plane on which man stands, confronted with an existence that crowds out all reliance on previous or future states and holds the individual in a lonely spot contemplating the prospects of having to make the best of his single moment isolated in time, cut off from purposeful movement. Within the perspective represented by Galdós, by contrast, the individual can dare to reach for a goal that lies, possibly only vaguely perceived, outside the restless uncertainty of the present moment.

The individual human being making his way amidst other individuals, with their help or with their hindrance, struggling, advancing, falling back, and advancing again—this is the solid, substantial human world that Galdós depicts for us. If we ponder the view that he leaves us, we must realize the impact of the good old-fashioned doctrine of the necessity of earning one's reward; and we can harmonize this thought with the currently prominent idea that man's total reality rests in his own hands. Past, present, and future are joined simply by admitting the concept of goal into the picture, the goal being to possess in the present moment a reality that is always past, present, and future at the same time. The Galdosian interpretation of life thus invites us to combine the old with the new and permits us to embrace the pressing demands and doubts

A late portrait. From Pérez Galdós: Spanish Liberal Crusader, *by H. Chonon Berkowitz. The University of Wisconsin Press, 1948. Courtesy of the publisher.*

of the present while supplying us with a firm basis for confidence. (pp. 3-9)

Sherman Eoff, "Galdós in Nineteenth-Century Perspective," in Anales Galdosianos, *Vol. 1, No. 1, 1966, pp. 3-9.*

JOHN DEVLIN   (essay date 1966)

[*Devlin is an American critic and translator. In the following excerpt, he examines Galdós's anticlerical views as exemplified in the novels* Gloria, Doña Perfecta, *and* La familia de León Roch.]

[The anticlericalism of Pérez Galdós] is intimately associated with his liberalism. It pivots largely on matters of an intellectual nature involving the acceptance of modernity, the "key" of which . . . is found more under education than under monarchical problems or republican controversies and aspirations. He was convinced that there were forces for good struggling beneath the surface of Spanish life and that these forces were being frustrated by various reactionary attitudes, especially clericalism. He fought these attitudes vigorously, wherever he found them, and . . . his position was historically justifiable. Unlike some writers . . . Pérez Galdós' anticlericalism is not antireligious. This fact is proved by his many characters who represent the author's anticlerical position and at the same time proclaim belief in and practise religion. Again, the author does not usually paint all his "clericalists" and clergymen as vicious, malicious scoundrels. Rather, in keeping with the artistic demands to depict life, he portrays the persons associated with the clerical position in a spectrum ranging from true interior dedication to the hard-bitten, *carlista* outlook.

The novel *Gloria* offers a glance at many of the various colors of the author's anticlerical palette. Juan de Lantigua, Gloria's father, is a *cristiano viejo* (an old Christian) as his name implies. He is too gentlemanly to be openly fanatical, but he is rooted in the sincere convictions of the particular brand of Catholicism which he inherited. "The contemplative turn of his mind led him to look upon religion not only as the governing principle of the individual's conscience, but as an official regulatory instrument which ought to direct all human affairs in their external manifestations." It would be difficult to find a more concise statement of the clerical mentality.

Don Angel, a bishop and Juan's brother, is of a different religious disposition—at least on the surface. "He was a man whose natural sentiments led him to see the good in everything. His studies and his work in the confessional had taught him that there were evil people in the world. . . . In dogmatic matters he professed the doctrine of tolerance." While Juan de Lantigua is firmly convinced of the necessity of the union of the Church and secular power, Don Angel tries to avoid getting involved in matters related to the political arena. He leaves this to his aides, Rafael Horro and Rev. Señor Sedeño. López Sedeño is the "ambitious ecclesiastic."

> [Don Angel] held his secretary, Doctor López Sedeño, in such high esteem that he never touched any serious problem without consulting him, for Sedeño was an eminent theologian and a great scholar of canon law. For some time the secretary had devoted himself assiduously to political affairs and reading on politics. At first this displeased Don Angel. But soon he became accustomed to it and ended up

by praising it, considering the fact that the times demanded taking up arms. . . . Others said that Sedeño was very proud and had aspirations to become a bishop . . . when Don Angel would be transferred . . . to a metropolitan see . . . and receive the red hat.

Still another type is the curate of Ficóbriga, Don Silvestre. He is neither all good nor all bad. He is worldy and boastful; he is anti-intellectual, engages in political pressurizing, and is not generous with people whom he considers weak. On the other hand, he is brave, hard working, and not unkind to the poor. The author lead us to conclude that Don Silvestre's type was not uncommon; that he belonged among those clerics whose vocations were stimulated by the material considerations of certain surviving medieval customs. "One day his father's voice penetrated his ears and caused him to realize the advantage of not losing the income of certain chaplaincies. Silvestre stuffed himself with Latin and became a priest. Things went quite well with him. He had forgotten a lot over the years, but not his congenital passion for hunting."

Pérez Galdós' anticlericalism can be isolated in the general area of Church-State relationships as they impinged on the educational-intellectual atmosphere. But its many facets both reflect and dart out against a variety of aspects of Spanish life. *Gloria,* by reason of its richness in characters, dialogue, and situations, affords a fairly composite view of the author's complex ideas on many overlapping areas. For example, a conversation between Don Horro and Padre Silvestre illuminates at least three matters related to anticlericalism: the Church's reliance on political power, her uneducated clergy, and religious hypocrisy. Don Horro is a "whitened sepulchre." Like Don Juan he believes in the necessity of intimate rapport between Church and State. But Juan would at least use the State to further spirituality. Rafael Horro, however, believes that spiritual practises help to further his particular type of state, even though his own personal beliefs are practically nonexistent. He says to Don Silvestre: "Let's understand one another, my good Father. I believe that society is impossible without religion. Where would the frenzy of the stupid, ignorant masses bring us were it not for the restraint of religion on their evil passions." Don Silvestre, despite his worldliness and ignorance, ventures that "in matters of belief there is something more than a restraint placed upon the ignorant." But Don Rafael insists that though he may "have some small doubts about what the catechism teaches" . . . he believes that "the Masses, sermons, offerings, and all the other rites and religious customs that have been invented should continue to assist the great work of the State and to surround with safeguards the powerful and intelligent classes." Don Silvestre agrees with the political principle but is too intellectually atrophied to enter another plea for spiritual value. His arguments dwindle off in the inane remark that he "could answer point by point" if he could remember what he had read in his books.

Pérez Galdós speaks his mind on education proper when dealing with Gloria and her contacts with her father. Gloria had received a stereotyped education of some years in a high school named after one of the most pious titles of the Blessed Virgin. She came back home with complete mastery of the catechism, a smattering of history (mostly Church history), and some confused notions about Geography, Astronomy, and Physics. She could mumble some French, without really having understood the basics of Spanish. She could recite "The Duties of Man" by heart and knew how to play the piano. Juan de

Lantigua decided to regulate his daughter's reading habits with his own thoroughgoing censorship. He recommended the great Quevedo's theological writings, but forbade his picaresque novel, the *Buscón.* Gloria—showing some of the latent fires of her personality that were to bring her to tragedy—rebelled and even managed to read *La Pícara Justina,* a novel about a woman of "easy virtue." In her long conversations with her father she gave further signs of the natural impulses she would later follow. Don Juan recommended the mystical writers of the Sixteenth Century. But Gloria found them not very interesting; she felt they never could be a guide for ordinary people because they were too difficult to understand.

The vital nucleus of Pérez Galdós' anticlerical position emerges in a conversation that the de Lantigua brothers have with Daniel Morton. Daniel is an English Jew who becomes Gloria's lover through chance. Using this conversation the author first isolates and then castigates what Conrad Bonacina called "the dogmatization of political energy." Morton first describes the Spanish Church as many have seen it:

> In no other country in the world is there less belief. And it should be noted that in no other country is there more pretending that there is belief . . . Belgian and French Catholics, Protestants, Jews . . . Mohammedans practise their faith with more fervor than the Spaniards . . . I am amazed at the lack of religion in the majority of well-educated people. With rare exceptions the entire middle class is indifferent . . . Women give themselves to devotions but men flee from the Church . . . Don't you understand that this gives you no right to say "We are the most religious people on earth?"

Don Juan is forced to agree. But he feels that the remedy lies in the realm of politics. He claims that the weakening of religion is due to "revolutionary excesses and the influence of foreigners who are jealous of the most religious nation on earth." The Church could easily cure the situation if it could "find a government pious enough to aid" in this work.

The central theme of the book, of course, is the inability of Gloria and Daniel to marry because of the conflict between their respective religious traditions. The de Lantigua brothers are unable to find an effective compromise. Daniel is admired for his excellent intellect but pitied for the impending damnation awaiting all Protestants. Gloria seeks out the advice of her uncle in the confessional. Don Angel advises her to "cast away this senseless passion, to suffocate it with an aspiration toward the one sovereign love." He refuses her absolution on the grounds of "latitudinarianism," or belief that non-Catholics can achieve salvation. When Daniel later says he is a Jew, the conflict reaches its climax and a terrible scene, with good splashes of Galdosian melodrama, ensues. Don Angel and Don Juan burst in. The father drops dread in shame; the bishop drops his genial mask of benevolence, and bares his claws and fangs. "Get out of here, you God-murderer!" he shouts.

In the anticlerical novels the author does not espouse any specific political cause. His position is limited to his objection to the extension of the influence of clericalism—or, indeed, any denominational attitudes which tend to separate mankind—in the conduct of human affairs. But he accurately observes the various nuances of the contemporary political scene. For example, republicanism was a *bête noire* in his early years as well as in the twentieth century. In *Gloria,* Bartolomé Barrabás, a village republican, was regarded with dark suspicion by the de Lantigua contingent. Horro pointed strongly critical remarks in this direction declaring that "a huge filthy, leperous pestilence was spreading over the social system. It is the so-called modern spirit, a dragon of one hundred deformed heads, that is fighting to dash down the standard of the Cross." In the second part of the novel a religious procession is described. The various external trappings of confessionalism are portrayed amid barbs of satire:

> Don Silvestre wore his pluvial cape with mundane elegance. Father Poquito, serving as deacon, was imprisoned in the dalmatic. Juan Amarillo went a bit behind, swollen with pride in finding himself in the fullness of his municipal functions.... He represented human authority protecting and fostering, with its guarding arm, divine authority. It was essential that his person should be equal to such a distinguished role ... When they passed by the casino the town band began to cut the throat of the Royal March.

Pérez Galdós' *Doña Perfecta* is perhaps even more widely read than *Gloria.* In *Doña Perfecta* the author's anticlericalism is double-pronged with two separate yet interwoven ideas:

1. The perennial conflict between liberalism and reaction.

2. The portrayal of a *beata*—that type of woman whose "piety" is out of proportion to her calling in life and occupied rather exclusively with the letter rather than the spirit.

The first theme is achieved by the plot of the story. Pepe Rey, in love with Perfecta's daughter, is the protagonist. He represents the modern struggle toward a new Spain which would rely upon the contributions of modernity and break away from narrow, intolerant provincialism and a mode of life which has passed into history. He is frank in his espousal of science which he has made his profession. Doña Perfecta, like the de Lantiguas represents the reaction against the modern spirit. In her mind Pepe's science is destroying faith and the life of the soul. Consequently, she equates his modernity with atheism. Unlike the de Lantiguas she does not have a good bone in her body. Pepe is not irreligious, but if his religious needs find fulfillment within the Catholic formula, it is certainly not the brand of Catholicism represented by Perfecta. In his second meeting with Rosario and in other scenes he firmly expresses his religious beliefs which seem to reflect the influence of Kraus and, in general, the optimistic pluralism of Giner and his followers, without much reference to any particular sectarian context. Doña Perfecta is determined to thwart Pepe by using her clerical friends. Chief among them is her confessor, Don Inocencio, a typical sacerdotal "lounge-lizard." He is a man of narrow views, inquisitorial, and intolerant, and he is not averse to using insinuation and half-truth. In the last analysis he is the ultimate cause of the conflict between Pepe and Perfecta— he wanted Rosario to marry his nephew, Jacinto.

The general lines of the conflict between Pepe and Perfecta, together with the nuances of the forces they represent, is summed up in the following conversation:

> "Ah, the fine understanding of your German mathematical and philosophic mind is not able to grasp the subtle thoughts of a prudent mother ... Ah, my boy, one does not get inside

the human heart by railway tunnels, nor plumb its depths by mine shafts. The conscience of another person cannot be read with the naturalist's microscopes nor can the guilt of one's neighbor be decided by balancing ideas with a theodolite."

> "For the love of God, dear Aunt!"

> "Why do you use God's name if you don't believe in Him?" Perfecta said in her solemn tones. "If you believe in Him, if you were a good Christian, you would not dare make wicked judgments on my conduct. I am a pious woman— do you get that? My conscience is at peace— do you get that? I know what I do and why I do it—do you get that?...

> "You are a mathematician. You can see what's in front of you and nothing else. You can see brutal nature, and nothing else—lines, angles, weights, and nothing else. You see the effect and not the cause."

This clash of seriously misunderstood value patterns brings about the tragic denouement. Perfecta's fanaticism mounts in intensity until she finally incites the braggart, Caballuco, to kill Pepe with a blunderbuss:

> Doña Perfecta moved forward a few paces. Her harsh voice vibrated with her terrible intent. She spat out these words, "Cristóbal, Cristóbal ... kill him." A shot was heard. Then another.

As can be seen from the foregoing, the author's picture of Doña Perfecta is unrelieved in its stark horror. Still possessing the remnants of physical beauty, the woman is despotic, cold, intransigeant, and fanatical. "She seemed like an anathema made into a woman." Yet, she is wax in the hands of the "penitenciary," Don Inocencio. The author wants to impress on his readers that the substructure of her character was an intense and terrible pride and he wishes to point up the effect of religious exaltation in a hard character which is devoid of native goodness. Rather than devoting herself to improving her spirit by meditation upon the beauty of the truths of her religion, which are beyond time and place, she seeks to arrange her own life and the lives of others by narrow formulas bounded by the limits of her own highly restricted horizons. This is what Pérez Galdós means when he appends these final lines to the novel: "This is about all we are able to say about people who seem good but really are not."

Objections have been made that the author erred artistically in this study of a *beata*. Critics have claimed that he created a character without any shades of psychological color—in short, a monster of abnormality. It has also been stated that this lack of proportion extends to the other characters and consequently to the book as a whole. Perfecta and the priest on the one hand, Pepe and Rosario on the other, become little more than opposing ideas thought out ahead of time and subsequently personified. The result is a stark contrast of black and white, lacking the ingredients of at least some good with evil, some imperfections with the good. César Barja asks, "What kind of a novel is a work in which good and evil are divided into absolute qualities?" And José Balseiro, speaking of both *Doña Perfecta* and Pereda's *Don Gonzalo González* (intended as a "reply" to Pérez Galdós' work) asks, "Is life as simple as presented to us in either work?'' In *Gloria* there is gradation between the separate individuals and much more psychological nuance within each character. And as will be seen in *La familia de León Roch*, a *beata*'s religious fanaticism can be complicated by very worldly wants indeed. Certainly, in *Doña Perfecta* Pérez Galdós has not probed as deeply into the psychological motivations of a *beata* as the contemporary Catholic author, François Mauriac. Mauriac, in his *La Pharisienne*, very competently analyzes deep, distorted religious convictions and self-righteousness that wreck the lives of many people. Certainly, also, Pérez Galdós has stacked the cards ahead of time. Perfecta and her clerical friends are entirely bad; Pepe and Rosario are all sweetness and light.

On the other hand, it should not be felt that Doña Perfecta's ''execution'' of Pepe Rey is beyond credence. Georges Bernanos, the late Catholic author, cites a real incident illustrative of the lengths to which the ''beatific'' spirit can go. The time and historical context are vastly different; the place is Mallorca; but it is a real example of fanaticism leading to crime as in the Inquisition:

> Yes, I have seen some strange things. There was an unmarried girl, thirty-five years old, who belonged to that inoffensive group that are called *beatas* down there. She was living quietly with her family after having left the novitiate. The time she did not spend in church she dedicated to the poor. Suddenly she fell victim of an unexplainable nervous terror; she spoke of possible reprisals and refused to go out alone. A very close friend of mine, whom I cannot name, took pity on her and hoping to restore her confidence, took her into her home. Sometime later the pious young lady decided to go back to her family. The morning of the day of departure her charitable hostess said to her affectionately: ''See here, dear girl. What can you possibly be afraid of? You're one of the Good Lord's little lambs. Who could be evil enough to wish death to a person as truly inoffensive as you?'' ''Inoffensive? You don't know what you're talking about, dear lady. You think I am incapable of rendering service to religion. And everyone thinks as you do. Make no mistake about me. Here's a bit of information for my lady. I have had eight men shot, Madame.'' Yes, there can be no doubt. It has been my lot to have seen strange, interesting things.

La familia de León Roch is another of Pérez Galdós' hard core anticlerical novels. Here the plot is centered in the tensions between a man and his wife—tensions that have been aggravated by religious fanaticism. A complicating factor—sometimes overlooked by critics who see it as a purely anticlerical work—is the presence of a ''triangle'' situation. León had never ceased to love Pepa Fúcar, even though he tried to disguise this love and sublimate it to the platonic level. He and María had been drawn to each other by strong physical attraction. When this ceased to be compelling, the religious problem rose to plague them. María tried desperately to recapture her husband's love and sexual interest and brought about her own death in the attempt. Pérez Galdós examines the couple's general psychological incompatibility rather than only their religious incompatability.

The work, however, has considerable importance for the anticlerical motif. María offers another study in the psychology of the *beata*. Unlike Perfecta she is more complicated and consequently less a monster. León has less religious conviction than either Pepe Rey or Daniel Morton and should be classed as an agnostic. María, however, accuses him of atheism: ''If only I were not married to you, an atheist. . . .'' Despite his agnosticism, however, he is able to pray in his own way for the recovery of Monina, the daughter of Pepa. In his calm and serene dedication to the intellectual life he seems to be a typical *ateneista*, whom the author might have met during hours spent at this center.

The anticlericalism of the novel is centered once again in a clash between religion and science, represented by the wife and the husband. María wishes León to be converted; he, reasonably, requests her to mitigate her ascetic practices and ''beatific'' observances. He proposes a *modus vivendi*. He promises to give up his studies and meetings with like-minded friends. He will wall up his library like Don Quijote's. There will be no conversation on science or history in his house and never a jocose or suspect word that might be taken with reference to the things of the spirit. For this concession León asks a similar one on María's part. ''I am sacrificing what you stupidly call my atheism (although it is something quite different); you will have to sacrifice what you call your piety, a dubious piety I am sure. You will have to give up your unending daily devotions, as well as your habit of going to confession every week to the same priest . . . You will go to Mass on Sundays and feast days.'' This bargain, was, of course, doomed to failure.

Closely associated with the theme of havoc engendered in family life through the abuse of religion is the thread of the confessor, Father Paoletti, who is presented in a striking uncomplimentary portrait. His familiarity with his penitent, María, disgusts León who is made to feel like an outsider in his own home. The baneful influence of Father Paoletti is augmented by María's brother, the tubercular seminarist, Luis Gonzaga, who, in his consuming fanaticism, appeals to his sister against her husband. Thus, though the theme of the novel is marital, the author introduces and bears heavily upon his anticlerical motif, insisting upon the harm that can be wrought in a home by an overinsistence upon the externals of religion. (pp. 82-92)

Like most Spaniards Pérez Galdós was a God-seeker and probably suffered several spiritual crises. Religion and religious preoccupations seem to press from the substructure of his subconscious mind to the forefront of his work. He seemed compelled to return again and again to the implications of religion (not only clericalism) in life. It is not essential that we probe his spiritual beliefs, but from knowledge of his own life and of the characters whom he permitted to represent him in his work, certain limited conclusions are rather evident. He believed in a supreme Deity; he reverenced Christ, but felt that His true image had been deformed by centuries-old formalisms and encrustations symbolized by Spanish reliquary art and outmoded religious customs. He was vigorously humanitarian (in the tradition of Kraus). His last brief play, *Santa Juana de Castilla* (1920), probably sheds very valuable light upon his deepest convictions. Here he depicts the later San Francisco de Borja as the comforter of Juana, whose *erasmista* tendencies were used as an excuse to consider her mad. Completely fictitious, the play none-the-less anticipates the modern re-evaluation of Erasmus. It also shows a longing toward the ecumenical spirit of Pope John XXIII and religious open-mindedness of the second half of the twentieth century. Certain it is, however, that the author, whatever his own beliefs might have been, is in no sense opposed to religion in general. He concentrates his fire on manifestations of any religious or denominational nature—or, indeed, of any social nature—which tended to separate rather than unite mankind. Because his own temperament was basically religious, he felt deformations of religion keenly—bitterly, at times. And his approach to clerical problems, strong as it is, is vastly different from that of certain other authors, who, it will be seen, have extended anticlericalism into an attempt to discredit all forms of religion.

At times some of the author's situations and characters may seem a bit extreme. At times some of the words and thoughts that Pérez Galdós puts into the mouths of his characters may seem, from our vantage point, to lie more in the realm of caricature. The de Lantigua brothers, for example—their ideas on church and state, the bishop's attitude toward people of other faiths. One has only to check back to the climate of opinion [in early twentieth-century Spain] to see that this is not caricature or distortion. Serious people writing in respectable publications or in carrying out the exercise of important offices spoke very similar words and thoughts. The views that Pérez Galdós' attributes to the "clericals" are practically direct quotations from real Spanish life. It may also be hard to believe that a religiously-inclined woman could stage a murder. Yet Bernanos knew an ex-novice who figured in eight murders in Mallorca during the first days of the Civil War. It may be hard to believe that a bishop could call a Jew a God-murderer. Yet the Church in its official public worship on Good Friday has only recently stopped praying "for the wicked Jews." And the entire problem of the collective guilt of the Jews in the Crucifixion of Christ has not (as of this writing) been finally disposed of by the Second Vatican Council. Doña Perfecta's attitude toward science and the young scientist Pepe may seem extreme—hard to believe. Yet the confrontation of Perfecta and Pepe has all the tell-tale signs of the larger confrontation of clericalism and sincere liberalism that was taking place in Spain, and that was to culminate eventually in the murder and bloodshed of the Civil War. (pp. 94-5)

> *John Devlin, "Anticlericalism in 'Belles Lettres' in Writers for the Most Part Associated with the Pre-Republican Era: Benito Pérez Galdós (1843-1920)," in his* Spanish Anticlericalism: A Study in Modern Alienation, *Las Americas Publishing Company, 1966, pp. 81-95.*

ALFRED RODRÍGUEZ   (essay date 1967)

[*In the following excerpt, Rodríguez discusses such elements as style, structure, characterization, and symbolism in the* National Episodes.]

The *Episodios nacionales* are historical novels; yet no "a priori" definition of that literary "genre" can satisfactorily include all forty-six volumes. These may only be classified therein if the term "Historical Novel" is broadened to include their special characteristics. But one finds, however, that the necessary process of classification blurs the most essential differences that might be thought to exist between Galdós' historical novels and the rest of his novelistic production.

Galdós treatment of History—a subject matter that holds the work within the broad category of historical fiction—is everywhere conditioned by the philosophical attitudes and artistic

perspectives of the realist writer, so that no inflexible definition of "Historical Novel," especially if based on the norms established by the literature of the Romantics, could possibly incorporate the *Episodios nacionales*. (p. 197)

It is their rigid formal outline, far more than any stylistic, thematic, or procedural criteria that might be applied, that distinguishes the *Episodios nacionales* from the rest of Galdós' work. Because they deal with a specific constant (historical time), and with a subject matter for which the novelist's perspective required a specific order of treatment, the *Episodios nacionales,* unlike any other segment of the novelist's work, are fixed into a set literary form: ten volume Series unit, progressive sequence of time, and prescribed quantitative limitations.

This external fixation of form can be quite misleading. In fact, the study of plot structure and development in the various Series reveals that the "set" formal outline of the literary unit may condition but rarely inhibits the novelistic variety or richness of the content. On the contrary, it is evident that the *Episodios nacionales* offer the widest range of novelistic forms encountered anywhere: objective narrations, memoirs, both immediate and retrospective, epistolary novels, and varied combinations of these. The flexibility of the individual Episodio, even within the formal outline of the Series, is extraordinary.

Galdós' use of varied novelistic forms to project the variety of historical circumstances, the specific and distinct character of each period, is an important factor in the success of the *Episodios nacionales*. One need only recall, in this connection, the novels of the Second Series which feature Bragas or those in the Fourth in which Santiuste is the protagonist. Nowhere else in Galdós are the alterations in literary temperament and expression so evident as in these forty-six volumes: from the epic drive of the first Episodios to the caricaturesque distortion of the last. And each stage of this evolution is made viable in the literary guise of a distinct form of novelistic expression.

The study of plot development also scores the progressive dissociation of novelistic content in successive literary units. This evolution within the formal outline of the Series, prompted both by qualitative variations in the historical subject matter and by the author's directed efforts to allow greater literary flexibility, accounts for the greater degree of novelistic complexity that enhances the artistic potential of each successive Series. This concept of progressive literary enrichment runs counter to most general evaluations of the *Episodios nacionales*. (pp. 198-99)

Another established view of Galdós' historical novel—its characterizational poverty—is disproved by a detailed analysis of character presentation and development in the *Episodios nacionales*. The novelist's primary interest in human development is definitely not diluted or altered when he approaches a historical subject. Whatever shift may take place between contemporary novelist and historical novelist—from people to events—is more than offset by the wealth of new characterizational possibilities opened by a perspective on the past.

In effect, the *Episodios nacionales* boast as wide a variety of characterizations as may be found anywhere in Galdós, even wider, in fact, if historical personages are included. Characters like Salvador Monsalud, "El Empecinado," José Fago, Trijueque, Maroto, Bragas, and Juan Hondón, to mention but a few of the myriad human patterns represented in the forty-six volumes, are both the product of one or more of Galdós' penetrating perspectives on human nature and the reflection, simultaneously, of some specific element of the historical situation depicted. And it is precisely this combination that accounts for the universal quality of a mere historical reconstruction.

In spite of the somewhat limiting representational function that most characters perform in the *Episodios nacionales,* these reveal characterizations that are comparable, in the quality of their presentation and development, to the better creations found in the *Novelas de primera época* or the *Novelas contemporáneas.* Fajardo, for example, experiences intensely dramatic human conflicts that make him one of the novelist's most memorable protagonists; and José Armengol or Navarro are as tragic in their fundamental human make-up as the Polo Corteses found in other segments of Galdós' work. As for feminine characterizations, always a specialty of the author, it was first in the *Episodios nacionales,* with Jenara, that the author sketched the prototype of his most expressive feminine creations. And any group of novels that boasts Pilar Loaysa, Domiciana Paredes, Teresita Villaescusa, and Sor Teodora de Aransis, to mention but a few, needs little defense in terms of feminine characterization.

The depiction of secondary figures, in which the characterizational opportunities offered by a perspective on the past are most readily implemented, represents one of Galdós' major successes in the *Episodios nacionales.* Characters almost too numerous to mention project the attitudes and feelings of every stage in Spain's nineteenth-century history, and they do so as believable human beings, anguished, overjoyed, or disheartened by the life that pulsates within or about them.

Here too the techniques are, to say the least, as varied as in any segment of Galdós' work: Pepe Pellejos, "Pujitos," Marcial, "Pelambres," and countless other types taken from Ramón de la Cruz or Mesonero Romanos; Hillo, "El Gran Capitán," Malespina, and innumerable other comical figures from the molds of Plautus and Cervantes; Lobo, the Requejos, Romo, and many others whose very physical being projects the twisted substance of their souls; and people like Negretti, Churi, and María Ignacia Emparán, whose cursory presentation as secondary figures suggests all the dense complexity of more extensively developed characters. (pp. 199-200)

Galdós' imaginative creativity is substantially less inhibited in the *Episodios nacionales* than elsewhere in his literary production. This, perhaps more than any single factor, makes the forty-six *Episodios* both a magnificent discovery for the reader of Galdós and an incalculably rich expression, perhaps the richest, of the novelist's creative abilities. This is true to a great extent, as we have seen, of plot development and characterization, but it is most evident in studies of specific areas of Galdós' historical novel.

A study of the comical elements in the *Episodios nacionales* reveals almost every conceivable degree and avenue of humor, a range and flexibility of comical devices and conceptions that is not found in Galdós' other novels. (pp. 200-01)

The study of symbolism in the forty-six volumes again reveals a remarkable diversity of practices and devices. Name symbolism—Galdós' most characteristic didactic device—prevails, as nowhere else, in the five Series, replete throughout with the most varied comical, illustrative, and characterizational functions. Galdós availed himself, for the purpose of symbolism, of every conceivable literary element: titles like *La segunda casaca, Un faccioso más y algunos frailes menos, De Oñate a la Granja, Los duendes de la camarilla, La de los tristes destinos,* and *De Cartago a Sagunto;* mock literary openings like that

which introduce the memoirs of Bragas or that which initiates Liviano's narration in *De Cartago a Sagunto;* and even animals, as many long passages from *Gerona*—and many shorter ones throughout the work—well indicate.

Moreover, Galdós' historical novel offers unique examples of an extraordinary ability to have believable characters and realistic plot situations (whole plots or segments thereof) project the qualitative essence and the human composition of specific historical moments. His artistic projection of historical relationships as concrete human problems and situations is his most effective illustrative device. But it is much more than that, for the characters and plot situations are themselves subtly affected by a suggestive association with transcendental historical realities. It is an esthetic interaction that endows the *Episodios nacionales,* and simultaneously, with a humanized historical transcendence and a visibly "historicized" human content.

A wealth of characters on all levels of development express, in the *Episodios nacionales,* the profound interest that Galdós reveals everywhere in the relatively hidden aspects of human personality. The difference is again a question of degree, of qualitative and quantitative flexibility. In no other segment of his work does the novelist accumulate a repertoire of "strange" characters like Leandra, Nelet, Fago, Churi, and Negretti. And the phenomenon is by no means restricted to the Third Series, for the following group of Episodios offers Fajardo, Santiuste, Binondo, and Miedes. Nowhere else does Galdós present such an impressive array of distinct enigmatic personalities, for each of those mentioned above—and many others besides—is a rule unto himself.

The subconscious externalizations and the aberrational behaviour that stem from Galdós' emphasis on the abnormal in the *Episodios nacionales*—yet to be studied with the care with which similar phenomena have been examined in the *Novelas contemporáneas*—are as rich and varied as any to be found in the novelist's work. As is usually the case in Galdós, dreams, hallucinations, and other psychic phenomena play important roles in characterization and plot development. In the *Episodios nacionales,* moreover, these are often made to reflect, in the crisis of an individual being, the turbulent character of a historical situation or the pathological condition of an entire age.

The study of Galdós' use of traditional literary themes and characters in the *Episodios nacionales* suggests that it may be necessary to modify certain widely held opinions:

> More important is the fact that Galdós' creative methods, especially in fictional materials as distinct from historical ones but even also in the *Episodios,* tended to use more recent personal experience and observation of his own rather than literary materials. [W. H. Shoemaker, "Galdós Classical Scene in *La de Bringas*"].

There are numerous indications of the novelist's use of a great variety of literary materials: primarily Spanish, to be sure, but with occasional foreign sources such as Shakespeare, Balzac, and Dickens.

Traditional Spanish themes and characters abound everywhere in the novelist's literary production: Don Quijote, Don Juan, the picaresque, Celestina, and Juan Ruiz. But it is in the historical novel, once again, that the full impact of Galdós' reelaboration of literary materials is felt.

The novelist's use of Cervantes, especially of the *Quijote*, has already drawn the attention of scholars. Nevertheless, the *Episodios nacionales* allow further comparative studies, particularly in connection with Cervantine works other than the *Quijote*. Most of these interesting re-elaborations have been overlooked by critics; yet themes like that of *Celestina* provide Galdós' historical novel with many characterizations and even an occasional plot outline.

Surprisingly enough, the Don Juan theme has not been studied in Galdós. When such a study is undertaken, the *Episodios nacionales* will undoubtedly figure prominently in it, for nowhere in Spanish literature, not even among the modern generations that have cultivated the Don Juan theme with special intensity, is there a repertoire comparable to the "byronized" Lord Gray, the pathetic Falfán de los Godos, the broken Nelet, the "calibanized" Churi, the genuine Gracián, the pathological Santiuste, and the fantastic Liviano.

The literary outline most employed by Galdós is the picaresque. This is especially true in the *Episodios nacionales,* in the study of which there has been occasion to note that the episodic character of novels that must incorporate widely dispersed historical events encouraged Galdós' use of the picaresque-like protagonist, rootless, and forever wandering. The fact is, however, that the picaresque stamp set upon numerous Galdosian characters entails something more than a mere literary expedient. More often than not the negative attributes of the rogue reflect the essential truth, off-repeated by modern thinkers, that a Spaniard without a vital "quehacer" ["objective"] instinctively reverts to a picaresque world-view.

The separate interpolations of these literary re-workings are always esthetically and functionally viable. Numerous pages in this study point out the realistic quality of a characterization or the essential verisimilitude of a plot outline, and indicate, as well, the important novelistic, characterizational, comical, stylistic, and symbolical functions they perform in the work. But it is the cumulative effect that is perhaps of greatest interest, for without its picaresque, donjuanesque, celestinesque, and quijotesque elements the *Episodios nacionales* would be completely altered. These elements constitute, if they are statistically arranged, a secondary background to the entire work, providing the primary historical background with unmistakable universal overtones.

Finally, the *Episodios nacionales* reveal a variety and range of geographical settings that is unique in Galdós. Nothing in the novelist's previous production, nor in that of the generation with which he is most often linked, prepares the reader for the foreign settings of the Fourth Series. In fact, one would have to go to Baroja or Valle-Inclán for anything comparable. Of course the uniqueness of this phenomenon—which is nevertheless meaningful and appropriate in the historical context of the *Episodios nacionales*—adds powerfully to the notion of Galdós' historical novel as that segment of his work in which he is least restricted in the conception and use of literary elements. (pp. 201-04)

> Alfred Rodríguez, *in his* An Introduction to the Episodios Nacionales of Galdós, *Las Americas Publishing Company, 1967, 222 p.*

WALTER T. PATTISON (essay date 1975)

[*Pattison is an American critic who has written numerous studies of Spanish literature, including two volumes devoted to the works of Galdós. In the following excerpt, he discusses the significance of characterization and setting in* Fortunata and Jacinta.]

Juanito Santa Cruz, an idle, pampered son of a well-to-do family of cloth merchants, is the man who links together the fortunes of the two women who give their names to the novel [*Fortunata and Jacinta*]. Fortunata is the girl of the common people whom Juanito seduces with promises of marriage; Jacinta is his cousin whom he marries.

On their wedding trip Jacinta little by little worms out of Juanito the story of his love affair with Fortunata, five months pregnant when he abandoned her. This is the beginning of the theme of maternity, which both divides and unites the two women. Jacinta is sterile and has a tremendous fixation on motherhood. In Madrid during trips into the slums on charity missions she meets Ido del Sagrario, whose diseased imagination creates a fiction that Fortunata's child by Juanito is living and is now in the care of Platón. To satisfy her great yearning for a child Jacinta buys the child from Platón and tries to get Juanito and his parents to accept it. It is proved, however, that Juanito's real son has died.

Now Maxi Rubín enters the tale. He "was rachitic, of a poor and lymphatic constitution, absolutely devoid of personal attractions," a youth given to daydreaming, who "lived two existences, that of bread, and that of chimeras," and who in his imagination envisioned himself the object of a great love. After meeting Fortunata he idealizes her, seeks her regeneration by a stay in a convent (Las Micaelas), and finally marries her. Maxi is sick on their wedding night, and soon Fortunata, who has never stopped loving Juanito, falls again into his power. When Maxi tries to remonstrate, Juanito beats him up, and the marriage is broken off.

In the convent Fortunata has seen Jacinta among a group of society women who sponsor the work of the nuns. The sight of her rival produces a strange mixed emotion in the sinner. "That woman had robbed her of what in her opinion belonged rightfully to her. But another very different and more pronounced feeling was amalgamated strangely with this one. It was a most keen desire to resemble Jacinta, to be like her, to have her air, her charming appearance of sweetness and nobility. Because of all the ladies she saw that day none seemed to Fortunata so much a lady as Mrs. Santa Cruz." The unpolished girl of the slums begins to gravitate toward the refined lady of the upper class, whom she sees as a victim of Juanito just as she is. Marriage, even to Maxi, she thinks will make her an "honest woman," hence more like Jacinta.

After the impossible marriage of Fortunata and Maxi has been patched up and the couple is living together, there occurs another revealing episode between the two women. A common friend (Doña Guillermina, about whom we shall say more later) who is trying to counsel Fortunata yields reluctantly to Jacinta's desire and permits her to eavesdrop on the interview from a hiding place in the next room. To the consternation of Doña Guillermina, Fortunata declares that she is really Juanito's wife because of his promise to marry her and above all because she bore him a child. Jacinta may be an angel, true, "but she has no children. A wife who has no children is not a wife." Soon after, Jacinta comes out of her hiding place and in an angry tirade abuses her rival in words which would be used by a woman of the common people. The civilized lady reveals an underlying natural stratum close to Fortunata's primitive emotional possessiveness.

During the interview Fortunata reveals that Juanito is pursuing her again and that she has an idea, not expressly stated, but that is something "which must be because it is so ordained." She goes back to her lover, exclaiming "it had to be. It's my destiny. . . . And I'm not sorry about it because I've got my idea here (in my mind), you know."

We learn exactly what her idea is when she becomes pregnant again. "You see how I achieved my idea." Her child will prove her claim that she is Juanito's real wife. The baby will, according to written law, have Rubín as his name, but by the law of nature he is a Santa Cruz. Nevertheless, Fortunata is distraught with another great anxiety. Juanito has taken another mistress (Aurora), and there is the possibility he will have other children by her. Fortunata rushes out to give Aurora a beating. Jacinta, for all her refinement, rejoices in Fortunata's act. And Fortunata declares that one of the reasons why she roughed up Aurora was that the latter had cast suspicion on Jacinta's virtue.

But the extreme exertion so soon after the delivery of her child brings Fortunata to the point of death. She sends the baby to Jacinta, tellng her in a note that this child is not false, like the first one Jacinta wanted to adopt, but "legitimate and *natural*, as you will see in his face," where Juanito's traits are visible. On receiving the child Jacinta was surprised "to perceive in her heart feelings which were something more than pity for the unfortunate woman, for there was perhaps, deep within her, something of comradeship, of fraternity, based on common misfortunes." Before long she thinks of herself as the flesh and blood mother of the baby and of Moreno Isla, her deceased platonic lover, as the father instead of Juanito, with whom she is no longer intimate.

Behind the misadventures of the two women lies the conflict between natural and social law, between free love and the institution of marriage. We must not take Fortunata's concept of free love as an endorsement for promiscuousness. Although she has had many men since the first episode with Juanito, she loves only Santa Cruz and regards him as her husband. "*You are my husband . . . (and) all the others, nothing at all.*" Even after her marriage to Maxi, she feels that her real husband is her first lover and that she is fatally united to him forever. So when Juanito calls her back she yields without hesitation, considering herself something "like a blind mechanism which is moved by a supernatural hand. What she had done she did, in her opinion, through the disposition of the mysterious forces which control the greatest things of the universe, the rising of the sun and the falling of heavy objects. She could not fail to do it, nor did she question the inevitable."

Her love is all impulse, essentially romantic, akin to the mating of animals. Santa Cruz describes her as "a cute little animal, a savage who didn't know how to read or write. . . . But a good heart, a good heart." For her "love redeems all irregular conduct, better said, love makes everything regular for it rectifies laws, annulling those which oppose it."

She is, of course, a representative of the common people, a class which Galdós now envisions with some of the mystique we see in the Russian novelists, specifically in Tolstoy's treatment of Platon Karataev. Guillermina Pacheco upbraids her mentally, thinking: "You have no moral sense; you can never have principles because you are before civilization; you are a savage and belong completely to primitive stages of humanity"; but, because Fortunata would never understand these concepts, she only says, "You have the passions of the common people, crude and like a block of unworked stone." Gal-

dós' comments on Guillermina's thought and speech: "This was true because the common people, in our (modern) societies, keep elemental ideas and sentiments in their rough plenitude, as the quarry contains marble, the matter (capable) of form. The common people possess great truths in block, and civilization has recourse to them as the little truths by which it lives are used up." In more specific terms, socialized love (marriage) cannot succeed without some of the primitive passion in which Fortunata believes. It is precisely because of this lack that her marriage to Maxi fails; he is capable of a profound and lasting love, but he is impotent. And should another elemental drive be frustrated (Jacinta's desire for children) that marriage is also incomplete.

Among the many secondary and minor characters that surround the central figure (Fortunata) we shall see a number who try to "civilize" her. There is, however, one who supports and reinforces her idea that nothing connected with love can be a sin. This individual is Mauricia *la dura* (the "toughie"), an alcoholic whom Fortunata met in the convent for fallen women, and toward whom she felt an instinctive, inexplicable attraction. Mauricia exercised a strange and powerful fascination on her friend who could never figure out just why. "Things of the spirit, that only God understands!" she exclaims and tells Doña Guillermina "something extraordinary happened to me respecting that woman. Knowing that she was very bad, I loved her . . . I liked her and I couldn't help it. When she told me the terrible things she did in her life, I don't know. . . . I enjoyed listening to her . . . and when she advised me [to do] bad things, it seemed to me, in my inmost mind, it seemed to me that they weren't so bad and that she was right in recommending them to me. How do you explain this?"

Mauricia can give her friend much information about the Santa Cruz family (she was reared in Doña Guillermina's house, next door to the Santa Cruz residence). Hence she can assure Fortunata that Juanito will return to her and that he has taken steps to seduce her the second time. Above all, on her deathbed she proclaims that Fortunata will not sin in loving Juanito. Mauricia, despite her Napoleonic countenance, her harsh voice, and her drunkenness, is Fortunata's authority in matters of love.

Doña Lupe, Maxi's widowed aunt, acts as a mother to her orphaned nephew, satisfying a strong maternal instinct as well as her dominant passion for directing other people's lives. When she discovers that Fortunata wants to learn, "that she is a savage who needs to be domesticated," her gifts as an educator and counselor are aroused. She accedes to the marriage, which she knows has almost no chance of success, simply because she thinks she can train Fortunata just as she is molding Papitos (her servant girl) and her nephew.

There is a great deal of educating and training to be done. Fortunata, like other women of her class, does not know the meaning of many fairly common words or the order of the months of the year. Even before Doña Lupe gets to know her Maxi has been teaching her how to write and the rudimentary facts generally known to a school boy. Doña Lupe sees that "She had to teach her everything: manners, language, conduct. The more poverty of education the pupil revealed, the more the teacher delighted in the perspectives and illusions of her plan."

But Fortunata runs off with Juanito soon after her wedding and for the time Doña Lupe's desires are frustrated. Shortly afterward, abandoned by her lover, she is taken in by Don Evaristo Feijoo, an elderly bachelor who leads a quiet, well-ordered existence, living on his pension as a retired colonel of the army. He becomes a half-father, half-lover to Fortunata, while at the same time he is the author's philosopher of free love. He recognizes that "it is a great stupidity to rebel against Nature. It has its laws, and he who ignores them, pays for it." One of these natural laws is the nonduration of love, so that infidelity in marriage is nothing but nature demanding its rights against social despotism. But one must compromise with the social rules, which means one must maintain appearances. This is the cardinal point in Don Evaristo's credo. Natural love, he agrees with Fortunata, is not a sin, but decorum must be maintained. "You must give the heart its bits of flesh; it is a wild beast and long hunger infuriates it; but you must also give society's beast the part which corresponds to it so it won't start a disturbance." With these words the retired colonel, soon incapable of sustaining the lover's role, is preparing Fortunata for a return to Maxi. In a sense he is half socializing her by advising her to kep her powerful natural love hidden, never ignoring "the holy appearances," the "external cult" of society "without which we would return to the state of savages."

In fact, after her return to her husband and the further civilizing influences of Doña Lupe, Fortunata does not forget the doctrine of appearances. Juanito seduces her for the third time and while she yields immediately to her fated love, she remembers Feijoo's advice. Had she not become pregnant (her way of proving her natural claim to be Juanito's wife) her relations with her lover could have continued indefinitiey.

A much more conventional socializing influence on Fortunata is exerted by Doña Guillermina Pacheco. This maiden lady has devoted her life to charity; her crowning achievement is the establishment of an orphan asylum for which she begs and wheedles alms from both friends and strangers.

In the structure of the novel she is a bridge between the lower classes, among whom she is constantly going on charitable missions, and the well-to-do. Her house adjoins the Santa Cruz residence and she is an intimate friend of the family. Jacinta accompanies her at times in her excursions into the slums or to the convent of Las Micaelas. Her nephew, the rich banker Moreno Isla, becomes a frustrated lover of Jacinta.

As Mauricia *la dura* lies dying, Guillermina cares for her, both attending to her physical wants and arranging for the proper religious rites. Fortunata also visits her dying friend; observing Guillermina's lively activity "she felt in her soul so much admiration for that woman that she would have kissed the hem of her dress." Guillermina becomes aware of Fortunata's identity after a chance meeting at Mauricia's flat between the two rivals, during which Fortunata abuses Jacinta. This leads to conferences between the saint and the sinner, in which Guillermina upholds the priority of social law over the impulses of the heart. But curiously, although Fortunata resents the advice Guillermina gives her, she identifies her with her deceased friend Mauricia and transfers to her "the mysterious sympathy" which the latter had inspired in her. This begins when Fortunata lies in bed in a twilight sleep and envisages the saint with Mauricia's features and voice. Significantly, it is at this very moment that the idea of proving her honorable place in society by bearing Juanito a son takes shape in Fortunata's mind. It is a subconscious melding of Mauricia's declaration that love cannot be a sin and Guillermina's exhortation to obey the canons of society. The net result of Doña Guillermina's advice is not what she intended. By upholding the rights of the legitimate wife she simply strengthens Fortunata's resolve

that she, too, has claims to an honorable status, based on the laws of nature, through maternity.

Compared to Fortunata, the woman of the common people, Jacinta is a rather pale figure, just as virtue and conventional conduct is always less exciting than vice and rebelliousness. But, of all the socializing influences on Fortunata, Jacinta, as a model, is the most powerful. The "mania of imitation" is so strong that Fortunata proposes to her husband that they adopt a child, if possible the very boy that Jacinta had tried to adopt. Again, "emulation or the imitative mania" makes her say that if her husband became very sick she would devote herself unreservedly to caring for him. "And then *that* woman would see if here (in me) there are perfections or not," she thinks, as her hatred of her rival combines with her admiration.

Jacinta, like any human being, has natural physical and emotional drives, especially her intense maternal instinct, which makes her try to save a kitten lost in a sewer or dream that she is nursing a baby. She feels extreme jealousy when she overhears Fortunata's claim to be the real wife of Juanito. While she is capable of imagining that Moreno Isla, not Juanito, is the father of the baby Fortunata gives her, she has always refrained from giving her admirer any positive indication of the esteem, bordering on love, which she felt for him. In other words, Jacinta's feelings are usually cloaked under social propriety. Living as she does in the household of Juanito's parents, she cannot talk to them about the infidelities of their son.

Aurora, at the time still Fortunata's friend, accuses Jacinta of having an affair with Moreno Isla, himself a great believer in social propriety. The effect of this slander of Jacinta on Fortunata is devastating. If the angel, the model of virtue has fallen, what difference is there between the paramour and the legal wife? Social law no longer exists, only love, the natural law, reigns.

Fortunata makes the mistake of telling Juanito that his wife is unfaithful and gets an angry denial for her pains. Soon afterward Aurora changes her story: Jacinta is virtuous although she may have looked at the banker with a certain sympathy. "What difference does it make to you if she is honorable or not? What matters to you is that he loves you more than her" says Aurora. "'Oh, no!' exclaimed Fortunata with her whole soul. 'If that woman were not honorable it would seem to me that there is no honor in the world'." So the woman who has declared that love is the supreme law now maintains that social law is of at least equal importance. Fortunata has come a long way toward society's standards.

Maxi's tragedy is that he is "all spirit" but only "half a man" physically. Doctor Augusto Miquis, had he been consulted, would have advised him peremptorily to remain unmarried. A dreamer, he sees "things through the lense of his own ideas," which made all appear as it ought to be and not as it is. He is of course another example of a person deluded by giving way to his imagination, and so he conceives that he has a "mission"—like the romanticists—to redeem the fallen woman.

If Galdós has often condemned imagination, he now sees its workings in a new and different light. The idea of a successful marriage with Fortunata was a mad, impossible dream, and Maxi was a fool to entertain it. "But he was not an ordinary fool; he was one of those fools who touch the sublime with their finger tips. It's true that they don't grasp it, but they *do* touch it." Imagination leads him out of reality into a dream world, but imagination also lets him see Fortunata as a human being, his equal, not an outcast from society. It is the faculty through which the spirit must operate, for all activity which originates within a person (not determined by outside causes) must be imagined as a first step toward its consummation. Galdós has given ground on his distrust of imagination; in later works he will give more and more value to the combination of imagination and spirit.

So Maxi is a kind of poet as he perceives a possible "honorability of the soul" in Fortunata and when he declares to his aunt that he feels "a very great force" within him which impels him to her salvation. Viewed from a different angle, Maxi's dream is to socialize his adored one. He counts on the force of his love, just as powerful and unswerving as Fortunata's for Juanito, as the agent which will ultimately make her his and give her an honorable place in society. For his love is the very core of his being. Wise Don Evaristo, urging Fortunata to return to her husband, tells her, "Don't you see he is like you a passionate, sentimental man? He idolizes you and those who love in that way, madly, are eager to forgive." Maxi himself tells her that "the world is worth nothing except through love" and Fortunata also realizes, even as she leaves him for the third time, that this "poor little fellow" is "the only one who has truly loved me, the one who has pardoned me two times and would pardon me the third . . . and the fourth."

Maxi goes literally mad from love and contemplates liberation through suicide. Fortunata's death removes the cause of his aberration so that after viewing her tomb he can calmly survey their relationship. He tells his friend: "I loved her with my whole soul. I made of her the capital object of my life, and she did not respond to my desires. . . . I made a mistake, and she did too. I wasn't the only one deceived; she was also. We defrauded each other reciprocally. We did not count on Nature, which is the great mother and teacher that rectifies the errors of her wayward children. We do a thousand foolish things and she corrects them for us."

These words are the author's summing up of the conflict between natural and social laws, represented by free love and marriage. Galdós was a realist in his philosophic outlook as well as in literature. He knew that many idealistic goals could not be reached in the Spain of his time, no matter how worthy they might be. (pp. 93-101)

Maxi's dream is condemned to frustration by the *données* in which the author states his problem. Not only is Maxi impotent (or at least very nearly so) but Fortunata cannot stop loving Juanito, no matter how badly he treats her. Consequently nature must necessarily overcome society, as Maxi finally realizes.

A couple of pages after his calm and sane evaluation of his marriage, at the very end of the novel, Maxi expresses the wish to retire to a monastery. They take him to Leganés, the insane asylum near Madrid. He exclaims: "These fools probably think they are deceiving me! This is Leganés. I accept it, I accept it and say nothing, as a proof of the absolute submission of my will to whatever the world wishes to do with my person. They will not shut my thought within walls. I reside in the stars. Let them put the man called Maximiliano Rubín in a palace or in a dung heap. . . . It's all the same."

This passage, which shows Maxi achieving a spiritual peace, indifferent to the material world, can be compared to a famous scene in *War and Peace*, in which Pierre realizes that there is a "force of life" which works against the deterministic law of history. A prisoner of the French, forced to march away from Moscow, poorly fed, and bivouacing in the cold, Pierre realizes "that just as there is no position in the world in which a man can be happy and perfectly free, so too there is no position in which he need be unhappy and in bondage." Sitting on the cold ground, leaning against a wagon wheel, he bursts into laughter, and says, "They have taken me—shut me up. They keep me prisoner. Who is 'me'? Me—my immortal soul! Ha, ha, ha!" For the present writer there is an undeniable similarity between Maxi and Pierre's reaction to imprisonment. Both come to the identical conclusion that spiritual peace is all that matters and that material conditions are of no importance.

Although of course there are numerous ways in which the two men differ, the spiritual naturalism of both authors is incarnated principally in these two figures. (p. 102)

Walter T. Pattison, in his Benito Pérez Galdós, *Twayne Publishers, 1975, 181 p.*

V. S. PRITCHETT (essay date 1979)

[*Pritchett is a highly esteemed English novelist, short story writer, and critic. Considered one of the modern masters of the short story, he is also one of the world's most respected and well-read literary critics. Pritchett writes in the conversational tone of the familiar essay, approaching literature from the viewpoint of a lettered but not overly scholarly reader. In his criticism, Pritchett stresses his own experience; judgment, and sense of literary art rather than following a codified critical doctrine derived from a school of psychological or philosophical speculation. In the following excerpt, he praises* Fortunata and Jacinta.]

Pérez Galdós is the supreme Spanish novelist of the 19th century. His scores of novels are rightly compared with the work of Balzac and Dickens who were his masters, and even with Tolstoy's. Why then has he been almost totally neglected by foreigners? One reason is that wherever Spanish city life had anything in common with Western European societies, it appeared to be out of date and a provincial parody; and where there was no resemblance it was interpreted by foreign collectors of the outlandish and picturesque. One of the anglicized characters in his longest novel *Fortunata and Jacinta* returns to England saying, bitterly, that all the British want from Spain is tourist junk—and this in 1873! One could read the great Russians without needing to go to Russia; their voice carried across the frontiers. To grasp Galdós—it was felt—one had to go to Spain and submit to Spanish formality, pride and claustrophobia. Few readers outside of academic life did so.

These objections no longer have the same force and it is more likely that the great achievement of Galdós can be recognized here today. A few years ago, his short novel *The Spendthrifts (La de Bringas)* was translated by Gerald Brenan and Gamel Woolsey and now we have Lester Clark's complete translation of the 1,100 pages of his most ambitious novel [*Fortunata and Jacinta*]. It takes its place among those Victorian masterpieces that have presented the full-length portrait of a city.

The originality of Galdós springs, in part, from the fact that he was a silent outsider—he was brought up in the Canaries under English influences. In time he learned how to drift to the Spanish pace and then, following Balzacian prescription and energy, set out to become "the secretary of history." He is reported to have been a quiet and self-effacing man and this novel gets its inspiration from the years he spent listening to the voices of Madrid. His intimacy with every social group is never the sociologist's; it is the personal intimacy of the artist, indeed it can be said he disappears as a person and *becomes* the people, streets and kitchens, cafés and churches. This total absorption has been held against him: the greatest novelists, in some way, impose—the inquirer does not. Yet this very passivity matches a quality in Spanish life; and anyway he is not the dry inquirer; his inquiry is directed by feeling and especially by tolerant worship of every motion of the heart, a tenderness for its contradictions and its dreams, for its everyday impulses and also for those that are vibrant, extreme—even insane. He is an excellent story-teller, he loves the inventiveness of life itself. Preaching nothing overtly, he is a delicate and patient psychologist. It is extraordinary to find a novel written in the 1880s that documents the changes in the cloth trade, the rise and fall of certain kinds of café, the habits of usurers, politicians and catholic charities but also probes the fantasies and dreams of the characters and follows their inner thoughts. Galdós is fascinated by the psychology of imitation and the primitive unconscious. He changes the "point of view" without regard to the rules of the novelist's game. We are as sure of the likeness of each character as we are of the figures in a Dutch painting and yet they are never set or frozen, they are always moving in space in the Tolstoyan fashion. The secret of the gift of Galdós lies, I think, in his timing, his leisurely precision and above all in his ear for dialogue; his people live in speech, either to themselves or to each other. He was a born assimilator of speech of all kinds from the rich skirling dialect of the slums or the baby-language of lovers, to the even more difficult speech of people who are trying to express or evade more complex thoughts.

The dramatic thread that runs through the panorama of life in Madrid in 1873 is the story of the love and destructive jealousy of two women. Fortunata is a beautiful and ignorant slum girl who is seduced by the idle son of rich shopkeepers before his marriage and bears him a son who dies. Jacinta becomes the young man's beautiful but pathetic wife, tormented less by her husband's love affairs than by the fact that she cannot bear children. The deserted Fortunata takes up a life of promiscuity from which a feeble and idealistic young chemist sets about rescuing her. She longs to be a respectable wife and is bullied into going into a convent for a time so that she can be reformed. But she cannot get over her love of her seducer and although she comes out of the convent and marries the chemist, she feels no affection for him. He is indeed impotent, and going from one philosophical or religious mania to another, ends by becoming insane and murderous in his jealousy of her first lover who has resumed the pursuit. It becomes a battle, therefore, between the bourgeois wife and the loose woman. Fortunata is a tragic figure of the people, a victim of her own sensual impulses who, in the end, has a second child by her seducer and regards herself as his true respectable wife because the other is barren. But her child is taken over by the rich and legitimate wife and Fortunata dies raging. The scene is overwhelming. The last time I wept over a novel was in reading *Tess* when I was 18. Fifty years later Fortunata has made me weep again. Not simply because of her death but because Galdós had portrayed a woman whole in all her moods. In our own 19th-century novels this situation would be melodramatic and morally overweighted—see George Eliot's treatment of Hetty Sorrel—but in Galdós there is no such excess. The bourgeois wife is in her limited way as attractive as Fortunata.

Among the large number of Fortunata's friends, enemies and neighbours, there are two or three portraits that are in their own way as powerful as hers. First there is Mauricia la Dura, an incorrigible, violent and drunken prostitute to whom Fortunata is drawn against her will in the convent. Mauricia attracts by the terror and melancholy of her face. She is a genuine Spanish primitive. There is a long and superb scene in which

she manages to get hold of some brandy in the convent and passes from religious ecstasy to blasphemy, theft and violence. It is a mark of the great novelist that he can invent a fantastic scene like this and then, later on, take us into the mind of the violent girl after she has got over her mania. Galdós knows how to return to the norm:

> "I was beside myself. I only remember I saw the Blessed Virgin and then I wanted to go into the church to get the Holy Sacrament. I dreamt I ate the Host—I've never had such a bad bout. . . . The things that go through your mind when the devil goes to your head. Believe me because I'm telling you. When I came to my senses I was so ashamed. . . . The only one I hated was that Chaplain. I'd have bitten chunks out of him. But not the nuns. I wanted to beg their forgiveness; but my dignity wouldn't let me. What upset me most was having thrown a bit of brick at Doña Guillermina, I'll never forget that—never—And I'm so afraid that when I see her coming along the street my face colours up and I go by on the other side so that she won't see me."

Doña Guillermina, a rich woman who has given up everything for the rescue work, is another fine portrait of the practical good-humoured saint, a sort of Santa Teresa who—and this shows the acuteness of the novelist's observation—can be frightened, a shade automatic, and sometimes totally at a loss. Against her must be placed Doña Lupe, a lower-middle-class moneylender. She is a miser who shouts to her maid:

> "Clean your feet on the next-door shoe-scraper . . . because the fewer people who use ours, the more we gain."

But at the wedding of Fortunata to her nephew we recognise Doña Lupe as more than a grotesque. Galdós is superior to Balzac in not confining people to a single dominant passion:

> Once back in the house, Doña Lupe seemed to have burst from her skin for she grew and multiplied remarkably. . . . You would have thought there were three or four widow Jaurequis in the house, all functioning at the same time. Her mind was boiling at the possibility of the lunch not going well. But if it turned out well what a triumph! Her heart beat violently, pumping feverish heat all over her body, and even the ball of cottonwool at her breast [she had had one breast removed] seemed to be endowed with its share of life, being allowed to feel pain and worry.

The final large character is Max, the husband of Fortunata. She dislikes him, but he has "saved" her. Puny and sexless, Max begins to seek relief in self-aggrandizement, first of all in prim and ingenuous idealism; when he realizes his marriage is null and that his "cure" of Fortunata is a failure, he turns to experimenting with pills and hopes to find a commerical cure-all. His efforts are incompetent and dangerous. The next stage is paranoia caused by sexual jealousy. He moves on to religious mania: thinks of murder and then invites his wife to join him in a suicide pact, in order to rid the world of sin. For a while he is mad and then, suddenly, he recovers and "sees his true situation"—but recovery turns him into a blank non-being. Here we see Galdós' belief in imitative neurosis, for in a terrible scene poor Fortunata is infected with her husband's discarded belief in violence. She declares she will love him utterly, if only he will go and murder her libertine lover. But Max has fallen into complete passivity: he enters a monastery where he will become a solitary mystic—and he does not realize that the monastery he has chosen is, in fact, an asylum.

It is surprising to find this Dostoevskian study in Galdós but, of course, Spanish life can offer dozens of such figures. They are examples of what Spanish writers have often noted: the tendency of the self to be obdurately as it is and yet to project itself into some universal extreme, to think of itself mystically as God or the universe. But usually—as Galdós showed in his portrait of the ivory-carving civil servant in *The Spendthrifts*—such characters are simply bizarre and finicking melancholics. Around them stand the crowd of self-dramatizers in the old cafés, the pious church-going ladies, the various types of priest, the shouters of the slums. What is more important is his ability to mount excellent scenes, and in doing so, to follow the feelings of his people with a tolerant and warm detachment. He is never sentimental. There is one fine example of his originality and total dissimilarity from other European novelists in his long account of Jacinta's honeymoon. The happy girl cannot resist acting unwisely: little by little she tries to find out about her husband's early love affair, mainly to increase the excitement of her own love. No harm comes of this dangerous love game, but we realize that here is a novelist who can describe early married life without reserves and hit upon the piquancy that is its spell. I can think of no honeymoon in literature to match this one. The fact is that Galdós accepts human nature without resentment. (pp. 152-57)

> *V. S. Pritchett, "Benito Pérez Galdós: A Spanish Balzac," in his* The Myth Makers: Literary Essays, *Random House, 1979, pp. 152-57.*

BRIAN J. DENDLE (essay date 1980)

[*Dendle is an English-born American critic and the author of several studies of Galdós's work. In the following excerpt, he examines the ways in which the* National Episodes *written after 1898 reflect Galdós's concern with Spanish politics of the time.*]

In part, Galdós uses the *Episodios* [written between 1898 and 1912] to comment directly on the concerns of his own day. The mark of 1898 is apparent in his warnings against fraternal strife, his disgust with rhetoric, and his hostility to Spanish involvement in foreign adventures. He for a while flirts with Costa's authoritarian solutions to Spain's problems. By early 1900, however, he openly satirizes the fatuous arrogance of self-appointed regenerators. Contemporary Liberal campaigns to submit the Church to a *Ley de Asociaciones* have their counterpart in the virulent anti-clericalism of certain *Episodios*. Such issues of the early twentieth century as the education of princes, the influence of *camarillas*, and Catalan claims to special treatment all provoke Galdós's remark. Portrayal of the past is affected by the politics of the present. Thus, the Revolution of 1868, grudgingly accepted in *Prim* (1906), is, after Galdós's conversion to Republicanism, harshly attacked in *La de los tristes destinos* (1907). Similarly, in novel after novel of the fifth series, Galdós lectures the Republicans of his own day on the shortcomings of their political ancestors.

Galdós's treatment of the past is selective and is strongly colored by hindsight. Within the individual *Episodio*, Galdós traces the reactions of those observing and participating in history. His overriding vision, however, reflects less the perceptions of the Spaniards of a previous age than Galdós's preconceived determination that the events he evokes are links in a chain leading to the "disaster" of the end of the century. The wealth of historical detail, the brilliant pastiches, the consistent, if pessimistic, vision of nineteenth-century Spain, will, I believe, deceive the reader anxious for enlightenment on Spain's past. The Spain so vividly created in the *Episodios* reflects the fertile imagination of a novelist, not the reasoned assembly of facts and arguments of a historian. Galdós's research for the *Episodios* was hasty; he sought from sources and correspondents colorful details rather than an understanding of the past on its own terms. Historical recreation was often accessory to the exigencies of a fictional narrative rooted in a moral vision of Spain.

Galdós's rejection of conventional histories is most apparent in the *Episodios* of the fourth and fifth series: "history" is now merely the symptom of an underlying reality, which is best expressed in terms of literary metaphor (the styling of periods or events as "tragic" or "comic opera," the recourse to symbolic characters and to fantasy). Indicative of his increasing aversion to a history based on facts are the "historians" he portrays in the later *Episodios:* the unstable Fajardo who seeks, in his history, an abstraction, the essential soul of Spain; the demented *Confusio*, who composes his "logical history" of Spain in a lunatic asylum; and Tito Liviano, who as narrator doubts his own existence.

Galdós's most marked bias in the later *Episodios* is that of an all-pervading pessimism. The hostility, and even contempt, with which he regards his compatriots is at times staggering. Galdós's Spain is but one step away from extinction: neglect of agriculture, racial degeneration, civil war, murder, suicide, and mindless despotism characterize a nation driven to self-destruction. The pages of the *Episodios nacionales* teem with whores, opportunistic politicians, degenerate aristocrats, Carlist savages, hypocrites, and the fatuous. Rare in these novels are those who, such as the Arratias, contribute in positive fashion to national life. But above all else, Galdós populates the *Episodios* with madmen: the schizophrenic Fago; the ranting, suicidal young Calpena; the hysterical Aura Negretti who sets out to kill her guardian; Nelet, murderer and suicide; Santiago Ibero, violent, superstitious, and afflicted by religious melancholia; Alonso de Castro-Amézaga, Montes de Oca, and General Ortega, quixotic dreamers whose idealism masks a suicidal urge; the Fajardo who, guided by his unconscious, murders Bartolomé Gracián; this same Gracián, forever seeking the impossible; a Lucila who, before her marriage, is homicidal and deranged; Santiuste, who acts compulsively and who ends his career in an asylum for the insane; the mentally unbalanced Santiago Ibero the younger; the homicidally insane Fernanda; Nicéfora, neurotically beyond the reach of any reason; and Tito Liviano, neurotic, fickle, a prey to panic terrors, reduced at times to idiocy.

Despite Galdós's constant strictures against abstract thought, the Spain of the later *Episodios nacionales* is at heart an abstraction. In his two historical novels—*El audaz* and *La fontana de oro*—Galdós had portrayed individuals caught up in a concrete historical situation. In the *Episodios,* however, novelistic characters embody aspects of the national soul; they symbolize (with corresponding loss of individuality), rather than respond to, the historical context. Thus, Galdós rarely seeks to explain the past by the interplay of historical forces or individual decisions. Instead, historical events are merely symptoms of an insanity that has afflicted Spanish life throughout the nineteenth century. The analysis of Spain's madness is consequently of greater concern to Galdós than the deeds of historic figures.

Because Spain's problems are rooted not in history but in the mind, Galdós's remedies are those of the alienist, not of the politician or of the social planner. There are no national solutions; an individual may with difficulty reform himself, but the reform of others is an impossibility. Ideology is irrelevant; behavior has primacy over thought. (Thus, our day-to-day activities, rather than our goals or beliefs, determined our mode of being.) Spaniards must avoid excessive excitement or—the reverse side of Quixotry—skepticism or depression. To this end, their activities must be ordered by intelligent direction, by the equivalent, indeed, of a parent or director of a lunatic asylum. The new Spaniard, "cured" by experience and by reflection of compulsive behavior, will view the world dispassionately. He will have self-knowledge (and the examination in the *Episodios* of Spain's past will reveal the self-defeating pattern of Spanish existence), will devote himself to work (and Fajardo's writing is presented as a form of therapy), and will be aware of and interested in others.

If we accept Galdós's initial premises—that nation may be assimilated to individual, that Spaniards, both collectively and individually, are insane—Galdós's prescriptions for moral reform are unassailable. In the Spain portrayed in the *Episodios,* however, Galdós's remedies are utopian and without practical consequences. Galdós, in any case, has little faith that a new Spaniard—aware, decisive, emotionally detached—will replace the old. The appeals for total revolution, which extend in the *Episodios* from *Mendizábal* to the final novel *Cánovas,* reflect disgust with the past and present behavior of Spaniards, not a vision of the future. The revolution, moreover, is not intended for the Spaniards whom Galdós so harshly castigates in the *Episodios:* Tito Liviano must be totally reconstructed before entry into the promised land is possible. Significantly, Galdós is unable to envision in a Spanish context those few Spaniards (the Calpenas and the Iberos, Teresa Villaescusa and Santiaguito Ibero) who do achieve spiritual health. Their moral growth takes place independently of history; they remove themselves from Spanish reality, fleeing to the never-never land of France. Paradoxically, those who have truly learned the lesson of experience can no longer contribute to Spain; thus, Santiaguito Ibero in 1868 immediately abandons the Revolution for which he had so long struggled.

I have been unable to discern in the *Episodios nacionales* the "benevolence" that other critics have perceived in these novels; indeed, Galdós's hostility to his fellow countrymen is often savage. Rather than benevolent, Galdós is evasive in his treatment of persons and matters that touch him closely: he is guarded in his judgments of such political figures of his own lifetime as Prim, Cánovas, and Sagasta; he manifestly shirks coming to terms, in *La vuelta al mundo en la Numancia,* with the agrarian problem; he is most reticent in the brief references in the fifth series to his own youth in Madrid. A similar pattern of retreat is evident in the behavior of the protagonists of the *Episodios:* involvement in political activity is followed by withdrawal, even flight. Furthermore, the "keys" with which Galdós explains Spanish history—national insanity, atavism, the preponderant role of the Church—represent an oversimplification, a refusal to treat in all its complexity a given historical situation.

I wish to conclude . . . on a note that, given the inadequacy of our knowledge of the man Galdós, must necessarily be speculative. In the later *Episodios,* Galdós has, I suspect, transferred

to the national scene a conflict that has its origins within his own psyche. At the most superficial level, Galdós offers soothing remedies for an overexcited nation: a calm detachment, self-awareness, therapeutic labor, the avoidance of fantasy, even at times the indulgent protection of a loving woman. When outside world and elements from within himself cannot be brought into harmony, Galdós takes refuge in evasion. But at a deeper level—and one that receives free rein in the later *Episodios*—Galdós is bitterly hostile and obsessed with themes of madness, of nightmare, and of catastrophe. The "Spain" that Galdós so unsympathetically analyzes in the *Episodios* is in part himself; the excesses against which he warns us—of the imagination, of a too great facility with words, of confusing word for deed—are his own; his "remedies" smack of personal defenses against internal demons. It is a common place that Galdós in part portrayed himself in Vicente Halconero (his youth in Madrid, his readings, his "half-will") and in Tito Liviano (his journalism, his seedy amorousness, his temporary physical blindness). It is possible also, I would suggest, that darker elements of Galdós's soul entered the portrayals of Halconero and Liviano: Halconero's suicidal thoughts (after amorous disappointment); Tito Liviano's melancholia, terrors, and depression. Similarly, Bartolomé Gracián's neurotic pursuit of the impossible, so vividly etched in *La revolución de julio,* is also Galdós's own; Gracián's murder, by Galdós's alter ego Fajardo, represents Galdós's brutal disposal of socially destructive elements existing within his own character. The therapeutic message of the *Episodios* was not only intended for the nation, it was also, in part, in Galdós's dialogue with himself. (pp. 182-86)

Brian J. Dendle, in his Galdós: The Mature Thought, *The University Press of Kentucky, 1980, 207 p.*

STEPHEN GILMAN   (essay date 1981)

[*Gilman is an American critic specializing in the study of Spanish literature. In the following excerpt, he examines Galdós's approach to writing historical novels through an analysis of the opening paragraph of* Fortunata and Jacinta.]

Meditation on a novel "afterwards" is a mournful task, but it does have one advantage over experiencing a novel in its immediacy as a "now." It permits unexpectedly illuminating comparisons with the assembled "afterwards" of other novels, primarily comparisons with those of the same novelist and secondarily with those of other novelists that we remember well enough to compare. Let us, therefore, begin by trying to recall whether the offhand and careless overture of *Fortunata y Jacinta* has precedents in prior or posterior novels of Galdós.

My first impression, subsequently confirmed by rapid rereading, is that our introduction to Juanito offers a more puzzling discrepancy than meaningful comparison with the beginnings of those "novelas contemporáneas" that readers of Galdós remember most vividly. Indeed, the first pages of *La desheredada, Tormento, El amigo Manso, Nazarín, La de Bringas,* and *Misericordia,* to choose virtually unforgettable examples, show their author to have been a past master of the art of arresting novelistic initiation. By "educating the responses and guiding the collaboration of the reader," they confirm Martin Price's observation that "the openings of novels serve to set the rules of the game to be played by the reader." Abrupt literary echoes (the mad monologue of Rufete, at once Cervantine and Zolaesque, or Ido's theatrically Romantic encounter with Centeno), elaborate emblematic descriptions (the two-faced church of San Sebastián or Bringas' myopic mosaic), and challenging disavowals of point of view (Manso's "yo no existo" ["I don't exist"] or the unidentifiability of the narrator of Nazarín's haphazard martyrdom) all contrive to remind us by means of surprise, provocation, or recollection that in each case we must once again try to learn the ever-changing rules of the novelistic game.

In *Fortunata y Jacinta,* however, Galdós employs an antithetical procedure. Rather than trying to guide us by catching our attention, he seems purposefully to be inviting our disinterest. Here is the long, first paragraph, which I reproduce for the benefit of those whose recollections of it may not be as sharply etched as mine:

> Juanito Santa Cruz
>
> The most remote information I have been able to gather concerning the person who bears this name came from Jacinto María Villalonga and dates back to the time when that friend of mine and his buddies, Zalamero, Joaquinito Pez, Alejandro Miquis, were to be seen in the lecture rooms of the University. They were not all members of the same class, and although they all met in Camus' course, they were at different levels when it came to Roman law. The Santa Cruz boy was a student of Novar's and Villalonga of Coronado's. Nor did they show the same degree of scholarly dedication: Zalamero, serious and solemn, was the sort of fellow who sits in the front row looking at the professor with an appreciative expression and nodding his head approvingly at every affirmation. Santa Cruz and Villalonga did just the opposite; they would sit as far up the aisle as possible, wrapped up in their capes, and looking more like conspirators than students. There they passed the time talking in low voices, reading novels, drawing funny pictures, or whispering the answer to each other whenever the professor would ask them a question. Juanito Santa Cruz and Miquis took a skillet one day (I am not sure whether to Camus' lecture or to that of Uribe's on metaphysics) and proceeded to fry some eggs. Villalonga has told me a lot more of such mischief, which I shall not repeat in order not to lengthen this account unnecessarily. All of them (with the exception of Miquis, who died in '64 dreaming of being worthy of Schiller's fame) took part in the celebrated scuffle of the night of Saint Daniel. Even goody-goody little Zalamero got excited on that noisy occasion and whistled and screamed like a wild man, for which he got his ears boxed by a veteran law officer but with no further consequences. Villalonga and Santa Cruz, however, had a harder time. The former was laid up by a saber thrust in the shoulder for two endless months, while the latter was caught on the corner by the Royal Theater and taken to the lockup with a group of other prisoners, students as well as various delinquents of shadier background. They kept him on ice there for almost twenty-four hours, and his captivity might have been longer if on the eleventh his papá, a very respectable person

with excellent connections, had not arranged for his release.

The technique employed at the very beginning of this passage is particularly curious. By using the name Juanito Santa Cruz as the chapter title and then referring to him in the text as "la persona que lleva este nombre" ["the person who bears this name"], Galdós projects into our minds a virtual image of the manuscript page and of himself laboriously composing it. When we come to the indentification we have to glance back and *up* to the title in order to understand it, a glance that makes us aware of the page itself as an undifferentiated unity. The title is not merely the author's name for a segment of narration (to be remembered subliminally during the reading process as if enclosed in brackets) but rather becomes a part of it, as if it were the heading of a report. This, in turn, tacitly defines the narrator as a reporter, a private detective, or a hired scholar, whose duty it is to collect and submit in writing information concerning an individual under investigation. Thus, also, the tone of carelessness, which disconcerts us in retrospect. . . . [The] narrator-reporter's collection of fragmentary facts and snippets of anecdotes seems even to him so boring and pointless that, before the paragraph has ended, he decides to omit data "para no alargar este relato" ["so as not to lengthen this story"]. Not only may the reader be put off by such stale stuff, but also the presumably mercenary "relator" himself does not hesitate to express his ennui.

Irony aside (the "relato" will, like the Restoration itself, continue to grow in spite of the "relator's" desire to stop it), what Galdós has accomplished is clear. He has used a facsimile of documentation, not to provide verisimilitude, but to diminish the interest of the opening statement. . . . [This stands in contrast to] the so-called documentary pretense (excitingly "true" manuscripts discovered in bottles, vaults, or flea markets and in more recent years excitingly "relevant" psychiatric tapes, dossiers, or trial transcripts) designed to help us suspend our disbelief. Galdós, on the other hand, by means of the somewhat paradoxical act of pretending to be the writer of his own document, cunningly subverts the age-old device. He has suspended our potential concern for what he has to tell us, and at the same time he has clearly distinguished the narrator from himself.

Why should he do so? In order to understand the malice of Galdós' unexpected return to and sardonic internalization of this novelistic pawn to Queen's four, further comparison is necessary. The documentary pretense is, if we stop to think about it, a primordial version of another, equally familiar opening gambit: that corresponding to what might be called the historical pretense. The opening sentence of Dumas' *Le Vicomte de Bragelonne* will serve to remind us of all the novels of this sort that we have loved and lost: "Towards the middle of the month of May, in the year 1660, at nine o'clock in the morning, when the sun, already high in the sky, was fast absorbing the dew from the ravenelles of the castle of Blois, a little cavalcade composed of three men and two pages reentered the city by the bridge. . . ." Nothing is new under the sun (meaning that I do not dare rule out categorically the possibility of examples prior to the nineteenth century), but it seems obvious that this—to us—standard beginning corresponds to Sir Walter Scott's view of history as an "elsewhere" to be excavated archaeologically and revived artistically. Accordingly, the historical novel does not begin with a birth (*Lazarillo de Tormes*), a self-introduction (*Moby Dick*), nor a generative action (the meeting of Calisto and Melibea) but with a threshold: an inviting entryway into another time and space. Instead of a physical document, documented history incites our belief and entices our participation.

The rise of the nineteenth-century novel from its Scottian origins requires no further presentation here, but it should be pointed out that the historical pretense with its initial threshold was not abandoned when novelists turned from the Middle Ages and the Scottish Highlands to the great cities of their own time. The "little cavalcade" and the "lone riders who might be seen" on the first pages of Western fiction were to become railroad passengers (***Doña Perfecta***, *The Idiot*) and even more recently lone couples getting undressed in suburbia. Once Scott and his emulators had shown how effective it could be to pinpoint a specific intersection of time and space other than ("elsewhere" than) the "now" of our watch and the "here" of our hammock, the practice became habitual. My point is obvious: it was precisely such a beginning accompanied by its customarily seductive expectations that Galdós, in launching ***Fortunata y Jacinta***, sought to avoid at all costs. Instead of the mysterious past of the Middle Ages or the mysterious present of the metropolis (as perilous and unexplored as Cooper's American wilderness), he chooses to introduce his reader to his own only-too-familiar and only-too-trivial Madrid. And for this a documentary pretense, suitably familiarized and trivialized, would serve far better than a "little cavalcade" of "señoritos" who might have been seen on their way to the University on a fine morning in the Spring of 1864.

Another factor to be considered is that the documentary pretense enables a fictional narrator to be present as writer or discoverer of the document whereas the historical pretense tends to eliminate him. Thresholds such as that of *Le Vicomte de Bragelonne* are usually presented without overt stylistic intervention on the part of the narrator's voice. The essential facts—location, date, time of day or night, weather conditions, mode of locomotion, personal identity or identities—are stated without irony, lyrical enthusiasm, or rhetorical intentionality of any sort. The reason is clear. The irresistible enticement of a surrogate world consists in its very existence, in that unquestioned illusion of reality, which would inevitably be diminished by the slightest intimation of an intrusion on the part of the storyteller. Indeed, the sooner we forget that Dumas or Scott (or their surrogates) exists, the sooner we are able to enjoy what Ortega y Gasset called our liberating "submersion" in the "then" and "there" of their novels. Instead of a fictional document discovered, glossed, or edited by a discoverer, commentator, or editor (activities) which necessarily imply interpretation), the page itself is presented as if it were documentary. It becomes a document, which the reader himself discovers in the act of opening the novel to its first page. Galdós, however, makes us aware of the pretense, and, in so doing (in spite of the growing unobtrusiveness of his narrator as the novel progresses), he is far closer to Defoe and the Cela of *Pascual Duarte* than he is to the historical and realistic novelists of his century.

In other words, it was what we might term inherent novelistic believability the comfortable habit of automatically attributing historical truth to fiction on the fragile basis of a date and a place name, that Galdós could not accept. He wants to be present and on the scene (in the persona of his bored narrator) in order to warn us against himself and against the easy magic he has at his command. Instead of letting us (with prefabricated naiveté and experienced "voluptuousness") believe in his "historia de dos casadas" ["history of two married women"]

just because it *seems* historical, he prefers to teach us to recognize it for what it is (or what it would be if it were): a compilation of more or less reliable and interesting facts by a more or less reliable and disinterested investigator. At the beginning of *La desheredada* Galdós indicates that all lives are potential novels; but now, having just finished *Lo prohibido*, he realized that biography, that is, personal experience understood historically, has no necessary significance. History for Scott and Balzac was a fascinating new revelation; for Stendhal and the mature Galdós, on the contrary, it represented the degeneration of the human condition in the nineteenth century. At best, in their view, it could be justified only when it challenged or "incited" the potential greatness of such exceptional individuals as heroes, villains, saints, and self-proclaimed angels.

The two characteristics just discussed, presentation of the prosaic Madrid that was familiar to his readers and self-presentation of the narrator as critic of his own narrative, inevitably remind us of the most famous of all novel beginnings. The flaunted carelessness, the tone of weary acquiescence, and the half-veiled scorn for the future hero and his world all amount to saying: "En un lugarón de España . . . no ha mucho tiempo . . . vivía un señorito de los de . . . de cuyas mocedades no quiero acordarme" ["In an overgrown village in Spain . . . not too long ago . . . there lived one of those dandies who usually . . . and whose youthful exploits I have no desire to recollect"]. Just as in the *Quijote*, the intentional insignificance of the initial documentation in ***Fortunata y Jacinta*** constitutes a negative point of departure for the immense significance that was waiting to be discovered and explored novelistically. At the same time, the critique of contemporary history as such (the wretched university ambiance, the ironical reference to "aquella célebre noche de San Daniel" almost as if it were an "anti-episodio") reveals tacitly a more fundamental similarity. Just as the *Quijote* on one level is a reply to those Romances of Chivalry that compensate for their exaggerations by pretending to be chronicles (the documentary pretence is inherent in the genre), so ***Fortunata y Jacinta***, as we remarked earlier, is to be an antihistorical novel. Not a parody, but an answer to the kind of fiction that began with Scott and seemed to have exhausted its authentic innovation—its "novelty"—with the saga of the Rougon-Macquarts.

I am not trying to suggest that Galdós did not dote on the major novels of his century, or that his considered opinion of their literary worth was as negative as that of the Cervantes of the Romances of Chivalry (who in the "escrutinio," in addition to applying critical theory, nevertheless revealed how hopelessly addicted he was to popular fiction). Rather ***Fortunata y Jacinta***'s nineteenth-century echo of "En un lugar de la Mancha . . ." ["In a village in La Mancha . . ."] corresponds to its author's intention to turn his immediate novelistic tradition inside out, to create a deicidal weapons-system capable of finishing off the latter-day divinity called history. Just as Cervantes satirized the Romances of Chivalry as a means of relieving his readers of the burden of their history and society (insofar as they conformed to stereotyped neo-chivalric roles), so Galdós in creating Fortunata proposed to relieve his readers of the burden of their historicism. . . . [Twelve] years ahead of his time, Galdós anticipates the Generation of '98 with a Cervantine attack on the central bastion of nineteenth-century awareness. Hence, a novel that is to end with ironic transfiguration and transcendence begins with what Roland Barthes might have called "le degré zéro de l'histoire," the deservedly forgotten, time-vulnerable reminiscences and anecdotes of a class reunion. (pp. 360-67)

> *Stephen Gilman, in his* Galdós and the Art of the European Novel : 1867-1887, *Princeton University Press, 1981, 413 p.*

BRIAN J. DENDLE   (essay date 1986)

[*In the following discussion of the first two series of* National Episodes, *Dendle concludes that, despite their essentially historical nature, the* National Episodes *can best be understood in terms of Galdós's purely literary and didactic aims.*]

In the first two series of *Episodios nacionales,* Galdós offers a starkly pessimistic vision of a nation teeming with beggars, rogues, religious fanatics, bestial mobs, degenerate aristocrats, political opportunists, corrupt clerics, undisciplined soldiers, demented revolutionaries, hypocritical *moderados,* naive *progresistas,* and *guerrilleros* who represent a throwback to more primitive times. Galdós seeks in the past, not so much the chain of cause and effect leading to Spain's present state, but rather examples of the same moral failings and erroneous behavior that he finds in his contemporaries. "Todos los disparates que hacemos hoy los hemos hecho antes en mayor grado" (All the absurdities that we commit today, we have done before to a greater degree). Dominating Galdós's thought is the inability of the Revolution of 1868 to establish in Spain stable liberal institutions; he thus inveighs time and time again against those elements in Spanish life that he considers most responsible for past and present disorder: the violence of an ignorant mob, the savagery of the Carlists, and the ingenuousness and self-seeking of Spain's liberals. Above all, Galdós attacks the moral and intellectual defects of his compatriots: demagoguery, indiscipline, fatuousness, irrationality, idleness, despotism, envy, theatricality, and the taking of form for substance. Spaniards suffer from selfishness *(egoísmo)* and an inability to perceive reality; thus, ideology and behavior are separate; there is no connection between Christianity and officially proclaimed "religion," nor between liberal pretensions and the petty envies and attempts at self-aggrandizement of Spanish reformers.

The vivid presentation of Spanish shortcomings at times obscures the positive elements of Galdós's teaching. For Galdós, the solution to Spain's ills is to be sought neither in abrupt change nor in ideology, which, he claims, always conceals a personal motivation. His remedies are a mixture of those of classical nineteenth-century liberalism (careful thought, the acceptance of personal responsibility, the preservation and strengthening of social order) and a compassionate form of Christianity. No true revolution is possible until Spaniards learn mutual respect, perseverance, the avoidance of excess, industriousness, self-control, and individual duty.

An important component of Galdós's teaching in the *Episodios* is the call to reason, to critical thought. The members of a mob, the masonic conspirators, the Carlist *guerrilleros,* and the proletarian household of *Un faccioso más y unos frailes menos* can, with their lack of rationality, only destroy. Throughout the *Episodios,* Araceli, Monsalud, Inés, the knife grinder Pacorro Chinitas, Amaranta, the mature Jenara, and others assume at times the exemplary role of *raisonneurs,* as they discuss and judge—rather than merely react to—the course of individual and national history. Gabriel Araceli, with his constant ironic undercutting of his own statements, obliges the reader to distance himself, to discriminate between the truth

and falsehood of his claims. Similarly, the divorce between Spanish reality and Spanish political rhetoric, whether absolutist or liberal, forces the reader to adopt an independent, critical position. Even two novels that ostensibly demonstrate Spanish heroism—*Trafalgar* and *Zaragoza*—have as undercurrent the insistent questioning of the utility of Spanish sacrifice.

Thought must also be accompanied by effort. The freedom of the liberal state, like the maturity of an individual, is not given but must be achieved. Instant, that is, revolutionary, solutions to national and personal problems are rejected. As Inés and Solita teach, there are no shortcuts to happiness and prosperity; we must accept our human limitations and, like the nation, merit our independence by unceasing endeavor. Much time is needed, both Araceli and Monsalud recognize, before national customs and habits of mind will change. Nevertheless, constant effort will bring success, as Araceli and Monsalud demonstrate as they learn to take responsibility for themselves and others. Even Benigno Cordero, a man of mediocre intellect, with perseverance attains prosperity and domestic happiness. A correct attitude is essential: thus, Santorcaz, who gives way to despair and resentment, accomplishes nothing; Araceli, Inés, Solita, and Benigno Cordero, on the other hand, despite occasional backslidings, have a basic cheerfulness and optimism that serve them well.

The social order, essential for the development of the individual and preservation of the nation, must be defended. Throughout the *Episodios,* Galdós approvingly presents examples of forceful leadership, scorns weak rulers, and attacks elements of disorder such as the mob and Carlist *guerrilleros.* Those who disturb the social order, like Lord Gray, Mosén Antón, Santorcaz, the revolutionaries with their bizarre speech, are to be pitied, not emulated; they are suffering from a form of madness and must be healed or destroyed. Inés and Solita preserve the values of society; thus, Inés refuses to elope with Araceli, knowing that defiance of societal rules will lead only to future unhappiness. Araceli, accepting responsibility not only for himself but also for others, defends society by challenging and killing Lord Gray. Nation and individuals are not inherently strong; they often need protection if they are to be guided to self-reliance. Thus, Spain needs leaders to prevent anarchy; Santorcaz depends on Inés to achieve sanity and peace; Monsalud, in his weakness, implores his mother and Solita to prevent his elopement with Jenara. In his defense of the fundamental values of society, however, Galdós is no supporter of the status quo. Numerous barriers that prevent the development of individual or nation must be removed: the rights of primogeniture, aristocratic privilege, repressive education, whether in the home or convent, the stranglehold of the Church on marriage, arbitrary or ineffective government, the ignorance and random violence that pervade the lower and rural classes of Spain.

As Francisco Pérez Gutiérrez has indicated, Galdós's moral teaching is Christian in its concern for others. The Spanish Church is condemned for its lack of spirituality and compassion, its encouragement of superstition, its repressive attitudes that lead to mania or sterile revolt, its venality, its meddling in politics, its warrior priests, the squabbling of religious orders. The other deviation from the norm of Christian love, the imbecilic anti-clericalism of Gallardo and the masonic conspirators, is equally condemned. Throughout the *Episodios,* there is reference to a higher moral law, expressed in the teaching and behavior of Inés and Solita and based on a compassion and a sacrifice of self that involve a heightening, and not a loss, of personality. Examples of the concern for others are many: Araceli and Inés protect Asunción; Solita cares for Sarmiento; Monsalud attempts to save his brother. Exemplary also is Inés's guidance of Santorcaz to a holy death, which demands his acceptance of reason and thus renunciation of revolutionary gibberish, abandonment of hatred and pride, and reconciliation with those he has offended. By way of contrast, those who give way to selfish passion—Lord Gray, Mosén Antón, Jenara de Baraona, Pepet Armengol, the Monsalud of romantic despair—bring only ruin on themselves and others.

An earlier generation of critics praised the *Episodios* above all for their accurate or "realistic" rendering of history. Galdós's presentation of historical events and characters is, however, superficial and heavily biased. The history is simplified, narrowly focused, presented at a high emotional level, and designed to appeal to the imagination rather than to give any understanding of the complexity of events or issues involved; no serious historian would, I suspect, consult the first two series of *Episodios* for insights into Spanish history of the period 1805 to 1834. Galdós's preparation for the *Episodios* was cursory: he read a limited number of historical works; although he frequently did not wait for a reply, he appealed to Mesonero and others for details of physiognomy and dress sufficient to provide local color and the appearance of historical accuracy. Despite Galdós's theoretical defense of "la vida interna," the history of the *Episodios* is linked to that of conventional nineteenth-century histories: battles, revolutions, the debates in the *Cortes*, the deeds of monarchs. Galdós's treatment of history is colorful, impressionistic, episodic, and markedly politicized. The caricature portraits of Riego, Fernando VII, the absolutists, and the masons would strain the credulity of even the most partisan of readers; similarly, the vision of a Spain divided between the forces of madness and those of enlightenment is dramatic and literary, rather than a "realistic" evocation of a historical moment. Furthermore, the characters of the *Episodios* are placed in a moral, rather than historical, universe; for this reason, Araceli and Monsalud often seem strangely detached from the Spain in which they live.

Rather than as novels of historical *vulgarización*, the *Episodios* should be treated above all as highly creative works of the imagination. Galdós's range in the *Episodios* is considerable. There are frequent changes of scene: both geographical (Cádiz, Madrid, Zaragoza, Gerona, Sevilla, Salamanca, the Carlist North, France, Catalonia) and social (the courts of France and Spain, bourgeois households, a convent, aristocratic salons, rogues' taverns, the stage, teeming cities, a medieval countryside). Characters are drawn from widely different social classes and origins: actors, peasants, countesses, *pícaros,* monarchs, politicans, sailors, army officers, clerics, nuns, farmers, Frenchmen, Englishmen, prostitutes, shopkeepers, the dregs of the proletariat. The mood varies greatly from one *Episodio* to another: there are novels of historical re-creation (*Trafalgar*), of claustrophobic narrowness (*Zaragoza* and *Gerona*), of intrigue (*La corte de Carlos IV*), of rogues (*Napoleón en Chamartín, Cádiz*), of thwarted lovers (*Zaragoza*), of high adventure and romance (*Juan Martín el Empecinado, La batalla de los Arapiles, Un voluntario realista*), of farce (*Memorias de un cortesano de 1815*), of savagery (*El terror de 1824*), of conspiracy (*La segunda casaca*).

The characters of the *Episodios* vary enormously in temperament. There are those who can to a large extent control their situations: the reasonable, like Padre Gracián, Araceli, and, on occasions, Monsalud and Jenara; the virtuous, like Inés, Solita, and Benigno Cordero; Araceli as the good-humored narrator; Bragas the opportunistic trimmer; the aristocratic intriguers of *La corte de Carlos IV;* and the rogues of *Napoleón en Chamartín* and *Cádiz.* But Galdós is above all drawn to those who are enslaved by a passion or mania: the obsessed defenders of Zaragoza and Gerona, the repressed religious fanatic Juan de Dios, the rancorous Santorcaz, the quixotic Santiago Fernández, the dangerous romantic Lord Gray, the envious Mosén Antón, the misers Mauro Requejo and Doña Restituta, the demented Sarmiento and Carlos Navarro, the suicidal Pepet Armengol, the passionate Andrea Campos. Even apparently "balanced" characters pass with ease into insanity: Gabriel Araceli spits at the heavens (*Cádiz*) and maniacally bites the earth and howls (*La batalla de los Arapiles*); Inés has attempted suicide; Jenara lashes trees and is murderously vengeful in her thwarted passion (*Los cien mil hijos de San Luis*); the "outsider" Monsalud is cruel and violent, the prey to nightmares and suicidal despair (*El Grande Oriente*).

Although Galdós etches with considerable skill scenes of social interaction—the intrigues of aristocrats and actors in *La corte de Carlos IV*, the meeting of the *Cortes* in *Cádiz*, the farcical plotting of the absolutists in *Memorias de un cortesano de 1815*—he is above all attracted to situations of narrow focus, even nightmare: the sieges that produce paranoia, the frequent scenes of imprisonment and escape, the headlong journey to rescue Inés (*Juan Martín el Empecinado*), the savagery of the mob and inquisitors (*El terror de 1824*), the violent and lonely passions of Jenara, Andrea Campos, and Monsalud, the insane medieval world of the Carlists, the dark conspiracies of the absolutists (*Los apostólicos*), and the melodramatic struggle between Monsalud and his half-brother. Characters also are often seriously distorted, at least if viewed in terms of a hypothetical "realism": the caricature portrayals of those for whom Galdós feels political aversion (Fernando VII, Riego, the Carlists), the grotesque assimilation of people to objects (*El terror de 1824*), the symbolism of names and events that prevents any illusion of "reality," and the constant overloading of character and situation. Thus, Carlos Navarro and Salvador Monsalud are not only psychologically motivated characters but also are symbols of a national fratricidal struggle; both Benigno Cordero and the nation await a signature in *Los apostólicos.*

The overloading of events and characters, the caricatures, the symbolic names, and the quite obviously biased vision of history immediately indicate that we are reading fiction, not historical recreation. As much as to the history of nineteenth-century Spain, the *Episodios* refer us to a world of literature: the drama within a drama and the *Arabian Nights* in *La corte de Carlos IV;* Martínez de la Rosa and Shakespeare in *Zaragoza;* the picaresque, Ramón de la Cruz, and the *costumbristas* in *Napoleón en Chamartín* and *Cádiz;* the *folletín* throughout the first series; exotic romanticism in *Cádiz* and *La batalla de los Arapiles;* the melodrama, in the fratricidal conflict of the second series; Larra in *El equipaje del rey José;* Miñano in *Memorias de un cortesano de 1815;* Moratín in the courtship of Benigno Cordero, who patterns his life on the works of Rousseau and who is himself named, ironically, after a character in Fernán Caballero's *Elia;* romantic rebellion in the all-devouring passions of Jenara, Andrea Campos, and Monsalud, who, at times, takes on the characteristics of a Balzacian hero. Throughout there is the all-pervasive influence of Cervantes in the humor and shifting perspective of the "narrator" Gabriel Araceli, in the quixotic Santiago Fernández, in the expurgation scene in *Napoleón en Chamartín,* in the Conde de Montguyon with his false, chivalric vision of Spain, and in the combination of madness and sanity in Sarmiento and Carlos Navarro.

The literary nature of the *Episodios* extends beyond our recognition of situations and characters from other fictional works. There is, for example, an ironic aspect to the first series that has escaped the attention of previous critics. In *La corte de Carlos IV* we enter a world of mirrors, as "life" (the play within the play, the court worthy of Haroun-al-Raschid), itself a fiction created by Galdós, interacts with "literature" to create a mystery that we must penetrate to reach a "reality" that, nevertheless, is also born of Galdós's imagination. Throughout the first series, there is a raveling and unraveling, a series of ironic juxtapositions that serve to alert the reader against a too uncritical acceptance of what is presented to him. Thus, Gabriel's protestations of honor in *La corte de Carlos IV* are followed by examples of his manipulations; the letter substitution device of this novel is repeated in *El 19 de marzo y el 2 de mayo*, as Araceli gives Juan de Dios's letter to Doña Restituta. The attack on romantic attitudes in *Cádiz* is accompanied by Gabriel's extravagant posturing; Mosén Antón's proud "Me basto y me sobro" becomes Araceli's own affirmation in *La batalla de los Arapiles*. Throughout, the narrator, Gabriel Araceli, draws our attention to the act of narration, and thus away from "history," through his discussions with the reader, through the obvious pastiches of the styles of the *costumbristas* and the *folletín,* through the constant Cervantine overtones, through the deliberate overwriting, through the curious attribution of botanical names to characters (*Trafalgar*), and through the casting of doubt on the existence of a character (Miss Fly), a procedure that destroys all possibility of verisimilitude in supposedly "historical" *memorias* but that transports us instead into a realm of the imagination. The ending to the first series is also ironic, belonging to "romance" rather than to "history," as Gabriel, who supposedly has established his moral worth, obtains a tongue-in-cheek "reward" in marriage to the long-lost daughter of the very nobility that he had earlier castigated for its futility. The play of mirrors, the reference to an outside world that is nonetheless fiction, is again evident in the introduction in the *Episodios* of characters from the nonepisodic works of Galdós (*La fontana de oro, El audaz, La desheredada, Doña Perfecta*).

In his moral teaching and in his analysis of Spanish shortcomings, Galdós is consistent throughout his career; his ideology—liberal, authoritarian, pessimistic about the Spanish present—is the same in the articles in the *Revista de España*, in the first two series of *Episodios nacionales,* in the political articles of *Cronicón* (1883-1890), and in the *Episodios* written in 1898 and later years. The darker tones of the second series of *Episodios* do not, I believe, represent any change in Galdós's vision of Spain, but merely Galdós's desire to treat a different type of protagonist, the brooding Monsalud rather than the jaunty Araceli. With a pessimism no doubt born of Spanish political failures following the Revolution of 1868, Galdós portrays Spanish defects with somewhat more force than possible remedies. At times, the teaching of the *Episodios* is paradoxical. Thus, work is extolled, but we never see Araceli at his trade of army officer; heroism is enthusiastically presented, but Galdós prefers prudence. Curious also is Galdós's nostalgia for simple values, his attribution of wisdom to the young and inexperienced like Inés and Solita, while more forceful women like Miss Fly, Andrea Campos, and Jenara de Baraona are dismissed as eccentric, neurotic, or immoral.

The defects—the repetitious nature of the teaching, Gabriel's ubiquity, the somewhat implausible changes of character in Monsalud and Jenara, the confusion that results from reading too many *Episodios* at once—noted by those critics who have taken as their basis of study an entire series of *Episodios* are less apparent if the unit of investigation is the individual novel. Galdós impresses with his versatility, his creative energy, his sense of irony, his ability to switch from scenes of humor to those of the blackest horror, his constant slipping from one layer to another, whether of literature (the play of mirrors) or of character (the obsessed worlds of the insane). The same speculative conclusions that I proposed in my earlier study of the later *Episodios* [see excerpt dated 1980] could, I venture to suggest, be applied to the earlier *Episodios*. There is in Galdós a creative tension between two forces: the madness, corruption, nightmare, and melodrama that he so frequently evokes in his novels; and the rationality, compassion, and good humor with which he struggles against the demons existing within himself and his compatriots. (pp. 158-66)

> *Brian J. Dendle, in his* Galdós: The Early Historical Novels, *University of Missouri Press, 1986, 184 p.*

ADDITIONAL BIBLIOGRAPHY

Berkowitz, H. Chonon. *Pérez Galdós: Spanish Liberal Crusader.* Madison: University of Wisconsin Press, 1948, 499 p.
    The most comprehensive biography available in English.

Calley, Louise Nelson. "Galdós's Concept of Primitivism: A Romantic View of the Character of Fortunata." *Hispania* 47, No. 4 (December 1961): 663-65.
    Maintains that Galdós's sympathetic treatment of Fortunata is related to her function as a representative of the "noble savage."

Cardwell, Richard A. "Galdós' *Doña Perfecta:* Art or Argument?" *Anales Galdosianos* 7 (1972): 29-47.
    Denies the charge that artistry is subordinate to polemics in *Doña Perfecta.*

Chamberlin, Vernon A. "The *Muletilla:* An Important Facet of Galdós' Characterization Technique." *Hispanic Review* 29, No. 4 (October 1961): 296-309.
    Discusses Galdós's use of the *muletilla,* or speech tag, to lend meaning and verisimilitude to his characterizations.

————. "A Soviet Introduction to *Doña Perfecta* (1964)." *Anales Galdosianos* 10 (1975): 63-81.
    Presents an English translation of K. V. Tsurinov's introduction to the Russian edition of *Doña Perfecta.* Tsurinov makes extensive use of Marxist philosophy in his interpretation of the novel and views Galdós as essentially sympathetic to socialism.

————. *Galdós and Beethoven.* London: Tamesis, 1977, 123 p.
    Develops the theory that significant structural similarities exist between *Fortunata and Jacinta* and Beethoven's *Third (Eroica) Symphony.*

Davidson, Ned J. "Galdós' Conception of Beauty, Truth, and Reality in Art." *Hispania* 38, No. 1 (March 1955): 52-4.
    Discusses Galdós's aesthetic philosophy.

Durand, Frank. "Two Problems in Galdós's *Tormento*." *Modern Language Notes* 79, No. 5 (December 1964): 513-25.

Discusses the function of social criticism in *Tormento* as well as Galdós's use of a novelist as one of the protagonists of the novel.

Elliot, Leota W. and Kercheville, F. M. "Galdós and Abnormal Psychology." *Hispania* 23, No. 1 (February 1940): 27-36.
Examines characters that clearly exemplify Sigmund Freud's description of the neurotic personality, pointing out that these characters were created by Galdós before the publication of Freud's work.

Engler, Kay. *The Structure of Realism: The "Novelas Contemporáneas" of Benito Pérez Galdós*. Chapel Hill: North Carolina Studies in the Romance Languages and Literatures, 1977, 193 p.
Study of the narrative techniques used to create a sense of realism in the *Novelas españolas contemporáneas*. Engler concludes that the realism of Galdós's fiction derives from his "comprehensiveness and coherence of vision."

Gillespie, Gerald. "Reality and Fiction in the Novels of Galdós." *Anales Galdosianos* 1, No. 1 (1966): 11-31.
Explores the nature of Galdós's realism.

Gogoza Fletcher, Madeleine de. "Galdós." In her *The Spanish Historical Novel 1870-1970*, pp. 11-50. London: Tamesis, 1973.
Extensive discussion of the *Episodios nacionales*.

Gold, Hazel. "Francisco's Folly: Picturing Reality in Galdós' *La de Bringas*." *Hispanic Review* 54, No. 1 (Winter 1986): 47-66.
Examines the symbolism of the cenotaph in *La de Bringas*.

Goldman, Peter B., ed. *Conflicting Realities: Four Readings of a Chapter by Pérez Galdós*. London: Tamesis, 1982, 145 p.
Comparative textual elucidations of Part III, Chapter IV of *Fortunata and Jacinta* by Galdós scholars Carlos Blanco Aguinaga, John W. Kronik, Peter A. Bly, and Goldman.

Hafter, Monroe Z. "Ironic Reprise in Galdós' Novels." *PMLA* 76, No. 3 (June 1961): 233-39.
Analyzes Galdós's use of repeated phrases to create irony.

Herman, J. Chalmers. *Don Quijote and the Novels of Pérez Galdós*. Ada: East Central Oklahoma State College, 1955, 66 p.
Examines the influence of the novel *Don Quijote* on Galdós's work.

Hispania 53, No. 4 (December 1970): 819-1031.
Special Galdós issue includes articles in Spanish and English and two major bibliographical essays.

Jones, C. A. "Galdós's *Marianela* and the Approach to Reality." *Modern Language Review* 56, No. 4 (October 1961): 515-19.
Suggests that the primary theme of *Marianela* is the vast difference in the way individuals perceive reality.

Kirsner, Robert. "Pérez Galdós' Vision of Spain in *Torquemada en la Hoguera*." *Bulletin of Hispanic Studies* 27, No. 108 (October-December 1950): 229-35.
Interprets the character of Don Francisco de Torquemada as an exemplification of Spanish culture.

——. "Galdós' Attitude Toward Spain as Seen in the Characters of *Fortunata y Jacinta*." *PMLA* 66, No. 2 (March 1951): 124-37.
Views Galdós's attitude toward Spain and the Spanish people as essentially benevolent despite the overt social criticism of the novels.

Mazzara, Richard A. "Some Fresh Perspectives on Galdós' *Doña Perfecta*." *Hispania* XL, No. 1 (March 1957): 52-5.
Discusses style, characterization, and major themes in *Doña Perfecta*, attempting to show that the novel is less flawed than is generally thought.

Nimetz, Michael. *Humor in Galdós: A Study of the Novelas contemporáneas*. New Haven, Conn.: Yale University Press, 1968, 227 p.

Explores Galdós's use of traditional fictional techniques to create humor. Includes analyses of diction, metaphor, and characterization.

Oliver, Walter. "Galdós' 'La Novela en el Tranvia': Fantasy and the Art of Realistic Narration." *Modern Language Notes* 88, No. 2 (March 1973): 249-63.
Contends that Galdós used fantasy to achieve psychological characterization in his fiction, using the short story "La novela en el Tranvia" as an example.

Pattison, Walter T. *Benito Pérez Galdós and the Creative Process*. Minneapolis: University of Minnesota Press, 1954, 145 p.
Attempts to discern Galdós's creative process by examining in detail the genesis of two novels, *Gloria* and *Marianela*.

Penuel, Arnold M. *Charity in the Novels of Galdós*. Athens: University of Georgia Press, 1972, 130 p.
Study of Galdós's use in his novels of nonsexual love to make ethical and social statements.

Percival, Anthony. *Galdós and his Critics*. Toronto: University of Toronto Press, 1985, 537 p.
Comprehensive secondary bibliography.

Pritchett, V. S. "Galdós." In his *Books in General*, pp. 31-36. London: Chatto and Windus, 1953.
Review of *The Spendthrifts*, which Pritchett considers "a brilliant, well-constructed comic novel."

Rodgers, E. J. "Religious Conflict and Didacticism in *Gloria*." *Anales Galdosianos* 1, No. 1 (1966): 39-51.
Discusses the theme of religious intolerance in *Gloria*, focusing in particular on the unintentional melodrama which results from Galdós's lack of experience at the time the novel was written.

Russell, Robert. "The Structure of *La Desheredada*." *Modern Language Notes* 76, No. 8 (December 1961): 794-800.
Examines the ways in which *La desheredada* exemplifies late nineteenth-century Spanish naturalism.

Santaló, Joaquín. *The Tragic Import in the Novels of Pérez Galdós*. Madrid: Coleccion Plaza Mayor Scholar, 1973, 176 p.
Analysis of themes and characters that indicate a predominately tragic vision in Galdós's fiction. Santalo maintains that Galdós was "thoroughly and continually absorbed in the tragic."

Scanlon, Geraldine M. "Heroism in an Unheroic Society: Galdós's *Lo Prohibido*." *Modern Language Review* 79, No. 4 (October 1984): 831-45.
Maintains that Galdós "sought to show that sublime actions and profound feelings could exist in ordinary everyday life, that heroism was accessible to every man and woman."

Schraibman, Joseph. *Dreams in the Novels of Galdós*. New York: Hispanic Institute of the United States, 1960, 199 p.
Analyses of how dreams further plot, reinforce characterization, and introduce elements of the supernatural in Galdós's fiction.

Schyfter, Sara E. *The Jew in the Novels of Pérez Galdós*. London: Tamesis, 1978, 127 p.
Examination of Galdós's depictions of Jewish characters. Schyfter concludes that Galdós's treatment of such characters is essentially sympathetic and that in his novels "the Jew serves to point out the deficiencies of Spanish culture."

Shoemaker, W. H. "Galdós's Literary Creativity: D. Jose Ido del Sagrario." *Hispanic Review* XIX, No. 3 (July 1951): 204-37.
Studies the reappearances and evolution of a single character in order to explore Galdós's use of recurring characters in the *Novelas españolas contemporáneas*.

Snow, C. P. "Galdós." In his *The Realists*, pp. 217-55. New York: Charles Scribner's Sons, 1978.

Biographical article in which Snow reveals some little-known facts concerning Galdós's private life.

Warshaw, J. "Galdós' Indebtedness to Cervantes." *Hispania* XVI, No. 2 (May 1933): 127-42.
Discusses Galdós's frequent use of Cervantine language and characters.

Weber, Robert J. *The* Miau *Manuscript of Benito Pérez Galdós: A Critical Study*. Berkeley: University of California Press, 1964, 155 p.
Compares the two extant manuscripts of Galdós's novel *Miau*.

Weber, Robert J., ed. *Galdós Studies II*. London: Tamesis, 1974, 68 p.
Includes five studies of Galdós's work by noted critics of Spanish literature.

Zaharias, Anthony. "The Tragic Sense in *Fortunata y Jacinta*." *Symposium* 19, No. 1 (Spring 1965): 38-49.
Considers Galdós's use of modern psychology in his creation of tragic characters.

Fernando (António Nogueira) Pessoa

1888-1935

(Also wrote under pseudonyms of Alberto Caeiro, Ricardo Reis, Alvaro de Campos, Alexander Search, Bernardo Soares, Baron de Teive, and others) Portuguese poet, essayist, and critic.

Considered the greatest Portuguese poet since the sixteenth-century poet Vaz de Camões, Pessoa is often described as an author whose works epitomize the themes and techniques of twentieth-century literature, specifically in his confrontation with the chaotic plurality of modern life and his experimental approach to poetic composition. This approach was based in large part on his creation of a set of literary alter egos, for which he coined the term "heteronyms," in order to explore the unstable nature of personal identity and to circumvent the limitations of a single literary persona. These heteronyms served Pessoa as a means of expressing disparate philosophical outlooks, the sum of which was intended to achieve a fuller and more objective account of reality than any single perspective could provide.

Pessoa was born into a cultured Lisbon family in which the arts were highly esteemed. His father, a music critic, died when Pessoa was five years old; a year later his mother married the Portuguese consul to South Africa, where Pessoa lived throughout the remainder of his childhood and youth. At the English secondary school he attended, Pessoa excelled in language study and became so proficient in English that he received the Queen Victoria essay prize in a competition with 900 other students. By the age of fifteen, he was composing sonnets in English that have been described as "ultra-Shakespearean" because they feature the kind of repetition, antithesis, and complex syntax characteristic of Shakespeare's sonnets, which Pessoa particularly admired. These poems were later collected and published as *35 Sonnets*. Returning to Portugal in 1905, Pessoa attended the University of Lisbon but left school after only a year of study. He used his fluency in English to secure a position as a business correspondent for Portuguese commercial firms, an occupation in which he remained for the rest of his life. Although he continued to write poetry, if was not until 1912 that Pessoa began composing poems in Portuguese. Around this time he also became associated with poets of the *saudosismo* movement, whose poetry was marked by a mood of nostalgia for, and glorification of, Portugal's past. By 1915 Pessoa was well known in the artistic and intellectual circles of Lisbon, establishing himself as a poet and critic who was in sympathy with the various modernist movements that flourished in Europe during the early years of the twentieth century and gaining renown as one of the founders of *Orpheu* and *Presença,* two major journals of modern Portuguese literature. Most of Pessoa's poetry published during his lifetime appeared in literary journals and remained uncollected in book form; with the exception of his English poems, only a single collection of his poetry appeared during his life. At the time of his death Pessoa's work was not widely known and his reputation is almost entirely based on posthumously published works.

Two subjects predominate in Pessoa's poetry: the shifting nature of personal identity and the limited extent to which an individual may apprehend reality. In order to explore these

related subjects in the most appropriate and comprehensive manner, he invented a variety of literary alter egos, each of whom would provide a different perspective. More specifically, Pessoa developed particular attitudes into separate personae which he called heteronyms. This term was used by Pessoa in contrast to the usual designation of "pseudonym." As he explained in a letter: "The pseudonymous work is by the author in his own person, except that he uses another name; the heteronymous is by the author outside his own person." By providing each heteronym with a fictionalized biography, philosophical outlook, and distinct literary style, Pessoa attempted to dissociate them from his own personality, thereby creating a more impersonal, and by implication more objective, body of work representing a multiplicity of viewpoints. Pessoa assumed a highly analytical attitude toward his own personality, considering each aspect of himself an independent facade unrelated to a controlling identity. This attitude is reflected in Pessoa's poetry in his frequent use of masks to symbolize fragmentation of the self. The repeated appearance of masks in Pessoa's poetry has often been noted in relation to his family name, which derives from the Latin word "persona," referring to the mask worn by an actor and by extension to the role an actor plays. That Pessoa was aware of this possible literal connotation of his name is made clear by his occasional punning on the word "pessoa," which in Portuguese means "person."

The first heteronym Pessoa created was Alberto Caeiro, whose philosophical views are those of a pagan materialist and whose poetic style is free verse. When writing as Caeiro, Pessoa repudiated all forms of supernaturalism and celebrated a natural existence in which appearances are accepted at face value. In "Guardador de Rebanhos" ("The Shepherd"), for example, Caeiro praises the senses as the only legitimate basis for knowledge, proclaiming: "I think with my eyes and with my ears." Also committed to an exclusively sensual reality was Pessoa's second heteronym Ricardo Reis, a neo-classicist whose "paganism" is derived in large part from his acknowledged master, Alberto Caeiro. Whereas Pessoa assumed the role of a naive pastoral poet as Caeiro, Reis is a sophisticated and world-weary fatalist who composes his poems in fixed forms rather than free verse. Reis's philosophy of resignation is illustrated in "Quando Lidia, vier o nosso outona" ("When, Lydia, Our Autumn Comes"), which admonishes the woman of the title to "seize the day" in view of the ephemeral nature of human existence. Pessoa's philosophical perspective changed again when he adopted the role of the modernist poet Alvaro de Campos. In the exclamatory free verse Pessoa wrote as Campos, critics have observed two contrary impulses. The first, seen in such poems as "Ode triunfal" ("Triumphal Ode") and "Ode maritima" ("Maritime Ode"), conveys a feverish desire to be everything and everyone, declaring that "in every corner of my soul stands an altar to a different god." The second impulse is toward a state of isolation and a sense of nothingness. In "Tabacaria" ("Tobacco Shop"), for instance, Campos is pictured alone in his room, questioning his own existence: "Just as those accustomed to invoke spirits invoke spirits / I invoke Myself and find nothing." In addition to these three major heteronyms, under which Pessoa wrote much of his poetry, he wrote a variety of works using numerous other heteronyms and "semi-heteronyms."

Pessoa also composed poetry under his own name, which he considered to be simply another literary alias, designating it as an "orthonym." Many of his best poems were written under this name, including those that reveal his preoccupation with occult studies. However, although he seriously pursued such subjects as astrology and secret societies, he remained uncommitted to any specific supernatural doctrine. Peter Rickard has observed that Pessoa "refuses to choose, to commit himself to any one god, for that would mean exchanging the reality for the appearance, the unlimited for the limited, and transcendent for the immanent, the occult for the positive, the soul for the surface." Nevertheless, Pessoa employed occult imagery to portray traditional esoteric concerns. Most prominently, he structured his poetry collection *Mensagem* (*Message*), which ostensibly depicts the legend of King Sebastian's resurrection as Portugal's savior, according to occult paradigms of an initiate's spiritual progress.

While Pessoa's works are undoubtedly among the most idiosyncratic in modern poetry, he is also considered a representative twentieth-century poet, especially for his concern with the problems and paradoxes of an individual's identity. As Alberto de Lacerda has written: "I shall venture to say that, given the tragic implacable light which Pessoa throws on identity, on responsibility, poetic and otherwise, on shifting the notion of sincerity from the lyrical impulse to intellectual and psychological honesty, he is not the greatest but the most emblematic poet of the Twentieth Century, as Baudelaire was for the Nineteenth Century."

PRINCIPAL WORKS

Antinous (poetry) 1918
35 Sonnets (poetry) 1918
English Poems. 3 vols. (poetry) 1921
Mensagem (poetry) 1934
*Obras completas de Fernando Pessoa. 11 vols. (poetry, criticism, essays, and philosophy) 1942-74
Selected Poems (poetry) 1971
Sixty Portuguese Poems (poetry) 1971
Fernando Pessoa: Selected Poems (poetry) 1974

*This edition of Pessoa's works is still in progress.

THE TIMES LITERARY SUPPLEMENT (essay date 1918)

[*In the following excerpt, the critic comments on* Antinous, *Pessoa's first poetry in English to be published.*]

Mr. Pessoa's command of English is less remarkable than his knowledge of Elizabethan English. He appears to be steeped in Shakespeare; and, if he is not acquainted with Daniel, John Davies of Hereford, and other Tudor philosophical poets, this affinity with them is even more remarkable than it appears. *Antinous* is not a poem that will appeal to the general reader in England; although the reflections of Hadrian over the dead body of his minion are interesting for what we should now call this Renaissance style and atmosphere, and the poetry is often striking. The sonnets, on the other hand, probing into mysteries of life and death, of reality and appearance, will interest many by reason of their ultra-Shakespearian Shakespearianisms, and their Tudor tricks of repetition, involution and antithesis, no less than by the worth of what they have to say.

A review of "Antinous: A Poem," in The Times Literary Supplement, *No. 870, September 19, 1918, p. 443.*

FERNANDO PESSOA (letter date 1935)

[*In the following excerpt from a letter to Adolfo Casais Monteiro, Pessoa discusses the genesis and characteristics of his three principal heteronyms.*]

I shall now turn to answering your question concerning the genesis of my heteronyms. Let me see if I am able to give you a full answer.

I shall begin with the psychiatric aspect. The origin of my heteronyms lies in the profound streak of hysteria which is existent within me. I do not know if I am purely and simply hysterical; or if I am, in more accurate terms, a hysteroneurasthenic. I am more inclined towards this second hypothesis because phenomena of abulia exist within me which are not to be found on the list of the symptoms of hysteria itself. Whichever it may be, the mental origin of my heteronyms lies in my organic and constant propensity towards depersonalisation and simulation. Fortunately, both for me and for others, these phenomena have been produced only within my own mind; I mean by this that they do not find expression in my daily life, in my external life, nor in my contact with others. They explode within my mind and I experience this phenomenon completely within myself. If I were a woman—for in the woman phenomena of hysteria burst forth in seizures and attacks of a similar nature—each poem written by Álvaro de Campos (the most hysterically hysterical within me) would cause alarm amongst the neighbours. But I am a man and in men hysteria mainly assumes configurations within the mind; and consequently everything terminates in silence and poetry . . .

This explains, *tant bien que mal,* the organic origin of my heteronyms. I am now going to give you the straightforward history of my heteronyms. I shall begin with those who have already died, some of which I can no longer recall, that is to say, those which lie deeply embedded in that remote part of my childhood that is almost erased from my memory.

Ever since I was a small child I felt driven to create a fictitious world around me and to surround myself with friends and acquaintances who never existed. (Indeed, I do not know if in reality it was they who did not exist or if it is I who does not exist. In these things, as indeed in all, we cannot afford to be dogmatic). Ever since I have known myself as being that to which I refer as "I", I can remember having imagined with great precision in my mind, various unreal figures—as far as appearance, movements, character and life history were concerned—who were so very visible to me and who were so much my own, as the things which we, abusively perhaps, call real life. This inclination and drive which has flourished within me ever since I can recall being an "I" has always been my companion, changing slightly the type of music with which it seduces me but never altering at all its manner of seduction.

In this manner I can recall that which seems to me to have been my first heteronym, or—more precisely—my first non-existent acquaintance—a certain Chevalier de Pas—when I was only six years old, for whom I wrote letters, by him to myself, and whose image, not entirely faint, still touches on that part of my affection which can be described as nostalgia. I can also remember, but less vividly, another image whose name I can no longer conjure up but it was also foreign, and who was, although I do not know in what respect, a rival of the Chevalier de Pas . . . things which happen to all children? Undoubtedly—or only perhaps. But I lived them to such a point that I am still living them—because I am able to recall them in such a way that an effort is required to make me realize that they were not realities.

This tendency to create another world within me, identical to this one but with different people, has never left my mind. This tendency went through various phases within which this is one which has already become of age. A witty remark which had been burgeoning within me, would occur to me, completely alien, for one reason or another, to that which I am, or to that which I suppose I am. I would say it immediately, spontaneously, as if it had come from a certain friend of mine whose name I would invent, on whose life history I would expand and whose physical appearance—face, stature, dress and mien— I would immediately see before me. And it was in this way that I invented and spread around various friends and acquaintances who had never existed but whom I still today, almost thirty years later, am able to hear, feel and see. I repeat: whom I can hear, feel and see . . . and I miss them.

(I only need to start to speak—and for me typing is the equivalent of speaking—and I have difficulty in putting on the brakes. Enough of the boring details for you, Casais Monteiro! I shall now delve into the genesis of my literary heteronyms, which is, after all, what you would like to know. In any case, what

has gone before provides you with the background to the mother who bore them.)

Around 1912, if I am not mistaken (which I never can be by much), the idea occurred to me to write some poems of a pagan propensity. I made a rough draft of a few items in irregular verse (not in the style of Álvaro de Campos, but in a more regular style) and then abandoned them. However, in an imperfectly matted penumbra, a vague portrait of the person who was doing the writing had become outlined within me. (Without my knowledge, Ricardo Reis had been born.)

I remember one day, eighteen months or two years later, playing a joke with Sá-Carneiro: namely, I were to invent a bucolic poet with a complicated nature and to introduce him—in a manner which I no longer recall—to Sá-Carneiro in any one kind of reality. I spent a few days developing a poet but I did not successfully achieve anything. On the very day I relinquished this task—it was March 8th 1914—I approached a high chest of drawers, and, taking a sheet of paper, I began to write, standing up, as I always write whenever I can. And I wrote thirty or so poems at a stroke in a kind of ecstatic trance, the nature of which I will not be able to define to you. It was *the* day of triumph in my life and I shall never succeed in living another like that. I opened with the title **"The Keeper of the Flock"** (**"O Guardador de Rebanhos"**); and what followed was that someone emerged from within me, and whom I christened that very moment Alberto Caeiro. Forgive me for the absurdity of the following sentence: my master emerged from within me. That was the immediate sensation that I felt. And thus, once that these thirty or so poems were written, I immediately availed myself of another sheet of paper and wrote— also at a stroke—the six poems which constitute **"The Slanting Rain"** (**"Chuva Oblíqua"**) by Fernando Pessoa. Immediately and totally . . . It was the throwback of Fernando Pessoa Alberto Caeiro to Fernando Pessoa himself. Or, in more explicit terms, it was the reaction of Fernando Pessoa against his non-existence as Alberto Caeiro.

Once that Alberto Caeiro had emerged, I immediately—both instinctively and subconsciously—undertook the task to find a few disciples for him. I extracted the latent Ricardo Reis from his false paganism, invented a name for him and adjusted him to himself because at that point I was already able to see him. And suddenly, from an origin opposed to that of Ricardo Reis, a new individual impetuously gushed forth before my eyes. In a jet, and on the typewriter, with neither interruption nor correction **"Ode Triunfal"** (**"Ode to Triumph"**) by Álvaro de Campos poured onto the page—both the Ode thus entitled and the man who bears that name.

I then created a non-existent *coterie.* I established it all in patterns of reality. I graded the influences, was aware of their friendships, heard within me the discussions and the differing of judgements and in all this it seemed to me that it was I, creator of everything, who had the least to do with it all. It seemed that everything took place independently of me; and it seems that this is still taking place in the very same way. If one day I am able to publish the aesthetic discussion between Ricardo Reis and Álvaro de Campos, you will see how much they differ from each other and how I am nothing in this matter.

A few more references to this matter are required . . . I *can* see before me, in the colourless yet real space of a dream, the faces and the miens of Caeiro, Ricardo Reis and Álvaro de Campos. It was I who fabricated their ages and their lives for them. Ricardo Reis was born in 1887 (I do not recall the exact day nor the month, but I do have them somewhere) in Oporto, is a doctor by profession and is at present in Brazil. Alberto Caeiro was born in 1889 and died in 1915. He was born in Lisbon but spent most of his life in the country. He did not have a profession nor any real education to speak of. Álvaro de Campos was born in Tavira on October 15th 1890 (at 1.30 pm, so I am informed by Ferreira Gomes; and it is certainly true as his horoscope for this hour confirms.) As you know, the latter is a naval engineer (from Glasfow University) but is now here in Lisbon, yet is not working. Caeiro was of medium stature and although in fact was of a very delicate disposition (he died of tuberculosis) he did not appear as delicate as he actually was. Ricardo Reis is slightly, yet only slightly, smaller in stature, is stronger and leaner. Álvaro de Campos is tall (1,75 metres—two centimetres taller than I am), thin and a little inclined to stoop. They all have clean-shaven faces: Caeiro was blonde, without much colour and blue eyes, Reis a vague opaque swarthy colour and Campos somewhere between white and brown ressembling slightly a typical Portuguese Jew; his hair, however, is straight and is normally parted at the side and he wears a monocle. As I have already said, Caeiro hardly received any education at all, only up to primary school level. Both his father and mother died early in his life and he just carried on living at home, surviving on a small income. He lived with an old aunt, a great-aunt. Ricardo Reis, educated in a Jesuit College, is, as I said, a doctor: he has been living in Brazil since 1919 when he spontaneously expatriated because he was a monarchist. He is a latinist as a result of the education he received from others and a semi-hellenist as a result of the education he gave himself. Álvaro de Campos received a common place secondary school education and subsequently was sent to Scotland to study engineering, firstly mechanical and then naval engineering. During one holiday period he undertook the journey to the Orient from which emerged *Opiário*. He was taught Latin by an uncle, a priest, from the Beiras.

How am I able to write in the name of these three . . .? Caeiro, out of pure and accidental inspiration, without knowing or even imagining what I was going to write. Ricardo Reis, after an abstract deliberation which suddenly becomes transformed into an "Ode". Campos, whenever I feel a sudden impulsion to write something, yet I know not what. (My semi-heteronym, Bernardo Soares, who, by the way, in many respects ressembles Álvaro de Campos, always appears when I am feeling tired or drowsy and appears in such a way that his qualities of reasoning power and inhibition are a little erratic; his prose is a continuous reverie. He is a semi-heteronym because, although not being my personality itself, it is not different from mine, but simply a mutilation of it. It is I less the reasoning power and the affectivity. His prose, with the exception of the tenuous *quid* which is present in mine, is the equal of mine, and from the language point of view the Portuguese is exactly the same. Whilst Caeiro wrote Portuguese badly, Campos of a reasonable standard but with odd slips, saying for example, "I, me" instead of "I myself". Reis writes better than I do but uses a purism which I consider excessive. What is difficult for me is to write Reis' prose—still unpublished—or Campos' prose. Simulation is easier, also because it is more spontaneous in verse form. (pp. 17-22)

Fernando Pessoa, in a letter to Adolfo Casais Monteiro on January 13, 1935, translated by Gillian Horrocks-Taylor and Maria Helena Rodrigues de Carvalho, in Fernando Pessoa: A Galaxy of Poets, 1888-1935, *edited by José Blanco, Portuguese Ministries of Foreign Affairs and Culture, 1985, pp. 17-22.*

PORTUGAL: AN INFORMATIVE REVIEW (essay date 1961)

[*In the following excerpt, the critic provides a retrospective appraisal of Pessoa's literary stature.*]

Twenty-five years after his death Fernando Pessoa has become a universal figure. He had foreseen the appearance in Portugal of a "super Camões" but his contemporaries thought this affirmation no more than the mere exaggeration of expression of an adolescent. In silence, almost anonymously, he had gone on, consciously and confessedly, with that "terrible and religious mission that every man of genius receives from God together with that genius." Did he in fact manage to reconcile these two statements, which he made at different periods of his life? Did he foresee the welcome which his message was to receive so many years later? Apart from his clear awareness of his own value, was he able to weigh and gauge the conscience of his time, listen to its still feeble murmurs of anguish, the crisis of reason, of internal disintegration, of its many-sidedness, so that he could identify himself as the spokesman of the generations which followed him? This is one more doubt to add to the many that make the poet's personality sphinx-like in its enigma. But of one thing we may be sure, and it is that his identification did in fact come to pass. The man of today feels himself mirrored in the poetry of Pessoa, just as the work of Camões expresses in its deepest symbology the man of the Renaissance.

It is still too early for us to give Pessoa his rightful place among Portuguese poets. It is even possible that, once the circumstances that determine new forms of living change, Pessoa will be brought down from the high pedestal to which he has risen. But this does not prevent him from being, par excellence, the poet of the present time, the one who lived the most complex vision of life in our time and who found the words that best define it.

He is a national poet, as none had been before or since Camões. His extreme subjectivism is situated at a certain moment of history and absorbs and clarifies a consciousness of the collective destiny which his contemporaries only vaguely and obscurely noted. Even so he did not sacrifice his inner feelings to external facts. In him, in fact, the external is transmuted and resolved on an inner plane. Everything around him, the cosmic and human panorama, becomes a dense inner nucleus, just like a many-sided crystal that absorbs light only to reflect it in a thousand different images. He was seized by the temptation to dissect and analyse, so that never could this supreme alchemist of the real and of the "ego" confine himself within the limited horizons of a personal, sentimental lyricism. His vision expands and widens to take in the most subtle metaphysical oscillations to which the "ego" is subjected. Thought and imagination almost fuse and generate an emotive intellectualism, lived dramatically, in which they make their appearance an infinite range of topics, from the most concrete to the abstract, from matters of daily moment to the most transcendental. Never could it be so just to speak of creative "richness" and fertility, were it not that the wear that such terms have undergone in literary criticism has made them easy words of empty praise. But let us be more precise. In him we find a richness of sensitivity, of captation of external suggestions, a richness of imagination which includes the subject matter of his poems, the richness of a thought which is transposed on to the plane of aesthetic emotion yet does not lose any of its density and depth, a richness of words to which he gives the magic power of communicability, a richness that is not even exhausted by its own multiplicity, for underneath all he says there is the suggestion of a greater richness that is merely touched on and hinted at, that of the unending, inexhaustible mystery of things and of beings.

It is for all these reasons that Pessoa is a very great poet. He deserves to be known throughout the world. We should add, too, that the characteristics that we have vaguely outlined take on in his work the most original development that poetry of subjective inspiration has ever attained, and this statement we make without fear of contradiction. That is why, in spite of the obstacles which hamper the divulgation of poets who write in Portuguese in foreign countries, he has been justly celebrated outside his own country. (pp. 35-6)

> *"Twenty-Five Years after the Death of Fernando Pessoa," in* Portugal: An Informative Review, *Vol. 5, No. 1, January-February, 1961, pp. 35-44.*

EDOUARD RODITI   (essay date 1963)

[*Roditi is a French-born poet, translator, and critic. In the following excerpt, he discusses Pessoa's English poems and the circumstances in his life that led to the composition of these works.*]

[Fernando Pessoa] spoke perfect English and wrote some of his earlier poetry in English. Pessoa's bilingualism may indeed be the cause of his extraordinary and almost psychopathic diversity as a Portuguese poet too. Not content with writing in two different languages and literary traditions, those of late Nineteenth-century English poetry and of post-Romantic or modernistic Portuguese poetry, Pessoa wrote and published his Portuguese works under six different names, in six different poetic idioms, each one of which constitutes a separate identity among what Pessoa and his Portuguese critics have called his *heterónimos*.

Denied any Wordsworthian spontaneity of expression because always forced to choose whether to express himself in English or in Portuguese, Pessoa made a virtue of the self-alienation imposed upon him by his having to hesitate between either of two languages that both remained, through this very choice, equally familiar and foreign to him. In either language, Pessoa had to pretend, at all times, to ignore the poetic traditions and conventions of the other, and in Portuguese to ignore each time the idioms that were particular to five other personalities of his own whom he repressed when he allowed the sixth to write.

Even Pessoa's name seems to imply this peculiar fate. Derived from the Latin word that means a character in a play or a mask, it now means, in spoken Portuguese, a mere person, in the very vaguest sense of the word. Long before his mental disturbances, Ezra Pound had thus chosen *Personae*, meaning masks, as the title of the early collection of his poems where he revealed, for the first time, the complexities of his own identity while hinting unconsciously at his own future alienation. To this very theme of the mask or person, Pessoa devoted one of the finest of the *35 Sonnets* (VIII) that he published privately in English in 1918.

But Pessoa was well aware of the limitations that fate and neurosis imposed on his genius. To be freed of these, he began, like a character in a Pirandello play, to lead his other lives, imaginary lives of imaginary poets, fictional characters whose very real works he wrote and published under these other names that are now his *heterónimos*. In the last of his *35 Sonnets*,

Pessoa justifies these playful mystifications by referring to the greater mysteries of astrology:

> With the higher trifling let us world our wit
> Conscious that, if we do't, that was the lot
>   The regular stars bound us to, when they stood
>   Godfathers to our birth and to our blood.

When he expressed himself in English, Fernando Pessoa generally clothed his metaphysical considerations and erotic fantasies in somewhat learned diction, creating for himself an idiom as personal as those of Edward Benlowes, William Blake, Hopkins or even Laura Riding. He was indeed one of the hermits of our language, a kind of Trappist of English poetry who wrote a language that he often read or imagined but rarely spoke or heard (see **"Sonnet VI"**).

It is odd that Pessoa, in his lifetime, should have published but one poem in England, in *The Athenaeum* of January 30, 1920; that his English writings, printed privately in Lisbon, should have attracted the attention, among English critics, only of two, unless I am mistaken, the critic of the *Times Literary Supplement* [see excerpt dated 1918] and of the *Glasgow Herald;* and especially that no critic or historian, whether English or Portuguese, should yet have taken the trouble, since the poet's death in 1935, to seek, among his literary remains, the three unpublished English poems, **"Prayer to a Woman's Body," "Pan-Eros"** and **"Anteros,"** which the author mentioned in a letter of November 18, 1930, to João Gaspar Simões but failed to include in the privately printed 1921 Lisbon edition of his *English Poems*. Pessoa admits, in this letter, that the three lost poems were already written; he even explains that they completed the cycle of erotic poems begun in **"Antinous"** and **"Epithalamium,"** both of which he had published. After celebrating, in these two published poems, the conceptions of love of the Greek and the Roman worlds of antiquity, he had expressed, in the three unpublished poems, the Christian philosophy of love, then that of the modern world and in the last, that of the future too.

In most of the Portuguese poetry that he published under his own name, Pessoa reveals himself as a late Romantic or a Symbolist rather than a Modern. Sometimes a bit decadent, like his friend the Portuguese poet Mario de Sá-Carneiro, Pessoa tended, after 1910, to be increasingly interested in occultism and, in this respect, was a precursor of the early Surrealists. Though a translator of Poe, Pessoa remembers his readings of Whitman too, but never as much as in the overtly pantheistic poetry that he published under two other names, Alberto Caeiro and Alvaro de Campos. At no time, in any of the poetry that he ever published in Portuguese under any of his various names, was Pessoa as intensely preoccupied with the wildly erotic visions that characterize much of his English poetry. On the contrary, he expressed as an English poet a personality as distinct as that of any of his Portuguese *heterónimos*. He seems indeed to have paradoxically chosen the language of his prim Anglo-Saxon school years to write the kind of poetry that some English poets dare write only in Latin or French.

As Ricardo Reis, one of the least prolific of his Portuguese personalities, Pessoa was consciously classical, a gnomic poet who remembered the *Odes* of Horace and perhaps also some of the more Olympian utterances of Goethe and even of Nietzsche, certainly the Augustan serenity of Alexander Pope as well as of the Eighteenth-century Portuguese poet Bocage. As Alberto Caeiro, Pessoa proved himself to be a modern Pantheist, a balanced and optimistic disciple of Whitman. Always more articulate than William Carlos Williams, less brash than Carl Sandburg, Pessoa was also more consciously complex, in his psychology and beliefs, than Whitman's French disciple Valéry Larbaud, the poet who created, after Gide's André Walter, his own *heterónimo,* A. O. Barnabooth, an imaginary poet of much the same race as Eliot's Prufrock too.

It is as Alvaro Campos, however, that Fernando Pessoa has attracted the most attention, both in Portugal and in France, where he has been excellently translated by the poet Armand Guibert. An imaginary Jew, a neurasthenic disciple of Marinetti's Futurism, a marine engineer who has lost faith in man and machines and no longer knows where he belongs, why he writes, Alvaro de Campos is almost like a character out of a Kafka novel:

> I have lived, studied, loved and believed,
> And today there is no beggar of whose fate I am not
>   jealous merely because he is not I.
> In each man I see the rage, the scars, the lies,
> And I think: "Perhaps you too have lived, studied,
>   loved, believed,
> (For it is possible to manipulate the reality of all this
>   without actually achieving any of it);
> Perhaps you have scarcely existed at all, like a lizard
>   that has had its tail cut off,
> And the tail severed from the lizard still quivers
>   endlessly. . . .

Writing free verse and remembering both Whitman and Baudelaire, both Marinetti and his own poems already published under the name of Alberto Caeiro whom Alvaro de Campos now claimed as his master, Pessoa went here much further, in some of the pseudonymous poems of Alvaro de Campos, than Guillaume Apollinaire ever did along those avenues of emotion and poetic expression that the French poet of *Alcools* also explored, especially in "Zone" and in the prose of *Onirocritique* and of *Les Mamelles de Tiérésias*. In a dreamlike world that was destined, a few years later, to become that of Surrealism, Alvaro de Campos stopped only at the very frontiers of hallucination, depersonalization, self-alienation:

> What do I know of what I shall be, I who do not know
>   what I am?
> To be what I think? But I think I am so much and so
>   much.
> And there are so many others who all think they are the
>   same and they cannot all be right. . . .

It is significant in this respect that Pessoa published under the signature of Alvaro de Campos the great prophetic manifesto where he defined the literature of the future, the poetry of an age in which the individual would cease to have any meaning or existence. Now that we are already living in a world that daily flouts, whether in the name of Marxism, Fascism or a panic-stricken democracy, the very principles of individualism on which our traditional conception of literature has always been founded, we begin to understand the nihilism and despair that once haunted the visions of Alvaro de Campos:

> I am nothing.
> Never shall I be anything.
> I cannot want to be anything.
> Apart from that, I bear within me all the world's dream.

Writing under the name of Bernardo Soares, Pessoa even allowed himself to be quite undistinguished, uninspired, a mutilated personality whom he treats with an affectionate indul-

gence. A competent accountant, Soares seems to be the kind of man that Pessoa's mother's second husband had wanted his problematic stepson to be. As C. Pacheco, Pessoa published only one work, a sample of highly intellectualized Futurism or Surrealism; as Antonio Mora, he wrote nothing at all but mentions himself under this name as the "intellectually pagan" imaginary master of his own imaginary C. Pacheco, much as Caeiro had already been the avowed master of Alvaro de Campos.

In an essay published in his *Paginas the Doutrina Estetica* Pessoa distinguishes clearly his various *heterónimos*:

> Bernardo Soares . . . is myself, minus my faculty of reasoning and my affectivity. His prose, except for the tenuous quality that my reasoning gives to mine, is equal to mine, in absolutely equivalent Portuguese; whereas Caeiro wrote bad Portuguese and Campos reasonable Portuguese, but with lapses . . . Reis wrote better than I do, with a purity of style that I consider exaggerated. It is difficult for me to write the prose of Reis, and that is why it is unpublished, or that of Campos. This kind of simulation is more easy, because more spontaneous, in verse than in prose.

All poetry, in Pessoa's eyes, was indeed simulation, and all poets, according to his faith, are most sincere when least sincere, most truthful when they feign with sufficiently convincing artistry.

When he formulated his famous equivocation about truth and beauty, Keats bequeathed to us an explosive belief. It produced, throughout the Nineteenth century, a critical chain reaction that still leaves victims of concussion in its wake today. The "ring of truth" has come, for some stupefied or feeble-minded critics, to be the only test for all those statements of poets that cannot be proven factually, I mean semantically, nor by checking them against other statements of the same poet, I mean syntactically. But this pragmatic test of the "ring of truth" involves one in all the absurdities of having to decide whether a poet is "sincere" and of then rejecting as "insincere" most poetry that seems artful or calculated instead of being spontaneous, blurted out artlessly, without a moment of hesitation, without a correction. Such a critique, in the long run, rejects most of the poetry of Dryden and Pope, of Milton, Donne and the Metaphysical poets, even of Arnold and Hopkins. It reduces its own scope, after the worst of Wordsworth and of Christina Rossetti, to the work of Eliza Cook and Jean Ingelow, Ella Wheeler Wilcox, Rita Frances Mosscockle and Wilhelmina Stitch. Most bad poetry is indeed disarmingly sincere, with the sincerity of the "simple soul" in the confessional or on the psychoanalyst's couch. Whether as confessor or as analyst, the critic often understands better than its author what the poem, a huge Freudian slip, is really trying to say.

Modern Portuguese poetry has fortunately been spared many of these critical heresies that spring from Keats, Shelley and Wordsworth, author of the "Idiot Boy," that least complimentary of all romantic self-portraits. In English and American literature, these heresies are the literary analogue of Methodism and, in the history of English Quietism, of the devotion of John Keble. On the continent of Europe, only German literature seems to have been at all infected with them and, after the advent of Tolstoi, Russian literature too. Elsewhere, especially in France, Italy, Spain and Portugal, the poet was still respected, until the revolution of Surrealism, for his skill, his art, his magic, his dazzling devices; and this explains why Poe, so long neglected in England and America, was so highly praised in France, where both Baudelaire and Mallarmé translated him, and in Portugal, where he was translated by Fernando Pessoa, one of the most outstanding Portuguese poets of the past hundred years, a literary magician, an artificer and a simulator of pyrotechnical brilliance.

Were one to set up a typology of poetry based on coincidental details of character, appearance and biography as well as on common topics and elements of style, Fernando Pessoa would pose a pretty problem. Like Camoëns, Baudelaire, Kipling and Roy Campbell, he has sailed the Indian Ocean. Like Baudelaire and Mallarmé, he has translated Poe. Like Baudelaire, he lost his father at an early age and experienced a second trauma when his beloved mother remarried soon after her bereavement. Like myself, he expressed himself in two languages and had a maternal grandmother whom the family was forced to intern in a mental home. Like Swinburne and Mallarmé, he seems to have had almost no relations with women. Like Proust and Baudelaire, he had the kind of eyes that become acutely self-conscious when they face a camera so that all Pessoa's photographs seem strangely tragic. This game might go on for a long while, but it has already proven our point: that Pessoa's character and private life placed him immediately among the *Sciagurati* of poetry, with Poe, Baudelaire, Swinburne and Mallarmé, rather than with Charles Kingsley, Kipling, Sandburg and Camoëns, among poetry's more muscular, healthy or adventurous representatives.

It was Pessoa's additional misfortune to express himself at times, as a foreign poet, in English. Had he chosen to write more regularly in French—he tried his hand at this language, without much success, in a couple of undistinguished lyrics—he might have achieved a considerable reputation in France, which has a long and great tradition of outstanding foreign-born writers who expressed themselves more or less frequently in French. One need but mention, in this context, the Uruguayan poet Jules Supervielle, the American poetess Renée Vivien, and Rainer Maria Rilke, an Austrian whose French poems immediately obtained in France the recognition they deserved. But we are unaccustomed, in England and America, to such phenomena. I myself, though American-born and educated in England and America, find myself again and again treated politely as a kind of literary freak because of my "foreign" name, because I generally live on the continent of Europe and because I also publish in French or German. The foreign poet who expresses himself in English indeed appears to be a rank outsider and remains, in most cases, shockingly neglected. Only two poets who regularly expressed themselves in our language seem to have concerned themselves at all with Pessoa's English poems: Roy Campbell [*see Additional Bibliography*] and I. A South-African Nationalist, Campbell was, of course, anxious to discover other South-African poets of distinction in order to propagate the notion of a South-African tradition in English literature; besides, Campbell happened to be an ardent admirer of the *Lusiads* of Camoëns and a regular reader of Portuguese literature. A kind of post-dated Levantine, I can only claim to feel great sympathy for all poets who, as I, have tried to remain linguistically as versatile as Dante or Milton: Pessoa remains, in this respect, obviously *"mon semblable, mon frère."* (pp. 372-79)

The Portuguese poet Fernando Pessoa's familiarity with the English tongue and with English and American poetry was . . .

so great that it astounded the few English men of letters who ever chanced upon him or his English writings. In a letter of January 1936 to Gerald Hamilton, the fabulous original of Christopher Isherwood's hilarious Mr. Norris, who had then left Berlin in a hurry and seemed anxious to shake the dust of Brussels and Paris off his weary feet too, the notorious English "nigromancer" Aleister Crowley suggested Lisbon as a quiet hide-out: "But if you can find Don Fernando Pessoa you will find him a really good poet, the only man who has ever written Shakespearean Sonnets in the manner of Shakespeare. It is about the most remarkable literary phenomena in my experience." In the same letter, Crowley asked for news of Spender and Auden. . . .

Nor is this but another of Aleister Crowley's many weird and rarely justifiable enthusiasms. The anonymous critic of the London *Times Literary Supplement* . . . had also pointed out their "ultra-Shakespearian Shakespeareanisms" [see excerpt dated 1918]. Today, in an era accustomed to nicer critical distinctions, we might detect, in these sonnets, much that is hardly Shakespearean or that we would attribute to other influences. Still, Pessoa had been awarded, as a boy, the Queen Victoria Memorial Prize for English compositon, in a school in Durban, in Natal [South Africa], and had then gone on to study at the University of the Cape of Good Hope in Capetown. Had he continued to express himself in English after 1920, he might well have become one of the more outstanding English poets of our age. Instead, he seems, a kind of Rimbaud, to have condemned his English self to total literary silence after 1921 and to have then expressed himself, until his death in 1935, only in Portuguese.

There may have been some psychoneurotic motivations to Pessoa's final rejection of English as a language of literary expression. He had learned it, as a boy, when his widowed mother, shortly after his father's death, had married a man who was appointed Portuguese Consul in Durban. A jealous child, Pessoa had resented not only this marriage but his subsequent exile from Portugal. For many years, his stepfather remained, in his eyes, an intruder; and Portugal, the lost Paradise of his childhood. In 1924, this stepfather, so much like the one who haunts Baudelaire's *Flowers of Evil,* finally died; early in 1925, the poet's mother died too. Pessoa's last **English Poems** had been published privately in 1921 and he neglected to publish, after that, any of those that should have completed the cycle and have now, it seems, been lost. The language that the accident of his mother's second marriage had forced Pessoa to learn was no longer of any importanace to him after his stepfather's death, perhaps because the poet no longer felt the need to flaunt, in the eyes of the man who had sent him as a boy to a commercial school in Durban and then expected him to outshine all Portuguese rivals in the utilitarian Anglo-Saxon world of business, an absurdly useless virtuosity in expressing himself in obscure and ornate English verse rather than in the less colorful English prose of trade and accounting.

In creating this unusual English idiom that is now his own, Pessoa seems to have been conscious of the syntax of Elizabethan verse, the casuistry of Shakespeare's *Sonnets,* the thought of Ben Jonson and of Milton, the wit of Pope, the richness of Keats, the energy of Byron, the moods of Shelley, the Deistic elevation of Wordsworth, the melody of Tennyson, the rhythms of Poe, the sensuality of Swinburne. One is even tempted, at times, to detect, in Pessoa's verse, alliterations and rhythms that might be improbable echoes of Hopkins:

"The God is dead whose cult was to be kissed. . . ."

"... in sad madness glad ..."

"The male milk that makes living ..."

"The rain again like a vague pain arose. ..."

But such alliterations are also the common heritage of all English poets since Lyly's *Cupid and Campaspe*.

The books that Pessoa chose as prizes at school in Durban give us some clues to his boyhood readings: Keats, Tennyson, Ben Jonson and Poe. From the autobiographical notes that he supplied in 1914 to his friend Cortes Rodriguez, we also know that he devoted much time to readings of Shakespeare, Milton, Pope, Byron, Wordsworth and Shelley.

In 1913, when Pessoa began to write the poems that he subsequently published in English, "the situation of poetry," to quote T. S. Eliot's preface to the *Literary Essays* of Ezra Pound, "was stagnant to a degree difficult for any young poet of today to imagine." In the England of the Georgian poets, of Rupert Brooke, James Elroy Flecker, Edward Thomas and Lascelles Abercrombie, only Yeats and a few unknown poets such as Wilfred Owen and Isaac Rosenberg were already writing verse that has the kind of texture that Pessoa sought to achieve. True, Pessoa's **"Antinous"** and **"Epithalamium"** show some symptoms of this stagnation, but they also prove their author to have been one of the outstanding erotic poets of our language, perhaps the greatest since the Restoration. There is, of course, a school-boyish obsessiveness that sometimes mars the erotic concepts of the **"Epithalamium"** and, in **"Antinous,"** a cloying outspokenness. But an erotic poetry, in an age that no longer has any Rakes or Bucks and has lost the tradition of the evil but dispassionate Dandy, is bound to seem adolescent, merely naughty.

One can detect, in the two published poems of this erotic cycle, an element of archaism that gives us a foretaste of the philosophies that Pessoa was probably destined to develop in the three unpublished poems that were intended to complete the cycle. Transcending Whitman in his pantheism, the Portuguese poet was already very close, in some respects, to D. H. Lawrence and Henry Miller but with a dash of decadence and of post-Romantic Satanism that would have shocked these latter-day apostles of a lower-middle-class Eros. Though Pessoa's English is often bookish and his syntax, every once in a while, a bit awkward, his expression remains, on the whole, scarcely more artificial than that of Sacheverell Sitwell or of many an American poet of our own more learned "English Department" tradition (See **"Epithalamium"** I).

Amateur psychoanalysts have gone to great lengths, in Portuguese literary journals whose readers have no great experience of orthodox Freudian methodology, to explain some of the complexities of Pessoa's cluster of personalities. Only João Gaspar Simões, in the two-volume work that he has devoted to Pessoa's life and works, seems to have detected some of the curious beliefs that helped Pessoa to escape from the involuntary hallucinations of mere madness into the voluntary simulations of art. Pessoa was haunted, from his early childhood, by the memory of his maternal grandmother's insanity and, after the death of his own father and his mother's remarriage to his stepfather, by doubts concerning his own identity, personality, character or idiosyncrasy. He overcame these fears and doubts by creating all the men that he might reasonably have been, including the English poet who developed out of the sexual repressions of his middle-class South-African schoolyears; and he acted out, as a separate literary figure,

each one of these in turn, even the rather unimaginative and methodical accountant, Bernardo Soares, whom his stepfather had hoped to see Pessoa become. In these necromantic experiments that brought to life those who might have died without ever having really been born, Pessoa was moreover guided by theosophical and astrological theories and all sorts of occultist beliefs and experiments. For Alberto Caeiro and Alvaro de Compos, for instance, he had invented dates of birth and drawn horoscopes so that the personality of each of them as a poet is determined by the actual position of the stars and planets at the hour of his fictitious birth. (pp. 380-83)

Perhaps too much attention has been devoted by Portuguese critics to the whole problem of Pessoa's masks, personalities or *heterónimos*. Actually, this device of creating fictional characters who may also happen to be poets, like their author, is but an extension of the dramatist's traditional art; to have been able to breathe an individual poetic idiom into each of these fictional characters proves only, in the final analysis, Pessoa's rare genius as a potential dramatist. In English poetry, such a gift is rare, but not utterly exceptional. Robert Browning, in his poetic monologues, often achieved something very similar; Pessoa only made a point of achieving more thoroughly and in lyrical verse a kind of poetic simulation that remains the basic device of all truly dramatic poetry. (p. 385)

Edouard Roditi, "Fernando Pessoa, Outsider among English Poets," in The Literary Review, *(Fairleigh Dickinson University), Vol. 6, No. 3, Spring, 1963, pp. 372-85.*

MICHAEL HAMBURGER (essay date 1969)

[*Hamburger is a German-born English poet, translator, and critic. His publications in each of these genres are recognized as distinguished, and his numerous studies of and translations from German authors are particularly esteemed. In the following excerpt, Hamburger regards Pessoa's heteronyms as a means of coping with the complexity of modern life and a varied literary tradition.*]

The most extreme case of multiple personality and self-division in modern poetry is that of the Portuguese poet Fernando Pessoa.... Like so many of his contemporaries—Pound and Eliot and Appollinaire are a few of them—Pessoa experienced a physical and cultural transplantation that may have something to do with his extraordinary development as a poet. (The term "transplantés" was used by Rémy de Gourmont and distinguished by him from the term "déracinés," which had become a term of abuse in the mouths of early believers in the "blood and soil mystique.") As a child, Pessoa was taken to South Africa, spending his formative years in Durban and at an English-speaking public school. His early poems were written in English and collected in three volumes in 1922, after two earlier books of English poems published in 1918. Most of his mature work, written in Portuguese, was never published in his lifetime, though Pessoa returned to Portugal in 1905.

A posthumous sketch explains Pessoa's desperate resort to a division even of his poetic self into four distinct authors—Alvaro de Campos, Alberto Caeiro, Ricardo Reis and Fernando Pessoa—each of whom was allowed to write a kind of poetry which the other three did not and could not write.

> The first stage of lyrical poetry is that in which the poet concentrates on his feelings and expresses them. If, however, he is a creature with mutable and multiple feelings, he will express a number of personalities, as it were, held to-

gether only by temperament and style. One further step, and we are confronted with a poet who is a creature with multiple and fictitious feelings, more imaginative than emotional, experiencing every state of mind more intellectually than emotionally. This poet will express himself in a variety of persons no longer unified by temperament and style, but by style alone; for temperament has been replaced by imagination, and emotion by intellect. One farther step on the way to depersonalization or, better, imagination, and we are confronted with a poet who becomes so much at home in each of his different states of mind that he gives up his personality completely, to the point where, by experiencing each state of mind analytically, he makes it yield the expression of a different personality; in that way even style becomes manifold. One last step, and we find the poet who is several different poets at once, a dramatic poet who writes lyrical poems. Each group of imperceptibly related states of mind thus becomes a personality with a style of its own and feelings that may differ from the poet's own typical emotional experiences, or may even be diametrically opposed to them. And in this way lyrical poetry draws close to dramatic poetry without assuming dramatic form.

This was Pessoa's way of coping with the conflicts and tensions common to the poets of his time. Alvaro de Campos, for instance, is an out-and-out modernist, deriving from Whitman and from the Futurism of Marinetti, with preoccupations extraordinarily close to those of Hart Crane. Alvaro de Campos wrote odes in long rhapsodic, exclamatory, irregular lines, syntactically free and elliptic. Tradition, on the other hand, was maintained by the pagan and classical poet Ricardo Reis, who wrote meditative poems in regular stanzas, as terse and spare as the odes are effusive. Both these potentialities also characterize the work of Hart Crane, but the need to contain both within a single poet's work led Crane into modulations and inconsistencies of style which Pessoa was able to avoid. Alberto Caeiro, "a bucolic poet of a complicated kind," as Pessoa called him, wrote seemingly traditional reflections on the simple life which reveal a sophisticated and very modern revulsion from the awareness of multiplicity. Like Gottfried Benn, who claimed that the burdened consciousness of modern urban man amounted to a biological hypertrophy of the brain that would destroy the white races, Alberto Caeiro, a swain and shepherd familiar with Nietzsche, developed his "metaphysic of not thinking":

O que penso eu do mundo?
Sei lá o que penso do mundo!
Se eu adoecesse pensaria nisso.

Que ideia tenho eu das coisas?
Que opinião tenho sobre as causas e os efeitos?
Que tenho eu meditado sobre Deus e a alma
E sobre a criação do Mundo?
Não sei. Para mim pensar nisso é fechar os olhos
E não pensar . . .

(What do I think about the world?
Do I know what I think about the world?
If I were to fall sick I should think about it.

What ideas do I have about things?
What opinions about cause and effect?
What conclusion have I reached about God and the soul
And about the creation of the World?
I don't know. For me, to think about that is to shut
  my eyes
And not think . . .)

This is the modern poetic scepticism—an irrational scepticism—first recorded by Keats, the "negative capability" so highly developed in Pessoa that he took the unprecedented step of inventing the authors of his poems, even writing prose dialogues in which one of them argues with another. In that poem by Caeiro another characteristically modern tendency emerges, the same tendency that prompted T. E. Hulme, Ezra Pound and others to evolve the theory of Imagism, out of a scepticism towards conceptual thought and a transference of faith to concrete visible phenomena. Caeiro's pantheism is one that can finally dispense wtih God, giving back God's attributes and glory to the visible world—much as Rilke did. (pp. 138-41)

Ironically enough, even confessional poetry—poetry of the empirical self—has its place in the rich and multifarious opus of the four poets that were Fernando Pessoa (whose own name means "person"—*persona*—mask!). Yet is was under his own name that Pessoa wrote his poem **"Autopsicografia"** (**"Autopsychography"**), concerned with the truth of masks, his true confession of the difficulty of telling the truth:

O poeta é um fingidor.
Finge tão completamente
Que chega a fingir que é dor
A dor que deveras sente.

E os que lêem o que escreve,
Na dor lida sentem bem,
Não as duas que ele teve,
Mas só a que eles não têm.

E assim nas calhas de roda
Gira, a entreter a tazão,
Esse comboio de corda
Que se chama o coração.

(Poets feign and conceal,
So completely feign and pretend
That the pain which they really feel
They'll feign for you in the end.

And he who reads what they've done.
Never senses the twofold pain
That's in them, only the one
Which they never feel but feign.

And so, to amuse our minds
Round again to the start
On its circular railway winds
That toy train called the heart.)

Stylistically that poem is indeed by an author quite distinct from Pessoa's three other poetic media, though he had the advantage of drawing on the experiences of all four of them in presenting a paradox highly relevant to the self-concealment which, in so much modern poetry, is the prerequisite of self-expression. The sceptical intelligence at work in **"Autopsicografia"** is to be found in all Pessoa's work, even in the production of Alvaro de Campos, whose Nietzschean vitalism is as ambiguous as Nietzsche's own or as Gottfried Benn's, since both Nietzsche and Benn were "intellectualists" in revolt against the intellect.

The **"Ode marítima,"** the most ambitious and most characteristic of the poems attributed to Alvaro de Campos, derives its power from an extreme tension between a sense of dynamic movement and an opposing sense of stasis—a tension also striking in the work of Gottfried Benn, who called one of his later collections *Statische Gedichte* (Static Poems), despite his cult of sheer energy. The **"Ode marítima"** vacillates between a vitalist, often brutalist, affirmation of the savagery not only of the sea itself, but of sailors, and a weary, gentle and tender return to an "inner ocean" forever at rest beneath the surface commotion. There is something morbidly masochistic about the intellectual's apostrophes to the sailors and his invocations of a "horrible and satanic God, the God of a blood-pantheism."

> Ah, torturai-me para me curardes!
> Minha carne—fazei dela o ar que os vossos cutelos
>   atravessam
> Antes de caírem sobre as cabeças e os ombros!
> Minhas veias sejam os fatos que as facas trespassam!
> Minha imaginação o corpo das mulheres que violais!
> Minha inteligência o convés onde estais de pé matando!
> Minha vida toda, no seu conjunto nervoso, histérico,
>   absurdo,
> O grande organismo de que cada acto de pirataria que
>   se cometeu
> Fosse uma célula consciente—e todo eu turbilhonasse
> Como uma imensa podridão ondeando, e fosse aquilo
>   tudo!

> (O, torture me in order to heal me!
> My flesh: make it the air that your knives slash
> Before they come down on heads and on shoulders!
> My veins the clothes pierced by your blades!
> My imagination the bodies of the women you violate!
> My intelligence the deck on which you murder!
> All my life—nervous, hysterical, absurd—
> The great organism in which each act of piracy when
>   completed
> Becomes a conscious cell—and the whole of me seethes
> Like a vast billowing putrefaction, being all that you
>   are!)

The "I" of the poem, who glorifies savagery in these terms, is described as "an engineer in Lisbon,—forced to be practical, sensitive to everything. / Unlike you, tied down to this place, even when I'm walking; / Even when I'm acting, inert; even when I have my way, feeble, / Static, broken, a cowardly defaulter from your glory, / From your great strident energy, hot and bloody." The interpolation of "Fifteen men on the Dead Man's Chest / Yo-ho-ho and a bottle of rum!' is drawn out into pure brute noises: 'Eh-lahô-lahô-laHO-lahá-á-ááá-àà. . . .'" In the spirit of the Futurists—rather than of Hart Crane, with his historical and mythical preoccupations—machines and the machine age are also celebrated in the **"Ode marítima,"** though unlike Marinetti, Alvaro de Campos ascribed the cult of machines to the waking and rational mind, not to daydream fantasies of a "blood pantheism," so that a crucial distinction is made between animal and mechanical energy. It is when the engineer recovers from his frenzy that he turns to "modern and useful things, / Freighters, steamers and passengers." The barbarous fantasies—threaded with erotic, passively homosexual overtones—are connected not with these modern phenomena but with an obsolete schooner; and this schooner, in turn, is associated with idyllic childhood remi-

niscences in stark contrast with the same violent fantasies. In its drastic modulations, therefore, the **"Ode marítima"** spans differences and distances as great as those between the productions of the four poets whose works were written by Fernando Pessoa; and the many potential identities available to Pessoa are at least intimated within the confines of this one poem. Yet the other poems of Alvaro de Campos add to those potential identities. The ode **"Grandes são os desertos, e tudo é deserto"** (**"Great Are the Deserts, and All Is Desert"**) is not only related in theme and imagery to T. S. Eliot's earlier poems, but as ironically understated as most of the **"Ode marítima"** is hyperbolical.

> Acendo o cigarro para adiar a viagem,
> Para adiar todas as viagens,
> Para adiar o universo inteiro.

> Volta amanhã, realidade!
> Basta por hoje, gentes!
> Adia-te, presente absoluto!
> Mais vale não ser que ser assim.

> (I light the cigarette to put off the journey,
> To put off all journeys,
> To put off the whole universe.

> Come back tomorrow, reality!
> Enough for today, gentlemen!
> Take a break, absolute present!
> Better not to be than to be like this.)

The whole poem is dominated by one question—to pack or not to pack the suitcase, to be or not to be; and its images, at once trivial and existential, give a new sardonic poignancy to a complex familiar since Baudelaire's and Laforgue's and Mallarmé's *poésie des départs,* a complex specifically recalled by the title of a related poem of Alvaro de Campos, **"Là-bas, je ne sais où"**:

> Vida inútil, que era melhor deixar, que é uma cela?
> Que importa? Todo o universo é uma cela, e o estar
>   preso não tem que ver com o tamanho da cela.

> (Useless life, better left behind, life is a cell?
> What if it is? All the world is a cell, and to the
>   imprisoned the cell's dimensions are not what
>   matters.)

Fernando Pessoa's disguises were assumed out of the conviction that "poetry is more true than the poet"—and it is not his practice alone that vindicates the conviction, though neither the practice nor the conviction could have occurred to poets immune to doubts about personal identity. With perfect sincerity Pessoa could write in a letter that "Ricardo Reis writes better than I do, but with a purism that I consider excessive." As in other poets before him, extreme doubts about personal identity turned into extreme doubts about reality itself. Again it is a poem by Alvaro de Campos, **"The Tobacco Shop,"** that combines the most minute concentration on an external reality, the tobacco shop itself, with a sense of dream-like unreality. Here Pessoa, or de Campos, anticipates not only existentialism but the *nouveau roman* and playwrights like Ionesco, by an identification of the poet with the tobacconist that effects a total break with Romantic-Symbolist conceptions of the poet: "He will die and I shall die / He will leave his sign and I, verses"; but, above all, by the deliberate accumulation of trivial or inconsequential details to produce an almost hypnotic effect. As in early poems by T. S. Eliot, irresolution and caprice yield new imaginative possibilities. The parenthesis "(If I married my washerwoman's daughter, / Perhaps I should be happy)" is one instance of Pessoa's encroachment here on the novelist's, as well as the dramatist's, preserves. As in the *nouveau roman*, seemingly fortuitious movements and actions are recorded as though for their own sake: "The man has left the shop . . . the tobacconist has smiled."

Pessoa's drastic resort to heteronyms gave him an extraordinary scope. Among other things, it enabled him to tell the whole truth about himself, about the multiple selves that elude biography. In his important letter of 19 January 1915 to Armando Cortes-Rodrigues he rightly insisted on the sincerity and truthfulness of his work. The poems of Caeiro-Reis-Campos, he writes, "are a literature that I have created and lived, sincere because it is felt . . . felt in the other's person; written dramatically, but as sincere (in my grave sense of the word) as what King Lear says, though Lear is not Shakespeare, but one of his creations." Under his own name, Pessoa could write poems of many kinds, including the mystical **"Initiation"** that concludes: "Neophyte, there is no death." He needed Alvaro de Campos to render the modern experience of death-in-life ("I am nothing. / I shall always be nothing"), just as he needed Ricardo Reis to produce pure poems, though in the same letter to Cortes-Rodrigues he wrote about "the terrible importance of Life, that consciousness which makes it impossible for us to produce art only for art's sake, and the consciousness of having a duty towards ourselves and towards humanity." Pes-

soa believed in "the civilizing function of all works of art." His sincerity, which required disguises and even at times "the expression of a general truth through a personal lie," is defined in the same letter by contrast with the insincerity of "things written to shock . . . and those which do not contain a basic metaphysical idea, through which there passes no sense of the gravity and mystery of life." He had no patience with the "decoratively artistic," with "those whose produce art for various inferior reasons, such as those who play, those who amuse themselves, those who decorate a drawing-room with good taste." Yet his practice rests on the discovery that the greatest artist "expresses with the greatest intensity, richness and complexity what in fact he does not feel at all."

Even that is a simplification, corrected in Pessoa's poem **"Autopsicografia."** It is the feelings of the empirical self which poetry enlarges, complements or even replaces with fictitious ones, but only because the empirical self is not the whole self, cramped as it is in its shell of convention, habit and circumstance. Pessoa's disguises did not impair his truthfulness because he used them not to hoodwink others, but to explore reality and establish the full identity of his multiple, potential selves. (pp. 142-47)

Michael Hamburger, "Multiple Personalities," in his The Truth of Poetry: Tensions in Modern Poetry from Baudelaire to the 1960's, *1969. Reprint by Methuen, 1982, pp. 110-47.*

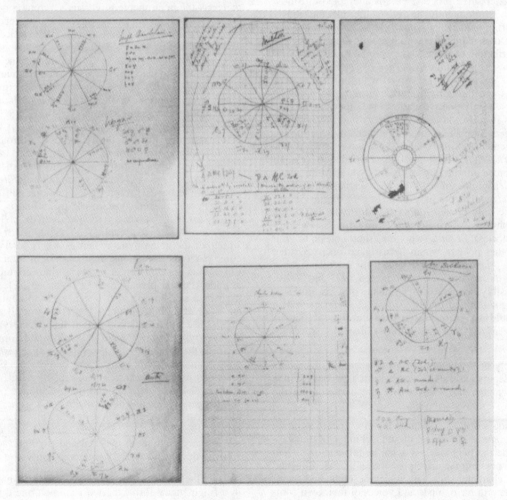

Horoscope made by Pessoa.

F. E. G. QUINTANILHA (essay date 1970)

[*In the following excerpt, Quintanilha examines the theoretical foundations of Pessoa's heteronyms and considers the unity of thought evident in Pessoa's works.*]

The heteronymic theory is based on the principle of the *impersonality of art*. Pessoa claims that the artist should be a synthesis of the varying personalities that go to make up his own character, and that he should reflect the thought of his own time. Thus, the greatest artist should be "the one who gives away his affiliations the least and the one who will write in the greatest number of literary genres, making use of paradoxes and dissimilarities. No artist should have only one personality. On the contrary, he should have several, each one from like states of mind which would discard the fictions that personality is one only and indivisible." Pessoa envisaged the replacement of thirty or forty poets of a given epoch by a mere two poets. Both would express themselves in as many as fifteen or twenty different personalities. Through these *alter egos,* they should attempt to go beyond the limitations of their own personality and time, and achieve a synthesis of the different ideological and aesthetic views of their time, and ultimately, represent what is common to Man throughout History. Thus, Art is the result of a process of development from the encounter of personalities, and from the synthesis of different aesthetics. This attitude demands considerable detachment on the part of the artist. In his creative process, Pessoa attempted to follow his theory of art. Consequently, he divided himself consciously into nineteen different names: *Fernando Pessoa* (he wrote some works under his own name, in accordance with the heteronymic technique of attributing to himself only specific types of thought and poems forms); the *Trilogy (Alberto Caeiro, Ricardo Reis,* and *Álvaro de Campos* were conceived within different ideological schemes and through different stylistic approaches: to Caeiro he allowed only poetry, while to the other two he permitted writings in prose on aesthetic theory and literary criticism); *C. Pacheco* (the author of a long poem anticipating the Surrealist movement); *Carlos Otto* (who wrote only a few poems); *Frederico Reis* and *António Mora* (Frederico Reis left fragments in prose on literary criticism, while Mora made speculations of a philosophical nature); *Vicente Guedes* and *Barão de Teive* (who wrote only in prose); *Bernardo Soares* (who also wrote only prose); *Rafael Baldaia* (who left a few notes on metaphysics); *Pero Botelho* (who wrote a few fragmentary short stories); *Eremita* (who left a short note on Logic); *A. March* (another poet to whom he assigned poetry written in Portuguese); *Alexander Search* and *Charles Robert Anon* (the authors of the poems he wrote between 1903 and 1909); *Jean Seul* (possibly conceived as an author for his works in the French language); and finally, *Miguel Otto* (conceived so that Pessoa could assign to him at least translations that he intended to do, as a manuscript amongst his papers reveals). (pp. xviii-xx)

With this variety of thought and form presented in his works and the total depersonalization which Pessoa advocates, one may wonder whether he achieved his aim of becoming the *Poet-Synthesis*.

Analysing Pessoa's works as a whole, it seems that, to a certain extent, he did achieve his aim. With the technique of the playwright, he made the *personae* say what he felt and also what he did not feel, obeying the principles of dramatic creation and keeping to the characteristics with which he embodied them. He expected them to have minds and voices of their own completely detached from his own personality and living in a world governed as much by reality as by fiction. Thus the heteronyms, created within the principle of decorum, were conceived differently from each other, either within the ideological structure which Pessoa imposed upon them, or representing various aesthetic attitudes.

A perusal of Pessoa's works, however, reveals that, owing to the fragmentary form of part of his output and difficulties in the fulfilment of the schemes he intended to impose on his creations, he was unable to develop the whole of his heteronymic theory. A complete detachment was never accomplished. The omnipresence of Pessoa is shown in attitudes common to all the heteronyms, therefore limiting them, and bringing to the fore Pessoa's real self. Some of the attitudes seem more relevant: *alienation,* typical of twentieth-century man, which is reflected in all his heteronyms who are *isolated islands* without the possibility of real communication, closed in upon themselves, analysing themselves, and looking at the external world from a critical and detached viewpoint. They remain strangers to the world, and by constant self-criticism they create a duality between observer and observed: *the principle of detachment* in which Pessoa tried to change subjective into objective poetry, which could stand on its own and live up to its own values; *intellectualism*—all the heteronyms reflect an intellectual attitude towards themselves and life, from which they banish the emotive element by dissecting their own thoughts in an ever-constant analysis; *consistency of metaphysical themes*—the main theme in Pessoa's output is not as varied as his heteronymic theory would suggest, and it concentrates mainly on a few themes concerning Man and Existence. Following a dialectical process based on different or even opposing attitudes of mind, the heteronyms seek to overcome metaphysical solitude and thus to discover the real essence of man in their inner self. They consider human life as a supreme mystery and the search they undertake assumes various aspects: either through a naïve positivism based on sensory knowledge (as in Caeiro), or a stoic and epicurean approach (as in Reis), or a decadent or an existential position (as in Campos), or through Occultism, or pure escapism in dreams or taking refuge in the world of childhood, or even by resorting to constant procrastination (as in Fernando Pessoa and Soares); through his *dialectical process* which is the basis of both these creations and their development, Pessoa makes constant use of antithesis, paradox, and syllogisms, which gives a certain unity to the style of his output when considered as a whole; *tendency towards the universal,* which all the heteronyms reveal as a way for Pessoa to overcome personal limitations, in a process of total acceptance of life, although never venturing into serious commitment. In this attitude, Pessoa reveals himself as an aesthete. He observes the world and himself, but never wants to commit himself to any type of definite thought. He repudiates all systems of beliefs, and feels dissatisfied with a superficial type of thought, always trying to go beyond it; finally, and common to all of them, is the *principle of artistry and craftsmanship*—this principle seems to be the great merit of Pessoa's output. All his creations reveal extreme care in artistic detail, and each heteronym shows a different and quite elaborate poetic attitude. If a deeper, systematic study of Pessoa's works shows certain ideological attitudes common to them all, such as those concerning life, death, love, religion, science, and politics, above all by the variations in metrical and rhythmic techniques and stylistic devices, it reveals great versatility and virtuosity.

Despite the fact that some of Pessoa's works have come to us in a fragmentary form, the works which one thinks he would consider complete reveal his greatness. One might venture to say that whatever the limitations of Pessoa's works, either because of his ideology or because of the fragmentary nature of his writings, they show a high intellectual and aesthetic conception, and attain a very mature poetic standard; they portray a man of immense stature, divided between a Faustian tradition with an intense intellectual curiosity, which makes him ready to exploit all trends of thought, and an ever-present Hamlet-like indecision, leading him to vacillate between any thesis and its antithesis; they also confront the reader with a vast cultural background, shown in the poet's attempt to blend the different ideologies—from the Ancient Greeks to the twentieth century—that he chose for the formation of the heteronyms, whether they reflect his own ideas or are merely a theme for a poem to be subsequently discarded; finally, they present Pessoa's extraordinary ability as a craftsman and a refined artist. All this has led many to consider Pessoa the finest Portuguese poet since Camões and has assured him a place amongst the most representative poets of Western Culture. (pp. xlvii-xlix)

> *F.E.G. Quintanilha, "Introduction: Fernando Pessoa, the Man and His Work," in* Sixty Portuguese Poems *by Fernando Pessoa, edited and translated by F.E.G. Quintanilha, University of Wales Press, 1971, pp. xi-xlix.*

OCTAVIO PAZ (essay date 1971)

[*An author of works on literature, art, anthropology, culture, and politics, Paz is recognized as one of the greatest modern Spanish-American poets. Early in his career he met André Breton, founder of Surrealism, and Paz's work shares the Surrealist quest for personal freedom and the high value placed on love relationships. Paz's poetry is characterized as visionary and experimental, and his critical writings on literature are regarded with respect. In the following excerpt, Paz analyzes Pessoa's heteronyms and discusses their significance individually and collectively.*]

Anglomanic, myopic, courteous, elusive, dressed in black, reticent and familiar, the cosmopolitan who preaches nationalism, *the solemn investigator of useless things*, the humorist who never smiles and makes our blood run cold, the inventor of other poets and self-destroyer, the author of paradoxes clear as water, and like water, dizzying: *to pretend is to know oneself*, the mysterious one who doesn't cultivate mystery, mysterious as the moon at noon, the taciturn ghost of the Portuguese midday—who is Pessoa? Pierre Hourcade, who knew him at the end of his life, writes, "Never, on taking leave of him, did I dare turn around; I was afraid of seeing him vanish, disappear in thin air." Anything else? In 1935 he died of a hepatic colon, in Lisbon. He left two "brochures" of poems in English, a thin booklet of Portuguese verse, and a trunk full of manuscripts. His complete works have not yet been published.

It all begins on March 8, 1914. But it is better to quote part of Pessoa's letter to Adolfo Casais Monteiro, one of the young men at *Presença*:

> Sometime around 1912, unless I'm mistaken (which couldn't be by very much), the idea came to me to write some poems of pagan character. I sketched out some things in free verse (not in the style of Álvaro de Campos but in my own normal style), and then abandoned the attempt. But in that dim confusion I made out the hazy outline of the person who was writing. (Without my knowing it, Ricardo Reis had been

> born.) A year and a half or two years later, I remember one day taking up Sá-Carneiro's challenge to invent a bucolic poet, of a complicated sort, and present him, I don't recall now how, as if he were really a living creature. I spent a few days working on him without getting anywhere. The day I'd finally given up—it was March 8, 1914—I went over to a high desk, and taking a piece of paper, began to write, standing up, as I always do when possible. And I wrote some thirty poems, one after another, in a sort of ecstasy, the nature of which I'm unable to define. It was the triumphant day of my life, and never will I have another like it. I began with the title, "**The Keeper of Sheep.**" What followed was the appearance in me of someone whom I named, from then on, Alberto Caeiro. Forgive me the absurdity of the sentence: in me there appeared my master. That was my immediate reaction. So much so that, scarcely were those thirty odd poems written when I took fresh paper and wrote, again without stopping, the six poems constituting *Chuva Obliqua (Oblique Rain)*, by Fernando Pessoa. Straight off and fully formed . . . It was the return of Fernando Pessoa-Alberto Caeiro to Fernando Pessoa himself. Or, better, it was the reaction of Fernando Pessoa against his nonexistence as Alberto Caeiro. Once Alberto Caeiro had appeared I instinctively and subconsciously tried to find disciples for him. Out of his false paganism I plucked Ricardo Reis, whose name I discovered and adapted to him, since I'd already seen him there. And suddenly, derived from and opposed to Ricardo Reis, there impetuously arose in me a new individual. At once, and on the typewriter, there surged up without interruption or correction, the "**Triumphal Ode**" of Álvaro de Campos—the ode so entitled together with the man so named [see excerpt dated 1935].

I don't know what there is to add to this confession.

Psychology offers a variety of explanations. Pessoa himself, who was interested in his own case, proposes two or three. One crudely pathological: "I'm probably an hysterico-neurasthenic . . . and this explains, more or less, the organic origin of the heteronyms." I'd say "less" rather than "more." The trouble with these hypotheses is not that they're false but that they're incomplete. A neurotic is an obsessive. But if he controls his disturbance, is he sick? The neurotic suffers his obsessions; the creative person masters and transforms them. Pessoa tells of living with imaginary people from the time he was a child. ("I don't know, of course, if it was they who didn't exist or if it was I who didn't: in such instances one shouldn't be dogmatic.") The heteronyms are surrounded by a fluid mass of semi-beings: Bernardo Soares, ghost of the ghostly Vicente Guedos; Pacheco, a poor copy of Campos. . . . Not all of them are writers. There's a Mr. Cross, the indefatigable contributor to charades and crossword-puzzle contests in the English magazines (an infallible means, according to Pessoa, of getting rid of the blues), Alexander Search, and others. All this—like his solitude, his discrete alcoholism, and other things—gives us hints about his personality but tells us nothing about his poems, which is the only thing that really matters to us.

The same is true of the so-called "occultist," whom Pessoa, being overly analytical, doesn't openly admit but never stops evoking. It's a well-known fact that spirits who guide the pen of mediums, whether of Euripides or of Victor Hugo, show a disconcerting literary torpor. Others believe this to be a matter of "mystification." The error is doubly vulgar: Pessoa is neither a liar nor is his work a fraud. There's something terribly mean-spirited about the modern mind. People who tolerate all sorts of debased falsehoods in real life and swallow every kind of worthless fact, won't accept the existence of the fable. And that's what Pessoa's work is: a fable, a fiction. To forget that Caeiro, Reis, and Campos are poetic creations is forgetting too much. Like every creation these poets are born out of play. Art is play—among other things. But there is no art without play.

The authenticity of the heteronyms depends on its poetic coherence, its verisimilitude. They were necessary creations because in no other way could Pessoa have devoted his life to living and creating them; what counts now is not that they were necessary for their author but that they are also necessary for us. Pessoa, their first reader, did not doubt their reality. Reis and Campos told what he perhaps would never tell. In contradicting him they expressed him; in expressing him they made him invent himself. We write to be what we are or to be what we aren't. In either case we are looking for ourselves. And if we are lucky enough to find ourselves—the sign of creation—we'll discover that we are an unknown person. Always the other, always he, inseparable, alien, having your face and mine, you who are always with me and always alone.

The heteronyms are not literary masks: "What Fernando Pessoa writes belongs to two kinds of works; we might call them orthonyms and heteronyms. We can't say they're anonyms or pseudonyms, because they aren't really. The pseudonymous work is by the author in his own person, except that he uses another name; the heteronymous is by the author outside his own person. . . ." Gérard de Nerval is the pseudonym for Gérard Labrunie: same person, same work. Caeiro is a heteronym of Pessoa's; impossible to confuse the two. Closer to home, the case of Antonio Machado is also different. Abel Martín and Juan de Mairena are not entirely the poet Antonio Machado. They are masks, but transparent masks; a piece by Machado is not distinct from one by Mairena. Also, Machado is not possessed by his fiction, they are not creatures he lives inside of, who contradict or deny him. Caeiro, Reis, and Campos, on the other hand, are the heroes of a novel which Pessoa never wrote. "I am a dramatic poet," he confided in a letter to J. G. Simões. Nevertheless, the relationship between Pessoa and his heteronyms is not the same as that between the dramatist or the novelist and his characters. He is not an inventor of poet characters but a creator of poet works. The distinction is crucial. As Casais Monteiro says, "He invented the biographies for the sake of the works and not the works for the sake of the biographies." Those works—including the poems by Pessoa written facing them, by means of as well as against them—are his poetic work. He himself turns into one of the works in his work. And not even he has the privilege of being the critic of this coterie. Reis and Campos treat him with a certain condescension; Baron de Teive does not always greet him; Vicente, the archivist, resembles him so much that when they meet, in some neighborhood eating-place, he feels a twinge of pity for himself. He is the bewitched enchanter, so totally possessed by his phantasmagorias that he feels them watching him, perhaps scornfully, perhaps sympathetically. Our creations do judge us.

"Alberto Caeiro is my master." This affirmation is the touchstone of all his work. And to this may be added that Caeiro's work is the only affirmation that Pessoa made. Caeiro is the sun in whose orbit Reis, Campos, and Pessoa himself rotate. In each are particles of negation or unreality: Reis believes in form, Campos in sensation, Pessoa in symbols. Caeiro doesn't believe in anything: he exists. The sun is life that is full of itself; the sun shines not because its rays are glances converted into heat and light; the sun is not aware of itself because for the sun thinking and being are one and the same thing. Caeiro is everything that Pessoa is not, and more—everything a modern poet could never be: a man reconciled to nature. Before Christianity, yes, but also before work and history. Before consciousness. Caeiro denies, by the mere act of existing, not just the Symbolist esthetic of Pessoa but all esthetics, all values, all ideas. Does nothing remain? Everything remains, clean of ghosts and the cobwebs of culture. The world exists because my senses tell me so; and by so telling me they tell me I too exist. Yes, I shall die and the world will die, but to die is to live. Caeiro's affirmation annuls death; by overcoming consciousness it overcomes nothingness. It doesn't affirm that everything is, since that would be to affirm an idea. It says that everything exists. And even more—it says only that is which exists. The rest are illusions. Campos sees to it that the *i* is dotted. "My master Caeiro was not a pagan; he was paganism." I would add, an idea of paganism.

Caeiro scarcely went to school. When he heard himself called a "materialist poet" he wanted to know what the doctrine was all about. When Campos explained it to him, he couldn't keep his surprise to himself. "That's a notion of priests without religion! You mean to say they say space is infinite? What space have they been looking at?" To his disciple's stupefaction, Caeiro maintained that space is finite. "What has no limits doesn't exist. . . ." The other replied, "Well, what about numbers? After 34 there's 35, then 36, and so on, consecutively. . . ." Caeiro stood there looking at him pitifully: "But those are only numbers!" adding, with crushing childlikeness, "Is there really in fact a number 34?" Another anecdote: they asked him, "Are you happy with yourself?" And he answered, "No, I am happy." Caeiro is not a philosopher: he's a sage. Thinkers have ideas; for the sage, living and thinking are not separate acts. For that reason it's impossible to express the ideas of Socrates and Lao Tse. They did not leave doctrines but a handful of anecdotes, enigmas and poems. Chuang Tse, more faithful than Plato, does not try to give us a philosophy but to tell us little stories; philosophy is inseparable from the story. It is story. The philsopher's doctrine incites refutation; the life of the sage is irrefutable. No sage proclaims that you can learn truth; what they all—or almost all of them—say is that the only truth worth bothering to live for is to experience truth. Caeiro's weakness is not in his ideas (actually, that's his strength); it's in the unreality of the experience he claims to be embodying.

Adam in some corner of a Portuguese province, with no wife, no children, and no antecedent; he has no consciousness, no job, no religion. One sensation among other sensations, one existence among other existences. The stone's a stone and Caeiro's Caeiro—for the moment. Later, each will be something else. Or the same thing. It's the same or it's different: everything is the same through being different. To be named is to be. The word for stone is not the stone but has the same reality as the stone. Caeiro does not propose giving beings any name, and so he never tells us whether the stone is an agate or a cobblestone, if the tree is a pine or an oak. Nor does he hope to set up relations among things; the word *like* doesn't figure in his vocabulary; everything is submerged in its own reality. If Caeiro speaks it's because man is a word-using animal, as the bird is a wing-using animal. Man speaks the way the river runs or the rain falls. The innocent poet doesn't have to name things; his words are trees, clouds, spiders, lizards. Not those spiders I see but these that I speak of. The idea that reality is ungraspable astonishes Caeiro: here it is, in front of us; touching it is enough. Speaking is enough.

It wouldn't be hard to demonstrate to Caeiro that reality is never graspable and that we must conquer it (though at the risk of its evaporating before us in the act, or of its being changed into something else—an idea, a tool). The innocent poet is a myth, but a myth that is the basis of poetry. The real poet knows words and things are not the same, and so in order to re-establish a precarious unity between man and the world, he names things with his images, rhythms, symbols, and comparisons. Words are not things; they are the bridges we set up between ourselves and them. The poet is the consciousness of words—that is, the nostalgia for the *real* reality of things. Words of course were also things before they became the names for things. This is what they were in the myth of the innocent poet, that is, before language. The opaque words of the real poet evoke speech prior to language, the scarcely glimpsed paradisaical covenant. Innocent speech: silence in which nothing is said because everything has been said, everything is bespeaking itself. The poet's language feeds on this silence, which is innocent speech. Pessoa, a real poet and a skeptical man, had to invent an innocent poet in order to justify his own poetry. Reis, Campos, and Pessoa speak mortal and dated words, words of loss and fragmentation; they are the presentiment of the nostalgia for unity. We hear them against the backdrop of the silence of that unity. It is no accident that Caeiro should die young, before his disciples begin their work. He is their foundation, the silence which sustains them.

The most natural and simplest of the heteronyms is the least real. Because of the excess of reality. Man, especially modern man, is not all real. He is not a compact entity like nature or things; his self-consciousness is his unsubstantial reality. Caeiro is an absolute affirmation of existence, whence his words appear to us to be truths from another time, a time when everything was one and the same. A sensate, untouchable presence: as we name it, it evaporates! The mask of innocence Caeiro turns on us is not wisdom: to be wise is to resign ourselves to knowing we are not innocent. Pessoa, who knows this, is closer to wisdom.

The other extreme is Álvaro de Campos. Caeiro lives in the timeless present of children and animals; the Futurist Campos, in the moment. For the former, his village is the center of the world; the other, a cosmopolitan, has no center, and is exiled in that no-man's-land which is everywhere. Yet they resemble one another: they both cultivate free verse; they both do violence to the Portuguese language; neither is afraid of being prosaic. They do not believe in anything they cannot touch, they're pessimists, love concrete reality, don't love their fellow creatures, scorn ideas, and live ouside of history—one in the plenitude of being, the other in extremest privation. Caeiro, the innocent poet, is what Pessoa couldn't be; Campos, the vagabond dandy, is what he could have been and wasn't. They are the vital, impossible possibilities of Pessoa.

Campos's first poem has a deceptive originality. "**Triumphal Ode**" is apparently a brilliant echo of Whitman and the Futurists. One can hardly compare the poem with those being written at the time in France, Russia, and other countries, before noticing the differences. (There was no one like him in Spanish till Lorca's and Neruda's generation. Yes, there was the prose written by the great Ramón Gómez de la Serna. In Mexico we had a modest beginning, but only a beginning, in Tablada. 1918 was when modern poetry really opened up in Spanish. But its initiator, Vicente Huidobro, is a poet of a very different cast.) Whitman really believed in man and machines; better yet, he believed that *natural man* was not incompatible with machines. His pantheism also welcomed industry. Most of his descendants do not agree with such illusions. Some see the machine as a marvelous plaything. I'm thinking of Valéry Larbaud and his Barnabooth, who resembles Álvaro de Campos in more ways than one. Larbaud's attitude toward the machine is Epicurean; that of the Futurists, visionary. They see it as the destructive agent of false humanism and, presumably, of *natural man*. They don't suggest humanizing the machine but constructing a new human species like it. An exception to this would be Mayakovski, and even he . . . "**Triumphal Ode**" is neither romantic nor Epicurean nor triumphant; it is a song of hate and defeat. And this is the basis of its originality.

A factory is a "tropical landscape" populated by huge, lascivious beasts. Endless fornication of wheels, pistons and pulleys. As the mechanical rhythm speeds up the paradise of iron and electricity turns into a torture chamber. The machines are the sexual organs of destruction: Campos would like to be torn to pieces by their furious helices. This strange vision is less fantastic than it seems and is not an obsession of Campos's alone. Machines are the reproduction, simplification, and multiplication of vital processes. They seduce and horrify us because they give us the feeling of intelligence and unconsciousness simultaneously; everything they do they do well, but they don't know what they're doing. Isn't this the image of modern man? But machines are one facet of contemporary civilization. The other is social promiscuity. "**Triumphal Ode**" ends in a scream; transformed into a bulk, a box, a package, a wheel, Álvaro de Campos loses the capacity to speak; he whistles, he squeaks, he chatters, hammers, explodes. Caeiro's word evokes the unity of man, stone, and insect; that of Campos, the incoherent noise of history. Pantheism and pan-machinism, two means of abolishing the consciousness.

"**Tobacco Shop**" is the poem of recovered consciousness. Caeiro asks himself, "What am I?" Campos, "Who am I?" From his room he studies the street: automobiles, passers-by, dogs, all real and all hollow, all of them close by and all of them far away. Across the way, sure of himself as a god, enigmatic and smiling like a god, rubbing his hands like God Almighty after his horrible creation, the Owner of the Tobacco Shop appears and disappears. Arriving at his combination lair-temple-shop is Stevens, the indifferent one, who speaks and eats "without metaphysics," has feelings and political opinions, and keeps the holy days of obligation. From his window—his consciousness—, Campos looks out at the two puppets and seeing them sees himself. Where is reality—in me or in Stevens? The Tobacco Shop Owner smiles and does not answer. Campos, the Futurist poet, begins by affirming that the only reality is sensation; a few years later he asks himself if he himself has any reality.

In abolishing his self-consciousness Caeiro eliminates history; but it is history that suppresses Campos. Marginal life: his brothers, if he has any, are the prostitutes, bums, dandies, beggars, the scum of high and low societies. His rebellion has no place at all for ideas of redemption or justice: "No, anything but being right! Anything but caring about humanity! Anything rather than give in to humanitarianism!'' Campos rebels against the idea of rebellion too. It's not a moral virtue, a state of consciousness—it's the consciousness of a sensation: ''Ricardo Reis is a pagan by conviction; António Mora, by intelligence; I am one by rebellion, that is, by temperament.'' His sympathy for shady characters is mixed with contempt, but it's a contempt he feels for himself above all:

I feel for all those people,
Especially when they don't deserve it.
Yes, I'm also a drifter and a sponger . . .
Being lazy and a beggar isn't being lazy and a beggar:
It's being outside the social hierarchy . . .
It's not being a Supreme Court Judge, a full-time
    worker, a prostitute,
Down and out, exploited proletarian,
Somebody with an incurable disease,
Hungry for Justice, or a captain in the cavalry,
It's not being, finally, one of those social characters
    invented by novelists
Bored stiff with literature because they've every right to
    pour on the tears
And rebelling against society because they've got more
    than enough reason to do so . . .

His vagrancy and beggarliness don't depend on any particular circumstance; they're incurable and unredeemable. To be vagrant that way is *to be isolated in one's soul*. And further, with a brutality that scandalized Pessoa: ''I don't even have the excuse of being able to have social opinions . . . I'm clear-headed. None of your damned humane esthetics: I'm clear. Shit! I'm clear-headed!''

The consciousness of exile has been a constant note in modern society for a century and a half. Gérard de Nerval pretends to be the Prince of Aquitaine; Álvaro de Campos chooses the mask of the vagrant. The shift is revealing. Troubadour or beggar—what hides behind the mask? Nothing, maybe. The poet is the consciousness of his historical unreality. Only if that consciousness withdraws from history, society founders in its own opaque abyss, turns into Stevens or the Tobacco Shop Owner. There's no lack of people to say that Campos's attitude is not ''positive.'' To critics of this sort, Casais Monteiro replied, ''Pessoa's work is *really* a negative work. It's not a model, it doesn't teach you to handle others or be handled. It's useful because it does just the opposite: it undisciplines the spirit.''

Campos doesn't rush ahead, like Caeiro, to become everything, but to be everyone and everywhere. The drop into plurality is paid for by the loss of one's identity. Ricardo Reis selects the other latent possibility in his master's poetry. Reis is a hermit as Campos is a vagabond. His hermitage is a philosophy and a form. The philosophy is a mixture of Stoicism and Epicureanism. The form, the epigram, the ode, and the elegy of the Neoclassical poets. Except that the Neoclassicism is a nostalgia, which is to say, a romanticism that either is unaware of itself or that disguises itself. While Campos writes his long monologues that come closer to being introspections than hymns, his friend Reis polishes little odes on pleasure, the flight of time, the roses of Lydia, the illusory freedom of man, the vanity of the gods. Educated in a Jesuit school, a doctor by profession, a monarchist, exiled in Brazil since 1919, a pagan and skeptic by conviction, a Latinist by education, Reis lives outside of time. He seems to be, but is not, a man out of the past. He has chosen to live in a timeless *sagesse*. Cioran re-

cently indicated that our century, which has invented so many things, has not created what is needed most. It is not surprising that some find it in Oriental tradition: Taoism, Zen Buddhism. Actually, those doctrines serve the same function that the moral philosophies of the classical period did. Reis's Stoicism is a manner of not being in the world, without actually leaving it. His political ideas have a similar significance: they are not a program but a negation of the present state of things. He neither hates Christ nor does he love Him: he abhors Christianity, although—esthete to the end—when he thinks of Jesus he admits that ''his pitiful suffering form brought us something that was missing.'' The true deity for Reis is Fate, and all of us, men and myths, are subject to its rule.

The form Reis uses, like all artificial perfection, is admirable and monotonous. One sees in those little poems, more than his familiarity with the Latin and Greek originals, a wise and distilled mixture of Lusitanian Neoclassicism and the Greek Anthology translated into English. The correctness of his language disturbs Pessoa: ''Caeiro writes Portuguese poorly; Campos does a reasonable job of it, though he falls into saying such things as *eu própro* for *eu mesmo;* Reis writes better than I but with a purity which I consider exaggerated.'' The somnambulist exaggeration of Campos is transformed by an altogether natural movement of contradiction into the exaggerated precision of Reis.

Neither form nor philosophy protects Reis; they protect a phantom. The truth is that Reis doesn't exist and he knows it. Brilliant, with a sharpness more penetrating than Campos' exasperation, he contemplates himself:

I do not know whose past I recall in me,
Since I was someone else then, nor do I recognize myself
When with my heart I feel that other heart
Which I remember I once felt.
We forsake ourselves from one day to the next.
Nothing truly ties us to ourselves—
We are who we are, and who we were
Is something we once glimpsed within.

The labyrinth in which Reis loses himself is that of his own self. The poet's looking-inward, something very different from introspection, brings him close to Pessoa. Though both use meters and fixed forms, it is not traditionalism that unites them because they belong to different traditions. The sense of time unites them—not as something which passes before us but as something that becomes us. Prisoners of the moment, Caeiro and Campos affirm being or absence of being in one decisive stroke. Reis and Pessoa lose themselves in the byways of their thought, catch up with themselves at a turn in the path and, fusing with themselves, embrace a shadow. The poem is not the expression of being but the commemoration of that moment of fusion. A hollow monument: Pessoa builds a temple to the unknown; Reis, soberer, writes an epigram that is also an epitaph:

Let luck deny me everything
Except to glimpse its workings,
For I, who am a Stoic but not obdurate,
Would see the sentence Destiny engraves,
And letter by letter savor it.

Álvaro de Campos would cite a remark of Ricardo Reis': ''I hate lying because it is not exact.'' The words could be applied to Pessoa, so long as you don't confuse lying with imagination or exactness with inflexibility. Reis' poetry is precise and simple as a line drawing; Pessoa's, exact and complex as music.

Complex and various, it moves in distinct directions: toward prose, towards poetry in Portuguese, and towards poetry in English (one must discount the poems in French as trivial.) The prose pieces, though all are not as yet published, can be divided into two big categories: those appearing over his name and those over his pseudonyms, mainly the Baron de Teive, a decayed aristocrat, and Bernardo Soares, a commercial clerk. In various passages Pessoa stresses that they are not heteronyms: "both write in a style that, for better or worse, is my own. . . ." It's not indispensable to linger over the English poems; their interest is literary and psychological, but they don't amount to much, it seems to me, as English poetry. The poetry in Portuguese, from 1902 to 1935, comprises *Mensage* [*Message*], the lyrical poetry, and the dramatic poems. The latter, in my opinion, have a marginal value. Even if they're put to one side, there remains an extensive poetic production. A primary distinction: the heteronyms write in one direction and on one temporal level; only Pessoa splits up like a delta with each arm giving us the image, the whole imagery, of a single moment.

The lyrical poetry branches out into *Mensagem*, the *Cancioneiro* (*Book of Ballads*) (with its unedited and scattered parts) and the hermetic poems. As usual, the classification doesn't correspond to reality. The *Cancioneiro* is a symbolist book and is impregnated with hermeticism, though the poet doesn't expressly resort to the imagery of the occult tradition. *Mensagem* is, above all, a book of heraldry—and heraldry is part of alchemy. Finally, the hermetic poems are symbolist in form and spirit; one does not have to be an initiate to get into them, nor does understanding them poetically require special knowledge. These poems, like the rest of his work, ask instead for spiritual understanding, the highest and most difficult there is. To know Rimbaud was interested in the Cabbala and identified poetry with alchemy is useful and brings us close to his work; but really to penetrate it one needs something more and something less. Pessoa defines that something else as sympathy, intuition, intelligence, comprehension, and—the most difficult—grace. Perhaps this list seems excessive. I don't see how, though, without these five conditions, one can read Baudelaire, Coleridge or Yeats. In any event, the difficulties of Pessoa's poetry are fewer than those of Hölderlin, Nerval, Mallarmé. . . . In all the poets of the modern tradition poetry becomes a system of analogies and symbols that parallels that of the hermetic sciences. Parallels but is not identical to: the poem is a constellation of signs with light of their own.

Pessoa conceived of *Mensagem* as a ritual; or, say, as an esoteric book. If one is looking for external perfection, it's his most complete book. But it's a contrived book, by which I don't mean that it's insincere but that it's born of the poet's speculations and not his intuitions. At first glance, it is a hymn of glory to Portugal and a prophecy of a new Empire (the Fifth) that will be not a matter of substance but of the spirit; its dominions will extend beyond historical space and time (any Mexican reader at once recalls Vasconcelos' "cosmic race.") The book is a gallery of historical and legendary characters, displaced by traditional reality and transformed into allegories of another tradition and of another reality. Without fully knowing what he was doing, perhaps, Pessoa violated the history of Portugal and, in its stead, presented another, purely spiritual, which is its negation. The esoteric character of *Mensagem* keeps us from reading it as a simple patriotic poem, as some official critics would like to do. One must add that its symbolism does not redeem it. For symbols to work effectively they must stop symbolizing and become palpable, live creatures, not be em-

blems out of a museum. As in all work where the will intervenes more than inspiration, few poems in *Mensagem* reach the state of grace that distinguishes poetry from *belles lettres*. But those few live in the very magical space of the better poems in *Cancioneiro*, side by side with some of the hermetic sonnets. It is impossible to define what this space consists of; for me it is poetry, properly speaking, its real, tangible territory, which *another* light illuminates. It doesn't matter that they are so few. Benn said: "Nobody, not even the greatest poets of our age, have left more than eight or ten perfect poems. . . . For six poems, thirty or fifty years of asceticism, of suffering, of fighting!"

The *Cancioneiro*, a work containing few creatures and many shadows. No women, the central sun. Without women the sensuous universe vanishes, there is no terra firma, no water, no incarnation of the impalpable. The terrible pleasures are missing, and also the prohibited ones. Also missing is passion, that love which is desire for a unique being, whoever it may be. There is a vague sentiment of fraternity with nature: trees, clouds, stones, everything fleeting, everything suspended in a temporal vacuum. The unreality of things, reflecting our unreality. There is negation, weariness and disconsolateness. In the *Livro do Desassossêgo (Book of Disquietude)*, of which only fragments are known, Pessoa describes his moral landscape: I belong to a generation without faith in Christianity, and which stopped having faith in all other beliefs; we were not enthusiasts of social equality, of beauty or progress; we did not look to the East or the West for other religious forms ("every civilization has an affiliation with the religion that represents it; on losing ours, we lost them all"); a few among us devoted themselves to conquering the quotidian; others, of nobler stock, abstained from public activity, seeking nothing and desiring nothing; still others got interested in the cult of confusion and noise; they thought they were alive when they listened, they thought they were in love when they bumbled up against the externals of love; others of us, "in the End-Race, the spiritual limit of the Dead Hour," live in negation, hopeless and unhappy. This is not a portrait of Pessoa but certainly of the background from which his figure stands out and with which he is confused at times. "Spiritual limit of the Dead Hour": the poet is a hollow man who in his helplessness creates a world in order to discover his true identity. All Pessoa's work is a search for lost identity.

In one of his most quoted poems he says that "The poet is a faker. He / Fakes it so completely, / He even fakes he's suffering / The pain he's really feeling." In telling the truth, he lies; in lying, he tells it. We are not dealing with an esthetic but with an act of faith. Poetry is the revelation of its unreality.

> Between the moonlight and the foliage,
> Between the stillness and the grove,
> Between night's being and the breeze,
> A secret passes.
> My soul follows as it passes.

That which passes—is it Pessoa or another? The question repeats itself all through the years and through the poems. He doesn't know if what he writes is his own. Or rather: he knows that though it may be, it isn't: "Why do I, who've been deceived, judge that mine which is mine?" The search for the self—lost and found and lost again—ends in loathing: "Nausea, the will to nothingness: existing not to die."

Only from this perspective can one perceive the full meaning of the heteronyms. They are a literary invention and a psychological necessity but also something more. In a certain way they are what Pessoa might have been or would have liked to be; in another, more profound sense, what he didn't wish to be: a personality. In the first instance, they make a tabula rasa of the idealism and intellectual convictions of their author; in the second, they show that innocent *sagesse,* public square, and hermetic philosophy are all illusions. The moment is uninhabitable, like the future; and stoicism is a remedy which kills. Nevertheless, the destruction of the self, which is what the heteronyms stand for, provokes a secret fertility. The true desert is the Self and not only because it encloses us in ourselves and thus condemns us to live with a ghost, but also because it withers everything it touches. Pessoa's experience, perhaps without his having himself intended it so, fits into the tradition of the great poets of the modern era, from Nerval and the German romantics on. The *I* is an obstacle, *the* obstacle. Which is why any merely esthetic judgment of his work is insufficient. If it is true that not everything he wrote has the same quality, all or almost all of it is marked by the traces of his quest. His work is a step toward the unknown. A passion.

Pessoa's world is neither this world nor the other. The word *absence* would define it, if by absence one understands a fluid state in which presence vanishes and absence heralds what?— a moment in which the present no longer exists and is encroaching on one which perhaps is hardly even dawning. The urban desert is covered with signs: stones say something, the wind speaks, the lighted window and the lone tree on the corner speak; everything is saying something, not the thing I'm saying but something else, always the same something else that is never spoken. Absence is not only privation but the presentiment of a presence that never shows itself entirely. Hermetic poems and songs coincide: in absence, in the unreality that we are, something is present. Astonished among people and things, the poet walks down a street in the old quarter. He enters a park and the leaves are trembling. They are about to say. . . . No, they've said nothing. Unreality of the world, in the last light of the afternoon. Everything is immobile, expectant. The poet already knows that he has no identity. Like those houses, half gilt, half real, like those trees suspended in the hour, he also takes leave of himself. And the other does not appear, the double, the true Pessoa. He will never appear: there is no other. It appears, it insinuates itself, the other, something that has no name, that is not spoken and that our poor words invoke. Is it poetry? No: poetry is what remains and what consoles us, the consciousness of absence. And again, almost imperceptible, a sound of something: Pessoa or the imminence of the unknown. (pp. 6-21)

> *Octavio Paz, "Introduction: Pessoa or the Imminence of the Unknown," in* Selected Poems *by Fernando Pessoa, translated by Edwin Honig, The Swallow Press Inc., 1971, pp. 1-21.*

PETER RICKARD   (essay date 1971)

[*Rickard is an English educator, translator, and critic. In the following excerpt, he discusses Pessoa's heteronyms and examines his originality as a poet and thinker.*]

Pessoa always insisted that his "other names" were no mere pseudonyms of the kind frequently adopted by authors for a variety of reasons—modesty, discretion, convenience or sheer caprice—and in no way affecting their manner of writing or their choice of subject. A pseudonym is merely the use of another name in order to continue to be the same person, in order to go on saying what one would have said in any case. But Álvaro de Campos, Alberto Caeiro and Ricardo Reis (not to mention other less productive heteronyms which appeared later) were, Pessoa maintained, not just names: they were personalities who produced poetry—and at times prose—in keeping with their education, their temperament, their preoccupations and their philosophy of life. On the other hand, he never tried to suggest seriously (though he sometimes joked about it) that any such persons existed in any material sense. Though he expresses himself on this vexed question in different ways at different times, it seems clear that they were in fact different facets or expressions of his own many-sided personality, or represented conceivable though at times debatable points of view which he could *imagine,* without necessarily approving of them. In intention, at least, and to a considerable extent in achievement, they were all different from each other, and different, individually and collectively, from "F. P. himself," to use Pessoa's own abbreviation. So it is understandable that he did not consider "pseudonyms" a suitable term. (p. 22)

The earliest heteronymic poems were written during the first half of 1914, and within a year . . . a few of those attributed to Álvaro de Campos had been published. On 19 January 1915, in a letter to the poet Armando Cortes-Rodrigues, Pessoa throws some light on this question. He speaks of his intention to launch, i.e. publish (for he had already written many of the heteronymic poems) the works of Caeiro, Reis and Campos, "a whole literature which I created and lived, and which is sincere because it is *felt.* . . . What I call insincere literature is not like that of Alberto Caeiro, Ricardo Reis or Álvaro de Campos. . . . Theirs is written *in the person of another:* it is written *dramatically,* but is sincere (in my serious sense of the word) just as what King Lear says is sincere, although he is not Shakespeare, but a creation of his. I mean by insincere those things which are done in order to astonish people, and also those things which . . . do not contain a basic metaphysical idea, i.e. are not inspired by a sense of the gravity and mystery of Life. For that reason, all I have written in the name of Caeiro, Reis and Campos is serious. In each of them I placed a profound conception of life, a serious involvement with the mysterious importance of Existence." He goes on to dismiss a poem like **"Quagmires"** as not serious, and to condemn his earlier attitude towards the public as that of a clown.

Much of what he said on this occasion is confirmed by a manuscript note which unfortunately cannot be dated: "For some psychological reason which I do not propose to go into, and which is unimportant, I constructed within myself several characters who are distinct from each other and from me, and to whom I attributed several poems which are not such as I, with my own feelings and ideas, would write. . . . Many of them express ideas I do not accept, and feelings I have never felt. They must simply be read for what they are." He further argues that no one would challenge Shakespeare's right to create Lady Macbeth on the grounds that he was not a woman, and he claims a similar right for the non-dramatic characters of fiction.

Twenty years later, when Adolfo Casais Monteiro, an admirer and disciple of his, wrote from Coimbra to ask him to account for the origin of the heteronyms, Pessoa replied at some length [see excerpt dated 1935]. This time we learn something about the "psychological reason" which he had earlier regarded as unimportant and had declined to enlarge upon. Pessoa attributes the need for heteronymy to the element of hysteria, or possibly hystero-neurasthenia in his make-up. He did not mention this in 1915, but he had read Freud, not to mention Max Nordau, and he may have fancied he recognized some of his own symptoms in their descriptions and analyses of hystero-neurasthentic types. It is not necessary to suppose that either Freud or Nordau turned Pessoa into a hystero-neurasthenic: one could perfectly well assume that they simply provided him with a label for something he knew or thought was true of himself. (pp. 22-4)

To his friend Rui Santos, Pessoa once confided that he saw no objection to using the expressions and ideas of others, if they seemed to him to be necessary, or beautiful, or both. We know that he was an omnivorous reader, that he had absorbed what is best in English, French and Portuguese literature, and that he had also read widely in the domains of occultism, theosophy, alchemy, astrology and even magic. He had digested Hegel's philosophy of history, and had found Nietzsche's amoralism, his cult of the superman, and his strictures on Christianity, very much to his taste. He had read Schopenhauer, but it is difficult to assess how far the German philosopher influenced Pessoa, and how far Pessoa found in him ideas which strikingly confirmed his own. For Schopenhauer, the terror of existence is the starting-point for all philosophy, and it is certainly a major preoccupation of Pessoa too. For Pessoa as for Schopenhauer, man is incapable of distinguishing between truth and error, incapable of seeing what lies beyond appearances, incapable of apprehending what Kant had called the *noumenon* or *Ding an sich,* incapable of knowing himself, save as the toy of fate, doomed to frustration and failure, and agonizingly aware of the passing of time. Misery and pain, for Schopenhauer as for Pessoa, are consubstantial with existence itself, hence perhaps the scepticism, particularly of Caeiro but in fact shared by all three heteronyms, about the value of any attempt to reform the world.

Yet Pessoa does not closely follow any one thinker or philosopher. From time to time we may hear an echo or sense an affinity, but it is as though the Portuguese poet, so far as he used other people's ideas or images, deliberately used them in new and startling ways. But what of his *poetic* originality? . . . [There] is much of Whitman in some of the early Campos poems, yet Pessoa is clearly far more interested in ideas, and far less exuberantly optimistic, than Whitman was. One of his best-known poems, **"Ela canta, pobre ceifeira"** (**"She sings, poor reaper"**), was certainly inspired by Wordsworth's "The Reaper" and contains verbal reminiscences of it: yet it also contains the typically Pessoan idea of something lacking, and the longing for the impossible. Wordsworth wants to know what the solitary reaper is singing about: for Pessoa, this is a matter of indifference. He wants to be the singer *and yet himself* at the same time. He wants to be, like the reaper, "blithely unaware," as he puts it, but at the same time *aware that he is blithely unaware.* And the appeal to sky, field and song with which the Portuguese poem ends, is quite lacking in Wordsworth. Caeiro may borrow one idea from Alice Meynell, yet the two poets are poles apart. Pessoa may personally have sympathized with the mystical element in Alice Meynell's verse, but it is anathema to his creation Caeiro. It is possible that the poem **"Night"** (**"Excerpt from an Ode"**) was inspired by Shelley's poem "To the Night" but Pessoa cannot have derived from it any more than the idea of a sustained apostrophe. It may be that the poem **"His mother's very own"** owes something to Rimbaud's sonnet **"Le dormeur du val,"** yet a comparison of the two poems shows that Pessoa's begins at the point where Rimbaud's sonnet ends. Rimbaud provides picturesque details of the spot where the "sleeper" is lying, but says nothing of his home and family, a major theme in the Portuguese poem. Both poems are extremely effective, but they make their effect in two quite different ways. Valéry, it seems, did not influence Pessoa, yet there are certain affinities between the two. In both, it could be said that the intellect kills spontaneity; both take refuge in abstraction; both are metaphysical minds who rise above the material level; both conceive of poetry as "the mathematics of feeling." Pessoa, like Valéry, could have said "Je me permets de penser qu'il y a de la pauvreté d'esprit à être toujours d'accord avec soi-même." (I venture to think it is a poor mind that is always in agreement with itself.) And he could have said with M. Teste "De quoi j'ai souffert le plus? Peut-être de l'habitude de développer toute ma pensée—d'aller jusqu'au bout en moi." (From what have I suffered most? Perhaps from the habit of fully developing my thought—of going all the way in myself.)

What were Pessoa's beliefs? In a postscript (dated 14 January) to the famous letter to Casais Monteiro of 13 January 1935 (a postscript which Pessoa asked him not to publish) he wrote: "I believe in the existence of inhabited worlds which are on a higher plane than ours; I believe in the experience of various degrees of spirituality, becoming more rarified until we arrive at a Supreme Being, which presumably created this world" . . . "I do not believe in direct communication with God, but, according to our degree of spiritual refinement, we shall be able to communicate with progressively higher beings." The means to this end could be magic, or mysticism, or alchemy, or occultism, and it was above all to the last of these that Pessoa turned as he grew older, for a hankering after the occult *is* a degenerate form of religious feeling—the religion of those who have no religion. For Pessoa, no single church or religion possesses the truth, but they all share in it, because they all assume an expression of the transcendental and a vision of the ineffable. This conviction he once vividly expressed through the mouth of Campos: "And in every corner of my soul stands an altar to a different god." For Pessoa, there is what he calls an *Além-Deus,* literally "Beyond-God," a notion which goes beyond all images and concepts of the divine. He refuses to choose, to commit himself to any one god, for that would mean exchanging the reality for the appearance, the unlimited for the limited, the transcendental for the immanent, the occult for the positive, the soul for the surface. Metaphysical speculation and qualified occultist belief are no mere occasional theme in Pessoa's poetry: they are fundamental to it. Take them away, and there would be little left. Every other kind of subject-matter takes second place, or indeed does not feature at all. This needs to be said, in case it should be thought extraordinary that the eight years he spent in South Africa should have left no trace in his poetry, and even more extraordinary that his everyday life in Lisbon, and that city itself, in which he spent all the rest of his life, should either not appear in his poetry at all, or appear as the vaguest, most shadowy backcloth to the adventures of his soul. A writer of fiction who had never been to Lisbon could describe it more convincingly than Pessoa does. But Pessoa's very nature, and his poetic instinct, prevented him from even attempting to describe contemporary reality at the superficial level. He does not evoke street scenes *à la* Cesário Verde. For him, the superficial level is quite literally that—the surface of things, their least interesting feature, the mere starting-point for speculation about what lies beneath or behind. It was for him as natural as breathing to imagine or believe in the depth and mystery below the surface. Pascal could be terrified by the silence of infinite space: Pessoa is capable of feeling a similar thrill of terror when he contemplates streets and passers-by, or merely the tobacco-shop on the other side of the street. The passers-by are not himself, but they are probably not themselves either, if only they knew it—just masks worn by Someone Else, sheets of paper on which Someone Else writes, pens and ink with which Someone Else writes, a canvas on which Someone Else paints a portrait, mouths uttering what Someone Else says: they do not really live, *they are lived,* by Someone Else. They are happy, because they do not know all this, or even suspect it, and Pessoa envies them, but *he* is doomed to go on thinking and speculating. Bricks and mortar seem inanimate enough, but who knows what reality lies behind the façade—another word for mask. "Reality," precisely because it has an infinite number of layers, is a thing of excitement and terror for the poet. Each thing suggests its opposite, inescapably: the real—the ideal; material existence—the soul; dreaming—waking; always the same exasperatingly limited Either-Or.

It is not surprising that the image of a *mask* should have suggested itself to Pessoa as a suitable one for conveying the idea of the difference between what seems and what is or may be. He uses it several times, and it is common to his heteronymic and to his orthonymic poetry. And there is more to it than that, for his very name *Pessoa,* meaning "person" in Portuguese, derives from the Latin *persona,* originally the mask worn by actors, and thus, by extension, "character" "part" "role." Pessoa certainly knew the origin of the family name, and it is curious indeed that the poet *par excellence* of the quest for lost identity, the poet who is convinced that one reality—or appearance—*masks* another, should have borne such a name. He occasionally played on the modern meaning of his name. *Pessoa* as a common noun is rather more frequently used in Portuguese than "person" is in English, and some at least of the poet's uses of the word read like deliberate puns.

His poetry expresses the torment of a man who is not content with things as they are, but this has nothing whatever to do with social reform. The things Pessoa is not content with are not the kind of thing which any human agency could alter. Indeed, he has been criticized, with some justification, for a lack of human warmth, a lack of sympathy for ordinary mortals, a lack of interest in their problems. It is rather that he has eyes and ears for only *one* problem, an eternal one which has nothing to do with such temporary accidents as political regimes or social conditions. It is a problem in which all men share to some extent, according to their degree of reflectiveness, or their awareness—usually though not necessarily through religion—of the transcendental. For most of us, however, the preoccupation with the divine or the transcendental is accidental and occasional, not constant or sustained. Most of the time, going about our everyday affairs, we are more like the little-girl-eating-chocolates-and-not-thinking, or the "unmetaphysical Esteves" of the poem "**Tobacco-shop.**" It is the problem of human identity. What is the self? And what is the relation of the self to everything which is not the self? Are we dreaming? How can we tell? What is the relation of the past to the present, in terms of the self? How can we be sure of *anything,* in the last analysis? We are torn between the intuition which believes, and the reason which denies; that is the agonizing dilemma which Pessoa presents so vividly in his verse. So far as man is capable of feeling religious unrest, so far as he is capable of sensing the mysterious element in life and in the universe, so far as he is capable of hungering for the Absolute, so far as he is not content with appearances, so far as he has ever sought and failed to find an overall pattern which makes sense of all its parts, Pessoa expresses our doubts, our fears and our aspirations in a quintessential form. If the intellect is not capable of arriving at the truth, might there not be something to

be said for falsehood? For dreams? For fiction? For poetry? If dreams can be a means of cognition, why not fiction and poetry too? But how reliable are dreams? In pessimistic moments he believes the dreamer cannot be right, in optimistic ones he thinks the dreamer is *more likely* (though *never certain*) to be right, while in sceptical moods he simply doubts the validity of dreams. This scepticism can be seen clearly in an English poem which he wrote when he was barely nineteen:

> What is true? What is't that seems—
> The lie that's in reality
> Or the lie that is in dreams?

Like Baudelaire, Pessoa considers it the role of the poet to *decipher* the baffling signs contained in the deceitful images which parade themselves before our eyes. An intuition that things are complex makes him hostile to any facile or one-sided interpretation of phenomena. The theories of Freud, or the theories of sociological determinism, may explain something, but they are a stimulus to our critical faculties rather than a final answer of absolute validity. This dissatisfaction with *one* explanation helps us to understand why he should have expressed himself in so many contradictory ways, notably, though not exclusively, through the heteronyms. At one level, the heteronyms are a mystification: at another, deeper level, they are a serious and profound attempt on Pessoa's part to view things from another angle in an endeavour to understand them or at least to gain some fresh insight into them and into himself. The poet tries to see himself from the outside, objectively; he is aiming at a kind of utopian abstraction of the self; through simulation, he hopes to find at least a negative definition of himself. *Fingir é conhecer-se,* he once wrote, "simulation is self-knowledge." And if poetry is indeed, as T. S. Eliot has suggested, "not the expression of personality, but an escape from personality," we have a further justification for the heteronyms, if one were needed.

From around 1913 to the end of his life, Pessoa showed a marked preference for the type of poetry in which the subject matter is vague and indefinite, yet lucidly expressed and viewed positively. He cultivates vague, musical qualities in verse, hazy analogues, ambiguous images, deliberately blurring the outlines of things and avoiding clear-cut distinctions. His intense and painful awareness of antithesis, of opposites, of the Either-Or, leads him to make frequent use of oxymorons such as "a silent cry," "dark brightness," "sees blindly," "the still movement of flowers" and "far-off anguish . . . near by." Some of the early poetry, written to demonstrate a theory and to make propaganda points, is extremely obscure and involved, though it contains brilliant flashes, but already in 1914 he was writing some of his best poems, such as "**Oh church bell in my village**" and "**Night**"; and with the exception of a small number of items of occultist inspiration, his later poetry can hardly be described as obscure, and still less as hermetic. He could be admirably lucid, even when expressing the ineffable and the esoteric. His strength lies in his ability to create a mood, to start a train of thought by suggesting an affinity, a *correspondance* between the material and the non-material world. He intellectualizes feeling, which is another way of saying what he himself makes Álvaro de Campos say: "All true emotion is false at the intellectual level, because that isn't where it happens. . . . Expressing oneself means saying what one doesn't feel." It is this idea which he also expresses in two of his English poems: "*Feeling, / I thought*—for feeling is unfeatured thought," and "Thought and feeling's endless schism," and, from one of his best-known Portuguese poems "What feels in me now is my thought.'' When he speaks of anguish and of longing, these ''feelings'' are usually to be related to various kinds of intellectual frustration, above all the frustration of being unable to remember, of being unable to relive earlier experiences, of having to choose between past and present, real and ideal, dreaming and waking. He excels in transposing the vocabularies and the images of emotion and of the intellect.

If there is one fundamental belief which is a presupposition and *sine qua non* of his poetry, it is his belief in the positive value of idealism, in the sense of "tendency towards the highest conceivable perfection" or "love for or search after the best and highest," even if some would regard such a quest as madness. He is also the poet of absence, of silence, of negation, for the cause of his sorrow is frequently presented, not as something positive, but as something which is absent, lacking, negated: dreams undreamt, music not heard, things which vanish when you turn to look at them. Even happiness has a negative definition for the poet: it is "not thinking." His poetry could be described as confidential, in that it is inspired by real emotions and sensations of his personality, but these emotions are expressed objectively, with reservations as to their validity, or are transmuted and intellectualized. His use of images, metaphors and other figures is anything but conventional: it rests on a fundamental principle of occultism, the idea of *correspondances,* and the links are subtle.

What does Pessoa stand for in the poetic tradition? He stands for the denial, not only of sentimentality, but even of sentiment itself as a matter of poetic content. He stands instead for the primacy of thought, intuition, vision and prophecy over sensibility and feeling. His literary ideas, as expressed in a large number of provocative articles, stand in the main for a questioning, a reappraisal, a deepening and heightening of the content of poetry, and for a search for new forms of expression. In his own practice, he introduced into Portuguese a new poetic syntax of the kind already achieved in French symbolist poetry, and he renovated the poetic vocabulary, carefully avoiding, except in parody, anything resembling the stock poetic diction of the accepted Portuguese literary tradition. For many of his contemporaries, this, indeed, and not the content of his verse, was his most remarkable achievement.

He was not a great philosopher, nor indeed any sort of philosopher, but a somewhat unsystematic thinker whose ideas might be termed early existentialist. He is of our time in his *Angst,* in his desperate struggle to make sense of himself and of his surroundings. All his work revolves round the mystery of existence. He has no solution to offer, however, to the problem of the immanence or transcendence of being. Instead, he can only struggle on, dissipating his thought in the complications and contradictions of a mind which feels doomed to absurdity, whatever it does. The only way out is resignation, an acceptance of nausea and tedium as our lot. We can delude ourselves for a while with feigned truths (for since we cannot know the truth, we might as well amuse ourselves by lying and pretending), but *náusea* and *tédio* are always in wait for us, just round the corner. Man comes from one unknown and is on his way towards another. Between him and the universe there is a relationship *of some kind,* but it is unverifiable. What man does, has no value. Obviously, what Pessoa has to say about man and the universe is not constructive: it contains no lessons for living. Man's choice is a limited one. He can shut his eyes to all but appearances, like Caeiro; he can discipline himself to expect nothing, and delude himself that that is happiness, like Ricardo Reis; or he can continue to speculate and

go round and round in a vicious circle, like Campos or Pessoa himself, convinced that there must be something there to know, but equally convinced that it is unknowable.

Can we explain the poetry in terms of the man? Or the man in terms of the poetry? Only to a very limited extent, and we would probably be wrong to try. One could imagine from the poetry that he had no aptitude for practical life. His life suggests that he had an aptitude for it, but a limited inclination. The fact remains that, more readily than most of his literary contemporaries in Lisbon, he undertook the practical tasks of editing and publishing, and carried them out with commendable efficiency. In his capacity of commercial correspondent, his advice was often sought in connection with complicated business deals, and it must be remembered that he also edited, with his brother-in-law, a journal of commerce and accountancy, to which he contributed highly technical articles. One would imagine from the poetry that he was a man torn by inner conflict, uncertain of his own identity, and doubting the reality of the world around him, doubting, indeed, even his own reality. And one would be justified. Yet the fact remains that those who knew him in everyday life were unaware of these conflicts and these doubts in him. The clue to this lies probably in his statement to Adolfo Casais Monteiro about his hystero-neurasthenic tendencies: they were purely internal and he did not allow them to manifest themselves outwardly, in his dealings with other people. Pessoa was certainly aware that he was different from other men, that he "saw" things that others did not see, or want to see, or take seriously, and to that extent, perhaps, we can say that he was "not understood." Or rather, in his poetry, he took the risk of not being understood, while in his life he did not, since he suppressed in contact with others those aspects of his personality which made him different, except his astonishing lucidity and intelligence, which he could not easily suppress. At all events, it is always refreshing to find a poet who does not complain that he is misunderstood by his fellow-men, or that he is being victimized by society. What Pessoa finds to complain about is the limitation, the sheer inadequacy of the human mind, primarily, it is true, on his own behalf, but also on ours. He is perfectly aware that the man in the street (or, once again, the little girl eating chocolates) is unconcerned with such problems and is thus far more likely to find happiness than he, Fernando Pessoa, but he accepts this as his destiny, just as he accepted his modest role in society as a commercial correspondent, and refused all offers of greater prosperity.

Not all Pessoa's poetry is of the highest quality, and it should be pointed out that Pessoa was himself for a long time diffident and fastidious about publishing it. Some of the poems have little substance, or make less effectively a point which has been better made in some of his other poems. Some are probably only rough drafts. Since the poet's preoccupations amount almost to obsessions, there is inevitably an element of repetitiveness in the arguments used, and even in the imagery, e.g. the mask, the well, the empty bucket, the door which is either closed or non-existent. Reis and Caeiro, in particular, make the same limited points over and over again, though of course in different words, different images and different arguments. There is an element of artificiality about the heteronyms, though the worst artificiality lies outside the poetry, in the ill-judged attempt to "dramatize" their relationship. There is a certain amount of logic-chopping in his way of presenting an argument, but that, again, is more noticeable outside his verse, and is certainly not always meant to be taken seriously. One of his critics, João Mendes, complained that "his poetic world is like shadows dancing on the wall of a sick-room," the point being presumably that Pessoa allowed his speculations to become a morbid obsession, out of touch with reality. But the same critic admits that for the analysis and presentation of these allegedly morbid preoccupations, Pessoa has no equal.

Above all, Pessoa has the merit of questioning our assumptions, of delving deeper into the things we take for granted, of making us think along new lines, and of presenting things to us in a different and startlingly unconventional way. Many poets have written about suicide, but who ever treated the subject as he has treated it? Many poets have apostrophized Night, but who has done so as Pessoa did? . . . Who has ranged so widely, so originally, so multifariously and at the same time so agonizingly and so poignantly over so many aspects of the mystery of existence and man's quest for identity? (pp. 47-56)

> *Peter Rickard, in an introduction to* Selected Poems
> by Fernando Pessoa, *edited and translated by Peter*
> *Rickard, 1971. Reprint by University of Texas Press,*
> *1972, pp. 1-61.*

MICHAEL WOOD   (essay date 1972)

[*Wood is an English writer, educator, and critic. In the following excerpt, he explores the relationships among Pessoa's heteronyms.*]

[Fernando Pessoa, Alberto Caeiro, Ricardo Reis, and Álvaro de Campos are] not masks, not other persons (Pessoas), but simply *others,* irreducibly different beings.

The relation Pessoa means us to take seriously is that of master and disciples: we are to see Reis, Campos, and Pessoa himself as sitting at Caeiro's feet. Caeiro, as Octavio Paz suggests, is the touchstone, the innocent poet, the founding myth, the necessary fiction which brings the poetry of the others into being. But this relation, it seems to me, was more important for Pessoa than it can be for us—something Pessoa tried to hint at, possibly, by having Caeiro die in 1915, at the nominal age of twenty-six, but only one year after his literary birth. Another relation, also given to us in the letter, but not insisted on, takes us further into Pessoa's work. It is a dialectical relation, a form of creation by antithesis: the innocent, primitive Caeiro releases the complicated, symbolist Fernando Pessoa; the classical Reis generates the modernist Campos. And this relation is present not only at the birth of the heteronyms but throughout their life—since Pessoa used both his own name and his heteronyms throughout his complete writing career, keeping even Caeiro, who "died" in 1915, writing until 1930.

That is, Pessoa in any one of his incarnations has the other three in mind, with the chances of correction and contradiction that they represent, and this is the way out of the trap created by the fact that all truths, however true, seem only half truths to Pessoa. It is his profound and constant habit to think in opposites. Am I happy or sad? he asks in one poem. My sadness consists in not knowing much about myself. But then my happiness consists in that too. . . . Twenty lost years, Campos cries out, only to catch himself up immediately: "but if they should be gained, what then?" "Contradiction is the essence of the universe," Pessoa once wrote. And again: "Paradox is the typical form of nature." (pp. 20-1)

[In an article] published in the Mexican magazine *Plural* in April and May of this year, [Roman] Jakobson explores a single poem by Pessoa and reveals a dazzling play of symmetries, mirror images, contraries, contradictions, and balanced cancellations. Pessoa's oxymorons, which critics always note, and

which are at the center of Jakobson's analysis, are particularly interesting to look at because in them we can follow the poet's progress very clearly. They go from purely formal figures of rhetoric (a motionless dance, a silent cry, the same differing fields, the old new flowers) through the expression of possibilities which can't find their way into ordinary language (shapes without shape, unthought thoughts, the dead body of a God who is alive, the king who dies but still lives) and into the expression of sheer impossibility (a door in a wall that has no door, the child you don't have sleeping peacefully at home).

These impossibilities are frequently ironic, but the sense of life they represent is perfectly serious, even desperate. Campos invokes night in one poem as "Our Lady of Impossible Things," and the line serves perhaps better than any other to characterize Pessoa himself. He is the poet not only of contradiction and paradox but of the categorically impossible; and it remains for us to look at the varieties of impossibility that are his special province.

In Caeiro the impossibility is Caeiro's very existence. He is a pastoral poet claiming not to have the complex, civilized worries which are the foundation of pastoral poetry. Nature is not beautiful, he says, "Beauty is the name of something that doesn't exist." In fact, there is no such thing as Nature, since Nature is a concept, and concepts are a sickness of the mind: "Nature is parts without a whole." Our great sin is thought, having theories, looking for meanings, wishing things were other than they are: "Beyond the immediate reality of things there is nothing."

Caeiro is the incarnation within literature of literature's absence, and it is not surprising that he should find this role something of a strain. Armand Guibert, Pessoa's French translator, writes of Caeiro's "*autoritaire douceur,*" but that's putting it mildly. Caeiro is a dull, heavy prose preacher, and he strikes far too many false notes. He is no more than a river or a tree, he says. "I laugh like a brook coolly babbling over stones" ("*Rio como um regato que soa fresco numa pedra.*" . . .) "I was never more than a child at play." These are things you can't say if they are true. More than that, if Caeiro were half the simple soul he says he is, he wouldn't be writing poetry at all, and especially not such predicatory poetry. Pessoa is aware of this of course, and gives Caeiro an occasional sense of his own phoniness, and even, now and then, a flicker of deadpan humor:

> The Tagus is fairer than the river flowing through my
>   village,
> But the Tagus isn't fairer than the river flowing through
>   my village
> Because the Tagus isn't the river flowing through my
>   village.

But the final result is a failed heteronym, the only one of the three to fail: a poet who interests us only because we know that Pessoa is behind him, and unlike him.

Reis, as much as Caeiro, is committed to what he can see and touch, to the "visible presence / Of my nearest gods." His gods, he says, "dwell not in Vagueness" but in fields and rivers, and like Caeiro he has nothing but scorn for people who seek something "better than life." Like Caeiro too, he professes indifference for the contemporary civilized world, for politics and suffering and injustice.

> I prefer roses to my country
> And I love magnolias more,
> Beloved, than glory or virtue.

The most obvious difference between Caeiro and Reis is the literary mode. Instead of a pastoral innocence, Reis chooses a Roman worldliness and hedonism, using Latinisms in Portuguese where he can, and creating intricate and artificial word orders which are a translator's nightmare and which drive [Pessoa translator Edwin] Honig to the straits of beginning a poem with the words, "I the roses love in the gardens of Adonis." But the more important distinction is the quality of the poems. They are false to the point of pastiche, of course; they belong in a world long since gone from us. But that is their point, and their charm. Their very impossibility is what they are about, that is, the style and stoic posture of Reis are what are impossible in the world Pessoa lived in, and Reis is fully aware of this. "I know what I am forgetting," he writes, "I sing in order to forget."

The poems are full of images of height, of standing straight, aloof, of making monuments to dignity. Let us have no grand passions, Reis says in a moving poem, no passions that raise their voice. Let us be quiet, Lydia, let us not wake the sleeping Fury. But the Fury will awake, however quiet we are. We shall care when our loved ones die, however much we try to dilute our love for them in their lifetime. Reis's denials of night and darkness are pathetic cries in a storm, a pretense that the wind will die down and life become possible again, when the poet and the poems know all too well that it won't.

There is something of Rimbaud in Campos, and a great deal of Laforgue. There is a recurrent regret for the lost innocence of childhood—"I know very well that in everyone's childhood there was a garden . . . and that sadness dates from today"—and the freely moving, mocking style suggests, as Laforgue's does, that there is so much more to say, that these poems, these poor half-finished lines, scarcely start to touch the subject.

Campos finds the familiar especially mysterious, is dazed by the thought that a man could enter a tobacco shop to buy tobacco, and come out slipping his change into his pocket. He lives with the sense that life is a bad dream, that this movie show, as he says, this circus, can't be all there is. He spends his life living, studying, loving, even believing, and then wonders whether he has ever done any of those things: "For we can do all this in reality without doing it at all." He is crippled by the sense of what might have been, he is Pessoa constantly longing to be another Pessoa:

In dreams I've achieved more than Napoleon.
I've clasped to my hypothetical breast more human races
     than Christ,
I've secretly devised philosophies no Kant ever wrote.

But even in dreams, he admits, his armies are defeated, and he will carry his compulsion to the point of sorrow at the thought that death will take away all the things he never even thought of being. The physically dead, he says, even my own dead past, may well live again in some metaphysical system or other,

But what I never was, what I never did, what I never
     even dreamed;
What I see only now that I ought to have done,
See clearly only now that I ought to have been—
It's *that* that's dead beyond the gods' recalling.

He compares himself to the damp in a corridor, to his childhood house now sold, to a burned-out match. He feels like something left behind on a seat in a tram. He is haunted by the sense,

impossible to render in normal grammar, that there is something better in himself than himself (*melhor em mim do que eu*), that something else has been substituted for his real self somewhere along the way. And yet his humor never leaves him, there is always an impudence lurking in his distress:

For I love what's finite, infinitely,
For I love what's possible, impossibly,
For I want everything or a bit more, if it can be done,
Or even if it can't. . . .

What is impossible for Campos is that life could really, seriously be as it is. But then he also finds it impossible that it could be otherwise.

Pessoa in the poems written in his own name is very close to Campos in many respects, and we probably need to distinguish between the heteronyms which are fictions, projections of what you are certainly not, although you might wish you were (Caeiro, Reis), and those which are doubles, second selves, agents of confessions or performances you could not bring off on your own but which are, nevertheless, yours (Campos). Like Campos, Pessoa is "serious about what is *not*," hurt, as he puts it in another poem, by what doesn't exist. But where the possibility of another life beyond this one, the possibility of waking from the bad dream, is for Campos merely a mockery of the life he is stuck with, for Pessoa it is a fragile, unkeepable promise—there *is* life on other astral planes, there is an immortality in myth, but there is no way in which we can penetrate those dimensions.

Pessoa hears voices sounding from the Islands of the Blessed, but as soon as he listens, they stop. In order for them to continue, he would have to hear without hearing, and the oxymoron becomes the emblem and instrument of a magical, inconceivable communication. In the poem Jakobson analyzes in *Plural*, Ulysses, the mythical founder of Lisbon, appears in a flurry of oxymorons: he *was* because he didn't exist (*Foi por não ser existindo*); without existing he was enough for us (*Sem existir nos bastou*); he came because he hadn't come (*Por não ter vindo foi vindo*); and more generally, although a mythical creature himself he created us (*nos creou*), the Portuguese, the live children of Lisbon.

The poet himself, in another poem, calls himself the last look of the last Moorish king leaving Granada, and suggests superlatively well what it means to be alive in the death of a former life:

What I am now is that imperial longing
For what I once saw of myself in the distance . . .
I am myself the loss I suffered . . .

And on this road which leads to Otherness
Bloom in slender wayside glory
The sunflowers of the empire dead in me . . .

(Hoje sou a saudade imperial
Do que já na distância de mim vi . . .
Eu próprio sou aquilo que perdi . . .

E nesta estrada para Desigual
Florem em esguia glória marginal
Os girassóis do império que morri . . .)

But if Pessoa writes of life in death—a favorite myth with him is that of Dom Sebastian, the young Portuguese king killed in Morocco in 1578 and fated, according to legend, to return again like Arthur, for his body was never found—he cannot do this without writing of death in life, and his poems all finally tilt that mournful way, nowhere more strikingly and beautifully than at the close of the Ulysses poem. The myth, Pessoa says, fades into legend, the legend fades as it touches reality (*"Assim a lenda se escorre / A entrar na realidade"*), and life, which is half of nothing, dies (*"a vida, metade / De nada, morre"*). The case is startling, since Pessoa is using a brutal oxymoron (life dies) to wipe out the magical realm of Ulysses' paternity created by the other oxymorons: dark, final magic to erase the magical promise.

Nothing, for Pessoa, crosses the gap from desire to the first taste of what you desire; all tastes are sour before your mouth reaches them. Dreams are real and reality is real but there are no roads across the frontiers. In the light of this it is not surprising that Pessoa's poems should be full both of royal imagery and abdications; not surprising that he should write the poems of **Mensagem**, dedicated to the dream of a broken, defeated past living in the promise of a resurrection. In the poems about Sebastian we are asked to admire not his future success but his heroic madness in hoping for it. In other poems thrones, dominions, kingdoms, castles become muffled allegories for a world that once was better.

There is an obvious analogy here with the world of childhood which haunts *all* Pessoa's poems, those of his heteronyms as much as his own. The empires and conquests of history; the palaces of metaphor; the lost garden of your childhood: three means of lighting up a crippled present. But it is the present that has the last word, and the dominant note of Pessoa's poems is the finality of failure, the clearly struck note of the impossibility of having anything you want. (pp. 21-2)

> Michael Wood, "Mod and Great," in The New York Review of Books, Vol. XIX, No. 4, September 21, 1972, pp. 19-22.

MARCIA SMILACK (essay date 1973)

[*In the following excerpt, Smilack analyzes the technique Pessoa employs in the poem "Tabaccaria," which was written under the heteronym Álvaro de Campos.*]

Álvaro de Campos' style in **"Tabacaria"** is a construction of contraries. He presents the juxtaposition of opposites only to diminish the importance of their differences by suggesting that in a universal context their differences are irrelevant—that in a universal context opposites are in fact indistinguishable. The poem's basic foundation of contrary statements naturally implies certain questions of truth and falsity which normally apply to contraries: that is, that one statement may be true or both may be false. However, in suggesting that opposites are indistinguishable, Álvaro de Campos removes their contrary characteristics and thus eliminates that question of validity. The question itself is not viable because its components, truth and falsity, are opposites of each other and are thus indistinguishable in a universal context. The irrelevance of distinguishing between entities is recognized by the man who realizes his insignificance in the universe. Unlike Borges and the transcendental poets, this man *unhappily* realizes the universal destiny of all men. He further realizes that seven thousand years of metaphysics have not helped him; rather, they have made him forget the feebleness of his own resources in dealing with reality. By sharing a common fate with other men, the character in the poem is anonymous even to himself; in his anonymity his writing or self-expression is a mere gesture. In this universal container of all men reality and illusion are indistinguishable; such a distinction does not affect the universal

condition anyway. The poem begins with his metaphysical thoughts as illusory in comparison to the nonmetaphysical world of the tobacco shop and the street outside his window. The poem ends with his realization that the street shares the same destiny of men—it will die unremembered by history. It too is unreal in the universal container.

A structural technique in the poem which effectively suggests the sameness of opposite entities is the interchange of distinguishing qualities of those entities. Metaphors, similes and oxymora suggest an equality between opposites, but those forms in themselves simply promote comparison between entities, they do not diminish the differences of their members nor produce the sense of balance found in **"Tabacaria."** When individual distinguishing qualities of an entity become interchangeable with individual distinguishing qualities of an opposite entity, the entities possess identical qualities and no longer appear opposite. One example of this interchange that appears throughout the poem is the simultaneous personification of physical objcts and the objectification of metaphysical thoughts of a person. In this way Álvaro de Campos shows the difficulty in distinguishing between "possible" reality (such as unconscious actions) and "impossible" illusion (such as dreams of unconscious actions):

> Dais para o mistério de uma rua constantemente cruzada
>   por gente,
> Para uma rua inacessível a todos os pensamentos,
> Real, impossìvelmente real, certa, desconhecidamente
>   certa . . .

> (You open on the mystery of a street that people are
>   constantly crossing,
> A street blocked off to all thought,
> A street that's real—so impossibly real, and right—so
>   thoughtlessly right . . .

The street which is "real" by virtue of being "blocked off to all thought," is at the same time "impossibly real." In being "thoughtlessly right," the street is not only free from illusory thought . . . the pun also implies a certain indifference in universal reality. As a poet, the character is torn between the reality of the universe and the illusion of his necessarily limited comprehension of the universe. The poem is developed through description of the simultaneous existence of reality and illusion.

In stanza thirteen, Álvaro de Campos describes his style and his dualistic theme in this poem:

> Sempre uma coisa defronte da outra,
> Sempre uma coisa tão inútil como a outra,
> Sempre o impossível tão estúpido como o real,
>   . . .
> Sempre isto ou sempre outra coisa ou nem uma coisa
>   nem outra.

> (Always one thing standing against another,
> Always one thing as useless as another,
> Always the impossible thing as stupid as the real thing,
>   . . .
> Always this thing or that, or neither one nor the other.)

The first line of this quotation parallels the poem's foundation of dichotomies. The other three lines show an equality between opposites and a futility in calling one thing "real" and its opposite "impossible." The poem begins with the character endorsing the "possible" and condemning the "impossible." By the time the poem reaches stanza thirteen, possible action is no better than impossible thought; because both are relative to the entire universe, they are insignificant and their distinction is unimportant.

The poem is developed with iterative images. As these repetitive images recur in each stanza they retain their previous meaning while they gain new meaning; in the final stanza they reflect all of the meanings attached to them throughout the poem. The theme, developed through these images, also reaches fruition in the final stanza. This accumulative pattern of imagery development in the poem is enclosed within a three-part plot structure. In the first part the character stands by his window, musing about his general condition, and he proceeds to consider his specific experience occurring during the composition of the poem ("today"). In the second part he retreats to his chair by the window and begins to answer his last question before sitting: "what should I think about?" As he turns his attention inward, he answers the "what" of his question. Part two provides him with consolation for the condition he described in part one. In the third part of the poem he rises from his chair and returns to the window, repositioning himself to the start of the poem. He leaves his thoughts resting in the chair and enters action, the opposite of thought—in this case, interaction with two other men.

Stanza one introduces all of the images which are repeatedly embellished with meaning in the poem:

> Não sou nada.
> Nunca serei nada.
> Não posso querer ser nada.
> À parte isso, tenho em mim todos os sonhos do mundo.
>
> (I'm nothing.
> I'll always be nothing.
> Not that I want to be nothing.
> But aside from that I contain all the dreams of the
>   world within me).

"I am nothing," wrote Álvaro de Campos—says the character to the reader. Yet "I," a pronoun referring to the man, is "something." By using the predicate nominative "nothing" rather than "no one," Álvaro de Campos personifies "thing" (from "no thing") and objectifies "I." Through conversion of implied animate and inanimate qualities, "I" and "thing" are not only grammatically equal but indistinguishable as well. The method of equating opposites which works throughout the poem is also exhibited in the first line: something is nothing. This suggests that reality (something) is equal to illusion (nothing). The character negates his identity in stanza one; the reader learns why the character has lost his identity in his discussion of persona in stanza eleven. The character does not "want" to be nothing, yet he is nothing. The verb "want" begins the repeated dichotomy of aspiring (dreaming) and completing the dreamed action (reality). His ineptness in becoming his dream of "something" suggests his lack of control in relation to the indifference of the universe. In believing he will "always" be nothing, he suggests a time that exists "always," an infinite time. The adverb "always" is picked up again and more fully exploited for its universal meaning in the quotation given from stanza thirteen. As he *contains* all the dreams of the world," the receptacle image begins its accumulative progression throughout the poem. As "nothing," he possesses dreams; as "something" would he possess elements of reality? The dichotomy of illusion and reality begins its poetic route of examination.

With stanza two, these images begin to accumulate further meaning and begin their explication of the illusion-reality theme.

The interchange of qualities which define objects and persons appears: the window of his room is personified, mystery lives under both "people and stones," and death spreads both "dankness on walls and white hair on heads." As death strikes both objects and persons, fate drives "each and every *thing* down *oblivion street*." Not only do men and things have a common destiny, but their path is oblivious (indifferent?) and perhaps arbitrary as well (he compares his "personal highway" to "drifting smoke" in stanza fifteen). As the character contains dreams in stanza one, his room contains him, and the street contains the room. The description of his room (consisting primarily of the window) sounds like a watchtower looking onto the street similar to the "garret" in stanza seven. His anonymity and unknown room foreshadow the realization of the macrocosmic container of both reality and illusion—the universe. At this point, the character believes the street to be the "real" container.

In stanzas three and four, the dichotomy of the physical and the metaphysical is represented by his "*brotherly* feeling for *things*" ("irmandade com as coisas"), by his "*nerve*-wracking, *bone*-creaking jerk" ("sacudidela dos meus nervos e um ranger de ossos"), and by the thoughts in his head—the house and the street. Using contrary statements to describe his mental state, he says that he is "clearheaded" and that he is "mixed up." While clearheaded his thoughts are associated with the street (earlier said to be real). He feels mixed up in the absence of thought. The first two stanzas suggest that he should feel clearheaded in the absence of thought and mixed up while thinking. As he is now torn between an allegiance to what he thinks to be reality (the tobacco shop) and his feeling that all is a dream, he later conquers in his dreams and finds the world strange upon awakening (stanza seven).

In stanza five he says "I failed in everything" ("Falhei em tudo") and then says "Maybe it [everything] was all really nothing" ("Talvez tudo fôsse nada"). He failed in everything and also failed in non-everything. These statements of opposite action suggest a strong feeling of futility in any action measured in terms of success—futility, as he is overwhelmed by his insignificance in relation to the universe. By slipping out the back window, he reinforces the idea that the front window looking onto the street is his connection with reality (after all, the reader knows from stanza one that *he* contains dreams).

As he begins answering the question "what should I think about" ("Em que hei de pensar?"), he invokes and possibly mimics Cartesian dualism. In discussing the difference between being and becoming ("I'll be," and "I am"), he suggests the difference between the physical object and the metaphysical person—in this case the difference between being a "thing" (such as a "genius" in stanza seven) and the process of thinking. Descartes defined his existence and negated his nothingness through the *process* of thought; this character ignores the process of thinking and clings to its result—thought. Because so many people call themselves "geniuses," the label "genius" cannot define an individual. He ignores the reality in the action of thinking and believes in the thought that he knows to be illusory. As in the first stanza when "I" is "nothing," in this stanza "I" is a "genius." Both predicate nominatives objectify the person by identifying him with a word . . . a word is a thing. Napoleon, Kant and Christ did not aspire toward action, they acted. He uses contrary statements to further this dichotomy of aspiration and action: he waits for the door (aspires) and he also waits for the non-door (reality of the situation). He aspires toward "something" (a door) but in reality he can only aspire toward "nothing" (there is no door). His first line was true—in reality, he is nothing, as he only contains dreams. He knows no action; as a "thoughtful man," he cannot eat chocolate "honestly" like the child innocent of thought. He has "promise" but like dreams, promise is only potential action; his reality is nothing.

The universal context of reality is implied in "a hundred thousand heads thinking they're geniuses like me" ("Cem mil cérebros se concebem em sonho gênios como eu"). The anonymity of his unknown room in the second stanza is reinforced through the large number of men named here. The suggestion of universal time through the names of men remembered by history reinforces his anonymity and reminds the reader of a single man's insignificance. This universal macrocosm and individual microcosm is furthered through new container images: the man contained in the chicken coop sings to infinity, the man contained in a sealed-up well sings to God, the cardiac cases are enslaved by the stars. The first stanza told the reader that the character contains dreams; the second stanza told the reader that the room contains the character. The reader now knows that the character, his dreams, and his room are all contained in the universe. This naturally suggests the reality of the universe and the illusion in one's limited comprehension of this universe—limited by the boundaries of his container. The character will always be the man in the garret though he does not live in one; he does not literally live in a garret perhaps, but his thoughts are as limited as the vantage point of man who does live in a garret. He knows what he will "never be" but ironically does not know what he is (stanza eight). He knows illusion but not reality.

He recalls the universal context again in stanzas nine and thirteen. Naming the muses suggests history; in saying "he'll die" (the tobacco shop owner) and "so will I," he notes universal destiny and suggests that like the tobacco shop owner, he too will be forgotten by history. The image of the container is further embellished: the signboard outside the tobacco shop contains the words which describe the owner's action (selling tobacco); the character's poems contain the words which describe his action (writing). The street contains the signboard and language contains words of poetry. The earlier reality of the street and the illusion of the character's thoughts are swallowed up together by the universe which contains both of them.

The last stanza summarizes the accumulated meaning of the dichotomies throughout the poem: an object and a person, aspiration and action, microcosmic individual life and the macrocosmic universe, and the illusion of metaphysical thought and the reality of physical action. The "divine instinct" of "unmetaphysical Stevens" suggests both the infinite time implied in "divine" and the honest action implied in "instinct" (rather than metaphysical thought). The universe is personified in its ability to reorganize itself, but it is objectified with its loss of "hopes and ideals."

In stanza eleven, the character discusses his persona. He differentiates between his real self (what he was) and his false self (what people took him to be). Having waited too long to remove his mask, it stuck to his face. Symbolically, his false self had coalesced with his real self. Since his two selves were no longer separate but both parts of the mask, in removing his false self, he also removed his real self. Since he threw his mask away (and thus his real self), and since he could no longer fit into the costume of his false self, he *was nothing* as he stated in the first line of the poem. He had no real self and no false self left. All that was left to him was sleeping in the

cloakroom, the container of his costume. In the dark of the cloakroom he is the imitation of his former mask—he has become a mask of his mask—the illusion of an illusion.

Why does he wish to write? In stanza eight, he says that he writes out of his bitterness of what he'll never be; the quick calligraphy of his lines is the broken archway to the "impossible." His writing is indeed a mere gesture when compared to a broken archway to illusion. His dream is to wear a clean shirt, but the only "possible" action is to throw away his dirty clothes and sit shirtless. He accepts his mediocrity in the universal context. He believes he will be one of the men unremembered by history.

The relationship between Álvaro de Campos and the narrator in the poem is variable. For the most part the character seems to be a creation of Álvaro de Campos espousing Álvaro de Campos' views. Yet in describing why he writes, he *says* "A caligrafia rápida *dêstes* versos" ("the quick calligraphy of *these* lines"), implying that the speaker is the writer of the lines. With this exception, the presumably speaking character is always "about" to write. Perhaps Álvaro de Campos is recording the words of his character, and he temporarily interrupts these words to mention his own work of calligraphy. Or perhaps in adopting the personality of Álvaro de Campos, Fernando Pessoa loses all of his own consciousness, regaining it momentarily with an interruption in his dictation that appears in the poem as "*these* lines." (pp. 113-19)

Marcia Smilack, "Opposition and Interchange: Resolution through Persona in Fernando Pessoa's 'Tabacaria'," in Luso-Brazilian Review, *Vol. X, No. 1, Summer, 1973, pp. 113-19.*

JONATHAN GRIFFIN   (essay date 1974)

[*Griffin is an English translator and critic. In the following excerpt, he analyzes the characteristics and function of Pessoa's heteronyms.*]

Fernando Pessoa is the extreme example of what may be the essentially modern kind of poet: the objective introvert. None has more consistently tried to find his real self with its multiplicity intact and to keep his poems impersonal. He accepted the dividedness of a human self so completely that he did something unique: wrote poetry under four names—his own and three "heteronyms." Not pseudonyms: they are imaginary poets with real poems in them. Fernando Pessoa was four poets in one: Alberto Caeiro, Ricardo Reis, Álvaro de Campos and himself; each strongly distinct from the others.

One is soon struck by an external difference between their poems. Those of Caeiro are in free verse; so (though very different in tone) are nearly all those of Campos; those of Reis metrical but unrhymed; Pessoa's own, except a few of the early ones, metrical and closely rhymed. This may have come about unconsciously, but was surely no accident. Pessoa was a poet who wrote poets as well as poems: he was two kinds of poet—dramatic, lyric. When he wrote as himself, he sang—in traditional metres, although the content of his songs is a modern mind caught at moments of self-confrontation, against a background of shadow. So he meets the present need for poetry that is both lyrical and searching, a poet who sings to our age. At the same time Pessoa was a dramatic poet who wrote poets instead of plays. One should enjoy the poems of the heteronyms as separate poems; but it is good sometimes to take them, instead, as lines or speeches in one of those three large-scale dramatic poems called ***Poemas Completos de Alberto Caeiro, Odes de Ricardo Reis*** and ***Poesias de Álvaro de Campos***. One then sees that Pessoa was the pioneer of a new kind of long poem, which would in fact answer certain twentieth-century needs—an open-ended dramatic monologue. Besides being a singer on a par with Yeats, Pessoa created three of this century's viable long poems. (pp. 9-10)

Pessoa's heteronyms coped with a problem which afflicts everyone writing now. "I must say that," one thinks, "and yet how, in this day and age, can I? It is me, but only part of me. A part, but still essential. It will be false if I write it as I." Any honest writer now has at times to make so many qualifications that they either overload his art or inhibit it, unless a *persona* enables him to explore without hedging. Pessoa set himself free by hiving off three great swarms of his thoughts and feelings, and by setting them free to grow into valid long poems, each the total output of an imaginary poet. *Personae* so real liberate readers as well as their author. The Douanier Rousseau embodied the myth of the innocent painter, and so became the *persona* which a group of innovating painters, among them Picasso, needed. Alberto Caeiro embodies the innocent poet, for Pessoa and for the rest of us.

"My master had appeared in me" is the really illuminating phrase. Pessoa meant it. He writes elsewhere:

> . . . Some act on men . . . like fire, which burns out all the accidental in them and leaves them bare and real, their own and truthful, and those are the liberators. Caeiro is of that race. Caeiro has that force . . . So, operating on Reis, who had not yet written anything, he brought to birth in him a form of his own and an aesthetic person. So, operating on myself, he set me free from shadows and tatters, gave my inspiration more inspiration and my soul more soul.

What in Caeiro could have this force? Pessoa imagined Campos writing a memoir of Caeiro, who had died, and saying in it: "My master Caeiro was not a pagan: he was paganism." And in some notes written in English Pessoa says:

> Even in our age . . . Caeiro . . . does breathe absolute novelty . . . To a world plunged in various kinds of subjectivisms, he brings Absolute Nature back again . . . Far from seeing sermons in stones, he never even lets himself conceive a stone as being a sermon. The only sermon a stone contains for him is that it exists . . . Out of this sentiment, or rather, absence of sentiment, he makes poetry.

In the memoir Campos is also made to say:

> And I suddenly asked my master Caeiro, "are you content with yourself?" And he answered: "No: I am content." It was like the voice of the earth, which is all and nothing.

I find a meaningful likeness between Alberto Caeiro and Francis Ponge. Monsieur Ponge said recently that each kind of animal proves its value simply by existing and being able to propagate, and that this, to him, is *le sacré*. The two do have much the same philosophy-religion: "absolute objectivism," Pessoa calls it. But their ways of conveying it are quite different. Francis Ponge is concrete and specific; but Caeiro does not tell us what kind of tree or flower he is speaking of; he

does not name, he rarely describes. And yet one of his poems ends with the line:

> And by the way, I was the only nature poet.

What achieves concreteness is Caeiro's teaching and—conveyed largely through it—the figure of the Master, teaching, painstakingly. In Wordsworth also there is a strange sparing of specific detail, and the reason could be that a really great nature poet has to be a sage, his essential business being not to describe, but to show nature as the open door to the meaning of life. The style of Caeiro is an unostentatious anti-poetry—this in 1914. His "poems" are the talk of a master to disciples as he walks along a hillside and rounds up sheep. His teaching—according to some notes in the name of Ricardo Reis—did for a moment seem to Pessoa "the one source of consolation" for those who feel like exiles in modern life. Such people need a shot of "the ancient serenity and grandeur" to save them from dangerous despair. The writers of Antiquity had no experience of our predicament, so that to read them makes things worse, "as if a child played near me, exasperating my adult illness by his too simple simplicity." Caeiro's **"Keeper of Sheep"** has "all the simplicity, all the grandeur the ancients had," all their "possession of things," but, being written in reaction against modern conditions, it "gives us now as balsam what in the others was merely coolness." Perhaps it does. When Octavio Paz says that Caeiro is "what no modern poet can be: a man reconciled with nature," I think he for once goes too far: Gary Snyder, for instance, makes a good bid to be a modern poet reconciled with nature. To the young men and women who want to get clean of the system and are seeking "serenity and grandeur" in perhaps the Zen way, the teaching of Caeiro, which expressed their purpose more than half a century before, has something to say.

The weakness of Caeiro lies, as Octavio Paz says shrewdly, not in his ideas, which indeed are his strength, but in "the unreality of the experience he says he embodies": he is an "Adam on a farm in the Portuguese countryside." Pessoa needed a capital city even when his life there seemed a banishment. For him Caeiro's simplicity in its turn proved, within three months, too simple. So Pessoa had to find a consolation for the failure of his consolation. And this, I think, was the main function of the output he created for Ricardo Reis. Caeiro is what Pessoa longed to be and could not: Reis is the nearest that Pessoa could come to being Caeiro. A disciple of Caeiro, Reis works paganism into an ethical doctrine, part epicurean, part stoic, yet conscious of, and kept clear of, a human environment conditioned by Christianity; a doctrine for people in the modern world to live by, so as to suffer as little as possible. This disciple is very different from his master: instead of the innocent poet, a highly sophisticated one; instead of the loping free verse, odes closely constructed with an air of ease in neo-classic metres. Many people find the work of Ricardo Reis much less fine and moving than the other heteronyms. I do not. He is cold, he is cooling it. Granted, some of the outward features—those metres reminding one of Horace but less varied, those addresses to Lydia, Neaera or Chloe—can be off-putting. But these work as alienation techniques: by depersonalizing, they set Pessoa free to say things he feels too deeply to say without distancing; and the classical convention enables him to say trite things again because true. Add the expressive syntax and the constant choice of the modest exact word, and the products are often poems of grace and strength, where the joy of the making comes through clear and pure. Some render with sad, calm straightforwardness a part of paganism which has its maximum meaning today: human dignity facing the shortness of life with no promise of anything beyond. And from some of them, suddenly, there emerges the authentic White Goddess presence. Yet the Reis vision of the Greek world excludes the Dionysiac elements, and quite a number of the Reis poems seem chill, merely perfect, like the typography of Bodoni in his last period.

But the repressed Dionysiac Pessoa did burst out: in modern dress, of course. The modern dress was Álvaro de Campos. Through Campos, Pessoa saved himself from settling down into Reis; it is as though Dionysus saved him from Apollo. The **"Triumphal Ode"** (1914) is Whitmanesque not only in its verse but in its "yes" to the modern city. The next year's vast **"Seafaring Ode"** is a passionately receptive voyage in the modern world. As sustained free structures, these are at least the equals of *Howl* and *Kaddish,* and I would say Campos has the bigger extrovert-introvert range. Campos is Whitman having a nightmare in which he wakes up to find he is Laforgue. He starts as an extrovert, ends as an introvert; starts determined "to feel all every way there is," and ends up obsessed, asking if he is real. He does sometimes seem to be only there to sign any poem of Pessoa's own that has demanded to be done in free verse. The trouble with open-ended long poems which remain works in progress is that the poet—in this case Pessoa—changes, and the work, confused by fresh starts, becomes a ragbag. Pound's *Cantos* come to mind. They remind us that the quality of the rags counts. Late Campos poems can be very fine.

As a poet in his own name, Fernando Pessoa matured fully almost as soon as his heteronym poets appeared. Caeiro the ideal; Reis the good second best; Campos doing Pessoa's travelling for him: but no escape from coming home to the real exploring. The essence of Pessoa was religion and scepticism. And Caeiro did give his soul more soul. On 19 January 1915, after much hesitation, Pessoa wrote a long letter to Armando Cortes Rodrigues, in which he speaks of himself as "fundamentally a religious spirit" and of his

> constantly greater awareness of the terrible and religious mission which every man of genius receives from God with his genius.

By this light he has come to detest "art merely for art's sake" and to see recent literary activities of his own as "only beginnings of my sincerity." This applies even to Intersectionism, the theory which the **"Chuva Obliqua"** poems had illustrated. It does not apply to Caeiro, Reis and Campos: his output in their names

> is written *dramatically,* but is sincere (in my grave sense of the word), just as what King Lear says is sincere, who is not Shakespeare but a creation of his . . . Into each of them I have put a deep conception of life, different in all three, but in all of them gravely alert to the mysterious importance of existing.

And so, "slowly but surely, in the divine inner obedience of an evolution whose ends are occult to me," he is raising his projects and ambitions "constantly more to the height of those qualities I have received." But this evolution was also taking him where the three heteronyms could not freely go, since they had to work out their conceptions along their own lines and to stay more or less in character. Pessoa had in him a "deep conception of life" which he could not hive off into a heter-

onym. There is a "take this cup from me" tone in the letter he wrote to Sá-Carneiro on 6 December 1915:

> I am physically besieged . . . The possibility that the truth may lie there, in Theosophy, *me hante.* You must not think I am on the path of madness . . . This is a grave crisis in a mind that is luckily able to take such crises.

He asks Sá-Carneiro to

> consider how Theosophy is an ultra Christian system—in the sense that it contains the Christian principles elevated to a point where they melt into some kind of beyond-God—and think of how much in it is fundamentally incompatible with my essential paganism.

This is the first element in his crisis, the second being that Theosophy, "because it admits all religions," is "just like paganism, which admits all the gods into its pantheon." So:

> Theosophy terrifies me by its mystery and occultist grandeur, repels me by its essential humanitarianism and proselytism . . . attracts me through having so much in common with a "transcendental paganism" (my name for the way of thinking which I had reached), repels me by having so much in common with Christianity, which I do not admit.

Pessoa was not a naïf: anything but. He was looking for a meaning, not ruling out any possibility and not liking what he thought he found. He believed as a man believes who wishes he did not:

> Why did you give what I asked, Holiness?
> I know the Truth, at last, of the real Being.
> Would it had pleased God I should know less!

But his scepticism practically never rested and was at times, apparently, the only thing he believed in: a point of honour, the one joy left. And, living "in the great oscillation between believing and half denying," the same honour in him insisted on his subjecting each poem of his own, especially the ones most disturbingly felt, to the mind's impersonal control. He thought, as Eliot said, that "the more perfect the artist, the more completely separate in him will be the man who suffers and the mind which creates"; indeed, several of his poems have this as their subject. In a letter to Francisco Costa he described Shakespeare as "the most insincere of all the poets there have been," a provocative expression for what Keats called "Negative Capability." Pessoa was one of the most thorough possessors and pursuers of negative capability since Shakespeare, not only because he wrote the poems of imaginary poets but also in most of his own poems.

This shifting conflict—between the religion he chose and the one which seemingly chose him, and again between religion and scepticism, patriotism and scepticism, scepticism and love—is the basic content of Pessoa's own poetry, from maturity till death. On the leading edge of modernism as Campos, as Pessoa himself he made new the old set forms of song and sonnet. I have found, in the close reading which translating is, that the variety of his songs is much greater than it seems at first. Although the language is limpid and fresh, Pessoa's negative capability enables him to leave intact all the "uncertainties, mysteries, doubts," all the ambivalences on which the whole truth of experience depends. And just because of his strict impersonal control, those poems which are surely personal—especially his highly original, sadly honest love poems—are intensely poignant. So, in poem after poem, the end-effect is a lucid mystery: in a closed form, an open content. In this, to my mind, Pessoa comes close to Dante (whom he seems to have disliked for his Christian proselytism). Like Dante, Pessoa was intellectual and passionate; he held together the strands of intricate, elusive thought, and sang like Schubert. He was an extraordinarily complex man who wrote simply. (pp. 14-23)

> *Jonathan Griffin, in an introduction to* Selected Poems
> by Fernando Pessoa, *translated by Jonathan Griffin,*
> *second edition, Penguin Books, 1982, pp. 9-23.*

MARILYN SCARANTINO JONES (essay date 1977)

[*In the following excerpt, Jones examines the role of the orthonym Fernando Pessoa, viewing it as a central figure in Pessoa's group of poetic alter egos.*]

In his critical writings, Fernando Pessoa insisted upon the distinction between autonymic-pseudonymic poetry and orthonymic-heteronymic poetry. An author's pseudonymic work differs from his autonymic production only in so far as a different name is attached to it. A heteronym, however, is not merely a name different from the author's but also a separate personality who expresses what the author does not or cannot.

Pessoa's reputation as a poet is based in large part upon the poetry of the heteronyms he created. It is unusual, even eccentric, for a poet to adopt pseudonyms; but Pessoa was not content with writing under names other than his own. He created biographies and even physical descriptions for the poet-characters who peopled the coterie responsible for much important modern Portuguese poetry. The principle heteronyms are three: Álvaro de Campos, Ricardo Reis, and Alberto Caeiro. The fourth member of the coterie is not a heteronym but an orthonym, one who shares the name Fernando Pessoa yet is not the Pessoa who created Caeiro, Reis and Campos. In his notes and diaries, Pessoa carefully distinguished between "F. P. himself" and the orthonymic Fernando Pessoa, the former being the creator of poet-characters while the latter is merely another member of the coterie. Why did Pessoa create an orthonym rather than another heteronym, and why did he so carefully distinguish between himself and that orthonym? His reasons for doing so are important in understanding the creation of the heteronyms and their usefulness in the totality of Pessoa's poetic expression. (p. 254)

Pessoa's heteronyms are more than *personae* or masks: they are poet-characters. Their creator lived their lives mentally; he did not only write their poetry. They are poets Pessoa became; and each of them is distinct in physical appearance, career, temperament, and poetic style. Pessoa, like all men, was basically egocentric; and thus his probings of the nature of identity began with himself. The heteronyms provided various perspectives from which he might view himself. Each of them was a man Pessoa might have been, and his insistence upon the distinct nature of each of the three can be seen as a way of augmenting the complexities of his nature which Pessoa was aware of and appreciated. The creation of poetic personalities was not, however, an accomplished feat for Pessoa but a dynamic process of continual probing and change. The poetry of each of the heteronyms reflects Pessoa's unending quest to embody the nature of elusive identity, an identity which had in his case been multiplied into three poetic personalities.

Pessoa was hostile to any attempt to simplify the complex, and he sought to intensify the complexity of his being through the creation and existences of his heteronyms. Their poetry must be accepted as the work of three different poet-characters who, like characters in a drama (an analogy Pessoa often used to describe the relationship of the heteronyms to their creator) are separate from each other and from their author. Yet, just as characters within a play interact, so do the heteronyms function together to express what none of them could separately. Each heteronym expresses doubts about the nature of his identity according to his own temperament and poetic style, but it is in *Cancioneiro,* the book of orthonymic poetry which Pessoa arranged shortly before his death that such doubts are given precedence over any other theme. The poetry of the orthonym Fernando Pessoa expresses a fission into a thinking-but-not-feeling Self and an Other capable of emotion but somehow estranged from the Self.

The three heteronyms also concern themselves with a fission that each senses, but their modes of existence allow them to avoid the continuous self-doubts that afflict the orthonym. The orthonym's poetic expression deals almost exclusively with the quest of the Other, the missing portion of his Self which appears to hold the key to his identity. Pessoa's orthonym seems to be his empirical self without any of the complexities that allow "F. P. himself" to become the heteronyms. The orthonymic Fernando Pessoa is not able to multiply himself into other personalities that offer various perspectives on the search for identity. The orthonym's search is strictly internal: it is the probing of Fernando Pessoa within his most basic self. The orthonym expresses poetically the doubts about identity which "F. P. himself" could express in no other way, not even in the privacy of his diaries. It would seem that Pessoa, an unusually complex man who contained elements of each of the three heteronyms, needed to express the doubts of his empirical self and could only do so in the poetry of an orthonym, one so close to "F. P. himself" that even their names were held in common.

The orthonym should not, however, be confused with that elusive "F. P. himself" who created the coterie. The orthonym Fernando Pessoa is distinct from his creator, and is as much a *persona* or mask as are Caeiro, Reis or Campos. The "true" Pessoa, "F. P. himself," may be nothing more than a composite of all of his various heteronyms; and the orthonym is only a portion of that composite. Yet, it is important to note that Pessoa created not only heteronyms but an orthonym, one who shared his name as well. In Portuguese, "pessoa" means a person in the very vaguest sense of the term. It is possible that Pessoa capitalized upon his name by creating a poet-character whose pervasive preoccupation is the nature of his identity, giving major importance to a concern expressed in each of the heteronym's poetry and a concern of their creator, too.

The orthonym expresses himself in his poetry, and it is only through his poetry that we can know him. The creator of the coterie carefully described the physical attributes and biographies of his heteronyms but never offered biographical data about the orthonym. It is tempting to reason that since Pessoa and his orthonym share a name, they share a biography as well. However, to do so would tend to eradicate that most basic and telling difference between the two: "F. P. himself" created a coterie of four poets while the orthonym exists only in his poetry. The orthonym is the portion of Pessoa that faces the problem of identity and probes it directly in his poetry. Pessoa's biography may help to explain why he found it necessary to create heteronyms and an orthonym, but the biography describes the coterie's creator and none of its members. (pp. 255-56)

Pessoa described his poetry as "the expression of a general truth through a personal lie." As Michael Hamburger points out: "Pessoa's disguises did not impair his truthfulness because he used them not to hoodwink others, but to explore reality and establish the full identity of his multiple, potential selves" [see excerpt dated 1969].

Pessoa often wrote about aesthetic doctrine in his diaries and journals. He discussed the relationship of the artist to his art, and much of what he wrote may be helpful in explaining his attitude toward his own poetry and may elucidate the reading of the heteronyms and the orthonym. When Pessoa says that the greatest artist expresses what he does not feel at all: "The artist expresses only those emotions which belong to others;" he is not speaking of the gratuitous creation of emotions but rather of an enlargement of the emotions of the empirical self." Pessoa was a highly self-conscious man who realized that his empirical self was not his entire self. He relied upon his poet-characters to allow him to escape the everyday world and all of the restrictions which it placed upon him.

The putting on of masks was, more than a disguise, a means of enlarging the scope of Pessoa's poetry. He thought of himself as a dramatic poet because he had achieved what he considered the highest level of poetic excellence, the ability to objectify emotion or to depersonalize it. He divided poetry into categories the most desirable being ". . . that one, the most rare, in which the poet, more intellectual and yet more imaginative too, enters into complete depersonalization. He not only feels, but lives, those states of being which he does not directly have." This is what Pessoa did when he wrote as his heteronyms; he did not merely feel the emotions of his *personae;* he lived them, and in living them he came to know them as poet-characters.

By moving out of his empirical self and into the persons of others, Pessoa broadened his perspective and attempted to generalize, generalization being the first maxim of art for him. "So, the first principle of art is generalization. The sensation expressed by the artist must be one that could be felt by all men who understand it." Pessoa condones art as a catharsis only when it can serve man in general and not the poet alone. The poet must express those emotions with which others can identify. If the reader cannot associate himself with the poet's state of being, he cannot participate in the poem and the poet has failed. The poet must serve those who read him, not himself.

> The artist does not express his emotions. His duty is not that. He expresses, among his emotions, those that are common to other men. Speaking paradoxically, he expresses only those emotions which belong to others. Humanity has no interest in his own private emotions. If an error in my vision causes me to see blue leaves, what importance is there in communicating this to others?

The expression of emotions untempered by the intellect was poor poetry at best to Pessoa. He defines the poem: "A poem is an intellectualized impression, or an idea made emotion, communicated to others by means of a rhythm." The collaboration of thought and feeling is basic to artistic expression from Pessoa's point of view.

All art is the result of a collaboration between feeling and thought; not only in the sense that reason works, in building the work of art, upon elements which feeling supplies, but also, and it is this that now concerns us, in the sense that the very feeling upon which reason thus works, and which is the matter on which reason puts form, is a special kind of feeling—a feeling within which thought collaborates.

The dual nature of art, the collaboration of thought and feeling, was of great importance to Fernando Pessoa because he considered it an essential criterion of art as indicated in his aesthetic theory and because he had difficulty in effecting that collaboration in his own work and life. For Fernando Pessoa, the Self and the Other represented thought and feeling. Although they are both part of the same man, they are somehow estranged in a schizoid relationship that can hold no hope for reunification.

As a poet, the orthonymic Pessoa experienced the schizoid relationship within himself. He bears his creator's name and expresses that most basic preoccupation. Alberto Caeiro found at least a temporary release from his self-doubts in the bucolic existence where just being was enough. Ricardo Reis found solace in the classical imitations he forged, while Álvaro de Campos's noisy poetry evidences his lashing out at doubt in an attempt, albeit futile, to eradicate it. The orthonym, however, is without recourse. The epigrammatic poetry of *Cancioneiro* probes deeply within the empirical self and finds none of the solutions which the Pessoa augmented by heteronyms achieves.

The orthonym may be viewed as the most important member of the coterie. It is he who poses the problem basic to all four poets and their creator, and it is he who surrenders to the futility of finding a solution. The heteronyms explore potential solutions and in a sense each satisfies himself at least in the trying. None of the three, however, satisfies "F. P. himself," and so the orthonym Fernando Pessoa's poetic voice encompasses the heteronym's voices and expresses what neither they nor their creator dared. (pp. 259-61)

> *Marilyn Scarantino Jones, "Pessoa's Poetic Coterie: Three Heteronyms and Orthonym," in Luso-Brazilian Review, Vol. 14, No. 2, Winter, 1977, pp. 254-62.*

RONALD W. SOUSA (essay date 1980)

[*Sousa is an American educator and critic. In the following excerpt, he examines the issue of Pessoa's sincerity in his works.*]

The controversy . . . begins with Pessoa himself. It is he who asks the question: "Am I being sincere in this present writing?" and it is he who offers implicit definitions for, and lines within, discussion of what he implicitly establishes as an intellectual problem regarding his "sincerity." His structuring of the problem is then taken up relatively uncritically by a number of his followers, primarily by the young poets of the *Presença* group, who saw in the fortyish Pessoa a predecessor and mentor. While several *presencistas* were involved in that transmission—prominent among them Pessoa's biographer, João Gaspar Simões—, the most important of them for the propagation of the "sincerity" issue was Adolfo Casais Monteiro, who would later become a well-known writer and scholar, one of the revealers of Pessoa's work to the critical world. Through his journalism and scholarship from the late 1930's on, he in fact propagates the main thrust of Pessoa's own structuring of debate on the subject of "sincerity."

Now the curious element in this propagation of the debate is the following: in apparent contradiction to the normal lucidity of the self-criticism that is a constant in him, Pessoa, when he comments directly on his "sincerity," usually limits the scope of the question to boundaries that separate it from other areas of his self-analysis, areas that in fact bear upon it in central ways. It would seem that in so doing he was in fact demarcating areas of the question that were of immediate interest to him as a working poet, not attempting a global approach to the matter. (It should be noted that much of his most-cited language in this regard comes from letters he wrote to other writers about his writing.) (p. 71)

Casais Monteiro, primarily in his well-known pamphlet *Fernando Pessoa, O Insincero Verídico* but also in his book of collected essays, *Estudos sobre a Poesia de Fernando Pessoa*, into which that pamphlet and other earlier work was inserted, and in subsequent works as well, draws out a problematic of Pessoa's "sincerity" seated virtually solely in the area of the methodology of artistic creation. He attacks biographical criticism and especially the practice in that criticism of seeing the poetic expression of emotion as a reflection of the biographical poet's actually-felt emotion. To that notion he counterposes the idea of a "poetic reality," in which he sees poetry as a discursive mode that creates a "reality" of its own and then operates within that "reality," appealing to the world external to it only for reference value in which to ground a creative use of the lexicon and for states of mind to be used as a set of raw materials. According to his idea, the poet—implicitly, the modern poet—knowingly cultivates this poetic reality by eschewing any notion of attempting to express his own emotions and instead exploring ideas, mental states, emotions, and so on, which are not his but which, rather, in their very impersonal nature, provide him with a means of seeing existence in more profound ways than mere reflection, in discourse, of actually-felt emotion can allow. According to Casais Monteiro, such a poet thus succeeds in speaking for "humanity" in general. Following Pessoa's precedent, he calls such impersonality "a sinceridade do poeta consigo mesmo," that is a "sincerity" that, to his way of thinking, is not biographically accurate and is therefore, paradoxically, "insincere" while attaining an outlook superior to that of biographical sincerity. Casais Monteiro cites Pessoa's poem **"Autopsicografia"** and his theories of a series of ascending levels of "depersonalization" in lyric poetic stance in support of his argument. And quite correctly, he points out the parallel between that notion of poetic impersonality and T. S. Eliot's theorization about the "objective correlative" and about the essential impersonality of poetic creation.

Now there are many problems with Casais Monteiro's elaboration of that analysis. For one, he is dealing with a notion of expression that, in a purely technical sense, is always true: language itself is, in strict terms, never mimetic; it must always create the sense that it represents actual emotional states, if such is in fact the purpose to which it is set. It is, therefore, always susceptible to the impersonalist argument; the differences between supposed "personal" and "impersonal" poetry must be analyzed as code differences, not differences between Monteiro's simplistic categories of, in essence, reflectionism and non-reflectionism. Misunderstanding of that issue leads him to confuse Eliot's notion of "impersonal emotion" with

actual thematic issues. (Too, his analysis bespeaks a frighteningly limited view of pre-Romantic poetics, to which he ascribes a reflectionism as he defines it.)

The major problem, however, lies in his performing, in part, in concert with Pessoa's lead, of a false isolation of the "sincerity" issue within Pessoa problematics. What results is a curious panorama that has been accepted by many commentors, either in a treatment of "sincerity" as though it were merely a methodological operation in poetic creation, or in a treatment of the core of the Pessoa problematic as one separate from the "sincerity" question. For all such commentors, the "sincerity" question seems first to betoken an impersonal harnessing of emotion to make a poetry that either is unreflectionist or, if it attempts apparent reflexion, does so with an awareness of the complex, "impersonalizing" nature of the undertaking. They then raise a pseudo-ethical question about the intellectual honesty of that process, a question that presumes as a norm a simple subjectivist poetics and too, rests on the false presumption that a poetics grounded in subjectivistic reflectionism is not susceptible to lack of intellectual honesty.

One of those who followed the lead of Pessoa and Casais Monteiro was the historian and sometimes literary scholar Joel Serrão, in his introduction to an edition of Pessoa's correspondence with the Azorean poet Armando Côrtes-Rodrigues. In an offhand remark in that introduction Serrão states that what seems to him to certify Pessoa's "sincerity" despite his various machinations is his continual preoccupation with the question "Am I being sincere?" That simple formulation, it seems to me, should have put a definitive end to the mixture of ranting and marvelling concerning the supposed ethical question about "sincerity." At the same time, that ingenuous remark opens up a line of questioning that leads to an integration of the "sincerity" problematic with the main body of Pessoa criticism.

Why does Pessoa ask the question "Am I being sincere?" so often? The answer goes well beyond a poetics involving the interplay of emotion and impersonal analysis. The basis of Pessoa's work is inquiry into the nature of human knowledge. In fact, when it is seen in terms of personal psychology, the notion of such inquiry provides a key to interpretation of Pessoa's work. The desire for a spontaneous ethics, for communion with essences that constitute the truth of existence, or lamentation of the impossibility of either for him, at their root pose the question of how one can achieve true knowledge and indicate the psychological anguish of a poet who is confronting that question with a basic sense either that it cannot be answered or that in fact there is something wrong with the question itself. In either case, there exist the dynamics of a frustrated seeker of some sense of validity about both himself and the world in which he finds himself. And while the language is abstract and intellectual, the problem is at its origin personal and psychological.

In the overall Pessoa problematic, then, "sincerity" is first and foremost a question. It has its origin in Pessoa's asking how he can be "sincere," that is how he can form utterances that are truly "his," that truly bespeak "him." . . . Pessoa's theorizing about the value of "impersonal" poetry, creation of a poetics built upon the "sincerity" problematic, and remarks on "sincerity" are constructs grounded in existential doubt. Pessoa, as is usual with him, sets forth such manifestations in highly schematic terms, that is, he creates a number of theories of poetry and poetic processes, and, in his poetry—I think specifically of **"Autopsicografia"**—, argues the problem abstractly. Further, those of his poems that express either lamentation of a state of benightedness or desire to transcend that state and reach a realm of true knowledge of one sort or another, while they do not involve the notion of impersonality directly, can be seen as fitting within Eliot's thinking about the psychological value of an impersonalizing poetics.

To be fair to Casais Monteiro, I should now return to a later work of his on the subject: a brief article entitled "Teoria da Impersonalidade: Fernando Pessoa e T. S. Eliot," published in 1969. In that piece, while still seeing "sincerity" as essentially synonymous with direct "poetic expression of the poet's subjectivity," he does follow Eliot's lead and begin to treat impersonality in terms of existential psychology, abandoning the notion of an autonomous "poetic reality." He clearly does not see the Existentialist need of authenticity in its proper terms, but citing Kierkegaard and Sartre, he in essence begins work toward unification of psychological and aesthetic-philosophical approaches—a direction in Pessoa criticism that I think fruitful and as yet not fully explored.

Let me now sum up the major points developed in my remarks. First, the "sincerity" problematic is a production of Pessoa's own tendency toward limited posing of the question and of propagation of it in similar contours by a number of people, principally Adolfo Casais Monteiro. Second, as a consequence, it has been treated in criticism as a phenomenon isolated from the rest of Pessoa problematics. Third, it is in fact of a piece with what amounts to Pessoa's existential dilemma.

Let me illustrate the final point by reference to a line that is touched on by almost everyone who deals with the subject. It is the first line of "Autopsicografia": "O poeta é um fingidor" ["The poet is a pretender"]. The unsaid precondition to the writing of that line is that, try as he will the poet can do no better, his writing has no verifiability, it is mere pretense, mere creation that has only aesthetic value. While "Autopsicografia" is a brilliant, compressed ars poetica, theory of a metaphor, and analysis of the nature of artistic creation and communication, it is also a poem that, if not itself deeply pessimistic, at very least arises from a sense of anguish about the position of the poet vis-à-vis knowledge and its expression. And too, it exists in a very complex relationship to its creator. The contours of that relationship throughout Pessoa's work are in the main unexplored by criticism.

The Eliot comparison, often cited, provides a fruitful illustration: in a passage where Eliot's poetic creation, J. Alfred Prufrock, after having demonstrated in dramatic terms his lack of cosmic centrality, shifts his exposition to questions of knowledge and of language—an area of a piece with Pessoa's treatment of the same existential problematic. In language very different from Pessoa's spare, abstract norm, Prufrock first observes: "I have heard the mermaids singing, each to each." He then forlornly adds: "I do not think that they will sing to me." He then goes on to sum up, in general terms, in the last stanza of the poem:

> We have lingered in the chambers of the sea
> By sea-girls wreathed and seaweed red and brown
> Til human voices wake us, and we drown.

What Casais Monteiro does not see—or only begins to see at the end of his life—is that the problematics of Pessoa's "sincerity," even when used as the basis of an ars poetica, generate very complex verbal formulations, ones set forth in, in Prufrock's Romantic terms, a very human voice—the voice of a poet who not only listens for the mermaids but also tells us so

in meditated artistic artifacts, all the while acutely aware that he is ever on the verge of drowning. And further, none of the elements of that tripartite act can be disassociated from the others. (pp. 71-3)

Ronald W. Sousa, "Adolfo Casais Monteiro and Pessoa's 'Sincerity'," in Selecta, Vol. 1, 1980, pp. 71-4.

JOANNA COURTEAU (essay date 1982)

[In the following excerpt, Courteau views Pessoa's work in the light of recent psychological theories of personal identity.]

Forty years after Fernando Pessoa's death, the mood of his critics has definitely changed. There is now a call among many critics to abandon the treatment of Pessoa as a case study and to initiate a concentrated examination of his poetic production. These critics argue that too much attention has been paid to Pessoa's subterfuge of the heteronyms as autonomous writers. (p. 93)

Perhaps not so coincidentally, this de-emphasis of Fernando Pessoa's heteronyms coincides with the great popularity in psychology of the "multiple personality" theory. One of its major proponents, Erving Goffman, claims that "there is no abiding self or personality, just an appearance generated afresh to meet each new social circumstance."

David Elkind, a figure well-known in the world of developmental psychology, considers Goffman's view to be consonant with that of other social scientists such as Chomsky, Erikson, and Piaget. In his review of Goffman's work, Elkind cites major social scientists who view Goffman's theory of personality as "the deepest insight into modern human condition provided by any novelist or social scientist writing today."

According to this multiple-personality theory, Fernando Pessoa's case, though slightly unusual, is not at all extraordinary. For in the poetry of "this traveller that got ahead of his fellow-travellers" it is easy to see the analysis of the phenomenon described by Sam Keen and Anne Valley in the popularized version of multiple-personality theory. To the authors of Telling Your Story, "Every I is a we" since we "each harbor the entire range of human possibilities. Within each of us there is a tribe with a complete cycle of legends and dances." The authors advise the lay reader to enrich his life by giving a voice to all the tribesmen and by hearing all the "multiple voices within yourself."

Fernando Pessoa's heteronymous and orthonymous poetry can be viewed as the expression of just such an attempt to give voice to the tribesmen within. Pessoa anticipated in art by sixty years the multiple-personality theory in science. He shows through the heteronyms and the orthonyms that it is possible to be aware of each member of one's tribe and to allow each to find a voice of his own. The heteronyms, then, could be interpreted as Pessoa's representation of man's attempt at listening to and expressing the various voices within.

Yet Pessoa is well aware that such constant attentiveness to the various voices within could prove to be frustrating and exhausting to the person having this experience. So he chooses the orthonymous poetry as the tool with which to analyze and convey such frustration. In the orthonymous poetry the poetic persona is often distraught at its inability to distinguish from among the many the one true voice of the real self. Listening to all the voices places the very existence of the one true self in doubt. This is clearly expressed in the orthonymous poems below:

> I know not how many souls I have.
> With each moment I have changed.
> Constantly I find myself strange.
> Never have I seen or found myself.
> Having been so much, I only have soul left.
> He who has soul has no calm.
> He who sees is only that which he sees.
> He who feels is not he who is.
>
> Attentive to that which I am and see,
> I become them and not me.
> Each of my dreams and desires
> Belongs to its source and not me.
> I am my own landscape,
> Spectator at my own passage,
> Diverse, immobile, and alone,
> I know not how to feel myself where I am.
>
> (pp. 95-6)

In these poems the poetic persona notes the fragmentary aspect and being of each self; all of the selves are strangers to one another. Attentive to each perceiving being, "Attentive to that which I am and see," he loses track of the one authentic being, for the being that he knows to exist in space has no awareness of its own: "I know not how to feel myself where I am." The other selves within the persona become alienated from the one true self: "I read, like pages, my own being." Whether it results from, or is engendered by, the self created anew from one moment to the next, the multiplicity of perception brings in its wake the constant sense of wonder and alienation, as evident in the persona's reiteration, "I look at them. Not a single one am I, being all." Here again Pessoa shows that the artist anticipates by far the scientist by realizing that there are moments when an individual has a basic, irreducible need for the one essential self. This he shows through the poetic persona's desperate desire to pause, to rest, and to get to know: "I wish, for a moment, here to pause / And rest in order to know."

In still other stanzas Pessoa shows even more strongly that parallel to the desire to allow expression to all the selves within, there is in man another desire equally (if not more) powerful to uncover among others the one voice of the true abiding self. It seems, in fact, as if the latter were the direct product of the former. It seems as if the very awareness, the wonder, the alienation before all the selves drives man to find the one true self. The poem **"Dia a Dia"** quoted above ends with the poetic persona's exclamation:

> My God! My God! Who am I, that I know not
> That which I feel I am? He who I want to be
> Lives, far away, where my being I forget,
> He departs, remote, in order not to have me.

Clearly Pessoa recognizes the need one has to know *who* one really is, to know which of all the voices is that of the real self. For throughout the orthonymous poetry he expresses over and over again man's need for this one definite self, man's search for the voice more true than the others.

> I unremember uncertainly. My past
> I know not who lived it. If it was I myself,
> It is confusedly unremembered
> I know not who I have been or who I am. I ignore
>   everything.
> There exists only that of mine which now sees me.

Yet simultaneously Pessoa shows his awareness of the fact that the only personality man can be sure of is his personality of the moment, the self that *now* perceives and is *now* perceived by surrounding reality: There exists only that of mine which now sees me.

As mentioned above, unlike the social scientist, the poet-philosopher intuits the need for the "abiding self" whose very existence is denied by Goffman. This intuition is expressed through the poetic persona's constant search in the orthonymous poetry. It can also be seen through the persona's emphasis on the idea that the very existence of reality depends upon the existence of the "abiding self." This dependence of reality upon being is explained by Benedito Nunes in his penetrating study, "Os Outros de Fernando Pessoa":

> In these conditions, the world that the imagination presents to him in the form of interior landscape, and which reason does not explain, the world, the objective aspects of which the subjective ends up by absorbing, depends on the I, the last support of a reality about to dissolve.

The frustration ensuing from such dependence is further summarized by Nunes in the following terms:

> The being itself of consciousness, the I, remade from moment to moment, without a definite form, becomes a vague and spectral entity. There is an hiatus, an interrelated vacuum between the I, which lacks identity, and the awareness of existence, inherent in the individual that remains.

Fernando Pessoa further intuits that the need for the one "abiding self" leading to the constant and frustrating search may occasionally result in an encounter with the self. This encounter may come not in the form of a dramatic recognition, but it may simply be an awareness of the self, as vague and illusory as the light in the abyss of nothingness which light tells a man that he exists. (pp. 98-100)

Pessoa conveys the idea that sometimes this awareness may simply consist of an obscure permanence at the core of one's being. The poetic persona's words, "There remains something obscure / In the center of my being . . ." could lead the reader to this variation of the Cartesian principle: I am but aware that I am, therefore I am.

Anticipating further the social scientist, Fernando Pessoa shows us in many poems that man might not be satisfied with the mere dim awareness of the self. Man might still continue looking beyond for that one true, abiding self. The search thus anticipated by Pessoa in his poetry is termed by the social scientists [Keen and Valley] as the "identity compulsion": "Identity is a repetition compulsion, a conspiracy to put a consistent face before the world, to cover up the glorious inconsistency of emotions and desires." The very creation of the heteronyms could be viewed as Pessoa's representation in poetry of that which is known as identity compulsion in psychology. Through the heteronyms Pessoa may be showing us that there is a way to organize into unified patterns of coherent perceptual behavior those multiple selves that resemble one another. The creation of heteronyms may have shown us the way for fitting into a coherent whole the bits and pieces of any one self: "As if one were to gather one's dispersed being / And tie it together with destiny."

While on one level Pessoa shows that the identity crisis can find at least a partial resolution in the creation of several coherent identities such as the heteronyms and the orthonym, he also shows us that basically we are dealing with an unresolvable crisis. Again, it is through the orthonymous poetry that he has chosen to express the hopelessness of such a search. Whether organized into patterns of coherent behavior or viewed as individual perceptions of reality, none of the many selves represents the real self. The real self simply and logically does not exist. Pessoa further speculates that perhaps even the dim awareness of the obscure permanence within is simply just another perception, another self, no more real than any of the others. Such speculation may be observed in the lines that follow:

All is unreal, anonymous and fortuitous.
. . .
And that which you know not now nor will ever know
Is that which is most real and most profound.

The last line, beyond the obvious, may mean also the fact that it is perhaps the one voice from within which one will never hear that may have the real story. It just may be that it is that self and that reality that is not within one's range of possibilities which is *the* real thing. But Pessoa continues speculating beyond this point. He goes on to consider the possibility that nothing at all is real and since that is so, there can be *no* real self to offer the one true perception of the one absolute reality.

Nothing is real, nothing in its vain motions
Pertains to a defined form,
A trace seen of a thing only heard.

In these lines Pessoa places the very nature and existence of reality in doubt. For how can we perceive, define, capture, and give form and meaning to a thing as intangible and inconceivable as the visible trace of a sound? "A trace seen of a thing only heard."

In completing his probe into the identity compulsion, Pessoa comes full circle. He shows that one may be dealing with an irresoluble quest having ended up with a totally reversible premise: reality not only depends upon the self that perceives but the self that perceives also depends upon reality. There can be no linear resolution to a problem thus posed in a circular fashion. (pp. 100-02)

> Joanna Courteau, "The Quest for Identity in Pessoa's Orthonymous Poetry," in The Man Who Never Was: Essays on Fernando Pessoa, *edited by George Monteiro, Gávea-Brown, 1982, pp. 93-107.*

ADDITIONAL BIBLIOGRAPHY

Bacarisse, Pamela. "Fernando Pessoa: Towards an Understanding of a Key Attitude." *Luso-Brazilian Review* 17, No. 1 (Summer 1980): 51-61.
    Argues that Pessoa's intentions in his poetry are essentially satiric.

Barrow, Geoffrey R. "The Personal Lyric Disguised: Fernando Pessoa's *Mensagem*." *Luso-Brazilian Review* 13, No. 1 (Summer 1976): 91-9.
    Observes a development in Pessoa's *Mensagem* from epic and historical poems to personal and lyrical poems.

Biderman, Sol. "Mount Abiegnos and the Masks: Occult Imagery in Yeats and Pessoa." *Luso-Brazilian Review* V, No. 1 (Summer 1968): 59-74.
    Discusses occult imagery in the poetry of W. B. Yeats and Pessoa. Biderman writes: "Pessoa, when he wears the mask of the mystic, believes, like Yeats, in the purifying nature of art and the rejoining of the soul to the universal Unity upon death."

Blanco, José, ed. *Fernando Pessoa: A Galaxy of Poets 1888-1935.* Lisbon: Servico Internacional da Fundacão Calouste Gulbenrian, 1985, 119 p.
    Catalogue of a London exhibition of books, manuscripts, paintings, and other material relating to Pessoa's life and work.

Campbell, Roy. "Portugese Poetry from King Sancho I to José Regio." In his *Portugal*, pp. 119-63. London: Max Reinhardt, 1957.
    Brief introduction to Pessoa's work.

Daghlian, Carlos. "Emily Dickinson and Fernando Pessoa: Two Poets for Posterity." *Emily Dickinson Bulletin*, no. 18 (Sept. 1971): 66-73.
    Compares the lives and poetry of Fernando Pessoa and Emily Dickinson.

Howes, R. W. "Fernando Pessoa, Poet, Publisher, and Translator." *The British Library Journal* 9, No. 2 (Autumn 1983): 161-70.
    Provides a well-documented overview of Pessoa's publishing history, association with literary movements, and role as a translator and publisher.

Josipovici, Gabriel. "Fernando Pessoa." In his *The Lessons of Modernism, and Other Essays*, pp. 26-50. Totowa, N.J.: Rowman and Littlefield, 1977.
    Discusses Pessoa as a poet whose work embodies "the essential spirit of modernism."

Losa, Margarida L. "Fernando Pessoa, the Saudosista." *Luso-Brazilian Review* 12, No. 2 (Winter 1975): 186-212.
    Detects elements of saudosismo, a literary movement founded on a nostalgia for Portugal's past and hopes for its future glory, in all of Pessoa's poetry.

Monteiro, George, ed. *The Man Who Never Was: Essays on Fernando Pessoa.* Providence: Gavea-Brown, 1982, 194 p.
    Contributions to this collection include the title essay by Jorge de Sena, "Pessoa and Portugese Politics" by Gilbert R. Cavaco, and "The Search for the Self: Álvaro de Campo's 'Ode Marítima'" by Francisco Cota Fagundes.

Parker, John M. *Three Twentieth-Century Portuguese Poets.* Johannesburg: Witwatersrand University Press, 1960, 43 p.
    Contrasts the functions of Pessoa's heteronyms.

Pilling, John. "Fernando Pessoa." In his *A Reader's Guide to Fifty Modern European Poets*, pp. 173-80. Totowa, N.J.: Barnes & Noble, 1982.
    Introduction to the poetry of Pessoa. Pilling concludes: "Pessoa is a deeply melancholic figure who, despite his unheroic stance, may be called a tragic poet; his condition permits of no permanent remedy, only limited and temporary relief."

Rabassa, Gregory. "Fourth Person Plural." *Parnasus* 1, No. 2 (Spring-Summer 1973): 133-39.
    Maintains that Pessoa presented his ideas through disparate and ultimately nonintegrated viewpoints.

Ramalho, Americo da Costa. "Fernando Pessoa: Portugal's Greatest Modern Poet." In his *Portuguese Essays*, pp. 47-84. Lisbon: National Secretariat for Information, 1968.

Biographical sketch interspersed with translations of Pessoa's poems.

Roberts, William H. "The Figure of King Sebastian in Fernando Pessoa." *Hispanic Review* 34, No. 4 (October 1966): 307-16.
Examines the importance of the King Sebastian legend in Pessoa's life and work.

Severino, Alex. "Fernando Pessoa's Legacy: The *Presença* and After." *World Literature Today* 53, No. 1 (Winter 1979): 5-9.
Traces Pessoa's influence on his contemporaries.

Sousa, Ronald W. "The Structure of Pessoa's *Mensagem*." *Bulletin of Hispanic Studies* LIX, No. 1 (January 1982): 58-62.
Argues that *Mensagem* is a poetry collection based on and unified by concepts from such occult systems as Freemasonry and Theosophy.

Ziomek, Henryk. "Dream and Vision in the Poetry of Fernando Pessoa." *Kentucky Romance* 20, No. 4 (1973): 483-93.
Analyzes Pessoa's use of dream imagery, noting the simultaneous presentation in his poetry of external and internal reality.

Alexey (Mikhailovich) Remizov

1877-1957

Russian folklorist, novelist, short story writer, dramatist, memoirist, and critic.

In the decade before the Bolshevik Revolution of 1917, Remizov emerged as one of the most prolific, versatile, and innovative writers in Russian literature. Best remembered today for his ornate prose style, which influenced a generation of Soviet writers, Remizov was the author of a diverse body of work that included fiction, mystery plays, religious parables, adaptations of folklore, recorded dreams, and experimental narratives combining historical chronicle, memoir, fiction, and literary criticism. Unifying modernist literary techniques with elements of the Russian oral tradition and nineteenth-century literary realism, Remizov's fiction served as a model for such writers as Yevgeny Zamyatin, Mikhail Bulgakov, and Alexey Tolstoy.

Remizov was the youngest of five children born to Mikhail Alexeevich Remizov, a Moscow merchant, and Alexandrovna Naidyonova, the daughter of a family of industrial entrepreneurs. According to Remizov's account, his mother had married his father "out of spite" after an unsuccessful love affair with another man and was unhappy throughout their marriage; when Alexey was two years old she left her husband, taking the children to live with her brothers. Scandalized by their sister's action, the wealthy Naidyonovs treated the Remizovs with disdain, offering them an old out-building in which to live and a limited allowance. The Naidyonovs later imposed their will in the children's upbringing—demanding, for example, that eight-year-old Alexey abandon his classical studies in favor of a business education—and Remizov later described his entire childhood as a period of "torment and maltreatment." Upon his graduation from secondary school in 1894, he rejected a position at the Naidyonov Trade Bank which his relatives had prepared for him and instead enrolled in Moscow University, where he attended courses in a variety of disciplines for the next two years. His studies were cut short in 1896, when he was arrested on the charge of instigating a political demonstration. Although Remizov disputed the charge, maintaining that he had been only a spectator at the affair, he was expelled from the university and exiled to the city of Penza, in eastern Russia. Before he had served his term he was arrested again, this time for attempting to unionize local workers, and after a lengthy period of deliberation by government authorities he was sentenced to three more years of exile in the northern cities of Ustsysolsk and Vologda.

During his exile Remizov read widely, translated works of literature and philosophy into Russian, and began to write sketches, stories, and poems. Although he was confined by the terms of his exile to a particular locale and was frequently under surveillance by police, his activities were unrestricted and he associated freely with the large communities of exiled intellectuals in these areas. As a result of their influence, and of the stimulation provided by his new surroundings, he developed a wide variety of interests which would shape his most characteristic writings. Exposure for the first time to the Russian countryside and peasantry initiated a lifelong fascination with folk culture, and Remizov incorporated into his prose

quaint and obsolete words, neologisms, and unusual slang gathered in his ethnographic studies. In Ustsysolsk he met Serafima Dovgello, a Ukrainian scholar specializing in the study of ancient writings, whom he married in 1904. His wife's work in paleography prompted an interest on his part in archaic forms of handwriting, and he began to affect an ornate calligraphy patterned after the style of 17th century Russian manuscripts. Remizov also kept abreast of developments in modern literature, both in Russia and the West. Particularly influenced by writers of the Russian Symbolist movement, he became interested in medieval religious mysticism, the occult, and erotica. Remizov received encouragement and advice in his literary pursuits from his fellow-exiles, who included Vsevolod Meyerhold and Anatoly Lunacharsky, and in 1902 and 1903 he saw his first works published in newspapers and Russian Symbolist journals. However, many of his early writings were rejected by editors who disliked the eccentric style and content of his work, and so were not published until several years after their completion.

After his term of exile ended in 1903, Remizov lived in Kherson, where he worked as a literary consultant, translator, and administrator for Meyerhold's theatrical company. In 1905 he settled in St. Petersburg and attempted to establish himself as a writer. For the next five years he wrote prolifically while earning a scant living from odd jobs, and by 1910 he had achieved widespread critical recognition. Remizov became a ubiquitous figure in St. Petersburg literary circles, earning notoriety for his amusing personal eccentricities. Remizov was a small, nearsighted man with a slightly hunched back, and commentators suggest that it was partly in compensation for his appearance, as well as in reaction to the traumas of his childhood and his arrest and exile, that he cultivated an exhibitionistic public persona, making himself known as a whimsical prankster. His most elaborate and long-running practical joke was the *Obezvelvopa*, "The Grand and Free Order of Apes," a mock-honorary society that he founded in 1916 and maintained for years afterward, issuing ornate hand-lettered membership certificates to virtually every notable writer, artist, and scholar in St. Petersburg.

Although he supported the basic principles underlying the Russian revolution, Remizov became disenchanted with life under the Soviet regime, and he and his wife seized the opportunity to emigrate in 1921. They stayed temporarily in Berlin, where Remizov found publishers willing to reprint nearly all of his previously published books. In 1923, the couple moved to Paris, where they remained for the rest of their lives. Although troubled by ill health during his final years, Remizov continued to write prolifically until his death in 1957.

Remizov's varied literary interests, influences, and goals resulted in a body of work characterized by diverse, sometimes contradictory elements. This tendency is particularly evident in the prose style for which Remizov became famous. Seeking to free written Russian from the "bookishness" that had traditionally dominated literary prose, he attempted to purge his writings of foreign linguistic influences and to pattern his prose on the vocabulary, syntax, and rhythms of spoken Russian. He approached this goal in part through the use of "skaz" narrative, a technique first popularized by Nikolai Leskov whereby stories are related in the words of a naive, often semiliterate narrator. Despite this populist tendency in his prose, however, Remizov's works contain so many archaic and exotic words incomprehensible to the average reader that many were published with glossaries. Furthermore, Remizov fashioned both exotic and colloquial Russian into an intricate and heavily mannered style far removed from spoken language. This eccentric style exerted a decisive influence on the works of Remizov's contemporaries; Remizov, along with Andrey Bely, is credited with initiating the Ornamentalist trend that dominated Russian prose of the 1920s.

Critics frequently divide Remizov's works into two categories, distinguishing his original works from his large body of writings derived from the Russian pagan and Christian oral traditions. Notable among the latter category are such folklore collections as *Posolon* and *Limonar*, in which Remizov sought to recreate primal myths by recasting fairy tales, children's games, pagan rituals, apocryphal legends, and other elements of folklore, which he considered vestiges of ancient mythology. Noted for their humor and poetic charm, Remizov's folklore collections are also praised by critics for accurately rendering the spirit of oral legends in written form. While these works exhibit a worldview drawing on both paganism and Christianity, some of Remizov's other derivative writings are more narrowly Christian in their focus. These include *Nikoliny pritchi*, a collection of parables from the life of St. Nicholas, *Plias Irodiady*, an adaptation of the legend of John the Baptist, and many of his dramas, which are frequently modeled after medieval mystery plays.

Remizov's original writings include numerous novels and short stories. His novels most often concern the trials of the downtrodden in a sordid world of cruelty and injustice, evidencing a preoccupation with grief and suffering similar to that of Fedor Dostoevsky, and several of his novels have been favorably compared to those of his more famous literary forebear. Realistic in style, Remizov's novels often focus on grim and grotesque aspects of their subjects; at the same time, critics note that their oppressive atmosphere is frequently mitigated by fantasy and humor. This combination of elements is exemplified in two of Remizov's most highly regarded novels: *Neoyomny buben (The Story of Ivan Semenovich Stratilatov)*, the tale of a provincial clerk, and *Piataia iazva (The Fifth Pestilence)*, a caricature of provincial life that both parodies and emulates Nikolai Gogol's drama *Revizor* (1836; *The Government Inspector*). Much of the critical commentary devoted to Remizov's novels has focused on their compositional complexity. Episodic in form, they eschew chronological narration in favor of a series of vignettes and lyrical digressions. While some commentators have criticized these works for excessive fragmentation, others have acclaimed them as models of craftsmanship, maintaining that the eccentricity of their form skillfully mirrors that of their content.

Like his novels, Remizov's short stories often concern the poor and oppressed, frequently depicting the spiritual dilemmas of individuals struggling to reconcile the injustice and brutality they encounter with Christian ideals of love and virtue. Many of his stories, including "Novyi god," "Emaliol," and "Krepost," portray the despair of exiles and political prisoners, expressing the anguish felt by individuals who have lost control of their lives to outside agents. In contrast to these works depicting the cruel realities of the adult world stand Remizov's stories concerning children. These stories, which constitute nearly a third of his short fiction, tend to be lyrical mood pieces that sympathetically describe a child's innocent view of the world. Remizov's short stories also demonstrate his fascination with supernatural folklore, demonology, and the occult. Devils, often of an impish rather than a satanic nature, appear frequently in his fiction; supernatural forces play a major role in "Zanofa," "Chertykhanets," and "Zhertva."

In the period following his emigration from the USSR, Remizov abandoned conventional fiction to develop what Alex M. Shane has described as "a highly subjective hybrid memoir genre which combined a chronicle of postrevolutionary Russia, reminiscences, autobiography, biographical sketches, essays on life and literature, and a fantasy dream world." One of his most significant achievements in this experimental narrative form, according to critics, is his autobiography *Podstrizhennymi glazami*. In this work, Remizov used a surreal technique that slurs distinctions between fact and invention to interlace the events of his life with fictional and mythological characters and incidents. Another notable work of this period is *Ogon veschei*, a Symbolist-influenced book of literary criticism which examines the role of dreams in the works of major 19th century Russian writers. Remizov's interest in dreams as literary artifacts also resulted in *Martyn Zadeka*, a collection of his own dreams.

During his lifetime, Remizov's works were extremely influential in the Russian literary world. Sona Aronian has written that during the last years of Remizov's life, "critics, . . . hailing the appearance of his works as major events in Russian literature, concentrated on each work as a new form with a new vision and on Remizov's *oeuvre* as a phenomenon that defied categorization.'' Despite this critical acclaim, Remizov's popularity with readers has been hindered by the eccentricity and occasional obscurity of his books. Furthermore, because Remizov's style is so dependent on its idiosyncratic use of the Russian language for its effect, it is difficult to translate, and only a few of his works are available in English. As a result, Remizov has remained unfamiliar to most non-Russian readers. In the Soviet Union, Remizov's writings were neglected for many years after his emigration, and much of the recent Soviet criticism of Remizov has concentrated on his social and political views. Most of the criticism in English, however, explores the diverse and highly individualistic nature of his writings. ''To get hold of the essence of Remizov's personality,'' observes D. S. Mirsky, ''or to realize the unifying principle of his work, is the most difficult and baffling of tasks, so elusive and many-sided is he.''

PRINCIPAL WORKS

Limonar (folklore) 1907
Posolon (folklore) 1907
Chasy (novel) 1908
    [*The Clock*, 1924]
Chortov log i polunoschnoe solntse (short stories) 1908
Prud (novel) 1908
Krestovye sestry (novel) 1910
Sochineniya. 8 vols. (novels, short stories, and folklore)
    1910-12
Piataia iazva (novel) 1912
    [*The Fifth Pestilence* published in *The Fifth Pestilence:
    Together with the History of the Tinkling Cymbal and
    Sounding Brass, Ivan Semyonovitch Stratilatov*, 1927]
Vesennee porosh'e (short stories and legends) 1915
Nikoliny pritchi (parables) 1917
Slovo o pogibeli zemli Russkoi (prose poem) 1918
Besovskoye deistvo (drama) 1919
Tragediya o Iude printse Iskariotskom (drama) 1919
Mara (short stories) 1922
*Neoyomny buben (novel) 1922
Plias Irodiady (prose) 1922
V pole blakitnom (novel) 1922
    [*On a Field Azure*, 1946]
Kukkha: Rozanovy pis'ma (prose) 1923
Skazki russkago narodna (legends) 1923
*The Fifth Pestilence: Together with the History of the
    Tinkling Cymbal and Sounding Brass, Ivan
    Semyonovitch Stratilatov* (novels) 1927
Olya (novel) 1927
Vzvikhrennaia Rus (memoir) 1927
Podstrizhennymi glazami (autobiography) 1951
Myshkina dudochka (memoir) 1953
Martyn Zadeka (dreams) 1954
Ogon veshchei (criticism) 1954

Translated selections of Remizov's works have appeared in *Russian Literature Triquarterly*, No. 18 (1985).

*This work was written in 1909.

JOHN COURNOS (essay date 1916)

[*Cournos was a Russian-born American novelist and critic. As a translator, he prepared the first English editions of works by*

several Russian writers, including Remizov's The Clock. *In the following excerpt Cournos characterizes Remizov's writing.*]

Aleksei Remizov must be classed among those artists who say an old thing in a new way. This is good, for it makes an old thing new, a dead thing living, and what once belonged to our fathers our very own again. (p. 28)

What I [have] said of Sologub—that he is a Russian soul with a French mind—is as true of most of the finer Russian writers to-day. It is also true of Aleksei Remizov.... [Remizov] is in the Dostoyevsky tradition. He loves the Russian word. The ''tendency to pity'' is strong in him. He penetrates into dark places by soft candle-light, and he gives us conversations and monologues which pass on the other side of the wall. He is primarily a writer of novels and short stories and poems in prose—and these are so beautiful as to be almost untranslatable.

This last word describes one of the chief differences between him and Dostoyevsky. Remizov loves his words. No Russian writer ever knew so many Russian words. And he loves to orchestrate them as a musician orchestrates his notes. The result he obtains is not always the same. Sometimes it is as simple as in his new version of the little folktale [**''The Betrothed''**] ... ; sometimes it is rather obscure in meaning, though extremely beautiful and suggestive as word music. (pp. 28-9)

> *John Cournos, ''Aleksei Remizov,'' in* The Egoist,
> *Vol. III, No. 2, February 1, 1916, pp. 28-9.*

LEV LUNTS (essay date 1920)

[*Lunts was a Russian dramatist, essayist, and critic. In the following excerpt from an essay originally published in 1920, he discusses three of Remizov's plays—*The Tragedy of Judas, The Pageant of Georgy the Bold, *and* Demonic Pageant—*and notes characteristic elements of Remizov's writing in these works.*]

Remizov has written three big ''pageants'' (*deistva*).... Of these three plays, the first **Demonic Pageant (*Besovskoe deistvo*)**, is *scenic* through and through. It is a parody of ancient Russian legends; everything depends on the action, on motion, on a punning series of comic situations. The play certainly should be successful in performance. When reading it, you lose not only the whole second act, but also the bright scenes with masks, the scene of the seduction and others. Finally, the central figures of the demons Aratyr and Timelikh, who are buffoons and punsters, cannot fail to produce uninterrupted bursts of laughter. Their saucy curses, chosen with typical Remizovian precision and pronounced in the most ''pious'' and ''sacred'' places, will no doubt strike the ''cultured'' spectator as blasphemy, but with a public which is naive and hungry for *spectacles* this play will have a huge success. (pp. 263-64)

The Tragedy of Judas, Prince of Iscariot (*Tragediya o Iude printse Iskariotskom*) and **The Pageant of Georgy the Bold (*Deistvo o Georgii Khrabrom*)** do not offer such scenic interest. They are made from the same material as the **Demonic Pageant,** but their approach is different. The **Demonic Pageant** is constructed as a parody, interlaced with purely comic show-booth numbers and insertions. It is enough to read the author's subtle, humorous footnotes to the last edition of the play to become convinced of this. The two other ''pageants'' are written in the same language and drawn from the same source, but they are profoundly serious. In **Judas,** Oriph and Ziph, playing roles analogous to the demons of **Demonic Pageant,** grow pale, lose their central position and become more like the traditional companions of the heroes. Yet even they now and then pepper their dialogues with curses, wink back and forth, tussle, play the show booth. *The Pageant of Georgy the Bold* finally gets rid of any crude buffoonery. As a result, the last two plays, especially *Georgy,* lose their scenic merits and cease to be pure "pageants." They should remain incomprehensible to the broad mass and, on the contrary, be accepted with condescension by the intelligentsia.

But in terms of literature, the last two plays are perhaps more interesting than the first. This is because we can trace Remizovian devices in them with surprising clarity. It would seem that *Judas* and *Georgy* are sewn together with obvious dark threads, and if you take these apart you leave nothing for analysis. The author himself encourages us in this view by graciously explaining how the works were made: the sources, the texts and aids from which he drew his material. He indicates all this. Remizov is a great expert on the nation's past, on all sorts of chants, legends and designs. And a good half of his stories are reworkings of these legends. But the "pageants" are weaved directly from them, as from patches. "For the writing of this tragedy, I made use of folk songs, chants, carols, lamentations and old traditions," says the author in his notes. The tragedy begins with a carol: "Ne zarya zareet. . ." ("Not the red sky reddens. . ."). Remizov provides the explanation: "Consult Potebnya." And other citations follow: This was taken from A. Veselovsky, this from Varentsov, this again from Potebnya, etc.

Such a compositional device is characteristic of the whole of Remizov's work. With good reason he wrote in the explanation of the title of his book *Vesennee porosh'e:* "The word *porosh'e* signifies minutia and dust, *Vesennee porosh'e* will be spring dust: the petals here of fallen flowers and all sorts of little leaves and birch aments and the blossom of the oak and little twigs and the tendrils of grasses." And every story, every novella by Remizov may be called such a *porosh'e.* In the "pageants," you can see in special relief how these little twigs and tendrils of grasses intertwine into one harmonious and shapely whole.

Likewise, in the material of the "pageants," you can pick out all of Remizov's favorite devices: (1) ancient and local words, which here play the role of "trans-sense" locutions (it's interesting that this predilection for words incomprehensible to the reader is realized with a full awareness, intentionally—the author appends glossaries of present words for the unknown words and expressions in his works); (2) alternation of short, one-worded replies and enormous, many-lined periods; (3) piling up of epithets and predicates; (4) enjambements; (5) alliterations; (6) doublings; (7) finally, countless repetitions and refrains. In this respect, the torture of the tsarevich in the second act of *Georgy the Bold* is remarkable. The tsarevich is tortured off-stage, and on-stage the tsar, prophet, tsarevna, images of the blessed, guards and elders exchange remarks, accompanying them with the same refrains. Each has his own strictly determined leitmotif. The elders express doubt in Georgy's invulnerability, the tsar hastens with the execution, the prophet incants, the images of the blessed pray for the tsarevich, the guards report on the course of the execution (in the same words), and, finally, the tsarevna from time to time invariably cries out: "Stop the execution!" (pp. 264-65)

Lev Lunts, "The Theater of Remizov," translated by Gary Kern, in Russian Literature Triquarterly, *No. 19, 1986, pp. 263-65.*

MOISSAYE J. OLGIN   (essay date 1920)

[*In the following excerpt, Olgin describes the sinister world depicted in Remizov's early fiction and offers brief characterizations of the novels* Sisters in Christ *and* The Fifth Affliction.]

A shocking world. Hideous details. Men and women seem ordinary human beings, yet each of them has a little mean devil in his brain. Every man and woman is committing or about to commit some unclean act. They are no criminals, yet a fetid ichor runs through their veins, and they experience malicious joy when they do vile mischief.

Such are the characters in Alexey Remizov's stories. Such is, in his perception, the population of his native land. A foul smell rises from the places he describes, an odor of decaying corpses, of suppurating ulcers, of ugly diseases, of sickening offal. A slimy substance is creeping through the land, through habitations of men, through their very souls, a heavy substance full of venom, license, rot, loathsome vermin, uncanny abomination. "A catalogue of turpitude," somebody called Remizov's stories.

His people are bored and intrinsically unhappy. Yet their conduct cannot be blamed on conditions alone. They have sinister instincts. They are cruel. They are drunken. They use the basest language. They indulge in vicious obscenity. They are sensuous in petty ways. They beat each other, they cripple the weak, they kiss the dust from the boots of the strong, they torture animals, they see ghosts, they are intermixed with demons, witches, monsters, and all the filthy creatures of an unhealthy imagination. Altogether it is a world in which every evil desire is given free swing, and the inhabitants would appear insane if they did not bear such a striking resemblance to the people we see every day in the ordinary pursuits of life.

It is this mixture of almost fantastic debasement with the most usual features of human character and occupation that makes Remizov's writings unique in Russian literature. Somehow one feels that he is not even exaggerating. He has only a keener eye for the ugly facts of life as they occur every day. He is appalled by the amount of real Russian, good-humored, matter-of-fact degradation, physical and mental, which is spread in every realm of life. His most favored image is a dragon, an unclean mystic serpent, wriggling slowly over the land. One must not forget that the time he appeared in literature was the time of Rasputins and Azovs, the time of cruel agrarian revolts accompanied by unwarranted atrocities, the time of Black Hundred outrages, punitive expeditions, scaffolds erected before dawn, summary shootings and pogroms. It is evident that most of his revolting details Remizov collected from news items in the daily press. One of his characters thus summarizes his views on Russia in the watchful hours of unhappy nights. "Injuries, violence, ruin, overcrowding, want, robbery, venality, murder, disorder, and lawlessness,—this is the Russian land. Unbalanced, unfriendly to each other, erratic in their ways, incoherent and inarticulate, eternally silent,—this is the Russian people. Who will save the Russian land, stripped, burned out, trampled bare, corroded, and devastated as it is? Who will break the untruth? Who will allay the hatred? Where are the straight, fearless thoughts, the untrembling heart?" Still, it must be noted that the scope of Remizov's pictures is much broader than mere social and political influences on human conduct. His scrutiny is directed into the souls of men. And it is there that he sees his dreadful visions.

In his effort to convey an adequate impression, Remizov often resorts to the fantastic. Devils, hobgoblins, all sorts of witchcraft, all manner of unnatural occurrences take place in his stories side by side with the facts of real life. It is sometimes difficult to discern whether the writer introduces these strange phenomena as part of the experiences of his persons, or gives them as an element of his own visions. Still, he is one of the staunchest realists in modern Russian literature. He knows a wealth of facts about the actual people in every walk of life. He knows such details as hardly any other man of letters has had an occasion to observe. He presents all this with unusual skill and in sharp outlines that impress themselves irresistibly on the mind of the reader. He seems to be grinning inwardly while unloading his mass of palpitating, glaring illuminated human material. He has done his work well, he seems to think. In fact, he came into the closest possible contact with the people. He acquired a vast knowledge of the people's tales, songs, conjurations, plays, beliefs, superstitions. He studied the people's toys, works of art, incarnations of the popular imagination. He drank from the fresh well of the people's mythology and mysticism, and the fantastic creations of the people's mind became almost a reality to him.

All this he embodies in his writings with relentless energy. He overwhelms by the number and variety of his facts. He makes one tired. Yet this very accumulation of colorful particulars creates the impression desired, the impression of a dreadful world.

Remizov seems to be objective. Yet through all his cruel pages a wounded soul is crying without words. Remizov is sick of life. Remizov is crushed by the horrors of life. It were easier if life were a tragedy. He might have found solace in the grandeur of conflicting forces. But life to him is abominable nonsense. Life is one protracted, agonizing nausea. And the miserable sadness of it all lingers at the bottom of his heart.

Sometimes he tries to be humorous. It seems as if a smile could give him relief. But he cannot detach himself from his world. He cannot be aloof. That's why his smile is more of a grin. He cannot even be funny. He is grotesque. He makes the grimaces of a clown. At times he looks as if he were a madman. There is no end to the twists of his caprices. Some of his pages would sound like a conscious mocking exaggeration if not for the repugnant horror that creeps through them. Altogether, Remizov's form is admirably suited to express just that perception of life which must drive a man into complete and incurable despair.

Just to catch his breath, Remizov sometimes leaves his cultured circles and goes back to folklore. Then he creates tales in the strain and in the language of the primitive people. It would be proper to call them ''tales of our times,'' because they combine the folklore with a modern conception of things. Remizov also writes stories for children,—very simple, very graceful, very sincere. Yet the careful reader will even here perceive the echoes of his dread of life. The same crooked nasty demons are playing their petty games everywhere.

Remizov is one of the unhappiest of modern Russian authors. Not one of the solutions offered by his fellow-artists comforts him. He is not religious in the higher sense of the word. He is close to the plain rugged men who believe, pray, worship, go to church, light a candle before holy images, and drink before and after. He often feels like one of them. But he is only in the grip of religious ceremonies without the elevation of real faith. In his worst moments he is inclined to mock even at God. These are, perhaps, the most painful spasms in the gray torture of his despair.

And no aid. And no way out.

Alexey Remizov is, perhaps, the greatest master of the Russian language in the present generation of writers. His vocabulary of popular expressions is amazing. His ability to adapt words to ideas is unsurpassed. He gives the impression of using naked words. His language is almost perplexing. With all this, he is not posing. He is genuine. A strange, unhealthy flower in the swamp of Russian life. (pp. 281-85)

[Remizov's novelette *Sisters in Christ* takes place in a] large tenement house in a poor section of Petersburg. Flats and rooms [are] packed with clerks, students, professional folk, and some of the working-class. Remizov goes from story to story, from door to door describing the inhabitants. In a few lines, he condenses the whole life of a person. And the life is always a hideous misery. As the descriptions grow in number and particulars, the reader is seized with fear. It seems as if a god with the qualities of a monkey had decided to distort the face of life, making it a mockery at harmony, happiness, justice. (p. 285)

[The novelette *The Fifth Affliction* takes place in a] provincial town. The portraits of all the notables are drawn with uncanny penetration. The elements of a society devoid of a higher human interest are presented with such clairvoyance as to make them look almost fantastic. Against this background is thrown the figure of a strong man longing for beauty and right. His protest against surrounding forces is silent but relentless. It is a gigantic struggle of one reticent man against the evil of a world absorbing even his own wife and children. In the tragic features of the hero, it is easy to recognize the author himself. (pp. 285-86)

> *Moissaye J. Olgin, ''Alexey Remizov,'' in his* A Guide to Russian Literature (1820-1917), *Harcourt, Brace and Howe, 1920, pp. 281-86.*

THE TIMES LITERARY SUPPLEMENT   (essay date 1924)

[*In the following excerpt the critic reviews several of Remizov's early works, stressing the originality and diversity of his writing.*]

Remizov is the foremost of Russian novelists under the age of fifty—not merely because of the intrinsic merit of his work, but also because of the enormous influence he has exercised on the prose writers of the following generation. With few exceptions all Russian literary fiction for these last ten or twelve years is either, like that of A. N. Tolstoy, Remizov-and-water; or, like that of Zamyatin, Pilnyak, and the whole of the younger group of St. Petersburg and Moscow, an exaggeration of certain of Remizov's peculiarities. . . .

Remizov is by far the most Russian of living Russian writers. Nearly all the most original and native currents of Russian literary tradition have met in his personality. His literary ancestors are Dostoevsky, Gogol, the old-Russian Apocrypha, and the Russian folk-tale—models, it must be admitted, various enough to lead us to expect a certain variety from one who has followed them. Indeed, Remizov's variety is astonishing, and even to many of his readers quite disconcerting. Few readers are sufficiently catholic to give an equal appreciation to all the aspects of his work. Add to this a very peculiar and whimsical humour (in the Jonsonian sense) both in his life and in his writings, and an unbending artistic honesty; he has never stooped to popularity or fashion, he has never courted success or curried the favour of either critics or public, he never writes but as his unique and capricious genius impels him to write. All this makes him a peculiarly difficult writer for the public to appraise. And it must be confessed that he is not widely read—he is still a writers' writer. This is, however, due to causes that are rather fortuitous than essential; there is little doubt that his popularity will grow (as it has steadily grown among the "inner circle"), for he has that width of human appeal which makes national classics, and that mastery of form which outlives generations. To the English reader at least one of Remizov's traits may appeal even more than it does to the Russian: this is his quaint humour and incurable, incalculable whimsicality. England has always produced, and recognized, writers whose characters, as Tristram Shandy has said, "do honour to our climate"; and she would gladly adopt, if he were made presentable to her, one who, in the wilfulness of his whims, outdoes both Sterne and Lamb. The trouble is, of course, the old trouble—*"traduttori traditori"* ["translator traitor"]. In the case of Remizov the translation demands particular care and skill. His Russian is unique in its quality, and something of a revelation. It has been said that Russian is the least bookish and the most colloquial of all literary languages, and this is to a great extent true. But Remizov has gone one better. His writings—at least his most characteristic writings—renounce the structure of written language altogether and adopt all the characteristics of colloquial speech; his syntax is based not on logical division but on the variety of spoken intonation, of which he has a marvellous command. He succeeds in producing the impression of actual speech, and those who have once heard his voice are haunted by its intonations from the first sentences, whenever they open one of his books. This gives an uncommonly fresh savour to all he writes. To do him justice in English would require a new school of translators who would be able to preserve his intonations (a thing by no means impossible).

This characteristic of Remizov's is seen at its best in the *Folk-Tales of the Russian People*. Heaven knows how much of them he has really overheard from the people or gleaned from printed collections, and how much he owes to his own mischievously inventive brain. They are brimful of a delightfully absurd humour, and, like real fairy-tales (as the Russian word *skazki* is usually Englished, though they have nothing whatever to do with fairies, who are unknown to the Russian imagination), they are quite beyond the laws of logic and consistency. Things happen in this world of Remizov's as they do in the genuine Russian fairy-tale, according to some entirely unknown laws of causation, as they do in dreams. For, as Remizov says in his preface, "fairy-tale and dream are brother and sister." And, like dreams, his fairy-tales have neither moral nor idea, though they are curiously—and rather elusively—pervaded by a certain philosophy of life, or one might say certain religious atmosphere. Remizov has also written down some genuine dreams of his—and certainly there are no more dreamlike dreams in the whole of human literature. To write about childhood from a child's point of view is a thing sufficiently difficult for a grown-up—still more difficult is it for the man awake to write about dreams from the point of view of the sleeper—without introducing his own logic and sense of consistency. Remizov's dreams have not been collected in a single book but are dispersed throughout most of his writings; these dreams have cost him more censure than even the naughtiest of his literary escapades (and some of these have been naughty enough); serious editors refused to disfigure their publications with such absurdities. But perhaps to the genuine Remizovite the dreams and the fairy-tales are worth all his more ambitious and "intellectual" works. To the English reader they would certainly come as one of the freshest breaths of air that ever came from Russia.

Sisters of the Cross and *The Fifth Plague* are less strikingly original and more conventional. The first of these stories gives a fair idea of that aspect of Remizov which is conspicuously absent from his fairy-tales. It is in the tradition of Dostoevsky; but it does not display either of that great master's supreme qualities—his narrative art and his art of character-creating; it is written in a tense and elaborate semi-poetical style, and it is mainly lyrical in appeal. It makes an effort to concentrate all the nameless horror and squalor of life in a single block of buildings—the Burkov house in St. Petersburg on the Fontanka. So it answers much better to the idea most English readers have made for themselves of what is Russian. Its *Leitmotiv* is a Dostoevskian intensity of compassion; and the book as a whole is decidedly painful. It is (a rare thing in Remizov) unrelieved by humour, and it is scarcely held together as a narrative.

The Fifth Plague is in yet another style. It also has in it elements of poetry. It rises at moments to poetical diction and emotion; but the bulk of the story is prose—Remizov's inimitable and racy Russian. It is a piece of grim and grotesque humour, a caricature of a Russian out-of-the-way, god-forsaken country town; a gallery of what Gogol would have called "pigs' snouts." It is very much in Gogol's tradition. The hero, Bobrov, who is contrasted with his ugly townspeople, is a public prosecutor; he is ashamed of being a Russian and obstinately calls himself a German; he is rigidly honest but cold and heartless. He has devoted the whole of his life to the law, which he applies to his fellow-creatures in all its rigid and heartless severity. Remizov's poetical justice makes him commit a glaring judicial mistake. And he perishes miserably in the pangs of lonely despair. *The Fifth Plague* belongs to a series of stories of provincial life which has been specially powerful in promoting Remizov's influence among the younger writers. The masterpiece of this genre is *The Story of Ivan S. Stratilatov,* one of the most terribly comprehensive and uncanny paintings of the Russian character. In the more conventional line *Stratilatov* . . . is Remizov's masterpiece. It produced an immense impression on the younger Russian novelists—and stories of provincial life in this grotesque and suggestive style almost swamped the Russian literary Press about 1913-1916. But Remizov has since turned to other ways—for he has never stooped to play the ape to himself. His later work, written since 1916, is freer and less conventional in composition. It almost ceases to be fiction. His stories of 1916 collected in *Mara* (a word difficult to translate—perhaps *fata morgana*) contain such a masterpiece of simple humanity as the **"Teapot,"** a story of pity and conscience told with a simplicity, a poignancy and a delicacy not to be found in Dostoevsky. *The Noises of the Town* is a chronicle of Petrograd life under the Bolshevists (1918-20). His latest work includes *The Chronicle of 1917* . . ., a curiously humorous, fantastic, tragical, poetical, and anecdotal account of the great Revolutionary year as he saw it.

We have by no means given anything like a complete outline of this extraordinary versatile genius. There remain his stories from the Apocrypha and lives of Saints, told in his simplest and raciest Russian, and containing more purely narrative interest than any other of his books; then there is *In a Field Azure,* a deliciously fresh, unpretending, and naive history of a little girl; and his purely poetical work, the grand and tragical *Lament on the Ruin of the Land of Russia,* written two months before the Bolshevist Revolution. Nor is this all. In fact, one is tempted to say (with but a small touch of exaggeration) that there are as many aspects of Remizov as there are aspects of the Russian mind and Russian life. But even if Remizov is not (though he probably is) the most comprehensive, he is certainly the most attractive and lovable, as well as the most original, of living Russian writers.

> *"Alexei Remizov," in* The Times Literary Supplement, *No. 1153, February 21, 1924, p. 108.*

JOSEPH WOOD KRUTCH   (essay date 1925)

[*Krutch is widely regarded as one of America's most respected literary and drama critics. Noteworthy among his works are* The American Drama since 1918 *(1939), in which he analyzed the most important dramas of the 1920s and 1930s, and "Modernism" in* Modern Drama *(1953), in which he stressed the need for twentieth-century playwrights to infuse their works with traditional humanistic values. A conservative and idealistic thinker, he was a consistent proponent of human dignity and the preeminence of literary art. His literary criticism is characterized by such concerns: in* The Modern Temper *(1929) he argued that because scientific thought has denied human worth, tragedy has become obsolete, and in* The Measure of Man *(1954) he attacked modern culture for depriving humanity of the sense of individual responsibility necessary for making important decisions in an increasingly complex age. In the following excerpt from a review of Remizov's* The Clock *and Boris Pilnyak's* Tales of the Wilderness, *Krutch criticizes the works of both writers for what he considers their lack of passion and intellectual substance.*]

Prince Mirsky begins his introduction to [Pilnyak's] *Tales of the Wilderness* [see Additional Bibliography] with the statement that the English reading public knows next to nothing of contemporary Russian literature and then, as he proceeds to discuss the prose writers since Chekhov, comes very near to saying that they are not worth knowing. Dismissing Merezhkovsky, Andreev, and Artsybashev as "second- and third-rate writers," he proposes Remizov and Pilnyak as representatives of the best which contemporary Russia has to offer; but of them and their school he says that they have little except a self-conscious and fastidious style to distinguish them. Both from this introduction and from [their writings] . . . we learn that they are devoted to meticulous, rather pointless studies of the mean and grotesque aspects of contemporary life and that, lacking the social ideas of their great predecessors, they have created a sort of inverted æstheticism which toys with ugliness without exactly knowing why it does so. A certain gift for clear-cut description they certainly have, but their stories are singularly barren of either intellectual or emotional content. (p. 163)

"Remizov," says Mr. Cournos [in the foreword to his translation of *The Clock;* see Additional Bibliography], "differs from the author of *Crime and Punishment* chiefly in that he is more conscious of his style"—a statement which would seem to imply that he is a greater Dostoevski. In reality he lacks almost completely the thing which makes the writer with whom he is so casually compared great; namely, his passion. However bad Dostoevski may have thought the world to be, he never ceased to resent with all his fierce soul the fact that it was not different. His despair was rung from him by the bitter results of his heroic efforts, but Remizov takes as a matter of course all that Dostoevski protests against, and he wrings no emotion from his tale because he is so far beyond struggle. At the beginning of his story his misshapen hero asked himself: "In general what was the use of life?" and the question is reiterated again and again. Innumerable other Russian authors have asked the same question, and it may very properly be the end of a great work. But it is not a good beginning, because if life is really without value then the only possible interest which it

can offer is the discovery of this fact. To start with it as an assumption is to destroy art along with life. Nearly all the stories of both the authors under discussion are emotionally static because the conflict is over before they commence, and the tragedy is not described because it is taken for granted. They are interesting as evidence of the state of mind to which the authors have descended, but they are strangely unmoving because nothing ever hangs in the balance. The characters have already lost all there is to lose, and the authors have descended to the lowest pit to which it is possible to descend.

The intense preoccupation with untranslatable niceties of language which is spoken of in the case of both as the distinguishing mark of their effort is probably . . . a sign of their barrenness of thought or feeling. They obviously find themselves at the close of a period, and having heard all they have to say already said they can do nothing except occupy themselves with ways of saying it. A writer must go up hill or down; he must be moving toward faith or toward disillusion, he must have an enthusiasm for either creation or destruction; and these writers have neither. (pp. 163-64)

> *Joseph Wood Krutch, "New Russia or Old?" in* The Nation, *New York, Vol. CXXV, No. 3110, February 11, 1925, pp. 163-64.*

PRINCE D. S. MIRSKY   (essay date 1926)

[*Mirsky was a Russian prince who fled his country after the Bolshevik Revolution and settled in London. While in England, he wrote two important histories of Russian literature,* Contem-

Portrait of Remizov by Boris Kustodiev.

porary Russian Literature *(1926) and* A History of Russian Literature *(1927). In 1932, having reconciled himself to the Soviet regime, Mirsky returned to the USSR. He continued to write literary criticism, but his work eventually ran afoul of Soviet censors and he was exiled to Siberia. He disappeared in 1937. In the following excerpt Mirsky offers an appreciative overview of Remizov's early writings.]*

Remizov's work is one of the most varied in the whole of Russian literature—to such an extent that few of his admirers can embrace the whole of it in their admiration. Those who value the "underground" Dostoevskianism of *The Pond* will find little interest in the studied naïveté of *On a Field Azure;* those who like the lyrical eloquence of the mystery plays or of *The Lament for the Ruin of Russia* will be disgusted by such privately printed uncensored tales as *Czar Dadon.* To get hold of the essence of Remizov's personality, or to realize the unifying principle of his work, is the most difficult and baffling of tasks, so elusive and many-sided is he. He is the greatest of humorists, and at the same time he shows now and again a curious lack of humour which induces one to classify him with the most hieratic of Symbolists. With this literary school his relations are unmistakable. He belongs to the same stratum in the history of Russian civilization. But there is more in him than mere Symbolism, and what marks him off from all the rest of his contemporaries is that he is firmly rooted in the traditional Russian soil. All the Russian tradition, from the mythology of pagan times through all the Russianized forms of Byzantine Christianity to Gogol, Dostoevski, and Leskov, has been absorbed and assimilated by Remizov. He is the most naturally Slavophil of modern Russian writers. (pp. 283-84)

Remizov is very largely a man of books and papers; it is not for nothing that he married a palæographist. No one in Russia has spoken of books with such sincere affection; in no one's mouth does the word *knizhnik* (bookman, lover of books) sound so caressing and laudatory as in Remizov's. A large proportion of his writings are adaptations of folk-lore matter or of ancient legends. One of his books, *Russia in Writ,* is a running commentary on certain ancient manuscripts in his possession. He is a very laborious writer, and in more senses than one. Not only is his work at his style as elaborate and patient as was Charles Lamb's (with whom he has certain points of resemblance), but his actual handwriting is a most elaborate and skilful revival of the cursive writing of the seventeenth century.

Remizov's work may be divided into what we may conveniently call his prose and his poetry. In actual metre he has written practically nothing, but the difference of diction and artistic object between his stories and, say, *The Lament for the Ruin* justifies us in speaking of his poetry and in distinguishing it from his prose. Both intrinsically and historically, his prose is more important than his poetry. It is by his prose that he has exercised such a profound influence on the young generation of writers. In spite of its great variety, it is unified by one purpose—which is to delatinize and defrenchify the Russian literary language and to restore to it its natural Russian raciness. Russian literary prose, since the beginning of letters in the eleventh century down to the existent forms of journalese, has never been free from foreign grammatical influence. The Greek influence of the Slavonic translations of Church books, the Latin influence of the schools in the seventeenth and eighteenth centuries, the French influence paramount since Karamzin and Pushkin, all lie in thick layers on the Russian literary language of to-day and make it so very different from the spoken Russian of the people and from the pre-schoolmaster Russian of the upper classes. The difference lies principally in the syntax, and

even writers who, like Tolstoy, were studiously colloquial in their diction could never go without a latinized and frenchified syntax. Only Rozanov in his "anti-Gutenberg" prose tried to create a more "spoken" form of written Russian. Remizov has gone farther in this direction. His prose, as I have already said, is *skaz,* that is to say, it reproduces the syntax and intonation of spoken language, and of the spoken language in its least literary and most native forms. He has a keen sense for words, for individual words and for grammatical composition. His prose, often very studious and elaborate, is always new and never falls into clichés. He has taught the Russian writer to value his words, to think of them as of independent beings and not to use them as mere signs, or as parts of ready-made verbal groups. He has gone often too far in this direction: he cannot resist the temptation of using a good old word he has chanced on in some old document, or of coining a new one to suit his needs. His action on the language has been largely parallel to that of the Futurists, who have also applied themselves to linguistic creation (Khlebnikov) and delatinizing the language.

Remizov's prose works consist of novels and stories of contemporary Russian life; of legends taken from the Prologue or from the Apocrypha; of folk-tales and fairy-tales; of dreams; of memoirs and diaries; and of commentaries on old documents.

He is not a story-teller in the true sense of the word, and his influence over the younger generation has greatly contributed to the disintegration of the narrative form. In his early stories the lyrical element is considerable. They are almost always concerned with the grotesque and the unusual, with a touch of Dostoevskian psychological weirdness. A typical example is **"Princess Mymra,"** one of the latest and best in the series, which tells of the cruel disillusionment of a schoolboy who fell platonically in love with a harlot. A Dostoevskian atmosphere of intense shame and humiliation dominates the story. Other of his early stories deal with the fantastic—with the familiar devils and goblins of Russian popular fancy, whom Remizov usually speaks of with a semi-humorous twinkle in the eye, but who, for all that, are sometimes very seriously mischievous. The largest works of his early period are *The Clock,* a story of provincial life which is only an imperfect sketch in comparison with the ones that followed it; and *The Pond,* a novel of Moscow, in which he drew on the impressions of his childhood. There is still a lot of the untidy, poetical *moderne* in *The Pond* which recalls the disagreeable manner of certain Polish and German novelists; but it produces a very powerful impression. The Dostoevskian intensity of pain, of compassion with another one's pain, and of morbid attention to pain wherever it is to be found, reaches in *The Pond* its most quintessential expression. The book is almost one uninterrupted paroxysm of pain and racking compassion. The filth and cruelty of life are portrayed with a ruthless realism that struck with horror even those who were accustomed to Gorky and Andreev. The same theme is taken up in *The Sisters of the Cross,* where the squalid misery of the inhabitants of a large block of buildings in Petersburg—"Burkov's house"—grows into a symbol of the world of misery. The principal theme of the book is the cruelty of fate to those "unanswering," defenceless, always unlucky and unsuccessful beings who come into the world to be the playthings of cruelty and treachery.

In 1909 Remizov wrote *The Story of Ivan Semenovich Stratilatov* (at first called *Neuyomny Buben—The Unhushable Tambourine*). In the way of formal fiction, it is his masterpiece.

It is a story of provincial life centred round the character of the clerk Stratilatov, one of the most striking and extraordinary creations in the whole picture-gallery of Russian fiction. Like most of Remizov's characters, he is an underworld character, but with such peculiar touches as are quite out of the line of Dostoevsky. The story is a masterpiece of construction, though the plan of it is not strictly narrative. Remizov alone of all Russian writers is capable of these weird, uncanny effects, quite free from anything apparently terrible or uncanny, but which convey the unmistakable impression of the presence of minor devils. *The Fifth Pestilence* is also a provincial story. It is more piercingly human and less weird: it is the story of a scrupulously honest but cold and inhuman, and consequently intensely unpopular, examining magistrate against a background of provincial sloth, filth, and spite. The hated man is gradually forced to commit a glaring and unpardonable judicial blunder, and Remizov's poetic justice makes his ruin come as an expiation of his cold and inhuman integrity. To the same period belongs "**Petushok**", the piercingly tragical story of a little boy killed by a chance shot during the suppression of the Revolution. It has become one of the most influential of Remizov's stories owing to the great richness of its "ornamentally" colloquial style.

In his later stories Remizov's style becomes chaster and less exuberant, always remaining as racy and as careful. The years of the war are reflected in *Marà (Fata Morgana)*, which includes "**The Teapot**," an extraordinarily delicate story of pity and sensitiveness. It is constructed with Chekhovian art, and belongs to a long series of stories of pity—characteristic of Russian realism—to which belong Gogol's *Greatcoat* and Turgenev's *Moomoo*. The Revolution and Bolshevik Petersburg are reflected in *The Noises of the Town*, which also contains many lyrical pieces and legends. His latest novel is *The Ditch*. . . . It contains a powerful piece of synthetic character-drawing in the person of the gloating pessimist, the "philosopher" Budylin, like Stratilatov, all in an aura of diabolical presences.

Somewhat apart from the rest of Remizov's fiction stands *On a Field Azure*. . . . It is the story of a girl, Olya, first at home in the country, then at school, and in the university, where she becomes an S.R. The story is one of his best: all the more so as he refrains in it from all the exuberance and originality of his style, but keeps its essential characteristic—the purity of colloquial diction. It is remarkable for the subtly produced atmosphere—thin and delicate—of the old-world country home, and for the charming drawing of the heroine's character. But it is not a novel—rather a series of glimpses of life, and of anecdotes.

In time Remizov grew always more willing to abandon the hard-and-fast limits of fiction, and to adopt freer forms. The most notable of these ventures are *The Chronicle of 1917*, a remarkably free and unjournalistic diary of his impressions during the Revolution; and *Rozanov's Letters*, a worthy tribute to the memory of that remarkable man who was his intimate friend, but a book which is written by a Russian for Russians, and will appear wildly unintelligible to the foreigner. The same tendency towards a freer and less formal expression appears in *Russia in Writ*, a book of commented documents, chiefly of the early eighteenth century. In all these and in other fragmentary memoirs, Remizov remains the wonderful stylist he is; nowhere does his mischievous and whimsical humour appear more freely and strangely. This twinkle in the eye, which is at times merely playful, but at times becomes unexpectedly uncanny, is perhaps the ultimate and truest expression of Remi-

zov's personality. It reappears in his *Dreams*, which are accounts of real, genuine, and quite ordinary dreams one sees every night, but which are revived with all their peculiar logic, so simply intelligible to the sleeping man and so wildly strange to him when he is awake. Introduced into *The Chronicle of 1917*, they give it that unique and peculiarly Remizovian touch which is so inimitable.

As dreams have a logic of their own, so also do folk-tales, and one which is very different from ours. This wonderful assimilation of the "fairy-tale" logic is the principal charm of Remizov's numerous and varied *skazki* (a word which it is customary but not quite exact to render by the English "fairy-tale." The German *Märchen* is a more exact equivalent). Some of these tales are his own and are connected with Olya, the heroine of *On a Field Azure*. They are perhaps the most delightful of all, so strangely and so convincingly alive are the hares, the bears, and the mice that inhabit them, so uncannily homely the goblins and devils, and so infectious their genuine dream-logic. These fairy-tales form a volume entitled *Tales of the Monkey King Asyka*. The same qualities, but without the same childlike atmosphere, reappear in *Tales of the Russian People*, which are founded on genuine folk-tales but become delightfully new in the hands of Remizov. The same style is reproduced in *St. Nicholas's Parables*, but these parables are more seriously meant and have a definitely religious object. The popular conception of the benevolent saint and miracle-worker Nicholas as a help in every work, who will even help to cheat and steal, and will always intercede before God for the poor man, is particularly near to the heart of Remizov. These *Parables* are a link between the fairy-tales and the legends. Some of the legends, especially those contained in *Travà-Muravà*, are merely humorous, complicated stories of adventures and wonders, in the style of the Greek romance—stories in which the absurdities of the narrative are brought out with affectionate emphasis. Such a story as *Apollo of Tyrus* is a delightful example in this manner, and a masterpiece of racy Russian. Other legends are more rhetorical and ornate, and have a more definite religious message. This religious message is very much akin to Rozanov's cult of kindness. Remizov dwells on the well-known legend of the Virgin's visit to hell, where she was so moved by the sufferings of the damned that she wished to share them, and finally obtained from God a release of all the damned souls from hell for forty days every year. This legend, of Byzantine origin, became especially popular in Russia, and Remizov sees in it the fundamental religious conception of the Russian people—the religion of pure charity and compassion. Most of Remizov's legends are from old Slavonic books, canonical or apocryphal, and ultimately of Byzantine origin. But he does not shun other sources. Some of his legends are of Western origin. Recently he has undertaken a series of adaptations from the folk-lore of various primitive nations and has already published folk-tales, in his recension, of Caucasian, Siberian, Tibetan, and Kabylian origin.

Remizov's legends are the connecting-link between his prose and his poetry. If *Apollo of Tyrus* is in his purest colloquial manner, the legends of the early *Limonar* are written in an elevated Slavonic style with a lyrical colouring. His "poetry" (with few exceptions, it is not in metre, but in rhythmical prose) is almost as various as his "prose." It includes the charming prose lyrics which together with the Asyka tales originally formed the book *Posolon*, and its sequel *To the Ocean Sea*. It includes also some of the best pages of *The Noises of the Town*, inspired by the life of Petersburg in 1918-1921, such as the wonderful "**Fences**," a lyric of spring after the "bestial" win-

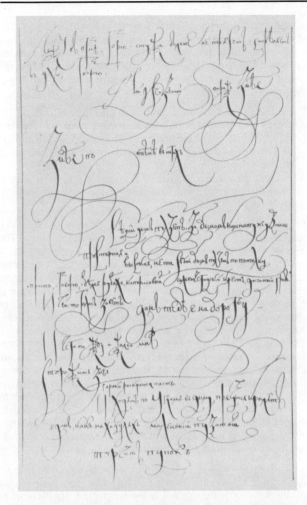

An example of Remizov's ornamental script. Reproduced by permission of Ardis Publishers.

ter of 1919-1920: walking in a suburb of Petersburg as the last fences were being taken down for fuel, he suddenly sees a vista opened on the infinite sea. Many of his prose lyrics are full of pathos and rhetoric, but the rhetoric is redeemed by the exquisite workmanship of words, and by the poignancy of the emotion. Such is the **Lament for the Ruin of Russia**. . . . It is full of passionate love and passionate suffering for his country.

But, on the whole, Remizov's poetry is "secondary," derivative; it is a "bookman's" poetry, which would not have been written without the ancient poetry contained in old books, canonical and apocryphal. This derivativeness is also apparent in his mystery plays, which are also founded on apocryphal and popular plays. Those who love Remizov the humorist will find little to their liking in **The Devil's Comedy,** in **George the Brave,** and in **Judas, Prince of Iscariot.** The plays are ritual and hieratic, and saturated with ancient lore and symbolism. Even **King Maximilian,** which is based on the amusing and absurd popular play of that name, is made into a mystery with profound symbols. Here more than anywhere is Remizov a contemporary of the Symbolists. The influence of his poetry and of his mystery plays has been as small as that of his prose style and of his provincial stories has been great. The principal difference between Remizov and his followers is that between the generation born before and after (roughly) 1885: the older generation in its greatest expression is mystical and symbolical—the younger

one is not. Remizov the craftsman, linguist, and realist has a numerous following—the poet and mystic remains barren of influence. (pp. 284-91)

Prince D. S. Mirsky, "The New Prose: Remizov,"
in his Contemporary Russian Literature: 1881-1925,
Alfred A. Knopf, 1926, pp. 281-91.

ALÉC BROWN   (essay date 1927)

[*Brown is the translator of* The Fifth Pestilence. *In the following excerpt from his preface to that work, he analyzes the portrait of humanity in Remizov's fiction.*]

Remizov must in the main be read slowly, in a quiet voice, not hastening, weighing the words in phrases, allowing the voice to cadence easily. He is not like Dostoyevsky, who may be read hastily, stormily, each successive overpowering idea borne along on the surface of a torrent.

Nor is he like Chekhov, relying mainly on an ungarnished ring of incident; for in Remizov, in whom Russian prose literature matures, the story has taken on the structure of mature, or classic, poetry, when every element is precalculated and mosaicked into a preconceived form.

Remizov's manner of telling a story derives more from Lyesskov—Lyesskov of the short stories, not of the diluted novels. (p. x)

If in his manner we may find a forerunner of Remizov in Lyesskov of *The Steel Flea,* in his content Remizov takes up the labours of none other than Dostoyevsky.

His main concern is with the burden of life; man suffering beneath this burden; and human warmth of heart—understanding, tolerance,—the healing balm.

The difference between the two writers is in this:

Dostoyevsky was concerned with demoniacal suffering (Raskolnikov, Myshkin, the Karamazov family), and a demoniacal or hysterical way out.

Remizov is concerned with the sufferings that are more terrible; the petty sufferings caused by puny desires tangled in webs of mean things—sorrows never elevated to the relief of catastrophe; the sufferings of desperation in which people are driven to seek forgetfulness of the wearying hours of life to which they nevertheless cling. Remizov is concerned with the misery of the great mass of mankind, whose happiness is gnawed by petty considerations, and for whom the slight oblivion of the cinema or the bottle is the paradise to which their daily activity is bent.

Whereas Dostoyevsky extended love to his fellow men in so far as they were demoniacal, Remizov extends it exactly because they are not demoniacal; and Bobrov, the *fifth pestilence,* cuckolded by his wife, soon deceived in his adolescent idealism by the mud of the life in a provincial townlet, perishes at the end, defeated, a secret drunkard; and falls, as a last despairing vodka bout kills him, to dreaming

of *Florry the Whore,*

of taking *the anointing balm of vice* with those
he despises for their vileness, in the club of
Stoudenets;

because he had stood against the human way of tolerance and understanding, become demoniacal, inhuman, living his solitary life, the incorruptible upholder of the unbending Law.

The *Social Club* of the provincial market town of Stoudenets, with its hardened tippling, its smutty stories, its indecent songs, its "sniggering and monkey guffawing"—this centre of moderate, but persistent vice,

> "At one o'clock every one goes home; it doesn't
> do to go *too* far,"

the picture of which cannot fail to disgust the reader (and perhaps frighten too by its alarming familiarity)—is this then preferable, is this then to defeat clean-handed, upright Bobrov, idealist upholder of the Law?

Fyodor Sologoub, in his novel *The Petty Devil,* described too the horrors of a provincial town—and let us remember that in its general qualities the provincial town is a summary of the meanness of our civilization. Sologoub, however, caricatures. His one comment would appear to be irony; "This is what civilization gives us," he would say, and, fearing contamination, turns disgusted aside and spits.

But Remizov's more realistic picture is not cloaked thus in irony; in place of Sologoub's gesture of disgust some readers may claim to detect even a smirk of approval in the more unpleasant passages. Is it then with resignation Remizov draws what seems at first a negative picture; petty vice triumphant?

It does not seem so. In *The Fifth Pestilence* he offers a choice. Here you have garbage—vile, debased men and women, savage, for here is the root of the savagery of which is spoken; but they are *human.* There you have an upright man of ideals, unbesmirched by vice—but *inhuman.* On the one hand the lowest of the low continuing their riot of life untouched; on the other, a man of hope, falling because he had learned to say in his heart *"people are at bottom coarse creatures,"* and held aloof. (pp. xi-xiii)

[But lest] it should be thought that Remizov sees naught but the beast in man, he who sees the beast with such clear eyes, and gloats on the unlit depths of old Ivan Stratilatov's mind, and on the vice of Stoudenets, let one more quotation be made.

In sketches written in Bolshevik Petersburg Remizov says:

> I have seen . . . the cement of kindliness by
> which the disjointed and impoverished world
> is held together . . . even amid *that* in man from
> which even the beasts turn aside.

It is this human understanding, this *cement of kindliness,* that is the key to Remizov; and raises the dirty old clerk Stratilatov to a lovable romantic idealist, and justifies the love with which the dark side of the town of Stoudenets is raked over, while incorruptible Bobrov is brought to a contemptible end.

In Remizov Russian prose literature finds maturity.

One characteristic common to all the great writers preceding him—Gogol, Gontcharov, Dostoyevsky, Tolstoy, Chekhov—is that these are not artists before everything else. Their first consideration is the propagation of a sociological theory, or the solution of a sociological problem.

Remizov, on the other hand, is always in the first place *the artist.* Further, he is the mature artist, for he is not only primarily concerned with the composition of as perfect a work of art as possible, but moreover concerned with it in a detached

manner, not allowing his emotions to interfere with the construction; selecting, moulding, and then mosaicking his material consciously. It is easy, in fact, to imagine him working as legend has made James Joyce work, with various coloured crayons for the various passages, to aid the mind in composing the preconceived pattern.

But although the first consideration is thus the *craft,* this does not mean that treatment of human affairs, what some would call the spiritual side of the book, is merely incidental. Remizov is no follower of the *l'art pour l'art* doctrine, in which, I take it, the material employed is of no consequence whatever, for the second great characteristic of Remizov's art is that it shall be immediately concerned with human affairs; that it shall, in other words, be utilitarian.

Remizov is a child of the Russian Symbolist movement, which grew to its full power in the first decade of this century. The theorist of the latter days of the movement, Vyatcheslav Ivanov, the most difficult, and perhaps profoundest, twentieth-century Russian poet, preached the essential need for literature to be utilitarian. In Vyatcheslav Ivanov's opinion *utilitarian* is to be understood somewhat as in the Middle Ages. That silent member of the Symbolist group, Professor E. Anitchkof, mediaevalist, continuing research into this matter, has clearly shown in a recent paper on the aesthetics of the Middle Ages that then literature was conceived of purely as a *spiritually utilitarian* occupation; that is, that aided the spiritual development of the individual, or helped him to approach the divine *principle.* This conception was widened by Vyatcheslav Ivanov, who taught that through and beyond the individual usefulness of literature there must be a more general, social usefulness; and that in this function of link between the *individual* and the *general* literature is myth-creating.

But if Remizov is said to be a child of the Symbolists, it must also be said that he has grown healthily free from his parental influences. While he retains, it appears to me, the Symbolist belief in the individually utilitarian nature of his art, he has clearly left the hazy religious strivings to which Symbolism led such writers as the poet Blok, and has turned towards a more real appreciation of the life around him.

He has approached nearer the spirit that animated Classic Poetry, that "human nature—whether viewed in action or thought—must stand out in clear relief."

From the preceding it should be easy to draw conclusions as to the composition of Remizov's work.

Surrounding human life is the principal material; matter from fable and mediaeval writers provides relief, comparison, contrast.

The material of life is apprehended never from any sociological point of view, but from that of the individual towards other individuals.

From selected material of real life the story is built up primarily as a work of art, and in a mature, classic, conscious manner.

To this end persons and events, though circumstantially *true to life,* for which reason Remizov appears at times to be a *realist,* are made symbolic in relation to the work as a whole.

In this way that dark-minded, dirty old villain, the clerk Stratilatov, jostling through the low Sunday night crowd on the boulevard, becomes, in contrast with this crowd, symbol of the ideal romantic lover; and, in *The Fifth Pestilence,* the strange affair of the ass's ears on the Police Captain's head, together with the incursion of worms proceeding widdershins and bearing a spiritual message, must be taken together with other extravagant things as symbolic events that contrast with the eternal slough of Stoudenets, its immovability, its *hearts and heads of oak quality*—and therefore as omens of impending misfortune. (pp. xv-xix)

> *Aléc Brown, in a preface to* The Fifth Pestilence, Together with the History of the Tinkling Cymbal *and* Sounding Brass: Ivan Semyonovitch Stratilatov *by Alexei Remizov, translated by Aléc Brown, 1927. Reprint by Payson & Clarke Ltd., 1928, pp. vii-xxv.*

MARC SLONIM (essay date 1953)

[*Slonim was a Russian-born American critic who wrote extensively on Russian literature. In the following excerpt he describes the style and themes that characterize Remizov's work.*]

In his formative years Remizov had been closely associated with the Symbolists, with whom he maintained personal ties of friendship and gratitude, but he gradually developed his own original manner. Although he always utilized certain of the Symbolists techniques—such as lyricism, rhythmic structure of sentences, systems of allusive images, and so on—the tone of his work was determined, in time, chiefly by two basic tendencies: his search for a "national style" based on folklore tradition and philological studies, and his interest in religious and moral problems. The source of his inspiration lies in the popular speech and the oral and written tradition of Kiev and Moscow, which had not been vitiated by Latin or French influences.

His knowledge of the living idiom was enhanced by historical research: a diligent and indefatigable reader and an interpreter of ancient texts and forgotten documents, he absorbed the Christian as well as the pagan traditions of the Russian language. To restore the freshness and vividness of the popular tongue and to liberate it from the trammels of bookishness and preciosity were among Remizov's aims, and no other Russian writer of the twentieth century proved to be a more national stylist than this "magus of the word." The verbal craft, the turn of a sentence, the effects a grouping of words can produce interested him beyond all else, and he evolved an amazing skill in and an extraordinary power over his medium.

His works present a maze of involved patterns, linguistic sleights, verbal and onomatopoeic play, and grammatical tours de force. His shifts from the lyrical to the colloquial and from the pathetic to the comic, the luxuriance of his vocabulary, the flexibility of his syntax, the bold twist of his sentences, the complex, tortuous, circuitous, or fragmentary structure of his tales—all the formal richness of this ornamental prose together with a weird sense of humor and the charm of a storyteller assures Remizov of a unique place in Russian letters.

Remizov's work (by contrast with Bely's mental acrobatics) is firmly rooted in folklore, from which he borrows not only his themes but his artistic devices. At the same time, like Bely, he imposes style upon reality. Art is for him a world of play and fantasy; the purpose of writing is not the representation of life but a transformation and "theatricalization" thereof. Only through an act of imagination do we acquire a deep sense of things and events and characters—the fairy tale, the grotesque, the dream, the whimsical flight are inseparable from the true creative effort. All the techniques of poetry are therefore justified in prose writing. Hence Remizov's devices and artifices

for producing a mingling of the real and the fantastic, his detailed descriptions of trivia, of insignificant occurrences followed by explosive displacement of the three-dimensional images. Devils, spooks, hobgoblins, and diverse animals, whether existing or mythical, abound in his stories; sometimes he merely tells his own dreams, which resemble the illuminations of medieval manuscripts or the woodcuts of the sixteenth century chapbooks: this universe of uncanny creatures and odd visions is depicted with the precision of a monastic miniaturist, who draws every line or curve with utmost meticulousness.

The peculiarities of Remizov's art naturally limit the number of his readers to those who can truly relish each phrase of the great craftsman. More respected than loved by the public at large, Remizov is often considered as a writer's writer and, as a matter of fact, he has exerted a profound influence on many of his contemporaries, among them such prominent Soviet novelists as Alexis N. Tolstoy, Michael Prishvin, Eugene Zamiatin, Viacheslav Shishkov, and a score or so of lesser storytellers.

Gogol and Dostoevsky were, of course, two of Remizov's masters. From Gogol he derived his banter (which often borders on mockery) and his fondness for contortions and grimaces. Critics maintain that Remizov is constantly sneering and scoffing; like a jester, he is forever inventing new quips and gibes, ridiculing his own heroes, and playing cat-and-mouse with his readers. He resembles a malicious sorcerer who delights in wonderful feats, yet can also cast weird spells and metamorphose men into beasts. (pp. 230-31)

Yet at the same time this grinning gnome who loved practical jokes and invented incredible stories about his friends always evinced a deep and sympathetic understanding of human grief and suffering. Like Dostoevsky, he explored with almost sadistic and masochistic curiosity the dark recesses of man's soul, and was always highly sensitive to pain. In the world he described—and it was usually the inane and senseless world of provincial monotony, of ugliness and monstrosity—the men and women are racked by poverty, injustice, and evil. "The Devil has spread himself all over the world like the shadow of a clock-tower, and God has forsaken His creatures"—this is Remizov's main theme, and he stresses again and again that man has been betrayed by the Almighty and cast into the abyss of loneliness, pain, and death. It was, therefore, quite natural for the French Existentialists to discover after World War II that Remizov was a kindred spirit.

There is, not infrequently, in the characters of Remizov a resemblance to Akaky Akakyevich, the poor and humble clerk of Gogol's *Overcoat*: Remizov is concerned with the fate of the little man, of the underdog, of defenseless "orphans of the earth" who are exposed to cruelty and frustration, and a profound sense of pity, a warm humanity which he loves to mask under various stylistic or symbolic disguises, forms the backdrop of all his work.

Dostoevsky's *Man from the Underground* also makes his reappearance in the stories of Remizov, who always portrays unhappy creatures who fear and tremble and are trampled down by the ruthless "masters of life." Why is man sentenced to pain and misery? And who has dared to claim that suffering has a purifying, sublimating effect? Here is one author who does not believe in it: "No, suffering and oppression gnaw at the heart; they distort and humiliate." And there is no justification for all the crosses on which living creatures are nailed during their brief passage through this earthly vale. The traditional theme of the "simple heart" who merits admittance into the kingdom of God, of the average man crushed by evil forces, runs through all of this strange writer's work; it is complemented by the recurrent images of a mild and melancholy Christ and of kind old Nikola the Miracle Worker—the favorite saint of the Russians. The religious strains in Remizov's writings are entirely humanized: his Christianity is but a major aspect of his keen feeling for the brotherhood of man.

The greatest impact of Remizov's works, however, lies not so much in the idea they convey as in the manner in which they are expressed. This highly subjective prose, which avoids conventional portraiture of characters but mingles realistic exposition with the author's lyrical or moral comments, dicta, and personal recollections, is undoubtedly a "slanted and stylized" prose. This was Remizov's main contribution—and most Soviet writers of the 'twenties, from Pilniak to Vsevolod Ivanov, learned their craft from him and from Bely.

Another, and by no means the least important, contribution of Remizov was his innovation of language. This he accomplished not by the invention of neologisms as the Futurists did, but by restoring the lost unity between the written literature of the intellectuals and the pure linguistic sources of the people. In this field his efforts were both national and democratic.

This Neo-Realist and friend of the Symbolists, whose progression was in the same direction as that of Blok and Bely, attempted to merge technical refinements that had originated in the West with the national trend represented by the Populists and the Writers of the Soil; he advanced the revival of an art based on folklore and the colloquial language of the masses. The fact that such a tendency could assert itself on the very eve of the Revolution constituted a decisive factor in the further development of Russian prose during the Soviet era. (pp. 232-33)

> Marc Slonim, "After the Symbolists," in his *Modern Russian Literature: From Chekhov to the Present, Oxford University Press, 1953, pp. 211-33.*

ALEX M. SHANE   (essay date 1972)

[*Shane is an American translator and critic specializing in Russian prose of the early twentieth century. In the following excerpt, he examines prominent themes in Remizov's short stories.*]

Remizov's first published works, **"Placha"** (**"Lament"**) and **"Bebka"** (**"Baby"**) represent the two basic categories of all his art, derivative and the non-derivative. I use the term derivative to designate the vast and varied store of folktales (Russian, Georgian, Armenian, Zyrian, Tibetan), canonical and apocryphal narratives, legends, letters, and mystery plays based upon existing literary monuments, written and oral, which encompass the entire Russian tradition from the mythology of pagan times through Russianized forms of Byzantine Christianity to nineteenth-century Slavophilism. **"Placha,"** the lamenting song of a Zyrian (komi) maiden on the eve of her wedding, was the first in a series of rhythmic poems (*poemy*) in prose based on the mythology and folk beliefs of the Zyrians, an Ugric tribe centered around Ust-Sysolsk, today named Syktyvkar and the capital of the Komi Autonomous SSR. The appropriateness of the piece as an author's maiden work testifies to Remizov's highly developed bookish consciousness, while the Zyrian cycle included in the collection *Polunoshchnoe solntse* (*The Midnight Sun*) was a direct product of his exile in Ust-Sysolsk, just as the cycles of Russian folktales, *Posolon*

(*Follow the Sun*) and *Kmoryu-okeanu* (*To the Ocean*) were largely inspired by his years of enforced travel through provincial Russian of Vologda and Penza. I do not mean to denigrate the literary sources of his folk-tales and legends, for Remizov was above all a dedicated bibliophile; however, the years in exile provided him with his first extensive contact with the "folk" of provincial Russia and the beginnings of his famous collection of folk memorabilia—children's toys, dolls, and other artifacts embodying folk beliefs.

On the other hand, **"Bebka"** belongs to Remizov's non-derivative works, which, as a group no less variegated and numerous than the derivative, include his novels, *povesti*, stories, sketches, lyric fragments, dreams, and a whole series of autobiographical works. Although at first glance the inclusion of fiction, dreams, and memoirs, under the same rubric may appear unorthodox, Remizov's development after 1917 demands it as many of his works present a curious, at times surrealistic blend of all three elements. . . . **"V plenu"** (**"In Captivity"**), the first work undertaken by Remizov, consisted of an amorphous series of fragments based on his experiences and impressions while in exile. The complex history of its composition provides an interesting insight into Remizov's creative technique. The work was dated 1896-1903, and a dozen fragments were published in various journals and newspapers between 1903 and 1907. At least three of these were incorporated into the 1908 edition of his novel *The Pond* (*Prud*), while the remainder was expanded and published as **"The White Tower"** (**"Belaya bashnya"**). A year later **"The White Tower"** was reworked, and then,—with the addition of another major fragment **"V sekretnoi"** (**"In Prison"**), the return of the segments temporarily loaned to *Prud,* and another thorough reworking—appeared finally as **"In Captivity"** in volume two of his collected works. The relatively free interchangeability of the component parts graphically illustrates one of Remizov's compositional peculiarities: segmentation. It is as if his works consist of building blocks which could be rearranged, detached, or supplemented without markedly altering the general effect. Perhaps this stems from his peculiar emphasis on individual words and "sounding phrases":

> Perception is sensation: what you feel, what scratches or pricks you. Articulating itself, thought will flash from feeling. The word stemming from the feeling, from the thought is not a fragment, but a sounding phrase. It will set the tone for the arrangement of words, for the construction of the verbal edifice. . . .

The predominance of lyricism, both in the sense of emotion and musicality, was also quite striking. Perhaps it stemmed from a surfeit of accumulated feelings and experiences during imprisonment, or perhaps it simply was the expression of Remizov's basic character (he claimed that he was not a storyteller, but a singer); in any case, **"In Captivity"** and the novel *The Pond* and by the avoidance of the first person singular in his stories: only two (**"In Captivity"** and **"Baby"**) of approximately twenty-five stories written before 1912 use a first person narrative, while after 1912 Remizov had, by and large, put aside his aspirations of further developing his novelistic skills in the area of traditional fiction genres and had already embarked along the path which ultimately was to lead him to a copious and unique memoir literature.

"Baby," a short narrative in which a political prisoner in the distant north describes his friendship with a small child, immediately established one of the most significant strains in

Remizov art: his loving attention to children and their world. Here, as in all his works devoted to children (more than a third of his stories), Remizov displays excellent powers of observation and a unique understanding of the child's world. There is considerable dialogue, which like the narrative itself, is successfully rendered in a simple, direct conversational style. Such stories frequently lack plot development; rather they represent mood pieces in which the author-narrator's ability to communicate with the child serves as the unifying element through which the reader perceives events. Remizov did not proceed to develop this direct memoir approach in which the author-narrator observes and interacts with the child until 1912-1913, when he penned nine charming stories: **"Alenushka,"** **"The White Rabbit"** (**Belyi zayats"**), **"The Miracle"** (**"Chudo"**), **"Murka,"** **"The Navel"** (**"Pupochek"**), **"The Stars"** (**"Zvezdy"**), **"The Little Apple Tree"** (**"Yablonka"**), **"The Little Bird"** (**"Ptichka"**), and **"Cherished Tales"** (**"Zavetnye skazki"**). All were couched in a limpid *skaz* and have a remarkably bright joyous tone. In some, however, the events depicted served to illustrate the author-narrator's point, usually a universal statement about human frailty. Thus the story of Nyushka (**"The Little Apple Tree"**), a four-year-old girl who is mercilessly beaten by her stepfather because she reminds him of his wife's dissolute behavior, serves as a vehicle for an authorial commentary of utter dismay at child beating and a lyric affirmation of the healing effect of children upon humans with lacerated souls. In **"The Navel,"** little Yura's willingness to give his navel to the narrator (who had once inadvertently frightened Yura by telling him he would eat it!) prompts a lyric eulogy on a child's willingness to give *everything* without typical adult constraint. Remizov's conception of children's role in life is perhaps best articulated in **"The Stars,"** where he describes the spontaneous joy, that wonderful love of life, which emanates from children, warming the soul of those who take the time to observe and bringing moments of happiness to a life which otherwise was "troubled, terrible, false, and uncertain." Later stories about children developed along similar lines, either simply describing incidents in a child's life, such as Tonya's theft of a pair of gloves in a story of that name (**"Perchatki"**) because instruction in Catechism had been abolished in her school due to the war or Shurka's fear of a Chinaman, or else utilizing a specific incident, such as Kostya's loss of all his toys due to a mean train conductor's whim in **"Blocks"** (**"Kubiki"**) as a vehicle for elaborating the author-narrator's philosophy, which in this instance was very similar to Ivan Karamazov's rebellion against God because of the injustices inflicted on innocent, defenseless children. In several stories the final focus shifted away from the child to an adult, frequently an old man or woman, devout and kind, who loves and understands children. This tendency was manifest in **"Lablon'ka"** where the old landlady Pakhomovna who rescued Niushka from her miserable family situation by finding good foster parents receives a just reward (Niushka's invitation to visit), and became quite pronounced in the stories **"Belyi zaiats,"** where the old general's life is full of good, warmth, and love because it has been dedicated to others, and in **"Svet nerukotvorennyi"** (**"Light Transcendant"**), where a woman's generous help to a shivering girl deeply affects the narrator and opens his eyes to the grief and unhappiness of all those whom he encounters.

Stories about children written in the third person with Remizov as an omniscient author rather than a participating narrator usually displayed a greater depth in the psychological analysis of the child protagonist and tended to have a more structured development of the action. In the earliest of these, **"Slonenok"** (**"The Little Elephant"**), Remizov successfully conveys the feelings and fears of eight-year-old Pavlushka, who has failed the first grade and is in danger of being expelled. Pavlushka's bright hope and various schemes for acquiring a little grey elephant locked in his teacher's cabinet are juxtaposed with thoughts of suicide (inspired by fear of expulsion) and of death and the devil (inspired by requiem services). Diverse threads become surrealistically intertwined in feverish dreams (he is ill with measles) where the devil appears in the form of a little elephant. Should this tale appear overly gloomy by comparison to those discussed earlier, we should remember that Pavlushka recovers in order to mischievously plan a new attempt at acquiring the elephant. And like most of Remizov's children, he displays unselfish generosity in giving his favorite toy, a little glass goat, to his friend Pugalo in order to soothe the latter's feelings at being mercilessly teased.

"Tsarevna Mymra" (**"Princess Mymra"**), the story of a young schoolboy's innocent infatuation with a lovely older woman and his subsequent disillusionment, rank among Remizov's best. Young Atya, who was born and raised by his grandfather in Votiak country north of the Kama River, loved nature and his grandfather's folk and fairy tales. His parents lived in Petersburg, where he joined them in order to attend secondary school. Due to financial difficulties, they rented a room to comely Klavdia Guryanovna, the kept woman of a government official. Sensing that she is someone special, Atya interprets two new words, mistress (*soderzhanka*) and prostitute (*prostitutka*), by means of a very plausible etymological derivation (via *soderzhanie* and *institutka*), to mean wealth and knowledge. This, coupled with the fact that her sole visitor is a most important Deputy of the Government Duma leads him to believe Klavdia Guryanovna to be his legendary princess. The story ends with his discovery that she is really quite ordinary, and although Atya is crushed by the loss of his princess, the reader feels the setback to be temporary, a normal development in an adolescent's maturation.

Four of Remizov's stories about children describe incidents in the life of Olya, the literary embodiment of his wife Serafima Pavlovna. In **"Maka"** he provides us with a description of the Dovgello castle and a large household centered around the activities of a charming but spoiled three-year-old child who has an imaginary friend. **"Bochenochek"** (**"The Little Barrel"**) adds an element of provincial excitement in describing the attack of a rabid dog, but Olya's father also seems to have been at the mercy of the charming little tyrant's whim. The best of the pieces is **"Tainstvennyi zaichik"** (**"The Mysterious Rabbit"**), which presents the death of Olya's kindly grandmother with affectionate tenderness and warm humor. The long biographical fragment, **"Zharkoe leto"** (**"The Hot Summer"**), depicts Olya as a young student on vacation and unlike **"Tainstvennyi zaichik,"** which approximated the bright tones of Remizov's narratives of 1912-1913, represented a typically segmented fragment structurally reminiscent of **"V plenu"** and Remizov's biographies written after emigration.

Unlike the rest of Remizov's stories dealing with children, **"Petushok"** (**"The Little Cock"**) ends tragically, and perhaps this element coupled with a trim structure and inexorable development of the action make it the most memorable. The world of chance (*sluchainost'*), of grief (*gore*), of misfortune (*beda*), of boredom (*skuka*), of senselessness (*bessmyslennost'*), of humiliation (*izdevatel'stvo*) and insult (*obida*), which had appeared obliquely in stories such as **"Iablon'ka,"** **"Kubiki,"** and **"Zvezdy"** now is shown full force as it destroys the child

Petka, affectionately nicknamed the little cock by his grandaunt with whom he lives in a small crowded room. The bright, mischievous little boy's dream of happiness consists of sailing in a balloon with his grandaunt and a little cock. Petak achieves part of that dream by placing a hen's egg under their barren old turkey, for the cock which hatches twenty-one days later immediately becomes a symbol of happiness for boy and grandaunt: "as if the secret of life, of life's happiness for him and his grandaunt were kept in the little cock." But that autumn Petka's father returns, a sinister figure with a twisted rheumatic arm and a face disfigured by elephantiasis. With his appearance, the grandaunt senses misfortune; and two months later he returns again demanding money. Not getting any he seizes the little cock which happens to be in the room, wrings its neck, throws it on the floor and leaves, just as Petka, while playing with some boys, darts out from the yard and is shot down by a passing patrol (the year in 1905). And having been dealt this final, bitter, fatal insult, the grandaunt accepted it and found solace in prayer to the Moscow wonder-working saints: Maxim, Basil and John. In this beautiful tale you have the felicitous juxtaposition of many of the major strains in Remizov's early stories: a poor hard life sparked by the presence of a joyous child; the kind love of an elderly, pious figure; a senseless, chance misfortune; suffering endurance alleviated by an unswerving faith in God.

Basically, the twenty-odd stories with child protagonists represent a bright and joyous chapter in Remizov's early works, which stands in distinct contrast to the dismal and hopeless world of his other stories. Half of his first twelve stories are taken from the life of prisoners or exiles. The world depicted in **"V plenu"** and **"Bebka"** is not at all frightening, but despair and disillusionment become key notes in **"Opera,"** **"Novyi god"** (**"The New Year"**), **"Serebrianye lozhki"** (**"Silver Spoons"**), and **"Krepost'"** (**"The Fortress"**). Although the incident described in **"Opera"** may at first glance appear to be trivial (Slyakin, a music buff in his fifth year of exile who is denied access to his seat because the performance has already begun, creates a scene and is arrested), the story represents a subtle study in human despair and desperation. Obviously a political prisoner, Slyakin has been exiled from Petersburg without his consent *(bez ego soglasiia)*, has missed the performance through ill chance *(nekhoroshaia sluchainost')*, and now his fate depends on the whim of the local police chief. The noisy scene Slyakin created at the opera house (it had been his first opportunity to see an opera in five years!) was not only a violent reaction against being denied access to the performance, but a symbolic protest against the conditions of his life, over which he himself had no control and which was ruled by blind chance and the whims of others. In **"Novyi god"** Remizov renders the protagonist's despair with considerably greater power and skill. Having endured three years of exile in a barren, isolated setting, Kudrin wishes to mark the new year's coming with something special, so he begins reading a work by the populist Gleb Uspensky aloud to his fellow exiles. But Uspensky's brave words, "the old world shall be conquered by human sacrifice, by human suffering, and a new immortal world shall come—a paradise on earth!" echo ironically as Kudrin's reading is interrupted and the gathering turns into a grotesque drunken debauch, after which Kudrin has nightmares and is reduced to moaning like a child. Human hopes and desires to win freedom for the people cannot withstand the perverse trauma of exile. Equally frightening, although less successfully rendered, is the fate of Pevtsov in **"Serebrianye lozhki,"** who gradually breaks down under the pressures of time and the accusation of being an informer, so

that at the tale's end he even believes himself to be a thief when so accused. In each of the above instances, the protagonist is presented as the victim of existing, impersonal circumstances, while the original cause of the exile or imprisonment remains unarticulated. However, the nameless protagonist in **"Krepost'"** [**"The Fortress"**], another one of Remizov's amorphous, segmented creations, visits a fortress and vows to avenge the trampled, hopeless existence of the inmates by seeking out those who perpetrated the torture. This instance comes closest to an accusation against a traceable human cause in Remizov's art; elsewhere torment, misfortune, and oppression seem to be an integral part of the human condition which can be countered only by submissive faith and self-perfection.

In later stories Remizov again returned to the theme of imprisonment and exile, posing the question of why it is man's lot to suffer. Khlebnikov, a meek man tormented by the falsity and anomaly of life, turns to politics and is arrested (**"Emaliol"**). In prison he comes to see that all men endure life as some sort of punishment, but there is no answer as to why man must suffer or be punished, other than fate or God's will. Although he almost becomes reconciled to his existence, ultimately he rebels against the mocking insult of such an existence. Perhaps the most pessimistic of all the prison tales is **"Kazennaia dacha"** (**"A Summer House at Public Expense"**). The protagonist Vasily Ptashkin, depressed by his humdrum daily existence, tries to fathom the purpose of living but is faced with a dilemma: if the purpose of living is the achievement of freedom from today's unfree existence, then what will be life's purpose when this freedom has been attained? Arrested and imprisoned for loitering, he instinctively wants to be released, and visualizes himself the victim of a huge omniscient cockroach that governs the lives of all men. The universality of this evil symbol is stressed in the denouement, when Ptashkin discovers that life outside the prison walls is no better than inside. We are doomed prisoners of an existence that devours our strength and thoughts, and then disgorges our mangled corpses into the grave, unless we have the strength to break free.

It is striking that Remizov consistently represents life as a senseless, tedious existence in most of his short fiction. In several stories, tedium explicitly motivates the actions of the protagonists: although Vinokurov's practical jokes in **"Sem' besov"** (**"Seven Demons"**) may not appear surprising due to the understandably boring life of those exiled to the distant north, in **"Bez piati minut barin"** (**"Almost a Gentleman"**) the destruction of all the windows in two railcars and the murder of four cossacks by the metal worker Senka out of boredom and the lack of anything to do indicates a frightening moral bankruptcy.

Senseless misfortune, like the quirk of fate which snuffed out little Petka's life in **"Petushok,"** seems to accompany relentlessly most of Remizov's adult protagonists, resulting in frustration, tragedy, or death. In **"Muzykant"** (**"The Musician"**) the protagonist Borodkin, an ugly, clumsy, inarticulate, shy tutor, has been doomed to eternal unhappiness because he has been endowed with a genuine love for music coupled with an ardent desire to sing, yet lacks the voice and confidence to do so. Chekhovian in its static composition and Gogolian in its grotesque, the story stresses the senseless contradiction between Borodkin's desires and abilities. In **"Sviatoi vecher"** (**"Holy Night"**) a Petersburg clerk's desire to celebrate Christmas eve with country traditions in his provincial home town is frustrated by delayed trains; and as he falls asleep on the train his thoughts and dreams focus on the figure of a brutal, red-bearded yard-keeper, symbol of the indifferent, hopeless fate which governs his life and that of all Russia. The story **"Pokrovennaia"** (**"The Protected"**) juxtaposes two women, Palageya Sergeevna and Nastasya, both of whom have been crucified by life's circumstances, but with one important difference: neither woman has forgotten her true love, but Palageya Sergeevna cannot understand why she betrayed her true love nor why the torments of the past forty years have been inflicted on her (and considers committing suicide), while Nastasya, whose crucifixion consisted of taking the sin of another upon herself, remembers the joy of her three days of happiness and finds inner peace through prayer to the Virgin of Protection. The idea of accepting the seemingly senseless vicissitudes of life as God's will finds sympathetic treatment in several stories, such as **"Petushok"**..., **"Za russkuiu zemliu"** (**"For the Russian land"**), where Olga accepts her husband's death with the words "God did not spare him," and **"Dnes vesna"** (**"Now It Is Spring"**), where the protagonist Andrei Pavlovich, having been deserted by his wife, stands before Dostoevsky's grave—a monument to burning grief—and brings to mind the kenotic tradition of passive suffering. But Remizov seems to have an ambivalent attitude toward Christian passivity, for elsewhere the protagonists rebel against the acceptance of God's Will, as has been mentioned in connection with **"Kubiki"** and **"Emaliol,"** and as is eloquently demonstrated in **"Sud Bozhii"** (**"The Judgement of God"**), an excellent story that ranks among Remizov's finest. Father Ilarion, a devout and revered monk in a Moscow monastery, was entrusted with the task of delivering a holy icon of the Virgin of Sorrows to the Bishop of Kiev. While enroute, the steppes' broad expanse and distant view gives him great joy and makes him think of leaving the monastery, a thought which he immediately interprets to be the Devil's temptation. A young fellow passenger asks him for advice: should he return to his beloved common-law wife and child in Moscow, or should he marry the unloved bride his parents have selected for him in Kiev? Father Ilarion immediately advises the former, but on second thought, fearful of human fallibility, places the choices written on lots in front of the icon (as was the custom at the monastery), and draws one—the opposite of his original advice. A week later he attends the young man's wedding in Kiev, only to see a coffin in place of the married couple. The vision passes, but Father Ilarion cannot reconcile what God has chosen to reveal: a marriage which defied common sense had taken place by His Will, and, by His Will, it was revealed that the marriage boded human suffering. Finding no justification, Father Ilarion abandons the monastery and becomes a wanderer. The rejection of passive acceptance has considerable weight because the reader's sympathies are with the protagonist, a good and devout man of God. However, since the idea of forsaking the monastery had originally been introduced as a temptation by the Devil, its realization endows the work with an irresolvable ambiguity that enhances its unique force.

Critics have considered Remizov a mystic who believed that the world was ruled by the Devil, but it would be difficult to build a convincing case on the basis of his short stories. Most of the works in which the Devil appears are not narrated directly by the author, whether as third person omniscient author or first person author-narrator, but are skillfully cast in a *skaz* narrative form, in which an intermediary narrator, ostensibly of provincial origins and considerably less sophistication than the bookish Moscovite Remizov, intrudes between the author and reader and becomes an individual, self-sufficient, fictional character. **"Zanofa,"** for example, begins with a colloquial

discourse on witches and local beliefs which the narrator presents objectively without qualification or evaluative commentary. The heroine Zanofa, a gay, lovely girl who falls while dancing and loses the use of her legs, becomes the object of village gossip and is branded a witch. Without dispelling the local interpretation, the narrator brings the story to its tragic close where Zanofa, incensed by the cruel and unjust punishment fate has meted her, crawls out into the garden because she imagines that her fiance is coming and is found strangled the next morning. The literal reader can accept the villagers' explanation of the incident (the Devil throttled her), but the discerning critic cannot help but notice that the final death scene is described through Zanofa's eyes and that the murderer could well have been a local villager who feared and hated the witch. A similar intentional ambiguity in interpretation can be seen in **"Zhertva"** (**"The Sacrifice"**) and **"Chertykhanets"** (**"The Cusser"**). In the former, Petr Nikolaevich Borodin, a provincial eccentric in the Gogolian tradition, has deadly-pale features, does not age, and exhibits a passion for gazing at corpses. As the story unfolds, the narrator even makes a point of stressing the implausibility of the reports upon which his tale is based: "As what concerns Petr Nikolaevich, people talked such utter nonsense in enumerating his peculiarities, that I even blush at repeating them." The death of the four Borodin children, three within a month's time (another example of senseless chance) lead his wife, Alexandra Pavlovna, to remember a prayer in which she had asked God to take her three older children, but to spare her husband. The rest of the story is presented from the point of a distraught, guilt-ridden woman and the final grisly scene in which the flesh falls from the bones of Borodin as he raises a knife against his wife and remaining daughter Sonia can be viewed as Satanic retribution by adherents of the Gothic tale, or as a realistic portrayal of unsupported rumors circulated by the servants (for the house and corpse were engulfed in flames leaving no tangible evidence). In **"Chertykhanets"** the protagonist Versenev, a dreadful bore whose sole conversational gambit consisted of a guttural squeak, a wave of the hand and the words—"the devil!", is finally deserted by his wife and children. Unable to bear the subsequent lonely existence on his provincial estate, he commits suicide. Although there is no overt intrusion of the supernatural, the Devil's presence is suggested by the confession of the protagonist's dying father and by the nurse's repeated admonishment that the Devil destroys those who invoke his name at inopportune moments. Here, as in other stories such as **"Glagolitsa"** (**"The Glagolitic Alphabet"**) and **"Chortik"** (**"The Little Devil"**), some of the characters have a firm and unshakable belief in the reality of the forces of evil, but the author, whether omniscient narrator or first person observer, as a rule remains neutral, unlike the novel *Prud*, where the Devil's demons appear in fact and are indisputably a part of the omniscient author's world view.

In retrospect, assertions stressing Remizov's alleged mysticism and allegiance to Symbolism should be carefully reexamined. Of the sixty pre-Revolutionary stories only three could be appropriately considered "typical" of the Symbolist mentality: **"V plenu,"** with its lyric introspection; the tedious mystical allegory **"Pridvornyi iuvelir"** (**"The Court Jeweler"**) in which Remizov denounces man's passion for unbridled freedom (... perhaps intended as a commentary on the events of 1905); and **"Pozhar"** (**"The Conflagration"**), an unusual and excellent combination of provincial folk mentality and the wrath of God, embodied in the towering figure of a stony-visaged monk in black who mercilessly destroys a debauched people. Although many Remizov's devices and techniques are a reflection of the

Remizov's drawing of Alexander Blok, 1926. Reproduced by permission of Ardis Publishers.

Symbolist aesthetic (preoccupation with the verbal texture, the studied use of recurrent motifs and refrains, a rhythmic prose, lyricism), his adherence to the conversational and colloquial intonations of a studied *skaz* bound him to the Russian earth and the nineteenth-century tradition of Gogol, Leskov, Melnikov-Pechersky and Dal. The Symbolist vision of another world, of which our daily reality is put a pale reflection, does not appear in Remizov's stories with perhaps the exception of **"Pridvornyi iuvelir."** Rather, he emphasizes the elements of chance, grief and insult in our senseless existence which, apparently, he cannot fully justify as being in accord with God's will. However, unlike Ivan Karamazov he does not reject God's world but seeks to express a compassion for the misfortunes of others and a call to Christian humility and kindness in human behavior. This world view, although the product of diverse elements and experiences, seems to have crystalized only after his arrest (a classic example of chance misfortune) and during his years of exile among the "unfortunates" of Russian society. Perhaps the words of Remizov's talented disciple, Evgeny Zamyatin, could be applied with even greater cogency to Remizov himself: "If I have any place in Russian literature, I owe it entirely to the . . . Police." (pp. 303-16)

Alex M. Shane, *"A Prisoner of Fate: Remizov's Short Fiction,"* in Russian Literature Quarterly, *No. 4, Fall, 1972, pp. 303-18.*

RENATE S. BIALY   (essay date 1975)

[*In the following excerpt, Bialy investigates elements of literary parody, philosophical polemic, and political satire in the novel* The Fifth Pestilence (Pjatalja jazva).]

Although Remizov's novels form a relatively small part of his overall literary output, they provide excellent models for studying his narrative technique. This is particularly true of the novels written between 1909 and 1911: *Neuemnyj buben, Krestovye sestry,* and *Pjataja jazva.* For one, these novels depend heavily upon literary allusions; in each case the predecessor determines the structure of the novel, and adds to its depth philosophically. For another, these novels have a steady undercurrent of the comic. Few critics have paid attention to this aspect in Remizov's writings, but its recognition is essential to a proper evaluation of his work. In *Pjataja jazva* these two features, literary allusions and the comic, combine to form parody. (p. 403)

[The protagonist of *Pjataja jazva*] is a rebel against his social order, a man who isolates himself from his fellowmen. The humanity that surrounds him is a Gogolian human zoo, and the reader sympathizes with the protagonist for rejecting this company. On the other hand, when the protagonist is called upon to show human compassion and fails to, we judge him. The protagonist errs, suffers intensely, and in the end dies. The central themes of the novel, those of crime and punishment, grow out of the profession of the protagonist; he is empowered by the state to prosecute transgressors. The development of these themes, however, depends upon intricately structured parody. Remizov refers to a variety of literary antecedents and manipulates them on three levels: as parody of the works themselves, as philosophical polemic, and as commentary on contemporary political events.

The novel is set in the provincial town of Studenec, where the protagonist Bobrov serves as judicial investigator (*sledovatel'*). He is the only character in the novel into whose background the reader gains insight. His father was well meaning but ineffectual, and his mother was sensitive to the point of morbidity. It is she who exerted the greatest influence on her son. Bobrov grew up an idealist, passionately devoted to the law—a concept of absolute justice that punishes evildoers with complete objectivity and is not concerned with human failings. The corollary to his idealism is a deep-seated disgust for the crudity and immorality of his fellow human beings, which causes him to withdraw from them both physically and spiritually. As the novel opens we find Bobrov maintaining only official contact with a citizenry that heartily detests him and retiring at night to his study to read over his literary composition of former days, a journal presenting his view of the history of the Russian people.

Bobrov used two seventeenth-century chronicles about the Time of Troubles as models for his journal: the *Vremennik* of Ivan Timofeev and the *Skazanie* of Avraamij Palicyn. Both of these works are records of the interregnum between the death of Tsar Fedor in 1598 and the ascension of Mixail Romanov in 1613. Both chroniclers—the first a cleric from Novgorod, the second a cleric and diplomat from the Holy Trinity and St. Sergius Monastery outside of Moscow—bring the same philosophical premise to the writing of their works: that the Time of Troubles was sent to the Russian people as a punishment for their sins. Palicyn identifies Russia's sinfulness with a gradual moral disintegration, beginning with crimes committed by Boris Godunov to secure his power; it culminated according to Palicyn, with the savagery of the civil war, visited by Russians upon Russians. For Timofeev the beginnings of sin lie further back in history. Though politically a legitimist, and therefore a supporter of the last annointed rulers of the House of Rjurik, Timofeev is still enough a son of Novgorod to condemn Ivan IV's brutal subjugation of that city. In his opinion Ivan bears the responsibility of unleashing immorality, not the least of his sins being the creation of the opričina. As the Tsar goes, so go the people. Timofeev lists, as in a sermon, the cancers on the moral body of Russia: pride, drunkenness and gluttony, fornication, ill-will towards one's neighbor, cupidity, and swearing.

Bobrov's chronicle begins with an accusation:

> And it was similar to what happened in the old times during the troubled years when the clerk Ivan Timofeev in his "Vremennik," reviewing the troubles, made his accusation against the Russian people

> the *wordlessly* silent one.

> And the monk from the Holy Trinity Monastery, Avraamij Palicyn, judged the Russian people

> for its *mad silence*.

It then echoes both Timofeev and Palicyn in its litany of sins. Like Timofeev Bobrov sees the origin of sin during the reign of Ivan IV; like Palicyn he dwells more on violence than on immorality. Living in a later age Bobrov extends his enumeration of crimes to include the present, apparently taking his examples from contemporary police dossiers. Bobrov uses the same tone of high seriousness as Timofeev and Palicyn. His concern is for the fate of the country; his horror of the violence which exists in society speaks from every page.

But Bobrov is not the only chronicler of the novel. A major part of the novel itself is a chronicle, narrated in a humorous and joking tone. To underscore the alienation of Bobrov from his fellow townspeople Remizov uses two narrative voices in the novel: a serious and omniscient narrator to relate Bobrov's life and provide insights into his thoughts; and a naive and bantering narrator, to tell in a light-hearted way about life in the town and the exploits of its disreputable citizens. This narrator's lack of sensitivity and discernment, his fascination with triviality, make him one with the world he describes; he is a voice out of the midst of Studenec. In the novel these two narrators alternate, the naive narrator echoing and distorting both the themes and the devices introduced by the serious narrator. The naive narrator becomes the vehicle for parody.

The novel begins with the naive narrator introducing the citizens of Studenec one by one, listing them in connection with their vices: the chief of police beats his servant; the doctor, the veterinarian, and the druggist drink; the judge, the priest, and the seminary teacher are impressive swearers; the town bum likes to expose himself; and the elder of the church "heals through fornication." The catalog of sins includes blackmail, bribery, and free-thinking; the townsfolk never miss an opportunity to do their neighbor a bad turn. This enumeration parodies Timofeev's list of sins, for quite unlike the historical chronicler, Remizov's narrator tells of the sins with great relish, dwelling on the sinners' enjoyment.

The narrator freely admits that the city is steeped in sin and foresees the punishment of hell for all the citizens of Studenec.

What follows next in the novel, however, is not punishment in hell but punishment on earth. Chapter 4 is devoted to the theme of retribution. The naive narrator begins in the following manner: "Is it for the sake of our many sins and falsehoods (as a chronicler would say) or perhaps for reasons having nothing to do with sin, for no reason at all, that many most marvelous occurrences took place in Studenec." As a self-respecting chronicler he should view the town's suffering as punishment for its sins. But he is prepared to doubt it and see no connection between one and the other: their burdens are sent to them "for no reason at all." Since the narrator and his fellow citizens expect to go to hell anyway, punishment on earth is unnecessary; they fail to see a connection between their suffering on earth and their sinful behavior.

The "marvelous occurrences" mentioned by the naive narrator correspond to the horrors of the Time of Troubles. In Studenec these occurrences range from the ridiculous to the farcical. Swarms of worms suddenly infest the town and disappear just as unexpectedly. This distasteful but trivial incident is described in great detail, reminiscent of a chronicle description of an approaching alien army. The reader learns what the worms look like and exactly how they crawl. Two worms are captured and placed in a bottle for posterity.

The next occurrence concerns the chief of police Antonov, who grows a pair of ass's ears (cf. Apollo's punishment of King Midas for preferring Pan's music to his). The only person who knows about his ears is the barber, who although sworn to secrecy cannot keep a secret. Knowing that he will be punished if he tells the secret, he whispers it into a hollow tree; rushes growing near the tree in turn whisper it to the winds. Remizov parodies the legend by keeping Antonov ignorant of why he received the ears. Like Midas Antonov seeks a confidant in his dilemma—not his barber, however, but the town veterinarian. The latter tries to convince Antonov of the benefits of his new acquisition: he will become part of Greek mythology or, with ass's ears, he has the necessary prerequisites for being Minister of Education. The veterinarian agrees in the end to treat his friend with a special salve to remove the ears, and the ears miraculously disappear. Although sworn to secrecy like the barber, at the club that night the veterinarian shouts the story "to the four winds."

No sooner has Antonov divested himself of his ears than the rumor spreads through town that the district governor will make a visit—a parody on Gogol's *Inspector General*. As in the play, rumor plays a decisive role in the action. Rumor turns the improvident Xlestakov into an inspector, whom the town officials royally entertain in hopes of evading punishment for their corruption, and he is exposed only because the postmaster snoops through the letters in the post office. When the real inspector is announced, the town's inhabitants freeze in terrified anticipation. Remizov rearranges these motifs to create high comedy. The telegraphist intercepts a personal cable announcing the visit of the governor by automobile. From the telegraph office the rumor spreads; all civil and clerical dignitaries are roused out of bed and assembled on the town square, where they stand in rigid expectation. The automobile arrives, and out of it step two of the town's most dissolute merrymakers. This gives a twist to Gogol's plot: the incident ends with the arrival not of the real but of the false inspector.

All the parodies have as their theme either threat of punishment (the army of worms, the inspector), or punishment itself (the ass's ears). The incidents all run their course and return their victims to the starting point. Because of this similarity in their resolution the parodies transcend the level of the purely literary. In probing the purpose and effect of punishment Remizov shows that punishment has no purpose: the victims do not know why they are being punished, or if they wonder about it they pick the wrong reason. In the end all is for naught; humanity reverts to its old sinful self.

The purpose of punishment is also explored within the plot of the novel. In this capacity as investigator Bobrov makes a judicial error: he orders the arrest of a suspected arsonist who is subsequently proven to be innocent. This is the first crack in Bobrov's superhuman, idealistic armor. His mistake unbalances his sense of right and wrong, and he no longer feels confidence in his judgment. Just as this point he faces Šapaev (the elder who "heals through fornication"). During a prayer session Šapaev attempts to rape one of the townswomen, a penitent sinner seeking religious guidance. She tears loose and runs to Bobrov. Bobrov's human inadequacy, his inability to satisfy human demands, is highlighted here: the woman asks for help and compassion, the attempted rape is a spiritual injury. Bobrov's response is dispassionate and legalistic: he summons Šapaev for questioning. Šapaev appears and is unrepentant, even unmoved, and totally uninterested in the legal aspects of the case. There is no crime, he claims, only sin, which is the inescapable lot of all humanity. Standing before the investigator he preaches the gospel of compassion and voluntary suffering: "Stand back and turn away from yourself, take upon yourself someone else's guilt, take on another's cross and carry that cross for him." This is a paraphrase of Dmitrij's statement in *The Brothers Karamazov,* where he decides to accept his cross. Bobrov rebels against this idea. If an innocent person will accept punishment for another's crime, what of the criminal? He might go free and commit more crimes.

In agreement with his protagonist, Remizov argues the case through the King Midas legend. The ass's ears are a punishment for error, and Antonov receives the ass's ears on the same day that Bobrov commits his judicial error: he "took on someone else's cross." Thus Antonov, whose only link to Bobrov is the law profession, suffers for a mistake he does not cause and about which he is ignorant. The absurd sequence of events proves that no one benefits from suffering by proxy, neither Bobrov nor Antonov. By Antonov's taking on Bobrov's punishment Bobrov is free to commit another error, namely, the mishandling of the rape-attempt case. It is true that Antonov does not accept his suffering voluntarily; he has very little choice for the ears simply appear. The incident suggests that punishment is meted out arbitrarily and quite uselessly.

Such punishment is also excessive. When Antonov discovers his ass's ears he tries to explain to himself why he is thus afflicted: perhaps because he had broken a promise given to his wife that he would not drink. "But to be so severely punished!" he moans *(Tak žestoko!).* This phrase is echoed towards the end by Bobrov as he lies dying; he tries to explain his suffering as God's sentence for making the judicial error. To him too the punishment seems excessive: "For one mistake, and so severely?" *(Za odnu ošibku, i tak žestoko?).*

Pjataja jazva is clearly a polemic with Dostoevskij. Remizov forms his ideas on a Dostoevskian pattern by creating an intellectual rebel with moral flaws. The moral flaws even bear the marks of Western decadence: Bobrov, for instance, denies his Russian heritage and claims to be German. It follows that his legal ideas are foreign and cannot prosper on Russian soil. The very unreliability of the judicial process is demonstrated by Bobrov's mistake. The man of intellect is then challenged

by the man of God; this recalls the juxtaposition of Ivan and Father Zosima. But here Remizov and Dostoevskij part company. Ivan is left in his dilemma, and Zosima's life story is offered as a Christian alternative, if not an answer, to Ivan's rebellion. Šapaev is no Zosima and hardly a faith-inspiring alternative to intellectual revolt; he preaches submission, although he certainly does not practice it. Moreover Remizov rejects the Dostoevskian concept of suffering, or—what amounts to the same thing to him as it did to Timofeev and Palicyn—of punishment. Through parody he shows that punishment is not only unjustified and useless but randomly distributed and therefore senseless.

It is fruitful to examine the novel also in the context of its time. Remizov suggests this by having the naive narrator mention the passing of Halley's Comet: "Last year . . . the ex-sailor Kočnov . . . in expectation of the comet tied himself with a rope to an anchor and buried himself in the ground." Halley's Comet passed in 1910, and all manner of doomsday predictions were circulated on the occasion. The world was expected to come to an end when the earth passed through the comet's tail in May. This apocalyptic theme is reflected in the title of the novel, and it is left to the naive narrator to explain the title. He transforms the Four Horsemen of the Apocalypse into "four pestilences," ruin, disaster, corruption, and desolation *(paguba, gubitel'stvo, tlja, zapustenie),* and adds as a "fifth pestilence" the very special divine punishment for the town of Studenec, the investigator Bobrov. The addition of Bobrov makes the enumeration slightly absurd. Through the naive narrator the apocalpytic theme is ridiculed. The end of the world is not imminent; the world is fated to continue its miserable course. It did not even come to an end in 1910!

The apocalyptic theme also figures in the chronicles of the Time of Troubles. Palicyn particularly, in the passages of his chronicle which he wrote during the civil war, considered the destruction of Russia to presage the end of the world. The final disaster was averted only by the election of Mixail Romanov in 1613. Timofeev saw this election as a sign that God had forgiven Russia. In other words Russia was saved by the advent of the Romanovs. These ideas were particularly relevant for 1911, the time of preparation for a mammoth tricentennial celebration of Romanov rule. Remizov's novel can be interpreted as an attack on the idea of celebrating the autocracy. The use of the chronicles of the Time of Troubles as a structural device suggests that the horror of those days has not ended but is still a part of Russian life. Since Timofeev and Palicyn considered the crimes of the Russian rulers to be initially responsible for the suffering of the land, the latter-day chronicler Remizov makes the same accusation, even if not explicitly. Celebration of Romanov rule is therefore a farce.

This oblique attack on the regime has interesting social and political implications. Studenec, steeped in immorality and corruption, stands for Russia. Anything that changes the accustomed flow of life is considered by its citizens as punishment from above, and ironically this includes both the bad and the good (Bobrov's idealism is probably the best thing that ever happened to Studenec). The citizens of Studenec seem to be incorrigible. They probably deserve the punishment that is visited upon them, but as to the question of guilt it is not clear that it is their fault they are sinful. In the novel's historico-political perspective it appears the citizens' moral state is a result of the rulers' immorality and the social and political conditions they instituted. So the people are indeed punished for something that is not their fault, and the naive narrator is right in claiming that punishment comes "for no reason at all." This too is ironic, for the naive narrator is shown to lack perception and be unenlightened. Should the suffering Russian people protest against the injustices which befall them? The only person to whom this occurs is Bobrov, who accuses the Russian people of acquiescence but does so in the privacy of his study, in a manuscript locked up in his desk. Remizov's target here is the liberal intelligentsia; his protagonist perfects his own ethics but remains remote from the common folk.

According to current superstition the world was coming to an end. But the events of the novel suggest that in spite of marvelous occurrences normalcy will prevail and the world will go on as usual. This is perhaps the most devastating truth of *Pjataja jazva*. There were those who might hope for the end of the world, at least the end of the autocratic system in Russia in 1911. The message for them is this: just as the advent of the Romanovs in 1613 did not bring relief to the Russian people, neither would a radical change in the twentieth century alleviate suffering and injustice. The recent past, the 1905 revolution and its aftermath, more than justified Remizov's pessimism. *Pjataja jazva* can thus be considered a part of a political polemic.

The parallels between the novel and the contemporary scene can be extended to the characters. An early review of *Pjataja jazva* suggested Bobrov is a parody of idealists in the judicial system such as the famous trial lawyer Anatolij Fedorovič Koni. Koni, whose career began with the Vera Zasulič case in 1878, was celebrated not only as an outstanding jurist and brilliant courtroom orator but also as the propagator of judicial ethics within the Russian legal system. In Bobrov the ideals of impartiality and concern for the rights of the individual are permuted into an inhuman coldness and commitment to absolute justice regardless of the human elements involved. Political implications can be drawn from this parallel. Becoming a model of incorruptibility Bobrov tried to change the moral tenor of Studenec; he was unable to effect any change. Legal reforms in real life are perhaps similarly doomed. But Remizov does not suggest that such reforms are desirable; like Dostoevskij (also Tolstoj) he believed that social ills cannot be solved by the judiciary process. As for Šapaev, in Russia in 1911 the figure of an immoral and dissolute "man of God" could only bring to mind Rasputin; and since Šapaev was endowed only with Rasputin's most scandalous characteristics (it was sexual excesses that made Rasputin the talk of St. Petersburg in 1911), he must also be considered a parody.

This examination of *Pjataja jazva* has shown that parody is a key to its interpretation. In view of Remizov's penchant for literary borrowings and for the comic, it is safe to assume that parody holds the clue to many more of his writings. (pp. 403-10)

> Renate S. Bialy, "Parody in Remizov's 'Pjataja jazva'," in Slavic and East-European Journal, *Vol. 19, No. 4, Winter, 1975, pp. 403-10.*

HAROLD B. SEGEL (essay date 1979)

[*Segel is an American translator and critic who has written extensively on Russian and Polish drama and dramatists. In the following excerpt from his study* Twentieth-Century Russian Drama: From Gorky to the Present, *he discusses Remizov's fusion of elements from folk, classical, and medieval literature in his* Devil Play *and* Tragedy of Judas.]

Remizov was steeped in Old Russian culture, both secular and religious, had a splendid command of the Old Russian language, and mined Russian folklore as a source of myth and style. These various elements combine to inform his theatrical works with a highly personal and unique flavor. In *Besovskoe deystvo* (*The Devil Play*) and *Tragediya o Iude, printse Iskariotskom* (*The Tragedy of Judas, Prince of Iscariot*) Remizov fused folk motifs and the medieval mystery for the purpose of conveying the spirit of Russian folk theater in which he was strongly interested. It was this same interest that led him in 1919 to write his own version of the famous Old Russian popular drama *Tsar Maximilian*.

Based on a legend in the medieval *Kievo-Pechersk Paterikon* (*Lives of the Saints of the Monastery of the Caves in Kiev*), *The Devil Play* is a macabre yet rollicking free-for-all of devils stalking souls for hell and the eventual salvation of a cave-dwelling ascetic monk who becomes their special target. There are scenes in hell that could just as well have come from the canvases of a Hieronymus Bosch and one stage direction that gives pause for thought—it calls for the onstage separation of a soul from its body and its transport to hell in the maws of a serpent who spews it out onto the hellfires. Of all the plays written by the Russian Symbolists in what they construed to be the spirit of the Middle Ages, none comes closer to the style and color of the popular medieval mystery and morality than Remizov's *Devil Play*.

The Tragedy of Judas, in some ways the more interesting of Remizov's theatrical works, dramatizes an apocryphal legend of Judas of unknown origin found in the Church of the Resurrection in Putivl, in the district of Kursk. Although new interpretations of various biblical events and personages resulted from the Christian revisionism of the *fin-de-siècle,* Remizov's version of Judas is indeed curious. The imminent betrayal of Jesus in Jerusalem comes only as a declared intention by Judas at the very end of the play. Until then, the *Tragedy of Judas* unfolds as a melodrama of dynastic rivalry involving the princes of the island of Iscariot—Judas and Stratim—and the scheming Unkrada, a distant relation from a far-off northern land, presumably Russia. Complicating the political intrigue is the fact that Judas is also the central figure in an Oedipal prophecy fulfilled in the course of the play. An exile from Iscariot in Jerusalem, Judas becomes the steward of Pilate's manor. While fetching golden apples for his master from an adjacent garden Judas kills the keeper of the miraculous orchard, marries his widow, and then discovers that the gardener was his father and that his wife is his mother who abandoned him at birth out of fear of a dreadful prophecy. Burdened with grief and self-loathing, Judas rushes out to find Jesus in order to expiate his sin by taking upon himself for the whole world—in the spirit of Christ's sacrifice—the "last and heaviest guilt" which Unkrada articulates as the betrayal of Jesus, the bearer of a "new order."

Remizov's play merits attention not only for the merging of the classical Greek myth of Oedipus and the New Testament account of Judas's betrayal of Jesus—which follows a pattern of medieval apocrypha—but also for its extensive use of folk elements. This folk stylization manifests itself especially in the speech of Judas's followers Orif and Zif who, like Pilate and the King of the Apes who appears in the play, wear half-masks throughout in a borrowing from antique theater as well as from the Italian commedia dell'arte. Furthermore, Judas himself is linked by name to ancient Slavic mythology, according to Remizov, since Yuda is a Slavic water divinity and is preserved in the person of the Russian fairy-tale hero Chuda-Yuda. Remizov has one of his characters explain, in fact, that the Slavic Yuda is from the Latin root *und* (as in the English "undine"). . . . Remizov's colorful mystery plays must be regarded as among the more fascinating Symbolist contributions to the drama. (pp. 68-70)

> *Harold B. Segel, "The Revolt against Naturalism: Symbolism, Neo-Romanticism, and Theatricalism," in his* Twentieth-Century Russian Drama: From Gorky to the Present, *Columbia University Press, 1979, pp. 50-146.*

SONA ARONIAN   (essay date 1985)

[In the following excerpt, Aronian summarizes criticism written in Russian on Remizov's works between 1907 and 1977.]

Alexei Mikhailovich Remizov is relatively unknown in the English-speaking world. Yet this brilliant writer, through his single-minded, life-long devotion to art, despite every conceivable adversity, published over eighty volumes and has been called by his countrymen "the most Russian of all Russian writers" and "the Picasso of Russian prose." Remizov's works were printed in the periodical press beginning in 1902 and his first three books appeared in 1907; when his collected works in eight volumes began publication in 1910, he was already recognized as a major writer. The critical response to Remizov's three major publications of 1907 set a pattern for what was to be typical of the literature on him for years to come. It contained an immediate perception of what was most striking in his work: superb craftsmanship that encompassed linguistic, thematic, stylistic, and compositional innovations which rendered his texts initially difficult to understand. These works were *Sunwise* (*Posolon'*), a unique cycle of lyric prose tales treating children's games and ancient folk rituals in mythic terms; *Leimonarion: The Meadow of the Spirit* (*Limonar'. Lug dukhovnyi*), a collection of recast Apocryphal legends; and *The Pond* (*Prud*), an autobiographical novel.

It is telling that a number of Russian poets should first respond, and with keen appreciation, to *Sunwise* and *Leimonarion*. Maximilian Voloshin, in his discussion of the linguistic treasures in *Sunwise,* created the image of Remizov the collector of words as precious gems; Andrei Bely stressed the musicality of Remizov's talent and his mastery of form; and Sergei Gorodetsky found convincing Remizov's portrayal of the imps and satyrs of folklore. A year later the cultural historian Mikhail Gershenzon claimed that Remizov had penetrated more deeply into the spirit of folk myths than had any other artist; and in the 1930s a Soviet scholar, B. Mikhailovsky, was to speak in retrospect of Remizov's use of transrational language (*zaumnyi iazyk*) and to apply the concept as well to the work's unmotivated plot (*stuzhetnaia zaum'*). Gorodetsky felt that in *Leimonarion* Remizov had captured the Russian spirit of the originally Byzantine legends; that he had, in his use of Slavic roots for neologisms, given expression to a "national idea"; and that his work would serve as a laboratory for new ideas and art forms in the coming decade. A few years later Georgy Chulkov, the poet and theorist of "mystical anarchism," noted that Remizov's reworked legends, filled with alliteration, repeated epithets, and rhythmic lines, had lost the ingenuous quality of the originals but had acquired a new poignancy.

The poetic charm of the *Sunwise* and *Leimonarion* pieces, their setting in the world of make-believe and the past may well have permitted reviewers to see Remizov's originality in a positive light which was not uniformly the case with his modernist novel *The Pond,* a vast mosaic composition set in a contemporary world where suffering, injustice, and cruelty have no apparent cause and where a mood of unmitigated gloom dominates. Bely insisted that the use of the lyric refrain as a compositional device was incompatible with the demands of the novel as a genre, and that it led in *The Pond* to such fragmentation as to make the work incomprehensible. However, when the novel appeared in a revised edition in 1911, the literary scholar and social critic R. V. Ivanov-Razumnik suggested that though the stylistic excesses of the 1907 edition had indeed been removed, it was not the technical flaws of the work that had provoked an initial negative reaction. For him Remizov's vision of life on earth as being devoid of any essential truth or permanent value and wanting of any evidence of God's presence was more difficult to accept than to grasp and that, therefore, the "God-seekers" among his contemporaries found him too unpleasant, the esthetes too complicated and the general reader too decadent. The poet Mikhail Kuzmin called the revised version one of the most remarkable works of contemporary Russian prose but asserted that the greater clarity achieved in the first part of the novel was missing in the second part which, with its preponderance of dreams, was inadequately motivated. Professor A. V. Rystenko, a specialist in Old Russian literature, drew attention to the makings of a twentieth century mythology in Remizov's use of cultural remnants of the past, citing among numerous other examples his depiction of monastery life at the beginning of the century by means of eschatological legends, the Old Russian oration (*slovo*), and hagiographical tales. The Dostoevsky scholar A. Dolinin pointed out the Dostoevskian legacy of pain in Remizov's work, and a popular critic of the time, Alexander Zakrzhevsky, discerned in *The Pond* the most vivid understanding and expression of suffering since Dostoevsky. His description of the novel as one filled with "the bestial horror of the underground kingdom and a satanic mockery of life" was to be widely quoted. Chulkov later contended that the theme of the underground could not be understood wholly within the context of a Dostoevskian affinity, for Remizov's nihilistic vision comprised but the content of the work which was subordinate to its form. For Chulkov the animating impulse in Remizov's art was the aesthetic, a transcendent value which emerged as the sole consolation in the underground.

The debate over form and content continued when *The Clock* (*Chasy*), Remizov's second and shorter novel (*povest'*) appeared in 1908. Bely stated that Remizov's mastery of form in the miniatures of *Sunwise* was still not evident in the novel form and that *The Clock* lacked unity of form and content, despite many stylistically brilliant pages. Gershenzon disagreed, claiming that the stylistic eccentricities of the novel were necessitated by and formed a unity with its content which was the source of offense to readers: downright ugly characters, a realistic story complicated by elements of the fantastic and the bizarre (*yurodstvo*), and a vision of mankind on the verge of destruction. Gershenzon viewed Remizov's creation of both the radiantly poetic short tales in *Sunwise* and the grand canvasses of despair in *The Pond* and *The Clock* as a sign of an unusual breadth of talent.

Remizov's collected stories of 1908, *The Devil's Lair and the Midnight Sun (Chortov log i polunoshchnoe solntse)* and of 1910, *Tales (Rasskazy),* elicited more uniformly enthusiastic critiques. For Bely the first volume was evidence that Remizov was the finest stylist of the period, and for him the stories were both rich in content and marked by clarity of style and lucidity of design. He singled out as most remarkable a work filled with elements of the grotesque and the fantastic, **"The Little Devil"** (**"Chortik"**), a story of children surreptitiously observing the strange behavior of their elders who are members of the Khlysts, a Russian religious sect. Chulkov was struck by Remizov's experimentation with form in the story **"The Fortress"** (**"Krepost'"**) which lacked the traditional elements of story, characters, significant dialogue or a well-defined idea, resulting in a fragmented depiction of reality. For him the story had a structure analogous to that of a dream, where the most unusual combinations of people, places, things, and situations appear plausible; and it was given unity and verisimilitude through its inner lyricism.

The second volume actually contained dreams as an independent genre, in a cycle entitled **"A Disastrous Lot"** (**"Bedovaia dolia"**). These prose poems celebrating moments of subconscious experience as a self-valuable and independent reality evoked some consternation. Kuzmin described the dreams condescendingly as nothing more than the non-sensical babbling of an old woman who had lost possession of her faculties. However, D. V. Filosofov, the writer and philosopher, analyzed one of the dreams by juxtaposing its seemingly senseless contents with several similar bizarre but real life events he found in contemporary journals. For him the dream exemplified a "higher reality"; it illuminated the absurdities of the epoch in a manner neither accessible to nor acceptable in a more conventional form. Alexander Blok was similarly impressed with the dreams as symbolic reflections of the contemporary psyche. Four other stories in the volume were cited by Blok as works of permanent value: **"Divine Judgment"** (**"Sud Bozhii"**), the story of a devout monk's traumatic confrontation with evil; **"Princess Mymra"** (**"Tsarevna Mymra"**), the tale of a young boy's disillusionment with love; **"In Transport"** (**"Po etapu"**), a political tale of deportation; and **"The Sacrifice"** (**"Zhertva"**), a fantastic tale of the intrusion of demonic powers into the life of a Russian family. For Blok Remizov was one of the most serious and profound writers of the period.

Remizov's next short novel, *Sisters in the Cross (Krestovye sestry)*, concerns the sufferings endured and seen by a petty clerk after losing his job because of a minor error in accounting. S. A. Vengerov, the well-known scholar, hailed the work as the biggest literary success of the year. Kuzmin was positively affected by the work's modernist emphasis on the isolated moment as opposed to chronological sequence but was bewildered by its unorthodox form, suggesting, puckishly, that it should be called a rhapsody, a chronicle, or a portrait gallery rather than a short novel (*povest'*). For the minor critic E. A. Koltonovskaya the work was a model of contemporary craftsmanship, and its central vision of life as pain and suffering was embodied in a frame image of ancient Rus. The element of ancient lore was seen by Rystenko, too, as centrally significant to the novel, especially the use of the motif of the apocryphal legend of "Mary's Journey Through the Torments." Rystenko went on to link Remizov's affinity to Dostoevsky (who had used the same motif in *The Brothers Karamazov*) to this legend as a common source of inspiration. Other echoes of Dostoevsky were examined in connection with *Sisters in the Cross*. Vladimir Khranikhfeld referred to the work as a set of variations on themes from *Crime and Punishment* and the writer Kornei Chukovsky as a first-rate treatment of the theme of the "little man" who discovers his "I" only through suffering. But Chukovsky emphasized that the meaning of suffering remained, in Remizov's work, a haunting, unanswered question, that life appeared to be a stupid empty

joke, and that Remizov responded to all this with a feeling of nausea (*toshnota*) that reached metaphysical dimensions. The existentialist dilemma of Remizov's vision convincingly detailed by Chukovsky was equally convincingly countered by the prominent critic of the prestigious *Messenger of Europe (Vestnik Evropy)*, S. Adrianov, who argued that though people stood alone in Remizov's world, without a higher power to turn to, both good and evil lay in their own hands; that it was a matter of inner will for them to be able to endure suffering without losing their sense of the joy of life. For Adrianov this union of suffering and joy was a tragic synthesis expressive not only of Remizov's temperament but also of the Russian cast of mind. And for him the dominant image in the work was not that of a traditional "hero" but of a "holy fool," and this feature, likewise, was characteristic of the timbre of Remizov's individuality and of the religious temperament of the Russian people.

Bely, who had previously praised only Remizov's short prose narratives, greeted his next short novel, *The Fifth Pestilence (Piataia iazva)*, with a burst of enthusiasm: "I read your book— I should say, rather, that I swallowed it. . . . I was deeply shaken by it. I simply couldn't tear myself away from it once I had opened it. It is colossal, something our literary decade can take pride in. *The Fifth Pestilence,* a Gogolian *tour de force*, pits an idealistic, self-righteous and crusading criminal investigator against his vulgar, corrupt and raucously jovial townspeople who are bent on ridding the town of him. The work's compositional complexity drew some typically negative complaints, but it was primarily the figure of Bobrov, the chief protagonist, that became the center of critical attention. A minor critic, P. Vladimirova, categorized Bobrov as an ideal hero in search of the truth. The Marxist scholar Lvov-Rogachevsky compared Bobrov, whom he found offensive, to Kozhemyakin in Gorky's *The Town of Okurov*. He maintained that though both men kept a "chronicle" of the misdeeds of the Russian people, only Bobrov came to hate his people. (This view as well as its specific points of comparison was to be repeated in Soviet criticism by S. V. Kastorsky.) Ivanov-Razumnik interpreted Bobrov as a tragic hero who had denounced the Russian people only to realize, belatedly, that there was no life outside the people.

The havoc that reigned in Russian from 1914 to 1921, the year Remizov emigrated, inevitably affected the cultural life of the country. Although Remizov was able to publish a few books and numerous shorter pieces in journals and newspapers and was still held in high regard, his work was not the subject of many new lengthy studies. In short reviews of his *Spring Trifles (Vesennee porosh'e)*, a volume of original and recast tales, and his *Buttress (Ukrepa)*, he was again berated for focusing excessively on senseless suffering or seen as having a keen perception of the joys of life. Furthermore, he was accused of expressing more sorrow for "sinful Russia" than pride in "Holy Russia." This fixation on the content of Remizov's work, especially as it touched upon the theme of Russia, reached a climax when his **"Oration on the Downfall of the Russian Land"** (**"Slovo o pogibeli Russkoi zemli"**), written on the eve of the October Revolution, was published in 1918. His longtime admirer Ivanov-Razumnik, though acknowledging the "Oration" to be one of the most remarkable and powerful works of the time, attacked Remizov as a philistine lamenting the destruction of Russia's traditional "Old World" values. Evgeny Zamyatin, agreeing only that Remizov had created a work of great power, responded with a scathing rejoinder. Zamyatin extolled Remizov as a true Scythian who had cried out against the philistines of the past in his eight-volume *Works,* and who had already discerned the signs of a new philistinism and criticized it in his "Oration."

Despite the vicissitudes of emigre life, Remizov's years abroad (1921-1957) were marked by the same extraordinary creative productivity as those in Russia. Almost all of his new publications were reviewed, predominantly in the emigre press, where a growing appreciation and understanding of the innovative aspects of his art and of the broader implications of his vision became apparent. Early reviews included those of his *Dance of Herodias (Plias Irodiady),* a recast Biblical legend concerning John the Baptist, based on Russian variants. One critic called attention to the erotic elements in the work and to Remizov's success in evoking the atmosphere of medieval Russia. For another critic, Alexander Bakhrakh, the work was a linguistically subtle and erudite presentation of the popular perception of the famous story, and its special charm lay in its primitive quality. Marc Slonim went on to say that Remizov's profound knowledge of Russian antiquity was the source of his success in reviving the devices, style, and rhythms of folk works in contemporary literature, as, for example, in his recast Byzantine tales and apocryphal legends in *Sward-Grass (Trava-Murava);* in the Siberian folk tales in *Chakhchygys-Taasu* and in the Caucasian folk tales in *Lalazar.* In addition Slonim reviewed Remizov's stories based on contemporary life in *The Eidolon (Mara),* seeing in them Remizov's continuing keen identification with human suffering and aspiration and his thematic concern with problems of conscience. Two Soviet critics focused on other aspects of this work. Nikolai Aseev interpreted it as a reactionary call to the past because of the recurrent theme connecting the stories, the demoralization of contemporary life stemming from a loss of respect for religious values. For the writer Veniamin Kaverin dreams were the central organizing device of the work, and its meaning was to be found in its image of Russia.

The poet Zinaida Gippius, reviewing *Echoes of Zvenigorod: St. Nicholas' Parables (Zvenigorod oklikannyi. Nikoliny pritchi),* discussed Remizov's unique talent for giving expression to both the practical, down-to-earth side of the Russian character and its more spiritual, enigmatic side. To depict the more intangible part of the Russian spirit Remizov indulged in much criticized literary eccentricities *(yurodstvo),* which Gippius defined as the combined use of elements of primitivism and fantasy. Another critic who commended Remizov's depiction of the Russian people added that Remizov was the "sacrist of the Russian language" because of his ability to express verbally the inarticulate thoughts of simple folk. A review of the St. Nicholas parables in *Three Sickles (Tri serpa)* recognized Remizov's montage technique of superimposing details from the contemporary life of Russian emigres in Paris on the Byzantine setting of the stories as a literary device to satirize the social-political issues of the day and took to task the oft-made statement that Remizov was a "writer's writer," insisting that the stories had popular entertainment value. Years later the emigre philosopher I. A. Ilin was to detect a note of blasphemy in these same tales where the blending of past and present produced a chaotic mixture of the sacred and the magical with Divine omnipotence placed on the same level as magic and technology. The eminent scholar Konstantin Mochulsky took issue moreover with the repeated claim that Remizov's retold tales were mere imitations or stylizations. For him Remizov was a first-person folk narrator with his own authentic voice, continuing the creation of a legend that had been in the making since the eleventh century.

Remizov's revised pre-revolutionary short stories that appeared in *Zga: Tales of Wonder (Zga. Volshebnye rasskazy)* were evaluated by G. Lovtsky in terms that anticipate Todorov's view of the fantastic. Commenting specifically on **"The Sacrifice," "The Little Devil," "Divine Judgment," "Zanofa"** (the story of a young girl deemed a witch by her community) and **"The Conflagration"** (**"Pozhar,"** the story of a prosperous, corrupt town completely destroyed by fire) Lovtsky proposed that Remizov's mastery in dealing with the fantastic lay in his ability to create in the reader a sense of expectation and the conviction that the demonic was present even though "natural" explanations abounded.

In a lengthy article reviewing the first decade of Russian emigre literature the Soviet critic D. A. Gorbov presented Remizov and the poet Marina Tsvetaeva as the two outstanding major writers who had had an impact on the post-revolutionary rebirth of Russian literature in the area of literary craftsmanship. Remizov, in Gorbov's view, had enriched the Russian literary language and influenced the technique of young Soviet writers including Zamyatin, Vsevolod Ivanov, and Leonid Leonov. However, Remizov's works published in emigration, *In a Field Azure (V pole blakitnom)* the story of his wife's childhood in the first part of a fictionalized biography; the volumes of the St. Nicholas legends; *Russia in the Whirlwind (Vzvikhrennaia Rus'),* a vast kaleidoscopic chronicle of the revolutionary years; and some excerpts from *Along the Cornices (Po karnizam),* fictionalized reminiscences of emigre life are categorically rejected in terms of any future influence they might have, allegedly because of their irrelevant content.

The emigre critics K. Mochulsky and D. S. Mirsky were unreserved in their praise of these same works. For Mirsky Remizov's creation of the demonic and the grotesque in numerous pre-revolutionary works and his creation of an idyll, of a lost paradise of simplicity in *Olya,* which included **"In Field Azure"** and a new section entitled **"With a Fiery Maw"** (**"S ognennoi past 'iu"**), the story of his wife's youth, was proof of the all-encompassing range of his craftsmanship. For Mochulsky Remizov's language was one of the most remarkable phenomena of contemporary Russian literature, and it was something completely new again in *Olya.* Mirsky judged *Russia in the Whirlwind* to be one of the finest works of the period as well as one of Remizov's finest and regarded his attitude in it toward the Revolution as ambivalent. Mikhail Osorgin commented additionally that the technical complexity of Remizov's works had never served so well as in *Russia in the Whirlwind,* for only a seemingly disjointed series of tales, scenes, digressions, and dreams, and the juxtaposing of experiences encompassing the mundane, the absurd, the lyrical, the destructive, the altruistic, and the romantic thrill of the cataclysmic could serve to depict Russia engulfed in revolution. Another modernist aspect of Remizov's complexity was taken into account by Mochulsky. For him Remizov was not only original but uniquely so in each new work, posing the problem for the critic of discovering anew a work's central organizing device without which it could not be understood. In Mochulsky's view Remizov's innovative use of the device of a first-person narrator in *Along the Cornices* made all previous use of the device in Russian literature pale by comparison, and it resulted in a truly amazing and peculiar "I" who was obviously in some instances the Russian writer Remizov and clearly in others some legendary figure living outside of time.

During the depression and war years Remizov published only in periodicals. Although there were no new reviews of his work, an entry did appear in the Soviet literary encyclopedia of 1935, where B. Mikhailovsky, dealing primarily with Remizov's pre-emigration works, summarized his literary themes and devices, and identified his literary genealogy and influences on early Soviet writers. In his final evaluation Mikhailovsky reckoned Remizov a reactionary because of his depiction of Russian reality, past and present, as a kingdom of lawlessness, violence, and stagnation, requiring an elemental revolt as an expiation and as a punishment to be endured as sacrificial suffering (*yurodstvo*). Subtle contradictory implications related to the theme of the revolution at work in *Olya* and *Russia in the Whirlwind* are completely ignored by Mikhailovsky.

Seventy-year-old Remizov's post-war literary output was an innovative as that of every other period of his life, if not more so. Critics, now hailing the appearance of his works as major events in Russian literature, concentrated on each work as a new form with a new vision and on Remizov's *oeuvre* as a phenomenon that defied categorization. In Remizov's *Dancing Demon (Pliashushchii demon)*, the narrator participates in ten centuries of Russian life. The writer Ariadna Tyrkova-Williams looked into the concept of reincarnation as the thematic organizing principle in the work which in her view was a depiction of Russia's orgiastic roots. In *With Clipped Eyes (Podstrizhennymi glazami)*, a haunting autobiography of Remizov's childhood and youth intertwined with a large body of historical and literary subtexts which destroy chronological verisimilitude, she located the main theme, the psychology of creativity, and the central link between forty separate episodes in the figure of the main character, a misunderstood, unhappy youth who grew up into an artist and turned his misfortunes into artistic materials. The writer Nina Berberova added the suggestion that *With Clipped Eyes* contained the key to understanding Remizov's *oeuvre* and that this "atonal text" was a subtle polemic against literary realism.

In an article dealing with the linguistic problems facing emigre writers the cultural historian Nikolai Andreev presented Remizov as an example of how a writer could survive outside his homeland. Calling Remizov a true preserve of the Russian language, Andreev read his memoir of life in Nazi-occupied Paris, *A Flute for Mice (Myshkina dudochka)* as a paean to the beauty of language which, through the act of language itself, has transformed humdrum everyday life into a poetic legend. For Andreev Remizov's use of pre-Petrine Russian within the framework of contemporary Russian had demonstrated for the first time in Russian literature how language could serve as a means of transcending time. In another article, one of the most penetrating ever devoted to Remizov, Andreev offered further that as with his linguistic experiments, Remizov's innovations in form such as the "destroying" of traditional genres by combining several of them into one new one were motivated by the demands of his thematic materials and were not ends in themselves. For Gleb Struve who placed Remizov in the front rank of emigre writers alongside Bunin these experiments in form had put *The Dancing Demon, With Clipped Eyes,* and *A Flute for Mice* outside the bounds of any established genre.

Remizov's major work of criticism, *The Fire of Things (Ogon' veshchei)*, a study of dreams in Pushkin, Lermontov, Gogol, Turgenev, Dostoevsky, and Tolstoy, appeared in 1954. In the view of the poet Yury Terepiano, it was essentially an investigation of the irrational principle in Russian literature, with the irrational perceived as the source of creativity. For Professor Zoya Yurieff, the section on Gogol brought to light new depths of meaning in his work and for the scholar Dmitri

Chizhevsky, Remizov's work was not only of fundamental importance for an understanding of Gogol, but also a completely unique and original contribution within the Symbolist tradition.

The two decades of posthumous Russian criticism on Remizov's works (1957-1977) is for the most part that of Soviet scholars engaged in a reevaluation of his pre-1921 publications, with an obsessive focus on his vision of pre-revolutionary society and his attitude toward the Revolution. When Ilya Ehrenburg reintroduced Remizov to Soviet readers in 1961 as the most Russian of all Russian writers and as a writer who had written critically of the old society, L. Usenko replied with a contumelious attack. For him Remizov had falsely depicted the Russian national character as devoutly pious or religiously fanatic, and his portrayal of revolutionaries and the Revolution was exclusively negative. More than a decade passed before the scholar V. V. Buznik brought forth an apologia. He said that Remizov's well-known compassion for human suffering had led him to an initial rejection of the Revolution in his *Oration on the Downfall of the Russian Land,* but that his attitude had been modified by the time he wrote *Russia in the Whirlwind* where he affirmed the Revolution's underlying idealism. In the finest Soviet commentary on Remizov V. A. Keldysh dealt with this theme from a psychological and aesthetic perspective. For him Remizov's short stories with a negative depiction of political exiles ("**The Opera,**" "**The New Year,**" "**The Silver Spoons**") and those with perception of the 1905 revolution as a cruel, blindly destructive force ("**Holy Night,**" "**The Fortress,**" "**Almost a Gentleman,**" "**The Court Jeweller**") did not reflect sympathy for the existing social order, already anathematized in *The Pond,* but the fatalistically pessimistic view of life that had grown out of Remizov's experiences as a political exile. And Remizov's style was an essential component of his tragic vision: his characteristic fragmentation of composition, his piling up of unmotivated episodes, and the indistinctly motivated actions of his often large numbers of characters embodied his concept of life as an existence ruled by an unknowable transcendent causality and devoid of any individual differentiated meaning.

In 1977, the centennial of Remizov's birth and the twentieth anniversary of his death, Yu. A. Andreev, in a commemorative article purporting to show why Soviets should read Remizov, arbitrarily dismissed everything Remizov had written after his emigration as incomparably inferior to what he had previously written. The post-1921 works, he averred, were dominated by mystical, irrational, and decadent tendencies while the earlier ones were realistically critical of the existing social order. Andreev blithely ignores the fact that most of Remizov's publications in the 1920s were of works either published or written earlier in Russia, thus making 1921 a meaningless date for the periodization of his *oeuvre*. The only other aspect of Remizov's work that received some attention from Soviet critics was his reworking of ancient tales. Ya. Lurie, referring to Remizov as the most original writer of the twentieth century (an idea that is echoed throughout almost all Soviet commentary on Remizov), compared his *Tale of Two Animals: Ikhnelat (Povest' o dvukh zveriakh. Ikhnelat)* to other extant versions and commented on the addition of details that created a clearly motivated plot and the modernist use of anachronisms which helped highlight those features of the medieval tale that had meaning for the modern reader. A comparison of Remizov's version of "**Pyotr and Fevroniya**" ("**Povest' o Petre i fevronii**") by R. P. Dmitrieva also shows the addition of psychological motivation to the plot as well as the centrality of fantastic elements that had been but motifs in the original, for example, Fevroniya is overthrown by the boyars not because she is of peasant birth, but because she is a witch.

It fell to the lot of emigre criticism to suggest the possibility of a continuing Remizov tradition in Soviet Russian literature. For the writer Roman Gul', Solzhenitsyn in his *One Day in the Life of Ivan Denisovich* displays a stylistic affinity not to Soviet literature but to the "school" of Remizov in a common interest in Old Russian word roots, popular or substandard pronunciation, new and striking acronyms, the mixing of the archaic with the contemporary language, *skaz* narrative, and some principles of sentence structure. And the recent Soviet emigre scholar, L. S. Fleishman, in the last major article of the Remizov centennial year, once again gave the innovative nature of Remizov's art its due through the analysis of one of his previously unexplored texts, *Kukkha: The Rozanov Letters* (*Kukkha. Rozanovy pis'ma*). In a superb reading of *Kukkha* which he counted among Remizov's most brilliant experiments in prose, Fleishman established the work's place in the Russian tradition of poetic epistles to the deceased and then enumerated Remizov's contributions to the genre. For Fleishman the letters together with the commentary on them constitute a parody on definitive scholarly editions that had begun to appear at the turn of the century in Russian philological studies. The Fleishman study returns Remizov scholarship to its still unfinished

Remizov's "Uchitel' muzyki." Reproduced by permission of Ardis Publishers.

task first set forth as a challenge by Mochulsky, that of ascertaining the principle of organization of individual texts. The larger issues that remain include an evaluation of Remizov's entire artistic achievement and its place in modern Russian literature. The work already done suggests that Remizov may yet take his place as the Russian Modernist par excellence. (pp. 3-13)

Sona Aronian, "The Russian View of Remizov," in Russian Literature Triquarterly, No. 18, 1985, pp. 3-15.

CHARLOTTE ROSENTHAL   (essay date 1986)

[*In the following excerpt, Rosenthal discusses Remizov's reworkings of folklore, analyzing in particular the adaptations in the collections* Sunwise *and* Leimonarium. *Translations in brackets are by Rosenthal.*]

In 1907 Remizov published two books that marked the beginning of a lifelong involvement with folklore: **Sunwise** (*Posolon'*) and **Leimonarium** (*Limonar*). A few years later he expanded both of these books and they became volumes six and seven of his **Works** (*Sochineniia*), published in 1911 and 1912 respectively. These four books serve as a good focus for discussing Remizov's involvement with folklore because they illustrate many aspects of this involvement as well as Remizov's evolving use of folklore between the years 1906 and 1912. Folklore played an enormous role in Remizov's creative life. It permeates the prose of these four books from individual stylistic components on the lexical, morphological, and syntactic levels to imagery and symbolism, from sources of character to entire narrative plots.

The clearest statement we have from Remizov himself on his procedure for using folklore in literature is found in a letter to the editors of the *Russian Gazette* in 1909. In his letter, Remizov divides folklore into two large categories—myth and folk tales. In working with folkloric material, he says, he has two different aims in mind. The first is "to recreate popular (*narodnyi*) myth, fragments of which I would recognize in rituals, games, *koliadki,* superstitions, omens, proverbs, riddles, charms, and apocrypha."

This first aim resulted in the books **Sunwise** and **Leimonarium**. At times what Remizov sees as a fragment of popular myth is only a name or a folk custom. He proceeds by collating various facts about this name or custom, and then by comparing these facts to similar ones from other peoples, "in order, finally, from the senseless and puzzling in the name or custom, to penetrate into its life and soul, which should be depicted."

Remizov does not really define "myth." Instead he gives us a list of phenomena which supposedly had evolved from myth. It is clear, though, that Remizov viewed myth as a phenomenon of the past which had left traces in the present. This view of myth, ultimately traceable to the English scholar Tyler, came to be labeled the "survival theory." According to this theory, "games, folk dances, and popular rhymes were presumed to be degenerate derivatives of original myths or even earlier rituals." But Remizov was to invert Tyler's hierarchy of values. Tyler approved of the ultimate demise of these useless cultural items as human society continued to march from savagery to civilization. Remizov, on the contrary, viewed this march of "progress" as a march toward destruction. He valued the vestiges of myth as cultural items reflecting prelogical human perception. Rather than looking with approval at its ultimate demise, Remizov wished to revive this folk culture and its revitalizing power.

Remizov's view of myth was reinforced by his reading. In the notes to **Leimonarium** and volumes 6 and 7 of his **Works,** two names keep reappearing—A. N. Afanasiev (1826-1871) and A. N. Veselovsky (1838-1906). In various publications, especially in *The Poetic Views of the Slavs on Nature,* Afanasiev saw remnants of ancient myth in the contemporary beliefs, practices, and language of the folk. It was from Afanasiev that Remizov got the idea that religious verse and apocrypha derive from myth.

It was primarily through the work of Veselovsky that Remizov became acquainted with Tyler's theory of survivals and the comparative method in folk-literary research. Veselovsky used the very comparative approach that Remizov outlines in his letter. It was also through Veselovsky that Remizov was exposed to some of the massive materials compiled by Frazer. Remizov most likely was attracted to the work of Afanasiev and Veselovsky and to the latter in particular, because of its suggestiveness. Their interpretations of folkloric symbolism must have prompted his imagination with its rich possibilities. Remizov did not necessarily adopt their interpretations, especially those of the "solar mythologist" Afanasiev. It was more the myriad possibilities for interpretation that these two scholars introduced him to.

In the same letter, Remizov explains that his second aim applies to folk narratives that are intact: he wants to render this material in an artistic retelling. He claimed to proceed by reading extant variants of the same tale, and, having chosen one, amplifying it "in order to render the folk tale in its conceivably ideal form." What the artist develops, declares Remizov, and what he leaves untouched, reveals his cleverness and mastery. Remizov's notion of an "ideal form" is an aesthetic one, and betrays an orientation toward written literature. As we shall see, to achieve this "ideal form" Remizov introduced changes in the language, structure, and characterization of the folk model.

Remizov's stated aims in dealing with folklore lead to the question of how he viewed the function of literature in general, and of folk literature in particular. Remizov believed that art enables man to cope with life through, among other things, the exercise of his imagination. This "message" is illustrated in a typically Remizovian way in a piece he contributed to the volume *Where Are We Headed?* of 1910. It is much more typical than the letter to the editors of the *Russian Gazette* because it contains a less direct answer to the question addressed. In fact, it is no answer at all but a "parable" (*pritcha*). He cannot, he says, reason about the matter. He illustrates this point with the following tale about Kot Kotofei, one of his characters in *Sunwise.* We follow Kot as he makes a trip to a godforsaken northern Russian town, where he gets stuck, so that he has to winter there. The town is described briefly but bleakly. Kot's landlady, Marya Tikhonovna, is as uninspiring as the town. One wonders how people can possibly live there. As the winter comes, and wears on, Kot requests his landlady to tell some folk tales. After the formulaic third such request, she consents, and the result is the following transformation of perception:

> The bedbug is biting you, the flea takes a nip
> or two, all over the walls cockroaches are
> swarming—you feel nothing, you hear nothing:
> you're flying on a magic carpet beneath the

very clouds to fetch the water of life and of death. Here's the water of life for you, and of death, too, and it's not Marya Tikhonovna, it's Vasilisa the Wise standing there, the princess is standing there and looking at Kot.

This "parable" is a unique mixture of realistic detail, satirically rendered, and the world of the folk tale. Remizov implies that the answer to the question of Russia's problems will not be found through reasoned discourse or education but through the accommodation with reality made possible through the workings of the human imagination as expressed in lore and literature.

It is the imaginative workings of the peasant's and child's mind that dominate *Sunwise.* It sings a paean to man's childhood and to children. This dual theme is introduced at the very beginning with its dual dedications to Vyacheslav Ivanov and Natasha, Remizov's young daughter. (pp. 95-7)

Although the two editions of this book vary in volume, contents, and order of presentation, these differences do not alter its nature. This is because of the kind of structure that *Sunwise* has: any individual part is not needed to make the whole book. It can be included or excluded. What holds the book together is a controlling point of view—the world as seen through the eyes of the primitive and the child. In this world there are no abstractions: a fear, a joy, a wish—all become concretized into three-dimensional creatures and things. This world is totally animated; Remizov's primary means for conveying this animism is personification.

Sunwise, as the name indicates, roughly follows the sun through the seasons from spring to winter. The pieces selected for each section generally have a connection with the specific season. Most of the pieces are based on what Remizov considered to be vestiges of ancient myths: children's games or toys, holiday celebrations, folk beliefs, charms, counting rhymes, words, and expressions. Remizov freely blends data from various regions of Russia, from Slavic areas outside of Russia, and even from non-Slavic peoples. He makes little attempt to distinguish present from past practices. The language, too, reflects a blend of different regions, historical periods, the language of children, and Remizov's colloquially oriented rhythmic prose. Remizov is not attempting to depict a specific locale at a specific period in its history.

The *Sunwise* pieces combine lyrical nature descriptions, full of personification, with extant "vestiges" of myths and with descriptions of pagan Slavic ritualistic practices and images from folk belief, folk tales, charms, sayings, and popular Christian mythology. The main actors in these pieces are children, pagan Slavs, supernatural creatures, folk-tale characters, and animate nature. Supernatural figures are the presumed sources of toys that come to life. They are also frequently the players in a game which may revert to the presumed original ritual.

The narrative in most of these pieces is quite minimal: a monk comes and hands out the first budding branches ("**The Little Monk**"); some widows perform the ritual eating and burial of a fertile hen ("**The Three-Brood Hen**"); during the passage of time from St. John's eve to the following dawn, many evil spirits appear and magic events occur ("**St. John Fires**"). The spare narrative is filled out through the workings of analogy between the peasant's syncretic world view and the child's. Some pieces are actually prose poems, lacking any semblance of story, and consisting almost wholly of pure lyricism and description ("**To Natasha,**" "**At the Fox's Ball,**" "**Kalechina-**

Malechina,'' "Indian Summer," "Korochun"). Throughout, the inanimate world is animated and nature is personified. It is the egocentric animistic world of the peasant primitive and of the child in which everything is perceived in terms of human life. There are exceptions to these generalizations, of course, as there always are in Remizov. A recognizable narrative structure turns up in such original stories as **"The Snake Kite"** (**"Zmei"**), **"The Hare Ivanych,"** and **"Kot Kotofeich."** Many of the pieces, both narrative and non-narrative, have an envelope (*kol'tsevoi*) structure: the final lines return to the opening ones. Throughout, Remizov uses a narrator who is best described as naive. In most of the pieces, the naive presentation is not undercut by irony. There are exceptions here, too, of course. The story **"The Snake Kite"** consists of a play-off between the naive and ironic points of view, represented by the grandmother and the child Petka.

One of the most prominent features of the *Sunwise* pieces is their theatricality. It derives in part from the nature of folklore itself. There is a definite dramatic performer-audience relationship in all "live" folklore, from the less obviously dramatic folk tale, to ritual and non-ritual play, and from the folk wedding ceremony to the more obvious folk drama proper and puppet theater. At times Remizov emphasized the dramatic quality of the *Sunwise* pieces by including in his notes specific instructions for reading certain passages aloud.

Sunwise begins in the spring. The pieces gathered together in this section consist primarily of descriptions of children's games. They are structured on an analogy between a child's game and a ritual. The course of the game becomes the basis of the plot. A player in the game, usually the one who is "it," becomes the main character. Indeed, play itself can be seen as a basic paradigm for much of Remizov's art. Play is a voluntary source of joy and amusement, carefully isolated from the rest of life. A game has only intrinsic meaning, proceeds under its own rules or by the power of "make-believe," a kind of free unreality. Remizov seems to be saying here that the "spirit of play is essential to culture," while "games and toys are historically the residues of culture."

In this spring section, an example of a children's game with an origin in Eastern Slavic ritual is **"Kostroma."** Remizov's source is Anichkov. Assuming that the figure of Kostroma symbolized the seed, Anichkov viewed the "burial" of Kostroma during the game as an echo of a magic ritual which guaranteed the future harvest. He saw in this game (under Veselovsky's influence) a vestige of a cult of the dying and reborn god, discussed at length by Frazer in *The Golden Bough.*

The game did retain vestiges of a vernal rite carried out between Trinity Day (fifty days after Easter) and St. Peter's Day (June 29), and therefore Remizov included it in the spring section. By Remizov's time the game had evolved quite a bit from its ritual origin. Usually the game was played by girls only. One of them depicted Kostroma, who would sit or lie in the center of a circle. Kostroma answered a series of questions put to her by the other players about her daily activities. The final questions and answers revolved around her health—she would fall ill and die. Then the other players, singing lamentations, carried her off. Kostroma would get away, and a game of catch ensued.

Whatever the various scholarly interpretations are, for Remizov Kostroma was a symbol of regeneration which comes with the warmth of spring. So he frames his piece with the refrain in rhythmic prose: "Teplyn'-to, teplyn', blagodat' odna!" ["The

warmth, oh the warmth, only abundance!"] Remizov depicts Kostroma as an animal harbinger of spring. This description is a Remizovian invention—perhaps suggested by a child—for Kostroma is never depicted as an animal in game or ritual. With Kostroma's rebirth, spring comes to nature and Remizov describes it. He adds other elements of what he considered the folk world view, e.g., the syncretic mixture of pagan and Christian elements in folk belief. For example, St. George (*Egorii*) appears in **"Kostroma"** because his name day comes in the spring, on April 23. For the Russian peasant, St. George was the protector of cattle. On this day the cattle would be put out in the field to graze for the first time. St. George, like Kostroma, symbolizes the renewal that comes with spring.

Remizov's slight narrative is structured around rhythmic refrains. There is the thematic refrain, already quoted. The two others include the anapestic lines: "Pomerla, Kostroma, pomerla" ["Has died, Kostroma, has died"] and "Ozhila, Kostroma, ozhila" ["Came alive, Kostroma, came alive"], as though, through the use of typographically isolated rhythmic lines, Remizov wanted to emphasize the most important dynamic events of the piece.

In his 1909 article Remizov stated that his first aim in working with folklore was to reconstruct ancient myths, and his second aim was to find an ideal form for folk tales. The 1907 edition of *Sunwise* contains only one example of this second aim, indicating that at this point in his career, the potential for myth-creation interested Remizov more. Remizov's source for this folk tale, **"The Hare Ivanych,"** was oral: he heard the tale in Solvychegodsk. **"The Hare Ivanych"** manifests some of the typical hallmarks of the fairy tale such as retardation through the repetition of motifs. Not only does the repetition of each sister's experience retard the narrative, it also serves to emphasize, by the time the third sister's turn comes, the great obstacles she is going to have to overcome. Here we also have the typical fairy-tale pattern of two attempts and two failures at overcoming an opponent and a third successful try, often by the youngest of three siblings.

Remizov's title is significant: he is not extending his sympathy to the captive sisters, but to their animal helper, the hare. The latter is quite taken with the third sister, and therefore willingly helps her, only to lose her company forever. Through the figure of the hapless hare, Remizov adds some melancholy lyrical moments. As he commonly does in his reworkings of all types of tales, Remizov individualizes his characters by the addition of psychological motivation: the bear is also more taken with the third sister than with the previous two, and is therefore put a little off guard, enabling Masha to escape.

When Remizov expanded *Sunwise* into volume 6 of his *Works,* he added new pieces to the original scheme and grouped them under the heading "Sunwise." He coupled this expanded "Sunwise" with an entirely new section, "To the Deep Blue Sea." Among the new pieces added to the book we find a tendency toward a more traditional narrative structure. This is true of **"The Pilgrimage"** and **"The Little Bear,"** both original stories told from a chid's point of view. It is also true of **"The Fingers,"** based on a South Slavic etiological legend, and **"A Tiny Wrinkle"** (**"Morshchinka"**), a retelling of an animal tale that Remizov heard. A further notable addition which appears only in the 1911 edition of this book is **"Plaint,"** a bride-to-be's wedding lament based entirely on a Zyrian model. It is the only piece in the book not partly based on Slavic materials. It indicates an early interest on Remizov's part not only in non-Slavic, but rather exotic folklore. Remizov placed his **"Plaint,"** a prose poem with an envelope structure, in the autumn section of "Sunwise," and followed it with **"The Three-Brood Hen"** and **"Dark Night"** (**"Noch' temnaia"**), all three pieces touching on marriage.

We find **"The Fingers"** in the winter section of the newly expanded "Sunwise." Remizov could have placed it anywhere in the book since it is not tagged to a specific season. It is entirely possible that he placed it here to ensure that the winter section, like the other three seasons, also contained seven pieces.

Remizov's source, a South Slavic etiological or explanatory legend, was related to the linguist Baudouin de Courtenay by an old man in a short, skeletal form, containing only seven sentences. Baudouin de Courtenay published it in Russian translation. Remizov has amplified this translated text so that his work is three times the length of the model. His amplifications include: (1) the typical fairy-tale opening of "Once upon a time . . ." ("Zhili-byli"); (2) a longer description of the fingers; (3) words of address when the fingers speak to one another; (4) the type of food they eat; (5) the arrival of their mother; (6) a description of the fingers asleep; (7) additional motivation for the fingers' behavior. All this amplification is in keeping with the basic metaphor of the model—the fingers are personified and given a mother. But the created narrator's amplifications and *skaz* style add a humorous tone to the story, as well as ironic distance from the author, that is absent in the source material. The original image of the human hand with its small tattletale finger becomes a universal symbol of human nature—Remizov reminds us that we all have pinkies, that is, all human beings have weaknesses in their character that are likely to cause trouble for them. In the original legend, Remizov saw a partially developed symbol and developed it into a full-scale commentary on what he saw as inherent in human nature.

In going from the oral performance to the written text, Baudouin de Courtenay already had recourse not only to the format used in playwriting, but also parenthetical comments as a substitute for the visual and aural effects of the oral performance. Remizov made further additions which compensate for the loss of the human voice (its intonation, pitch, loudness, accent, etc.), gesture, and mime.

The new section, "To the Deep Blue Sea," has a plot framework—a journey to the sea undertaken by Alalei and Leila—that tenuously connects its various episodes, which, like the pieces in "Sunwise" were written at different times. All the works in "To the Deep Blue Sea" date from a later period than those in the "Sunwise" section: most were written in the years 1907-8. Like the new additions to "Sunwise," this new section tends toward a greater use of narrative. Most of the folkloric material still falls in the area of folk belief.

Alalei tells Leila of **"The Penduline Tit"** (**"Remez—pervaia ptashka"**), about which Remizov learned partly from Potebnia's discussion of a ritual song (*koliadka*) concerning this bird, and partly from the entry in Dal's dialect dictionary. As in many of the pieces in "Sunwise" and "To the Deep Blue Sea," the folkloric materials in this work do not form the basis of a plot dynamics. The plot here is minimal—Alalei and Leila find a place to spend the night. The folkloric material serves thematic purposes: the primitive's and child's apprehension of the world. This view, transmitted by Alalei and Leila, is represented by various folk beliefs about the penduline tit. Leila displays the wide-eyed wonder of the child. Again the repetition of certain phrases or leitmotifs formally holds the piece

together. The opening lines: "A strange forest. And nighttime too," become the closing "It's scary in the forest. Night keeps getting closer, comes nearer now." Leila's line, "The stars are so large," is amplified and repeated by the narrator ("And the stars, the stars are so large").

Also in "To the Deep Blue Sea" is **"The Vampire,"** based on a local belief legend. Remizov's source was a scholarly ethnographic study about the belief in vampires in Russian Galicia. The ethnographer included several local legends about vampires and transcribed them in the local dialect. To create his ideal form in this case (in contrast to **"The Hare Ivanych"** or **"The Fingers"**), Remizov completely transformed the model. He treated the legend as a total fiction: he provided it with an atmospheric winter setting; the ordinary folk of the model become a fairy-tale prince and princess who live in never-never land. Although Remizov follows the plotline of the model very closely, he dramatizes it by the greater use of dialog. He also individualizes his characters by the addition of psychological detail. As in so many of the works in this book, **"The Vampire"** comes to a close by returning to the beginning, here—the winter setting.

In our discussion of **"The Fingers"** we mentioned that it was based on an etiological or explanatory legend. Since the Russians have few such legends and Remizov was quite fond of them—they constitute the folk's explanations for natural phenomena—he had to use models from non-Russian sources. This is true of **"The Fingers."** **"A Dog's Lot"** (**"Sobach'ia dolia"**) which Remizov included in "To the Deep Blue Sea" has Russian and Ukrainian sources from Afanasiev's *Russian Folk Legends*. **"A Dog's Lot"** is an etiological tale that attempts to explain why rye has the form it has today—a long stalk with a tiny ear.

Incorporating this work into "To the Deep Blue Sea" Remizov provided the model with a narrative frame. A certain Belun is playing host to Alalei and Leila. He has a dog named Belka, and it is through the dog motif that the tale is introduced. "'We're eating Belka's lot,' the old man said once, 'a man has a dog's lot.'" There follows the explanation of what he means by this statement. Once there was abundance and rye had only an ear, no stalk. Then abundance came to an end and the appearance of rye changed too. Only because the dogs (or Remizov's Belka) begged the Lord to leave an ear of rye for them do we have this grain at all. So today, man has a dog's lot, i.e., a small ear of rye. No doubt this story, like **"The Fingers,"** appealed to Remizov because of its potential symbolism. It accorded with his view of the human condition, a condition no better than a dog's lot.

Although Remizov provided "To the Deep Blue Sea" with a plot framework, it was a loose one, and allowed for the inclusion of all sorts of works, many of them with little story at all, such as **"The Penduline Tit,"** and others completely storyless. An interesting example of the latter is **"The Begetter"** (**"Rozhanitsa"**). In it Remizov fuses pagan and Christian elements with the theme of Russia. After opening with a reference to the pagan Slavic belief that each star in the sky represents a living human soul, Remizov then addresses the Virgin Mary in prayerful tones. Mary notably is appealed to as "Most Holy Mother" (*Mat' presviataia*). Herein lies her connection to the title **"The Begetter."** The *rozhanitsa*, or more commonly, the plural *rozhanitsy,* were female beings believed by the pagan Russians to preside over birth. At the time of birth, they believed, each person was allotted his destiny. The concepts of birth and destiny, then, were bound up in the *rozhanitsy.*

As the bearer of God, or mother, Mary became identified with the *rozhanitsy* as early as the Kievan period of Russian orthodoxy. It is to this syncretic figure that Remizov's narrator addresses his prayer for Russia. He offers to Mary that same repast that the pagan Russians had offered the *rozhanitsy:* bread, cheese, and meat; not on his own behalf, but on behalf of the Russian land. The gist of the prayer is the request that Russia's bad fortune (*Obida, Nedolia, Gore, Kruchina, Likha*) be changed into good fortune, *Dolia.* Only their desperation, caused by misery, has driven the Russians to plunder and theft, he claims. Their good intentions have always ended badly. This must be their destiny, this lot must have been adjudged to them at the birth of their nation. If only, says the narrator, referring to numerous Russian legends and folk tales about Fate-Fortune (*Sud'ba-dolia*), some one could be found who would rid us of this accursed fate in the manner it is made to vanish in our lore.

Besides bringing in the figure of fate from East Slavic folk tales, Remizov confounds the image of the Mother of God with other folk-tale images—the wise maiden, or the prophetic swan who reads in the book of magic—and with the pagan Slavic cult of Mother Earth.

In "The Begetter" Remizov achieved a rhetorical tone through the use of his favorite device, anaphora, and, as in "Plaint," the use of the imperative mood. What is most striking about "The Begetter," unique in this volume of his *Works,* is the way in which the pagan and Christian elements are readily mixed with the theme of Russia's fate. Often in addressing himself to the question of Russia—its destiny, its national character, its place in world history—Remizov was to do so using syncretic pagan and Christian imagery taken from popular lore.

The book *Leimonarium* . . . forms a companion piece to *Sunwise:* both contain examples mostly of what Remizov understood to be "myth-recreations." If *Sunwise* treats the folk calendar, *Leimonarium* mixes folk etiology with mythology: five explanatory tales on the origin of various natural phenomena and one apocryphal tale, full of folklore, about the crucifixion. Again, as in *Sunwise,* Remizov presents a syncretic pagan and Christian view of the world. Yet all the works in *Leimonarium* have a narrative core. As we noted before, Remizov considered apocrypha to contain remnants of myth, so he would have considered this book too part of his myth reconstruction activity. To create these six stories, Remizov had recourse to various folkloric and bookish materials: etiological legends, spiritual verses (*dukhovnye stikhi*), rituals and ritual songs (*koliadki*), charms, folk beliefs, laments, the folk puppet show (*vertep*), apocrypha, and old Russian literature. The child's presence is not felt in *Leimonarium.* Instead there is a greater contribution from the unofficial, popular version of Christianity.

Formally, both early books display signs of experimentation, though *Sunwise* to a much greater extent. The latter is much more oriented toward oral performance. "On Herodias' Frenzy" in *Leimonarium* stands out precisely because it is more experimental than others in that collection. Like the *Sunwise* pieces, "Herodias" exhibits a marked theatricality. It too is based on folkloric materials, primarily Eastern Slavic and Romanian *koliadki* and the Eastern Slavic folk puppet theater (*vertep*). Its narrative core is the explanation for the natural phenomenon of the whirlwind. But this pagan explanation is surrounded by popular and official Christian interpretations of the subject matter.

A dialog version of the Russian folk puppet (*vertep*) play, *The Death of King Herod,* forms the basis of Remizov's plot. To flesh out this plot Remizov used the same technique of analogy that figured so often in *Sunwise.* He found suggestions for these analogies primarily from Veselovsky's *Inquiries,* but he also made use of folklore from Potebnia, Shchegolev, and Shein that had become associated with the Christian Yuletide celebration. This pagan Slavic folklore revolves around the ancient festivities in honor of the winter solstice and the onset of the new year. One of the old calendar rites reflected in "Herodias" was *koliado-vanie.* Groups of young people would go from house to house singing special songs called *koliadki.* Originally songs to honor and guarantee the welfare of each household, the traditional *koliadki* eventually died out and were replaced by songs glorifying the birth of Christ.

If in other parts of his narrative Remizov has recourse to all sorts of apocryphal materials—primarily Romanian, but also Ukrainian, Belo-russian, Byzantine, German, and Catalonian—the scene at Herod's makes the greatest use of ritualistic pagan practices from all over Europe, but particularly from Byzantium and the three eastern Slavic countries. Remizov found that he could motivate the inclusion of unadulterated pagan elements more readily here than anywhere else. Most of this material comes from Veselovsky. Remizov introduces us to Herod's court with a description of the palace, paraphrasing the Great Russian *koliadka.* The narrator (*vertepnik*) informs us that Herod is celebrating the New Year with a harvest feast (*zhatvennyi pir*), a Byzantine ritual, during which the emperor regaled the public. It was accompanied by a bellicose dance of mummers. This "dance" gives Remizov the opportunity to introduce a series of Russian pagan New Year's practices. These include entertainers and a series of mummers. The mummers dance, invoke the plough, personified by Remizov, and greet the one whose name day it is, *Ovsen',* also personified. These latter details are taken from *koliadki. Ovsen'* can occur as a refrain in these songs. Remizov sees *Ovsen'* as an echo of a divine figure.

If the Russian folk puppet play *The Death of King Herod* shifted the focus of attention in the Christmas legend from the birth of Christ to the story of Herod, then Remizov made one more shift—from Herod's story to that of his daughter, Herodias (Irodiada). Remizov's source for this elaboration was again Veselovsky. From his research Remizov derived the psychological motivation for Herodias' actions: her love for John the Baptist. Remizov has amplified this motivation: it is Herodias, not her father Herod, who demands John's head because John has spurned her love. Remizov devotes some of his best writing to the details of this motivation. The prose here is markedly rhythmical. Herodias dances to an amphibrachic line: "I pliashet neistovo, bystro i besheno—pannastrela" ["And she dances unrepressedly, swiftly and frenetically—Madame arrow"].

In punishment, Herodias is turned into a whirlwind, fated to dance till the end of time. This is the explanatory element of the legend. At this point Remizov picks up another detail reported by Veselovsky: Herodias has a red line around her neck. Even without the notes the symbolism of the red line is suggestive. In other cases, one finds that Remizov's inclusion of details, culled from his research, is perplexing rather than enriching.

"On Herodias' Frenzy" displays features typical of both *Sunwise* and *Leimonarium.* In its theatricality, its unique form, and its use of pagan folkloric elements it resembles the former. But it is closer to the latter cycle in the presence of a storyline, in the explanatory core of the story, and in the use of Christian figures. Remizov seemed fascinated by the popular version of the Christian legend, with its focus on the persecutors of Christianity. Stimulated by his reading of Veselovsky, Remizov included the tragic theme of frustrated love and revenge, subjects he was to return to on other occasions.

There are also signs of formal experimentation in another *Leimonarium* story, "**Mary of Egypt.**" The etiological element here is the explanation for the origin of the moon and stars. A lovely narrative based on Romanian folklore, "**Mary of Egypt**" also has an envelope structure: it begins and ends with the narrator's rhetorical address directed to the reader. Also marking off the opening and closing of the legend is the use of negative parallelisms, a device found frequently in Russian folk poetry: "Ne ot tsvetov beleiut luga. . . ./Ne ot tumana sereiut gory. . . ." ["Not from the flowers do the meadows look white. . . ./Not from the mist do the hills look silver. . . ."]. Remizov has endowed this prose narrative with the envelope structure he used in such *Sunwise* pieces as "**Plaint,**" "**The Little Monk,**" "**The Vampire,**" and "**The Penduline Tit.**"

When Remizov enlarged *Leimonarium* to create volume 7 of his *Works,* published in 1912, he did so by adding more narratives, not based on etiological legends, but on spiritual verses, religious legends, folk sayings and the folk calendar, pre-Petrine church literature, and apocrypha, both Russian and non-Russian. He divided this volume into two parts, "Leimonarium" and "Paralipomenon."

One addition was "**Nick the Saint**" ("**Nikola Ugodnik**"), based on folklore—the folk calendar, folk sayings, and a religious verse (dukhovnyi stikh)—and Nicholas' official saint's life (*zhitie*). St. Nicholas combined two prominent features which Remizov saw as the main reason for his popularity in Russia: his compassion and readiness to help those in need and his ability to perform superhuman miracles. "**Nick the Saint**" was the first of a long series of works that Remizov was to adapt from folkloric sources which concerned St. Nicholas. Remizov felt that St. Nicholas had a special place among the Russians as proven by the numerous folk narratives that he had inspired. So his stories about St. Nicholas often explore questions about Russia itself—its destiny, its past, and its popular heritage. His "**Nick the Saint**" refers to Russia as St. Nicholas' "land."

The first two parts of "**Nick the Saint**" are almost plotless pictures of the saint—first on earth and then in heaven—compiled from official and apocryphal church sources and from Russian folklore, especially from the folk calendar and folk sayings. The third part shows St. Nicholas as an intercessor, this time on behalf of a non-Russian group of seafaring monks. There is more narrative in this part. The source is folkloric, a religious verse. The inclusion of this third part broadens the perspective on St. Nicholas. He is shown not only as the patron saint of Russia, but as an intercessor for non-Russians as well. The piece ends with a reiteration of the opening theme of Nicholas as the "intercessor for the Russian land." Through his cycle of St. Nicholas stories, Remizov explored the Russians' high regard for charity and their hope for justice through miraculous intervention. Remizov's exploration of the popular view of St. Nicholas in sayings, religious songs, and legends was a search for shared values at a time when the social fabric of Russia was being torn asunder (1905-17).

An example of a religious legend (*legenda*) in "Leimonarium" is "**Job and Magdalene**" ("**Iov i Magdalina**"). Although Re-

mizov lists three different sources for his adaptation, the plot, details, and language come entirely from Onchukov's collection of folk narratives. In constructing his "ideal text," Remizov usually did not arrive at a composite, but rather at a version that was a reworking of only one of the texts that he consulted. There are two major themes that run throughout the different versions of this folk legend: the theme of charity toward the poor, and sometimes, toward the physically ugly, and the theme of a just fate. In his version, Remizov underscores the idea of humility present in the folk legend: all the characters who meekly accept their fate receive some form of deliverance.

Four of the six stories in "Paralipomenon" are religious *legendy,* and like "**Job and Magdalene**" deal with moral issues. There are two exceptions: the folk tales "**The Dread Skeleton**" ("**Ligostai strashnyi**") and "**King Solomon**" ("**Tsar' Solomon**"), the last two pieces in volume 7. Remizov offsets the serious theme of death in "**The Dread Skeleton**" with the humorous, occasionally ribald, "**King Solomon.**" This is a typical Remizovian juxtaposition: the theme of human mortality next to a comic presentation of earthly justice—the tragicomedy of existence.

The theme of the folk tale "**The Dread Skeleton**" is man's inability to come to terms with his own death. In general Remizov's changes create a more leisurely literary tale. Some of the changes he made include: the elimination or elucidation of dialect words; the replacement of non-standard morphology and syntax by the standard; the use of an idiosyncratic word order; a prose made more rhythmic through verbal and syntactic repetitions; a more consistent use of alliteration and assonance. Remizov fills in the narrative a great deal; some of this additional verbal material, however, simply makes up for the non-verbal material of a live performance such as intonation, gesture, and mime. By far the greatest "defects" in the folk tale, from a literary viewpoint, are its abrupt transitions. Remizov carefully motivates the transitions and plot sequences. As usual, Remizov individualizes his characters to a greater extent: the hero is endowed with a pious and good nature. But the process of individualization most affects the figure of death. The latter, although repeatedly called fearsome (*strashnyi*) is a carnavalesque figure with chattering teeth and a grimacing face.

"**King Solomon**"—published seven times—must have been one of Remizov's perennial favorites. He thus opens and closes volume 7 with two symbolic figures—St. Nicholas, the figure of divine justice, and King Solomon, of earthly justice. They are figures which inspire hope and a good-humored compassion. In both cases Remizov has taken stock figures from folk literature and elaborated them into personal symbols. But because these figures derive from popular lore, they signify also supra-personal concepts. Through the use of such figures Remizov was able to combine a cluster of ideas and attitudes from the pre-logical past with the modern world.

"Paralipomenon" marks a shift in Remizov's work with folkloric materials. In the first place we find a thematic concern with moral issues. In the second place, they are pure narratives and exemplify Remizov's expressed aim of finding an ideal form for such material. Furthermore, most of this material can be classified as folk legends. And it was the folk legend, more than any other type of folk literature, that was to dominate Remizov's adaptations. He often chose the legend because of its direct revelation of popular views of the world and man's place in it.

All of Remizov's subsequent involvement with folklore was presaged in some form by volumes 6 and 7 of his *Works*. After their publication, Remizov devoted most of his subsequent efforts to the creation of ideal texts, whether narrative or dramatic. In choosing which folk literary works to adapt, Remizov selected his models, for the most part, not on the basis of availability, but on suitability. Thus, since there are few etiological legends to be found in the Russian repertoire, Remizov's fondness for this genre led him to Ukrainian, Romanian, and other sources. The changes we noted between Remizov's adaptations and his models generally fall into two categories: changes necessitated by the shift from the oral to the written medium and consequently a shift in audience, and changes effected because of his own sensibility as a writer.

We have also noted certain tendencies in chronology and in the type of folklore that most interested Remizov. In the two 1907 publications, *Sunwise* and *Leimonarium*, Remizov found the greatest stimulation in what he perceived to be remnants of myth, actually evidences of a syncretic pagan-Christian belief system among the peasantry, which he wove into short prose works, many with no or minimal narrative framework. What held them together was a controlling point of view, a primitivism born of the peasant and of the child. By the time that Remizov expanded these two books for inclusion into his multi-volume *Works*, a shift occurred away from such "myth recreation" to the creation of "ideal forms." The works created with either aim in mind display the marks of experiment in prose through the exploitation of poetic devices: progression through analogy, an abundance of symbolism and imagery—especially personification, repetition of leitmotifs, syntactic parallelism, rhythm, alliteration, and assonance.

The varied means and manner of expressive folklore penetrated into almost everything Remizov wrote. His involvement with folklore formed part of an examination of the Russian cultural heritage in particular, and of the general cultural heritage of twentieth-century man. Whether he was attempting to recreate myth or to render the ideal form of a folk narrative, Remizov modernized the folkloric material, enabling this traditional culture to enter contemporary culture. He must have thought that the expressive lore of the folk could and should speak to us "non-folk," made accessible through intermediaries such as himself. Folklore was a means by which to explore essential truths, not through logical or scientific discourse, but through alogical, analogical, and symbolic means. The products of the folk imagination, less subject to the limitations of scientific and rationalistic thought, could speak to modern man about the tragic tenor of life and its incomprehensibility, but also about the joy of existence which is ours if we give free range to our imagination and look at the world with wide-eyed wonderment and ready humor.

Ultimately the results of these endeavors must be judged on their own merit as literature. They form part of Remizov's contribution to modernist prose. As such they display features of formal experiment, a concern with consciousness and perception, a weakened narrative structure and unity compensated for by poetic means, and, often, a *skaz*-like narrator or multiple points of view, and the measurement of the passage of time by the non-scientific sign-posts of folk and church holidays and the seasonal agricultural cycle. Some of these works stand today as minor literary masterpieces because they integrate vision, structure, and language. Folklore did not so much shape Remizov as a writer, as he shaped folkloric materials to suit his own sensibility. (pp. 98-109)

Charlotte Rosenthal, "Remizov's 'Sunwise' and 'Leimonarium': Folklore in Modernist Prose," in *Russian Literature Triquarterly*, No. 19, 1986, pp. 95-112.

VALERIE TERRELL   (essay date 1986)

[*In the following excerpt, Terrell examines fantastic elements in the autobiography* With Clipped Eyes.]

At first reading, [*Podstrizhennymi glazami (With Clipped Eyes)*] appears to be a poetic autobiography, a variation of Proust's *A la recherche du temps perdu*, firmly anchored in the present and focusing on the past as the author looks back on his life and his career as a writer, weighing successes and failures and affirming his aesthetic credo. The child, the young novice, and the mature artist confront one another in Moscow, Saint Petersburg and Paris along a series of ellipses traced by memory. However, it soon becomes apparent that a current of pure fiction is conspiring against the conventions of the genre. All of Russian literature, German Romanticism, and a vast body of myths, legends and tales furnish the material for innumerable comparisons and metaphors. In the course of evoking his past, the narrator links people he knew with those he encountered in his readings. Insidiously, fictional characters such as Pushkin's Dead Princess ("Mertvaia Tsarevna") and Gogol's Kopeikin invade the memoir. More striking still are the temporal and spatial rifts, going far beyond mere flashbacks, in which the narrator is witness to the fiery execution of Avvakum, the blaze that destroyed the first Printing House in Moscow and the exorcism of Solomoniya. The boundary between the real and the imaginary vanishes. Indeed, *With Clipped Eyes* owes much to the fantastic genre. However, Remizov's fantastic world is not one of stereotypes. It bypasses the outworn repertoire of gothic clichés such as ghosts, werewolves and vampires, and the use of typical motifs such as magic objects remains but a superficial manifestation.

Ever since Boris Eikhenbaum's famous study of Gogol's novella "The Overcoat," it has been generally acknowledged that the role of the narrator largely determines the composition of a literary work. Accordingly, Tzvetan Todorov, defining the fantastic genre in his essay *Introduction à la littérature fantastique*, designates the first person narrative as one of the essential characteristics of the genre. Subtly gaining the reader's confidence, the first person narrator presents supernatural phenomena as part of his experience, thus giving them a semblance of authenticity. Remizov makes use of this device to a great extent. Yet the truly supernatural events, such as the amazing sequences in "The Sleepwalkers" ("Lunatiki"), are surprisingly few and may mislead the reader into overlooking what is more profound and not so readily noticeable. In fact, Remizov's fantastic world emerges almost entirely from the narrative structures themselves.

An outstanding example is to be found in the chapter "The Hungry Abyss" ("Golodnaia Puchina"). The story (fabula) centers on the wedding of Pavel Safronov, the coppersmith first introduced in the chapter "Bedeviled" ("Porchenyi"). A master story-teller himself, Safronov initiated the Remizov children into the world of Apocrypha and took them to the notorious Simonov Monastery, where they watched the exorcism of the possessed. Safronov has a nimbus of mystery and enchantment in the mind of the hero for several reasons: first, he is closely associated with Nikolas, a young painter who introduces the boy to the magic of colors, and second, because he appears at Easter, which in Remizov's world is as much Walpurgisnacht as Orthodox holiday. Safronov's story is enriched and complicated by the fact that he identifies with Saint Alexei, a figure immortalized in folk traditions around the world and in a work by Mikhail Kuzmin, *About Alexei the Man of God (O Aleksee cheloveke Bozhem),* a tragic account of the conflict between duty and conscience. Forced to marry by his family, Saint Alexei must forsake his bewildered bride in order to follow his religious calling. Safronov, seeking to pattern himself on his pious idol, weds the with intention of abandoning his bride and fleeing to a monastery. The wedding takes place and in the last scene of the chapter Safronov relates the story of Saint Alexei to his young wife, who fails to see the similarity and, instead of guessing what is in store for her, begs him to scratch her back. If this were all, ''The Hungry Abyss'' would be just an amusing parody, but Remizov takes it beyond caricature. While remaining within the context of the autobiography, the author enlarges the scope of the plot (sujet) to truly fantastic proportions by means of a series of carefully timed narrative devices.

The first hint of something diabolical comes in the statement that the young couple met at the eerie Simonov Monastery, but it is promptly dispelled by extensive literary commentary, only to be subtly reiterated as the narrator compares the church where the ceremony is to be held to the illustrious haunted chapel in Gogol's *Vii.* This a typical example of Remizov's literary sleight-of-hand. Briefly summarizing Gogol's novella, he evokes the seminary student, Foma Brut, and the beautiful Ukrainian Panna, turned witch, introduced as it is, the comparison between Gogol's pair and Remizov's engaged couple is perhaps not immediately evident, but the association is left in the mind of the reader and serves as the foundation for the extraordinary literary edifice that is to take shape.

The devilish undercurrent surfaces in the description of the snow-storm that engulfed Moscow on the day of the wedding. Again it is preceded by a reference to the world of literature, this time to Pushkin, Tolstoi, and Blok and their portrayals of the unleashed natural fury of the Russian *metel'.* The narrator states that the Russian blizzard is Gogolian and, as the plot progresses, the allusions to *Vii* form a leitmotif.

Another dimension appears as the scene shifts from the snow-covered church to the house where the reception is to take place. The point of view is no longer that of the ''writer'' (not necessarily Remizov) but that of the boy, who is slowly filled with foreboding, fearing that the dreadful night will never end. His anxiety mounts as he learns that the bride is an orphan and observes the woebegone face of her aunt and guardian. Then the two points of view intersect. The narrator evokes ''A Scandalous Story'' (''Skvernyi anekdot''). As with all the narrator's ''asides'' this one is far from haphazard. It is intended to call forth Dostoevsky's grotesque novella about a nightmarish wedding party in which the uninvited guest starts by planting his foot squarely in a dessert set on the stoop to cool and ends by humiliating himself and everyone present. Knowing as we do from the previous chapter that Safronov disappeared shortly after the nuptials, this allusion serves as a danger signal, foreshadowing the ruined marriage and the imminence of nightmare.

The overlapping points of view blend description and references to the poetry of Baudelaire and Nekrasov, and Gogol's *Vii,* this time to evoke the hideous monster itself and its imperious command ''Raise my eyelids!'' Here the association is left deliberately vague for the purposes of suspense. The

point of view again shifts from the writer to the child, who is overwhelmed by the primal chaos of the universe as he listens to the howling gale. Like a refrain, nagging phrases cross his mind again and again: ''Nothing ever ends,'' ''A night without dawn.''

Suddenly the nightmare begins to unfold. The sole musician, an accordion player, leaves in a huff and a chanting rises to accompany the dancers. The rhythmic beat of the chant, the pounding feet, the shrieking wind and the heat take effect, and suddenly the narrator slips into a world between dream and reality by means of the ambiguous phrase: ''Either I dozed off or I was absorbed in listening. . . .''

The nightmare is all the more horrible because it is so realistic, like a haunting memory: ''It was as if I had once been she, Solomoniya.'' The narrator is at once participant and witness, reliving the rite of exorcism with this ethereal girl who was married at fourteen, roughly used by her shepherd husband and driven by horror to madness. Her inhuman screams plunge the boy still further into his dreamlike trance. He hears the voice of another woman, a gypsy, whose song is full of life's ''insouciant, blind, absent-minded sweetness,'' but also of its ''insidious venom, unexpressed guilt, and hidden sin.'' The third panel of this triptych is composed of a stone stairway rising ever higher to an open window. On the sill there is a pot full of a thick and bitter lunar substance. Outside the window appears a sparkling white star.

These visions, seemingly irrelevant to the plot, are in fact what gives emotional depth to the story. The symbolism of the third sequence can only be understood by relating it to the preceding ones and to Remizov's work in general. Solomoniya is conjured by association with the Simonov Monastery and the possessed. The gypsy song is in keeping with the raging elements and the ill-omened love of the young couple. In the last vision, the moon appears in the form of a lunar-green substance. Throughout the book, the moon is a potent magical force, causing all manner of unusual events and gradually becoming an ambiguous female character who exerts a hypnotic fascination over the hero. As for the star, it is closely linked to the divine and merciful figure of Mary, the Mother of God, in Remizov's *Zvezda Nadzvezdnaia. Stella Maria Maris.* The three sequences taken together constitute a kaleidoscopic view of womanhood, inspiring ambivalent feelings of fear, pity and reverence. More than just an anecdote, the story of Safronov's wedding confronts the boy with the many facets of love.

At this point the door of the house sweeps open and the narrative returns to the wedding party and Safronov's dilemma: how to bring off his ''escape.'' The narrator's point of view fuses with that of Safronov who is also pursued by inhuman voices from Simonov Monastery and *Vii.* As the chapter comes to an end, Safronov, in his fear and indecision, is unable to distinguish between his hallucinations and his bride. The chimes of a bell give way to the screeches of the possessed and the cries of the wind.

In this typically dense chapter, a number of situations develop within the autobiographical framework.

1. The funeral ceremony in *Vii*
2. The wedding party in ''A Scandalous Story''
3. The tragedy of Solomoniya
4. The marriage of Saint Alexei
5. The wedding of Pavel Safronov

There is something disturbingly similar about these apparently unrelated events and when their salient elements are juxtaposed an unexpected coherence comes to light: each one has three main characters, a *man*, a *woman*, and a *catalyst*, whose intrusion determines the *outcome*. . . . As for the outcome, it is death in *Solomoniya* and *Vii*, scandal and ruined lives in "A Scandalous Story," *Alexei the Man of God* and "The Hungry Abyss," where Safronov's disappearance confirms the worst fears of the bride's guardian. The common factor in all five cases is the irrevocable estrangement of the man and woman.

In effect, the plot incorporates five superimposed quadrilaterals. Each of the characters and the outcome have five different levels where autobiography, fiction and dream intertwine. Safronov, by association, takes on all the attributes of the characters projected on him: he is at once the devout and imaginative coppersmith, the mystic, the poor seminarist who falls prey to the witch, the downtrodden civil servant at the mercy of his superiors and in-laws, and, interestingly enough, the brutish shepherd whose lack of sensitivity brings on his wife's madness. The same may be said of the female character. She is the penniless orphan who weds Safronov, the devout Mastridiya, the dangerous enchantress of *Vii*, the capricious shrew Mlekopitayeva and the tormented Solomoniya. The union of the two is rendered impossible by all the forces of the universe, from the divine to the diabolical.

The tension created by the attraction and repulsion of these two poles is only to be resolved in the final passage of "Snow White" ("Belosnezhka"). In this chapter, the hero, now a young man, glimpses and falls in love with a pale, dowerless girl, whom he calls "Snow White." Although they never become acquainted, he is unable to forget her. Then unexpectedly he meets Iroida, who is engaged to one of his friends. She so resembles "Snow White" that in his mind the two become one. He secretly longs to take her away from her dull surroundings. Amid discussions of Russia's destiny, Pushkin and Sar Péladan mysteriously appear in Moscow. These two unlikely rivals embody two trends in Russian letters: Classicism and Decadence. As the chapter comes to an end, the two are mocked and humiliated. In the final sequence, half dream and half reality, the hero lures "Snow White" away and she responds to his love for her by revealing a precious secret.

Whereas in "The Hungry Abyss" the dynamic is due to a conflict between the godly and the demoniacal, in "Snow White" there are three parameters: the world of fairy tale versus reality, a controversy over political philosophy and the opposition of literary schools. In both chapters Remizov makes use of the same narrative techniques. Autobiographical anecdotes form the basis of the plot and passages of literary criticism serve as a springboard for fantastic digressions. The diverse narrative planes are connected by allusions to "A Scandalous Story" and two poems by Pushkin, "The Fiancé" ("Zhenikh") and "The Dead Princess." From the world of folklore comes the motif of the unmasked imposter. Just as in "The Hungry Abyss" dreams interrupt and echo the plot.

In "The Hungry Abyss," the supernatural element is limited to the telepathic communication between the narrator, Safronov, and the possessed. In "Snow White," identities are jumbled, ordinary people are transformed into famous figures from literature and history or into animals. Yet in contrast to classics of the fantastic genre, the intrusion of supernatural forces takes place only in the realm of recollection, dream and delirium. Clearly, Remizov's fantastic world cannot be defined in traditional terms. Reality and illusion are not at odds; rather they are interwoven in the fusion of memoir and fiction. As a craftsman, Remizov draws on an assortment of literary devices borrowed from his precursors, Gogol, Dostoevsky, and E.T.A. Hoffmann.

Gogol's influence is felt in the use of the yarn and pathetic declamation. The technique of slanting the narrative through a gullible raconteur goes back to Gogol's *Evenings on a Farm near Dikanka* (*Vechera na khutore bliz Dikanki*) and his *Petersburg Stories*. It is especially memorable in "The Overcoat," where it is unclear whether something truly supernatural takes place or whether it is merely the narrator's penchant for hyperbole that conjures visions of phantoms. Dostoevsky employs the same legerdemain in *The Demons (Besy)* and Remizov makes use of it in several chapters of *With Clipped Eyes,* including "Nikolas," "The Dwarf Monk" ("Karlik Monashek") and "Poor Yorick" ("Bednyi Iorik"), where the comings and goings of the characters take on an uncanny air owing to the neighbors' speculations and the narrator's credulity. In a truly remarkable passage of the "The Cold Corner" ("Kholodnyi Ugol"), the popular imagination transforms the governor of Moscow, Prince Dolgoruky, into a mechanical man with detachable parts. Remizov is able to don the proper mask thanks to the nature of the narrator, who reverts to childish innocence at will. The reader, confronted with heresay and recurrent phrases such as "it seemed to me," loses track of reality.

As for the pathetic declamatory style, in *With Clipped Eyes* it expresses a deep undercurrent of sorrow and anxiety. At its lightest it transforms a potentially burlesque scene into black humor, as in "Poor Yorick" where the narrator repeats Hamlet's famous soliloquy to lament the clown's improbable and unnecessary suicide. At its bitterest, this style calls to mind the desperate rage of Ivan Karamazov, especially in the passages devoted to the death of Yegorka, the little boy crushed by the flywheel at the Naidyonov factory. Here the narrator is no longer an actor; instead he expresses the deeper sentiments of the author, whose fears and misgivings provide the dark dimension so essential to the fantastic genre.

Like Hoffmann in *Kreisleriana* and *Fantasies in the Manner of Jacques Callot,* Remizov adopts the essayist's tone to reflect upon art and artists, meanwhile cunningly returning to the narrative, thereby creating mysterious links between historical figures, famous characters from literature, and his own inventions. In the chapter "A Happy Day" ("Schastlivyi Den'"), Zakhary, the school doorkeeper, accompanies the Remizov children to a funeral. The narrator compares him to the repugnant Murlyka, a character from Anton Pogorelsky's novella *The Poppyseed-Cake Seller from Lafertovo (Lafertovskaia makovnitsa).* As the two characters gradually overlap, the autobiographical narrative veers off into pure fiction.

Just as changes of tone and style are a fundamental part of Remizov's fantastic world, so is the multidimensional effect obtained by the frequent departures into the irrational. Unlike Gogol and Dostoyevsky, Remizov was neither prey to his obsessions nor to the "grand mal," yet he was fascinated by the separate reality vouchsafed to the mad and the ill. It is perhaps for this reason that he felt such a special kinship with Hoffmann, for whom literature was above all a diversion, a means of escaping the banalities of everyday existence. The hero of *With Clipped Eyes* occupies a privileged position, slipping easily into the world of the afflicted and the pariahs, for whom the author invariably shows special compassion. In the chapters "Colors" ("Kraski"), "White Fire" ("Belyi Ogon'"), "A

Happy Day'' and ''The Herb Fufyrka'' (''Travka-Fufyrka''), the child experiments with colors, literature, alcohol and a mysterious herbal concoction, all means of entering twilight spheres open only to those endowed with his empathy and imagination. Above all, the boy's ''clipped eyes,'' so-called because they have been shorn of their protective lashes, give him insight into the world around him. In an essay devoted to the works of Dostoevsky, Remizov explains the significance of this image:

> Normal reality no longer exists, all that remains are rags and tatters. And this exposed reality, if we look at it with our everyday eyes, is incredible, improbable, difficult to distinguish from a dream. But, and this is the oddest thing, it turns out that the more improbable reality becomes, the more it is ''for real''.... It is the reality of ecstasy, the reality of epilepsy, the reality of religious trances, and of the possessed. And it is quite possible, I feel it to be so, that this unfathomable reality is the source of all life.

The hero's singular way of looking at his surroundings allows him to partake of this fantastic reality.

Like Gogol and Dostoevsky, Remizov uses dream sequences in the narrative as a means of erasing the boundary between the real and the imaginary. Nightmare is ever present. An abrupt change of point of view alone can signal the onset of a dream as in ''The Incendiary'' (''Podzhigatel''') and ''White Fire.'' At times the passage from reality to dream is imperceptible, suggested by the appearance of the moon, as in ''Knots and Twists'' (''Uzly i zakruty''), ''The Dwarf Monk,'' ''The Sleepwalkers'' and ''Poor Yorick.'' The moonlight, bringing silence and stillness, creates an eerie melancholy that leads one to suspect illusion.

However, Remizov's use of dreams varies greatly from that of Gogol and Dostoevsky, in whose works the dreamer's point of view remains constant. In *With Clipped Eyes,* dream and reality interpenetrate. The narrator is both story-teller and hero and has the disconcerting ability to ''become'' the other characters as well. Different points of view overlap, permitting flashbacks and telepathic phenomena that span centuries. In these passages, the narrator seems to be reincarnated as the scribe (''The Incendiary''), the martyr Fyodor Stratilatov (''White Fire'') and Solomoniya (''The Hungry Abyss''). The characters, too, undergo sudden transformations or have several identities at once. Those characters that issue from the autobiographical substrata are reduced to a few outstanding traits and become polyvalent, fitting into narrative patterns suggested by their functions. Like archetypes, they have no psychological depth and may be superimposed on characters from other works. As in ''The Hungry Abyss'' and ''Snow White,'' allusions crystallize around the autobiographical anecdotes; one situation comes to contain a multitude of others. To some extent, Remizov's views are reminiscent of Jung's, in that both consider the dream as a subjective expression of the collective unconscious, whose archetypes underlie world mythology. According to Jung, dream images are symbols of inner aspects of the dreamer himself: ''The dream is the theater where the dreamer is at once scene, actor, prompter, stage manager, author, audience and critic.''

The dream sequences in *With Clipped Eyes* are baffling in their highly surreal quality. Their relation to the narrative is obscure because they add a poetic dimension rather than information vital to the plot. In ''The Hungry Abyss,'' as in Gogol's ''The Portrait,'' the dreamer ''awakes'' from one dream into yet another, so that it is impossible to disentangle dream and reality. However, in ''The Portrait'' the diabolical presence is confirmed and clarified in the denouement, whereas the forces at work in the destiny of Pavel Safronov are merely intimated. This ambiguity is precisely what gives a fantastic dimension to *With Clipped Eyes.* According to Todorov, uncertainty is the key to differentiating the fantastic genre from the related genres of the *marvelous* and the *strange.* The *marvelous* includes the world of fairy tale, legend and myth, where the supernatural is the rule rather than the exception. The *strange* includes those works in which the fantastic reigns until the end when the illusion of supernatural events is dispelled by a rational explanation. The true fantastic genre, however, is a labyrinth where reality and illusion are indistinguishable.

Perhaps Remizov's most original device is his distinctive use of the double narrator. In effect, he is two characters in one: the wide-eyed boy and the wizened old man. The prelogical perceptions of the one color the mature reflections of the other, allowing changes of style and point of view as well as numerous anachronisms as the two contemplate one another across an expanse of some fifty years. Thus *With Clipped Eyes* is a veritable anamorphosis, a double perspective where memory acts as the distorting mirror, producing one optical illusion after another. It is indeed a curious juxtaposition of structures, that of the autobiography, in which the first person narrator and the hero are logically one, and that of myth, legend and folktale, in which the narrator and hero are necessarily distinct. This double perspective corresponds to a twofold quest; first, that of the child seeking his way in an occult and hostile world, and second, that of the writer, the aesthete whose goal is to experience the unique perceptions of the child. By recreating his childhood, the author is able to retrace the genesis of his own artistic temperament and the development of his aesthetic views. There is thus a double movement in time.

It has been said that the prerevolutionary fantastic literature of Russia sprang from a foreboding of the Apolcalypse. Remizov's fantastic world then would appear to mirror a world already shattered by catastrophe. The social and patriotic preoccupations that have motivated Russian writers from Pushkin to Maximov are overshadowed in Remizov's work by those of a very personal and intimate nature. The author of *With Clipped Eyes* is not so much concerned with the destiny of his country as with his own.

Remizov's fantastic world is one of form as well as content, sparked by the collision of memoir, essay, folktale, romantic novella and surrealistic free-association. The resulting plot is disjointed and multileveled, and the narrative structures themselves form the labyrinth. The narrator's role is more complex than just facilitating identification between himself and the reader. Instead he takes the reader on a journey through dimensions of time and literature.

Firmly rooted in the Russian tradition of Gogol and Dostoevsky, Remizov's fantastic world is comparable to that which is found in the works of his contemporaries Zamyatin (''About the Most Important Thing,'' ''O Samom Glavnom'') and Bulgakov (*The Master and Margarita),* where the fantastic elements are also the result of intertwining narrative planes.

Eminently modern, *With Clipped Eyes* is essentially an experiment with modes of fiction and as such can be likened to the writings of Borges *(Ficciones)* and Barth *(Lost in the Fun-house)*. (pp. 228-36)

> Valerie Terrell, "Fantastic Elements in the Narrative Structure of 'With Clipped Eyes'," in Russian Literature Triquarterly, No. 19, 1986, pp. 227-37.

ADDITIONAL BIBLIOGRAPHY

Bailey, Jo Ann. "Patterns of Ambiguity in the Function of A. M. Remizov." *Proceedings of the Pacific Northwest Council on Foreign Languages* XXVII, Pt. 1 (April 22-24, 1976): 146-9.
  Analyzes three aspects of Remizov's pre-Revolutionary fiction: language, plot and characterizations, and philosophical viewpoint.

Carden, Patricia. "Ornamentalism and Modernism." In *Russian Modernism: Culture and the Avante-Garde, 1900-1930*, edited by George Gibian and H. W. Tjalsma, pp. 49-64. Ithaca, N. Y.: Cornell University Press, 1976.
  Proposes that the Ornamentalist style used by Remizov, Andrey Bely, Velimir Khlebnikov, and other Russian writers of the pre-Revolutionary era was a direct parallel to the Modernist movement in the West.

Cournos, John. Foreword to *The Clock*, by Alexey Remizov, translated by John Cournos, pp. vii-x. London: Chatto and Windus, 1924.
  Impressions of Remizov and his works.

Hackel, Sergei. "Three Catalysts: Remizov." In his *The Poet and the Revolution*, pp. 171-77. Oxford, England: Oxford at the Clarendon Press, 1975.
  Examines Remizov's influence on the imagery and structure of Aleksandr Blok's poetry.

Holthusen, Johannes. "Aleksei Remizov." In his *Twentieth Century Russian Literature: A Critical Study*, pp. 59-61. New York: Ungar Publishing Co., 1972.
  Brief overview of Remizov's life and works.

Jackson, Robert Louis. "A. M. Remizov's 'Sisters in the Cross'." In his *Dostoevsky's Underground Man in Russian Literature*, pp. 117-19. The Hague: Mouton and Co., 1958.
  Relates themes in Remizov's novel to their origins in Dostoevski's seminal work *Notes from the Underground*.

Mirsky, D. S. Introduction to *Tales of the Wilderness*, by Boris Pilnyak, pp. vii-xxxi. 1925. Reprint. Freeport, N. Y.: Books for Libraries Press, 1971.
  Discusses Remizov in a survey of Russian fiction from 1904 to 1923. Mirsky considers Remizov's originality and importance to lie in his idiomatic prose style and grotesque yet sympathetic portraits of humanity.

Pyman, Avril. "Aleksei Mikhailovich Remizov and Nikolay Efremovich Andreyev." In *Poetry, Prose, and Public Opinion: Aspects of Russia, 1850-1970*, edited by William Harrison and Avril Pyman, pp. 299-320. Letchworth, England: Avebury Publishing Co., 1984.
  Reprints, with commentary, some letters exchanged by Remizov and Andreyev, a scholar specializing in Russian culture.

————. "Revolution and the Old Gods." In her *The Life of Aleksandr Blok: Vol. I, The Distant Thunder, 1880-1908*, pp. 196-99. Oxford, England: Oxford University Press, 1979.
  Mentions Remizov and his literary circle in St. Petersburg.

Rannit, Aleksis. "Remizov, a Mannerist Drama." *New Directions in Prose and Poetry* 38 (1979): 47-51.
  Introductory notes to ten drawings by Remizov, reproduced on pages 52-61. Rannit maintains that "Remizov's intention" in his art "is *comic*—he is a nonsentimental Cyrano de Bergerac, staging a parody of oratory, his joke lying precisely in the contrast between the serious, or even sacred, nature of the subject and its conversion into the ludicrous."

Reavey, George. Introduction to *On a Field Azure*, by Alexey Remizov, translated by Beatrice Scott, pp. 1-6. Westport, Conn.: Greenwood Press, 1946.
  Short summary of Remizov's career.

Russian Literature Triquarterly 19 (1986): 65-312, 405-10.
  Contains biographical and critical essays on Remizov by twelve critics, including Natalya Reznikova ("Reminiscences: Alexei Remizov in Paris"), John E. Bowlt ("Colors and Words: The Visual Art of Alexei Remizov"), and Sona Aronian ("The Hidden Determinant: Three Novels of Remizov").

Shane, Alex M. "Remizov's *Prud*: From Symbolism to Neo-Realism." *California Slavic Studies* VI (1971): 71-82.
  Examines how changes Remizov made in the second published version of *Prud* reoriented the novel's style from Symbolism to Neo-Realism.

Shane, Alex M. "An Introduction to Alexei Remizov." In *The Bitter Air of Exile: Russian Writers in the West, 1922-1972*, edited by Simon Karlinksy and Alfred Appel, Jr., pp. 10-16. Berkeley: University of California Press, 1973.
  Summarizes Remizov's career and contributions to Russian literature.

Slobin, Greta Nachtailer. "The Ethos of Performance in Remizov." *Canadian-American Slavic Studies* 19, No. 4 (Winter 1985): 412-25.
  Observes ways in which Remizov transformed his life and literary career into a type of theatrical performance.

West, J. D. Introduction to *The Fifth Pestilence*, by A. M. Remizov. 1912. Reprint. Lechtworth, England: Bradda Books, 1970, 99 p.
  Demonstrates how *The Fifth Pestilence* shows many of the characteristics of Remizov's somewhat paradoxical literary personality.

Jóhann Sigurjónsson

1880-1919

Icelandic dramatist and poet.

Sigurjónsson is recognized as one of the leading figures of modern Icelandic drama and a significant contributor to the early twentieth-century renaissance in Icelandic literature. In *Eyvind of the Hills* and other works, he drew subjects and characters from national folk literature to present neoromantic dramas endowed with modern psychological and philosophical insights.

Born into a wealthy family in Laxamýri in northern Iceland, Sigurjónsson was educated in Reykjavik before moving to Copehagen in 1899 to attend university. There he became increasingly interested in literature, especially in drama, which was flourishing in Denmark at the time. An honor student in veterinary medicine, Sigurjónsson soon abandoned his studies to pursue a career as a dramatist, composing his earliest works in Danish in order to reach a wider audience than his native language would afford. Recalling his early struggle for recognition, Sigurjónsson later wrote: "To begin with, I had to write in a language not my own. And then, what knowledge I had of human nature was limited to a most incomplete knowledge of myself and of a few college chums of my own age." His initial success was made possible when Norwegian dramatist Bjørnstjerne Bjørnson recommended his work to a prominent publisher in Copehagen, who issued Sigurjónsson's first drama, *Dr. Rung,* in 1905. While *Dr. Rung* and his next work, *The Hraun Farm,* received only moderate praise, critics recognize in them the developing dramatic and lyric skill that characterizes such later works as *Eyvind of the Hills* and *The Wish.* He subsequently wrote alternate Danish and Icelandic versions of each of his works, often substantially altering the plotline or ending in the second version. He produced several dramas ranging from grim tragedy to romantic idylls before his death from tuberculosis in 1919.

Sigurjónsson's dramas are often based on the romantic legends of Icelandic folklore, using traditional characters and motifs to examine modern themes. *Eyvind of the Hills,* for example, is patterned after the story of a legendary eighteenth-century outlaw and his wife. In Sigurjónsson's drama, the pair are pursued into exile in a mountainous region of Iceland where their love is tested by physical and psychological hardships, including isolation from society and starvation. Translated into numerous languages, produced in several countries, and filmed by Swedish director Victor Sjöström, *Eyvind of the Hills* is Sigurjónsson's best known work. In *The Wish,* based on a tale collected by Jón Arnason in *Icelandic Folktales and Fairystories* (1864-74), Sigurjónsson updated the tale of a young man who employs magic in an attempt to murder his pregnant lover. Recognized as an outstanding lyric drama and his most accomplished work, *The Wish* also exemplifies the underlying theme of all Sigurjónsson's writings. As Einar Haugen has explained, Sigurjónsson's dramas present "the ambitious man's challenge to the laws of the universe, a basically Nietzschean and Dostoievskian theme. Each of his heroes is endowed with a will to exceed his grasp, and this becomes his tragic downfall."

Although several English translations of Sigurjónsson's plays are available, his international reputation is generally limited to scholars of Scandinavian literature. His importance within his own national literature, however, remains great: he was instrumental in the growth of professional drama in Iceland and an inspiration to generations of writers who followed.

*PRINCIPAL WORKS

Dr. Rung (drama) [first publication] 1905
Bóndinn á Hrauni (drama) [first publication] 1908;
    published in Danish as *Gaarden Hraun,* 1912
    [*The Hraun Farm* published in *Modern Icelandic Plays,*
    1916]
Bjoerg-Ejvind og hans hustru (drama) 1911; published in
    Icelandic as *Fjalla-Eyvindur,* 1912
    [*Eyvind of the Hills* published in *Modern Icelandic Plays,*
    1916; also published as *Eyvindur of the Mountains,*
    1961]
Ønsket (drama) 1915; published in Icelandic as *Galdra-*
    Loftur, 1915
    [*Loftur,* 1939; also published as *Loft's Wish* in journal
    Poet Lore, 1940; also published as *The Wish* in *Fire*
    and Ice, 1967]
**Modern Icelandic Plays* (dramas) 1916
Løgneren (drama) [first publication] 1917; published in
    Icelandic as *Lygarinn,* 1939
Smaadigte (poetry) 1920
Rit. 2 vols. (dramas, poetry, essays, and letters) 1941-42

*With the exception of *Bóndinn á Hrauni* and *Rit,* the titles listed here are Danish.

**This work contains English translations of *Gaarden Hraun* and *Bjoerg-Ejvind og hans hustru.*

HENRY GODDARD LEACH (essay date 1916)

[*An American critic and autobiographer, Leach was an authority on Scandinavian culture. In the following excerpt, he discusses Sigurjónsson's major dramas.*]

Sigurjónsson's first drama, **Dr. Rung,** was written in Danish and published in 1905. This tragedy presents a young Copenhagen physician, Harold Rung, who is endeavoring to find a specific against tuberculosis. In order to test the effect of his serum, he decides to inoculate himself with the disease, and the pleading of Vilda, who loves him, fails to shake him from his purpose. The remedy proves a failure; the young scientist goes mad, giving Vilda poisoned grapes.

The Hraun Farm was published in Icelandic in 1908 (**Bóndinn á Hrauni**), and in Danish in 1912 (**Gaarden Hraun**). In rewriting the play for the Copenhagen stage, Sigurjónsson gave it a happy ending, thus changing a tragedy into a pleasant dramatic idyl of contemporary country life in Iceland. It is the familiar Scandinavian theme of the struggle of human love with love of the homestead. An old farmer, Sveinungi, is a veritable patriarch living at the edge of the "hraun," the lava-field. His only daughter, Ljot, he has destined for a sturdy neighbor's son, who will keep up the estate. But the girl falls in love with a young geologist and arouses her father's wrath, until the play ends with a scene in which Sveinungi is won over by Jorunn, his persuasive wife. The action is interrupted by an earthquake. The dialogue is well maintained and rises to heights of lyrical splendor. In point of dramatic effectiveness, *The Hraun Farm* may be regarded as only a preliminary study compared to the next play, but its picture of pastoral Iceland makes it a fitting companion-piece to the greater drama in the present volume.

All other work of Sigurjónsson and the younger Icelandic dramatists pales beside *Eyvind of the Hills,* written in Danish and published in 1911. The high sky of dramatic vision, the simple nobility of the characters portrayed, and the poetry of exalted passion raise above the ordinary in this stern tragedy of natural lives in the wilderness. Eyvind is a man of heroic mould, who was forced by circumstances and hunger to the state of a common thief. When outlawed, he fled to the mountains. Seeking human companionship, he now descends into a valley where his identity is unknown and takes service with Halla, a rich young widow. She learns of his disguise only to fall in love with his real character. Persecuted by her brother-in-law, who wishes to marry her, and possessed by a great love, she insists on sharing the outlaw's lot and escapes with him to his old haunt in the mountains. Here they have two children, but she is obliged to sacrifice them both in turn, and to flee ever farther away. The last act finds the outlaw and his wife facing each other in a lonely hut, in the midst of a snowstorm which has shut off every avenue of sustenance. Although the beautiful reality of love is there, they are tormented by hunger and utter need into doubts and mutual reproaches, and at last seek death in the snow.

According to the historical facts upon which the story is based, a stray horse found its way to the hut of the starving couple, and so their lives were saved. Sigurjónsson used this ending when he rewrote the last scenes of the fourth act for Fru Dybvad, who played the part of Halla in Copenhagen, concluding with Halla's exclamation: "So there is then a God!" With *Eyvind,* as with *The Hraun Farm,* we can thus take our choice of two endings.

The Wish (*Önsket*), Sigurjónsson's latest play, was published in 1915. Gloomy and terrible, but strong and restrained, it is built on a theme of seduction, remorse, and forgiveness in death, woven about the legendary figure of Galdra-Loftur, who lived in Iceland at the beginning of the eighteenth century. It ends with an intensely dramatic scene in the old cathedral church at Hólar.

In addition to these four plays, Sigurjónsson has also written some beautiful verse. (pp. ix-xi)

Georg Brandes, the veteran Danish critic, though not given to over optimism, has recognized Sigurjónsson's distinction, and the Icelander is acclaimed by the public who best know Ibsen and Strindberg, in Copenhagen, Stockholm, and Christiania. *Eyvind* has been successful also on the German stage. "Poetic talent of high order," says Brandes, "manifests itself in this new drama, with its seriousness, rugged force, and strong feeling. Few leading characters, but these with a most intense inner life; courage to confront the actual, and exceptional skill to depict it; material fully mastered and a corresponding confident

style!" And the French critic, Leon Pineau, concludes a long account of Sigurjónsson's production with the following estimate of *Eyvind of the Hills:* "In this drama there is no haze of fantasy, no bold and startling thesis, not even a new theory of art—nothing but poetry; not the poetry of charming and fallacious words, not that of lulling rhythm, nor of dazzling imagery which causes forgetfulness, but the sublimely powerful poetry which creates being of flesh and blood like ourselves—to whom Jóhann Sigurjónsson has given of his own soul." (pp. xi-xii)

Henry Goddard Leach, in an introduction to Modern Icelandic Plays: Eyvind of the Hills, The Hraun Farm *by Jóhann Sigurjónsson, translated by Henninge Krohn Schanche, 1916. Reprint by The American-Scandinavian Foundation, 1929, pp. vii-xii.*

HANNA ASTRUP LARSEN   (essay date 1916)

[*In the following excerpt from a review of the translation* Modern Icelandic Plays, *the critic focuses on* Eyvind of the Hills.]

Finished dramatic art is the most surprising feature of the *Modern Icelandic Plays* by Jóhann Sigurjónsson. . . . Rugged strength we naturally expect from the author's Norse ancestry and the environment of his childhood in Iceland. Primitive passion we look for in the land where "volcanoes burn under the snow," to use his own words. Visions and dreams might well spring to life on the lonely farm where mountains spurred on the imagination while hemming it in. But the fusion of all these into an organic drama like *Eyvind of the Hills,* where every word falls into its place like a hewn stone, while windows are opened on what seem illimitable vistas, this is an art that is almost startling when we remember that Iceland does not even possess a stage except for an amateur dramatic society. Marvelous, too, is the psychological insight shown by this young writer, who says of himself that when he began to write his knowledge of human nature "was limited to a most incomplete knowledge of myself and a few college chums of my own age." Early familiarity with the sagas may in part account for his style, but as we penetrate more deeply into his work we can only say that he is one of the very few whose genius seems to drink from the eternal fountains without being influenced by their outward condition.

The play opens with a picture of life on the farm of the rich young widow, Halla. The time is the eighteenth century, but we may surmise that customs have not altered much with the changing generations. It is a homely, pleasant life, with rude comforts, with a democratic relation between mistress and servants, and a hearty hospitality which does not scan too closely the record of the stranger. The people feed their minds on the old sagas, and we find echoes of them in such sententious bits as these: "Distance makes mountains blue and mortals great," or: "You live and fill your place. That is enough to make enemies." Halla's childhood dreams have been fired by the story of Grettir, the outlaw, whose fate she thought it would have been glorious to share. As yet her days flow as peacefully as a river in a sunny plain. Her warmth of heart spends itself in little daily kindnesses. Her instinct for revolt has only colored her dreams, but the element of disturbance is there in the person of her servant, Kari, whom she has put in a trusted position, in spite of the fact that no one knows his origin. Kari's strength, his fleetness of foot, and his love of the wilds somehow mark him out from the others. "I have lived where I could not touch the roof over my head with my clenched fists, and I have lived where my eyes could not reach it.'' These words suggest that Kari has a past, and what it is we learn through the wiles of Halla's brother-in-law and suitor, Björn, who finds out that Kari's real name is Eyvind, that he has been sentenced for theft, and escaped to the hills, where he has lived as an outlaw.

These revelations change Halla's love for Kari from a hearthstone flame to a sacrificial fire. The true grandeur of her nature shines out—''like a blue mountain rising from the mist,'' her lover rapturously exclaims. When discovery draws near, she insists on fleeing with him, and in the third act we find them domesticated in the hills. With fine simplicity Sigurjónsson has pictured how they order their lives—drinking tea of mountain herbs by the fire, playing with their little girl, planning how to procure food and medicine and to hide their stores from the relentless people of the valleys. In the presence of mountain and glacier, their every-day existence gains a wild, free strength, and Halla's and Kari's love has the exaltation of the wind-swept hills.

Perfect as their union seems, there is already the first light shadow falling across it. Arnes, their fellow-outlaw, feels it and ventures to tell Halla that he loves her better than her husband does. ''It seemed to me that you and I were more akin in our souls. That we had more of the wilds in us.'' She repels him passionately, but her subconscious sense that something is gone from Kari's love is shown in her words: ''It is queer about the waterfall. . . . At first I was almost afraid of it. Then I began to love it, and now I should only miss it if it were not here any more. We mortals are strange.''

The inner cleavage, for which Sigurjónsson has prepared us by subtle suggestion, is apparent in the last act, where husband and wife sit alone in a mountain hut, perishing of hunger, and bitterly reproaching each other. Their devotion has not borne the strain of suffering and the loneliness that meant absolute dependence on each other. The difference between their two natures has come to the surface. Halla is by instinct a revolutionist. She has followed Kari to the hills on an impulse, which she now begins to doubt. She has killed her two children to save them from a worse fate. Her nature rises in revolt against the unjust laws and the cruelty of organized society. In the difference between this desperate woman and the Halla of the first act we get the full measure of her suffering. She clutches at her love, demanding of herself and Kari that it be all in all to them, and begs him to take her hand and lie down by her side to die rather than let hunger tear the fine web that time had spun between them.

Kari is no revolutionist. He has broken the law once, in pity for his starving little sisters and brothers, but by that very act he has come to feel the sacredness of law. He has tried to atone by the courage and patience with which he has borne his banishment, and now he wants to go out into the raging snowstorm to seek food, in obedience to what he regards as the divine law of life. Halla, with her more primitive impulsiveness, replies: ''The storm writes many laws in the sand.'' She is longing for a word of love from him and resents his clinging to a faith and a standard outside of himself and herself. Kari cannot understand the sudden collapse of the wife whose strength of soul he has learned to depend upon in all these years and is repelled by her wild outbursts.

In the first edition, Sigurjónsson makes Kari turn to her in a softer mood to tell her what she has been to him: ''No woman was ever greater in her love than you. When the sun strikes the rim of the glacier, it takes on the loveliest hues, though in

truth it is nothing but colorless clay. So your love has been the sunlight of my life, and I love you—have always loved you.'' These words the author has ruthlessly cut out of the later edition, demanding of his readers that they shall believe in the reality of Kari's tenderness underneath his harshness. (pp. 346-49)

Sigurjónsson's art is perhaps never greater than in this last act. His people never lose their warmth or solidity in all the psychological play and interplay of emotion. Something is lacking in realistic presentation. His characters are not sharply individualized in speech or outward appearance. This may be due in part to the fact that he is writing Danish, which is not his mother tongue, and in so far it makes translation into another language less difficult, but more is probably due to the fact that he cares little for this outward realism. Kari's speech, quoted in the paragraph above, is not the language of a common peasant, but a great poet's interpretation of a soul which in real life, perhaps, was inarticulate. We willingly dispense with the idiomatic flavor and gain the poetry instead. (p. 349)

Hanna Astrup Larsen, ''Eyvind of the Hills,'' in The American-Scandinavian Review, *Vol. IV, No. 6, November-December, 1916, pp. 346-49.*

THE NATION, NEW YORK   **(essay date 1917)**

[*In the following excerpt, the critic praises* Eyvind of the Hills *as a representative drama of the twentieth-century renaissance in Icelandic literature.*]

During the past year the American-Scandinavian Foundation has added two volumes—numbers five and six—to its series of Scandinavian Classics. In what sense the very recent Icelandic plays by Sigurjónsson can be regarded as classics it is hard to see. With such significant time-tested works, for example, as Paludan-Müller's *Adam Homo* or J. P. Jacobsen's *Niels Lyhne* and *Fru Marie Grubbe* practically unknown to American readers, it is a little disappointing to find this series transformed into another agency for translating the latest plays into English.

To be sure, **Eyvind of the Hills** is an unusually stirring tragedy. The author is one of a group of young Icelandic writers who bear witness to the existence of a well-defined intellectual and literary renaissance in the birthplace of the most characteristic Old Norse writing. In the work of this coterie some of the sternness and majesty of that remote mediæval literature persists. This is true especially of **Eyvind of the Hills**. (p. 682)

The play is more than a story in dramatic form. True, some romantic interest is contributed to the tragedy by the strange, picturesque spots in which the scenes are laid and the extraordinary situations in which the characters find themselves. The author, however, shows himself a true dramatist in the way in which he reduces these situations into the mere setting for the struggle among human beings. In the last act, in particular, he shows a psychological realism and directness that proves him an inheritor from Ibsen. Yet this incisive method is applied to characters in whom flows the blood of the men and women of the heroic sagas. The play establishes in our minds the persistence in modern Iceland of Old Norse modes of action and thought and the conviction of the essential humanity of this man and woman suffering almost superhuman anguish. It is thus at once romantic and realistic. . . . If not a Scandinavian classic, **Eyvind of the Hills** is at least an unusual and moving contemporary drama.

The Hraun Farm, the other play in the volume, is of much less importance. It is a love story of pastoral Iceland told with little dramatic skill. The successful effects are produced by the presentation of distinctly Icelandic scenery and events, such as the earthquake which drives the farmer and all his household to live in tents and finally shakes down his farmhouse in ruins. This drama is clearly the product of the author's "'prentice hand.'' (p. 683)

> *"Translations from the Scandinavian," in* The Nation, *New York, Vol. CIV, No. 2710, June 7, 1917, pp. 682-83.*

W. W. WORSTER   (essay date 1924)

[*In the following excerpt, Worster discusses the subjects, themes, and artistic merit of Sigurjónsson's major dramas.*]

Jóhann Sigurjónsson . . . inclines to subjects of a somewhat gruesome character. *Dr. Rung* shows us a medical man who, while nobly using his own body for dangerous experiments, incomprehensibly falls in love with a girl—and kills her. The play is pathological as literature, and the effect is heightened by the overstrained lyrical tone of the dialogue.

There is less gratuitous horror and more dramatic power in *Bjærg-Ejvind.* . . . It is the best known, though not the best, of the author's works. The dramatic effects are external applications rather than the outcrop of inherent potentialities. Only the last act is pure character-conflict. In *Gaarden Hraun,* the acting turns on the attachment of the *bonde* or yeoman type to the soil and stead that have held his life and his life's work. Sveinungi stands as the last representative of an old school of thought, overpowered by the new. The theme has, of course, been dealt with often before, but the setting here is admirably suited to the subject.

Artistically, Sigurjónsson's best work is *Önsket (The Wish).* The subject here is nothing less than black magic; time, early 18th century. Loftur, son of the Bishop of Holar's steward, is studying for holy orders; at the same time reading occult works and carrying on an intrigue with Steinunn, one of the maids. She, however, represents, as far as *his* feelings are concerned, merely the lust of the flesh. In Disa, the Bishop's daughter, he finds an uplifting angel—and Steinunn is thenceforward an encumbrance. After a violent scene with Steinunn, Loftur utters the words of a spell he has found for causing the death of a person by a wish. Within a few hours, Steinunn is found drowned. Technically, it is a case of suicide, with grave moral responsibility on the part of Loftur; he, however, sees it as the direct result of his wish. The last act shows him in the cathedral, conjuring up an evil shade. Disa strives with him in vain; Loftur is now frankly mad, and when the shade appears, he falls dead.

Loftur is a medieval character in a medieval setting. His thirst for knowledge and his dabbling in occult sciences are the product of an age when all science was occult, and all knowledge was forbidden fruit. So, too, his passion for Steinunn and his worship of Disa are but the expression of that inhuman and unnatural duality which marked the cloistered view of womankind in the days of flagellant celibacy and the cult of the Madonna. The play as a whole stands out among Sigurjónsson's work as a piece of pure craftsmanship, of genuine power well controlled. It is a drama that should rank among the Faust plays; and the theme that inspired so various temperaments as those of Marlowe and Goethe, Grabbe and Lenau, seems here to have reached its height *as* an inspiration; the poet's gift,

hitherto feeling vaguely for its proper form, crystallizes at the touch, and becomes firm, ordered, definite.

Lögneren (The Liar) suffers by comparison with the pure, determined line of *The Wish.* The theme is taken from the story of Burnt Njal; a difficult subject to stage, and the burning scene at the end does not make it easier. Skarphedinn's final words "we burn, we burn as beacons on the shore of eternity," are hardly well chosen as a substitute for those of the saga. The characters, however, especially those of Maar and Skarphedinn, are drawn with sympathetic insight. (pp. 347-48)

> *W. W. Worster, "Four Icelandic Poets," in* The American-Scandinavian Review, *Vol. XII, No. 6, June, 1924, pp. 346-51.*

EINAR HAUGEN   (essay date 1967)

[*Haugen is an American linguist and critic who specializes in Scandinavian languages and literature. In the following excerpt, he discusses characteristic traits of Sigurjónsson's dramatic work and traces the sources of* The Wish *in literature and folklore.*]

It is a striking fact that all five of the plays which Jóhann Sigurjónsson managed to complete and publish in his short but intense creative period ended with the tragic death of the chief character. That the first of these, *Dr. Rung,* should have dealt with tuberculosis and that he himself should have died of the same dread disease fourteen years later is perhaps no more than a coincidence. But there runs through his work a sense of the profound tragedy of life, which is the more intense because he was one who loved life and enjoyed it to the full. In an essay entitled, **"I Love Life,"** he ecstatically confessed: "I love life, as a man loves a woman: I follow it helplessly, it enchants me with irresistible force. . . . I love it as a lovesick man desires a cold, disdainful dancer, and if I should lose this love, I would do so with distress, like the king of old who took the life of his beloved because he was afraid of losing himself." Friends from his days in Copenhagen describe him as a man of sudden and unpredictable moods, who could shift from light-hearted gaiety to the blackest despair. Professor Arni Pálsson, who had known him then, wrote in 1920 that many thought of him as "a vacillating and unreliable enthusiast." But they agreed that "he was unlike all others, and that in his best moments sun and summer shone around him."

This dual emphasis on the beauty and the tragedy of life is projected into all of Jóhann's writings. "When I was a child," he once wrote, "I promised the Lord that if He would give me the gracious gift of poetry, I would use it to honor Him and His work. In those days His heaven was so wondrously near and there could be no doubt that all He did was good. Later the firmament grew larger and colder and the conditions of life were harder to understand. But however this might be, the inmost nerve in all my creation is the same as when I was a child: to shape in the ringing metal of language something of the flowing eternity of life, in simpler and if possible in more beautiful images." Beauty, as this is seen in the simple things of life, is one of the keys to his work. He found it in nature, especially the nature of Iceland, which is the setting of all but one of his plays. He found it in women and children, who are pictured with tenderness and insight. He found it above all in love, here coupled with tragedy in each of his plays. His thoughts, as one also sees from his published letters, circled around a man's inescapable need for love, his fear that love might not come, and his equal fear that if it did, it would lead only to tragic upheaval and death. His temperament was in many ways more lyric than dramatic, but he had set himself the goal of becoming a great dramatic author. He was borne on the wave of drama that had been stirred up by Ibsen, Bjørnson, and Strindberg, but his work was more nearly akin to that of his immediate predecessors, the Norwegians Gunnar Heiberg and Knut Hamsun, in whose plays the irresistible force of love and the tragic edge of happiness were basic themes. (pp. 13-14)

The central theme of all [Jóhann's] plays may be formulated as the ambitious man's challenge to the laws of the universe, a basically Nietzschean and Dostoievskian theme. Each of his heroes is endowed with a will to exceed his grasp, and this becomes his tragic downfall. Dr. Harald Rung burns to produce a vaccine for the cure of tuberculosis and goes to the length of trying it on himself. To a friend who remonstrates with him he says: "Couldn't you want something so passionately that you would buy it with your life?" Sveinungi, the farmer at Hraun, defies an earthquake that threatens to destroy his farm, a possession more important to him than life itself. In the end it is not the earthquake that destroys him, however, but his own daughter. Her love for a man whom her father despises makes the farmer's life valueless and his efforts vain, and so he chooses to be destroyed with the farm. In [*Fjalla-Eyvindur (Eyvind of the Hills)*] it is the woman, Halla, who defies nature. She joins the man she loves in voluntary outlawry among the inhospitable mountain wastes of the interior. To one of the characters she says, "May not a strong will turn the tide of fate?" But in the end fate catches up with her also, when the hounding of the community and the inclemency of the elements bring out the basic cowardice of the man she loves. She loses her faith in her own love for him and rather than face emptiness she walks out into the snow to her death. In [*Ønsket (The Wish)*] Loftur embodies perhaps more fully than any of the rest man's defiance of his limitations, here symbolized by the secret lore which Loftur seeks beyond and above the knowledge that his school conveys.

The reception of *Eyvind* was enthusiastic, and foreign critics like Georg Brandes in Denmark and Léon Pineau in France acclaimed Jóhann as a worthy successor to the great dramatists of the preceding generation. Brandes described him as having "poetic talent of a high order" and Pineau spoke of his "sublimely powerful poetry."

The Wish appeared in Danish as *Ønsket* and in Icelandic as *Galdra-Loftur (Loftur the Magician)*. . . . The latter name is one that was applied to his hero Loftur because of his practice of the magic arts. Even before the appearance of *Eyvind*, Jóhann was thinking of this play. In a letter dated August 2, 1911, he wrote to his fiancée, "The play lives in my soul as one long, beautiful song, *The Wish*. The individual scenes come into the light one by one, like a landscape emerging from the dark. The people who live there are becoming my friends,—what a joy to try to create something beautiful, but also a torment, often a frightful torment, when discouragement and doubt fill my soul." When the play finally appeared, Jóhann was already a celebrity. *Eyvind* had been a sensation, but *The Wish* was something less than that. It was well received, however, and over the years it has proved to be rather more enduring. The Danish critic Anders Thuborg wrote at the time of Jóhann's death: "*The Wish* constitutes the culmination of the author's life work." (pp. 16-18)

Jóhann described the relation of his play to its source as being that of a "free fantasia." This is not far from the truth, since the play is essentially one more embodiment of his own basic

concern with man's relationship to the universe. Loftur reflects the author himself and carries his message to the audience. But much of the story and the central character are also historical, or at least legendary. Jóhann is known to have been familiar with the story of Galdra-Loftur from childhood, since it appeared in the most widely read collection of Icelandic folklore, Jón Arnason's *Islenzkar Thjóðsögur og æfintýri (Icelandic Folktales and Fairystories*, Leipzig, 1864-74), a work which was also the source of his preceding play, *Eyvind*. Jón Arnason's tale is derived from a written source, but builds on popular narrative reflecting contemporary notions on the nature of academic activities. Loftur is reported to have been a pupil at the cathedral school in Hólar in the north of Iceland, and a ringleader in the secret practice of witchcraft indulged in by some of the pupils. Although no dates are given in the story, historical persons mentioned in it lived in the first half of the eighteenth century. Various tricks which Loftur performed with his magic are mentioned, but the only one that Jóhann found use for in his play was the following:

> Another time Loftur got a servant girl on the farm with child and then killed her by witchcraft. She had the job of carrying containers of food in and out of the kitchen. To speed up this work they used trough-shaped trays on which they put several containers at once. Loftur opened a passage for her right through the wall so that she went in through this. But because the girl was frightened and hesitated, the magic worked and caused the wall to close again. A long time later, when the wall was torn down, the skeleton of a woman was found standing in it, with a tray of containers in her arms and the bones of an unborn child in her womb.

It is clear that this poor little story was no more than a springboard for the poet's imagination, and he found much more to his use in *Anne Pedersdotter*, a play that had been successfully performed in Copenhagen in 1909. This play [translated into English by John Masefield as *The Witch*] was by the Norwegian playwright Hans Wiers-Jenssen, and was performed with the same Johanne Dybwad in the main role who was to play his Halla in *Eyvind* three years later. Anne Pedersdotter was a woman of sixteenth-century Bergen, the widow of a bishop, who was accused of having killed her husband by witchcraft and was eventually burned at the stake for her supposed crime. As Wiers-Jenssen presented the theme, her sin was much the same as Loftur's: she wished her husband's death because she loved another. . . . The connection between this play and *The Wish* has been demonstrated by Professor Steingrímur Thorsteinsson, but as he has also pointed out, the essential psychological content is deeper in *The Wish*. This play reflects to the full the personality and inner experience of its author.

Even though the hero's dilemma is therefore less a part of the legend of Loftur than it is of the author's own experience, Jóhann returned to the legend for the final, dramatic scene of the play. This concerns Bishop Gottskalk the Grim and his powerful book of magic, the *Rauðskinna (The Red Book*, lit. "Redskin"). Gottskalk appears to have been one of the last Catholic bishops of Iceland, having died in 1520. That people believed, even as late as the eighteenth century, that the clergy and their pupils practiced witchcraft is abundantly clear not only from legends of this kind, but from actual court records of cases in which they were publicly accused of witchcraft and compelled to clear themselves if they wished to save their

necks. This is that same early modern world of Christian superstition which we know from Arthur Miller's *The Crucible*.

Loftur is said to have frightened one of his schoolmates into
joining him in an attempt to raise all the dead bishops of Hólar
from their rest under the ground. The friend was asked only
to stand in the church steeple and hold the bell cord until Loftur
gave him a signal to ring the bell. Loftur had learned all he
could from the book called *Gráskinna, The Gray Book,* which
legend said was used as a textbook at the cathedral schools,
and now he wanted to lay his hands on the more advanced
Rauðskinna. His explanation to his friend of the reasons for
this is of interest:

> Those who have learned magic, as I have, can
> only use it for evil, and they will all be de-
> stroyed when they die. But if a person learns
> enough, the devil will no longer have power
> over him, but will have to serve him without
> getting anything in return, just as he served
> Sæmundur the Wise. Anyone who learns that
> much is free to use his knowledge as he pleases.
> This kind of knowledge cannot be acquired in
> our days since the Black School was disbanded,
> and Bishop Gottskalk the Grim had the
> *Rauðskinna* buried with him.

In the play this is reflected in Loftur's words to the girl Dísa,
who has replaced his schoolmate in the legend: "Only one path
is open to me. I have to go on into darkness. I have to gain
so much knowledge that I can win power over Evil. If I can
then abstain from ever wanting anything for myself, I will be
forgiven in the hour of my death." But the Loftur of our play
is placed in a modern, Nietzschean context: "When I make
use of Evil to promote the Good—what is then Good and what
is Evil?"

In the legend Loftur enters the pulpit and conjures the bishops
up into the moonlit church one by one; the oldest of them says
to Loftur, "Stop this, thou evil man, while there is time." In
the play these words are elaborated and turned into the "voices
of conscience." In the legend Loftur finally succeeds in raising
Bishop Gottskalk, with the red book in his right hand. "Well
have you sung, my son, and better than I expected," he says,
"but you will not get my *Rauðskinna.*"

> Loftur was seized by a veritable fury and frenzy,
> and conjured as he had never done before. He
> turned the words of benediction and the Lord's
> prayer against the Devil; the whole church shook
> and trembled. It looked to the schoolboy as if
> Gottskalk came nearer to Loftur and was re-
> luctantly handing him one corner of the book.
> So far the boy had been brave, but now he
> shook with fear and all turned black before his
> eyes. It seemed to him as if the bishop turned
> the book as Loftur thrust forth his hand. He
> thought that Loftur was giving him the signal
> and he grabbed the bell cord. Immediately ev-
> erything vanished into the floor with a tremen-
> dous crash. Loftur stood a moment as if frozen
> in the pulpit and laid his head in his hands.
> Then he stumbled slowly down and found his
> companion, groaned and said, "This went worse
> than it should have."

The legend goes on to let Loftur explain that it was his own
impatience and anger in grabbing for the book that had caused

the boy's error. Loftur does not die immediately, as he does
in the play, but his mind is beclouded and he knows that his
fate is sealed. In spite of the friendship and vigilance of a local
priest, he vanishes into the sea one day, having been seized
by a large, hairy hand.

The material as Jóhann found it in Jón Arnason's book was
certainly tempting as material for dramatic reworking. The play
has often been referred to as an Icelandic *Faust*, but there are
more differences than similarities. The emphasis here is not
on knowledge as knowledge, rather on the passion for knowledge which can become so overpowering that it crushes the
humbler passion of love. Bishop Gottskalk tells Loftur: "In
the darkness, before thou wert born, Evil cleft thy will." Loftur's curse is his divided will, or in psychological terms, his
schizophrenia, which is symbolized in the two women he loves.
The evil wish that kills Steinunn and gives the play its name
is an expression of deep and mysterious forces within himself
which he is unable to master and which are his fate. "In the
beginning was the wish," he cries, apparently in conscious
rejection of Faust's "Im Anfang war der Tat." (pp. 18-22)

> *Einar Haugen, in an introduction to "The Wish,"
> in* Fire and Ice: Three Icelandic Plays by Jóhann
> Sigurjónsson, David Stefánsson, and Agnar Thór-
> darson, *edited by Einar Haugen, The University of
> Wisconsin Press, 1967, pp. 13-23.*

ADDITIONAL BIBLIOGRAPHY

Chandler, Frank W. "Björnson and the Minor Scandinavians." In his
Modern Continental Playwrights, pp. 39-63. New York: Harper &
Brothers, 1931.
> Includes plot summaries of *Eyvind* and *Hraun* and general eval-
> uation of Sigurjónsson's work. According to Chandler: "What
> attracts in Sigurjónsson is neither his philosophy nor his technique.
> It is rather the freshness of his material, and the poetic power
> with which he bodies forth simple situations and primitive char-
> acters."

Einarsson, Stefán. "Literature of the Soul—The Danish-Icelandic
Writers." In his *History of Icelandic Prose Writers: 1800-1940,* pp.
123-55. Ithaca, N.Y.: Cornell University Press, 1948.
> Biographical and critical sketch characterizing Sigurjónsson's
> contribution to his national literature. According to Einarsson:
> "Among his countrymen [Sigurjónsson] stands out for his tow-
> ering ambitions, his fiery temperament, his keen sense of dramatic
> conflict and his profound psychology. His meticulously polished
> style usually has a warm lyrical quality and is often interspersed
> with symbolical similes of great beauty and phrases that have
> become proverbial."

Johnson, Jakobina. "Jóhann Sigurjónsson." *Poet Lore* XLVI, No. 2
(Summer 1940): 147-49.
> Outlines Sigurjónsson's career. Johnson concludes that "it may
> be seen that Icelandic folk-lore and saga supply the themes for
> Sigurjónsson's most noted works. Eyvind and Loft are both tra-
> ditional figures. . . . But the dramatist touches them with the magic
> wand of poetic imagination, until little remains of the original,
> except the name and the setting. And through his treatment these
> traditional figures become deeply symbolical."

Leach, Henry Goddard. "Outlaws." *American Scandinavian Review*
IV, No. 6 (November-December 1916): 350-54.
> Examines several Icelandic legends involving outlaws, attempting
> to separate the facts from the folklore. Leach concludes that "Sig-
> urjónsson had at his disposal a variety of conflicting anecdotes
> about the great eighteenth-century outlaw, Eyvind, and his wife.
> The historical facts are few."

Magoun, Jr., Francis P. "Jóhann Sigurjónsson's *Fjalla-Eyvindur:* Source, Chronology, and Geography." *PMLA* LXI, No. 1 (March 1946): 269-92.

   Examines compositional elements of Sigurjónsson's best known drama. According to Magoun: "With an almost classical simplicity *Fjalla-Eyvindur* treats of the universal emotions of love, devotion, and loyalty, especially as displayed under highly trying circumstances."

Review of *Modern Icelandic Plays* by Jóhann Sigurjónsson. *Spectator* 118, No. 4624 (10 February 1917): 176.

   Appreciative review stating that *Eyvind of the Hills* and *The Hraun Farm* "have not only dramatic power but literary distinction of a high order."

Woodbridge, Homer E. "A Flood of Foreign Drama." *The Dial* LXII, No. 734 (25 January 1917): 67-70.

   Includes a favorable review of *Modern Icelandic Plays: Eyvind of the Hills, The Hraun Farm.* Woodbridge recommends both plays as "notable for their spontaneity and freshness; the strong clear wind of the north blows through them. They deserve a wide reading."

A(nton) H(ansen) Tammsaare

1878-1940

(Pseudonym of Anton Hansen) Estonian novelist, dramatist, short story writer, and essayist.

The central figure of modern Estonian literature, Tammsaare is best known for his five-volume novel *Tõde ja õigus,* in which he combined elements of psychological realism and social satire to create what critics consider a comprehensive and perceptive account of rural Estonian life during the late nineteenth and early twentieth centuries.

Tammsaare was the fourth of twelve children born to a poor Estonian farm family. He began his education at the local village school but later transferred to a boarding school in the nearby town of Väika-Maarja, where he studied under the direction of the noted Estonian poet Jakob Tamm. An extremely bright student, Tammsaare published his first novel, *Tähtis päev,* while still in high school; upon graduating in 1903 he was offered a position with one of the leading Estonian newspapers, *Teataja.* During his five years at the newspaper, Tammsaare continued to publish novels and short stories, but he also wished to resume his formal education, and in 1908 he enrolled in the college of law at the University of Tartu. However, he was forced to abandon his law studies when he developed severe tuberculosis in 1911, and he spent the next six years recuperating in various rural retreats.

Faced with an abundance of leisure, Tammsaare began to devote himself more seriously to literature during this period, but it was not until he settled in the city of Tallinn in 1917 that he produced the works for which he is known today—the drama *Juudit* and the novels *Tõde ja õigus* and *Põrgupõhja uus Vanapagan (The Misadventures of the New Satan).* These works earned Tammsaare not only the reverence of the Estonian people, for whom he was a source of great national pride, but also the respect of the international literary community, and at his death in 1940 he was hailed as one of the most accomplished Eastern European authors.

Critics generally divide Tammsaare's work into three periods, corresponding with his high school and journalism days, his stay at the university, and his residence in Tallinn. The writings of the first period are considered immature and reflect Tammsaare's background in their concern for the activities of Estonian farmers. The writings of the university period are more consciously intellectual, particularly the novels *Pikad sammud, Noored hinged,* and *Üle piiri,* which recount the activities of a group of students and contain a number of lengthy philosophical discussions. In the mature works of his third period, Tammsaare succeeded in integrating his various concerns and theories into a unified vision, most notably in the work which is considered his masterpiece, *Tõde ja õigus.* Influenced by the social criticism of Nikolai Gogol, the bucolic satires of Ivan Turgenev, and the psychological novels of Fedor Dostoevski, Tammsaare sought to present in *Tõde ja õigus* a comprehensive and realistic view of rural Estonians which would clearly reveal both their strengths and their shortcomings. Critics agree that Tammsaare was entirely successful in this endeavor, noting further that the message of the novel is greatly enhanced by Tammsaare's fluid, lyrical prose style.

Translated into several languages, including Swedish, German, and Dutch, *Tõde ja õigus* is considered to be the masterpiece of Estonian literature. Although Tammsaare's reputation in English-speaking countries has been limited by a lack of English translations of his works, he remains a major figure in his native country and throughout much of Europe.

PRINCIPAL WORKS

Tähtis päev (novel) 1903
Pikad sammud (novel) 1908
Noored hinged (novel) 1909
Üle piiri (novel) 1910
Poiss ja liblik (short stories) 1915
   [*Miniatures,* 1977]
Kärbes (novel) 1917
Varjundid (novel) 1917
Juudit (drama) 1921
Kõrboja peremees (novel) 1922
Tõde ja õigus. 5 vols. (novel) 1926-33
Elu ja armastus (novel) 1934
Kuningal on külm (drama) 1936
Põrgupõhja uus Vanapagan (novel) 1939
   [*The Misadventures of the New Satan,* 1978]

Kogutud teosed. 14 vols.　(novels, short stories, essays, and dramas)　1978-

---

ELIZABETH JUDAS　(essay date 1938)

[In the following excerpt from a dissertation written in 1938, Judas discusses the influence of Russian authors on Tammsaare's work.]

Before considering the major Russian influences upon Tammsaare, something must be said of his relations to Tolstoy. While the great master of the Russian novel did not exert a permanent force upon him, Tolstoy's influence cannot be overlooked in any examination of Tammsaare's development. [Mihkel] Kampmaa, the noted authority on Estonian literature, tells us that in high school days a struggle raged in the soul of Tammsaare between the forces exerted on him by the two Russian novelists, Tolstoy and Dostoevsky. He had read and analyzed most of the masterpieces of these writers. In 1914 he translated Tolstoy's *Death of Ivan Illich* (1886). He did not yet know in his own mind which was the greater, and he wanted to settle that issue for his own sake. He carried this problem in his mind for many years. In pre-war days *War and Peace, Resurrection,* and many other works of Tolstoy were very popular, but he gradually lost his popularity because of his quietistic attitude, the so-called "Tolstoyism," and because of his opposition to the church. In Estonia as in Russia the decline of Tolstoy's vogue would have been greater had the Russian Holy Synod not blundered in insisting on the writer's excommunication. It would have been wiser to ignore the Count's whim and leave him unmolested. The excommunication caused a sensation and Tolstoy posed as a persecuted martyr, with increased influence.

The Estonians took up the question of Tolstoyism with interest. The Estonian gymnasiums began to fight the movement. Conservative to the core, they taught lessons of religion on the basis of the Bible. From this standpoint they had no difficulty in showing that Tolstoy was wrong in many of his ideas and that he did not live up to his own teachings. For instance, he did not admit the right of personal property or other possessions, either land or books. Nevertheless, he retained his large estate to the day of his death; and though he did not profit personally from his copyrights, his family did, and his wife was known as a good business woman in her dealings with publishers.

Russian influence on the work of Tammsaare was exerted mainly by the three writers: Gogol', Turgenev, and Dostoevsky. Their importance for Tammsaare follows in this order chronologically. Gogol's themes and spirit show their effect during the school years and the years of earliest literary apprenticeship, Turgenev's importance begins at the university, while that of Dostoevsky belongs to the period of maturity, following the stay in the Caucasus.

The first period opens with the short story now called **"Kuresaare vanad"** (**"The Old Folks of Kuresaare"**). When first published in 1901, the title read **"Mäetaguse vanad"** (**"The Old Folks of Mäetaguse"**). However, nothing but the title has been changed. This simple tale of old Mats and his aged wife takes us to an Estonian bath-house ("saun" or "banya"), where the old folks lived. The reader will not go far astray if he regards the location of this "saun" as the Põhja-Tammsaare farm, the author's boyhood home. The couple are very old.

Nothing happens in the story. The reader is introduced to a lazy old man who does nothing but sleep and quarrel with his wife; he does not realize that he is lazy, but considers himself a very hard worker. Although the couple have spent their whole married life quarreling with one another, still, as old Mats is dying, they shake hands for the last time and tell each other how thankful they are that they have always been such good friends.

The form of the story reminds one forcibly of Gogol's "Old-Fashioned Landowners," also a simple, almost plotless story, which treats of an old couple who lived in a low-roofed Russian cottage. Its main interest to the reader is in Gogol's description of an idle life. Here also the old folks do not themselves realize that the life they are living is idle. The only difference between the two stories is that the Estonian couple quarrel, while the Russian people lived in peace. Both sketches are charming in their humorous realism.

The other story of this period which recalls Gogol' is **"Kakspaari ja üksainus ("Two Couples and a Single")"**, written in 1902. This is simply a neighbor-story, as was Gogol's "How Ivan Ivanovich Quarreled with Ivan Nikiforovich" (1831).

Tammsaare introduces us to two rural families of Estonia. Two couples named Laiad and Kaasid are neighbors, and they quarrel every Lord's Day. Then if the husbands are not fighting with each other, the wives are at it. However, these neighbors do not take their quarrels very seriously, and even violent disputes are soon forgotten. One day Tiina, the wife of Kaasi, stands outside the window of her neighbor, Viiu, scolding her and calling her names. Viiu is about to give birth to a child and is in labor. She needs help and sympathy, but instead gets only abuse. The next day, however, Tiina brings gifts to the new-born child and nothing is said about the "swine" and other harsh words of yesterday. Then finally the day comes for one of the families to move away. The couples part in sorrow, declaring that they have always been good friends and that they have never had a real quarrel.

The difference between Tammsaare's treatment and that of Gogol' is seen only in the conclusion. Gogol' has the quarrel end quite differently. In his story the two Ivans are nearing reconciliation, but when one of them says to the other: "Permit me to observe in a friendly manner that you took offence because I called you a goose," the quarrel breaks out anew. On account of the word "goose" the two Ivans continue to quarrel to the end of their lives.

In both cases Tammsaare has borrowed the situation and the motives from Gogol', and has reproduced something of the atmosphere of satire with which the Russian author surrounds his characters. Tammsaare has given the theme an Estonian setting and has in both cases put more vigor into the plot.

The second period of Tammsaare's development as a novelist brings him under the influence of Turgenev. The Russian writer affected his art both in the delineation of character and in the shaping of his style. We cannot speak here of a direct borrowing of material. . . . It is rather a subtle influence exerted by Turgenev's language; the delicacy of the art with which he selects situations, and the limpid and musical style in which his impressions are recorded.

The frame in which Tammsaare places his stories is one which he introduces into Estonian literature. The type that he uses has been called the "city novel," for the modern city is the milieu of the narrative in the group of works that we shall now consider. Urban life, with its sophistication and complex interplay of character, affords the author an opportunity for unfolding his great wealth of imagination and especially for the creation of full-blooded youthful types in conflict with the modern complexities of life.

His most successful novels of this period are: *Pikad sammud* (*The Long Steps*); *Noored hinged* (*Young Souls*); and *Üle piiri* (*Across the Borderline*). By combining the titles of these three novels, we get the sentence: "Noored hinged lähevad pikkade sammudega üle piiri" ("The young souls are going with long steps across the borderline"). This picturesque expression takes the reader involuntarily from Tammsaare to Russia, back into the atmosphere of Turgenev's analysis of problematic characters.

One of the most typical creations of the great Russian is his *Rudin* (1855), and this is the novel that set its stamp most definitely on Tammsaare's technique in the works just mentioned.

The contents of *Rudin*, Turgenev's first long story, is briefly as follows: The hero, Dmitry Nikolaevich Rudin, is a type of the progressive idealist of the eighteen-forties. Through a friend he makes the acquaintance of Darya Mikhailovna, a distinguished and wealthy noblewoman, the widow of a privy councillor. This lady is accustomed to withdraw each summer from Moscow to her country estate. Here, with her daughter, Natalya, aged seventeen, and two young sons, she keeps open house for the neighborhood; "that is to say, she received men visitors, especially bachelors—country ladies she could not endure." The immediate circle consists of the old French governess, the tutor of the boys, and three neighbors: Alexandra Pavlovna Lipin, a wealthy, childless widow; her brother, Sergey Volyntsev, a retired captain of cavalry; and an odd character, Pigasov, who was self-taught and embittered toward the world, especially toward women.

In this group Rudin now makes his appearance. With his accustomed detail Turgenev puts him before us as a man of thirty-five, somewhat round-shouldered, curly-haired, with an irregular but expressive and intelligent face, a faint gleam in his dark blue eyes, a straight, broad nose and finely chiseled lips, and a rather shrill voice which contrasted strikingly with his stature and broad chest. He has been well educated at home and abroad. As a welcome member of the circle Rudin shows himself a fluent talker, and much of our interest in the novel lies in the long discussions which take place, and especially in the long monologs which reveal the character of this idealist. These deal with his adventures abroad, with scholarship and science, with love and the problems of life, all set forth in the manner of one who is less concerned with details than with the philosophy of life which underlies human actions.

Darya Mikhailovna's guests understood little of what he said, but they were astonished and delighted with his flow of words and listened to him with close attention. Especially the younger members of the group, Bassistov, the tutor, and Natalya were fascinated. He talked long and often of love and of the freedom and sacrifices which it demands, and here Natalya hung on his words until her wonder and admiration turn to affection and she gives him her heart.

In this crisis the hero shows himself a helpless idealist. Love for Natalya has also awakened in his heart, but he is a man of words, not of actions. When he learns from Natalya that her mother is determined not to give her to him, all Rudin's eloquence about freedom and sacrifice turns out to be empty phrases.

He can only say to Natalya, "Submit! Submit!" So the lovers part forever; Rudin "drew the cord too tight, and it broke." He withdraws and later is killed in Paris, July 26, 1848, just as the workingmen's revolution, in which he has taken a part, comes to an end. Natalya marries Captain Volyntsev, who had loved her before Rudin came on the scene.

In Tammsaare's novel *Pikad sammud,* the action takes place in the Estonian capital, Tallinn. Two friends, journalists, Heinrich Orisoo and Otto Leisner, are in love with the same girl, Olga, but they keep it a secret from each other. Olga also betrays to neither her relationship with his friend and visits each of them separately at their attic apartment. When finally the secret is revealed, the three separate, and something new then develops in the personality of each. Otto is an idealist, but never acts in accordance with his ideals. He reminds the reader of Turgenev's Dmitry Rudin, with the exception that Otto plays with the affections of Olga for his own selfish pleasure while Rudin acts in all sincerity with Natalya. Heinrich is honest and sincere, somewhat the type of Turgenev's Lavretsky in *The Nest of Nobles* (1868). He has loved Olga sincerely, but when he finds that she is carrying on an affair with his friend, he turns away from her for good. Olga, who has been playing with both of them, now falls in love with Heinrich, but it is too late, for nothing can be done to bring back Heinrich's love. Otto urges him to trust Olga, but all in vain. The story ends with a meeting of all three friends at Heinrich's apartment, where he is planning to give a definite explanation to Olga in the presence of Otto. However, his introduction is so long that Olga can stand no more. She realizes how foolish she has been, and without saying a word, runs out of the room. Otto follows her immediately, but Heinrich stands in the middle of the room, like a fool, scolding himself for his attempt at explanation. Otto overtakes Olga and makes her stop and listen to him. He feels that now he really loves her and asks her to marry him, but she loves only Heinrich, and since she cannot have him, she will have no one else, and runs away. Otto, half crazed, looks around and begins to run too, as if trying to catch the thief of his love. In Olga we have something of the character of Turgenev's Natalya in *Rudin*.

Tammsaare's second novel, *Noored hinged* (*Young Souls*), pictures the psychology of a student's life at the university. The hero, Arthur Kulno, is a dreamer, skeptical and introspective. Many boys and girls visit him. They also have drinking parties. One of the girls, Aino Võsand, a former student, pretends to be interested only in making men suffer and then ridiculing them. "Laugh a man's heart from his bosom and make his head bend from his shoulders," seems to be her motto, but in reality she is a virtuous girl. Aino draws hearts of all the boys after her, but the fervid eloquence of Kulno makes her fall in love with him. Kulno is a master of words, but not of action. He finally falls in love with Aino too, but does not know how to seize the moment to propose to her. Aino leaves for St. Petersburg, and they never meet again!

The story is a harsh criticism of modern young people in all their capriciousness and heartlessness. Here again Turgenev's influence appears. Aino reminds us of his Natalya in *Rudin*, and Kulno has much of the ready eloquence of Rudin. He pictures the outer and inner life of the fully emancipated students, touching on questions like free thought, love and self-love with almost Rudin's words. He is so "full of fire and enthusiasm that the other students listen to him with a feeling of admiration," but he cannot act.

In *Üle piiri,* the third novel of the series, the principal character is a beautiful and very virtuous girl-student at the gymnasium, Hedvig Stern, the daughter of a wealthy business man. She falls in love with Robert Muidu, a fellow-student who is younger than she and much less mentally developed. He declares that he is suffering from erotic passion. Again we recall Turgenev's Rudin, for Robert, like he, overflows with good nature, "that special good nature," as the author tells us, "of which men are full who are accustomed to feel themselves superior to others." Hedvig falls in love with him out of sympathy. After the two have become intimate, Hedvig discovers that she has no real love for him. So she leaves him, and immediately thereafter makes the acquaintance of a young physician, Dr. Kalamaa. Soon they become engaged. Then Kalamaa discovers that Hedvig is expecting to give birth to a child, the result of her affair with Robert. At first he thinks of giving her up, but he loves money, and Hedvig's father is wealthy. So he forgives her, keeping her father's wealth well in mind. But here Hedvig's pride asserts itself. She drops the materialistic doctor, sets herself against all men, and resolves to go through life single, with her baby.

Hedvig has a certain similarity to a character of Turgenev's *Liza* in *The Nest of Nobles.* There is the important exception that Liza is so ideally virtuous that it is hard to conceive of such a person in real life. Hedvig, disappointed in love and socially dishonored, sets herself against all men; her ideal now is to live only for her child. Turgenev's Liza, after an unhappy love affair with Lavretsky, a married man, enters a convent.

Tammsaare had great and deserved success wtih his new type of novel. In the manner of Turgenev in his portrayal of Rudin, he shows his characters from the outside and not from within. He puts the character before the reader, not through soul analysis but by means of the impression that he makes on others. This is just the technique of Turgenev, whose idea is not to uncover the souls of his heroes by subjective analysis. They are to become known to the reader by the way in which they affect others, which is the way one discovers character in real life. Although Rudin does not amount to much when it comes to action, he is a master of words and through his flowing oratory we remember him as if he were an old acquaintance. This is just the method employed in the novels of Tammsaare in this period.

Kampmaa says that Tammsaare in his early youth, having been inspired by Tolstoy's *War and Peace,* thought of writing a similar novel, using his home surroundings for a setting. He intended to picture Estonian characters and to use the beautiful countryside as a background. This dream came true only after a long number of years, and after the paradoxes in Tolstoy's philosophy had caused his influence on Tammsaare to be supplanted by that of Dostoevsky's masterpieces, *Crime and Punishment* (1868), *The Idiot* (1868), *The Possessed* (1871-72), and *The Brothers Karamazov* (1880). Life's struggle and cruelty in general are as keenly felt by Tammsaare in his *Truth and Justice,* as by Dostoevsky in his great works. Here, even more than in the case of Turgenev, the Russian influence on Tammsaare is of a stimulating character. It provided the inspiration under which the writer began to create new ideas. These are far more important than any borrowing or imitation of situations and motives.

The third period of Tammsaare's literary work unrolls before his readers the problem of "truth and justice." This had already been long in his mind when he finally chose it as the title for his great five-volume novel *Tõde ja õigus* (*Truth and Justice*).

The idea is an old one, but it is always of vital interest to humanity and always invites fresh treatment. The issue was fundamental for Tammsaare because of experience interwoven with early life. His father and neighbors had fought for justice in the courts regarding the settlement of the lands about them. Tammsaare has introduced his own father and mother as characters in the story, and has hid himself in his hero, Indrek Paas. The action takes place at Vargamäe. Here the author pictures the farm of his father, although he uses his imagination freely in describing the scenery as well as in his character delineation, according to the exigencies of the novel. (pp. 93-105)

Even the casual readers of *Truth and Justice,* who also know Dostoevsky, must feel how deeply the Russian novelist has impressed Tammsaare and how definite his influence was upon his work. It is not merely in the employment by the Estonian master of motives like the conversations on religious and philosophical problems in *The Brothers Karamazov* nor the story of Nellie and the marriage conflict in *The Insulted and the Injured.* It is not even chiefly in the similarity of the views of the two writers on moral topics. It lies rather in the identity of their conception of the fundamental problems of man's relation to God, to nature, and society, in the question of the search for the key to real happiness in human life. Tammsaare is a realist who refuses to close his eyes to things bitter or ugly, but rather looks deeply into them because he is convinced that in everything there is some good. This is also characteristic of Dostoevsky. The writers share the belief in the necessity for religion in the battle of life. The more clearly they realized mortal misery and sin, the more firmly they believed in God. In contrast with many other writers, they do not essay to show the reader what is insane in the sanest of man, but rather they seek to find the sanity of the insane.

Dostoevsky and Tammsaare are aware that suffering exists, that no one is guilty, that one thing follows upon another in a perfectly simple fashion, that everything proceeds from something else, and that everything works out as in a mathematical equation. But this is not enough for them. They feel the need of compensation and retribution, not sometime in infinity, but now on this earth, so that they may see it themselves.

Both have a profound sympathy with humanity. This is nowhere more evident than in their attitude towards the suffering of little children. They understand that retribution may be demanded for the sins of men, but they cannot understand the idea that suffering is God's punishment for children, for a child has not yet had time to sin. Tammsaare sends all of the children away from Vargamäe as soon as possible, leaving the parents to suffer and continue their fight against nature alone. In his *Truth and Justice* he has given a deeply sympathetic picture of all human suffering. This, perhaps, more than anything else gives it its unique position in Estonian literature.

Truth and Justice is indeed a marvelous panorama of human life and is entitled to a high position in the world's literature. The author's dependence on Dostoevsky in no sense diminishes his claim to originality. On the background of the nature and society of a small nation, just become conscious of its own national culture, he has drawn the picture of the struggle for true happiness with a sovereign hand. Little Estonia can indeed be proud of her master of the novel, Anton Hansen Tammsaare. (pp. 136-38)

Elizabeth Judas, in her Russian Influences on Estonian Literature: A Study of Jakob Tamm and Anton

H. Tammsaare, *Wetzel Publishing Co., Inc., 1941, 159 p.*

ARVO MÄGI (essay date 1968)

[*In the following excerpt, Mägi discusses Tammsaare's major works.*]

Anton H. Tammsaare started writing as a schoolboy in the realist tradition of the turn of the century. He described the conflict between generations on Estonian farms of that time as an inevitable fate for which neither party was responsible.

In 1908-1917 he published a number of longer narratives about young intellectuals, estranged from their families as well as from bourgeois society. Their days are devoted to philosophical discussions and to erotic philandering. Tammsaare's style in this his early work is already full of indirect references, syntheses and ironic aphorisms. Apparently incidental occurrences lead frequently to fatal consequences.

Tammsaare returned to village life in his novel *Kõrboja peremees* (*Farmer on Kõrboja*). It describes the tragical love between the educated daughter of a wealthy farmer and the stubborn, dare-devil son of a poor farmer. The man, disabled in a quarrying accident, considers himself unworthy of marrying the heiress of a rich farm and commits suicide. The novel, full of the tension of an inevitable tragedy, is also thoroughly aware of surrounding nature.

The *magnum opus* of Estonian fiction is Tammsaare's five-volume novel *Tõde ja õigus* (*Truth and Right*). The first volume, partly autobiographical, describes village life at the end of last century. Two neighbouring farmers—severe, hard-working Andres and the prankster Pearu—keep quarrelling and starting lawsuits against each other. Andres, the hard worker, fights the eternal (and, in the view of the author, hopeless) battle of all peasants of the world against a surfeit of water, stones and brushwood. The younger generation leaves the farm because of unremitting toil and because of the prevailing gloom. This latter is partly due to a sense of guilt from which Andres and Mari, his second wife, suffer because of an imagined adultery. All Andres's toil does not bring him closer to the fulfilment of his dreams, and his children refuse to carry on his work.

In the second volume, which is also partly autobiographical, Andres's son, Indrek, moves to Tartu to study at Maurus's private school. Teachers and pupils alike spend endless hours in an intense search for a theory of life. The novel abounds with lengthy dialogues and monologues analysing (and occasionally turning up-side-down) all problems imaginable. Indrek loses his faith in God but is forced to admit that miracles are possible when a crippled girl suddenly regains her ability to walk. Maurus, the owner of the school, is a complex personality and a pedagogue with his own peculiar brand of logic.

The action of the third volume takes place during the Russian revolution of 1905. The author is deeply disappointed with the longed-for liberty. The insurgents are incapable of making any other use of their short freedom than egoistical transactions or senseless destruction. This short freedom is brutally suppressed: Indrek's brother is shot and his father, Andres, beaten up by Tsarist punitive troops. Indrek gives his mother Mari, suffering from incurable cancer, a killing drug out of compassion with her. His beloved drowns herself when she learns that her father has been an agent of the Tsarist political police.

The fourth volume of the novel is basically the most pessimistic one. It describes the parvenus in Estonian towns in the twenties, their lack of culture, their careerism, avarice, blind superstition and sexual anarchy. The last-mentioned is represented by Indrek's wife, Karin, and by her insatiable erotic curiosity. Indrek shoots and wounds her when he catches her in the act of adultery—above all because she accuses him of matricide. Indrek is acquitted while Karin is killed by a tram.

In the fifth volume Indrek returns voluntarily to his native farm to dig ditches. Much has changed in the village since the events described in the first volume. Andres has now grown into a gentle philosopher. Before his death he sees the fulfilment of his great dream—the start of a large scale drainage project. Pearu tries, half forcibly, to acquire for his farm the "blood" of Andres's first wife, Krõõt, Pearu's secret love. Indrek's former maid, Tiina (the girl who regained her ability to walk in the second volume), follows him to the village. Tiina's almost superhuman goodness calls forth only evil among her fellow men. The novel ends with Indrek's and Tiina's departure from the farm for a new life together.

The entire novel is based upon a psychological intrigue the consequences of which bind together the five volumes (Andres's and Mari's illicit love). The outer scope of the novel is extensive: it describes suggestively a number of social milieus during half a century. A couple of hundred characters come alive under the author's pen. The novel's problems are deep-reaching and its psychological analyses penetrating. The whole is permeated with a sense of the inevitable. In the later volumes one can feel nostalgia for the "good old days." The author's indirect, humoristic and ironical comments, his plenitude of aphorisms and of psychological observations, make his style thoroughly enjoyable.

The most interesting of Tammsaare's later work is his last novel, *Põrgupõhja uus Vanapagan* (*The New Old Nick of Hell's Bottom*). Tammsaare, balancing on the borderline between reality and fantasy, uses here the folk tale motives of a gawky Old Nick and a clever Kaval Ants. His sympathies are with the former, he shows how the intelligent, but egoistical and heartless Kaval Ants exploits the simple-minded Nick and his family. Nick's blind revolt in the concluding chapters of the novel is but senseless destructiveness and arson. The general mood of the novel is gloomy, its imagery starkly grotesque.

Tammsaare, a penetrating novelist, is one of the central personages of Estonian literature. In *Tõde ja õigus* he has created a whole "Tammsaarean" world. Beginning with Vol. II of this his major work, he characterises his personages and presents his ideas largely in the form of dialogue. His literary models include, possibly, Fedor Dostoevsky and Joseph Conrad. (pp. 54-7)

> *Arvo Mägi, "Neo-Realism of the Independence Period," in his* Estonian Literature: An Outline, *translated by Elga Eliaser, The Baltic Humanitarian Association, 1968, pp. 48-68.*

ENDEL NIRK (essay date 1970)

[*In the following excerpt, Nirk examines the themes and techniques that unify Tammsaare's work.*]

A. H. Tammsaare made his literary debut in the early years of the century with short prose items depicting country life. The young writer seemed to continue the realistic trend familiar from the works of Vilde and Kitzberg. Nevertheless, already in his writings of that period there was something which was new and promising. This was a special striving and ability to see the complexity of and the contradictions inherent in human nature and to depict them in a subtly modulated manner. Inspired by the great Russian realists, Dostoevski in particular, Tammsaare saw his primary task in the true-to-life and manifold description of the psychology of his characters. In consequence Tammsaare deliberately concentrated all his attention on human strivings and aspirations with social conflicts forming a more remote background. Tammsaare's earlier stories do indeed contain some downright naturalistic descriptions of abject poverty and the reader can just sense its social causes. The author does not, however, confine himself to this, but lays special emphasis on something quite different: the coarseness and drabness of everyday drudgery and the tragicomical senselessness of continuous bickering (**"Two Couples and the Single One"**), the tragic lack of understanding and the conflict between generations (**"The Old and the Young"**). Some of his stories were written under the immediate influence of the revolutionary events of 1905.

Subsequently Tammsaare gravitated towards the *Noor-Eesti* group, although he never became one of the more active members. His interest now shifted to an analysis of the inner workings of the human soul. The more extensive stories of the period (***Long Steps, Young Souls, Across the Border***) are concerned mainly with immature young intellectuals and their often ill-defined moods and cravings, their somewhat aimless aspirations and fanciful ratiocinations, their defiance of a petty-bourgeois mode of life. In these stories everything external, even the plot, is neglected and the writer's entire attention is focused on the impressionistic rendering of the psychological background to various youthfully exuberant discussions. This necessary intermediate stage in the writer's evolution led to greater successes in the stories **"Nuances"** and **"The Fly"** (both in 1917). Here an impressionistic depiction of moods and feelings is synthesised with increasingly realistic character studies, thus providing a foretaste of the author's work in his prime. Tammsaare's artistic fairy tales and miniatures (in the anthology *The Boy and the Butterfly*), written under the influence of O. Wilde, are among the finest achievements of Estonian neo-romantic literature.

A writer disposed to live like a philosopher-recluse, Tammsaare's poor health also compelled him to lead a life of retirement. During those long years full of mental tension and tireless self-development his epic talent matured. In his later years as well, Tammsaare remained aloof from political and social life, although he closely and critically followed events in Estonia and throughout the world. He sought to maintain his independence as a creative personality in order to serve only what he considered to be truly great literature and his own humanistic ideals in the field of art. The subsequent writings of the author, who had by then attained self-confidence and a high degree of mastery, constitute the best works of the period.

Known until then exclusively as a prose writer, Tammsaare surprised the reading public with a play ***Judith,*** in which a biblical story repeatedly dealt with in world literature received a new, unexpected and contemporary interpretation. Unlike the heroine in the Bible (and also in F. Hebbel's tragedy of the same name) Tammsaare's Judith utters her patriotic phrases merely to camouflage her true motives. Frustrated in her feminine and maternal instincts, she is impelled to go over to the hostile camp by her ambition to win the love of the military hero Holofernes, and then to incite him to seek the royal throne,

thus enabling her to become the ancestress of a new dynasty. It is only when the famous general, who has long felt a repugnance for power and glory, is sobered by the woman's ambitions and rejects her, that the jilted and enraged Judith decides to kill Holofernes in revenge. It is thus that the writer deprived Judith of the aureole of heroism and, at the same time, produced a work that condemns speculation with ideas, a work with a humanitarian resonance directed against war, violence and despotism. With the diversity and psychological interest of its character studies and its precise as well as pithy wording, ***Judith*** is a work that could be compared with some of the plays of G. B. Shaw, whom Tammsaare esteemed so highly.

In his novel ***The Master of Kõrboja Farm*** the author returned to a subject particularly close to his heart, namely to that of rural life, the mentality of country folk, the theme of struggle against the force of circumstances and against one's own inner nature. If in Tammsaare's stories about intellectuals the characters were usually removed from their social environment and placed, as it were, in a chamber for psychological experiments, then in this novel the evolution of human destinies is shown as the result of the dialectical interplay of external and internal forces. The novel is the tragic love story of a young man from the country, strong-willed and determined, but unrestrained in temperament and defiantly proud, and an educated young woman who longs to return to country life. The complex psychology of both characters is presented in a masterly fashion. The novel provides ample evidence of the extent to which the author's realism had become artistically more subtle and refined. Dealing as it does with problems of general human interest and owing to its inherent poetic tonality, ***The Master of Kõrboja Farm*** is one of the most charming novels in Estonian literature. It is here that the author's peculiar manner of expression with its suggestivity and abundant use of repetitions may be seen at its best.

After the success of ***The Master of Kõrboja Farm*** Tammsaare felt he could begin the realisation of a plan which had taken shape over the years, that of writing a lengthy epochal novel ***Truth and Justice***. This work in five volumes appeared in 1926—1933, and made the author a classic already in his life-time. It also permits him to be regarded as one of the most original thinkers and novelists in Europe during the period between the two World Wars. The novel ***Truth and Justice*** is more deeply rooted in Estonian life and reflects the Estonian character better than any previous work of literature. Despite its concrete local subject-matter the novel also deals with many of the crucial issues of our time. The latter include above all such problems as the essence and significance of the human struggle for existence, the foundations of and the preconditions for the development of a truly humanitarian culture, the possibilities of checking the erosion of human values by the evils of bourgeois civilisation.

A close study of the life of his own people in all its manifestations led Tammsaare to the conclusion that culture cannot be mechanically taken over or copied, but that it has to be created independently. In order to do this the same intensity, earnestness and depth of thought, feeling and action are necessary as are characteristic of the more advanced nations of Europe. Tammsaare believed—somewhat idealistically, of course—that he could find all this above all in the peasantry which constituted the bulk of the Estonian nation, and which had until then been the embodiment of its vitality. It is from among the farmers and the intellectuals of rural stock that Tammsaare selected the protagonists of the ideas dearest to his heart; and whom he contrasted to characters warped by a capitalist sense of property or rendered shiftless and paltry by superficial urbanisation. Such contrasts are not the result of any dislike of progress or a nostalgia for the past. They are due first and foremost to the author's endeavour to ascertain the foundation on which the life of his people is based and on which alone one could build something really lasting. This is the basic problem underlying all the parts of *Truth and Justice*. In each volume, however, it is dealt with in a different setting and from a different aspect. Each volume, moreover, has its own special problems. The novel as a whole constitutes a broad panorama of the destinies and aspirations of several generations of rural and town life, peasants and intellectuals, revolutionary circles and the upstart bourgeoisie, the ideas and social relations of an entire period in all their complexity. The author, a keen observer of life, has also woven numerous comic threads into the serious web of the novel and there is room for humour and irony as well. Tammsaare appreciated wise scepticism, but he certainly did not disdain lyricism.

The first three volumes of *Truth and Justice* contain much that is autobiographical (early life on a farm, secondary school days in Tartu, the years spent as a journalist in Tallinn), whereas the last two volumes constitute a sequel based on more general observations of life. Nevertheless the author's imagination remoulded and enriched the subject-matter of the first volumes in accordance with the overall artistic conception of the work. Tammsaare himself characterised the different parts of the novel as follows: part one describes man's struggle with the land, part two—his struggle with God, part three—man's struggle with society, part four—his struggle with himself, and his search for happiness, part five depicts resignation. But Tammsaare also emphasised that this should be understood only as the domination of a certain idea in a given part of the novel, in reality all the ideas referred to are intertwined and they underlie the work as a whole.

The struggle with the swampy and stony land, the age-old struggle and endless toil of the peasant to wrest a living from the stingy soil, is interpreted in *Truth and Justice* as the primeval basis of all progress and culture. It is in this struggle that the writer sees true human depth and seriousness of purpose, as well as genuine intensity of feelings and aspirations. As a great realist and keen-sighted analyser Tammsaare also depicts the contradictions in the evolution of the personality of his hero Vargamäe Andres, the bitterness caused by excessive toil and boundary disputes with a spiteful neighbour, the stern reticence resulting from the incomplete realisation of one's plans and from a variety of tribulations, estrangement from one's children as well as disillusionment with religion. Despite everything, however, the indefatigable workman remains true to his ideals; a society infected with the spirit of speculation and profiteering does not succeed in remoulding him. The knowledge that despite occasional lapses he has, on the whole, engaged in a righteous struggle for truth and justice gives the old farmer profound satisfaction and lends a noble poetic radiance to the decline of his life.

Matters are different in the case of those who lack a serious purpose in life and who are inwardly warped. These are people who do not seek truth but specious justice, and who do not value creative work but only property and the privileges it confers. Such traits are conspicuous in Andres's neighbour Oru Pearu. Tricky by nature and fond of litigation, he is one of the most complex and interesting characters in the novel whose

ostentatious individualism and egocentricity drag him unawares towards an inevitable dead end. One cannot but feel downright pity for the floundering Maurus, the secondary school headmaster, who has destroyed his own personality by adapting himself to the abnormal conditions created by reactionary Czardom and with whom equivocation and paradoxical utterances have become second nature. When depicting town life Tammsaare now draws downright sarcastic portraits of representatives of the upstart bourgeoisie who have lost touch with everything that is healthy and creative, and whose greed is as repellent as their wastefulness (especially in Part 4 which deals with the early period of the bourgeois republic).

The central character in *Truth and Justice* is Vargamäe Andres's son Indrek Paas, who leaves the countryside in pursuit of knowledge in town. The life story of this young man passes through the whole novel. In the course of his education Indrek overcomes the religious prejudices of the peasant environment in which he grew up and finds his way to materialism and atheism. Like the majority of his contemporaries Indrek is attracked by attempts to modernise society and he takes part in revolutionary events, being repelled, however, by violence and the spontaneous human urge to destroy. Indrek is not a man of action, but rather an introvert who tends to ponder over the meaning of life and to seek for truth and justice in the contradictions of the period in which he lives. His attempt to find shelter from the harsh realities of life in marriage and bourgeois prosperity proves illusory. It is inevitable that there can be no lasting trust or mutual understanding between a man of his kind and a woman that is restless and thirsty for life, and who is attracted by a society actuated by avarice, the pursuit of pleasure, corruption and careerism. Disillusioned and mentally unhinged, Indrek returns to his father's farm where in simple labour and direct contact with the land he endeavours to find himself anew and gathers strength to resist the ravaging influence of a profit-seeking society that has rejected the true values of life.

A. H. Tammsaare's *Truth and Justice* with its search for humanist ideals may be included among the period novels of the early 20th century, the most outstanding of which were written by R. Rolland, Th. Mann and J. Galsworthy. There are certain differences as regards artistic perfection (e.g. parts of the novel are marred by prolix discussions and the verbosity of some of the characters); on the other hand, however, the Estonian writer has drawn on his own life experience and introduced a great deal of such material that is lacking in the works of the urbanised West-European authors.

Immediately after completing his main work, Tammsaare produced two more novels (*Life and Love, I Loved a German Girl*) in which a psychological study of love is interwoven with social as well as ethical problems and with a criticism of bourgeois morality and culture. The last period of the writer's life is marked by new ideas and a new artistic quality in the play *The King Feels Cold* and in the novel *The New Vanapagan of Põrgupõhja*. In these works Tammsaare's philosophy and criticism of society assume a conventional and allegorical guise which lends them greater force and broader applicability. Developing the biblical theme of an old king who suffers from the cold, Tammsaare in his satirical play transfers him to a non-existent European state and turns him into a symbol of the crisis of the bourgeois social system and in human relations generally. In the shape of a new religious movement, whose idol is a double-headed calf, the author provides a grotesque generalisation of fascist demagogy and its influence. This witty satire of various anti-democratic manifestations is evidence that Tammsaare embarked on a new course in drama at the same time as B. Brecht. Tammsaare's critical pathos reached its culmination in the novel *The New Vanapagan of Põrgupõhja*. This book is a merciless indictment of bourgeois society with its injustice, selfishness and demagogy. A peculiarity of the work is the ingenious manner in which it makes use of elements of folklore and mythology. Such an approach reinforces the tone of the novel and gives the latter the semblance of a myth that generalises the fundamental conflicts of the period. The author succeeded in showing that even a trustful and simple-minded drudge endowed with superhuman physical strength finally recognises who is his real enemy in this world full of lies, injustice and hypocrisy, and that all the moralising as well as religious and patriotic demagogy of the oppressors cannot save them from their doom. The lasting popularity of this novel is due to its originality of treatment, masterly delineation of characters, interplay of scathing satire and inimitable humour, as well as to its underlying keen sense of justice and profound humaneness.

In addition to his work as a writer of fiction Tammsaare was also for many decades a prolific publicist and essayist. He wrote a large number of articles on the most varied subjects. In these articles he developed the democratic and humanitarian ideas on which his entire literary production is based, and he did this with characteristic thoughtfulness, a marked capacity for dialectical analysis and a wittiness interspersed with paradoxes.

A. H. Tammsaare is the greatest epic talent that Estonian literature has ever known. He gave much serious thought to the crucial problems confronting mankind, he possessed extraordinary powers of discernment and literary self-expression. He carried on from where E. Vilde, the first distinguished Estonian critical realist, had left off; he received impulses from the neo-romantic trend and from various movements that sought to develop realism in other countries. It was thus that Tammsaare led Estonian critical realism to its culmination in the '20s and '30s of this century, and his literary heritage has continuously gained in significance ever since both at home and abroad. (pp. 208-18)

> *Endel Nirk, "Prose Fiction and Its Principal Representatives," in his* Estonian Literature: Historical Survey with Bibliographical Appendix, *translated by V. Hain, A. R. Hone and O. Mutt, Eesti Raamat, 1970, pp. 204-39.*

ILSE LEHISTE   (lecture date 1972)

[Lehiste is an Estonian-born American critic and linguist. In the following excerpt from a lecture delivered in 1972 and later published in the volume Baltic Literature and Linguistics, *she provides an analysis of* The Misadventures of the New Satan.]

Far from people and their habitations, in a lost corner of the woods, was a solitary farm called Põrgupõhja: Hell's Bottom in Estonian. Everybody thought that it was empty, and had been empty for years, since the old farmer had died and a new one had not been found to take his place. But one fine day a chance passer-by noticed smoke coming from the vent-hole of Hell's Bottom farm. Somebody had evidently moved in: Hell's Bottom had a new master.

This is the beginning of Anton H. Tammsaare's last novel, *Põrgupõhja uus Vanapagan (The New Devil of Hell's Bottom)*, written in 1939, one year before his death. The novel occupies a special place not only in Tammsaare's rich epic production, but in all of Estonian literature. It constitutes no more and no less than a negative counterpart to the story of Faust and Mephistopheles, the inverse of the story of salvation.

The novel starts with a prologue in Heaven. (The prologue was not published in 1939; it was first included in the fifth edition, published in 1954.) The Devil shows up at the gate to complain that the supply of new entrants to Hell has dried up. St. Peter explains that God is having second thoughts about his creation of mankind: it just might be possible that man, as God has created him, is not able to live in such a way as to merit heaven. Therefore it would be unfair to condemn him to hell. God makes the Devil a new proposition: the supply of condemned souls will recommence, if the Devil will agree to become human and demonstrate that it is possible to live on earth in such a way as to merit heaven. As far as forgiveness of sins is concerned, salvation just does not count anymore. The Devil agrees and becomes human: he is the new master of Hell's Bottom, and the only purpose of his life is to deserve heaven.

This is what I mean by the inverse of the story of salvation: the Devil becomes mortal, not in order to save sinners, but to guarantee that they will go to hell as before. And the way to achieve it is for the Devil to merit heaven. Tammsaare's complex novel shows how he both succeeds and fails. While Goethe's Mephistopheles was a spirit who always intended evil, but created good, Tammsaare's Devil desires nothing but to do good, and yet he creates evil. Assuming human nature, he, too, is unable to merit heaven, and the question whether man would be able to do so remains untestable.

This cosmic question is embedded in a form that blends myth and fairy tale with fierce social satire. A special cycle of Estonian folk tales deals with the relationship between the Devil and a shrewd farmer named Ants. The Devil is depicted in these tales as a hulking brute, with superhuman strength, but subhuman intelligence. The clever farmer Ants is always able to outwit the Devil. The Devil's name in these stories is Vanapagan, which literally means "Old Heathen"; it has been speculated that the purpose of the stories was to strengthen Christianity by ridiculing the Devil as representative of the old heathen religion. I think it more probable that we are dealing with a verbal taboo: the name "Old Heathen" was used in order not to mention the Devil by his true name, and its use reflects a still real belief in the Devil's powers. Nevertheless, the storyteller's sympathy was with Ants; the Devil's superior strength is of no avail, the weaker one wins. Tammsaare's Devil resembles the devil of these folk tales. He is a barrel of a man, somewhat taller than average, but almost as broad as tall; he has a broad face, low forehead, and a red curly beard that seems to continue down his neck and chest. His strength is literally that of a bear; he kills two of them in paw-to-paw combat. As far as intelligence is concerned, he is even worse off than the Old Heathen of the folk tales, since he has to contend with modern society (modern in 1939, that is). The clever weakling Ants appears in Tammsaare's novel as a modern operator, who starts out as a farmer, but soon expands into other business, amassing a fortune through deceit and falsehood. Ants presents himself to the Devil as a friend and benefactor and wins his complete trust. He uses it to entangle the Devil in illegal machinations and debt, so that he slaves day and night to increase the wealth of Ants. The law does not protect him, for the laws are made by Ants and people of his ilk. In spite of superhuman labors on the farm, the Devil and his family fall deeper and deeper into misery. Yes, the Devil has a family; in fact he even has two wives for a while. The first is Lisete, the wife he brought with him from hell; the other is Juula, an earthly woman who is a match for him in both strength of body and simplicity of mind. When Juula announces to Lisete that she expects twins, the first wife lies down in bed, refuses food and drink, and dies. When her coffin is dug up a few weeks after the funeral, it is found to contain only stones; the Devil explains that she has gone straight to hell as she had promised, but he finds few believers.

The humanness of the Devil becomes most evident in his concern for his children, who are destroyed one after another by Ants and his household—a son driven to suicide by his daughter, a daughter seduced by his son, who persuades her to attempt a lethal abortion by false promises of marriage. The Devil is sustained by his conviction that the more he labors and suffers, the more certain he is of meriting heaven. His wife dies, and he is left mourning with the youngest child, a daugher named Riia, still too young to have been corrupted by Ants and the forces of society he represents. Ants entangles the Devil in another lawsuit, as a result of which he is to be thrown out of Hell's Bottom, the farm on which he has labored so hard and long. Driven to the limit of endurance, the Devil finally explodes in a blind rage. He throws Ants across the fence on a heap of stones, cracking his skull; then he burns down his own farm and sets fire to that of Ants. Nobody is able to subdue him as he rages in the midst of the flames. His body is found unburned, and Tammsaare gives him a fitting funeral. He is buried by a drunken quartet of men, consisting of a stonecutter, a ditchdigger, a peatcutter, and a latrine cleaner. The child Riia has escaped from the burning farm and follows the coffin, hugging her black cat to her breast. She falls asleep in the graveyard, her head on the grave; the wife of a church steward picks her up and carries her home.

Tammsaare delights in paradoxes, and in *The New Devil of Hell's Bottom* he has presented many of them. In the New Testament, God sent his son to become man, and men crucified him. Here, God sends the Devil, and society crucifies him too. The purpose of Christ was to save mankind; the Devil's purpose is to condemn them. No matter: men treat both in the same way. While the folk tale sided with Ants against the Devil, Tammsaare compels us to sympathize with the latter. The Devil tries to lead a saintly life, and perishes; Ants is the incarnation of evil, yet he flourishes and prospers, and all his undertakings are crowned with success. The Devil tries his utmost to merit heaven, and yet he murders, burns, and commits adultery. The minister of God, with whom the Devil has many and varied dealings, considers him an idiot, and nevertheless draws strength from the Devil's unshakable faith. After all, if there is a Devil, there must be a God.

In the epilogue, the Devil is again knocking at the gates of Heaven: he would like to know whether he has succeeded in meriting heaven during his earthly life. Centuries go by, but God cannot make up his mind. The Devil feels that his life on earth had been in vain; but St. Peter consoles him, saying that at least now he has hope. He can hope that he will be deemed worthy of heaven and thus may continue in charge of Hell.

Tammsaare's novel never indulges in sentiment. The elements of folklore incorporated in the narrative are of a robust, earthy kind; especially in the beginning of the novel, Tammsaare's wit and verbal humor make it possible to assume that the author

had little else in mind than the retelling of a funny folk tale. An undercurrent of tragedy gradually comes to the surface, becoming stronger and stronger in the second half; but even the final revolt of the tormented Devil is grotesque rather than heroic. Tammsaare's misanthropy extends to the Devil in man's body. It is only the presence of the child Riia that lends a note of warmth and tenderness to the conclusion and saves us from nihilistic despair. (pp. 69-72)

Ilse Lehiste, "Tammsaare, Kangro, and the Devil," in Baltic Literature and Linguistics, *edited by Arvids Ziedonis, Jr. & others, Association for the Advancement of Baltic Studies, Inc., 1973, pp. 69-74.*

FELIX J. OINAS (essay date 1986)

[*Oinas is an Estonian-born American critic who specializes in the study of Baltic languages and literature. In the following excerpt, he examines the motif of the scapegoat as it appears in Tammsaare's drama* Juudit.]

The theme of the scapegoat is one of the most dynamic in the history and literature of antiquity. It concerns overcoming distress caused either by war, an epidemic, hunger or some other calamity. As James Frazer and Walter Burkert have amply demonstrated, the essence of the scapegoat theme involves selecting a victim, who is then adorned and sent out into a desert to perish or is killed outright. Its death eliminates the cause of the danger. The scapegoat is thus a material vehicle by which the evils of the community are sent beyond its boundaries. According to Claude Levi-Strauss' formula, the scapegoat is the mediator who brings about the reversal from common danger to common salvation: the situation "community endangered" versus "individual distinguished" is turned into "individual doomed" versus "community saved."

The Old Testament reports that on the day of Atonement (Yom Kippur) two goats were selected, one of which was to be sacrificed to Jahve and the other to his opposite Azazel. After confessing the sins of Israel, the high priest placed the sins on the head of the second goat and sent it to its doom in the desert. The scapegoat could also be a person. In the Greek Thargelia festival of Apollo, a repulsive person becomes the scapegoat (*pharmakós*), is garlanded, fed, and then mistreated and destroyed.

Animals and human beings could also be sent to the enemy. This was done in the case of war or plague (which was thought to be sent by a god of the enemy). The Hittites, e.g., crowned a ram and sent it to the land of the enemy. A similar action, motivated either by the enemy's impending attack or a plague, is also known in Ancient India, Ancient Greece and Rome. In all of them, the act of sending forth an animal or human to perish amidst the enemy called forth disorder and panic. The country that accepted this animal or human also accepted the loss of the war or the onset of the plague.

A variation of this theme involves a female who voluntarily becomes a scapegoat. Usually the girl has a love affair with the enemy commander or some other dignitary, who pays for his lechery with the loss of the war. In this instance, it is more appropriate to speak of "self-sacrifice" rather than "scapegoat," as Erich Neumann has suggested.

Burkert, in his investigation of this pattern, gives a few typical examples. Polycrite, by her self-sacrifice, saves her native island of Naxos in Greece. She has been left behind in a sanctuary of Apollo, when the troops from Miletus and Erythrae invade the island. The enemy commander Diognitos has a love-affair with her. Polycrite exploits the situation by keeping her brothers informed about the enemy. During a festival celebration, the unsuspecting enemy is attacked and routed. Upon her triumphant return home, Polycrite is welcomed with so many garlands, girdles and shawls that she expires under their weight. After her death, a special cult is established in her honor.

In antiquity, this pattern became quite common. Victory was guaranteed, if females simply fell into the hands of the enemy, where they were mishandled. For example, the virgins of Leuctra, *Leuctrides parthénoi,* had been treacherously raped by Spartan soldiers and had afterwards killed themselves out of shame. Epaminondas of Thebes, fighting against Sparta, paid homage to their tomb and through this act alone guaranteed his victory over the Spartans.

We can even attribute the final loss of the Trojan war to the abduction of Helen by Paris—with the help of Aphrodite in her role as pimp—and the Trojans' acceptance of her. After the end of the war, she was about to fall under Menelaus' sword, but she saved herself through "the spell of the eternal feminine" by taking off her clothes and displaying her bare breasts and her beauty. While this episode is not included in Homer's poems, it occurs in others (Euripides, Pausanius, etc.) that describe the fall of Troy. Thus, Helen was a kind of metaphorical Trojan horse, precipitating the doom of the Trojans.

In contrast, the fate of Tarpeia in Roman mythology might have been called the "scapegoat reversed." Tarpeia joined the attacking Sabines to betray the Capitol in exchange for golden bracelets. According to some reports, the king of the Sabines, Tatius, accepted her erotic charm, but not her services as a traitress, and she was killed when they threw golden and silver trinkets at her. Killing her saved the Sabines; thus, only the acceptance of the scapegoat is fateful for the receivers, but not their refusal.

The Biblical apocrypha story of Judith and Holofernes fits perfectly into the pattern of the self-sacrificing female. The city of Bethulia is about to succumb to the army of Nebuchadnezzar, commanded by Holofernes. Judith, a wealthy and beautiful widow of noble descent, decides to save the city. After fasting and prayer, she discards sackcloth and the garments of widowhood and puts on her finest apparel: "she decked herself bravely, to beguile the eyes of all men that should see her." She goes to the camp of Holofernes, accompanied by her maid. Her extraordinary beauty grants her access to the commander. On the evening of the fourth day, Judith appears to yield herself to Holofernes, by joining him at a private banquet. "Holofernes' heart was ravished and his soul was moved, and he desired exceedingly her company; and he was watching for a time to deceive her, from the day that he had seen her." Holofernes' erotic excitement and the subsequent remark that "Holofernes took great delight in her," suggest how the evening was spent. After drinking much wine, Holofernes falls asleep and Judith cuts off his head with his own sword. Together with her maid, she takes Holofernes' head to her native town. On seeing the head, a great shout of triumph arises. After panic breaks out in the Assyrian army at finding their beheaded commander, the men of Bethulia pursue the enemy and take great spoils. Judith is revered as the savior of the city and is celebrated with a psalm of thanksgiving.

Tammsaare, a classic of Estonian literature, in his drama *Juudit* uses the scenery of the Biblical story as the background for the personal tragedy of a love-thirsty woman. The basic plot of Tammsaare's play is the same: Juudit, accompanied by her maid, Susanna, arrives at Olovernes' camp, is admitted, spends a memorable but disappointing night with Olovernes, kills him, and brings his head back to Petuulia. But although the main dramatis personae are basically the same (except for Nameless in Tammsaare), the motives for their actions are different. Tammsaare's Juudit goes to Olovernes' camp not to save her home town (as she at first declares) but to consummate her passion for the famous commander. The chief elder, Osias, sees through her, when he says: "You are talking about Petuulia and Israel, but your thoughts are circling around yourself, your lusts encircle Olovernes . . . Your flesh is burning, your female beauty is in flame for Olovernes." Juudit's husband Manasse was impotent and her body craved a man's touch. While lying next to Manasse, she "hungered for life and for the joy of desires."

Preparing for her journey to Olovernes' camp, she makes her body a "fragrant flower." When she steps before Olovernes and falls down before him, she confesses to Susanna: "For the first time in my life I felt that I was really worshipping a live divinity . . . I would have liked to have remained face down." Madness overcomes her when she thinks about the women who can conceive children by him, and she decides that she, too, must have his child. "I'll become the mother of Olovernes' child, or I don't know what I'll do."

Whereas the Biblical Holofernes burns with passion for Judith, Tammsaare's Olovernes remains sober and calculating, inclined to skeptical philosophizing. Sitting cozily at Juudit's knees and feeling the warmth of her body, he feels like a child who is near his mother. And when he asks her to extinguish the chandelier, it is so they can go to bed not as man and woman, but as mother and child: "The child wants to sleep with you, the child would like to go to sleep, since he is drunk of wine and of you, mother." Because of the mother-child complex, Olovernes cannot have an erotic affair with her, although he refers to it in passing: "You are young, you are beautiful, I almost regret that you are my mother."

After the mother-child episode, their talk turns to Olovernes' greatness and fame. Juudit would like to see him still greater, and encourages him to strive for Nebukadnetsar's (Nebuchadnezzar's) throne: "Demand your right, you have the right to your father's throne. . . ." Juudit's ambition is revealed in her monologue: "Then the world will be at your feet! Then I and my kindred people will not be mistaken, awaiting you as the king. We'll go up to Jerusalem, and the knees of all will bend before you in the temple. I'll walk ahead of you and proclaim you to all creation."

Carried away by her fantasy, Juudit has completely forgotten her people. She is willing to take the enemy into her own country, in order to share his fame. Her wishful thinking soars like that of the old woman in the fairy tale "Fisherman and His Wife," in which the old woman cannot restrain the wishes guaranteed to her by the golden fish. With special vividness, the extent of Juudit's wishes appears in the following passage: "Olovernes! Olovernes! I desire you as prince of the world, king of kings, so as to look the more humbly up to you, to worship you. Today I felt for the first time as if in the proximity of God."

Juudit has revealed her secret wishes, but they do not appeal to Olovernes. He realizes that Juudit sees and hears only his name, and she would like "to make it even more glorious in the eyes of the world, so as to share in its splendor." Just as in the fairy tale of the fisherman and his wife, after the greedy old woman expresses her last unachievable wish (to become goddess), so a full twist of fate also happens with Juudit. Olovernes tells her frankly: "I would like you better, if you were not so ambitious." Juudit's wish to have a child by him, expressed by hints, is decidedly rejected: "You are young and beautiful. Nebukadnetsar is arriving soon; there is still place in his harem for quite a few who wish to bear the king's sons and daughters." Olovernes is tired and would like to go to sleep, since "Olovernes does not forget his duties because of a woman."

Olovernes' rejection strikes Juudit like a thunderbolt. "My virginity has once more become a laughing stock," she complains to Susanna. Utterly offended by her misfortune and Olovernes' apathy, she instigates Nameless (Nimetu) to kill him. When Nameless refuses and, instead, commits suicide, Juudit in anger and revenge cuts Olovernes' head off with his sword. Not having had him in life, she passionately kisses his lifeless head, like Oscar Wilde's Salome.

When Juudit returns home with Olovernes' severed head, she is received with jubilation as the savior. The Assyrian troops, left without a leader, take to flight. But in the midst of the triumph, Juudit breaks down "under the burden of sanctimoniousness and murders." Her love for the dead Olovernes erupts like a volcano and makes her hurl her sins and crimes before the people. She confesses that it was not the fate of her hometown, but "the desire, wild desire," that sent her to Olovernes' camp. In the past as she had not only awakened lust in young men, "who had enough virility," but also had baited her husband with them. Manasse had died as a result. As a murderess and adultress, Juudit demands that she be stoned to death and her body be thrown over the wall. Shouts are heard: "Take her out! Out of the gates! Beyond the wall!"

The crowd begins to move with Juudit to the gates to execute her. But at this moment Osias, frustrated by his loss of Juudit and the vacillation of the masses, kills himself, and thus turns the people's attention away from her. With her house pillaged, she is taken in by old Siimeon to live with his dog in a corner of his hut.

The final act of Tammsaare's *Juudit* at the city wall is permeated with carnivalistic features. "Here everything is unexpected, out of place, incompatible and impermissible if judged by life's ordinary, 'normal' course." First of all, we have here the most typical characteristics of carnival—crowning and decrowning. Juudit performs the role of the carnival queen. Having arrived with Olovernes' head, she is received as the Savior. This is apparent from the following dialogue:

> AKIOR. (*chief of Ammon, falling down before Juudit*): Great are you and great is your God . . .
>
> VOICES. Long live Juudit!
>
> OSIAS. (*chief elder of Petuulia*): Do run, shout, blow trumpets, roll the drums, rattle the weapons, so that all will hear and will come. Announce to everybody: Juudit has beaten the Assur!

> AKIOR. You have killed the mightiest of all men whom my eyes have seen.
>
> OSIAS. Rejoice, Juudit, be glad, for all generations will praise you blessed from now on: you have saved Israel.

Soon after that comes the fall of Juudit from her regal pedestal. After she has confessed her sins, the elder of Petuulia, Kabris, takes the floor:

> KABRIS. Men and women of Petuulia, it is not good that young wives begin to kill their old husbands because of their desires; it is not good that the men of Israel have to worry for their life in the marriage bed.
>
> VOICES. (*of men and women pell-mell*): That's right! . . . Kabris has spoken well . . . Juudit has to die! Death! Death!
>
> VOICES. Juudit has killed her husband! Juudit is guilty of her husband's blood! His blood should come upon us and our children!
>
> VOICES. Take her out! Out of the gates! Beyond the wall! Out!

In the fate of Juudit, we see the carnivalistic rise and fall: from the height of the carnival queen she comes crashing down to earth, having debased and decrowned herself. This fall has been preceded by another fall, which foreshadowed, as it were, the latter, viz. the crashing of the imagined throne of the one standing next to Olovernes, his mother or his favorite wife.

This scene has numerous other carnivalistic traits as well. The carnival square is represented here by the square at the city wall. This place corresponds to the threshold in carnivalistic works, from which paths lead to the city and beyond the wall, controlled by the enemy. Here, heterogeneous people—the elders, the rabbi and the mob—are in free, familiar contact and listen to the sensational news. Here Juudit unveils her past and her most intimate secrets to acquaintances and strangers alike, as is usual in carnivalistic literature. The people are flabbergasted by what they hear and are not sure what to think of it. Their reaction undergoes sudden shifts according to what their leaders say. When the elder Kabris comes out with his suggestion that Juudit is guilty, the mob agrees and demands that she be stoned.

This is a scandal scene typical of carnivalized works. Carnivalization is especially characteristic of Dostoevskij; it is found—as Baxtin has demonstrated—in his major novels (*Crime and Punishment, The Brothers Karamazov,* etc.) and in short stories ("The Village of Stepančikovo and Its Inhabitants," etc.). Tammsaare was profoundly interested in Dostoevskij. It is not impossible that in the carnivalization of the last act of *Juudit* Dostoevskij's influence may be manifested.

Concerning *Juudit,* critics have repeatedly raised the question: what was the reason for Juudit's tragedy—the drama of unsatisfied passions or ambition and greed for power? H. Siimisker writes: "Observing the logic of Juudit's behavior, we can agree with both of these assertions." Siimisker is obviously right. Lust had accumulated in Juudit for years. It increased after Olovernes' approach to Petuulia and her dreams about him. A visit to him could satisfy her passions and—as importantly—also her ambitions. The possibility of erotic involvement with one of the world's most powerful men added a special attraction to the prospect of meeting him.

A comparison of the Biblical story and Tammsaare's version of the drama reveals essential differences. In the Bible, the victim offers herself to a lecherous man. In Tammsaare, a lecherous woman is treated by the man not as the object of erotic love, but as a mother figure. In both cases the man, literally, loses his head—in the first for the sake of the woman's hometown, in the second as the victim of a woman scorned. In both, the woman is received with hosannas for her heroic deed, but in Tammsaare's work she barely escapes stoning.

Let us now examine the structure of the stories of women's self-sacrifice to win a war. (Tarpeia, and perhaps Helen are exceptions.) The pattern that emerges, excluding Tammsaare's *Juudit,* is as follows:

1. The female goes to the enemy, viz. Polycrite from Naxos to the Erythraeans; Biblical Judith from Bethulia, Israel, to the Assyrians; Tarpeia from Rome to the Sabines; and Helen from the Achaians to Troy.

2. The woman has an erotic encounter with the enemy commander or other dignitary; Polycrite with Diognetus, a general of the Erythraeans; Judith with Olofernes; Tarpeia with the ruler Tatius; and Helen with Paris, son of king Priam.

3. She renders decisive military help to her army, either by sending information or giving a sign (Polycrite, Helen), or killing the enemy commander, her sexual partner (Judith).

4. Her action guarantees victory for her army. Thus, the enemy of the island of Naxos is beaten as a result of Polycrite's deed and the army of the Assyrians is routed because of Judith's feat.

5. The female is occasionally killed or condemned by her own people, but since this happens after the victory, it has no effect on the outcome of the war. Polycrite perishes after her return, by being buried under the garlands and trinkets hurled at her. Helen, destined to die at the hands of her husband, survives only because of her feminine wiles. If, however, the enemy repudiates the girl and kills her, as is the case with Tarpeia, then her action has no effect on the outcome of the war.

This pattern has been persistent in legends and literature for thousands of years, perhaps because of the thrill and power engendered by the sacrifice of a female for a high cause. She goes out alone into a hostile environment to accomplish an enormous task, one which seems to be in the powers of gods alone—to ensure victory and freedom for her country. With her charm and skill, she is expected to obtain victory from a lecherous commander or other dignitary. The only commodity she has to offer is sex or, if she is a virgin, her virginity, the most valuable of her possessions. There is, furthermore, the possibility of losing her life. But despite the risks, she undertakes the mission.

As Burkert has shown, this theme is rooted in the real, unritualized situation, in which a group, pursued by predators, has to sacrifice one of themselves, in order to save the rest. For example, in the tale about travelers whose sleigh is pursued by hungry wolves, when the horse tires, some passengers are thrown out to save the others. The situation is likewise present in stories about the becalmed boat which can be set in motion

only with the sacrifice of one of the crew. Or, during war, a small detachment is left behind in a fort to cover the retreat of the main force. Being anchored deeply in real life and folklore, this story has enjoyed undiminished interest in legend and literature for ages. Saad Elkhadem, for instance, lists fifteen authors (not knowing Tammsaare), who have used the Biblical story of Judith since the tenth century.

Tammsaare's drama only partially fits into the self-sacrifice pattern. Juudit goes to the enemy camp (1), kills the commander (3), brings about the victory for Israel (4), and is finally taken behind the city gates to be stoned to death (5), although she is saved by an unexpected occurrence.

Tammsaare has, however, made an essential change in the pattern—he lets Juudit spend a night in Olovernes' company without eroticism (move 2). It is obvious that eroticism is the chief trade mark of the self-sacrifice pattern. What does Tammsaare offer instead? Just a lengthy conversation on two topics: the child-mother relationship, and the spread and increase of Olovernes' power. The child-mother topic and the assumption of the role of the naive child is unfitting for a ladies' man commander, who is known to have virgins procured for him. He even confesses to Juudit that "the warmth of your body is sweeter than wine," "the warmth of your body dazes me," and "I attacked the peoples with war chariots, in order (to be able) to touch your trembling limbs and to hear your whispering voice." (But, nevertheless, he does not touch her, because of the idea that she is his mother!)

Why did Tammsaare bring the mother-child relationship into the drama? Mihkel Kampmaa writes: "Realizing that Juudit is a woman who loves the child in a man, Olovernes too wants to be Juudit's big and beloved child." When Juudit is first taken before Olovernes, it is true, she refers to woman as the mother. We cannot, however, believe that these casual remarks could have impressed Olovernes so strongly as to direct his talk to the mother-child topic a few days later. I would rather assume here the influences of Friedrich Hebbel's drama *Judith* (1841), which Tammsaare had read around 1910. In Hebbel's drama, Holofernes mentions a friendly relationship between the child (=Judith) and the lion (=Holofernes). But—according to Holofernes—this relationship changes, when the child "becomes big and wise." It is especially important that the discussion of the mother-child in Tammsaare occurs in the same scene as the reference to the child-lion relationship in Hebbel's *Judith*—at the beginning of their conversation. It could be recalled that Hebbel's influence on Tammsaare's drama is found elsewhere, too, viz. in the abnormality of Juudit's marriage, in Juudit's dream, and most likely, in the scene of putting out the chandeliers.

If the discussion of the first topic—the mother-child relationship—occurred at Olovernes' initiative, then it was Juudit who introduced and developed the discussion of the second theme—of Olovernes' power. We can hardly restrain our surprise at Juudit's bravery not only in leading the conversation to the increase of Olovernes' authority and power (as if they were not big enough), but for suggesting that he take away Nebukadnetsar's crown, conquer the world, and—with her at his side—march into Israel. This topic, just as the first one, sounds unnatural. Despite the author's intentions and efforts, the conversation does not compensate for the expected night of passion and fire in the camp of the commander. Therefore, Tammsaare's drama does not have as strong an impact on readers or spectators, as it would have had, had the drama followed the classical scheme or replaced the love scene with a dynamic episode. It also shows how hard it is to modify the plot of a story established during myriad generations. (pp. 12-19)

Felix J. Oinas, "The Problem of the Scapegoat and Tammsaare's 'Juudit'," in Journal of Baltic Studies, *Vol. XVII, No. 1, Spring, 1986, pp. 12-20.*

ADDITIONAL BIBLIOGRAPHY

Harris, E. Howard. "Neo-Realism." In his *Literature in Estonia*, pp. 62-68. London: Boreas, 1943.
    Brief discussion of Tammsaare's best-known works, focusing on *Tõde ja õigus*.

Kross, Jaan. "The Great Estonian." *Soviet Literature*, no. 1 (1978): 103-09.
    Discusses Tammsaare's life and literary career.

Edith (Newbold Jones) Wharton

1862-1937

American novelist, short story writer, critic, autobiographer, and poet.

The following entry presents criticism of Wharton's novella *Ethan Frome*. For a discussion of Wharton's complete career, see *TCLC*, Volumes 3 and 9.

Wharton is best known as a novelist of manners whose fiction exposed the cruel excesses of aristocratic society at the turn of the century. From an upper-class perspective, she observed power and wealth shift from the hands of New York's established gentry to the nouveau riche of the Industrial Revolution. Wharton considered many of the newly rich, whose obsession with economic status overshadowed personal and moral concerns, to be cultural philistines, and she later drew several of her richest fictional characters and situations from this group. Yet in *Ethan Frome,* perhaps Wharton's most widely read work, she chose an uncharacteristic milieu, portraying instead the frustration and limitations imposed on individuals by poverty and adherence to a strict social code. As explained by K. R. Srinivasa Iyengar: "In some of her novels . . . [Wharton] tried to show how excessive opulence could start in its insensitive beneficiaries the corrupting and rotting process of physical and moral degeneration,'' while in *Ethan Frome* she demonstrated "that mere poverty and the shifts to which it condemns its victims, are no guarantee either that moral sensitiveness will remain uncorroded.''

In her autobiography, *A Backward Glance,* Wharton recorded the origin of *Ethan Frome.* After her marriage in 1885 to Edward R. Wharton, she and her husband travelled widely in Europe. While living in Paris she engaged a language tutor who suggested that she compose written exercises before each lesson. Predisposed to work in fiction, Wharton began the story of a love triangle involving a New England farmer, his wife, and his wife's cousin. The notebook containing the French "Ethan Frome'' was set aside when the lessons ended, and Wharton was not reminded of the story until several years later, when she visited the New England hill country which served as its setting. She subsequently reworked the narrative in English, making numerous structural and stylistic changes, most notably the addition of a framing device. Unlike the French version, the English story is narrated by a visitor to the aptly named New England village of Starkfield. When Frome is first introduced, he is fifty-two years old, and, although striking in appearance, physically crippled. The narrator, who has hired Frome as a driver, is fascinated by him and seeks information about his history from the villagers. The principal narrative is comprised of the narrator's speculations on the circumstances that have shaped Frome's bleak existence. Whether the narrative is truly the story of Frome's life or solely the imaginings of the narrator has become the subject of critical debate. Most critics believe that the story is an accurate representation of Frome's past; others disagree, however, including Joseph X. Brennan and Cynthia Griffin Wolff, who emphasize the role of the narrator as the creator of an imaginative "vision'' of Frome's life.

Twenty-four years before the narrator encounters him, Frome and his hypochondrical wife Zenobia ("Zeena'') share their

home with Zeena's destitute young cousin, Mattie Silver. As time passes, Mattie and Ethan are drawn together. Frome, bound by a sense of duty to his jealous wife, reluctantly accepts her decision that Mattie must leave. As he drives Mattie to the train station, they profess their love for each other and impulsively decide to go sledding. Mattie, unable to accept the idea of a lifetime of separation from Ethan, suggests that they commit suicide by crashing their sled into an elm, but as they travel down the hill, Ethan's attention is diverted by a vision of his wife, and he fails to steer the sled squarely into the tree. The principal story concludes as the pair are regaining consciousness—injured but not dead. The frame resumes with a description of the scene in Frome's house during a visit by the narrator: Mattie, an ill-humored invalid, querulously snaps at Zeena, who has acted as her nurse since the "accident." Because of their poverty and immobility, Ethan, Zeena, and Mattie are trapped indefinitely, spending nearly every hour together in the kitchen of the decaying farmhouse.

Numerous critics, including Wharton herself, have commented on the use of the framing device and the function of the narrator in *Ethan Frome*. According to Wharton: "I was severely criticized by the reviewers for what was considered the clumsy structure of the tale. I had pondered long on this structure, had felt its peculiar difficulties, and possible awkwardness, but could think of no alternative which would serve as well in the given case; and though I am far from thinking *Ethan Frome* my best novel . . . , I am still sure that its structure is not its weak point." For the most part, critics have found the frame an effective device for conveying both the reasons for, and the results of, the characters' actions.

Although Wharton is generally better remembered as a chronicler of aristocratic society, *Ethan Frome* is considered typical of her works in many ways, especially in its vision of discontented married life. Several commentators have alluded to Wharton's own unhappy marriage and her intimate relationship with journalist Morton Fullerton in suggesting an autobiographical basis for the novella. In *Ethan Frome,* as in several other works, she presents a world in which no satisfactory escape from a loveless marriage exists, and infidelity invariably leads to further unhappiness. Several critics have examined the themes of the novella through an analysis of imagery and symbolism. Relentless images of darkness, coldness, and inarticulateness surround Frome and his desolate existence in Starkfield; Mattie, conversely, is conjured through images of warmth and light. Sexual imagery and symbolism are considered important to plot advancement in the novella, most notably in the associations surrounding Zeena's prized pickle dish, a wedding gift that is unused until Mattie and Ethan use it in Zeena's absence.

Many critics have protested the grim conclusion of *Ethan Frome,* especially condemning its apparent inevitableness and the helplessness of its victims. An early reviewer found it "hard to forgive Mrs. Wharton for the utter remorselessness of . . . *Ethan Frome,* for nowhere has she done anything more hopelessly, endlessly grey with blank despair." This judgment has been echoed by modern observers, most notably by Lionel Trilling, who has described the novel's world as incomprehensible in its random brutality. In his view "between the moral life of Ethan and Mattie and their terrible fate we cannot make any reasonable connection. Only a moral judgment cruel to the point of insanity could speak of it as anything but accidental." Kenneth Bernard, on the other hand, has concluded that the suffering and injuries sustained by Mattie and Ethan represent, in the world they inhabit, just punishment for their infidelity. Other critics have viewed the moral outlook of the novella more moderately. In David Eggenschwiler's analysis, for example, "Wharton will have it both ways, showing that man does determine his life in a universe that is not chaotic, but also showing that his lot is hard, his choices difficult, his sacrifices many, his strengths inseparable from his weaknesses, and the consequences of his actions often different from what he had expected." Although the bleakness of the vision conveyed in *Ethan Frome* made its success unaccountable even to Wharton, the novella became a popular favorite, and it received renewed attention in the 1930s when a dramatic version was produced. In the decades since, *Ethan Frome* has become perhaps Wharton's best known work of fiction and a standard text for generations of students of American literature.

(See also *Contemporary Authors,* Vol. 104; and *Dictionary of Literary Biography,* Vol. 4: *American Writers in Paris, 1920-1939;* Vol. 9: *American Novelists, 1910-1945;* and Vol. 12: *American Realists and Naturalists.*)

THE NATION, NEW YORK   (essay date 1911)

[*In the following essay, the critic offers a favorable review of* Ethan Frome, *praising the plot, characterization, and structure of the novel.*]

More than ten years ago Mrs. Wharton published a short story called **"The Duchess at Prayer."** Since that time we have cherished an estimate of her powers which no intermediate accession to her repertory has raised, nor even, to speak truth, quite justified. Practised, cosmopolitan, subtle, she has seemed, on the whole, to covet most earnestly the refinements of Henry James. In spite of her habit of a franker approach, her consistent rating of matter above manner, and the gravitation—we should hesitate to say transfer—of her interest from exotic to native themes; we might have been reasonably content to rank her as the greatest pupil of a little master, were it not for the appearance of *Ethan Frome*. This startling fulfilment recalls not only the promise of the early story, but its revelation of a more potent influence—the inspiriting example of a greater novelist to whom Mr. James's *devoirs* have been paid in the phrase, "The master of us all." Exactly how much the inception and execution of **"The Duchess at Prayer"** owed to Balzac's "La grande Bretèche" is beyond our present point, which is, specifically, that the excellence of Mrs. Wharton's work in this case outstripped the charge of imitation, and allied her with that company of splendid talents whom neither magnificence nor the catastrophes of passion can abash.

There is certainly no imitative strain in *Ethan Frome*. The style is assured and entirely individual, the method direct and firm in its grasp upon substantial fact. Yet here is the companion-piece to the **"Duchess,"** a variation upon the same theme of triumphant malice and tortured love, evoking the same emotions. And here as there the genius of a place presides, and the scene and the hour conspire to meet the racial temper. But there is this great difference: in the place of sumptuous memories, decaying under the sultry oppression of Italian noon, she was, at heart, a stranger; whereas she writes now of New England as one writes of home, plainly, and with a wealth of understanding and familiar allusion. Even the arrangement of the narrative is designed to fit the life described and its probabilities rather than to satisfy any precious scruples. A winter-bound stranger in an out-of-the-way Massachusetts hamlet recognizes in the limping figure of Ethan Frome the "ruin of a man," and apprehends some singular misfortunes behind his obvious plight. The sparse comment of a community respectful of privacies and little indulgent to curiosity yields but scanty information. Out of the native's penury come at length hours of enforced companionship, the daily rides to the station during which "Frome drove in silence, the reins loosely held in his left hand, his brown, seamed profile, under the helmet-like peak of the cap, relieved against the banks of snow."

"It was that night," explains the visitor, "that I found the clue to Ethan Frome, and began to put together this vision of his story." Such an approach could not be improved, forbearing, as it does, to violate the seal of silence; nor could, we think, the conclusion of village confidences be spared, with its ultimate breaking down of reserve between the initiated, its natural cadence of secret curiosity, and its softening echo of unavailing human sympathy.

Surely, the melancholy spirit that haunts the remoter byways of rural New England has entered into this chronicle; over all its scenes breathe the benumbing and isolating rigors of her winters, a sense of invisible fetters, a consciousness of depleted resources, a reticence and self-contained endurance that even the houses know how to express, retired from the public way, or turned sideways to preserve a secluded entrance. Yet it is with a softly-breathed strain of native romance that the drama opens. As well try to transplant arbutus from its native habitat as to dissociate this exquisite burgeoning of passion from its homely circumstances and the inflexible trammels of a local speech meant for taciturnity rather than expression. Thriving on meagre opportunities and pleasures—the coasting, the picnic, the walk home from the ''church sociable''—and on the sharing of frugal household cares, the love between the young farmer and the little dependent who inefficiently ''helped'' in his home, spread like a secret flowering too innocent and too fragrant to escape the wife's malicious eye. The brave and fragile figure of Mattie Silvers is not an idealized one, although this is the type of New England girlhood whose modesty and touch of fairy grace have been the subject of much poetry.

The wife who stands for fate in this drama is a curious and repugnant figure. She introduces the same vein of close-mouthed malignity which darkens local history. The helpless fear and loathing she inspires in her husband is the essence of supernatural terror without its obsolete husk of ignorance. By showing this instance of a hypochondriac roused by jealousy out of a ''sullen self-absorption'' and transformed into a mysterious alien presence, an evil energy secreted from the long years of silent brooding, Mrs. Wharton touches on a very radical identity. We realize that the same gloating satisfaction that made the wife smile upon the parting lovers, had something to do with her capabilities as a nurse. Her pleasure at the sight of pain she had inflicted—was it, perchance, from such an evil spring that her strength was drawn for the long years of drudgery between two cripples?

No hero of fantastic legend was ever more literally hag-ridden than was Ethan Frome. The profound irony of his case is that it required his own goodness to complete her parasitic power over him. Without his innate honesty and his sense of duty he could have escaped her demands and her decrees, refused the money for her nostrums and ''doctor books,'' followed the vision of a new free life ''out West.'' In his submission to obligation and in his thwarted intellectual aspirations he typifies the remnant of an exceptional race whose spiritual inheritance has dwindled amid hard conditions until all distinction is forfeited except that of suffering; but which still indicates its quality, if only by its capacity for suffering.

The wonder is that the spectacle of so much pain can be made to yield so much beauty. And here the full range of Mrs. Wharton's imagination becomes apparent. There is possible, within the gamut of human experience, an exaltation of anguish which makes a solitude for itself, whose direct contemplation seals the impulse of speech and strikes cold upon the heart. Yet sometimes in reflection there is revealed, beneath the writhing torment, the lineaments of a wronged and distorted loveliness. It is the piteous and intolerable conception which the Greeks expressed in the Medusa head that Mrs. Wharton has dared to hold up to us anew, but the face she shows us is the face of our own people. (pp. 396-97)

> *A review of "Ethan Frome," in* The Nation, *New York, Vol. XCIII, No. 2417, October 26, 1911, pp. 396-97.*

THE SATURDAY REVIEW, LONDON (essay date 1911)

[*In the following excerpt, the critic presents an unfavorable review of* Ethan Frome, *maintaining that the novel is flawed by its ending.*]

[*Ethan Frome*] is a novel in that it unfolds completely to our view the lives of its few people; but it is a short story in that the mood is throughout the same; and that the interest is from first to last fastened upon the one terrible incident of the story's climax. Also it is a short story because the story is short—it can be read easily at a sitting. For many reasons it is worth reading. The writing is singularly beautiful. It has passed through flame of the author's imagination. Yet, having read the story, we wish we had not read it. The error is in the end. There are things too terrible in their failure to be told humanly by creature to creature. Ethan Frome driving down with the girl he loved to death—here there is beauty and a defiance of the misery of circumstance which may sadden, but uplift, the reader. But these lovers could not die. They must live horribly on, mutilated and losing even the nobility of their passion in the wreck of their bodies. Had Mrs. Wharton allowed her creatures to die as they intended *Ethan Frome* would be high indeed among our shorter tales—high as ''The Tale of Chloë.'' She has marred her work with no motive we can discover. With Mrs. Wharton it could not have been the mere craving for the exaggerated terror which in art must always defeat itself. The end of *Ethan Frome* is something at which we cover the eyes. We do not cover the eyes at the spectacle of a really great tragedy.

> *A review of "Ethan Frome," in* The Saturday Review, *London, Vol. 112, No. 2925, November 18, 1911, p. 650.*

EDITH WHARTON (essay date 1934)

[*In the following excerpt from her autobiography,* A Backward Glance, *Wharton recalls the circumstances under which she began writing* Ethan Frome.]

[The] book to the making of which I brought the greatest joy and the fullest ease was *Ethan Frome*. For years I had wanted to draw life as it really was in the derelict mountain village of New England, a life even in my time, and a thousandfold more a generation earlier, utterly unlike that seen through the rose-coloured spectacles of my predecessors, Mary Wilkins and Sarah Orne Jewett. In those days the snow-bound villages of Western Massachusetts were still grim places, morally and physically: insanity, incest and slow mental and moral starvation were hidden away behind the paintless wooden house-fronts of the long village street, or in the isolated farm-houses on the neighbouring hills; and Emily Brontë would have found as savage tragedies in our remoter valleys as on her Yorkshire moors. (pp. 293-94)

Ethan Frome shocked my readers less than *Summer*; but it was frequently criticized as ''painful,'' and at first had much less success than my previous books. I have a clearer recollection of its beginnings than of those of my other tales, through the singular accident that its first pages were written—in French! I had determined, when we came to live in Paris, to polish and enlarge my French vocabulary; for though I had spoken the langauge since the age of four I had never had much occasion to talk it, for any length of time, with cultivated people, having usually, since my marriage, wandered through France as a tourist. The result was that I had kept up the language chiefly through reading, and the favourite French authors of my early youth being Bossuet, Racine, Corneille and La Bruyère, most of my polite locutions dated from the seventeenth century, and [Paul] Bourget used to laugh at me for speaking ''the purest Louis Quatorze.'' To bring my idioms up to date I asked Charles Du Bos to find, among his friends, a young professor who would come and talk with me two or three times a week. An amiable young man was found; but, being too amiable ever to correct my spoken mistakes, he finally hit on the expedient of asking me to prepare an ''exercise'' before each visit. The easiest thing for me was to write a story; and thus the French version of *Ethan Frome* was begun, and carried on for a few weeks. Then the lessons were given up, and the copy-book containing my ''exercise'' vanished forever. But a few years later, during one of our summer sojourns at the Mount, a distant glimpse of Bear Mountain brought Ethan back to my memory, and the following winter in Paris I wrote the tale as it now stands, reading my morning's work aloud each evening to Walter Berry, who was as familiar as I was with the lives led in those half-deserted villages before the coming of motor and telephone. We talked the tale over page by page, so that its accuracy of ''atmosphere'' is doubly assured—and I mention this because not long since, in an article by an American literary critic, I saw *Ethan Frome* cited as an interesting example of a successful New England story written by some one who knew nothing of New England! *Ethan Frome* was written after I had spent ten years in the hill-region where the scene is laid, during which years I had come to know well the aspect, dialect, and mental and moral attitude of the hill-people. The fact that *Summer* deals with the same class and type as those portrayed in *Ethan Frome*, and has the same setting, might have sufficed to disprove the legend—but once such a legend is started it echoes on as long as its subject survives. (pp. 295-96)

> *Edith Wharton, in her* A Backward Glance, *D. Appleton-Century Company Incorporated, 1934, 385 p.*

BLAKE NEVIUS (essay date 1951)

[*In the following excerpt, Nevius examines prominent themes in Wharton's fiction, using illustrations drawn from* Ethan Frome.]

Although much—perhaps too much—has been made of that minor classic of our literature, *Ethan Frome*, as a picture of New England life and as a triumph of style and construction, its relation to Edith Wharton's more characteristic and important stories has never been clearly established. *Ethan Frome* is not a ''sport.'' It belongs to the main tradition of Mrs. Wharton's fiction, and it has a value, independent of its subject and technique, in helping us to define that tradition. (p. 197)

Beginning with *The Fruit of the Tree* (1907), the argument of Mrs. Wharton's novels focuses with varying depth but remarkable consistency on a single problem, which she once defined (although not with reference to her own work) as ''that immersion of the larger in the smaller nature which is one of the mysteries of the moral life.'' Many well known novels—*The Scarlet Letter, The Portrait of a Lady,* and *Of Human Bondage* among others—have explored the problem in their own way. It is strikingly present in George Eliot, whom Edith Wharton, no less than Henry James, regarded as one of the masters of her art. It provides the central theme in Proust as Mrs. Wharton defines it: ''the hopeless incurable passion of a sensitive man for a stupid uncomprehending woman.'' But few novelists have exploited it as persistently as she did. Although it is prefigured in her early novelettes *The Touchstone* and *Sanctuary,* it is not until we are confronted in succession by *The Fruit of the Tree, Ethan Frome,* and *The Reef* that we are able to appreciate its centrality.

A glance at the principal relationships in some of the stories may help confirm my point. In each case the emphasis falls on the baffling, wasteful submission of a superior nature to an inferior one, a phenomenon which Edith Wharton, no more than George Eliot or Henry James, was able to explain, but which presented intriguing possibilities to the novelist who believed that it was moral issues principally that guaranteed the life of fiction. In *The Fruit of the Tree,* John Amherst's humanitarian program is hampered by the petty social aims of his first wife Bessy; and then, by an ironic inversion, the happiness of his second wife, Justine, is threatened by the limitations of his own moral vision. Ethan Frome is morally victimized by Zeena, Ralph Marvell (*The Custom of the Country*) by Undine Spragg, Ann Eliza Bunner (*The Bunner Sisters*) by her sister Evelina. . . . The examples can be multiplied to include every novel Edith Wharton wrote after *The House of Mirth* with the exception of *A Son at the Front,* in which the usual relationship is reversed.

How do these unequal partnerships come about? Invariably they originate in a sentimental error on the part of the destined victim. Amherst, in love with Bessy Westmore, is deluded into thinking that she shares his interest in reform. Ethan Frome, grateful for Zeena's devoted nursing of his parents, marries her. Ralph Marvell, naïvely fancying himself a Perseus, rescues his corn-belt Andromeda from the clutches of rich, lecherous, pop-eyed Peter Van Degen. . . . The motive in each case is high-minded, and the act calls for a generous, if vain, display of altruism.

In the anti-romantic tradition, none of the love affairs in Edith Wharton's novels acquires interest or significance until one or both the partners is married. Once she has her characters ensnared as a result of their sentimental miscalculations, she is able to introduce a second, contingent theme. In all of the stories I have mentioned, she proceeds directly to the question: What is the extent of one's moral obligation to those individuals who, legally or within the framework of manners, conventions, taboos, apparently have the strictest claim on one's loyalty? This question occupies the center of Edith Wharton's moral consciousness as it reveals itself in fiction. It is the great question posed by *Ethan Frome*. There is no doubt in her mind regarding the prior assumption that a sense of individual responsibility is the only basis of social order and development. But she is seeking the most liberal interpretation of that axiom consistent with her inherited notions of fair play and respectability. (pp. 197-200)

As might be expected, the moral implications of divorce are debated endlessly in Edith Wharton's fiction. The traditional prejudice of her class outlawed it. It was one of the convenient arrangements introduced by the *nouveau riche* invaders of her old New York, and partly because of her instinctive hostility to this group she rejected it (in her fiction, at least) as a solution. In spite of the latitude with which she discusses certain moral problems, she generally rests her case on the status quo. There is a pronounced straining at the seams of conventional morality, and an occasional triumph of open-mindedness, as in the treatment of euthanasia, in *The Fruit of the Tree*; but in her fiction, as in her life, flat rebellion is usually disparaged or at least shown to be futile.

There is of course a reason for this, which is rooted in the puritan sub-soil of Edith Wharton's nature. The morality of an act is evaluated in terms of its cost to others. (p. 202)

Given the notion of individual responsibility, no human destiny can be detached from those it touches, directly or indirectly, and the ramifications of a selfish or thoughtless act are indefinitely extended. The individual justification . . . is forced to yield to the larger question of the act's effect on the social structure as a whole. (pp. 202-03)

Edith Wharton's attempt to define the limits of responsibility is an act of mediation . . . between the claims of passion and duty. She is not a problem novelist. Except in some of the early short stories, her themes never become merely problems, demonstrations, propositions. The dilemmas of her characters, however much light they may shed on the nature of the conflict, are never resolved, unless, as I have remarked, by a return to the status quo—witness *Ethan Frome, The Reef, The Age of Innocence.* Her own experience, we must believe, was a perpetual testing-ground for her situations, but it provided no final answers. Her separation and divorce from Edward Wharton were not followed, as might have been anticipated, by a rationalization of the act in fiction: there is no discernible compromise in her attitude toward divorce. (p. 203)

But to return to *Ethan Frome*: The final, lingering note of the story it seems to me, is one of despair arising from the contemplation of spiritual waste. Ethan himself sounds it just before his last, abortive attempt to escape his destiny:

> Other possibilities had been in him, possibilities sacrificed, one by one, to Zeena's narrowmindedness and ignorance. And what good had come of it? She was a hundred times bitterer and more discontented than when he had married her: the one pleasure left her was to inflict pain on him. All the healthy instincts of selfdefence rose up in him against such waste. . . .

And taking Mrs. Wharton's novels as a group, that note swells into a refrain whose burden, as George Darrow in *The Reef* formulates it, is "the monstrousness of useless sacrifices." Here is the ultimate result of that "immersion of the larger in the smaller nature which is one of the mysteries of the moral life." As a theme, the mutility of self-sacrifice is merged repeatedly with the primary theme of the limits of individual responsibility. A realization of "the monstrousness of useless sacrifices" encourages the characters' selfish, passional bent, while the puritanical assertion of responsibility opposes it. For Ethan, as for most of Edith Wharton's protagonists who are confronted by the same alternatives—Ann Eliza Bunner, Newland Archer, Charlotte Lovell, Kate Clephane, Nona Manford, Martin Boyne—the inherited sense of duty is strong enough to conquer, but the victory leaves in its wake the sense of futility which self-sacrifice entails.

How and to what degree does the situation in *Ethan Frome* embody this conflict? No element in the characterization of Ethan is more carefully brought out than the suggestion of his useful, even heroic possibilities. He had longed to become an engineer, had acquired some technological training, and is still reading desultorily in the field when the narrator encounters him. This is one aspect of his personality. There is still another which helps explain why Edith Wharton is predisposed to treat his case with the utmost sympathy:

> He had always been more sensitive than the people about him to the appeal of natural beauty. His unfinished studies had given form to this sensibility and even in his unhappiest moments field and sky spoke to him with a deep and powerful persuasion.

Add to these qualities his superior gifts of kindness, generosity, and sociability, and his impressive physical appearance ("Even then he was the most striking figure in Starkfield, though he was but the ruin of a man"), and it is evident that Edith Wharton set about, as Melville did with Ahab, to invest her rather unpromising human material with a tragic dignity.

It is in view of his potentialities that Ethan's marriage to Zeena is a catastrophe. By the time Mattie Silver appears on the scene, he is only twenty-eight but already trapped by circumstances and unable to extend the horizon of his future beyond the family graveyard. Mattie, once she has become the victim of Zeena's jealousy, offers a way out which Ethan is quick to follow. But immediately his plans are set afoot, things begin to close in on him again: farm and mill are mortgaged, he has no credit, and time is against him. Moreover, even in the heat of his resentment he cannot disregard Zeena's plight: "It was only by incessant labour and personal supervision that Ethan drew a meagre living from the land, and his wife, even if she were in better health than she imagined, could never carry such a burden alone." His rebellion dies out, only to be rekindled the next morning as Mattie is about to leave. Suddenly it occurs to him that if he pleads Zeena's illness and the need of a servant, Andrew Hale may give him an advance on some lumber. He starts on foot for Starkfield, meets Mrs. Hale enroute, is touched by her expression of sympathy ("You've had an awful mean time, Ethan Frome"), continues toward his rendezvous—and is suddenly pulled up short by the realization that he is planning to appeal to the Hales' sympathy to obtain money from them on false pretences. It is the turning point of the action:

> With the sudden perception of the point to which his madness had carried him, the madness fell and he saw his life before him as it was. He was a poor man, the husband of a sickly woman, whom his desertion would leave alone and destitute; and even if he had the heart to desert her he could have done so only by deceiving two kindly people who had pitied him.

Although he is neatly hemmed in by circumstances, it is Ethan's own sense of responsibility that blocks the last avenue of escape and condemns him to a life of sterile expiation.

In *Ethan Frome* the themes I have mentioned are developed without the complexity that the more sophisticated characters and setting of *The Fruit of the Tree* and *The Reef* require; they are reduced to the barest statement of their possibilities. To a person of Ethan's limited experience and capacity for straightforward judgments, the issues present themselves with the least ambiguity or encouragement to evasion; and in this, I believe, we have the measure of the subject's value for Mrs. Wharton. As her characters approach her own sphere, their motives disentangle themselves with increasing difficulty from her own and their actions are regulated by a closer censure; they become more complex and are apt to lose their way amid fine distinctions and tentative judgments. They are aware, like Woburn in the short story **"A Cup of Cold Water,"** of the impossibility of basing a decision upon absolutes:

> Was not all morality based on a convention? What was the stanchest code of ethics but a trunk with a series of false bottoms? Now and then one had the illusion of getting down to absolute right or wrong, but it was only a false bottom—a removable hypothesis—with an-

other false bottom underneath. There was no getting beyond the relative.

Ethan Frome is closer than any of her characters to the source of the ideas which underlie Edith Wharton's ethical judgments. Puritanism has lost very little of its hold on that portion of the New England mind which he represents and its ideas have not been weakened, as they have in the more populous industrial and commercial centers, by two centuries of enlightenment based on what Bernard Shaw calls the Mercanto-Christian doctrine of morality. It is not surprising that many persons unacquainted with Edith Wharton's biography associate her—and not wholly on the strength of *Ethan Frome*—with Boston or with New England as a whole. Whatever the influences exerted by her New York origin and background and her long career abroad, it is the moral order of Ethan Frome's world that governs the view of reality in all her novels. (pp. 204-07)

> Blake Nevius, "'Ethan Frome' and the Themes of Edith Wharton's Fiction," in The New England Quarterly, Vol. XXIV, No. 2, June, 1951, pp. 197-207.

J. D. THOMAS (essay date 1955)

[*In the following essay, Thomas discusses narrative inconsistencies in* Ethan Frome.]

Edith Wharton in *Ethan Frome* performed a real artistic service in imaging that isolated world of snowdrifts, sledges, and weary struggle for the mere survival of man and beast which until yesterday was the lot of over half the American people during nearly a half of their lives. It is regrettable that she felt obliged to narrate her story from a masculine point of view. To think of the contrived Mr. Lockwood against the infinitely human Nelly Dean is to take the measure of the ability of even a highly intuitive authoress to fathom male psychology. Mrs. Wharton, of course, had vastly more experience of men than Emily Brontë, but it counted for little in a book like *Ethan Frome*. The men she knew intimately were men in society, where the established controls drive behavior and speech toward a feminine norm. Thus she was deluded into supposing that an engineer in the field would observe that "outcroppings of slate . . . *nuzzled up* through the snow like animals pushing out their noses to breathe." This figure could not possibly occur spontaneously to a man of action (one may as well say, to any man), though the phrase might be self-consciously employed in an effort to please a drawing room.

An evident uncertainty of the author about the occupational concerns of men leaves the "job connected with the big powerhouse at Corbury Junction," which accounts for her narrator's presence in Starkfield, the shadow of a wraith. But she cannot totally ignore the daily affairs of Ethan Frome; her efforts to describe them sometimes veer between the ludicrous and the pathetic, depending on the precise cast of the reader's sympathies. Ethan's main source of cash income is his sawmill, and during Zeena's "therapeutic excursion" to Bettsbridge he is engaged in hauling several loads of lumber to Starkfield. At least they begin as "lumber," but presently are termed "logs" and even "tree trunks . . . so slippery that it took twice as long as usual to lift them and get them in place on the sledge." Exactly what Andrew Hale, a carpenter and house builder, would want with logs, or in any event how sawed lumber could be reconverted to tree trunks, is not revealed. On this delivery of lumber (logs?), Ethan asks Hale for a "small advance" of fifty dollars. If from the word *small* we have a right to assume

that he is now creditor to the builder for perhaps a few hundred dollars, we are bound to question the financial crisis two days later, when "he knew that without security no one at Starkfield would lend him ten dollars. . . . There was no way out—none." Probably Edith Wharton had never had occasion to hypothecate or discount a note, but the shift certainly would have occurred to the well-experienced Ethan—who "six months before . . . had given his only security to raise funds for necessary repairs to the mill"—as a natural alternative to catastrophe.

Mrs. Wharton's vagueness about the common affairs of life is not wholly limited to men, for she once attributes to her narrator's chief informant, Mrs. Ned Hale, a singular obtuseness. Following an account of Ethan's attempted suicide with Mattie, Mrs. Hale remarks that "the folks here could never rightly tell what she and Ethan were doing that night coasting, when they'd ought to have been on their way to the Flats to ketch the train." Now, any small-town woman would know that "the folks" have a sure instinct for scandal, and that there would be no doubt whatever in the collective mind of the village—especially in its female lobe—as to the general situation between Ethan and his wife's cousin. Here Mrs. Wharton is betrayed by a fundamental ignorance of rural life, which she thought she understood after watching it for a few seasons from the windows of a villa. What real country woman, in telling a story, would allow the moon to set and rise at approximately the same hour on successive nights?

The plot of *Ethan Frome* involves an interesting, if perhaps unimportant, problem of chronology. Ethan and Zeena have been man and wife for seven years. They were married following the death of his mother, who "got queer and dragged along *for years*" after the death of his father. These clear and coherent data are unreconcilable with a report at the beginning of the main action of the story that "*four or five years earlier* he had taken a year's course at a technological college at Worcester," especially when read in conjunction with an accompanying explicit statement: "His father's death, and the misfortune following it had put a premature end to Ethan's studies . . .".

In all probability the inconsistency of dates is to be explained as a simple *lapsus calami aut memoriae,* and if so is inconsequential. However, the book raises a much more fundamental problem that cannot be so summarily dismissed. The principal moral crisis occurs on the day after Zeena's return from Bettsbridge. Faced with the certainty of his loss of Mattie, Ethan goes into Starkfield determined to find some way out of his difficulties: "He had made up his mind to do something, but he did not know what it would be. . . ."

> Suddenly it occurred to him that Andrew Hale, who was a kind-hearted man, might be induced to reconsider his refusal and advance a small sum on the lumber if he were told that Zeena's ill-health made it necessary to hire a servant. . . .
>
> The more he considered his plan the more hopeful it seemed. If he could get Mrs. Hale's ear he felt certain of success, and with fifty dollars in his pocket nothing could keep him from Mattie. . . .

The expected sympathy of Mrs. Hale is quickly forthcoming, and Ethan is hurrying on to present his request to her husband when suddenly scruples of the most remarkable character assail him. The ethical situation would seem clear enough. He had willingly married a relative older than himself, a woman with whose character he was more intimately acquainted than most bridegrooms with that of their brides, and whose only new faults revealed after marriage where chronic ill health (no doubt genuine enough) and chronic lamentation about it. On her side, she certainly had enough hardship to bear, and at least she showed some virtue of forbearance, for we learn that she had never once quarreled openly with her husband until the pretty face of Matt came between them. Such considerations might give him pause before the house of Andrew Hale, but his actual thoughts are very different:

> . . . he pulled up sharply, the blood in his face. For the first time, . . . he saw what he was about to do. *He was planning to take advantage of the Hale's sympathy to obtain money from them on false pretences*. That was a plain statement of the cloudy purpose which had driven him in headlong to Starkfield.

Only as an afterthought does the real ethical problem occur to him, and then obliquely and in relation to the forced issue of his dun of Mr. Hale for payment of a legitimate debt:

> With the sudden perception of the point to which his madness had carried him, the madness fell and he saw his life before him as it was. He was a poor man, the husband of a sickly woman, whom his desertion would leave alone and destitute; and *even if he had had the heart to desert her he could have done so only by deceiving two kindly people who had pitied him*.

> He turned and walked slowly back to the farm.

This extraordinary passage could be interpreted as an ironical revelation of the moral darkness into which a man can wander, but there is no indication that it is so intended. From the author's point of view, the fictional problem was to force the story at this point into a tragic resolution. If the genuine moral issue had been threshed out in Ethan's mind, it would have been necessary for him either to repent or to yield openly and knowingly to temptation. Repentance would have meant walking "back to the farm" for good and ever. Yielding could have led easily enough to the catastrophe of the sled, but it doubtless would have destroyed the empathy of most readers for the runaway lovers. To make illicit love attractive is simple enough, but to make it seem right is difficult. Mrs. Wharton solves the problem by a dodge that we must agree is clever, whatever we may think of the intention behind it. (pp. 405-09)

> *J. D. Thomas, "Marginalia or 'Ethan Frome'," in* American Literature, *Vol. 27, No. 3, November, 1955, pp. 405-09.*

LIONEL TRILLING   (lecture date 1955)

[*A respected American critic and literary historian, Trilling was also an essayist, editor, novelist, and short story writer. His exploration of liberal arts theory and its implications for the conduct of life led Trilling to function not only as a literary critic, but as a social commentator as well. A liberal and a humanist, Trilling judged the value of a text by its contribution to culture and, in turn, regarded culture as indispensible for human survival. Trilling focused in particular on the conflict between the individual and culture, maintaining that art had the power to "liberate the individual from the tyranny of his culture in the environmental sense and to permit him to stand beyond it in an autonomy of perception and judgement." In the following lecture, Trilling*

maintains that Ethan Frome *is a morally bankrupt work that fails to meet the precepts of Aristotelean tragedy.*]

A theological seminary in New York planned a series of lectures on "The Literary Presentations of Great Moral Issues," and invited me to give one of the talks. Since I have a weakness for the general subject, I was disposed to accept the invitation. But I hesitated over the particular instance, for I was asked to discuss the moral issues in **Ethan Frome**. I had not read Edith Wharton's little novel in a good many years, and I remembered it with no pleasure or admiration. I recalled it as not at all the sort of book that deserved to stand in a list which included *The Brothers Karamazov* and *Billy Budd, Foretopman*. If it presented a moral issue at all, I could not bring to mind what that issue was. And so I postponed my acceptance of the invitation and made it conditional upon my being able to come to terms with the subject assigned to me.

Ethan Frome, when I read it again, turned out to be pretty much as I had recalled it, not a great book or even a fine book, but a factitious book, perhaps even a cruel book. I was puzzled to understand how it ever came to be put on the list, why anyone should want to have it discussed as an example of moral perception. Then I remembered its reputation, which, in America, is very considerable. It is sometimes spoken of as an American classic. It is often assigned to high-school and college students as a text for study.

But the high and solemn repute in which it stands is, I am sure, in large part a mere acccident of American culture. **Ethan Frome** appeared in 1911, at a time when, to a degree that we can now only wonder at, American literature was committed to optimism, cheerfulness, and gentility. What William Dean Howells called the "smiling aspects of life" had an importance in the literature of America some fifty years ago which is unmatched in the literature of any other time and place. It was inevitable that those who were critical of the prevailing culture and who wished to foster in America higher and more serious literature should put a heavy stress upon the grimmer aspects of life, that they would equate the smiling aspects with falsehood, the grimmer aspects with truth. For these devoted people, sickened as they were by cheerfulness and hope, the word "stark" seemed to carry the highest possible praise a critical review or a blurb could bestow, with "relentless" and "inevitable" as its proper variants. **Ethan Frome** was admired because it was "stark"—its action, we note, takes place in the New England village of Starkfield—and because the fate it describes is *relentless* and *inevitable*.

No one would wish to question any high valuation that may be given to the literary representation of unhappy events—except, perhaps, as the high valuation may be a mere cliché of an intellectual class, except as it is supposed to seem the hallmark of the superior sensibility and intelligence of that class. When it is only this, we have the right, and the duty, to look sniffishly at starkness, and relentlessness and inevitability, to cock a skeptical eye at grimness. And I am quite unable to overcome my belief that **Ethan Frome** enjoys its high reputation because it still satisfies our modern snobbishness about tragedy and pain.

We can never speak of Edith Wharton without some degree of respect. She brought to her novels a strong if limited intelligence, notable powers of observation, and a genuine desire to tell the truth, a desire which in some part she satisfied. But she was a woman in whom we cannot fail to see a limitation of heart, and this limitation makes itself manifest as a literary and moral deficiency of her work, and of *Ethan Frome* especially. It appears in the deadness of her prose, and more flagrantly in the suffering of her characters. Whenever the characters of a story suffer, they do so at the behest of their author—the author is responsible for their suffering and must justify his cruelty by the seriousness of his moral intention. The author of *Ethan Frome*, it seemed to me as I read the book again to test my memory of it, could not lay claim to any such justification. Her intention in writing the story was not adequate to the dreadful fate she contrived for her characters. She indulges herself by what she contrived—she is, as the phrase goes, "merely literary." This is not to say that the merely literary intention does not make its very considerable effects. There is in *Ethan Frome* an image of life-in-death, of hell-on-earth, which is not easily forgotten: the crippled Ethan, and Zeena, his dreadful wife, and Mattie, the once charming girl he had loved, now bedridden and querulous with pain, all living out their death in the kitchen of the desolate Frome farm—a perpetuity of suffering memorializes a moment of passion. It is terrible to contemplate, it is unforgettable, but the mind can do nothing with it, can only endure it.

My new reading of the book, then, did not lead me to suppose that it justified its reputation, but only confirmed my recollection that *Ethan Frome* was a dead book, the product of mere will, of the cold hard literary will. What is more, it seemed to me quite unavailable for any moral discourse. In the context of morality, there is nothing to say about *Ethan Frome*. It presents no moral issue at all.

For consider the story it tells. A young man of good and gentle character is the only son of a New England farm couple. He has some intellectual gifts and some desire to know the world, and for a year he is happy attending a technical school. But his father is incapacitated by a farm accident, and Ethan dutifully returns to manage the failing farm and sawmill. His father dies; his mother loses her mental faculties, and during her illness she is nursed by a female relative whom young Ethan marries, for no other reason than that he is bemused by loneliness. The new wife, Zeena, immediately becomes a shrew, a harridan and a valetudinarian—she lives only to be ill. Because Zeena now must spare herself, the Fromes take into their home a gentle and charming young girl, a destitute cousin of the wife. Ethan and Mattie fall in love, innocently but deeply. The wife, perceiving this, plans to send the girl away, her place to be taken by a servant whose wages the husband cannot possibly afford. In despair at the thought of separation Mattie and Ethan attempt suicide. They mean to die by sledding down a steep hill and crashing into a great elm at the bottom. Their plan fails: both survive the crash, Ethan to be sorely crippled, Mattie to be bedridden in perpetual pain. Now the wife Zeena surrenders her claim to a mysterious pathology and becomes the devoted nurse and jailer of the lovers. The terrible tableau to which I have referred is ready for inspection.

It seemed to me that it was quite impossible to talk about this story. This is not to say that the story is without interest as a story, but what interest it may have does not yield discourse, or at least not moral discourse.

But as I began to explain to the lecture committee why I could not accept the invitation to lecture about the book, it suddenly came over me how very strange a phenomenon the book made—how remarkable it was that a story should place before us the dreadful image of three ruined and tortured lives, showing how their ruin came about, and yet propose no moral issue of any kind. And if *issue* seems to imply something more precisely

formulated than we have a right to demand of a story, then it seemed to me no less remarkable that the book had scarcely any moral reverberation, that strange and often beautiful sound we seem to hear generated in the air by a tale of suffering, a sound which is not always music, which does not always have a "meaning," but which yet entrances us, like the random notes of an Aeolian harp, or merely the sound of the wind in the chimney. The moral sound that *Ethan Frome* makes is a dull thud. And this seemed to me so remarkable, indeed, that, in the very act of saying why I could not possibly discuss *Ethan Frome*, I found the reason why it must be discussed.

It is, as I have suggested, a very great fault in *Ethan Frome* that it presents no moral issue, sets off no moral reverberation. A certain propriety controls the literary representation of human suffering. This propriety dictates that the representation of pain may not be, as it were, gratuitous; it must not be an end in itself. The naked act of representing, or contemplating, human suffering is a self-indulgence, and it may be a cruelty. Between a tragedy and a spectacle in the Roman circus there is at least this much similarity, that the pleasure both afford derives from observing the pain of others. A tragedy is always on the verge of cruelty. What saves it from the actuality of cruelty is that it has an intention beyond itself. This intention may be so simple a one as that of getting us to do something practical about the cause of the suffering or to help actual sufferers, or at least to feel that we should; or it may lead us to look beyond apparent causes to those which the author wishes us to think of as more real, such as Fate, or the will of the gods, or the will of God; or it may challenge our fortitude or intelligence or piety.

A sense of the necessity of some such intention animates all considerations of the strange paradox of tragedy. Aristotle is concerned to solve the riddle of how the contemplation of human suffering can possibly be pleasurable, of why its pleasure is permissible. He wanted to know what literary conditions were needed to keep a tragedy from being a mere display of horror. Here it is well to remember that the Greeks were not so concerned as we have been led to believe to keep all dreadful things off the stage—in the presentation of Aristotle's favorite tragedy, the audience saw Jocasta hanging from a beam, it saw the representation of Oedipus's bloody eyesockets. And so Aristotle discovered, or pretended to discover, that tragedy did certain things to protect itself from being merely cruel. It chose, Aristotle said, a certain kind of hero; he was of a certain social and moral stature; he had a certain degree of possibility of free choice; he must justify his fate, or seem to justify it, by his moral condition, being neither wholly good nor wholly bad, having a particular fault that collaborates with destiny to bring about his ruin. The purpose of all these specifications for the tragic hero is to assure us that we observe something more than mere passivity when we witness the hero's suffering, that the suffering has, as we say, some meaning, some show of rationality.

Aristotle's theory of tragedy has had its way with the world to an extent which is perhaps out of proportion to its comprehensiveness and accuracy. Its success is largely due to its having dealt so openly with the paradox of tragedy. It serves to explain away any guilty feelings that we may have at deriving pleasure from suffering.

But at the same time that the world has accepted Aristotle's theory of tragedy, it has also been a little uneasy about some of its implications. The element of the theory that causes uneasiness in modern times is the matter of the stature of the hero.

To a society based in egalitarian sentiments, the requirement that the hero be a man of rank seems to deny the presumed dignity of tragedy to men of lesser status. And to a culture which questions the freedom of the will, Aristotle's hero seems to be a little beside the point. Aristotle's prescription for the tragic hero is clearly connected with his definition, in his *Ethics,* of the nature of an ethical action. He tells us that a truly ethical action must be a free choice between two alternatives. This definition is then wonderfully complicated by a further requirement—that the moral man must be so trained in making the right choice that he makes it as a matter of habit, makes it, as it were, instinctively. Yet it *is* a choice, and reason plays a part in its making. But we, of course, don't give to reason the same place in the moral life that Aristotle gave it. And in general, over the last hundred and fifty years, dramatists and novelists have tried their hand at the representation of human suffering without the particular safeguards against cruelty which Aristotle perceived, or contrived. A very large part of the literature of Western Europe may be understood in terms of an attempt to invert or criticize the heroic prescription of the hero, by burlesque and comedy, or by the insistence on the commonplace, the lowering of the hero's social status and the diminution of his power of reasoned choice. The work of Fielding may serve as an example of how the mind of Europe has been haunted by the great image of classical tragedy, and how it has tried to lay that famous ghost. When Fielding calls his hero Tom Jones, he means that his young man is not Orestes or Achilles; when he calls him a foundling, he is suggesting that Tom Jones is not, all appearances to the contrary notwithstanding, Oedipus.

Edith Wharton was following where others led. Her impulse in conceiving the story of Ethan Frome was not, however, that of moral experimentation. It was, as I have said, a purely literary impulse, in the bad sense of the word "literary." Her aim is not that of Wordsworth in any of his stories of the suffering poor, to require of us that we open our minds to a realization of the kinds of people whom suffering touches. Nor is it that of Flaubert in *Madame Bovary,* to wring from solid circumstances all the pity and terror of an ancient tragic fable. Nor is it that of Dickens or Zola, to shake us with the perception of social injustice, to instruct us in the true nature of social life and to dispose us to indignant opinion and action. These are not essentially literary intentions; they are moral intentions. But all that Edith Wharton has in mind is to achieve that grim tableau of which I have spoken, of pain and imprisonment, of life-in-death. About the events that lead up to this tableau, there is nothing she finds to say, nothing whatever. The best we can conclude of the meaning of her story is that it might perhaps be a subject of discourse in the context of rural sociology—it might be understood to exemplify the thesis that love and joy do not flourish on poverty-stricken New England farms. If we try to bring it into the context of morality, its meaning goes no further than certain cultural considerations—that is, to people who like their literature to show the "smiling aspects of life," it may be thought to say, "This is the aspect that life really has, as grim as this"; while to people who repudiate a literature that represents only the smiling aspects of life it says, "How intelligent and how brave you are to be able to understand that life is as grim as this." It is really not very much to say.

And yet there is in *Ethan Frome* an idea of considerable importance. It is there by reason of the author's deficiencies, not by reason of her powers—because it suits Edith Wharton's rather dull intention to be content with telling a story about people who do not make moral decisions, whose fate cannot have moral reverberations. The idea is this: that moral inertia, the *not* making of moral decisions, constitutes a very large part of the moral life of humanity.

This isn't an idea that literature likes to deal with. Literature is charmed by energy and dislikes inertia. It characteristically represents morality as positive action. The same is true of the moral philosophy of the West—has been true ever since Aristotle defined a truly moral act by its energy of reason, of choice. A later development of this tendency said that an act was really moral only if it went against the inclination of the person performing the act: the idea was parodied as saying that one could not possibly act morally to one's friends, only to one's enemies.

Yet the dull daily world sees something below this delightful preoccupation of literature and moral philosophy. It is aware of the morality of inertia, and of its function as a social base, as a social cement. It knows that duties are done for no other reason than that they are said to be duties; for no other reason, sometimes, than that the doer has not really been able to conceive of any other course, has, perhaps, been afraid to think of any other course. Hobbes said of the Capitol geese that saved Rome by their cackling that they were the salvation of the city, not because they were they but there. How often the moral act is performed not because we are we but because we are there! This is the morality of habit, or the morality of biology. This is Ethan Frome's morality, simple, unquestioning, passive, even masochistic. His duties as a son are discharged because he is a son; his duties as a husband are discharged because he is a husband. He does nothing by moral election. At one point in his story he is brought to moral crisis—he must choose between his habituated duty to his wife and his duty and inclination to the girl he loves. It is quite impossible for him to deal with the dilemma in the high way that literature and moral philosophy prescribe, by reason and choice. Choice is incompatible with his idea of his existence; he can only elect to die.

Literature, of course, is not wholly indifferent to what I have called the morality of habit and biology, the morality of inertia. But literature, when it deals with this morality, is tempted to qualify its dullness by endowing it with a certain high grace. There is never any real moral choice for the Félicité of Flaubert's story "A Simple Heart." She is all pious habit of virtue, and of blind, unthinking, unquestioning love. There are, of course, actually such people as Félicité, simple, good, loving—quite stupid in their love, not choosing where to bestow it. We meet such people frequently in literature, in the pages of Balzac, Dickens, Dostoievski, Joyce, Faulkner, Hemingway. They are of a quite different order of being from those who try the world with their passion and their reason; they are by way of being saints, of the less complicated kind. They do not really exemplify what I mean by the morality of inertia. Literature is uncomfortable in the representation of the morality of inertia or of biology, and overcomes its discomfort by representing it with the added grace of that extravagance which we denominate saintliness.

But the morality of inertia is to be found in very precise exemplification in one of Wordsworth's poems. Wordsworth is preeminent among the writers who experimented in the representation of new kinds and bases of moral action—he has a genius for imputing moral existence to people who, according to the classical morality, should have no moral life at all. And he has the courage to make this imputation without at the same time imputing the special grace and interest of saintliness. The poem I have in mind is ostensibly about a flower, but the transition from the symbol to the human fact is clearly, if awkwardly, made. The flower is a small celandine, and the poet observes that it has not, in the natural way of flowers, folded itself against rough weather:

> But lately, one rough day, this Flower I passed
> And recognized it, though in altered form,
> Now standing as an offering to the blast,
> And buffeted at will by rain and storm.
>
> I stopped, and said with inly-muttered voice,
> It doth not love the shower nor seek the cold;
> This neither is its courage nor its choice,
> But its necessity in being old.

Neither courage nor choice, but necessity: it cannot do otherwise. Yet it acts as if by courage and choice. This is the morality imposed by brute circumstance, by biology, by habit, by the unspoken social demand which we have not the strength to refuse, or, often to imagine refusing. People are scarcely ever praised for living according to this morality—we do not suppose it to be a morality at all until we see it being broken.

This is morality as it is conceived by the great mass of people in the world. And with this conception of morality goes the almost entire negation of any connection between morality and destiny. A superstitious belief in retribution may play its part in the thought of simple people, but essentially they think of catastrophes as fortuitous, without explanation, without reason. They live in the moral universe of the Book of Job. In complex lives, morality does in some part determine destiny; in most lives it does not. Between the moral life of Ethan and Mattie and their terrible fate we cannot make any reasonable connection. Only a moral judgment cruel to the point of insanity could speak of it as anything but accidental.

I have not spoken of the morality of inertia in order to praise it but only to recognize it, to suggest that when we keep our minds fixed on what the great invigorating books tell us about the moral life, we obscure the large bulking dull mass of moral fact. Morality is not only the high, torturing, dilemmas of Ivan Karamazov and Captain Vere. It is also the deeds performed without thought, without choice, perhaps even without love, as Zeena Frome ministers to Ethan and Mattie. The morality of inertia, of the dull, unthinking round of duties, may, and often does, yield the immorality of inertia; the example that will most readily occur to us is that of the good simple people, so true to their family responsibilities, who gave no thought to the concentration camps in whose shadow they lived. No: the morality of inertia is not to be praised, but it must be recognized. And Edith Wharton's little novel must be recognized for bringing to our attention what we, and literature, so easily forget. (pp. 34-44)

> *Lionel Trilling, "The Morality of Inertia," in his* A Gathering of Fugitives, *1956. Reprint by Harcourt Brace Jovanovich, 1977, pp. 34-44.*

KENNETH BERNARD   (essay date 1961)

[*An American dramatist, poet, short story writer, and critic, Bernard is the author of* Night Owl and Other Plays *(1971), a collection of nontraditional dramas in which plot and characterization are abandoned in the pursuit of metaphorical action. In the following excerpt, he analyzes imagery and symbolism in* Ethan Frome.]

A common criticism of Edith Wharton's *Ethan Frome* is that it is too contrived. In the last analysis, the characters seem peculiarly unmotivated, put through their paces in a clever, but mechanical, way. Such an opinion can only be the result of a cursory reading. It is true that the book has a kind of stylistic and organizational brilliance. But it is not merely a display; it is invariably at the service of plot and character. The nature of her subject imposed certain difficulties on Wharton, particularly her characters' lack of articulation. How could she, without over-narrating, get at a deep problem involving such characters when they do not speak enough to reveal that problem? Frome's character and his marital relationship are at the heart of the novel, but they are revealed only indirectly. Wharton solved her difficulty in a masterful way by her use of imagery and symbolism. It is in her use of imagery and symbolism that the depths of the story are to be found. Without an understanding of them, a reader *would* find the characters unmotivated and the tragedy contrived. For easy discussion, the imagery and symbolism may be divided into three parts: the compatibility of setting and character, the uses of light and dark, and the sexual symbolism. A survey of these three parts in the novel will, it is hoped, clarify the real story in *Ethan Frome* by adding a new dimension of meaning.

The beginning of this new dimension of meaning is the first mention of the New England village—Starkfield. On many levels the *locus* of the story is a stark field. The village lies under "a sky of iron," points of the dipper over it hang "like icicles," and Orion flashes "cold fires." The countryside is "gray and lonely." Each farmhouse is "mute and cold as a grave-stone." This characterization of Starkfield is consistent throughout the book. Frome, in all ways, fits into this setting. On several occasions his integration with it is described. The narrator, upon first seeing him, sees him as "bleak and unapproachable." Later he says of Frome, "He seemed a part of the mute melancholy landscape, an incarnation of its frozen woe, with all that was warm and sentient in him bound fast below the surface . . . he lived in a depth of moral isolation too remote for casual access." Frome, unhappily married to Zeena, and pining for her cousin Mattie, is indeed parallel to the Starkfield setting. Everything on the surface is hard and frozen. His feeling, his love, for Mattie cannot break loose, just as spring and summer are fast bound by winter's cold. Mattie, appropriately, has the effect of loosening the rigid physical and emotional landscape. At one point, when she speaks, "The iron heavens seemed to melt down sweetness." Again, she is "like the lightning of a fire on a cold hearth." Frome, however, who has suffered "the profound accumulated cold of many Starkfield winters," does not thaw easily. He remembers when his feelings were free, or, as he puts it, when he was once in Florida, climatically (and emotionally) the opposite of Starkfield: "Yes, I was down there once, and for a good while afterward I could call up the sight of it in winter. But now it's all snowed under." Finally there is Frome's inarticulateness. Not only are his feelings locked, frozen; his very speech is also, beyond the natural reticence of the local people. Neither he nor the landscape can express its warm and tender part. When Mattie once pleases him immensely, he gropes "for a dazzling phrase," but is able to utter only a "growl of rapture: 'Come along'." Later he is again thrilled by her: "Again he struggled for the all expressive word, and again, his arm in hers, found only a deep 'Come along'." He is truly a man of "dumb melancholy."

The separation of feeling from its expression, the idea of emotion being locked away, separated, or frozen, just as Starkfield is bound by ice and snow, is demonstrated also by the Frome farm. The house seems to "shiver in the wind," has a "broken down gate," and has an "unusually forlorn and stunted look." More important, though, is the "L." Wharton gives a full description of the New England farm "L":

> that long deep-roofed adjunct usually built at right angles to the main house, and connecting it, by way of store-rooms and tool-house, with the wood-shed and cow-barn. Whether because of its symbolic sense, the image it presents of a life linked with the soil, and enclosing in itself the chief sources of warmth and nourishment, or whether merely because of the consolatory thought that it enables the dwellers in that harsh climate to get to their morning's work without facing the weather, it is certain that the "L" rather than the house itself seems to be the center, the actual hearth-stone of the New England farm.

Frome casually mentions to the narrator that he had had to take down the "L." Thus Frome's home is disjointed, separated from its vital functions, even as he is. The narrator, not unnaturally, sees in Frome's words about the "diminished dwelling the image of his own shrunken body." Just as Frome is emotionally trapped, just as Starkfield is frozen in the winter landscape, just as Frome's home is cut off from its vitals, so too is he cut off physically from his former strength, trapped in his crippled frame. Images of being caught, bound, trapped are frequent. "He was a prisoner for life." "It seemed to Ethan that his heart was bound with cords which an unseen hand was tightening with every tick of the clock." "I'm tied hand and foot, Matt." Although Mattie is described with flight images like "the flit of a bird in branches," and birds making "short perpendicular flights," the last such image describing her is of her lashes beating like "netted butterflies," and her last "twittering" is her pitiful cry after the unsuccessful suicide attempt, when she is a broken, pain-racked body. Even Mattie, Frome's one hope of escape, is trapped. On top of this, Frome mentions that before the railroad came to a nearby town the road by his farm was a main route, implying that business was better: "We're kinder side-tracked here now." The farm, too, is separated from its former economic vitality. Thus the setting of the novel, the landscape and the farm, is parallel to Frome's condition and serves to illuminate it. But Wharton does not stop at this point.

There is hardly a page throughout the book that does not have some reference to light and dark. Wharton uses all of them with effect. The supreme light image is Mattie Silver, as her name implies. She is in contrast to everything in Starkfield; her feelings bubble near the surface. Frome, on the other hand, is all dark. He lives in the dark, especially emotionally. At the beginning of the novel, when he has come to meet Mattie, she is dancing gaily in a church filled with "broad bands of yellow light." Frome keeps "out of the range of the revealing rays from within." "Hugging the shadow," he stands in the "frosty darkness" and looks in. Later he catches up to her "in the black shade of the Varnum spruces," the spot from where they finally begin the attempted suicide that cripples them. He stands with her in "the gloom of the spruces," where it is "so dark . . . he could barely see the shape of her head," or walks with her "in silence through the blackness of the Hemlock-shaded lane." Blackness is his element. As they walk back to the farm he revels in their closeness. "It was during their night walks back

Title page for Ethan Frome.

to the farm that he felt most intensely the sweetness of this communion." Their love is a bloom of night. "He would have liked to stand there with her all night in the blackness." He does not see Mattie so much as sense her: ". . . he felt, in the darkness, that her face was lifted quickly to his." "They strained their eyes to each other through the icy darkness." Frome's favorite spot is a secluded place in the woods called Shadow Pond. On their last visit there "the darkness descended with them, dropping down like a black veil from the heavy hemlock boughs." Frome cannot seem to get out of the dark. And often, as in quotations above, the dark is pregnant with suggestions of death and cold. Frome's kitchen, on their return from the village, has "the deadly chill of a vault after the dry cold of night." As Ethan settles in his tomblike house, Mattie's effect on him dies away. He lies in bed and watches the light from her candle, which

> sending its small ray across the landing, drew a scarcely perceptible line of light under his door. He kept his eyes fixed on the light till it vanished. Then the room grew perfectly black, and not a sound was audible but Zeena's asthmatic breathing.

Without Mattie's "light" he is left with the ugly reality of his wife. In numerous small ways also Wharton makes the light and dark images work for her. When Mattie relieves Ethan's jealousy at one point, "The blackness lifted and light flooded Ethan's brain." When Mattie is told by Zeena she must go, and she repeats the words to Ethan, "The words went on sounding between them as though a torch of warning flew from hand to hand through a dark landscape." Before their suicide plunge, "The spruces swatched them in blackness and silence." A bitter argument between Ethan and Zeena is "as senseless and savage as a physical fight between two enemies in the darkness." After, Zeena's face "stood grimly out against the uncurtained pane, which had turned from grey to black." The cumulative effect of all these images is to tell us a great deal about Frome and his tortured psyche.

The most important thing the images of light and dark reveal about Frome is that he is a negative person. Frome is a heroic figure: nothing less than the entire landscape can suffice to describe him effectively; his agony is as broad and deep as that of the winter scene. But he is not tragic because he is a man of great potential subdued and trapped by forces beyond his capacity. His tragedy is entirely of his own making. He is weak. His character never changes. Both before and after the accident he is the same. Like his environment he has a kind of dumb endurance for harsh conditions. There are several indications of his weakness besides his identity with darkness. Frome married Zeena because she had nursed his mother through her final illness. He was twenty-one and she twenty-eight. He married her less because he loved her than because he needed a replacement for his mother. Certainly it is Zeena who cracks the whip in the household, and Ethan who jumps. What Zeena says, goes. Frome "had often thought since that it would not have happened if his mother had died in spring instead of winter . . .". When he and Mattie are about to attempt suicide, Mattie sitting in front of Ethan on the sled, he asks her to change places with him. She asks why. Quite sincerely he answers, "Because I—because I want to feel you holding me." He wants to die being cuddled and comforted, leaving to Mattie the role of protecter and shelterer.

Throughout the book, Frome recognizes his futility and accepts it rather than trying to fight his way out of it. He does not ever realistically reach for a solution. His love inspires little more than dreams. He thinks of another man who left his wife for another woman and invests the event with fairy tale qualities: "They had a little girl with fair curls, who wore a gold locket and was dressed like a princess." Once he imagines Zeena might be dead: "What if tramps had been there—what if . . .". When he spends his one night alone with Mattie, instead of thinking of a way to achieve permanence for their relationship he "set his imagination adrift on the fiction that they had always spent their evenings thus and would always go on doing so . . .". Ironically, this is just about what he achieves by crippling instead of killing himself and Mattie. He did not, however, envision that Zeena would be a necessary part of the arrangement, as a nurse to Mattie.

The negation, the blackness, in his character is revealed also in his funereal satisfactions. When Mattie says she is not thinking of leaving because she has no place to go, "The answer sent a pang through him but the tone suffused him with joy." He rejoices in her helplessness; he is pained and thrilled at the same time because she has nowhere to go, because she too is trapped. Looking at the gravestones on his farm that have mocked him for years ("We never got away—how should you?"), he rejoices: ". . . all desire for change had vanished, and the sight of the little enclosure gave him a warm sense of continuance and stability."

"I guess we'll never let you go, Matt," he whispered, as though even the dead, lovers once, must conspire with him to keep her; and brushing by the graves, he thought: "We'll always go on living here together, and some day she'll lie there beside me."

The finest thought he can have is of the triangle going on forever, and then lying in the earth next to Mattie: "He was never so happy with her as when he abandoned himself to these dreams." Frome's aspirations do not finally go beyond darkness. His final acceptance of suicide is the culmination of his negative instincts: death is the blackest blackness.

Although the meaningful use of light and dark is pervasive in the book and is illuminating, it is the sexual symbolism that cuts deepest. The sexual symbolism is more dramatic than the two elements already discussed because it revolves around the key scenes in the book, Ethan and Mattie's night together and Zeena's return. It is also more significant because without an understanding of it the source of Zeena and Ethan's estrangement and antagonism remains unknown. After all, what *is* the deep gulf that lies between them? There is no explicit revelation in the book. In part, Wharton's use of symbolism to clarify the book's central problem is compatible with the inarticulateness of the characters. But perhaps also it represents a reticence or modesty of the author's. Ethan and Mattie's night together is ostensibly a mild affair. Wharton might well have revealed then the true relationship between Frome and his wife and demonstrated overtly Mattie and Ethan's transgression. But was it really necessary for her to do so? Even as it is, the evening progresses with the greatest of intensity. Every action, every word, even every silence quivers. It is because these apparently innocent actions and words exist in such intensity that they must be scrutinized. There are disproportions of feeling, particularly centering around the pickle dish, that are revealing. (pp. 178-82)

Barrenness, infertility, is at the heart of Frome's frozen woe. Not only is his farm crippled, and finally his body too; his sexuality is crippled also. Zeena, already hypochondriac when he married her, has had the effect of burying his manhood as deeply as everything else in him. In seven years of marriage there have been no children. Within a year of their marriage, Zeena developed her "sickliness." Medicine, sickness, and death are, in fact, rarely out of sight in the book. The farm itself, with its separation of its vital center, its regenerative center, suggests of course the sexual repression. The name Starkfield also connotes barrenness. However, Ethan and Zeena's sexual relationship is suggested most by the incident of the pickle dish, a dish which, unless understood, lies rather unaccountably at the very center of the book.

The red pickle dish is Zeena's most prized possession. She received it as a wedding gift. But she never uses it. Instead she keeps it on a shelf, hidden away. She takes it down only during spring cleaning, "and then I always lifted it with my own hands, so's 't shouldn't get broke." The dish has only ceremonial, not functional, use. The sexual connotations here are obvious. The fact that the wedding dish, which was meant to contain pickles, in fact never does, explains a lot of the heaviness of atmosphere, the chill, the frigidity. The most intense scenes of the book, the most revealing, center around this dish. For example, Zeena never does discover an affair in the making between Ethan and Mattie, nor does she ever say anything, except for one hint not followed up, that reveals such knowledge. Her only discovery (and it is *the* discovery of the book) is of her broken (and used) pickle dish. It is this which brings the only tears to her eyes in the entire book. When Zeena is gone for a day, Mattie, significantly, brings down and uses the pickle dish in serving Ethan supper. Only if the dish is properly understood can it be seen how her violation is a sacrilege, as Zeena's emotions amply testify. The dish is broken, and Ethan plans to glue it together. Of course the dish can never be the same. This kind of violation is irrevocable. Zeena does not discover that the dish is broken until she gets, again significantly, heartburn, the powders for which she keeps on the same private shelf as the pickle dish. The scene following is a symbolic recognition of the fact that Mattie has usurped her place, broken her marriage, and become one with Ethan, though in fact it was the cat (Zeena) who actually broke the dish. The fact that Zeena never truly filled her place, acted the role of wife, and is herself responsible for the failure of the marriage does not bother her. Ethan is hers, however ceremonially, and she resents what has happened. Her emotion transcends any literal meaning the dish may have, so much so that other implications of the dish force themselves on the reader. Speaking to Mattie, she says,

> "... you waited till my back was turned, and took the thing I set most store by of anything I've got, and wouldn't never use it, not even when the minister come to dinner, or Aunt Martha Pierce come over from Bettsbridge.... I tried to keep my things where you couldn't get at 'em—and now you've took from me the one I cared for most of all—" She broke off in a short spasm of sobs that passed and left her more than ever like the shape of a stone.... Gathering up the bits of broken glass she went out of the room as if she carried a dead body....

The passage reveals most clearly the gulf between Ethan and Zeena. The body she carries out is the corpse of her marriage. The evening that Mattie and Ethan spend together, then, is not as innocent as it seems on the surface. That Mattie and Ethan's infidelity is so indirectly presented, whether because of Wharton's sense of propriety or her desire to maintain a minimum of direct statement, does not at all lessen the reality of that fact. If the overt act of infidelity is not present, the emotional and symbolic act is. The passage is full of passion; the moment, for example, when Frome kisses the edge of the piece of material Mattie is holding has climactic intensity.

The sterility of their marriage, Frome's emasculation, is represented elsewhere. For example, just before Zeena leaves for the overnight trip to a doctor, she finishes a bottle of medicine and pushes it to Mattie: "It ain't done me a speck of good, but I guess I might as well use it up.... If you can get the taste out it'll do for pickles." This is the only other mention of pickles in the book. Significantly, it is the last word in the chapter before the one devoted to Ethan and Mattie's night together. The action might be interpreted as follows: after Zeena has exhausted the possibilities of her medicine for her "trouble," she turns to sex—but she passes on that alternative to Mattie. Mattie may use the jar for pickles if she wishes. The action is a foreshadowing of Mattie's use of the pickle dish. In a sense, Zeena has urged her to that act, for she is abdicating the position of sexual initiative.

Again, in *Ethan Frome* each word counts. But there are some descriptions, obviously very particular, that do not fit in with any generalizations already presented. However, in the light of an understanding of the pickle dish incident, they are clar-

ified. When Frome first points out his home, the narrator notes "the black wraith of a deciduous creeper" flapping on the porch. Deciduous means shedding leaves, or antlers, or horns, or teeth, at a particular season or stage of growth. Frome has indeed shed his manhood. Sexually he is in his winter season. Later, another vegetation is described on the porch: "A dead cucumber vine dangled from the porch like the crape streamer tied to the door for a death ...". A cucumber is no more than a pickle. The pickle dish is not used; the cucumber vine is dead. That it should be connected with crape (black) and death is perfectly logical in the light of what has already been discussed about Frome. Frome's sexuality is dead. There is, of course, in all this the suggestion that Frome could revive if he could but reach spring, escape the winter of his soul. Mattie is his new season. At one point, where Mattie "shone" on him,

> his soul swelled with pride as he saw how his tone subdued her. She did not even ask what he had done. Except when he was steering a big log down the mountain to his mill he had never known such a thrilling sense of mastery.

Mattie, as Zeena never does, makes Ethan feel the springs of his masculinity. But he never overcomes the ice of accumulated Starkfield winters. His final solution is to merge himself with winter forever.

Thus Ethan Frome, when he plunges towards what he considers certain death, is a failure but not a mystery. His behavior is not unmotivated; the tragedy is not contrived. The very heart of the novel is Frome's weakness of character, his negation of life. Behind that is his true, unfulfilled, relationship with Zeena. Wharton's economy of language in the novel is superb. There is hardly a word unnecessary to the total effect. Her final economy is the very brevity of the book. It fits the scene and character. There were depths to plumb; her people were not simple. To overcome the deficiencies of their natural reticence (and perhaps her own), to retain the strength of the severe and rugged setting, particularly the "outcropping granite," she resorted to a brilliant pattern of interlocking imagery and symbolism, three facets of which have been outlined here, to create a memorable work. The reader of *Ethan Frome*, then, need not find it merely a technically successful work, a virtuoso performance. With an understanding of the imagery and symbolism he can look into the heart of the book and see characters as full-bodied people in the grip of overwhelming emotional entanglements. He is also in a position to see the book's true dimensions as tragedy. (pp. 182-84)

> *Kenneth Bernard, "Imagery and Symbolism in 'Ethan Frome'," in* College English, *Vol. 23, No. 3, December, 1961, pp. 178-84.*

K. R. SRINIVASA IYENGAR   (essay date 1962)

[*Iyengar is an Indian man of letters, spiritual advisor, and critic who writes in English. In* Indian Writing in English *(1962) and other works he has sought to familiarize readers with Indian literature and thought and has written on such various topics as the relationship between Indian and English literature, the nature of beauty, and the administration of education in India. In the following excerpt, Iyengar praises the craftsmanship and psychological insight of Wharton's presentation of a simple plot and compares* Ethan Frome *with Ford Madox Ford's* The Good Soldier *(1927) and Rabindranath Tagore's* The Garden *(1933).]*

If in some of [Edith Wharton's] novels (*The House of Mirth* and *The Custom of the Country,* for example) she has tried to show how excessive opulence could start in its insensitive beneficiaries the corrupting and rotting process of physical and moral degeneration, in *Ethan Frome* she is at pains to demonstrate that mere poverty, and the shifts to which it condemns its victims, are no guarantee either that moral sensitiveness will remain uncorroded. If luxury is a drug, an opiate,—for the more one feeds on it the more is one's appetite for it roused,—then penury is a dull force that benumbs the moral sense, atrophies it, or reduces it to a condition of fatalistic listlessness and suicidal apathy. Under such circumstances one doesn't exist, one merely suffers the disease that is life. (p. 168)

Detaching the story from its cunningly contrived framework in the novel, we see that it is but one more variation of the "love triangle"—only here the tale ends, not with a bang, but a prolonged, almost unending, whimper and drone. Ethan Frome a man of more than average tastes and abilities is obligated to linger in his farm, first to look after his father, then his mother, and finally his invalid wife Zeena. When Mattie, Zeena's poor cousin, comes to live with them, Ethan and the young girl are slowly drawn together—though no word is spoken to which one can take exception. Zeena's suspicions, however, are aroused at last and she decides to send Mattie away and hire some other help. Ethan is impotent with rage, but he feels "tied hand and foot": he can only submit to his fate. This one year's sunshine after the fog of the seven years of marriage is a mere dream that must be forgotten. When he is taking Mattie in his sleigh to catch the train, they stop on the way, and yielding to an erratic impulse they decide to use a sled to go down the slope of the hill, just avoiding the big elm on the way. The night, the exhilaration of the descent, and the growing sense of desperation suddenly drive them into each other's arms. . . . Although the clock jerks them back to reality, having now really found each other, they cannot separate; "What's the good of either of us going anywheres," he asks, "without the other one now?" Mattie has a mad idea which she puts into words: they should slide a second time, but hit "right into the big elm . . . so 't we'd never have to leave each other any more." It is the woman who sees this way out of the despair in which they find themselves engulfed; and, indeed, Mattie seems to Ethan "the embodied instrument of fate." They make the mad attempt, of course, but the suicide compact fails; they are battered, not dead. They are duly picked up, given first aid, and Zeena receives them back. . . . The "smash-up" changes the sweet-tempered Mattie into a sour woman; and as for Zeena, she had never been sweet: and, poised between the two, Ethan plays his silent role. (pp. 169-71)

There is both craftsmanship and psychological insight in Mrs. Wharton's management of this simple plot and in the telling of this painful story. Nature, as in Hardy's novels, is a grim spectator. The Shadow Pond is almost a person, an observer, a silent wayside chorus. The "elm tree" is both tree and symbol. Ned Hale and Ruth kiss under the tree, and they almost run into the tree. "The elm *is* dangerous. . . . It ought to be cut down," Mattie says at one stage of the story to Ethan. Later Ethan concedes: "That's an ugly corner down by the big elm. If a fellow didn't keep his eyes open he'd go plumb into it." Yet it is the same Mattie that, in her extremity of anguish, insists that Ethan should run her into the tree. The pickle-dish is another symbol. The only time it is made use of, it crashes down—as Ethan and Mattie, the only time they come so close together, sweep down past the elm and mangle themselves for life. Ethan and Zeena—their sad seven years together—the year

of Mattie's bright sojourn with them—and then the smash-up, followed by the twenty-four years of their huddled-up graveyard life, like the broken fragments of the pickle-dish placed on the shelf edge to edge, to create the semblance of a form that they do not really have: Ethan's romance and the china's active life have alike been a transient mockery and no more.

The pickle-dish fiasco is what Mrs. Wharton would call an *illuminating incident* in the novel. In her monograph, *The Writing of Fiction* . . . , she refers to such incidents as "the magic casements of fiction, its vistas on infinity." The pickle-dish incident, the coasting, and the final crash against the elm-tree are such "vistas on infinity" in *Ethan Frome.* The only time the lovers have really come close is also the occasion when they plan the crash against the elm-tree. "When the novelist has been possessed by a situation, and sees his characters hurrying to its culmination," writes Mrs. Wharton, "he must have unusual keenness of vision and sureness of hand to fix their lineaments and detain them on their way long enough for the reader to recognize them as real human beings." Mrs. Wharton herself is so possessed by the imagined situation of the fateful crash of the lovers against the elm-tree that she is able to portray the whole drama of their mad endeavour and total failure with clarity and convincing detail and a sense of utter inevitability. We are awed and almost crushed by the event, but we do not question the veracity of the recital.

Mr. Lionel Trilling is not altogether just when he says that *Ethan Frome* "isn't a great book, or even a fine book. It seemed to me a factitious book, perhaps even a cruel book" [see excerpt dated 1956]. He says further: "The moral sound that *Ethan Frome* makes is a dull thud. . . . [It] presents no moral issue, and no moral reverberation." Mr. Trilling apparently finds Ethan, Zeena and Mattie guilty of "moral inertia." What they do they cannot help doing. They are not "free" agents. There is neither courage nor choice, only necessity, behind their actions. Is this, then, the whole truth about *Ethan Frome*? Merely a "factitious" and "cruel" book.

It would be an oversimplification to say that the chief characters in *Ethan Frome* are only moved by blind necessity. Ethan himself is by no means a cipher. He has had dreams of a technical career. Even in the days of his decline he is not lacking in impressiveness:

> He seemed a part of the mute melancholy landscape, an incarnation of its frozen woe, with all that was warm and sentient in him fast bound below the surface.

Zeena is capable of positive malice; her power is the power of the strong-minded over the weak, and she mercilessly uses it. When she declares that Mattie must go, Ethan but wriggles in vain: "All the long misery of his baffled past, of his youth of failure, hardship and vain effort, rose up in his soul in bitterness and seemed to take shape before him in the woman who at every turn had barred his way." Of course he could desert Zeena and run away with Mattie. There *are* ways and means, but after weighing them he decides *not* to make the attempt:

> With the sudden perception of the point to which his madness had carried him, the madness fell and he saw his life before him as it was. He was a poor man, the husband of a sickly woman, whom his desertion would leave alone and destitute; and even if he had had the heart to desert her he could have done so only by deceiving two kindly people who had pitied him.

There is far more than just "moral inertia"—"the morality imposed by brute circumstance, by biology, by habit, by the unspoken social demand"—in Ethan's decision. Again, there is more than mere inertia in Ethan's deciding—in defiance of Zeena's opposition—to take Mattie to the station himself, instead of sending her with Jotham:

> . . . Ethan strode down after him (Jotham) a-flame with anger. The pulses in his temple throbbed and a fog was in his eyes. He went about his task without knowing what force directed him, or whose hands and feet were fulfilling its orders. . . .

All that he obscurely hopes for is a good last ride together, a display of some affection and consideration when the girl who has meant so much for him leaves his farm for good. They go round the Shadow Pond, with its pleasant associations. It is only when, after questioning her, he realizes how bleak life for her without him is going to be, even as he knows how his own future without her must be—only then, and as much for her sake as for his own, he starts obscurely figuring a future *together,* even if only in terms of annihilation. As the sun sets and the dusk spreads, they make a full avowal of their mutual love, and this comes with a shock of glorious recognition to both of them. Seeing the village children with sleds, the idea comes to Ethan that, after all, he and Mattie might "coast" this last time together. When the sled stops after its heady descent, the events of the evening are too much for them, and they feel that they simply cannot part now. There is no normal future for either of them alone, or for them together; but if they cannot live together, they can at least die together. A crazy decision it may be—even a mad one—but it is by no means an expression of mere "moral inertia." To equate their decision with the fall of the "small celandine"—

> This neither is its courage nor its choice,
> But its necessity in being old—

is entirely to misread the actual course of events.

It is true, of course, that Ethan and Mattie fail: even death eludes them. But while the failure is the fact, it is no less clear that, with a little luck, they *might* have succeeded in their limited aim of co-destruction. Ethan is known to be clever enough to have "fetched it." The fact of failure should not make us withhold our startled and pained admiration for their decision to die together because they feel they cannot live and love together. Zeena, desiring the separation of Ethan and Mattie, starts a chain-reaction that finally ties them up together in the trance of death-in-life. Desiring a nurse that is safer and more useful than Mattie, Zeena has to forego all help and herself become Mattie's nurse for life. Mr. Trilling says that moral inertia proceeds, not from reason and choice, but from habit and biology. This is not wholly true of the characters in **Ethan Frome**. Zeena reasons in her own way and makes her choice, both when she decides to send Mattie away and when she receives her back. Ethan reasons and makes his choice when he decides not to borrow money under false pretences and use it to run away with Mattie and make a start elsewhere. And even under the pressure of violent emotion, and although enveloped in the double darkness of the night without and the despair within, Ethan and Mattie do reason after a fashion before resolving what to do. They cannot live and love, and so they will die. Mrs. Wharton's rendering of the tangle of circumstances in Ethan's farm is stark, realistic, "relentless and inevitable"; granted this, Mr. Trilling asks: What is her

"moral intention" in projecting this tableau from Hell before us? Perhaps it is simply to emphasize that to fail in love—in charity—even in elementary humanity—is to set up evil currents that must, sooner or later, draw in and engulf oneself, and others too besides oneself. The theme is Zeena, her hardness, her incapacity for love of any kind. She can only think of herself, not of the other—or of others. First she feeds her ego by dieting on her ailments: later, after the smash-up, she forges an armour of rectitude for herself by nursing Mattie, certainly without love, but not without thought or choice. Of course Mrs. Hale says that "there was nowhere else for her to go," but if Zeena could say only a day or two earlier that "it's somebody else's turn now" (to maintain Mattie), she might have taken the same callous attitude after the smash-up also. If she takes the mangled Mattie back, it is because such is her choice now, and she is prepared to face the consequences. It is not the moral inertia of custom and "duty" alone, but also the sense of satisfaction in having the detested rival back in a condition of helplessness, that determine her reasoning and choice.

Zeena is indeed rather like Leonara Ashburnham, the Wife in Ford Madox Ford's *The Good Soldier,* which appeared four years after **Ethan Frome**. If Leonara is Zeena transplanted into a European setting, Edward is Ethan grown old, and Nancy is another Mattie. But whereas Mattie has lived with the Fromes for barely a year, Nancy has as it were grown from girlhood to young maidenhood with the Ashburnhams over a period of eight years. Leonara and Edward and Nancy, unlike the Fromes and Mattie, are sophisticated and complicated in their natures, and are quite unpredictable most of the time. Further, in Ford's novel, Edward's "past" and the fact that the narrator, Dowell, also loves Nancy introduce other elements of complexity. In the end, separated from an estranged Nancy, Edward cuts his own throat with a pen-knife, and Nancy, reading the news in a paper at Aden, goes mad. Leonara marries again, and it is left to Dowell to look after the mad Nancy and to tell this "saddest story." (pp. 171-75)

Like its complicated and sophisticated characters, in its technique too *The Good Soldier* is far more cunningly contrived with an "intricate tangle of references and cross-references" than the more austerely constructed **Ethan Frome**. Each is of a piece with its theme, the characters, the background. *The Good Soldier* shifts uneasily from Nauheim in Germany to Stanford in the States or Branshaw Teleragh, with its oaks and clumps of gorse, in England. There is variety in scene, in situation, in character, in mood, in talk. But Starkfield in **Ethan Frome** is, well, "stark"—notwithstanding its "sweet-fern, asters and mountain-laurel." Winter snow covers up everything. Again, in *The Good Soldier,* the narrator is himself one of the actors in the drama, and has been intimately (though half-unconsciously) involved in the happenings over a period of almost ten years. But he does his best to present the different "points of view"—Leonara's, Edward's, Nancy's, his own wife Florence's—though all suffer some unavoidable distortion being refracted through his own "central intelligence." The design of the novel is certainly more complex than that of **Ethan Frome,** in which the narrator comes into the story 22 years after the "smash-up" and even so only as an observer, a recorder. No difference, according to Mrs. Hale, between the Fromes at the farm and the Fromes at the graveyard—between death-in-life and total oblivion. In *The Good Soldier,* too, the final scene is Dowell and Nancy sitting at the dining table, with the old nurse standing behind her; and what does it amount to?—"nothing—. . . a picture without a meaning."

Darkness at noon, death in life, Nothingness amidst Everything!

It is clear that Mrs. Wharton (when she wrote *Ethan Frome*) and Ford (when he wrote *The Good Soldier*) were both wrestling with Despair (for whatever reason). While not equating the two novels (for it may be readily conceded that Ford's is the richer book and the finer masterpiece), it is still permissible to say that both novels are about people who passionately desire to live but purblindly embrace a living death: both novels are about people who are betrayed partly by themselves and partly by chance. . . . It is likely . . . , that Mrs. Wharton's unhappy marriage (her husband was afflicted with a progressively deteriorating mental disease) was responsible for the bleakness of novels like *Ethan Frome* and *Bunner Sisters*. When Mrs. Wharton was at last able to escape to Europe (leaving her husband in the care of an attendant), she felt less constricted, less oppressed, less doomed. On the other hand, with the removal of the pressures of frustration, the tension of the art relaxes too—and neither Ford in his later Tietgens books nor Mrs. Wharton in her later fiction (except, perhaps, *The Age of Innocence*) quite recaptures the fierce concentration and feeling of fatality that we have in *The Good Soldier* and *Ethan Frome*.

In a short novel of Tagore's also, *The Garden* . . . , the central situation recalls that of both *Ethan Frome* and *The Good Soldier*. Niraja is the sick wife of the well-to-do florist, Aditya. After ten years of happy married life, Niraja falls sick, and Aditya sends for Sarala to help him with his work in the flower garden. Like Mattie, Sarala too had known better days, but her uncle has now left her destitute, and it was at her uncle's that Aditya had apprenticed himself as a florist and first met Sarala. Like Edward and Nancy (though less explosively), like Ethan and Mattie (though less consciously), Aditya and Sarala feel drawn to each other—not only as ardent florists but also as man and woman—and this provokes the jealousy and hatred of the wife, Niraja. Ultimately, in all three stories, it is the wife who by her words and actions sets the incipient love of the husband and the other girl into a blaze of passion. If in *Ethan Frome* Zeena hopes that her rival, Mattie, would marry Denis Eady and thus be out of the way, so also, in *The Garden*, Niraja hopes that Sarala would marry Ramen and remove herself from the scene. When later the wife in sheer desperation tries to effect the separation of the lovers, Ethan cries: "You can't go, Matt! I won't let you!"; and Aditya likewise declares: "I will not allow you to be snatched away from me—no, never." All three wives—Leonara, Zeena, Niraja—are terribly possessive, and that is why in the final reckoning they lose all. (pp. 175-77)

We have in all three novels (notwithstanding differences in emphasis) the same "classic" predicament: When a chasm yawns between wife and husband, and the husband is drawn towards another, what is the way out? In Mrs. Wharton's novel, it is clear that at no time love had held husband and wife together; in *The Good Soldier*, again, we are meant to see through the narrator's ambiguous surmises and contradictory asseverations and conclude that there was really no love lost between husband and wife. In *The Garden*, however, we are to draw the inference that it is sickness that has soured Niraja and turned her love into jealousy. In all three novels, the girls— Mattie, Nancy, Sarala—are presented as pure unspoilt girls, and the eruption of jealousy, and the lava flood of passion let loose by it, overwhelm them all—Mattie is maimed for life, Nancy is rendered insane, and, as for Sarala, she is saved apparently only by the final collapse of Niraja.

In *Ethan Frome*, it is the jealous wife that takes determined action to separate the lovers. In *The Good Soldier*, Leonara seems actually to pimp for her husband, telling Nancy that she should "belong" to Edward to save his life and at the same time systematically poisoning the girl's mind against him, thus brandishing like an athlete a double-edged sword. In *The Garden*, Niraja see-saws between protest and acquiescence, and her moods and words and actions only bring to the fore the passions that might otherwise have lain dormant. This, then, is the conclusion of the matter: where love is absent, or where love has turned to resentment and hate, nothing can save the situation. Love failing, there is only death—or, what is even worse, the nightmare death-in-life. (p. 178)

> K. R. Srinivasa Iyengar, "A Note on 'Ethan Frome',"
> in Literary Criterion, Vol. V, No. 3, Winter, 1962,
> pp. 168-78.

MARIUS BEWLEY (essay date 1964)

[*Bewley was an American educator and critic. In the following excerpt, he refutes Lionel Trilling's interpretation of* Ethan Frome *(see excerpt dated 1956). In discussing the relationship between the novel and Wharton's life, Bewley incorrectly states that Wharton wrote* Ethan Frome *in the year of her divorce. The novel was written several years earlier.*]

A few years ago in an essay on *Ethan Frome* Lionel Trilling said, a little severely, of Mrs. Wharton: ". . . she was a woman in whom we cannot fail to see a limitation of heart, and this limitation makes itself manifest as a literary and moral deficiency of her work, and of *Ethan Frome* especially" [see excerpt dated 1956]. He bases his judgment on what he takes to be her cruelty, even (one gathers) her sadism, in her attitude towards her characters, whom she submits to needless and gratuitous suffering—gratuitous because in the given situation they are incapable of acquiring moral knowledge from their pain. Speaking of that last horrifying scene in which we see the three principals trapped, as it were forever, in that impoverished New England kitchen, Mr. Trilling says: ". . . all that Edith Wharton has in mind is to achieve that grim tableau . . . of pain and imprisonment, of life-in-death. About the events that lead up to this tableau, there is nothing she finds to say, nothing whatever." . . .

Against this reading of *Ethan Frome* it is possible to oppose a quite different reading in which the movement and meaning of the whole narrative depend on two crucial moral decisions made by Ethan, the second of which cancels the first and entails tragic consequences because it is the *wrong* decision. The two moral decisions are painstakingly prepared for in the text, and given as sharp a focus as possible. The first decision is made when Ethan, tormented by his love for his wife's young cousin Mattie, plans to run away with her, and for that purpose considers the possibility of securing money from the Hales on false pretenses:

> He started down the road toward their house, but at the end of a few yards he pulled up sharply, the blood in his face. For the first time . . . he saw what he was about to do. He was planning to take advantage of the Hales' sympathy to obtain money from them on false pretenses. That was a plain statement of the cloudy purpose which had driven him in headlong to Starkfield.

With the sudden perception of the point to which his madness had carried him, the madness fell and he saw his life before him as it was. He was a poor man, the husband of a sickly woman, whom his desertion would leave alone and destitute: and even if he had had the heart to desert her he could have done so only by deceiving two kindly people who had pitied him.

He turned and walked slowly back to the farm.

Ethan's second choice, which reverses the one that has been quoted, is to die with Mattie rather than to face the intolerable pain of parting from her forever. It is not a rational choice in the sense that the first decision was. As Mrs. Wharton finely presents it in the last chapter but one, it is the result of an all but irresistible compulsion of love and despair—almost irresistible, but not quite, for in that *first* decision of Ethan's that Mrs. Wharton rendered for us with such clarity, she showed us a will and a moral intelligence capable of overcoming even this last temptation.

In the sled crash that brings the main action of the story to a close, Ethan and Mattie are not killed but hopelessly crippled. As Ethan painfully regains consciousness under the great elm towards which he has steered the sled, Mrs. Wharton gives us an extraordinary paragraph:

> The sky was still thick, but looking straight up he saw a single star, and tried vaguely to reckon whether it was Sirius, or— or—. The effort tired him too much, and he closed his heavy lids and thought that he would sleep. . . . The stillness was so profound that he heard a little animal twittering somewhere near by under the snow. It made a small frightened *cheep* like a field mouse, and he wondered languidly if it were hurt. Then he understood that it must be in pain: pain so excruciating that he seemed, mysteriously, to feel it shooting through his own body. He tried in vain to roll over in the direction of the sound, and stretched his left arm out across the snow. And now it was as though he felt rather than heard the twittering; it seemed to be under his palm, which rested on something soft and springy. The thought of the animal's suffering was intolerable to him and he struggled to raise himself, and could not because a rock, or some huge mass, seemed to be lying on him. But he continued to finger about cautiously with his left hand, thinking he might get hold of the little creature and help it; and all at once he knew that the soft thing his hand had touched was Mattie's hair and that his hand was on her face.

Ethan's half-delirious desire to help the little animal he imagines he hears is not the reaction of a morally lethargic character; but apart from its immediate effectiveness in deepening still more our sense of his humanity, the passage rises to a bleak revelation when he becomes aware that the agonized *cheep* is not from an animal in pain but from the crushed body of the only person who has ever satisfied his instinct to love. The presence of the little field mouse does not act as a reductive agent on the dignity, the suffering, or the moral natures of Ethan and Mattie, nor does it suggest that they exist on a *sub-*tragic level; rather, it precipitates them into a non-human void beyond tragedy where the sufferings of mice and men are one, where moral decisions and love and decency are obliterated in a blank indifference.

But this was a resolution which, however strongly she may have felt impelled towards it, Mrs. Wharton would not accept any more than she accepted Ethan's *second* moral decision to find an escape in self-imposed death with Mattie. The horrifying closing scene in the kitchen in which Ethan, Mattie, and Zeena seem to confront one another forever is not suffering wantonly imposed on her characters by an embittered female writer, but a punishment that grows ineluctably out of a moral action deliberately performed, and the punishment is meant to exist as an evaluation of that action. In the prologue to *Ethan Frome* the narrator of the story exclaims when he first sees Ethan's face: "He looks as if he was dead and in hell now." One might plausibly argue that *Ethan Frome* is a moral parable, and the sequel played out in the farmhouse kitchen is really meant to be an epilogue in hell.

Since the purpose of these comments is not to offer a critique of the novel but to suggest a relation between Mrs. Wharton's biography and her art, it will be necessary to glance quickly at her situation during the several years that preceded the publication of *Ethan Frome*. . . .

In 1908, according to [biographer] Wayne Andrews . . . , Mrs. Wharton's husband, "who had already developed symptoms of neurasthenia, suffered a severe nervous breakdown." Two years later he was placed under the care of a psychiatrist. Something of the blackness of the period comes through in a letter Henry James wrote to her at the time, and from which Mr. Andrews also quotes: "Only sit tight yourself *and go through the movements of life*. That keeps up your connection with life—I mean of the immediate and apparent life, behind which, all the while, the deeper and darker and unapparent, in which things really happen to us, learns under that hygiene, to stay in its place."

Mr. Andrews gives us for these same years quotations from Mrs. Wharton's unpublished diaries that reveal the passionate intensity of her love for Walter Berry, not more than hinted at in *A Backward Glance* or in Percy Lubbock's *Portrait*. His excerpts are immensely more moving than passages of this kind commonly are, and they reveal a woman who has little apparent relation with the "official" Edith Wharton. They also reveal a human being with a hopeless sense of entrapment. Returning from Paris to her husband, mentally ill at their home in Lenox, Massachusetts, she entered in her journal, which seems to be addressed to Berry:

> I heard the key turn in the prison lock. That is the answer to everything worth-while!
>
> Oh, Gods of derision! And you've given me twenty years of it!
>
> *Je n'en peux plus.*
>
> And yet I must be just. I have stood it all these years, and hardly felt it, because I had created a world of my own, in which I had lived without heeding what went on outside. But since I have known what it was to have some one enter into that world and live there with me, the mortal solitude I come back to has become terrible. . . .

It requires no very ardent effort of the imagination to conceive the possibility that *Ethan Frome* may well have grown out of the double ordeal that Mrs. Wharton went through between 1908 and 1911 when the novel was published. All the constricting circumstances in which Ethan finds himself entrapped, Mrs. Wharton may have carried over, suitably disguised, from her own situation, to scrutinize and question in the pages of her novel. But the ultimate resemblance between her situation and that depicted in *Ethan Frome* is a moral one. From neither situation does there appear to be a possible issue in terms of happiness. Even though Mrs. Wharton was divorced in 1913, she remained apart from Berry, and the moral decision she made in her own life would appear to correspond more or less to the first moral decision made by Ethan—the one which she punished him so severely for forsaking.

There is no intention of suggesting here that Mrs. Wharton was vulgarly capitalizing on her private experiences in *Ethan Frome*. Despite what may be a personal origin, her art is at last a highly impersonal one. But her own moral crisis appears to be reflected with remarkable fidelity in *Ethan Frome*, and one might even venture to suggest that it may have become for her, as she wrote it in the year of her divorce, a moral laboratory in which she tested creatively the alternatives that confronted her in her impossible situation. If she was cruel, the cruelty was in the severity with which she judged herself. So far from indicating a limitation of heart, *Ethan Frome* would seem to be, if the relation between Mrs. Wharton's art and life that has been conjectured here is true, the expression of a remarkably sensitive moral nature. (p. 8)

Marius Bewley, "Mrs. Wharton's Mask," in The New York Review of Books, *Vol. 111, No. 3, September 24, 1964, pp. 7 9.*

R. BAIRD SHUMAN (essay date 1971)

[*In the following excerpt, Shuman discusses the symbolism in* Ethan Frome *as the novel's most pervasive single element.*]

The critics have had many quarrels with *Ethan Frome*. Lionel Trilling, certainly a discerning reader and perceptive critic, wrote that he recalled *Ethan Frome* "... as not at all the sort of book that deserved to stand in a list which included *The Brothers Karamazov* and *Billy Budd, Foretopman*. If it presented a moral issue at all, I could not bring to mind what that issue was" [see excerpt dated 1956]. He continued to say that "My new reading of the book, then, did not lead me to suppose that it justified its reputation, but only confirmed my recollection that *Ethan Frome* was a dead book, the product of mere will, of the cold hard literary will." Another critic, J. D. Thomas, notes that there are many factual inconsistencies in *Ethan Frome*, such as the fact that Ethan has been married to Zeena for seven years, yet he speaks of having attended a technolocigal school before his marriage, some five or six years ago [see excerpt dated 1955]. Such minor inconsistencies definitely pervade the novel, but they have not been so great as to reduce the popularity of the work, and this [essay] is concerned with attempting to account for the continued acceptance of a novel which is manifestly weak in many respects.

Henry Seidel Canby calls *Ethan Frome* a "... piece of perfect craftsmanship" [see Additional Bibliography], and in doing so seems to be praising the book; however, many works which demonstrate fine craftsmanship are not widely read or easily readable—Pater's *Marius, the Epicurean* is a case in point— so it is not this quality alone which accounts for the rather

general acceptance of *Ethan Frome*. Indeed, other critics than Mr. Thomas would dispute Canby's statement altogether. Such critics would point to obvious inconsistencies of fact and would consider these akin to structural weakness. However, viewing structure more broadly, one would be inclined to agree with Blake Nevius that "Edith Wharton's imagination could occasionally be roused to symbol-making activity by the conjunction of a theme and a setting both deeply cherished and understood. In *Ethan Frome* her theme is enhanced by every feature of the landscape ... only in *Ethan Frome*, however, is the symbolism sustained by every element in the setting" [see excerpt dated 1951].

There is probably no more pervasive single element in *Ethan Frome* than the symbolism. Nevius and other writers have pointed out specific examples in which the landscape and the Frome dwelling are clearly related to the action of the story and to the development of characters within it. However, other symbolic elements have not been fully explored and these should be noted, because they are central to the work on a psychosexual level, and this level is very important to the novel because of the underlying sexual tensions which motivate its three central characters. Through the use of carefully chosen symbols, Mrs. Wharton consistently emphasizes problems which are basic to the central action, and she also gives a very strong clue regarding the basis of Zeena Frome's hypochondria.

One of the most notable symbols in *Ethan Frome* is the symbol of the elm tree into which Ethan and Mattie crash their sled during their ill-fated suicide attempt. It is evident that this tree might have been used by Mrs. Wharton, either with conscious intent or subconsciously, as a phallic symbol. Note that the reader is told of the tree long before the suicide attempt is made and is thus prepared for what is later to happen. However, such advanced preparation is not entirely necessary; enough is said of the elm just before the accident to convince the reader of the danger it presents to anyone sledding down the slope which it partially obstructs. Mattie, speaking to Ethan about the elm, says, "Ned Hale and Ruth Varnum came just as *near* running into the big elm at the bottom. We were all sure they were killed. . . . Wouldn't it have been too awful?" Read on a symbolic level, and in light of the fact that later in the narrative the reader is told that Ethan had seen Ned Hale and Ruth Varnum kissing under the Varnum spruces, there is a clear indication, that the elm stands as a representation of sexual temptation, that it draws to it those whose resistance is weak enough that they might violate the puritanical moral codes of a small New England community. Ned and Ruth, though tempted by love, are not pressed to the point that they violate the community mores. But Ethan and Mattie, though their love has not transgressed these mores in any physical sense, cannot long resist their physical natures and will soon be sufficiently dominated by these natures to violate the established codes.

Physical reality is hard and relentless; Mrs. Wharton, in her introduction, warns the reader that it is with this "harsh and beautiful land" that she will concern herself. The harsh moral structures of this land prevent Ethan and Mattie from finding fulfilment for their love, and even the fulfilment of a death together is denied them. They collide head-on with the symbolic tree, and are doomed to a life of unbearable agony, both physical and mental. . . . The means which Ethan and Mattie chose for their suicide woud lead a sensitive reader to expect some symbolic shadings to be apparent. These shadings are quite evident both in the fact of what the tree itself represents and in the fact that Ethan and Mattie run into it on a borrowed sled, on a sled which technically they have no right to, any more than Ethan technically has a right to Mattie's love, nor she to his.

There is, throughout the novel, an emphasis upon the barrenness of the Fromes' lives and surroundings. The graveyard is constantly, mockingly in the background. Very early in the novel, the reader is told that Ethan has had to take down the "L" from his house, and Mrs. Wharton, in a lengthy paragraph, tells that the "L" in a New England house is the center of all life, the hearth-stone of the dwelling. Zeena, presumably, is barren, and her barrenness pervades the atmosphere of the house and is constantly in direct contrast to Mattie's vitality. The illusion of barrenness is supported by such statements as "Zeena always went to bed as soon as she had had her supper, and the shutterless windows of the house were dark." And the statement which immediately follows this one is directly applicable to Ethan: "A dead cucumber-vine dangled from the porch like the crape streamer tied to the door for a death." The Freudian overtones of the shutterless windows and of the dead cucumber-vine are clearly apparent. Death surrounds Ethan; the graveyard is a constant reminder of death's inevitability; and even as he looks ahead, there is no hope. He is the last of the Fromes. The future of his family, the hope of continuance, have been killed by his marriage to Zeena. Mattie presents a momentary hope of something wholesome and satisfying, but Ethan knows that she is what might have been, not what might ultimately be.

Although Mattie is not overly strong, she appears strong in contrast to Zeena. The reader is told that she has gained a great deal of strength during her year at Starkfield. She is often described in terms of the strong color red and its variations: "Mattie came forward, unwinding her wraps, the colour of the cherry scarf in her fresh lips and cheeks." ". . . through her hair she [Mattie] had run a streak of crimson ribbon." "Her [Mattie's] cheeks burned redder." "She [Mattie] looked so small and pinched, in her poor dress, with the red scarf wound about her." However, before Ethan's passion for Mattie had developed, she was sallow; and when she is described in terms of color, the color is more moderate: "You were as pretty as a picture in that pink hat." Red is also used symbolically in relation to the sun: "The sunrise burned red in a pure sky." "Now, in the bright morning air, her [Mattie's] face was still before him. It was part of the sun's red and of the pure glitter of the snow." This use of "red" and "pure" in the same sentence would seem almost to provide an element of mockery, for Mattie is the pure, the virginal figure, but the red heat of passion is intruding upon her life and is leading her irresistibly into a hopeless situation.

Perhaps the most telling symbolic element in *Ethan Frome* is the cherished pickle dish which Zeena received as a wedding gift and has never used. When Zeena goes to Bettsbridge and leaves Mattie andd Ethan alone overnight, Mattie takes this pickle dish from its accustomed place and uses it for its intended purpose. The cat, used symbolically throughout this part of the book to represent Zeena's inescapable presence, knocks the dish to the floor, and it is smashed. Zeena, almost immediately upon her return, discovers what has happened to the dish and blames Mattie for having used it. For the first time in the book, Zeena shows true emotion. "Her voice broke, and two small tears hung on her lashless lids and ran slowly down her cheeks."

This is a major tragedy for Zeena as Mrs. Wharton presents the episode. The question, of course, arises of why this particular incident should be given such play. The smashing of the dish is not used as a pretext for sending Mattie away; Zeena has already reached the decision to do this. The incident might have been used as a turning point in the action of the novel, but it occurs after any turning point with which it might be directly associated. It is not used for characterization, because the characterization has been achieved as fully as it is to be by this point. However, on a symbolic level, it serves as explanation for Zeena's hypochondria and insecurity. The dish was a wedding gift and this, in itself, is significant. The fact that it was red and that it was a *pickle* dish adds to the sexual connotations which it might possess as a symbol. And the fact that Zeena cries because it is broken would point to the fact that Zeena is bemoaning her lost virginity and that her hypochondria is attributable to her fear of her husband's, and perhaps her own, animal nature. Zeena finds that her marriage has placed her in conflict with the codes which her New England upbringing instilled in her; her inhibitions have become so great that she is made pathological by them. Zeena is a pitiable woman. For one reason or another, she has never been able to find fulfilment. Her life is barren. Her future is dark. She reacted well to the responsibility of caring for Ethan's mother, because it was necessary to Zeena that she be needed. But with the death of Ethan's mother, there was a gap in Zeena's life. This gap might have been filled had she had children, but she was denied this satisfaction. Hence, her concern turned inward and her hypochondria, which apparently had moderated when she began caring for Ethan's mother, returned in full force.

To an extent, Zeena was rewarded for the suffering which she endured during the first seven years of her marriage when Mattie and Ethan were injured and needed Zeena to look after them. Zeena—like Ethan—is strongly masochistic throughout the novel. Her hypochondria provided her with masochistic satisfaction, just as her leaving Ethan and Mattie alone for the night did. But when she could become the martyred servant of the sharp-tongued wretch which Mattie became after the accident, her masochistic satisfaction found its greatest fulfilment. She could simultaneously feel that she was needed, that she was morally superior, and that she had been sinned against but had had the humanity to be forgiving. (pp. 257-61)

[The] character of Zenobia Frome represented a controlling principle in the novel at hand, for in this character Mrs. Wharton represents in a single person the generalized, warped manifestation of New England puritanism in its most unwholesome extremes.

Alfred Kazin has quoted Edith Wharton as saying that "Life is the saddest thing next to death." Yet in *Ethan Frome* life has become much sadder than death. Starkfield, the name of which sounds funereal, is a cemetery for those who are still physically alive. There is not "much difference between the Fromes up at the farm and the Fromes down in the graveyard; 'cept that down there they're all quiet, and the women have got to hold their tongues."

The question still remains of what has caused *Ethan Frome* to be so generally accepted and read over the years since its publication in 1911. To begin with, the novel is appealingly brief; it can easily be read in a single sitting, and because it is so brief and is the product of a noted American author, it is often assigned reading in classes on both the secondary school and college levels. But brevity alone does not account for its continued acceptance. The book presents a domestic situation which is very interesting to young people who are concerned with marriage and its problems. Indeed, it has been suggested [in *Essays on the Teaching of English,* edited by E. J. Gordon and E. S. Noyes] that the novel can be taught at the high school level not as a literary work, but as a novel "to teach the concepts and values of family relationships."

However, the book is such a mixture of good and bad writing technique, that it is a valuable book to use for discussions of writing. One who reads it can be guided through it toward the establishment of critical principles by which he might judge much that he reads. The book is notable for its symbolism, much of which is on a different level from that discussed in this paper. The irony not only of the total situation, but of the smaller situations within the book, might be very rewardingly discussed. The development of character is well handled, and the adaptation of the physical properties used in the book—the landscape, the buildings, the town—to the total moral environment demonstrates that the author does not waste any detail that she brings into the story at this point.

On the other hand, there are digressive passages such as that in which Ethan recounts his meeting with Mattie at a picnic during the previous summer. This passage does not aid in the development of the novel, nor does it significantly enhance the reader's understanding of the basic situations involved in the work. The inconsistencies which occur in the novel also raise an interesting point of criticism.

Regardless of considerable adverse criticism, *Ethan Frome* remains a monument in the Edith Wharton canon. It is probably valid to say that it is the Edith Wharton novel which has been most read in the past two or three decades. It retains a freshness in dealing with the problem of the marriage triangle from a relatively impersonal viewpoint. Nature and life and moral codes move steadily forth, drawing with them such as Ethan and Mattie. Mrs. Wharton does not sentimentalize; indeed, she cannot sentimentalize if she is to achieve her end of producing a work which will counter the sweetness and light in which other novelists had steeped New England. In a very real sense, *Ethan Frome* is a novel in the spirit of *The Scarlet Letter,* although its literary stature is far below that of the Hawthorne classic. (pp. 261-63)

> R. Baird Shuman, "The Continued Popularity of
> 'Ethan Frome'," in Revue des langues vivantes, *Vol.*
> *XXXVII, No. 3, 1971, pp. 257-63.*

GEOFFREY WALTON (essay date 1971)

[*In the following excerpt, Walton discusses the fatalism and frustration presented in* Ethan Frome.]

[*Ethan Frome*] is especially closely written, the narrator being made to assume the role of editor; he says he coordinates, which is perhaps a better expression, as he produces a continuous story and not a collection of anecdotes, which might at first sight have been more naturalistic; Edith Wharton had, however, carefully thought out reasons in terms of both subject and story-telling technique for using the method she borrowed from Balzac's "La Grande Bretêche." Within his role, the narrator is the omniscient author; he interprets what he has been told; no one could have told him some of the details that he puts into his "vision." The name Starkfield is all too suitable for the remote Massachusetts village, and the landscape is as carefully chosen as any of Hardy's. One is not made strongly aware of the religious background as a body of doctrine but one has a sense of a narrow world, whose foundations are religious, closing in on the inhabitants and of poverty, sickness,

and inescapable unhappiness. Only little breakaways at rare intervals are possible; it is appropriate to the place as well as to Puritan tradition that Endurance has been a women's name. The opening sentence sets the tone; it is informal, businesslike, and utterly detached:

> I had the story, bit by bit, from various people,
> and, as generally happens in such cases, each
> time it was a different story.

The implication is, as Edith Wharton wished to suggest, of rural inarticulateness and exasperating inconsequence, which the narrator has ordered and disciplined. One is then confronted with Frome, "the ruin of a man," crippled by an accident, and one infers the existence of a hypochondriac wife; "'. . . he's been in Starkfield too many winters. . . . Most of the smart ones get away'" sums up the two basic features of the scene and its influence, the numbing rather than bracing cold and the difficulty of communications. Frome, however, is not a clod; he preserves an interest in science from early days at a Technical College. When at the climax of the introductory section the narrator is snowbound at the Frome farm, even the house looks appropriately "stunted" because Frome has pulled down the wing linking it to the farm buildings. . . . The impression that everything has been contrived and the impression of spontaneous happening are just about equally strong, and the plan of the book as a whole, with its carefully arranged flashbacks, accentuates both this more literary quality in a narrow sense and also the essential fatalism. It is a tale of gratuitous and unavoidable frustration of natural impulses, of revolt, and of suffering. There is again no social conflict; human and inanimate environment seem all one. We already know that Ethan Frome has married the cousin who nursed his senile mother. We learn later that Zeena was once a "smart" and lively bride, but she has become both the supreme product and, for Frome, the ever-present representative of that environment, a silent brooding power from which he cannot escape. She represents no one particular oppression, such as Puritan tradition, but the whole range of suspicions, obligations, and restrictions, large and small, that arise in an isolated and impoverished community, stiffened by Calvinism. There is a decided element of caricature in the treatment of Zeena. With "her hard perpendicular bonnet" and the "querulous lines from her thin nose to the corners of her mouth," she appears as the very incarnation of dyspepsia and uncharitableness. We are shown Frome torn between the exacting dominance of this presence and his natural attraction to Mattie Silver, *her* young and destitute cousin—Mattie's story is all of a piece with the rest—who has been brought to help in the house. This domestic situation is cunningly but effectively sandwiched into an account of Ethan Frome fetching the girl back from a dance; the contrast brings out his emotional situation with simple forcefulness. References to Mattie's incompetence and her vague intellectual sympathy add to the sum of "temptations," which are so inevitable that they seem merely part of his fatal environment; circumstances, action, sensation, and wishful thinking are clearly and naturally related in the description of their return home:

> For the first time he stole his arm about her,
> and she did not resist. They walked on as if
> they were floating on a summer stream.
>
> Zeena always went to bed as soon as she had
> had her supper, and the shutterless windows of
> the house were dark. A dead cucumber-vine
> dangled from the porch like the crape streamer
> tied to the door for a death, and the thought

flashed through Ethan's brain: "If it was there for Zeena—" Then he had a distinct sight of his wife lying in their bedroom asleep, her mouth slightly open, her false teeth in a tumbler by the bed.

When, between the presentation of this situation and the consequence, Ethan Frome and Mattie are thrown together, he is totally inhibited by his opportunity, but a trivial accident results in Mattie's departure in favor of a "hired girl," which implies financial ruin as well as emotional stagnation for Frome. Zeena's state is summed up with a grimly comic reference and an ominous suggestion:

Almost everybody in the neighbourhood had "troubles," frankly localized and specified; but only the chosen had "complications." To have them was in itself a distinction, though it was also, in most cases, a death-warrant.

Each succeeding episode increases the feeling of inevitability, and images of small disasters, such as "netted butterflies," increase the pathos. . . . Though the final act is described as "some erratic impulse," one feels that it is the last of a sequence. The last "coast" down the frozen hill and the suicide pact that fails are a symbolic culmination, very powerfully rendered, of the main theme of head-on frustration. The image of Zeena, obtruded in Frome's consciousness just before the crash, reminds us of the theme of infidelity. This is a minor element, however; there has been no real moral any more than social conflict. Ethan Frome's actions are the product of his environment and his natural temperament and the author does not blame him; Zeena calls Mattie "a bad girl" for breaking a plate, but the moral overtone, though implied, is not very important. One "accident" partly helps them; the next, their survival, is disastrous.

The epilogue presents a state of death in life and life in death, the two cripples looked after by the ex-hypochondriac in a setting of direst poverty; Zeena has developed thus far morally. One of the narrator's informants, a character comparable to Nellie Dean, registers the grimness and the pathos and Frome's surviving pride. There is no suggestion of either punishment or release, simply of continuous pain.

It is not difficult to criticize *Ethan Frome*. Despite, indeed perhaps because of, Edith Wharton's skill, one feels it is a little too inevitable. The contrasts are a little too sharp, the setting a little too bleak, the characters almost caricature—of a grim kind, the disaster melodramatic, and the end unrelievedly wretched. Apart from the formal derivation from Balzac, the construction and the atmosphere in fact remind one more of Hardy than of Emily Brontë; the book lacks both the delicacy and the power of *Wuthering Heights*. One sees a certain kinship between Frome with his thwarted intellectual ambition and Jude Fawley. It is a peasant tragedy in an American setting. Ultimately one probably agrees with Trilling's criticism [see excerpt dated 1956], but one must recognize the distinction of the story, as he recognizes the stoic virtues it offers for our admiration, the endurance and self-respect in the face of hopeless odds. It has something of "the bare, sheer, penetrating power" that Arnold attributed to Wordsworth's "Michael" and comparable poems. Insofar as he rebels, Ethan Frome seems to rebel against life itself—as it exists at Starkfield—rather than against vestigial Puritanism or the social system, but his self-respect and independence, preserved at any cost, are fundamental middle-class qualities, masculine equivalents of the Miss Bunners' little gentilities [in *Bunner Sisters*].

In both cases tragedy culminates in an all-out assault on these values, the last refuge of the individual, and, limited as the scope of it, one feels the ultimate human significance of what is involved in the particular and the class situation. Miss Bunner saves nothing for certain but her self-respect; Ethan Frome keeps his economic independence also, but in conditions that almost nullify it. Edith Wharton has recorded certain social facts, the resignation and pathetic conservatism, the personal pride and desperate individualism of a large number of people of a certain type and class background. She invites us to admire, but to realize the misery to which devotion to these values may lead. Her picture does not fit into any version of the class struggle except as an embarrassing problem, but one should be grateful to her for showing it, as one is to her for showing that tragedy is possible also among the merely well-to-do. (pp. 78-83)

> *Geoffrey Walton, in his* Edith Wharton: A Critical Interpretation, *Fairleigh Dickinson University Press, 1971, 216 p.*

MARGARET B. McDOWELL   (essay date 1976)

[*An American educator and critic, McDowell is the author of* Edith Wharton, *a biographical and critical study of Wharton and her works. In the following excerpt from that book, she examines the narrator as a structural element in* Ethan Frome.]

In *Ethan Frome* Edith Wharton emphasizes the differences between the present and the recent past by using the young narrator, Lockwood, who must look back twenty-five years. Distressed by the duration into late spring of snow drifts and intense cold, he imagines himself in the place of these people in the recent past when hardship was even more acute and isolation more complete. While Ethan is twenty-eight during the main part of the story in Lockwood's retrospective narrative, he is already fifty-two and prematurely aged by toil and by the bitter climate when Lockwood first sees him.

Isolated from the world, Ethan Frome's wife, Zeena, naturally chooses to be sick because sickness promises adventure in its possible complications, sudden cures, and relapses. The patent medicines she receives in the mail provide her only excitement and her only relief from a paralyzing spiritual monotony. She resents Mattie Silver's vitality and her tendency to daydream more than she fears Ethan's interest in her. Zeena is tired and needs household help, but Mattie, the hired girl, lacks efficiency. Zeena is not seen simply as part of Ethan's curse, as some critics have implied, but as a deprived woman who grieves over lost beauty when the cherished red pickle dish she has saved since her wedding is used by Mattie and broken.

The book is fraught with such ironies: the dish that is treasured is the one that is broken; the pleasure of the one solitary meal that Ethan and Mattie share ends in distress; the ecstasy of the coasting ends in suffering; the moment of dramatic renunciation when Ethan and Mattie choose suicide rather than elopement ends not in glorious death but in years of pain. The lovely Mattie Silver becomes an ugly, querulous woman cared for by Zeena, who, again ironically, finds strength and companionship by caring for her former rival. (p. 66)

[Wharton] regarded the book as the fruition of her long search for technical mastery and artistic maturity and contended that she had modulated carefully her structure to the requirements of her materials. The characterization is subtle, strong, and masterful. Her three chief figures have achieved, in the years since it was written, a mythic dimension and seem to be extensions of the grim landscape itself. The ardent lover turned cynic, the beautiful woman turned a soured cripple, and the protective mother figure emerging as a sinister dictatorial presence are all illuminating and arresting conceptions. The very texture of the prose elicits admiration, particularly in the accomplished use of imagery to sustain a moral judgment or to comment implicitly on a character or situation. The blighted apple trees, the rocks sticking out of the soil, the neglected cemetery, the broken cut-glass pickle dish that was a wedding present too good to use, the false teeth that Ethan hates to see beside Zeena's bed, the misshapen remodelled farmhouse that reminds Lockwood of Ethan's crippled back—all are vivid and compelling metaphors in this tale of spiritual deprivations. Yet these deprivations, endured stoically, form the vision of life that Lockwood creates. We cannot, then, separate the technical felicities of the novel—its compelling characterization and its vital imagery—from the experience that Mrs. Wharton sought to enlarge in the work.

Since life was stark rather than rich for her characters, Edith Wharton felt that she must avoid the leisurely elaboration inherent in the novel form and utilize instead the bluntness possible in short fiction. Writing an introduction to a new edition of *Ethan Frome* in 1922, she realized that this conviction conflicted with her usual view that the novel provided the most appropriate genre for any narrative spreading over two generations. In the case of this narrative, she had instinctively realized that the shorter form could alone express the unadorned strength of Ethan Frome and that exhaustive analysis would tend to nullify the stark effect for which she was striving. To encompass Ethan's situation persuasively, she saw that she must present it "without an added ornament, or a trick of drapery or lighting."

In the earliest version of *Ethan Frome*, written in French, she used no character as narrator. In the final version, Lockwood, as narrator, provides a frame to the story and a complicated time scheme by means of which she could dramatically envision the contrast between the bleak existence of her characters in the present with their youthful expectations in the past. Lockwood, more sophisticated than the people he observes, learns gradually about the tragedy from several simple, relatively inarticulate persons; for each of the villagers tells him as much about the situation as he can understand. His more sophisticated intelligence, then, synthesizes these complicated and mysterious fragments into a single *vision* which gives order to the myriads of facts and impressions that others have presented to him. Possessing "scope enough to see it all," he is, in effect, a kind of artist in his own right. Lockwood's own character is important in helping him fulfill his task. He is never the factual reporter; he is the curious, meditative, expansive sensibility who feels ready sympathy for the wasted Ethan Frome when he first observes him and who associates the bleakness in Ethan's face with his own reaction to the harsh winter. In Lockwood's endeavors to withstand the benumbing influence of coldness and isolation upon his own spirit, he finds strength in actively sympathizing with Ethan, Zeena, and Mattie. His human warmth, perhaps, prevents his own spiritual relapse.

As an engineer who constantly daydreams, Lockwood can identify with Ethan who had attended a technical school and who had found the beginnings of a sustaining illusion in his work in the laboratories. But, as an outsider and a member of another generation, Lockwood is remote enough from Ethan's tragedy to see it in perspective, much as it appalls him. Lockwood's seeing Ethan's youthful promise at a distance deepens the implications of his tragedy because time only dulls Ethan's wounds but does not cure them. He has had to learn to endure, and time has only accentuated his suffering instead of alleviating it. Because the tragedy continues to ramify from the past into the present through the sensibilities of an imaginative narrator, mundane survival for Ethan and Mattie becomes more horrible in its impact than their sudden death would have been. As a result of their suicide pact, Mattie and Ethan exchange a hoped for life-in-death for a demeaning death-in-life when their attempt fails. How overwhelming their defeat has been, Mrs. Wharton fully actualizes by presenting it obliquely through the eyes of a young stranger. (pp. 67-9)

Margaret B. McDowell, in her Edith Wharton, *Twayne Publishers, 1976, 158 p.*

DAVID EGGENSCHWILER   (essay date 1977)

[*An American educator and critic, Eggenschwiler is a contributor to numerous literary journals. In the following excerpt, written in response to essays by Lionel Trilling (see excerpt dated 1956) and Kenneth Bernard (see excerpt dated 1961), he discusses the moral and emotional responses elicited by* Ethan Frome.]

The narrative frame story that opens [*Ethan Frome*] provides us, if we are so inclined, with the makings of an allegory. The winter storms are pitiless armies that besiege the remote village of Starkfield, and through this symbolically frozen wasteland Ethan Frome limps like a bound Samson: "it was the careless powerful look he had, in spite of a lameness checking each step like the jerk of a chain." And when a villager says that Ethan is one of the few smart ones who did not "get away," the pattern quickly becomes clear: Ethan is a strong, intelligent man who would have escaped this "negation" of life (the term is the narrator's) had he not been pathetically destroyed by circumstances (later identifiable as fate, accident, or the moral inertia of his society) or tragically destroyed by his own flaws (weakness of will, sexual impotence, habit). But even within the frame story the novel requires much trimming to fit such a pattern. The predominant militance of winter is lightened by glittering snow, blazing blue sky, and crystal clearness—images that will recur throughout the novel to complicate the chill of sleet storms and the entrapping snow drifts. And when we recognize that Ethan's grave dignity is inseparable from the harsh weather and granite outcroppings of this countryside, we should also suspect that the forces, both from within and without, that have lamed him have also helped to give him "the bronze image of a hero." When Ethan surpasses his agreement and drives the narrator ten miles in a snowstorm and when, returning, he struggles through a blizzard, he shows that such elemental strength to endure requires adversity, as it does with Wordsworth's old shepherds and soldiers or with Oedipus, blind at Colonus rather than full of bread at Thebes. So, as we go into the past to find, as the narrator says, "the clue to Ethan Frome," we should already suspect that the clue will not be as simple as a literary, ethical, or psychological detective might wish.

In the first chapter on Ethan's past the narrator mentions the scientific studies that Ethan had followed before his father's death forced him to return home, and the narrator does not make those studies as solemnly ideal as an allegorist would like. He says that Ethan "dabbled in the laboratory" and that the courses had "fed his fancy and made him aware of huge cloudy meanings behind the daily face of things.'' The tone here is ambivalent: while it suggests the touching stirrings in a mute, inglorious Milton, it also condescendingly suggests the fuzzy longings of a Jude Fawley or a James Gatz. Throughout the novel Ethan's dreams of escape call for such ambivalent responses because they mix admirable desires for knowledge, beauty, and freedom with such triteness and sentimentality, and the narrator repeatedly points out this mixture by his ironic tone. So, for example, he describes the response to natural beauty that distinguishes Ethan and Mattie from the more practical people around them: "And there were other sensations, less definable but more exquisite, which drew them together with a shock of silent joy: the cold red of sunset behind winter hills, the flight of cloud-flocks over slopes of golden stubble, or the intensely blue shadows of hemlocks on sunlit snow. When she said to him once: 'It looks just as if it was painted!' it seemed to Ethan that the art of definition could go no farther, and that words had at last been found to utter his secret soul . . .''. Surely we are to accept these sensations as exquisite and to be touched that a secret soul has at last found expression and understanding, but are we not also to smile at the naive, dated remnant of the picturesque tradition in which the characters find that expression? Wharton points out in her introduction that "the looker-on is sophisticated, and the people he interprets are simple''; this perspective encourages the mixture of admiration and condescension that is often provoked by pastoral literature (at least as Empson defines it) from a comedy of *As You Like It* to the tragedy of *The Return of the Native*.

Mattie Silver herself is a perfectly imagined object for Ethan's confused desires. She dances gaily in the church basement, wears red scarves, flirts coyly with the village gallant, walks with a light step, admires sunsets, and is becomingly modest when Ethan makes his embarrassed gestures of affection; as a silver girl, she is the "bit of hopeful young life'' that has come to the Fromes' cold hearth. But Mattie is not solid silver; she has less glittering qualities that also appeal to Ethan. After her bankrupt parents died, she was left alone to make her way in the world: "For this purpose her equipment, though varied, was inadequate. She could trim a hat, make molasses candy, recite "Curfew shall not ring tonight,'' and play "The Lost Chord'' and a pot-pourri from *Carmen*. When she tried to extend the field of her activities in the direction of stenography and bookkeeping her health broke down, and six months on her feet behind the counter of a department store did not tend to restore it.'' This description makes the orphan seem not only pathetic but also a bit silly. The narrator is obviously amused at the "equipment'' of this spoiled daughter of a nouveau-bourgeois father, and his ironic account of her venture into the world seems less appropriate to a bit of hopeful young life than it does to some of the anemic heroines of Tennessee Williams. Accordingly, Mattie is too weak to do all of her work at the farm, so that, to protect her from criticism, Ethan must secretly scrub floors and churn butter like an emasculated Hercules among the handmaidens of Omphale. And Ethan is attracted by her deficiencies, for her weakness makes him feel strong, her ignorance makes him proud of his knowledge, and her dependence makes him feel authoritative in small matters. Repeatedly he boasts and swaggers, enjoying moments of male vanity when a slight gesture—eavesdropping at the dance, talking of steering a sled, reassuring her about the broken dish—has overcome his usual shyness with her. Obviously in both her strengths and weaknesses the girl is the opposite of Zeena, the ugly old woman who scornfully dominates her husband, and just as obviously we sympathize with Ethan in his attraction to that opposite. Yet the characters and motives are too complex

to produce the clear patterns of life versus death, freedom versus imprisonment, that would make the novel more easily explainable. How could such patterns render fully enough our mixed impressions of Ethan's feelings as he stands outside the dance, treasuring the sensibilities that unite him with Mattie and distinguish him from other villagers, envying and scorning the brash son of a successful grocer, feeling as loutish as he used to when, a country-bred student, he tried to jolly city girls? Here are rudimentary touches of one of Joyce's favorite character types as seen in Little Chandler or Gabriel Conroy: and the similarity should remind us that, even if we do not find Joyce's sharp, detached irony in this novel, we should be careful not to sentimentalize Ethan's longings for beauty, love, and knowledge any more than Wharton does.

If Mattie is complex, Ethan's fancies about her are even more so, as an early passage amusingly implies. Mattie has been described as lively, sensitive, forgetful, and dreamy, as a girl having no natural turn for housekeeping; all of these qualities appeal to Ethan's romantic side because—like science, sunsets, and Florida—they suggest the opposite of his tedious farm life. But "Ethan had an idea that if she were to marry a man she was fond of the dormant instinct would wake, and her pies and bisquits become the pride of the country.'' You cannot take the country out of the boy; as he dreams of his silver girl, he can still imagine her at the oven and perhaps with blue ribbons at the county fair. Throughout the novel his fancies about Mattie vacillate between romantic adventure and domestic stability; sometimes amusing, sometimes touching, sometimes chilling, these pointed contrasts reveal and evaluate Ethan's opposing needs.

As the potential lovers walk home through the "irresponsible night,'' Ethan presses the girl against him, steals his arm about her, and feels so excited by her touch that he can think afterwards that he should have kissed her. But he feels subtly different as they pass the Fromes' graveyard. In the past the graves had mocked his restlessness, warning him that he would not escape, yet as he walks by with Mattie they seem comforting:

> But now all desire for change had vanished, and the sight of the little enclosure gave him a warm sense of continuance and stability.
>
> "I guess we'll never let you go, Matt,'' he whispered, as though even the dead, lovers once, must conspire with him to keep her; and brushing by the graves, he thought: "We'll always go on living here together, and some day she'll lie there beside me.''

The overt point of Ethan's meditation is obvious and traditional: love can transform a prison, even the grave, into paradise. But one is tempted to reply that none can there embrace, for Ethan has shifted disturbingly from exhilaration to a sense of continuance and stability, from a potentially illicit relationship to an image of domestic peace, from the warm pressure of the girl at his side to the chaste twin beds of the graveyard. We would distort the scene to talk of morbidity and the negation of life here, for we must not ignore the moving sense of fulfillment that this restless man feels; we must not ignore major effects to exaggerate minor ones. But we should feel troubled that, as with the imagined pies and bisquits, Ethan has again confused his adventurous conception of Mattie.

We might feel less troubled when, finding that he will have a night alone with the girl, Ethan looks forward to their spending a quiet evening "like a married couple''; a comfortable kitchen,

Wharton in Paris, post World War I. Collection of American Literature, Beinecke Rare Book and Manuscript Library, Yale University.

although not a bedroom, is not a grave either, and only an unkind Lawrentian would scorn Ethan's substituting a warm stove for the dark fires of the blood. As Ethan imagines them together, "he in his stocking feet and smoking his pipe, she laughing and talking in that funny way she had," we are prepared to indulge sentimentally in that domestic idyll. Whatever we recognize of Ethan's psychological evasions (and Wharton will make us recognize some), we must still remember that the warm, shy, gentle relationship between the lovers that evening suggests the kind of life that Ethan ought to have. But he cannot have such a life because seven years earlier he had married Zeena, trying blindly to fulfill some of the same desires that still torment him. And the narrator reminds us of this when, in the midst of Ethan's quiet joy, he says, "he set his imagination adrift on the fiction that they had always spent their evenings thus and would always go on doing so."

The narrator also disrupts this idyll with momentary surges of passion and conscience to remind us what motives are precariously balanced in this scene, which is not, after all, the innocent evening of a newly married couple. No sooner has Ethan set himself adrift on the "illusion of long-established intimacy which no outburst of emotion could have given," than he says, "this is the night we were to have gone coasting." Coasting with Mattie, which Ethan mentions on each of the four evenings of the main story, suggests to him excitement, danger, a night

"as dark as Egypt" (which outdoes Florida for pat associations), and masculine domination (again he swaggers and swells with authority). To prolong his feeling of authority he adds, "'I guess we're well enough here,'" and so he reabsorbs the excitement into the "warm lamplit room, with all its ancient implications of conformity and order." Yet even in this room he refers roguishly (and, he immediately fears, vulgarly) to having seen a friend of Mattie being kissed, and he makes shy, guilty gestures of love with the material she is sewing. But she remains modest and he tactful; the next morning he can be glad "he had done nothing to trouble the sweetness of the picture" of what life with her might be.

Ethan's moral scruples in the scene are even more troubling than his shifts from passion to propriety. There is some value in his conventual, even habitual, fidelity and in his possible sense of Mattie's morally delicate position in the household. But there is also neurotic violence in his guilt, which tortures him more histrionically than the facts warrant. Twice during the evening he sees Zeena's image replace Mattie's as the girl performs simple acts that the wife had done. If one were fond of psychological case studies one could make much of the fact that Zeena has replaced Ethan's mother as the invalid who keeps him on the farm, but it seems enough to note that Ethan's fidelity and duty are tainted with an unmanly fear of his shrewish, self-righteous wife. Perhaps we are to understand that the sensitive, honorable nature is easily victimized by the insensitive, dishonorable one and that Ethan's weakness is a defect of his virtue, but the weakness is not entirely excusable, for all that.

In following scenes between the climax of the novel (Mattie's banishment) and the catastrophe (the abortive suicide attempt) Ethan continues to vacillate emotionally; and Wharton shows precisely that his impulses to escape and to stay are both caused by good and bad motives. Again Wharton shows that Ethan's circumstances make conflicting demands on him, that Ethan has conflicting desires, and that each of these desires has noble and ignoble forms. She is not being morally vague or ambiguous by avoiding a simple pattern of guilt or victimization; she is exactly manipulating the reader to produce the complex moral and emotional responses that most good fiction requires.

When Ethan confronts his wife over Mattie's dismissal, his ineffectualness is vexing and sometimes embarrassing, but in part it results from admirable traits. When, for the first time in their seven-year marriage, they fight openly, the narrator sympathizes with Ethan's squeamishness: "Through the obscurity which hid their faces their thoughts seemed to dart at each other like serpents shooting venom. Ethan was seized with horror of the scene and shame at his own share in it. It was as senseless and savage as a physical fight between two enemies in the darkness." The narrator's imagery and the characters' dialogue do present a horrible scene, and we can appreciate Ethan's shame at fighting with this coarse, vindictive woman: "Ethan felt as if he had lost an irretrievable advantage in descending to the level of recrimination. But the practical problem was there and had to be dealt with." What telling irony! If one ignores practical consequences, Ethan's sensibilities *are* a moral and psychological advantage; they exist because he is an intelligent, gentle man. Also his pride in them has helped to protect him for years against Zeena's attacks and has probably served as a weapon, vexing her as she repeatedly has failed to provoke his anger. But at what cost this advantage! Never refusing her, never asserting his needs, Ethan has allowed Zeena's bitter willfulness and domination to grow, while he has found comfort in a moral superiority. We should be reminded of Ethan's standing in the shadows outside the dance two evenings before, treasuring his sensitivity and scorning the gregarious grocer's son who dances with Mattie.

Defeated by his wife, Ethan retreats to his makeshift study to thrash about. For a while he thinks of going west with Mattie to make his fortune. (The West has become the enchanted land of his conventional fancy, replacing the City, which has become the unholy place where a million bread-seekers would crush the exiled girl.) But as moral and financial problems occur to him, he vacillates with half-pathetic, half-ludicrous abruptness between hope and despair. The next day, realizing that he must act, he decides to lie to his neighbor, Andrew Hale, secure an advance on the lumber he supplies, and run away with Mattie, leaving Zeena to her relatives and eventual alimony payments. Although the scheme is desperate and poorly planned, Ethan is acting and making a choice that circumstances have required. He has been scrupulous in considering the moral issues of running away—Zeena's financial state, his inability to help her emotionally, Mattie's dependence—and his decision seems right in a situation in which no decision can be guiltless. But on the way to the contractor's he meets Mrs. Hale, who pities him for his misfortunes (an uncommon act in Starkfield), and he is unable to deceive the two kind people who have pitied him. Again the scene calls for a complex response. Ethan's sudden reversal, his extreme feelings ("with a sudden perception of the point to which his madness had carried him"), and his readiness to despair—all suggest that he is hypersensitive and unable to assume the burden and consequences of acting. Yet we should not scorn Ethan, because his reason for not deceiving the Hales is both honorable and emotionally understandable. Earlier, when he had thought of asking Hale for an advance, although with no thought then of cheating him, Ethan soon backed down because of a habitual pride. The later scene is different. There he shows not pride but humility, not a habitual, conventual sense of honor but gratitude and affection. Appreciating Ethan's reaction to unusual kindness, we cannot say confidently that his refusal to lie is wrong.

Ethan's refusal to cheat Andrew Hale is his last decisive act in the novel; from now on, he abandons himself to circumstances, acting weakly to postpone and avoid. He insists on driving Mattie to the railroad but only to prolong their last hours together; he stops by Shadow Pond to reminisce about their summer picnic; and when he suggests that they go coasting, he does so merely to postpone the last part of their drive to the railroad. Up to the moment of the collision he continues to vacillate, from proudly exulting in his ability to steer on the dangerous slope to childishly clinging in his despair at losing Mattie, from recoiling in horror at her plea for suicide to finally acquiescing in it. Even the time of day reflects his ambivalence: "it was the most confusing hour of the evening, the hour when the last clearness from the upper sky is merged with the rising night in a blur that disguises landmarks and falsifies distances." In such confusion Mattie must control Ethan and force the last actions of despair. Even as he sits in the sled he almost springs out again; even as they coast toward the tree he again imagines Zeena's face and momentarily swerves from the path. And even the attempt at suicide is not a decisive choice but another evasion, an admission that no course of action seems tolerable among the complicated circumstances and contradictory desires.

The immediate aftermath of the collision, as experienced through Ethan's semiconsciousness, is painfully pathetic; and the consequent twenty-four years of suffering are so grim that no one could reasonably consider Ethan's and Mattie's fate to be deserved. We have sympathized too much with these characters and understood too well their difficulties and confusions to speak righteously about moral flaws and deserved tragedy. But Trilling was wrong when he said that "only a moral judgment cruel to the point of insanity could speak of [their fate] as anything but accidental." Fate, as Oedipus or Michael Henchard could testify, often scorns proportion, and this fate is excessive; but it is not accidental. In fact, it is mercilessly, ironically precise in giving the three characters appropriately metaphorical sufferings. Ethan, whose moral and emotional conflicts kept him from acting decisively, is chained with lameness. Mattie, whose birdlike frailty made her dependent on others, is made a complete invalid. Zeena, who secured Ethan in marriage by nursing his mother and playing on his sense of obligation, must dutifully nurse the girl whom she had once scornfully evicted and who is now a permanent guest. Throughout the concluding pages of the frame story there are ironic, and sometimes grotesquely comic, variations on past themes. Remembering Zeena's continuous search for healing, we are amused at Ruth Hale's comment that Zeena rose up as if by a miracle when the call came to her after the injuries. Remembering the times when Ethan guiltily imagined Zeena's face in place of Mattie's, we see how appropriate, if cruel, it is that

Mattie has become so much like Zeena in her shrill complaining. And if we are especially shrewd in our humor, we might find irony in Ruth Hale's references to the Frome's "troubles." Nearly half a novel earlier the narrator explained the difference between troubles and complications: "People struggled on for years with 'troubles,' but they almost always succumbed to 'complications'"; so we can assume that if Ethan and Mattie had had complications they would have died in the crash, but with mere troubles they must struggle on for years. Whether or not Wharton intended this grim joke, she obviously intended the irony with which Mrs. Hale's comments end the novel. Remembering Ethan's wishes that he and Mattie could go on living in their farmhouse and then lie together in the Fromes' graveyard, we hear of his wishes symbolically fulfilled and telescoped; "'and the way they are now, I don't see there's much difference between the Fromes up at the farm and the Fromes down in the graveyard; 'cept that down there they're all quiet, and the women have got to hold their tongues'."

These punishments and ironically fulfilled wishes in the concluding frame story can give contradictory impressions, as shown by Trilling's opinion that Ethan's universe is cruelly incomprehensible and by Bernard's opinion that it is just. If one ignored the symbolic precision of the punishments and the partial responsibility of the characters, one could see the characters' fate as perverse and the novel as excessively cruel. If one ignored the extreme pathos and the sympathy that Ethan and Mattie stimulate throughout the book, one could see the conclusion as symbolically appropriate like the punishments in Dante's *Inferno* or Ovid's *Metamorphoses,* in which outward form and action horribly express mind and soul. But Wharton will have it both ways, showing that man does determine his life in a universe that is not chaotic, but also showing that his lot is hard, his choices difficult, his sacrifices many, his strengths inseparable from his weaknesses, and the consequences of his actions often different from what he had expected. And this is not a perversely ambiguous position, but a strictly classical one. Nor is it a moral demonstrated in a pat conclusion; it is essential to Wharton's method throughout the novel. When she shows that suffering both sours and ennobles, that longings for knowledge and beauty can be both admirable and silly, that a strong sense of duty can be honorable and neurotic, that man can long for both freedom and stability and try confusedly to combine the two, when she shows characters suffering in situations over which they have only partial control and creating painful situations out of conflicting motives, and when she makes the reader appreciate these complexities by manipulating his sympathy and detachment, making him feel compassionate, amused, and vexed, then she does the hard work of making a coherent and complex novel. We must be careful to respect both the coherence and complexity and not obscure them in our rage for another, simpler kind of order. (pp. 237-45)

> David Eggenschwiler, "The Ordered Disorder of
> 'Ethan Frome'," in Studies in the Novel, *Vol. IX,*
> *No. 3, Fall, 1977, pp. 237-46.*

RICHARD H. LAWSON (essay date 1977)

[*Lawson is an American linguist and critic whose works reflect his interest in twentieth-century language and literature. His studies include* Edith Wharton and German Literature (1974) *and the critical biography* Edith Wharton. *In the following excerpt from the latter work, Lawson examines characterization and style in* Ethan Frome, *noting parallels between the novel and Wharton's life at the time she wrote it.*]

In a time of despair over her husband and her marriage, over her relationship to Walter Berry and her love affair with Morton Fullerton, Edith Wharton wrote—or rewrote—*Ethan Frome*. The first, fragmentary version, a few pages in French, she had written some four years previously as practice material for private lessons in French that she was taking in Paris. . . . The final version, although it deals with poor and simple people in the Massachusetts back country, is a crucible into which she poured, as R. W. B. Lewis declares [see Additional Bibliography], "deep and intense private emotions." Whether it is her best novel or not, it is quite likely her best known—although she could not see why. And it certainly marks a turning point in her career as a writer, in that from then on her own strongest feelings were to go into her fiction rather than her poetry.

Ethan Frome is a frame story. It is ostensibly related by an engineer, whom we may guess to be in his thirties, after he had obtained the story in bits and pieces during an enforced stay in late winter in the village of Starkfield. (The stay is caused by a strike. Are Wharton's patrician sympathies with the striking carpenters? Rare for her time, she issues no invectives against strikes, which were in those days commonly thought to be criminal.) The narrator is "pulled up sharp" by the most impressive figure in Starkfield, though the latter "was but the ruin of a man," lame, bleak, and seemingly unapproachable. Ethan Frome has looked and acted thus ever since his sled crashed twenty-four years ago. (pp. 67-8)

The fifty-two-year-old Ethan, despite his added misery, his suffering when Zeena and Mattie "get going at each other," and his face that would break one's heart, is not now essentially different from what he was in the first years of his marriage. Even then he had an immense tolerance for suffering (like Edith Wharton); even then he was capable of cheerfulness and a close personal relationship with a responsive person, that is, Mattie. Now his tolerance for suffering has been tested longer; now he is still capable, though with greater difficulty, of sympathetic human interaction with an interested person, that is, the fictive narrator.

The distance between Ethan and the narrator is at first only "bridged for a moment." It is bridged for a longer period when Ethan finds the narrator's lost book on bio-chemistry and agrees he would like to borrow it. Then Ethan volunteers to drive the narrator through a snowstorm to enable him to keep an appointment. And finally, the ultimate gesture of friendliness and openness: on the return trip Ethan invites the narrator to spend the stormy night in his house. As we know, it is not a happy house, and a less sympathetic man than Ethan Frome would hardly have risked exposing its spiritual and material impoverishment to a virtual stranger. To be sure, the narrator is probably the only stranger in twenty years to set foot in the house. But our point is: Ethan remains, in all his misery, capable of reacting in a friendly and sympathetic way.

Zeena, as we see her ill-naturedly ministering to the needs of the invalid Mattie and the partial cripple Ethan, is a replica of the Zeena who nursed Ethan's mother thirty-two years ago. And both Zeenas, the early and the recent, are consistent with the intervening hypochondriac Zeena, who was preoccupied with nursing herself. Wharton implies a still earlier hypochondriac stage, as she insists on the relationship of the nurse with the hypochondriac, which is in fact psychologically valid: ". . . her [early] skill as a nurse had been acquired by the absorbed observation of her own symptoms."

Mattie's personality is the only one that has basically changed. When Mattie, the outsider, arrived in Starkfield, she was vital and light-hearted in a community typified by, and given to, "deadness." Mattie wore bright red ribbons in her hair in a locale characterized by a "sky of iron," by ice, snow, gray, and black. However inevitably, however innocently, Mattie became the third point in a domestic triangle. However agreeable her disposition, Mattie was a threat to the Fromes' marriage, and Zeena knew it. Finally, Mattie had to live, or half-live, with the realization that only as a hopeless cripple was she acceptable under Zeena's roof. (Of course Zeena took her back when Mattie was no longer a threat, and when her presence could only make Ethan's life more miserable.)

Mattie must now contend with Zeena's meanness at close range—only on summer days can Mattie be moved out of the house for a few hours. In short, Mattie's is a ruined life in every way, and she is compelled to reexperience that ruin every day of her life in the house with Ethan and Zeena.

As the characterizations are complex, free of cliché, believable, and even gripping, Edith Wharton's best characters yet, so the style of *Ethan Frome* is her best yet—perhaps best ever—taut, precise, unpretentious. Realism is suggested by leitmotiv: "deadness," "sky of iron," rather than by lists of details. Wharton refrained from moralizing, and from pointing out the theme. And that theme must be simply: tragedy. Some people—Ethan Frome and Mattie above all, but also Zeena—are fated for suffering.

Gradations of morality play no role and are probably irrelevant critical impositions on the novel. Ethan and Mattie sin against certain moral codes in their illicit but hardly profligate passion and in their willingness to commit suicide. Zeena does not break these codes; but Zeena fails the test of humaneness.

The morality of Starkfield as a whole is not even alluded to, but there is generous mention of the suffering of Starkfield's inhabitants. The unhappy fact of being fated for suffering makes itself known well before fate itself descends. And nothing can be done, either early or late, to avert it—witness the appearance of Zeena's face before Ethan's eyes, between the speeding sled and its target, the elm tree. That the face is a manifestation of Ethan's mental state only underscores the fated nature of the outcome.

There is a persuasive parallel between Wharton's tormented life at this period and the tormented life of Ethan Frome. Despite her declaration that her characters always "arrived" in her novels bearing their own names, the fact is that Ethan Frome did not have that name in earlier versions of the story. He attained his final name only after Wharton's intense personalization of the original story idea. This was possibly a consequence of Wharton's despair over her unrequited love for Walter Berry, but more likely a consequence of the end of her affair with Morton Fullerton.

Parallels between Wharton's circumstance and that of Ethan come readily to mind. Both are trapped in hopeless marriages to uncongenial spouses. Both are married to spouses of uncertain health, who are, moreover, given to excessive contemplation of their states of ill health, real and imagined. Both spouses—Teddy Wharton and Zeena Frome—incline at various times and in varying degrees to irrationality. Both Edith Wharton and Ethan Frome are drawn to sweethearts more congenial than their spouses, but in each case marriage to these sweethearts cannot be achieved. Ethan even considers fleeing to the west with Mattie, but cannot, owing both to poverty and to conscience, any more than Edith could flout her society by fleeing to Egypt with Walter Berry (who helped her a good

deal in the writing of *Ethan Frome*) or by establishing a permanent liaison with Morton Fullerton.

Of course these parallels are broad and basic. Perhaps for that reason they are the more convincing. Wharton may not have been aware that she was writing about herself. This hypothesis has the advantage of offering an explanation, more intrinsic than those based on locale or structure, of why *Ethan Frome* is regarded—correctly—as somehow "different" from her other works. It may perhaps even explain why, throughout the years—beginning in the 1930s—*Ethan Frome* has been the most read and best liked of Wharton's novels, despite her own misgivings about its primacy. (pp. 70-4)

> *Richard H. Lawson, in his* Edith Wharton, *Frederick Ungar Publishing Co., 1977, 118 p.*

CYNTHIA GRIFFIN WOLFF (essay date 1977)

[*An American educator and critic, Wolff is the author of* A Feast of Words: The Triumph of Edith Wharton. *In the following excerpt from that work, she presents a close analysis of the novel, characterizing the narrator as guide to his own fantasy of Frome's history.*]

[Wharton's early French version of *Ethan Frome*] is short, only eight printed pages, and it is skeletal by contrast with the finished novel. There are but three characters: Hart, his wife Anna, and her cousin Mattie. When the tale opens, Hart and Mattie are conversing intently as they walk through the woods; we soon discover that they are lovers and that Mattie has been asked to leave Hart's home. The story begins with Hart's voice: "'Tu as raison... je ne puis rien pour toi... mais ne me quitte pas, chère petite. Je serai raisonnable, tu verras...' balbutia-t-il, comprenant que, pour la retenir et pour effacer le souvenir des paroles échangées, le seul moyen était de reprendre courageusement son rôle de frère ainé." The tale is told by an omniscient narrator; there is no frame story and no first-person narration. The events central to the final novel are scarcely anticipated, and only one or two short passages (which we shall remark later) find their way into the longer fiction. Hart and Mattie continue their walk home, arriving to discover that Anna, who is sickly and complaining, plans a trip to the doctor in a neighboring town. The next day she makes the trip, and Hart, who is embarrassed and timid, stays at a local tavern until late in the evening when he returns rather tipsy. The next day Anna comes home announcing that she has found a job for Mattie in a city some distance away. Hart protests mildly, but in the end he submits. The tale concludes as he is putting Mattie on the train. Now the tone of the French version is flat, the sense of longing and of frustration muted; the desolation of the sledding accident and of the resultant eternal, infernal triangle is simply not there. What we have in the Black Book *Ethan* is only the germ of an idea—a lengthy donnée that has not yet been explored and shaped and wrought into a focused fiction. That would come only three or four years later.

In her introduction to the Modern Student's Library edition of the novel, Wharton . . . [comments on] her interest in the novel's structure. "I make no claim for originality in following a method of which 'La Grande Bretèche' and *The Ring and the Book* had set me the magnificent example." (Despite the pellucidity of its prose and its apparent simplicity, *Ethan Frome* is a tantalizingly literary work; certainly Wharton's careful planning of it followed a complex tradition, of which the works by Balzac and Browning are only two examples.) In both "La Grande Bretèche" and *The Ring and the Book*, it is not the "facts" themselves which are of primary importance in the end, but the collection of facts and—perhaps above all—the impact of these facts upon the mind of the observer. In *Ethan Frome*, Wharton reminds us, "only the narrator of the tale has scope enough to see it all, to resolve it back into simplicity, and to put it in its rightful place among his larger categories." It is the *relation* of the tale of the narrator's larger categories that must be our primary interest, the focus of the story as Wharton has defined it. Other writers, the venerable regionalists of New England, had already given us the surface view that Wharton scorned: a prettified spectacle of billboard art, a pastoral land seen through awestruck eyes. Wharton would look through the surface to discover what was timeless in the human mind, just as Browning had done before her. (pp. 161-62)

It helps our understanding of *Ethan Frome* to have this literary kinship dangled before us (perhaps that was Wharton's reason for agreeing to write a preface to the work). But it is not necessary. There are literary affinities inherent in the work itself that force themselves upon us. Outside of *Ethan Frome*, for example, there is no other Zenobia in American literature save Hawthorne's heroine in *The Blithedale Romance;* one of the changes that Wharton made from the [early French version of] *Ethan* was the change of Anna's name to Zeena (Zenobia), though Mattie's name was left unaltered. Hart's name was changed to Ethan. If we wonder why, we might plausibly connect this change with Hawthorne as well, for the only other notable Ethan in American literature is Ethan Brand of Mount Graylock (a geographical neighbor of Wharton's Lenox and psychological kin of the villagers in Starkfield—amongst whom Wharton lived in imagination for ten years). Ethan Brand had found the Unpardonable Sin in a willed isolation from the brotherhood of humanity. Wharton was not interested in sin, but she was interested in the effect of isolation upon the workings of man's emotional life: thus Ethan Frome is related to Ethan Brand; but his deadening isolation is in the cold world of unloved and unloving inner emptiness—a world of depression, loneliness, and slow starvation. Why, in the end, would Wharton be interested in so deliberately suggesting an affinity between her work and the tales of Hawthorne? Again, we must look to the structure of the novel and the role of the narrator for our answer. In much of Hawthorne (and in that most "Hawthornian" of Edith Wharton's stories—"The Eyes"), we follow the tale principally as a revelation of the teller. *The Blithedale Romance* is, ultimately, about Coverdale. Just so, *Ethan Frome* is about its narrator.

The novel begins with him, begins insistently and obtrusively.

> I had the story, bit by bit, from various people, and, as generally happens in such cases, each time it was a different story.

> If you know Starkfield, Massachusetts, you know the post-office. If you know the post-office you must have seen Ethan Frome drive up to it, drop the reins on his hollow-backed bay and drag himself across the brick pavement to the white colonnade; and you must have asked who he was.

> It was there that, several years ago, I saw him for the first time; and the sight pulled me up sharp.

We must ask why Wharton would begin thus, assaulting us with the narrator's presence in the very first word. It is a decidedly unusual way to open a fiction. Only two like it come

readily to mind: *Wuthering Heights* and "Bartleby the Scrivener." Wharton has informed us that she was consciously indebted to Brontë's work when she wrote *Ethan Frome*; and her preoccupation at the time with the techniques of Hawthorne suggests that she may have had Melville's tale in mind as well. What does all of this suggest? First of all, an extraordinarily literary self-consciousness. Second, a focus on the narrator (for however intricate Brontë's story is, however compelling Melville's vision, it is the *narrator's reaction* that must be deemed the ultimate "subject" in both fictions).

Bearing this fact in mind, let us rush momentarily ahead—to that point in the novel where the "real subject" is generally assumed to begin. An astounding discovery awaits us: the man whom we come to know as the young Ethan Frome is *no more than a figment of the narrator's imagination*. Wharton's method of exposition leaves no doubt. We are not permitted to believe that the narrator is recounting a history of something that actually happened; we are not given leave to speculate that he is passing along a confidence obtained in the dark intimacy of a cold winter's night. No: the "story" of Ethan Frome is introduced in unmistakable terms. "It was the night that I found the clue to Ethan Frome, and began *to put together this vision* of his story . . ." emphasis mine). Our narrator is a teller of terrible tales, a seer into the realms of dementia. The "story" of Ethan Frome is nothing more than a dream vision, a brief glimpse into the most appalling recesses of the narrator's mind. The overriding question becomes then—not who is Ethan Frome, but who in the world is this ghastly guide to whom we must submit as we read the tale.

The structure demands that we take him into account. Certainly *he* demands it. It is *his* story, ultimately his "vision" of Ethan Frome, that we will get. His vision is as good as any other (so he glibly assures us at the beginning—for "each time it was a different story"), and therefore his story has as much claim to truth as any other. And yet, he is a nervous fellow. The speech pattern is totally unlike Wharton's own narrative style—short sentences, jagged prose rhythms, absolutely no sense of ironic control over the language, no distance from it. Yes, the fellow is nervous. He seems anxious about our reaction and excessively eager to reassure us that had *we* been situated as *he* was, catching a first horrified glimpse of Ethan Frome, we "must have asked who he was." Anyone would. Frome is no mere bit of local color. He is, for reasons that we do not yet understand, a force that compels examination; "the sight pulled me up sharp." (It would pull all of you up sharp, and all of you would have done as I did.)

Certain elements in Wharton's story are to be taken as "real" within the fictional context: Ethan Frome is badly crippled; he sustained his injuries in a sledding accident some twenty-four years ago; he has been in Starkfield for most of his life, excepting a short visit to Florida, living first with his parents and then with his querulous, sickly wife Zeena; there is a third member of the household, his wife's cousin, Miss Mattie Silver; she too was badly crippled in the same sledding accident that felled Ethan. To these facts the various members of the town will all attest—and to *nothing more*. Everything that the reader can accept as reliably true can be found in the narrative frame; everything else bears the imprint of the narrator's own interpretation—as indeed even the selection of events chronicled in the frame does—and while that interpretation *might* be as true as any other, we dare not accept it as having the same validity as the bare outline presented above. Even at the end of the narrator's vision, in the concluding scene with Mrs.

Hale, Wharton is scrupulously careful not to credit the vision by giving it independent confirmation.

At this point the narrator himself is still probing. He has now spent a long winter's night in the Frome household, where no one outside the family has set foot for many years, and he is an object of some interest. He responds to that interest by attempting to use it to gain information. "Beneath their wondering exclamations I felt a secret curiosity to know what impressions I had received from my night in the Frome household, and divined that the best way of breaking down their reserve was to let them try to penetrate mine. I therefore confined myself to saying, in a matter-of-fact tone, that I had been received with great kindness, and that Frome had made a bed for me in a room on the ground-floor which seemed in happier days to have been fitted up as a kind of writing-room or study." Despite this tactic, the narrator elicits nothing that he has not already known. Mrs. Hale agrees that "'it was just awful from the beginning. . . . It's a pity . . . that they're all shut up there'n that one kitchen'." And these fervent platitudes fall so far short of assuring the narrator that he has touched upon the truth that even as they come tumbling inconsequently from her lips, he withdraws into himself. "Mrs. Hale paused a moment, and I remained silent, plunged in the vision of what her words evoked." Her words, vague generalities—driving the narrator back ino his own "vision."

If we return now to the opening of the story, we must remind ourselves that the status of the narrator is doubly significant: we are surely meant to credit the information that is given to us in the frame as "true" (and the contrast between the validity of the contents of the frame and the unreliability of the contents of the internal story is clearly signaled by the recurrence of that key word, vision); however, since it, too, is reported by the narrator who has thrust himself before us in the first word of the first sentence, we must recognize that it is biased information and that evaluations and judgments have been built even into the language and choice of incident which make it up. Wharton does not do what Conrad often did, open with a reliable omniscient narrator only to introduce her talkative character when the "facts" have already been established. Instead she forces us to traffic only with the narrator from the beginning; if we are to do that effectively, we must weigh his introduction as carefully as we measure his vision, for only by doing so can we understand, finally, why the vision is so important.

The obsessive anxiety of the narrator's opening statements reveals his need to assure us that we would have reacted just as he did. He wants to elicit our confidence; perhaps he also wants to reassure himself that he is part of our company.

Many of his preliminary remarks about Ethan have a double thrust, carrying the strong implication that he is (or seems) one way, but that he might be (or might at one time have had the option of being) quite dramatically different. It is, indeed, striking how often the narrator's conjuration of Ethan manages to conflate *two* images. "He was the most striking figure in Starkfield, though he was but the ruin of a man. It was not so much his great height that marked him, for the 'natives' were easily singled out by their lank longitude from the stockier foreign breed: it was the careless powerful look he had, in spite of a lameness checking each step like the jerk of a chain." For clarity's sake we must dissect fantasy from fact: Ethan is tall, as are most natives, and he walks with a pronounced limp; yet these simple attributes havebeen elevated by the narrator's language—"the most striking figure in Starkfield," "but the

ruin of a man," "careless powerful look," "each step like the jerk of a chain." Ethan Frome becomes, in the eyes of the teller of his tale, an emblem of vanquished heroism, defeated strength, and foreclosed potentiality—not merely a crippled man, but Manhood brought low. (pp. 163-67)

The contrast preys upon the narrator's mind, and he finds himself compelled to pry into the matter. Relentlessly he questions those taciturn New Englanders, and he gets a series of enigmatic and taciturn replies. "Harmon drew a slab of tobacco from his pocket, cut off a wedge and pressed it into the leather pouch of his cheek. 'Guess he's been in Starkfield too many winters. Most of the smart onces get away.' 'Why didn't *he*?' 'Somebody had to stay and care for the folks. There warn't ever anybody but Ethan. Fust his father—then his mother—then his wife'." Too many winters. The phrase becomes a key to the puzzle. (p. 167)

The narrator offers this phrase to us as a central clue to Ethan's dilemma and to his own investigation; then abruptly, the distance between those two narrows. The narrator becomes implicated in Ethan's fate, and his investigation must be presumed to include himself as well. "Before my own time there was up I had learned to know what that meant. . . . When winter shut down on Starkfield, and the village lay under a sheet of snow perpetually renewed from pale skies, I began to see what life there—or rather its negation—must have been in Ethan Frome's young manhood. . . . I found myself anchored at Starkfield . . . for the best part of the winter." Was the speaker interested in Ethan Frome's history before he (like Ethan) had been constrained to spend a winter at Starkfield? There is no way, really, of knowing, for the entire tale is told retrospectively (and of course, the narrator is insistent—perhaps too insistent—that *anyone* would have felt an interest in the man, the interest that he felt immediately upon seeing him).

Who is the narrator? A busy man—we see the energy that he pours into his quest—a man of affairs: "I had been sent up by my employers on a job connected with the big power-house at Corbury Junction, and a long-drawn carpenters' strike had so delayed the work that I found myself anchored at Starkfield." Nothing else would have brought such a man up here. Even marooned as he is in this desolate spot, he does what he can to keep his routines regular: he hires Denis Eady's horses to take him daily over to Corbury Flats where he can pick up a train, and when Eady's horses fall sick, he hires Ethan Frome. The man has a visionary side; we have already seen it in the language of his opening remarks. But surely he is at heart an active man, a man who is part of the larger world, a man who keeps his options open, a man who bears no essential similarity to these poor folk among whom he has been thrust. Spending one winter in Starkfield will surely mean nothing to such a man. "During the early part of my stay I had been struck by the contrast between the vitality of the climate and the deadness of the community"—the observation of a confident outsider.

And yet, slowly, something within him begins to succumb to this insidious environment.

> Day by day, after the December snows were over, a blazing blue sky poured down torrents of light and air on the white landscape, which gave them back in an intenser glitter. One would have supposed that such an atmosphere must quicken the emotions as well as the blood; but it seemed to produce no change except that of retarding still more the sluggish pulse of Stark-

field. When I had been there a little longer, and had seen this phase of crystal clearness followed by long stretches of sunless cold; when the storms of February had pitched their tents about the devoted village and the wild cavalry of March winds had charged down to their support; I began to understand why Starkfield emerged from its six months' siege like a starved garrison capitulating without quarter.... I felt the sinister force of Harmon's phrase: "Most of the smart ones get away."

And as he begins to "feel" the force of the phrase—and of the environment which sucks his confidence and his independence away from him—and as his tale draws closer and closer to that crucial moment of transition when we move into the "vision," a peculiar thing begins to happen to his language. The brave assertion of heroic contingencies falters; what he limns now is capitulation, and at the heart of the experience is an unavoidable and dreadful image—"cold" and "starved."

Doggedly, the narrator persists in his quest. He sounds the finer sensibility of Mrs. Ned Hale, who rises only to the platitude that she seems fated to reiterate without explanation: "'Yes, I knew them both ... it was awful ...'."

And yet, it is not entirely clear what *would* satisfy him. He does not want facts alone; he wants something less tangible, something deeper. "No one gave me an explanation of the look in his face which, as I persisted in thinking, neither poverty nor physical suffering could have put there." He wants an explanation for his own inferences and his own suppositions—we might call them the projections of his own morbid imagination. Harmon Gow, who is more loquacious, can be prodded to speak. The "facts" as he sees them look only to those causes which the narrator has already rejected as insufficient, poverty and physical suffering. But the language in which he speaks, language which the narrator records more completely than any other utterance in the frame, addresses itself to the deeper meaning and heightens the horror of the narrator's speculations by reinforcing those images of starvation:

> "That Frome farm was always 'bout as bare's a milkpan when the cat's been round; and you know what one of the old water-mills is wuth nowadays. When Ethan could sweat over 'em both from sun-up to dark he kinder choked a living out of 'em; but his folks et up most everything, even then, and I don't see how he makes out now.... Sickness and trouble: that's what Ethan's had his plate full up with, ever since the very first helping."

The narrator's next description of Ethan—drawn during their initial intimate contact as Frome drives him for the first time to the railroad junction—brings all of these themes together. The sight of Frome still calls up visions of ancient heroism and strength; but superimposed upon these images and ultimately blotting them out is a picture of Ethan Frome as the embodiment of some deep mortal misery. Not poverty, merely; not hard work, merely. But something intrinsic to human existence, something imponderable and threatening—something that might swallow up everything else.

> Ethan Frome drove in silence, the reins loosely held in his left hand, his brown seamed profile, under the helmet-like peak of the cap, relieved against the banks of snow like the bronze image

of a hero. He never turned his face to mine, or answered, except in monosyllables, the questions I put, or such slight pleasantries as I ventured. He seemed a part of the mute melancholy landscape, an incarnation of its frozen woe, with all that was warm and sentient in him fast bound below the surface; but there was nothing unfriendly in his silence. I simply felt that he lived in a depth of moral isolation too remote for casual access, and I had the sense that his loneliness was not merely the result of his personal plight, tragic as I guessed that to be, but had in it, as Harmon Gow had hinted, the profound accumulated cold of many Starkfield winters.

And, as we have already observed, this is a winter of the soul that the narrator must now share.

We can see the narrator attempting to assert a distance between himself and this foreboding figure; but in the palpable cold of the region of Starkfield, all things seem to contract. Instead of discovering reassuring distinctions, the narrator finds disconcerting and unexpected similarities.

> Once I happened to speak of an engineering job I had been on the previous year in Florida, and of the contrast between the winter landscape about us and that in which I had found myself the year before; and to my surprise Frome said suddenly: "Yes: I was down there once, and for a good while afterward I could call up the sight of it in winter. But now it's all snowed under." ... Another day, on getting into my train at the Flats, I missed a volume of popular science—I think it was on some recent discoveries in bio-chemistry—which I had carried with me to read on the way. I thought no more about it till I got into the sleigh again that evening, and saw the book in Frome's hand. "I found it after you were gone," he said.... "Does that sort of thing interest you?" I asked. "It used to." ... "If you'd like to look the book through I'd be glad to leave it with you." He hesitated, and I had the impresion that he felt himself about to yield to a stealing tide of inertia; then, "Thank you—I'll take it."

The winter landscape reduces the world and obliterates casual surface distinctions. The snow-covered fields lie about the two men, "their boundaries lost under drift; and above the fields, huddled against the white immensities of land and sky, one of those lonely New England farm-houses that make the landscape lonelier." Unknown affinities emerge when everything that fleshes out man's daily existence is taken away—like the ice-age rocks that unpredictably thrust their noses through the frozen ground during winter heaves—shared mortal problems and shared mortal pain. A man must comfort himself in such a world, and the narrator is brought to this terrible task in his journey with Ethan Frome. Frome is his Winterman, his shadow self, the man he might become if the reassuring appurtenances of busy, active, professional, adult mobility were taken from him.

The narrator is a man of science; he knows the meaning of cold. Cold is an absence, a diminishment, a dwindling, and finally a death. Everything contracts in the cold. The "place" of the novel is defined by this contraction: from the world to Starkfield; from Starkfield to the thickening darkness of a winter night, "descending on us layer by layer"; from this "smothering medium" to the "forlorn and stunted" farmhouse that is a castrated emblem of its mutilated owner. This relentless constriction of place accompanies a slow shedding of adult personae and leads finally to a confrontation with the core of self that lives beneath these and that would emerge and engulf everything else should the supporting structures of the outside world be lost, somehow. To this point is the narrator reduced—to the edge of nothingness: without identity, without memory, without continuity, without time. All these are outside and beyond. Now there is only the farmhouse. The two men enter it, enter into a small, dark back hallway. The movement is inescapably decreative, and it is captured in a perverse and grotesque inversion of the terms of birth. They move through the hall to the door of a small, warm room. Slowly, the door is opened, and as it opens, the narrator, who is poised on the threshold, starts to "put together this vision" of Frome's story. The fantasy begins.

The fantasy begins with an involuntary echo of the narrator's own world: Ethan Frome, a young man striding through the clear atmosphere of a winter night, "as though nothing less tenuous than ether intervened between the white earth under his feet and the metallic dome overhead. 'It's like being in an exhausted receiver,' he thought"—an association that is plausible in the young Ethan Frome, who had been, so the fantasy postulates, at a technological college at Worcester, but which is much more probably related to the consciousness of the storyteller, who has been sent to Starkfield to work on a power plant. Perhaps the principal thrust of the image is to assert the similarities between the two. They are surely placed similarly. The story brings Ethan to the church where Mattie Silver has gone to dance. He waits for her—poised just outside and looking in—and his position recapitulates the modalities of the narrator's own placement in the framing story, the cold without and the warmth within. However, the implication here is inverted: in young Ethan's life the warmth of the dance represents gaiety, freedom, and love.

The motif of the threshold renders one of the most significant themes of the novel. The narrator's vision begins while he is poised at the edge of the kitchen with the door beginning to swing open. The long fantasy is spun out; it concludes with the terrible, abortive sledding accident, and we return to the framing world of the narrator. "The querulous drone ceased as I entered Frome's kitchen. . . ." The entire fantasy has been formulated in the instant that marks the passage from hall to kitchen—that timeless eternity of hesitation upon the threshold. In its essential formulation, the story is about that transition (or the failure to make it). The narrator's fantasy about young Ethan begins by placing him at the juncture of two worlds. Over and over again he is pictured thus. Ethan and Mattie return to the farmhouse, and they are greeted at the threshold by Zeena. "Against the dark background of the kitchen she stood up tall and angular, one hand drawing a quilted counterpane to her flat breast, while the other held a lamp. The light, on a level with her chin, drew out of the darkness her puckered throat and the projecting wrist of the hand that clutched the quilt, and deepened fantastically the hollows and prominences of her high-boned face under its ring of crimping-pins." The next night, after Zeena has gone, the vision is reenacted with Mattie:

> So strange was the precision with which the incidents of the previous evening were repeat-

ing themselves that he half expected, when he heard the key turn, to see his wife before him on the threshold; but the door opened, and Mattie faced him. She stood just as Zeena had stood, a lifted lamp in her hand, against the black background of the kitchen. She held the light at the same level, and it drew out with the same distinctness her slim young throat and the brown wrist no bigger than a child's. Then, striking upward, it threw a lustrous fleck on her lips, edged her eyes with velvet shade, and laid a milky whiteness above the black curve of her brows.

Since these threshold scenes with Zeena and Mattie are the only two significant passages that have been preserved from the [original version of] *Ethan*, we must infer that Wharton chose to use them again because *only these* were appropriate to the story as it is told by the narrator, for only these echo his own spatial position and his own psychological dilemma. (pp. 168-73)

[Central to the world of *Ethan Frome*] is an inability to communicate: its habitants are inarticulate, mute; and like the patient farm animals they tend to, they are helplessly bound by their own incapacities. The narrator has already experienced Ethan's parsimonious conversation, and his vision repeatedly returns to it. Ethan, walking with Mattie, longing to tell her of his feelings, admiring her laughter and gaiety: "To prolong the effect he groped for a dazzling phrase, and brought out, in a growl of rapture: 'Come along'." Again and again Ethan "struggled for the all-expressive word"; and again and again he fails to find utterance.

Speech is the bridge that might carry Ethan Frome to a world beyond Starkfield, the necessary passport to wider activities and larger horizons. Without it, he is literally unable to formulate plans of any complexity because all such determinations are beyond his limited powers of conceptualization and self-expression. Because he cannot think his problems through in any but the most rudimentary way, he is as helpless as a child to combat the forces that bind him. It is not that he does not feel deeply, for he does. However, one mark of maturity is the ability to translate desire into coherent words, words into action; and Ethan Frome is incapable of all such translations. (p. 174)

It is not too much to say that the entire force of Ethan's life has been exerted merely to hold him at the level of primitive communication he does manage; and the balance of his life, even as he leads it, is precarious and dangerous. A more fully developed capacity to express himself might open avenues of escape. Any further dwindling of his limited abilities would lead in the opposite direction, propelling him down pathways that are both terrifying and fascinating. Further to lose the power of expression would be a diminishment of self; but though loss of self is an appalling specter, there is at the same time a sensuous attraction in the notion of annihilation—of comforting nothingness.

Why had he married Zeena in the first place, for example? Left with his mother after his father's death, Ethan had found that

> the silence had deepened about him year by year. . . . His mother had been a talker in her day, but after her "trouble" the sound of her voice was seldom heard, though she had not lost the power of speech. Sometimes, in the

long winter evenings, when in desperation her son asked her why she didn't "say something," she would lift a finger and answer: "Because I'm listening." . . . It was only when she drew toward her last illness, and his cousin Zenobia Pierce came over from the next valley to help him nurse her, that human speech was heard again in the house. . . . After the funeral, when he saw her preparing to go away, he was seized with an unreasoning dread of being left alone on the farm; and before he knew what he was doing he had asked her to stay there with him.

Yet Ethan's own habitual tendency to silence is not relieved by Zeena's presence. The deep muteness of his nature seems to have a life of its own, spinning outside of him and recreating itself in his environment. After a year or so of married life, Zeena "too fell silent. Perhaps it was the inevitable effect of life on the farm, or perhaps, as she sometimes said, it was because Ethan 'never listened.' The charge was not wholly unfounded. When she spoke it was only to complain, and to complain of things not in his power to remedy; and to check a tendency to impatient retort he had first formed the habit of not answering her, and finally of thinking of other things while she talked."

He knows that his silence (so like the silence of his mother who had been "listening" to unearthly voices) is but a short step from pathology. He fears that Zeena, too, might turn "queer"; and he knows "of certain lonely farm-houses in the neighborhood where stricken creatures pined, and of others where sudden tragedy had come of their presence." But his revulsion from silence is ambivalent, for beyond insanity, there is another vision—the close, convivial muteness of death. Ethan feels its attractions each time he passes the graveyard on the hill. At first the huddled company of gravestones sent shivers down his spine, but "now all desire for change had vanished, and the sight of the little enclosure gave him a warm sense of continuance and stability." On the whole, he is more powerfully drawn to silence than to speech. Over and over again, the arrangements of his life reinforce that silence. If his consciousness recoils from it in terror, some deeper inclination perversely yearns toward it.

It is always easier for Ethan to retreat from life into a "vision" (the word is echoed within the fantasy in a way that inescapably reinforces the narrator's deep identification with him). If Ethan is not able to talk to Mattie during that walk home from church, the deprivation is more than compensated for by his imagination. "He let the vision possess him as they climbed the hill to the house. He was never so happy with her as when he abandoned himself to these dreams. Half-way up the slope Mattie stumbled against some unseen obstruction and clutched his sleeve to steady herself. The wave of warmth that went through him was like the prolongation of his vision." The force of such visions is indescribable: it is the appeal of passivity, the numbing inertia that renders Frome impotent in the face of real-world dilemmas. Like a man who has become addicted to some strong narcotic, Frome savors emotional indolence as if it were a sensual experience. In the evening he spends alone with Mattie he is ravished by it. They sit and talk, and "the commonplace nature of what they said produced in Ethan an illusion of long-established intimacy which no outburst of emotion could have given, and he set his imagination adrift on the fiction that they had always spent their evenings thus and would always go on doing so. . . ." In truth

he is not listening to Miss Mattie Silver with any greater attention than he gives to Zenobia; he is listening to the mermaid voices within himself. Afterwards, the vision lingers. "He did not know why he was so irrationally happy, for nothing was changed in his life or hers. He had not even touched the tip of her fingers or looked her full in the eyes. But their evening together had given him a vision of what life at her side might be, and he was glad now that he had done nothing to trouble the sweetness of the picture." As always, the uncompromised richness of the dream is more alluring than the harsher limitations of actual, realized satisfactions.

In electing passivity and a life of regression, Ethan Frome has chosen to forfeit the perquisites of manhood. The many images of mutilation throughout the story merely reinforce a pattern that has been fully established well before the sledding accident. Ethan flees sexuality just as he has fled self-assertion. When he loses his mother, he replaces her almost without a perceptible break in his routines; and the state of querulous sickliness to which Zeena retreats after a year of marriage might plausibly be seen as a peevish attempt to demand attention of some sort when the attentions more normal to marriage have not been given. It is not Zenobia's womanliness that has attracted Ethan: "The mere fact of obeying her orders . . . restored his shaken balance." Yet the various components of this wife-nurse soon grate upon Ethan Frome's consciousness. "When she came to take care of his mother she had seemed to Ethan like the very genius of health, but he soon saw that her skill as a nurse had been acquired by the absorbed observation of her own symptoms." Ethan and Zeena have been brought together by their mutual commitment to the habits of care-taking; now they have become imprisoned by them.

At first, Ethan's affection for Mattie seems to have a more wholesome basis. However we soon realize that the sensual component in that relationship is of a piece with the sensuality of death. It thrives on exclusions and cannot survive in the rich atmosphere of real-world complexities. Ethan features Mattie as someone who can participate in his visions, and he does not allow the banality of her actual personality to flaw that supposition. One evening they stand watching the blue shadows of the hemlocks play across the sunlit snow. When Mattie exclaims: "'It looks just as if it was painted!' it seemed to Ethan that the art of definition could go no farther, and that words had at last been found to utter his secret soul . . . .". His imagination can remedy the deficiencies of genuine conversation; if worse comes to worst, he can ignore genuine conversation altogether (as he has in his realtionship with Zeena) and retreat to the more palatable images of his fancy.

By far the deepest irony is that Ethan's dreams of Mattie are not essentially different from the life that he has created with Zeena; they are still variations on the theme of dependency. Mattie "was quick to learn, but forgetful and dreamy. . . . Ethan had an idea that if she were to marry a man she was fond of the dormant instinct would wake, and her pies and biscuits become the pride of the country; but domesticity in the abstract did not interest her." The fantasies here are doubly revealing. As always he substitutes make-believe for reality— loving his vision of Mattie rather than Mattie herself. However, even when Ethan is given full rein, even when he can make any imaginary semblance of Mattie that he wants, he chooses a vision that has no sexual component. He does not see her as a loving wife to warm his bed in the winter. No. She is, instead, a paragon of the kitchen, a perfect caretaker, someone who can fill his stomach—not satisfy his manhood. She is, in short, just what he had imagined Zeena might be. And there is no reason, even at the beginning of the tale, to suppose that Mattie Silver would be any better in the role than Zeena.

Ethan and Mattie are never pictured as man and woman together; at their most intimate moments they cling "to each other's hands like children." At other times, they envision a life in which they exchange the role of caretaker and protector: if Mattie might become the best cook in the county; Ethan longs "'to do for you and care for you. I want to be there when you're sick and when you're lonesome'." When they finally do come together in their momentous first kiss, even that physical contact is described in terms that remove it from the world of adult passion and reduce it to the modalities of infancy: "He had found her lips at last and was drinking unconsciousness of everything but the joy they gave him."

The sled ride is a natural climax to all of the themes that have been interwoven throughout the story. It is, or ought to be, a sexual culmination—the long, firm sled; the shining track opening up before them; the swift, uneven descent, now plunging "with the hollow night opening out below them and the air singing by like an organ," now bounding dizzily upward only to plunge again with sudden exultation and rapture past the elm until "they reached the level ground beyond, and the speed of the sled began to slacken." The description of their long, successful first ride gives some intimation of the possibilities before them. Nevertheless, the language does not remain fixed; the vision is not steady. By this time the story has achieved such a palpable air of veracity that the reader is apt to accept this language as a more or less adequate description of what "really happened." Of course it is not. Even at this point— especially at this point—we must recollect that Ethan's world and all of the decisions in it (all the language that renders those decisions) is no more than the narrator's vision. We have finally reached the heart of that vision—the ultimate depths of the shadow world in which the narrator has immersed himself— and the inescapable implications of it crowd about us like the shades that gather dusk together and enfold the world in night.

The story becomes a veritable dance around the notion of vision. Ethan's eyesight is keen. "'I can measure distances to a hair's breadth—always could'," he boasts to Mattie. And she echoes his thought: "'I always say you've got the surest eye ...'." Yet tonight "he strained his eyes through the dimness, and they seemed less keen, less capable than usual." Other visions are competing against his clear-eyed view. The couple discovers that each has ached throughout the long six months before, dreaming of the other, dreams defying sleep. This, too, is a climax; for the mingling of their love-fancies becomes the most explicit bond between them. It is a more compelling vision even than the long, smooth, slippery track before them, a vision that is compounded by the potent imagery of Mattie's despair. "'There'll be that strange girl in the house ... and she'll sleep in my bed, where I used to lay nights and listen to hear you come up the stairs ...'." Vision calls to vision, and Ethan, too, succumbs to the stealing softness of his own dreams. "The words were like fragments torn from his heart. With them came the hated vision of the house he was going back to—of the stairs he would have to go up every night, of the woman who would wait for him there. And the sweetness of Mattie's avowal, the wild wonder of knowing at last that all that had happened to him had happened to her too, made the other vision more abhorrent, the other life more intolerable to return to. ..."

It is Mattie who suggests death (though her plea has the urgency of a lingering sexual appeal): "'Ethan! Ethan! I want you to take me down again!'" and he resists her—as he has always resisted any action.

In the end, he is seduced by the vision; her words do not even penetrate. "Her pleadings still came to him between short sobs, but he no longer heard what she was saying. Her hat had slipped back and he was stroking her hair. He wanted to get the feeling of it into his hand, so that it would sleep there like a seed in winter." Not the violence of passion, but the loving, soothing release of sleep. Never has the silence been more profound (her words lost entirely into the cold and empty ether—that exhausted receiver of sky inverted over earth). The close conviviality of the grave has overwhelmed his imagination at last: "The spruces swathed them in blackness and silence. They might have been in their coffins underground. He said to himself: 'Perhaps it'll feel like this ...' and then again: 'After this I sha'n't feel anything ....'." The indivisible comfort of nothingness.

The delicate balance has swung finally to the side of retreat; time and space rush forward, and Ethan Frome lapses back into the simplicities of childhood, infancy. Words will not suffice to reach him now. Nothing does, save one sound—"he heard the old sorrel whinny across the road, and thought: 'He's wondering why he doesn't get his supper ...'." Food—and then sleep—the very oldest memories, the persistent, original animal needs, nothing more. Mattie urges him, but he responds only to the "sombre violence" of her gesture as she tugs at his hand. Slowly they take their places. But then, Ethan stops. "'Get up! Get up!'" he urges the girl. "But she kept on repeating: 'Why do you want to sit in front?' 'Because I— because I want to feel you holding me,' he stammered, and dragged her to her feet." This is how he must go, cradled in the embrace of her arms.

The ride begins. Down the hill—no farewell but the gentle neighing of the sorrel. Down and down again, a "long delirious descent [in which] it seemed to him that they were flying indeed, flying far up into the cloudy night, with Starkfield immeasurably below them, falling away like a speck in space." "We can fetch it"; he repeats the refrain as the sled wavers and then rights itself toward the looming elm. "The air shot past him like millions of fiery wires, and then the elm. ..."

Afterwards, there seems nothing left but silence; silence at first, and then "he heard a little animal twittering somewhere near by under the snow. It made a small frightened *cheep* like a field mouse. ... He understood that it must be in pain. ... The thought of the animal's suffering was intolerable to him and ... he continued to finger about cautiously with his left hand, thinking he might get hold of the little creature and help it; and all at once he knew that the soft thing he had touched was Mattie's hair and that his hand was on her face." He has come to the very verge, but he has not managed to go over. His own final threshold remains uncrossed. He has not quite died. He has only been reduced, irretrievably reduced, to the sparse simplicities of animal existence.

Having plunged thus far from the world of adult possibilities, having brought Mattie and Zeena with him, he is doomed, after all, to wait for the end—possibly to wait for a long time. The last words of the vision measure the level of reality to which he has consigned himself. "Far off, up the hill, he heard the sorrel whinny, and thought: 'I ought to be getting him his feed ...'." Thus the vision concludes, and the narrator steps finally through the kitchen door into the unchanging world of Ethan Frome, his wife, and Miss Mattie Silver. The condition of static misery that he infers, the life that has been Frome's scant portion, is an inevitable consequence of those dark impulses that lead past madness to the edge of oblivion.

We leave the narrator reflecting upon the tale he has told. It is not "true" except as an involuntary expression of his own hidden self; nevertheless, this purgatory of the imagination becomes ominously insistent, and the "self," having had life breathed into it, grows stronger even as the narrator assembles his story. Mrs. Hale's banal chatter falls upon deaf ears: he heeds her no more than Ethan has heeded Zeena or Mattie; and like Ethan, he has a parsimonious way with conversation. "Mrs. Hale paused a moment, and I remained silent, plunged in the vision of what her words evoked." (pp. 175-81)

The literary device of the "frame" in this story makes an important assertion: the narrator's "vision" is just that, a vision. The life of the young Ethan Frome that he has conjured is *not* a description of necessary human hopelessness; it is no more than a private nightmare. . . . Beyond it and outside is a whole world—made "real" by multitudinous possibilities.

Finally, *Ethan Frome* is a statement of Edith Wharton's coming of age as a novelist. What had she meant when she said that "it was not until I wrote *Ethan Frome* that I suddenly felt the artisan's full control of his implements"? One thing she might have meant was that she had finally learned to distinguish between a "vision" and a "fiction." By her own admission: "No picture of myself would be more than a profile if it failed to give some account of the teeming visions which, ever since my small-childhood, and even at the busiest and most agitated periods of my outward life, have incessantly peopled my inner world." A vision must be hammered into shape. It is, perhaps, the germ of a fiction; but it is not yet a fiction. A vision is a primitive expression of self; a fiction is the creation of an independent world that stands apart from self. Within *Ethan Frome* the narrator lapses into a vision (the tale of Ethan which is, as we have seen, a terrified expression of the narrator's latent self—his *alter ego,* his "Winterman"). The *novel, Ethan Frome,* focuses on the narrator's problem: the tension between his public self and his shadow self, his terror of a seductive and enveloping void. (pp. 183-84)

> *Cynthia Griffin Wolff, in her* A Feast of Words: The Triumph of Edith Wharton, *Oxford University Press, 1977, 453 p.*

ALLEN F. STEIN (essay date 1984)

[*In the following excerpt, Stein discusses* Ethan Frome *as "Wharton's fullest treatment of the disasters that can occur when one attempts to leave even a repellent marriage."*]

In Edith Wharton's short story **"The Introducers,"** Tilney, a supremely knowing fellow, asserts in his most knowing manner, "It takes a pretty varied experience of life to find out that there are worse states than marriage." As a paean to domesticity, this is hardly in the same league with old chestnuts of the "it takes a heap of living to make a house a home" variety, but it is as close to an impassioned defense of marriage as Wharton ever presents explicitly in her fiction. At least once in her conversation, though, she went well beyond Tilney's tepid affirmation. Percy Lubbock reports that he was present one day when Wharton in the course of a discussion of *Middlemarch* "spoke out, 'Ah, the poverty, the miserable poverty,

of any love that lies outside of marriage, of any love that is not a living together, a sharing of all!'" Such an outburst is, of course, more than a little surprising given the failure of Wharton's own marriage, the predominantly bleak tenor of her work generally, and the fact that the bleakness inheres most strongly in her marriage stories, which, as Geoffrey Walton notes aptly, convey "a stronger feeling of pathos and even tragedy" than do her other works. Clearly, a glance at most of the marriages Wharton presents, a group that includes such infelicitous matings as those of the Fromes, Dorsets, Marvells, and deChelleses, might lead one to find even Wharton's wry avowal of faith in matrimony in **"The Introducers"** a bit improbable. Yet neither Tilney's comment nor the emphatic assertion recorded by Lubbock is finally at odds with the over-riding outlook on marriage that Wharton presents in her works. Though she knows that all too few marriages offer the perfect "living together" and "sharing of all" that she so passionately envisions—and, to be sure, presents no marriages of this sort— she also knows full well that there are indeed "worse states" outside marriage, states verging on the "miserable poverty" of emotional, moral, and spiritual chaos. And her defense of marriage is not merely negative, for she stresses throughout her career that even unfortunate marriages can have worth for the individual and society. Positive as it tends to be, though, her defense is almost invariably a somber one, as even her best marriages are successful usually only insofar as they lead married folk to see the bleakness of life and the depth of human folly. (pp. 209-10)

Wharton's fullest treatment of the disasters that can occur when one attempts to leave even a repellent marriage is *Ethan Frome.* Perhaps no other character in Wharton's work is tied to a more insensitive mate than is poor Ethan. Indeed, so unremitting is his pain throughout his long marriage that some have suggested that this work is not much more than a nasty little horror show. Lionel Trilling, for one, asserts that it "presents no moral issue at all" and merely reveals Wharton's limitation of heart [see excerpt dated 1956]. Though Trilling's reading is admirably responsive to Ethan's suffering, it seems to miss the point when it implies that the loveless Frome marriage is only a means by which Wharton indulges virtually sadistic tendencies in herself by tormenting her protagonist. Actually, Wharton's tale does present a discernible counsel on how best to face life in a universe that apparently cares little for those who inhabit it.

In Ethan's small New England town, one sees a way of life with none of those genteel trappings that in polite society shelter people from a daily confrontation with the grimmer facts of existence. Perhaps the grimmest of these is that people are often victimized irremediably by forces over which they have no control. Gary H. Lindberg, in fact, sees Wharton as essentially deterministic in her outlook in that her characters generally seem to be caught up in a "flow of destiny" in which their private schemes "generated by personal lines of intention are simply dwarfed." It is not, he notes, a "scientific formulation of biological and environmental determinism but rather a configuration of moral inevitability posited by the conjunction of a given choice and the social world within which that choice is made." Lindberg's point about Wharton's determinism is well-taken, though in this particular case the crucial conjunction is not that of a "given choice" and the "social world" but of a choice (itself not quite freely made) and the very nature of things, of which the dense social world usually seen in Wharton's works is merely a manifestation. Though the context here is cosmic rather than social, the configuration of moral imperatives that inevitably takes shape is no different from that to be seen in Wharton's tales of marital entrapment that are set in circumstances less bereft of social relations.

That Ethan's marriage is an unhappy one for him is well known and needs no rehearsal here. What may be less obvious, though, in the narrator's account of things is that both his decision to marry Zenna and his subsequent attempt to escape the marriage through suicide with Mattie grow out of a deep, almost childish fear of loneliness, a fear instilled in him, in great measure, by the bleak landscape itself and all that it seems to symbolize about the bleakness of the universe. Ethan proposed to Zeena because he had an "unreasoning dread of being left alone on the farm." This dread evoked, substantially, by the wintry scene around him led him to overestimate Zeena's capacity for human feeling. Reflecting on his error, Ethan "often thought since that it would not have happened if his mother had died in spring instead of winter . . .". Showing more fully that Ethan was a good deal less than a free agent when he married are the references to the landscape about him as having been shaped by the huge, timeless pressures exerted on it, these references serving as an implicit reminder that those who people this landscape are similarly shaped by elements larger than themselves. Thus, the "ledge of granite thrusting up through the ferms," which seems to unroll the "huge panorama of the ice age and the long dim stretches of succeeding time," forces one to see Ethan's story in a larger context than the one in which one normally thinks Wharton's tales operative—forces one, in other words, to see Ethan in a universe of powerful and inevitably enigmatic forces that buffet people about uncaringly and probably unknowingly.

Positing implicitly this central vision, then, the narrator's account of the disaster of Ethan establishes as a central issue the problem of ascertaining how one is to confront life in a bleak, indifferent universe in which one's options are severely limited. The young Ethan's inability to cope with the pressures in his life in no way indicates that means of coping cannot be found; rather, it is an index to his own sentimentality and immaturity as he childishly sees Mattie as embodying virtues and as linked to a happiness that are, quite obviously, well removed from the world we all know. As Cynthia Griffin Wolff notes, "It is always easier for Ethan to retreat from life into a 'vision'" than to face what must be faced. He is, Wolff goes on to say, invariably too receptive to the "appeal of passivity and a life of regression" [see excerpt dated 1977]. The childishness of his attempt—typically bungled, of course—to regress to a state of ultimate passivity through suicide is brought out by the very form that the attempt takes: a downhill ride on a sled. One can imagine few others in Frome's village who would have chosen such a ride.The Powells, Hales, and their ilk, glimpsed briefly through the narrative, are there, in part, to offer an instructive contrast to the dreamy, dissatisfied Frome. They go quietly about their business and in the routine they establish create a little realm of order and responsibility in the midst of a stark wintry scene, an order that Ethan's crack-up crudely violates.

One possibility in this work that cannot, of course, be overlooked is that the facts as presented by the narrator may not accord with the events that occurred. The narrator's vision of Ethan's past is just that—a vision, and Joseph X. Brennan suggests, therefore, that *Ethan Frome* must be judged "in terms of the special character of the narrator's mind" and, further, that "since the narrator has had to imagine almost the whole of Ethan's history and the most important traits of his character as well, in many respects, inevitably, the sensibilities of the two are indistinguishable." So indistinguishable might they be

that one cannot be sure that the real Ethan Frome ever felt anything akin to what the narrator attributes to him or did the things he did for the reasons the narrator either consciously or inadvertently offers. What *is* objectively verifiable does not necessarily reinforce one's sense of the narrator's accuracy. For example, the picture of Ethan, Mattie, and Zeena with which Wharton closes the work calls into question much of what has been offered previously as a probable version of the past. Though Mrs. Hale asserts that before the crash she "never knew a sweeter nature than Mattie's," whereas Zeena was, she says, "always cranky," in evidence nevertheless as the narrator enters the Frome farmhouse are Mattie's "querulous drone" and Zeena's quiet patience in ministering to this irritable invalid. Inevitably, this makes one wonder whether Mattie was ever quite so good or Zeena quite so bad as the narrator envisions them to have been. On this central question as elsewhere, the narrator may well be indulging his propensities for the exaggerated and the romantic that he reveals throughout the work. Indeed, were the narrator not an exceedingly romantic fellow, even something of a sentimentalist, he would not involve himself in an extensive reverie about thwarted dreams and longings in the first place, nor would he construct the monolithic (and perhaps reductive) image patterns he does in contrasting Mattie and Zeena before the sledding disaster. As Brennan notes [see Additional Bibliography], the narrator consistently links Mattie with lovely and delicate objects in nature, such as birds and field mice, whereas he characterizes Zeena throughout with stifling imagery of the indoors and the artificial and through ties to such predators as cats and owls (which, of course, have an innate yen for field mice and small birds). Moreover, the narrator's liking for such phrasing as "in a sky of iron the points of the Dipper hung like icicles and Orion flashed his cold fires" and Ethan "had found Mattie's lips at last and was drinking unconsciousness of everything but the joy they gave him" further reveals the presence here of an exceedingly romantic sensibility and, consequently, must lead one to question the accuracy of his vision of the past.

Whatever the case, however, whether the narrator's vision is a valid one or not, Wharton's allegiances are clear. An accurate telling implies, whether the perhaps too romantic narrator is aware of it or not, that Frome was, as I have noted, a sentimentalist who could not face up to the facts of his existence. If it is an inaccurate account, then it is the narrator who stands indicted as a mawkish sentimentalist (or, as Wolff puts it, one with a "ghastly" mind) who indirectly and inadvertently makes a powerful argument for living up to such commitments as those he envisions the young Ethan as trying to escape. Finally, if one concludes, as one well might, that *Ethan Frome* is irresolvably ambiguous, Wharton's position is no less clear. In a world in which the truth is nebulous, perhaps impossible to glean with certainty, one must, she teaches, strive for order, even self-imposed order; and this must be carried out even in the face of the determinism that she sees as operative, for, rightly or wrongly, she does not regard moral responsibility as incompatible with a restricted will. The establishment of routine, of order, by carrying out ordering responsibilities imposed by the severe demands of marriage is thus a goal to strive for, one that either Ethan or the narrator (or both) could not perceive as valuable. Without such order, Wharton believes, a difficult existence can only be made more difficult. (pp. 225-30)

Allen F. Stein, "Edith Wharton: The Marriage of Entrapment," in his After the Vows Were Spoken: Marriage in American Literary Realism, *Ohio State University Press, 1984, pp. 209-30.*

ADDITIONAL BIBLIOGRAPHY

Bjorkman, Edwin. "The Greater Edith Wharton." In his *Voices of Tomorrow: Critical Studies of the New Spirit in Literature*, pp. 290-304. New York: Mitchell Kennerly, 1913.

    Calls *Ethan Frome* essentially a social rather than a personal tragedy, characterizing it as "above all else a judgment on that system which fails to redeem such villages as Mrs. Wharton's Starkfield" [see excerpt dated 1913 in *TCLC*-3].

Blackall, Jean Frantz. "The Sledding Accident in *Ethan Frome*." *Studies in Short Fiction* 21, No. 2 (Spring 1984): 145-46.

    Finds Frome's insistence that he sit in front of Mattie on the suicide run consistent with his idea of love as represented throughout the novella. According to Blackall: "Ethan's idea of love is nurture. He wants to sit ahead of Mattie on the sled so that he, not Mattie, will hit the elm tree first. Perhaps his solicitude is misplaced since their objective in common is to commit suicide."

Blankenship, Russell. "Rise of Realism: Edith Wharton." In his *American Literature as an Expression of the National Mind*, pp. 502-08. New York: Henry Holt & Co., 1931.

    Introductory sketch noting Wharton's literary relationship to Henry James and Sinclair Lewis. Blankenship also discusses Wharton's novels, concluding of *Ethan Frome* that "volumes of explanation could not adequately describe the high pitch of the story, the passion which animates it, and the grim, lingering punishment of the end. *Ethan Frome* is to be read, not discussed."

Bloom, Lynne G. *Ethan Frome: A Critical Commentary*. New York: American R.D.M. Corp., 1964, 40 p.

    Handbook designed for classroom use, including a biographical sketch of Wharton, analyses of plot structure and characterization, critical appraisal, summary of characters, suggested study topics, and bibliography.

Brennan, Joseph X. "Ethan Frome: Structure and Metaphor." *Modern Fiction Studies* 7, No. 4 (Winter 1961-62): 347-56.

    Detailed textual analysis of *Ethan Frome*, noting the importance of the work's narrative framework and elaborate metaphorical patterns [see excerpt dated 1961-62 in *TCLC*-3].

Burgess, Anthony. "Austere in Whalebone." *Spectator*, No. 7171 (3 December 1965): 745.

    Reviews *Ethan Frome, Custom of the Country*, and *Summer*. According to Burgess: "The utter pessimism of *Ethan Frome*—the Immortals sporting in a frigid new England—is too bad to be true; it is Hardyesque self-indulgence; a tragic thesis takes over and manipulates chess-characters."

Canby, Henry Seidel. "Edith Wharton." *Saturday Review of Literature* (New York) XVI, No. 17 (21 August 1937): 6-7.

    Retrospective essay occasioned by Wharton's death. Canby characterizes *Ethan Frome* as Wharton's "one important departure from society and New York" and as "a striking footnote to her career. For in this famous story she turned to another dying class, inhibited and unstrung by different causes, but equally futile, equally doomed—the ethical New Englander."

Cooper, Frederic Taber. Review of *Ethan Frome*. *The Bookman* (New York) 34 (November 1911): 307-13.

    Comments that "it is hard to forgive Mrs. Wharton for the utter remorselessness of *Ethan Frome*, for nowhere has she done anything more hopelessly grey with blank despair. . . . Art for art's sake is the one justification of a piece of work as perfect in technique as it is relentless in substance."

Davis, Owen, and Davis, Donald. *Ethan Frome: A Dramatization of Edith Wharton's Novel*. New York: Charles Scribner's Sons, 1936, 260 p.

    Includes a foreword by Wharton in which she notes her appreciation and approval of the Davis's adaptation of her work and expresses the hope that her "poor litle group of hungry, lonely New England villagers will live again for a while on their stony hillside before finally joining their forbears under the village headstones."

Deegan, Dorothy Yost. "What Does the Reader Find?: The Synthesis—Portrait in Miniature." In her *The Stereotype of the Single Woman in American Novels*, pp. 40-126. New York: King's Crown Press, 1951.

    Places Mattie Silver in the literary tradition of the "single-woman character who is brought to an unfortuante position largely because of her lack of fitness to make her way with economic independence."

Follett, Helen Thomas, and Follett, Wilson. "Edith Wharton." In their *Some Modern Novelists: Appreciations and Essays*, pp. 291-311. New York: Henry Holt and Co., 1919.

    Characterizes *Ethan Frome* as a striking example of an intermediate literary form—a new kind of novel that grew out of the long short story. The critic contends that none of Wharton's other works "has quite the hard shapeliness, the smooth enameled finish, the exquisite inward adjustment part to part, of this tragic idyll of New England."

Herron, Ima Honaker. "The Town, the Brahmins, and Others." In her *The Small Town in American Literature*, pp. 100-45. New York: Pageant Books, 1959.

    Discusses the note of universal tragedy struck in *Ethan Frome* and *Summer*. Herron concludes that "in neither of these portrayals of the decaying village does Mrs. Wharton dally with an ethical thesis. She simply represents human beings as being surrounded by forces quite beyond their own powers to control or defy."

Jessup, Josephine Lurie. "Edith Wharton: Drawing-Room Devotee." In her *The Faith of Our Feminists: A Study of the Novels of Edith Wharton, Ellen Glasgow, Willa Cather*, pp. 14-33. New York: Richard R. Smith, 1950.

    Sees a "feminist victory celebrated in *Ethan Frome*." According to Jessup, the novella depicts "an acute case of frustration, but frustration for Ethan alone; the women manage to have their own way, if only to the extent of ordering one man between them."

Lewis, R. W. B. "Ethan Frome and Other Dramas." In his *Edith Wharton: A Biography*, pp. 294-313. New York: Harper & Row, 1975.

    Relates *Ethan Frome* to events in Wharton's life during the period in which she wrote it. Lewis states that "*Ethan Frome* portrays [Wharton's] personal situation, as she had come to appraise it, carried to a far extreme, transplanted to a remote, rural scene, and rendered utterly hopeless by circumstance."

Lyde, Marilyn Jones. "The Artistic Value of the Theory of Morality and Convention." In her *Edith Wharton: Convention and Morality in the Work of a Novelist*, pp. 141-79. Norman: University of Oklahoma Press, 1959.

    Includes references to *Ethan Frome* in a discussion of Wharton's use of "crucial moments" to illustrate moral conflicts between the individual and society.

MacCallan, W. D. "The French Draft of *Ethan Frome*." *The Yale University Library Gazette* 27, No. 1 (July 1952): 38-47.

    Transcription of Wharton's French text. In an introductory sketch, MacCallan remarks that "concerning the relation between the manuscript and the final version of *Ethan Frome* the most important observation is the lack, in the French draft, of the tragic accident—or rather the attempt at suicide. . . . In all other respects the final version is little more than a careful expansion of the French draft, to which has been added the mechanism for the narration of the story by a suitably sensitive observer."

"Three Lives in Supreme Torture." *New York Times Book Review* XVI, No. 40 (8 October 1911): 603.

    Review of *Ethan Frome*. According to the critic: "Wharton has . . . chosen to build of small, crude things and a rude and violent event a structure whose purpose is the infinite refinement of torture. All that is human and pitiful and tender in the tale—and there is much—is designed and contrived to sharpen the keen edge of that torture."

Overton, Grant. "Edith Wharton." In his *The Women Who Make Our Novels,* pp. 324-42. New York: Dodd, Mead & Co., 1928.
    Surveys Wharton's works to 1928 and concludes that "there can be no doubt that *Ethan Frome* is one of the masterpieces of American literature."

Quinn, Arthur Hobson. "Edith Wharton." In his *American Fiction: An Historical and Critical Survey,* pp. 550-81. New York: Appleton-Century-Crofts, 1936.
    Proposes that "it is not misery . . . that makes *Ethan Frome* a fine novel. It is the struggle of Ethan to taste one moment of happiness, and the iron logic of the situation in which a nature like his could not abandon a duty, even if it wrecked his life."

Ransom, John Crowe. "Characters and Character." *American Review* VI, No. 3 (January 1936): 271-88.
    Examines the function of the narrator in *Ethan Frome* and finds fault with the structure of the novel, considering it too short and undeveloped. According to Ransom: "The book is half long enough, or less; it is a 'study,' a well-proportioned first draft or outline for the real circumstantial thing that was to come, that would have been fiction" [see excerpt dated 1936 in *TCLC*-3].

Scott-James, R. A. "Editorial Notes: Edith Wharton." *London Mecury* XXXVI, No. 215 (September 1937): 417.
    Obituary tribute to Wharton concluding that "her best book was that short novel, *Ethan Frome,* in which for once she let herself go and attained a passionate intensity which she reached in no other work."

Appendix

The following is a listing of all sources used in Volume 27 of *Twentieth-Century Literary Criticism*. Included in this list are all copyright and reprint rights and acknowledgments for those essays for which permission was obtained. Every effort has been made to trace copyright, but if omissions have been made, please let us know.

THE EXCERPTS IN TCLC, VOLUME 27, WERE REPRINTED FROM THE FOLLOWING PERIODICALS:

The Academy, v. XXXIV, July 28, 1888; v. XLVII, October 20, 1894.

American Literature, v. 27, November, 1955. Copyright © 1955, renewed 1983, Duke University Press, Durham, NC. Reprinted by permission of the publisher.

The American-Scandinavian Review, v. IV, November-December, 1916; v. XII, June, 1924.

Anales Galdosianos, v. 1, 1966. Reprinted by permission of the publisher.

Ariel (The University of Calgary), v. 3, October, 1972. Copyright © 1972 The Board of Governors, The University of Calgary. Reprinted by permission of the publisher.

The Athenaeum, n. 2164, April 17, 1869.

Australian Literary Studies, v. 7, October, 1976 for "The Craftsmanship of Lawson Revisited" by Livio Dobrez; v. 11, October, 1983 for "'The Loaded Dog': A Celebration" by Ken Stewart. Both reprinted by permission of the publisher and the respective authors.

Books Abroad, v. 38, Summer, 1964. Copyright 1964 by the University of Oklahoma Press. Reprinted by permission of the publisher.

Bulletin, August 29, 1896.

College English, v. 23, December, 1961 for "Imagery and Symbolism in 'Ethan Frome'" by Kenneth Bernard. © 1961 by The National Council of Teachers of English. Reprinted by permission of the publisher and the author./ v. 25, April, 1964. © 1964 by The National Council of Teachers of English. Reprinted by permission of the publisher.

The Critic, New York, v. XXXVIII, May, 1901.

Critical Quarterly, v. 29, Summer, 1987. © Manchester University Press 1987. Reprinted by permission of Manchester University Press.

The Dial, v. XV, December 1, 1893; v. XVI, June 16, 1894.

The Double Dealer, v. II, December, 1921.

The Egoist, v. III, February 1, 1916.

English Literature in Transitions: 1880-1920, v. 28, 1985 for ''An Assessment of Wilfred Owen'' by Richard Hoffpauir. Copyright © 1985 *English Literature in Transition: 1880-1920.* Reprinted by permission of the publisher and the author.

Essays in Criticism, v. IV, January, 1954.

Germano-Slavica, n. 2, Fall, 1979. Reprinted by permission of the publisher.

Harper's Bazaar, v. XXVIII, November 2, 1895.

Hermes, November 20, 1894.

Hispania, v. III, October, 1920.

The International Review, v. VII, September, 1879.

Jahrbuch Für Amerikastudien, v. 6, 1961, for ''Tragedy and 'The Pursuit of Happiness': 'Long Day's Journey into Night'''' by Alan S. Downer. Reprinted by permission of the Literary Estate of Alan S. Downer.

Journal of Baltic Studies, v. XVII, Spring, 1986. Copyright © 1986 by the Association for the Advancement of Baltic Studies, Inc. Reprinted by permission of the publisher.

Literary Criterion, v. V, Winter, 1962. Reprinted by permission of the publisher.

Literary Digest, New York, v. LXVI, September 18, 1920.

The Literary Review (Fairleigh Dickinson University), v. 6, Spring, 1963. Copyright © 1963 by Fairleigh Dickinson University. Reprinted by permission of the publisher.

The London Mercury, v. XXXII, June, 1935.

The London Quarterly Review, v. CXLV, January, 1926.

Luso-Brazilian Review, v. X, Summer, 1973; v. 14, Winter, 1977. Copyright © 1973, 1977 by the Board of Regents of the University of Wisconsin System. Both reprinted by permission of The University of Wisconsin Press.

Meanjin, v. 7, Winter, 1948; v. XVI, December, 1957.

The Modern Language Journal, v. LXVII, Autumn, 1983. © 1983 *The Modern Language Journal.* Reprinted by permission of The University of Wisconsin Press.

Modern Language Quarterly, v. XXI, March, 1960. © 1960 University of Washington. Reprinted by permission of the publisher.

The Nation, New York, v. XCIII, October 26, 1911; v. CIV, June 7, 1917; v. CXXV, February 11, 1925; v CXXIX, December 4, 1929.

The Nation and the Athenaeum, v. XLIV, February 2, 1929.

The New England Quarterly, v. XXIV, June, 1951.

The New Statesman & Nation, n.s. v. XII, October 24, 1936.

The New York Review of Books, v. III, September 24, 1964; v. XIX, September 21, 1972. Copyright © 1964, 1972 Nyrev, Inc. Both reprinted with permission from *The New York Review of Books.*

The New York Times, February 19, 1956. Copyright © 1956 by The New York Times Company. Reprinted by permission of the publisher.

The New York Times Book Review, May 11, 1924. Copyright 1924 by The New York Times Company. Reprinted by permission of the publisher.

The North American Review, December, January, February, 1925-26.

THE EXCERPTS IN TCLC, VOLUME 27, WERE REPRINTED FROM THE FOLLOWING BOOKS:

Angoff, Charles. From an introduction to *The Temptation*. By Vincas Krévé, translated by Raphael Sealey. Manyland Books, 1965. Copyright, 1965, by Manyland Books, Inc. All rights reserved. Reprinted by permission of the Literary Estate of Charles Angoff.

Baker, James. From *Literary and Biographical Studies*. Chapman and Hall, Limited, 1908.

Bell, Aubrey F. G. From *Contemporary Spanish Literature*. Alfred A. Knopf, 1925.

Benson, E. F. From *Our Family Affairs: 1867-1896*. Doran, 1921. Copyright, 1921, by George H. Doran Company. Renewed 1948 by Kenneth Stewart Patrick McDowall. Reprinted by permission of the Literary Estate of E. F. Benson.

Blunden, Edmund. From *War Poets: 1914-1918*. The British Council, 1958.

Bogard, Travis. From *Contour in Time: The Plays of Eugene O'Neill*. Oxford University Press, 1972. Copyright © 1972 by Oxford University Press, Inc. Reprinted by permission of the publisher.

Brainina, Berta. From a foreword to *Cement: A Novel*. By Feodor Gladkov, translated by Liv Tadge. Progress, 1981. English translation © Progress Publishers 1981. Reprinted by permission of the publisher.

Brenan, Gerald. From *The Literature of the Spanish People from Roman Times to the Present Day*. Second edition. Cambridge University Press, 1953.

Britt, Albert. From *The Great Biographers*. Whittlesey House, 1936.

Brown, Aléc. From a preface to *The Fifth Pestilence, Together with the History of the Tinkling Cymbal and Sounding Brass: Ivan Semyonovitch Stratilatov*. By Alexi Remizov, translated by Aléc Brown. Wishart and Co., 1927.

Brown, Edward J. From *Russian Literature Since the Revolution*. Revised edition. Collier Books, 1969. Copyright © 1963, 1969, and 1982 by Edward J. Brown. All rights reserved. Reprinted by permission of the author.

Bryer, Jackson R. From " 'Hell Is Other People': 'Long Day's Journey into Night'," in *The Fifties: Fiction, Poetry, Drama*. Edited by Warren French. Everett/Edwards, Inc., 1970. Copyright © 1970 by Warren French. All rights reserved. Reprinted by permission of the publisher.

Budd, Kenneth. From *The Last Victorian: R. D. Blackmore and His Novels*. Centaur Press, 1960. © Kenneth G. Budd 1960. Reprinted by permission of the publisher.

Burris, Quincey Guy. From *Richard Doddridge Blackmore: His Life and Novels*. University of Illinois Press, 1930.

Chabrowe, Leonard. From *Ritual and Pathos—the Theater of O'Neill*. Bucknell University Press, 1976. © 1976 by Associated University Presses, Inc. Reprinted by permission of the publisher.

Chothia, Jean. From *Forging a Language: A Study of the Plays of Eugene O'Neill*. Cambridge University Press, 1979. © Cambridge University Press 1979. Reprinted with permission of the publisher and the author.

Clurman, Harold. From a review of "Long Day's Journey into Night," in *The Divine Pastime: Theatre Essays*. Macmillan, 1974. Copyright © 1974, 1971 by Harold Clurman. All rights reserved. Reprinted with permission of Macmillan Publishing Company.

Cohen, Joseph. From *Owen Agonistes*. Revised edition. N.p., 1966. Reprinted by permission of the author.

Coombes, Archie James. From *Some Australian Poets*. Angus and Robertson, 1938.

Courteau, Joanna. From "The Quest for Identity in Pessoa's Orthonymous Poetry," in *The Man Who Never Was: Essays on Fernando Pessoa*. Edited by George Monteiro. Gávea-Brown, 1982. Copyright © 1981 by George Monteiro. Reprinted by permission of the publisher.

Dendle, Brian J. From *Galdós: The Early Historical Novels*. University of Missouri Press, 1986. Copyright © 1986 by The Curators of the University of Missouri. All rights reserved. Reprinted by permission of the publisher.

Dendle, Brian J. From *Galdós: The Mature Thought*. University Press of Kentucky, 1980. Copyright © 1980 by The University Press of Kentucky. Reprinted by permission of the publisher.

Quintanilha, F. E. G. From "Introduction: Fernando Pessoa, the Man and His Work," in *Sixty Portuguese Poems*. By Fernando Pessoa, edited and translated by F. E. G. Quintanilha. University of Wales Press, 1971. © University of Wales Press, 1971. Reprinted by permission of the publisher.

Raleigh, John Henry. From *The Plays of Eugene O'Neill*. Southern Illinois University Press, 1965. Copyright © 1965 by Southern Illinois University Press. All rights reserved. Reprinted by permission of the publisher.

Rickard, Peter. From an introduction to *Selected Poems*. By Fernando Pessoa, edited and translated by Peter Rickard. Edinburgh University Press, 1971. © 1971 by Peter Rickard. All rights reserved. Reprinted by permission of the publisher.

Roderick, Colin. From *Henry Lawson: Poet and Short Story Writer*. Angus and Robertson, 1966. Copyright 1966 Colin Roderick. Reprinted by permission of Angus & Robertson Publishers.

Rodríguez, Alfred. From *An Introduction to the Episodios Nacionales of Galdós*. Las Americas, 1967. Copyright © 1967 by Las Americas Publishing Co. Reprinted by permission of the publisher.

Saintsbury, George. From *The English Novel*. J. M. Dent & Sons, Ltd., 1913.

Sassoon, Siegfried. From "Wilfred Owen—A Personal Appreciation," in *A Tribute to Wilfred Owen*. Edited by T. J. Walsh. N.p., n.d.

Segel, Harold B. From *Twentieth-Century Russian Drama: From Gorky to the Present*. Columbia University Press, 1979. Copyright © 1979 Columbia University Press. All rights reserved. Reprinted by permission of the publisher.

Seldes, Gilbert. From an introduction to *All About Lucia: Four Novels*. By E. F. Benson. Doubleday, Doran & Company, 1936. Copyright 1936, renewed 1963, by Doubleday, Doran & Company, Inc. All rights reserved. Reprinted by permission of Doubleday, a division of Bantam, Doubleday, Dell Publishing Group, Inc.

Senn, Alfred. From "Vincent Krėvė, Lithuania's Creator of Heroes," in *World Literatures*. By Joseph Remenyi and others. © 1956 University of Pittsburgh Press. © 1984 Joseph Remenyi. Reprinted by permission of the publisher.

Silkin, Jon. From *Out of Battle: The Poetry of the Great War*. Oxford University Press, 1972, Routledge & Kegan Paul, 1987. © Jon Silkin 1987. Reprinted by permission of Routledge & Kegan Paul PLC.

Slonim, Marc. From *Modern Russian Literature: From Chekhov to the Present*. Oxford University Press, 1953. Copyright 1953 by Oxford University Press, Inc. Renewed 1981 by Tatiana Slonim. Reprinted by permission of the publisher.

Slonim, Marc. From *Soviet Russian Literature: Writers and Problems 1917-1977*. Second revised edition. Oxford University Press, 1977. Copyright © 1964, 1967, 1977 by Oxford University Press, Inc. Reprinted by permission of the publisher.

Stein, Allen F. From *After the Vows Were Spoken: Marriage in American Literary Realism*. Ohio State University Press, 1984. Copyright © 1984 by the Ohio State University Press. All rights reserved. Reprinted by permission of the publisher.

Steuart, John A. From *Letters to Living Authors*. United States Book Co., 1890.

Struve, Gleb. From *Soviet Russian Literature*. Routledge & Kegan Paul Ltd., 1935.

Sutton, Max Keith. From *R. D. Blackmore*. Twayne, 1979. Copyright 1979 by Twayne Publishers. All rights reserved. Reprinted with the permission of Twayne Publishers, a division of G. K. Hall & Co., Boston.

Tabachnick, Stephen Ely. From *Charles Doughty*. Twayne, 1981. Copyright 1981 by Twayne Publishers. Reprinted with the permission of Twayne Publishers, a division of G. K. Hall & Co., Boston.

Taylor, Walt. From *Doughty's English*. The Clarendon Press, Oxford, 1939.

Treneer, Anne. From *Charles M. Doughty: A Story of his Prose and Verse*. Jonathan Cape Ltd., 1935.

Trilling, Lionel. From "The Morality of Inertia" in *A Gathering of Fugitives*. Beacon Press, 1956, Harcourt Brace Jovanovich, 1977. Copyright © 1956 by Lionel Trilling. Renewed 1984 by Diana Trilling. Reprinted by permission of Harcourt Brace Jovanovich, Inc.

Tynan, Kenneth. From *Curtains: Selections from the Drama Criticism and Related Writings*. Atheneum Publishers, 1961. Copyright © 1961 by Kenneth Tynan. All rights reserved. Reprinted by permission of the Literary Estate of Kenneth Tynan.

Walton, Geoffrey. From *Edith Wharton: A Critical Interpretation*. Fairleigh Dickinson University Press, 1971. © 1970 by Geoffrey Walton. Reprinted by permission of the publisher.